THE OXFORD COMPANION

TO

MARK TWAIN

The writing of books and magazine matter was always play, not work. I enjoyed it; it was merely billiards to me.

—*Mark Twain*

THE OXFORD COMPANION

 TO

MARK TWAIN

GREGG CAMFIELD

ADVISORY BOARD

Lou Budd   Jim Cox

Shelley Fisher-Fishkin

Sue Harris   Bob Hirst

OXFORD
UNIVERSITY PRESS

2003

OXFORD
UNIVERSITY PRESS

Oxford   New York

Auckland   Bangkok   Buenos Aires   Cape Town   Chennai
Dar es Salaam   Delhi   Hong Kong   Istanbul   Karachi   Kolkata
Kuala Lumpur   Madrid   Melbourne   Mexico City   Mumbai   Nairobi
São Paulo   Shanghai   Singapore   Taipei   Tokyo   Toronto

Published by Oxford University Press, Inc.
198 Madison Avenue, New York, New York, 10016
http://www.oup-usa.org

Oxford is a registered trademark of Oxford University Press

Library of Congress Cataloging-in-Publication Data

The Oxford companion to Mark Twain / editor, Gregg Camfield.
p.   cm.
Includes bibliographical references and index.
ISBN 0-19-510710-1
1. Twain, Mark, 1835–1910—Handbooks, manuals, etc. 2. Authors,
American—19th century—Biography—Handbooks, manuals, etc. I. Title:
Companion to Mark Twain. II. Camfield, Gregg.
PS1331 .O97 2003
818'.409—dc21

The essays "Censorship," by Nat Hentoff, "Etiquette," by Judith Martin,
"Performance," by Arthur Miller, and "Realism," by Frederik Pohl
are excerpts from the authors' introductions to volumes in
The Oxford Mark Twain series, and appear with
the permission of the authors.

Printing number: 9 8 7 6 5 4 3 2 1

Printed in the United States of America
on acid-free paper

Contents

Preface

Like most people, I had heard about Mark Twain before I had read any of his works. I visited Disneyland the summer before I turned seven, so I had seen one fantasy version of "Tom Sawyer's Island." At another extreme, my grandfather's homilies in financial management often included the story of Twain's bankruptcy. So when Scholastic Book Services listed a slim collection of Twain short stories in its catalog for junior high school readers, my seventh-grade self had a vague sense that he must be somebody; maybe the book was worth a look. I counted out my money and took the plunge. When the book arrived, I first plunged into "How I Edited an Agricultural Newspaper," a confusing blur that made no sense to me. I put the book down. But when I had finished the other volumes I had ordered—such fare as *Two-Minute Mysteries* and a bunch of ghost stories—I had nothing new left except this book by Twain. I tried again. Then I realized that he was supposed to be funny, and the scales fell from my eyes. I have been reading and studying and teaching Twain's words ever since. Whenever I begin a class on him, I always ask my students what they know of Twain and why they want to study him. Many tell me they already love his works and want to learn more. Of these, many were introduced to Twain directly by a family member—usually one who read aloud *The Adventures of Tom Sawyer* or *Adventures of Huckleberry Finn*; others discovered Twain accidentally, some in the very volume in which I first found him. Still others simply have heard of him, seen his many photographs, or watched movies supposedly based on his books, and want to find out something more. My own introduction to Twain, I've thus learned, was merely one variation on a theme that has replayed itself for generations in America and throughout much of the world: Twain is always around, ready to be found.

Has any other American writer commanded so much attention for so long? Each year brings forth a flood—in English and a multitude of other languages—of articles, essays, books, films, and adaptations about Twain and his writings by scholars, journalists, pundits, novelists, actors, and filmmakers. When the world wants a quintessentially American point of view, it turns to Twain, though what exactly constitutes that Twainish-American viewpoint is and always has been hotly debated. People of radically different political and ethical orientations glibly cite him as an authority to buttress their positions. And as much as Twain is used, he is read even more. In dozens of guises, from the cheap paperback to the leather-bound gift set to the scholarly edition, Twain's books find their way into the minds and hearts of countless readers.

We have designed this *Companion* primarily for those readers. This book is an effort to distill a century of interpretive tradition and historical study into a single volume that will help a reader more fully to understand and enjoy Twain's works. It is designed as much for interested nonspecialists as for scholars and teachers. Secondarily, the volume reflects on the world out of which Twain's writings grew and which they still inhabit. As much as he was a central figure in late nineteenth-century intellectual and political culture, study of his works and life teaches us much about his world—and ours.

Approach

William Dean Howells, reviewing the "Uniform Edition" of Twain's works in 1897, wrote, "Nothing is more characteristic of a great talent (and I believe Mark Twain's one of the greatest) than its refusal to be illustrated by anything short of its whole range" (*Harper's Weekly,* 13 February). I would endorse that statement by going further; I don't believe that Twain's talent can be illustrated without putting it into its many contexts—personal, social, intellectual, political, and even that of its posterity. I have tried in the pages that follow to illustrate the "whole range" of Mark Twain not only by examining a variety of his works but also by looking beyond his writing to his life, times, and enduring impact.

While it has been exhilarating, this has not been an easy task. I have come over the course of planning and writing and revising this book to envy Shakespearean scholars—they have so little biographical information about their subject that they can fill in the blanks with whatever ideas fit their needs and desires. The scholar's task is more difficult with Twain. Collectively we know too much, both about his life and his times. So the scholar must take a line through the material, must build a thesis in order to make sense of some of the mass of information. Enough scholars have been doing this long enough that we can put the pieces together into a larger whole, like, to use one of Twain's favorite similes, an impressionist painting. In this book I've tried to use the insights of many scholars as so many dabs of color on one canvas in order to create a whole picture. Or, to use a perhaps more apt metaphor, I have woven many strands of thought together, connecting various themes and ideas, facts and interpretations, in order to create a rich tapestry of Twain in his times and ours.

Such a picture is difficult to compose because it must be a moving one. As Twain himself put it in a paper he presented to the Hartford Monday Evening Club on 2 December 1884, "What is the most rigorous law of our being? *Growth.* No smallest atom of our moral, mental or physical structure can stand still a *year.* . . . In other words, we *change*—and *must* change, constantly, and keep on changing as long as we live." Twain certainly did, and I have tried to account for that change. Still, in many ways he remained true to form and character throughout his life, and I have tried to capture that too.

I have, of course, drawn on the works of literally hundreds of scholars of American literature and culture, and I have called on the formidable collective wisdom of an ideal advisory board. As a scholar relying on the work of so many excellent scholars, I have tried to be true to the facts as they are known. I have also had the good fortune to find access to many relatively obscure writings of Twain, so I have included generous quotations from these throughout in hopes that these lessknown writings will flesh out the larger picture. (Twain does, after all, speak extraordinarily well for himself.) But as much as I have been responsible to and have tried to foreground matters of fact and interpretive consensus, I have concentrated on the controversies and puzzles with which Twain's works struggle. This is, after all, meant to be a *reader's* companion. I hope to open the kinds of questions a reader of Twain would wish to explore. I hope to bring the reader into the largescale cultural conversations that Twain himself engaged with and that have continued to engage serious readers in the generations following his death. Thus, in addition to a number of entries that give background information, I have also written many essays that are primarily intended to explore difficult, often open-ended questions posed by reading Twain.

In the final analysis, the picture presented in this book is mine. I have not tried for bland neutrality here. Rather, I have attempted to give a sense of the dynamic presence Twain had and still has, and therefore I have kept an interpretive presence in this book throughout. No doubt readers will disagree with my particular emphases and interpretations in many places, but that, it seems to me, is what a reader's *companion* demands. For balance and richness, this book also includes the points of view of other scholars and writers—Louis J. Budd, Susan K. Harris, Nat Hentoff, Judith Martin, Bruce Michelson, Arthur Miller, Frederik Pohl, David L. Smith—in their study and interaction with Twain. The resultant picture that emerges is one, I hope, of great breadth and variety, one that will help any reader better appreciate not only Twain but the world his works inhabit.

Given the extraordinary richness and range of materials by and about Twain, I planned this book around three large categories: his life, times, and works.

Life. Biographical essays cover significant events in Twain's life, his characteristic attitudes and outlooks, and significant people and places that left their impression on him and his writings. Mark Twain, of course, is a pseudonym, a persona created by and ultimately inhabited by Samuel L. Clemens. In looking at the life, I attend to the period of Clemens's life before he invented the Mark Twain persona as well as to his life-long identity as citizen Clemens of Hartford, Connecticut, and the world. There are thus entries on the Clemens family, on the family's social circle, on Clemens's personal friends and business associates, and on the significant political, artistic, and intellectual figures with whom Clemens had contact or against whose ideas he reacted. But the biography of Clemens includes the virtual second life of Mark Twain as a professional writer's alter ego, as a stage persona, as a creative muse, and as a psychological counterweight to Victorian seriousness. Many of Clemens's most important human connections, such as his friendship and professional collaboration with Howells, were carried on as much by Clemens being Twain as by Clemens being Clemens. Yet even as he played with his dual identity, and as much as he himself sometimes found it difficult to separate the two, he took the distinction seriously. For the sake of the many times when the distinction is important to interpreting Twain's works, I try to use these two names to identify different facets of the Clemens-Twain life. Still, the difficulty scholars regularly have in drawing the distinction attests to the degree to which Clemens came to inhabit rather than merely perform the Twain identity, and I therefore beg the indulgence of the reader for my difficulties in separating the two identities.

Times. Even though Clemens knew of fin-de-siècle artistic movements, art for art's sake was as foreign to Clemens's motivations as possible for a serious writer. Clemens drew on his world not for the sake of art but for the sake of influencing that world. It is impossible to understand fully these works without recognizing how he understood the main intellectual and political issues of his day. Many of the entries, then, give the reader quick access to fundamental historical questions about religion, politics, economics, science, technology, and so forth.

Works. Of course, readers of Twain have many of his works in hand, but to know the entire corpus is beyond the ability of all, including the most dedicated of scholars. Twain was so prolific that it is unlikely we will ever even find all of his writings, and many that we do have are so obscure as to be available only to specialists. As one such specialist, I have tried here to give important background information and to sketch out the central interpretive questions about all of Twain's major works against the backdrop of minor works as well. But no single volume could treat all of what is available. Consequently, as well as providing many entries devoted to major works, I also include larger entries on genres in which Clemens regularly wrote, such as "Sketches" and "Letters." To help readers know what specific pieces I have excluded, the appendices include a substantial primary bibliography of Mark Twain's writings. After all, this *Companion* is meant not only to help a reader understand what most people have read but also to encourage further reading.

Ultimately, these three broad categories served my purpose in deciding what would be in the *Companion*, but they are not the organizing principle. After all, these categories blur easily, and the primary principle of the *Companion* is to show interconnections. Thus, essays tend to be larger in this *Companion* than in most single-volume encyclopedias, and even these longer entries invite a reader to move on to others in order to develop a larger picture.

How to Use This *Companion*

Essays in this volume are arranged alphabetically. When seeking the largest and most obvious topics, a reader should first turn to the body of the book. Readers can easily access major works, figures, and intellectual movements that way. Occasionally, blind entries will lead a reader from a likely title to the one of several that I've chosen. For instance, a reader looking for the novel *Huckleberry Finn* will find a blind entry leading to the full title, *Adventures of Huckleberry Finn*. Topics not covered in separate entries are best found in the index.

I have tried to make each entry an essay complete unto itself. For those readers who wish to use the *Companion* to create a large picture of Twain's life and times, however, there are three ways to combine single essays into networks of related entries:

Asterisks appear in front of words that are titles to other entries. The article "Religion," for example, includes asterisks leading the reader to obviously related entries, such as "Calvinism," and to less obviously related entries such as "Social Class." Generally, these asterisked entries fall into clusters that develop a larger treatment of a topic that cuts across many other subtopics.

Major works are regularly cited in essays to illuminate how Twain used ideas, events, and so on as raw material in his writing. Most of these have entries of their own. They will not be marked by asterisks, but the reader is encouraged to follow these connections as well.

Cross-references appear at the end of many entries in order to suggest further connections that are not apparent from the body of the essay. The entry on "Inventions," for example, ends with cross-references to the larger context of the "Industrial Revolution" and to the personal context of Clemens's "Business Ventures."

This book does not have a list of references for each individual topic, not only because the secondary bibliography on Twain is so substantial that it would overwhelm the essays if included along the way, but also because any such bibliography would be outdated almost as soon as it was issued. Two essays fill this gap. In the body of the book an essay entitled "Critical Reception" gives a historical overview of the development of Mark Twain studies. Included is a list of titles of many of the most important critical works on Twain. Given how quickly the secondary bibliography on this subject grows, the book also includes, as an appendix, an essay on researching Twain. This piece gives information on regularly updated scholarly bibliographies of Twain research, internet resources for Twain studies, and a short bibliography of historiographical resources.

Acknowledgments

This book is the product of a community of scholars. I have relied on much more scholarship than would be possible to document, and I thank all of those whose work has supported my own. Beyond my general debt to the tradition of Twain scholarship, I owe particular and personal debts to a handful of the most generous scholars I have ever known—Lou Budd, Jim Cox, Shelley Fisher-Fishkin, Sue Harris, and Bob Hirst. These were the five eminent scholars Oxford University Press recruited to be my advisory board—what I came to think of as my dream team.

Other scholars and friends, too, have helped with drafts, research, conversation, and emotional support. Among these, I would like especially to thank Bruce Michelson; Larry Howe; Robert Reagan; Douglas Tedards; Cynthia Dobbs; all of the editors and staff of the Mark Twain Papers, but especially Ken Sanderson and Vic Fisher; the members of the Mark Twain Forum, especially Barbara Schmidt; and the Special Collections staff at the University of the Pacific.

Two scholars I wish could read their names in this list will not be able to. Just after I finished going through the copyediting of this book, I learned that revered Twain authorities Everett Emerson and Hamlin Hill died. Like all Twain scholars, I owe a substantial debt to their work, to their support of Twain scholarship, and, though I did not have the good fortune to study under the tutelage of either, their friendship.

All of this help would have gone for naught had I not been able to carve out the time to write. For this I thank the University of the Pacific for a sabbatical leave and the Graves Foundation for funding at a crucial time in drafting the manuscript.

For helping me turn the manuscript into a book, I thank the production crew at Oxford University Press in New York: Maggie Hogan and Dan Geist for copyediting; Adams Holman, Dan Geist, and Ryan Sullivan for proofreading; Mary-Neal Meador for a lovely design that includes initial caps from Mark Twain first editions and first magazine appearances to begin each alphabetical section; Kathleen Lynch for a striking cover; Martin Coleman for putting all the pieces together; Liza Ewell for securing the book and Casper Grathwohl for following through after Liza left Oxford; and finally, Nancy Toff, for being a hands-on, brilliant, and wonderful producer of the whole show.

I have had the good fortune to find in Peter Meyer a friend whose work lies outside academe but who nevertheless—or perhaps therefore—has for nearly twenty years encouraged my professional development as much as has any scholar. Near the end of this project, when I was tearing my hair out over the bibliography, Peter Meyer rescued me. While he takes his generosity as a matter of course, I do not; I know how to value it for the rarity it is.

Finally, I want to thank Eileen, Isabella, and Michael Camfield. In the seven years since I signed the contract to write this book, Eileen has moved with me across the continent, has supported me in a new job, has borne Isabella and Michael, and has kept her sense of humor through it all. It amazes me to see how much more complicated our lives have become since we decided that I should take on this project. And somehow, I have been able to make time to keep going, which I could not have done without Eileen's help with the research, with the organization, with the manuscript, and with the motivation. Oddly, Isabella and Michael have been both tangible distractions *and* inspirations. They have very much helped me better understand Mark Twain, or at least to understand one of his sources of fun. In his *Autobiography*, Twain asked repeatedly of life, "What's it all for?" When I think of Eileen, Isabella, and Michael, I have my answer to that question.

Gregg Camfield
Stockton, California
September, 2002

A Thematic List of Entries

Entries and headings in SMALL CAPITALS are the titles of essays in the *Companion*. All can be found at their place in the alphabetical run, except for those for which a page number is given.

Works:

Novels:

ADVENTURES OF HUCKLEBERRY
  FINN
ADVENTURES OF TOM SAWYER,
  THE
AMERICAN CLAIMANT, THE
CONNECTICUT YANKEE IN KING
  ARTHUR'S COURT, A
GILDED AGE, THE

PERSONAL RECOLLECTIONS OF JOAN
  OF ARC
PRINCE AND THE PAUPER, THE
PUDD'NHEAD WILSON AND THOSE
  EXTRAORDINARY TWINS
"THREE THOUSAND YEARS AMONG
  THE MICROBES"
TOM SAWYER ABROAD

Travel Narratives:

FOLLOWING THE EQUATOR
INNOCENTS ABROAD, THE
LIFE ON THE MISSISSIPPI

ROUGHING IT
TRAMP ABROAD, A

SKETCHES and Tales:

"AWFUL ---- TERRIBLE MEDIEVAL
  ROMANCE, AN"
"BLUEJAY YARN"
CELEBRATED JUMPING FROG OF
  CALAVERAS COUNTY, AND OTHER
  SKETCHES
"CHRONICLE OF YOUNG
  SATAN"
"CORN-PONE OPINIONS"
"EXTRACT FROM CAPTAIN
  STORMFIELD'S VISIT TO
  HEAVEN"
"FABLE, A"

"FACTS CONCERNING THE RECENT
  CARNIVAL OF CRIME IN
  CONNECTICUT, THE"
"FACTS IN THE GREAT LANDSLIDE
  CASE, THE"
"FENIMORE COOPER'S LITERARY
  OFFENSES"
"GREAT DARK, THE"
"HOW TO TELL A STORY"
"JUMPING FROG, THE"
LETTERS FROM THE EARTH
"MAN THAT CORRUPTED
  HADLEYBURG, THE"

Styles and Genres:

Collaborations

Condensed Novels

Detective Stories

Frame Narrative

Naturalism

Realism

Romance

Science Fiction

Language:

Dialect

Profanity

Slang

Humor:

Amiable Humor

Burlesque

Comic Journalism

Irony

Off-color Humor

Parody

Practical Jokes

Satire

Southwestern Humor

Scholarship and Criticism:

Bibliography (p. 675)

Collecting

Critical Reception

Mark Twain Journal

Mark Twain Circle

Mark Twain Forum

Mark Twain Papers

Researching Mark Twain
 (p. 665)

Reputation

Life:

Clemens, Samuel Langhorne

Mark Twain

Family:

Clemens, Henry

Clemens, Jane Lampton

Clemens, Jane Lampton (Jean)

Clemens, John Marshall

Clemens, Langdon

Clemens, Olivia Langdon

Clemens, Olivia Susan (Susy)

Clemens, Orion

Crane, Susan Langdon and
 Theodore

Gabrilowitsch, Nina Clemens

Langdon, Jervis and Olivia Lewis

Langdon, Charles Jervis

Moffet, Pamela Clemens and
 William A.

Samossoud, Clara Clemens
 Gabrilowitsch

Webster, Annie Moffet and
 Charles L.

Wright, William

Thematic List of Entries

Friends and Acquaintances:

Aldrich, Thomas Bailey
Burlingame, Anson
Gillis, James N. (Jim) and
    Steve
Hay, John
Howells, William Dean
King, Grace

Nast, Thomas
Rogers, Henry H.
Slote, Dan
Trumbull, James Hammond
Twichell, Rev. Joseph
Wakeman, Capt. Edgar (Ned)
Warner, Charles Dudley

Clubs:

Aquarium Club, The
Monday Evening Club

Saturday Morning Club

Finances:

Business Ventures
Charities
Economy

Money
Webster and Company

Professional Associates:

Ashcroft, Ralph W.
Bliss, Elisha
Browne, Charles Farrar
Cable, George Washington
Conway, Moncure
Fairbanks, Mary Mason
Goodman, Joseph T.
Grant, Ulysses S.
Harte, Bret
Harvey, George Brinton
    McClellan

Locke, David Ross (Petroleum
    V. Nasby)
Lyon, Isabel
Osgood, James
Paine, Albert Bigelow
Reid, Whitelaw
Riley, John Henry
Servants
Warner, Charles Dudley
Wright, William

Printing and Publishing Industry:

Censorship
Copyright
Illustrations

Mark Twain Company and Mark
    Twain Foundation
Subscription Publishing

Work:

Work Ethic

Work Habits

Places:

CALIFORNIA
CANADA
CITIES
DOMESTICITY
ELMIRA, NEW YORK
EUROPE
HANNIBAL, MISSOURI

HARTFORD, CONNECTICUT
HOUSES
MISSISSIPPI RIVER VALLEY
NEVADA
NOOK FARM
SUMMER RESIDENCES
WASHINGTON, D.C.

TOURS:

QUAKER CITY

READING, CLEMENS'S:

AGE OF REASON, THE
ARABIAN NIGHTS ENTERTAINMENT,
THE
BIBLE

GULLIVER'S TRAVELS
HISTORY
PUNCH
SHAKESPEARE, WILLIAM

CELEBRITY:

ARNOLD, MATTHEW
BARNUM, PHINEAS T.
BEECHER, HENRY WARD
INTERVIEWS
LECTURE CIRCUIT

LECTURES
PERFORMANCE
PUBLIC IMAGE
SEVENTIETH BIRTHDAY DINNER

Contemporaries:

DARWIN, CHARLES
DICKENS, CHARLES
DICKINSON, ANNA
DOUGLASS, FREDERICK
FIELDS, ANNIE AND JAMES T.
FREUD, SIGMUND
GREELEY, HORACE
HARRIS, GEORGE WASHINGTON
HARRIS, JOEL CHANDLER
INGERSOLL, ROBERT G.
JAMES, HENRY

JAMES, WILLIAM
KIPLING, RUDYARD
LECKY, W. E. H.
MOORE, JULIA
PRESIDENTS
RILEY, JAMES WHITCOMB
ROBBER BARONS
SPENCER, HERBERT
STOWE, HARRIET BEECHER
WHITMAN, WALT

Social Attitudes Toward:

ADAM AND EVE. Adam and Eve are among the most frequently mentioned characters in all of Mark Twain's works; surprisingly, though, coming from a religious skeptic with a propensity to burlesque, not all of the references are satiric or even comic. Granted, such quips as the Pudd'nhead Wilson's Calendar entry, "Adam and Eve had many advantages, but the principal one was, that they escaped teething," express a skeptical irreverence toward these biblical figures, and his bathetic weeping over Adam's tomb in *Innocents Abroad* not only challenges the truth of the story but mocks the literal-mindedness of many believers in the Bible. A similar perspective underlies Clemens's joking petition for "A Monument to Adam" (collected in *The $30,000 Bequest*):

> I once suggested to Rev. Thomas K. Beecher, of Elmira, New York, that we get up a monument to Adam, and . . . Mr. Beecher favored the project. . . . Mr. Darwin's *Descent of Man* had been in print five or six years, and the storm of indignation raised by it was still raging in pulpits and periodicals. In tracing the genesis of the human race back to its sources, Mr. Darwin had left Adam out altogether. . . . Jesting with Mr. Beecher and other friends in Elmira, I said there seemed to be a likelihood that the world would discard Adam and accept the monkey, and that in the course of time Adam's very name would be forgotten in the earth.

While Beecher and Clemens easily accepted Darwinian theory, they enjoyed teasing the orthodox who would not read biblical stories figuratively. Clemens took the joke fairly far, even drafting a petition to Congress. But his friend and fellow *Monday Evening Club member Joseph R. Hawley, then a member of the House of Representatives, at the last moment refused to present the petition, fearing that "it was too gushy, too sentimental—the House might take it for earnest." The earnestness of believers in the literal truth of the Bible was part of the fun Clemens found in his irreverent play with Adam and Eve.

Nonetheless, the figurative meanings of Adam and Eve's story captured Clemens's imagination. Like his contemporaries, Clemens wanted to know about human origins, and he found the idea of an original, compressed into the name "Adam," a convenient shorthand for speculations about human beginnings. Whether referring to the idea of evolution or creation, he referred to the original human being as Adam. His ultimate preference for the idea of evolution made him skeptical of even the radical originality of this "Adam" itself. As he has Hank Morgan put it in

Illustration by Lester Ralph (1877–1927), from *Eve's Diary: Translated from the Original MS by Mark Twain*, New York: Harper & Brothers, 1906, p. 38.

chapter 18 of *Connecticut Yankee*: "All that is original in us, and therefore fairly creditable to us, can be covered up and hidden by the point of a cambric needle, all the rest being atoms contributed by, and inherited from, a procession of ancestors that stretches back a billion years to the Adam-clam or grasshopper or monkey from whom our race has been so tediously and ostentatiously and unprofitably developed." In identifying a nonhuman ancestor as Adam, Mark Twain shows how far he can stretch a figurative reading of a story.

In describing human character as the product of evolution from some non-human Adam, Clemens absolved human beings of guilt, blamed God for virtually all terrible things that happen to human beings, and, sometimes, praised human love as an antidote for all the sufferings inflicted on humanity by a dispassionate or even malignant universe. In interpreting the creation this way, Clemens returned repeatedly, almost obsessively, to the Genesis story in his later years. He published a number of maxims about Adam and Eve in Pudd'nhead Wilson's Calendar in *Pudd'nhead Wilson* and in Pudd'nhead Wilson's New Calendar in *Following the Equator*. He also published "Eve's Diary" and "Extracts from Adam's Diary," and wrote but did not publish many other Adam family papers, including the posthumously published "Adam's Soliloquy" and various manuscripts collectively titled "Papers of the Adam Family," edited by Bernard DeVoto in his collection of Twain pieces, *Letters from the Earth* (1962).

The leitmotif of these works is that human beings are fundamentally innocent of all crimes attributed to them because human nature entails certain consequences, consequences they should not be held accountable for, as *history invariably shows. Furthermore, many evils in the world—violence, disease, hunger, toil—are natural, not the fault of human intervention. When Eve complains that tigers do not look happy as herbivores, Twain metaphorically explains that the myth of Eden does not fit with the natural order of things. In the face of pain and suffering, Mark Twain describes human companionship as the only solace. In his interpretation of the Adam and Eve story, this is Twain's main point. In "Eve's Diary," the fall from grace has its compensation: "The Garden is lost, but I have found *him,* and am content. He loves me as well as he can; I love him with all the strength of my passionate nature, and this, I think, is proper to my youth and sex. If I ask myself why I love him, I find I do not know, and do not really much care to know. . . . This love is not a product of reasonings and statistics. It just *comes*—none knows whence—and cannot explain itself. And doesn't need to." Adam, less voluble and longer lived, gives his version of the same idea "At Eve's Grave": "Wheresoever she was, *there* was Eden." As Mark Twain's public comment on how much he valued his wife, he makes clear to the world the metaphoric power of the story of Adam and Eve.

♦ SEE ALSO Bible; Domesticity; Reverence.

ADVENTURES OF HUCKLEBERRY FINN (1884 English edition; 1885 American edition). One of the greatest literary works in the English language, *Adventures of Huckleberry Finn* has also frequently been subject to *censorship, almost from the moment of its publication to the present. Its detractors have attacked the book variously on three grounds—the morality it promotes, the language it uses, and its approach to *race relations. Ironically, the book's supporters have argued for its greatness based on these same three points. All of them grew in importance in Clemens's mind as he wrote the book, as the history of its composition shows.

Writing Huckleberry Finn

Clemens began writing *Huckleberry Finn* in the flush of excitement over finishing *The Adventures of Tom Sawyer.* William Dean *Howells's praise for *Tom Sawyer* extravagantly suggested that it might be Twain's masterpiece, the apex of an already exceptional career. Clemens enjoyed the praise, but before he even let Howells see the manuscript he already had a sense of opportunities lost: "I have finished the story & didn't take the chap beyond boyhood. I believe it would be fatal to do it in any shape but autobiographically—like Gil Blas. I perhaps made a mistake in not writing it in the first person" (to Howells, 5 July 1875). This observation is the first description of *Huckleberry Finn*'s structure and Clemens's initial intention to describe the transition from boyhood to adulthood.

Later, Howells criticized the closing chapter in *Tom Sawyer,* about Huck's life at the widow's, which Howells believed did not fit the novel. Clemens cut it as suggested, but rather than let such a good subject for comedy go, he combined it with his earlier idea of writing a bildungsroman in the first person. When he turned to writing Huck's story in the summer of 1876, he wrote with great energy and gusto, but burned himself out by summer's end: "Began another boys' book—more to be

3

at work than anything else. I have written 400 pages on it—therefore it is very nearly half done. It is Huck Finn's Autobiography. I like it only tolerably well, as far as I have got, & may possibly pigeonhole or burn the MS when it is done" (to Howells, 9 August 1876).

He opted for the pigeonhole. No one knows what he disliked about the tale, but perhaps it was the structural detail of having Huck and Jim run south on a raft past the Ohio River. The idea of a slave running south to freedom is patently absurd, which Clemens himself acknowledged in chapter 20 when Huck exclaims, "Goodness sakes, would a runaway nigger run *south*?" Yet for Clemens to have his characters leave his well-known Mississippi River for the unknown Ohio may have been beyond his ability to imagine. Be that as it may, he came back to the book in either 1879 or 1880, carrying it to the end of chapter 21 before shelving it again. When he did return energetically and consistently to the book in 1883, he finished a draft of the complete tale and made significant changes in the earlier sections, including the addition of chapters 12–14, by summer's end. As he wrote to his English publisher, Andrew Chatto, "I've just finished writing a book; & modesty compels me to say it's a rattling good one, too" (1 September 1883). But over the course of composing this one novel, Twain explored many of its themes in different contexts in three other books—*A Tramp Abroad, The Prince and the Pauper,* and *Life on the Mississippi.* The explorations he made in and the reaction he received to those books significantly expanded and enriched his efforts in *Huckleberry Finn,* turning it into the masterpiece that he knew *Tom Sawyer* had finally failed to become.

Part of the difficulty Clemens had in writing this book was the same he had with all of his novels—he was less interested in plot than in character, and so his stories tended to drift through episodes until he could no longer plausibly resolve the plot without violating either the characterization or the tone. But as much as the plot of *Huckleberry Finn* deviled him, the moral situation he had concocted was at the center of his intellectual life at the time, and far too rich to abandon.

Morality

Twain's 1874 reading of W. E. H. *Lecky's *History of European Morals* galvanized his already strong interest in ethics, but moved him to reflect on causes. He had already found Thomas Paine's *Age of Reason* and Oliver Wendell Holmes's works to be convincing arguments for rationalism, and as he interpreted the rationalism of the day, it required a belief in the mechanical nature of human mentality. As such, he came quickly to accept, in theory, utilitarian ethics.

In Lecky he found a beloved opponent of *utilitarianism with whom he argued in energetic marginalia. When Lecky wrote in support of *sentimentalism that human beings have "innate moral perceptions," Clemens shot back: "All moral perceptions are acquired by the influences around us; these influences begin in infancy; we never get a chance to find out whether we have any that are innate or not." At another

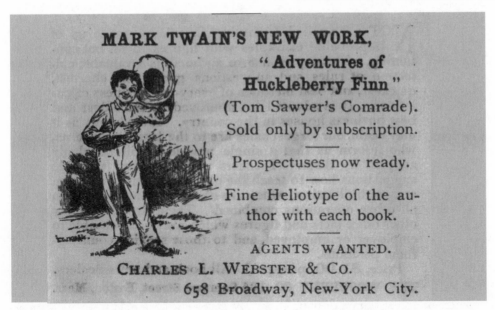

MARK TWAIN'S NEW WORK,

" Adventures of
Huckleberry Finn "

(Tom Sawyer's Comrade).

Sold only by subscription.

Prospectuses now ready.

Fine Heliotype of the au-
thor with each book.

AGENTS WANTED.

CHARLES L. WEBSTER & CO.

658 Broadway, New-York City.

A prospectus for the first edition of *Huckleberry Finn*, with an illustration from the book by
Edward Windor Kemble (1861–1933).

point, Lecky summarized the utilitarian position in order to attack it: "A desire to
obtain happiness and to avoid pain is the only possible motive to action. The reason,
and the only reason, why we should perform virtuous actions, or in other words, seek
the good of others, is that on the whole such a course will bring us the greatest
amount of happiness." Clemens underscored this entire passage, bracketed the
"should," and responded, "Leave the 'should' out—then it is perfect (& true!)."

Clemens engaged this position with increasing intensity beginning with *Tom
Sawyer*. As late as January 1876, when he wrote "The Facts Concerning the Recent
Carnival of Crime in Connecticut," he merely allegorized the consequences of three
different ethical positions without choosing between them. In *Adventures of Huckleberry Finn* he attempted to make his utilitarianism clear, beginning in the earliest
written parts and with greater clarity and energy during each return to writing over
the years 1876–1884, when he finally finished drafting and revising. Clemens's two
main points are that Huck's conscience contains nothing but learned morality and
that Huck always makes his moral choices to minimize discomfort or maximize
comfort. Huck always couches his moral decisions in terms he learns from pap,
from the Calvinist biblical literalist Miss Watson, from the sentimentalist Widow
Douglas, or from Jim. He never has an unmediated moral feeling, and he makes his
choices selfishly to satisfy his moral feelings, as is perhaps most concisely illustrated
when Huck tries to save the outlaws he has stranded on the wreck of the *Walter
Scott:* "I couldn't rest easy till I could see the ferry-boat start. But take it all around,
I was feeling ruther comfortable on accounts of taking all this trouble for that gang,

5

for not many would a done it. I wished the widow knowed about it. I judged she would be proud of me for helping these rapscallions, because rapscallions and dead-beats is the kind the widow and good people takes the most interest in" (chapter 13). In acting cold-bloodedly, here Huck cares more about his feelings than about the consequences of his action. When Huck learns that his efforts were too late and the outlaws probably drowned, he merely "felt a little bit heavy-hearted about the gang, but not much, for I reckoned if they could stand it, I could."

But as much as Clemens argued with Lecky, he partially agreed with him, per-haps because the very conception of *childhood that he cherished worked its way into Huck's moral agency. As early as a 24 May 1884 letter to his nephew and pub-lisher, Charles Webster, he called Huck "an exceedingly good-hearted boy," an impossibility according to the strict utilitarianism he thought he advocated. He explained to himself the existence of this good heart in terms borrowed not from Lecky but rather from Charles *Darwin and Herbert *Spencer. Both tried to show that human beings had developed a moral sense as a product of evolution. Darwin's chapters on the evolution of morality in *The Descent of Man* held Clemens's atten-tion—they are the only part of his copy of *The Descent of Man* that have marginalia and show heavy use. Darwin suggested that we evolved an instinctive sense of altruism, though Clemens argued in the margin, "Selfishness again—not charity not generosity (save toward ourselves)." But Twain agreed with Darwin that human beings are fundamentally gregarious. Darwin suggests that social instincts are the root of sympathetic morality, and Clemens's comments in the margins—for exam-ple, "Sheep eat with the heads all turned the same way on the hillside—cows mostly too"—show his interest in Darwin's arguments. This interest found its way into *Huckleberry Finn* when Judith Loftus quizzes Huck about animal behavior in chapter 11: "'If fifteen cows is browsing on a hillside, how many of them eats with their heads pointed in the same direction?' 'The whole fifteen, mum.'"

What matters here is that Clemens does see potential congruence between social feelings and the capacity to do right. Many readers interpret *Huckleberry Finn* as Clemens's total, Romantic rejection of society—"Sivilization"—in favor of a natural life on a raft. But Huck despises isolation in nature and only feels alive in society—even if it is the society of a single fellow outcast, Jim. In society, any society, Huck habituates himself to his circumstances. He acculturates to the widow's strictures, even to the school to which she sends him: "At first I hated the school, but by and by I got so I could stand it. Whenever I got uncommon tired I played hookey, and the hiding I got next day done me good and cheered me up. So the longer I went to school the easier it got to be. I was getting sort of used to the widow's ways, too, and they weren't so raspy on me. . . . I liked the old ways best, but I was getting so I liked the new ones, too, a little bit" (chapter 4). Kidnapped by pap, he gets used to dirt and anarchy. When he lives with the Grangerfords, he accepts their ways with-out a murmur, even though he once would have bridled against their formality. In fact there he tries to read, without prompting, "'Pilgrim's Progress,' about a man that left his family it didn't say why" (chapter 17). Huck always has a reason for leaving the society of anybody, and that reason is usually to escape violence. This explains why he never leaves Jim; Jim never hurts him and usually helps him feel good about himself.

While this ultimate bond of compassion and reciprocal benefit becomes the foremost reason why Huck sticks by Jim, it is not the first. Rather, Huck remains because he feels dead without company. Repeatedly in the book he equates "lonesome" feelings with death, and his escape to nature on Jackson's Island is no escape at all from the virtual death of isolation:

> When it was dark I set by my camp fire smoking, and feeling pretty satisfied; but by-and-by it got sort of lonesome, and so I went and set on the bank and listened to the currents washing along, and counted the stars and drift-logs and rafts that come down, and then went to bed; there ain't no better way to put in time when you are lonesome; you can't stay so, you soon get over it.
>
> And so for three days and nights. No difference—just the same thing. (chapter 8)

Alone, Huck just "mainly . . . wanted to put in the time," but the moment he discovers Jim on the island he says, "I was ever so glad to see Jim. I warn't lonesome, now." While the two wrangle over social position and experience tension and fear in each other's company, Huck's life begins anew in conversation, and his moral growth dates from his commitment to this conversation. As much as the novel is about an individual's moral development, it is a novel not about preserving natural innocence, but about training human compassion in society, and while Huck may serve his own feelings in his moral decisions, they grow risky to him; he satisfies his heart in defiance of merely utilitarian calculations of self-interest.

So in spite of his intention to argue that morality is really selfishness, Clemens moves to a middle-ground position. This was not an academic question to Clemens; he was concerned with the basis of morality because he was concerned about the relationship between moral intentions and consequences. Sentimentalists emphasized intention while utilitarians stressed consequences. Clemens's appreciation of utilitarianism may have stemmed from his pragmatic concerns over moral actions rather than mere feelings.

Race Relations and Language

In no other moral question did Clemens find consequence more important than in the issue of race relations. *Huckleberry Finn* does not address slavery per se—after all it had been practically abolished by the Civil War and legally abolished with the passage of the Thirteenth Amendment in 1865—but one does need to understand the race roles that evolved under slavery in order to understand the characterization of Jim. Clemens accurately reports the kind of subterfuge necessary for a slave to get by in white society. Whenever in the presence of any whites but Huck, Jim's language becomes stilted in its self-deprecation. Initially he is subservient with Huck too. But Jim also plays inside jokes on Huck to show that he is not fully beholden, as when Huck reports, in chapter 8, "Jim said bees wouldn't sting idiots; but I didn't believe that, because I had tried them lots of times myself, and they wouldn't sting me." Jim calls Huck an idiot without Huck even realizing that he has been insulted. The longer the two are alone together, the more direct Jim becomes with Huck, but the moment they are once again in the company of adult whites, Jim returns to a state of verbal and physical self-deprecation. Such behavior was required of blacks under slavery; the issue for Clemens over the course of writing the book was what behavior was required of the ostensibly free blacks of the post-Reconstruction South.

This issue did not arise immediately in *Huckleberry Finn*. When Jim first made his appearance in the book it was to serve as a foil for Miss Watson's literalistic Christianity. In showing Jim's superstition as a way to manipulate those around him—he uses his supposed witch ride to glean money from other enslaved blacks— and in setting up Jim's superstition as parallel to Miss Watson's Christianity, Clemens suggests not only that Christianity is mere superstition, but that its advocates use it for their own ends. As the third advocate of religion, Widow Douglas stands in opposition to these two by interpreting her beliefs figuratively rather than literally, and by being generous rather than selfish.

According to Victor Doyno, who has studied the manuscript of *Adventures of Huckleberry Finn* extensively, Clemens did not originally plan to keep Jim in the story. But when Huck's ennui on Jackson's Island made a companion a structural necessity, Clemens, like Huck, discovered Jim. The manuscript suggests that until the last possible moment Clemens himself did not know who the stranger on Jackson's Island was going to be. When he decided to make it Jim, the story took off and both characters began to grow.

Clemens had already shown himself adept at challenging stereotypes about African Americans in "A True Story"; here was a larger canvas to build a story about two characters who Clemens later said were "close friends, bosom friends, drawn together by community of misfortune." Such was the tale Clemens wrote at first; later, after his 1882 trip to the Mississippi River valley in preparation for writing *Life on the Mississippi*, he came to address a larger political question, the virtual re-enslavement of African Americans.

He learned about the conditions of blacks in the South substantially from George Washington *Cable, whom he met in New Orleans in April 1882. Cable, a former confederate soldier, had during Reconstruction decided both that the racial hierarchy of the South made the South backward and that racism was intrinsically wrong. His work as a southern crusader for equal rights made him an expert on the treatment of blacks. It had also earned him the enduring enmity of the South, ultimately forcing him to live in the North where he was no longer able to speak to the community that he wanted to enlighten. Cable taught Clemens not only what was going on but the dangers of addressing the problem directly. Clemens decided to treat the problem allegorically by having Jim become progressively more trammeled just as he begins to know freedom. By the time Huck and Jim learn that Jim is technically free, Jim has just endured the worst captivity of his entire life.

As an allegory for the situation during what historians call the nadir of conditions for African Americans, the "evasion" chapters of *Huckleberry Finn* promote racial equality. But Clemens was not willing to risk his livelihood on the cause, so he hid his message behind slapstick humor. Such was the point of the book's illustrations. After commissioning a series of illustrations from Edward W. Kemble, Clemens reviewed the work, offering suggestions and even excising some that too pointedly reinforced the book's satire. Ironically, he seemed to like some that he cut, while complaining about the ones he retained. And while he expressed displeasure that the caricatures made all the characters into grotesques, he accepted them. These comic illustrations provide a countertext to all levels of the satire, but most especially, in depicting Jim as a stereotypical minstrel-show darkey, the illustrations soften the satire against racial bigotry.

Today, the focal point for the battle over race in the book is Clemens's use of the word "nigger," held by many to be fundamentally demeaning when uttered by a white person, even if used ironically to attack the attitudes held by white racists. Early detractors of the book also attacked the book's language, not so much for its use of a single word, but for its general use of the *dialect of an ignorant, rural, Missouri boy—a vernacular far from the refined standards held to be a part and parcel of morality by Victorian stylists.

Clemens, like many of his contemporaries, had long experimented with dialect, but he usually protected himself from attack by using a conventional *frame narrative. In *Huckleberry Finn*, he leaves no more frame than a frontispiece illustration of "Mark Twain" and Huck's opening comments: "You don't know about me, without you have read a book by the name of 'The Adventures of Tom Sawyer,' but that ain't no matter. That book was made by Mr. Mark Twain, and he told the truth, mainly. There was things which he stretched." As much a sales pitch for the earlier novel as it is a narrative frame, this opening does not validate an elite position by which the reader can judge Huck. It does not provide enough frame to satisfy the conventional readers of local color that Huck's dialect is, for all of its debased quality, still going to serve the purpose of moral uplift.

Clemens took the risk in part in reaction to Joseph T. *Goodman's criticism of *The Prince and the Pauper*, in which Goodman told Clemens to stick to "existing people and things" (29 January 1882). Subsequently, Clemens systematically revised his work in progress to lower Huck's language, to make it more accurately represent the speech of a person in his time and place. In fact, he went so far as to try to distinguish between different characters by showing consistent differences in their dialects according to diction, grammatical inflection, and pronunciation. His notebooks for the period show him working with variant spellings in an effort to capture dialect effectively, as when he tried five different spellings for Jim's variant of the word "something": "suffin," "sumfin," "sumf'n," "suthin," and the spelling he settled on, "sumfn."

Publication and Public Response

As much trouble as Clemens took with the details of *Huckleberry Finn*, to the extent of establishing his own publishing firm so that he could control publication, the book still often slipped his grasp. He had hired Charles Webster to run the firm, and the two neophytes in publishing made several mistakes that affected the final book. One was the effort to convince the American Publishing Company to allow Webster and Company to sell *Huckleberry Finn* with *Tom Sawyer*. Not surprisingly, Clemens's former publisher and now competitor was not cooperative, but Webster convinced Clemens that *Huckleberry Finn* had to be shortened in order to sell with *Tom Sawyer*. He suggested that Clemens excise the raftsman chapter, previously printed in *Life on the Mississippi* as an advertisement for the forthcoming book. Clemens, preoccupied by other concerns, concurred. When the book was ready to print, negotiations with the American Publishing Company finally fell through, eliminating the reason for excising an important chapter, but coming too late to make its reinclusion financially prudent.

Other difficulties intruded later. When the book was being printed, a press-operator either deliberately or accidentally defaced the illustration of Silas Phelps meeting Huck (captioned "Who do you think it is?") so that it appeared as though Uncle Silas had an erection sticking out of his pants. Such an illustration would have ruined Clemens, especially considering the risks he was already taking with his satiric jibes at Christianity and white racism. Victorian America could forgive political satire even against such sacred cows, but it would not forgive obscenity. Salesmen were required to cut the offending page out of publishers' prospectuses; the edition, already in press, was delayed for correction. Offending illustrations were cut out of already bound volumes and corrections tipped in; unbound volumes had new signatures printed. The corrections delayed issue of the American edition until 18 February 1885, well after the crucial Christmas season. The smaller English edition was corrected more quickly, allowing it to issue nearly on schedule in December 1884.

Production difficulties notwithstanding, the book sold very well—51,000 copies in America by May 1885. This success convinced Clemens that he had correctly decided to publish his own books, and that he should not only sustain but expand Webster and Company. This decision would ultimately have dire consequences for his *finances.

Huckleberry Finn's wide public success did not protect it from early and continuing attacks. Reviewers often found its depiction of life squalid and mean, and worried that it would teach children to emulate Huck's abilities to lie and steal, as well as to avoid church. Later, the book was attacked as promoting racial stereotypes. True, many African-American critics have supported the book, some on the grounds that it shows accurately how blacks had to adjust to the political conditions of the times. Some, like Ralph Ellison, argued that it discovers possibilities that transcend racism:

> If the ideal of achieving a true political equality eludes us in reality—as it continues to do—there is still available that fictional vision of an ideal democracy in which the actual combines with the ideal and gives us representations of a state of things in which the highly placed and the lowly, the black and the white, the northerner and the southerner, the native-born and the immigrant are combined to tell us of transcendent truths and possibilities such as those discovered when Mark Twain set Huck and Jim afloat on the raft. (Author's Introduction to the 1982 edition of *Invisible Man*)

Nonetheless, others, most notably Chicago educator Dr. John Wallace, who calls the book "the most grotesque example of racist trash ever written," concentrate more on what ideas and attitudes about race children *might* learn from the book.

Such criticism all revolves around interpretations of what imaginative literature should do, either tell us how things are so we can choose what not to do, or tell us how things should be so we can conform to an ideal. Clemens himself never knew which purpose literature should serve, and as much as his confusion between utilitarianism and sentimentalism—between realism and idealism—manifests itself in *Adventures of Huckleberry Finn*, his confusion inspires the debates that engulf his most important novel.

◆ SEE ALSO Webster, Annie Moffet and Charles L.

ADVENTURES OF TOM SAWYER, THE (1876). *The Adventures of Tom Sawyer* is Mark Twain's most popular book, enchanting generations of children and adults alike as a book not only for children but also about *childhood. While scholars consider other Twain books "deeper," none does a better job of creating a mood that transcends its particular time and place, and none has gone so far to create images of America.

Tom Sawyer had its earliest beginnings in Twain's western journalism in pieces attacking sentimental ideas of childhood, such as "Those Blasted Children," and in his parodies of didactic fiction, such as "The Story of the Good Little Boy Who

Did Not Prosper" and "The Story of the Bad Little Boy." But marriage, and correspondence with his friends about marriage, changed his bias. In reply to a letter from childhood companion William Bowen, Clemens wrote, "Your letter has stirred me to the bottom. The fountains of my great deep are broken up & I have rained reminiscences for four and twenty hours" (6 February 1870). The following pages of reminiscences show, in part, that Bowen was as much the model for Tom Sawyer as Clemens himself. They also show Clemens's willingness to indulge a sentimental *nostalgia that he recently had deprecated. Without this change, he could not have written *Tom Sawyer*.

Not until the summer of 1872, however, did Twain begin to turn these childhood memories into a book. He first had to clear other projects, including *Roughing It* and a collaborative work on South African diamond mines. The death of his collaborator, John Henry *Riley, ended that plan but not the contract with American Publishing Company to provide a book under the Mark Twain name; *Tom Sawyer* ultimately satisfied the terms. But even after its beginnings in 1872, the book's planning and writing were sketchy and slow, interrupted by yet another project, *The Gilded Age*, cowritten with Charles Dudley *Warner. Clemens was certainly working on *Tom Sawyer* in January 1873 when he wrote the first draft of the whitewashing scene, but he occupied most of the next several months writing the collaborative novel.

After finishing his part of *The Gilded Age*, Clemens was free to work on *Tom Sawyer* but began another project instead. Traveling twice to Britain in 1873, Clemens began planning a a satirical book about England. Caught up in a whirl of social activity that changed his mind about writing a satire of a country he came to love, he never wrote the England book. Instead, he found himself thinking often about his childhood, as Charles Warren Stoddard, Clemens's hired companion and secretary during his November trip to England recalled in a 1903 memoir: "I learned much of his life that is unknown even to his closest friends—of his boyhood, his early struggles, his hopes, his aims. I trust I am betraying no confidence when I state that a good deal of the real boy is blended with the 'Story of Tom Sawyer.'" Clemens often acknowledged as much, perhaps too much. He sometimes appropriated from fiction events that he claimed happened in his own life in order to absolve himself of the charge of plagiarism. But several episodes, both in plot and in detail, derive from other fiction, such as the grave-robbing scene from Charles Dickens's *A Tale of Two Cities* or the doughnut stealing from B. P. Shillaber's Mrs. Partington tales. *Tom Sawyer* is, ultimately, a piece of fiction that draws on and transmutes many sources.

Central to the way Clemens developed that fiction of childhood was his growing sense of parenthood. By the time of his November 1873 conversations with Stoddard, Clemens's first child, Langdon, had been dead over a year and his second, Susy, was alive, thriving, and in that fascinating stage of development between ages one and two. In watching Susy, Clemens began to see childhood in fact, rather than through cultural lenses of what childhood is supposed to be. Naturally, it made him think as much about what childrearing should entail, and the contrast that formed with his own experience. Specifically, the contrast between Calvinist ideas of childrearing and the reality of communal love for children—the painful battle between discipline and indulgence—inspires the novel. As Polly puts it in the opening chapter: "I ain't doing my duty by that boy, and that's the Lord's truth, goodness knows. Spare the rod and spile the child, as the Good Book says. I'm a-laying up sin and suffering for us both *I* know. He's full of the Old Scratch, but laws-a-me! he's my own dead sister's boy, poor thing, and I ain't got the heart to lash him, somehow. Every time I let him off my conscience does hurt me so, and every time I hit him my old heart most breaks." As Susy developed, so did Clemens's interest in his novel; he finally turned to writing in earnest in 1874. That summer saw him writing at a steady clip before he finally ran out of inspiration, as he explained in a letter to Dr. John Brown: "I have been writing fifty pages of manuscript a day, on an average, for sometime now. . . . But night before last I discovered that that day's chapter was a failure . . . and so I must burn up the day's work and do it over again" (4 September 1874). But rather than return immediately, he let the manuscript lie, in accordance with his preferred *work habits, until the following year, probably after a visit from William Dean Howells in March. "I got intellectual friction enough out of your visit," he wrote Howells, "to be able to go to work Monday. Which turned out to be correct—I wrote 4000 words yesterday" (16 March 1875). He may, here, have been referring specifically to "Old Times on the Mississippi," which the *Atlantic* was then running in installments, but the burst of writing carried through to the novel. Sometime in spring 1875 he got back into the swing of *Tom Sawyer*, finishing the remaining two-fifths of the manuscript by the end of June and beginning serious revisions through the summer. He delivered the manuscript for production on 5 November 1875, but kept revising the novel through the fall of 1876, making numerous changes in the proofs.

Clemens wrote the book without a clear sense of audience, writing more out of his own nostalgia for childhood and thus with himself as the audience. In thinking of childhood experience from an adult point of view but without any loss of feeling for the subjectivity of the child, he wrote a story that is indulgent, rather than judgmental, in its humorous attitude toward childhood, but that clearly relishes adulthood. In this sense, his first plan was to have the book be for adults, not children: "It is *not* a boy's book, at all. It will only be read by adults. It is only written for adults." (to Howells, 5 July 1875).

When he told Howells of the book during the latter's visit to Hartford in June 1875, Howells encouraged him, even asking to serialize it in the *Atlantic*. But on reading a copy of the manuscript, Howells saw what Clemens did not, that the book could work best as a children's book, expanding the potential audience appreciably:

> I finished reading Tom Sawyer a week ago, sitting up till one A.M. to get to the end, simply because it was impossible to leave off. It's altogether the best boy's story I ever read. It will be an immense success. But I think you ought to treat it explicitly *as* a boy's story. Grown-ups will enjoy it just as much if you do; and if you should put it forth as a study of boy character from the grown-up point of view, you'd give the wrong key to it. (21 November 1875)

When his wife agreed with Howells, Clemens went about editing in earnest to make the book suitable for children, cleaning up mild profanity in various places and cutting some images that would require embarrassing explanations to an audience of children. In his 18 January 1876 letter to Howells thanking him for his editorial help, Clemens wrote:

> I finally concluded to cut the Sunday-school speech down to the first two sentences, (leaving no suggestion of satire, since the book is to be for boys & girls; I tamed the various obscenities until I judged that [they] no longer carried offense. . . . There was one expression which perhaps you overlooked. When Huck is complaining to Tom of the rigorous system in vogue at the widow's, he says the servants harass him with all manner of compulsory decencies, & he winds up by saying "and they comb me all to hell." . . . Since the book is now professedly & confessedly a boy's & girls's book, that dern word bothers me some nights, but it never did until I had ceased to regard the volume as being for adults.

The word came out, of course, as did much overt satire, though some subtler social commentary remains.

None of these alterations changed the book's appeal to adults, for all really good children's books appeal as deeply, albeit for different reasons, to the adults who read them to children. *Tom Sawyer* does that particularly well because its initial focus was not clearly on children, so there is none of the saccharine condescension and mistargeting of a child's capacities that mar so many children's books.

Part of the compound appeal of the book lies in the complexity of its moral themes. While the book is substantially an exercise in nostalgia—"a hymn," as Twain called it in a 8 September 1887 letter, "put into prose form to give it a worldly air"—it does also suggest something of a boy's growth in moral consciousness, though not into adult responsibility. Because Tom never has adult responsibilities to give his behavior any significant consequences, his moral growth is halting and capricious, but the book is nonetheless a Bildungsroman with a moral lesson. It describes the gradual dawning of Tom's moral sense through the exercise of sympathetic imagination.

In this interest in moral development, Clemens showed his continuing concern with sentimentalism as an ethical system, especially as he learned of it through his reading of W. E. H. *Lecky's *History of European Morals*. Twain's works show continued development of this theme in concurrent and later projects, such as "The Facts Concerning the Recent Carnival of Crime in Connecticut" (1876), which Clemens wrote while revising *Tom Sawyer*, and *Adventures of Huckleberry Finn*, which he began while *Tom Sawyer* was in press but did not finish until nearly a decade later. In each of these cases, he examines the development of conscience as a collaboration of experience and imagination, rather than as an implanted and absolute sense of right and wrong. The question that vexed him was the degree to which one could rely on conscience in this collaboration to create a truly viable moral compass. In *Tom Sawyer* he argued that it could, even in the case of someone as self-absorbed as Tom.

In having Tom learn his own moral code, the book argues against the Calvinist notion of innate depravity. Twain even has Tom's Aunt Polly, superficially an orthodox Calvinist, state the book's case when she believes Tom has drowned: "He warn't bad, so to say—only mischeevous. Only just giddy, and harum-scarum, you know. He warn't any more responsible than a colt. He never meant any harm, and he was the best-hearted boy that ever was" (chapter 15). In seeing a good heart behind bad behavior, she goes further than John Locke ever did in describing the child as a blank slate; she attributes basic goodness to him.

The degree to which Twain has Polly speak his own position becomes clear in an episode in which Tom takes Becky's punishment for tearing the frontispiece of the schoolmaster's prized anatomy book (chapter 20). At first when Tom realizes she will suffer the consequences of her crime, he shrugs it off as unfortunate but of no real concern. When he sees her fear upon imminent discovery, however, his reaction changes: "Tom shot a glance at Becky. He had seen a hunted and helpless rabbit look as she did, with a gun leveled at its head. Instantly he forgot his quarrel with her. Quick—something must be done!" Tom's change of heart arises not from his own sense of the shame of punishment, but from his sympathetic imagination, which gives him insight into the depths of Becky's fear.

Tom cannot understand Becky's fear because he is unaware of his culture's expectations regarding feminine innocence of all things sexual. But by having Becky tear "a handsomely engraved and colored frontispiece—a human figure, stark naked," Twain suggests what is really at stake here: a knowledge of sexuality, which Victorian children were not supposed to have. In staving off Becky's exposure for her crime, Tom protects Becky's reputation for innocence, a reputation that Twain shows as correlating with reality. After all, Becky's curiosity is truly innocent, much as Tom's transgressions throughout, lacking the intention to sin, are fundamentally innocent. Twain thus demonstrates that children begin amoral and rise to self-consciously ethical adulthood by becoming conscious of the fears and desires of other people only after having experienced fears and desires of their own. It is a sentimental ethics, one that preaches self-sacrifice as the defining trait of moral action, but one that advocates a larger range of childhood experience as its basis.

But a countertext to this theme is the pleasure a child takes in his amoral state, and the greater pleasure the world takes in participating vicariously in that moral freedom. Tom builds his world on fantasy without drawing distinctions between benign play and harmful lies. The community relishes the show of Tom's imagination, and all participate, with greater or lesser degrees of willingness, in the exercise of "showing off." In most of the book's episodes, characters treat each other as means to selfish ends; Tom's superiority invariably has to do with his superior chicanery, his capacity to make others serve his ends better than they make him serve theirs. In his preface, Twain says that he plans in part "to pleasantly remind adults of what they once were themselves." In the nostalgic glow of such remembered childhood, St. Petersburg's mutual yet competitive utilitarianism seems merely quaint and amusing, and the reader is comfortably allowed to stand superior to all the characters in using them for his or her own pleasure. But the moral danger of that kind of voyeurism turned into a problem for Twain, as he began to develop it in *A Tramp Abroad* and *Huckleberry Finn*, both of which turn away from the comfortable rationalizations that make Tom's, and the town's, moral failings enchanting.

While *Tom Sawyer* ultimately became Mark Twain's best-selling book, its initial sales were relatively weak. The economic depression of 1873–1880 partly explains the slow sales, but the bungling of the timing of the American publication, abetted by Clemens, contributed even more. Elisha Bliss's American Publishing Company delayed production significantly in spring 1876, but Clemens compounded the delays by a deliberate decision to wait for the holiday market, even though Howells had already written a review for *The Atlantic Monthly*'s May issue:

> Bliss made a failure in the matter of getting Tom Sawyer ready on time—the engravers assisting, as usual. I went down to see how *much* of a delay there was going to be, & found that the man had not even put a canvasser on or issued an advertisement yet—in fact that the *electrotypes* would not all be done for a month! . . . When I observed that my Sketches had dropped from a sale of 6 or 7000 a month down to 1200 a month, I said *this* ain't no time to be publishing books; therefore, let Tom lay still till autumn, Mr. Bliss, & make a holiday book of him to beguile the young people withal." (to Howells, 26 April 1876)

Still, wasting publicity was not the main problem. The real mistake was to go ahead with the British and Continental editions. Chatto and Windus brought out the English edition, without illustrations or any of Clemens's last-minute editorial changes, in June. Canadian publisher Belford Brothers pirated that edition and flooded the American market with copies in late July, over four months before the first authorized American edition came out on 8 December. Not surprisingly, sales of the authorized edition, and consequently royalties to Clemens, languished. First-year sales amounted to only 23,638, which compared atrociously to *Innocents Abroad* (69,156), *Roughing It* (65,376), and *The Gilded Age* (50,325). On the basis of this experience Clemens resolved to seek alternatives to the American Publishing Company, ultimately founding his own publishing firm of *Webster and Company.

Contrary to tradition, while the popularity of the Canadian piracy robbed *Tom Sawyer*'s author of royalties, it did not rob *Tom Sawyer* of publicity. The book was well reviewed in England, and many American journals either reviewed the book in advance by excerpting British reviews or using the British text, or reviewed it early in 1877 after the American edition came out. The book was indeed a critical as well as a popular success from the beginning. It shows no signs of losing popularity, and indeed its star is likely to shine until the day that Tom Sawyer's whitewashing scam falls out of favor as one of America's favorite myths.

AFRICAN AMERICANS. In his autobiography, Clemens describes his contact with slaves on his uncle John Quarles's farm in Missouri: "It was on the farm that I got my strong liking of his [i.e. of "Uncle Dan'l," one of the slaves Quarles held] race and my appreciation of certain of its fine qualities. This feeling and this esti-mate have stood the test of sixty years and more and have suffered no impairment. The black face is as welcome to me now as it was then" (*North American Review*, 1 March 1907). Here Clemens allows *nostalgia to cover a more complex reality, to rewrite his own much less generous history. His early attitudes toward African Americans were like those of many in the slave-holding South. He had regular, familiar interactions with blacks, but on terms that required their subservience and gave a tenuous sense of superiority to the whites. Clemens acknowledged as much in his autobiography: "All the negroes were friends of ours, and with those of our own age we were in effect comrades. I say in effect, using the phrase as a modifica-tion. We were comrades, and yet not comrades; color and condition interposed a subtle line which both parties were conscious of, and which rendered complete fusion impossible." Certainly in situations beyond the familiar, Clemens as a young man drew that line as boldly and strenuously as possible, expressing anxiety about his place and condition in a culture in turmoil over both race and slavery. The dif-ference between Clemens and other men of his era, however, was that he changed. Over the course of his lifetime, he developed an increasing social consciousness of the wrongs done to African Americans and acted on that consciousness to become a public and private activist for the rights and social improvement of blacks not only in America, but also throughout the world.

Such a journey would have been difficult to predict from his earliest public pro-nouncement on the subject. In his first known letter, a 24 August 1853 missive from New York City to his mother in Hannibal, Missouri, and published in Orion

*Clemens's *Hannibal Journal*, he wrote, "When I saw the Court House in Syracuse, it called to mind the time when it was surrounded by chains and companies of soldiers, to prevent the rescue of McReynolds' nigger, for in these Eastern States niggers are considerably better than white people." He refers here to a failed attempt to enforce the Fugitive Slave Act in favor of a Hannibal-area slave owner, John McReynolds. In 1851, Jerry McHenry, a slave who had escaped from McReynolds, was captured in Syracuse, where he had lived for several years. The police tried to hold him for a time before an angry abolitionist mob forced McHenry's release. Clemens's attitudes here, facing for the first time a majority of abolitionists, reacted defensively, suggesting doubts about his sense of racial superiority.

Such defensiveness persisted through the 1860s, even after he had become a supporter of the Union cause in the Civil War. His "Mark Twain on the Colored Man," a report about San Francisco's Fourth of July parade of 1865, displays a vulgar attitude toward blacks who marched:

> I was rather irritated at the idea of letting these fellows march in the procession myself, at first, but I would have scorned to harbor so small a thought of it had I known the privilege was going to do them so much good. There seemed to be a religious-benevolent society among them with a banner . . . and all hands seemed to take boundless pride in it. The banner had a picture on it, but I could not exactly get the hang of its significance. It presented a very black and uncommonly sick looking nigger, in bed, attended by two other niggers—one reading the Bible to him and the other one handing him a plate of oysters; but what the very mischief this blending of contraband dissolution, raw oysters and Christian consolation, could possibly be symbolical of, was more than I could make out.

In fact, 1865 was the first year blacks had been invited to march in Fourth of July parades in California cities. Such invitations met with wide and vociferous protest, and in Stockton and Placerville blacks declined the invitations in order to prevent riots. But in San Francisco, they marched—last in parade order—and were enthusiastically applauded by the onlookers. Most protesters boycotted the parade.

Clemens had by this time an open friendship with the black editor of the San Francisco *Elevator*, but in a common pattern for southerners, he distinguished easily between personal friendship and public sentiment. His sketch gives little sign of his changing political opinions about African Americans, but that little may indicate the dawning of a satirical bent in attacking in others the prejudicial feelings he knew well in himself: "The 'damned naygurs'—this is another descriptive title which has been conferred upon them by a class of our fellow citizens who persist, in the most short-sighted manner, in being on bad terms with them in the face of the fact that they have got to sing with them in heaven or scorch with them in hell some day in the most familiar and sociable way, and on a footing of most perfect equality." Here Clemens takes a swipe at the predominantly Irish protesters against the inclusion of blacks in the parade. His animosity toward the Irish overcame his anxiety about blacks, leading in a grudging and ironic way to an acknowledgment of racial equality.

Over the next ten years, Clemens steadily dispensed with his grudge. In renouncing the South, in seeing northern industry and wealth as a correlate of northern mores, he also renounced his racism against blacks. In particular, his courtship of Olivia Langdon put him in the company of upstate New York racial liberals, people who had actively resisted slavery and who courted the society of men like Frederick *Douglass. By the time he developed a friendship with William Dean *Howells, whose father, too, was an active abolitionist, and who himself worked throughout his life for the improvement of conditions for African Americans, Clemens had struggled hard to change his attitudes. Howells encouraged Clemens's change in conversation, letters, and publishing. He accepted with great enthusiasm Clemens's "A *True Story" for the 1874 *Atlantic Monthly* and asked for more such stories. While Clemens produced none similar, he did combat stereotypical notions of African Americans in small ways. For instance, in the "Bluejay Yarn" in *Tramp Abroad* (1880), Jim Baker describes the blue jay's Herculean labor with the comparison, "he worked like a nigger." Given the commonly held stereotype that all black people were lazy, such a simile works against the grain in a positive way, especially given the *social class of a narrator who uses the pejorative epithet "nigger."

In his personal life, Clemens in the 1880s actively supported individual blacks and African-American institutions. In 1884, for instance, he began paying for the board of Warner T. McGuinn, one of Yale Law School's first black students and ultimately a successful civil rights lawyer who mentored Thurgood Marshall. Clemens explained his charity in a 24 December 1885 letter of inquiry to the Yale Law School's dean:

> Do you know him? And is he worthy? I do not believe I would very cheerfully help a white student who would ask a benevolence of a stranger, but I do not feel so about the other color. We have ground the manhood out of them, & the shame is ours, not theirs, & we should pay for it.
>
> If this young man lives as economically as it is & should be the pride of one who is straitened, I would like to know what the cost is, so that I may send 6, 12, or 14 months' board, as the size of the bill may determine.

Clemens ended up paying for a year and a half's board, covering the remainder of McGuinn's time at Yale.

Such conscience money shows as much about Twain's attitudes toward whites as toward blacks. Perhaps more revealing is a 27 February 1881 letter to Howells describing a charity reading Clemens was scheduled to give for an African-American church:

> On the evening of March 10th, I am going to read to the colored folk in the African church here, (no whites admitted except such as I bring with me,) & a choir of colored folk will sing Jubilee songs. I count on a good time, & shall hope to have you folks there, & Livy. I read in Twichell's chapel Friday night, & had a most rattling high time—but the thing that went best of all was Uncle Remus's Tar Baby—I mean to try that on my dusky audience. They've all heard that tale from childhood—at least the older members have.

Despite his best intentions, he still demonstrated a persistent condescension about racial difference.

This attitude never wholly disappeared, though he turned it into a counter-racism by which he came, out of guilt and embarrassment, to dislike his own race:

> Mrs. Clemens has said a bright thing. A drop letter came to me asking me to lecture here for a <baptist> church debt. I began to rage <as usual> over the exceedingly cool wording of the request, when Mrs. Clemens said "I think I know that church; & if so, this preacher is a colored man—he doesn't know how to write a polished letter—how should he?"
>
> My manner changed so suddenly & so radically that Mrs. C said: "I will give you a motto, & it will be useful to you if you will adopt it: 'Consider every man colored till he is proved white.'" (to Howells, 17 September 1884)

The particular context here of making allowances for a man not trained in the nuances of Victorian etiquette spilled outward in his life as a more general motto about the value of the two races. By the time he wrote *Following the Equator*, he said he preferred nonwhites to whites, turning the symbolic "white" skin into a disability by contrast:

> The white man's complexion makes no concealments. It can't. It seems to have been designed as a catch-all for everything that can damage it. Ladies have to paint it, and powder it, and cosmetic it, and diet it with arsenic, and enamel it, and be always enticing it, and persuading it, and pestering it, and fussing at it, to make it beautiful; and they do not succeed. But these efforts show what they think of the natural complexion. . . . The advantage is with the Zulu, I think. He starts with a beautiful complexion, and it will last him through. And as for the Indian brown—firm smooth, blemishless, pleasant and restful to the eye, afraid of no color, harmonizing with all colors and adding a grace to them all—I think there is no sort of chance for the average white complexion against that rich and perfect tint. (chapter 41)

Many of Clemens's readers would consider such statements race treason in the late nineteenth century.

In part such taste signaled Clemens's growing cosmopolitanism, but the attack on white complexion suggests something akin to the guilt and shame expressed in his letter inquiring about McGuinn. This guilt allowed him not only to glory in dark skin pigmentation, but also to indulge positive stereotypes of blacks like those promulgated by Harriet Beecher *Stowe a generation earlier. In her racialist argument against slavery, Stowe saw African Americans as innately religious, gentle, and patient in contrast to the "martial" character of "Anglo-Saxons." While she inverted the usual argument that tropical peoples are passionate in contrast to the "rational" coldness of races from northern climes, she still argued that blacks and whites were essentially different. Since Clemens suggested, embracing *utilitarianism, that "training is all there is to a person" (in *Connecticut Yankee*) and "training is everything" (in *Pudd'nhead Wilson*), it is hard to see how he could make blanket statements about racial characteristics. But he did, even in his autobiography. Again describing his childhood contact with blacks on his uncle's farm, Clemens wrote:

> We had a faithful and affectionate good friend, ally and adviser in "Uncle Dan'l," a middle-aged slave whose head was the best on in the negro quarter, whose sympathies were wide and warm, and whose heart was honest and simple and knew no guile. He has served me well, these many, many years. I have not seen him for more than half a century, and yet spiritually I have had his welcome company a good part of that time, and have staged him in books under his own name and as "Jim," and carted him all around—to Hannibal, down the Mississippi on a raft, and even across the desert of Sahara in a balloon—and he has endured it all with the patience and friendliness and loyalty which were his birthright.

Although his autobiographical statements distort the past, his fundamentally realistic perception, one of the attributes that helped make him such a gifted writer, enabled him in his fiction to challenge such simplistic attitudes, instead giving black characters a wider range of actions and motivation. For instance, Jim in *Adventures of Huckleberry Finn* is not the "Dan'l" of the autobiography, though he may have been the "Dan'l" of fact. He used his intelligence to carve out what freedom and dignity he could in oppressive circumstances, manipulating Huck even as he cared for him. Similarly, in the figure of Roxana in *Pudd'nhead Wilson*, Clemens gives a black character a heart far from simple, honest, and guileless.

One of Twain's most powerful black characters, Jasper in the unfinished novel *Which Was It?*, reveals a calculating and vengeful black man who, when finally in possession of information by which he can blackmail an influential white man, brilliantly turns the tables, making himself the master and the white man the slave. In such fictional depictions of blacks, Clemens shows attributes of patience and apparent guilelessness as the necessary superficial adaptations African Americans made to white power, but he does not suggest these accurately reflect reality. In *Which Was It?*, just before Jasper reveals his anger and desire for revenge for all the indignities he suffered even as a putatively free black man in the slave-holding South, the narrator sardonically observes, "The whites imagined that the negroes did not mind it. They judged by the negro's outside, and forgot to inquire within."

Perhaps in his personal dealings with African Americans he looked beyond the outsides—we will never know. But when he wrote what professed to be nonfiction, he often retailed superficial stereotypes. In his fiction he was more likely to inquire deeply within; in his fiction he found it easier to overcome the habits of his time and place.

AFTERLIFE. While Samuel Clemens remained perpetually in doubt about the existence or nature of God, he had no questions whatsoever about the nonexistence of an afterlife. As a popular writer, he rarely allowed himself the luxury, however, of making that statement public, primarily because in the early years of his career, he discovered the emotional power of the idea of heaven in the enormous popularity of Elizabeth Stuart Phelps's *The Gates Ajar*. Phelps, following the basic principles of Anglican Bishop Joseph Butler's *Analogy of Religion*, argued that one could extrapolate the existence and character of heaven on the basis of life as known in the world. In a country still dominated not by the deism, Unitarianism, or pantheistic transcendentalism of the New England elites but by fundamentalists who took the promises of heaven quite literally, Phelps's vision resonated, precisely because she promised

Illustration by Daniel Carter Beard (1850–1941), from *Following the Equator*, Hartford: American Publishing Company, 1897, p. 240.

heaven for all. With the deaths of so many in the Civil War holding heaven in the nation's consciousness, the promise of nearly universal salvation appealed broadly.

Clemens's absolute contempt for what he called in his *autobiography Phelps's "mean little ten-cent heaven about the size of Rhode Island" led him to write an elaborate reductio ad absurdum not only of Phelps's idea of heaven but of the idea of heaven itself. Clemens first drafted "Captain Stormfield's Visit to Heaven" in 1868, completely rewrote it between 1878 and 1880, and added to it in the early 1900s. But he suppressed the story for fear of insulting and alienating his public, as well as his wife. After his wife's death, and after years of public debate over the implications of evolutionary theory, the literal belief in heaven had apparently waned enough for Clemens to come forward with his "*Extract from Captain Stormfield's Visit to Heaven." He published it in *Harper's Monthly in two install-ments in 1907–1908 and in a single volume—Twain's last in his lifetime—in 1909.

Fear of ostracism may have restrained his making strong public statements against conventional ideas of heaven, but privately he railed against heaven as at best the delusion of a mad species, at worst the hypocrisy of a race of charlatans. In a piece written in 1885 probably intended to be read to, but never delivered at, the *Monday Evening Club, Twain called it a lie "that there is something about [man] that ought to be perpetuated—in heaven, in hell, or somewhere." In "Letters from the Earth," Twain has Satan describe the human concept of heaven as a product of a grotesquely silly human imagination:

> He has imagined a heaven, and has left entirely out of it the supremest of all his delights, the one ecstasy that stands first and foremost in the heart of every individual of his race—and ours—sexual intercourse!
>
> It is as if a lost and perishing person in a roasting desert should be told by a rescuer he might choose and have all longed for things but one, and he should elect to leave out water!
>
> His heaven is like himself: strange, interesting, astonishing, grotesque. I give you my word, it has not a single feature in it that he *actually values*.

Such energetic condemnation Twain kept in private, with posthumous publication finally revealing the strength of his beliefs.

In public, Twain stated his opinion less directly, as in his 1895 "Contract with Mrs. T. K. Beecher," published in *Munsey's Magazine*:

> If you prove right and I prove wrong,
>   A million years from now,
> In language plain and frank and strong
>   My error I'll avow
>   To your dear waking face.

If I prove right, by God His grace,
 Full sorry I shall be,
For in that solitude no trace
 There'll be of you and me.

A million years, O patient stone,
 You've waited for this message.
Deliver it a million hence;
 (Survivor pays expressage.)

Humbler in stance, this verse would likely offend fewer than would such direct denunciations as those Twain kept private. In other cases, Twain's indirect satire shielded him from the scorn he anticipated, as when in *Adventures of Huckleberry Finn*, he has Huck want to go to "the bad place" because he wants to be with Tom Sawyer. The joke's literalness and naïveté protected Twain, as did his stance of joker who could praise, without deeply challenging the existence of either, "heaven for climate, hell for society."

♦ SEE ALSO Ingersoll, Robert G.; Religion.

AGE OF REASON, THE. Dictating for his *autobiography on 15 May 1908, Twain recalled his first reading of Thomas Paine's deist philosophy: "It took a brave man before the Civil War to confess he had read the *Age of Reason* . . . and yet that seems a mild book now. I read it first when I was a cub pilot, read it with fear and hesitation, but marveling at its fearlessness and wonderful power. I read it again a year or two ago, for some reason, and was amazed to see how tame it had become. It seemed that Paine was apologizing everywhere for hurting the feelings of the reader." Yet without that apologetic tone, young Samuel Clemens would not have been able to read it. Even though his father, John Marshall *Clemens, was a deist, young Clemens was more influenced by the *Calvinism of his mother and community. Not until he began his piloting apprenticeship in 1857 was Clemens ready to entertain other points of view. Already a voracious reader whose intellectual ramblings reinforced a nascent skepticism, he found his reading of Paine's philosophy to be an intellectual watershed, broadening his horizons at precisely the point in his life when his social circumstances allowed him to take advantage of it. No more would the biblical literalism of his mother's teaching hold him abjectly in its power; instead he found in Paine a cogent belief in a deistic universe, put in motion by a distant God whose purposes did not run to vindictive punishment of sinners. Human life was in human hands under the dictates of nature. While Clemens did not maintain the optimism of Paine's deism for his entire life, he never left Paine's intellectual universe, accepting Paine's ideas not only about God, but about *religion as a human artifact, government's appropriate role in securing human happiness, and the importance of dissent.

♦ SEE ALSO Politics; Reading, Clemens's; Revolution.

ALCOHOL. In *Hannibal, Missouri, in the 1840s, a number of bars and at least one distillery flourished as energetically as did a large *temperance movement. With two models before him, the adolescent Clemens, setting out from Hannibal for the first time in search of work as a compositor, took the temperance pledge, promising his mother that he would not drink. But in just over a decade, passing through his careers as a printer and steamboat pilot, his attitudes and practices changed. By Christmas Eve 1863, he got so drunk while visiting Charles Farrar *Browne that, when Browne said, "I can't walk on the earth. . . . I feel like walking on the skies, but as I can't I'll walk on the roofs," Twain followed him (quoted in Joseph P. Goodman, "Artemus Ward: His Visit to the Comstock Load," San Francisco *Chronicle*, 10 January 1892, p. 1).

The temperance promise was broken but not forgotten, and by 1868, when Clemens began courting Olivia Langdon, he was ready to reseal his bargain. Langdon was the daughter of dedicated temperance crusaders, who were anxious about Clemens's reputation as a drinker. Clemens's earnest and simultaneous pursuit of temperance and Christian conversion marked his efforts to regain control over his life as well as to secure him a wife, and on both counts he proved successful. He never again drank with the same intensity and regularity as in his far western days, but neither did he stick to the narrow path of strict abstinence. He soon was telling his new wife how to mix old-fashioneds for him, and before long, she, too, was drinking ale.

It is no wonder, then, that alcohol figures so prominently in Twain's fiction, though it is somewhat surprising that drunkards are usually fools or worse. The constant joking about drinking in his California and Nevada journalism, as in "The Unreliable" or "The Launch of the Steamer Capital," implies he relished alcohol. In most of the writing after his marriage, the censoriousness of temperance tracts makes an appearance. Muff Potter in *Tom Sawyer*, Tom Canty's father in *Prince and the Pauper*, and pap, the king, and the duke in *Adventures of Huckleberry Finn* all suggest the degree to which Twain either agreed with or pandered to temperance opinion. Even writing for himself rather than for the public, Clemens in his later years created characters whose evil was correlated to drinking, as in the case of Adolph and Wilhelm Meidling in the first of three *Mysterious Stranger* manuscripts. Meidling, normally a paragon of human decency, runs to the bottle when he loses the affections of his fiancée. Only under the influence does his melancholy turn to murderous rage. No matter how difficult a time he had hewing to the path of abstemiousness, Twain seemed to agree that alcohol could be either sign or cause of evil.

Twain's work, however, does not accept the usual conjunction of Christianity with self-control, but rather often equates drunkenness with religiosity. As early as

Roughing It, Twain suggests that a facile belief in the promises of an ordered, predestined universe is akin to alcoholic delusion. In chapter 53, inebriated Jim Blaine tells the assembled boys that "prov'dence don't fire no blank ca'tridges," even though a dog, in its clear-sighted realism, "can't be depended on to carry out a special providence." Years later, having reread Jonathan Edwards's "On the Freedom of Will," Clemens wrote in a letter to Rev. Joseph *Twichell that it was like being "on a three day's tear with a drunken lunatic."

Out of the contrariness of humor, he could call sobriety the real social evil, as in a letter to Augustin Daly: "Excuse me to Miss Dreher for that I went away without saying good-night—I mean good morning—& explain that I always act like that when sober, & am always remorseful for it as soon as I get normal again" (25 April 1887). More frequently and importantly, he links fantasy and to some degree liberation with drunkenness. Hank Morgan in *Connecticut Yankee* says he has no imagination, but his unreliability as a narrator has as much to do with the amount of alcohol he consumes before beginning his story as it does with his extraordinary lack of self-knowledge. In declaring himself to be a man barren of sentiment and imagination, Hank creates a fantasy self at odds with the power of his imagination. To a degree, alcohol here is a sign of imaginative power. The same is true in *Those Extraordinary Twins*, where Angelo's temperance seems dull and flat beside Luigi's passion. Angelo grows most interesting, though less fortunate, when Luigi gets him drunk.

Thus, as much as Mark Twain depicted alcohol conventionally as a destructive power, a source of anarchy and disorder, he also depicted it as a creative power in its very liberation from order. The preface of *Roughing It*, with its reference to the author as "tight" when writing, is a tribute to creativity, and several characters in the book suggest the same. For instance, the "Admiral" (chapter 62), who begins each day with three tumblers of whiskey, dominates all conversation out of the well of his irrepressible imagination. Imagination meant much to a humorist with a metaphysical bent, tumbling out toward the end of his career in strange fantasies such as "The Great Dark" and "Three Thousand Years among the Microbes," the plots of both of which depend on the creative energy unleashed by drink.

ALDRICH, THOMAS BAILEY (1836–1907). Aldrich, one of the most scintillating members of William Dean *Howells's literary circle, was also a friend of Clemens. Some propose that Aldrich's *The Story of a Bad Boy* (1869) was one of the literary models for Twain's *The Adventures of Tom Sawyer*, though the two took radically different stylistic and narrative paths. In a letter to Olivia Langdon (27 December 1869), Clemens said he was reading *The Story of a Bad Boy*, "but for the life of me I could not admire the volume much." Regardless of the degree to which Aldrich's book actually influenced Twain's, Aldrich, as a respected poet, journalist, and writer, helped pave the way toward respectability for books that challenged simplistic notions of childhood innocence. Twain's own books of boyhood owe much to that path, if not to the model itself.

Aldrich, like most men of letters of the nineteenth century, considered his poetry to be his most important work, though it was as a war correspondent during the Civil War and as the man who succeeded Howells as the editor of The *Atlantic Monthly (1881–1890) that he made his major public marks. He took the *Atlantic* back into a conservative literary path after Howells's expansive and creative leadership, suggesting a growing rift between conservative sentimental realists of the New England school and other writers of the period.

Among his acquaintances and friends, Aldrich was perhaps best known for his conversation, which was very different from Clemens's: Aldrich was known for, in Howells's words, "his heat-lightning shimmer of wit" rather than for his storytelling. In the first published installment of his *autobiography, Twain wrote, "Aldrich has never had his peer for prompt and pithy and witty and humorous sayings. None has equalled him, certainly none has surpassed him, in the felicity of phrasing with which he clothed these children of his fancy. Aldrich was always brilliant, he couldn't help it, he is a fire-opal set round with rose diamonds; when he is not speaking, you know that his dainty fancies are twinkling and glimmering around in him; when he speaks the diamonds flash." But the friendship that Clemens wished to cultivate with such a star of conversation—an art Clemens held in high esteem—never flourished as his friendship did with Howells, substantially because Aldrich married a woman Clemens could not stand. The feeling was in all likelihood reciprocated. In any event, Clemens's animosity began in the winter of 1871–1872 when Aldrich spontaneously invited Clemens to his house to meet his wife and share a family dinner. Clemens's unfashionable clothing and drawling speech appalled Lilian Woodman Aldrich. Assuming he was drunk, she refused to serve dinner. While she did express regret when she learned that Clemens was completely sober, she never could forgive Clemens his outrages against conventional *fashion. For his part, Clemens never forgave the initial snub.

In parts of his autobiography he did not publish, Clemens explained the impossibility of pursuing the friendship between the families when he considered Mrs. Aldrich "a strange and vanity-devoured, detestable woman! I do not believe I could ever learn to like her except on a raft at sea with no other provisions in sight." Clemens nonetheless maintained his professional and, to some degree personal, connection with Aldrich, even—despite reservations and resentments—appearing as the final speaker at a ceremony dedicating an Aldrich memorial library in Portsmouth, New Hampshire.

AMERICAN CLAIMANT, THE (1892). Clemens first planned this novel in 1884 in a notebook entry, "Turn Sellers play into a novel." This note refers to a farcical *drama written in *collaboration with William Dean *Howells in 1883. But when Howells withdrew his support for the venture, Clemens dropped the idea temporarily as business pursuits crowded writing out of Clemens's schedule. When on the verge of bankruptcy in the early 1890s, Clemens returned to writing with a vengeance, in order to make money. That is when, with Howells's permission, Twain converted the play to a novel by fleshing out descriptions and adding political material, by which he converted a simple farce into a bizarre commentary on democracy and culture.

Not surprisingly, most of the tales turned out in the frenetic early 1890s are even more uneven than the bulk of Twain's oeuvre, and much of this work, including *The American Claimant*, has been neglected by book buyers and literary critics alike. *Claimant* does, however, speak provocatively to many of Clemens's main concerns. As both a counterpoint to *A Connecticut Yankee in King Arthur's Court* and a commentary on Clemens's business and financial troubles, it shows much about his emotional and artistic resiliency.

By having crazy Colonel *Sellers believe that he has found a way to rematerialize the dead and so provide cheap labor for American industry, Clemens gives himself a comic counterpoint to the book's serious discussion of the *labor movement. At the same time, Twain finds a comic exorcism of his rage at the failure of the *Paige typesetter, in which Twain invested heavily, to live up to its promise, to replace human typesetters whose high skill level made them an expensive part of the publishing industry. In a sense, Clemens may have seen himself as a Sellers-like character, investing in dreams that turned out to be pure nonsense. But in the character of the irrepressible Sellers, Clemens postulated an alternative to despair at failure. That this alternative is a kind of madness hints at Clemens's desperation, but that it is comic entails a kind of redemption.

Clemens's appreciation of comedy is the greatest value of this short novel. In discussing the intractability of political problems in *Connecticut Yankee*, Clemens has Hank Morgan lament that his revolution ended when the nobility collectively frowned at the masses, and the masses, cowering in abject terror at the disapproval of their ostensible superiors, returned to their stations. In *Claimant* he suggests, instead, the power of laughter. In the words of his American skeptic, Barrow, "There isn't any power on earth that can prevent England's thirty millions from electing themselves dukes and duchesses to-morrow and calling themselves so. And within six months all the former dukes and duchesses would have retired from the business. . . . Royalty itself couldn't survive such a process. A handful of frowners against thirty million laughers in a state of eruption: Why, it's Herculaneum against Vesuvius" (chapter 11).

Clemens concentrates primarily on the political consequences of this kind of laughter. In particular, he defends the American press against the attacks of Matthew *Arnold:

Well, the charge is, that our press has but little of that old world quality, reverence. Let us be candidly grateful that it is so. . . . Our press is certainly bankrupt in the "thrill of awe"—otherwise reverence; reverence for nickel plate and brummagem. Let us sincerely hope that this fact will remain a fact forever; for to my mind a discriminating irreverence is the creator and protector of human liberty—even as the other thing is the creator, nurse, and steadfast protector of all forms of human slavery, bodily and mental. (chapter 10)

In this political dimension, Clemens supports laughter's seriousness in satire.

In *Claimant* he also finds the personal value of humor. Berkeley, in despair over his inability to find work, finally gets a job he *can* do—daubing comic paintings. He begins this work only after finding that viewing the paintings of his soon-to-be partners gives him his first good laugh in months. But he still will not consider stooping to the level of working as a humorist. When he finally does, he finds himself "obliged to confess to himself that there was something about work—even such grotesque and humble work as this—which most pleasantly satisfied something in his nature which had never been satisfied before, and also gave him a strange new dignity in his own private view of himself" (chapter 17). In a way, this is Clemens's own history recapitulated. He began his career as a humorist concerned that it was a "poor, pitiful business," but finally came to see the value of laughter, not merely as a calling or even as a political weapon, but ultimately as an outlook on life.

♦ SEE ALSO *Colonel Sellers*; Finances; Inventions; Monarchy.

AMERICAN PUBLISHING COMPANY. SEE Bliss, Elisha.

AMIABLE HUMOR

AMIABLE HUMOR is a product of Enlightenment optimism, the belief that all things human, created by a benign God, serve beneficial purposes. Laughter, according to its great defender, eighteenth-century Scottish philosopher Francis Hutcheson, arises out of our sense of incongruity, out of our awareness that the world is filled with people and things that are at odds with our ideals, standards, and expectations. Rather than seeing this incongruity as a sign of human weakness, he describes it as an opportunity to extend an ennobling sympathy over as many different kinds of people as possible. Thus, to Hutcheson, the exercise of the sense of humor was in harmony with the *moral sense and the sense of sympathy.

By the mid-nineteenth century, Hutcheson's explanation of humor had more or less supplanted earlier classical and Renaissance understandings of humor as a mode of attack, perhaps best encapsulated in philosopher Thomas Hobbes's definition as the exultation of a victor in battle. Hutcheson built his entire and highly influential system of moral philosophy, the first part of which was a series of essays on humor, in opposition to Hobbes's pessimism. Hutcheson's definition of the sense of humor was, arguably, the most historically important step in the rise of *sentimentalism, even though sentimentalists by Mark Twain's time had come to value tears over laughter as a mark of refined sensibility.

Often, amiable humorists tried to combine a sense of underlying pathos with surface humor, a delicacy of touch by which painful circumstances are partially transmuted. This is the humor of much of Charles *Dickens (one of the most important literary influences on Clemens as a young man), many of Harriet Beecher *Stowe's local color sketches collected in her *Sam Lawson's Old Time Fireside Stories*, and much of the work of two of Twain's early literary mentors, Bret *Harte and Charles Dudley *Warner. Twain often used such a mixture, as in "The Californian's Tale," "A True Story," or, perhaps most compellingly, "*Bluejay Yarn" from *A Tramp Abroad*. The opening maxim of chapter 10 of *Following the Equator* (1897) puts Twain's understanding of this union of sensibilities most succinctly: "The secret source of Humor itself is not joy but sorrow. There is no humor in heaven." Or, as he put it in his *autobiography in a dictation of 22 May 1908, "an absolutely essential part of any real humorist's native equipment is a deep seriousness and a rather unusually profound sympathy with the sorrows and sufferings of mankind."

While such a union of sentiments might have been the dominant use of amiable humor, the idea that it binds different classes and types of people into community without requiring homogenization and conformity remained an important concept right up to the end of the nineteenth century. Amiable humor ostensibly enables an appreciation of difference. Laughter at the unusual was considered a necessary step in allowing us to extend sympathy to those unlike us, but in whose eccentricities we find possibilities for individuality. Thus, amiable humor is the comedy of character rather than of wit.

One of the dominant genres of humor, then, is the character *sketch, a short piece that may or may not entail plot, but rather turns not so much on the revelation of character in the sense of moral fiber as on the exposition of a character in the sense of eccentricity. In the American tradition, scholars usually cite Washington Irving as the first important practitioner of character sketches in his *The Sketch Book of Geoffrey Crayon*. Irving's Crayon is a man who admits his eccentricities and failings in a humor that cannot keep the traditional proportions of things in mind. Tinged throughout with melancholy but able to laugh at the characters he meets on the way, Crayon is both a source of laughter, and more importantly, a mediator between the reader and what Crayon describes as the Europe of "storied and poetical *association," that will refine and elevate the reader who knows how to embrace its humor as well as to thrill with awe at its grandeur. The interplay between European refinement and American roughness in stories like "The Angler" or "Rip Van Winkle" introduce further "characters" in *frame narratives, protecting the reader from vulgarity while allowing sympathy, with, say, the "virtuous poverty" of the angler himself. While not all amiable humor uses frame narration or third-person narration to provide a buffer between the "character" under view and the reader, such techniques were common ways to elevate vulgarity. The humorous sympathy Hutcheson held to be intrinsically ennobling was usually not fully trusted by amiable humorists.

Of course, the genteel concern for elevation through the exercise of sensibility, even the sense of humor, and the ideal of liberal compassion behind the philosophy of sensibility is a source of comic incongruity all by itself. In developing the comedy of character, Clemens discovered this early on in such sketches as that of Scotty Briggs and the parson in *Roughing It*. "Stalwart Rough" Scotty Briggs, whose fractured grammar and fractious personality are as far from the sphere of gentility as can be imagined, is embraced through the reach of humor as a pure-hearted gentleman-in-the-rough, with the laughter extending simultaneously back toward both the minister and Mark Twain as genteel narrators. The laughter in the sketch gently ridicules all forms of social snobbery and inflexibility in order, finally, to endorse a large sense of common humanity. But the use of a frame narrative is essential to maintaining genteel standards at the same time that it extends the range of sympathy. Over time, Clemens saw the limitations of such a controlled sympathy, and began to use the comedy of character for more satiric purposes, as in *Adventures of Huckleberry Finn*, in which he more or less drops the frame. Not surprisingly, *Huckleberry Finn* came under immediate attack for its coarseness. In pushing the boundaries, Clemens tests the capacity of humor to extend sympathy beyond easy stopping points.

ANGELFISH. SEE Aquarium Club, The.

ANIMALS. When on 15 August 1862, Samuel Clemens wrote home from the mining fields near the Nevada-California border, he listed his partner's dog as among the camp's significant inhabitants. And when he further listed their domestic chores, he described himself as lazier than the dog, who at least "scratches up the dirt floor of the cabin, and catches flies, and makes himself generally useful in the way of washing dishes." Here Clemens developed a typical motif in his life and writings, to include pet animals as part of society, not only for the company they offer but for the commentary they could provide on human behavior.

In fact pets were always a significant part of his life. Over the years he and his family regularly kept pet dogs and cats, and much of his literature mentions these animals as part of the normal backdrop of family life. In *Pudd'nhead Wilson*, he says, "A home without a cat—and a well fed, well petted, and properly revered cat—may be a perfect home, perhaps, but how can it prove title?" Clemens's home, while perhaps not perfect, at least always had well-fed, well-petted cats, who decorously suffered under the names Clemens gave them: "Sin" for a black cat, and "Sackcloth" and "Ashes" for her gray kittens. When in Hartford, the family had pet collie dogs, as well as garden ducks and a pony in the stable.

Not surprisingly, in his later years, when the burgeoning Anti-Vivisectionist League (of which Jean Clemens, Twain's daughter, was a member) and the Society for the Prevention of Cruelty to Animals organized protests, Twain turned his pen to aid the cause. Pieces such as "A Dog's Tale" and "A Horse's Tale," both of which Clemens wrote upon request, are fairly straightforward propaganda in service of these crusades. A similar complaint against human beings as the cruelest of animals appears in "The Chronicle of Young Satan," when a dog, injured by its drunken master, nonetheless tries to get help for that same master. The protection of animals became a pet Clemens cause.

More importantly, animals become significant characters in Twain's writing as foils for human behavior. Often he wrote animal fables, as in the bluntly named "A *Fable," or interpolated in larger works, as the coyote and town dog story in chapter 5 of *Roughing It*. More often, he told stories about human beings interacting with animals in ways that reveal the nature of the human beings themselves. For example, a character who alternately appears as Dick Baker and Jim Baker in *Roughing It* and *A Tramp Abroad* tells animal stories that reveal his nature and, by extension, allegorize on the human condition. In *Roughing It*, chapter 61, Twain has Baker describe his cat, Tom Quartz, in order to suggest something of Baker's conservatism, his worry about the potential damage caused by industrial technologies as he paradoxically pursues wealth as a miner in a bucolic setting. His own mining disrupts that setting even as his self-defeating money management repeatedly forces him back into near-isolation in a desolate, rustic setting. While Baker himself mentions none of this, in describing his cat's "sagacity" in understanding mining practices and his wise refusal to update those practices, his yarn to Twain tells us much about his paradoxical character. Later, in Baker's "*Bluejay Yarn," chapters 2 and 3 of *A Tramp Abroad*, Twain uses Baker's animal tale to reveal how work can yield a dangerous misanthropy unless mitigated by humor.

In creating such characters, Clemens showed that he recognized the intellectual and moral danger of projecting human virtues and vices onto animals, yet he persisted in doing so himself, especially given his belief in Charles *Darwin's theory of the descent of man. In this context, his animal references suggest at least a latent and often explicit misanthropy, as when in chapter 18 of *Connecticut Yankee* he has Hank Morgan claim human degeneracy through evolution. In this vein, his posthumously published "Man's Place in the Animal World," and "Was the World Made for Man?" argue that *evolution has diminished moral purity, inverting Darwin's postulate that the exclusively human moral sense is the apex of evolution. On the other hand, "In the Animal's Court" and *"Three-Thousand Years among the Microbes" try to exonerate humanity by proving that human beings cannot be held culpable for their crimes, much as we would not hold any other animal culpable for nature's cruelty. In either case, Twain worships animals for their ignorance of moral dilemmas, turning them, along with children, into symbols of innocence in a fallen world.

♦ SEE ALSO Religion.

ANTI-SEMITISM. Of the different ethnic prejudices prevalent in nineteenth-century America, the one against Jews was probably the least virulent; it was certainly mild by European standards. To be sure, many Americans who thought of themselves as Christian did discriminate. Perhaps most famously, James Russell Lowell cut Bret Harte for his half-Jewish parentage and Samuel Clemens because he thought Clemens looked Jewish. But for the most part, American Jewish communities in Philadelphia, Newport, New York, and other cities had long histories of fairly peaceful coexistence with their Christian neighbors. Partly this was due to small numbers—the total population of Jews living on the eastern seaboard had risen from about 3,000 in colonial times to only about 250,000 in 1870, mainly through immigration from German-speaking central Europe.

More importantly, popular Protestant theology contributed to the mildness of anti-Semitism in America. *Calvinism took quite literally the Christian injunction that not one jot or tittle of the law would be suspended before Christ's second coming. Consequently, many Calvinist sects hewed closely to the Mosaic laws found in Genesis and Deuteronomy. The proximity in practice between such Christians and Jews emphasized commonality, not difference. And since they did not indulge, as Europeans often had, in a ritual blaming of Jews for Christ's death, Americans had little to inflame religious intolerance against a religion that did not argue points of Christian doctrine. Protestant Americans reserved their most energetic religious hatred for "papists."

Likewise, most American Jews up to the 1880s were from western Europe, primarily Germany and England, and had integrated culturally so that they were not conspicuous. American social *clubs tended to have no membership policies against Jews, who were often prominent members of the most prestigious, eastern clubs.

All of that changed in the 1880s and 1890s, when anti-Semitism, fiercely debated by social elites, came to dominate thinking at all points of the social spectrum. Deepening xenophobia in the face of massive immigration, which for the first time in the 1880s included large numbers of Jews from eastern Europe after Russia began a series of pogroms in 1881, contributed to this change.

Clemens's reactions to Jews in general were based on ignorance. He reports in his autobiography the arrival in Hannibal, Missouri, of a Levin family, whose Judaism he found fascinating but not fearsome. Such naive interest characterizes his treatment of Jews in *Innocents Abroad*. But with the rise of anti-Semitism in the 1880s,

33

Clemens had no qualms about taking sides, even if his ignorance remained deep. He berated Bret Harte for trying to hide his half-Jewish heritage. He supported Émile Zola in the international *cause célèbre* of the Alfred Dreyfus affair. His "Stirring Times in Austria" condemns virulent Austrian attacks on Jews. He wrote "Concerning the Jews" explicitly to fight anti-Semitism, though his acceptance of stereotypes about Jews as shrewd businessmen may have done more harm than good, and as an assimilationist, he had little interest in or tolerance for Judaism culturally, or for traditions of and arguments about Talmudic interpretation.

While much of his reaction to anti-Semitism was abstract, his stay in Vienna from 1897 to 1899 brought it home more personally, when his regular companionship with Jewish intellectuals and musicians made him the target of the popular anti-Semitic press. His reaction was to pillory the Christian socialist leader Karl Luegar in *"Chronicle of Young Satan," as well as to pen two other *unfinished works, "Newhouse's Jew Story" and "Randall's Jew Story." While he shelved these pieces, his defense of Jews culminated in his "Concerning the Jews," published in *Harper's Monthly* in September 1899. He foresaw, in a 26 July 1898 letter to H. H. Rogers, that "neither Jew nor Christian will approve of it," not surprisingly for the stereotypes it contains and its deep misanthropy: "All I care to know is that a man is a human being—that is enough for me: he can't be any worse." Such an opening hardly makes a good defense of any group of human beings.

♦ SEE ALSO Gabrilowitsch, Nina Clemens; Race Relations.

APHORISMS. SEE Maxims.

APPRENTICESHIP. SEE Labor Movement.

AQUARIUM CLUB, THE. In 1908 Clemens wrote the bylaws of the Aquarium Club, one of his many burlesque social clubs. The rules made him perpetual "admiral," and, excepting himself, all members had to be female and of "school-girl age" (membership expired automatically at age sixteen). The business of the club was to correspond and visit. An enamel pin in the shape of an angelfish signified membership.

This organization was Clemens's semijoking way of maintaining his correspondence with a group of girls whom he started "collecting" on a visit to Bermuda in 1906. The first of these, fourteen-year-old Dorothy Butes, responded to Clemens's loneliness; his daughter Susy had been dead for a decade and his living adult daughters spent little time with him. Butes appreciated Clemens's attendance on her in Bermuda, delighted in his pet name of "angelfish," and maintained the friendship in correspondence and in a visit, with her mother, to New York City. The pleasure he took in this surrogate parenthood, or grandparenthood as the case may be, prompted him to, as he put it in his autobiographical dictations, "collect pets: young girls—girls from ten to sixteen years old; girls who are pretty and sweet and naive and innocent." In 1906 alone he "collected" a dozen such young friends, and by 1908, when he devised the rules of the club, he was building much of his social life around his planned activities and correspondence with these girls.

Clemens's motivations in these activities have been the subject of controversy. Some scholars have suggested that Clemens had prurient interests, but most see him as trying merely to compensate for loss by retreating into an innocent fantasy world, one akin to his purified recollection of his best years in Hartford. In any case, the record of his correspondence—about three hundred letters to the various girls—shows Clemens at his most sentimental, quite opposite from the traditional image of a bitter and cynical Clemens late in life.

♦ SEE ALSO Childhood.

ARABIAN NIGHTS ENTERTAINMENTS, THE. Clemens read this book early and often, and tapped it regularly in his writing. Often he merely mentioned it in passing as a point of comparison, but in some cases he used *Arabian Nights* tales as raw material for his fiction. This is explicitly the case in the long burlesque, "1002d Arabian Night" (1883). William Dean *Howells advised him not to publish, but he pressed ahead, sending the manuscript to his publisher James Osgood. He then retrieved it shortly thereafter when he founded his own publishing firm. Perhaps because the illustrations were lost in transit between publishers or perhaps because he had second thoughts, he did not bring it out in his lifetime. It finally saw print in 1967 in *Mark Twain's Satires and Burlesques*.

The *Arabian Nights* play two especially significant roles in *Adventures of Huckleberry Finn*. In the opening chapters, Tom Sawyer makes repeated reference to the *Nights* only to have Huck debunk the magic of books. Huck's resistance places common sense above fantasy. Later, as the relationship between Huck and Jim develops, Twain again turned to the *Nights* to further add moral depth to this point, this time making Huck the supporter of fantasy and Jim the advocate of common sense and decency. Specifically, Twain exploited the *Nights* tale, "The Story of Noureddin Ali and Bedreddin Hassan." Bedreddin, separated from his wealthy and powerful family for ten years, has made a new life as a baker's servant. When his family accidentally discovers him in this role, it plays on him a series of cruel practical jokes intended to heighten the effect of their reunion. The final joke is to convince Bedreddin that all of his sufferings were but a dream. After struggling to adjust to this idea, he is confronted by physical evidence that his "dream" did, in reality, occur. Rather than growing angry at any of these jokes or their perpetrators, however, "the joy Bedreddin felt in finding himself surrounded by so many persons, deservedly dear to him, made him ample amends for his past suffering; and in their beloved society he passed pleasantly the remainder of his life." Significantly, the whole point of this tale is to propitiate the Caliph Haroun al Rashid so that he will put to death neither a man who murdered his wife nor the "black slave" who ostensibly precipitated the murder. The story that begins seriously ends in the tale of a practical joke leading to pardons and parties all around.

Such an ending shows a remarkable shift in tone from angry seriousness to happy frivolity. It comes as no surprise that Twain would fish, to whatever degree of consciousness, in such a book for incidents to use in *Huckleberry Finn*. More important, however, is the degree to which parallels between a story he read and a story he wrote are transmuted through his own imagination. In choosing to burlesque a story that shifts from seriousness to comedy, his mind, working as usual through contrast, inverts the emotional progression of the original. Thus, in landing the story of Noureddin Ali, Twain found his own novel's moral seriousness.

In having Huck play a similar practical joke on Jim—declaring Jim's past misfortunes to be just a dream—Twain gives Jim the opportunity to assert the importance of reality, the reality of his suffering and the reality of his dignity. Many readers find Huck's joke, Jim's reaction, and Huck's repentance the first important episode in developing the book's morality. It sets up Huck's recognition of Jim as a human being and makes possible his grand gesture to "go to hell" in an effort to free Jim. But the same tale also makes possible the deep irony of the book's ending. In having Tom Sawyer take over the story at the end, Twain returns to the original *Nights* tale, with Tom planning to make everything up to Jim by giving him a grand torchlight procession and reuniting him with his family and friends. In inverting the first part of the story, that is, by saying "no" to the humor of the practical joke, Twain creates an ironic denouement. In giving the old ending straight, he challenges readers to choose between the fantasy ending of redemption, or the more likely, but more painful, sense that the crimes of the past cannot be atoned for so easily.

♦ SEE ALSO Reading, Clemens's; Work Habits.

ARISTOCRACY. SEE Monarchy.

ARNOLD, MATTHEW (1822–1888), British poet and cultural critic, best known and reviled in the nineteenth-century United States for his stinging criticism of American culture.

In his criticism, Arnold became a champion for a conservative ideal of culture as an elite intellectual movement designed to balance the crudeness of mass culture in an increasingly democratic age. As such, he took the United States as his object lesson, especially in his *Discourses in America* (1885) and his essay "Civilization in America," published in the April 1888 issue of *Nineteeth Century* just days before he died of a heart attack. After Lorettus Metcalf, editor of the journal *Forum*, asked prominent writers to rebut Arnold's criticism, Clemens wrote about one hundred manuscript pages in response, but chose to suppress them, perhaps out of respect for the recently deceased. Certainly it would have been a tactical blunder to have published then, as Arnold's particularly galling criticism of American journalism and humor was that they had no sense of *reverence, which Arnold held to be essential to any high civilization.

While Clemens held his immediate response, the gist of his reply found its way into *Connecticut Yankee* and *The *American Claimant,* both of which defend the irreverence of the press as a necessary counterweight to the powers of nobility and privilege. Arnold's criticism of American culture came at a time when Clemens's own reservations about democracy temporarily took a back seat to his hopes for it, so the energy of his response to Arnold was not an indicator of his antagonism to Arnold himself. Indeed, when the men met—the Clemens family even hosted Arnold for tea in Hartford in 1883—they seemed to enjoy each other's company. Clemens's good friend and neighbor, Joseph Twichell, commented in his journal on the occasion that Arnold seemed more sympathetic than one would have expected from his writings. The same could be said of Clemens himself, especially as regards the energy of his criticism of Arnold's work.

♦ SEE ALSO Democracy; Etiquette; Patriotism; Style.

ARTEMUS WARD. SEE Browne, Charles Farrar.

ASHCROFT, RALPH W. (1875–1947). Clemens's relationship with Ashcroft typifies the volatility of his connections with business associates. He met Ashcroft in 1903 when Ashcroft was treasurer of the American Plasmon Company, which manufactured a processed milk powder and in which Clemens had invested. Clemens eventually felt that the company had taken advantage of him, and Ashcroft helped him negotiate complex legal dealings with it. Merely on the basis of this contact, Clemens hired Ashcroft as a business advisor in about 1907, ultimately giving him, along with Clemens's private secretary Isabel *Lyon, power of attorney over his business affairs. In March 1909, Ashcroft and Lyon married, perhaps at Clara Clemens's urging to quell her fears that Lyon wanted to marry Clemens. Perhaps again at Clara's urging, perhaps out of his own paranoia, Clemens turned against the couple, accusing them of abusing their powers over his *finances. Clemens wrote a long manuscript detailing his charges against the two, though no solid evidence of wrongdoing exists. In fact, Ashcroft's advice to establish in 1908 a Mark Twain Company, securing a trademark for the name "Mark Twain" and exercising control over that name as a commercial property, served Clemens and his estate well. Even today, the income from the company's successor, the Mark Twain Foundation, helps fund, in a modest way, various Mark Twain memorials, including the Mark Twain Papers. Still, the speed with which Clemens came to trust a man whose greatest recommendation was his deference to Clemens shows much about Clemens's gullibility and instability in financial dealings.

♦ SEE ALSO Business Ventures.

ASSOCIATION. According to sentimentalist psychology, the mind converts the impressions of the senses to ideas, and through unified action of memory and imagination, combines simple ideas into complex ones. Thus, association of ideas is the trace of memory, and the power of one memory to evoke a train of recollections was a central intellectual feature of sentimental literature.

Mark Twain's writing certainly demonstrates this, though he often juxtaposes incompatible ideas to make a comic rather than serious association. For both humorous and serious passages, Mark Twain's literature depends on the association of ideas, as he admits in his *autobiography:

> A man can never know what a large traffic this commerce of association carries on in his mind until he sets out to write his autobiography; he then finds that a thought is seldom born to him that does not immediately remind him of some event, large or small, in his past experience.... Sometimes a thought, by the power of association, will bring back to your mind a lost word or a lost name which you have not been able to recover by any other process known to your mental equipment. (*North American Review*, 2 August 1907, 696)

A recurring idea in the autobiography, it is also a structural principle by which Twain sought to free-associate on news of the day or on memorabilia from his past in order to start a train of associated memories that would reveal the truth about his life.

Such trains of association were central to Twain's work as a writer throughout his career. His Mississippi writings, for instance, spilled forth substantially in response to his correspondence with his childhood friend Will Bowen:

> My heart goes out to you just the same as ever! Your letter has stirred me to the bottom. The fountains of my great deep are broken up & I have rained reminiscences for four & twenty hours. The old life has swept before me like a panorama; the old days have trooped by in their old glory, again; the old faces have looked out of the mists of the past; old footsteps have sounded in my listening ears; old hands have clasped mine, old voices have greeted me, & the songs I loved ages & ages ago have come wailing down the centuries! (6 February 1870)

While the language makes Clemens sound like a septuagenarian, he was at the time just thirty-five and newly married. Association through memory always invokes *nostalgia.

A chain of association also justifies the digressive, meditational style that Twain turned into a formula for humor. As long as he worked by association, by allowing unconscious cerebration through association to lead him on a digressive path, his writing was not bound by conventions of narrative linearity or plausibility. Association as a principle of composition freed Twain to meditate and joke in a rambling fashion.

Association for Twain, as for his contemporaries, was not merely a mechanical mnemonic device; it also served as a conduit for moral imagination. In responding to the vividness of Twain's "*Old Times on the Mississippi," friend and fellow writer John Hay praised Clemens for having "memory and imagination," the two greatest gifts a writer could have. Obviously, imagination does not so much capture facts as render them significant, and this is the purpose of mental association according to sentimental aesthetics. By tying memories, especially for physical objects, to emotional states, sentimental association turns simple memory into a moral experience. Such, at least, were the expectations of readers who enjoyed Twain's "serious" word-paintings as much as his comic writing. Consider, for example, the description of the Sphinx in *Innocents Abroad*:

> It was stone, but it seemed sentient. If ever image of stone thought, it was thinking. It was looking toward the verge of the landscape, yet looking *at* nothing—nothing but distance and vacancy. It was looking over and beyond every thing of the present, and far into the past.... It was the type of an attribute of man—of a faculty of his heart and brain. It was MEMORY— RETROSPECTION—wrought into visible, tangible form. All who know what pathos there is in memories of days that are accomplished and faces that have vanished—albeit only a trifling score of years gone by—will have some appreciation of the pathos that dwells in these grave eyes.

Associating individual memory with an image, Twain turns a statue into an allegory, connecting a work of stone with the idea of history itself.

♦ SEE ALSO Work Habits.

ASTRONOMY. Born in a year when Halley's comet was visible and predicting that he would die in the year it next returned, Twain used popular fascinations with extraordinary celestial events to bolster his public image, and the terminology of astronomy as metaphor in his literature. At least twice he used astronomical discoveries to float comic sketches, in "A Curious Pleasure Excursion" (1874) and "The New Planet" (1909). But astronomy was not merely a commercial property for Clemens; he read frequently in the subject because the vastness of the universe— the idea of the light year struck him as particularly compelling—filled him with an almost religious awe. Such a feeling did not bolster his belief in conventional religion; rather, his reading in astronomy served his skepticism about Christianity.

Clemens's use of astronomy as a defense against Christianity comes most pointedly in his courtship letters with Olivia Langdon, whose willingness to correspond with him in the first place was contingent on their relationship as a devout Christian trying to serve the conversion of an aspiring one. In his role as penitent, Clemens inveigled his way into Langdon's heart, but once the wedding date was set and secure, Clemens launched into a report of his readings in astronomy, in which he discovered the temporal and spatial vastness of the universe as an argument against conventional Christianity:

> I have been reading some new arguments to prove that the world is very old, & that the six days of creation were six immensely long periods. For instance, according to Genesis, the *stars* were made when the world was, yet this writer mentions the significant fact that there are stars within reach of our telescopes whose light requires 50,000 years to traverse the wastes of space & come to our earth. . . . Did Christ live 33 years in each of the millions & millions of worlds that hold their majestic courses above our heads? or was *our* small globe the favored one of all? . . . I do not see how astronomers can help feeling exquisitely insignificant, for every new page of the book of the Heavens they open reveals to them more & more that the world we are so proud of is to the universe of careening globes as is one mosquito to the winged & hoofed flocks & herds that darken the air & populate the plains & forest of all the earth. If you killed the mosquito would it be missed? Verily, What is Man, that he should be considered of God? (8 January 1870)

In his conclusion he quotes the Bible to imply that his humility is orthodox, but in doing so, he undercuts conventional faith. The traditional answer to that biblical question is that humans are the product of the hand of God, lord of God's creation, made in his image. Clemens implies, rather, that we should not be considered of God at all.

Nine years later, he read Amedée Victor Guillemin's *The Heavens* while working on the manuscript he would ultimately publish as *"Extract from Captain Stormfield's Visit to Heaven." His marginalia in Guillemin's book all support his religious skepticism, which worked its way into "Extract" in a broad satire of human arrogance for even believing in eternal salvation.

♦ SEE ALSO Science.

ATLANTIC MONTHLY, THE. For most of Clemens's life, *The Atlantic Monthly* was the premier literary journal in the United States. Founded in 1857 by a coterie of New England writers with a common interest in New England culture and abolitionism, the magazine called itself a journal of politics, science, literature, and the arts. The word "Atlantic" suggests the editorial bias toward England and European standards of taste. Under the editorship of James Russell Lowell, with contributions by important arbiters of New England culture, the *Atlantic* quickly built a reputation for moral seriousness and aesthetic and intellectual quality. Its influence was disproportionate to its relatively small and distinctly regional circulation.

Purchased by Ticknor and Fields in 1859, the *Atlantic* passed the editorship to James T. Fields in 1861. After the Civil War, Fields decided to try to expand circulation by broadening the journal's regional focus, intending to make a national journal by capitalizing on its reputation for quality. He hired William Dean *Howells as his assistant editor in 1866 to carry out his plan. Howells did so, looking to western, southern, and European writers, both for contributions to the journal and as subjects for the journal's reviews. Under this policy, the *Atlantic* began publishing contributions by Bret Harte and reviewing the works of a newly arrived western humorist, Mark Twain.

The *Atlantic*'s highly laudatory review of *Innocents Abroad* was, in Clemens's eyes, the ultimate praise, so much so that he made a pilgrimage to the *Atlantic*'s offices to offer thanks. There he met Howells, who had penned the review, and thus began a friendship and literary partnership that would last for the rest of Clemens's life.

Howells was promoted to the editorship of *The Atlantic Monthly* in 1871, where, for the next ten years, he not only continued to review Twain's books favorably, but also invited Twain to become a contributor. Initially, Clemens did not want to publish his first such piece, "A *True Story," under his nom de plume, fearing that the *Atlantic*'s hallowed pages needed a serious story by a man of letters, not a low comic tale by a notorious joker. Clemens's next contribution, at the insistent urging of Howells, was a series of articles, *"Old Times on the Mississippi." With this, Clemens reached the apex of American literary culture, publishing a multi-installment work under his pseudonym in the august *Atlantic*.

While the *Atlantic* continued to publish Twain's works, his relationship with the journal remained vexed by the concern that, as a westerner and a humorist, he was less a bona fide contributor than a licensed clown. His ostensibly disastrous performance at the *Whittier Birthday Dinner, arranged in 1877 by the *Atlantic*, heightened this feeling. In fact, the *Atlantic* did much to bolster Twain's status. Still, inasmuch as the *Atlantic* represented something toward which Twain aspired but which he felt he could never attain, it became a source of anxiety, though one of the central, shaping anxieties of his literary career.

♦ SEE ALSO Fields, Annie and James T.

AUTOBIOGRAPHY. Although Clemens was convinced that his autobiography would be the most important work of his life, he published only a small fraction of it in his own lifetime. No full edition has yet been published, and two of the four existing editions deliberately violate the book's basic design. The reasons for these anomalies have to do with the autobiography's peculiar structure and overwhelming size. This structure has led to a divergence of opinion about the value of the book, with some critics, including two who have edited editions, finding the digressiveness and verbosity self-indulgent. They admit the existence of gems, but believe these need to be extracted and set into a new order. Fans of the autobiography have been thwarted by its simple bulk, which, in typescript, occupies three file-cabinet drawers in the Mark Twain Papers. Only a set of bound volumes, or perhaps a compact disc or some other electronic medium, could encompass the entire mass, and whether the economics of publishing would ever allow such an endeavor remains an open question.

The autobiography as it exists in that file cabinet begins with one of Clemens's early efforts at self-description, but that very beginning proved to Clemens the inadequacy of traditional narrative memoir. He came to believe that as long as the autobiography tried to construct a coherent narrative, the result would be too literary, too dead:

> Narrative is a difficult art; narrative should flow as flows the brook down through the hills and the leafy woodlands, its course changed by every boulder it comes across and by every grass-clad gravelly spur that projects into its path; its surface broken but its course not stayed by rocks and gravel on the bottom in the shoal places; a brook that never goes straight for a minute, but *goes*, and goes briskly, sometimes ungrammatically, and sometimes fetching a horseshoe three-quarters of a mile around and at the end of the circuit flowing within a yard of the path it traversed an hour before; but always *going*, and always following at least one law, always loyal to that law, the law of *narrative*, which *has no law*. Nothing to do but make the trip. . . .
>
> With a pen in the hand the narrative stream is a canal; it moves slowly, smoothly, decorously, sleepily, it has no blemish except that it is all blemish. It is too literary, too prim, too nice; the gait and style and movement are not suited to narrative. That canal stream is always reflecting; it . . . can't help it. Its slick shiny surface is interested in everything it passes along the banks, cows, foliage, flowers, everything. And so it wastes a lot of time in reflections. (31 January 1904)

So rather than waste time in polish, Clemens chose to write the bulk of his autobiography by dictating it to a stenographer, usually Josephine Hobby. Often in the presence of Albert Bigelow Paine, his biographer, and Isabel Lyon, his private secretary, Clemens would follow a stream of *associations that would begin with the day's news, a recent event, a family artifact, or, sometimes, the last idea of the previous day's dictations.

The result is a radically digressive account that moves much as the brook he describes, busily, noisily, at different paces and moods on different days and ideas, letting audience, occasion, and memory conspire to make anecdotes, jokes, tender reminiscences, scathing denunciations, and tall tales. Many events come up repeatedly, and each time, there is a different cast to the event from a different point of view, a different set of facts remembered, a different mood from which Clemens tells the tale. After each day's dictations were transcribed to typescript, Clemens went over them, sometimes on different copies, making minor changes in style, adding new ideas, using his own text for further free association.

Clemens's autobiography is a remarkably wide-ranging and fanciful text, but it is revealing too, the one thing Clemens hoped it would be. Besides finding the literary autobiography too polished, he also found it deceptive. He believed that the polish itself would make the narrative overwhelmingly fictional, rather than revelatory: "Without intending to lie [the autobiographer] will lie all the time, not bluntly consciously, not dully unconsciously, but half-consciously—consciousness in twilight; a soft and gentle and merciful twilight which makes his general form comely with his virtuous prominences and projections discernible and his ungracious ones in shadow" (31 January 1904). Not only did Clemens discover this to be the case in his own "attempts to do the autobiography," but in every autobiography he had ever read—and he relished memoirs as a genre. Believing that no fully honest autobiography had ever been written, Clemens dared his notoriously honest brother to try his hand at the impossible task, writing an honest memoir. Two times in his own autobiography he refers to Orion Clemens's effort:

In the other room you will find a bulky manuscript, an autobiography of my brother Orion, who was ten years my senior in age. He wrote that autobiography at my suggestion, twenty years ago, and brought it to me in Hartford, from Keokuk, Iowa. I had urged him to put upon paper all the well remembered incidents of his life, and to not confine himself to those which he was proud of, but to put in also those which he was ashamed of. I said I did not suppose he could do it, because if anybody could do that thing it would have been done long ago. The fact that it has never been done is very good proof that it can't be done.... I urged Orion to try to tell the truth, and tell the whole of it. I said he couldn't tell the truth of course. (23 February 1906)

Orion wrote his autobiography and sent it to me. But great was my disappointment; and my vexation, too. In it he was constantly making a hero of himself, exactly as I should have done and am doing now, and he was constantly forgetting to put in the episodes which placed him in an unheroic light. I knew several incidents of his life which were distinctly and painfully unheroic, but when I came across them in his autobiography they had changed color. They had turned themselves inside-out, and were things to be intemperately proud of. (6 April 1906)

Clemens hoped that his random and unreflective approach would help him avoid this deceptive attribute of an autobiography, not because it would keep him from lying, but because it would be harder for him to lie well enough—consistently enough—to be truly deceptive.

Any autobiography, he felt, would ultimately reveal the truth of a character to some degree, because the autobiographer "will tell the truth in spite of himself, for his facts and his fictions will work loyally together for the protection of the reader; each fact and each fiction will be a dab of paint, each will fall in its right place, and together they will paint his portrait; not the portrait he thinks they are painting, but his real portrait, the inside of him, the soul of him, his character" (31 January 1904). A digressive, energetic, dictated autobiography would protect the reader better because it could wind up telling the same story over and over again, with enough variations to be revealing. As a technique, it works well. Many anecdotes get developed one day in such a way that Clemens comes out the hero, but whenever he does this, the story nags at him until he comes back to it from a different angle. He may again make himself a hero, but the discrepancies between versions create lacunae that the reader can easily fill in. No matter how much he distorts the events of his life, how he felt about it shows clearly. He described this clarity as the morality behind his method when he said in a 15 January 1906 dictation, "I don't mind excursioning around in an autobiography—there is plenty of room. I don't mind it so long as I get things right at last, when they are important."

Again, what he means by right is less the facts of a particular incident than the fact of his character. One aspect of his character he reveals is his violently unstable ability to pass judgment on his own actions. In describing his *Whittier Birthday Dinner speech, an event he considered one of the most humiliating of his life, he changes his mind many times. The part published in the *North American Review* and republished many times as "The Story of a Speech" has Twain declaring how much he now sees that speech as brilliantly funny and completely inoffensive. If he had that same audience before him with the confidence of *his* old age to support him, he "would take that same old speech, deliver it, word for word, and melt them till they'd run all over that stage. Oh, the fault must have been with me, it is not in the speech at all" (11 January 1906). Yet this opinion was not his final autobiographical judgment about that speech. His 23 January 1906 dictation reverses his ground: "[I] have changed my notion about it—changed it entirely. I find it gross, coarse—well, I needn't go on with particulars." Then, at the bottom of the page, in holograph, is the notation, "May 25 . . . day before yesterday . . . I gave it a final & vigorous reading—aloud—& dropped straight back to my former admiration of it. MT."

The point he tries to make by revealing his vacillations is that he cannot really know himself, but that by revealing his own mental processes, he can enable others to know him:

How do I account for this change of view? I don't know. I can't account for it. I am the person concerned. If I could put myself outside myself and examine it from the point of view of a person not personally concerned with it, then no doubt I could analyze it and explain to my satisfaction the change which has taken place. As it is, I am merely moved by instinct. My instinct said, formerly, that it was an innocent speech, and funny. The same instinct, sitting cold and judicial, as a court of last resort, has reversed that verdict. I expect this latest verdict to remain. [then the asterisk leading to the 25 May revision] I don't remove the speech from the autobiography, because I think that this change of mind about it is interesting, whether the speech is or not, and therefore let it stay. (23 January 1906)

Such repetitions are to some readers as interesting as they were to Clemens, but to others, they are a source of frustration. Looking for a more literary book, one that carefully selects from experience in order to make a coherent and direct narrative, they see such variations in repeated stories a mark of confusion and lost intellectual power.

Such readers prefer the apparently factual evaluations Clemens gives of his early years, of his family and friends, and, especially, the definite judgments he passed on those contemporaries—business associates, fellow writers, and politicians—for whom he had contempt. Clemens was not afraid to deal in wholesale denunciation in the autobiographical dictations, in part because he rightly expected such diatribes to be suppressed until well after his death. Again, he justified his unusually candid opinions as an exercise in honesty, not about those whom he denounces, but about himself:

It is not my purpose, in this history, to be more malicious toward any person than I am. I am not alive. I am dead. I wish to keep that fact plainly before the reader. If I were alive I should be writing an autobiography on the usual plan. I should be feeling just as malicious toward Webster as I am feeling this moment—dead as I am—but instead of expressing it freely and honestly, I should be trying to conceal it; trying to swindle the reader, and not succeeding. He would read the malice between the lines, and would not admire me. Nothing worse will happen if I let my malice have frank and free expression. The very reason that I speak from the grave is that I want the satisfaction of sometimes saying everything that is in me instead of bottling the pleasantest of it up for home consumption. (31 May 1906)

Such diatribes are perhaps the most self-indulgent part of the autobiography, but as gossip dealt by a master wordsmith, they have an enduring fascination.

Clemens did not keep his promise to speak only from the grave, publishing substantial selections from the ongoing project as "Chapters from My Autobiography" in the *North American Review* in 1906 and 1907. Nor did he keep his promise to be fully candid in the parts he published, which carefully select episodes from many different days' dictations, rarely insulting anyone living or with living immediate family members. In these published chapters he does not give his most candid self-portrait, either, but does remain true to his method, which is, as he says in the very first installment, a "method whereby the past and the present are constantly brought face to face, resulting in contrasts which newly fire up the interest all along." The chapters published in the *Review* have only recently been republished, once as *Mark Twain's Own Autobiography* in 1990, and again as *Chapters from My Autobiography* in 1996 in the Oxford Mark Twain.

Three other editions compiled by various editors have been published since Clemens's death. Twain's first literary executor, Albert Bigelow Paine, published a version simply as *Mark Twain's Autobiography* (1924). In two volumes—each over 350 pages long—this edition is the only one to follow the original order of the dictations, preserving the feel, if not the entirety, of the autobiography as it exists in the Mark Twain Papers. Paine cut the scope of the autobiography in part by including nothing after the 19 January 1906 dictation, even though Clemens continued dictating, on and off, into 1909. Paine also excised any passages that would compromise the image he was trying to craft of Mark Twain as a kindly gentleman.

Bernard DeVoto, Paine's successor as literary executor of the Mark Twain Papers, published the next collection of autobiographical writings, in part to counter Paine's image of a genteel, benign Twain. Titling his collection *Mark Twain in Eruption*, after one of Twain's favorite literary images of himself as satirist, DeVoto printed a number of diatribes Paine left out. But DeVoto thought that the structure of the autobiography was not worth preserving. He instead organized passages he found interesting according to topic, and while he noted the date of composition at the head of each new passage, the overall effect is very unlike that of the original.

Charles Neider published the most complete and yet most shamelessly mauled edition of the autobiographical writings in 1959 as *The Autobiography of Mark Twain*. Absolutely rejecting Clemens's approach to memoir but not having the honesty to segregate discrete passages by date of composition, Neider put the pieces together into as tight a chronology as the material allows, making this rendition a fairly conventional autobiography. Whatever one's opinion of the success of Clemens's original efforts, they are nonetheless the experiments in stream-of-consciousness of a major American literary figure, whose challenge to linear narrative precedes that of the modernists by at least two decades. As such, they deserve honest and fair presentation.

♦ SEE ALSO Work Habits.

"Awful ---- Terrible Medieval Romance, An." This *condensed novel, written in 1869, first published in the Buffalo *Express* in January 1870, and later collected in *Sketches, New and Old* (1875), is one of Twain's earliest stories that addresses three interrelated concerns of great importance in his oeuvre. First, as the very title makes clear, Twain is mocking Victorian *medievalism, which had not yet reached its peak in Britain or America. Here he merely mocks the simplicity of Victorian historical *romance without understanding or addressing the deeper political concerns, namely Victorian anxiety over modernity and a longing for an alternative in an idealized past. Second, he plays with the theme of mistaken *identity, especially gender identity. Third, Clemens develops one of his pet concerns, the unfinishable story, the pleasure of which he explains at the end of chapter 2 of *Following the Equator* (1897). Through most of his life, however, the unfinishable story gave him pain rather than pleasure. He found it difficult to wrap up too many of his tales with conventional happy endings, because such endings too often violate realistic plausibility and because the logic of his stories often worked more toward tragedy than comedy. Yet the demands of his profession as a humorist forced him to deny that logic.

Here he finds a way to make the conflict between the logic of a story and the demands of his genre generate comedy, not in a happy ending but in the complete lack of an ending. In denying the conventional happy ending here quite directly and honestly, Twain almost attacks his readers for demanding the impossible. What he overtly does here foreshadows the covert endings of many other stories. In particular, the happy endings of *Adventures of Huckleberry Finn* and *Pudd'nhead Wilson* ironically challenge the audience expectation for pleasant resolution to all human difficulties. Here he merely mocks the expectation; in these later books, he uses that expectation to develop complex ironic meanings.

♦ SEE ALSO Work Habits.

BANQUETS. SEE Speeches.

BARNUM, PHINEAS T. (1810–1891). Clemens met America's most famous showman in 1872 at a birthday celebration for Horace *Greeley, but the two were never friends. Clemens's suspicions of hucksters as well as a degree of professional jealousy precluded much more than casual social contact when their paths crossed. Barnum did, however, help pave the way for Clemens's career by helping to legitimize public entertainments and teach public figures how to promote themselves using the mass media.

Barnum's primary claim to fame was developing his American Museum in New York City and taking pieces of his exhibition on the road. He masked a basic circus and freak show with the rhetoric of moral improvement, turning a marginal entertainment into a vaguely respectable one. His famous comment, "There's a sucker born every moment," taken out of context, does not acknowledge how willingly his viewers were duped. Barnum's pretenses of moral probity allowed everyone to wink at the real value, that is, pure entertainment value, of his shows. While a correspondent from New York for the San Francisco *Alta California*, Mark Twain wrote of his visit to the American Museum: "Now that Barnum is running for Congress, anything connected with him is imbued with a new interest. Therefore I went to his museum yesterday, along with the other children. There is little or nothing in the place worth seeing, and yet how it draws!...Barnum's Museum is one vast peanut stand now, with a few cases of dried frogs and other wonders scattered here and there, to give variety to the thing" (9 April 1867). This pretty much set the tone for all of Twain's references to Barnum.

Barnum appears, usually as a target of criticism, in numerous Twain works. Most notably and explicitly, "Barnum's First Speech in Congress" (1867) reveals Twain's contempt for Barnum's over-reaching self-promotion. Less explicit references occur in "General Washington's Negro Body-Servant" and in *A Connecticut Yankee in King Arthur's Court*. In the first of these, Twain alludes to Barnum's exhibition of an old African-American woman whom he fraudulently claimed was Washington's childhood nurse. In the second, when Hank Morgan first views Camelot, he asks if it is Bridgeport, Connecticut, the location of Barnum's fantastically arabesque mansion. Thus does Morgan suggest that the whole of knight errantry was a fraud worthy of Barnum.

♦ SEE ALSO Confidence Games; Leisure; Spectacle.

BEARD, DANIEL. SEE Illustrations.

Illustration from "When Mr. Beecher Sold Slaves in Plymouth Pulpit," *Harper's New Monthly Magazine, Harper's Magazine Advertiser* (supplement), November 1896.

BEECHER, HENRY WARD (1813–1887). One of the most prominent American clergymen of his day, Beecher occupied the pulpit of Brooklyn's Plymouth Church, which he brought to prominence through his charismatic preaching and social activism. As James Parton described the church in a January 1867 article in *The *Atlantic Monthly*, "If we had a foreigner in charge to whom we wished to reveal this country, we should like to push him in, hand him over to one of the brethren who perform the arduous duty of providing seats for visitors, and say to him: 'There, stranger, you have arrived; *this* is the United States, the New Testament, Plymouth Rock, and the Fourth of July,—*this* is what they have brought us to. What the next issue will be, no one can tell; but this is about what we are at present'" (41).

A son of Lyman Beecher and younger brother of Harriet Beecher *Stowe, Henry Ward Beecher made his fame as a powerful preacher against *slavery. He used to "auction" young escaped slave women to his congregation in order not only to raise the money to buy their freedom, but also to dramatize the horrors of slavery. He concentrated especially on the dangers to young women in slavery, in which they were often treated as sexual property.

Ironically his use of Victorian sexual morality as a tool in the fight against slavery ultimately became his undoing. Having worked quite closely with one of his parishioners, Elizabeth Tilton, Beecher was sued by her husband, Theodore Tilton, for "alienation of affections." A hung jury acquitted Beecher, but his case became a touchstone for the debate over sexual morality and *women's rights. Members of the radical wing of the suffrage movement used the scandal to dramatize their belief that sexual relations between men and women were a primary component in women's subjugation. Beecher denounced women's sexual rights in public, they said, but hypocritically practiced "free love" in private. His scandal was a wedge issue for the more radical branch of nineteenth-century feminism.

Clemens's home, in *Nook Farm, was in the heart of Beecher country, and he naturally took great interest in the controversy, which split the community as well as the country. At first, most of the respectable folk in Nook Farm defended Beecher, with the notable exception of Isabella Beecher Hooker, who was, as a feminist crusader, more loyal to her cause than to her brother. The community mostly ostracized her for her opinion.

Clemens, like most of his neighbors, initially sided with Henry. But while attending the trial in April 1875, Clemens came to believe in Beecher's guilt. This is around the same time that he likewise changed his mind about women's suffrage. Because Clemens kept his opinions about Beecher's conduct more or less private, however, it is impossible to know if the Beecher-Tilton controversy affected Clemens's ideas about sexuality and women's rights.

♦ SEE ALSO *Innocents Abroad, The*; Lecture Circuit.

BIBLE. In chapter 51 of *Roughing It*, Twain quotes Philippians 4:7 to characterize the editor of Virginia City's new literary weekly:

> Once while editor of the *Union*, he had disposed of a labored, incoherent, two-column attack made upon him by a cotemporary [*sic*], with a single line, which, at first glance, seemed to contain a solemn and tremendous compliment—viz.: "THE LOGIC OF OUR ADVERSARY RESEMBLES THE PEACE OF GOD,"—and left it to the reader's memory and after-thought to invest the remark with another and "more different" meaning by supplying for himself and at his own leisure the rest of the Scripture—"*in that it passeth understanding.*"

Twain's Mr. F., in reality Thomas Fitch, comfortably relied on his audience's absolute familiarity with the Bible; Twain, on the other hand did not. In so doing, Twain acknowledged other purposes for literacy beyond merely reading and memorizing the Bible, though to many Americans well into the nineteenth century, such a concept was anathema.

Twain's references to the Bible must also have been anathema to some people, for his intense familiarity with it—he had read the book in its entirety, including the apocrypha, while still young—made him a sharp critic. Publicly, that criticism came in the form of attacks on the uses of the Bible and on its interpretations, rather than its content. But throughout his life, he directed his animosity toward what he called the Bible's "uncleanliness," that is, the sexual mores it expresses, as well as toward the image of God it depicted, especially in the Old Testament. The degree to which Twain treated that image as the product of human imagination, rather than accepting the Bible's God as real and therefore culpable, shifted from work to work, meditation to meditation. In any case, Clemens mostly held his anti-Bible vituperation for private consumption.

For instance, the autobiographical dictations for 19–20 June 1906 begin, "Our Bible reveals to us the character of our God with minute and remorseless exactness. The portrait is substantially that of a man—if one can imagine a man charged and overcharged with evil impulses far beyond the human limit; a personage whom no one, perhaps, would desire to associate with, now that Nero and Caligula are dead." The following fourteen pages of typescript show Clemens at his angriest, denouncing just about every aspect of Christianity as it flows from the Bible. At the top of the first page for each day's dictation, he wrote in hand: "Not to be exposed to any eye until the edition of A.D. 2406. SLC." He indulged such frankness only under the cloak of nearly absolute privacy.

On 20 June, the dictation speaks not of the Bible, but of "Bibles," the plural signifying that each is merely a testament of belief, not of truth, and is fully a human product. He sees that "an almost pathetic poverty of invention characterizes them all. . . . Each pretends to originality, without possessing any. Each borrows from the other, and gives no credit, which is a distinctly immoral act." In talking of the congruence between different mythological systems and the religions on which they depend, Clemens organizes his thoughts around the ideas he first found in *The *Age of Reason*, and which he confirmed over a lifetime of study and travel. In *Following the Equator*, he publicly espoused a more tolerant position with respect to the human origins of religion, summed up in his maxim, "True reverence is reverence for another man's god." But in private, the human origin of *religion was yet another source of anger and apparent disappointment.

That disappointment stemmed from a hope that life would be meaningful in a transcendent way, that the question repeatedly asked in *Chapters from My Auto-biography*, "What is it all for?" would have a generous, positive answer. Yet the leit-motif in much of his work, "verily, what is man that he should be considered of God," suggests that Clemens saw God as too distant to provide such meaning. If, he believed, human beings could provide themselves no better meaning than that contained in their Bibles, then they are truly damned, not by God, but by their own lack of imagination.

Thus, many of Twain's posthumously published references to the Bible interpret biblical stories in light of human history or figurative possibilities, in order to discern a divine purpose behind human existence. For instance, those pieces collected by Bernard DeVoto as the Adam Family Papers in *Letters from the Earth* examine the cycles of human history against a curiously ambiguous divine plan. The "Letters from the Earth" themselves, on the other hand, view the creation from the point of view of an angel, Lucifer, who visits earth to see what is becoming of God's "experiment in morals." Two of the so-called mysterious stranger manuscripts,

*"Chronicle of Young Satan" and "Schoolhouse Hill," approach this question from opposite but equally fanciful angles. The first shows a morally perfect angel committing atrocious crimes, tinkering with cosmic dimensions in ways wholly inappropriate to human needs. The second, quite brief, has a perplexed angel coming to earth to try to figure out what went wrong. In both cases, the heavenly point of view is so out of sympathy with human needs as to be at best irrelevant, at worst malignant.

Other of Clemens's posthumously published fulminations against the Bible have to do with human uses of it, as in "Colloquy between a Slum Child and a Moral Mentor," "Little Bessie," and "Mamie Grant, Child Missionary," each of which shows biblical ideas grossly inapplicable to human situations.

None of these direct attacks on the Bible saw the light of day in Clemens's lifetime. When he treated the Bible under the name Mark Twain, he did so with a light touch, attacking the Bible indirectly through comic irreverence. Often, he reinterprets various biblical stories using inappropriate language that casts their moral value in a different light. In his newspaper correspondence from the Middle East, for instance, he depicts Joseph as an opportunistic investor who corners the market in grain in order to secure himself—and Pharaoh—hefty returns on their investments. In *Adventures of Huckleberry Finn*, he has Miss Watson misinterpret Matthew 6:6 when she takes Huck into the closet, that is, a pantry, to pray. She has no sense that words have shifted meaning from the early seventeenth century when the King James Bible was translated; she reads the words literally. In juxtaposing Miss Watson's misinterpretation of the Bible with Huck's and Jim's superstitions, Twain may suggest that the Bible itself is a set of superstitions, but by distancing the attack in the person of an illiterate and unreliable narrator, Clemens tried to distance himself from reproach. He took a similar approach in the earlier tale "The Scriptural Panoramist" and in his sketch of Captain Edward (Ned) *Wakeman—scarcely hidden under the pseudonym Captain Blakely—in *Roughing It*.

Whether secretly denouncing it or publicly teasing its devotees, Mark Twain was, like his contemporaries, steeped in the stories and language of the Bible, and his continuous reference, while usually couched in *irony, shows how thoroughly the Bible shaped his consciousness whenever he confronted the spiritual, ethical, and scientific questions of his day.

♦ SEE ALSO Adam and Eve; Censorship; Moral Sense.

BLISS, ELISHA (1821–1880). In November 1867, Bliss, as secretary of the American Publishing Company, took the risk of inviting Clemens to publish *The Innocents Abroad* through his *subscription publishing firm. This was a risk for both of them actually. Subscription publishing had made its money on serious nonfiction, and Clemens, who had only limited experience with book *publishing, knew nothing about the company. The contract Bliss secured with Clemens began their dozen-year battle of wills. Bliss, a shrewd businessman who had begun as a dry-goods merchant and later sold lumber, always tried to keep control over his author, while Clemens thought himself far too important for this business yet acted far too self-important to keep from upsetting the business.

As a subscription publisher, Bliss worked on the edge of legality and far into the gray areas of morality as a matter of course. Still, he could be generous and support-ive of his authors. Marietta Holley, the humorist Bliss discovered shortly after his success with humorous writing in *Innocents Abroad*, considered him a mentor. With Clemens, however, Bliss could never keep the emotional upper hand, precisely because Clemens had such a large base of literary contacts on whom he could rely for support and guidance. He did not need Bliss, as Holley did, and Clemens was at least as shrewd as Bliss in judging the literary market.

Clemens developed a degree of anger at Bliss virtually unmatched in his history of emotional extravagance. His ire was directly proportional to his dependence on Bliss and Bliss's willingness to humiliate and badger Clemens. During the writing of *Roughing It*, for instance, Bliss seemed to belittle Clemens's literary abilities. Clemens had already coerced Bliss into hiring Orion *Clemens. With his older brother in Bliss's office daily, by the spring of 1872 Clemens received information convincing him that Bliss regularly cheated him, giving him needed leverage against Bliss's attacks. Clemens then wanted out of his dealings with Bliss, but he had contracted for several future books with the American Publishing Company and was absolutely hooked on the financial power of the firm's subscription system.

Such was the dynamic that fueled Clemens's animosity, which still boiled hot as late as a 23 May 1906 autobiographical dictation: "As a liar [Charles H. Webb] was well enough and had some success but no distinction, because he was a contempo-rary of Elisha Bliss and when it came to lying Bliss could overshadow and blot out a whole continent of Webbs like a total eclipse. . . . Bliss told the truth once, to see how it would taste, but it overstrained him and he died." Yet the entire thrust of sub-scription publishing was to use high-pressure sales tactics of dubious probity to con-vince people to buy books they could barely afford, and then, after subscription sales dwindled past profitability, to "dump" the remainder on the trade market. Whether publishers or agents did the dumping first, the practice violated their contracts of exclusivity, yet the practice was part of the business. Clemens, through Bliss, profited from such practices, and in his battles with Bliss, Clemens not only whetted his anger, but also learned the business well enough to set himself up as a publisher.

♦ SEE ALSO Webster and Company.

"BLUEJAY YARN." Spanning chapters 2 and 3 of *A Tramp Abroad* (1880), Jim Baker's "Bluejay Yarn" is one of Twain's most frequently reprinted pieces. But in extracting the story from its context, most editors cut out the significant opening in which Twain describes his rambles in the Neckar hills of Germany, where he put himself in the mood to believe in magic. He recalls that the moment he fully believed, he began to hear the ravens in the trees talking about him, criticizing his clothing and chasing the huffy Twain out of the forest. Only then does Twain begin the "Bluejay Yarn" with the ironic "animals talk to each other of course."

Such an opening calls attention to the human capacity to project feelings onto the world, showing not the congruence between nature and humankind, but rather the overwhelming self-importance of humanity in trying to make the world conform to its image. In so doing, Twain primes us to see animal fables in a new way. We expect them to present us with easily identifiable allegorical figures, *animals representing particular character types or forces immanent in nature. We are conditioned to know how to read animals—a fox represents craft, a dog loyalty, and so on. Such tales are not about their third-person narrators, but rather about the traits under discussion. By contrast, Twain's opening sends us into a *frame narrative in which we first are given reason to question the outside narrator's reliability. This in turn prepares us to challenge the inside narrator. Reading the story's moral, then, occurs only after we have interpreted the inside narrator's limitations.

When we see that the inside narrator, Dick Baker, does not endow the blue jay with a single characteristic, but rather with every human characteristic, we wonder less about jays than about Baker. He compliments the jays on their linguistic abilities and sense of humor, but every other trait he ascribes to them is despicable. If we recognize, then, the jay as an analog to human beings (as Baker wants us to), we see humanity as profoundly depraved. If, on the other hand, we learn our lesson from the frame and see the animal portrait as a projection, then Baker becomes a misanthrope and the tale's cautionary figure, rather than the jay.

Baker's story itself explains why. He has failed as a miner, and now lives in a worked-out district in California in nearly complete isolation. Undoubtedly he had promised himself not to return "to the states" until he made his fortune, and he has resigned himself never to go home again. In implying that California is still a territory, Baker reveals how long he has been gone. But in the story itself, Baker reveals a solution to his problem, though one he either cannot see or simply will not take. The jay, like Baker, has set himself an impossible task, but rather than stick to it and turn sour in failure, he shares his grief in order to find a way out. In that sharing, while the jays offer "[l]eather headed" answers to the conundrum Baker poses, "[H]ow could I have nothing to show for my work?," the jays in community stumble onto the answer, that Baker had set himself an impossible task. With this discovery, they transmute the pointlessness of the *work* into the point of a joke, making the labor meaningful and valuable. The capacity to laugh is also closely allied to the ability to perceive beauty; without these, work destroys the worker.

♦ SEE ALSO Gillis, James N. (Jim) and Steve; Humor; Work Ethic.

BOER WAR. "The very ink with which all history is written is merely fluid prejudice." Thus in the epigraph to chapter 69 in *Following the Equator* does Twain explain the bald rationalizations for the Jameson Raid, which led ultimately to the Anglo–Boer War of 1899–1902. In carefully examining the raid, Clemens developed his systematic opposition to *imperialism, which manifested itself in his participation in the Anti-Imperialist League and his overt rejection of the imperial depredations of almost every European or American power in the rest of the world.

The Boer War officially began in 1899, but Clemens knew by 1896 that it was already unofficially underway, and his writings were remarkably prescient regarding the ways the British would ultimately fight the war. As he remarks with caustic understatement in "Pudd'nhead Wilson's New Calendar" (*Following the Equator*, chapter 67), "First catch your Boer, then kick him." When Britain formally entered the war, however, Twain restrained himself in his public criticism. Clemens was convinced that the British war against the Boers was a war of conquest by a great imperial power over a lesser one, but his lack of sympathy for the Boers themselves—he disliked their treatment of the indigenous Africans—coupled with his sense of realpolitik—he preferred British colonial rule to the rule of other European powers—encouraged him to temper his opposition. Nonetheless, he expressed his outrage over Britain's invention of the modern concentration camp in "A Salutation Speech from the Nineteenth Century to the Twentieth" and "To the Person Sitting in Darkness."

♦ SEE ALSO War.

BROWNE, CHARLES FARRAR (1834–1867). The real name of Artemus Ward, comic journalist and humorous lecturer. Browne met Clemens in Virginia City in 1863. The two hit it off, sharing the pleasures of yarn spinning and heavy drinking. As Twain wrote in "A Reminiscence of Artemus Ward" about the day of their meeting, "I breakfasted with him. It was almost religion, there in the silver mines, to precede such a meal with whisky cocktails. Artemus, with the true cosmopolitan instinct, always deferred to the customs of the country he was in, and so he ordered three of those abominations."

Clemens and Browne maintained their connection via letters until Browne's death by tuberculosis in England. Browne had a significant impact on Clemens's career, primarily in showing Clemens how to develop a stage presence in comic lecturing. In his exposition of the American "art" of humorous yarn-spinning, "*How to Tell a Story," Twain describes Artemus Ward's mode of comic indirection and apparent aimlessness as the perfection of comic delivery.

Browne also encouraged Clemens's writing career. As Twain wrote on 26 February 1865, upon his return to San Francisco after a three-month stay in the California goldfields, "find letters from 'Artemus Ward' asking me to write a sketch for his new book of Nevada Territory travels which is soon to come out. Too late—ought to have got the letters 3 months ago. They are dated early November." Clemens wrote back; Ward pleaded for a submission; Clemens failed to comply until, after at least a third request, Clemens got around to writing and sending "The *Jumping Frog" in October 1865. It arrived in New York too late for the book, but later appeared in Henry Clapp's *Saturday Press*. The tale catapulted Twain into national *celebrity and showed him the possibilities of vernacular expression to challenge the authority of the genteel *frame narrative. This change of published venue may have proved fortunate, because it allowed the story to stand on its own, instead of being buried within Browne's book. Browne, after all, was one of the "mere humorists" who, Twain noted in his autobiographical dictations, had "perished" as a popular author. Better, perhaps, that Twain's tale began in a journal, rather than in a book by a humorist whose reliance on comic techniques such as "eye dialect" and whose political and social conservatism bound his humor very much to a moment.

♦ SEE ALSO Alcohol; Comic Journalism; Humor; Lecture Circuit.

BUFFALO EXPRESS. SEE *Express*, Buffalo.

BURLESQUE. Unlike *amiable humor and *satire, burlesque has no moral purpose. Primarily a form of play, it indulges the anarchy of *humor to yield the pleasure of disrupting conventional ideas. It usually aggressively mocks a target and in that aggression can easily be misconstrued as satire. The mockery of burlesque, however, not only offers no moral alternative to its target, but manifests knowledge of and often even affection for the target. Celebratory "roasts" are perhaps the most common example of burlesque.

Literary burlesque is a cousin of *parody. Parody plays off of a specific work; burlesque more broadly mocks a *type* of writing, playing off of the tropes and conventions of a genre. As such, burlesque, like other modes of humor, cannot readily be defined by its own tropes and patterns, as it always takes its form from the target of mockery. Still, it does have some characteristic devices. It usually develops humor through some combination of overstatement (especially emotional overstatement, as in bathos), caricature, inversion, and incongruous juxtaposition. Burlesque usually creates broad *irony with these devices. The humor, while sometimes emerging through character, arises substantially out of a rambunctious tone. Not surprisingly, burlesque plots often turn on drunkenness, a fitting symbol for burlesque as a whole.

Much of Twain's early work is burlesque, occasionally, as in the *Burlesque Autobiography* (1871) or the unfinished and posthumously published *Burlesque Hamlet*, self-consciously so. But rarely does his burlesque name itself as such. Like his hoaxes, Twain's burlesques usually begin from a stance of earnestness. For example, his "Advice to Correspondents" burlesques the advice column genre by creating inappropriate questions and answers: "MARY, *Rincon School*.—Sends a dainty little note, the contents whereof I take pleasure in printing, as follows, (suppressing, of course, certain expressions of kindness and encouragement which she intended for my eye alone): 'Please spell and define *gewhilikins* for me.'" Similar emotional discrepancies occur in "The Scriptural Panoramist," a story of a "fellow travelling around ... with a moral religious show—a sort of scriptural panorama" whose pianist played absurdly appropriate music for each picture. The showman introduced a picture of

> "one of the most notable events in bible History—our Savior and his disciples upon the Sea of Galilee. How grand, how awe inspiring are the reflections which the subject invokes! What sublimity of faith is revealed to us in this lesson from the sacred writings! The Savior rebukes the angry waves, and walks securely upon the bosom of the deep!"
>
> All around the house they were whispering: "Oh, how lovely! how beautiful!" and the orchestra let himself out again:
> "Oh, a life on the ocean wave,
> And a home on the rolling deep!"

This tale was framed in "'Mark Twain' on the Launch of the Steamer 'Capital'" (1865), in which Twain gets diverted from his task of reporting on the launch in a round of drunken, maudlin storytelling. The entire sketch works through a series of misdirections and inversions, with inappropriate emotions characterizing each one. Such is the comic thrust of Twain's burlesque.

In the burlesques of the early period, Twain developed his habits of emotional extravagance and inverting even the most serious story line—or for that matter inverting the most nonsensical story line—a propensity that wrought havoc on his efforts to rise in literary stature. Twain caused trouble for himself, for instance, by burlesquing New England's literary giants at the *Whittier Birthday Dinner. His habit of inversion was both a source of constant inspiration and real imaginative difficulty, especially when he worked on novels where the demands for coherence in tone, character, and plot were easily disrupted by the anarchic power of burlesque.

A Connecticut Yankee in King Arthur's Court began as burlesque, the idea of a man out of time and place providing comic contrasts. Like the book salesman of the *Burlesque Hamlet*, Hank Morgan's emotional being is at odds with the time and place where he finds himself. Even though the juxtaposition quickly turned satiric, burlesque elements remain, as in Hank's experiences with armor, or in Arthur's knights riding to the rescue on bicycles.

The novel perhaps most controversially touched by burlesque is *Adventures of Huckleberry Finn*, the ending of which often comes under attack for its inappropriateness to the rest of the novel. The ending, though, is not where burlesque first enters the narrative. Arguably, even some of the book's seriousness comes from Twain's habit of inversion, turning over a story to look at it from another point of view. When he writes of Harney Sheperdson and Sophia Grangerford escaping their families' feud, Twain revisits the story of Romeo and Juliet, but has the title characters escape and the families annihilate one another. Rather than allow that happy ending to work satisfactorily, however, Twain leaves Huck behind to witness the carnage and pay the psychological price: "I ain't agoing to tell *all* that happened—it would make me sick again if I was to do that. I wished I hadn't ever come ashore that night, to see such things. I ain't ever going to get shut of them—lots of times I dream about them" (chapter 18).

An emotional climax such as this needs confirmation, not another inversion, but burlesque intrudes shortly down-river when the King and Duke, newly arrived on the raft, practice outtakes from Shakespeare, including a rendition of the balcony scene from *Romeo and Juliet*. The bathetic treatment of the lovers' angst and the inappropriate image of a bearded old man playing the youthful Juliet seems to mock the emotional intensity of the earlier presentation of the same material. Such burlesque inversions move the plot, but do so in ways that disrupt the novel's emotional coherence. Twain always used burlesque as a window into humor, but often at the risk of destroying the moral purposes he hoped his humor would serve.

BURLINGAME, ANSON (1820–1870). "Envoy extraordinary and minister plenipotentiary from the United States to China" from 1861 to 1867, Burlingame met and befriended Clemens in Honolulu in June 1866. Burlingame helped Clemens get his most famous reportorial scoop: Burlingame, while interviewing the just-rescued survivors of the wrecked ship *Hornet,* allowed Clemens to take notes. Clemens then wrote up the story and shipped the manuscript to the Sacramento *Union*. Clemens used Burlingame's entrée with the survivors to gain the confidence of the *Hornet*'s captain and two passengers, and from his use of their diaries, Clemens wrote an extended account of the disaster, "Forty-Three Days in an Open Boat," published in the December 1866 issue of *Harper's Monthly*.

Burlingame also offered to further Clemens's career by inviting him to Peking (Beijing), where he could exercise his talents as a travel writer. While Clemens declined the invitation in favor of his European tour, later, when Burlingame resigned his ambassadorship and was hired by the Chinese government as an envoy to the European powers, Clemens wrote, comically but with some serious intent, that he would like to become part of Burlingame's entourage: "*Don't* neglect or refuse to keep a gorgeous secretaryship or a high interpretership for me in your great embassy—for pilgrim as I am, I have not entirely exhausted Europe yet, & may want to get converse with some of those Kings again, by & bye. . . . I think I shall want to be an interpreter. I always *did* want to be an interpreter. It is the only ambition I have" (19 February 1868). Twain's letter reveals both his persistent wanderlust of the 1860s—he wrote to his brother Orion that he expected to join Burlingame in Europe, though he ultimately did not—and his remembrance of a conversation with Burlingame, who advised Clemens not to waste his talents but instead to exercise his ambition: "Avoid inferiors. Seek your comradeship among your superiors in intellect and character; always *climb*."

BUSINESS VENTURES. Writing his brother Orion *Clemens from St. Louis on 21 November 1860, Samuel Clemens complained about his speculations in commodities:

> The New Orleans market fluctuates. If any man doubts this proposition, let him try it once. Trip before last, chickens sold rapidly on the levee at $7.00 per doz—last trip they were not worth $3.00. Trip before last eggs were worth $35 @ 40c per doz—last trip they were selling at 12 1/2—which was rather discouraging, considering that *we* were in the market with 3,600 dozen, which we paid *15* cents for—together with 18 barrels of apples, which were not worth a d—m—we *expected* to get $6 or 7 per bbl. for them. We *stored* the infernal produce, and shall wait for the market to *fluctuate* again. But in the meantime, *Nil desperandum*—I am deep in another egg purchase, *now*.

This account capsulizes the history of his business ventures: itching to spend the money he made at something he did well, he misjudged a market, invested more than he could afford, took a beating, then went back for more.

These speculations in commodities, funded by his salary as a steamboat pilot, were just the beginning. Clemens went into the prospecting business in the 1860s, living off his savings from piloting and from the meager salary his brother drew as a government official in Nevada. Given the disruption of river traffic by the Civil War, such a turn of business practices made a kind of sense. But when his stint as a miner found him broke and despondent in 1862, he found his real vocation as a writer. Still, he behaved as if this steady-paying work was merely a sideline as he went from mining per se to investing in mining stocks. Not only did he not realize long-term capital gains, but mining stock holders were regularly assessed additional payments in order to fund mining operations before the ore came in—if it ever came in. Clemens invested in eight shares of Hale and Norcross stock, for example, half of which he put in his brother Orion's name. When the company assessed twenty-five dollars per share in September 1864, the two had trouble paying the cost on Orion's shares: "Orion, the H & N assessment is not delinquent until the 1st Nov, & I may be able to pay all of it myself" (28 September 1864). He did, but given that he was earning twenty-five dollars per week on the San Francisco *Call* and twelve dollars per article for the *Californian* at the time, that assessment pinched.

Certificate of Incorporation of the Clemens Gold & Silver Mining Co. Original in California State Archives, Sacramento, California. This print taken from a facsimile in the Mark Twain Papers, Bancroft Library, University of California, Berkeley.

Nonetheless, Clemens continued to invest in stocks and bonds, usually in highly speculative companies not yet earning a dime. One such, a prospective insurance company that turned out to be a fraud, saw Clemens invest heavily, but for a rare change, actually get his money back. He received something a bit more, too, in his delightful "Accident Insurance, etc.," the speech he gave to introduce Cornelius Walford, the company's principal. Similarly, his participation in business in general yielded literary returns far beyond the direct returns he expected; the highly successful book *Roughing It* is perhaps the best example.

Sometimes he invested well, seeking both dividends and capital gain. His *notebooks usually record his investments, revealing the remarkable extent of his speculations by the 1880s. One such entry for the summer of 1882 lists about $100,000 of such investments in twenty-three different stocks and bonds. At the same time he was investing heavily in the Kaolatype engraving process and beginning to invest in the *Paige typesetter. Not afraid to gamble on the market, he often bought stocks on margins. In January 1883, for example, he purchased on margin two hundred shares worth fifteen thousand dollars in the Oregon and Transcontinental Company. When the prices fell, he bought another one hundred shares in September, ultimately unloading the lot in May for twelve dollars per share (*N&J* 3:29).

Given that Clemens needed to work full time as a writer to afford his hobby as a businessman, he naturally relied on the business sense of others to manage his financial affairs. He hired a number of lawyers to oversee different aspects of his businesses, and also hired, from very early on, a series of managers. When working as a freelance journalist and lecturer in the late 1860s, he hired Frank Fuller to handle his affairs. In the 1870s she entrusted much of his business to Dan *Slote, in whose Kaolatype he had invested, and whom he used to produce and market Mark Twain's self-pasting scrapbook. He had a British business agent in Moncure Conway from about 1876 to 1881. But no more important agent crossed his path than his nephew by marriage, Charles *Webster, whom Clemens hired to manage the Kaolatype business and ultimately run not only his publishing firm, *Webster and Company, but also his investments in the Paige typesetter. A capricious taskmaster, Clemens broke Webster, and then hired Fred Hall to carry on with the business as it headed toward bankruptcy in the early 1890s.

Clemens did not have a cool head for business: His letters to Orion when in Nevada are often profanity-laced expostulations about how to manage money; his notebooks show obsessive tinkering with ideas for investments, contracts, and analyses of markets. He hired business managers with a euphoric sense of trust, worked them capriciously, and then fired them in fury. He regularly sued former collaborators and partners, or would turn former targets of lawsuits into collaborators. When he finally came to know his weakness in the mid-1890s and entrusted his affairs to Henry H. *Rogers, he found, for the first time in his life, a manager who could manage him. Rogers helped Clemens merely for fun and friendship. He was the rare manager of Clemens's business ventures on whom Clemens did not turn. Even after Rogers straightened out the mess of Clemens's bankruptcy, however, Clemens returned predictably, obsessively, to the icon of *money, blaming his behavior on his "instinct to speculate." No wonder he breathed such life into his character *Colonel Sellers; the motto of both was "there's millions in it." For posterity's sake, it's just as well that Clemens had imagination but no discernment; had he been as good a businessman as he imagined himself to be, he would have written precious little, and only a failed businessman could have written the *"Bluejay Yarn."

Of course, *publishing itself was also a business, indeed one of the most important industries of the nineteenth century. But publishing in America relied on an artificial distinction between the genteel art of writing and the rough and tumble world of the market. Book publishers were in the market, but, before about 1850, they paid writers precious little beyond vanity, assuming that writers were otherwise gainfully employed or independently wealthy. Of course, in the absence of international *copyright, it was cheaper for publishers to steal the work of European writers than to pay American writers well. The reverse was equally true: European publishers stole the product of American writers, as Clemens came to know. Thus, it was difficult for professional writers to build a substantial career out of book publishing, though over the course of the nineteenth century, with the rise of *leisure and a growing literary nationalism, writing did become professionalized.

Journalism served as an important transitional occupation in this rise of professional authorship. It occupied a middle ground between the practical and genteel, with writers very much earning their livings in contact with the larger economy but still maintaining a higher *social class standing for working in the world of letters. Indeed, given the Clemens family's social class pretensions even in the face of economic hardship, the vaguely genteel aura surrounding journalism may explain why Samuel Clemens and his two brothers apprenticed in the print trades.

Be that as it may, Clemens began seriously writing at the moment when modern communications media had turned the writer's task into a commercially lucrative one. While early in his career Clemens could tell Mary Mason *Fairbanks that he could not afford to marry while working as a journalist, because he could not "turn an inkstand into Aladdin's lamp" (12 December 1867), he did learn how to make writing pay, far better than his more genteel friends like William Dean *Howells and Thomas Bailey *Aldrich. He did so by first rejecting the idea that writing should not be a business. As he wrote to Howells,

> No doubt you & I both underrate the <value>worth of the work far enough; but that you are warrior enough to stand up & charge anything above a week's board is gaudy manliness in a literary person. Our guild are so egotistically mock-modest about their own merits.—We make a wretched bargain— caressing our darling humility the while—& then when we come to think how much more we could have got, we go behind the house & curse.—By George I admire you. I suppose "consuling" is not without its uses—it breeds common sense in parties who would otherwise develop only the uncommon. (15 July 1874)

Clemens was right about Howells; Howells adroitly charged the best rates he could get for his writing, making a comfortable career as an author. Still, Howells usually needed to supplement his income with editorial work. Ironically, of the two, Clemens was the one who discovered how to make writing a more lucrative profession, properly assessing the larger market available to him in *subscription publishing, and then developing that market by seeking and exploiting *celebrity. He knew that a writer had to be both a businessperson and something finer; he knew that he needed a reputation as a thinker beyond the pursuits of mere business if he was to make the business of writing work.

In that he was successful beyond the dreams of most writers of his day. He meshed his *lectures with his writing, feeding each by the publicity of the other, and he manipulated the press with the artfulness of an insider. Thus, as much as he squandered his earnings venturing into speculations where he had no business, he was one of the pioneers who turned the art of writing into a viable business of its own.

♦ SEE ALSO Finances.

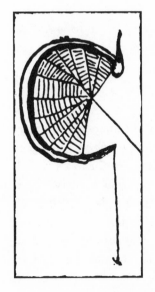

CABLE, GEORGE WASHINGTON (1844–1925).
Born and raised in New Orleans and one of the foremost authorities on the city and its surroundings,
George Washington Cable fought for the South in the
Civil War, was injured twice, and returned to his unit
both times. Unlike many other southern young men, in
the early 1870s Cable turned against the cause and began
to view *slavery as a crime and the war itself as an egre-
gious wrong committed by the South. These beliefs
fueled his writing, and his work caught the eye of a
northern publishing house, Scribners, through which he
commanded a substantial national audience for his tales
of southern life. But Cable's essays attacking racial prejudice were also published in the southern press. It took
courage to denounce slavery and racism in New Orleans,
a hotbed of the organized extralegal violence that effectively re-enslaved blacks in
the post-Reconstruction South. Snubbed by most in his community and even
threatened by extremists, Cable ultimately moved to Massachusetts in 1885.

Clemens admired Cable's writings, calling him in chapter 44 of *Life on the
Mississippi*, "The South's finest literary genius." The two met briefly in Hartford,
Connecticut, in 1881, and developed a strong friendship on Twain's Mississippi trip
in 1882. Cable was Clemens's tour guide in New Orleans and gave Clemens much
of his information about conditions in the South. Cable profoundly influenced
Clemens's ideas about the treatment of former slaves. Clemens's depictions of slavery—de facto as well as de jure—in *Adventures of Huckleberry Finn*, *Pudd'nhead
Wilson and Those Extraordinary Twins*, *A Connecticut Yankee in King Arthur's Court*,
and the unfinished *Which Was It?* owe much to Cable.

Cable visited the Clemens house in Hartford in 1883 and went on a reading tour
with him from November 1884 to February 1885, making more than one hundred
appearances together. (Clemens originally proposed including William Dean
*Howells and Thomas Bailey *Aldrich on the tour, too, but only Cable took him up
on the idea.) The tour's manager, James B. Pond, billed them as "Twins of Genius,"
but they behaved more like the antithetical twins in *Pudd'nhead Wilson*—they disagreed in almost all their personal habits. Cable indulged in neither *alcohol nor
*tobacco, and his abstemiousness exasperated Clemens. But neither of these good
habits bothered Twain as much as Cable's piety. Clemens complained often about
Cable's refusal to travel on Sundays and insistence on attending multiple religious
services. At trip's end, Clemens wrote to Howells: "Cable's gifts of mind are greater
& higher than I had suspected. But— . . . You will never never know, never divine,

guess, imagine, how loathsome a thing the Christian religion can be made until you come to know & study Cable daily & hourly. Mind you, I like him . . . but in him & his person I have learned to hate all religions. He has taught me to abhor & detest the Sabbath-day & hunt up new & troublesome ways to dishonor it" (27 February 1885).

♦ SEE ALSO Censorship; Collaborations; Race Relations; Reform.

CALIFORNIA. In the 1860s, California was rapidly transforming itself from a state based on the simple boom-and-bust economy of mining to one with diversified interests in finance, transportation, logging, and agriculture. As Clemens would discover during his first trip to San Francisco in May 1863, San Francisco was already a city of nearly 150,000 people, no longer a mere stopping place on the way to the California goldfields. Having spent nearly two years as first a miner then a reporter in Nevada and just over the border in California, Clemens arrived in an urbane, bustling, boisterous city, and for the first time since the outbreak of the Civil War, was able to indulge his idea of high living. Clemens was so impressed by the city during his 1863 trip that a year later, when his editorial indiscretions nearly precipitated a duel and left him persona non grata among the society of Virginia City, Nevada, he headed not back home to the Mississippi Valley, but on west to the heart of California culture, San Francisco, where he lived for most of the next three and a half years.

In spite of California's position in the full stream of American industrialization, urbanization, and modernization, the state's image back east was as an outpost on the frontier. Partly the image had simply not caught up to reality, but partly many Californians helped to maintain that image because it paid. When citified dandy Bret *Harte started selling his local color stories of California, he created an image of mining camps filled with rustic adventurers, stage-coach drivers, and prostitutes with proverbial hearts of gold. Joaquin Miller, one of the most notorious Californians of the late 1860s and early 1870s, toured the East and England in the persona of a wild frontiersman. Like Benjamin Franklin one hundred years earlier wearing a coonskin cap in the French salons, Miller wore boots, bandanna, and slouch hat in the drawing rooms of Victorian England. The eastern public ate up his act, easily played by a man who had in fact once been engaged in Indian warfare in northeastern California, alternately fighting with and against the Modoc. (Clemens met Miller in London in 1873.)

When Clemens arrived in the East in January 1867, he too adopted this role. Indeed, since his slender East Coast reputation derived from "The *Jumping Frog," easterners were already predisposed to see Twain as a frontiersman. This stereotyping of Californians, based on his own sketch, bothered him at first; he complained to his mother and sister, "To think that after writing many an article a man might

Illustration from Samuel Williams, "The City of the Golden Gate," *Scribner's Monthly Magazine*, July 1875, p. 268.

be excused for thinking tolerably good, those New York people should single out a villainous backwoods sketch to compliment me on!" (20 January 1865). But the cachet was too alluring, and when he lectured in the East, he was billed as the "Wild Humorist of the Pacific Slope." Throughout his career, he would play this wild-man pose when it suited his interests, either to create a little profitable notoriety or to offend snobs whose good opinion Clemens did not value. In many ways, he played the part of Simon *Wheeler in the Jumping Frog story, himself, demonstrating to provincial easterners that their stereotypes get in the way of seeing a more complex reality.

But the wildness of California was not all image. Clemens knew that it was at least a part of the reality. Not only did he worry when mining on the California-Nevada border in 1862 about the ongoing battles between white ranchers and *Native Americans, but he had seen and fallen in love with much of the West's stunning beauty. He wrote to his mother in August 1863 that Lake Tahoe "seems more supernaturally beautiful now than ever. It is the masterpiece of the Creator." Of course, its wildness was not purely natural; already in 1863 an opulent hotel, the Lake Shore House on Tahoe's eastern shore, had opened, and Clemens found it "crowded with the wealth & fashion of Virginia [City, Nevada], & I could not resist the temptation to take a hand in all the fun going" (19 August 1863). The human wildness of civilized fun was a part of Clemens's West, as were the privations of mining in the nearly abandoned towns of California's gold country. In all, Clemens's visits to the eastern Sierra from Nevada and his three-year sojourn in California left a strong impression on Clemens, giving him not only a literary pose, but also endless anecdotal material for his books, sketches, and speeches. These run the gamut from the simple patriotic mention of Lake Tahoe in *The Innocents*

Abroad, to the calculated contrast between the urbane and profane in the *Whittier Birthday Speech's imaginary encounter with a California miner, to the sentimentality of "The Californian's Tale," to the profound humor of the *"Bluejay Yarn" from *A Tramp Abroad*. In most of these post-California sketches, Clemens depicts the rough edges; only in *Roughing It* did Twain willingly capture both Californias.

CALVINISM. In his autobiographical dictations, Clemens mocked the Calvinism in which he was raised, suggesting that it encouraged extreme egotism by teaching each believer to construe everything, no matter how tenuously pertinent, as a message from God. Describing how he had been discharged from his berth as a reporter for the San Francisco *Call* forty years earlier, he facetiously suggested that the San Francisco earthquake was God's punishment of the *Call's* proprietor:

> I was educated, I was trained, I was a Presbyterian, and I knew how these things are done. I knew that in Biblical times, if a man committed a sin, the extermination of the whole surrounding nation—cattle and all—was likely to happen. I knew that Providence was not particular about the rest, so that He got somebody connected with the one He was after. I remembered that in the *Magnalia* a man who went home swearing from prayer meeting one night got his reminder within the next nine months. He had a wife and seven children, and all at once they were attacked by a terrible disease, and one by one they died in agony till at the end of a week there was nothing left but the man himself. I knew that the idea was to punish the man, and I knew that if he had any intelligence he recognized that that intention had been carried out, although mainly at the expense of other people. (13 June 1906)

Having had his view of the world transformed by reading Thomas Paine's *The *Age of Reason*, and having found enough in science to back up his deism, Clemens found the tenets of Calvinism absurd. Still, the rigor of the religion left its mark in his imagination, shaping much of his response not only to the idea of God, but to ideas of *childhood character, human nature, and the prevalence of sin.

These tenets of Calvinism, as codified in the Westminster Confession (1640), describe the progress of the human soul according to five general ideas. The first of these is original sin, the fall of Adam near the beginning of creation. Adam had a covenant of works with God, by which he would remain blessed so long as he obeyed simple commandments. In disobeying, he was cast out of grace. According to the interpretation of the *Bible favored by Calvinists, Adam's disobedience imputed his sin to all of his descendants.

The second principle has each person born in a state of complete and total depravity. No natural attribute was left untainted in Adam's fall, and therefore human beings have no resources on which to rely should they wish to find redemption. The corollary here, and the one that proved the rock on which Calvinism foundered, was the idea of infant damnation. If born sinful, a child who had not experienced a conversion—and conversion was usually not accepted by a congregation until a child attained the ability to understand the principles of Calvinism itself—was damned. Twain's early writings show his belief in childhood evil, as his sketch "Those Blasted Children" (1864) suggests in the title alone, with "Blasted" euphemistically replacing "damned." Early on he saw girls as somehow outside the purview of original sin, but he persisted in seeing boys as fundamentally malicious much longer, writing from New York to the *Alta California* about an asylum for blind girls: "It was the saddest place I ever got into. I don't mind blind boys—they ought all to be blind, for that matter—and deaf and dumb, and lame and halt and paralyzed, and shaken up by earthquakes and struck by lightning—just to make them behave themselves, you know—but I felt so sorry for those girls" (14 July 1867). Clemens's persistent sense of boys' guilt ran deep enough to color his ultimate picture of boyhood innocence, capturing in *Adventures of Huckleberry Finn* the sense of shame that *religion inculcates in even the best-hearted boys.

Given the Calvinist idea of total human debasement, the idea that only God, through his grace by way of the sacrifice of Jesus, can save human beings was a logical corollary. This third principle of salvation through grace alone separates Calvinism from many other schools of Christian thought in denying any redemptive power to good works. Instead, Calvinists emphasized God's power and freedom in suggesting that God elected from among the human population those sinners whom he would redeem as saints. Election is an act of God's will and a mark of his plan, with all events foreordained and meaningful. The believers' task is to interpret all events in order to discern not only his or her own spiritual state, but to understand God's plan for his or her life. This is one aspect of Calvinism that Twain's works repeatedly mock, yet an aspect of Clemens's consciousness that merely resurfaced in a secular version of *determinism.

Once elected into this covenant of grace, the redeemed would feel their natural selves die, only to be replaced in a rebirth in grace. This feeling of being born again, the Westminster Confession's fourth point called "saints' regeneration," was the primary mark of election, but such a simple mark was not enough for a human being. Even though granted grace, the challenge of the born-again saint was to persevere in grace by following the original covenant of works, that is, by being totally obedient to all of the commandments of God, in both testaments of the Bible. Thus, this fifth point, "saint's perseverance," stresses a literal interpretation of the Bible and complete obedience to its many rules.

Besides mocking the faith such obedience required, Twain's writings often savage the workings of those principles. Rather than seeing any opportunity for doing good to others in doing good works, says Twain, the elect are concerned with a narrow interpretation of the letter of the law, not the spirit, in order to be sure that they preserve their own status as elect. This is the basis of his attacks on "The

Saints" in *The Innocents Abroad*. More pungently, in "Letter from the Recording Angel" Twain suggests that someone already elected to heaven has no incentive for improvement, and that therefore any demonstration of piety is merely show. To Clemens, the heart of religion had to be selflessness, but in seeing no generosity in Calvinism, he revealed how convinced he was by the second principle of Calvinism: complete and total depravity, a belief he could best express in his denunciations of Calvinism itself. As he put it in "Moral and Intellectual Man," an unpublished essay from 1907, "Man thinks he is not a fiend. It is because he has not examined the Westminster Catechism which he invented." Clemens did not, however, accept the idea that human beings were to blame for their perversity. As he put it in a late notebook entry, "Damn these human beings. If I'd invented them, I'd hide my head in a bag."

♦ SEE ALSO Progress; Sentimentalism.

CANADA. Although Clemens visited Canada many times on various lecture tours, used Vancouver as his point of departure from North America on his final around-the-world lecture tour in 1895, and regularly crossed to Canada when living in Buffalo, New York, from 1869 to 1871, the country figured in Clemens's life primarily as the home of Belford and Brother's Publishers, the Canadian firm that specialized in literary piracy. Clemens at first tried to prevent such piracy by having his books *copyrighted in Britain. *The Adventures of Tom Sawyer* proved the worthlessness of that tactic. When Belford flooded the American market with cheap copies of *Tom Sawyer* printed after the Chatto and Windus British edition but before the American Publishing Company's American edition, Clemens asked Chatto to sue Belford for violating British imperial copyright. Belford defended his actions by claiming that the Canadian Act of 1875 superseded imperial law. Thus, Clemens would have to take out Canadian copyright to secure his royalties. From then on, Clemens began to spend two weeks in Canada per book, beginning with *The Prince and the Pauper* in 1881, in order to establish residence before securing Canadian copyright.

CELEBRATED JUMPING FROG OF CALAVERAS COUNTY, AND OTHER SKETCHES. Mark Twain's first book was mostly a collection of *sketches written for the *Californian*, the Sacramento *Union*, and the Virginia City *Territorial Enterprise*, with the addition of a few sketches published in eastern journals including the title story. Written originally for inclusion in Charles Farrar *Browne's *Artemus Ward: His Travels* but sent to New York too late for inclusion, the Jumping Frog sketch was first published in Henry Clapp's *Saturday Press* and gave Clemens a national reputation. Charles Henry Webb, Clemens's California friend and one-time publisher of the *Californian* who had moved to New York

City, thought the story's vogue would float a book on the trade market. He suggested that Clemens put together a collection of sketches that could be brought out quickly enough to capitalize on the celebrity of the Jumping Frog story.

Clemens, with help from Webb, selected sketches from his earlier journalism with an eye to what he thought was the superior refinement of an eastern audience. Even after selecting less rambunctious sketches, he edited the remainder, again with Webb's help, careful not only to elevate the diction, but also to remove profanity, references to alcohol and sex, and even allusions to death.

When finished, he presented the manuscript to Browne's publisher, George W. Carleton, who responded brusquely. As Twain wrote years later,

> For two or three minutes I couldn't see him for the rain. It was words, only words, but they fell so densely that they darkened the atmosphere. Finally he made an imposing sweep with his right hand, which comprehended the whole room and said,
>
> "Books—look at those shelves! Every one of them is loaded with books that are waiting for publication. Do I want any more? Excuse me, I don't. Good morning." (*North American Review*, 21 September 1906, 451)

Webb then undertook publication himself, seeing the book through the production process while Clemens toured the Midwest in the spring of 1867. Webb promised the book for a mid-April release, but first copies were not bound and shipped until the beginning of May.

Clemens was understandably proud of and anxious about his first book, but Webb's resources were not equal to the task of promoting it. While Clemens admitted in 1870 that he had "fully expected the 'Jumping Frog' to sell 50,000 copies . . . it only sold 4,000" (to Francis S. Drake, 26 December 1870). This financial failure may have been one of the reasons that Clemens subsequently chose to publish by subscription, persisting in the practice long after he had made a more substantial name for himself and after *subscription publishing had passed the apex of its profitability.

The book's financial failure does not fully explain, however, his deep embarrassment about it. As proud as he was of it upon issue, he grew to hate the book. As he put it in a letter to Olivia Langdon, "*Don't* read a word in the Jumping frog book, Livy—*don't*. I hate to hear that infamous volume mentioned. I would be glad to know that every copy of it was burned, & gone forever" (31 December 1868). He even went so far as to buy out Webb's interest in order to, as he wrote Mary Mason *Fairbanks, "melt up the plates" (17 December 1870). Of course, at virtually the same time, he proposed to Elisha *Bliss that the American Publishing Company reprint the volume as a pamphlet, so it is important not to overstate the case. These different reactions to two different kinds of audiences suggest the deep ambivalence

Clemens felt about his role as a humorist. That the book did not sell well in the trade served to confirm Clemens's worry that his writing was not refined enough for eastern tastes and that his crudeness would forever leave him on the cultural margins. No success ever fully alleviated this anxiety, but his willingness to republish this book through the lucrative subscription publication route suggests that he was willing to swallow his pride if he thought he could turn a healthy profit.

♦ SEE ALSO "Jumping Frog, The."

CELEBRITY. The development of print media as the world's first mass media made mass culture and celebrity in the modern sense of the word possible. Beginning in the late eighteenth century, such international hits as Johann Goethe's *The Sufferings of Young Werther* and the cult of personality developed by the poet Lord Byron intimated things to come, but it was not until the nineteenth century that writers like Sir Walter Scott and America's Washington Irving figured out how to translate the new media attention into a good living. With the next generation of writers, like Charles *Dickens and, almost by accident, Harriet Beecher *Stowe, the term "celebrity" gained its modern definition, just in time for Clemens to learn not only how to use the media to create his own star, but also how to push the boundaries further than anyone had gone before. By the time Clemens died in 1910, he had exploited print media and the new technologies of *photography to turn his Mark Twain persona into an icon that, still flourishing nearly a century later, shows no signs of losing its luster.

He began modestly, learning as a reporter how the newspapers worked. He quickly discovered that the kind of news that sells, sensational news, as often needed to be manufactured as found, and that colorful characters with local reputations furnished endless pages. Moreover, he learned that touring celebrities on the *lecture circuit could use newspapers to promote their shows, mingling news and entertainment in a provocative kind of advertisement that did not appear to be advertisement. His introduction to Artemus *Ward in Nevada was his first object lesson, not so much in deadpan humor, but rather in the promotional capacities of flamboyant behavior.

Later, Twain billed himself as "The Wild Humorist of the Pacific Slope," and his promotional materials often showed a caricature of Twain decked out in loincloth and feathers. While he did not show up on stage in that manner, he did affect some strange garb, wearing western string ties, to the dismay of his friends and family, and an outrageous sealskin coat and hat, a *fashion so outré that William Dean *Howells blushed to be seen near it. Howells attributed such clothing to Clemens's "keen feeling for costume" and his pleasure in "the shock, the offence, the pang which it gave the sensibilities of others." What Howells missed was how such "shock" served as advertising. Clemens himself observed this astutely when in

London in 1873, he played second fiddle to Joaquin Miller, whose insistence on acting the part of the rough American delighted the English by confirming their stereotypes. Miller's publication was slim; his presence, dressed in "the picturesque and untamed costume of the wild Sierras" (autobiographical diction, July 1907) and augmented by a conversation laced with braggadocio and western slang, was more than enough to make him the toast of literary London.

At about the same time, Clemens made the mistake of not encouraging newspaper notice for *Roughing It*, fearing that bad press would kill the book. What he learned instead was that any press is better than none. By the end of 1875, then, even though his early years of married life had been an exercise in taming him to eastern gentility, Clemens had learned that Mark Twain as a commercial property needed an edge. As much as anything, his flamboyant dress—the white suit in his old age, wearing his Oxford gowns at every possible opportunity—is of a piece with his other violations of Victorian respectability. They were commercial actions taken to create media buzz.

Still, the nineteenth century was an era of print culture, and not until the end of the century did photography have a significant influence on print culture itself. Granted, the electronic medium of the telegraph allowed newspapers instantly to exchange stories over long distances so that a mass culture could extend beyond the borders of even the largest city, but the only way to distribute even electronically transmitted information was through the press. Hence, the cult of celebrity included much more than actors and stage performers—even the shyest of writers could be celebrities. To Twain, a writer who made his fame substantially as a performer, the modesty of some writers remained a mystery. His remarks on Charles Dodgson (Lewis Carroll), whom he met in England in 1873, and on Joel Chandler *Harris, express astonishment:

> We met a great many other interesting people, among them Lewis Carroll, author of the immortal "Alice"—but he was only interesting to look at, for he was the stillest and shyest full-grown man I have ever met except "Uncle Remus." Dr Macdonald and several other lively talkers were present, and the talk went briskly on for a couple of hours, but Carroll sat still all the while except that now and then he answered a question. His answers were brief. I do not remember that he elaborated any of them. (*North American Review*, 16 November 1906, 970)

Nor were all celebrities entertainers or even politicians. Charles *Darwin was among the celebrities Twain met, and in his jesting newspaper columns about New York City in 1868, he could drop the names of Louis Agassiz and John Ericson—important names in *science—on the assumption that great thinkers were as much celebrities as were actors, poets, novelists, or politicians.

Illustration from "Prominent Americans," *New York Home Life* and in New York *Commercial Advertiser*, 22 December 1900.

One of the ways to build celebrity in the nineteenth century, as today, was to associate with celebrities, either in mutual admiration or mutual denigration. Either way, it received press. The public love-fests usually were organized as banquets, always set up as much with an eye to the press as to the guest of honor. Twain attended innumerable banquets, and his *speeches at these semipublic feasts—some organized as fund-raisers, others primarily as advertising—kept him in the public eye in countless newspaper reports. Often celebrities met at other public events, such as at the university ceremonies at which Clemens received *honorary degrees, and celebrities tended to celebrate each other, too, inviting one another to private dinners at which no more than a dozen guests would be invited. In such contexts, friendships could develop that would lead to significant correspondence or even to business collaborations, creating a small world of influence and fame. Often, new celebrities in many different fields would invite Twain to join them so that they could bask in his celebrity as much as the other way around. In these contexts, Clemens met almost every famous person of his day, including: Henry M. Stanley, R. L. Stevenson, Matthew *Arnold, much of Europe's nobility, Bram Stoker, Thomas Alva Edison, Ulysses S. *Grant, Philip H. Sheridan, William T. Sherman, most American *presidents, Andrew Carnegie, John D. Rockefeller, George Bernard Shaw, Rudyard *Kipling, Oliver Wendell Holmes, Henry Wadsworth Longfellow, Ralph Waldo Emerson, Charles Darwin, J. M. Barrie, Helen Keller, Charles "Artemus Ward" *Browne, Bret *Harte, John Hay,

Horace *Greeley, Harriet Beecher Stowe, Henry Ward *Beecher, Frederick *Douglass, Anna *Dickinson, David "Petroleum Nasby" *Locke, Wendell Phillips, Henry "Josh Billings" Shaw, Schuyler Colfax, P. T. *Barnum, Henry Irving, Herbert *Spencer, Charles "Hans Breitman" Leland, Robert Browning, Wilkie Collins, George MacDonald, Charles Kingsley, Edwin Austin Abbey, Augustus Saint-Gaudens, Robert *Ingersoll, George Washington *Cable, Grace *King, Sarah Orne Jewett, Annie *Fields, Mary Wilkins Freeman, Elinor Glynn, Julia Ward Howe, Edward Everett Hale, Thomas W. Higginson, James R. Lowell, Edward Bellamy, Kaiser Wilhelm II, Edward prince of Wales, James Whitcomb *Riley, James McNeill Whistler, Winston Churchill, Booker T. Washington, H. G. Wells, Auguste Rodin, Saint-Saens, Woodrow Wilson, and many others. As he exclaimed to his daughter Susy, "Whom *haven't* I met?"

Of course, many of the people he met, once prominent, would now seem obscure, as media-born celebrity rarely lasts. Twain has retained his fame on the basis of two distinct talents. He was a widely popular writer, with successes in novels, magazine fiction, *essays, newspaper *sketches, and even popular *drama. He also was a gifted stage performer and talker, easily able to make a celebrity based on his personal presence. This combination gave him the tools to build an extraordinarily enduring popularity, especially in the last fifteen years of his life when, after bankruptcy, he needed to use his celebrity to maximum effect in order to recoup his losses. With the gradual demise of subscription publication in the 1890s, he could no longer expect the huge returns on his books that he had counted on early in his career. Increasingly he turned to magazine fiction and trade publication and used his public persona to keep himself constantly marketable.

He also mastered the newspaper *interview. Wherever he went, he turned his journey into a spectacle and made sure to take time out to talk to the press. And his flamboyant grooming and garb, always noted and subject to caricature, became especially photo-worthy when technologies for printing photographs in daily newspapers improved rapidly with the development of half-tone printing, which came into widespread use in 1897. Long accustomed to using his image on lithographed postcards, and even longer fascinated by photography, Twain was well prepared to capitalize on this new advance. The enduring legacy remains all around us; few other nineteenth-century figures are still so readily identifiable and so widely used.

CENSORSHIP. Mark Twain has the distinction of having two titles among the fifty most banned books in America in the 1990s, *Adventures of Huckleberry Finn* and *The Adventures of Tom Sawyer*. The American Library Association's *Intellectual Freedom Manual* describes four common motivations behind challenges to books. The first three are primarily conservative: censors regularly appeal to "traditional" family values, saying a book is corrupt; they may appeal to religion, calling a book sacrilegious; or they may attack a book for having subversive political views. The fourth kind of challenge comes from the other end of the political spectrum, attacking traditional books for denigrating a group or race.

While *Tom Sawyer* may get a few knocks for the hero's lying, cheating, and stealing, Twain's most frequently attacked book, *Huckleberry Finn*, takes its lumps for its frequent use of the vernacular term "nigger," and, in a larger sense, for its characterization of Jim. Since the early 1960s, public high schools have included *Huckleberry Finn* in their curricula, and the post–civil rights movement awareness of racism has made *Huckleberry Finn* the target of many challenges. Many districts have responded by removing the book from required reading lists, others by removing it entirely from the curriculum. A longer standing tradition of censorship occurred silently in the use of editions bowdlerized for school use, in which much offensive *language and behavior was removed without comment. Many schools still circulate such editions as if they were the real *Huckleberry Finn*, even though many new editions carefully explain contexts and invite students to participate in the debate over the value of the book.

Twain would probably have expressed surprise over the grounds of attack today, though he would not have been surprised *that* the book is attacked. In his own time, *Huckleberry Finn* was also subject to censorship challenges, not over the book's representations of race and racism, but because many considered it vulgar. The Concord, Massachusetts, public library, for instance, removed it from circulation almost immediately after acquiring it. As the Boston *Evening Transcript* reported on 17 March 1885:

> The Concord Public Library committee has decided to exclude Mark Twain's latest book from the library. One member of the committee says that, while he does not wish to call it immoral, he thinks it contains but little humor, and that of a very coarse type. He regards it as the veriest trash. The librarian and the other members of the committee entertain similar views, characterizing it as rough, coarse and inelegant, dealing with a series of experiences not elevating, the whole book being more suited to the slums than to intelligent, respectable people.

Twain put a bold public face on the matter, thanking the library for increasing the book's sales, by increasing the number of people who could not get the book any other way and providing such excellent advertising. Privately, however, he fumed. He had long faced standards of literary taste that excluded vernacular voices as debasing, but his own circle of trusted advisors, primarily William Dean *Howells and especially Joseph T. *Goodman, confirmed his own instincts that real American speech was of great literary value.

Up to this point, the power of censorship as a voice of opprobrium had uncolored his language and deflected his writing from topics that interested him. From Bret *Harte and Mary Mason *Fairbanks discouraging his use of slang and the frequent complaints of vulgarity his humorous works received, to British pirate publisher Hotten editing slang out of his works (changes Twain later accepted when he republished in Britain), Twain had been under pressure to elevate his style to conform to values appropriate to family journals and books. His works are replete with references to his adherence to those standards even as he bridled against them. In *"Old Times on the Mississippi," he complained in the beginning of the sixth installment, "Writers of all kinds are manacled servants of the public. We write frankly and fearlessly, but then we 'modify' before we print." In chapter 50 of *A Tramp Abroad*, Twain contrasts the writer's plight with that of painters:

> I wonder why some things are? For instance, Art is allowed as much indecent license to-day as in earlier times—but the privileges of Literature in this respect have been sharply curtailed within the past eighty or ninety years. Fielding and Smollett could portray the beastliness of their day in the beastliest language; we have plenty of foul subjects to deal with in our day, but we are not allowed to approach them very near, even with nice and guarded forms of speech. But not so with Art. The brush may still deal freely with any subject, however revolting or indelicate.

Twain's own effort to invigorate his language in *Huckleberry Finn* led him to the condemnation he received at the hands of the Concord Public Library. While he had many defenders in the press and in other institutions, he knew he was pushing the limits with Huck's graphic speech.

Later, he made censorship an implicit theme of his "Stirring Times in Austria," when he began the piece by condemning the active censors who suppressed much of the Austro-Hungarian Empire's newspaper reporting. He assumed his American and British readers would be scandalized at such suppression, but a few pages later, he begins to show the degree to which his American publishers exercised their own censorship:

> Remark flung across the House to Schonerer: *"Die Grossmutter auf dem Misthaufen erzeugt worden!"* It will be judicious not to translate that. Its flavor is pretty high, in any case, but it becomes particularly gamy when you remember that the first gallery was well stocked with ladies. . . . At one sitting an angry deputy turned upon a colleague and shouted "_____ _____ _____ _____ _____ _____!" You must try to imagine what it was. If I should offer it even in the original it would probably not get by the Magazine editor's blue pencil; to offer a translation would be to waste my ink, of course. This remark was frankly printed in its entirety by one of the Vienna dailies.

According to Clemens, a press boxed in by an official government censor had more liberty in some regards than a magazine protected by a constitutional guarantee of freedom.

Complain as he might about such standards, mostly tending toward prudery and "elevation" of language, Twain surrendered, sometimes grudgingly, but sometimes willingly censoring his own writing. As he put it in the epigraph to chapter 20 of *Following the Equator*, "It is by the goodness of God that in our country we have three unspeakably precious things: freedom of speech, freedom of conscience, and the prudence never to practice either of them." Twain exercised much self-censorship in writing or in suppressing books that he had written but deemed socially unacceptable. Among these are many of his *posthumous publications and *unfinished works.

Among the works published under his name, many were edited against Twain's wishes. When Hotten both pirated and edited Twain's works, of course, Twain had absolutely no control over the results. But proofreaders and editors who should have supported Twain's works often censored them through either minor or major editing. Most conspicuously, in publishing *Tom Sawyer Abroad*, the editors of *St. Nicholas* magazine ruthlessly elevated the style, even though the book is supposed to be in Huck's vernacular voice. This treatment angered Twain greatly, but he did not let the dispute get into the public eye. Worse, after Twain's death, his literary executor, Albert Bigelow *Paine, published many silently edited books purporting to be Twain's work. While Paine's editions of Twain's letters and notebooks, the collection of short works *Europe and Elsewhere*, and his version of the *autobiography are replete with editorial excisions and alterations, the worst travesty is in the bowdlerized The *Mysterious Stranger*.

The steady and careful editing of Twain's works by both the Mark Twain Project and independent scholars is slowly correcting most of this editorial censorship, and only time will tell whether public schools will ultimately retain or remove *Huckleberry Finn* from their curricula. Still, the remarkable thing is not that Twain's works are frequently challenged, but that they are not challenged more frequently and on broader grounds. In one work or another, Twain's satire cuts most cherished American traditions. *Huckleberry Finn* in particular lambastes fundamentalist Christianity with great gusto. Given how often people challenge books for ostensibly supporting Satanism, it is surprising that book burning parties have not been held to execrate *The Mysterious Stranger*, in which an angel named Satan comes to earth to expose the absurdity of human ideas of religion, or *Letters from the Earth*, in which Lucifer handles the same task. To some extent, Twain's status as an American icon has protected him from the very critics he feared most, those whose wrath he feared when he suppressed *"Extract from Captain Stormfield's Visit to Heaven" for decades, restricted publication of *What Is Man?*, and held in private a number of late texts attacking religion. Partly because one never knows whence the attacks will come, pursuing freedom of speech is never easy. As Twain himself

Continued on page 81

Censorship

Nat Hentoff

The boy who remained inside Mark Twain, hoping against hope to be free of all the Aunt Pollys in "sivilization," would have agreed wholeheartedly with one of Twain's more resounding lines: "In the first place God made idiots. This was for practice. Then he made School Boards."

I expect that Twain might have been beguiled by the use of that line by two high school students in Beaver Falls, Pennsylvania, not long ago. The students' adventure speaks to the continual resonance of Twain's view of the follies of official adults. And it also tells of the punishments in store for some of Twain's young readers: not only being deprived of *Adventures of Huckleberry Finn* because of the word "nigger"—which is also in *Tom Sawyer Abroad*—but the kinds of sanctions inflicted on Jessica McCartney and Heidi Schanck, seniors at Blackhawk High School in Beaver Falls.

The two teenagers were considered sufficiently trustworthy to read school announcements over the public address system. To enliven the broadcasts, school officials gave them *A Teacher's Treasury of Quotations*. Looking through the anthology, the students found Twain's observation about idiots and school boards. Since there had been some recent controversy concerning the local school board, the young women thought that the quotation had a certain topical interest and read it over the public address system.

The principal was not amused. Charging the students with "disrespectful behavior," he punished them with three-day in-school suspensions. Furthermore, he commanded them to write letters of apology to each member of the school board, the teachers, and their fellow students. Until this crime, the perpetrators had had clean records. God made school boards *and* principals.

Eventually, having been sharply criticized by the local newspaper as well as some parents and a number of Mark Twain admirers, the principal reduced the suspensions to two days and expunged the record of the students' transgression against common decency. Like Huck Finn, Jessica McCartney and Heidi Schanck would just as soon have escaped from civilization. And the author of *Tom Sawyer Abroad* would not have been at all surprised at the solemn stupidity of their principal.

Indeed, Mark Twain had experienced the solemn stupidity of censors himself, most egregiously with the bowdlerization of *Tom Sawyer Abroad* by Mary Mapes Dodge, who not only "purified" some of the language but even insisted that the illustrators put shoes on Huck—an act he might well have protested as violating his Eighth Amendment right to be free of cruel and unusual punishment if Dodge had been an agent of the state.

79

There is something about that other novel by Twain, *Adventures of Huckleberry Finn*, a story full of the surprises of growing up and out, that has encouraged feverish censorship since its publication. Whatever the reasons that drive quite diverse people to want to exile Huck, the fundamental cause, it seems to me, is fear of his immediate honesty, which leads to his impatience with hypocrisy and pretense, and that leads to his irreverent independence of all pressures to conform. And many people, of all backgrounds, are deeply suspicious of incorrigible nonconformists. While nonconformists make some of us acutely uncomfortable, no civilization that cares about freedom can afford not to have them. We cannot afford to banish Huck.

Continued from page 78

explained in a paper titled "Consistency," delivered to the Hartford *Monday Evening Club in 1887, "The surest way for a man to make of himself a target for almost universal scorn, obloquy, slander, and insult is to stop twaddling about these priceless independencies, and attempt to *exercise* one of them."

♦ SEE ALSO Public Image; Work Habits.

CHARITIES. In "The *Facts Concerning the Recent Carnival of Crime in Connecticut" (1876) one of the narrator's greatest conundrums is what to do about the large number of beggars who come to his door asking for food or money. As a tourist in north Africa and the Near East in 1868, Clemens expressed disgust at the commonplace mendicancy that demonstrated the deep destitution of large percentages of the populations there. His feelings found their way into *The Innocents Abroad* in his remarks on the moral failure of these lands for not promoting the technological and material progress that would end poverty. But his own destitution in California and Nevada, and his family's destitution when he was a child, might have added to his aversion; often those who have climbed out of a situation do not wish to be reminded of it. Be that as it may, when the panic of 1873 hit America, Clemens's comfortable belief in progress came face up against the realities of working-class poverty. He wrote to his wife from England, "There will be such hard times this winter that here will be a multitude of tramps & prowlers about. Send Father Hawley a cheque for $50; have all tramps treated kindly but *sent to Hawley*; give them soup-tickets when they ask for food" (21 November 1873). With that fifty dollars having the buying power of about one thousand dollars today, one

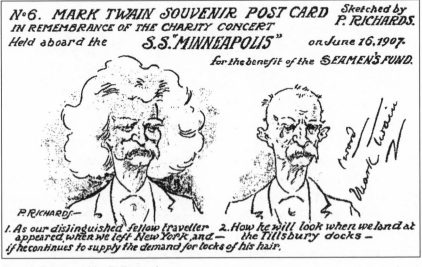

Postcard designed by P. Richards, 1907.

recognizes that Clemens took his charity seriously even if there is a conspicuous gap between the act of alms-giving and the spirit of philanthropy itself.

By the time Twain wrote "Carnival of Crime" a bit over two years later, the depression had not eased and the problem was no closer to resolution. Clemens was not alone in his exasperation; the basic charity that he and members of his *social class considered an obligation was simply not enough to solve the problem or to assuage their guilt. But such charity was the nation's primary response to systematic poverty and other ills, and just as the charity industry today relies on *celebrity participation, Twain was constantly involved in fund-raising activities. He gave time, money, or endorsements to everything from soup kitchens, a relief fund for Walt *Whitman, and the Fisk University Jubilee Singers, to Helen Keller's campaign for schools for the deaf. While these charities wanted his money, they more readily wanted him to help them raise money by giving benefit lectures.

Twain instigated some of his own charitable activities, as when he helped Warner T. McGuinn through law school or when he donated many of his own books to the Redding, Connecticut, Public Library in 1908. More often, charities solicited his participation. In spite of his frequent participation, he not surprisingly grew suspicious of the motives of many operatives. His suspicions manifested themselves in his writing, most conspicuously in "Carnival of Crime" and *Adventures of Huckleberry Finn*'s depiction of the King and Duke working charity scams. Nonetheless, Clemens remained committed to charity as a fundamental action of a socially conscious citizen to the end of his life.

♦ SEE ALSO African Americans; "Man That Corrupted Hadleyburg, The"; Missionaries; Reform.

CHILDHOOD. In *Following the Equator* Twain criticizes Christian missionaries in South Africa for their scrupulous adherence to orthodox rules about salvation: "They are particular about babies. A clergyman would not bury a child according to the sacred rites because it had not been baptized. The Hindoo is more liberal. He burns no child under three, holding that it does not need purifying." Such a statement from Twain in his sixties would hardly have been imaginable thirty years earlier, when he accepted *Calvinism's proposition that human beings are born depraved and children—at least male children—are diabolical agents. He moved a long way toward entertaining the sentimental notion of childhood innocence, though he vacillated between embracing the utilitarian and romantic notions of childhood derived from the same sentimental conception of human character. In both his rejection of Calvinism and his ambivalence over the alternative, Clemens's positions mirror Victorian culture, and his literature participates energetically in Victorian arguments about children's nature and how best to bring that nature into moral adulthood.

This historical shift in childrearing practices derived from, but also fueled, the shift in American religious practice from Calvinism to *sentimentalism. Clemens, raised in a Calvinist environment but surrounded by a culture that had mostly made the shift, tended to pay little attention to children in his early writings. When he did, he usually mocked sentimental notions of childhood. His "Those Blasted Children" (1864) bars no holds in suggesting childhood depravity and shocks readers through its antigenteel extremism, but given Twain's propensities for comic exaggeration, it is doubtful that Clemens's feelings about children ran so deep. More likely, as a bachelor writing primarily for an audience of men in western journals, his propensity for shock *newspaper journalism simply spilled over into a new topic when he turned his attention to the growing field of children's literature and to the subject of childhood itself.

If a shocked reaction was what he sought, he received it almost immediately. Although he published "Those Blasted Children" in the New York *Sunday Mercury*, an eastern weekly well known for its humor, he was chastised in local print by Ada Clare in the San Francisco *Golden Era* for his failure to understand "God's little people." Perhaps such a response provided Twain with incentive enough to continue in this same groove for several more years, with "Advice for Good Little Boys" (1865), "Advice for Good Little Girls" (1865), "The Christmas Fireside" (1865), "Mamie Grant, Child Missionary" (written 1868, *posthumously published), "The Story of the Good Little Boy Who Did Not Prosper" (1870), and "Wit-Inspirations of the 'Two-Year Olds'" (1870).

Strongest reactions came from the growing segment of the population that had adopted new methods of childrearing, designed not to break a child's will but to form it, predicated not on an idea of depravity that needed curbing, but on an innocence that needed both protecting and cultivating. As Lydia Hunt Sigourney, one of the American pioneers of sentimental ideas of motherhood, put it in her best-selling *Letters to Mothers* (1838): "How entire and perfect is this dominion over the unformed character of your infant. Write what you will upon the printless tablet with your wand of love. Hitherto your influence over your dearest friend, your most submissive servant, has known bounds and obstructions. Now you have over a new-born immortal almost that degree of power which the mind exercises over the body." Sentimental childrearing was less harsh than the preceding mode, but the degree of surveillance and control implicit in this model was very much part of the repressive nature of Victorian culture. Indeed, while always describing such motherhood as a process of love, advocates of a sentimental model of childrearing often use language in which power lurks beneath the surface or erupts into public view, as in William Ross Wallace's ditty "The Hand That Rocks the Cradle Is the Hand That Rules the World."

More happily, one of the byproducts of this new view was the development in the nineteenth century of children's literature. With the purpose of uplifting young minds by giving them appropriate *associations on which they could exercise their sensibilities, writers for the first time produced articles and books geared specifically toward the capacities and interests of children. Much of this literature was didactic and explicitly religious, commissioned for use in *Sunday schools. But some was not so close to homily, designed instead as recreational reading for home. While in retrospect much of this literature seems geared to an adult's conception of what children should be thinking, the beginning of children's literature stimulated a concurrent interest in child psychology. Both of these trends had a profound impact on the writings of Twain, whose first reaction regarding the new approach toward schooling was to reject it as too flowery, as in his "Report to the Buffalo Female Academy." Soon, however, when ensconced in his own family and watching his wife rear his own children, Twain turned his hand to writing first about childhood and then, often, even for children.

For Clemens, this shift began not with the birth of his own children, but with his marriage. At that time, he turned his mind nostalgically to his own early years, beginning his initial attempts to recapture his childhood that would eventually lead to *The Adventures of Tom Sawyer*. These first efforts showed how shallow Clemens's Calvinistic belief in childhood depravity was. After marriage, his *nostalgia became conventionally romantic, seeing childhood imitations of adult behavior as essentially innocent and as sanctifying adulthood itself. In this, his wife Olivia's own Romantic notions of family pushed Clemens away from the social practices of a Calvinism he had long since dropped as an active faith. In Olivia's nickname for him, "Youth," she endorsed his fundamental goodness in spite of all of his social flaws and emotional volatility.

The reality of childrearing, however, did not at first lend easy support to Clemens's newly accepted romantic notion of childhood innocence. The brief, unhappy life of his sickly, colicky son exasperated Clemens beyond all measure, doing nothing to endear him to children. No wonder, then, that one of his nicknames for Susy, his second child, was "the Modoc," after a northern California native tribe the existence of which was popularized by Joaquin Miller's accounts of his experiences living with and fighting them. Miller's depiction of a tribe of passionate, warlike natives fit Anglo-America's idea of barbarism, and in nicknaming his daughter after Miller's idea, Clemens playfully expressed his sense of her fundamental wildness. As he put it tongue-in-cheek to Mary Mason *Fairbanks in a 6 July 1873 letter, "The Modoc is able to stand alone, now. She is getting into a habit of swearing when things don't suit. This gives us grave uneasiness." Clearly the term "Modoc" was one of endearment and the uneasiness was veiled pride in his daughter's willfulness. Indeed, he began keeping a record of his children's precocious sayings, a practice he had mocked as late as 1870 in his "Wit-Inspirations" essay. At any rate, as he watched Susy grow, Clemens found himself often able to step briefly outside of cultural expectations of childhood to see instead the difficult task of acculturation that each human being experiences. In this, he began his intellectual movement toward cultural relativism that would culminate in *Following the Equator* and in his anti-imperialist writings of the twentieth century.

Clemens was in the position to observe his children's acculturation precisely because his wife was primarily responsible for raising them, as he gleefully documented. In an 1878 notebook, for instance, he records a conversation between Susy and the landlord at Heidelberg's Schloss-Hotel: "Mr. Albert—Why your papa would let you have [wine]. *Susie*—Yes—but we do as mamma says." In 1885, he took his wife's techniques for raising children public in a 16 July letter to the *Christian Union* on how to spare the rod and still not spoil the child. He describes Olivia's technique of having the children choose their own punishments. Essentially, she used guilt over shame or violence to inculcate morality. Here Clemens explicitly observed children's selfishness being molded to conventional ideals of social responsibility, and in that molding he developed the insights that would guide him in his treatment of childhood in *Adventures of Huckleberry Finn*, in which a child is neither simply innocent nor fundamentally depraved, but caught in the difficult task of following his needs to belong to human community.

As an observer of childrearing rather than as a participant, Clemens was left with the pleasant task of entertaining his children and sympathizing with them as they confronted the difficulties of learning the complex moral and social patterns of Victorian society. He designed his games with the children not only to spark their imaginations, but to spark his as well. He used the audience of his children and of the *Saturday Morning Club to test ideas for literature, and he used amateur theatricals with his children to help him gauge the suitability of various works for dramatization. In a sense, being a father was an extension of Twain's professional life, helping him to understand how to tap the new audience for children's literature. His market research stood him in good stead—few of the many other Victorian writers of children's literature are still read with the same avidity as Twain over a century later. In that sense, his careful observations of children helped him extend the possibilities of children's literature.

But all of his practical development of children's literature notwithstanding, Clemens became deeply invested in an ideal of childhood innocence that became more important to his literature in later years, even as his conception of the worldly cost of innocence grew more tragic. Later works, such as *Personal Recollections of Joan of Arc* or the unfinished *"Chronicle of Young Satan," suggest that childhood innocence will always be sacrificed to the immoral needs of the adult world, or even of the divine plan. In this mood, the nostalgic praise of childhood that dominates the portions of his *autobiography that he published in his own lifetime rise above a mere tribute to one lost child and instead become a tragic tribute to the impossibility of innocence living. Thus did the cynical part of Twain derive as much from his culture's romanticism as from his own early Calvinism.

CHINESE IN AMERICA, like other nonwhites, were subject not only to discrimination, but to overt extralegal harassment, humiliation, and intimidation. This was especially true in the West where, in the 1860s and 1870s, governments encouraged immigration to provide cheap labor for railroad construction and support services in mining operations. But throughout the West, as competition for unskilled labor increased, especially among other immigrant groups like the Irish, the Chinese were regularly beaten and even lynched. Conscience over such treatment of the Chinese seems to have sparked Clemens's own growth away from the racism he imbibed in his youth.

Ironically enough, Clemens's conscience about racial matters began in racism. In a letter to fellow Virginia City *Territorial Enterprise* reporter William *Wright, he said that he and Steve Gillis, rooming together in a house that overlooked San Francisco's Chinatown, used to hurl empty beer bottles on the tin roofs of the houses below in order to "see the poor Chinamen scatter like flies" (15 July 1864). Given the audience, this account could very well be fiction, but in suggesting that such behavior is funny, Twain reveals his own bias. Yet while in San Francisco in 1864, as a reporter for the *Morning Call*, he came across a common racial incident:

> One Sunday afternoon I saw some hoodlums chasing and stoning a Chinaman who was heavily laden with the weekly wash of his Christian customers, and I noticed that a policeman was observing this performance with an amused interest—nothing more. He did not interfere. I wrote up the incident with considerable warmth and holy indignation. . . . I sought for it in the paper next morning with eagerness. It wasn't there. . . . The foreman said Mr Barnes had found it in a galley proof and ordered its extinction. And Mr. Barnes furnished his reasons— . . . and they were commercially sound. He said that the *Call* was . . . the washerwoman's paper—that is, it was the paper of the poor. . . . The Irish were the poor. They were the stay and support of the *Morning Call* . . . and they hate the Chinamen. (autobiographical dication, 13 June 1906)

Clemens's own dislike of the Irish, going back to his earliest political beliefs as a Know-Nothing party supporter, in part spurred his defense of the Chinese in such articles as "What Have the Police Been Doing" (1866), "Disgraceful Persecution of a Boy" (1870), "John Chinaman in New York" (1870), and "Goldsmith's Friend Abroad Again" (1870–1871). In these pieces, he describes a cultured people trying to mind their business in spite of barbaric treatment from lower-class whites. His defense in *Roughing It* of California "ladies and gentlemen" from the charge of anti-Chinese racism implicitly continues his attack on the Irish as the riff-raff who do persecute the Chinese. His newly dawning racial tolerance did not extend very far in 1872, nor do his stereotypical descriptions of the Chinese show great cultural sensitivity. But his willingness to see a civilized people where many Euro-Americans saw barbarians became one of his primary moral traits.

His pro-Chinese attitudes helped him fit into Hartford's *Nook Farm community, which not only tended to support the rights of blacks, but also found other racial causes to espouse. One of Nook Farm's most influential clergymen, Rev. Joseph *Twichell, took on the plight of the Chinese in America as one of his ministerial causes, helping to found and preserve Hartford's Chinese Educational Mission, which funded the education in America of young Chinese men. No doubt Clemens's familiarity with the large western Chinese communities was a point of common interest for the two men. Given their friendship and Clemens's ever increasing cosmopolitanism and racial tolerance, it is no surprise that Clemens continued to defend the Chinese, especially toward the end of his career when his adamant opposition to European and American imperialism manifested itself in defense of the so-called Boxer rebellion, especially in "To the Person Sitting in Darkness." While Twichell and Clemens shared their abhorrence of anti-Chinese racism, they did not come at it with the same intentions. Twichell saw his humanitarianism as part of an evangelical purpose; Clemens disparaged the idea of spreading Christianity to the Chinese, as can be seen in "The *United States of Lyncherdom."

♦ SEE ALSO Gillis, James N. (Jim) and Steve; Newspaper Journalism; Race Relations.

CHRISTIAN SCIENCE (1907). In the last ten years of his life, Clemens devoted considerable attention to Christian Science, writing numerous articles, which he ultimately collected in *Christian Science*, and beginning several literary fantasies in which Christian Science figures prominently. *Christian Science* begins in a light-hearted way, teasing the inconsistencies out of Christian Science doctrine but never denying the humane value of faith healing for those whose ailments are susceptible to mental control. He seemed to encourage his daughters to investigate Christian Science—Clara ultimately joined the church.

In the unpublished fragments "The Secret History of Eddypus, the World Empire" and *"Three Thousand Years among the Microbes," however, Clemens expressed paranoid fantasies about the power, duplicity, and cupidity of the church, sardonically imagining, in "Eddypus," a century-spanning totalitarian theocracy built on an ecclesiastical court combined from Christian Science and Roman Catholicism. "Three Thousand Years among the Microbes" is more tolerant of the value of belief in the church, but still dismisses it as a patent fraud, bent on fleecing susceptible young women. The reasons for Clemens's fascination and fear are not readily apparent a century later, as Christian Science never has boasted more than one out of four hundred Americans among its followers. Still, it grew astronomically in the late nineteenth and early twentieth centuries, and its blend of the language of mysticism with the language of *science did touch a chord that still res-onates in American culture, though outside of the intense ecclesiastical control that Mary Baker Eddy established for the church she founded.

Christian Science is an American-born harmonial *religion, that is, as historian Sydney Ahlstrom puts it in *A Religious History of the American People*, one that "encompasses those forms of piety and belief in which spiritual composure, physical health, and even economic well-being are understood to flow from a person's rap-port with the cosmos." The church had its origins in the 1830s when mesmerism and other early forms of *spiritualism were making their mark in America. Phineas Parkhurst Quimby, a Maine spiritualist who had a successful practice as a faith healer, coined the terms "science of health" and "Christian Science" in his practice, which he felt went behind the forms of mesmerism to the fundamental ideas of divinity. His cures, he alleged, were similar to those of Jesus Christ, because he had discovered that human beings, as spiritual beings, needed merely to have an imme-diate connection to God's mind to attain worldly perfection.

The similarity, here, to Emersonian transcendentalism and to other forms of mysticism shows how close Quimby was to the center of American religious prac-tice. His greatest success was in curing Mary Baker Glover Patterson, a woman whose ill health throughout her life led her to seek morphine treatments as readily as spiritualist healers. Widowed once and ill-married to an itinerant dentist, she had good psychological reasons for her invalidism, and when Quimby cured her, he released a pent-up life's worth of energy. On Quimby's death in 1866, Patterson had a deep relapse, hurting her back in a fall on the ice, from which she cured herself by reading Matthew 9:2 about Christ healing a paralytic by forgiving his sins. Patterson dated the founding of Christian Science from that moment.

She took over Quimby's mission and, especially after the death of Patterson in 1873, devoted herself single-mindedly to that work, first founding a church and col-lege, and later organizing it to reflect her complete authorization of the church's message. She married Asa Gilbert Eddy, a collaborator in her mission. (Inci-dentally, Asa Eddy died in 1882. Mary Baker Eddy's marital history explains Mark Twain's quip in *Christian Science* that Eddy was a "widow in the third degree.") She said that she had received divine enlightenment about how to read the scripture, and her *The Science of Health with Key to the Scriptures* promoted that revelation, with her position as medium central to the message.

The church did prosper quickly under her charismatic leadership, with 85,000 declared adherents by 1906 and over 200,000 twenty years later. Most of these adherents were relatively wealthy, educated urban women, who found appealing both the church's message and its inclusion of women in its organization. Eddy's influence spread even further through sales of her book: 50,000 copies by 1891, 400,000 by her death in 1910. Eddy's message, that all ill results in life were merely the failure of an individual to believe strenuously enough, fit into a particularly American form of optimism. Ironically, Eddy herself built her reputation in part through her reclusiveness, working much of her organizational magic through agents. She hid herself away, anxious about her own ailments—for which she regularly took morphine—believing that her pain was the result of the mesmeric influence of her enemies. Fears notwithstanding, she amassed significant power within her church and significant wealth through it; she left an estate worth over two million dollars to her church. Somehow, Clemens seemed in touch with Eddy's paranoia and megalomania, believing in her power as a master player of *confidence games, even as he was skeptical of her doctrine.

◆ SEE ALSO Health and Disease.

"CHRONICLE OF YOUNG SATAN." This is the gold mine from which editors Albert Bigelow *Paine and Frederick Duneka extracted The *Mysterious Stranger, though they left behind much good ore in their effort to turn a scathing satire into an innocuous romance. The entire lode has been available since 1969 with the publication of the *Mark Twain Papers volume The Mysterious Stranger Manuscripts.

Clemens wrote this work in three installments—from October 1897 to January 1898, May to October 1899 while living in Vienna, and June to August 1900 while living in London—before abandoning it. He did not write for publication but for catharsis during one of the most bitterly painful periods of his life. He had just faced and cleared himself from bankruptcy; at the same time, one daughter, Olivia Susan (Susy), died and another, Jean, was diagnosed with epilepsy. His wife's deteriorating health further depressed his spirits, and his awareness of political events throughout the world merely added to his gloom. In a notebook entry of 10 November 1895 he wrote, "It is the strangest thing that the world is not full of books that scoff at the pitiful world, and the useless universe and violent, contemptible human race—books that laugh at the paltry scheme and deride it. . . . Why don't I write such a book? Because I have a family." "Chronicle of Young Satan" carries the same tone and served the same emotional needs. As he wrote in a 22 January 1898 letter to William Dean *Howells, "I couldn't get along without work now. I bury myself in it up to the ears. Long hours—8 & 9 on a stretch, sometimes. And all the days, Sundays included. It isn't all for print, by any means, for much of it fails to suit me: 50,000 words of it in the past year. It was because of the deadness which invaded me when Susy died." In an effort to relieve his "deadness," Clemens wrote a parable of suffering and enlightenment.

Undoubtedly, "Chronicle" scoffs at the pitiful world. The story makes reference not only to medieval religious bigotry and inquisitions, but also to current political events. Appalled by the rising *anti-Semitism he saw in Vienna, he modeled his story's villain, Father Adolf, on Karl Lueger, the charismatic mayor of Vienna and head of Austria's anti-Semitic Christian Socialist party. The intolerance and hypocrisy in the story's opening pages is powerful enough *satire, but the piece really pulls out all the stops when Satan arrives in Eseldorf (German for "Donkeyville"). Everything he does serves to highlight human incompetence, limitation, and depravity. In particular, the little theater of war that Satan helps the boys manufacture mocks late nineteenth-century militarism, which becomes a leitmotif of the entire tale. As Satan later explicitly puts it, "In that day the lands and people of the whole pagan world will be at the mercy of the sceptered bandits of Europe, and they will take them. Furnishing in return, the blessings of civilization ... then the pagan world will go to school to the Christian; not to acquire his religion but his guns. The Turk and the Chinaman will buy those, to kill missionaries and converts with." The angel Satan's all-encompassing contempt appears unanswerable.

Oddly, what Clemens discovered as he wrote was not human depravity and the cosmos' contempt for it, but the need for human beings to care less for their place in the universe and more for each other. If human beings are so depraved, Clemens reasoned, it is not their fault but the fault of their creator. As he put it in a 12 May 1899 letter to Howells, "Damn these human beings; if I had invented them I would go hide my head in a bag." Satan is so proud of his powers and so contemptuous of human beings that it never occurs to him to be ashamed of *himself* as an agent of that creation. Unfortunately, most of the human beings he meets also do not think to ignore divine power in favor of caring for one another. Whenever Satan appears, human beings defer to him, neglecting and harming one another. The tale's narrator, though, does reach this understanding, as he complains about the inappropriateness of Satan's standards: "He had never felt a pain or a sorrow, and did not know what they were." Without sympathy, the divine power is irrelevant to the human condition. Thus, the satire that begins as an attack on human beings turns back on the gods, and in so doing demands of human beings that they become their own measures of morality. Only in a compassion that arises from self-concern and experience, suggests Clemens, can human beings find their own salvation.

♦ SEE ALSO Unfinished Works.

CITIES. "I have at last," Twain wrote from New York City to the San Francisco *Alta California* in June 1867, "after several month's experience, made up my mind that it is a splendid desert—a domed and steepled solitude, where the stranger is lonely in the midst of a million of his race." Such is the conventional lament of a nineteenth-century American in the big city. Many held to the agrarian ideal preached by eighteenth-century writers such as Thomas Jefferson and Hector St. John de Crèvecouer as an alternative both to the putative barbarism of the frontier and the corrupt over-sophistication of the big city. This type of vision has held powerful sway over the American imagination, leading to the development of sub-urbs, which create the illusion of space and independence for Americans whose livelihoods depend on the commerce and industry of cities.

In some ways, given that Clemens grew up in a very small town on the rural edge of American culture, one would expect Twain's writings to reflect this anticity note. They do not. Whenever Clemens had the choice, he chose city vice over country virtue, in part because he, like an ever increasing number of Americans in the post–Civil War period during which the growth of the great cities far out-stripped the growth of the rural population, preferred the excitement and economic opportunity of urban life. He also rejected the idea that the city was intrinsically the abode of corruption. Clemens was born in a small town, but in a town nonethe-less, and while he spent some summers on his Uncle Quarles's farm, his orientation as a craftsman in the publishing industry was toward the urban world.

From early in the eighteenth century, artisan laborers equated the traditions and skills of crafts labor with the alleged independence and virtue of the yeoman farmer so celebrated by Jefferson. Clemens inherited that ethos in his printing apprentice-ships, and as such gravitated toward cities all his life. His first trips from home took him to St. Louis; New York; Philadelphia; Washington, D.C.; and Cincinnati, where he may have failed economically but discovered an appetite for broader work and *leisure opportunities than those offered in rural America. His second career as a steamboat pilot familiarized him with New Orleans, and his subsequent career as writer saw him living at various times in San Francisco; Washington, D.C.; Buffalo; *Hartford; Paris; Berlin; Vienna; London; and, repeatedly, New York, as well as visiting major cities around the world.

Most of his travel narratives and short fiction deal with contemporary life in cities, and while he returned regularly to small town and country life in his works set in the *Mississippi River valley, his depiction of the country is usually an effort to debunk the myth of the virtuous agrarian life. The Mississippi countryside he depicts in *Tom Sawyer, Huckleberry Finn*, and *Life on the Mississippi* is one of unjust privilege supported through violence and maintained through ignorance. In par-ticular, *Life on the Mississippi* praises the North as progressive and the South as regressive in proportion to which the North is home to more industrial cities. In Twain's work, with few exceptions, the city is the locus of *progress, based in part on technology and *education.

Nevertheless, Clemens did to some degree accept the American ideal of a middle state between the frontier and the city. He and his family chose to settle in suburban developments in large *houses with significant grounds. He even bought a neighboring empty parcel in Hartford to prevent anyone else from building too close to his home. His family usually summered at Quarry Farm outside of *Elmira, New York. But like most American suburban dwellers, Clemens's liveli-hood was based in the industries of cities, and he withdrew to the country not to farm, but to spend some time in pastoral withdrawal. The idea of country and nature as an amusement park or as a subject worthy of *nostalgia is yet another byproduct of urbanization. In this way, Twain's local color *realism is of a piece with the urbanization of his time.

◆ SEE ALSO Labor Movement.

CIVIL WAR. If one were to extend west through Missouri the Mason-Dixon Line, the surveyor's mark dividing Pennsylvania from Maryland and mythically the North from the South, one would find that *Hannibal lies almost on the line, just about where Clemens stood when the Civil War broke out. As a boy, he developed strong *patriotism for the United States, writing home to his family from Philadelphia, for instance, with pride in the "revolutionary associations" (28 October 1853), including the room in which the "mighty Declaration of Independence was passed by Congress, July 4th, 1776. When a stranger enters this room for the first time, an unaccountable feeling of awe and reverence comes over him, and every memento of the past his eye rests upon whispers that he is treading upon sacred ground" (4 December 1853). His letters show little of his political leanings in the years immediately preceding the war, but his niece reported that he voted for John Bell in the presidential election of 1860, suggesting that he favored both the Union and the southern system on which he was economically dependent as a steamboat pilot in the St. Louis-to-New Orleans trade.

Family tradition and one midwar letter from his mother indicate that Clemens was violently opposed to his boyhood friend Will Bowen's ardent secessionist sympathies, going so far as to fight him on the steamboat they were both piloting. Nonetheless, when the war broke out, he sided with Missouri and the secessionists rather than with the Union. His niece, Pamela Moffett, recalled,

> In the spring of 1861, when I was eight years old, Uncle Sam returned home to St. Louis, his occupation of pilot lost forever. He came on the last boat from New Orleans to get through the Union lines. He was obsessed with the fear that he might be arrested by government agents and forced to act as pilot on a government gunboat while a man stood by with a pistol ready to shoot him if he showed the least sign of a false move. He was almost afraid to leave the house. (*Mark Twain, Business Man*, 60)

In contrast, Horace Bixby, who trained Clemens in piloting, served as a Union pilot through the war, and Will Bowen, whose Confederate sympathies remained hot, also served as a Union pilot but used the opportunity to carry mail for the Confederacy.

Moffett continues, "[Clemens] loved his country's flag and all that it symbolized, and it hurt him to see even [a] cheap little flag insulted. I know he would gladly have given his life for his country, but he was a Southerner, his friends were all

Southern, his sympathies were with the South" (62). Hence, when invited back to Hannibal to join a Confederate militia, he left St. Louis, perhaps as much to avoid being drafted as a Union pilot as to fight *for* the South. At all events, he kept his visit to Hannibal secret from his brother Orion *Clemens, whose ardent support of Abraham Lincoln's election and the Union cause would have opened Samuel to reproach. After a brief stint as a Confederate militiaman, partially fictionalized in "The *Private History of a Campaign That Failed," Clemens decided not to make his participation formal or enduring. He instead accepted his brother's offer to leave for Nevada territory, where Orion was bound as the newly appointed Union secretary to the governor.

Such, say most critics, was the extent of Clemens's involvement in the salient political event of his lifetime, a limited role that made him a virtual outsider to the American scene. Certainly his experience with the patriotic pressures put on a person in time of war may have affected his patriotism, leading him to become skeptical about the connections between self-sacrifice and one's country. To this extent he may have been unusual, though the number of men who did not enlist would suggest otherwise—ambivalence characterized America's response as much as passionate commitment. Still, to say that Clemens did not participate in the war is to assume the impact of the war was felt only by those on the battlefield.

Twain himself may have helped create this idea by writing in chapter 45 of *Life on the Mississippi* of the truly profound impact the war had on those whose homes it destroyed, but he also makes clear in that chapter that the Civil War was as much about ideas as battles. In this sense, there was no escaping the Civil War in fleeing west. Indeed, the importance Lincoln's administration placed on the West as a source of money for the war and as a region that would help bind the Union led to the appointment of a territorial administration in the first place. (Orion Clemens's design for the seal for Nevada territory included "a motto expressing the two ideas of loyalty to the Union and the wealth to sustain it, '*volens et potens*'.") Those on the ground in the new territory kept up the political battle, with the war of words often threatening to break out into something more, as in the border dispute with California over the Aurora mining district near Mono Lake. The California contingent was made up primarily of Confederate sympathizers (even though California was securely in the Union camp), who threatened to prevent the Nevada territorial government from ruling over them. Their use of the border dispute to resist the power of the Union government erupted into low-level violence.

Feelings ran high enough that Clemens expressed his views on the war only circumspectly in his letters. Yet careful reading of them shows at most a lukewarm support of the Union cause. One of the most notorious incidents of his time in Nevada suggests his real hostility to the northern cause of ending *slavery. While working for the Virginia City *Territorial Enterprise*, he wrote a squib accusing the Sanitary Commission (a precursor of the Red Cross) of collecting funds to support a "miscegenation society." The ensuing brouhaha forced Clemens out of Nevada as persona non grata. He claims that the publication of the squib was an accident, and that he wrote it merely as a private joke when under the influence of *alcohol. Yet even as a jest, or perhaps especially as a jest, it reveals his biases.

Still, the North gradually won the war for Clemens's heart and mind. He became a real convert to the Union cause, substantially because he came to change his mind about slavery. By the time he courted Olivia Langdon, a member of a family of ardent abolitionists and unionists, Clemens wanted to join her circle in part because he was coming to embrace her family's politics. In a 1 November 1876 letter to an old Missouri friend, Jacob H. Burrough, Clemens wrote of his change:

> As you describe me I can picture myself as I was, twenty-two years of age. The portrait is correct. You think I have grown some; upon my word there was room for it. You have described a callow fool, a self-sufficient ass, a mere human tumble-bug. . . . Ignorance, intolerance, egotism, self-assertion, opaque perception, dense and pitiful chuckle-headedness. . . . That is what I was at 19-20; & that is what the average Southerner is at 60 to-day.

As William Dean *Howells puts it in *My Mark Twain*, "The part of him that was Western in his Southwestern origin Clemens kept to the end, but he was the most desouthernized Southerner I ever knew. . . . [He] was entirely satisfied with the result of the Civil War, and he was eager to have its facts and meanings brought out at once in history" (chapter 9). To some degree Clemens even helped to bring out those meanings. For instance, in chapter 45 of *Roughing It*, he revised his estimate of the Sanitary Commission's efforts.

In a very real sense, as much as the war began long before the firing on Fort Sumter in 1861, the Civil War did not end with Lee's surrender at Appomattox in 1865. Radical Reconstruction attempted to make permanent in the federal Constitution and the administration of state governments the victories that the North had won on the battlefield. Nonetheless, while the passage of the thirteenth through fifteenth amendments altered the Constitution, the disputed election of Rutherford B. Hayes in 1876 basically ended Reconstruction and the hopes of northern radicals for a total victory, not only to save the union of the states, but also to create a union of the people by ending legal racial discrimination. At this point, the Civil War turned into a symbolic battle, one to which Clemens was totally committed. He helped wage this battle by publishing the memoirs of Ulysses S. *Grant and in much of his own writing, including "A *True Story, Repeated Word for Word as I Heard It," *Life on the Mississippi*, *Adventures of Huckleberry Finn*, *Pudd'nhead Wilson and Those Extraordinary Twins*, and "The *United States of Lyncherdom."

CLASS. SEE Social Class.

CLEMENS, CLARA. SEE Samossoud, Clara Clemens Gabrilowitsch.

CLEMENS, HENRY (1838–1858). In later years, Clemens always described his younger brother as the good son, in contrast to his own rebelliousness. Yet in a family that honored a strong *work ethic as the central component of a fine character, Samuel was the good, diligent son in contrast to Henry's wicked laziness. At least Clemens implies this in the letters he wrote home in the 1850s, which frequently refer to his younger brother's family reputation as the lazy, sloppy worker. For instance, in an 1853 letter from New York City to Pamela Clemens Moffett in which Clemens proposes a way to help Orion, his older brother, and Henry prosper as printers, Clemens says his plan would easily work "if $5.00 for 25,000 [typeset words] (per week) could beat a little work into (no offence to him) Henry's lazy bones!" (8 October).

Clemens was always looking out for the financial interests of all of his siblings. In 1858, as an apprentice steamboat pilot, he found a situation for Henry as a "mudclerk" on a steamboat, once again saving Henry the work of putting his own life together. Henry died shortly thereafter in a steamboat accident. Clemens blamed himself for his brother's death. Thus, when Clemens said that his relationship with Henry was the model for that between Tom and Sid Sawyer, he strangely distorted reality. Certainly, their relationship was often fractious, especially when the older brother resented Henry's ability to ditch work and responsibility, but such rivalries do not explain Clemens's sense of moral inferiority. More likely, Clemens's own overly developed sense of responsibility, coupled with the impossibility of ever living up to the ideal of the good son, made him mischievously exalt his dead brother as the family's "good little boy."

♦ SEE ALSO Moffett, Pamela Clemens and William A.

CLEMENS, JANE LAMPTON (1803–1890). "When I was younger," Twain wrote in his autobiography, "I could remember anything, whether it had happened or not; but my faculties are decaying now, and soon I shall be so I cannot remember any but the things that never happened" (*North American Review*, 1 March 1907, corrected according to original manuscript). His remarkably accurate memory made this quip an ironic cover in most cases, but in the case of his mother, it is remarkably true. For a man who usually based his fiction on fact, his memories of his mother follow the opposite pattern: they are based primarily on fiction. For instance, he said he had based Aunt Polly in *The Adventures of Tom Sawyer* on his mother, but most of the salient episodes that he claimed were from his own childhood actually came from B. P. Shillaber's Mrs. Partington stories.

In a work of fiction multiple derivations are no problem, but when such incidents get cited as reality, biography suffers. When interviewing Clemens for *Mark*

Twain: A Biography, Albert Bigelow Paine took Clemens's characterization of his mother at face value, translating Clemens's stories into ostensible fact:

> Her sense of pity was abnormal. She refused to kill even flies, and punished the cat for catching mice. She would drown the young kittens, when necessary, but warmed the water for the purpose. On coming to Hannibal, she joined the Presbyterian Church, and her religion was of that clean-cut, strenuous kind which regards as necessary institutions hell and Satan, though she had been known to express pity for the latter for being obliged to surround himself with such poor society. (chapter 9)

Again, the story of warming the water before drowning kittens comes from Shillaber, who, like Clemens, tried to sentimentalize the Calvinist past by presenting Calvinist women as torn between soft hearts and wrong-headed principles.

Clemens's efforts to expunge the religious intensity of his own mother and the other women from his past suggest some ambivalence toward them and that past. Ambivalent or not, however, Clemens never rejected his mother. In fact, as his career became the most permanently successful of any of Jane Lampton Clemens's surviving three children, he supported her until her death. All the while, his experiences in the world were so far beyond her horizons that the simplest of pleasures—such as theater or dancing—to which he introduced her evoked in her a mixture of astonishment and censure. To have become a writer of comic fiction and drama—worldly lies in the minds of the orthodox Calvinists of the first third of the nineteenth century—Clemens had to outgrow, if not reject, his mother. But as a public figure whose livelihood depended on an image as a family man, his growth beyond her sphere had to be colored in a satisfactorily sentimental way. And he was fond of her—he dedicated *The Innocents Abroad*, his first major book, to her. But his development as a writer required him to fictionalize that relationship in ways that make it difficult for us fully to know.

What is known about Jane Lampton Clemens is that she was born in 1803 in Lexington, Kentucky. In 1823, after breaking off an engagement to Richard Barrett, she quickly married John Marshall Clemens, perhaps out of spite. Their marriage was neither warm nor close, though it did yield seven children. She outlived all but three—Orion, Pamela, and Samuel—who provided for her after her husband's death in 1847 until her own death in 1890.

Immediately after her husband's death, Jane Clemens and her surviving children, Orion, Pamela, Samuel, and Henry, remained in Hannibal. Individual members left over the years, however, with first Pamela marrying and moving to St. Louis, and then Samuel leaving to become an itinerant printer in various cities around the country. When Orion moved to Muscatine, Iowa, in 1853, Jane Clemens moved with him and lived in his home. When Orion moved again the next year to

Keokuk, Iowa, Jane Lampton Clemens did not follow. She moved instead to the home of her daughter and son-in-law, successful St. Louis merchant William A. Moffett.

During these years, Samuel saw her frequently, especially when he became a riverboat pilot. As a pilot, Clemens quickly grew away from his mother's moralistic and narrow orbit, but he tried to bring her along. Not only did he see her and correspond with her regularly, but he also took her on a trip to New Orleans by steamboat in 1861. There he teased and cajoled her about her strictures against entertainment, keeping her up late to watch him dance with several young women:

> Ma was delighted with her trip, but she was disgusted with the girls for allowing me to embrace and kiss them—and she was horrified at the Schottische as performed by Miss Castle and me. She was perfectly willing for me to dance until 12 o'clock at the imminent peril of my going to sleep on the after watch—but then she would top off with a very inconsistent sermon on dancing in general; ending with a terrific broadside aimed at that heresy of heresies, the Schottische. (to Orion Clemens, 18 March 1861)

This letter to his brother reveals Clemens's sense of his mother as a conflicted audience to his high spirits. His portrait of his mother as moving away from the strictures of her Calvinist beliefs may have had a fundamental reality even as he fictionalized the circumstances. In fact, as much as she may have spoken the religious line, she apparently was rather high-spirited in her own youth and always had a robust sense of humor.

Certainly, Clemens's relationship with his mother over the next several years was one of playful banter. His letters home from Nevada territory intimate that he was pushing the boundaries of decency in ways that would induce her to sermonize, but that show him never actually crossing those boundaries beyond a limit of which she tacitly approved. Furthermore, the very joking about idleness and bad language against a backdrop of hard work and creative prose shows that he had not transgressed at all—or so he wanted her to believe. Many of his other letters from the years in Nevada suggest otherwise. In correspondence with men his own age, Clemens reveals himself as a profane, impatient, hard-drinking man who in fact had crossed his mother's line more than once.

From that point on, even as he tried to redeem himself by the civilized standards of eastern gentility while courting Olivia Langdon, and even as he took the burden of supporting his mother off the hands of his economically flailing brother and recently widowed sister, he never was close to his mother again. He did try to find her and his sister Pamela a place to live near enough for him to visit regularly. Shortly after moving to Buffalo, New York, Clemens moved them to Fredonia, New York, in 1870. But they were as unhappy in upstate New York as he was, and his business and lack of interest kept him an infrequent visitor. For that matter, his mother visited him in his Hartford home rarely, perhaps only twice. Jane Clemens moved back to Orion's house in Keokuk in 1883, where she lived until her death in 1890.

As much as Clemens fairly early grew beyond his mother's intellectual and moral sphere, her influence on his writing is seminal and enduring. His obsessive and pervasive concerns with questions of divine justice and personal rectitude were, of course, congruent with the concerns of his age, but the particularly puritanical inflection in his treatment of these issues points back to his earliest days. More importantly, perhaps, as the recipient of many letters from the eastern seaboard and from the far West, Jane Clemens was the primary early audience for Clemens's comic writing. In this context, her censorious puritanism was only partly a constraining influence; while it may have forced Clemens to tone down his most vigorous writing, it made the rich humor possible in playing constraint against desire, limitation against possibility, control against license. She was the first in a series of female readers whose sense of humor and susceptibility to shock provided the frisson that Clemens needed in order to find his best voice and richest humor.

♦ SEE ALSO Calvinism; Moffett, Pamela Clemens and William A.

CLEMENS, JANE LAMPTON (JEAN) (1880–1909).

The youngest of Samuel and Olivia Langdon Clemens's four children, Jane Lampton Clemens was named for her paternal grandmother, but was called Jean to distinguish her from her namesake.

As much as the Clemens household revolved around the children in the 1870s and 1880s, Jean was farther from the center than her sisters. Neither as precocious as Susy nor as entertainingly willful as Clara, and significantly younger than either, Jean occupied the position of perpetual baby in the family, a situation solidified by her precarious health. When two years old she contracted scarlet fever, from which her recovery was slow and perhaps never complete. As early as age ten, she began having mysterious episodes that were finally diagnosed, six years later, as epilepsy, which may have been a long-term consequence of her earlier fever. After her diagnosis in 1896, the then transient Clemens family spent much time, effort, and money trying to find a cure, seeking new treatments wherever they were. They even moved to Sanna, Sweden, to try Jonas Kellgren's treatments in 1899. But the symptoms steadily worsened, and Jean spent much of her life after her mother's death in 1904 in various sanatoriums, especially after her attacks became increasingly violent. In the winter of 1905–1906, two of her attacks turned so violent that housekeeper Katy Leary felt that Jean had tried to kill her.

Certainly in the years during which Isabel *Lyon ran Clemens's household, Jean had little contact with her father, partially because Lyon kept Jean's letters from

Clemens, ostensibly to protect him, perhaps to isolate him. With Clara living in Europe and Susy and Olivia dead, Clemens and Jean were equally lonely and often depressed over their isolation. Jean, of course, was furious over her perceived abandonment, but as much as Clemens thought Jean's institutionalization was for the best, he felt guilty for her isolation, and he missed her company. Their separation was tragic for both.

The pain of this separation was all the more poignant considering the difficulties Jean had experienced in growing up. While Susy and Clara came of age in Hartford in a stable home, Jean reached young adulthood during the turbulent years of the 1890s when financial failure kept the Clemens family moving from one temporary home to another. As both her parents shared horror at the dissolution of the family's financial stability, they hung on to their daughters ferociously. They impeded the development of the romantic life of each of their daughters, and gave mixed signals about the development of their daughters' vocations. But while all three suffered under this dark turn in the family's fortunes, Jean suffered the most. Having no obvious talents that demanded cultivation and a debilitating illness that impeded normal development, as well as being younger and less strong-willed than her sisters, Jean more or less retreated into the role of perpetual child.

She did try, however, to make a fulfilling career out of charity work and *reform activity. In particular, she joined the nascent animal rights movement. (It was at her request that Clemens wrote "A Dog's Tale" and "A Horse's Tale.") Such charity was, for many women, a conventional alternative to professional work, not to *domesticity. Naturally, then, when Olivia's death and Clara's departure left Samuel and Jean as the remaining family, Jean expected to be with him. Her enraged letters attest to the depth of her anger and disappointment that she was ostracized from the family.

When Clara finally intervened and forced Lyon's ouster from the Clemens household, Clemens took Jean back home to serve as his private secretary in April 1909. This arrangement apparently worked, or at least it did not have time to sour. Jean died on Christmas Eve 1909. She apparently suffered a seizure while taking a bath and either died of a heart attack or of drowning. Clemens, suffering from congestive heart disease, was too ill to attend Jean's funeral in Elmira. It was then he penned his last significant piece of writing, "The Death of Jean."

♦ SEE ALSO Health and Disease.

CLEMENS, JOHN MARSHALL (1798–1847). John Marshall Clemens, Samuel Clemens's father, was born in Virginia but spent too little time there for his recollections to be anything more accurate or less powerful than the nostalgia of a child. On his own father's death in 1805, his mother moved the family to Kentucky where she remarried in 1809. It is unclear how traumatic he found the loss of his father, but the reports of his lifelong pride in his Virginia ancestry and the history

of his teen years suggest that it was a watershed event leaving him emotionally scarred. As a teenager he worked as a clerk while studying law, and when he came of age, he actually paid his stepfather for the costs of raising him.

As an adult he moved frequently in search of better prospects, first to Tennessee in 1825, two years after marrying Jane Lampton. Over the next several years, he moved his family repeatedly, all the while accumulating substantial holdings of land in eastern Tennessee. In 1835, he moved his family to Florida, Missouri, following his brother-in-law, John Quarles. Active in politics and land promotions as well as in his dry-goods business and law practice, he proved himself remarkably unlucky as a businessman, and relocated yet again, to *Hannibal, Missouri, in 1839. He died of pneumonia there in 1847.

The flightiness of his business dealings seems unlikely given his character. Twain describes him in *Following the Equator* as "a refined and kindly gentleman, very grave, rather austere, of rigid probity, a sternly just and upright man, albeit he attended no church and never spoke of religious matters, and had no part nor lot in the pious joys of his Presbyterian family, nor ever seemed to suffer from this deprivation" (chapter 38). Clemens thus compresses much about his father and his father's relation to his family in a kind of shorthand. His father prided himself on his Virginia background, believing in the aristocracy of the first families. Born in the eighteenth century, he shared the Enlightenment's religious skepticism, though living in the trans-Allegheny West for most of his life, he was surrounded by the newly kindled Calvinist religion of rural America. His skepticism made him unusual, but his rigid probity, like that of so many freethinkers, was designed to prove that religion was not a necessary precondition for moral behavior.

According to his son, however, his moral rectitude was not allied with compassion or demonstrations of feeling. His "kindliness" did not manifest itself in warm connections to his children or his wife. His was a life of pride and duty, not of love and pleasure. By contrast, Pamela Clemens *Moffett disagreed with her brother's assessment; she felt that her father was perfectly normal in his demonstrations of affection. Nonetheless, Samuel Clemens's consistent reports of his father's coldness must be taken seriously. Critics have long speculated that the conspicuous absence of fathers in Twain's fiction derives as much from John Marshall Clemens's emotional absence from his family before his death as from his death itself. Samuel Clemens may have lived his life in awe of his father's commandingly upright behavior, but he rejected that stern rigidity in favor of humor, anger, and other intense emotional states.

CLEMENS, LANGDON (1870–1872). The first child and only son of Samuel and Olivia Langdon Clemens, Langdon came into the world in less than auspicious circumstances. His mother had just witnessed the death from typhoid fever of her friend Emma Nye in her house in Buffalo. Suffering nervous exhaustion, Olivia nearly miscarried in October 1870. Shortly after she prematurely gave birth in

November, she and the boy contracted typhoid as well. Astonishingly, he recovered, only to succumb to diphtheria a little over a year later.

Late in life, Clemens blamed himself for his son's death, accusing himself of taking the boy out for a ride in cold weather and paying little attention to his son's needs, allowing his blankets to slip. The resultant cold, said Clemens, killed the child. The facts appear to be otherwise, as the infant's constant and inconsolable crying likely indicate an outward manifestation of his nearly constant sickness. Fighting for life, the child's development was backward; he had not, for example, learned to walk by the time he died at nineteen months. His yielding to a common childhood disease three months after his infant sister was born had nothing to do with Clemens's behavior, or at least nobody close to the family suggested as much. On the contrary, many family friends thought the child's death was a blessing. For example, Susan Warner, one of Olivia's earliest and dearest Hartford friends, wrote, "Of course everybody thinks what a mercy that he is at rest—but his poor devoted mother is almost heart-broken. It is always so, I believe—those children that are the most delicate & th[at] needs the most care—that everybody else want to have die—are the most missed & mourned by their mothers." In blaming himself for Langdon's death, Clemens in all probability was blaming himself for sharing Warner's and others' sentiments. His correspondence of the period shows how distressing he found the child's incessant crying, and he seemed almost pleased to get away from it on a lecture tour in the winter of 1871–1872. Even his efforts to assure his wife that he loved his son suggest her knowledge that he did not: "Bless your heart, I appreciate the cubbie & shall, more & more as he develops and becomes vicious & interesting" (15 November 1871).

CLEMENS, OLIVIA LANGDON (1845–1904).

One of the oldest canards in Twain criticism is that his wife Olivia Langdon Clemens stifled Twain's robust humor under a blanket of eastern respectability. No doubt she did help edit Twain's works, but the true nature of her influence is suggested in Clemens's 27 October 1879 letter to William Dean *Howells:

> Speaking of [John] Hay, I said "the presence of such a man in politics is like a vase of attar of roses in a glue-factory—it can't extinguish the stink, but it modifies it." Mrs. Clemens said, "That will apply to Gen. Hawley, too—take it out of your letter & put it in your speech when you introduce Hawley to his audience—your speech *needs* a snapper on the end of it, for it flats out, as it is at present—& just say *stench*, that is strong enough." It was pretty good advice, & I followed it.

A woman who could ask her husband to add a comment like that to a public introduction of a prominent political figure was hardly an impediment to Twain's humor, despite the minor modification of "stink" to "stench." Clearly his nickname for her, "my little gravity," was substantially a jest. Twain himself is responsible for giving the world a very narrow, conventional picture of Olivia in his *autobiography, but the gap between the complex reality of their life together and the picture Twain gives speaks more to his own sense of self and idealized vision of women than it does to Olivia's real influence.

The woman who would become one of Twain's most valued literary advisors, his primary audience in helping him judge the quality of his work, was born in *Elmira, New York, shortly after her parents moved there from Ithaca. Her father's speculations in lumber, coal, and railroads made him one of the town's richest residents, giving Olivia a life of material ease. But her life was not without difficulty; by age fourteen she had contracted an illness, probably tuberculosis of the spine, that made her an invalid by age sixteen. She recovered enough to become active (Twain claims a faith healer gave her the strength to get out of bed), but her health was always precarious. Although her father helped to found the Elmira Female College to provide a school for Olivia, she in fact was never healthy enough to attend more than sporadically, instead taking private lessons from professors employed by the school. She read widely and avidly, with as much interest in science as in the belle lettres more conventionally associated with Victorian womanhood.

She also grew up deeply immersed in a powerfully religious atmosphere. Not surprisingly, her faith was central to her self-conception, and the gap between the aspirations for service promoted by her family's brand of Christianity and her own physical power was a source of much anxiety. As she wrote in a letter to her good friend Alice Hooker:

> If I only grow in Grace and in the knowledge of our Lord and Saviour I am content. You may know how with all the tokens of affection from friends is renewed the desire to be to them all I can, to cultivate day by day all the powers that are given me, that will be of pleasure or service to them—Yet I feel more and more keenly, that of my Self I am utterly incompetent to do *any thing*. But I hope that I am learning more and more where to look for strength. (28 November 1867, quoted in Susan K. Harris, *The Courtship of Olivia Langdon and Mark Twain*)

Twenty-two-year-old Olivia, firmly ensconced in the protective embrace of her family as the weak and cherished younger daughter, pined for some active way to express her identity but despaired of finding it. As such, she was very susceptible to the impetuous courtship of Samuel Clemens.

Olivia's brother, Charles Jervis *Langdon, had shown Clemens a miniature portrait of Olivia while on board the *Quaker City*. In later years, Clemens claimed he fell in love on the spot. His letters suggest something else. Even after meeting Olivia in New York at a Charles Dickens reading on 31 December 1867, Clemens's letters are full of references to other young women. An 8 January 1868 letter to his mother mentions a New Year's Day visit in which a courtship began, but not necessarily of Olivia:

> I started to make calls, New Year's Day, but I anchored for the day at the first house I came to—Charlie Langdon's sister was there (beautiful girl,) & Miss Alice Hooker, another beautiful girl, a niece of Henry Ward Beecher's. We sent the old folks home early, with instructions not to send the carriage till midnight, & I just staid there & deviled the life out of those girls. I am going to spend a few days with the Langdon's, in Elmira, New York, as soon as I get time, & a few days at Mrs. Hooker's in Hartford, Conn., shortly.

Clemens's visit to the Hooker family came later that month whereas his visit to Elmira did not take place until 21 August, lasting three weeks. In that time, Clemens apparently fell in love with Olivia and declared his affections, was gently repulsed, and finally given permission to write letters to Olivia as if she were his sister.

On the day of his departure, Clemens wrote a fulsome letter explaining his hopes in terms perfectly designed to open Olivia's heart:

My Honored "Sister"—

The impulse is strong upon me to say to you how grateful I am to you and to all of you for the patience, the consideration & the unfailing kindness which has been shown me ever since I came within the shadow of this roof, and which has made the past fortnight the sole period of my life unmarred by a regret. Unmarred by a regret. I say it deliberately. For I do not regret that I have loved you, still love & shall always love you. I accept the situation, uncomplainingly, hard as it is. Of old I am acquainted with grief, disaster & disappointment, & have borne these troubles as became a man. So, also, I shall bear this last & bitterest, even though it break my heart. I would not dishonor this worthiest love that has yet been born within me by any puerile thought, or word, or deed. It is better to have loved & lost you than that my life should have remained forever the blank it was before. For once, at least, in the idle years that have drifted over me, I have seen the world all beautiful, & known what it was to hope. For once I have known what it was to feel my sluggish pulses stir with a living ambition. The world that was so beautiful, is dark again; the hope that shone as the sun, is gone; the brave ambition is dead. Yet I say again, it is better for me that I have loved & do love you; that with more than Eastern devotion I worship you; that I lay down all of my life that is worth the living, upon this hopeless altar where no fires of life shall descend to consume it. If you *could* but—

But no more of this. (8 September 1868)

Clemens could not have contrived a more effective piece of rhetoric. It appeals to a young woman whose ambition is to serve but who lacks the power to do so directly. He offers her the chance to inspire a man of talent and energy to a better life. Clemens's clever quotation of Isaiah 53:3 ("He was despised and rejected by men; a man of sorrows and acquainted with grief"), conventionally interpreted in Christian doctrine as a foreshadowing of Jesus, suggests that Clemens's is a Christian martyrdom. Olivia would have likely responded to his veiled suggestion here that he is trying to become Christian by imitating Christ. As significantly, he also quotes from Alfred, Lord Tennyson's "In Memoriam": "It is better to have loved and lost than never to have loved at all." His courtship was distinctly literary, and her response suggests a deep affinity, a shared love of literature that would stand them in good stead through a life centered on Clemens's literary aspirations.

Olivia took little time to fall under the onslaught of Clemens's letters and frequent brief visits, falling not only to Clemens's plan to reform himself into a Christian under her tutelage, but also to the romantic impetuousness of his courtship. By November, they were engaged to be married, and Clemens began making arrangements to buy into a newspaper as an editor in order to provide a more stable household than he could have as a reporter and lecturer. The prospect of such a household made Olivia somewhat ambivalent about her engagement; she feared having to live up to her dreams of usefulness in a life of her own rather than merely as a child in her parents' home. As she put it in a letter to Clemens in December:

> I think that you must have scared me a little, yesterday, talking about the home in Cleveland, because to-day I have been feeling sad at the thought of ever leaving this home of mine, ever going out from among those who have always made a part of my life. *To think of having them grow used to my being absent from them, so that at last they would cease to miss me*, MADE ME FEEL AS IF I WANTED FATHER TO PUT HIS ARMS ABOUT ME & KEEP ME NEAR HIM ALWAYS. (24–25 December 1868, quoted in *Samuel Clemens to Mary Mason Fairbanks*)

Not surprisingly, Clemens scrapped Cleveland, shifting his attentions instead to Hartford, where his efforts to buy into the *Courant* were rejected. He settled, finally, with the generous financial support of his soon-to-be father-in-law, on Buffalo, a town with which Jervis Langdon had strong business connections. Part of the key, then, to Clemens's courtship of Olivia was his willingness to fall into the orbit of Jervis and Olivia Lewis Langdon's home. Indeed, even though Jervis died soon after Samuel and Olivia were married, the couple maintained close connections with the Elmira homestead, ultimately burying all of their children and having themselves buried in the Langdon family plot there.

The couple announced their engagement in February 1869 and married one year later, on 2 February 1870 in Elmira. In the interim, they continued their courtship, substantially from afar, as Twain's travels on the *lecture circuit and editorial work on the Buffalo *Express* kept him far from Elmira most of the time. They shared books, marking them up for one another and corresponding over their common reading. Most significantly, Clemens had Olivia read Coventry Patmore's *Angel in the House* as a model for a woman's role. In spite of the pressures put on her to conform to this Victorian model of womanhood, she expressed some reservations, which would ultimately stand Twain in good stead as Olivia became to a large degree his literary collaborator.

The transition to housekeeper was difficult for Olivia, whose education and health had kept her dependent. Neither she nor her husband was particularly good with *finances, and as they spent over their budget regularly, generous gifts from Olivia Lewis Langdon kept the Clemenses' books balanced. Financial concerns remained a perennial issue for the couple; both worried over debt but neither had the self-control to resist the kind of spending that made their houses typical of Victorian *fashion. According to Victorian ideals of *domesticity, Olivia was primarily responsible for overseeing childrearing and served as the last court of refuge for moral teaching in the family, even over Samuel himself. Nonetheless, their relationship became much more of a modern partnership than the ideology they both professed would have comfortably allowed. Olivia became actively involved in developing the public role of *Mark Twain, not only serving as audience and editor for his writing, but also as part of the domestic team that turned the *Hartford house into a business office and hotel. The parade of guests that came through included visiting dignitaries in politics and the arts. This visiting was not completely social—it was an essential activity for building Twain's reputation. Clearly, the Victorian myth that a family maintained a firewall between the public and private was one that vanished in the reality of Twain's career.

Olivia's health, never robust, nevertheless held through four children and family bankruptcy. But in 1902, just as the family's finances, under the direction of Henry H. *Rogers, had recovered enough for them to buy a house in Tarrytown, New York, her health collapsed. Before they could occupy the new house, they moved, under medical advice, to a warmer climate, choosing Florence, Italy, in 1903, where Olivia died on 5 June 1904. Devastated by the loss, Twain then turned to creating in his autobiography a simplified, purified picture of a moral paragon who fit the ideal of Patmore's Angel. But his richer tributes to Olivia, in the diaries of *Adam and Eve, while not denying the ideal of perfection, suggest something more of the creative tension between the two, a tension very real but never enough to challenge Clemens's love.

♦ SEE ALSO *Personal Recollections of Joan of Arc*; Temperance.

CLEMENS, OLIVIA SUSAN (SUSY) (1872–1896). The second of Samuel and Olivia Clemens's children, but the first to live past infancy, Olivia Susan Clemens, called Susy to distinguish her from her mother, was her father's favorite child. From Samuel's point of view, after the disappointment of Langdon, whose constant crying he found alienating, Susy was a delightful alternative, and given his preference for girls over boys in the first place, he easily fell in love with her. From Olivia's point of view, Susy's very presence was a substantial consolation after Langdon's death. In effect, Susy occupied the role of first child, redefining the family dynamic and becoming the focal point for family activities, tasks, and energy. The shift in Clemens's attitudes about *childhood—a shift that allowed him to write compellingly about children—took place over the first years of Susy's life.

Being the family cynosure was not easy for Susy. She exhibited early a marked intellectuality, and the Clemens family worked hard to develop it. From early on they taught her languages, hiring a German nursemaid, for instance, to teach her German. As Clemens wrote in a letter to William Dean *Howells: "Poor Susie! From the day we reached German soil, we have required Rosa to speak German to the children—which they hate with all their souls. The other morning in Hanover, Susie came to me (from Rosa, in the nursery,) & said, in halting syllables, 'Papa, wie viel Uhr ist es?'—then turned, with pathos in her big eyes, & said, 'Mamma, I wish Rosa was made in English'" (4 May 1878). Typically, Clemens could find pity for his daughter's travails, but had little inclination to act on it or to let her grow at her own pace. While he let Olivia discipline and educate the children, he stood back as an observer, taking great joy in their innocent errors. In a notebook entry from the same period, for instance, he records a conversation with Susy and Clara (nick-named Bay):

> Bay—When the waiter brought my breakfast this morning, I spoke to him in Italian.
> *Mama.*—What did you say?
> B—I said, "Polly voo fransay."
> M—What does it mean?
> B—I don't know. What does it mean, S?
> *Susie*—It means "Polly wants a cracker." (*N&J* 2:234)

Always on stage, Susy developed an acute sensitivity. From his position as father, Clemens was her consoler, entertainer, and confidant, and they developed an exceedingly close relationship. Susy's childhood effort to write a biography of her father documents this closeness. Clemens himself used the biography as a focal point for the autobiographical dictations he published in the *North American Review*:

When Susy was thirteen, and was a slender little maid with plaited tails of copper-tinged brown hair down her back, and was perhaps the busiest bee in the household hive, by reason of the manifold studies, health exercises and recreations she had to attend to, she secretly, of her own motion, and out of love, added another task to her labors—the writing of a biography of me. She did this work in her bedroom at night, and kept her record hidden. After a little, the mother discovered it and filched it, and let me see it; then told Susy what she had done, and how pleased I was, and how proud. (*North American Review,* 19 October 1906)

This passage shows the difficulty Susy had in keeping anything private and the degree to which family members performed for one another as well as the rigors of the life the Clemenses set for Susy.

Naturally, the relationship between Clemens and his daughter was fraught with emotional difficulties. Susy grew into a high-strung young woman whose very temperamental nature may have been patterned on Clemens's own. Certainly her character was affected by Clemens's temper. As she put it in her biography of her father, "He *has* got a temper, but we all of us have in this family." About this same time, Clemens learned that she feared that temper, or so he said in a letter to Howells:

I found that all their lives my children have been afraid of me! have stood all their days in uneasy dread of my sharp tongue & uncertain temper. The accusing instances stretch back to their babyhood, & are burnt into their memories: & I never suspected, & the fact was never guessed by *anybody* until yesterday. Well all the concentrated griefs of fifty years seemed colorless by the side of that pathetic revelation. That list is closed, that record is ended; if I live seventy-five years yet, it will still remain without an addition. (12 December 1886)

The characteristic exaggeration of this passage suggests that Clemens was neither so surprised nor so dismayed, but undoubtedly the relationship between father and daughter included an element of fear along with emulation.

Susy had great trouble breaking away from her family as she approached adulthood. When she went off to attend Bryn Mawr College in the autumn of 1890, she was stricken by homesickness. As Clemens wrote in a letter to his sister, "The last time I saw her was a week ago on the platform at Bryn Mawr. Our train was moving away, & she was drifting collegeward afoot, her figure blurred & dim in the rain & fog, and she was crying" (12 October 1890). It is difficult to say who felt the separation more acutely. Clemens visited many times to "comfort" Susy, but revealed in a letter to Howells on 10 February 1891 that he missed her terribly and worried that she would grow to accept their separation: "Mrs. Clemens has been in

Philadelphia a week at the Continental Hotel with Susy (who, to my private regret is beginning to love Bryn Mawr) & I've had to stay here alone. But this is the last time this brace of old fools, old indispensables-to-each other, are going to separate themselves in this foolish fashion." Here Clemens admits his fear of isolation, suggesting that he and his wife would have to become closer as the children grew up and left home. But neither parent readily allowed Susy to grow up. In a letter Dixon Wecter solicited from one of Susy's college companions as he prepared to write a biography of Clemens, he learned that Clemens and his wife were too quick to visit. Evangeline W. Andrews, a sophomore when she met the freshman Olivia, as Susy chose to call herself at school, wrote,

> At the time it seemed to us very natural that Olivia like ourselves should be coming to college, but later I realized how strong was the tie between her and her father, how much they minded being separated, and also how eager Mrs. Clemens was that Olivia should be happy in a new environment, leading an independent life of her own as a college student among girls of her own age, free from the limiting influences of home. . . . Mrs. Clemens would come down occasionally for a short stay, I think in order to keep Mr. Clemens from coming, because she told me that he would make anything an excuse, even to bringing down Olivia's laundry! (26 February 1949; original in Mark Twain Papers)

Susy's mother readily made her husband the scapegoat, but also persisted in visiting, keeping the cord short. As Susy adjusted to Bryn Mawr, she developed a deep attachment to another student, Louise Brownell, which served as a partial excuse for her parents to discourage her continued attendance at Bryn Mawr. With her homesickness and poor health contributing to the decision, she withdrew from Bryn Mawr in April 1891.

Then, with the family *finances so precarious, the Clemenses decided to live in Europe to economize. Susy accompanied the family, studying with private tutors rather than being in the company of her contemporaries. But when Clemens went bankrupt in 1894 and chose to recover his fortunes by making an around-the-world *lecture tour from 1895 to 1896, Susy opted to stay behind, living in Hartford. Before she could make anything definite out of her growing efforts to separate from her family, she contracted spinal meningitis, of which she died, in the Hartford house, with neither parent present, on 18 August 1896.

Susy's death devastated both of her parents, and their decision never to return to the Hartford home was predicated on their grief. They ritually observed the anniversary of Susy's death until Olivia died eight years later; for the first anniversary of Susy's death, Clemens wrote one of his few poems, "In Memoriam, Olivia Susan Clemens," which he published in *Harper's Magazine* in 1897. His most eloquent tribute, though, he saved for his *autobiography, not only movingly describing the "dumb sense of vast loss," but using the autobiography itself to make her live in his own literature. But while the autobiography praises the value of Susy's life, it is likewise replete with the depth of grief caused by her death. Clearly Clemens missed the mark when he prophesied to Howells that learning about his daughter's fear of his temper was the apex of grief; within a mere decade, his list of griefs had an overwhelming addition.

♦ SEE ALSO *Adventures of Tom Sawyer, The*; Poetry.

CLEMENS, ORION (1825–1897). It is difficult to get a clear picture of Samuel's older brother, Orion Clemens, because Samuel mocked, berated, and belittled Orion in letters and his *autobiography as a foolish, inconsistent, extravagant dreamer, so little in touch with the real world that he raised both laughter and pity: "Did you ever see," Samuel wrote to William Dean *Howells on 9 February 1879, "the grotesquely absurd & the heart-breakingly pathetic more closely joined together?" But whatever picture of his brother Twain bequeathed to posterity, the more complex reality of their relationship significantly shaped Samuel's life. Without the powerful influence of Orion on Samuel's adolescence and early adulthood, Mark Twain's fictional resources and Samuel Clemens's character would have been extremely different.

Born in Tennessee before the Clemens family made its move to the Mississippi River valley, Orion was the oldest of John Marshall and Jane Lampton Clemens's children. When old enough to begin work, Orion set the pattern for the surviving male children by apprenticing himself to the printing trade. Unlike Samuel and Henry later, however, Orion left home for his apprenticeship, moving to St. Louis, probably in 1842, to work in Thomas Watt Ustick's print shop, where he set type for the St. Louis *Evening News*. After finishing his apprenticeship, Orion's wages helped support the rest of the family back in Hannibal, especially after their father died in 1847. In spending the better part of a decade away from home, Orion was a distant figure to his younger brothers, all the more so given their great disparity in age. But when in 1851 Orion returned to Hannibal to go into the publishing business for himself, he took on the position of surrogate father, proving to be as stern as the deceased real one.

Orion served as Samuel's moral and political guardian, preaching religion, temperance, and Whig politics. Orion's print shop was geared toward the respectable task of producing a paper, which in antebellum American *newspaper journalism usually meant supporting a political position as well. In the name he gave his paper, the *Western Union*, he highlighted his pro-Union politics. In the wake of the infamous Fugitive Slave Act of 1850, when sectional rivalries flourished, especially in Missouri, Orion's significant early investment in what would become the *Republican party's antislavery, pro-union platform did not earn him wide favor in proslavery Hannibal. Orion soon bought out the failing Hannibal *Journal* and combined it with the *Union*, using the *Journal* as the new paper's name, but such a gesture could not stave off Orion's failure in Hannibal for long. In 1853, he sold out and moved instead to Muscatine, in the free state of Iowa, which ardently supported the Union when the *Civil War broke out.

Orion not only provided food for the family but also training in a trade for both his younger brothers, Samuel and Henry. In 1851 Samuel was already apprenticed to Hannibal's competing newspaper's publisher, Joseph P. Ament. At first, he was happy to leave what he considered Ament's tyranny for what should have been an easier berth with his brother. But Orion proved a rigid taskmaster, ultimately driving Samuel away in June 1853, first to St. Louis and then east. Yet Samuel continued to write letters for Orion's newspaper, and Orion continued to publish them, complete with boasting introductions. For instance, Orion prefaced a 31 August 1853 letter of Samuel's from New York in which Samuel discussed his work in one of New York's most important printing houses, with praise of his own talents as an instructor of printers: "The following letter is some encouragement to apprentices in country printing offices, as it shows that it is practical to acquire enough knowledge of the business in a Western country office, to command the best situations, West or East. There are a great many who suppose that no mechanical business can be learned well in the West" (Hannibal *Journal*, 10 September 1853).

While Samuel skipped town before Orion moved to Muscatine—indeed, Samuel's letters home indicate surprise at Orion's move—Samuel joined his brother and mother in Muscatine in late spring 1854, where Samuel once again worked for his brother's print shop. This was a more auspicious location for Orion's work, in a larger Mississippi River city of about 5,500 people in a free state. Yet the tether between the brothers was broken enough that Samuel spent little time in Muscatine, quickly moving on to St. Louis. Still, his politics were enough influenced by Orion that Samuel continued to write for his brother's Muscatine paper, expressing his political sympathies with Orion's nativist politics.

Orion, however, was beginning to show the signs of itinerancy that Samuel so often mocked in later years. Orion married Mary Eleanor (Mollie) Stotts of Keokuk, Iowa, and rather than have Mary move with him to the larger town, he moved to the smaller, selling out his interest in the Muscatine *Journal* and establishing the "Ben Franklin Book and Job Office," which undertook, among other ventures, to publish a local directory. Samuel in turn moved to Keokuk from St. Louis, working steadily in the print shop for nearly two years before deciding that Orion's prospects were poor.

But even as Samuel found a new career as a steamboat pilot and thus became the family's primary breadwinner, Orion's efforts in unionist politics, eventually working for the nascent Republican party, put him in a position to aid his younger brother again. When the war broke out in 1861, Orion was able to maneuver himself into a political position as secretary to the newly appointed governor of Nevada territory. Samuel, not wanting to participate in the Civil War, departed with his brother for the silver fields of Nevada. Their relationship then became much closer, oriented around neither Orion's work nor the household they shared with their mother, but instead around the necessities of their close interactions in a land alien to both and far from the rest of the family.

The two constantly plotted mining and financial speculations, getting in each other's way as often as not, and in this time they developed mutual frustrations with one another's tendency to go off half-cocked. But while Samuel dashed around the countryside digging holes, Orion stuck to his task as a civil servant, often acting as governor when the governor was absent, earning the respect of a diverse group of fortune-hunters throughout the territory for his probity and forthrightness. He could have had a political career, and certainly his access to power in the territory made his younger brother a good catch as a reporter for the Virginia City *Territorial Enterprise*, to which Samuel turned when he found himself deeply in debt after failed efforts at mining. The *Enterprise* probably would not have been as interested in employing Samuel and teaching him the ropes of professional journalism without Orion's connections in the territorial government.

But territorial secretary was Orion's high-water mark. Too unwilling to compromise to make a career in politics, too emotionally mercurial to develop the career in law to which he aspired after he left the government, and too much a dreamer to stick to any trade for long, Orion degenerated into the caricature of a man that Samuel depicted in his letters and autobiography. Over the years Samuel substantially supported his brother, either indirectly by finding him work as a clerk for the American Publishing Company, or directly by giving him a pension—under the guise of a loan—of up to six hundred dollars per year for the rest of his life. He died in Keokuk in 1897.

Clemens wanted to blame much of Orion's failure on his marriage and his wife Mary, telling Howells,

> He is a printer, but she [Mary] won't allow him to work at his trade because she can't abide the thought of being a mechanic's wife. She prefers to keep boarding-house & make him let on to be a lawyer. He wrote piteously once, how the governor or somebody gave a blow out, with a broad general invitation to lawyers & their wives to be present, & she made him go, & take her,—& it was the year that he didn't have a case or make a cent, & those people all knew it. Moreover, he hadn't any decent clothes, for she gobbles all the money & buys clothes & new wigs for herself with it. The only way we can keep him from being ragged is to send him money distinctly for *himself* occasionally. (9 February 1879)

Samuel found her a convenient scapegoat, because in Orion's emotional volatility, susceptibility to grand schemes, and capacity to waste money, Orion bore an uncomfortably strong family resemblance to Samuel himself.

CLEMENS, SAMUEL LANGHORNE (1835–1909). In many respects, this entire book is the biography of Samuel Clemens; this entry presents in short scope some of the important events and influences of his early life, before fame made his every movement a subject of public scrutiny. The man who became the celebrated Mark Twain, dinner companion of kings and plutocrats, spokesman for the common person, maker and waster of fortunes, began life in the quiet northeastern Missouri settlement of Florida on 30 November 1835. Just four years later, he moved with his family to *Hannibal, Missouri, on the Mississippi River, another hamlet in a growing area not far removed from the frontier of Anglo-American civilization. Hannibal itself would not legally be chartered as a town until 1845.

In Hannibal in the 1840s, young Samuel Clemens had to deal with the virtually loveless marriage of a cold, morally rigorous, atheistic father and a passionate though not affectionate, equally morally rigorous, Calvinist mother as the sixth child in a family of seven children, three of whom died before Samuel turned seven years old. He noted in his autobiography that by 1858, he "had never seen one member of the Clemens family kiss another one—except once. When my father lay dying in our home in Hannibal he put his arm around my sister's neck and drew her down and kissed her, saying, 'Let me die.'" (*North American Review,* 19 April 1907)

His father's immediate fortunes were never good. He had to deed his Hannibal property in payment of a debt in 1841, just two years after he bought it, and in 1846 the family sold much of its furniture to raise money. Still, his father's large holdings of Tennessee property were a golden promise of future fortunes worthy of a well-born family. This land, Twain later wrote,

> influenced our life in one way or another during more than a generation. Whenever things grew dark it rose and put out its hopeful Sellers hand and cheered us up and said, "Do not be afraid—trust in me—wait." It kept us hoping and hoping during forty years and forsook us at last.... It is good to begin life poor; it is good to begin life rich—these are wholesome; but to begin it poor and *prospectively* rich! The man who has not experienced it cannot imagine the curse of it. (*North American Review,* 1 March 1907)

Certainly the poverty of his early days influenced him, but the idea of prospective wealth played almost as large a role in Mark Twain's literature as the worry over *money played in Clemens's life. He used, for example, his father's fantasy of a rise in fortunes to more than compensate his losses as a central plot element in *The Gilded Age,* and he created a story of people whose lives were ruined by the promise of a legacy in "The *Thirty Thousand Dollar Bequest."

Strapped for cash, the Clemens family sent Samuel off to his Uncle Quarles's farm near Florida for summers from 1843 to 1847. His reminiscences about the farm, among those parts of his *autobiography that he published in his lifetime, contain nothing but positive comments about his time there: "It was a heavenly place for a boy," where he ate well, had eight cousins and "fifteen or twenty negroes" to learn about, and a creek with "swimming pools ... which were forbidden to us and therefore much frequented by us. For we were little Christian children, and had early been taught the value of forbidden fruit" (*North American Review*, 1 March 1907). He explained that "Uncle Dan'l" on Quarles's farm provided the model for Jim in *Adventures of Huckleberry Finn*, and that the farm itself "has come very handy to me in literature, once or twice. In 'Huck Finn' and in 'Tom Sawyer Detective' I moved it down to Arkansas. It was all of six hundred miles, but it was no trouble, it was not a very large farm. . . . And as for the morality of it, I cared nothing for that; I would move a State if the exigencies of literature required it" (*North American Review*, 1 March 1907).

These years in Hannibal and at the Quarles farm provided the raw materials for much of Mark Twain's Mississippi writings, most particularly *The Adventures of Tom Sawyer* and *Huckleberry Finn*. The former of these books, though undoubtedly dealing in some frightening episodes, captures much of the positive side of growing up in a small river town on the edge of a virtually untamed forest. Young Clemens undoubtedly had great freedom to explore the community and its surroundings, giving him a wealth of experiences on which to draw and a chance to develop his imagination. The latter book captures the bleaker side, not merely in the financial difficulties of his family, but in the turbulence of antebellum America in the South and West.

Clemens himself usually whitewashed his past, only bringing out the dirt through association when following some literary track. While in his autobiography, for instance, he says that he never learned anything against *slavery and therefore, "I was not aware that there was anything wrong about it" (*North American Review*, 1 March 1907), in fact there was energetic antislavery agitation in Hannibal, enough for Sam's older brother to become an ardent abolitionist by 1860. For that matter, Clemens himself flirted with Know-Nothing politics and likely disagreed with slavery. Certainly, though, he knew the likely consequences of outspoken abolitionism. While there had been a secret and active underground railroad stop in Hannibal, whenever any resident was found participating, he was run out of town. One time in 1841, three men were accused of grand larceny for inciting some Hannibal area slaves to run off. All three were found guilty and sentenced to twelve years in the penitentiary. John Marshall Clemens, Samuel's father, was a member of the jury.

Slave owners from the border states thought of themselves as humane, at least by the standards of deep-south plantation slavery. To some degree that was true, and as a boy, Clemens's proximity to slaves as part of the Quarles family put him in touch with an oral tradition that would bear fruit in his literature. Still, in an era when even blood relations in families were regularly subjected to corporal punishment—"Spare the rod; spoil the child"—slaves were regularly beaten. In *Following the Equator*, Twain witnessed a German strike a valet who had failed to perform some duty:

> [This] carried me back to my boyhood, and flashed upon me the forgotten fact that this was the *usual* way of explaining one's desires to a slave. . . . When I was ten years old I saw a man fling a lump of iron-ore at a slave-man in anger, for merely doing something awkwardly—as if that were a crime. It bounded from the man's skull, and the man fell and never spoke again. He was dead in an hour. I knew the man had a right to kill his slave if he wanted to, and yet it seemed a pitiful thing and somehow wrong, though why wrong I was not deep enough to explain if I had been asked to do it. Nobody in the village approved of that murder, but of course no one said much about it. (chapter 38)

People may have preached in favor of slavery and taken its abuses for granted, but there remained an undercurrent of horror and guilt. The context of slavery partly explains the tortured conscience that bedeviled Clemens all his life, a conscience he has *Huckleberry Finn represent. Certainly the moral problem of slavery came up repeatedly in Twain's works, from *Huckleberry Finn* right up to the unfinished novel *Which Was It?* in which the guilt of persecution is expiated when an ex-slave blackmails his boss into a role-reversal.

Slavery, however, was not the sole motive for Clemens's perpetually active sense of guilt; he had other sources for his hyper-conscientiousness. Hannibal was a breeding ground for revivalist religion, and evangelists regularly embraced moral reform. Nothing young Clemens ever did was worthy by the exacting standards of his mother's religion. And in the community around him, he had numerous examples of people who had gone wrong and paid the price. The notes he drafted in 1897 about Hannibal residents of 1840–1843 list numerous people whose choices to resist "reform" had pernicious consequences:

> *Blankenships.* The parents paupers and drunkards; the girls charged with prostitution—not proven. Tom, a kindly young heathen. Bence, a fisherman. These children were never sent to school or church. Played out and disappeared. . . .
>
> *Sam* [Bowen]. Pilot. Slept with the rich baker's daughter, telling the adoptive parents they were married. The baker died and left all his wealth to "Mr. and Mrs. S. Bowen." they rushed off to a Carondolet magistrate, got married, and bribed him to antedate the marriage. Heirs from Germany proved the fraud and took the wealth. Sam no account and a pauper. Neglected his wife; she took up with another man. Sam a drinker. Dropped pretty low. Died of yellow fever and whisky on a little boat with Bill Kribben the defaulting secretary. ("Villagers 1840-3")

Such disasters needed no interpretation in young Clemens's mind:

> Mine was a trained Presbyterian conscience and knew but one duty—to hunt
> and harry its slave upon all pretexts and on all occasions, particularly when
> there was no sense nor reason in it.... My teaching and training enabled me
> to see deeper into these tragedies than an ignorant person could have done. I
> knew what they were for. I tried to disguise it from myself but down in the
> secret deeps of my troubled heart I knew—and I *knew* that I knew. They were
> the inventions of Providence to beguile me to a better life. (*North American
> Review*, 3 May 1907)

Certainly he observed tragedy enough to blame himself. Between violent deaths by
accident or design, self-inflicted deaths from alcoholism, and death by disease, it is
a wonder that Hannibal ever grew.

The most eventful death of young Clemens's life was that of his father in March
1847. After this, Clemens had to learn a trade and provide his own bread. But for a
family with pretensions to gentility, not just any trade would do. Printing, with its
vaguely literary associations and honorable historical background, seemed to fit the
bill, so Clemens was, like his brothers Orion and Henry before and after him,
apprenticed to the *printing trade. He learned to be a fairly good—very good by rural
Missouri standards—compositor working for Joseph Ament, publisher of the
Missouri Courier in Hannibal. But before he finished his apprenticeship, he changed
masters. His brother Orion had begun the Hannibal *Western Union* and needed cheap
labor; Samuel provided it from 1851 until he virtually ran away to St. Louis in 1853.
Intermittently from 1853 to 1856 he worked for Orion first in Muscatine and then in
Keokuk, Iowa, where Orion had moved in an effort to make his printing business pay.

In spite of later efforts to paint his boyhood as a time of pranks and pratfalls,
contrasting himself to his younger brother Henry's almost saccharine goodness,
Samuel seems to have been the diligent member of the family. As such, his older
brother took advantage, recalling in 1880, "He was as swift and as clean as a good
journeyman. I gave him tasks, and if he got through well I begrudged him the time
and made him work more. He set a clean proof, and Henry a very dirty one. The
correcting was left to be done in the form the day before publication. Once we were
kept late, and Sam complained with tears of bitterness that he was held till midnight on Henry's dirty proofs" (*Mark Twain: A Biography*, chapter 17). When
Samuel finally ran out on his brother, he traveled as an itinerant compositor, first to
St. Louis, then on to the great cities of the East, New York and Philadelphia. In
Philadelphia in particular, he noted with great reverence his visit to the tomb of
Benjamin Franklin. No doubt he noticed interesting parallels between his own life
and that of Franklin.

During his travels, Clemens sent correspondence to his brother for inclusion in
the newspaper, so the break was never clean enough to violate family unity, at least

not as long as his mother remained the center of the family. His correspondence from the East shows that he kept his promises to his mother to avoid drink, swearing, or any amusements that might degrade his character. In one letter he wrote that "the printers have two libraries in town, entirely free to the craft; and in these I can spend my evenings most pleasantly. If books are not good company, where will I find it?" (to Jane Lampton Clemens, 31 August 1853).

In this early travel correspondence, he already shows the reporter's eye. He covers the expected ground with careful detail, changing emotional pace quickly and effectively. The same skill appears in his personal correspondence, and he complained to his sister that his family's correspondence did not live up to the standards he had set: "I have received one or two letters from home, but they are not written as they should be; and know no more about what is going on there than the man in the moon. One only has to leave home to learn how to write an interesting [letter]" (5 December 1853).

Clemen's first trip east ended badly, as the competition for work was fierce and in a printing market depressed after Harper and Brothers publishers had a major fire, the young man could not make a reasonable living. He returned to his family, dispersed between Orion's homes in Iowa and his sister's home in St. Louis, but could not make a comfortable life with either sibling, inducing him to take to the road again. Thus began a pattern of mobility that he never shook. Later, when in 1867 working on a successful career as a reporter and on the verge of his trip on the *Quaker City* to Europe and the Holy Lands, he wrote a bitter letter to his mother about his failings as a son and correspondent. It culminates,

> All I do know or feel, is that I am wild with impatience to move—move—
> *Move!* Half a dozen times I have wished I had sailed long ago in some ship
> that wasn't going to keep me chained here to chafe for lagging ages while she
> got ready to go. Curse the endless delays! They always kill me—they make me
> neglect every duty & then I have a conscience that tears me like a wild beast.
> I wish I never had to stop *anywhere* a month. I do more mean things, the
> moment I get a chance to fold my hands & sit down than ever I can get for-
> giveness for. (1 June 1867)

Of course, by then he had long since lost the comfort that came from following his mother's wishes. He had ceased to be the good boy and had come more to resemble the prodigal son before he returned home.

This transformation began in 1857 after a stint in Cincinnati, Ohio, as a typesetter. Tired of the grind, he decided instead to enter a trade that, while less genteel, promised more money. He chose to travel to the Amazon basin via New Orleans in order to deal in coca, then a legal drug used in patent medicines. On the way, he decided instead to become a steamboat pilot, arranging an apprenticeship with Horace Bixby, half the cost of which would come out of his wages when

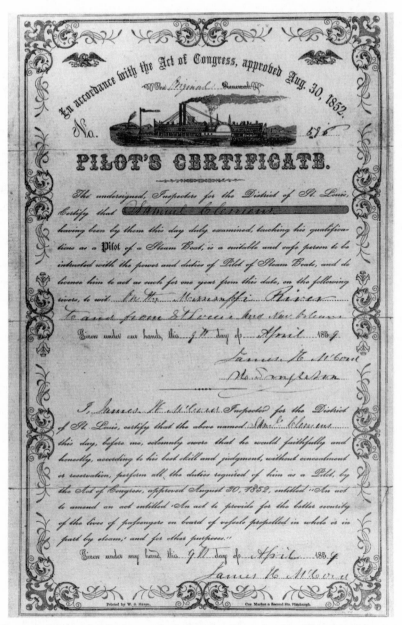

Samuel Clemens's riverboat pilot's license. Now in the Mariner's Museum, Newport News, Virginia.

certified, half of which would be paid up front. After arranging with his brother-in-law William A. *Moffett, to loan him the down payment, Clemens embarked on a new career. Not only did his new profession satisfy his wanderlust and need for money, but it also opened new horizons of cosmopolitanism for a young man who had seen many places but not much of the world. When the Civil War closed down the river, Clemens went west with his brother Orion, newly appointed secretary to the governor of Nevada territory. While the two held opposing views of the war, Samuel's commitment to the southern cause was so weak that he preferred to set out for the silver mines of the West than become involved, more intent on fortune and adventure than on the glories and discomforts of a war in which he did not fully believe.

In Nevada, Clemens began his career as *Mark Twain, but before he turned to journalism, he tried mining, expecting to return home flush or not at all. In a letter to Orion's wife, Mollie, he explained in jest what he held in his heart to be true— that his happiness and future depended on making not merely a living, but substantial sums: "I am not married yet, and I never *will* marry until I can afford to have servants enough to leave my wife in the position for which I designed her, viz:—as a *companion*. I don't want to sleep with a three-fold Being who is cook, chambermaid and washerwoman all in one. I don't mind sleeping with the female servants as long as I am a bachelor—by *no* means—but *after* I marry, that sort of thing will be 'played out,' you know (But lord bless you, Mollie, don't *hint* this depravity to the girls)" (31 January 1862). He worked franticly as a miner, but when nothing panned out, he considered suicide. *Newspaper journalism was the alternative. Not surprisingly, when desperate in the West he became a hard-drinking, hard-swearing, hard-living man, far from the good boy his mother had tutored him to be. With his energetic conscience reminding him how far he had come from his days in Hannibal as a Temperance Cadet, Clemens lived his life in cycles of remorse and rebellion, a pattern he would never shake.

Remorse and rebellion are traits of a passionate personality. By all accounts, Clemens was such, making strong friendships and equally strong antipathies. Such antipathies often arose from the friendships, into which he entered too quickly and too trustingly. While some few of those friendships—most notably with William Dean *Howells and Rev. Joseph *Twichell—remained fast, others became the focal points for Clemens's periodic rages. As Howells put it,

> He was apt to wear himself out in the vehemence of his resentments, or, he had so spent himself in uttering them that he had literally nothing more to say. You could offer Clemens offenses that would anger other men and he did not mind; he would account for them from human nature; but if he thought you had in any way played him false you were anathema and maranatha forever. Yet not forever, perhaps, for by-and-by, after years, he would be silent. There were two men, half a generation apart in their succession whom he thought equally atrocious in their treason to him, and of whom he used to talk terrifyingly, even after they were out of the world. He went farther than Heine, who said that he forgave his enemies, but not till they were dead. Clemens did not forgive his dead enemies; their death seemed to deepen their

crimes, like a base evasion, or a cowardly attempt to escape; he pursued them to the grave; he would like to dig them up and take vengeance upon their clay. (*My Mark Twain,* chapter 17)

But as much as he vented his resentments and bitterness in writing or strong speech, Clemens likewise gave regular expression to his positive feelings and his sense of humor. He was a devoted family man, though his temperament made him exasperating to his wife and alternately captivating and terrifying to his three daughters.

Endlessly entertaining to those for whom he would perform, the creative spark that went into Mark Twain made Clemens a scintillating host or guest. But while behind the mask of Mark Twain he could find a comfortable freedom for his antics, in the sober mornings as Clemens, remorse weighed him down. The passionate alternation between extreme moods, the doubts and determination that were born in the first thirty years of his life before he even donned the cover of Mark Twain, were the characteristics that made Twain, in all his duality and insight, possible. Conflicted, passionate, dynamic, given to sulks, imaginative, extreme in all ways, Clemens grew into the twentieth century with the birthmark of the West still on him.

CLEMENS, SUSY. SEE Clemens, Olivia Susan (Susy).

CLUBS. When a lonely old man, Clemens began the *Aquarium Club in order to secure himself some surrogate grandchildren. Such a gesture would not have surprised Alexis de Tocqueville, who, in *Democracy in America*, noted that Americans, highly mobile and lacking traditional social structures, flocked to voluntary organizations in order to give themselves a sense of belonging in an otherwise fluid society. Chief among these groups was the church, but not far behind were various trade organizations, fraternal societies, political parties, societies dedicated to some sort of reform (temperance, antislavery, civil service reform, or anti-imperialism, for example), and educational societies. By the end of the *Civil War, de Tocqueville could have added many leisure societies to the list as well, with the flourishing of British-style social and sports clubs, too.

Clemens belonged to virtually every kind of social organization, for varying reasons. Church membership was always low on his list. While he was a tithing member at the Elmira Park Church, of which his father-in-law was a founding member, and for several years rented a pew in Rev. Joseph *Twichell's church in *Hartford, religious groups were not at the center of Clemens's sense of community. Early in his life, his primary memberships were professional. He belonged to the typesetter's organization wherever he worked, not only relying on his membership to set wages and working conditions as one would expect from a labor union, but to use the organizations' social and educational facilities as well. Similarly, his membership in the Western Boatman's Benevolent Association served him both financially and socially in his career as a riverboat pilot. His participation in freemasonry—he belonged to the St. Louis Polar Star Lodge from December 1860 to October 1869—was a bit more complicated. It connected him to one of the most influential fraternal societies in nineteenth-century America, one that justified itself, as Clemens formulaically put it in his letter of application, as an "Institution" that would encourage him in his "desire of knowledge and a sincere wish of being serviceable to his fellow creatures." The ritualistic association gave members instant community wherever they traveled in the United States. Clemens found this to be the case in both California and Nevada, where he attended lodge meetings in Carson City and Angel's Camp in 1862 and 1865 respectively.

But he dropped his membership when he moved east because he felt freemasonry was incompatible with his *social class aspirations. Instead, he turned his energy to the educational *Monday Evening Club and its girl's auxiliary, the *Saturday Morning Club. Later in life, he willingly joined his name to various reform efforts, actively participating, for example, in the Anti-Imperialist League. All of these clubs had a marked impact on his writing, but none affected his professional development more than the Pall Mall–style gentleman's club. Long popular in England, these exclusive men's clubs became exceedingly popular in America after the Civil War.

Such clubs, part of a greater move toward *leisure, were part of an American cultural Anglophilia, and as such emphasized social class. Some of the best clubs built mansions for clubhouses; others purchased ones sold by bankrupt businessmen. Either way, appointments tended toward opulence and, consequently, clubs became collective patrons of the arts. They traded on exclusivity, and while they invited entertainers like Twain, often granting them free memberships, they primarily served to keep the well-to-do in regular contact with one another. They regularly organized banquets at which people like Twain gave *speeches; some, like the Lotos Club, published books. Twain's "Encounter with an Interviewer," for instance, was an invited contribution to *Lotos Leaves*, compiled by the club and published in 1874. Mostly, though, they were places for members to talk, drink, smoke, read, eat, and play billiards and cards.

Exclusively male in membership, these social clubs were a strange variant of *domesticity. Not only did clubs serve food, but they also usually had bedrooms for overnight stays. Clemens frequently lodged at the Player's Club in New York City in the early 1890s. Other rooms in these clubhouses were very much in keeping with the expectations for a Victorian mansion. Members could come and go at will, simply relaxing with the latest newspapers or books, or finding congenial company at most any time of the day or night. Thus, they served the putative function of domesticity as a "haven in a heartless world" of work, and cut out the familial responsibilities of home life as well. This attribute helped to make these clubs attractive; absent women and children, members could relax conventional decorum of speech (though not of manners generally), addressing topics taboo in mixed company. One of the reasons clubs kept humorists like Twain in so much demand, and Twain so enjoyed performing in them, was that Twain could indulge himself in racy *humor which he was not allowed as a family man or public writer. The club served as a quasi-public forum in which humor was given greater license than in the larger public to which Twain usually had his eye turned.

COLLABORATIONS. When Judge Oliver in chapter 27 of *The Innocents Abroad* retreats into evening solitude to "dig poetry out of himself," Twain mocks the image of the solitary romantic artist whose isolated existence creates ghastly poetry or nonsensically florid prose. He often made fun of this stereotype precisely because he never was this kind of writer. Granted, most writing is done alone and Twain spent many an hour with no company but the characters in the stories he wrote, but his ideal for composition was to write in collaboration with some convivial spirit. Twain's was a social imagination; his writing worked best in the frisson of conversation. Even when he wrote by himself, he wrote with particular people and particular conversations in mind.

This collaborative approach should come as no surprise given that he learned to write not as a poet or novelist, but as a newspaper journalist, sitting in the editorial offices of the Virginia City *Territorial Enterprise* alongside of his editor and mentor Joseph T. *Goodman and the paper's other reporters. Writing in these circumstances, Twain received immediate feedback from interested readers, including creative suggestions and editorial corrections. This situation was quite convivial, with shared yarns, *tobacco, *food, and *alcohol enlivening what could otherwise be a quiet, isolated activity. He recreated this context in San Francisco with Bret *Harte and the staff of the San Francisco *Golden Era*, but once he left San Francisco, he lost the immediate community of a journal's staff to give him the kind of collegial atmosphere in which he thrived. Instead, his career as a professional writer forced him into a life of quiet isolation.

He did as much as he could over the years, however, to break up that quietness. In part, he created out of family and friends an audience that would listen to each day's literary output. But he also often sought the more concrete, reciprocal community that comes from direct collaboration. In fact, he collaborated on more works than most novelists, though usually collaboration was a dream for him, a fantasy of communal labor that helped give him strength to write.

This fantasy manifested itself most conspicuously, perhaps, in 1871. Having struggled mightily with *Roughing It* for months, Twain was near despair when he invited Goodman to visit him at his in-laws' Quarry Farm residence. Goodman provided careful critical reading and support on Twain's work. More than anything, though, having Goodman, "who writes at my side every day up at the farm" (30 April 1871) in the study working on his own writing gave Twain strength. At this time, he proposed a more direct collaboration with Goodman on a book about national politics. As he explained to his brother, Orion *Clemens: "Joe [Goodman] & I have a 600-page book in contemplation which will wake up the nation. It is a thing which I have talked over with David Gray a good deal, & he wanted me to do it right & well—which I couldn't without a man to do the accurate drudgery and some little other writing. But Joe is the party. This present book will be a tolerable success . . . but the other book will be an *awful* success" (30 April 1871). Like many of Twain's planned collaborations, nothing came of this immediate idea, but it still inspired him.

Most of Twain's aborted plans for collaborative literature were meant seriously but failed for reasons beyond his control. For instance, when his brother-in-law Charles Jervis *Langdon was to go on a grand around-the-world tour in the company of a tutor, Professor Darius R. Ford, Clemens proposed a collaboration with Ford to write a series of travel articles for the Buffalo *Express. As noted by Twain in the 12 February 1870, issue, "These letters are [to be] written jointly by Professor D. R. Ford and Mark Twain. The former does the actual travelling, and such facts as escape his notice are supplied by the latter, who remains at home." Ford's primary purpose on the travels, though, was to help Langdon overcome a taste for alcohol and frivolity, and the sideline of writing letters was not something on which Ford expended much time. Twain wrote several letters under this guise before any of Ford's actually reached him in Buffalo, and the planned trip was cut short when Langdon came home from Japan after learning that his father had developed stomach cancer. Nonetheless, two Ford letters did make their way into the *Express* complete with Twain's comic commentary. But in disposition, the two writers were so different that they could not agree on how to make the collaboration work.

The very idea of a series of travel letters by proxy was inherently absurd and thus an appropriate vehicle for comedy, but once Twain got the idea in his head, he began to take it seriously. He soon contracted with his friend John Henry *Riley to collaborate on a book on the South African diamond mines. With a contract and a two-thousand–dollar advance from the American Publishing Company in hand, Riley set off for Africa in January 1871. He developed cancer, however, and could not fulfill his part of the contract. The idea lapsed, only to be recovered in self-mocking form in chapters 30 and 35 of *A Tramp Abroad*.

Other collaborations also died before producing anything, as in Twain's idea, proposed to William Dean *Howells, of a collaborative novel with many "literary big-fish" as contributors. The plan for what Twain called a "Blindfold Novelette" was to create a skeleton plot and serialize a novel with chapters contributed by multiple authors (to Howells, 12 October 1876). It was surprising that Twain would take such an idea seriously, considering how thoroughly he had mocked it in chapter 51 of *Roughing It*, but Twain's imagination often worked to turn mockery to seriousness and back again. Indeed, he infected Howells with the same cycle of enthusiasm, followed by remorse, followed by enthusiasm. Howells, while not acting on Twain's initial suggestion in 1876, ultimately organized such a collaborative novel, *The Whole Family*, for publication in *Harper's Bazaar* in 1906, but Twain, for once, declined to participate.

Twain constantly suggested writing ideas to Howells that they could either share or that Howells could realize alone, though Howells usually either ignored or politely declined such plans. Twice, however, the collaboration went further—once merely a business venture editing and publishing *Mark Twain's Library of Humor*, the other writing a joint play, *Colonel Sellers as Scientist*. The two had, as Howells put it in *My Mark Twain*, "A jubilant fortnight in working the particulars of these things out.... We would work all day long at our several tasks, and then at night, before dinner, read them over to each other. No dramatists ever got greater joy out of their creations" (chapter 6). The enthusiasm carried to the point where they actually prepared the play for production, but by then, Howells developed cold feet, quailing before the burlesque absurdities of the plot and characterization. The two actually had to pay their way out of their stage contract in order to satisfy Howells's desire to kill the play.

Their work together did not end their friendship, which is more than can be said for Twain's and Bret Harte's collaboration on the play *Ah Sin*. In this case, Twain tried to recapture some of the magic of the old days, when the two planned an extravagant burlesque of California poets. But the trajectories of the two were headed in opposite directions in 1876, with Harte frittering away his talents and abandoning his family, while Clemens assiduously developed his skills and became a devoted family man. The strain of working together while Harte lived in the Clemens house destroyed the friendship and contributed to a dramatic flop.

Twain did have some successful collaborations. *The Gilded Age* ended up being the Washington novel he originally wanted to share with Goodman; instead, he wrote it with Charles Dudley *Warner, with modest help from James Hammond *Trumbull. The novel was reasonably successful and spawned a play that proved extraordinarily lucrative. In a less conspicuous way, he collaborated regularly with Rev. Joseph *Twichell, who, though he never shared the writing with Twain, still served him well as the conversational companion Twain needed to inspire him in writing *"Old Times on the Mississippi," "Some Rambling Notes of an Idle Excursion," and *A Tramp Abroad*.

♦ SEE ALSO Cable, George Washington; Nast, Thomas; Newspaper Journalism; Work Habits.

COLLECTING. In the chapter from his *autobiography published in the *North American Review* on 21 September 1906, Twain refers to a newspaper article about the sale of some of his old *letters. He brags that his letters bring more than those of Ulysses S. *Grant, declaring, "I can't rise to General Grant's lofty place in the estimation of this nation, but it is a deep happiness to me to know that when it comes to epistolary literature, he can't sit in the front seat along with me." Knowing that his papers were becoming valuable, he gave away many of his manuscripts in his own lifetime as tokens of appreciation. For instance, he delivered several manuscripts to the American Academy of the National Institute of Arts and Letters in New York City when it inducted him as a charter member in 1904. Most famously, Twain presented the first half of the manuscript of *Adventures of Huckleberry Finn* to James Fraser Gluck, a Buffalo New York collector. Gluck had solicited the manuscript for the Buffalo and Erie County Public Library. Twain sent one half, which ended up in the library. The other half he sent under separate cover. This second part was lost until 1990 when it turned up in an old steamer trunk in a Los Angeles attic, where Gluck's heirs had unwittingly kept it for years.

Twain saved most of his valuable literary remains as part of his children's inheritance. Most of these materials remained with the estate after all survivors died, forming the nucleus of the *Mark Twain Papers. Much of the collection was sold off, however. When Clara Clemens Gabrilowitsch *Samossoud, Samuel and Olivia Clemens's second daughter and the only child to outlive her parents, needed to raise funds, she simply sold some books or papers out of her father's library or allowed Albert Bigelow *Paine to manage the sales. These articles have been distributed among collectors and many are now lost to the public.

Not all private collecting has been a public loss, however. Collectors essentially saved Twain's letters, and when a private collector buys one that has long been lost, he or she usually has it authenticated by the Mark Twain Papers for the simple fee of a photocopy to go into the collection and the text eventually into the edition of Twain's letters. Moreover, many lifelong collectors have willed their collections to various libraries, which give public access to this material. Libraries around the country have collections of original letters and manuscripts. The largest of these— the Mark Twain Papers, the Mark Twain House, the New York Public Library, and the Morse Collection at Yale—watch dealers' catalogues closely and increase their holdings whenever possible. In short, without private collectors' selling, buying, and preserving his literary remains, we would know far less about Twain and his times.

COLONEL SELLERS (1874). Twain spent a fair amount of time writing *drama because of the commercial success of *Colonel Sellers* which, ironically, was written substantially by someone else. It began as an unauthorized dramatization of Twain's and Charles Dudley *Warner's novel *The Gilded Age*. San Francisco drama critic G. B. Densmore pirated certain elements of the successful novel mainly as a comic vehicle for actor John T. Raymond. While Densmore's five-act melodrama cribbed freely from the novel, it had a plot structure of its own, a structure that deprived the play of much of the novel's satiric bite. Densmore's play, titled *The Gilded Age*, was actually produced in San Francisco in April 1874 before Twain learned of it and threatened legal action against it. He then paid Densmore for the script, reworked it to some extent, allowed John T. Raymond to continue performing the starring role, and put the play into production in New York City. It ran from 16 September 1874, to 9 January 1875 in New York City's Park Theatre, then six more weeks in the summer of 1875. It went on a national tour and was revived almost annually from 1876 to 1888. It became a cash cow for Twain during the period in which he wrote *The Adventures of Tom Sawyer*, diverting his attention from literature as an art in its own right in favor of seeing literature as a prelude to drama. This may in part account for the theatricality that so many critics find in this novel. Certainly the play gave Clemens incentive to think in this groove; as he wrote to William Dean *Howells on 11 October 1876, "Check for 1,616.16 has just arrived— my clear profit on Raymond's first week in Philadelphia. Write a drama, Howells." As much as the money provided a powerful incentive, it did not provideTwain with the knowleldge he needed to be an effective playwright; he never again had such a success with a play.

COMEDY. SEE Humor.

COMIC JOURNALISM. In an era when newspapers rarely distinguished between news and "features," comic pieces were used often as filler. These ranged from a single line, such as "A man with a pot of green paint can stand where he pleases on a ferry-boat," to substantial anecdotes and even *sketches. Many of these were written expressly for newspapers, either by local reporters or taken from newspaper exchanges. The habit of newspapers simply to borrow from other journals in defiance of *copyright meant that much material from comic magazines, such as B. P. Shillaber's *The Carpet-Bag* or William T. Porter's *The Spirit of the Times*, also found its way into newspapers. Much of America's best as well as best-known *humor was this anonymous kind of filler comedy, or so thought Clemens and his coeditors William Dean *Howells and Charles Hopkins Clark when they selected several newspaper squibs for inclusion in *Mark Twain's Library of Humor*.

Newspapers in fact spawned many of America's best humorists as well as its best humor. Clemens himself counts among these. His first contact with newspaper humor was as the compositor who set into type several humorous pieces borrowed from *The Carpet-Bag* to fill columns in Orion Clemens's Hannibal *Journal*. No wonder, then, that young Samuel sent his first comic piece for national publication, "The Dandy Frightening the Squatter," to Shillaber's *Carpet-Bag*, where it appeared in 1852.

Newspapers created an entire subcategory of literary humor in the United States, written by a group of comic writers who have come to be known collectively as literary comedians. Notable among these, and all known to Clemens either as models for his early writing or in person, were Shillaber himself, John Phoenix and Squibob (George Derby), Q. K. Philander Doesticks (Mortimer M. Thompson), Petroleum V. Nasby (David Ross *Locke), Orpheus C. Kerr (Robert Henry Newell), Artemus Ward (Charles Farrar *Browne), and Josh Billings (Henry Wheeler Shaw). Many were also stage performers, wrote for both magazines and newspapers, and collected their sketches into books. But the newspaper gave them birth and the newspaper shaped their characteristics.

Dialect humor, predicated on misspellings and grammatical errors, was the most conspicuous characteristic of comic journalism. American elites already attacked newspapers for their vulgar language, especially the use of *slang. As Robert Herrick and Lindsay Todd Damon put it in chapter 14, "Barbarisms, Slang, and Newspaper English," of their 1899 high school textbook, *Composition and Rhetoric for Schools*, "Students . . . will do well to look for their models elsewhere than in the popular magazines and newspapers; it is always easy to let one's style down to a col-loquial level; it is not easy, if one has habitually used slipshod, careless English, to get pure, exact, dignified English when required." Against a backdrop of such cen-soriousness, deliberate solecisms are funny, and many of the comic journalists played on the pleasure of defying rigid conventionality. Adopting the persona of the cracker-barrel philosopher, many of these journalists trotted out witticisms that take their spice from the contrast between form and content, as in Josh Billings's aphorisms: "An Amerikan aristokrat iz the most ridikilus thing in market. They are generally ashamed ov their ansesstors; and, if they hav enny, and live long enuff, they generally have cauze tew be ashamed ov their posterity." Or consider Artemus Ward's note at the beginning of his "Fourth of July Oration": "I delivered the fol-lerin, about two years ago, to a large and discriminating awjince. I was 95 minits passin' a given pint. I have revised the orashun, and added sum things which makes it apporposser to the times than it otherwise would be. I have also corrected the grammars and punktooated it. I do my own punktooatin nowdays. The Printers in *Vanity Fair* offiss can't punktooate worth a cent." Many of Billings's and Ward's misspellings are phonetic spellings of normal pronunciation. Such so-called "eye-dialect" indicates mere marginal literacy, as opposed to a genuine regional vernacu-lar. Thus, the characterization of such a persona is limited to the range of observations within the sphere of an unlettered person, denying to the humorist any learned allusions or any comic device but the contrast between ignorance and normal standards of education. Many of Clemens's earliest *pseudonyms and per-sonas follow in these tracks; *Mark Twain served Clemens better by not being caught in the formulaic stance of the unlettered sage.

CONDENSED NOVELS. A *parody genre developed and popularized by William Thackeray in his association with the British humor magazine *Punch*, the condensed novel comically captures characteristics of particular novels or particular kinds of novels in the scope of a short story. It became a favorite genre of Bret *Harte, whose *Condensed Novels and Other Papers* (1867) was not only his first book but one of his best.

Under Harte's tutelage in San Francisco, Clemens learned about the genre and published some of his efforts—like "Lucretia Smith's Soldier" and "The Christmas Fireside"—in literary magazines such as *The Californian*. Other early condensed novels, including "Mamie Grant, Child Missionary" and "Burlesque *L'Homme Qui Rit*," have been published posthumously. All of these are little more than bare plot outlines that suggest a characteristic style while describing the crises of exaggerated, one-dimensional characters. Pacing is quick, development abbreviated by the condensation of a novel's plot into the scope of a short story, and plots usually have absurd twists on convention.

For a while after he moved east, Twain continued to publish condensed novels, such as "The Legend of the Capitoline Venus," and "An *Awful ---- Terrible Medieval Romance." While Twain usually gave such works a mocking tone, occasionally he used the form not to undercut the model he followed but to borrow its prestige, as in "Goldsmith's Friend Abroad Again," which recasts the satiric force of Oliver Goldsmith's *Citizen of the World* into an American context.

The techniques of condensation that he learned in the *burlesque short form show their traces in many of Twain's full novels. In *The Gilded Age*, *Pudd'nhead Wilson and Those Extraordinary Twins*, and *The *American Claimant*, for example, the strange pacing, flat characters, and tendency toward parody as a crude form of *satire all stem substantially from Twain's early practice as a writer of condensed novels.

CONFIDENCE GAMES. Folk literature from most human cultures is replete with instances of trickery and chicanery, but nineteenth-century American culture raised the confidence game as a literary and cultural subject to the level of obsession, one amply demonstrated in Twain's works. Americans moved so frequently that the kinds of social structures that protect people from fraud in stable societies were merely distant memories in many communities, especially on the frontier or in large, anonymous *cities. In the words of Simon Suggs, con-man hero of Johnson Jones Hooper's tales in the tradition of *southwestern humor, "It's good to be shifty in a new country," and the major city was as much a new country as was the frontier. More importantly, the development of a market economy blurred the lines between shrewd bargaining and outright chicanery. In the early days of American capitalism, the idea that all is fair in the love of making *money still seemed shocking, and much of the literature of confidence games questions the new economics.

Not surprisingly, moralists denounced all kinds of fraud and deceit, attacking everything from the theater to the full-blown confidence man as manifestations of a moral decline, the end of genuineness in character. Most major American authors

"I AM THE LATE DAUPHIN."

Illustration by Edward Windsor Kemble (1861–1933), from *Adventures of Huckleberry Finn*, New York: Webster & Company, 1885, p. 165.

of the nineteenth century tended to address the confidence game in a more complex fashion, seeing, as for example in Edgar Allan Poe's "Diddling" or Herman Melville's *The Confidence Man*, not merely a threat to social order but also a source of individual power and pleasure in deception. Melville in particular raises the question of the confidence man's "masquerade" to a metaphysical level, suggesting the necessity of deceit and mutual faith in one another's deceptions as a precondition not only for society but even for individual happiness.

Living in constant motion alternately on the frontier and in the city, and always out to make his fortune, Clemens followed the path that gave rise to this literature. Naturally, the confidence game appears frequently in his works. Indeed, his first national hit, "The *Jumping Frog," turns on the tale of a confidence game in the making of a practical joke. In this piece, Twain's elaborate *frame narrative becomes a parable of the need to take a new country on its own terms, to abandon the eastern idea of stable character marked by definite external trappings of dress and language. In this sense, what happens to narrator Mark Twain is a cautionary tale advising us to embrace the modern, democratic, fluid society and economy of the West. But the internal tale of Jim Smiley has a conflicting message, namely that an obsession with gambling—that is, with participating in the new market economy in an effort to get rich quick—opens one up to becoming the mark in a confidence game. Similarly, the "Professor's Yarn" from chapter 36 of *Life on the Mississippi* describes an educated, bright, but socially rigid eastern professor learning to abandon his old system of morality by watching the ways of western gamblers.

The ambivalence came legitimately from Clemens's own experiences. As a reporter, he was in the business of drumming up readership, which he did by exploiting Americans' ambivalence over the confidence game. He would as readily expose frauds with a sense of moral outrage as he would retail stories of clever cons—sometimes simultaneously. Usually, however, the stories of various frauds were a counterpoint in his travel writings to his more serious descriptions of interesting places, people, or events. The shifts back and forth from the different moods of belief to skepticism were very much part of the technique of *newspaper journalism. In the process, he developed his lifelong habit of extending the idea of a fraud to social and political hypocrisy.

While he simply used confidence games as grist for his journalistic mill, his attitudes toward fraud became more complicated and morally charged over the years as his greater involvement in *business ventures brought home to him the costs of confidence games. His dealings began before his writing career, back when he had a more than adequate income as a riverboat pilot and had begun speculating in agricultural commodities. He usually lost money, but according to his letters, he never blamed anyone for duping him. But once he headed west in 1861, cutting himself off temporarily from the idea of steadily earning money at a legitimate profession, he turned to the world of pure speculation in the minefields of Nevada and California. There he allowed himself to be whooped into a frenzy by the machinations of newspapers working in cahoots with developers; there he had a mining claim jumped and discovered the entanglements of the law as a vehicle not for securing justice but for arguing cases. Then, when he began working for a newspaper, he learned even more about the political machinations of a legislature selling rights to franchises such as tollroads, and about the economic machinations of a newspaper itself in promoting a bubble economy. Indeed, much of *Roughing It* celebrates these boom times, and chapters 42 and 44 in particular outline the journalist's role in this massive confidence game. Given that chapters 40 and 41 describe Twain's ultimate failure to be duped by the con, the turn toward celebration in subsequent chapters is ironic, especially given that, within weeks of the book's publication, he received information that his publisher, Elisha *Bliss, was in fact cheating him.

Of course, the entire business of *subscription publishing, with its high-pressure sales tactics, was one that blurred the line between legitimate sales and fraudulent practices. Clemens at this early stage knew little about subscription publication and felt that author and publisher should be on the same side. But Bliss was one of those businessmen whose shrewdness crowded out morality. Clemens repeatedly confronted Bliss, but somehow managed always to feel as if he were the mark in a con game.

Not surprisingly, then, his next book, the collaborative *Gilded Age*, takes as its theme the interlocking frauds of government subsidies for business at public expense and the major business frauds of railroads and land speculations. In this book, the outrage against chicanery rises to a fever pitch, with no celebration of the speculative spirit, no celebration of confidence games because every con causes significant damage.

That measure of harm done, coupled with the questions of power or the moral character of the target of the con, became the standards by which Twain's works either attack or celebrate the con. In pieces such as "The Professor's Yarn," the targets of the con are not people worthy of sympathy, allowing the reader to celebrate the performance of the con artist. But in chapter 39 of *Life on the Mississippi*, the everyday folk dragged down by the con games of the traveling salesmen force the reader to blame the clever con artists. When Twain turned the games into fiction, the ambivalence remains. Huckleberry Finn in *Adventures of Huckleberry Finn* engages in many cons, from trying to buy off Jim with a fraudulent quarter, to depriving his father of money to which he is legally entitled by "giving" his fortune to Judge Thatcher for "a consideration," to fooling the town into believing in his death, to manufacturing different identities for himself. In most of these cases, he does no harm to deserving people. On the contrary, he merely protects himself, taking a modicum of power from a world that would otherwise overwhelm him. As such, his shiftiness is laudatory (although contemporary reviewers often condemned the book precisely on the grounds that it promoted deceit). Pap, on the other hand, is merely repugnant in his conning the new judge, or in his efforts to con money out of Huck and Judge Thatcher. The King and the Duke move between these two extremes. At first they are objects of sympathy, then of our admiration as we see how they connive to make a living off of a corrupt society; finally, we see that their alternative to pious convention is even more corrupt in its willingness to harm the weak.

The character Hank Morgan in *A Connecticut Yankee in King Arthur's Court* reveals the depth of Twain's ambivalence. The very term "yankee" disparaged the New England traveling salesman, notorious for cheating. In time, the term also came to be used in praise of shrewdness and ingenuity. In the *Civil War, both valences were in play, depending on the political orientation of the person using the term. So by the time Hank Morgan became the Connecticut Yankee, Twain could use the term to express both sides of this showy, shrewd, and megalomaniacal character, hero and villain of the story.

The reporter in Twain justified his exposes of con men as a socially useful practice in alerting the public to the need for skepticism and vigilance. The creative artist in Twain embraced a more complex attitude. This side of Twain asks readers to suspend skepticism in order to appreciate the rich show the con man puts on—at least as long as we can watch from a safe distance.

♦ SEE ALSO Tricksters.

CONNECTICUT YANKEE IN KING ARTHUR'S COURT, A (1889).

Connecticut Yankee is not only the most ambitious novel Twain published in his lifetime, but also, excepting *Pudd'nhead Wilson and Those Extraordinary Twins*, the most fragmented of his major works. The shift in conception and tone from novel's beginning to end parallels the usual shifts in Twain's long works as his imagination played its way through plot by way of a series of reversals, but the magnitude of the shifts in this book marks a change much more profound. In *Connecticut Yankee*, Twain thought he was writing a paean to progress, only to discover—not fully consciously perhaps—the limits of his optimism and the depths of his cynicism.

Clemens's initial idea for *Connecticut Yankee* came to him in December 1884 when on a lecture tour with George Washington *Cable. Cable called Clemens's attention to Sir Thomas Malory's *Mort D'Arthur*, and the two relished the book's archaic English. Clemens's burlesque imagination went to work, and on 3 December he jotted in his notebook the germ of a new story:

> Dream of being a knight errant in armor in the middle ages. Have the notions & habits of thought of the present day mixed with the necessities of that. No pockets in the armor. No way to manage certain requirements of nature. Can't scratch. Cold in the head—can't blow—can't get at handkerchief, can't use iron sleeve. Iron gets red hot in the sun—leaks in the rain, gets white with frost & freezes me solid in the winter. Suffer from lice & fleas. Make disagreeable clatter when I enter church. Can't dress or undress myself. Always getting struck by lightning. Fall down, can't get up. See Morte DArthur.

Caught up in other matters, including the lecture tour; the publication of *Adventures of Huckleberry Finn*, which was the first book to issue from his own publishing firm, *Webster and Company; investments in the *Paige typesetter; and other ideas for novels, including the germ of *The American Claimant*, Clemens had plenty to keep him from executing this idea. He only sketched notes for the book over the course of the following year. Some of those notes suggest much of what would finish the book: the battle of the sand-belt and the narrator's suicidal tendencies on returning to England in the nineteenth century after wishing for the England in which he was so prominent. But all of the notes have the same comic feel as the first, suggesting that *burlesque—including burlesque sentimentality—was at the heart of his initial conception.

Certainly the high humor of burlesque suited Clemens's basic outlook in 1885. Things had rarely looked better for Clemens. Early sales of *Huckleberry Finn* were stellar; the lecture tour had netted Clemens about sixteen thousand dollars; and he successfully negotiated to have his publishing company secure the book of the decade, the *Personal Memoirs of U. S. Grant*. The first chapters of *Connecticut Yankee*, written sometime in late 1885 or early 1886, display a confident comic energy. Partly he sustained the joy of writing in the belief that he was no longer writing for the public. As early as the winter of 1885–1886, his daughter Susy recorded in her biography of her father: "Mama and I have both been very much troubled of late because papa, since he had been publishing General Grant's books, has seemed to forget his own books and works entirely; and the other evening . . . he told me that he didn't expect to write but one more book" (quoted in *Mark Twain: A Biography*, p. 840). Given how often he had struggled to finish his books—he ended *Huckleberry Finn* with Huck saying, "If I'd a knowed what a trouble it was to make a book I wouldn't a tackled it and ain't agoing to no more"—it comes as no surprise that Clemens hoped to make a living in other ventures and no longer have to write. By the time he finished *Connecticut Yankee*, he explicitly told William Dean *Howells, "It's my swan-song, my retirement from literature permanently" (24 August 1889). Not surprisingly, he did not hurry his work on such a book.

But he did use those opening chapters at an 11 November 1886 public appearance on Governor's Island for the Military Service Institute. He read some chapters and sketched out the book in the rest of his talk, describing the story of a Yankee swindler conniving his way through Arthur's Britain. As sketched, it remained a burlesque. Constant references to the Yankee as a showman—the reference to Bridgeport, Connecticut, in "A Word of Explanation" draws the connection to Phineas T. *Barnum—are lighthearted, almost Tom Sawyerish as Tom is depicted in his own *Adventures*, not with the serious concern evinced in his return in *Adventures of Huckleberry Finn*. But the Yankee's slanginess and irreverence far exceed Tom's. Clemens's friend Mary Mason *Fairbanks got wind of these early chapters and the book's early plan via extensive newspaper coverage of this military event, and evidently expressed her concern that Clemens was reverting to the crudeness of his early journalism. Clemens wrote back that he had written few chapters, expected to take his time—thirty years, he said—and never expected to publish the results. More importantly, he told her the book was not to be a "satire peculiarly. It is more especially a *contrast*. It merely exhibits under high lights, the daily life of the Arthurian times & that of today. . . . Of course in my story I shall leave unsmirched & unbelittled the great and beautiful *characters* drawn by the master hand of old Malory" (16 November 1886).

What happened between this letter and the following summer has as much to do with Clemens's unconscious flow of ideas as with any deliberate change in focus. He took the book to Elmira in late June, and in about six or seven weeks wrote nearly three hundred manuscript pages, covering chapters 5 to 20, excepting chapter 10. He wrote to Charles *Webster on 3 August 1887, "the fun, which was abounding . . . up to three days ago, has slumped into funereal seriousness, and this will not do—it will not answer at all." But as much as he may have regretted the book's turn toward seriousness, he adjusted to it, discovering that as a swan song, a serious *satire gave him an outlet for all of his pent up political, social, and philosophical ruminations, especially as they had changed over the preceding fifteen years. *Connecticut Yankee* became an attack on reactionary *medievalism, on Matthew *Arnold's ideas about the political value of *reverence and conformity, on *religion, on American business practices, and, finally, on the Victorian idea of character itself.

Following his reading in Charles *Darwin and Herbert *Spencer, much of the book argues that human character is not free, not morally responsible, that it is merely the product of "heredity and training" (chapter 18). Here he took his *utilitarianism to its moral extreme—and found the result painful. Even as he argued himself into a nearly complete determinism, he found a longing for a different idea of *identity, one that had a center, a soul: "And as for me, all that I think about in this plodding sad pilgrimage, this pathetic drift between the eternities, is to look out and humbly live a pure and high and blameless life, and save that one microscopic atom in *me* that is truly me: the rest may land in Sheol and welcome, for all I care" (chapter 18). For all of the Yankee's subsequent swagger, a deep misanthropy, a deep cynicism about human possibility, colors the rest of the book, alternating with a sentimental longing for something better.

Early notes included the Yankee's sentimentality, but clearly burlesque it, and the opening chapters, in creating a contrast between the Yankee's own self-image as a "practical" man "barren of sentiment" on the one hand and his melancholy and heavy drinking on the other, sets the stage for this book of time-travel as mere fantasy. As the book turned serious, Clemens sometimes dropped the mask of his narrative persona, letting himself speak directly through Hank, but he never fully lost the sense that the plan makes Morgan quite unreliable. *Connecticut Yankee*, then, is a drunkard's fantasy; as such, it is the imposition of modern desire on the past, an imposition that romanticizes the past precisely because it is immune to the power of the present.

In this context, Clemens was criticizing those of his contemporaries who romanticized the past even as he understood their longing. In *Idylls of the King*, for example, Alfred, Lord Tennyson created a fantasy of the past that evolved from an idealized vision of the present. Hank Morgan does much the same thing, but the contrast between his vision and that of Tennyson not only shows the failings of Tennyson's vision, but also the failings of Morgan's. His longing at the end is for the illusion of power and importance that a drunkard living in England, haunting the museums of the feudal past, might relish. The fantasy ending, therefore, is the most important marker of Hank's inadequacy as an interpreter of the past, or the past's meaning and value. One must keep in mind that Clemens's original conception for the book was of a dream story, not of real time-travel, and the introduction makes the likelihood of illusion very high. Only after the book took its serious turn did Clemens discover the poignancy of Hank's misinterpretation of the past, that his own idea of *progress is as much a fantasy as is Tennyson's hope for regression.

Such a feeling came over Clemens by the time he carried Hank Morgan to Morgan LeFay's dungeons in chapter 18. From this point on, the theme of imprisonment haunts the book, and human actions are shown as constrained by environment as much as by politics, church, and law. Ultimately the king and Morgan are enslaved. While Clemens took the description of slave life from *Slavery in the*

United States: A Narrative of the Life and Adventures of Charles Ball, a Black Man, Who Lived Forty Years in Maryland, South Carolina and Georgia, as a Slave (1837), he meant it more as a universal symbol of the *slavery into which every person, from king to serf, is ultimately born. The very oxymoron of a "man factory" that Morgan uses to create independent adults out of "human sheep" reveals Clemens's fear that independent adulthood is impossible. But in this argument for determinism, he contradicted the moral urgency that also fills the book. If humanity is merely a product of circumstance, then all of his moral anxiety is wasted energy; human beings are not free and therefore not morally responsible. But as much as he argued this position, he simultaneously suggested that human beings should be free and independent, should resist conformity, should be moral agents.

This contradiction, reconcilable only in nihilism, provided the energy that drove Clemens to finish the book, now apparently delighting in its serious turn. While he had hoped to take thirty years to finish it and keep it private, money troubles again pushed him to publish. In particular, with Webster and Company needing to keep up its cash flow and the Paige typesetter consuming money—thousands of dollars each month—he hoped that *Connecticut Yankee* would provide the last capital needed to put him beyond ever having to write again. He wrote a few chapters in the summer of 1888, probably up to chapter 24, but decided to continue through the autumn in hopes of finishing. His friend Joseph *Twichell let him use an upstairs room in his house so that Clemens could avoid the inevitable distractions of his own home, and in spite of the noise of Twichell's family, Clemens boomed away on the manuscript into October. He hoped to finish the manuscript that month: "I want to finish the day the machine finishes, and a week ago the closest calculations of that indicated Oct. 22—but experience teaches me that their calculations will miss fire, as usual" (to Theodore Crane, 5 October 1888). Some critics have speculated that the divided feelings the book evinces respecting technology as a measure of progress can be traced to his alternating euphoria and frustration with the Paige typesetter.

In putting the book into production in the spring of 1889, Clemens had to secure *illustrations. He began to look for an artist even before he finished the manuscript in March, and ultimately settled on Daniel Carter Beard in July. Beard asked for three thousand dollars (one thousand more than E.W. Kemble had taken to illustrate *Huckleberry Finn*) for over 250 illustrations, but was willing to take less for cruder work. Clemens accepted Beard's terms: "I prefer this time to contract for the very best an artist can do. This time I want pictures, not black-board outlines & charcoal sketches. If Kemble's illustrations for my last book were handed me today, I could understand how tiresome to me that sameness would get to be, when distributed through a whole book, & I would put them promptly in the fire" (to Fred J. Hall, 19 July 1889). Clearly, as much as Clemens decided to publish *Connecticut*

Yankee to make money, he was not interested in cutting corners. This was to be the best *subscription book he had ever made—perhaps the best anyone had ever made.

Even though Clemens had written a scathing satire, he hoped at first that Beard's illustrations would soften the blow, instructing him, "I have aimed to put all the crudeness and vulgarity necessary in the book, and I depend upon you for the refinement and scintillating humor for which you are so famous" (late July or August 1889). But Beard's interpretation of the book stressed the political allegory and thus did little to soften Clemens's vulgarity, even though the illustrations were exquisite. Clemens did not complain, but rather praised everything Beard did. On reviewing the last illustrations, Clemens wrote to Beard: "Hold me under permanent obligations. What luck it was to find you! There are a hundred artists who could illustrate any other book of mine, but there was only one who could illustrate this one. Yes, it was a fortunate hour when I went netting for lightning-bugs & caught a meteor. Live forever!" (11 November 1889). After publication, he wrote to L. E. Parkhurst, "To my mind the illustrations are better than the book—which is a good deal for me to say, I reckon" (20 December 1889).

Beard's illustrations pick up as much on Clemens's anxiety about the political impact of speculative wealth—ironic given Clemens's speculations as he wrote the book—as on the satire of England, past and present. In canvassing the book in the United States, however, Webster and Company stressed its patriotic Americanness. As Fred Hall wrote to Clemens in a letter asking for approval of the canvassing prospectus, "Whatever makes fun of royalty and nobility, and the idea of a government by an aristocratic class, we have put in, as that will suit the American public well" (16 October 1889). Clemens approved this approach, not only for its commercial soundness, but for its truth to at least one side of *Connecticut Yankee's* satire. Ironically, once published, some American reviewers saw both sides of the satire, whereas the English saw only the attacks on their country. While some progressive British reviewers appreciated the work, many English readers fumed over Clemens's treatment of the Arthurian legends.

The book was a financial disappointment. Not only did it sell significantly less well than *Huckleberry Finn*, its much greater production expenses, coupled with Webster and Company's great need for funds, kept Clemens from realizing any money from the book's American sales. It sold about fifteen thousand copies in England, which was par for the first-year sales of a Twain book there, but the negative publicity dampened sales of all of his books there for the next several years. English royalties accounted for a significant portion of Clemens's income, so he felt the effects quite severely, especially in the run-up to his eventual bankruptcy in 1894.

Although early sales were disappointing, the book has become one of Twain's popular and critical favorites. Critics recognize the ambition of the book, and see in its ending a prescient glimpse not only into modern warfare, but into Clemens's own increasing iconoclasm. To a twentieth-century critical establishment bent on finding the serious in Twain, *Connecticut Yankee* was surpassed only by *Huckleberry Finn*, and to a current critical audience as interested in the discontinuities in literature as in artistic wholeness, *Connecticut Yankee* is equaled only by *Pudd'nhead Wilson*.

The popular reaction to *Connecticut Yankee* has been enthusiastic, though for opposite reasons. Somehow, the fantasy element and the incongruity have captured stage and screen, with radically bowdlerized versions being produced numerous times. Richard Rodgers and Lorenz Hart's 1927 musical version had a run of more than four hundred performances. Hollywood has produced at least four film versions, including Disney's recent *A Connecticut Kid in King Arthur's Court*; the best known is a Bing Crosby musical version of 1949. In this, the political content is drained out, replaced by one song in which the king, out of his castle for the first time in years in order to see his people, breaks into song with Hank (played by Crosby) warbling "We're busy doing nothing." Only the Warner Brothers animated version, *Bugs Bunny in King Arthur's Court*, starring Bugs Bunny as Hank and Daffy Duck as King Arthur, comes remotely close to capturing the anarchic violence and satiric thrust of the original. But perhaps it would be too much to expect any interpretation to capture the full range of meanings in the book. Even Clemens himself recognized that no book, not even the *Connecticut Yankee* he wrote, could do all he wanted it to do. As he said in a letter to Howells shortly before publication: "Well, my book is written—let it go. But if it were only to write over again there wouldn't be so many things left out. They burn in me; & they keep multiplying & multiplying; but now they can't ever be said. And besides, they would require a library—& a pen warmed up in hell" (22 September 1889).

CONSCIENCE. SEE Moral Sense.

CONWAY, MONCURE (1832–1907). A Virginia-born minister and journalist, Moncure Conway moved to England in 1863 while lecturing in support of the Union cause. He was offered a pastorate in a London suburb, and stayed the rest of his life. Having written for many influential American journals, and having edited *The Dial*, Conway was better known as a journalist than as a minister, and he continued this work throughout his life, writing for both British and American newspapers and magazines.

He met Clemens in London in September 1871, beginning a long and cordial friendship carried out primarily through correspondence. We know of forty-two letters Clemens wrote Conway between 1872 and 1905; Clemens saved fifty-five of Conway's letters.

Conway ardently promoted Twain's writing and speaking engagements in England, so much so that Clemens hired him to act as his publishing agent in

England in the late 1870s. He was especially active in the British publication of *The Adventures of Tom Sawyer*. Probably because he acted more out of friendship than out of a need for business, Conway was one of the few agents to remain on good terms with Clemens.

♦ SEE ALSO Business Ventures.

COPYRIGHT. Solid copyright protections for intellectual property are relatively recent inventions, especially international copyright agreements, which governments have passed only slowly as they adapt to the needs of the *publishing industry. As authorship became professionalized in the nineteenth century and publishing became a lucrative industry, it was often cheaper for publishers to pirate literature—that is, to reprint unauthorized editions and sell them without giving the author any royalties—than to solicit and pay for new material. While this practice was outlawed fairly early in most countries, the absence of international copyright agreements made international piracy perfectly legal. American publishers in the eighteenth and nineteenth centuries were among the worst literary pirates, knowing that established European authors tended to sell better in the United States than unknown American ones. Thus, the absence of international copyright was one of the great impediments to developing a national literature in the United States.

Had authors seen themselves as professional writers first, they might have lobbied sooner and more effectively for stronger copyrights and for international agreements, but well into the nineteenth century, most authors of books and stories had other professions. Writing was a genteel sideline, not expected to make significant money. With the explosion of literary interest and a marketplace in America after the Civil War, this de facto disparagement of the commercial aspect of writing faded fast, but the corresponding legal developments were slow to follow. Many publishers themselves continued to profit from literary piracy and therefore lobbied effectively to prevent any copyright law that might become the basis for an international agreement.

Certainly Clemens discovered this almost immediately to his dismay when he began to make a name for himself as a writer only to find his newspaper sketches and speeches printed throughout the country by newspaper exchanges. When working as a reporter, this exchange increased his marketability, but when trying to control the sales of his works in literary magazines and books, he found that the exchanges damaged his sales. He did not take such piracy quietly; he aggressively sued anyone he thought was breaching his copyright and loudly voiced his opinions of any newspaper that would use the excuse of public interest or newsworthiness to copy literature. A 5 July 1875 letter to William Dean *Howells touches on both points: "Osgood & I are 'going for' the puppy Gill on infringement of trademark.

Thomas S. Nast (1840–1902), famous caricaturist for *Harper's Weekly*, used the occasion of Clemens traveling to Canada to secure Canadian copyright for *Prince & the Pauper* to support international copyright agitation. From *Harper's Weekly*, January 1882.

To win one or two suits of this kind will set literary folks on a firmer bottom. The New York *Tribune* doesn't own the world—I wish Osgood would sue it for stealing Holmes's poem. Wouldn't it be gorgeous to sue Whitelaw R[eid] for *petty larceny?* I will promise to go into court & swear I think him capable of stealing pea-nuts from a blind peddlar." William F. Gill and Company had published an anthology, edited by John Brougham and John Elderkin, that pirated Twain's "Encounter with an Interviewer." Clemens sued the publisher rather than the editors as part of his strategy to take the profit out of piracy. The fantasy suit against the *Tribune* refers to Oliver Wendell Holmes's "Grandmother's Story of Bunker Hill Battle," published by James R. Osgood with Holmes's explicit request that it not be reprinted anywhere else. The *Tribune* promptly violated that request. Clearly, American copyright laws had weak teeth. From suing over trademark infringement to imagining an indictment for petty larceny, Clemens tried to find ways to make intellectual property worth something.

Merely pestered by domestic pirates, Clemens was positively plagued by international ones. The first was British publisher John Camden Hotten, who collected many of Twain's earliest writings, edited them, and sold them without authorization and without paying Clemens a penny. Hotten may actually have helped Clemens in the long run, however, by building up Twain's English reputation and then, conveniently, dying. Clemens had tried to sell his books through Routledge in order to thwart Hotten, actually traveling to England on the eve of publication of *The Gilded Age* in order to establish the residency required to secure British copyright, but Routledge was too slow in its scrupulousness to make any money for Clemens, nor did the arrangement really stop Hotten. When Hotten died, his associate, Andrew Chatto, contracted with Clemens to serve as his official British publisher. This relationship proved useful and profitable to both, with Clemens's English sales usually accounting for about one third of his book royalties.

Canadian publisher Belford Brothers was not the first to pirate Twain's material, but the worst from Clemens's point of view, since Belford could republish Twain's works in cheaper form and ship the product back to the United States, significantly undermining Clemens's home market. Clemens eventually learned that he could secure copyright throughout the British commonwealth if he were to establish residency in Canada and publish there before he published in the United States. He took this course of action for several of his books after *The Adventures of Tom Sawyer*.

But no matter what he did to slow the pirates, Clemens could not stop them until copyright laws themselves had enough teeth to protect his work. In *Clemens* v. *Belford*, the court ruled that Belford was legally entitled to reprint various sketches by Twain as long as they were accurately attributed to Twain and Clemens had not registered a copyright for the sketches. In the face of such a legal precedent, Clemens's alternatives were to seek other means of employment or to lobby for changes in copyright laws. He did both, in part pursuing his various *inventions and investments in other *business ventures, in part by turning to *drama. As he put it in a 13 December 1876 letter to Moncure Conway, then his British business agent, "We find our copywright [sic] law here to be nearly worthless, & if I can make a living out of plays, I shall never write another book." This was during the extraordinary success of the play *Colonel Sellers*, so Clemens's alternative did not seem absurd at the time.

As for lobbying for changes in the laws, Clemens tried in 1875 to get Howells to help him circulate a petition among American authors asking for the national legislature to secure copyright on all literature written by Americans or Europeans. But strangely, when in 1886 he had a chance to help pass a newly proposed law that would strengthen domestic and secure international copyright, his passion for the cause waned. He did contribute time, money, and a brief statement to the American Copyright League, but he did not lobby vigorously. He had decided that there was a political advantage to a freer American press, and that cheap, pirated editions of literary masterpieces from all over the world helped to develop the intellectual capacities of the average American citizen: "Morally, this is all wrong—governmentally it is all right; for it is the *duty* of government . . . to be selfish, & look out simply for their own. . . . Even if the treaty *will* kill Canadian piracy, & thus save me an average of $5,000 a year, I'm down on it anyway" (30 October 1880). Still, he benefited from the passage of the Chace Act in 1891, and when Congress revisited copyright in 1906, the speaker of the house invited Clemens to Washington to address the legislature on copyright. His address lacked substance, but made the kind of show that helped the cause. The revised copyright law of 1909 came out of the negotiations that Clemens helped stimulate and also helped Clemens secure copyright for all of his major works for over fifty years after his death.

"CORN-PONE OPINIONS." Written in 1901, first published in an edited, slightly abridged version by Albert Bigelow *Paine in *Europe and Elsewhere* (1923), and frequently reprinted in this edited version, this short essay was conceived as embracing *determinism in like fashion to *What Is Man?* Yet the emotional thrust of the piece implies that, in discerning that opinions mostly come to us from the outside, we can resist outside influences. There is a thwarted Romanticism here not that different from Hank Morgan's statement in *A Connecticut Yankee in King Arthur's Court* that there is "some microscopic atom" of individuality to a person worth developing.

Not surprisingly, this feeling arises as much from the beginning of the essay as from the exposition. The opening vignette describes a slave man, forced to work as a wood sawyer, who has discovered ways to avoid some of his compelled labor, and whose satirical reflections have afforded him a degree of mental freedom. As a slave, he metaphorically represents Twain's thesis that we are in *slavery to fashion and compelled to think as the world requires, but as satirist and escape artist, he stands for Twain's diminished hope of freedom, a hope that freedom lies in consciousness rather than in physical reality.

The best text can be found in the University of California Press edition of *What Is Man? and Other Philosophical Writings* (1973).

COURANT, HARTFORD. Founded in 1764 as the *Connecticut Courant*, this newspaper was a moderate Know-Nothing journal in the 1850s and became a moderate Republican paper after Lincoln's election in 1860. Joseph Hawley, active in politics and a founder of the *Republican party, established the Hartford *Evening Press* as an alternative to the *Courant* in 1857, and in 1860 hired Charles Dudley *Warner to edit it. The two principals of the *Evening Press* purchased the *Courant* in 1867, merged the papers, and made the *Courant* a Radical Republican newspaper. As one of the nation's oldest and most respected papers, with a new lease on life as a major mouthpiece for the dominant branch of the dominant political party in the nation, the *Courant* was not merely a Hartford newspaper; it was a national trendsetter.

Clemens tried to buy an interest in it in 1869 but was refused. Later, when his first best-seller *The Innocents Abroad* made him both widely known and respectable, Warner tried to get Clemens to buy the interest he had earlier been refused. Clemens described the event in a 27 December 1869 letter to his then fiancée, Olivia Langdon:

> To-day we came upon a democrat wagon in Hartford with a cargo in it composed of Mrs. Hooker & Alice [a good friend of Olivia's] ... Mrs. Warner & another lady. They all assailed me violently on the Courant matter & said it had ceased to be a private desire that we take an ownership in that paper, & had become a public demand. Mrs. H. said Warner & Hawley would do anything to get me in there (this in presence of Mrs. W. who did not deny it by any means,) & Mrs. H. said she had been writing to Mr. Langdon to make us sell out in Buffalo & come here. (It afforded me a malicious satisfaction to hear all this & contrast it with the insultingly contemptuous indifference with which the very same matter was treated last June, (by *every one of them*.).

Clemens did not invest in the paper because his experience in Buffalo had soured him on daily journalism. Still, Warner used it to puff Clemens's books, and the pages were open to Clemens when he wished to write on matters of interest to Hartford.

♦ SEE ALSO Newspaper Journalism.

CRANE, SUSAN LANGDON (1836–1924) AND THEODORE (1831–1889).

Susan Langdon Crane was Olivia Langdon *Clemens's sister, adopted by Jervis and Olivia Lewis Langdon in 1840, five years before Olivia was born. Susan Langdon married her father's business partner, Theodore Crane, in 1858. When her father died in 1870, she inherited one of his two *Elmira homes, Quarry Farm, where Clemens himself lived briefly in 1871 before moving to *Hartford. Olivia was very close to her sister throughout her life, with Susan attending at the births of all of Olivia's children and accompanying the Clemens family on a European tour in 1891. Susan was also very fond of all her Clemens nieces, going out of her way to spend time with them. She was one of the few family members who attended Olivia Susan (Susy) Clemens during her terminal illness in 1896.

The Crane family was extraordinarily generous to the Clemens family, offering a permanent invitation to spend summers in Elmira at the Quarry Farm homestead. Clemens did much of his best writing at Quarry Farm. The Cranes built a detached octagonal study on their property so that Clemens could have uninterrupted solitude for his work. At the end of each work day, he would return to the house, where he would share his day's output with his wife, children, and in-laws. The Cranes had a well-stocked library on which Clemens could draw, and his discussions with Theodore Crane about Clemens's *reading were an important spur to his creativity. Crane introduced him to, and conversed with him over, W. E. H. *Lecky's *History of European Morals*, one of the most influential books on Clemens's career. Clemens also likely discussed his reading of Charles *Darwin with his in-laws.

CRITICAL RECEPTION. Literary criticism is an argument about values mediated through a discussion of literature, so any history of Twain criticism must also be a thumbnail sketch of American intellectual history from 1910 to the present. The professional practice of literary criticism in modern, as opposed to classical, languages, began not in colleges and universities, but in newspapers and magazines, where it still exists in reviews of contemporary writers. Much of the tone of Twain criticism was set by influential reviewers who spoke at large to the American public. Certainly when Twain was alive, most critical reaction was in newspapers, and while many reviewers took Twain's work seriously as important literature, most reviewed him as a humorist, that is, as a person without much staying power.

After Twain's death, H. L. Mencken frequently made a powerful case for Twain's *humor as something significant in its own right, praising him for helping to tear down Victorian culture. Most significantly, Mencken's "The Burden of Humor" in *The Smart Set* (13 February 1913) declared Mark Twain

> the noblest literary artist, who ever set pen to paper on American soil, and not only the noblest artist, but also one of the most profound and sagacious philosophers. . . . He dealt constantly and earnestly with the deepest problems of life and living, and to his consideration of them he brought a truly amazing instinct for the truth, an almost uncanny talent for ridding the essential thing of its deceptive husks of tradition, prejudice, flubdub and balderdash. No man, not even Neitzche, ever did greater execution against those puerilities of fancy which so many men mistake for religion, and over which they are so eager to dispute and break heads. No man had a keener eye for that element of pretense which is bound to intrude itself into all human thinking. . . . And yet, because the man had humor as well as acumen, because he laughed at human weakness instead of weeping over it, because he turned now and then from the riddle of life to the joy of life—because of this habit of mind it is the custom to regard him lightly and somewhat apologetically, as one debarred from greatness by unfortunate infirmities.

In this article, Mencken struck many of the central themes of much twentieth-century criticism of Twain' writings: he elevated humor, attacked *religion and conformity, used Twain to articulate an ideal of American distinctiveness (especially in *language), and, in describing Twain's "irrepressible maleness," made an argument against Victorian ideas of civility and gentility in favor of something more aggressive, more individualistic.

In that crusade, Mencken shared the spotlight with public intellectuals who crossed the increasingly sharp distinction between professional academic literary criticism and journalism—people like George Santayana, Constance Rourke, Van Wyck Brooks, and Bernard DeVoto. Santayana's attack on the "genteel tradition" praised Twain in a lukewarm way for breaking down Victorian conventionality, which he construed as the feminization of the intellect. Brooks, in *The Ordeal of Mark Twain* (1920), used Freudian psychology to make the opposite case; he argued that Twain may have attacked Victorian culture, but ultimately surrendered to it. Bernard DeVoto, in *Mark Twain's America* (1932), replied to Brooks's charge that eastern respectability castrated Twain's genius by writing a social history of the robust frontier, which, in his thesis, gave Twain his birth and more than enough strength to resist the bland eastern establishment. While he disagreed with Brooks's idea that eastern and feminine respectability had constrained Twain, his argument accepted the early twentieth-century belief that American culture should be robust and "masculine." While Rourke had no such gendered agenda in her *American Humor: A Study of the National Character* (1931), her thesis that American humor helped Americans differentiate themselves from their European forebears helped validate notions of American distinctiveness and the inappropriateness of adopting European ideas of gentility.

For each of these authors, Twain the iconoclastic humorist fit a larger cultural agenda. This agenda overlapped nicely with those of many modernist writers, who turned to Twain especially for his experimentation with language and his confrontation with American materials from an American perspective. Writers as varied as T. S. Eliot and Ernest Hemingway wrote in praise of Twain.

Academic criticism of Twain's works followed a bit more slowly, not really blossoming until after World War II. College positions in modern languages were still new when Twain's writing began appearing, and literature professors then tended to concentrate on European works on the assumption that first, Americans could read their own contemporary literature without help, and second, that there was little in it of proven quality. While the works of Nathaniel Hawthorne, Washington Irving, James Fenimore Cooper, and the Fireside Poets were made exceptions to that general policy, American literature as a subject worth special consideration took much longer to come in its own. While college professors of modern literature sometimes agreed with the nationalistic agenda of the more public intellectuals, their task of setting a clear line between high and low literature and seeing American works in the great traditions of literature militated strongly against inclusion of anything very new, and certainly against humor.

Now, of course, Twain's works are among the most frequently studied in colleges and universities. The turning point, perhaps, was the publication in 1941 of F. O. Matthiessen's *American Renaissance: Art and Expression in the Age of Emerson and Whitman*, even though the book discusses Twain only peripherally. Matthiessen, a professor at Harvard from 1929 to his death in 1950, published extensively on American literary figures, but his *American Renaissance* became an absolute trend-setter in the academy. It went far toward legitimating a study of American literature as a distinctive body of writing, and with the swelling of American colleges and universities in the postwar period and a corresponding nationalism during the cold war, American literature began to rival British as a course of study in college English departments. In such a context, Twain was ripe for discovery by the aca-demic establishment.

Twain had not been completely ignored before. A trickle of books came from his literary executors Bernard DeVoto and then Dixon Wecter, and a steady number of articles were published in academic journals from the 1930s to the 1950s. Nor did Twain's entry into the so-called "canon" of great writers come without contest. But the very contest itself was legitimating; the 1950s debate waged in the pages of *College English*, *The American Scholar*, and *American Literature* about whether *Adventures of Huckleberry Finn* is a great novel brought sustained scholarly attention to this book. The upshot of this controversy was an outpouring of works in the early 1960s, mostly from major academic presses and by major scholars, legitimat-ing not only *Huckleberry Finn*, but also Mark Twain generally.

While nationalistic conditions were ripe for this outpouring, they did not end debate on what exactly constituted the American character and how Twain repre-sented it. Philip Foner's popular account in *Mark Twain: Social Critic* (1958) put him in the vanguard of cultural critics, a person so far out in front of his contemporary mores and politics that he could have taught the Bolshevik revolutionaries a thing or two. Louis J. Budd, on the other hand, in *Mark Twain: Social Philosopher* (1962), showed how even Twain's most seemingly extravagant positions were usually anchored in fairly conservative ideas about human nature and politics. Henry Nash Smith's *Mark Twain: The Development of a Writer* (1962) saw Clemens as more progressive, but still in a liberal, not radical, line. Smith's Twain was a committed liberal humanist whose individualism pitted American common sense *realism against the rigid hierarchical idea of culture borrowed from Europe. He saw Twain as successfully freeing American culture from Europe's long shadow. In this, he shared in the Rourke thesis, which had been picked up by Walter Blair in *Native American Humor* (1937; revised edition 1960) and *Mark Twain and Huck Finn* (1960). The Brooks-DeVoto controversy influenced all of these critics to some

Continued on page 151

Critical Reception

David Lionel Smith

The September 1975 issue of *National Geographic* featured as its lead article a piece by Noel Grove called "Mark Twain: Mirror of America." This essay combines reflections on Samuel Clemens's life and public career as Mark Twain with the author's own yearlong pursuit of Twain, including an excursion down the Mississippi River encountering the contemporary small towns and so-called common folk of America's heartland. As might be inferred from the article's title, Grove sees Mark Twain, with his contradictions, adventures, narrations, ambitions and presumptions, triumphs and nightmares, as the quintessential American. The article ends with a caption quoting William Dean Howells's assertion that Twain was "the Lincoln of our literature." In its combination of clarity and ambiguity, this description by Howells perfectly captures the paradox of Mark Twain. His myth and reality are inseparable, and his life and work, transcending literature, have become inescapable in our reflections about what it means to be American.

Making a nineteenth-century writer the subject for a lead article in *National Geographic*, the journal of contemporary exploration, might seem anomalous but is actually entirely apt. Mark Twain, a name culled from the jargon of riverboat pilots, was never a strictly literary identity. The term itself means two fathoms, a depth at which pilots could assume smooth sailing. By extension, it is a name that connotes the constant plumbing of depths in the course of a river journey, calling attention to both hidden dangers and skillful navigation. It explores the unknown while luxuriating in the pleasures of safe sailing. This simultaneous attentiveness to both depths and surfaces is a self-advertisement implicit in the name that Clemens chose for his literary self. Adventurer, engineer, journalist, raconteur, and literary artist, Twain was tailor-made for *National Geographic*.

Grove's article represents Twain's stature in the broader realm of popular culture. It is also paradigmatic of a well-established genre in which discussions of Twain become excursions in pursuit of him and quickly evolve into meditations on the American self. In this respect, Twain was amazingly successful at defining the terms of his own legacy and even the means by which his legacy would be discussed. Through a kind of wizardry worthy of Hank Morgan, Clemens has managed to entice his posterity to pursue Mark Twain, to imitate him, and even to imitate his characters. This latter point is redundant, of course, since Twain is himself obviously a character created by Clemens—in effect, Clemens's greatest fiction. Even the dissident voices that rise to challenge Twain's iconic status often have the unintended effect of instead reiterating his stature as an icon.

Indeed, the pursuit of Twain, virtually a patriotic ritual now, has become an ever-expanding industry. There are three Mark Twain houses, in Hannibal, Missouri; Elmira, New York; and Hartford, Connecticut, which attract tens of thousands of visitors annually. Although *Adventures of Huckleberry Finn* sometimes incites local controversies when taught in high-school English classes, these brouhahas have inadvertently reinforced the iconic status of the work and its author. Community festivals such as Hartford's "Mark Twain Days," celebrating the author and his writings, continue to proliferate, replete with costumed Toms and Beckys, Hucks and Jims, raft rides and Mark Twain impersonators. Twain impersonators may not outnumber the Elvis ones, but their numbers are substantial. Furthermore, they often acquire a detailed knowledge of their subject, including highly refined skills of characterization, that would be superfluous in Elvis impersonation. Countless Twain consumer products, from cheap souvenirs to sculptures and special-edition fountain pens costing thousands of dollars, are produced and marketed each year. A number of scholarly works have examined Twain's pervasive presence. *Lighting out for the Territory: Reflections on Mark Twain and American Culture* by Shelley Fisher Fishkin (1998) is one notable example. Now, as during his own lifetime, the amazing popularity of this author is a lucrative international phenomenon.

The allure of our demotic bard has seduced even high-brow intellectuals. A quarter century after Grove's article in *National Geographic*, the *New York Times Magazine* commissioned the fiction writer Richard Ford and the cultural critic Stanley Crouch to ride down the Mississippi River together and reflect on Twain, race, and *Huckleberry Finn*. This contrived encounter paired two writers who had virtually nothing in common except their utter dissimilarity from Mark Twain. Nonetheless, the conception of the project did reveal how irresistible the siren song of Huck Finn's raft remains.

At around the same time, Ken Burns was beginning to work on his Twain documentary, which would eventually appear on PBS in January 2002 in two, two-hour installments. Like his previous examinations of the Civil War, baseball, and jazz, he intended this documentary to illuminate a quintessentially American subject. With Burns's characteristic blend of ambition, thoroughness, broad historical perspective, and intellectual passion, the documentary presents Twain's entire career, always within the context of American social and cultural history. Although he covers Twain's whole life, Burns shrewdly emphasizes aspects of it that are not as familiar to the general audience. The film provides a detailed treatment of Clemens's early career as a journalist in California and his triumphs in travel writing—*Roughing It* and *The Innocents Abroad*—that made Twain an international celebrity. As Burns skillfully shows, this period also included the beginning of Twain's extraordinary career as a public lecturer. This stage persona became a crucial asset during the last two decades of his life, when he was obliged to return to the lecture circuit in order to resurrect himself from bankruptcy. These final two decades, darkened by personal tragedies and increasing bitterness, are for the general public perhaps the least known period of Twain's life. Burns's decision to make them the primary focus of his documentary constitutes the most distinctive and controversial aspect of this excellent and troubling film.

Like many of his predecessors, Burns represents Twain as "the American": the individual who most clearly embodies our national experience in his epoch. On this point, the consensus may well be valid. Burns understands Twain as more than a supreme comic—as a man who accrues cogent, albeit cynical, wisdom through his various experiences. By extension, Burns also offers a vision of America as a maturing nation, not a perpetually youthful innocent. Consequently, he aligns himself with critics who regard Twain as a self-conscious dissident against contemporary racist dogmas and not as just another smug white guy who echoes the attitudes and ambiguities of his time. Implicit in this difference of perspectives is an ongoing political conflict between a progressive attitude that insists on the importance of critical consciousness and moral self-improvement over time, and a conservative, essentially complacent attitude that regards the status quo, both personal and social, as sufficiently virtuous. This latter view vindicates the enjoyment of existing group identities and personal circumstances, and it is currently resurgent in our political culture. Mark Twain would surely relish the irony that both camps in the culture wars claim him as an ally. One side perceives him as a great humanist, a staunch critic of racist and imperialist attitudes. The opposing camp views Twain as a humorist plain and simple, not a social reformer. Burns is obviously in the humanist camp, and his emphasis on Twain as an older cynic implicitly rebukes the politics of complacency. That his film provoked such heated responses is thus not at all surprising.

Inevitably, there are some critics who consider Twain and *Huckleberry Finn* to be overrated. The novelist Jane Smiley declared this view in an essay published in *Harper's Magazine* in 1996. While recovering from a broken leg, Smiley reports, she decided to re-read *Huckleberry Finn*, which she had not tackled since her adolescence. Although she acknowledges Twain's technical skills as a writer, she finds the novel unworthy of its reputation for greatness. Smiley believes that the author demanded too little moral maturity from his preadolescent protagonist. Furthermore, she finds the portrayal of Jim morally and aesthetically repugnant. She follows these dubious but defensible judgments with the astonishing assertion that Harriet Beecher Stowe's *Uncle Tom's Cabin* is a better and greater novel, a work that she would much prefer to have her children read. Obviously, *Uncle Tom's Cabin* is a novel that, at this point in history, only an ideologue can love. Nonetheless, Smiley's literary talent commands respect, and one might excuse her *Harper's* essay as the result of painkillers and ill-considered reactions in a stressful moment. However, such condescending absolution is undermined by Smiley's publication in 1998 of

The All-True Travels and Adventures of Lidie Newton, a work designed to one-up *Huckleberry Finn.* In this novel, Lidie, a twenty-year-old Yankee abolitionist woman, enters the dangerous frontier world of "Bloody Kansas" in the 1850s and commits various acts of astonishing heroism against overwhelming odds. Thus far, *Adventures of Lidie Newton* has not threatened to displace *Huckleberry Finn* from the literary canon. It is, however, tangible evidence of the enduring power of Twain's masterpiece that, as recently as 1996, it could propel a highly respected, Pulitzer Prize–winning novelist toward such a bizarre tangent.

The most important and insightful book on the cultural status of *Adventures of Huckleberry Finn* published in recent years is Jonathan Arac's *Huckleberry Finn as Idol and Target* (1997). *Idol and Target* is by turns illuminating and frustrating. On each particular, Arac gives clear and incisive commentary. There are, however, many topics, and their sequencing derives from a set of theoretical presuppositions that the book does not forthrightly articulate. Consequently, most readers would probably have difficulty discerning the logical structure of the book.

Broadly speaking, Arac's perspective might be described as left, postmodern skepticism, a philosophical tendency embodied in the 1980s by the journals *Social Text* and *boundary 2.* This outlook places Arac at odds with (though not necessarily antagonistic to) the vast majority of Mark Twain scholars. *Idol and Target* is meant to be a public intellectual's contribution to the ongoing debate about *Huckleberry Finn* in secondary school classrooms. Yet at the same time, it is also a critique of canon formation and a complicated argument against many of the implicit premises that have informed the major tendencies in Mark Twain criticism. Despite the blunt rhetoric of its title, this is a subtle and difficult book.

Idol and Target was inspired by public debates over teaching *Huckleberry Finn* in secondary schools. Arac was puzzled and troubled by the apparently universal presence of *Huckleberry Finn* in secondary school curricula ("hypercanonization") and by what he perceived as an "excessive media response in defense of *Huckleberry Finn,*" which he calls "idolatry" (p. vii). In Arac's view, *Huckleberry Finn* is simply "one very good book among other books" (p. 138). Thus, *Idol and Target* is a brief against idolatrous hypercanonization. To make its case, it traces the history of *Huckleberry Finn's* reception by critics, other novelists, and the general public. Arac begins with his sympathy for black parents who find Twain's novel offensive. Interestingly, however, his book ends with a coda that meditates on the special status of *Huckleberry Finn* as "not only a cultural treasure, but also a resource for power" (p. 213). In this meditation, those aggrieved parents are tellingly absent.

It is surprising that Jonathan Arac, who is primarily known as a literary theorist, came to write this book at all. As he explains:

> I am not an Americanist by professional formation, and as in the 1980s I
> came to focus my teaching and reading in American literature, I was struck by

what seemed to me, compared with other national literatures I knew or had studied, a state of hypercanonization. By hypercanonization I mean that a very few individual works monopolize curricular and critical attention: in fiction preeminently *The Scarlet Letter*, *Moby-Dick*, and *Huckleberry Finn*. (p. 133)

Huckleberry Finn is what the various sections of *Idol and Target* have in common, and as Arac follows the novel through its encounters with various constituencies, he becomes immersed in a critical odyssey that necessarily affirms the centrality of Twain's novel, despite Arac's explicit intentions to decenter it. This might have been a book about the place of literature in public education or the theory of literary history or the nature of literary critical debates and influence. Instead, it is a book about *Adventures of Huckleberry Finn*, and it takes its shape from its subject.

In his "Coda," Arac makes a final attempt to break the spell of Twain's text. After explaining why *Huckleberry Finn*, a narrative of memory, resonates so deeply for Americans, Arac shifts the terms of his argument, criticizing those who equate literary texts with political acts. Literary works, he argues, are not substitutes for political actions, and they should not be asked to carry a burden that they cannot bear. "The Lincoln of our literature," he asserts, "must yield to the Lincoln of our politics" (p. 218). Nonetheless, Arac makes this point by quoting from Lincoln's speeches, not by citing Lincoln's political acts. If Lincoln's texts count as political acts, why can't Twain's? In fact, the relationship between words and deeds is a pervasive concern of *Huckleberry Finn*. In its closing passage, for instance, the novel presents the uncertain relationship between freedom as a concept and freedom as lived experience. In spite of himself, Arac concludes his book very much as *Huckleberry Finn* concludes—with a discussion of "principles and actions," racism and citizenship.

The ironic complexity of its closing scene reflects the greatness of this novel. *Huckleberry Finn* is great because it is true. Its language is true, its social observations are true, and its characterizations are true. The author was true to the work and did not distort it with personal tics or extraneous agendas.

Beyond this greatness, *Huckleberry Finn*, like much of Twain's work, is appealing and pertinent even now. The book embodies fundamental values that Americans and others continue to embrace: honesty, fairness, intelligence, accurate perception, practicality, compassion, good humor, and a love of fun. We professional critics do not like to speak in such terms, but to speak accurately about the achievements of this novel, we need to use such terms.

Twain's commitment to depict Huck honestly, without deference to proprieties and ideological dogmas, shows in his rendering of Huck's celebrated crisis of conscience as a comic moment. Huck concludes that he will go to hell rather than betray Jim. Huck's heroic choice of risking hellfire is excessive and thus comic. His honest heart triumphs over his training. But his decision is nothing new. He declared the same at the beginning of the novel when he stated that he'd rather go to hell than be in heaven with dull, pious old ladies. Twain, even in this morally serious moment, is having fun as he depicts the gap between what a preadolescent boy can feel and what he can express adequately in words. In this passage, Huck recalls images of Jim's acts of friendship, but he does not deliver a verbal essay on friendship, as Stowe's characters would. His realization is mostly nonverbal. This is honest writing, unlike the absurd speeches of Little Eva from Uncle Tom's Cabin. It is true to the virtues and limitations of the character.

Unfortunately, we can pursue Twain without pursuing his fundamental values, especially his unflinching honesty. We can relish his humor without embracing the truthfulness on which he predicated that humor. Such pursuit and imitation is flattery but not a compliment. It mimics the outer form of the author while ignoring his substance. Ironically, the perpetual circulation of this image, the creation called Mark Twain, can reify a depthless surface, an artifice without art. Whether the ongoing allure of Mark Twain will yield a more visible artist or an empty fetish remains to be seen.

Continued from page 144

degree, each coming down on the side of DeVoto not only in overall assessment of Twain's common sense connection to American realism, but also in theoretical approach, grounding Twain's work in social rather than psychological contexts.

While the oversimplification Brooks used served as a caution, psychological criticism of Twain did not disappear under this deluge of historical criticism. Most notably, James M. Cox's *Mark Twain: The Fate of Humor* (1966) handled the interweaving of biographical and psychological criticism deftly, substantially by recognizing the psychological differences inherent in the generic distinctions between humor, wit, and *satire. Cox's book came out in the same year as Justin Kaplan's popular psychobiography *Mr. Clemens and Mark Twain* (1966), giving new strength to this type and line of criticism.

Also at about this time, the publication of many previously suppressed *unfinished works coincided with rising anti-establishment feelings in the late 1960s and 1970s, with Twain at first becoming a hero of protest, and then a target of attack as a symbol of the establishment idea of American culture. This argument is still being waged. Thus, after a fairly brief period in which Twain was generally accepted as a "canonical" author, Twain's work has once again become the subject of intense controversy about literary and cultural value. What particular values are being addressed, however, ranges over a much wider field than before, and certainly with many more voices joining the conversation. Through the 1980s and 1990s, several books and dozens of articles per year have been published by academic presses and in academic journals.

With the introduction of numerous new theoretical perspectives on literary study over the course of the 1970s, 1980s, and 1990s, the entire field of Twain studies fragmented. Few studies anymore attempt to see Twain as a monolithic emblem of American values, but instead now try to take into account the complexities and fractures in Twain's works and in the culture to which he belonged. Given the yearly output in Twain studies, it is impossible to pick out which will be most influential, but without doubt, questions of gender, race and *social class receive regular treatment, usually revising earlier consensus opinions. The most extreme example of such revisionism is Jonathan Arac's *Huckleberry Finn as Idol and Target: The Functions of Criticism in Our Time* (1997). Arac complains that *Adventures of Huckleberry Finn* has been "hyper-canonized," even though, he says, it is neither great art nor great politics. But not all revision goes to Arac's lengths; indeed, much is designed to recanonize Twain's works on different grounds.

In particular, a number of books have addressed the question of whether Twain is indeed the paragon of "irrepressible maleness" postulated by Mencken. Hamlin Hill's biography of Twain's last years, *Mark Twain: God's Fool* (1973), in which he argued that Twain's work was better under Olivia *Clemens's critical eye, broke the path for this line of thought. Laura-Skandera Trombley's *Mark Twain in the*

Company of Women (1994) and Susan K. Harris's *The Courtship of Olivia Langdon and Mark Twain* (1996) both show the positive influence on Twain's creativity in his interactions with significant women in his life.

Racial issues persist as one of the hottest topics in Twain criticism and the issues over which agreement seems least likely. Henry Nash Smith, Leo Marx, and other major critics of the 1960s saw Twain as a racial progressive, and praised *Huckleberry Finn* precisely in that regard. But their position has never rested comfortably, and many scholars, both black and white, have weighed in on both sides of this question. Among the most interesting books addressing this question is a collection of essays, *Satire or Evasion: Black Perspectives on Huckleberry Finn* (1992), which has an excellent annotated bibliography on the topic of race in Twain. Other notable works include Shelley Fisher Fishkin's *Was Huck Black? Mark Twain and African-American Voices* (1993), Jocelyn Chadwick-Joshua's *The Jim Dilemma: Reading Race in* Huckleberry Finn (1998), and Elaine and Harry Mensh's *Black, White, and Huckleberry Finn: Reimagining the American Dream* (2000). These books address not only the abstract question of whether or not *Huckleberry Finn* is racist or antiracist, but also the practical question of whether and how to teach the novel in public schools.

Another significant topic under revision is the nature of Twain's humor and its relation to cultural patterns of performance. Most notably, Bruce Michelson's tour de force *Mark Twain on the Loose* (1995) insists that humor is not about fitting in, but about stretching the boundaries. In that sense, humor is not a manifestation of national character nor of American realism, but instead a gesture of resistance not only to cultural forms but to the very form of self-hood. Michelson sees Twain as fundamentally creative and anarchic, challenging the Enlightenment conception of character on which modernity depends and, in so doing, giving readers a glimpse of freedom and relief from the regular patterns of culture. Few other critics take humor so far, with recent work informed instead by a persistent effort to see how Twain's performances fit within cultural patterns. Notable among these is Lawrence Howe's *Mark Twain and the Novel: the Double-Cross of Authority* (1998), which shows much of the same struggle Michelson describes but sees in it a more difficult challenge.

All the while, the Mark Twain Project continues to produce volumes of Twain's letters as well as carefully annotated editions of his works. These, while presented quietly and without any thesis to make them controversial, are a deeply informed kind of historical scholarship. The information unearthed by these splendid volumes informs much of the best new scholarship about Mark Twain.

DAN DE QUILLE. SEE Wright, William.

DARWIN, CHARLES (1809–1882). Samuel Clemens met Charles Darwin in 1879 in England's Lake District. Clemens later recalled that the meeting was quite awkward. Darwin, the British naturalist credited with originating the first non-Lamarckian theory of *evolution in his *The Origin of Species* (1859), was a reluctant *celebrity in his own day and no doubt disliked Clemens's adulation. Darwin knew his theory of natural selection would challenge orthodox Christianity. His fear that the moral consequences of such a challenge would lead to social upheaval prompted him to suppress his theories until forced to publish or risk losing credit for his own work.

Once published, Darwin's theory quickly became both celebrated and condemned, as well as used to justify predatory social practices, much to Darwin's chagrin. Despite the frequent misuse of his ideas, Darwin continued to publish, not only elaborating and modifying his theory, but also challenging these so-called social Darwinists. He wrote *The Descent of Man* (1871) in part to show that social Darwinism misreads the divine purpose of evolution, which to Darwin was the evolution of the *moral sense, a sensibility that set human beings above the amoral imperatives of natural selection.

Clemens read Darwin's works avidly and referred to his theories in works too numerous to list. Generally these references are positive, and they grow increasingly admiring over the course of Twain's career. While most readers concentrated on Darwin's theory of physical evolution, Clemens was at least as interested in Darwin's speculations about moral evolution. Darwin's claim that moral progress depends on an increasing ability to distinguish between subjectivity and objectivity appealed to Clemens, though by the late 1890s he did wonder if moral progress were possible in Darwin's terms.

In spite of his admiration, Clemens did not clearly understand the most important aspect of Darwin's theory. Like his contemporary Herbert Spencer, a chief proponent of social Darwinism, Clemens espoused a Lamarckian theory of evolution while attributing its proof to Darwin. Regarding Darwin's defense of the moral sense in *The Descent of Man*, Clemens's marginalia show him arguing against Darwin, insisting that Darwin's model of selflessness, in fact, showed the inherent selfishness of human beings.

Darwin read Twain equally eagerly, and reportedly kept Twain's works at his bedside. It is unknown whether Darwin misinterpreted Twain.

♦ SEE ALSO Adam and Eve.

DEATH. If *Innocents Abroad* really does, as the preface says, "suggest to the reader how *he* would be likely to see Europe and the East if he looked at them with his own eyes instead of the eyes of those who travelled in those countries before him," then the reader would see a land of the dead. When in Paris, Twain pays uncommon attention to the grotesqueries of the morgue, not only wallowing in the morbid details of a distended and distorted corpse, but hypocritically criticizing the Parisians who go to the morgue for entertainment. When in Venice, he meditates at length on the Bridge of Sighs; in Rome, the Coliseum, the mummies in the Vatican, and the bare-bones (protominimalist?) art of the Capuchin Convent. We get descriptions of martyrs and relics everywhere. The climax of Twain's old world tour is, of course, the visit to the tomb of Adam, a monument designed to elicit the tears and simultaneously allay the fears of thousands of pilgrims.

In part, *Innocents Abroad* is about the burden of history, about how a young culture is to make sense of the past. The repeating refrain of Twain and his friends, "Is he dead?" is young America's question to Europe. Insofar as the answer is "yes," Twain is telling his readers to see the world anew, afresh, vitally. In this sense, one expects Twain merely to satirize an interest in death. Lest we think, however, that the sarcastic tone shows Twain's disdain for a world spending its living time meditating on death, he admits that his own emotional life is filled with fantasies of death and ghosts. In one instance, he recounts in minute detail the time he spent a night with a corpse in his father's office.

This obsession with death pervaded Twain's career. The early sketch "A Curious Dream" satirizes American towns that do not properly memorialize their dead. The plot of *Tom Sawyer* turns around the gothic horrors of a midnight murder in a graveyard and the potential living entombment of Tom Sawyer and Becky Thatcher. *Huckleberry Finn* seems torn between Huck's refusal to "put . . . stock in dead people" and its mockery of the Sheperdson-Grangerford self-fulfilling death wish on one hand, and its sense of Huck's isolation as a kind of death—"I was so lonely I most wished I was dead"—on the other. *Connecticut Yankee* mocks the violence of chivalry in contrast merely to the efficient means of killing at the disposal of the modern world. "The Californian's Tale" tells of a ritual celebration of the anniversary of a beloved woman's death. Twain wrote this tale in 1892 and first published it in 1893, long before the Clemens family had to deal with the death of Susy Clemens in 1896, which they observed every year as if they were the characters in the story. In short, as much as Clemens may have mocked America's morbid fascination with mortality, his mockery grew out of a deep fascination of his own.

This connection to the concerns and interests of his contemporaries helped to make Clemens such a successful writer, and there is no question that much of his motivation in writing about the catacombs or the Parisian morgue was his knowledge that death sells. It sold well in the late 1860s not merely because strong emotion catches people's interest, but also because American attitudes toward death changed along with its attitudes toward religion.

Christianity had, in the belief that mundane life is not the real life, always required believers to meditate on mortality. The martyrdom of Jesus Christ, according to Christian doctrine, means the eternal salvation of all believers, and in imitating Christ, believers were expected especially to contemplate the meaning and value of sacrifice. Bearing one's cross while meditating on one's end was the emotional scourge to wean believers from the damning seductions of this world. St. Jerome's death-head was only the most extreme *memento mori*; every good Christian was supposed to keep mortality in mind at all times.

Calvinist Americans were no different in this regard than Continental Protestants and Catholics. Every town had its church, every church its graveyard, and every graveyard contained its tombstone inscriptions, such as the following, common in Puritan cemeteries:

> Look on me as you walk by
> Where you are now so once was I
> Where I am now so you will be
> Think on death and follow me

Of course, the plainness of this verse suggests that American Calvinists were not fully in league with European Catholics in approaching death. In inscribing tombstones in this way, Puritans stressed the mnemonic and didactic functions of verse over the aesthetic. The American Calvinist tradition, with its fear of holding false images up before God, intended to strip away the art of death. Puritan graveyards are, like Puritan churches, monuments to simplicity.

Over the course of the first half of the nineteenth century, as part of the same intellectual and moral sea change that began in America's cities, this Puritan way of death altered. The rigors of Calvinism, in its refusal to allow grief, gave way under the pressures of *sentimentalism to a more compassionate approach to death. At the same time that sentimentalists were opening American culture to secular music, novels and poetry, painting, architectural ornament, and to ornament in dress, they began to change American patterns of grieving. Rejecting the Puritan idea that resignation was the sign of pure faith and thus grief was a sin, the sentimentalists believed that earthly objects of love were designed to lead us to heaven through attachment, not renunciation. Believing in childhood innocence and the possibility of universal salvation, sentimentalists changed the contemplation of death from a duty to a pleasure. That is, they believed that by cultivating grief, they were maintaining their bonds to loved ones whose presence in heaven would help pull the living to that heaven.

Responding to this shift in belief, American funeral customs became more elaborate and artistic, and the graveyard—once located either in the church or on a family's grounds—became a cemetery park, disconnected from any specific church, given spacious grounds, and landscaped to be evocatively beautiful rather than somber, regular, and simple. Such parks became refuges in cities, and, when new, were treated as tourist attractions. Monuments became individualized and as elaborate as one's means allowed. In this sense, as in many other cultural and artistic ways, American Protestant rituals grew closer to the Roman Catholic forms that Puritan Protestants had long held anathema. While the tendency toward a more elaborate kind of funeral began early in the nineteenth century and can be traced broadly to Romantic and sentimental theories of art, emotion, and faith, in America the shift had a powerful impetus in the years following the Civil War. Those who had lost sons, husbands, and brothers needed to make sense of sacrifice. The popularity of Elizabeth Stuart Phelps's *The Gates Ajar* was fed by this need, and in turn the book sped the spread of sentimental ideas of grief, mourning, and art.

As his satiric parody of *The Gates Ajar* in *"Extract from Captain Stormfield's Visit to Heaven" shows, Clemens distrusted this sentimental approach to death. His essentially Puritan outlook toward *religion and art explains to some degree his anxiety about European death mementos as well as new American funeral rituals. His anti-Catholic bias shows clearly not only in his dispatches from Europe, but also in his attack on undertakers in New Orleans in *Life on the Mississippi*. A similar anxiety about ostentation in death arises in the description of Buck Fanshaw's funeral in *Roughing It* and in his mockery of Emmeline Grangerford and of Peter Wilks's funeral in *Huckleberry Finn*.

But of course, his own loss of faith in a resurrection made his discomfort with ostentation a matter of aesthetics rather than of faith. In his agnosticism he found a conflicting impulse toward a complex funerary art. To some degree, as his faith fled, he began to see funeral anniversaries and rituals as a kind of immortality in the classical sense: *ars longa, vita brevis*. His own efforts to memorialize his dead daughter—such as his poem "In Memoriam: Olivia Susan Clemens" and those parts of his autobiography that use recollections of Susy as the occasion for extended meditations on the meaning of life and death—serve not only to console him over her loss, but also to perpetuate her memory.

Clemens's loss of faith in Christian immortality further explains some of his commentary on death, as his mentions of heaven and martyrdom are often derisive. The story of Jim Blaine and his grandfather's ram from *Roughing It*, for example, mocks Christian beliefs in predestination, special providences, martyrdom, and the importance of meditating on mortality. But his loss of faith and his derision of traditional Christian consolation did not break his lifelong habit of meditating on death or even of worshipping it as a translation of the soul from this life of suffering. In "The Five Boons of Life," in parts of *"Chronicle of Young Satan," and in numerous other works of his last twenty years, Twain expressed his occasional belief that death was the ultimate gift, for the peace and end to suffering that it brought. Old habits die hard.

♦ SEE ALSO Afterlife; Health and Disease.

DEMOCRACY. As the son of an impoverished yet elitist Whig politician, Clemens easily gravitated toward rather conservative positions about political democracy; as a child of the socially egalitarian West, he easily adopted democratic social ideals. The conflict between these two attitudes is one of the central tensions driving Twain's satire.

Politically, Clemens grew up believing in a limited franchise and oligarchic rule, ideas central to the Whig party and its heirs, the Know-Nothings and finally the Republicans. Pervasive worries about the ability of a pluralistic culture to cohere, about the Roman Catholic church dominating American *politics through Catholic immigrants, and about the "rabble" debasing the moral tenor as well as the efficiency of government characterized these parties. Clemens, for all of his early southern sympathies and western manners, easily fit into the Republican haunts of New England in that he shared these attitudes—at least until around 1880.

He predicated his early opposition to *women's rights on the idea of an elite male ruling class, and his ultimate conversion to woman's suffrage also sprang from his belief, as he put it in "The Temperance Insurrection" (1874), that "our last chance . . . to save the country" would be for "women to be raised to the political altitude of the negro, the imported savage, and the pardoned thief, and allowed to vote." His belief "that in a moral fight woman is simply dauntless" encouraged him to posit that the elite would govern if women were given the vote.

His conservative attitudes about democratic rule manifest themselves most clearly in "The Curious Republic of Gondour," published anonymously in the October 1875 *Atlantic Monthly*. A short utopian sketch, "Gondour" complains that universal suffrage "had seemed to deliver all power into the hands of the ignorant and non-tax-paying classes; and of a necessity the responsible offices were filled from these classes also." He suggests as an alternative not to restrict the franchise of the poor and ignorant, but to dilute it by giving additional votes to the rich and, especially, to the educated: "Learning being more prevalent and more easily acquired than riches, educated men became a wholesome check upon wealthy men, since they could outvote them. Learning goes usually with uprightness, broad views, and humanity; so the learned voters, possessing the balance of power, became the vigilant and efficient protectors of the great lower rank of society." Clemens seemed to take this reform seriously as a beneficial alternative, which is all the more remarkable since he himself had little formal education. But surrounded by the mildly reformist but elitist, mostly college-educated, well-to-do Republicans of the *Nook Farm community, he readily believed in the moral power of wealth and education.

During this period, he also attacked popular journalism in an essay presented to the *Monday Evening Club, "The License of the Press" (1873), in part because it encouraged the basest of human passions, playing into the powers of mob rule at the hands of demagogues. Demagoguery in the face of mass ignorance was the theme of "The Great Revolution in Pitcairn" (1879), written originally for *A Tramp Abroad* but cut and published separately in the *Atlantic*. An American, Butterworth Stavely, intrudes upon a primitive and bucolic community, where he "sow[s] the seeds of discontent among the people. It was his deliberate purpose, from the beginning, to subvert the government." First fomenting unrest by creating parties and factions, he ultimately gets the chief magistrate thrown out of office and himself elected. From that position, he declares himself emperor. Every step of the way he makes the lives of the people more difficult, always in the name of *reform, until they finally cast him aside, returning to their earlier simple republic under the flag of the British Empire. The tale is an allegory of how easy it is to abuse democratic powers, and as such is a foreshadowing through opposition of *Connecticut Yankee*.

Part of the problem of democracy, as Clemens saw it, was that electors had to vote in public. Not until 1889 did ten states adopt the secret ballot. Since voters had to declare their votes in public, they were susceptible to retribution. As he put it in an 1876 letter to a Missouri correspondent, "I think I comprehend the position there—perfect freedom to vote just as you choose, provided you choose to vote as *other* people think—social ostracism otherwise" (to Burrough, 1 November). Clemens felt just such pressure during the presidential election of 1884, in which Nook Farm's Republicans, excepting Clemens and Rev. Joseph *Twichell, backed James G. Blaine. Clemens and Twichell took public stands as *mugwumps, vowing instead to vote for Cleveland. Both were attacked in person and in print. In his autobiographical dictations, Clemens remembered, perhaps inaccurately, that Twichell's livelihood was damaged by his taking such a public stand against his party. Despite the community pressure, Clemens did vote for Cleveland, explaining his reasoning to William Dean *Howells: "You know now that they [the charges against Blaine] are proven, & it seems to me that that bars you & all other honest & honorable men (who are independently situated) from voting for him" (17 September 1884). It took an independent situation to enable *political* independence.

Such glitches in the mechanisms of democracy notwithstanding, by the time he wrote *Connecticut Yankee* nearly a decade after "Pitcairn," Clemens had changed his political principles to favor radical democracy. The man who had in 1880 called the French Revolution "beneficent but hideous" (*A Tramp Abroad*, chapter 26) wrote to Howells on 22 August 1887:

How stunning are the changes which age makes in a man while he sleeps. When I finished Carlyle's French Revolution in 1871, I was a Girondin; every time I have read it since, I have read it differently—being influenced &

changed, little by little, by life & environment (& Taine, & St. Simon): & now I lay the book down once more, & recognize that I am a Sansculotte!— And not a pale, characterless Sansculotte, but a Marat. Carlyle teaches no such gospel: so the change is in *me*—in my vision of the evidences.

Following that change, *Connecticut Yankee* praises *revolution to supplant *monarchy with democracy, and celebrates Hank Morgan for fomenting such a change. Part of Morgan's arsenal is the press, the license of which Clemens had come to respect rather than denigrate.

While *Connecticut Yankee*'s prognosis for democracy in the face of aristocratic power is grim, in *The American Claimant* (1892) Clemens postulated a democratic polity arising from democratic social behavior. He saw the democratizing power of the American working and middle classes stemming from their ability to laugh at the pretensions of rank and privilege. His worker hero, Barrow, shows Berkeley, the British aristocrat who wishes to become a democrat, that political power is a matter of perception and manners. Barrows says that the British people could end aristoc-racy in six months by "electing themselves dukes and duchesses to-morrow and calling themselves so. . . . Royalty itself couldn't survive such a process. A handful of frowners against thirty million laughers in a state of eruption: Why, it's Hercu-laneum against Vesuvius" (chapter 11). By this point in the novel, Berkeley has already discovered that his rigid training in aristocratic behavior inhibited his dem-ocratic ideals; he here learns that if he is to change his attitudes, he needs to learn to laugh at himself.

As much as Clemens attributed his own change in political beliefs to his age and his *reading, he also owed much to his own manners as a westerner. Throughout his time in the East, his social manners were at odds with that region's relatively courtly behavior, and his relish of Nook Farm depended in part on its relative relax-ation of the norms of social interaction. Even there, though, Clemens's openness was unusual. As Charles Dudley Warner described Clemens in the first (July 1871) of his "Backlog Studies": "He is the person who comes in without knocking, drops in in the most natural way, . . . and not seldom in time to take the after-dinner cup of tea before the fire. Formal society begins as soon as you lock your doors, and only admit visitors through the media of bells and servants. It is lucky for us that our next-door neighbor is honest." Warner's simultaneous delight and worry over this western freedom echoed the reaction of many of Clemens's eastern friends, as it did, for that matter, Clemens's own internal reaction; he did, after all, hope to stand well in the eyes of the eastern establishment at the same time that he wanted to be true to himself. As much as this tension manifests itself throughout Twain's works, it also contributed to his developing sense of the value of democratic politics.

♦ SEE ALSO Meritocracy.

De Quille, Dan. see Wright, William.

Detective Stories. In an 1896 notebook Clemens wrote, "What a curious thing a 'detective' story is. And was there ever one that the author needn't be ashamed of, except 'The Murders in the Rue Morgue'?" Twain wrote this at about the time he was publishing "Tom Sawyer, Detective" and shortly after he had published *Pudd'nhead Wilson and Those Extraordinary Twins.* He was acknowledging a certain degree of shame for having produced potboilers designed to capitalize on the popularity of detective fiction, and for his own intense interest in a genre that was half pseudoscience, half horror story.

The genre was indeed born with Edgar Allan Poe's Dupin stories "The Murders in the Rue Morgue" and "The Purloined Letter." Typically, they are in the gothic tradition, countering *sentimentalism by playing on negative rather than positive emotions, while still accepting the psychology of sensations on which sentimentalism was built. Rather than stressing faith in human order and love, gothic tales wallow in disorder; instead of stressing the benefits of personal freedom and the capacity to choose a life path in accordance with positive emotions, gothic tales develop a fear of freedom, suggesting that negative emotions lead people to make destructive choices through overwhelming compulsion. Poe's detective stories are very much in this vein, and even with Dupin restoring an ordered universe by his actions, his capacity to do so depends very much on his status as a brilliant outsider, one who disdains the new methods of what was becoming modern police work in favor of the capacity to understand sympathetically the mind of a criminal.

But the genre that quickly evolved out of Poe's stories lacked his self-consciousness of the ambiguity of human motives. Instead, accounts of detective work published by Alan Pinkerton, founder of the famous American detective agency, stress completely methodical and rational methods of detective work even as they allow readers to wallow in lurid and stereotypical ideas of what a criminal is and how he acts. Pinkerton and other pseudoscientific students of criminology in the early days of the developing detective industry believed in physiological causes of crime, and as such, their stories reinforced ideas of *social class and hierarchical *race relations. Pinkerton's stories are simplistic accounts of the restoration of an order threatened not by one's own impulses, but by the impulses of dangerous outsiders. And Pinkerton's stories, ostensibly true, helped develop an entire genre of detective stories, some fiction, others parading as true, few of which ever rose above the level of potboilers.

Twain early on took the bait of burlesquing this genre, writing a play and then a novel, *Simon Wheeler, Amateur Detective*, beginning in about 1873 and culminating in a draft that was written in a flurry of creative energy around 1877. While he eventually abandoned the story, the ideas found their way into numerous published stories, first in chapters 11 and 24 of *The Adventures of Tom Sawyer*. In chapter 11, the town quickly concludes Potter's guilt and the sheriff promises quick apprehension of the criminal. The reader already knows Potter is innocent; Twain is mocking the people and police for their gullibility, as well as for their fascination with the crime itself. Twain's long-standing feud with the police in San Francisco may have been one deep source of his skepticism about detective work done by the police. But his disdain for the hired private detective was even greater. In chapter 24, he writes, "One of those omniscient and awe-inspiring marvels, a detective, came up from St. Louis, moused around, shook his head, looked wise, and made that sort of astounding success which members of that craft usually achieve. That is to say, he 'found a clew.' But you cant hang a 'clew' for murder, and so after that detective had got through and gone home, Tom felt just as insecure as he was before." Of course, Twain's own novel follows the general path of detective fiction—and most other gothic and sentimental fiction for that matter—in having Tom's insecurity disappear when order is restored at novel's end. Yet that restoration stirred Twain's skepticism.

When he finished writing *Simon Wheeler, Amateur Detective* as a play, he tried to turn it into a novel, but, as he told William Dean *Howells in a 21 January 1879 letter, "I have given up writing a detective novel—can't write a novel, for I lack the faculty. . . . I was going to send you that Detective play, so that you could re-write it. I didn't do it because I couldn't find a single idea in it that could be useful to you. It was dreadfully witless & flat." But he refused to give up the idea of mocking detective fiction entirely. As he put it in the same letter, "When the detectives were nosing around after Stewart's loud remains, I threw a chapter into my present book [*A Tramp Abroad*] in which I have very extravagantly burlesqued the detective business—if it *is* possible to burlesque that business extravagantly." Alexander T. Stewart was a wealthy New York merchant whose body was stolen from a vault in November 1878. Sensational accounts of the efforts of the police and private detectives to recover the body filled the newspapers. Twain quoted many of these accounts directly in his chapter, but turned the stolen object from a corpse into a white elephant. Worried about the literary quality of such a burlesque simply because he found the target unworthy of attack, he eventually dropped this chapter. Still, he found the impulse to attack the genre so compelling that he published it as a separate tale under the title "The Stolen White Elephant" (1882).

Clemens did not dislike everything about the genre. The possibility that scientific knowledge and technique could solve crimes fascinated him. His *Pudd'nhead Wilson* has Wilson succeed in solving a murder by using the new technology of fingerprinting. But Twain never found himself comfortable with the idea that the social order "restored" in detective stories was really worth restoration. The ending of *Pudd'nhead Wilson* burlesques the entire idea of resolution on which the conventional detective story turns. In that sense, Twain's novel is much more in line with the feeling of the original Poe detective stories than with the genre as it developed in Twain's own day.

In particular, Arthur Conan Doyle developed the genre to blend the characteristics of Poe's Dupin with the conventional techniques of "scientific" detecting in a way that undercut the emotional ambiguity of Poe's stories. Sherlock Holmes mixed careful observation and ratiocination with an intuitive sympathy with the criminal mind to make the irrational process of sympathy seem perfectly scientific. The promise is one of a perfectly ordered world in which a perceptive mind can make out deep patterns, and in so doing, thwart chaos.

For a mind such as Clemens's that thrived on chaos and used humor to discover alternate conceptions of reality, Doyle's detective was a profound affront. Moreover, the popularity of Doyle's Holmes stories, beginning in 1887 with *A Study in Scarlet* and continuing with a flurry of short stories, collected in *The Adventures of Sherlock Holmes* (1892) and *The Memoirs of Sherlock Holmes* (1894), was a serious threat. As much as Twain tried to cash in with "Tom Sawyer, Detective," used a detective motif in the unfinished novel "Which Was It?" and wrote an extended but ultimately *unfinished parody in "Tom Sawyer's Conspiracy" (1897), his animus comes out most flagrantly and humorously in *A Double-Barreled Detective Story* (1902). In this tale, Sherlock Holmes appears as an arrogant but incompetent idiot whose cousin, Fetlock Jones, explains that the only way Holmes ever solves a crime is to arrange it in advance. On the other hand, the character Archy Stillman is able to find any man because he possesses a preternatural nose, able to track like a bloodhound. It is an outrageous send-up of the more extravagant devices of detective fiction, and its occasional passages of purple prose, including a description of a landscape over which "a solitary oesophagus slept upon motionless wing," lambaste the stylistic excesses of the genre. Apparently Twain found a way to burlesque a genre that he found self-parodying by using his chaotic sense of humor to challenge the limits of parody itself.

DETERMINISM. Newtonian science promises a predictable universe governed by strict laws of cause and effect. Writers and thinkers who extrapolated these ideas to life itself gave birth to a scientific determinism that dominated nineteenth-century philosophy. The absolute determinism of scientism was the rock on which William *James foundered as a thinker, leading him ultimately to develop his pragmatism, which allows for the possibility of multiple truths and cultural relativism. Twain, less systematically and almost in spite of himself, followed a similar path.

In such works as "The Turning Point of My Life" and *What Is Man?* Twain directly proposed what he implicitly suggested in *A Connecticut Yankee in King Arthur's Court* and *Pudd'nhead Wilson and Those Extraordinary Twins*, that "training is everything" because human beings are merely machines influenced by outside forces and inner compulsions. Through this idea, Twain developed a position that inner temperament—that is, the structure of the human machine—coupled with environmental influences—which he, following Herbert *Spencer's misreading of

Charles *Darwin, felt were inheritable—caused all human behavior. Under these influences, human beings had only the illusion of free will.

This philosophy seems to echo Clemens's early Calvinist beliefs. Indeed many of the era's most ardent naturalistic determinists had a quasi-religious bent to their attacks on the idea of free will. In Clemens's case, though, his determinism seems as much as anything an effort at self-exculpation, a way to escape from his powerful conscience and the sense that everything that happened to him was the consequence of his own evil or, at least, error. As he puts it in his *autobiography, "Mine was a trained Presbyterian conscience and knew but the one duty—to hunt and harry its slave upon all pretexts and on all occasions, particularly when there was no sense nor reason in it." The religious determinism of *"Chronicle of Young Satan" shows the close linkage between Twain's material determinism and his Presbyterian origins.

But as much as he adamantly articulated a determinist position, he also explored cultural relativism in *Following the Equator*, the possibility of an intellectual superiority to determinism in *"Corn-Pone Opinions," and even solipsism in *"No. 44, The Mysterious Stranger." In this last work, Twain explores the possibility of perfect mental freedom, a freedom that also exculpates him from his sense of wrongdoing. So inasmuch as his motives for embracing any of these philosophical positions were personal, Twain found that determinism did not take him far enough from his early training to satisfy his needs.

DIALECT. Twain's writings have elicited much praise in the twentieth century for enabling American writers to use an American voice, to discover the artistic value of their own dialects. Twain took many risks by using the vernacular, but he was not alone in so doing. He wrote in an age of dialect writing, much of which adhered to time-honored conventions of using "low style" to denigrate characters, but some of which was engaged in exploring the artistic and political possibilities of American regional and class dialects.

Two strong aesthetic traditions of classical rhetoric and sentimental *taste militated against this late-nineteenth-century shift to validating dialect. According to classical rhetorical teachings, all rhetoric must adhere to styles appropriate to the social condition of the characters and the circumstances of the piece of rhetoric. Arising out of Renaissance readings of Horace and Aristotle, distinctions between high, middle, and low styles were commonplaces of education in rhetoric well into the nineteenth century. By these rhetorical rules of propriety, low-style dialect was used to depict characters of low social status and limited intellect. Low style was considered appropriate for most comic genres and especially for satire.

Well into the middle of the nineteenth century such proprieties were observed as a matter of course, such as in James Russell Lowell's *Biglow Papers*, written originally to oppose the Mexican-American War, which used dialect characters to convey in earthy words fundamental political ideas. Lowell's anxiety about common people being subject to demagoguery comes through especially in his letters from Birdofredum Sawin, a stupid man whose willingness to volunteer as a soldier ends in his mutilation. In his second letter, unable to do any practical work after the war, he decides to run for president as a war hero. In his words:

> Then you can call me "Timbertoes,"—thet's wut the people likes; / Sutthin' combinin' morril truth with phrases sech ez strikes; / Some say the people's fond o' this, or thet, or wut you please,—/ I tell ye wut the people want is jest correct idees; / "Old Timbertoes," you see, 's a creed it's safe to be quite bold on, / There's nothin' in 't the other side can any ways git hold on; / It's a good tangible idee, a sutthin' to embody / Thet valooable class o' men who look thru brandy-toddy; / It gives a party Platform, tu, jest level with the mind / Of all right-thinkin' honest folks thet mean to go it blind; / Then there air other good hooraws to dror on es you need 'em, / Sech es the ONE-EYED SLARTERER, THE BLOODY BIRDOFREDUM; / Them's wut takes hold o' folks thet think, ez well ez o' the masses, / An' makes you sartin o' the aid o' good men of all classes. (pp. 110–11)

Comedies of manners, too, often took dialect as their characterizing style, as in B. P. Shillaber's famous Mrs. Partington stories, a significant source for Twain's depiction of Aunt Polly in *The Adventures of Tom Sawyer*. Partington's malapropisms come to the reader comfortably framed by a genteel narrator:

> As she mused, in harmony with her clicking needles, her thoughts took form in words.
>
> "How the world has turned about, to be sure!" said she; "'t is nothing but change, change. Only yesterday, as it were, I was in the country, smelling the odious flower;—to-day I am in Boston, my oilfactories breathing the impure execrations of coal-smoke, that are so dilatory to health. Instead of the singing of birds, the blunderbusses almost deprive me of conscientiousness." (*Knitting Work* 11)

Shillaber's tactic of using a *frame narrative to drive home how we are to read the contained dialect is a typical early-nineteenth-century approach to satire, though occasional variants appeared even before the Civil War. For instance, Frances Miriam Whitcher's *Widow Bedott Papers* (1855) ruthlessly satirizes the social climbing Priscilla (Silly) Bedott in the form of her letters, given to us without the orienting frame of a genteel narrator. With such models before him, Twain could choose to frame his dialect stories or not, but he would find it difficult to endorse dialect as a positive character attribute even as he used it for satire.

In his efforts to do so, he was breaking new ground. As early as 1872, with *Roughing It*, Twain cautiously walked the same path as his contemporary, Marietta Holley, whose enormously popular Samantha Allen novels were unframed first-person dialect narratives in which Samantha is both an object of ridicule and admiration for her homespun ignorance and equally homespun common sense.

Those who would use dialect to validate American vernacular had a second barrier to overcome in the aesthetics of *sentimentalism, which argued that any exercise of *taste is ennobling. By contrast, then, any exercise in vulgarity is corrupting. Against this standard, use of slang or vernacular had a moral valence, and usually writers put slang in the mouths of characters they wanted to denigrate or at least condescend to. In *Uncle Tom's Cabin*, for example, Harriet Beecher *Stowe characterizes the slave trader Haley through a comic slang that reveals his lower-class origins and tastes even as it shows his economic power. Stowe thus uses dialect to reveal a moral class hierarchy that may not correspond to an economic one, but, in her mockery, she reveals which she holds to be more important.

But ironically it was in the sentimentalist's desire to extend sympathy across social barriers that much of the impetus to redeem dialect arose. Usually using a frame narrator to guide the reader's evaluation of the worthiness of a dialect-speaking character, dialect writers often revealed a "heart of gold" in a lowly position, such as in Bret *Harte's "The Luck of Roaring Camp" or as Stowe does with Uncle Tom in a book subtitled *Life Among the Lowly*. Each time she has Tom speak in his dialect, she uses a frame narrator to endorse Tom's sentiments in spite of his language.

Later in the century, under the influence of local color *realism, such efforts to capture dialect as a way of preserving regional peculiarities improved the social status of dialect, but again, usually under the ministrations of a genteel frame narrator whose perfect grammar and polished syntax signal that his or her valuations are trustworthy. Perhaps in no other book of the nineteenth century is this more true, and ultimately more troubling, than in Joel Chandler *Harris's *Uncle Remus: His Songs and Sayings*. Harris made a concerted effort to capture the folktales of African Americans, and by most accounts he succeeded admirably, but in order to make these tales palatable for a white audience, he created a stereotypical "plantation darky" to tell the tales to a little white boy. The white boy's speech is rendered in standard English, despite the fact that he, too, would have had an accent, while Uncle Remus's speech is rendered in spelling that takes much effort to unravel:

> Presently Uncle Remus looked at him in a sad and hopeless way, and asked:
> "W'at dat long rigmarole you bin tellin' Miss Sally 'bout yo' little brer dis mawnin?"
> "Which, Uncle Remus?" asked the little boy, blushing guiltily.
> "Dat des w'at I'm a axin' un you now. I hear Miss Sally say she's a gwineter stripe his jacket, en den I knowed you bin tellin' on 'im."
> "Well, Uncle Remus, he was pulling up your onions . . ."

Harris's narration extends sympathy to Remus only by trivializing him. The dialect still serves to convince the reader to condescend. Unless the frame disappears or is set up to cast doubt back on the frame narrator's authority, dialect supports, rather than bridges, class distinctions.

One of the most extravagant pieces of dialect *humor that may have influenced Twain, George Washington *Harris's *Sut Lovingood Yarns*, does exactly that. By pushing the boundaries of dialect to the point that readers must learn new spellings and pronunciations as if they were a foreign language, Harris makes the arbitrariness of language itself a fundamental part of the experience of reading. Coupled with the dynamic battle between the frame narrator George and inside narrator Sut, the class battle highlighted becomes a self-conscious part of the reading experience, preventing the reader from assuming the superiority of his or her own ostensibly standard dialect. For example, when Sut interrupts George's storytelling, complaining that George takes too much time setting the scene to get to the story, Sut says,

> "Oh, komplikated durnashun! That haint hit. . . . Yu's drunk, ur yure sham'd to tell hit, an' so yu tries to put us all asleep wif a mess ove durn'd nonsince, 'bout echo's, and grapes, an' warnit trees; oh, yu be durn'd! Boys, jis' gin me a hoult ove that are willer baskit, wif a cob in hits mouf, an' that ar tin cup, an' arter I'se spunged my froat, I'll talk hit all off in English, an' yu jis' watch an' see ef I say 'echo,' ur 'grapes,' ur 'graveyard' onst." (pp. 115–116)

Sut attacks George's educated artistry as over-refinement, calling into question the conventions of classical rhetoric.

Harris's stories raise some of the most difficult questions concerning written dialect. How does one capture colors of speech in written form? Is it possible to do any more than hint at dialect? Even in spoken form, dialects are easily misconstrued by hearers who have no experience with them. A New York reviewer once confused Twain's southern drawl for a Maine accent: "With his calm self-possession and winning geniality of manner, added to a slight 'Down East' accent, he is the impersonation of the shrewd, fun-loving, genuine 'live Yankee'" (George W. Elliot, "Mark Twain Lecture," *Mohawk Valley Register*, 25 December 1868, 3). How much more difficult, then, to capture sound from print. Often, dialect writers succumb to a worthless use of "eye dialect," misspelling words in ways that give no hints about pronunciation, as when Harris spells "complicated" with "k" instead of "c." If Sut were ostensibly writing his stories, such mistakes would be sensible markers of his level of education, but as George is merely transcribing Sut's tales, such solecisms do nothing, really, to reveal character or sound. But perhaps it is not possible to reveal sound through English orthography, because with no standard dialect to use as a basis for pronunciation, there is no regularly accepted correspondence between letters and sounds.

Hence, any representation of American dialects requires the imagination of the reader as much as it requires the ear of the writer. Twain said that he "amend[ed] dialect stuff by talking & talking and *talking* it till it sounds right" (to William Dean *Howells, 20 September 1874) but what those right sounds are must forever remain a mystery in the absence of voice recordings by Twain himself. Still, even if his renditions of dialect cannot realistically capture the sound of vernacular speech, his dialect representations tend to work quite well at validating dialect. Twain mastered the ability to challenge the frame or to cut the dialect loose from the frame in order to suggest that dialect can carry sentiment as effectively as can polished, educated language.

Twain perhaps learned this when he wrote the interpolated story of Scotty Briggs and the parson in *Roughing It*, in which, as in *Sut Lovingood's Yarns*, all dialects are put on a more or less even footing, regardless of the double framing of the story. In *Adventures of Huckleberry Finn*, Twain abandoned the frame altogether, allowing a vernacular character freedom to validate his own sentiments in spite of social pressures to the contrary. In giving Huck this voice, Twain knew he was running a risk—one that has in fact borne fruit through years of efforts to *censor the book because of its dialect. Still, in letting a vernacular character speak for himself, Twain became perhaps the most influential of many late-nineteenth-century writers who validated American vernaculars as legitimate, artistic media.

♦ SEE ALSO Amiable Humor; Irony; Leisure; Satire; Social Class; Style.

DICKENS, CHARLES (1812–1870).

In his autobiographical dictation of 10 October 1907, Twain recalls Charles Dickens:

> I heard him once in that season [1867]; it was in Steinway Hall, in December, and it made the fortune of my life—not in dollars, I am not thinking of dollars; it made the real fortune of my life in that it made the happiness of my life; on that day I called at the St. Nicholas Hotel to see my *Quaker City* Excursion shipmate, Charley Langdon, and was introduced to a sweet and timid and lovely young girl, his sister. The family went to the Dickens reading, and I accompanied them. It was forty years ago; from that day to this the sister has never been out of my mind nor heart.

In typical misdirection, Twain teases us into imagining the professional link between himself and the other most influential nineteenth-century male English-speaking writer, only to talk about a personal and fully accidental link. But such misdirection does not deny the influence.

Clemens, like most readers in the English-speaking world, avidly read Dickens's works. His early letters in particular are full of laudatory references. And like most writers in Dickens's wake, Clemens shaped his style in imitation and defiance of Dickens's: Twain's grappling with the moral engagements of *sentimentalism was influenced as much by Dickens as by any other writer. Under the tutelage of Bret *Harte, Twain trained in a Dickensian style of comic characterization, mingling humor and pathos, and made use of typical Dickens subject matters—especially the poverty-stricken child whose heart is as good as gold. While echoes of Dickens abound in Twain's works, Twain, not surprisingly, often resisted that influence through parody and *burlesque, as in his mockery of Dickens's *Pictures from Italy* in the "Ascent of Vesuvius" chapters of *The Innocents Abroad*.

♦ SEE ALSO Clemens, Olivia Langdon; Europe; Lecture Circuit; Reading, Clemens's.

DICKINSON, ANNA (1842–1932). One of the most popular attractions on the lecture circuit in 1868 when Clemens first met her, Anna Dickinson was known for her energetic antislavery speeches and was one of the few widely popular feminists. She was admired for her pluck at pulling herself up out of poverty and, in defiance of cultural norms, by standing on the public platform to argue—energetically, forcefully, with compelling logic—for *women's rights. Her charisma and panache helped her overcome the usual scorn given to the public articulation of women's rights in the middle of the nineteenth century. In fact, she became one of the most highly paid performers on the lecture circuit, earning twice Twain's one hundred dollars per night in 1868.

Dickinson had already befriended the Langdons by 1867, and her influence on Olivia Langdon *Clemens provoked Olivia to wonder about her proper role in a marriage. In 1868, knowing Olivia's appreciation for Dickinson and admiring her platform style and success himself, Clemens became a partisan of Dickinson, even though he disagreed with her position on women's rights. His admiration was, perhaps, politic given that he worried she would not approve of him. His fears were well founded. She wrote to her sister of her astonishment "how the flower of their house, Olivia, as frail in body as she is clear of mind & lovely of soul ever married the vulgar boor to whom she gave herself.—I hear of him all about the country at wine suppers, & late orgies,—dirty, smoking, drinking—" She considered his popularity as an author, in contrast to that of more refined authors, repellant: "'Tis enough to disgust one with one's kind" (to Mary E. Dickinson, 14 March 1873).

As much as he admired Dickinson's rhetorical power, Clemens grew to dislike her. He may very well have intended Laura Hawkins's lecture performance at the end of *The Gilded Age* as a criticism of Dickinson's politics, and in January 1877 he went so far as to gloat in *The Atlantic Monthly*'s "Contributor's Club" column over Dickinson's failure as an actress. By this time he had come to agree with Dickinson's position on women's rights, so the animosity was clearly personal, not political.

♦ SEE ALSO Taste.

DOMESTICITY. In chapter 47 of *Roughing It*, Scotty Briggs's best evidence that Buck Fanshaw was a good man is that "he never *throwed off* on his mother," meaning he always provided for her. Even though saloon-keeper Fanshaw, whose backing was needed by every successful politician, . . . had been the proprietor of a helpmeet whom he could have discarded without the formality of a divorce," Briggs suggests that Fanshaw was a gentleman because he remained true to his mother. Twain here mocks the validity of this common cultural claim, that a mother's love is the center of all morality and statesmanship. But in this mild disagreement, Twain was merely quibbling with part of a newly dominant *sentimental ideology, one that had taken over from the land's once regnant Calvinist patriarchy; one that had fueled the moral fervor of the era's most popular book, Harriet Beecher *Stowe's *Uncle Tom's Cabin*; one that had as its anthem the 1823 song "Home, Sweet Home"; one that went variously under such names as "the cult of true womanhood," "domestic science," "home economics," or, perhaps most tellingly, the "cult of domesticity."

Each of these terms suggests much about the character of this sea change in domestic organization that took place from the late eighteenth through the middle of the nineteenth century as America's political, economic, and theological conditions altered. Politically, American republicanism espoused a middle-class citizenship based on a cultivated gentility that centered in individual families. Alexis de Tocqueville, in his celebrated *Democracy in America*, highly praised the family as the institutional structure that would make democracy in such a large land a real possibility. Tocqueville was not alone in praising America's familial focus, but his praise makes clear how radically different such a focus was from that of the European communities from which many Americans traced their origins. The idea of a domestic center built around a marriage based on love between equals, rather than on economic exchange, was the idea around which American gentility was built. And in order for such an idea of equality and freedom of choice in marriage to have developed in the first place, Calvinist patriarchy had to have been softened and the economic structures that necessitated arranged marriages had to shift. These gradually did, theoretically allowing for a much greater degree of freedom among young people to choose mates and for love to create a feeling of companionship and equality in marriage.

The reality, of course, was far more complex, with *women's rights a vexed feature of domesticity from the beginning. Even though influential British philosophers postulated complete political equality between men and women as early as the 1750s, the translation of such ideas into American family life happened slowly and only through an intervening step, the development of a belief that women and men had separate but equal spheres of dominion in which they would exercise naturally feminine and masculine proclivities. Both social progressives, who found the idea of women having a sphere of their own liberating, and conservatives,

Continued on page 179

The Dream of Domesticity

Susan K. Harris

In 1870, Samuel Clemens and Olivia Langdon were married in the sumptuous parlor of her parents' home in Elmira, New York. At least once during their courtship, that house and the woman in it had appeared in Clemens's dreams as a vision of near-unobtainable bliss. From his meeting with Langdon in 1868 to the end of his life in 1910, houses and what they represented of the pleasures and tragedies of family life would become central to him in both his life and writings. Clemens's fascination with houses reflects his class and his era; the way that fascination appears in his writing conveys his own vision of the relationship between domesticity and loss.

The elder Langdons' wedding gift to Langdon and Clemens actually *was* a house, in Buffalo, New York, where Clemens had just bought into the Buffalo *Express*. Their friend Charles Dudley Warner recorded that the house was not only fully furnished and staffed, but it also came with "a hot supper on the table and a horse and carriage with their monogram on the panel" (to George Warner, 14 February 1870, Katharine S. Day Collection, Stowe-Day Library, Hartford). Early letters from the young couple show them happily playing house, with Langdon asking her mother to send her old flannels and Clemens trying on the role of married man. But this idyl quickly turned to a nightmare as the couple sustained a series of deaths and illnesses and the premature birth of a sickly first child. After fifteen months they quit Buffalo, sojourning first with relatives in Elmira, then to a rented house in Hartford, Connecticut, while they built a mansion that reflected their joint idea of what a home should be. An examination of the ways the Clemenses lived in this house during their children's formative years gives us a window first into life among the wealthy literati in the second half of the nineteenth century, and second, into the ways that houses and families function in Mark Twain's fiction.

For nineteenth-century men and women, especially among the upper classes, the material bases of good living lay in the house and its arrangements. This was the era of "The Home," when domestic architecture suddenly blossomed as the most popular art form, when Andrew Jackson Downing became a hero to the middle classes and Louis Comfort Tiffany a hero to the rich. It was also the era of "The Family," forerunner to twentieth-century obsessions with parent-child relations. We tend not to think of Mark Twain in these terms, primarily because he has been presented within a historical construction of nineteenth-century masculinity that figures men as antithetical to domestic space. This framework is not useful for studying Mark Twain. Rather, it is important to recognize that although men on the whole worked outside the house, and women on the whole worked inside it (and even this generalization shatters if we look at men's and women's work patterns across class and race), many nineteenth-century men were involved not only in childrearing but also in domestic practices such as designing, furnishing, and decorating houses. Beneath the nineteenth-century clichés about men's and women's spheres lay a pattern of domestic practices that reveal nineteenth-century home life to be an imaginative act that was deeply engrossing to men and women alike, an act that helped them surf the turbulence of a society that was both thrillingly and frighteningly mobile.

Both Clemens's letters and those of his wife show that he was deeply involved with family life, despite his often frantic public career as Mark Twain. At least from his early marriage, Clemens was far more responsive to his domestic environment than his public image suggested, at first because the material pleasures wealth can bring were new to him, later because they had become indispensable. While the Buffalo idyl lasted, he was enchanted by the house his in-laws had provided: "Our home," he wrote them two weeks after the wedding,

> is the daintiest, & the most exquisite & enchanting that can be found in all America—& the longer we know it the more fascinating it grows & the firmer the hold it fastens upon each fettered sense. It is perfect. Perfect in all its dimensions, proportions & appointments. It is filled with that nameless grace which faultless harmony gives. The colors are all rich, & beautiful, & all blended with & interchanged & interwoven without a single marring discord. Our home is a ceaseless, unsurfeiting, feast for the eye & the soul, & the whole being. It is a constant delight. It is a poem, it is music—& it speaks & it sings, to us, all the day long. (20 February 1870)

Even discounting Clemens's audience (the gift of the house came on top of the $25,000 his in-laws had already lent him to buy into the Buffalo *Express*), this letter shows Clemens as far more responsive to his domestic surroundings than we generally imagine Mark Twain capable of being. What is particularly interesting here is the way that he characterizes the pleasure he took in the presence of beautiful objects by using words suggesting absence: "nameless," "faultless," "ceaseless," "without discord." While his intention is certainly to convey ecstatic appreciation, the linguistic tension between substance and absence suggests illusion—what he calls "enchantment." Like the music to which he compares it, the magic of the house can cease at any time.

When it did stop, the couple, in true American fashion, decamped. Their choice of Hartford signaled their ambitions: Hartford was a far more established and conservative town than Buffalo. The choice also signaled their acceptance of financial risk: unlike in Buffalo, where Clemens had bought into a thriving newspaper and was assured of a steady income, in Hartford he was dependent on royalties, lecturing fees, flat pay for periodical publications, and the money that Langdon, wealthy in her own right, regularly received from her shares in her family's business. The couple began, as always, optimistic, seeing their future clearly as they planned their new home: "We will put if it is necessary the $29000 into the house, grounds, and what new furniture we may need," Langdon told Clemens on 2 December 1871:

> If we wait to know whether we can afford it we shall wait eight years, because I do not believe we shall know whether we can afford to live this way until the end of the copartnership—Charlie [her brother] says I can perfectly well have from there five hundred dollars a month—You may lecture *one month* in New England during the Winter, that will give you $2000.00. . . . The three hundred dollars a month with what your regular work will bring you will be plenty. (*Mark Twain Letters* 4:510–511)

A year later they took the plunge: "Have just bought the loveliest building lot in Hartford 544 feet front on the Avenue & 300 feet deep (paid for it with first six months of 'Roughing It' hows' that?)," Clemens first wrote, then crossed out, in a letter to Whitelaw Reid (13 and 17 January 1873). Time would prove their optimism ill-founded; the house cost far more to run than they had anticipated and by the next decade they were deeply in debt. Although Clemens's declaration of bankruptcy in 1894 is generally attributed to his investments in the Paige typesetter, the fact is, as Kenneth Andrews pointed out in *Nook Farm: Mark Twain's Hartford Circle* (1950), most of his neighbors were in debt too. For the upper middle class, especially those dependent on writing for their livelihoods, the dream of domesticity was a very expensive proposition.

Building the Hartford house engaged both Langdon's and Clemens's energies, although Langdon, on location while Clemens was on the lecture circuit, formulated most of the initial designs. Her own mother had superintended a massive renovation and expansion of her Elmira home in 1865, and Langdon's confidence in her own abilities to design a house reflected her mother's calm assurance. Lilly Warner, the Clemenses' neighbor and friend, who with her husband George was also building on the Nook Farm subdivision, took note of some of Langdon's plans: "[We walked] home through the grove past our house," she told her absent husband on 14 January 1873.

> Mrs. Clemens took me, and though most of my eyes were for our houses, we both did a good deal of looking at the spot where hers is to be. It *is* beautiful, there's no question about it. She said as we passed ours . . . that "Mr. Clemens says we must have the red paste too, for ours." She came yesterday to show me her plan—drawn roughly—"because Mr. Clemens knew nothing about

houses on paper & she *must* talk with somebody about it as she went along."
She . . . wishes to keep the interior just as she has always planned, & . . . to get
the right windows in the right rooms etc. . . . she wants to get it all drawn out
before they see [an architect]. (Mark Twain Papers.)

Eventually the Clemenses engaged Edward T. Potter, who listened to them carefully
before designing the nineteen-room, five-bath mansion that would be their home
for the next twenty years. There they would entertain family, close friends, and
acquaintances, many of whom would leave memoirs celebrating Langdon as a particularly gracious hostess.

Having built this opulent stage for enacting Victorian domesticity, the
Clemenses performed it in part through intensive parenting of their three children:
Susy, born in 1872; Clara, born in 1874; and Jean, born in 1880. (Their first child,
Langdon, born in Buffalo in 1870, died in Hartford at the age of sixteen months.)
Here Olivia Langdon was the primary parent though not necessarily the primary
caregiver—the Clemenses employed full-time childcare as well as other servants.
Katie Leary, also an Elmira native, joined the household staff as Langdon's personal
maid in 1880 and stayed as housekeeper until Clemens died in 1910; it was in her
arms that Susy Clemens died of meningitis in 1896, while her parents were on the
global lecture tour that redeemed them from bankruptcy. Additionally, nursemaids
and governesses (all the children were home-schooled) formed the children's constellation of domestic adults.

Even though she may not have changed many diapers, Langdon's maternal
supervisory duties—like her housekeeping duties—nevertheless were complex. She
was responsible for the *shape* of her children's lives as well as the material conditions
for performing them: she oversaw everything from clothing to birthday parties,
governesses and tutors. She also did a considerable amount of primary teaching,
especially basic literacy and physical science. Although adolescent illness disrupted
her own formal education, she had read widely and received tutoring in French,
chemistry, and physics prior to her marriage. Like other women of her class, she
continued to read and study even after taking on marital responsibilities. Her
diaries and letters of the 1870s and 1880s show her conducting daily reading and
science lessons with her young daughters, and observing and evaluating their
progress under their tutors a few years later.

Clemens's contributions to his daughters' education was less formalized, more
pleasurable. Langdon read to them; he told them stories and urged them to create
their own. At times he helped them write or adapt plays and he occasionally acted
in them (at least once in drag). He also invented a yard game to teach them English
history. During the summers, which the family spent at Langdon's sister's farm
outside Elmira, Langdon and the children collected insects and studied entomol-
ogy, while Clemens and the children collected rocks and attempted to build a

tower. Together, Langdon and Clemens worked to foster an atmosphere that would produce well-read and self-possessed young women for an elite and socially conservative society. When one died at the age of twenty-four, another developed epilepsy at sixteen, and the third insisted on a musical career, Clemens saw (rightly according to the ethos under which he and his wife had labored) that he and Langdon had failed as parents. Unable to bring himself to blame his wife, he generally blamed himself.

Much of this atmosphere—the houses and the childrearing practices—is reflected in Twain's fiction, though often its social existence is signaled, paradoxically, by absence. On the one hand, families are everywhere in his stories, from the McWilliamses' panicking over a child with membranous croup to Hank Morgan's proclaiming his happiness with his sixth-century wife and child. On the other hand, as even these examples show, few of the families portrayed are intact, and those that are tend to convey a tremendous sense of deprivation. Many of these portraits, especially those written in the last twenty years of his life, clearly reflect Clemens's own family and his latter-day sense that domestic bliss was a paradise that had been forfeited. In the very late "Which Was the Dream?" manuscripts, the male narrator repeatedly records his loss of wife, children, and home. The typical plot in these stories begins with a man at the height of good fortune, financially and socially successful, with a loving and gracious wife and lovely, responsive children. Something happens (in one version he contracts with the "Superintendent of Dream" to enter the microscopic world of a drop of water and then can't get back home) and he loses everything. By the manuscript's conclusion—in the few cases where they are concluded—the protagonist no longer knows whether the life he is living or the one he remembers is the dream.

Clearly, the tragedies accompanying the Clemenses' married life fueled these stories. By the late 1890s, when he began composing them, Clemens must have felt that the domestic bliss of his middle years was a cruel hoax by a malicious deity. But even before his major tragedies, there is something about Clemens's fictional houses and families that suggests the unreality of the domestic idyl. Certainly Hank Morgan of *A Connecticut Yankee in King Arthur's Court*, mourning the wife and child left behind when he is transported from sixth-century England to the "civilization" of the nineteenth-century United States, anticipates the late works in the suggestion that such contentments are only possible in a dream. Although the 1889 novel reflects many of Clemens's financial frustrations, it still was written well before the deaths of Susy, Olivia, and Jean.

I suspect that the biographical was only the most potent fuel for the fire of Twain's doubts. Twain's dream of domesticity was shared by his contemporaries; the entire setup, from the house to the family reading circle, was dreamed into existence by a culture struggling to create touchstones of stability in an increasingly unstable world. Victorian domesticity was deeply fulfilling when it worked, but it was a hard act to pull off. I am not arguing that Twain's domestic life—or the lives of any of his contemporaries, for that matter—was unhappy; rather, I am suggesting that their representation of that life through words was itself an act of faith, an attempt to create by describing. For, as nearly all biographers have pointed out, Twain's dream of domesticity was always deeply flawed, and not because Langdon was a prude (she wasn't) or because Clemens had less than total reverence for the proprieties. The flaws lay in the dream itself, in the way that nineteenth-century Anglo-Americans declared women miracles of housewifely efficiency, men bedrocks of financial and emotional support, and children models of sensitive and obedient subordination, against all the evidence that women were often disorganized and grouchy, men incompetent, and children rude and rebellious.

Living together is difficult. It is especially difficult if you live in a culture that celebrates the individual and makes a cult of solitude. We need to remember that the cult of American domesticity arose at the same time as the cult of the American isolato; rather than seeing them as paired opposites, as we usually do, it may be most useful to see them as dual responses to a crisis of identity in a new nation, role-playing for fledgling nationals. By the time the Clemenses were enacting their domestic play, the popular image of "The Individual" (created by writers such as James Fenimore Cooper and transformed by those like Henry David Thoreau) had degenerated into the Western Cowboy; soon, Theodore Dreiser would transform it once more into the Business Tycoon. Over the same time span, the cult of community, especially as embodied in "The Family," attained equal cultural currency. Although some contemporaries and many later critics have attempted to characterize Mark Twain as the individual, in fact he was most attracted to the family. But he discovered that acting out the role of the family is more difficult than portraying the role of the individual.

Twain found that Victorian domesticity, especially among the wealthy, was a very complicated play to enact, perhaps most importantly because it asked more of any individual than he or she was capable of producing, and therefore led to a great deal of dissimulation on all levels. For instance, despite her considerable staff, Langdon's role demanded that she mentor each member of her family. The games that could entail were complex: Take, for example, her role in monitoring her children's moral behavior, which required continual surveillance and interrogation. The fact that the children were aware that this was an ongoing process also meant that they could manipulate the scenery. In 1885, when the two older Clemens girls were in their early teens, Langdon recorded an incident in her journal in which it is clear that not only was she monitoring her children's thinking, but that the children were also monitoring each other and calculating how to impress their mother.

Today as we were reading in the Bible together I took Clara's Bible from her to look at something and a poor uneven little piece of paper fell out, written closely on both sides. I saw at a glance that it was of interest to me, that some of the child's thoughts were on it. She picked it up and evidently did not want it seen—but I insisted until she gave it to me—Susy saying too "why Clara it is real sweet I saw it in your bible the other day." I read it and later when Clara stepped out of the room Susy said "that little piece of paper made me know Clara better than I ever did before." This is what was on the paper— exactly except that I can not copy the dear little irregularities of the childish hand.

"Be good to Susy, be not rude, overbearing, cross or pick her up. Be considerate of Eliza (the nurse) and put yourself in her place. Be as sweet and generous to Jean as Susy is and even more so, and be not selfish with the donkey but think how much you like to ride her and Jean enjoys it just about as much. Be sweet to Mamma and when you see that she is tired you ought to ask her as few questions as you can not to bother her. Be not cross and unmannerly to Julie even if you do think her queer, perhaps she thinks you queer. Be good always." There were places where she was troubled with the 3rd person form, would at first use the 1st person and then write over it. It is a precious little document and I wish that I could [word illegible]. She asked for it tonight. I told her I would give it to her tomorrow, and [word illegible]. I do hate to have it lost. It has to me a real a Kempis ring about it. (Olivia Langdon Clemens Diary, Mark Twain Memorial at Watkinson Library, Trinity College, Hartford, Connecticut)

Here we see Langdon performing the parental duty of scrutinizing her daughter's thoughts, much as Mrs. Darling, in J. M. Barrie's *Peter Pan*, tidies up her children's minds after they have fallen asleep. Clearly, this kind of surveillance was expected of Victorian parents. Here the fact that not only Langdon but also older sister Susy feel the right—the obligation, even—to read Clara's private papers is simply a threshold into a family dynamic in which the children, knowing that anything they commit to paper is open to scrutiny, leave self-valorizing "evidence" for their mother to find. In this scenario, everyone is performing: Langdon as the loving but watchful parent; Susy as the generous and appreciative older sibling; Clara as the young aspirant to selflessness. Langdon's analysis of her daughter's prose is exactly right. Clara's outmoded syntax ("Be not"), her parallel structures, and her self-admonitions show her writing herself into the role of fledgling saint. What is most interesting here is the role of reading and writing in creating this family dynamic. Along with the Sermon on the Mount, Thomas à Kempis's ever-popular *Imitation of Christ* is the model for Clara's prose style and themes; the Bible is the "location" where her vows are found, and the vows are written, not enacted. Rather than *doing* goodness, Clara writes it, and both her mother and her older sister take the writing as revelatory of her "real" self. Here writing *creates* goodness; it enacts the activity and the personality behind it.

So too with much of Victorian domesticity. The amount of writing *about* it, generally in didactic or self-celebratory tones, suggests both that it was constructed and extremely difficult to maintain. Domestic advice books, which originated and proliferated during this period, give step-by-step instructions on both the material and the psychological (which they would characterize as the spiritual) creation of good living; at the same time, however, they signal its internal tensions. *The American Woman's Home* (1869), a revision by Catharine Beecher and Harriet Beecher Stowe of Beecher's earlier *Treatise on Domestic Economy for Use of Young Ladies at Home and at School* (1841), featured, in addition to detailed chapters on topics such as "Stoves, Furnaces, and Chimneys" or "Home Decoration," one on "Good Temper in the Housekeeper." Here the authors freely admitted that "there is no class of persons in the world who have such incessant trials of temper, and temptations to be fretful, as American housekeepers" (p. 213). Nevertheless, the book insists that only a woman "who is habitually gentle, sympathizing, forbearing, and cheerful" (p. 212) creates the right atmosphere for the kind of moral growth ("for all to do right") that is the ultimate goal of the American home. Enjoining silence rather than sharp words, and recommending much prayer and trust in Providence, the advice book overtly contextualizes the home within the framework of "the reality of a life to come, and of its eternal results" (p. 218). The implication here is not only that the home should emulate heaven but that the ideal home will be as difficult to achieve as salvation. Parents' manuals proffered similar advice about training children, especially girls, to habits of self-abnegation and control; the strident tone of their demands suggests the difficulty of the task. Andrew Jackson Downing's manuals for householders, which virtually created the American suburb, reveal another kind of tension: on the one hand, they create a taste for distinctive architecture among the middle class; on the other, their careful listing of costs suggests the financial risks such tastes entail. Finally, as the Clemens family's tragedies illustrate, no amount of material comfort or loving relationships could stave off illness and premature death.

All of this speaks to the sense of loss and disillusionment that underlies portrayals of domesticity in Twain's writings. Perhaps the House Beautiful, from *Adventures of Huckleberry Finn*, best shows its early manifestation: like the beautiful fruit that Huck discovers to be made of chalk, the loving ties that bind the Grangerford family are strained by disobedient children and set in relief by outward violence. Huck is deeply impressed by the material conditions of the house and the family rituals enacted within it, but in the end human factors—passion, hatred, possessiveness, and revenge—destroy the illusion of family that the house and its rituals had created. In most of Twain's major works, intact nuclear families simply do not exist. Aunt Polly, the Widow Douglas, Huck Finn and his Pap, the orphaned Wilks girls, Hank's lost Sandy, the nonexistent father of Roxy's child—in their implicit or explicit pathos, all suggest the ideal family only by demonstrating its absence. What whole families do exist seem more like parodies than affirmations: Colonel Sellers has a wife, who, true and loyal woman that she is, sticks by him through all his financial vagaries; Tom Canty has a mother and two sisters, all of whom their father regularly beats. In *Joan of Arc*, the heroine grows up in what amounts to a nineteenth-century middle-class family transported to the fourteenth century; the narrator of her story, however, is an orphan who envies the d'Arc family's warmth and painfully notes the fact that Joan must forfeit home in order to be a martyr for France. Several of the "Which Was the Dream?" manuscript fragments begin with a woman recording the preparations for a children's birthday party before turning over the narration to her husband, who proceeds to tell how he lost that joyous crew. Throughout, images of houses and families are linked to themes of destruction, deprivation, and failure. The overriding motif is that successful domesticity is itself a dream.

Words are the instruments that create and destroy the dream. Mark Twain knew that his ability to write his world—to create fictional environments and people them with characters so powerful that they still live in popular iconography more than one hundred years later—gave him godlike powers of creation and destruction. In his works he rehearses his personal experiences of domestic bliss and its loss. But in a wider context, one that examines Twain's writings within his culture as well as within his own biography, we see that he shared his fear that domestic harmony is an illusion with his contemporaries. As his family life shows, Victorian domesticity was an imaginative construct, a play, complete with props and staged by affluent members of a culture who were trying to create a sense of community and stability in a world where "place," whether social or geographical, was highly unstable. Twain's writings reveal the realities behind the illusions: his words do not describe a scene but create it, and when the words stop, the stage goes dark.

Continued from page 169

who saw women's sphere as a way to keep women in their "proper place," embraced this idea energetically.

That "place" was built around a set of ideas about the "natures" of men and women, namely that women were morally superior to men because they were more spiritual, less physical, and more emotional, and that they expressed these attributes most completely in the home tending to their children. In the cult of domesticity, woman was placed on a pedestal, but only as a matron making a home for her own family. Not until the ideology of domesticity was developed did this cult of motherhood make the spinster an object of derision. In earlier eras, the economic power of a woman who could devote her full time to spinning made her a respected and useful member of an extended household.

In retrospect, it is easy to see that the shift to a middle-class ideal of gentility depended on different economic as well as political circumstances. Only with the rise of commercial textiles could the spinster's role in a family's economy be degraded; only with machine production of many goods could people create enough surplus wealth to allow the nuclear family to replace the extended family as an economic and political unit. Over the course of the nineteenth century in America, the *industrial revolution created such conditions, changing the work of both men and women from an artisan-based to a factory-based system, encouraging the development of financial instruments, and creating an extensive marketplace not only for goods but also for labor outside the home. The cult of domesticity was as much about creating a "masculine" sphere of work outside the home as it was about creating the home as a "haven" from the "heartless world" of business.

Clemens very much felt the pressure to earn large sums of money substantially because he aspired to this new ideal of domesticity. As he put it in a letter to his sister-in-law while mining in Nevada, "I am not married yet, and I never *will* marry until I can afford to have servants enough to leave my wife in the position for which I designed her, viz:—as a *companion*. I don't want to sleep with a three-fold Being who is cook, chambermaid and washerwoman all in one" (to Mary E. Clemens, 29 January 1862). A few years later, he had given up on the dream of striking it rich, working instead as a journalist and lecturer, both of which required long hours and an itinerancy at odds with domesticity. He responded to his friend Mary Mason Fairbanks's suggestion that he marry because "a good wife would be a perpetual incentive to progress" with a frustrated

> & so she would ... progress from house to house because I couldn't pay the rent.... But seriously, Madam, you are only just proposing luxuries to Lazarus. That is all. I want a good wife—I want a couple of them if they are particularly good—but where is the wherewithal? It costs nearly two letters a

week to keep *me*. If I doubled it, the firm would come to grief the first time anything happened to the senior partner. . . . I am as good an economist as anybody, but I can't turn an inkstand into Aladdin's lamp. (12 December 1867)

He needed a more stable and lucrative position to support a spouse.

Clemens responded to this pressure in typical fashion, beginning work as an itinerant laborer, mostly in *cities, and finally settling in an urban community. The social and economic changes creating this new cult of domesticity were urban before rural, creating a values gulf between educated middle- and upper-class city dwellers and farmers—and, for that matter, the working classes of the cities themselves. Only a family with enough economic clout could sequester women into the role of "Angel in the House," the title of the poem by Coventry Patmore that Clemens used to court Olivia Langdon.

This idea of a woman's spiritual and moral superiority to men completely inverted the old Christian idea, endorsed by American Calvinism, that women, in keeping with Eve's curiosity about evil, were men's moral inferiors. But under the new sentimental Christianity, not only were homes the moral centers of the republic, but mothers were the moral centers of homes. Hence the conservative insistence on keeping women "pure" and "innocent," an agenda Twain's works almost always promote, and the progressive sense that women's moral purity should be tapped as a social force in the public arena, an idea Twain came to support in his acceptance of women's rights. Furthermore, the idea that women were the best suited to raise children created a social need to educate women and, in turn, to open schoolteaching to women as well.

The corollary to women's purity is men's corruption—that in working in the world men taint themselves, but their innately debased character in comparison to that of women makes them suitable for such work in the first place. This idea comes up repeatedly in Twain's work, either in full acceptance of it or in defense of masculinity as a source of clear insight into the ways of the world. Boys in Twain's work range from the merely mischievous in *Tom Sawyer*, to the good-hearted Huck, to the inquisitive Clarence in *Connecticut Yankee*. Each character redeems himself not because he is "good," in the sense that this term can be applied to Twain's girl characters, but because each has a skeptical eye that allows him to see behind corrupt social practices. The boy's eye to Twain does not have an innocent girl's faith, but may be better for the world because its skepticism is cleansing. Still, in all of these cases, Twain seems to worry that the boys will become men, and as such become dangerously violent and self-serving. Twain clearly accepts that women are innately self-sacrificing and that men are calculating and selfish, demonstrated, for instance, in the difference between Joan of Arc and almost any of the men with whom she deals in *Personal Recollections of Joan of Arc*.

♦ SEE ALSO Adam and Eve; Association; Houses; McWilliams; Off-color Humor; Social Class; Work Ethic.

DOUGLASS, FREDERICK (1817–1895). The most celebrated black man of his day, Frederick Douglass escaped from slavery as a young man and spent the rest of his life working to better the conditions of African Americans. He came first to public notice as an antislavery orator working for William Lloyd Garrison, but soon broke with the Garrisonians, in part because he came to advocate using the ballot as a tool in the antislavery fight. A powerful orator, writer, political thinker, and politician, he at various times worked as the editor of a newspaper (*The North Star*) and as a civil servant, most notably as U.S. minister to Haiti from 1889 to 1891.

Clemens met Douglass through the Langdons, who befriended him after he escaped from slavery. In some ways, Clemens's reactions to Douglass were a test case for the Langdons of how far Clemens had changed from quondam states' rights partisan. In a 15 to 16 December 1869 letter to Olivia he wrote,

> Had a talk with Fred Douglas[s], today, who seemed exceedingly glad to see me—& I certainly was glad to see *him*, for I do so admire his "Spunk." He told the history of his child's expulsion from Miss Tracy's school, & his simple language was very effective. Miss Tracy said the pupils did not want a colored child among them—which he did not believe, & challenged the proof. She put it at once to a vote of the school, and asked "How many of you are willing to have this colored child be with you?" And they *all* held up their hands!

Clemens reveals a vestigial condescension here, though he willingly continued the Langdon's task of supporting Douglass's career, helping him secure a position in the James Garfield administration as the District of Columbia's recorder of deeds, a position Douglass held from 1881 to 1885. The two maintained cordial if infrequent contact for the rest of Douglass's life.

♦ SEE ALSO Race Relations.

DRAMA. Throughout his career, Clemens enjoyed writing plays, in part because he liked the *spectacle of drama, in part because he liked the potential financial rewards. His knowledge of drama developed as a reporter for several western newspapers in the 1860s, for whom Twain covered the *theater. His interest in drama, then, began from a critical, rather than a technical, point of view. Mark Twain commented as much on the social arrangements of theaters and the fashions of theatergoers as on performances themselves, and even when commenting on scenery or acting, he did so without any apparent knowledge of the technical aspects of theatrical performance. In other words, he lacked the insider's knowledge that would enable him to be a successful dramatist. Nonetheless, he tried repeatedly to write drama, substantially because of the success of *Colonel Sellers. Indeed, that play's success threatened to distract Twain from all other literary tasks, as he suggests in his correspondence to his British agent Moncure *Conway: "We find our copywright [*sic*] law here to be nearly worthless, & if I can make a living out of plays, I shall never write another book" (13 December 1876).

His letter to Conway exaggerates. Certainly the subscription book was lucrative, too, so in spite of his frustration with the lack of international *copyright—which damaged his income from books—he began to see the writing of literature for press and stage as intimately connected. He copyrighted a stage version of *The Adventures of Tom Sawyer* in 1875, and conceived of *The Prince and the Pauper* first as a drama before writing the book and then overseeing its adaptation to dramatic form. Twain initially wrote *The *American Claimant* in *collaboration with William Dean Howells as a play, *Colonel Sellers as Scientist. Huckleberry Finn, Connecticut Yankee, Pudd'nhead Wilson,* and *Joan of Arc* were all adapted into plays with Twain's permission, and in the case of *Pudd'nhead Wilson* (which ran successfully starring Frank Mayo), with Twain's help.

Twain's efforts to produce a dramatic hit equal to *Colonel Sellers* were most intense in the 1870s but never fully succeeded, especially when he crafted a story from the outset as a play. His *Simon Wheeler, Amateur Detective* (written in 1876), for instance, never worked as a play, in part because he tried to develop it as a platform *lecture, that is, as the expression of a single character. This more or less followed the model of *Colonel Sellers,* but its success depended as much on the talents of John T. Raymond, the actor who played the title role, as on the writing. The anomalous success of *Colonel Sellers,* combined with Twain's own success on the platform, convinced him to play from his strong suit without really learning the craft of a dramatist. He confessed as much in a letter to Howells, in reply to Howells's news that he had satisfactorily finished writing a play.

> So the comedy is done, & with a "fair degree of satisfaction." That rejoices me, & makes me mad, too—for *I* can't plan a comedy, & what have you done that God should be so good to you? I have racked myself baldheaded trying to plan a comedy-harness for some promising characters of mine to work in, & had to give it up. It is a noble lot of blooded stock & worth no end of money, but they must stand in the stable & be profitless. I want to be present when the comedy is produced, & help enjoy the success. (9 August 1876)

Perhaps Twain had just received a letter from Charles Reade, who turned down Twain's initial idea for the Simon Wheeler play with the admonition, "I beg to acknowledge your detecting plot. It is full of Brains but improbable on the stage and not popular. . . . Put in a story" (6 August 1876. Quoted in *Mark Twain's Satires and Burlesques,* University of California Press, 1968, p. 217).

Still, Twain persisted, inviting Bret *Harte to his Hartford home that fall, where the two collaborated on *Ah Sin: The Heathen Chinee,* a play built around a character Harte had used in several of his works. The play—along with the friendship—flopped in production in 1877, but even after its weak opening in May, Twain persisted in his work as a playwright, returning to his Simon Wheeler idea that summer. While he finished a script and copyrighted it that year, no producers were willing to take it up. Undeterred, he worked on a burlesque of *Hamlet* in 1881, and collaborated with Howells on *Colonel Sellers as Scientist,* which they wrote in 1883 and arranged to have produced, only to have Howells back out at the last minute. Howells turned the copyright over to Twain, who tried to produce the play in 1887 under the title *The American Claimant,* but the play failed.

With enough failures under his belt, and in spite of the modest success of professional adaptations of *The Prince and the Pauper* in 1889 and *Pudd'nhead Wilson* in 1896, Clemens finally decided that he was not a dramatist, letting his writing and then his publishing and other business concerns take precedence. Drama instead became an amateur passion, with the family, for example, doing its own staging of *The Prince and the Pauper.* He also wrote *Meistershaft* (1887) to serve as a lesson in the German language for his children. Not until after his bankruptcy in 1894 did Twain return seriously to drama. As he explained to H. H. Rogers, he had been approached by an Austrian playwright, Sigmund Schlesinger, to cowrite plays:

> I resolved to stop book-writing and go at something else. Just then an Austrian professional dramatist came along and proposed to write an American comedy with me (woman in politics) on half-profit basis. And between-times I have written a comedy by myself, entitled, "Is He Dead?"—and I put on the finishing touches to-day and read it to Mrs. Clemens, and she thinks it is very bully. I think, myself, that for an ignorant first attempt it lacks a good deal of being bad. I am learning the trade pretty fast—I shall get the hang of it yet, I believe. I shall stick to the business right along until I either turn out something real good or find out I can't. (5–6 February 1898)

By 28 August 1898 he wrote to Rogers: "*Put 'Is He Dead?' in the fire.* God will bless you. I too. I started in to convince myself that I could write a play or couldn't. I'm convinced. Nothing can disturb that conviction." But his late letters show him negotiating to have professional dramatists adapt many of his works, and his literature has continued to serve as the basis for successful dramatizations as well as film adaptations.

DREAMS. When writing "A Curious Dream: Containing a Moral" in 1870 in order to shame the city of Buffalo, New York, into taking better care of a cemetery, Twain incidentally mocked an Emersonian conception of dreams. According to Ralph Waldo Emerson's *Nature* (1836), "a dream may let us deeper into the secret of nature than a hundred concerted experiments." Anti-Romantic in its thrust, Twain's piece suggests a mechanistic view of dreams: "At that very moment a cock crowed, and the weird procession vanished and left not a shred or a bone behind. I awoke, and found myself lying with my head out of the bed and 'sagging' downwards considerably—a position favorable to dreaming dreams with morals in them, may be, but not poetry." The entire fable presumes on the idea that dreams are a connection to spiritual veracities, and that they are a source of divine inspiration, ideas as old as humanity itself but with a renewed currency through the avatars of Romanticism. While serious thinkers like Emerson could carefully distinguish between an analogical or symbolic truth and a physical truth, the more literal-minded believers of *spiritualism (which was very popular in 1870) accepted the idea that the dead actually talked directly to the living in dreams and other altered states of consciousness. At this stage of his career, Twain saw such beliefs as irrational bunkum. In chapter 15 of *Adventures of Huckleberry Finn*, Huck's prevailing upon Jim to imagine the trip in the fog as a dream and Jim's interpretation of that dream is another effort to show dream interpretation as a manifestation of superstition.

But the late nineteenth century also witnessed the beginnings of serious scientific study of psychology, that is, the study of the human mind not merely through introspection but through observation of the thoughts, feelings, and behavior of others. Scholars with approaches as different as those of William *James and Sigmund *Freud began to investigate such altered states of consciousness as dreams, assuming them to be essential to the processes of the human mind. However much they professed to be objective observers, though, no major thinkers of the period were fully freed of the Romantic conception of dreams as metaphorical reflections of hidden meanings, either universal or subjective.

Late in his career, having read James's *Principles of Psychology* and other works and Sir John Adams's *Herbartian Psychology*, Clemens became aware of theories of levels of consciousness, and in reading eighteenth-century mathematician Georg Christoph Lichtenberg's writings on dreams, he began to take seriously the psychological importance of dreams. But as befit the rationalist who earlier rejected symbolic interpretations of dreams, he was never sure whether to take these altered states of consciousness as realities or as symbolism.

Clemens often played with the idea that dream states were in fact as real—literally, tangibly (though spiritually) real—as waking states. In his letter to Susan Crane of 19 March 1893, for instance, he assumes that his real life could be just another dream: "I dreamed I was born, and grew up, and was a pilot on the Mississippi, and a miner and journalist ... and had a wife and children ... and this dream goes on and on and *on*, and sometimes seems so real that I almost believe it *is* real. I wonder if it is." Much of Twain's writing of this period professes this idea, including the *unfinished works "The Great Dark" and "Which Was the Dream?" as well as the *posthumously published "My Platonic Sweetheart" (written about 1898; published in 1912). This latter makes the serious statement that "in our dreams—I know it!—we do make the journeys we seem to make; we do see the things we seem to see; the people, the horses, the cats, the dogs, the birds, the whales, are real, not chimeras; they are living spirits, not shadows; and they are immortal and indestructible." Such an idea makes up a significant part of the action of *"No. 44, The Mysterious Stranger," as well, though in this work Twain also suggests something more metaphysically symbolic and less literal. At the end of the piece, when No. 44 explains that life itself is a dream, or rather a thought, Twain plays with philosophical solipsism to suggest that dreams are a manifestation of divine creativity. In this sense, they are merely projections of creative intelligence, shadows that are neither immortal nor indestructible.

Like those who were investigating dreams scientifically at about the same time, Twain's explorations of dreams were substantially an effort to arrive at an understanding of personal *identity. Taken by Adams's *Herbartian Psychology*, Clemens corresponded with Adams, hoping he would shed some light on these questions: "Meantime, *which is I and which is my mind?* Are we two or are we one?" (5 December 1898). In this sense, Twain's examination of dreams was in keeping with Emerson's, trying to decide whether the universe is essentially dualistic, divided between matter and spirit, or monistically physical. These late dream works postulated dualism, but other works that postulate *determinism, such as *What Is Man?* or that hew to a *utilitarian morality argue for monism. As with many of the major philosophical and social questions of his era, Twain was able to entertain both sides of the issue, but was finally unable to decide between them.

♦ SEE ALSO Crane, Susan Langdon and Theodore.

 **ECONOMY.** In his September 1870 *Galaxy Magazine* sketch "Political Economy," Twain parodies this earliest of the social sciences, suggesting that even while "political economy is the basis of all good government" and "the wisest men of all ages have brought to bear upon this subject the ... richest treasures of their genius," the economy is really about confidence men selling too much, too often, to the ignorant. *A Connecticut Yankee in King Arthur's Court* and to some degree *The American Claimant*, the two books that deal most extensively in economic theory—which is to say not very extensively at all—have pretty much the same tenor. For the most part, as much as Clemens took seriously the economy's impact on real lives, he wrote little about economics, accepting his own ignorance and proclaiming the ignorance of all who would hold themselves up as experts. Toward the end of his career, for example, he wrote in *"Corn-Pone Opinions,"

> Men think they think upon great political questions.... In our late canvas half of the nation passionately believed that in silver lay salvation, the other half as passionately believed that that way lay destruction. Do you believe that a tenth part of the people, on either side, had any rational excuse for having an opinion about the matter at all? I studied that mighty question to the bottom—and came out empty. Half of our people passionately believe in high tariff, the other half believe otherwise. Does this mean study and examination, or only feeling? The latter, I think. I have deeply studied that question, too—and didn't arrive.

Given Twain's skepticism regarding anyone's ability to understand the economy, it is no wonder that few economic issues intrude on his literature, despite the fact that the *realism and *naturalism of his day dealt almost obsessively in such issues.

The appearance of such concerns in much of the literature of the period is not surprising. The growing complexity of the economy, and the increasing participation of even the smallest farmers in an international market, confused many and quickly outstripped the power of any government to intervene effectively in order to, as the U.S. Constitution commands, "promote the general welfare." The failings of the government were ones of both will and understanding. Many authors wrote thinly veiled economic and political advocacy built around economic theory, as, for instance, Edward Bellamy's best-selling *Looking Backward: 2000–1887*. Clemens called Bellamy's book "the last and best of all the bibles." But excepting Hank Morgan's ruminations about speculation and wages and prices in *Connecticut Yankee* and the mechanics club speeches in *The American Claimant*, Clemens neither took part in this advocacy and theorizing, nor tried to cash in by imitating it.

His avoidance of large-scale economic theories is all the more remarkable given the enormous impact of the business cycle on his own life. The economic contraction of the late 1830s and 1840s helped bankrupt his father, forcing young Clemens into the print shop as an apprentice. Later, his fortunes rose and fell nearly in tandem with the nation's business cycle. The panic of 1873 resulted in a seven-year-long depression that cramped both his wife's income from investments and his income from book sales. The recession of 1884–1885 did not hurt Clemens appreciably, though its long-term consequences on the financial health of his publishing firm, *Webster and Company, founded in 1884, cannot be estimated. Perhaps if Clemens had launched the firm during a stronger economy, it might have been better capitalized and thus better prepared for the next downturn, which began with the panic of 1893. This panic itself forced the undercapitalized Webster & Company to the verge of bankruptcy when tight money made it impossible for Clemens to borrow from any bank. The ensuing depression, lasting until 1897, sealed Webster's fate, and with it, the immediate fortunes of the Clemens family.

All of these events loomed large in the life of the Clemenses, taking up significant space in their letters. For instance, in an 1873 bread-and-butter letter to his new English friend, Dr. John Brown, Clemens jokingly wrote, "The financial panic in America has absorbed about all my attention & anxiety since Monday evening when I laid down this pen. However, I feel relieved, now—of £600 sterling, & so am able to take up my letter again & go on & finish it" (22 and 25 September). Losing six hundred pounds, equal to about three thousand dollars (about sixty thousand dollars in today's *money) is hardly a joking matter. It was still less funny considering that Clemens was in Europe, unable to get to his funds in his New York bank, Henry Clews and Company, when it suspended payments on 23 September. (It did not resume fully making payments until January 1874.) Naturally, these events interrupted the Clemens family's travel plans, but more importantly, they briefly threatened the family's entire sense of station. Olivia's letter to her mother on 25 September registers more of this anxiety:

> Last night when we returned from the theater we had a notification that our bankers had suspended payment—After we went to bed Mr Clemens could not sleep, he had to return to the parlor and smoke and try to get sleepy—He said the reason that he could not sleep was that he kept thinking how stupid he had been not to draw out our money after he heard that J. Cook & co. had failed, said he kept thinking what the "boys" (meaning Mr Slee, Theodore, & Charlie [the partners in Olivia's family business, J. Langdon and Company]) were saying at home—"Well, it is 24 hours since J. Cook suspended and Clemens will have drawn his money out of the bank—now it is 48 hours since

J. Cook failed and of course Clemens is all safe, he will have his money drawn out &c &c." ... We fortunately have by us the £200 that Charlie sent for you and £43 that Pamela sent—but we owe several quite heavy bills and shall have to have more money from home unless Clews & co resume payment in a few days. Mr Clemens is inclined to think they will—If they do not you will probably get a dispatch from us before this reaches you— ... We do wish that we knew how you are all feeling at home financially, it seems as if this *terrible* panic must effect [*sic*] all business men.

In letters throughout Clemens's life, such comments on "the times" show up regularly.

The topic made few appearances in his literature, however. Despite all of his putative determinism, all of his intellectual belief in forces larger than individuals, his imagination ran in a more personal groove. If Clemens could not attach a person to the event, it made little or no sense to him. He blamed, for example, Theodore Roosevelt for the panic of 1907, assuming that a single person had such power over complex, large-scale events. The one exception to this way of thinking about the economy was Twain's perspective on the *labor movement. But again, it was through his personal involvement in labor organizations as a printer and steamboat pilot that he found his understanding of the larger power of concerted action. If he did not have a personal connection to it, an idea for Clemens remained a cold abstraction; as he put it in *Connecticut Yankee*, "How empty is theory in the presence of fact." To Clemens, the economy was theoretical, and as an individualist, he preferred to personalize its macroscopic actions and the related political decisions. In that regard, his idea of political economy was tinged with *nostalgia, even for the simple contact between a small-time confidence man and his mark.

♦ SEE ALSO Finances; Robber Barons; Rogers, Henry H.

EDDY, MARY BAKER. SEE Christian Science

EDUCATION. Samuel Clemens's formal education was, to paraphrase Thomas Hobbes, nasty, brutish, and short. Beginning in 1840, his family paid for him to attend at least four different schools, first that of Elizabeth Horr, second with Mary Ann Newcomb, then for the longest time with Samuel Cross, and finally, in the year after his father died, with John Dawson. When no longer able to afford his schooling, his mother apprenticed him, in 1848, to the printer's trade.

Clemens's experience was fairly typical for a young person in a small antebellum American town. Most towns had an educated or partially educated man or woman setting up school, and while towns sought to invite teachers and subsidize their efforts, schooling was seen primarily as an exercise in the rudiments of knowledge. Few students had any hope of attending college; those who displayed extraordinary ability might learn Latin with the schoolmaster, but most studied reading, writing, and "'rithmetic." Such primary training was handled under an authoritarian regimen, with scholars of many ages and abilities grouped into a single room. Lessons were communally taught, with older children helping younger in a pyramid with the master at the top. Parents had to choose to send their children to school; it was neither mandatory nor free, even when sponsored by a town or county. Most families relied on children's labor for some part of their income, so education usually took place around agrarian or industrial work cycles. College was reserved for the wealthy few or for those who intended to go into the ministry.

The wealthy often employed private tutors rather than sending their children to school. The rest paid tuition to either the common schools, to religious schools, or to tonier "academies" and "seminaries." Beyond using primers, schools rarely graded their curricula to a child's capacity. Not until the 1830s, with the publication of McGuffey's readers and other texts by educational reformers (including Catharine Beecher and Harriet Beecher *Stowe) did the idea of a child-appropriate curriculum slowly emerge. At about the same time, women were breaking into the teaching profession. Frugal schoolboards readily accepted this change because they did not have to pay women as much as men. No wonder then that Twain quipped in *Pudd'nhead Wilson's New Calendar*, "In the first place God made idiots. This was for practice. Then he made school boards." (*Following the Equator,* chapter 61).

Twain depicted these typical American common schools remarkably well in *The Adventures of Tom Sawyer*, in which he modeled the schoolmaster on his last teacher, John Dawson. The novel accurately shows the practice of corporal punishment as an inducement to scholarship; the miracle is that any love of learning ever survived such practices. Despite this negative portrayal, Clemens—and Americans more broadly—deeply valued education both as a foundation of national politics and for personal promotion. "Self-culture" was the buzzword, and it began with an education in early childhood. Americans considered college the apex of education. Of course, collegiate education was not, essentially, self-culture, but since most schools were not designed to prepare students for college, the college-bound child had to prepare himself, either by attending a special Latin grammar school or through an individual program of study. As a college education was out of reach for most, people valued alternatives, such as the *lecture circuit, which proved so important to Twain's career. The public lecture's popularity provides a good index of how widespread was the interest in education among people of all ages and walks of life.

Beyond basic training in reading, writing, and elementary arithmetic, one's real education was usually facilitated by different voluntary associations. In Clemens's case, the printer's associations to which he belonged in St. Louis, New York, and Philadelphia supported libraries, debating societies, and other educational pastimes. Most trades and professions had the equivalent, connecting general education with professional training. Indeed, excepting the ministry and medicine, most trades regulated education not through colleges or trade schools, but through apprenticeships and voluntary organizations.

In a country with such broadly based education, a national public culture evolved through both the lecture circuit and print. These were the real schools Clemens attended. He read as widely as he possibly could, and participated further in such voluntary educational groups as the Hartford *Monday Evening Club, where he listened to the ideas of others and tested his own. In this context, he undertook numerous courses of study. For instance, he taught himself French while working as a riverboat pilot. At other times he set himself to learn about music, painting, history, science, drama, and poetry, both reading avidly and seeking the company of others who shared his interests.

Still, Clemens had doubts about his education. Hobnobbing with as many college-educated men as he did in Hartford, he developed a profound respect for collegiate education. In "The Curious Republic of Gondor," he suggests that the franchise should be expanded for those who have advanced formal educations, and in writing *The Gilded Age*, he deferred to college-educated Charles Dudley *Warner's ideas of education. Later, in *Pudd'nhead Wilson*, the townspeople's stupid response to college-bred Wilson's sophistication suggests that Clemens feared the untrained mind. Likewise, his joyous pride over his *honorary degrees indicates how much he relished formal acknowledgment of his own self-directed education. Nonetheless, he was not awed by college. As he put it in a 1908 notebook entry, "All schools, all colleges, have two great functions: to confer, and to conceal valuable knowledge. The Theological knowledge which they conceal cannot justly be regarded as less valuable than that which they reveal. That is, if, when a man is buying a basket of strawberries, it can profit him to know that the bottom half of it is rotten" (5 November 1908).

During his adulthood, Clemens participated actively in educational *reform—one of the great movements of the last half of the nineteenth century—by sponsoring the Hartford *Saturday Morning Club, a debating society for girls designed to expand intellectual opportunities for women. Mostly, though, he used the tools of the wealthy to have his children educated privately, hiring governesses to teach his children languages and instructors in music to give voice lessons. His eldest daughter, Olivia Susan (Susy) *Clemens, briefly attended Bryn Mawr College, though Clemens's efforts to sabotage her success suggest that he did not want her to have the full independence of a collegiate education. This may have been one of the boundaries to Clemens's belief in equal rights for women.

While securing higher education for women was an important advance in the late nineteenth century, common school education remained at the center of most reforms, with reformers demanding more professional teaching and, most importantly, universal childhood education at public expense. At the same time, reformers pushed laws making education mandatory, in effect crimping child labor, a cause

Clemens endorsed. In a 23 November 1900 speech to the annual meeting of the Public Education Association of New York, Twain said:

> Now, this same Russian plan of retrenchment was brought up once in a township on the Mississippi River when I was a boy. The town was short of money and it was proposed to discontinue the common schools. At a meeting where the scheme was being discussed, an old farmer got up and said: "I think it's a mistake to try to save money that way. It's not a real saving, for every time you stop a school you will have to build a jail. What you gain at one end you lose at the other. It's like feeding a dog on his own tail. It wouldn't fatten that dog. (Paul Fatout, *Mark Twain Speaking* [1976].)

Nonetheless, in 1900, universal education remained a crusade, not a foregone conclusion; not until 1918 did the last state, Mississippi, finally make childhood education compulsory. Thus, even at his death in 1910, Clemens's lack of formal education was still common.

◆ SEE ALSO Childhood; Reading, Clemens's; Sunday School.

ELMIRA, NEW YORK. As the home town of Clemens's wife, Olivia Langdon *Clemens, and residence of his in-laws, Susan Langdon and Theodore *Crane, Elmira became Clemens's most frequented *summer residence. He used the writing studio his in-laws built for him to produce some of his best work, including substantial stretches of *The Adventures of Tom Sawyer*, *Adventures of Huckleberry Finn*, and *A Connecticut Yankee in King Arthur's Court*.

Elmira was not the stuffy, conservative, eastern establishment town that scholars have often painted it to be. It was, rather, a newly prosperous city connected through rail and canal to northeastern industry, and it shared in upstate New York's tumultuous history of religious, political, and social *reform movements. Like most upstate New York towns, it began its life as an agricultural community in the early nineteenth century. Originally given the too-common name "Newtown," it was renamed "Elmira" in 1828 just before the opening of the Erie Canal transformed upstate New York in 1833. While the canal gave birth to major cities right along its main route, towns far from its orbit needed to find ways to connect. Elmira built a spur, the Chemung Canal, which connected the timber and coal regions of the Susquehanna River valley with the country's main trans-Allegheny shipping route, the Erie Canal.

Still, Elmira was a relative backwater through the 1840s when Jervis Langdon was laying the grounds for his fortune in lumber and coal. With the coming of the railroad in 1851, Elmira became a transportation center, allowing transshipment of coal and lumber more easily throughout the northeast. Langdon was instrumental in building this railway, and ultimately Elmira became such a successful shipping center that the Erie, Lackawanna, Lehigh Valley, Delaware, and

Western railroads all had lines or spurs connecting Elmira to the main eastern population centers. Like many other upstate New York towns rich in natural resources, the railroad created an industrial boom: Elmira boasted steel, engine and boiler, bridge, fire engine, and woolen manufactories, as well as warehouses and coal and lumberyards. So while as late as 1847, humorist Frances Miriam Whitcher could describe Elmira as a village not altogether different from the *Hannibal, Missouri, Clemens knew as a boy, by the time he first saw Elmira after the Civil War, it was a booming industrial town of about 16,000, making it the 93rd largest city in the United States.

When the Langdons moved there in 1845, Elmira was beginning its growth and poised to help an aggressive entrepreneur make a fortune. It was also a fit ground for Langdon's aggressive reformist tendencies. Throughout the country, interest in the issues of religious orthodoxy, antislavery, temperance, and other assorted reform movements grew in intensity from the 1830s through the 1850s especially true in what became known as the burned-over district of upstate New York, an area where religious revivals of various sects swept like wildfires, and where the revivalists preached sobriety and hard work as much as salvation. Upstate New Yorkers particularly took to heart the question of antislavery, with countless towns serving not only as stops on the underground railroad but also as sanctuaries. The Langdons actively supported the underground railroad, and their opposition to slavery made them instrumental in establishing the antislavery Park Church in Elmira, after their local congregation—true to American form in the 1840s and 1850s—split over the issue of slavery. Under the guidance of Thomas K. Beecher, brother of Henry Ward *Beecher and Harriet Beecher *Stowe, Park Church developed a more sentimental Christianity, one comfortable with scientific discoveries and more interested in moral reform than in doctrinal controversy.

In these ways, Elmira was right in the mainstream of northeastern culture, promoting *progress as a combination of moral education and the technological advances of the *industrial revolution. During the Civil War, Elmira, with its railroad connections, was important to the Union war effort both as a staging ground for troops and as the site of a notorious prisoner-of-war camp. Before, during, and after the war, Elmira was a main stop on the *lecture circuit, as well as on the performance circuit for musicians and actors, giving this small city a cosmopolitan flavor. After the war, immigrant groups settled there in large numbers to work in the factories. This, coupled with the African-American population attracted to Elmira for its role in the underground railroad, changed the homogeneous nature of Elmira in ways once again typical of the industrial North. In its intense adherence, too, to the *Republican party's dual identity as both the party of reform and antislavery and the party of big business, Elmira shared the fundamental social and political contradictions of the Gilded Age. As such, Clemens, when he married into Elmira society, did not find himself in rustic seclusion during his summers there;

rather, he found himself in a small city that gave him a window onto one part of the modern America he so often took as his subject matter.

Today, Elmira is home to the Center for Mark Twain Studies, operated out of Elmira College (originally founded in 1855 as Elmira Female College, with the Langdons among the original promoters). The center owns the original Quarry Farm home where Clemens spent so many summers, as well as many family papers. The town has also developed regular summer festivities to celebrate its connection to Twain, with theatrical adaptations of Twain works and events from his life.

♦ SEE ALSO Langdon, Jervis and Olivia Lewis.

ESSAYS. While the essay took its name and some of its best models from Michel de Montaigne in the sixteenth century and found its first major English practitioner in Francis Bacon at the beginning of the seventeenth century, the form achieved its broadest appeal at the beginning of the eighteenth century with the rise of an energetic daily journalism. Montaigne and Bacon gave legitimacy to the essay as a form of meditation or argument, but journalism allowed this genre to flower in a multitude of directions, taking anything from politics, manners, and art, to morality, metaphysics, and religion as subjects, and developing those subjects through argument, criticism, homily, exhortation, meditation, or *sketch.

Both newspapers and magazines proved perfect venues for the familiar essay, so it is not surprising that Twain produced so many. As a newspaper correspondent in the 1860s, Twain built columns out of numerous short essays and sketches strung together; in these he usually tried to develop several different feelings over the course of the entire column by shifting approaches from section to section. In doing so, he sometimes mingled fiction with fact. This style, not surprisingly, informed his travel narratives, but once Twain made the leap to writing books, journalism ceased to be his mainstay. No longer producing regular correspondence, Twain wrote essays either to make a specific political point, often in newspapers, or to write for magazine publication. These more sustained essays are the ones that are most often reprinted and anthologized. By the end of his career, Twain's output was increasingly published in magazines before being collected in books. He consequently turned to shorter forms, among them the essay. Perhaps his greatest output of essays was between 1890 and his death in 1910.

Twain's essays cover all of the traditional forms, ranging from political advocacy to metaphysical meditation, with everything in between. While many are humorous, and tend toward exaggeration, such as "About Barbers" (1871) and "Taming the Bicycle" (1886), others are quite serious, ranging from the grandiloquent "The New Dynasty" (1886), written for the *Monday Evening Club, to the angry "To the Person Sitting in Darkness" (1901) or "The United States of Lyncherdom" (1901). Especially given the number of political crusades he took on in his later years, the intensity of his essays during this time is not surprising, though he did not write political exhortations alone. He also continued to cover the range of possible approaches and topics, as for instance a homiletic about manners in *"Corn-Pone Opinions" (1901), much literary criticism, as in *"Fenimore Cooper's Literary Offenses" (1895) and "William Dean Howells" (1906), and even metaphysical meditation as in "The Turning Point of My Life" (1910).

The energetic and direct mode of argumentation he used in many of these essays gives the impression that Twain was fully committed to the positions he develops. The frequent and clear bitterness of many of these later essays, in contrast to the more ambiguous arguments of his earlier fiction, helps create the simplistic portrait of the elderly Twain as a deeply pained cynic. While Twain did have a cynical streak throughout his career, it is important not to put too much weight on any single expression of his opinions—whether in his essays or his fiction—in trying to abstract his essential outlook on life. He took to heart the idea of the essay, using them as attempts to explore what he should believe. One should not read Twain's essays as his last word on any subject, but rather as one of his opportunities to examine the puzzles and contradictions of life as he found it.

ETIQUETTE. In May 1879, Clemens jotted in his notebook an idea of a burlesque "book on Etique[tte] & Complete Letter Writer," for which he took notes over the next two years. William Dean *Howells encouraged him in the project, writing on 5 March 1881, "The idea struck me as enormously good. Don't give it up. Such a book . . . put into the trade would go like wildfire. Think what a chance to satirize the greed, solemn selfishness and cruel dullness of society! It's a wonderful opportunity, and you were made for it." This push moved Clemens to turn some random notes, such as an entry for "Rules for Com[mitting] Suicide for Love," into almost one hundred pages of manuscript (much of which is published in *Letters from the Earth*) before abandoning the project. In these pages, Twain gives rules for deportment at funerals, billiard games, fires, and dogfights, and, most of all, for the proper use of that strangest of social inventions, the calling card. In place of calling cards, he suggests using playing cards, intimating that the social rituals by which one negotiated the high society of America's fashionable cities was a form of high-stakes gambling for wealth, prestige, and power.

While Twain did not complete this book, the subject of etiquette was never far from the center of his literary concerns, precisely because it was never far from the center of middle-class America's social concerns. Howells was convinced the book would sell precisely because real etiquette books were perennial best-sellers in America, and had been since the early years of the republic. Before Twain began on his burlesque, he purchased a number of real etiquette books in order to find particular passages to parody, and his manuscript even directly quotes at times in order to mock not only the content but the tone and style of these manuals.

Such manuals were popular in America because the problem of etiquette went right to the heart of America's cultural identity. Before independence, the eastern colonies relied on a European idea of etiquette, based on deference to social superiors, and therefore predicated on forms of submission or condescension. In such a system, different rules of etiquette were enforced between ranks and within them, and used not only to maintain separation but to symbolize class ranks. After the revolution, Americans questioned this function of manners, and especially in the trans-Appalachian West, new ideas of deportment developed, with manners coming to mark egalitarian instead of hierarchical ideals. A dichotomy within America grew between West and East, which served as the basis for much of Twain's comedy in his early journalism and, most significantly, in *Roughing It*. Whether such a democratic system of openness was a leveling down, however, and whether America could develop a mannerly society without rank, remained an open question in the nineteenth century.

Americans were especially stung by the published remarks of many European travelers that Americans lacked manners entirely, that the gaucheries of a classless society proved that America would never have a culture at all. In response, the American middle class developed an obsession with proving Europe's aristocratic America-bashers wrong by developing a gentility based on deportment rather than birth. Precisely what this would entail, however, was debated well into the twentieth century.

Certainly Twain registered these concerns in all of his accounts of European travel. Following in the footsteps of that first American literary traveler, Washington Irving, he sometimes took a stance of false humility in ostensibly agreeing to the superiority of European polish even as he attacked European pretensions:

> It will not do for me to find merit in American manners—for are they not the standing butt for the jest of critical and polished Europe? Still I must venture to claim one little matter of superiority in our manners: a lady may traverse our streets all day, going and coming as she chooses, and she will never be molested by any man; but if a lady, unattended, walks abroad in the streets of London, even at noonday, she will pretty likely to be accosted and insulted—and not by drunken sailors, but by men who carry the look and wear the dress of gentlemen.... Even the most degraded woman can walk our streets unmolested, her sex and her weakness being her sufficient protection. She will encounter less polish than she would in the old world, but she will run across enough humanity to make up for it. (*A Tramp Abroad*, chapter 47)

Continued on page 204

Etiquette

Judith Martin

The device that makes the plot of *The Prince and the Pauper* possible is, of all things, an etiquette book. The look-alike pauper, Tom Canty, stranded in the clothes, persona and apartment of the prince, stumbles upon a book "about the etiquette of the English court. This was a prize. He lay down upon a sumptuous divan and proceeded to instruct himself with honest zeal" (chapter 7). And arose from it a more or less properly behaved prince.

The book he read would most likely have been *The Babees Book* of 1475, which was specifically addressed to the princes of the English royal family, in an attempt to teach them the newly popular concept of restraining in public their natural inclinations, such as spitting, yawning, whispering, and picking the nose. It could also have been Erasmus's *De Civilitate morum puerilium libellus*, published in 1526 and known at Henry VIII's court, although the philosopher aimed his similar instructions at less socially privileged students, with the radical plan of creating an intellectual elite that would be presentable (and therefore, he hoped, influential) in the highest circles of government.

Etiquette books present part of a larger Renaissance response to the age-old philosophical question of what constitutes proper human behavior. The history of manners is a constant swing of the pendulum between the artificial and the natural—or, as these styles of behavior are termed by their respective detractors, the affected and the disgusting. During a time of elaborate conventions, people yearn for simplicity; during a time of frank crudeness, they yearn for refinement. Thus, Renaissance philosophers were promoting artificial improvements on the natural medieval manners to which people were sick of being exposed; Victorians reacted to what they considered the artificiality of the eighteenth century with the cult of what they called "sincerity," the twentieth century reacted to what was seen as *Victorian* artificiality with the cult of "honesty"; and here we are now beginning to have had enough of the twentieth century's idealized naturalness and are again receptive to the idea of a little unnatural politeness.

What makes *The Prince and the Pauper* a novel of manners, rather than merely a novel of cultural advantages, is its contribution to this debate, particularly to its most troubling aspect—that outward forms do not necessarily reflect inner character. The realizations that a virtuous heart does not ensure pleasant manners and that an evil heart can be disguised by them so dismay modern moralists that they can hardly bear to contemplate the very subject of manners, even though it was of such importance to their most distinguished predecessors.

Far from being stymied by that alarming paradox, this tale begins from the opposite assumption—that interior virtue is naturally linked to outward politeness. Both boys are depicted as being of exceptionally good character, and at the book's opening, each demonstrates that his manners transcend the roughness of his particular background. Tom exhibits gentleness and dignity that are conspicuously lacking in his associates, and the prince is sensitive and hospitable in a way lacking among his. Thus, both the prince and the pauper illustrate the idea that a good heart inspires a gracious manner.

Yet in the course of the book, they both have dangerous etiquette problems. Etiquette turns out to be much more of a problem for the prince, who tries to use his royal manners among common people, than for the commoner willingly acting as a prince, but both of them arouse suspicion and antagonism. This suggests that meaning well is not enough if one is not familiar with the etiquette specific to the circumstances in which one finds oneself.

In addition to their relationship to morals, manners are therefore a force in the plot, in that they are a device to place individuals within the society. Mistaken identity depends on similarity, and when the author posits the mix-up of two boys from the extreme ends of the social scale, it is not enough to make them look alike. They must behave in unfamiliar worlds in such a way that neither is identified as what he really is.

The setting takes for granted a world in which conditions and behavior vary widely but everyone is etiquette-conscious. Both spheres, palace and slum, are filled with people very much alive to transgressions of the standards they know and expect. While they have different notions of what constitutes offensive behavior, they share the concept that certain attitudes and conventions must be observed.

The poor, harboring a high sense of their own etiquette, are no less condemning of pretension and arrogance, and no less concerned with hierarchy and suitable demeanor, than the rich. They are quick to make charges of rudeness, and they are right, given their assumption that Edward is one of them, in thinking that he is badly behaved. What is majestic in an acknowledged prince is arrogant among equals.

The prince's inappropriate attitude to his presumed position, as well as his attempts to enforce a protocol that turns common practice upside down by demanding that grown-ups show deference to a youngster, earn him life-threatening condemnation. While Tom keeps improving his new position by learning to behave like a prince, Edward keeps bringing disaster on himself by refusing to behave any other way. The consequences of etiquette transgression are also more severe in the lower and criminal classes than among courtiers—and not only because the former are given to blunter expression of disapproval while the latter have the habit of enforced tolerance and flexibility from dealing with those who outrank them and recognizing that royalty can make its own rules.

That etiquette is a sorer point with the ruffians in the street than with the proud dignitaries of the prince's court may surprise some readers. As in our own streets, etiquette is always a more volatile subject among those who cannot count on being treated with respect than among those who have the power to command deference. When Tom infringes courtly etiquette by publicly scratching his nose it passes unnoticed, because the assembled courtiers observe the highly sophisticated etiquette conventions of pretending that they failed to notice, and then of explaining away the supposedly unnoticed errors with the timeless excuse of illness and overwork.

This is not the response that Tom's peers would have made to an etiquette error. They would have responded with ridicule or violence, and through long experience Tom knows how to deal with both. Edward has to learn these techniques the hard way when, not knowing or caring that very different rules of etiquette prevail in his new surroundings, he deliberately or inadvertently violates them.

We see that at court it is considered rude to satirize people's (or maybe just princes') inadvertent transgressions. Whether that is praiseworthy, or merely reflects the humorlessness of a court where the teenaged Princess Elizabeth and Lady Jane Grey "forbid their servants to smile, lest the sin destroy their souls," is not clear. At any rate, the humor practiced in ordinary life also works to the displaced prince's advantage. Edward's manners may be subjected to blatant satire—"Ho, swine, slaves, pensioners of his grace's princely father, where be your manners?" responds the first boy he addresses with royal condescension; "Down on your marrow bones, all of ye, and do reverence to his kingly port and royal rags"—but the prince's survival, when he insists on the prerogatives of royalty among those who assume him to be a fellow pauper, turns out to hang implausibly on his protector's willingness to treat apparent insults as jokes and eccentricities.

In the end, the prince finds protocol used against him. As a presumed intruder who is thought impudent to royalty when he forces his way before the ersatz prince, Edward is made to realize that he is dependent for protection not on the enforcement of royalty-respecting law but on the virtue of Tom. A rule dear to the royal heart, "Up, thou mannerless clown! Wouldst sit in the presence of the king?"— which Edward has been trying to enforce on others throughout the book—does not sound quite so reasonable when directed at himself. The valuable point is thus made that rote etiquette, like law untempered with justice, is dangerous when not accompanied by the judgment to adjust it for motivation and circumstance.

Of course, one has to judge Edward mercifully, as well. One could say that a crown prince in a society that believes in the divine right of kings might have a handicap when it comes to learning to consider the feelings of others. At least until recently, royalty did not noticeably worry about the popularity polls, however many examples history offers that this might have been a good idea.

When Tom is catapulted into his new position, he has much less trouble adapting his manners to changed circumstances, and not only because a court etiquette book is available, whereas there was no such introduction to the etiquette of the streets. Unlike Edward, Tom seems to know from the beginning that etiquette is dependent on context. Therefore, he actually has less to learn: he has only to change his surface behavior, while the prince needs—but fails—to learn how manners operate as a force in society.

Tom's sophistication in this matter seems to arise from a healthy (and suspiciously American) sense of the possibility—however farfetched the reality may be—of social mobility. In order even to feel etiquette anxiety—which Tom does but Edward does not—one needs to know that behavior is different at different levels of society, and to believe that it is worth learning the practices of higher levels because one might be able to leave one's native circumstances and move up.

This assumption has less to do with the Tudor period, in which the book is set, than with the Victorian period, in which it was written. The anachronistic tip-off is Tom's recurrent anxiety about dining implements: "Poor Tom ate with his fingers mainly" and feared "the ordeal of dining all by himself with a multitude of curious eyes fastened upon him and a multitude of mouths whispering comments upon his performance—and upon his mistakes, if he should be so unlucky as to make any." The fear of exposing social ineptitude by "using the wrong fork" is a quintessential Victorian preoccupation, oddly surviving into our own time, when the nineteenth century's sudden proliferation of specialized flatware has vanished. It could hardly have existed before, however. At this sixteenth-century royal court, the fork was all but unknown.

Another etiquette concept, periodically popular but especially exciting to those involved in the social upheavals of the Industrial Revolution, is even more significant to the story of prince and pauper. That is the idea that a gentleman may be defined by his behavior rather than his birth. When William of Wykeham articulated this idea in the fourteenth century as "Manners maketh the man," it suggested that gentlemen—which is to say, men of gentle birth—should behave themselves, not that gentle behavior could earn one the birthright status of gentleman. It takes on new meaning, however, whenever an important change in the economic system raises the possibility of genuine social mobility.

Of course, money, not gentility, was, as it usually is, the major requirement for improving one's social fortunes in the nineteenth century. The connection between the two was a great deal more sordid than suggested by the rush to manners of that period. Etiquette, in one of its least pleasant aspects, was blatantly being brandished by those of high but decaying circumstances as a weapon against the social advancement of the new rich. True principles of manners were jettisoned as the inside knowledge of details of behavior—often deliberately complicated forms, freshly devised for use as social markers—was trickily employed as a test of eligibility.

However viciously used, this ploy—ever with us as groups at all levels seek to distinguish insiders from outsiders—is always ultimately unsuccessful against financial reality. Moneymakers, familiar with the combative use (or rather, misuse) of etiquette from their own efforts to distinguish themselves from their circles of origin, either learn the new rules or, at the least, provide their children with the leisure to do so. These dynamics remain familiar as a staple of the Victorian novel, where aristocratic but financially embarrassed parents are finally persuaded to admire and accept the industrial heiress their son coincidentally loves, because even they have to admit that she is beautifully behaved, in spite of the parents they deem so crude. At the end, everyone is happy—the young lovers, who have each other; the bride's parents, who gain rank for their descendants (whom they are expected to enjoy from a distance); and the bridegroom's parents, who get their hands on that despised money.

This sort of thing was going on in America, too, as well as between rich Americans and financially strapped European nobles. As befits an egalitarian society, however, America maintained the ideal that the moral principles underlying etiquette (along with a few virtues outside the domain of etiquette, notably hard work and American ingenuity) counted for everything, and inherited advantages for nothing.

The Prince and the Pauper is very much of this way of thinking. We are given to understand that the son of a thief, because he has a kind and honest heart, can make an easy transition not just to the very top of society but above it, convincingly, if temporarily, as its ruler. History to the contrary, this presumes that moral merit is the key qualification for the job.

Omitting our historical knowledge that the real Edward VI would not live through another year, the story ends on the promise that he is bound to be a king of stature. From the start, it is demonstrated that he has instincts above his origins, as it were. Not only does he rescue Tom from the palace guard and invite him for a visit, as if he were an equal, but he thoughtfully protects his visitor from scrutiny— again so that Tom will not be ashamed of his table manners: "The prince, with princely delicacy and breeding, sent away the servants so that his humble guest might not be embarrassed by their critical presence."

All this indicates a deep feeling for the principles of manners, especially the classic touchstone of hospitality, which also figures in the major religions as a moral test. When a god appears disguised as a pauper, those who turn him away will be punished and those who take him in rewarded. Excuses about who they thought he was or how little they had to share make no difference. Under the surface rules of the situation in this novel, the ejection of a scruffy intruder who has penetrated the security of the palace would be routine and reasonable, but Edward will not allow such a thing to happen. Later, on his own behalf, he keeps a running account of whom to reward and punish, based on how they treated him when his identity was not known.

Notwithstanding the prince's devotion to this principle of courtesy, the suspicion is bound to arise that it is the restrictions of court etiquette that have prevented him from understanding and feeling the life of his own realm, with all the tragedies and injustices to which his eyes are finally opened. His royalty itself stands in his way, and he becomes worthy of the throne only when he has left the protected environment that has shielded him from the complexities of life, and has been exposed to Tom Canty's world. The author is taking the position that a true king must be a man of the people—which, however politically laudable, is puzzling in the context of monarchy.

This populist proposition seems to be confirmed by the reaction of the sensible Tom when he is first exposed to court etiquette, and finds it is not only bewildering, but stifling, ridiculous, and boring. Remember that this is the boy who has admired and aped royalty all his life, now, on first contact, rejecting its ways because he realizes that they are not as straightforward as those of the simple life he found so distasteful. Immediately on finding himself living his dream of becoming a prince, he yearns to escape; and so he does at the end, when he happily turns the realm back to its true owner. The implication is that no right-thinking person would stand for such an elaborate life if not condemned to it by birth.

Something odd happens in between, however. Tom begins to get a taste for the royal way of life—and not just for the adulation directed toward his person, but for the ritual he at first misjudged because it was not practical; not just for the glamour, but for the power to do good. Neither he nor anyone reading about his pre-palace existence is likely to romanticize the slums as being more vital or authentic. The temptation to hang on at the top, perhaps with the rationalization that he would be doing so for the sake of what he could accomplish for the people, might have felled a less virtuous boy. Having denied his mother, Tom has it within his power to deny the true claimant and make the throne his forever. He is ultimately too good to do this. Recoiling from that first dastardly act, he cannot do the second.

Was he in danger of being corrupted by the surrounding web of privilege from which the real prince's sabbatical saved him? Was Edward so ensnared in complicated etiquette that it would have stifled his innate goodness but for his adventure? Is etiquette actually the villain of the novel, threatening to blind the boys to pity and social justice? Have they both had lucky escapes—Edward temporarily, Tom permanently—from a force that would have killed their inborn sense of decency and humanity?

To think so requires assuming that a king is restricted by etiquette. *The Prince and the Pauper* amply illustrates not only that etiquette also pertains to all levels of society, perhaps more rigidly and certainly more dangerously at the bottom than at the top, but that kingship, if anything, frees one from etiquette, and in ways that are not good for the soul. Far from being bound by the principles of manners, a secure prince is free to expect courtesies he has no intention of bestowing, and to operate without fear or consideration of the feelings of others. He is also free, at will or whim, to break or change any rules of etiquette, even his own, prevailing in his own court. Bound by etiquette? He is the one person who can eschew it with impunity, because he is above it.

That is what is corrupting. Edward, exposed to etiquette but never restrained by it, must have his behavior judged by others before he can understand the troubles of ordinary people who must live at the sufferance of one another and of their king. It is only when Tom experiences what it is to be above the laws of manners that he can test his own virtue against temptation. And so, as the pauper acquires a whiff of polish and the prince acquires a touch of humility, a common ideal standard emerges, in which goodheartedness, through study and experience, is honed into something socially useful.

♦ SEE ALSO Monarchy; Social Class.

Continued from page 196

In this excerpt, Twain suggests that the essence of manners is decent deportment toward all women. As such, he participates in the Victorian American ideal of manners as a way of marking gender rather than class distinctions. Indeed, Twain's works often set up a dichotomy between women as the teachers and enforcers of manners and boys and men as either the victims or the beneficiaries of female control. Most conspicuously, much of the instruction in etiquette—for good or ill—in *The Adventures of Tom Sawyer* and *Adventures of Huckleberry Finn* comes from female characters.

While the basic thrust of Twain's commentary about etiquette deals with this idea of gender, much of it also has to do with politics. In *The Gilded Age*, for example, Twain and Charles Dudley *Warner challenge the pseudoaristocratic pretensions of high society in a culture in which wealth is the primary marker of clout. This attack takes the form of a rather elitist denunciation of parvenus in favor of educated "gentlemen," but Twain and Warner's standard of gentility does not rest on education alone. Instead, they offer an ideal of gentility based not on birth, as in the case of what they called the "Antiques," nor on wealth, as in the case of the "Parvenus," but rather on a cultivation that includes an ideal of masculine political activism as well as of refined private behavior: "These gentlemen and their households were unostentatious people; they were educated and refined; they troubled themselves but little about the two other orders of nobility, but moved serenely in their wide orbit, confident in their own strength and well aware of the potency of their influence. They had no troublesome appearances to keep up, no rivalries which they cared to distress themselves about, no jealousies to fret over" (chapter 33). In *The Prince and the Pauper* and *The American Claimant*, Twain offers further criticism of the idea of etiquette based on either money or birth, again suggesting an ideal of refinement beyond ostentation, based on respect and democratic values. In this, Twain embraced a mainstream American concern, which saw the increasingly aristocratic pretensions of the Gilded Age as a threat to American values even as it failed to recognize the fundamental conflict between republican simplicity and refinement.

♦ SEE ALSO Fashion; Social Class; Style; Taste.

EUROPE. European abuse of America began early, most notably with French naturalist L. L. Buffon's *Epoques de la Nature* (1778), in which he postulated that the climate of the United States made all people living there degenerate. Although Buffon spoke primarily of physical attributes, other European travelers focused on the moral and aesthetic qualities of American civilization, and excepting the few admirers like Alexis de Tocqueville, the chorus was decidedly and snobbishly negative. From Frances Trollope through Charles *Dickens on to Matthew *Arnold, European visitors to America decried the United States as a land of boors. As Dickens put it in *American Notes* (1842),

> It would be well...for the American people as a whole, if they loved the Real less, and the Ideal somewhat more. It would be well, if there were greater encouragement to lightness of heart and gaiety, and a wider cultivation of what is beautiful, without being eminently and directly useful.... They certainly are not a humorous people, and their temperament always impressed me as being of a dull and gloomy character.... In travelling about, out of the large cities, ... I was quite oppressed by the prevailing seriousness and melancholy air of business: which was so general and unvarying, that at every new town I came to, I seemed to meet the very same people whom I had left behind me, at the last. Such defects as are perceptible in the national manners, seem, to me, to be referable, in a great degree, to this cause: which has generated a dull, sullen persistence in coarse usages, and rejected the graces of life as undeserving of attention. (chapter 18)

In short, Americans were shopkeepers rather than gentlemen and ladies.

Educated Americans' reactions expressed a deep anxiety about American culture in the face of Europe's historical importance. On the one hand, many replied defensively, suggesting that America's lack of refinement was superior to the snobbish, hypercultivated, decayed, and impractical European culture. On the other, many agreed that America's masses really were degenerate, but that America's best classes were worthy of European respect and admiration for carving small enclaves of European-style culture out of a raw, new nation. Either way, Americans accepted Europe as the world's cultural center.

Twain's works take both tacks in different places. On the one hand, *The Innocents Abroad* and *A Tramp Abroad* dismiss European art, legends, and music, while *A Connecticut Yankee in King Arthur's Court*, *The American Claimant*, and "On Foreign Critics" attack feudalism, *reverence, and the idea that Europe historically is anything greater than America. On the other hand, works such as "The Great Revolution on Pitcairn" and chapters 27 and 28 of *Life on the Mississippi* agree with European charges against America. Like other Americans of his class, his reactions to Europe show a complex anxiety about what constitutes civilization, generally accepting European standards precisely because America's literature, art, and music derived from European models. Without a homegrown alternative, and given that America's system of *education taught European *history and forms as the center of America's own culture, Americans had little choice but to define their culture against the standards of Europe. As much, then, as Twain found poetry in American dialects and beauty in American landscapes, he always articulated that value against implicitly or explicitly stated European standards. Even as a steamboat pilot on the Mississippi River before the Civil War, Clemens followed a common cultural pattern when he undertook a study of the French language in order to elevate himself.

Of course, Clemens became cosmopolitan in ways far beyond the range of possibility for most Americans, even the educated and wealthy. As a celebrated writer, he had entry into European society in ways that ultimately gave him more than the superficial traveler's understanding of Europe. With America's growing economic clout in the post–Civil War era making travel in Europe relatively inexpensive, Europe became a regular retreat for the Clemens family, whose heavy expenses in housekeeping in Hartford made periodic retrenchment a necessity. In Europe they could live in equal opulence for far less expense.

As Twain's career developed and he spent ever more time in Europe, the continent ceased to be a mythic standard and more a fact of life. In demystifying it for himself, he increasingly turned his analytic, humorous, and satiric powers not on Europe as a whole or as an ideal, but on individual European nations and cultures as matters of fact (always excepting France, which remained an abhorrent abstraction to him). By the end of his career, repatriated in America after the death of his wife, Twain finally could become the ultimate American by becoming the ultimate cosmopolitan. As a brash young journalist, he published *Innocents Abroad* as a declaration of independence—but he protested too much. Not until he had visited Europe repeatedly and lived for years in various parts of the continent could he finally put Europe in perspective—seeing America by contrast as no exception at all, neither in boorishness nor virtue—and engage his political imagination globally in the fight against *imperialism.

EVE. See Adam and Eve.

EVOLUTION. The idea of evolution as progress toward perfection was not new in the western world in 1859 when Charles *Darwin published his *On the Origin of Species by Natural Selection*. Indeed, the medieval and Enlightenment idea of a great chain of being, hierarchically organized, is readily adapted to an idea of *progress from bottom to top, especially given the Christian belief in a soul's progress through this hierarchy from a state of matter to a state of spirit. So in spite of the biblical account of the creation and the scientific codification of that idea in Carolus Linnaeus's taxonomy, an abiding hope for progress made the idea of evolution accessible to the western mind.

With the eighteenth-century development of the *science of geology, along with the discovery of fossils, belief in fixed species was challenged, and by the early nineteenth century, a comfortably optimistic idea of evolution gained some prominence. French naturalist Jean-Baptiste Lamarck postulated an idea of evolution as the inheritance of learned traits. According to Lamarck, an animal adapts to new conditions, or finds a better way of adjusting to old conditions, and passes on this change to its offspring. In keeping with the idea of the soul's progress from a lower to a higher spiritual condition, this idea of evolutionary progress has a clear sense of creative agency, an optimistic focus on directed movement toward a superior state.

Darwin, for the most part raised in a conventionally religious environment, knew of these theories, in part because his grandfather, Erasmus Darwin, subscribed to them and promulgated them in verse. But not content with a comfortable linking of Christian progress and physical evolution, Darwin found that the work of Sir Charles Lyell, the seminal influence in modern geology, called into question the congruence of biblical accounts of creation and the natural record. Darwin was early torn, then, between an idea of fixed species and evolution, and when he began his voyage on HMS *Beagle*, he was open to new explanations about the diversity of animals. As much as he gets credit for "discovering" evolution, he developed his ideas in contact with a community of fellow researchers, including Lyell, Thomas Henry Huxley, and Alfred Wallace. Wallace arrived at similar conclusions shortly after Darwin, and it was under Huxley's pressure to beat Wallace to the punch that Darwin, despite his fear of what his theory would do to religious faith, published *The Origin of Species*.

Darwin's insistence on the common origins of all species and thus the lack of human exceptionalism, and the Malthusian and potentially random basis of selection, made his theory different and controversial. Darwin and his fellow evolutionists, lacking a detailed paleontological record and knowing neither the genetic mechanisms of selection nor the time scale available for evolution, needed to compress the evolutionary scale, insisting on exaggerated similarities between humans and not only other apes, but other mammals. As such, they argued that human racial groups were part of the evolutionary hierarchy, playing into a burgeoning racism in the West over the course of the nineteenth century. They also, confusing the use of signs by animals with human symbolic language, argued that animals have incipient language. Certainly the idea of talking with the animals had been a human fantasy from time immemorial, but Darwin's theory made it seem plausible. In any event, the evolutionists' insistence on common animal origins enraged the religious orthodox, who declared that human beings could not be mere monkeys, that God had not created human beings in the image of an ape, and so forth.

The less understood implications of the Malthusian basis of evolution were more disturbing to the thoughtful. In seeing selection as the victory of the strongest in a battle for survival, Darwin's theory threatened not only the grounds of faith in God, but also the Enlightenment hope that self-interest is congruent with altruism. Darwin's theory seemed to sanction aggressive materialism, class warfare, race warfare, and an ethics of self-seeking.

The theory also had its scientific detractors, among them the towering figure in physics, William Thomson, Lord Kelvin. Kelvin weighed in late with his disagreement, arguing (incorrectly it turns out) from the laws of thermodynamics that the earth could not be old enough to allow for evolution by natural selection. Under Kelvin's criticism, Darwin backtracked from his own greatest insights, readopting some Lamarckian ideas.

In fact, in the popular dissemination of evolutionary theory, Lamarck remained more influential in the nineteenth century than Darwin, even though Darwin received the credit. Herbert Spencer, the great popularizer of evolutionary theory, actually hewed to Lamarck's line while justifying his positions on the strength of Darwin's reputation. Others put together their own peculiar mixes of evolutionary, religious, and political theory. Many such popularizers existed, and they received their greatest support in America. With their long tradition of perfectionism, Americans were open to evolutionary arguments and quickly came to accept Darwinian theory, despite powerful resistance from some religious leaders. Even many clergymen, such as Thomas K. Beecher, embraced these ideas, though often as modified by Darwin's promoters, most of whom ignored the elements of chance and circumstance that Darwin saw as central to natural selection.

Two influential American popularizers, both well known by Clemens, agreed that evolution was not random, but beyond that, saw Darwin through quite different lenses. John Fiske, best known for his evolutionary tract *The Meaning of Infancy* (1883), argued that evolution was divinely inspired to reach the goal of perfection. He believed that God acted "through time," instead of accepting the orthodox idea that God's miracles acted supernaturally "from all time." He argued that evolution itself developed altruism and sympathy (as did Darwin himself in *The Descent of Man*). Clemens disagreed, noting in the margin of his copy of *Descent* that, no matter how Darwin couched it, as long as the motive to other-regarding behavior was one's own pleasure, it is "selfishness again / —not charity / not gene / rosity / (save to- / ward our-selves.)" (p. 78).

In seeing evolution as a process of pursuing self-interest, Clemens followed Yale professor (and frequent visitor to Hartford) William Graham Sumner, who argued that human morality is irrelevant to natural *determinism, the fated development of superior human beings through competition. He argued from this position that the free market, untrammeled by any government regulation, was the best way to achieve a superior civilization. In this position, Sumner became the intellectual father of determinism in American literature and culture as well as the academic apologist for the excesses of big business during the Gilded Age. While Clemens never was comfortable with social Darwinism, he did develop a deterministic philosophy in many ways congruent with Sumner's, whose work he knew not only through the *Monday Evening Club's discussion of Sumner's ideas, but from Sumner himself.

In fact, Twain reacted to all of these promoters of evolution, not merely to Darwin alone. His initial responses to the theory were cautious, sometimes derogatory, of a piece with his brief skepticism about science. The end of "Some Learned Fables for Good Old Boys and Girls" (1875), for example, admonishes scientists to "not go prying into the august secrets of the Deity." The quondam miner who had read Lyell's *Principles of Geology* to better understand the Darwinian argument was not likely to retain this attitude for long, but fairly soon found himself comfortable with, indeed predisposed to, scientific explanations of natural events. As Clemens's career progressed, he embraced evolution, primarily from a Spencerian point of view. His remarks in *Connecticut Yankee* and *The American Claimant* about inherited characteristics show the depth of his agreement, and his argument about the nature of morality shows a constant engagement with evolutionary theory as a means of understanding the development of morality. In this way, he followed Darwin's discussion of the genesis of morality in *Descent* and incorporated some of Darwin's ideas about the social nature of sympathy into *Adventures of Huckleberry Finn.*

Late essays show that Clemens continued to follow the controversy. "McFarlane" (written about 1894, published posthumously in *Mark Twain's Autobiography*, ed. Albert Bigelow *Paine), "Man's Place in the Animal World" (written in 1896, published posthumously as "The Lowest Animal" in *Letters from the Earth*), and "Was the World Made for Man" (written in 1903 or later, published posthumously in *Letters from the Earth*) all show that Clemens's early caution about evolution gave way to a wholehearted agreement. The last of these shows his willingness to take positions within the controversies of evolution, accepting the full implications of Darwinian selection against the teleological arguments of some evolutionists. Specifically, he argues against Alfred Wallace, who in his *Man's Place in the Universe* proposes that earth is the only habitable world and thus the real center of the universe. Clemens used the theory of evolution exactly as the orthodox feared people would—to attack religious ideas regarding the importance of human beings and the existence of a deity.

♦ SEE ALSO Adam and Eve; Religion; Robber Barons.

***EXPRESS*, BUFFALO.** A daily newspaper with an editorial policy that in the 1870s supported the Republican party, the *Express* was the newspaper with which Clemens was last affiliated as he tried to make a full-time career out of *newspaper journalism. He began his work there as coeditor in August 1869, having purchased a third share in the paper with $25,000, half of which he borrowed from his future father-in-law, Jervis Langdon. In working as editor of the *Express* Clemens hoped to make it an exemplary newspaper that would not sell itself on lurid typography and more sensational reporting:

> I am simply working late at night in these first days until I get the reporters accustomed & habituated to doing things my way. . . . I simply want to educate them to modify the adjectives, curtail their philosophical reflections & leave out the slang. I have been consulting with the foreman of the news room for two days, & getting *him* drilled as to how I want the type-setting done—& this morning he has got my plan into full operation, & the paper is vastly improved in appearance. I have annihilated all the glaring thunder-and-lightning headings over the telegraphic news & made that department look quiet & respectable. (To Olivia Langdon, 19 August 1869)

In spite of such early efforts, his editorial duties were merely ornamental additions; the paper's political editor Josephus N. Larned and business manager George H. Selkirk managed nicely whenever Clemens failed to keep up his share of the paper's management. At first that happened rarely, as Clemens kept regular business hours while contributing stories and sketches. Later, when Clemens went on a lecture tour in the winter of 1869–1870 and his contracts to submit humorous work to *The Galaxy* and to write *Roughing It* for the American Publishing Company took up much of his time, he became an absentee editor. By March 1871 he left Buffalo permanently, selling his interest in the paper for fifteen thousand dollars. The ten thousand dollar loss on his investment is a substantial measure of how painful the newspaper business, as well as Buffalo, had become for him.

"Extract from Captain Stormfield's Visit to Heaven."

Begun in 1869, "Stormfield's Visit to Heaven" took longer to find its way into print than any piece Clemens published in his lifetime. It took so long partly because Clemens was worried that the tale could be construed as blasphemous and that it would therefore damage his public image and partly because he could not find the right form to match the story's purpose.

In retrospect, Clemens said the sketch was based on a dream Capt. Edgar (Ned) *Wakeman described in 1868, shortly before he began writing in 1869. The 1869 intention was not only to mock common conceptions of heaven, but also to attack the reasoning that justified a belief in heaven. In attacking Elizabeth Stuart Phelps's very popular *The Gates Ajar*, Clemens went after the literal idea of heaven that Phelps had proposed. She based her ideas on Bishop Joseph Butler's *Analogy of Religion*, an influential piece of moral philosophy that explained the existence of all earthly matter and experience as imperfect analogies to corresponding states in heaven. Clemens found such egotism absurd, especially after reading a book on astronomy, Amédée Victor Guillemin's *The Heavens*. Thus he parodied Phelps's notions by adding the appropriate cosmological distances, the number of other worlds likely to be populated throughout the heavens, and a complex heavenly bureaucracy necessary to administer that vastness. In doing so, Clemens reduces the very idea of an analogy between heaven and earth to the absurd. His concern over this potential blasphemy did not depend solely on the popularity of Phelps's book, but also on its intellectual underpinnings, which were essential parts of much of the liberal Christianity of the post–Civil War years.

Clemens drafted the work at least three times between 1869 and 1878, tinkered with it some more in the 1880s, and returned to it in the early 1900s, probably after his wife's death in 1904. He added significantly to the piece, but with a different purpose, instead suggesting his loneliness by describing characters whizzing through the vastness of space in nearly complete isolation. When he then decided to publish, he cut all of the new material and some of the passages about the futility of family reunions in heaven, changed Wakeman's name to Stormfield, and renamed the piece, coyly suggesting that more might follow. The money he earned from publication in part paid for his new house at Redding, Connecticut, which he in turn dubbed "Stormfield," after his daughter Clara complained about its original name, "Innocence at Home."

♦ SEE ALSO Afterlife; Censorship; Death; Religion; Work Habits.

"Fable, A." Written in 1906 and published in *Harper's Magazine* in 1909, this animal fable is usually interpreted as Twain's effort to show that truth is relative. In fact it shows just the opposite. While it does suggest that belief is relative to the believer, it argues that truth itself is absolute; while all of the animals in the story see a work of art only according to their own lights, the tale posits an objective reality that transcends the self-interest, egotism, and training of each individual.

It is perhaps best to construe this work, then, as an exercise in literary criticism and as an intervention into politics. The fable's stylistic mimicry of Rudyard *Kipling's *Just So Stories* suggests that the artist whose work is misinterpreted is Kipling. Twain believed that those political readers who wanted to use Kipling's stories to bolster their particular kinds of *imperialism missed Kipling's irony. Specifically, the satiric "The White Man's Burden" denounces the United States for its hypocrisy in annexing the Philippines after years of chastising Europe for imperialism, but was regularly misconstrued as praise for the United States's willingness finally to take up the cause of spreading Christianity and "civilization." While Kipling advocated a *pax Britannica*, he did so in hopes of preserving separate cultures, not of Christianizing other lands. When living in Vermont in the early 1890s, he decided that the United States was not politically mature enough to protect other cultures under its control and so could not participate in his proposed imperial protectorate. As a satirist critical of America's war in the Phillipines, Twain was not only sensitive to Kipling's critique, he was annoyed that so few readers could understand the point. Yet Clemens probably did not himself understand Kipling's pro-imperialistic side. As an anti-imperialist, Clemens himself stood in the way of the mirror of the imagination as he perceived only half of Kipling's message.

"Facts Concerning the Recent Carnival of Crime in Connecticut, The." This piece began as an essay for the January 1876 meeting of the Hartford *Monday Evening Club. In inviting William Dean *Howells down from Cambridge, Massachusetts, to attend the meeting, Clemens described his essay as an "exasperating metaphysical . . . extravaganza" (18 January 1876) that would "bring out considerable discussion among the gentlemen of the Club" (11 January 1876). It certainly did; the discussion carried over for months, with William Hammersley delivering a rebuttal essay titled "Conscience" to the club's March meeting.

The essay is exasperating because Clemens refuses to take a definite stand about what exactly constitutes conscience. In the debates of moral philosophy, how one defines the agency that promotes moral behavior determines the philosopher's system of moral regulation. As an amateur philosopher with great interest in such issues, Clemens had been reading W. E. H. *Lecky's *History of European Morals* (1869) and the passages on the evolution of morality in Charles *Darwin's *The Descent of Man* (1871). He had also heard fellow club members converse about prominent moral philosophers, such as John Stuart Mill, and on various applications of ethical theory. Clemens was raised to know the Calvinist conception of conscience. He thus had before him three conflicting models of moral motivation in *Calvinism, *utilitarianism, and *sentimentalism. Calvinists believe conscience is an external spiritual power castigating human beings for their turpitude; utilitarians believe that conscience is merely calculation of greatest individual pleasure in a complex world; sentimentalists believe that there is an innate *moral sense that discerns the moral qualities of actions. In his essay, Twain's incarnated conscience embodies all three models—ones that should be mutually exclusive.

While Clemens planned to make the piece exasperating, it turned out to be one of his most delightful and best-loved short pieces. According to Joseph *Twichell's diary, Clemens's immediate audience loved it. Howells quickly published it in *The *Atlantic Monthly*, and it has been reprinted in numerous anthologies. Part of its protracted appeal lies in the pleasure and horror of its fantasized freedom from social regulation.

"Facts in the Great Landslide Case, The." The earliest version of this piece appeared under the title "A Rich Decision" in Mark Twain's 30 August 1863 letter to the San Francisco *Morning Call*. More reportorial in nature than subsequent versions of his other writings, the account describes an actual mock trial that took place in Virginia City, California, in February 1862. Twain transmuted his report into a fine *sketch for the Buffalo *Express* of 2 April 1870, during Clemens's brief period as an editor and part owner of that newspaper. He characteristically compares western and eastern attitudes toward *social class and prestige, using the *practical joke as an *initiation rite. In this respect, this work is similar to "The *Jumping Frog." Its use of a court of *law as a dramatic setting is, again, very much in the mainstream of Twain's interests.

Twain incorporated this piece, with minor changes, into *Roughing It* as chapter 34, an interpolated tale that breaks up the flow of his own narrative with this allegory of initiation. What stood alone before instead becomes a counterpoint that thematically strengthens a much larger narrative. Twain typically reworked old material in new ways. This piece also highlights how slippery Twain was in working conventional genres to accommodate his own comic vision.

♦ SEE ALSO Work Habits.

FAIRBANKS, MARY MASON (1828–1898). A close friend of Clemens from their meeting on the *Quaker City* in 1867, Fairbanks journeyed alone on that ship while serving as newspaper correspondent for the Cleveland *Herald*, of which her husband was part owner. A mere seven years older than Clemens and a fellow newspaper correspondent, she obscured their common interests by playing the role of "mother" to his "prodigal son" or "cub." According to their game, she was to advise him in matters of propriety, both social and literary, and he was to give her opportunity to do so.

Their correspondence, especially in the years immediately following the *Quaker City* cruise, was substantial, with Clemens writing letters in which he deliberately teased her about his improprieties, all the while swearing he was reformed, reforming, or unreformable. The pattern probably began on shipboard, but the first record we have appears in his letters of December 1867. In the wake of his article in the New York *Herald* in which he blasted the journey, calling the trip a funeral excursion without a corpse, he wrote to fellow passenger Emma Beach that most passengers were piqued by his parting shot and that "even Mrs. Fairbanks felt hurt about that best-natured squib that was ever written . . . & scolds—scolds hard—but she can't deceive this Prodigal Son—I detect the good nature & forgiveness under it all" (5 December 1867).

In his letter to Fairbanks three days earlier, addressed to "My Dear Forgiving Mother—" he offered an extended, tongue-in-cheek apology for breaking his promise to her not to attack the "pilgrims." "I never keep a promise," he explains, "I don't know how." He closes the letter, "Give me another sermon! Yr. Improving Prodigal, Sam L. Clemens" (2 December 1867).

Clemens's teasing continues with reports of his drinking, using slang, and breaking social taboos, and even goes to the point of trying to spark jealousy in Fairbanks. In a letter he wrote to her from her cousin's house, where Clemens stayed briefly during his 1868 lecture tour, he states,

> I am here, the guest of Judge Mason—& happy. Mrs. Mason is *so* good, & so kind, so thoughtful, so untiring in her genuine hospitality, & lets me be just as troublesome as I want to, that I just love her, & it seems as if she were *you*— or your double. She lets me smoke in the house, & bring in snow on my boots, & sleep late, & eat at unseasonable hours, & leaves my valise wide open on the floor & my soiled linen scattered about it just exactly as I leave it & as it *ought* to be to make life truly happy. I tell you I *like* that. It is being at *home*, you know. . . . Don't you wish *you* were here? But we have two pleasant young ladies, & so we don't need you & haven't got any use for you, mother mine. (12 December 1868)

At this point, Fairbanks had already encouraged Clemens to settle down in a marriage, and had even written to Olivia Langdon's family, after Langdon and Clemens had fallen in love, to assure them of Clemens's fundamental decency of character. The flirtation here is obviously fraudulent in a playful way.

Still, Clemens clearly admired her, even to the point of revealing some of that admiration in one of his letters to Olivia: "Livy, was *ever* the love of an ill-matched couple born of both heart & brain? Do superiors ever *love, revere, & honor* inferiors with the brain's consent? Hardly, I think. Mrs. Brooks & Mrs. Fairbanks, brilliant women both, have married away down below them—& it would be hard to convince me that they did not love first & *think* afterward" (4 December 1868). Such a tribute to Fairbanks is all the more conspicuous given that, in spite of his contempt for Abel Fairbanks, Clemens was then trying to purchase a share in the Cleveland *Herald* in order to establish a settled life for himself and Olivia.

The strategies of teasing and contrition developed in his correspondence with Fairbanks parallel in remarkable fashion the kinds of letters he wrote to Olivia when he started courting her, substantially by letter, in late 1868 and 1869. His mock flirtation with Fairbanks served as preparation for real courtship, and he used Fairbanks as his confidante and advisor while he pursued Langdon.

From the beginning, Clemens's exchanges with Fairbanks included a professional component, which maintained its tone over their nearly thirty-year correspondence, long after the mock flirtation disappeared. From shipboard days, Clemens allowed Fairbanks to edit some of his letters, and later when Clemens was composing *The Innocents Abroad*, Fairbanks supplied him with her travel writing in order to help him recollect details of the journey. For years thereafter, he wrote to her about his work, sometimes apologetically for his irreverence. His playing "prodigal" to her "mother" was merely a cover for a different game, however; her secret approval under the guise of disapproval was the kind of response he used to judge how far he could push the bounds of humor.

FALSE ATTRIBUTIONS. When then–Vice President Dan Quayle conspicuously and publicly miscorrected a school child's correct spelling of "potato," he was reviled in the national press as an idiot, until he quoted Twain for purportedly saying that only those who lack imagination stick with conventional spelling. Whether the story died down because Twain bailed out Quayle or because the story had already grown old is uncertain, but Quayle's effort to lean on Twain's authority for exoneration is unquestionably an American tradition. This practice explains, perhaps, the equally widespread tendency to ascribe apt witticisms to Twain, whether he said them or not.

In many cases, now unknown contemporaries of Twain coined these famous bons mots, but still they live on under the umbrella of the perennial favorite. "Politics makes strange bedfellows" and "Everyone talks about the weather but nobody does anything about it" were both coined by Clemens's neighbor and one-time literary collaborator Charles Dudley *Warner. In his *autobiography, Clemens quoted fellow comedian Bill Nye when he wrote that "Wagner's music is better than it sounds."

Many other quotations commonly attributed to Twain probably did not come from him. Examples include "When I was a boy of fourteen, my father was so ignorant I could hardly stand to have the old man around. But when I got to be twenty one, I was astonished at how much the old man had learned in seven years." "Patriot: the person who can holler the loudest without knowing what he is hollering about." "We all live in the protection of certain cowardices which we call our principles." "The coldest winter I ever spent was last summer in San Francisco." And "When I feel the urge to exercise, I lie down until it passes away." None of these has been found anywhere in Twain's writings.

They may, however, have been said by him in conversation and then passed on from there. Twain gave so many newspaper *interviews, spent so many evenings at formal banquets where bons mots were de rigueur, and passed so many visits with famous people who would preserve his best repartee, that it is not possible to say categorically that none of these came from Clemens. Many of them reflect things he did say, so these false attributions are often actually gradual distortions of lines that, in other contexts, did not quite resonate as well. Certainly this is the case of one of the most famous false attributions, "The reports of my death have been greatly exaggerated," which is false merely in the sense that it slightly alters Twain's exact words: "The report of my illness grew out of his illness; the report of my death was an exaggeration."

Given how easy it is, though, to ascribe one's opinions to Twain, many of the quotations passing as his are pure fabrications, designed to give the imprimatur of America's most famous indigenous sage to whatever fad, fancy, product, or political agenda is in the limelight at any given moment. The reports of Twain's ubiquity are greatly exaggerated.

♦ SEE ALSO Critical Reception; Public Image.

FASHION. When he wrote "Clothes make the man; naked people have little or no influence in society," Twain engaged in his frequent class leveling, saying not that *fine* clothing matters, but that *some* clothing matters to make one's position in society. From the sociologist's position of dispassionate distance, Twain frequently commented on clothing as a system of social symbology, a way of making oneself conspicuous within one's peer group. In this, he was distancing himself from the Victorian *taste for relative drabness in adult clothing among classes striving for respectability. Throughout his career, Twain called attention not merely to Victorian plainness in dress, but also to the Victorian obsession with what dress means, in direct contrast to the ostensible value of plain clothing.

Still, he himself was also caught between Victorian material opulence and puritan simplicity. His interest in the social rituals of fashion and the symbolic meanings of kinds of clothing arose when, as a young man, he shifted from village simplicity to working-class cosmopolitan and dandy as a steamboat pilot, then to western rough as a silver miner, to San Francisco bohemian, and finally to eastern gentleman. In each incarnation, his behavior commented on clothing as a marker of status change, and he often fought against the strictures of those changes. For instance, he continued wearing the thin black "string" neckties fashionable in the far West after he moved to Hartford in the early 1870s. In an 18 December 1874 letter to William Dean *Howells, Clemens remarks on his change in fashion:

> You & Aldrich have made one woman deeply & sincerely grateful—Mrs. Clemens. For months—I may say years—she has shown an unaccountable animosity toward my neck-tie, even getting up in the night to take it with the tongs & blackguard it—sometimes going so far as to threaten it. When I said you & [Thomas Bailey] Aldrich had given me two *new* neckties, & that they were in a paper in my overcoat pocket, she was in a fever of happiness until she found out I was going to frame them; then all the venom in her nature gathered itself together—insomuch that I, being near to a door, went without, perceiving danger. *Now* I wear one of the new neck-ties, nothing being sacred in Mrs. Clemens's eyes that can be perverted to a gaud that shall make the person of her husband more alluring than it was aforetime.

Here Clemens made a great game out of conformity, recognizing that the point of fashion was to call attention to one's self by *not* calling attention to oneself.

He, on the other hand, often resisted fashion to call attention to it as much as to himself. In *My Mark Twain*, Howells recalled first meeting "Clemens . . . wearing a sealskin coat, with the fur out, in the satisfaction of a caprice, or the love of strong effect which he was apt to indulge in life. In spite of his own warmth in it, [it] sent the cold chills through me when I once accompanied it down Broadway, and shared the immense publicity it won him." But as much as Howells found discomfort in a breach of convention, Twain knew and called attention to the ways in which people suffered discomfort for the sake of fashion. In *The Adventures of Tom Sawyer*, for instance, he describes the young men and ladies who served as Sunday School teachers wearing excruciatingly uncomfortable clothing, including collars that cut the neck and boots with toes absurdly "turned sharply up, in the fashion of the day, like sleigh-runners—an effect patiently and laboriously produced by the young men by sitting with their toes pressed against a wall for hours together" (chapter 4). He similarly describes missionary efforts in Hawaii to get locals to wear clothing, which they do "incorrectly," if one assumes that the correct purpose of clothing is to cover one's nakedness. But Twain points out they have found another, truer point of clothing: "They only wanted it for grandeur. . . . They gazed at each other with happy admiration, and it was plain to see that the young girls were taking note of what each other had on, as naturally as if they had always lived in a land of Bibles and knew what churches were for; here was the evidence of a dawning civilization" (chapter 67). In passages such as these, Twain mocks the ostensible symbolism of Sunday clothing, suggesting that in spite of respectably muted coloring, such clothing was designed not to show humility before God but ostentation before neighbors.

Twain was also acutely aware of the class implications of clothing. In *Roughing It*, the contrast between eastern swallowtail coats on the one hand, and flannel shirts over pantaloons stuffed into boot tops on the other, marks the passage from East to West, from refined to rough. The chapter on Scotty Briggs and the parson contrasts the lower-class flamboyance in bright red flannels to the somber black and white of the college-educated minister. Twain depicts this contrast not as one of real hierarchy so much as of fashion, and he makes the implicit statement that the bland propriety of the aristocratic easterner will win no converts in the democratic West.

In this spirit, Twain, the "Wild Humorist of the Pacific slope," persisted in his affectations of western fashion after he moved East. He implicitly criticized propriety when he pretended to an absentmindedness, or even unconsciousness, to fashion. His wife played into this game, as his autobiographical story about the reception he went to for President Grover Cleveland recounts. When Clemens's wife put a note in his vest pocket to remind him to take his galoshes off before seeing the president, he presented the note to the president's wife.

Howells believed that these breaches were in part Clemens's "keen feeling for costume which the severity of our modern tailoring forbids men; yet he also enjoyed the shock, the offence, the pang which it gave the sensibilities of others" (*My Mark Twain*). While Howells did understand Clemens's iconoclastic side, he failed to recognize the internal struggle Clemens's fashion rebellion included—his breaches of propriety apparently cost him many a pang. As much as he admired colorful clothing, he could not easily resist the compulsion to conform, as he explains in the posthumously published "Corn-Pone Opinions":

> A new thing in costume appears—the flaring hoop-skirt, for example—and the passers-by are shocked, and the irreverent laugh. Six months later everybody is reconciled; the fashion has established itself; it is admired, now, and no one laughs. Public opinion resents it before, public opinion accepts it now, and is happy in it. Why? . . . The instinct that moves to conformity did the work. . . . What is its seat? The inborn requirement of Self-approval. But as a rule our self-approval has its source . . . in the approval of other people.

Clemens wanted the approval of others, but only approved of himself if he had the courage to defy fashion. Not surprisingly, then, when large-scale iconoclasm cost him and his family too dearly, he turned to the symbolic resistance of odd clothing. But while at the end of his life he wished to wear bright colors, the most he could do was wear a white suit in the winter. As usual, Twain was more the rebel in imagination than in fact.

Feminism. see Women's Rights.

"Fenimore Cooper's Literary Offenses." Published in 1895 in the *North American Review and ultimately one of Twain's best-known pieces of literary criticism, this is the single work most readily cited to prove that Twain advocated and practiced literary *realism and its cousin, plain *style. After all, in the essay Twain promotes a literary art that depends on careful observation, consistency, thorough plotting, plausibility, and "a straightforward style." Yet Twain himself violated most of these tenets, sometimes deliberately for the sake of humor, other times under the impression that he was writing realistic dialogue in love scenes—for example in *The American Claimant*, written about the same time as his Cooper essay.

The animosity in the Cooper essay, then, comes from some other source than mere concern over the form of American literature; it seems, in fact, to have emerged from Clemens's own love-hate relationship with James Fenimore Cooper's works. As a child and young man, Clemens read Cooper avidly, but in his early adulthood he began a lifelong reaction against Romantic literature for promoting falsely idealistic standards of human behavior. The energy of Clemens's attack attests to his deep disappointment, a sense that he had been conned into a dangerous idealism. Such became a repeating motif in much of his literature, from *The Innocents Abroad* and *Roughing It*, in which the "innocent" narrator is repeatedly disabused of his romantic preconceptions, to *The Gilded Age* and *Adventures of Huckleberry Finn*, in which questions of what and how to read are central to the plots. In this sense, Twain advocated not so much a literary realism as a moral realism, which makes his Cooper essay so powerful.

♦ see also Reading, Clemens's.

Fields, Annie (1834–1915) **and James T.** (1817–1881). Annie and James T. Fields were an influential couple at the center of the American literary world. James, a publisher, writer, and editor, served as editor in chief of The *Atlantic Monthly* from 1862 to 1871. On assuming control of the magazine, he attempted to expand the *Atlantic*'s readership and influence beyond its New England base in order to make the journal truly national in scope and influence. Under his direction, it began to review, accept, and solicit work from western writers, including Twain. Annie Fields, in a position to observe and influence the inner workings of the literary community, preserved much of her insight in her own writing, including literary biographies and a revealing account of her own position in *Memories of a Hostess*. In this autobiography, she recounts her impression of Clemens in 1875: "It is curious and interesting to watch this growing man of forty—to see how he studies and how high his aims are," suggesting that Clemens was still following Anson *Burlingame's advice always to strive to improve himself.

FINANCES. After a childhood spent in poverty, Clemens not surprisingly pursued *money energetically throughout his life. Despite this preoccupation with wealth, Clemens had little sense of how to keep it, was never able to live for very long within his means, and rarely kept track of his income and expenditures with any great care. He spent money with a free hand, even when he did not have it. Such a person easily goes bankrupt, but not every bankrupt spendthrift ends his life worth half a million dollars (equivalent to the buying power of about ten million dollars today).

Clemens began his earning life in St. Louis in 1853, working at piecework wages, as typesetters traditionally did. While compositors in St. Louis had a strong union, with most skilled typesetters earning around twelve dollars a week, Clemens was so green that he could work only fast enough to earn about eight or nine a week. This amount put him ahead of the average laborer (who earned roughly a dollar a day for a six-day week), so even as an inexperienced typographer he managed to make a living wage. Still, he moved on to the big cities of the East to try to do better, only to find himself working for even less and losing money all the time. He returned to his brother Orion *Clemens's shop in Iowa in 1854 before setting out on a second career as a riverboat pilot.

Clemens first experienced prosperity beginning in 1859 when he earned his pilot's license. By June 1860, he bragged in a 27 June 1860 letter to Orion about being able to "'bank' in the neighborhood of $100 a month." After living expenses, then, Clemens was *saving* over four times the average worker's wages, putting him very much in the aristocracy of labor. This is all the more astonishing given that the average gap between skilled and unskilled labor in 1850 was only about 50%, rising to a high of 300% by the 1880s. Clemens had found one of the few laborer's jobs that could put him into America's financial upper-crust, though these wages were still nothing compared to what he would earn later as a writer. His reaction was to speculate in various ill-considered *business ventures; despite these, by the time the Civil War drove Clemens out of piloting in March 1861, he had saved enough to finance his trip to the West and several months of silver prospecting. When he gave up the prospecting in August 1862, he was in debt, and his mother and brother were pushing him to return to piloting. His own image of overwhelming wealth, however, kept him in the West:

> What in thunder are pilot's wages to me? which question, I beg humbly to observe, is of a *general* nature, and not discharged particularly at you. But it is

singular, isn't it, that such a matter should interest Orion, when it is of no earthly consequence to me? I never have *once* thought of returning home to go on the river again, and I never expect to do any more piloting at any price. My livelihood must be made in this country—and if I have to wait longer than I expected, let it be so.... Do not tell any one that I had any idea of piloting again at present—for it is all a mistake. This country suits me, and it *shall* suit me, whether or no. (to Pamela A. Moffet, 15 August 1862)

Protesting too much, he turned that September to working as a reporter for the Virginia City *Territorial Enterprise* at twenty-five dollars per week.

In *Roughing It*, Twain describes Nevada's flush times of the 1860s as a period when he did not need to draw his salary because money was so free. Even discounting the exaggeration, he did have the money to invest heavily in mining stocks while working as a reporter, and by all accounts, he lived higher than his mere salary would justify. But by the time he moved to San Francisco, his investments were draining his coffers, and his income as a writer was barely enough to sustain him and his investments. Not until he became a traveling correspondent and lecturer in 1866 did he find himself earning a steady enough income to keep out of debt, though he worried perpetually about money.

His marriage to Olivia Langdon did nothing to ease his concerns. Even though the overwhelmingly large sales of *The Innocents Abroad* and his very successful lecturing put him in an acceptable financial situation to court the heiress of a coal fortune, he felt pressure to sustain the income. Hence, he returned to journalism, seeking an ownership position on a major daily newspaper. Looking especially in Cleveland and Hartford, he finally settled on Buffalo under the advice of and with the financial support of his soon-to-be father-in-law, Jervis Langdon. Olivia herself had nothing but theoretical training in housekeeping. While she sketched out budgets in her journals, she had no clue how expensive her tastes were, and each time she made out a budget, she exceeded it substantially.

When Buffalo turned out to be unsatisfactory, Olivia and Samuel moved to Hartford (losing significant money on the sale of their Buffalo house, given to them by Langdon, and on Clemens's interest in the Buffalo *Express*), but the demands of their style of living made it imperative not only for Clemens to write more books, but to lecture throughout several winter seasons. As Olivia wrote in a 25 September 1873 letter to her mother, "Lecturing is what Mr C. always speaks of doing when there seems any need of money." He could earn two thousand dollars a month lecturing, and with his roughly three hundred dollars a month in royalties and Olivia's three to five hundred dollars a month from her share of the family business, they should have been able to live like royalty and stay within their means. In fact, they often had to have their income supplemented by large checks of up to a thousand dollars from Olivia's mother.

Despite an economic downturn in 1873 that lasted for years, and their feelings of poverty, the couple had and spent money the likes of which most American workers would never know, and about which Samuel himself could only have dreamed as a young man. When the depression finally eased at the end of the 1870s, and prosperity returned in the early 1880s, Clemens finally lived without financial concern. At this point, beyond supporting his brother and his mother, he began investing heavily, not only in his own publishing company, *Webster and Company, and in the *Paige typesetter, but also in many other stocks. Even Clemens's by then formidable income could not sustain the strain. He spent $3,000 a month alone on the Paige machine, which ultimately cost Clemens $200,000. Webster and Company also swallowed cash. After the firm's early high-flying successes selling Ulysses S. Grant's memoirs and *Adventures of Huckleberry Finn*, business went downhill. By July 1893, a financial statement disclosed $62,000 in uncollected installment accounts on the firm's albatross, the Library of American Literature. At the same time, the firm's liabilities totaled nearly $200,000, mostly to Olivia Clemens, who had sunk much of her estate in the firm. When the company went into receivership in April 1894, 101 creditors, not counting Olivia, filed claims totaling nearly $80,000.

Fortunately for Clemens, in 1893 a friend put him in contact with Henry H. Rogers, one of the principals of the Standard Oil Company and an ardent admirer of Twain's work. Rogers took over Clemens's finances, and when Webster & Company entered bankruptcy proceedings, Rogers negotiated for Clemens. He insisted that Olivia Clemens be considered the preferred creditor, assigning her all of Twain's copyrights. A typical post-bankruptcy year's copyright statements from Chatto and Windus and Harper and Brothers show the wisdom of that plan, with Chatto and Windus paying the Clemenses over £181 (worth about $25,000 current U.S. dollars) and Harper and Brothers, $1,500 (worth about $31,000 current dollars). Royalty statements from the American Publishing Company no longer exist, but would presumably have been substantial, too. Even though many creditors fought the assignment of Twain's copyrights, Rogers's name, deep pockets, and hard negotiating carried the day. With the most valuable assets protected, most creditors agreed to take little immediately in favor of receiving full compensation over time, though a few did settle for their share of existing assets. These few never did receive full payment, the myth that Twain paid back every dollar of his debt notwithstanding.

On 1 September 1897, Bainbridge Colby, the attorney who managed the receivership, issued his final report in a letter to Rogers, showing Clemens fully out of debt. Clemens's grueling around-the-world *lecture tour, coupled with Rogers's handling of Clemens's investments, put the Clemens family back on a solid financial footing, enabling them to live up to their accustomed style. Without Rogers, the family probably would have had to change its way of life. Clemens knew he did

223

not have the skill to manage his own accounts. As he put it in a 25 August 1894 letter to Rogers, written while the publishing house was in receivership, "She keeps the accounts; and as she ciphers it we can't get crowded for money for eight months yet. I didn't know that. But I don't know much anyway." Considering, however, that Olivia knew little more about finances, it is fortunate that in a time of financial trouble, they could rely on someone of Rogers's acumen.

♦ SEE ALSO Langdon, Jervis and Olivia Lewis.

FOLLOWING THE EQUATOR (1897). The verse from Ecclesiastes "Of making books there is no end, and much study is a weariness of the flesh" encapsulated Clemens's attitude toward writing many of his books, but none so much so as *Following the Equator*. Clemens confronted the task in a bleak frame of mind and found the pull through the book colored by extraneous events. In fact, the extraneous prompted the book in the first place. Having gone into bankruptcy in 1894, Clemens decided to recoup his losses by going on an around-the-world *lecture tour and writing a book about the voyage. He had lectured previously when he needed to raise money quickly, and in writing a travel book, he was returning to the pattern of his first success, *The Innocents Abroad*, interpreting the world for his stay-at-home compatriots. He contracted with the American Publishing Company to produce a subscription book. He also tried to negotiate with various magazines to provide articles about his tour, but eventually rejected their offers because of the difficulty of handling the tour, the book, and the journalism. He made this choice even though the American Publishing Company offered a minimum return on the book of ten thousand dollars with a likely return of thirty thousand, while *The Century Magazine* offered a sure twelve thousand dollars for a mere twelve articles.

Clemens explained his decisions in a 15 June 1895 letter to Henry H. *Rogers:

> I have a good reason for inclining to Bliss at this time: I can write a *subscription* book of travels without any effort, but to write travels for *serial* publication is hideous hard work. I am not committed to any magazine yet—and I believe it will be wisest to remain unfettered. The Century people actually proposed that I *sign a contract to be funny* in those 12 articles. That was pure insanity. Why, it makes me shudder every time I think of those articles. I don't think I could ever write one of them without being under the solemnising blight of that disgusting recollection.

As much as he rebelled against the thought, what he recognized in the magazine proposal was that his very insolvency made for good publicity. People watched the famous author avidly to see if, in his age and circumstances, he could pull himself out of the hole, and publishers were willing to pay him top dollar to get a piece of the action.

Such morbid world-girdling curiosity about Clemens's fate made his lecture tour a possibility even as his creditors also used publicity to undermine Clemens's position. Repeatedly sued by creditors, and threatened with public humiliation as a cheat who was trying to sequester property while his creditors waited to be paid, Clemens was aware that the success of his tour required that he appease the reporters dogging his story, along with his creditors. Rogers wanted to play hardball, Olivia wanted to satisfy her honor by paying off the creditors, and Clemens kept the eye on the prize—the resuscitation of his reputation as a commercial property. Once on his tour in July, he found himself a cynosure as never before, despite his celebrity since publishing *Innocents Abroad* nearly thirty years earlier.

Hounded by questions about his financial dealings, and advised by his lawyers to pay all of his debt—regardless of any possible lesser settlement that might be sanctioned by bankruptcy law—he needed to make sure the publicity went his way. As he wrote to Rogers, he promised to pay his debts in full and "as long as the promise must be made, it was necessarily well to make it *public*" (17 August 1895). So he arranged an interview in Vancouver with his nephew, Samuel A. Moffett, a reporter for the San Francisco *Examiner*. Moffett and Twain together managed to get much of the interview published in the New York *Times*, giving broad publicity to Clemens's promise to pay his debts and those of his publishing firm, including those he was not legally bound to pay:

> It has been reported that I sacrificed, for the benefit of the creditors, the property of the publishing firm whose financial backer I was, and that I am now lecturing for my own benefit. This is an error. I intend the lectures, as well as the property, for the creditors. The law recognizes no mortgage on a man's brain, and a merchant who has given up all he has may take advantage of the rules of insolvency and start free again for himself; but I am not a business man, and honor is a harder master than the law. It cannot compromise for less that a hundred cents on the dollar, and its debts never outlaw. (*Times*, 17 August 1895)

So ended the North American phase of his lecture tour through the northernmost tier of the United States and Canada, accompanied by his wife, daughter Clara, and James B. Pond, who arranged the North American section of the tour. Playing to excellent crowds almost everywhere, he finished this leg with a public relations coup that would set himself up well for the rest of the journey.

He then embarked from Victoria, British Columbia, to begin a tour of the British Empire. He had hoped to revisit Hawaii first, but a quarantine prevented this, so he continued his voyage west, stopping in Australia, New Zealand, India, Ceylon (Sri Lanka), and South Africa before ending in London. Throughout the trip, indeed even before the trip began, Clemens's health showed signs of age and worry. He had been troubled by rheumatism in his writing arm for years. By 1895, he suffered from gout and skin ulcers as well. As he put it in a letter to Rogers on the eve of departure for the lecture tour, "I am progressing. There is more Clemens than carbuncle, now. This is a considerable improvement. It puts the balance of importance where it belongs" (11 June 1895). But the work and worry load encouraged relapses, and he suffered throughout the tour, adding debilitating coughs to his list of ailments.

Perhaps the one uplifting aspect of the tour was that his audiences greeted his effort to recover his losses as an act of heroism. He was treated as a visiting dignitary, and his *celebrity enabled him to see people and places that would otherwise have been denied to him. The resulting book is in part a testament to the kindness of his audiences, but he remained cool enough to the blandishments of his hosts to deal out criticism as readily as praise. Not surprisingly, *Following the Equator* is Clemens's most mature travel book, and while all of them gain their spice from balancing enthusiasm with criticism, the tone of this book is milder even as the criticisms are more profound.

Throughout the tour, Clemens kept notebooks, but his plan of writing on shipboard did not pan out. His health and the work he did perfecting his lectures impeded his progress. He consequently planned to hole up in London for the winter of 1896–1897 in order to write the volume. He expected to be joined by his daughters Susy and Jean in England, allowing him to have his family together, yet before he could fairly settle in London, news of Susy's illness reached him. Olivia and Clara immediately returned to America, leaving Clemens behind in London, where he received word of his daughter's death. Still under contract, Clemens turned to the task of producing a subscription book of typically generous proportions. The circumstances could not have been less auspicious, but the quick result was Clemens's largest work, 712 printed pages. In the gloom of mourning, Clemens discovered something not mentioned in Ecclesiastes, that in making books, there is a loss of consciousness from other difficulties that are not new under the sun.

Writing, then, from October 1896 to May 1897, he compiled an enormous manuscript, which was larger originally, including such excised sections as "The Enchanted Sea-Wilderness" and "Newhouse's Jew Story." Frank Bliss, without Clemens's permission, cut more, issuing the elaborately illustrated volume in November 1897. Meanwhile, Clemens's English publisher produced a different version, keeping the material that Bliss had cut and issuing the longer volume under the title *More Tramps Abroad* in late 1897.

The book's financial returns did not meet expectations in America, selling only twenty thousand copies by the end of 1897. The decline of *subscription publishing itself contributed to the problem; sales simply could not reach the volume Clemens had attained with earlier subscription books. Since Clemens had received a ten thousand dollar advance, he got little more from the book. While disappointed, he found that the money did what it needed to do; it gave Rogers funds to invest, and money to work with in paying off Clemens's debts.

Neither exceptionally popular in its own day nor reprinted regularly since, *Following the Equator* has only recently become the focus of much critical attention. Late-twentieth-century interest in the literature of the colonial and postcolonial period has called attention to this book, in which Clemens sardonically discovers the great crimes of *imperialism even as he does little to challenge the one empire he admired—the British. But as much as his audience included the British, and as much as he felt that British rule was preferable to that of any other European imperial power, he still attacked imperialism per se. For instance, he writes, "All the territorial possessions of all the political establishments in the earth—including America, of course—consist of pilferings from other people's wash" (chapter 63), satiric understatement all the more devastating for suggesting that colossal and destructive wrongs were committed for trivial ends.

Clemens rooted his attack on imperialism in a much deeper philosophical position. Like many thinkers of his era, he began with a comfortable belief in the moral as well as technological superiority of European civilization, but in the very process of comparing cultures, he discovered cultural relativism. He came to see what most Europeans, locked in a static idea of moral value, could not—namely that Europeans did not recognize their own moral failings because they had become commonplace, too obvious: "A crime persevered in a thousand years ceases to be a crime, and becomes a virtue. This is the law of custom, and custom supersedes all other forms of law" (chapter 63).

Clemens himself, though, was unwilling to abandon a belief in some transcendent morality. Without it, he could not call European "virtues" crimes, nor could he have denied European superiority in his often quoted line, "There are many humorous things in the world; among them the white man's notion that he is less savage than the other savages" (chapter 21). He clearly continued to believe in savagery; he just no longer believed that any people had transcended it. In drawing this conclusion, Clemens found an emotionally and intellectually valuable way to define civilization and savagery both. He looked behind a culture's mores to the impulses undergirding them, allowing him to see morality not in the simple rules a culture follows but in the moral quality of having rules at all. For instance, when describing the sentiment of modesty, he writes,

Without doubt modesty is nothing else than a holy feeling; and without doubt the person whose rule of modesty has been transgressed feels the same sort of wound that he would feel if something made holy to him by his religion had suffered a desecration. I say "rule of modesty" because there are about a million rules in the world, and this makes a million standards to be looked out for. Major Sleeman mentions the case of some high-caste veiled ladies who were profoundly scandalized when some English young ladies passed by with faces bare to the world; so scandalized that they spoke out with strong indignation and wondered that people could be so shameless as to expose their persons like that. And yet "the legs of the objectors were naked to mid-thigh." Both parties were clean-minded and irreproachably modest, while abiding by their separate rules, but they couldn't have traded rules for a change without suffering considerable discomfort. (chapter 50)

While cultural rules differ, says Clemens, the feelings behind them do not, so no culture can legitimately judge the rules of another. After all, as necessary as they are, "all human rules are more or less idiotic" (chapter 50).

By this standard, Clemens describes true civilization as respect for the moral impulses of any culture even if one cannot respect the particular rules of other cultures. Beginning with the text, from *Pudd'nhead Wilson's New Calendar*, "True irreverence is disrespect for another man's god," chapter 53 of *Following the Equator* explains his idea of civilization. First describing his audience with a Hindu holy man who had "attained to what among the Hindus is called the 'state of perfection'" and is therefore considered to be a god, Clemens explains the similarities between Hindu and Christian renunciation of the "vanities and comforts of the world" in order to further their spiritual quests. Yet he notes the contempt Christians have for the Hindu devotee, in whom they see

merely a crank. . . . The ordinary reverence, the reverence defined and explained by the dictionary, costs nothing. Reverence for one's own sacred things—parents, religion, flag, laws, and respect for one's own beliefs—these are feelings which we cannot even help. They come natural to us; they are involuntary, like breathing. There is no personal merit in breathing. But the reverence which is difficult, and which has personal merit in it, is the respect which you pay, without compulsion, to the political or religious attitude of a man whose beliefs are not yours. You can't revere his gods or his politics, and no one expects you to do that, but you could respect his belief in them if you tried hard enough; and you could respect *him*, too, if you tried hard enough.

By this standard, Clemens pleads for a culture of respect, not so much for individual behavior as for the impulses that make living in this difficult world possible. In such an attitude, Clemens was clearly generations ahead of his time.

♦ SEE ALSO Finances; Patriotism; Reverence; Tours.

FOOD. At the end of the eighteenth century, in "What Is an American," Hector St. John de Crèvecoeur described the basis of American *patriotism not as connection to a common culture, king, or ideal of nation or state, but rather as the love of

American prosperity: "What attachment can a poor European emigrant have for a country where he had nothing? The knowledge of the language, the love of a few kindred as poor as himself, were the only cords that tied him; his country is now that which gives him his land, bread, protection, and consequence; *Ubi panis ibi patria* is the motto of all emigrants."

Where one's bread is, there is one's country. If the number of comments Twain makes in his travel writings is any indication, this was certainly his primary idea of patriotism. At least, the kinds of panegyrics many of Twain's contemporaries spent on an ideal of country, he spent on America's food.

Early on, of course, he heaped praise not on America's food but rather on the country food of Missouri. Young Clemens, on his first visit to the eastern seaboard in 1853, wrote longingly home about the foods he missed. Albert Bigelow Paine in his biography of Twain says that Clemens "had been accustomed to the Southern mode of cooking, and wrote home complaining that New-Yorkers did not have 'hot-bread' or 'biscuits,' but ate 'light-bread,' which they allowed to get stale, seeming to prefer it in that way." Later as a steamboat pilot, Clemens acquired more cosmopolitan tastes, and when working as a miner in the West, he learned to eat bacon and beans one month, oysters and champagne the next. Such wide-ranging experience of American food found its way into his writings throughout his life. In "No. 44, The Mysterious Stranger," for example, he speaks of food with almost religious intensity:

> Hot corn-pone from Arkansas—split it, butter it, close your eyes and enjoy! Fried spring chicken—milk-and-flour gravy—from Alabama. Try it, and grieve for the angels, for they have it not! Cream-smothered strawberries, with the prairie-dew still on them—let them melt in your mouth, and don't try to say what you feel! Coffee from Vienna—fluffed cream—two pellets of saccharin—drink, and have compassion for the Olympian gods that know only nectar!

Typically, he concentrates mostly on homely American foods, excepting only the Vienna coffee, which he discovered in the 1890s while living in Austria.

In singling out Vienna coffee, Clemens marked a radical change from his 1879 opinion about the typical European brew. In the penultimate chapter of *A Tramp Abroad*, when he puts the capstone on his incessant criticism of European food by comparing the European article with the American, he begins with the coffee:

> In Europe, coffee is an unknown beverage. You can get what the European hotel keeper thinks is coffee, but it resembles the real thing as hypocrisy resembles holiness. It is a feeble, characterless, uninspiring sort of stuff....
> The milk used for it is what the French call "Christian" milk—milk which has been baptized. After a few month's acquaintance with European "coffee,"

one's mind weakens, and his faith with it, and he begins to wonder if the rich beverage of home, with its clotted layer of yellow cream on top of it is not a mere dream, after all. (chapter 49)

Thus he begins a course-by-course criticism of a day's food on the continent, which illustrates his point that "a man accustomed to American food and American domestic cookery would not starve to death suddenly in Europe; but I think he would gradually waste away, and eventually die." He follows this with a two-column list of his favorite American foods, particularized by locality when possible, covering nearly every region and its specialties. He includes such things as "Fried Chicken, Southern style," "Virginia bacon," "Philadelphia terapin soup," "Connecticut Shad," "Missouri partridges," "Brook trout, from Sierra Nevadas," "Boston bacon and beans," "Saratoga potatoes," and, of course, "Apple pie."

He gives this list in full knowledge that he speaks out of a kind of patriotism. He vaunts his provinciality, even as he acknowledges that other countries would have reciprocal narrowness: "Foreigners cannot enjoy our food, I suppose, any more than we can enjoy theirs. It is not strange; for tastes are made, not born. I might glorify my bill of fare until I was tired; but after all, the Scotchman would shake his head and say, 'Where's your haggis?' and the Fijian would sigh and say, 'Where's your missionary?'" The flippancy of his remarks belies his deeper sense of patriotism in leveling the cuisines of civilization and savagery alike. No need, suggests Twain, for Americans to be embarrassed about their homely but tasty and plentiful food. No need to bow before the haute cuisine of European *tables d'hote*. He subtly makes a similar point at the end of chapter 17 of *Roughing It* when he says, "Nothing helps scenery like ham and eggs." In other words, refined appreciation cannot begin until one is fed. Later in life, during an interview over breakfast, he played on the same theme in stating that "bacon would improve the flavor of an angel," once again putting the low over the high.

In this implicit rejection of American inferiority to all things European, Twain shows his proximity to Crèvecoeur's remarks. In no place does he better demonstrate this than in *Adventures of Huckleberry Finn*. Huck's famous praise of the raft as a place where one feels "mighty free and easy and comfortable" follows his first food in a day: "Jim he got out some corn-dodgers and buttermilk, and pork and cabbage, and greens—there ain't nothing in the world so good, when it's cooked right" (chapter 18). The country way, Huck implies, is just right, and Twain behind Huck gives the civilized standard of experience by which Huck's opinion is legitimized.

Much of *Huckleberry Finn* is about food. Even the first name of the title character comes from the common name for a wild blackberry that grows primarily in the northeastern United States. When once a reader begins thinking in this course, the name "Finn" easily conjures the fish that Huck so often catches and fries. As early as the third paragraph of his narrative, Huck tells us:

The widow rung a bell for supper and you had to come to time. When you got to the table you couldn't go right to eating, but you had to wait for the widow to tuck down her head and grumble a little over the victuals, though there warn't really anything the matter with them. That is, nothing only everything was cooked by itself. In a barrel of odds and ends, it is different; things get mixed up, and the juice kind of swaps around, and the things go better. (chapter 1)

In many ways this passage sets the stage for a subtle commentary on American culture that pervades the book. In his concern that literature be realistic, Twain refers to food not only to add realistic details but also to insist on honesty about the importance of food in the daily lives of people. Although Huck here dislikes having to come to supper "to time," throughout his story he marks time by his meals. Time and again, when relating some event, Huck describes when it happened by the meal he has just eaten. For instance, chapter 10 begins with the words "After breakfast," and the duration of pap's reformation at the hands of the new judge is marked by the meals pap finagles: "So he took him to his own house, and dressed him up clean and nice, and had him to breakfast and dinner and supper with the family, and was just old pie to him, so to speak. And after supper he talked about temperance." (chapter 5).

Much of Victorian culture emphasized character and soul at the expense of the body. Twain's Huck rejects such idealism. His emphasis on ingestion is not merely realistic; it also serves broadly symbolic ends. Huck repeatedly reveals that his tastes are as homespun as is he. He prefers potluck to a seven-course meal, partly because formal manners require him to be "all cramped up." Symbolically we see Huck as a natural democrat, averse to the constraints of *social class distinctions because people rigidly separated become insipid. Huck is well aware of these class distinctions and ironically accepts them as legitimate. When eating the bread cast upon the waters to find his body, he remarks, "It was 'baker's bread'—what the quality eat—none of your low-down corn-pone" (chapter 8). He seems to appreciate the expense lavished on his low-down, ornery self. He does not, however, say that white bread *tastes* good. He reserves that high praise for the corn-pone he eats again and again throughout the novel. In fact, when he praises food, it is usually the food of the common person: "cold corn-pone, cold corn beef, butter and butter-milk—that is what they had for me down there, and there ain't nothing better that ever I've come across yet" (chapter 17).

It has often been said that *Adventures of Huckleberry Finn* is America's successful declaration of literary independence. The book's references to food support such a claim. Clemens knew his European history, and in chapter 14, speaking of "Louis Sixteenth that got his head cut off," he implicitly reminds us that hunger helped precipitate the French Revolution. Furthermore, in chapter 19 when he mentions

"Marry Antonette," he calls to mind the story that she earned her death by supposedly telling the hungry poor of Paris to eat cake. In his running commentary on class distinctions, and as critical as he is of the American—or at least southern—insistence on hierarchy in spite of democratic ideals, Huck's comments on food remind Americans of what really matters. Huck runs away from brutality; he runs toward good food and good company. *Ubi panis, ibi patria.*

♦ SEE ALSO Domesticity; Speeches.

FRAME NARRATIVE. An ancient and common literary structure by which one story is told within another, the frame narrative is especially common in Twain's oeuvre, including such pieces as "Jim Smiley and his Jumping Frog," "A *True Story, Repeated Word for Word as I Heard It," "Cannibalism in the Cars," "The Whittier Birthday Speech," numerous interpolated stories in all of the travel narratives, *A Connecticut Yankee in King Arthur's Court*, and many of the unfinished works of Twain's later years, such as *"Three Thousand Years among the Microbes," in which the frame narrator masquerades as a translator. While Clemens knew many frame stories in world literature, as in his beloved *Arabian Nights*, he was particularly interested in the tradition of *humor in which the frame narrator buffers the reader from the interior narrator, a low-class comic character.

Perhaps most famous of these in *southwestern humor is T. B. Thorpe's "Big Bear of Arkansas," which begins with the account of a gentleman narrator traveling on the Mississippi River. This narrator tells us precisely how to react to the vernacular narrator of the framed hunting tales. When the inside narrator rudely bursts upon the scene, the gentleman frame narrator says, "Some of the company at this familiarity looked a little angry, and some astonished; but in a moment every face was wreathed in a smile. There was something about the intruder that won the heart on sight. He appeared to be a man enjoying perfect health and contentment; his eyes were as sparkling as diamonds, and good-natured to simplicity. Then his perfect confidence in himself was irresistibly droll." In his condescension, Thorpe's outside narrator is the reader's surrogate. As the outside narrator dismisses the rudeness in order to appreciate the rustic "simplicity," so, too, does the reader. This is the typical formula for framed narration in the short fiction of Twain's day.

Sometimes Twain followed that formula, but often he pushed it beyond its usual borders, destabilizing the comfortable surety of the outside narrator and thus of the reader as well. For instance, in "The *Jumping Frog," the outside narrator, Mark Twain, a man with no sense of humor, tells us that inside narrator Simon Wheeler "had an expression of winning gentleness and simplicity upon his tranquil countenance." The reader follows the cue of Twain's condescension, but by story's end, it becomes clear that Twain's own genteel prejudices have led him into a trap, set by his "friend" and sprung by Wheeler. Whether Wheeler is in on the joke cannot be determined from the story itself, but hints of Wheeler's sensitivity to confidence games, especially in the subject matter of his internal narrative, suggest that "gentleness and simplicity" are not his essence.

In attacking the superiority of the outside narrator, Clemens ironically inverts the usual function of the frame and thereby challenges the superior point of view the reader wishes to bring into the reading. That disruption is not only a source of humor through incongruity between a reader's expectations and the way the story pans out, but also a potential source of deep *satire by disrupting a reader's complacency, a tactic Twain would use in frame stories like "A True Story."

FRENCH REVOLUTION. SEE Revolution.

FREUD, SIGMUND (1856–1939). Although Twain lived in Vienna for several years in the late 1890s and shared many mutual acquaintances with Sigmund Freud, there is no direct evidence that they ever met. Freud, however, did attend at least one performance by Twain in February 1898 (and may have attended others); read Twain regularly and persistently; and referred to Twain in many of his books, including *The Psychopathology of Everyday Life* (1904), *Jokes and Their Relation to the Unconscious* (1905), *The Uncanny* (1919), and *Civilization and Its Discontents* (1939).

GABRILOWITSCH, NINA CLEMENS (1910–1966). The only grandchild of Samuel and Olivia Clemens, Nina Clemens Gabrilowitsch was born to Clara Clemens Gabrilowitsch *Samossoud in Clemens's house in Redding, Connecticut. After living her first three years in Europe, she was raised in Detroit, Michigan; educated at Barnard College; and moved in 1936 to Los Angeles to pursue her career in acting and photography. In 1944, her mother established a trust fund for her, on which she lived for the rest of her life. When her mother died in 1962, she contested the will that had cut her off from any further inheritance from the Twain properties. Samossoud's lawyers settled, giving Gabilowitsch a significant portion of the royalties from Twain's works. Long battling drug addiction, spending time in and out of sanatoriums, she died of an overdose of barbiturates.

While she did marry and divorce, she had no children. Thus, there are no surviving direct descendants of Samuel and Olivia Clemens.

GAMES. Games were, of course, nothing new in Clemens's lifetime, but the scope of organized *leisure did change, with games becoming a regular part of the cultural landscape. Baseball, for instance, became the nation's sport in these years. Developed as a gentleman's sport in the 1840s, taken up by Civil War soldiers as a pastime, and diffused throughout the country by veterans, the sport quickly spread in popularity after the war, with professional play beginning in 1869. Thus, the intrusion of baseball into *A Connecticut Yankee in King Arthur's Court* serves as more than a burlesque element; it represents symbolically the American spirit. Hank Morgan says he introduced the "experiment" of baseball "to replace the tournament with something which might furnish an escape for the extra steam of the chivalry, keep those bucks entertained and out of mischief" (chapter 40), but Twain's juxtaposition of baseball and business chicanery in the story was more than accidental. Baseball as practiced in the early days was rough and tumble, hardly a game of rules at all. As historian J. C. Furnas puts it in *The Americans*, "The atmosphere of a baseball game accepts the stacking of all decks—pretty much the atmosphere of Wall Street c. 1870—and of that other American-grown diversion, poker, based on dead-panned deception." In what other game is "stealing" sanctioned? So in having his knights emulate the American spirit through baseball, Twain set the stage for the short step to Lancelot's "manipulation in the stock market." Lancelot's modernity, then, starts the civil war that brings the end not only to Arthur's reign, but also to Morgan's modernization.

Clemens did not frown on such deceptive sports, but rather merely did not accept the confused moral position of Americans on their practices of work and play. The American interest in athletic games received moral sanction by the advice of such spokesmen as Oliver Wendell Holmes, who advocated sport as a way of ensuring physical fitness. In the last half of the nineteenth century, colleges and universities saw the rise of interscholastic sporting competition, with crew, baseball, football, and other games garnering increasingly widespread participation and acceptability. Yet much of the real motivation behind athletic competition remained gambling, in spite of a generation of moral outrage and legislative prohibition against all "games of chance."

Twain kept that reality before his readers, mocking simultaneously the impulse to moral *reform and the wholesomeness of games. In some cases, he discreetly implied the presence of gambling, as when in *Roughing It* he has Ballou renounce card playing as intrinsically vicious even though he never gambles. Of course, the point of the attack on card playing was that such games were *always* the basis for gambling. More often, he was explicit in referring to gambling, as in "Science vs. Luck"; the "Whittier Birthday Speech"; passages in his autobiography regarding games as diverse as billiards, bowling, and shuffleboard; and, perhaps most importantly, Twain's first nationally known and acclaimed work, "The Jumping Frog," which takes gambling as its text and deceit as its moral. No matter how much, then, the growing American acceptance of leisure was a part of Twain's success, he never let the roots of those games of leisure get too far from the moral center of his writing.

♦ SEE ALSO Work Ethic.

GILDED AGE, THE (1873). When toward the end of his life Twain described how he and Charles Dudley *Warner came to write *The Gilded Age* together, Twain said that he and Warner were complaining to their wives about the debased and demoralizing state of contemporary fiction. Their wives challenged them either to write a better novel or to stop complaining. As professional writers and, at the time, good friends, the two rose to the challenge, satirizing false models of heroism and sanguine expectations of easy success. Other accounts of the novel's genesis, while less dramatic, corroborate Albert Bigelow *Paine's report that the idea to burlesque contemporary fiction was one of the original impulses behind the novel's creation. The other main impulse grew out of the political activism of both authors. Given his experiences as a Washington newspaper correspondent, Clemens had for some time promised to write a book about Washington; Warner's intense interest in politics made him a natural coauthor. Their political interests quickly carried them beyond the limited and mildly satirical intention of burlesquing contemporary fiction to writing what they subtitled "A Story of Today," a wide-ranging satiric assault on the political and economic excesses of the post–Civil War period to which the novel gave its name.

In late 1872 or early 1873 when the two authors decided to collaborate, Twain was a new literary light in an old New England center of literary, religious, and political culture. At the time, Warner had a wide reputation as an essayist; as editor of the influential Hartford *Courant*, the premier journal of a founding branch of the Republican party, he had a stature that Twain lacked. Twain, on the other hand, had surrendered a career in journalism as editor and part owner of the Buffalo *Express* to make a career as a full-time writer of books, determined to follow the successes of *The Innocents Abroad* and *Roughing It* with a string of lucrative volumes. However, he also wanted the high status of people like college-educated, well-connected Warner and therefore used Warner as a mentor of eastern values, gradually expanding his circle of literary peers beyond the western ones such as Bret *Harte and Joseph T. *Goodman.

In collaborating with Warner, Twain attached himself to a man who had access to important eastern journals and whose writing easily pronounced judgment on all things artistic. Warner's "Back-Log Studies" essays in *Scribner's Magazine*, for instance, categorically denounce novels, "written by women," that are

generally immoral in tendency, in which the social problems are handled, unhappy marriages, affinity and passional attraction, bigamy, and the violation of the seventh commandment. These subjects are treated in the rawest manner, without any settled ethics, with very little discrimination of eternal right and wrong, and with very little sense of responsibility for what is set forth. Many of these novels are merely the blind outbursts of a nature impatient of restraint and the conventionalities of society, and are as chaotic as the untrained minds that produce them. (June 1872)

Thus, when the two came to write *The Gilded Age*, one of their primary purposes was to describe what they saw as a proper use of literature, one connected to fundamental ethics and social responsibility. While the specific ideas of what ethics literature should teach and what constitutes social responsibility continued to change over the course of Twain's career, these are thematic concerns that Twain treated repeatedly, most importantly, perhaps, in *Adventures of Huckleberry Finn*.

From the central idea that proper use of reading builds moral character and a true idea of citizenship, the novel spilled quickly outward into a *satire of contemporary events. The recent revelations of Kansas Senator William Pomeroy's attempts to purchase his Senate re-election, the Credit Mobilier scandal, and the wide-scale political corruption in the Tammany Hall machine in New York City provided the authors in early 1873 with plenty of raw material to write a powerful denunciation of political and economic corruption. Their novel reads in part as a political *roman à clef*, with Senator Dilsworthy as a lightly masked rendition of

Pomeroy, and the entire Salt Lick railroad extension a parody of the political and economic machinations involved in financing the Northern Pacific Railroad through the Credit Mobilier.

Both authors also infused substantial amounts of personal experience into the novel, with each writer inventing parts of the plot line around details of his own experience. Twain used his frontier midwestern childhood and collection of crazy, scheming relatives to provide the characters of the Hawkins and Sellers families, while Warner, from his New England, college-educated, law school background, created the experiences of Philip Sterling, Henry Brierly, and the Montague and Bolton families. Both authors had traveled extensively—Warner as a railroad surveyor, Twain as a prospector, both as journalists—and the experience of each found its way into the novel, with Warner providing the details of engineering and surveying, Twain of steamboat racing, mining, and Washington social life, and both an acute understanding of politics during Reconstruction.

In burlesquing what was known as "sensation fiction," the complex plot contains most of the elements of such works, including disasters, unknown parentage, seduction, betrayal, jealousy, murder, self-sacrificing devotion, and courtroom drama. The authors built their wild, multilayered plot around two love triangles: the genteel one of Philip Sterling, Ruth Bolton, and Alice Montague, and the rough-and-tumble one of Laura Hawkins, Henry Brierly, and the bigamist Colonel Selby. Participants in both are driven as much by the quest for lucre as for love. In addition, Twain sweetened the plot through the wild-card Colonel *Sellers, the blow-hard comic villain of the piece, the man whose dreams of fortunes were always so large that present realities disappeared in a haze of speculative glory.

In the course of composition, Twain began the book, developing his characters and his part of the plot until he ran out of steam. He then turned it over to Warner, who developed his characters for the next several chapters until he too needed a rest. The two then tossed the book back and forth, progressively interfering more and more with each other's story lines. When at a point of confusion over plot or character development, they would often write alternative sections, present the possibilities to an audience of their wives, and allow the audience to choose.

Naturally, such an approach was not conducive to coherence, leaving the final result at least as chaotic as those novels that Warner so roundly denounced in *Scribner's*. Twain later admitted as much in a 9 March 1883 letter to George MacDonald, in which he said the novel's "ingredients refused to mix, & the book consisted of *two* novels—& remained so, incurable & vexatiously, spite of all we could do to make the contents blend." In this after-the-fact analysis, Twain incorrectly implies that the two authors had divergent intentions; at the time their intentions were convergent, they just did not know how to execute them collaboratively. At one point, for instance, the novelists began to doubt whether to stick with their original intention to kill off Ruth Bolton through overwork and thus allow the heroic Alice Montague to marry Philip Sterling. This was in keeping with the novel's original plan to mock conventional melodrama by defying expectations. At the last minute, however, they changed their minds, allowing Ruth and Philip the conventional happy ending in a bathetically exaggerated burlesque of melodramatic convention. They never did decide how they wanted to go about developing their satire, through ironic understatement or extravagant reductio ad absurdum.

This confusion of rhetorical position carried through to the last touch in the novel, the parody chapter mottoes. Such mottoes were standard fare in nineteenth-century fiction, usually cribbed from German, French, and Italian as well as English authors. To mock the pretentiousness of such shows of erudition in multi-lingual epigraphs, Warner and Twain enlisted the aid of their friend and neighbor James Hammond *Trumbull, head of the Watkinson Library at Hartford's Trinity College. Trumbull provided mottoes to all chapters and the title page not only in the usual languages, but in Sanskrit, Chinese, various Native American languages, Arabic, and other languages undoubtedly inaccessible to the book's readers. No translations were provided until the 1899 Authorized Uniform Edition of the Writings of Mark Twain. As an extravagant parody of the business of mottoes, unknown languages serve the point nicely, but the authors had Trumbull actually find quotations that would speak to the content of each chapter. If they had intended absolute parody, then nonsense would have served better. Instead, they merely increased the sense of elitism that they intended to mock.

In spite of such rhetorical inconsistencies, core thematic concerns do come through quite clearly. Laura's trial for the murder of her seducer, Colonel Selby, serves as a commentary on political corruption of the legal process, both through the politicization of judgeships and through the jury system. The description of "selling" appropriations bills to Congress effectively attacks the power of special interests to bilk the public. And the repeated examples of the consequences of read-ing, either alone or in the context of a society of readers, suggests the power of literacy to affect the moral vision of individuals for good or ill. The treatment of literacy is perhaps the most perplexing feature of the book. *The Gilded Age* reads as something of a tract against fiction, complaining that music hall dramas and cheap novels were corrupting America's youth with visions of easy success and absolute entitlement. As a writer of fiction, Twain himself was open to the charge of pro-moting escapism, and indeed he came to recognize that his position as a humorist kept people from taking him seriously. This recognition, substantially developed in the wake of the public's response to *The Gilded Age*, forced Twain into repeated examination of his artistic principles, the first consequence of which was that he shifted from Warner's tutelage to that of William Dean *Howells, who was so instrumental in developing American literary *realism.

The authors wrote the novel quite quickly, between mid-January and mid-April 1873, and submitted it to the American Publishing Company in early May, expecting a fall publication date. But production moved slowly, as did canvassing. *Sub-scription publication depended as much on advance sales as on production, and as the search for customers began during a major financial dislocation—substantially caused, ironically, by the Credit Mobilier scandal that Twain and Warner so roundly satirized—sales were not as substantial as Twain had hoped. The book was not released until late December. As Twain put it in a letter, "The fearful financial panic hit the book heavily, for we published it in the midst of it. But nevertheless in the 8 weeks that have now elapsed since the day we published, we have sold 40,000 copies; which give £3000 royalty to be divided between the authors. . . . But for the panic our sale would have been doubled, I verily believe. I do not believe the sale will ultimately go over 100,000 copies" (to Dr. John Brown, 28 February 1874). Indeed, only about another ten thousand copies sold within the remainder of the year. Twain, used to large sales of his humorous books, may have hoped for more, but Warner, unused to such a large audience and such large profits, was delighted. As he put it in a letter to poet Helen Hunt, "There is no doubt . . . that 'by subscription' is the only way for the author to make any money. I will tell you. The copyright just to Clemens and myself . . . on 50000 Gilded Age has been eighteen thousand dollars" (20 July 1874; quoted in Bryant French, *Mark Twain and* The Gilded Age, 1965).

The critical success of the book did not match its commercial success, partly because many reviewers were surprised by the book's content and tone. Perhaps from our perspective, the most surprising thing about the early reviews is how surprised the reviewers were that the book was satirical. We now know Twain primarily as a satirist, but even the book's favorable reviews tell us that as late as 1874 this was not the case. Consider, for example, the review in *Hearth and Home* on 17 January 1874:

> It is sometimes very annoying to begin reading a book under the impression that it is an excellent thing of one sort, and discover that it is an excellent thing of quite a different kind. But such occurrences are not always annoying, by any means, and we have just had an experience of the kind which was one of unmixed pleasure. . . . We confidently expected a treat, and we were not disappointed, though the book turned out to be as unlike what we expected it to be as was possible. We imagined it an extremely funny exaggeration of life with here and there a touch of Mr. Warner's dainty humor, and thought the whole would prove an inimitable burlesque of the modern novel peculiarly rich in the characteristics of both its authors. We find . . . instead . . . the satire of the book is pungent enough to have grown on a red-pepper plant, and the accuracy of aim with which it is delivered is not excelled by that of a Wimbledon prize-fighter.

The reviewer speaks of expecting the merely funny, based on either Twain's "exaggerations" or Warner's "dainty humor," but neither of these categories accounts for the book's cutting edge. In fact, in *The Gilded Age* Twain was learning the serious side of his trade.

At the same time, he learned the dangers of leaving *humor for *satire. In an era in which most journals were affiliated with political parties, political satire did not go unchallenged. Many journals attacked the book to defend their patrons, even though the reviews avoided the book's charges in favor of assaults on the moral character of the authors. The *Chicago Tribune*'s review of 1 February 1874 called the book a fraud that "abused the people's trust" in Twain's reputation as a good-natured humorist. The Boston *Literary World*, in its review of January 1874, basically charged the authors with hypocrisy: "The book has a strong savor of lucre; it was evidently written to sell, and in the hope of gaining a liberal heap of that money, whose worship it purports to ridicule." There was some truth to this, as Twain convinced Warner to publish the book by subscription in order to gain a wider circulation and make money, and both were pleased by the financial results.

But the personal attacks the book generated threatened Twain's reputation, and as long as he wrote to make a living, he could not afford to have his reputation sullied. Perhaps most difficult for him to manage were the attacks on satire itself as a legitimate mode of expression. The *Literary World*, for instance, claimed that any criticism of corruption required a tone of high seriousness because "neither a buffoon nor a bumpkin can successfully lead a reform" (January 1874). As little as two years later, Twain wrote to Howells, "When a humorist ventures upon the grave concerns of life he must do his job better than another man or he works harm to his cause" (23 August 1876). Twain's caution to veil his satire in subsequent books and to suppress publication of others, and his increasingly careful efforts to control his public image, were his reactions to the volleys launched at *The Gilded Age*.

Today, of course, Twain's moral seriousness earns him his stature, and *The Gilded Age* tells us much about Twain's developing powers as a satirist. It also tells us much about Twain's weaknesses as a writer. He here discovered the problems he would continue to have in plotting long, serious novels. His journalistic style and preference for inversions and burlesques always made his plots less a vehicle for meaning than an excuse for ironic vignettes.

The Gilded Age is also worth reading to see Twain's social conservatism at this stage in his development. In calmly acceding to Warner's attack on *women's rights and expressing his own whiggish concern about too broad a franchise, Twain seems unlike the champion of democratic values he ultimately, though always ambivalently, became. For several years, though, he had been following Anson *Burlingame's advice to "seek your comradeships among your superiors in intellect and character; always *climb*," and his acceptance in Hartford suggested to him that he was nearing the top. He adopted the republicanism of his neighbors along with their membership in the Republican party. But as Twain returned over the ensuing decades to this book's concerns with class distinction, women's rights, and democratization, he became progressively less elitist. *The Gilded Age* in many ways stands as a milepost on Twain's journey into moral and political advocacy, as well as a stage in his development of a kind of realistic fiction.

The book's popularity, however, has dwindled partly as a consequence of Twain's success in advocating a different kind of fiction. The melodramatic novels of his day grew less popular as serious literature over the course of his own lifetime, giving way to social realism and *naturalism. No longer recognizing the literary conventions that Twain and Warner parodied, audiences now find the literary burlesque silly rather than biting. The political components of the novel still work, but without a suitable medium they are now read more often in history classes as primers on the mores of an era than as enjoyable fiction. Still, it is a rare book that names an era—the appropriateness of the name and the argument that supports it give the book an enduring interest beyond what it tells us about Twain himself.

♦ SEE ALSO Copyright.

GILLIS, JAMES N. (JIM) (1830–1907) AND STEVE (1838–1918). The
Gillis brothers were part of a family that moved to California during the gold rush and stayed on in the West. Steve, trained as a compositor, was the foreman for the Virginia City *Territorial Enterprise* when Clemens began work there as a reporter in 1862. The two became fast friends, notwithstanding Gillis's proclivity for fighting. Indeed, Gillis served as second to Clemens in his aborted duel with William R. Laird of the Virginia City *Union* in May 1864. When Clemens left Nevada in disgrace in the wake of that dispute, Gillis accompanied him to San Francisco, where both of them found berths on the *Morning Call*. The two roomed together, drank together, and footed each other's bills. When Gillis was arrested for brawling, Clemens posted bond for him and the two fled, Steve to Nevada, Clemens to a cabin in Jackass Gulch, Tuolumne County, California, the home of Steve's brothers, Jim and William, and their mining partner, Dick Stoker. In all, Steve helped keep Clemens's stay out West interesting, introducing him to many incidents and characters that found their way into Twain's works.

The influence of Jim, though brief since Clemens stayed with him a scant three months beginning in December 1864, was substantial. In his autobiography (26 May 1907), Twain credited Jim Gillis with originating the "Tom Quartz" stories in *Roughing It*, the "Bluejay Yarn" from *A Tramp Abroad*, and "The King's Camelopard" from *Adventures of Huckleberry Finn*. Such attributions are overstated, however, as the evidence of Twain's notebook for the period suggests. But Twain did hear many tales from Jim Gillis, who was, by all accounts, a gifted raconteur and yarn spinner from whom Twain learned much about humor.

♦ SEE ALSO Off-color Humor.

GOODMAN, JOSEPH T. (1838–1917). Joseph Goodman was the first in a series of mentors who helped Clemens develop the discipline and self-consciousness of a professional writer. Goodman, like Clemens, learned the printing trade as a youth. Unlike Clemens, however, he stuck persistently to the path longer and detoured less significantly. He was apprenticed to the trade in New York, where he not only took his education in the print shop but also developed a taste and knack for writing poetry. His move west from New York in 1854, however, exposed him to a different set of influences, learning the more free-handed and rambunctious journalism of the far West. He worked as a compositor on various San Francisco newspapers before moving to Nevada, where he bought into and edited the Virginia City *Territorial Enterprise*. He was in the right place at the right time: When the silver boom hit Nevada, he and his partner were able to build the *Enterprise* into a lively, very profitable newspaper.

Clemens's work as a full-time professional writer began while employed by Goodman for the *Enterprise* in 1862. Goodman taught Clemens the ropes of regular reporting, sending him to Carson City to write about the territorial legislature, as well as having him cover regular beats in Virginia City. More importantly, Goodman recognized Clemens's creative talents, giving him a remarkably free hand to write satires, burlesques, and hoaxes. Of course, the journalism of the day was not as fastidious as twentieth-century journalism pretends to be, so that Clemens's creativity was not out of bounds for daily newspapers. Still, Goodman's willingness to cultivate Clemens's talents was fundamental to Clemens's ultimate success. And Twain gave credit where it was due in his portrait of Goodman in *Roughing It*.

Goodman remained a lifelong friend and literary advisor to Clemens. He visited Clemens in 1871, helping to galvanize the writing of *Roughing It* when Clemens had lost confidence in the material and his ability to handle it. The two maintained correspondence through the years, with Goodman expressing strong opinions about the kind of literature that should come under the name Mark Twain. When Twain published *The Prince and the Pauper*, in part to satisfy the urgings of his family and Hartford friends to "do something fine," Goodman wrote a letter upbraiding him for selling out: "If I had obeyed my impulse, I should have written immediately to thank you for the beautiful copy of 'The Prince and the Pauper,' with its affectionate inscription; but before I had fairly finished reading it I was seized with toothache, and earache, and eye-ache, and sore throat, and neuralgia, and all the other evils that flesh is heir to, so that my thankfulness will lose half its grace from being expressed so tardily." Goodman then enumerated his complaints before writing:

> I don't want you to think, pray, because I have put forward wholesale what was disappointing to me in the book that I am insensible to its many beauties, its picturesque situation, the morals it inculcated, or the valuable information interwoven in it. It would be impossible for you to write a story not garnished

with somewhat of all this; but why voluntarily seek conditions where these are the be-all and end-all, when you might crown them with that royal and familiar play with human nature, character, customs, times and locality which render "the Gilded Age" and "Tom Sawyer" the most entertaining of books? Your forte is existing people and things. No one but a mere romancer should travel out of his age. (29 January 1882)

We do not have a direct record of Clemens's response, though we do know that shortly thereafter, he systematically revised *Adventures of Huckleberry Finn* to lower Huck's diction and make it more consistent with "existing people and things."

Like Clemens, Goodman could make fortunes but found it difficult to keep them, losing the money he made when he sold the *Enterprise* and then turning back to journalism and book writing in San Francisco. To help Goodman get back on his feet, Clemens published Goodman's *The Big Bonanza*, a history of mining days in Nevada, through Webster and Company. Later, when Goodman had reestablished his fortunes by farming grapes near Fresno, California, he tried to help Clemens through the financial woes of funding the Paige typesetter by trying in 1890 to get some Nevada mining capitalists to help Clemens back the machine.

Such was the long-distance devotion the two had for each other, based in part on the intense experience of a few years together in Virginia City. From that experience and from reading Clemens's works as they came out, Goodman knew that Clemens was a major talent. In a 9 March 1881 letter, Goodman assured Clemens that humor alone was not what made Twain great:

I have always prized your faculty of clear statement and your incomparable use of pure English above even your humor—unexampled as I esteem that to be. I never envied any man anything, but I have come near envying you your—shall I call it?—biblical force and simplicity of language. Take my word for it, you will live as a classic after you have ceased to sway people as the foremost humorist. Other people will come after you who will write in a strain that will better catch the fancy of the hour, but no one can come whose sorcery of speech shall so captivate the cultivated taste of all time.

♦ SEE ALSO Collaborations; Newspaper Journalism; Work Habits.

GRANT, ULYSSES S. (1822–1885). Ulysses Grant's *celebrity stemmed from his status during and after the Civil War as the general who preserved the Union. His popularity as a war hero made him a natural choice as the *Republican party's presidential nominee in 1868 after Andrew Johnson's divisive administration. But as much as he helped to consolidate his party, Grant was not up to the political machinations of the postwar world. He was a weak president in the face of a strong Congress, and his administration was plagued by scandals.

During that time Clemens worked as a reporter in Washington, D.C. (1867–1868), frequently visited the capital city over the next four years, and wrote a Washington book that exposed political corruption, including references to many of the scandals that rocked Grant's first term. Despite this, a close and friendly connection developed between Clemens and Grant. In a country that had fallen in love with celebrity, public events brought them together often enough to allow the two to discover mutual respect, and mutual benefit in the connection.

In an autobiographical sketch he wrote for his nephew Samuel Moffet to publish, he referred to himself in the third person: "In June [1861] he joined the Confederates in Ralls County, Missouri, . . . and came near having the distinction of being captured by Colonel Ulysses S. Grant."[1] This was merely Clemens's fancy way of saying that they were in the same state at the beginning of the war, in order to exaggerate their connection. Their first meeting really was in 1867 when Senator William Stewart of Nevada, for whom Clemens was at the time working, introduced them. Clemens reports that meeting, though he gets the dates wrong, in chapter 2 of *Following the Equator*. They did not meet again until 1879, when Clemens had become as famous as Grant and was asked to participate in a banquet held in Grant's honor in Chicago. There he delivered a speech on "The Babies" in which he flirted with irreverence by calling attention to the reality that their revered and honored guest was once a baby. But he delivered the speech with perfect composure and timing, not only encouraging the assembled company to laugh but getting the publicly impassive Grant to participate, too. This success helped compensate him for his feelings of humiliation after the *Whittier Birthday Dinner. Subsequently, Clemens shared the limelight with Grant in October 1880 and June 1881 when Grant visited Hartford.

Grant's career after his public life was no more fortunate than his career before the Civil War. He was invited to use his name for a brokerage firm in New York City, but his partner embezzled funds and left Grant broke in 1884. Grant turned to writing his Civil War memoirs for the *Century Magazine* in order to pull his family out of debt. About that time, he learned that he had throat cancer. Clemens was just entering the publishing business with *Webster and Company when he learned about Grant's situation, and he immediately began negotiating with Grant to publish the memoirs. When Grant ultimately decided to go with Twain's firm, Clemens coddled his prize author, fighting the clock in order to get the memoirs finished before Grant died. When Grant died while the book was in production, Clemens succeeded in capitalizing on the nation's grief, turning *The Personal*

---

1. Mark Twain's previously unpublished words are © 2002 by Richard A. Watson and the Chase Global Private Bank as Trustees of the Mark Twain Foundation, which reserves all reproduction or dramatization rights in every medium. Quotation is made with the permission of the University of California Press and Robert H. Hirst, General Editor of the Mark Twain Project.

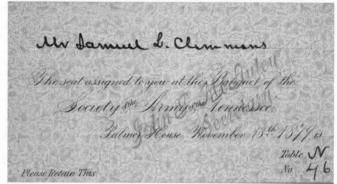

Tickets to two of the events for the Army of the Tennessee's
Reunion in November 1879.

Memoirs of U. S. Grant into a best-seller. Initial sales of the first volume, issued in December 1885 five months after Grant's death, allowed Twain personally to present to Grant's widow a royalty check for $200,000. Grant's family ultimately received $400,000 on sales of the two-volume set.

Clemens grew so involved in publishing Grant's memoirs that he let his own writing temporarily languish, prompting his family members to complain of his neglect. But when his own fortunes failed less than a decade later, Clemens turned to the figure of Grant to explore some of his own feelings of isolation and guilt attendant on financial ruin. The main character of the *unfinished work *Which Was the Dream?*, General X, brings out the parallels between Grant's bankruptcy and Clemens's, suggesting how closely Twain's sense of success was tied to his connection to Grant, and implying his hope that somehow he, too, would redeem himself from the disgrace of failure.

♦ SEE ALSO Business Ventures; Presidents; "Private History of a Campaign That Failed, The."

"GREAT DARK, THE." An *unfinished work of novella length written mostly in 1898, "The Great Dark" is one of Twain's late fantasy fictions in which he combines his deep interests in the psychology of consciousness and the new science of microbiology, all in the comic context of a burlesque of sea fictions. In all likelihood, he wrote the bulk of the piece after abandoning the novel *Which Was the Dream?*. The comic thrust of the piece, though, suggests a gradual lightening of Twain's mood. The story's theme of life as a dream turned suddenly nightmare became a leitmotif in Twain's letters of the 1890s when the *Paige typesetter, which was the objective correlative for Clemens's dreams of perpetual wealth, proved to be an empty one, dragging Clemens into a nightmare of financial ruin. In describing this turn of events in "The Great Dark," Twain personifies the impulse to dream in the "Superintendent of Dreams," a *trickster figure suggesting the amoral and chaotic nature of the universe. This figure, in conjunction with the idea of microbial life, became a bridge in Twain's imagination between possibility and *determinism, between a controlled machine of a universe and one of infinite flexibility and creativity. As such, "The Great Dark" shares a heady ambivalence with *"Three Thousand Years among the Microbes" and *"No. 44, The Mysterious Stranger."

♦ SEE ALSO Dreams.

GREELEY, HORACE (1811–1872). One of the towering figures of the Civil War era, Horace Greeley founded and edited the New York *Tribune*, one of the nation's most influential daily newspapers, notable for its Radical Republican bent. Greeley continued to espouse the radical cause after the war, supporting the rights of the freed slaves and of labor and promoting the Homestead Act. His populist tendencies caused him to break from the *Republican party over its increasing support of the Civil War plutocracy. His unsuccessful run for the presidency under the banner of a splinter group, the Liberal Republican party, which joined forces with the Democratic party in opposing Ulysses S. *Grant, was virtually his last public act. He died shortly after losing the election, having already suffered extreme grief at the death of his wife earlier in the year.

Clemens wrote frequently for Greeley's *Tribune* in 1867 and 1868, though his contact with Greeley himself was limited to a few letters and one meeting. Staff writer John *Hay inadvertently provided the occasion for Clemens's meeting with Greeley, as Clemens recalled in his autobiographical dictations:

> I met Greeley only once and then by accident. It was 1871 [more likely December 1870], in the (old) *Tribune* office. I climbed one or two flights of stairs and went to the wrong room. I was seeking Colonel John Hay.... I rapped lightly on the door, pushed it open and stepped in. There sat Mr. Greeley, busy writing, with his back to me.... It was not a pleasant situation for he had the reputation of being pretty plain with strangers who interrupted his train of thought. The interview was brief. Before I could pull myself together and back out, he whirled around and glared at me though his great

spectacles and said:

"Well, what in hell do *you* want!"

"I was looking for a gentlem——"

"Don't keep them in stock—clear out!"

I could have made a very neat retort but didn't, for I was flurried and didn't think of it till I was downstairs. (From a manuscript titled "Horace Greeley," probably written in 1898. Published in Bernard DeVoto, ed., *Mark Twain in Eruption*, 1940.)

Such treatment may have spurred a mild sort of revenge in Twain's two extended references to Greeley in *Roughing It*, chapters 20 and 70, where he mocked Greeley's notorious intensity and his miserable handwriting as well as his formidable influence. Then again, he rarely needed a motive to mock anything, as his 1868 sketch, "Private Habits of Horace Greeley," also makes fun of his handwriting: "He hired out once, in his young days, as a writing master, but the enterprise failed. The pupils could not translate his marks with any certainty. His first copy was 'Virtue is its own reward,' and they got it 'Washing with soap is wholly absurd.'"

♦ SEE ALSO Newspaper Journalism; Reform; Reid, Whitelaw.

GULLIVER'S TRAVELS. Not surprisingly, one of America's greatest satirists read and admired the work of Jonathan Swift, but the way he expressed his admiration suggests his knowledge of the dangers of *satire. In his 2 March 1869 letter of courtship to Olivia Langdon, he remarked,

> I have been reading—I *am* reading—Gulliver's Travels, & am much more charmed with it than I was when I read it last, in boyhood—for now I can see what a scathing satire it is upon the English government; whereas, before, I only gloated over its prodigies & its marvels. Poor Swift—under the placid surface of this simply-worded book flows the full tide of his venom—the turbid sea of his matchless hate. You would not like the volume, Livy—that is, a part of it. Some of it you would. If you would like to read it, though, I will mark it & tear it until it is fit for your eyes—for portions of it are very coarse and indelicate.

In brief, Clemens here unknowingly predicted the course of his own career, having his satire misconstrued as simple romance for children except when it was attacked as coarse and indelicate.

Still, Twain never did comfortably accept his own capacity to hate, nor did he find satire the only expression of his literary creativity. When in *"Three Thousand Years among the Microbes" he calls his narrator "Huck," he names Huck's nemesis "Lem Gulliver" and makes his danger lie in his cynicism.

♦ SEE ALSO Reading, Clemens's; Taste.

HANNIBAL, MISSOURI. Hannibal figures frequently in Twain's fiction, but the image he presents ranges widely from the nearly idyllic St. Petersburg, Missouri, of *The Adventures of Tom Sawyer* to the morally corrupt Dawson's Landing, Missouri, of *Pudd'nhead Wilson and Those Extraordinary Twins*, to the hellish Bricksville, "Arkansaw," of *Adventures of Huckleberry Finn*. All were part of Clemens's *childhood—the freedom and beauty, the crimes and guilt, the alternating boredom and terror.

Hannibal, when the Clemens family moved there in 1839, was a new hamlet on the Mississippi River. As such, it was trying to build its livelihood as a commercial depot for the growing region's farmers and sawyers to ship their goods via the Mississippi. As much as the flow of people into the *Mississippi River valley came from east to west, giving the adjacent states of Missouri and Iowa a distinctly different flavor, the geography made the region economically tied around the nation's major internal highway, the river itself. Hannibal's identity as a southern town blurred with its overlapping identity as a western river town. In other words, Hannibal, like most Mississippi River towns, had a multiple personality depending on whether it saw itself on an east-west or north-south axis.

As people settled the interior, Hannibal grew, developing not only wharves and warehouses, but distilleries, slaughterhouses, and tanyards. Because Missouri was a slave state, it also had auction houses for human chattel. The town grew enough to be chartered in 1845, and while the Clemens family found it difficult to make a living, the town itself, in spite of the wild ride most frontier towns had during the economically turbulent 1830s and 1840s, grew simply because of its ideal position on the riverfront of a growing agricultural region. As dependent as it was on agriculture, it was a town, and Clemens's basic attitudes about life were formulated not as a farm boy, but as a child connected to the commercial values of the city. In Clemens's life, the farm was usually a bucolic retreat from urban cares, either in youthful summers at his uncle's farm or later in life at his in-law's Quarry Farm, but his pastoral impulse was always that of a city-dweller for whom the farm's work rhythms are alien and exasperating. Usually when Twain depicts farmers, he depicts them as bumpkins. And usually, when Twain depicts himself in contact with the country—in his "How I Edited an Agricultural Newspaper" for example, or in his many contacts with horses—he describes himself as a city dandy whose knowledge of country ways is woefully inadequate. Clearly he exaggerated for effect, but his own childhood experience was not that of the typical American child born in the 1830s on a farm, but that of the general movement of Americans toward towns and *cities over the course of the century.

Of course, as a new town, Hannibal was hardly urbane, and its crudeness, violence, and social mobility figure prominently in Twain's works. So, too, does the social battle over propriety. Throughout the trans–Allegheny West in the first half of the nineteenth century, Americans were in a new kind of society—fluid, raw, marked by a conspicuous need to cooperate in order to build new communities, but at the same time moved by the most individualistic of impulses. In these dynamic social environs, the old aristocratic social *etiquette of the former English colonies was clearly inappropriate, but what would replace it was unclear until late in the century. Hannibal, like most new western towns, was the meeting place of aristocratic values of people like John Marshall *Clemens, and radical democrats, who scorned pretense. The intense *social class consciousness Twain depicts in his Mississippi writings—as well as in *Roughing It*—accurately describes a fundamental American concern of the nineteenth century. But these concerns did not simply play themselves out in polite debates about what kind of etiquette would be appropriate for a new democracy; the West was often a place where clashes of values turned violent. No wonder that the evangelical revivals of the 1830s through 1850s emphasized moral *reform, with revivalists crusading against dueling, *alcohol, tobacco chewing, cursing, idleness, etc. When these crusades reached Hannibal, they swept up young Clemens, giving him an early taste of the enthusiasm of reform and the sour taste of repentance that soon followed. Again, the matter of Hannibal, as critics have called it, is not exclusively that of one small town; it is typical of larger American concerns that Twain powerfully worked in his writings.

Similarly, the question of *slavery was central to Hannibal's existence, as it was to the nation as a whole. While Hannibal had its slave market and many domestic slaves, it also had an underground railroad stop and an active—though clandestine because illegal and socially unacceptable—antislavery movement. Often, antislavery advocates who made their views public or were exposed to the public were run out of town by angry mobs. But such behavior was not exclusive to southern towns. Cincinnati, Ohio, for instance, had major race riots when Harriet Beecher Stowe lived there, with angry white mobs destroying the printing press of an antislavery newspaper and murdering free blacks. Again, it is important to see Hannibal not as some magical and exclusive place that gave birth to Twain's best writing, but instead as a typical American town, caught in the complex crosscurrents of a dynamic culture.

That confusion persists today as recent protests have called to mind the inadequacy of Hannibal's self-representation as Mark Twain's boyhood home. Civic leaders have for years put on "Tom Sawyer Days" festivities for the Fourth of July, celebrating the idyllic Hannibal as an American archetype. The absence of African

Americans in this recreated history has led several people to challenge the legitimacy of those celebrations. Under these challenges, part of the more complex history of Hannibal is beginning to appear, but whether it remains no more than a lurking underground reality or comes into its rightful prominence only time will tell.

◆ SEE ALSO Public Image.

HARPER'S NEW MONTHLY MAGAZINE AND HARPER'S WEEKLY: A JOURNAL OF CIVILIZATION. Harper and Brothers Publishers, one of America's oldest and largest publishing houses, devoted itself primarily to religious books until 1850, when it jumped into the *magazine market with one of the most successful and enduring entries: *Harper's New Monthly Magazine*. Hiring George William Curtis, one of the editors and owners of the respected *Putnam's Monthly*, to edit their own magazine, the well-known Harper's firm was able quickly to establish a position of prestige while outstripping the older magazines in circulation.

Following on the heels of their success with the monthly, Harper's began a weekly in 1857, moving Curtis to the editor's chair there. Curtis, always politically active, found the weekly format very congenial to political reporting. He thus developed the new journal into a staunchly Union voice during the war and a forum for political *reform thereafter. The heavy use of illustrations in both journals was one reason for the magazines' success, and when the weekly hired Thomas *Nast as one of its political cartoonists, the journal developed a powerful formula for political advocacy. Its circulation of 160,000 by 1872 made it one of the most influential American magazines.

Twain published sparingly in Harper's journals until relatively late in his career, when both had seen a period of decline in the 1890s and were looking for ways to bolster their sagging fortunes. Clemens, too, was seeking a way to build his wealth, and linking himself to a publishing house that could produce his books as well as many of his shorter pieces in their journals seemed like the ideal situation. But the formula did not work fully until George Brinton McClellan *Harvey helped reorganize Harper's, bringing his talents as a publicist to bear on the venerable publishing firm.

HARRIS, GEORGE WASHINGTON (1814–1869). Mark Twain knew of George Washington Harris from Harris's comic *Sut Lovingood's Yarns*, a collection of *dialect sketches in the tradition of *southwestern humor, many of which were published in the 1850s in William T. Porter's *Spirit of the Times* magazine. Twain wrote from New York to the *Alta California* in 1867 that Harris's book "abounds in humor, and is said to represent the Tennessee dialect correctly. It will sell well in the West, but the Eastern people will call it coarse and possibly taboo it" (14 July 1867).

In its persistent life over the last hundred years, the book has been damned more than once, perhaps most famously in *Patriotic Gore* by Edmund Wilson, who called it the "most repellent book of any real literary merit in American literature." The book that could generate such an attack is the most Rabelaisian American book of the nineteenth century, one that insists that bodily urges are the human essence; that attacks church, law, marriage, school, and respectability of all kinds with anarchic vigor; and that exaggerates with a gusto that surpasses late twentieth-century animated cartoons. Its profound cynicism reflects Harris's advocacy of the Confederate cause during the Civil War and his disillusionment with politics in the war's aftermath.

The degree of influence that Harris's writings had on Twain is not clear. Twain's willingness to write and print scatological and sexual tales was limited. Certainly Harris's disruption of the *frame narrative to emphasize the value and importance of the inside narrator and Harris's distrust of conventional standards of cultural propriety, however, as well as Harris's cynicism, have their counterparts in Twain's works.

HARRIS, JOEL CHANDLER (1848–1908). Joel Chandler Harris was one of Clemens's favorite American authors for the way Harris related African-American folktales in *Uncle Remus: His Songs and Sayings*. Harris's complex work is an interesting indicator of Clemens's own attitudes toward *race relations, authorship, and *celebrity.

As an illegitimate child raised by his mother in the small Georgia town of Eatonville, Harris developed a painful shyness around whites. His career as a journalist began at age thirteen when he apprenticed to the printing trade on Turnwold, the plantation of Joseph Turner, who published the only plantation newspaper in America. Turner owned slaves but had unusual ideas about slave labor, adopting an approach not that different from the paternalism of some northern factory owners. It was here that Harris developed close relationships with *African Americans, learning their folkways so completely that he was more at home among blacks than whites—always excepting his family. A life working as a journalist allowed him to develop his avocation, that of anthropologist, under a mask more palatable to his reading public.

After the Civil War, Harris worked for the Atlanta *Constitution*, which, in promoting the "New South," tried to mitigate the virulent racism of most southern whites while suggesting to northern capital that there was no labor problem in the South. In following this policy, Harris invented "Uncle Remus" as a stereotypical "darkey." But when Harris turned to writing his first book of Remus stories, he found the mask allowed him to express a greater complexity in race relations, in part because he related with great accuracy stories that went to the heart of the African-American experience in its fusion of African, Native American, and

European folk motifs. And above all, Harris tried to be as true as he could to the language of the African Americans of a particular region.

In these tales, published in 1880, Twain found a model for some of what he was then trying to do with dialect in *Adventures of Huckleberry Finn*, and found another white who had grown up in the South immersed in black dialect stories. No wonder the tales impressed him. But as much as a shared sense of guilt and fascination with African-American life piqued Clemens's interest, he never could understand how someone who could write so well could not live out his celebrity in person. Having fallen in love with the book, Clemens wrote to Harris suggesting that he join him on a lecture tour. When they met in New Orleans in 1882, it became clear to all that such a plan was impossible. As Twain put it in chapter 47 of *Life on the Mississippi*, "It turned out that he had never read aloud to people and was too shy to venture the attempt now. Mr. Cable and I read from books of ours, to show him what an easy trick it was; but his immortal shyness was proof against even this sagacious strategy, so we had to read about Brer Rabbit ourselves." Twenty-five years later, Twain declared in his *autobiography, "he was the bashfulest grown person I have ever met" (*North American Review*, 16 November 1906).

♦ SEE ALSO Style; Vernacular Humor.

HARTE, BRET (1836–1902). Francis Bret Harte was among Twain's most influential mentors, helping, as a fellow writer and as editor of the *Californian*, to cultivate Twain's wilder western humor and teach him much about *style at the same time. As Clemens put it in a letter to Thomas Bailey Aldrich on 28 January 1871, "He trimmed and trained and schooled me patiently until he changed me from an awkward utterer of coarse grotesquenesses to a writer of paragraphs and chapters that have found a certain favor in the eyes of even some of the very decentest people in the land."

Harte himself was, through the 1860s and 1870s at least, the best known western writer in both the eastern United States and Europe, building a reputation on the basis of his Dickensian sketches of western life, particularly "The Luck of Roaring Camp." While slightly younger than Clemens, he seemed always a jump ahead in developing his career, and as such served both as a role model and as a target of envy for Clemens. But while Harte's attention to conventional forms, modes, genres, and writing styles helped him to teach Clemens about the conventions of writing, Harte himself could never rise above mimicry to the point of developing a unique style. And ironically, while he taught Clemens much about the discipline of writing, he himself lacked discipline, succumbing to both his own lack of depth and his alcoholism as his career went on, squandering tremendous opportunities and becoming known in America by the 1880s as a wasted talent. In William Dean

*Howells's words, "After repeated and almost invariable failures to deal with the novel characters and circumstances which he encountered [in his travels in the East] he left off trying, and frankly went back to the semi-mythical California he had half discovered, half created, and wrote Bret Harte over and over as long as he lived." (Howells, *Literary Friends and Acquaintance* p. 299)

None of this was even a premonitory shadow in Clemens's eyes as the two men came to know each other in California in the mid-1860s. In a letter of 20 January 1866 to his mother and sister, he expressed not only his admiration of Harte's work, but his sense of pleasure in working with him:

> Though I am generally placed at the head of my breed of scribblers in this part of the country, the place properly belongs to Bret Harte, I think (late editor of the "Californian"), though he denies it, along with the rest. He wants me to club a lot of old sketches together with a lot of his, & publish a book together.... And ... we are going to burlesque a book of poems which the publisher, Bancroft, is to issue in the spring. We know all the tribe of California poets, & understand their different styles, & I think we can just make them get up & howl.... Then you'll hear these poetical asses here tear around worse than a pack of wildcats.... I am willing enough to go into this thing, because there will be *fun* in it.

As Clemens's career advanced, the *Californian*, for much of the time under Harte's editorship, sedulously reprinted Twain's sketches, helping burnish his West Coast reputation no matter how far afield Clemens went.

But there were flies in the ointment early on, as Harte's book of sketches was accepted and published by Carleton and Company at about the same time that Twain's *The Celebrated Jumping Frog* was rejected. Two years later, Harte's review of *The Innocents Abroad* included criticism of the book's "lawlessness and audacity" and its "lack of 'moral or aesthetic limitation' in its humor" (*Overland Monthly*, January 1870). Harte's success at this point in his career depended on his ability to mimic the style and standards of a more reputable literary class, and in pursing this class, he was willing to sacrifice his friend.

Still, Twain counted Harte as a friend and potential collaborator, inviting Harte to his Hartford house in 1876 to collaborate on a play, *Ah Sin*, based on Harte's celebrated poem, "The Heathen Chinee." While there, Harte not only violated all the rules of propriety of a household that was itself remarkably relaxed by Victorian standards, he also showed up drunk to give a lecture to the Hartford girls' reading group, the *Saturday Morning Club. The difficulties in collaborating on *Ah Sin* coupled with Harte's social breaches ended the friendship between the two so violently that Harte became Twain's benchmark for literary and character flaws. He often condemned Harte's writing as wordy, pompous, and derivative, and in his attacks on

Harte's character, he barred no holds. As he put it in a 27 June 1878 letter to Howells on learning that Harte had been given a consulship to Germany, "Harte is a liar, a thief, a swindler, a snob, a sot, a sponge, a coward, a Jeremy Diddler, he is brim full of treachery, & he conceals his Jewish birth as carefully as if he considered it a disgrace. . . . If he had only been made a home official, I think I could stand it; but to send this nasty creature to puke on the American name in a foreign land is too much." Clemens's opinions did not soften with time, though the mollifying memory of the good times in San Francisco ultimately rounded his portrait of Harte. In his autobiographical dictations of 14 June 1906, in which he continued to attack Harte as "showy, meretricious, insincere," he also remembered "a happy Bret Harte, a contented Bret Harte, an ambitious Bret Harte, a hopeful Bret Harte, a bright cheerful, easy-laughing Bret Harte, a Bret Harte to whom it was a bubbling and effervescent joy to be alive. That Bret Harte died in San Francisco." More likely, the same Bret Harte existed all along, but the bohemian life of San Francisco is one that Clemens himself grew out of as he adjusted to a more settled life back East, whereas the free and easy life of San Francisco is the only one that Harte could occupy with any success. Harte earned Clemens's enmity not only by insulting him but by serving as a reminder of where he once thought his own life was going.

◆ SEE ALSO Anti-Semitism; Collaborations; Condensed Novels; Taste.

HARTFORD, CONNECTICUT. Founded in 1636 by Thomas Hooker's congregation of Puritans, Hartford, the capital of Connecticut, grew into a thriving commercial city of about forty thousand by the time Twain first saw it in 1868. He came to the city to pursue a contract with Hartford's *American Publishing Company, but was immediately in awe of the prosperity of a city with three major industries—publishing, arms manufacturing, and insurance—in addition to the business of state government. In 1868, Hartford was still a legitimate cultural and mercantile rival to New York and Boston, and yet its relatively small size made it seem primmer, tidier, more the ideal northern city in the eyes of the longtime traveler. As he described it in his correspondence to the *Alta California*, "They have the broadest straightest streets in Hartford, that ever led a sinner to destruction, and the dwelling houses are the amplest in size, and the shapeliest, and have the most capacious ornamental ground about them. This is the center of Connecticut wealth. Hartford dollars have a place in half the great moneyed enterprises of the union" (25 January 1868). On a longer visit later that year, he again wrote to the *Alta* about the wealth of the town: "To live in this style one must have his bank account of course. . . . Where are the poor in Hartford? I confess I do not know. They are 'corralled' doubtless—corralled in some unsanctified corner of this paradise whither my feet have not yet wandered, I suppose" (August 1868). He supposed correctly, and his dream of residence was connected not to that unknown corral but rather to the bank account. His hopes for prosperity and residence converged when he and Olivia moved to Hartford in 1871, where they lived in two *houses. After renting for a while, they planned and built a house of their own, into which they moved in 1874. Clemens's residency in Hartford's *Nook Farm neighborhood was his longest in any of the many places he lived.

HARTFORD *COURANT*. SEE *Courant*, Hartford.

HARVEY, GEORGE BRINTON MCCLELLAN (1864–1928). One of the young men who helped Joseph Pulitzer build his publishing empire in the early 1890s, Col. George Harvey purchased the venerable *North American Review* in 1899 and began a reorganization of Harper and Brothers as its new president that same year. He began editing *Harper's Weekly* in 1901. Twain's contract with Harper's put him in contact with Harvey, who became one of Clemens's best friends and most important literary advisors after Olivia Langdon *Clemens's death in 1904. In particular, Harvey helped Clemens edit the selections from the *autobiography that were serialized in the *North American Review* from 1906 to 1907, under the title "Chapters from My Autobiography."

Harvey was a brilliant publicist as well as editor, one of the shapers of the new mass journalism coming into play in the early part of the twentieth century. While Twain himself was very adept at manipulating the press in order to further his own image, Harvey was equally skillful at keeping that image alive after Twain had recovered his fortunes. As a Pulitzer acolyte, Harvey recognized that notoriety was as commercially useful a kind of fame as any, and let Twain use the *North American Review* to publish some of his hard-hitting, and therefore controversial, statements against *imperialism.

HAY, JOHN (1838–1905). Raised in southern Illinois nearly directly across the Mississippi River from Hannibal, Missouri, John Hay had a distinguished career as a statesman, journalist, and man of letters. Best known to posterity as secretary of state under President William McKinley, in which capacity he formulated America's "Open-Door" policy to China, he began his public career as private secretary to President Abraham Lincoln. After the Civil War and several diplomatic posts, he became an assistant editor for the New York *Tribune* under Whitelaw *Reid, serving frequently as editor in Reid's absences.

Clemens and Hay had a long and warm friendship, beginning either in 1867 with a meeting in New York City, or, less likely, in 1871 at the *Tribune*. They shared a common interest in *dialect writing and a common rivalry with Bret Harte, whose writings many considered to be without equal but which both Twain and Hay disliked. Hay's best known literary work, *Pike County Ballads*, was written not in imitation of Harte's "Plain Language from Truthful James" but as a corrective to it.

Sharing Hay's midwestern origins, Clemens admired Hay's success at conquering the manners and mores of the East. As a graduate of Brown University and as an international diplomat: "He had a charm about him of a sort quite unusual to my Western ignorance and inexperience—a charm of manner, intonation, apparently native and unstudied elocution, and all that—the groundwork of it native, the ease of it, the polish of it, the winning naturalness of it, acquired in Europe where he had been Charge d'Affairs some time at the Court of Vienna. He was joyous and cordial, a most pleasant comrade" (*North American Review*, 15 February 1907).

Clemens and Hay corresponded frequently and praised each other's works, most notably in Hay's reaction to *"Old Times on the Mississippi." Clemens's most public praise for Hay's work came after Hay's death. In his *autobiography, Twain credits Hay with giving Twain the impetus and some insight into the value and method of autobiography itself (*North American Review*, 15 February 1907).

HEALTH AND DISEASE. In his 26 May 1867 letter to the *Alta California* from New York City, Twain wrote under the title "Information for the Cholera":

> You know how the telegraph thrilled us every day, a year ago, with accounts of the scourging of the great plague here, in Cincinnati, St Louis and other places. I find now—at least they tell me—that respectable people did not die from it. The term is a hard one, but it describes well. Only the poor, the criminally, sinfully, wickedly poor and destitute starvelings in the purlieus of the great cities suffered, died, and were hauled out to the Potter's field—the well-to-do were seldom attacked. It seems hard, but truly humiliation, hunger, persecution and death are the wages of poverty in the mighty cities of the land. No man can say aught against honest poverty. The books laud it; the instructors of the people praise it; all men glorify it and say it hath its reward here and will have it hereafter. Honest poverty is a gem that even a King might feel proud to call his own, but I wish to sell out. I have sported that kind of jewelry long enough. I want some variety. I wish to become rich, so that I can instruct the people and glorify honest poverty a little, like those good, kind-hearted, fat, benevolent people do.

This is just one of a multitude of places in which disease, both as a biological and social fact, is a central subject in Twain's works. "How to Cure a Cold" (1863); "Lucretia Smith's Soldier" (1864); "Official Physic" (1867); "The Experience of the McWilliamses with the Membranous Croup" (1875); "The Invalid's Story" (1877); chapter 23 of *Adventures of Huckleberry Finn* in which Jim describes his daughter going deaf from scarlet fever; "Aix, the Paradise of Rheumatics" (1891); "At the Appetite Cure" (1898); "Man's Place in the Animal World" (1896); "Christian Science and the Book of Mrs. Eddy" (1899) and *Christian Science*; "Was It Heaven, or Hell?" (1902); *"Three Thousand Years among the Microbes"; chapter 1 of "Little Bessie Would Assist Providence" (1908–1909); and Letter 7 from *Letters from the Earth* provide just a fraction of the list, covering the range of Twain's years, genres, and moods. He even went so far as to credit getting the measles as the first important step leading him to a literary career in "The Turning Point of My Life" (1910).

Nineteenth-century Americans granted health and disease an importance difficult to imagine today. People were susceptible to a far greater number of devastating diseases, but the promise of treatment was for the first time in human history becoming something more than a confidence game—though distinguishing between the new medicine and the old was a challenge fraught with error and obscured by superstition.

When Twain was born in 1835, the state of medical knowledge had not advanced significantly since the middle ages. As Twain describes doctoring in his *autobiography,

> I remember two of the Florida doctors. . . . They not only tended an entire family for $25 a year, but furnished the medicines themselves. Good measure, too. Only the largest person could hold a whole dose. Castor-oil was the principal beverage. The dose was half a dipperful, with half a dipperful of New Orleans molasses added to help it down and make it taste good, which it never did. The next standby was calomel; the next rhubarb; and the next, jalap. Then they bled the patient, and put mustard-plasters on him. It was a dreadful system, and yet the death-rate was not heavy. The calomel was nearly sure to salivate the patient and cost him some of his teeth. There were no dentists. When teeth became touched with decay or were otherwise ailing, the doctor knew of but one thing to do: he fetched his tongs and dragged them out. If the jaw remained, it was not his fault. Doctors were not called in cases of ordinary illness; the family's grandmother attended to those. Every old woman was a doctor, and gathered her own medicines in the woods, and knew how to compound doses that would stir the vitals of a cast-iron dog. And then there was the "Indian doctor"; a grave savage, remnant of his tribe, deeply read in the mysteries of nature and the secret properties of herbs; and most backwoodsmen had high faith in his powers and could tell of wonderful cures achieved by him. . . . We had the "faith doctor," too, in those early days—a woman. Her specialty was toothache. . . . She would lay her hand on the patient's jaw and say "Believe!" and the cure was prompt. (*North American Review*, 1 March 1907)

In this list, Twain enumerates not only kinds of cures, but, implicitly, attitudes toward disease.

Many attributed disease to supernatural causes. Hard-core Calvinists, for instance, believed every disease, as well as every benefit, emanated from the hand of

God. Calvinists did not hold a monopoly on supernatural explanations. In the same general league, Pennsylvania Dutch country's "pow-wows"—that is, faith-herbal healers who combined the medical traditions of European, African, and Native American folk medicine—attributed illness as readily to devils, and faith healers of many stripes, including late century's Christian Scientists, considered disease less a matter of body than of spirit.

The "physic's" alternative explanation was not much better. Believing disease to be an imbalance of four bodily humors—bile, blood, lymph, and choler—healers who thought of disease as physical were little more likely to help their patients than were faith healers. Indeed, given that the three kinds of medicine—allopathic, homeopathic, and hydropathic—resorted to therapies that put extraordinary stress on the body, physicians probably killed more patients than they cured until about 1880 or 1890. As Twain put it in "Official Physic," "Some sarcastic people, justified by the saying of the well-known Oliver Wendell Holmes, may be of the opinion that more people get well in spite of the doctors than by their help, and that a doctor is as likely to be famous from the number that he kills as from that which he cures." Physicians could maintain their reputations since expensive allopathic physicians, who usually treated patients with bleedings and purges, were not called in until other treatments had failed; thus, they always had the excuse, when their patients died, that they came too late.

The incredible herbal pharmacopoeia at healers' disposal likewise had a hit-or-miss flavor to it. Quinine was discovered as a good treatment for malaria, but the use of mercury for any number of diseases, venereal or otherwise, was about as dangerous as the heavy use of toxins like foxglove and jimsonweed, or drugs like morphine and cocaine. Such medicines were usually mixed in solutions of up to 50 percent alcohol. For the common frontier complaint of "milk sickness," caused by drinking the milk or eating the meat of cattle that had been feeding on white snakeroot, taking alcohol-laced potions actually helped since alcohol neutralizes the snakeroot toxin. On the other hand, when such elixirs were used as treatments for alcoholism, the results were anything but comic. Yet Twain managed to turn such cures into the meat of humor in "Curing a Cold" or in Tom Sawyer's dosing the cat with "Pain-killer" in *The Adventures of Tom Sawyer.*

The extremity of the treatments (though to be honest, the kinds of poisons we use on diseases like cancer and AIDS and the drugs we use as anesthetics for invasive surgery must also be seen as extreme) merely reflects the range and number of common diseases, which Twain conveniently lists in "Man's Place in the Animal World":

Mumps, measles, whooping cough, croup, tonsillitis, diphtheria, scarlet fever ... colds, coughs, asthma, bronchitis, itch, cholera, cancer, consumption, yellow fever, bilious fever, typhus fevers, hay fever, ague, chilblains, piles, inflammation of the entrails, indigestion, toothache, earache, deafness, dumbness, influenza, chicken pox, cow pox, small pox, liver complaint, constipation, bloody flux, warts, pimples, boils, carbuncles, abscesses, bunions, corns, tumors, fistulas, pneumonia, softening of the brain, melancholia and fifteen other kinds of insanity, dysentery, jaundice, diseases of the heart, the bones, the skin, the scalp, the spleen, the kidneys, the nerves, the brain, the blood; scrofula, paralysis, leprosy, neuralgia, palsy, fits, headache, thirteen kinds of rheumatism, forty-six of gout, and a formidable supply of gross and unprintable disorders of one sort and other. Also—but why continue the list?

This list may not be any shorter, now, but it is much less serious. Cholera, scarlet fever, consumption (tuberculosis), yellow fever, whooping cough (pertussis), diphtheria, smallpox, polio, leprosy, and the bacterial infections that cause earaches and toothaches are all either preventable through vaccination or treatable (at least for now) with antibiotics. In Clemens's day, something as simple as a toothache could lead to life-threatening abscesses, and a compound fracture of an arm or leg called for amputation to prevent fatal infection. Almost any bacterial disease took the sufferer weeks to shake and weeks longer to recover energy and strength. Not surprisingly, people watched their health carefully, taking doses of supposedly prophylactic medicines, and indulging themselves when experiencing psychosomatic illness for fear of the real thing. At any rate, Twain capitalized in "The Invalid's Story" on the power of imagination to make one sick.

Many of these real diseases swept over great swaths of the land in virulent outbreaks. Typhoid fever and cholera, both water-born, broke out in cities frequently in the summers, leading the wealthy to develop the practice of summering outside of cities. But there was really no full escape from summer sicknesses, as malaria and yellow fever—both imported from Africa by way of the slave trade, both carried by mosquitoes—were as common in the country as in the cities. The very term "malaria," meaning "bad air," gave rise to many phony preventatives, but the association of "bad air" with swamps did at least lead to draining swamps as an early, significant, and effective public health measure. Still, ignorance gave disease the upper hand. Some major epidemics were not even known as such until the turn of the century. Hookworm, for instance, epidemic in the South among the poor, was discovered by Dr. Charles Wardell Stiles of the U.S. Public Health Service in 1902. The cause of milk sickness was not discovered until 1920.

Clemens's own experience with illness was not out of the ordinary for a man of his day, but was certainly devastating. His father's death, either from pneumonia or, as his brother Orion would have it, from too heavy use of patent medicines, was not the first—Clemens also lost two older siblings to childhood diseases. Later in life, his wife nearly died of typhoid fever after nursing her friend, Emma Nye, who did die of it. His father-in-law succumbed to stomach cancer. His son died in infancy of diptheria. One of his daughters, Olivia Susan, died of meningitis; another suffered epilepsy so severe that it made her occasionally insane. His wife, Olivia Langdon *Clemens, suffered throughout her life from Pott's disease, a tuberculosis infection of the spine, and may have died of its complications—with more than a little help from heart and lung disease exacerbated by breathing second-hand smoke. Of course, Clemens himself suffered from various respiratory, digestive, and skin disorders, and suffered intense rheumatism and gout—diseases making the physical act of writing for hours at a time inordinately painful.

This was not the only way in which disease interfered with his professional life. When the copyist he had hired did not send her portion of the manuscript of *Life on the Mississippi* to the publisher on time, Clemens "went to my copyist's house this morning to see what was the delay, and found she is laid up with the persistent enemy of this book, *scarlet fever*. But they said my MS had been removed from her room and disinfected with carbolic acid as soon as the disease was determined. So I brought it away and expressed it to you. . . . May be you had better give it another good disinfecting before you meddle with it, or let your children get hold of it. Will you telephone Fairchild that we are in quarantine?" (to James *Osgood, 29 December 1882).

Dealing with their own ailments, the Clemens family, particularly in the 1890s and 1900s, traveled regularly to various spas for treatments, including spending time in Sanna, Sweden, to try Heinrick Kellgren's hydrotherapy for Jean's epilepsy, and to baths in Kaltenleutgeben, near Vienna, Austria, for Olivia. Twain's late fascination with Christian Science is easily explained by the family's search for useful therapies for the many maladies they suffered. None, however, proved more than temporarily useful. The kinds of regimens his family undertook, without enduring success, may explain Twain's autobiographical quips about health programs: "There are people who strictly deprive themselves of each and every eatable, drinkable and smokable which has in any way acquired a shady reputation. They pay this price for health. And health is all they get for it. How strange it is; it is like paying out your whole fortune for a cow that has gone dry" (*North American Review*, 1 March 1907).

The discoveries of microbiology and the attendant progress made in medicine did not, as one would expect, give Clemens a dose of good humor about the state of his, his family's, and the world's health. Instead, it turned him energetically to thinking and writing about religion. Given his early background in which disease was often attributed to God, this is not surprising, especially since the tenor of so many of these pieces is to try to supplant the idea of providence with the idea of an impersonal, mechanical world. *Letters from the Earth*, for instance, has a long passage on disease that he uses to mock the biblical account of the Flood. Satan explains that consistency would require human beings to acknowledge that disease germs were the real freight of Noah's ark. Moreover, he explains that human efforts to blame God for disease might make sense, but for cures, they really ought to re-examine their idea of God:

> Shem was full of hookworms. It is wonderful, the thorough and comprehensive study which the Creator devoted to the great work of making man miserable. . . . Many poor people have to go barefoot, because they cannot afford shoes. The Creator saw his opportunity. I will remark, in passing, that he always has his eye on the poor. Nine-tenths of his disease-inventions were intended for the poor, and they *get* them. The well-to-do get only what is left over. . . . The poor's only real friend is their fellow man. He is sorry for them, he pities them, and he shows it by his deeds. He does much to relieve their distresses; and in every case their Father in Heaven gets the credit of it. (Letter 7)

As much as Twain's satiric approach blames people for believing in such a conception of God, the underlying anger is for the creation itself, and for the creator that must have made it. In this sense, both "Three Thousand Years among the Microbes" and "Little Bessie Would Assist Providence" reach an extreme conclusion in which Twain combines science and Calvinism to redefine the creation. In chapter 1 of "Bessie," the title character mimics the religious line that diseases are sent by heaven for a benign purpose:

> All troubles and pains and miseries and rotten diseases and horrors and villainies are sent to us in mercy and kindness to discipline us; and he says it is the duty of every father and mother to *help* Providence, every way they can; . . . brother Eddie needs disciplining, right away; and I know where you can get the small pox for him, and the itch, and the diphtheria, and bone-rot, and heart disease, and consumption, and—*Dear* mamma, have you fainted. . . . Now *this* comes of staying in town this hot weather.

In "Microbes," the cosmos is a chain of beings infesting one another, from greatest to smallest, with none immune from a universal plague. Implicitly in both, Twain rewrites the gospel to say that God is disease.

♦ SEE ALSO Summer Residences.

HEAVEN. SEE Afterlife.

HELL. SEE Afterlife.

HISTORY. Twain's interest in history began in the usual vein of the travel writer, mentioning historical anecdotes on par with legend as a source of *associations that would create interest. Most American travel writers, fearing that the United States was too new and raw to have, as Washington Irving puts it in the opening of *The Sketchbook*, "storied and poetical association," looked to *Europe for the shared icons of cultural meaning. "There," Irving continues, "were to be seen the master-pieces of art, the refinements of highly cultivated society, the quaint peculiarities of ancient and local custom." In this sense, history is mere antiquarianism, a part of the refinement developed by those of high *social class. Twain rebels against such ideas in *The Innocents Abroad*, arguing that American experiences are appropriate grounds for culture. Europe, according to the brash American, should be seen directly rather than through the mists of poetry and history. If we want to develop the poetry of history, Twain turns us to the history of the United States. The *nostalgia of *"Old Times on the Mississippi" fits this tradition of associations, merely substituting American scenes, traditions, and bygone conditions for European. Striking the sublime note, Twain describes the natural and human history of the Mississippi River valley to give *Life on the Mississippi* the substance he thought he would need to make the book a standard.

Not merely a marker of refinement, history was also a fundamental liberal art, one of the acquisitions expected of an educated citizen. History was considered the repository of knowledge, the source of examples and models that would guide a person's life. By the time Clemens moved to Hartford, he began a study of history that would fit him for citizenship by such standards, and like the educated men who helped guide his reading, he studied European history.

He so enjoyed the study that he turned to history for some of his favorite pleasure reading, revisiting David Hume's histories of England, Thomas Carlyle's history of the French revolution, and W. E. H. *Lecky's works repeatedly. He also read very pointedly to prepare to write many of his own books, not only the historical novels like *The Prince and the Pauper*, *A Connecticut Yankee in King Arthur's Court*, and *Personal Recollections of Joan of Arc*, but also for his travel narratives, especially *A Tramp Abroad* and—looking at American history—*Life on the Mississippi*, as well as *Following the Equator*.

Earlier in his career, Clemens accepted history as the clear record of what had happened and why. In *Adventures of Huckleberry Finn*, much of the humor stems from the contrast between Huck's jumbled history and the generally accepted truth of the matter. Twain's defense of America in *Connecticut Yankee* was based on an idea of historical *progress, contrasting the America of the nineteenth century, often criticized by Europeans, with the reality of Europe's past. The goal was to debunk, using James Hammond *Trumbull's *True History of the Blue Laws* and Lecky's *History of European Morals*, the European idea of its superiority to America simply because of its greater age.

But the book's argument turned on Twain. What began as a manifesto of progress instead, in part under the influence of theories of *evolution, came to be a lament that history is an insufferable burden. No present fails to carry the complex legacy of the past in deterministic ways. In this sense, Twain's study of history pushed him toward *determinism at times in pieces like "The Turning Point of My Life" (1910).

At the same time, another possible way of looking at history opened itself to Twain's imagination. He wrote himself into discovering that history may be less a matter of fact than of interpretation. He came to see that historians construct conclusions to support political positions, that such conclusions are contingent and always debatable, and that the very facts on which scholars base such conclusions are easily subject to distortion. This realization coincided with his growing doubt about the possibility of moral progress. Combined, these two shifts in intellectual outlook led to Twain's conclusion in chapter 69 of *Following the Equator* (1897) that "the very ink with which all history is written is merely fluid prejudice" by which the powerful justify their privileges.

These two conflicting possibilities pushed Twain away from supporting the idea of progress. Still, the kinds of writing he did following each vein resulted in radically different styles, subjects, and approaches. On the one hand, he indulges cynicism, saying in his *autobiography:

> It is not worth while to try to keep history from repeating itself, for man's character will always make the preventing of the repetitions impossible. Whenever man makes a large stride in material prosperity and progress he is sure to think that *he* has progressed, whereas he has not advanced an inch.... He is richer than his forebears but his character is no improvement upon theirs. Riches and education are not a permanent possession; they will pass away, as in the case of Rome and Greece and Egypt and Babylon. (15 January 1907)

The corollary to this cynicism is nostalgia, such as that in which he indulged in a historical vein in *Joan of Arc*.

On the other hand, the sense that history may be a fiction, while morally disturbing in the somber anti-imperialism of *Following the Equator*, allowed Twain a sense of play in certain *unfinished works in which he explodes history as a burden through one comic device or another. In "The Secret History of Eddypus," puns crumble the seriousness of historical investigation. In *"No. 44, The Mysterious Stranger," the "Assembly of the Dead," created after No. 44 makes time run backward, turns history into a circus. While the narrator finds the radical disruptions of his comfortable frames of reference frightening, No. 44's message is one of hope, that the playfulness of imagination can release human beings from their bonds, including those of time and precedent.

♦ SEE ALSO Reading, Clemens's.

HONORARY DEGREES. Although self-educated, Clemens earned a place in the world of letters and won several honorary degrees. The first of these, an honorary Master of Arts from Yale University in 1888, was proposed and supported by Joseph Twichell, who was an active alumnus. In 1901, Yale conferred an honorary Doctor of Literature. In Hartford, Clemens had many friends who were also connected to the university, and he knew several Yale professors, so these first honorary degrees were in many ways a celebration of the esteem in which his immediate community held him. Much the same can be said for the University of Missouri granting one of the most celebrated sons of the state an honorary Doctor of Law in 1902. But the honorary degree that gave Clemens the most pride was the Doctor of Letters he received from Oxford in 1907. As he wrote in his *autobiography, in the dictations of May 1907, "I am quite well aware—and so is America, and so is the rest of Christendom—that an Oxford decoration is a loftier distinction than is conferrable by any other university on either side of the ocean, and is worth twenty-five of any other, whether foreign or domestic." No wonder he missed no opportunity to wear his scarlet Oxford robes, including at his daughter's wedding.

♦ SEE ALSO Education; Spectacle.

HOUSES. For a culture that had as one of its unofficial theme songs "There's No Place Like Home," that pointed with pride to the ease of home ownership among many classes, and that saw *social class substantially in material terms, homes were very important symbolically. Twain worked that symbolic importance in much of his literature, using descriptions of homes as markers of states of civilization and culture. He certainly had a breadth of experience on which to draw in his depictions. Clemens lived in dozens of houses and hotels around the world, from frontier shanties to opulent mansions. Many of these—covering the gamut from shack to palace—still exist, four as museums open to the public.

Two of these are from his earliest years, the house in which he was born in Florida, Missouri, and his boyhood home in Hannibal, Missouri. The first has been moved from its original site to the shores of an artificial lake, making it fraudulently picturesque, but the second is on its original site in a part of Hannibal that has been turned into a museum. This modest wood-frame house is an example of the then-new kind of construction, the "balloon frame" house, that cut costs so significantly that Americans of even modest means could own decent housing. The double log cabin of Clemens's uncle John Quarles's Missouri farm no longer exists, except in the pages of Twain's books. As a style of house, the log cabin took advantage of America's ample forests, enabling frontiersmen to build substantial structures, lending a certain solidity to the claims of gentility of even the rawest communities. Twain makes use of such structures in *The Gilded Age*, *Life on the Mississippi*, and *Adventures of Huckleberry Finn*. Both kinds of construction were also true to

American form in that they decayed easily; indeed, the ephemerality of American neighborhoods, a common theme in nineteenth-century literature, makes its way into Twain's works as well, most especially in *The Gilded Age* and *Roughing It*. Certainly the most transient of structures still parading itself in Twain's name is the rebuilt cabin on Jackass Hill, Tuolumne County, California. The canvas lean-tos he describes in *Roughing It* are of course gone, but so are the boardinghouses in which he lived in San Francisco.

Clemens's most important attempt at permanence was the brick and wood house he and his wife built in Hartford, Connecticut, in 1873. In buying a five-acre lot in Hartford's most desirable residential neighborhood, Nook Farm, the Clemenses hoped to find stability. They extended themselves to the edge of their means to build a mansion in accordance with—or perhaps a touch beyond—the standards of the neighborhood. As Olivia put it in a letter to Samuel:

> We will put if it is necessary the 29000 into the house, grounds, and what new furniture we many need—If we wait to know whether we can afford it we shall wait eight years, because I do not believe we shall know whether we can afford to live in this way until the end of the Copartnership—Charlie [her brother] says I can perfectly well have from three to five hundred dollars a month—You may lecture *one month* in New England during the winter, that will give you 2000.00 that will give you what money you want for Ma and other incidental matters—The three hundred dollars a month with what your regular work will bring you will be plenty. If after a time we find that the estate is not worth a living to us, we will change entirely our mode of living [but] we need now the comfort of a convenient home, while our babies are young and needing care. (2 December 1871, published in *Mark Twain's Letters* 4: 510–511)

Their income did prove sufficient, in spite of a recession in 1873. Still, they pushed their expenditures to the limits of their means, paying $31,000 for the land, $70,000 for the house, and $21,000 for the furniture.

The house expresses their joint idea of the material side of *domesticity in a *fashion of opulence and a machine-tooled exuberance of ornamentation. Within a few years, they renovated to include hand-painted wallpaper and other ornaments from Tiffany's. As much as Twain's literature about the West recaptures the material culture of his earlier houses, his later literature also expresses the cultural attitudes embodied in his Hartford house. Indeed, these attitudes are not that different in principle so much as scale. In all cases, the house is an external sign of economic aspiration; whether it is a clapboard house on the frontier denoting rising wealth or the brick house announcing arrival, the basic idea of the American dream is central to Twain's visions of prosperity and uprightness.

It is the contrast between the home of the Widow Douglas and pap's shack in *Adventures of Huckleberry Finn*.

Their hopes of permanence notwithstanding, Olivia and Samuel Clemens did not live out their lives in the three-story, nineteen-room mansion they had built according to Olivia's plans and put into reality under the hand of architect Edward T. Potter. While they stayed in Hartford from 1874 to 1891, the high price of maintaining the house, which included entertaining in appropriate style, proved too much through the financial vicissitudes of the 1890s. They closed the house in 1891 and moved to Europe. Their daughter Susy, while visiting Hartford in 1896, contracted meningitis and died in the house. That apparently dissuaded Olivia and Samuel from returning, though they did not put the house on the market until 1902. Theirs was not the only Nook Farm fortune suffering reversal; all of the original residents at one time or another suffered serious financial difficulties. And the city's growth around the neighborhood ultimately devalued the community itself. When they finally sold the house in 1903, the Clemenses received a mere $28,000. The house was used briefly as a private residence, a school, a warehouse, a library, and a rooming house before the Mark Twain Memorial Foundation finally purchased and renovated the building, turning it into a museum.

The Clemens family was itinerant from 1891 until well after Olivia's death in 1904, trying out a number of houses, none of which they found ultimately congenial. Fully out of debt, Clemens decided toward the end of his life to try to recover the feeling of stability that the Hartford home represented by building another house, this time in Redding, Connecticut, where he had purchased nearly 250 acres of land in 1906. In 1907, he commissioned John Mead Howells, son of William Dean *Howells, to design the house, and allowed, or perhaps even encouraged, daughter Clara to participate in planning and overseeing construction. Built on the money he earned on *"Extract from Captain Stormfield's Visit to Heaven," he named the house "Stormfield" and lived there until his death in 1910. Clara sold the house many years after her father's death. When the house burned down, its owners built a near replica, which remains in private hands.

This late effort to find stability was only partly successful since the family had already dispersed. Ironically, the most stable home of Clemens's life was one that he did not own, the Crane's house at Quarry Farm, *Elmira, New York. Given the enduring familial connections to that homestead, it is no surprise that the entire Clemens family is buried not in Hartford, where it lived longest, but in Elmira, where its roots were deepest.

♦ SEE ALSO Crane, Susan Langdon and Theodore; Finances.

HOWELLS, WILLIAM DEAN (1837–1920).

In a 23 March 1878 letter to William Dean Howells, Twain wrote, "I owe as much to your training as the rude country job printer owes to the city boss who takes him in hand & teaches him the right way to handle his art." While this tribute is perhaps exaggerated, it is true that, with the exception of Olivia Langdon Clemens, no other person had a greater impact on Twain's works than Howells. The central literary figure of his age—prolific writer, wide-ranging reader, and national arbiter of taste for much of his career—Howells generously supplied his time and talent helping Clemens to shape the voice and develop the ideas that became the works of Mark Twain.

Like Clemens, Howells grew up west of the Appalachians, a distinction in the literary world of mid-nineteenth-century America that branded Howells as a westerner, though his boyhood in Ohio must have been significantly different from Clemens's in Missouri. Still, they both grew up next to major rivers, glorified steamboating, idolized steamboat pilots, and began their working lives in print shops—in Howells's case, that of his father, the editor of a country newspaper. In this common "western" experience they found a bond early in their friendship. At least Howells, for all of his aspirations to eastern respectability and propriety, could appreciate the untrammeled language of different places and social classes as he read and edited Twain's writings. Although Howells had dropped the dialect of the West in cultivating gentility, he "gladly recognized the phrases which [Clemens] employed for their lasting juiciness and the long-remembered savor they had on his mental palate" (*My Mark Twain*, chapter 4).

Still, the differences of their experiences are equally significant. Howells followed his father's intense abolitionism. He wrote a campaign biography of Abraham Lincoln for the 1860 presidential election, and was rewarded with an appointment as U.S. Consul in Venice. Clemens's father held slaves, and for all of Samuel's exposure to abolitionism from his brother Orion, he did not grow fervent in his abolitionism until the point was made moot by the Union victory in the Civil War. While both Howells and Clemens missed directly participating in the most momentous public event of their lifetimes, they did so for opposite reasons. Howells's job as consul during the Civil War kept him in Italy, where his aspirations toward gentility and his studies both received environmental encouragement. Clemens deserted from the war to head west, working for himself as a miner and journalist in Nevada and California. In the 1860s, their movements in social respectability were diametrically opposed.

On the strength of poetry he had published in 1860 and journalism in eastern newspapers and magazines in 1863 and 1864, Howells returned to America, married to Elinor Mead, a well-connected New England woman. He worked first for the New York *Times*, then as an assistant editor for *The Nation*, the newly established Radical Republican journal of politics and the arts. He moved to Boston to take up a position as assistant editor for *The *Atlantic Monthly*, which he joined in 1866, the same year he published his first travel writing, *Venetian Life*.

At the *Atlantic*, Howells's task was to walk a fine line between New England propriety and a more ecumenical opening onto a larger world of letters. It became his job, ultimately, to discover and print new writers from around the country. In this capacity, especially when he was promoted to the editorship of the *Atlantic* and later as a contributing editor at *Harper's* from 1886, Howells introduced to America many of its—and the world's—most important writers. Among these were not only French realists like Émile Zola, but authors beyond America's usual English, French, and Italian horizons: Leo Tolstoy, Fyodor Dostoyevsky, and Henrik Ibsen, among others. On the American scene, Howells's early advocacy of such new writers as Stephen Crane, Sarah Orne Jewett, Harold Frederic, Charles W. Chesnutt, and others too numerous to mention here helped shape the development of American literary realism. Gaining favorable public notice from Howells could launch a career for an American author. Howells's move from the Boston area to New York in 1888 symbolized the shift in the nation's cultural center from Boston to New York, which he memorialized in *A Hazard of New Fortunes* (1890).

Clemens first met Howells in 1869, before Howells had become eminent. Howells had just written a favorable notice of *The Innocents Abroad*, and Clemens visited the offices of the *Atlantic* to pay his thanks. This began a friendship that served the professional, intellectual, and social interests of both, though only for a brief time near the end of Clemens's life when he lived in New York City did the two live near enough to spend much time together. They built their friendship on an intense correspondence and on more intense visits of several days either in Clemens's Hartford home or in the Boston area where Clemens often had literary business.

Both men looked forward to such meetings, though the restrained Howells sometimes found Twain's contact overwhelming and unusual:

> He used to give me a royal chamber on the ground floor, and come in at night after I had gone to bed to take off the burglar alarm so that the family should not be roused if anybody tried to get in at my window. This would be after we had sat up late, he smoking the last of his innumerable cigars, and soothing his tense nerves with a mild hot Scotch, while we both talked and talked and talked, of everything in the heavens and on the earth, and the waters under the earth. After two days of this talk I would come away hollow, realizing myself best in the image of one of those locust-shells which you find sticking to the bark of trees at the end of summer. (*My Mark Twain*, chapter 3)

But as exhausting as the visits must have been, with interminable late night bouts of drinking, smoking, billiards, and conversation, Howells kept coming back, lured by Clemens's creative energy, which pulled Howells into its orbit. The two often conspired late at night to work together on the most impossible of projects, though the cold light of day usually found Howells in a more conventional mood.

Fortunately, the record of their forty-year friendship has been preserved in their copious and often brilliant correspondence, which shows the wide range of intellectual and personal interests they shared, as well as the professional concerns that brought them together in the first place. Primarily this relationship began with Howells's acting, appropriately, as Clemens's editor:

> I had become editor of *The Atlantic Monthly,* and I had allegiances belonging to the conduct of what was and still remains the most scrupulously cultivated of our periodicals. When Clemens began to write for it he came willingly under its rule, for with all his wilfulness [*sic*] there never was a more biddable man in things you could show him a reason for. He never made the least of that trouble which so abounds for the hapless editor from narrower-minded contributors. If you wanted a thing changed, very good, he changed it; if you suggested that a word or a sentence or a paragraph had better be struck out, very good, he struck it out. His proof-sheets came back each a veritable "mush of concession," as Emerson says. Now and then he would try a little stronger language than *The Atlantic* had stomach for, and once when I sent him a proof I made him observe that I had left out the profanity. He wrote back: "Mrs. Clemens opened that proof, and lit into the room with danger in her eye. What profanity? You see, when I read the manuscript to her I skipped that." It was part of his joke to pretend a violence in that gentlest creature which the more amusingly realized the situation to their friends." (*My Mark Twain,* chapter 5)

Howells, walking the line between what he called Clemens's "Elizabethan breadth of parlance, which I suppose one ought not to call coarse without calling one's self prudish" (*My Mark Twain,* chapter 1), and the crisp, indeed prudish standards of the literary elite, helped Clemens negotiate those standards without destroying the power of Clemens's own language and imagination. Howells's own sense of humor aided him in negotiating that difficult line, and the catholic taste that came out of his humor undoubtedly made him an astute critic and editor.

Certainly Twain relied on Howells's taste often, not only in the early days when contributing his first pieces to the *Atlantic*—when Howells legitimately "scarified," to use Clemens's phrase, Twain's pages—but later, when publishing his books. Howells read drafts, edited manuscripts, and even corrected proofs for most of Twain's books, all while working on his own extremely heavy writing load. But the criticism frequently laid on Howells that he restricted and damaged Twain's genius does not hold up. Often, Howells was more enthusiastic about Twain's draft works or ideas than was Twain himself. For instance, when Howells saw the bulk of the manuscript of *"Extract from Captain Stormfield's Visit to Heaven" in the early

1880s, he advised Clemens to publish. Clemens held back, fearing that publication would damage his reputation.

Howells was, of course, a prolific writer in his own right, publishing not only regularly as editor and columnist for major literary magazines, but also numerous volumes of novels, poems, essays, and memoirs. Notable among these are his travel sketches *Venetian Life* (1866) and *Italian Journeys* (1867); his novels *A Modern Instance* (1881), *The Rise of Silas Lapham* (1885), *A Hazard of New Fortunes* (1890), and *A Traveller from Altruria* (1894); and his literary memoirs, *My Literary Passions* (1895), *Literary Friends and Acquaintance* (1900), and *My Mark Twain* (1910).

Clemens's and Howells's shared interest in politics stands out in their correspondence. Like so many Radical Republicans, Howells had come from a background of utopian political activism. But it was tinged with a certain *noblesse oblige*. Howells's radicalization after the Haymarket riots of 1884 put him in a much better mood to understand and appreciate Clemens's own less focused, less cultivated, less traditional iconoclasm. Clemens, in turn, supported Howells and praised his work, as in a 21 January 1879 letter about *The Lady of Aroostook*: "It is all such truth—truth to life; everywhere your pen fall it leaves a photograph." In 1882, commenting on a passage from *A Modern Instance*, Clemens praises and teases simultaneously: "That's the best drunk scene—because the truest—that I ever read. There are touches in it which I never saw any writer take note of before. And they are set before the reader with amazing accuracy. How very drunk, & how admirably drunk you must have been to enable you to contrive that masterpiece!" (22 June). Here Clemens articulates the literary aesthetic of realism that the two authors were developing in the 1870s and 1880s. Of course, the disciplined Howells was better able to assess social realities than the more energetically imaginative Clemens, but Clemens's ear was far better at capturing the real rhythms of speech. Had they been able to collaborate, perhaps they could have created a realistic fiction. But their abortive efforts on the play *Colonel Sellers as Scientist* proved that their dispositions as writers were too disparate for them to collaborate fruitfully.

Their shared intellectual interest in realism was, however, a powerful connection, binding the two in a desire to create a moral fiction, as well as being the common ground for their moral and political inconsistencies. Certainly Howells was an ambivalent reformer. On the one hand he said publicly in *Criticism and Fiction* (1891) that the realist's fiction is profoundly moral because the realist "feels in every nerve the equality of things and the unity of men." On the other he noted in a private letter to his father, William Cooper Howells, that he was a "theoretical socialist," but "practical aristocrat" (2 February 1890). Clemens, too, had an inconsistent relationship to democratic values, an inconsistency that provided much of the creative tension in many of his best, as well as worst, works.

Howells's inconsistent relationship to democratic values explains his puzzling reaction to Clemens. As much as Howells admired Twain's writing, it also, to some degree, embarrassed him. One cannot know how much Howells let Clemens know this, but he certainly admitted it in his memoir of Clemens, of whose writing he said, "I was often hiding away in discreet holes and corners the letters in which he had loosed his bold fancy to stoop on rank suggestion; I could not bear to burn them, and I could not, after the first reading, quite bear to look at them. I shall best give my feeling on this point by saying that in it he was Shakespearian." More than his writing, Clemens's "relish for personal effect" enchanted a horrified Howells. Howells, whose own efforts to fit into the eastern establishment made him seek an inconspicuous propriety of manner in spite of the prominence of his position, often found the way Clemens "enjoyed the shock, the offence, the pang which" his "love of strong effect ... gave the sensibilities of others" too much to bear (*My Mark Twain*, chapter 1). It was he, perhaps, who magnified the offense of Twain's speech at the *Whittier Birthday Dinner in Clemens's own mind.

Clemens certainly knew that he embarrassed many of the literati. When, for instance, Howells did not carry through on their plan to have Howells use his magazine connections to begin a collaborative novel including installments from many prominent writers, Twain wrote to Howells, "I see where the trouble lies. The various authors dislike trotting in procession behind me. I vaguely thought of that in the beginning, but did not give it its just importance. We must have a new deal. The blindfold Novelettes, must be suggested anonymously" (12 October 1876). Clemens's ambivalence about that judgment led him alternately to perform his outrages iconoclastically and then to recoil in horror at the effect. Howells served him both as enthusiastic and censorious audience to these ambivalent performances.

Clemens's own hankering toward respectability perhaps explains his public and private admiration of Howells as a literary stylist. In an autobiographical dictation he left unpublished, Twain said, "Fine thought and perfect wording are a natural gift with Howells" (9 July 1908). In public he wrote for a *Harper's Monthly* essay entitled "William Dean Howells," "In the sustained exhibition of certain great qualities— clearness, compression, verbal exactness, and unforced and seemingly unconscious felicity of phrasing—he is ... without peer in the English-writing world. ... In the matter of verbal exactness Mr. Howells has no superior, I suppose. He seems to be almost always able to find that elusive and shifty grain of gold, the *right word*" (July 1906). Twain goes on to praise Howells through a series of homey metaphors, including the suggestion that Howells's writing includes a "pemmican quality of compression." showing more of Twain's stylistic power than of Howells's. Indeed, the one attribute of Howells's writing that made him a target of his successors in the 1920s was his Victorian orotundity. For this style and for his moral exactness, he was dethroned as America's reigning writer for the first half of the twentieth century. Rediscovered by academics in the 1950s and 1960s, he is today admired for his keen moral perceptions and aesthetic and structural innovations, but his writing remains in its rhetorical complexity a barrier to a widespread appeal.

"HOW TO TELL A STORY." Twain wrote this exercise in literary criticism, one of his most widely reprinted pieces, on 8 February 1894 while living in the Players Club in New York City. His family was living in Europe, but he was in New York tending to business, which was collapsing around him. As exhausted as he was, he still managed to toss off this tight essay, though he did not place it for some time. It first appeared in *Youth's Companion* on 3 October 1895.

It is a deceptive essay. On the surface it seems merely to describe, with an American bias, oral storytelling traditions, labeling them as typically American and contrasting them to European forms of comedy, which Twain calls comic and witty. But too many commentators have taken this essay only at face value. Twain knew that there was a substantial appetite for American "humor" in Europe and that its very "Americanness" made it sell, but that European pleasure in coarse American comedy came with a degree of condescension. And in fact, much American comedy did play on frontier crudeness, often the comedy of elites mocking the lower classes, though sometimes with the comedy celebrating, rather than denigrating, crudeness. Regardless, Europeans considered American humor a natural excrescence, a primitive ebullition, rather than an art.

What Twain does is turn the tables. He insists that American humor is genial and—especially—artful. In his definition, he taps the European tradition of *amiable humor, which is often the humor of character rather than wit. It is a tradition that promised to promote political liberalism, a cause Twain certainly held dear at this point in his career, and that implicitly lies in this essay. In proclaiming such humor as uniquely American, he disingenuously co-opts a long English tradition of artistry; in grafting it to American folkways, he elevates folk art over the art of cultivation.

HUCKLEBERRY FINN. When Twain introduced Huckleberry Finn's character in chapter 6 of *The Adventures of Tom Sawyer*, Huck was little more than a symbol, a social type, a touchstone by which Tom Sawyer's straining against authority could be authenticated. He was the forbidden child of an alcoholic tramp, and as such was "admired" and "envied" by "every harassed, hampered, respectable boy in St. Petersburg." But as a marginal character, Huck moved into the center of Twain's consciousness precisely because Huck's imperfect socialization made him a test case for Clemens's moral ruminations and a perfect foil for numerous aspects of American culture. The shift began at the end of *Tom Sawyer* when Huck becomes a moral agent on his own in rescuing the Widow Douglas from Injun Joe's revenge. At that point, Twain began to write much about Huck's experiences in becoming "civilized." William Dean *Howells suggested he cut this material from *Tom Sawyer*, which he did, only to use it as the opening of *Adventures of Huckleberry Finn*.

In narrating this ostensible sequel to *Tom Sawyer* in Huck's voice, Twain created not the "idle, lawless, vulgar and bad" character first introduced in the earlier book, but instead a character Twain came to call a good-hearted boy. As he put it when introducing the "Small-pox and a Lie Save Jim" sequence of his standard lecture in his world tour of 1895, "In a crucial moral emergency a sound heart is a safer guide than an ill-trained conscience. I should support this doctrine with a chapter from a book of mine where a sound heart & a deformed conscience come into collision & conscience suffers defeat." The key for Twain is the internal battle between training and temperament that was at the center of his moral thinking in his examinations of *sentimentalism and *utilitarianism.

Most of the other characters Twain returned to repeatedly over his career—Colonel *Sellers, *Tom Sawyer, *Joan of Arc, and *McWilliams—represent one character trait or stance almost to the exclusion of all others, creating conflict external to the characters in depicting them against a cultural or social backdrop. Huck internalizes conflict, and as such, Huck became the character in which Twain invested himself most heavily.

That investment does not show in the published sequels to *Adventures of Huckleberry Finn*, namely *Tom Sawyer Abroad* (1894) and *Tom Sawyer, Detective* (1896). In each of these, Huck is the first-person narrator, but in neither does Twain maintain the same moral intensity he discovered in *Huckleberry Finn*. In each of these tales, Huck seems awestruck by Tom's authority, which is frozen in place despite the ostensible lessons Huck learned at the end of his own novel. In neither does the narrator develop his own character, serving instead more as a shallow audience to Tom's antics. In both of these short novels, published in the 1890s when Twain was strapped for cash and writing quickly to earn it, Twain seems to have decided to sell out depth for a flashy surface.

But Twain maintained his investment in Huck's character in other ways, not least of which in his lecture tour of 1895. Huck makes his way, too, into the book that came out of that tour, *Following the Equator*. In chapter 53, when Twain has an audience with a Hindu holy man who has attained the state of perfection, he writes,

> He proposed an exchange of autographs, a delicate attention which made me believe in him, but I had been having my doubts before. He wrote his in his book. . . . It contains his voluminous comments on the Hindu holy writings, and if I could make them out I would try for perfection myself. I gave him a copy of Huckleberry Finn. I thought it might rest him up a little to mix it in along with his meditations on brahma, for he looked tired, and I knew that if it didn't do him any good it wouldn't do him any harm.

Here Twain ironically levels himself with a holy man, suggesting something of the moral wisdom he finds in Huck's travails. Later, he creates a Huck alterego in the *unpublished work *"Three Thousand Years among the Microbes," the narrator of which takes the name Huck after he is transmogrified into a microbe inhabiting the body of a drunken tramp. Again, the character stands outside the norms of society, seeks a comfortable conscience, and finds it difficult to reconcile his social needs with morality. Such was the plight of Clemens himself; no wonder that Huck was one of his favorite characters.

HUCKLEBERRY FINN, ADVENTURES OF. SEE *Adventures of Huckleberry Finn.*

HUMOR. Definitions of humor abound but that nomenclature has changed from generation to generation and place to place, making it difficult to anatomize Twain's humor. The basic psychology of humor may be the best starting point. Humor usually stems from perception of incongruity, from sudden recognition that the world is not as expected. Incongruous dislocations, when they cause no immediate pain and when psychologically distant enough to feel safe, force us into laughter, into a suspension of action in favor of aesthetic contemplation. When in such a state of suspended activity, we are alive to other possibilities, to alternative modes of thought that could entail new modes of action.

But humor implies no action of its own. It is part of a dialectic between choices and choosing. Made choices require repression of alternatives in order to suspend incessant recrimination. Humor provides a way to second-guess without consequences, to wallow in alternatives without recrimination. Perpetual humor would entail perpetual passivity, just as humorlessness would entail dogmatically inflexible pursuit of goals. The problem for the human mind is to move from the openness of humor to the directed behavior of seriousness, from the amorphous and amoral nature of a mode of perception to finding value and thus purpose in such perception. Humor's form and value come from its social contexts, which try to direct humor's anarchic potentials through conventional forms, such as parody, *burlesque, anecdote, tall tale, hoax, comedy of manners, *amiable humor, *satire, and so on. To understand Twain's uses of humor, then, it is important to understand how his culture tried to shape humor and how he understood that shaping.

While most historical theories of humor that were accepted during the 1800s agreed that humor arises from a perception of incongruity, the value of that perception was hotly contested. That contest, in turn, impinged on Clemens's own exercise of his sense of humor. When Clemens finally committed himself to a career as a writer of humorous literature, in a 19 October 1865 letter to his brother Orion, he did so with a remarkable degree of self-denigration:

> I never had but two powerful ambitions in my life. One was to be a pilot, & the other a preacher of the gospel. I accomplished the one & failed in the other, because I could not supply myself with the necessary stock in trade— *i.e.* religion. I have given it up forever. I never had a "call" in that direction,

anyhow, & my aspirations were the very ecstasy of presumption. But I *have* had a "call" to literature, of a low order—*i.e.* humorous. It is nothing to be proud of, but it is my strongest suit.

His sense that humor was unworthy of his attentions persisted through much of his life; his letters are replete with disparaging references to "mere" humor, even when he was surprised to find that others appreciated his writings. For instance, in a letter to Olivia shortly after he met Rev. Joseph *Twichell, he wrote, "The idea of that party of ministers at [Twichell's] house the other night thanking me fervently for having written & published certain trash which they said had lit up some gloomy days with a wholesome laugh was a surprise to me. I had not flattered myself before that a part of my mission on earth was to be a benefactor to the clergy" (30 October 1868). Early in his career, he was told repeatedly about the value of his work, but only grudgingly endorsed it. As he put it in a letter to Mary Mason *Fairbanks in which he described his newest lecture, "The American Vandal Abroad," he noted, "I *think* it will *entertain* an audience, this lecture. I *must not* preach to a select few in my audience, lest I have only a select few to listen, next time, & so be required to preach no more. What the societies *ask* of me is to *relieve* the heaviness of their didactic courses—& in accepting the contract I am just the same as *giving my word* that I will do as they ask" (12 October 1868). This defense of his contract comes in a letter in which he explains to Fairbanks that he will not offend with his humor, and will thus be worthy of his gifts and of the audience's higher feelings and principles.

The context of the letter alone suggests that the simple value of entertainment was not enough to supply him with a sense of mission. In his autobiographical dictation of 31 July 1906, he returned to the theme of his 1865 letter to Orion. In comparing his work to that of other humorists, he stressed his own moral purpose:

> In this mortuary volume I find Nasby, Artemus Ward, Yawcob Strauss, Derby, Burdette, Eli Perkins, the "Danbury News Man," Orpheus C. Kerr, Smith O'Brien, Josh Billings, and a score of others, maybe two score, whose writings and sayings were once in everybody's mouth but are now heard of no more and are no longer mentioned. . . . Why have they perished? because they were merely humorists. Humorists of the "mere" sort cannot survive. Humor is only a fragrance, a decoration. . . . Humor must not professedly teach, and it must not professedly preach, but it must do both if it would live forever. . . . I have always preached. That is the reason that I have lasted thirty years. If the humor came of its own accord and uninvited, I have allowed it a place in my sermon, but I was not writing the sermon for the sake of the humor. I should have written the sermon just the same, whether any humor applied for admission or not.

Obviously, Clemens could not comfortably resign himself to the exercise of his gifts as a humorist because he did not find value in those gifts themselves, though he did come to appreciate them as a medium.

Such an assessment was not peculiar to his place and time, in part because he was a child of American Protestantism, which in its most rigorous forms distrusted all *games and amusements, and cited biblical passages to enjoin laughter, joking, raillery, and play. The gospel of Luke begins the New Testament assault on laughter in chapter 6, verses 21 and 25: "Blessed are ye that weep now, for ye shall laugh" in the kingdom of heaven, and "Woe unto you that laugh now! for ye shall mourn and weep." These verses in part justified a cultural preoccupation with the literature of pathos over the literature of laughter.

More elaborate in its denunciation of laughter, Paul's letter to the Ephesians compares those who laugh with some of the most despicable of sinners:

> But fornication, and all uncleanness, or covetousness, let it not be once named among you, as becometh saints; neither filthiness, nor foolish talking, nor jesting, which are not convenient: but rather giving of thanks. For this ye know, that no whoremonger, nor unclean person, nor covetous man, who is an idolater, hath any inheritance in the kingdom of Christ and of God. Let no man deceive you with vain words: for because of these things cometh the wrath of God upon the children of disobedience. (5:3–6)

Overall, fundamentalist American Protestants followed the advice of the book of James: "Be afflicted and mourn, and weep: let your laughter be turned to mourning, and your joy to heaviness" (4:9), and "Is there any among you . . . merry? let him sing psalms" (5:13). Clemens, whose psychological roots lay in the fundamentalist Presbyterianism of the 1830s and 1840s, obviously imbibed these sentiments, and the continuing religiosity of his age and community throughout his years in Hartford would not so much have imposed a sense of the impropriety of laughter as reinforced it.

Partly the religious elites could point to a folk humor and to a journalistic variant of that folk literature to support their contention that humor was at best idle, at worst immoral, in that so much folk comedy revels in violence, scatology, and bawdry. As long as this comic tradition existed, it is easy to see the roots of Twain's anxiety about the status of comic writing. Indeed, early in his career as a humorist, people categorized Twain's writing as less than genteel. Some labeled the early work as *southwestern humor or *comic journalism, or more simply as the product of the West, as the *Overland Monthly* put it in its review of *Roughing It*:

> As Irving stands, without dispute at the head of American classic humorists, so the precedence in the unclassical school must be conceded to Mark Twain. About him there is nothing classic, bookish, or conventional, any more than

there is about a buffalo or a grizzly. His genius is characterized by the breadth, and ruggedness, and audacity of the West; and, wherever he was born, or wherever he may abide, the great West claims him as her intellectual offspring. (June 1872, 580–581)

This reviewer saw ruggedness and audacity as virtues, when so many Americans would see them as vices, but few would argue that the early Twain wrote out of such a tradition.

The reference to "classic" humor as opposed to western humor suggests yet a third strand influencing Clemens's work, and ultimately the standard by which Clemens could find his moral voice and his justification of humor. America is as much a product of the Enlightenment as it is of the Reformation or of folk culture. Consequently, Clemens developed an understanding of the Enlightenment's defense of laughter in the creation of the entire idea of a sense of humor.

The concept of a sense of humor was a product of the psychology of *sentimentalism with its emphasis on mental sensitivities to the internal qualities of persons, things, and events. As such, sentimentalists held that each person had an innate capacity to sense and find pleasure in incongruities. Sentimentalists believed that the capacity to see incongruities was a saving grace against seriousness, which, while the essence of life, if pursued too rigorously would lead to mental and emotional exhaustion, despair, and inutility. To the serious moralists of the Enlightenment, then, the sense of humor was a counterweight to the serious sensibilities, such as the *moral sense or the sense of *reverence. Those Christian ministers of the nineteenth century who tried to alleviate the rigors of *Calvinism, then, turned to sentimental ethics to justify humor as a relief. Clemens's San Francisco friend Rev. Whitney Bellows, for instance, argued that humor was the "inner side of laughter," which in its regular exercise improved the serious faculties of the mind: "The intellect that plays a part of every day, works more powerfully and to better results, for the rest of the time; the heart that is gay for an hour, is more serious for the other hours of the day" (*The Role of Public Amusements to Public Morality,* 1857).

The health-giving capacity of humor was its more common justification in America, with the clergy tapping not only Enlightenment moralists but also the Old Testament for support. The proverb, "A merry Heart Doeth good like a medicine," and writings from Ecclesiastes endorse the idea that there is a time for all things, even humor. At least the American Publishing Company, in advertisements of 11 December 1871 to promote *Roughing It,* quoted the latter: "'There is a time to laugh,' and all who read this book will see clearly that time has come."

The value of humor as recreation was less important to the European philosophers who promoted it than was humor's capacity to liberalize social interaction. Renaissance thinkers held that our capacity to laugh at "humorists"—those whose behavior was eccentric in proportion to which their dispositions were dominated by a single humor—coerced them back to normalcy under the pressure of scorn and satire. Enlightenment philosophers suggested that there was an amiable humor, one that enabled us to indulge and appreciate eccentricity and incongruity as a way to escape conformity.

While such a description of the role of humor does not necessitate formal genres, it does lead to certain structural peculiarities that allowed writers to distinguish between humor and wit as well as humor and satire. Clemens, though he often violated them, accepted such distinctions, as can be seen in his description of humor in "How to Tell a Story":

> The humorous story depends for its effect upon the *manner* of the telling; the comic story and the witty story upon the *matter*. The humorous story may be spun out to great length, and may wander around as much as it pleases, and arrive nowhere in particular; but the comic and witty stories must be brief and end with a point. The humorous story bubbles gently along, the others burst. . . . The humorous story is told gravely; the teller does his best to conceal the fact that he even dimly suspects that there is anything funny about it; but the teller of the comic story tells you beforehand that it is one of the funniest things he has ever heard, then tells it with eager delight, and is the first person to laugh when he gets through. And sometimes, if he has had good success, he is so glad and happy that he will repeat the "nub" of it and glance around from face to face, collecting applause, and then repeat it again. It is a pathetic thing to see.

No wonder, then, that comedians of all stripes and inclinations tried to attach to their work the name "humor" in order to elevate its prestige, but no wonder, too, that reviewers of humor constantly quibbled over whether it is in fact vulgar and denigrating, or fine and uplifting, as they certainly did in reviewing Twain's books. Clemens always paid attention to such reviews and tried to strike a balance between genteel humor, which would win the applause of the cultural elites, and the more energetic humor of the folk and journalistic traditions, which would help him sell books to the masses.

Perhaps that is why Clemens found the value of his humor in its didacticism. But there is an irony here in that didacticism tends not to value the free play of humor so much as the constructive use of humor either in sympathy or ironic satire. Both derive their comedy from exploiting incongruities, but the essential difference between "humor" and "irony" as comic attitudes may be in the humorist's faith in what incongruity means. Satiric *irony entails negation, whereas humor tends to be optimistic about indulging incongruity, about seeing its way out of difficulty, conflict, or pain. Humor usually ends happily. With the pleasure of construction and optimism, humor tends to be playful, even behind the screen of didacticism. The didacticism is what nineteenth-century Americans valued above all, and that is the attribute of his own work that Clemens assumed gave his comedy staying power. As he once wrote on a scrap of paper (now tipped into a copy of *Mark Twain's Library of Humor in the Lilly Library), "The function of humor is that of the screw in the opera glass—it adjusts one's focus"[1]—a view of humor stressing its use rather than its pleasure. Yet in comparison to the humorists he listed as having "died," many, like Orpheus C. Kerr and Petroleum Nasby were more "preachy" than Twain. Sermons alone do not give Twain's works their staying power. Perhaps they last because Twain had a deeper capacity for play, a more liberal and encompassing comic imagination, a more profound humor, than most of his contemporaries.

---

1. Mark Twain's previously unpublished words are © 2002 by Richard A. Watson and the Chase Global Private Bank as Trustees of the Mark Twain Foundation, which reserves all reproduction or dramatization rights in every medium. Quotation is made with the permission of the University of California Press and Robert H. Hirst, General Editor of the Mark Twain Project.

IDENTITY. The question of personal identity in western cultures has long been tied up with the idea that each person has a unique soul, that identity is fundamental, intrinsic, and immutable. But the history of western literature is replete with masquerades in which class and gender identities are confused, only to be sorted out by tale's end, and Twain's literature is no exception. The plots of "An *Awful ---- Terrible Medieval Romance" and *The Prince and the Pauper* turn on swapped identities, and Huck's multiple disguises ultimately end in his exchanging roles with Tom Sawyer. Likewise, Hank and the King masquerade as commoners in *A Connecticut Yankee in King Arthur's Court*, and Tom's cross-dressing compounds the central plot problem of the changelings in *Pudd'nhead Wilson and Those Extraordinary Twins*. Joan also cross-dresses as a soldier in *Personal Recollections of Joan of Arc*. Conventionally in western literature, the masquerade is resolved in favor of an immutable reality; disguises are all uncovered as accidental while a person's real self comes through as essential in the climax of a comic story.

Twain's stories often work on this same pattern, but the stakes seem much higher, suggesting something of a larger cultural anxiety about identity that was leading to major shifts in conception of human personality over the last half of the nineteenth and first half of the twentieth centuries. Scientific theories about the orderliness of the universe and the distance of God challenged comfortable ideas of the soul, and the conception of the mind as a blank slate came to suggest that personality was a product of experience. Thus, many thinkers began to suggest that identity is not intrinsic but contingent on culture and training. At the same time, however, the bourgeois idea of individual freedom, spawned in the sixteenth century and the basis of a concept of character on which nineteenth-century business culture depended, required an idea of the intrinsic value and uniqueness of the individual as the *sine qua non* of political freedom. Thus, the conditions of modernity created an uncomfortable tension between faith in the individual and skepticism that individuality even exists.

This background makes Twain's play with identity all the more poignant. On the one hand, Twain's works argue on the whole that, as he put it in *Connecticut Yankee*, "training is everything" (chapter 18). In such a context, a human being is merely surface, the presentation of self that sociologists in the twentieth century came to argue constitutes identity. As such, the many masquerades of Twain's works, mirroring the many shifts in stature and role that Clemens himself experienced in his various careers and habitations, suggest that a person can shift according to circumstance to become anything socially necessary. Some of Twain's tales suggest that such a condition is one of freedom and independence.

Yet Twain never was comfortable with this modern definition of identity as much as he often tried to argue for it. At the same time, he seems worried that a selfhood based on such shifting sands while free is also shifty, a source of *confidence games and immorality. As such, he always struggled against himself to find an essential identity, "that one atom of me that is me" as Hank Morgan puts it (chapter 18), that can persist in spite of social mores and the exigencies of any immediate circumstance. Only such a continuous identity could be a source of moral direction, Twain felt, as did so many of his Victorian peers.

Twain's perplexity in part fueled his late belief, expressed in such works as *What Is Man?*, "The Turning Point of My Life," and the various diaries of *Adam and Eve, that identity was a combination of circumstance and temperament, the latter intrinsic and immutable, the former extrinsic and variable. The combination, as Twain came to see it, made for a tortured human psychology, caught between the honesty of impulses too selfish to reveal and social needs too powerful to endure. As such, he denied the idea that identity is completely malleable, but also rejected the belief that the immutable part of one's identity provided any useful moral bearings.

♦ SEE ALSO Determinism; Dreams; Sentimentalism; Utilitarianism.

ILLUSTRATIONS. Few twentieth-century editions of Twain's writings do his work full justice because they omit the original illustrations, which were almost as much a part of the conceptual content as the words themselves. More than a century later, in a culture that sees visual and print media as opposed, such an assertion might seem extreme, but in the nineteenth century, print was the mass medium and illustrations provided quick entrée for mass audiences into the pleasures of reading. Indeed, illustrations provide the first, and often the most compelling, interpretation of a book.

Still, the level and nature of illustrations varied among kinds of printed matter. Trade books, the apex of status in the publishing industry, tended to have few if any illustrations, and newspapers and journals usually had more the larger the circulation they hoped to have. Subscription books occupied a middle ground, reaping the benefits of production technologies developed for journalism, while capitalizing on the formality and pretension of the book itself.

Illustrations were the most expensive part of publishing, primarily because technologies of production were more labor- and skill-intensive than for print alone. Over the course of the nineteenth century these technologies changed, from wood cuts to various techniques of photo-engraving (Clemens himself invested in and lost money on an ingenious but short-lived advance in lithography, the

Kaolatype process), but while each change improved the process, improvements in text-only printing far outstripped those for illustrations. Thus, the costs of illustration remained a limiting factor in the cost of book and journal production.

As with commercial art today, the balance between art and commerce was dynamic and complex. Daniel Carter Beard, one of Twain's favorite illustrators, learned illustration, against his parents' wishes, in the workshop of his brother, a commercial illustrator who worked for both journal and book publishers in New York City. Beard, like many commercial illustrators, pursued commercial art to satisfy his desire to live an artist's life while earning a living. He learned quickly that the commercial elements of the trade stressed speed over artistry:

Illustration of Merlin using the face of Tennyson as a model, Daniel Carter Beard (1850–1941), from *A Connecticut Yankee in King Arthur's Court*, New York: Webster & Company, 1889, p. 41.

All the pictures were drawn on wood, and the blocks handed over to the wood engraver, who engraved them. As soon as the engraving was done the original pictures, of course, were lost. Boxwood was used for the blocks which were coated with white lead, so that the picture could be drawn upon the block with lead pencil.... All the pictures had to be drawn backwards; that is, if a man were represented whittling something or using a stick or a hammer, he must be doing it with his left hand, because when it was engraved and printed the impression was reversed and the man would then be using his right hand. The artist signed his name backwards, and some illustrators became so expert that it was said that they could write their names backwards better then they could forwards. (*Hardly a Man Is Now Alive*)

Nonetheless, Beard pursued the artistic side quite admirably, finally working in book illustration where his product would not necessarily be destroyed in the production. The Mark Twain Papers hold many of the original pen-and-ink drawings Beard did for *A Connecticut Yankee in King Arthur's Court*.

Illustration of Mark Twain being shaved, by True Williams (1839–1897), from "About Barbers," *Sketches New and Old*, Hartford: American Publishing Company, 1875, p. 257.

Most of the illustrations attending Twain's works were done for subscription books, from *The Innocents Abroad* through *Following the Equator*. Such books were copiously illustrated to appeal to a mass market. As George Ade put it, "The publisher knew his public, so he gave a pound of book for every fifty cents, and crowded in plenty of wood-cuts and stamped the outside with golden bouquets" ("Mark Twain and the Old Time Subscription Book," *Review of Reviews*, June 1910). Clemens began publishing books hoping merely that they would be illustrated. After the success of *Innocents Abroad*, which taught him that illustrations contributed significantly to sales, Clemens worked energetically to control as best possible the production of the illustrations. He worried, rightfully, about the quality and appropriateness of the illustrations, as one of the tricks of the illustration game—then for books as now for television and film—was to keep stock images on hand. Twain wanted pictures that went with his text; he often received generic illustrations. The frontispiece in *Innocents Abroad*, for instance, was a recycled picture of a ship at sea, not an illustration of the *Quaker City*. Elisha Bliss may have justified this decision on expedient grounds, namely that production of the illustrations lagged and if the book were to be out in a timely fashion corners had to be cut faster than new illustrations could be. But Bliss also saved money by reusing the old. Indeed, there was an after-market in illustrations between publishers, allowing all of them to pool resources, saving money and time.

Bliss saved money in another way, too, by hiring inexpensive illustrators. Among these were untrained artists whose work was not up to the standards of tonier magazines and books. Often Bliss's illustrators were alcoholics, who would alternately work and drink in binges. The most important of these for a reader of Twain's work was True Williams (1839–1897), who had a hand in illustrating every subscription book Twain published with the *American Publishing Company. A self-taught artist, Williams's marketability suffered from his drinking as much as from his lack of training. As Clemens put it in a letter to William Dean *Howells about the illustrations for *The Adventures of Tom Sawyer*, "Williams has made about 200 rattling pictures for it—some of them very dainty. Poor devil, what a genius he has, & how he does murder it with rum. He takes a book of mine, & without suggestion from anybody builds no end of pictures just from his reading of it" (18 January 1876). Here Clemens damns with faint praise, as the illustrations for *Tom Sawyer* were not up to Williams's best standards. They often stray from the text and the drawings of various characters are not consistent from one illustration to the next. But Clemens, who usually oversaw the illustrations in a book, kept his hands off Williams in this case, perhaps for fear of putting the artist into a sulk which would further slow down the book's production. In any event, after the relative failure of *Tom Sawyer* on the market, Twain tried in the future to control illustrations more carefully, first by choosing his own illustrator for his next book with the American Publishing Company and then by leaving the company entirely. Certainly Twain felt that Bliss, in hiring such workers, may have employed economies that cost more in the long run, as contracted illustrations often came in late or were poorly done.

Such idiosyncracies notwithstanding, Williams and the other illustrators hired by Bliss got the job done in a remarkably effective way. As much as Twain complained in a 24 March 1874 letter to Thomas Bailey *Aldrich about the "Execrable illustrations" attendant on subscription publishing, the very crudeness of the illustrations was often appropriate to the rambunctiousness of Twain's humor. Perhaps most importantly to the development of Mark Twain as a literary persona, Williams and the others included many caricatures of Twain in *Innocents Abroad*, *Roughing It*, and *Sketches, New and Old*.

In this sense, Twain was beholden to the illustrators for the very creation of his public being—no wonder then that he would want to exercise more creative control over the illustrations. He had always done so to some extent, collecting portraits and landscapes for his illustrators to use as models, and sometimes even providing his own drawings, as in *The Gilded Age,* in which he sketched Colonel Sellers's railroad map. After *Tom Sawyer,* Clemens tried to capture that control in his travel book *A Tramp Abroad.* Touring Europe, ostensibly in part to learn to draw, Twain contributed a few sophomoric sketches himself, but for the bulk of the illustrating, he hired an American, Walter Francis Brown. Brown had left America and his career as a commercial illustrator to study painting in France. When offered a major commission as an illustrator by Clemens, he accepted, with the understanding that he would not only do the drawings but would also oversee the production of the plates in Europe. Thus Clemens could supervise Brown and control both the drawing and production. The task proved more than they could handle. Ultimately most of the plates were engraved in Hartford, and many of the illustrations were done by American artists, including, once again, True Williams. Under the pressure of production deadlines, the American Publishing Company bought or pirated already existing work, which could be fitted into the finished book. These irregularities further convinced Clemens of the editorial value of choosing and controlling his own illustrators.

These mishaps all led to Twain's ultimate decision to found his own subscription publishing company, giving him the opportunity to control all aspects of publication, including illustration. The two books most significantly affected by this editorial oversight were *Adventures of Huckleberry Finn* and *Connecticut Yankee,* illustrated by Edward W. Kemble and Daniel Beard respectively.

Kemble, whose meager artistic schooling in New York City supplemented his self-instruction, was beginning his career as an illustrator, working for the New York *Daily Graphic* and *Life* magazine. On the strength of this work, Clemens offered Kemble his first commission to illustrate a book. Kemble's advantage over Williams was his consistency in creating identifiable characters, but Clemens was never exactly sure whether or not he approved of Kemble's work. Kemble created all of his characters off of a single model, an Irish-American boy, Cort Morris. Clemens complained that Kemble made Huck look "too Irishy." Later, when Kemble depicted the king at a revival meeting kissing a young woman, Twain struck the picture from the book, exclaiming that while excellent, it was too lurid for illustration. In these comments, one can see Clemens's editorial principle at work. He had written a biting satire, but knew that he sold best when packaged as an amiable humorist. The illustrations, then, needed to provide a genial counterpoint that would take the sting out of the satire. The pictures needed to posit Huck as a sympathetic hero and almost everybody else as too silly to be taken seriously. Kemble was especially effective in belittling the character of Jim. No matter how urgently the text of the story invests Jim with his full humanity, the grotesque caricatures of him in the illustrations return him to minstrel show status. (Kemble went on to make a career out of such illustrations, selling books of them under the titles *Kemble's Coons* and *Comical Coons.*)

In hiring Beard to illustrate *Connecticut Yankee* five years later, Twain took the opposite editorial tack. Convinced that his investments in the Paige typesetter would set him free of commercial writing, Twain let his satiric temperament have freer range in *Connecticut Yankee* than in any previous book. Assuming *Connecticut Yankee* would be his "swan song," he deemed it worthy of the most opulent treatment physically, including excellent illustrations. Beard proved ideal; he pushed the satiric meaning of the book to its extreme in a series of allegorical political cartoons, the inscriptions of which brought the text home to many contemporary political issues. His choices of famous people as models for many of his illustrations—Albert,

Illustration by Edward Windsor Kemble (1861–1933), a portrait of Colonel Grangerford, from *Adventures of Huckleberry Finn*, New York: Webster & Company, 1885, p. 143.

Lord Tennyson for Merlin, Queen Victoria for a pig princess, Jay Gould for a slave driver—pleased Clemens as much as they offended many contemporary readers. No matter, Clemens was delighted enough to hire Beard again to illustrate *The *American Claimant* and **Tom Sawyer Abroad*, as he considered Beard "the only man who can correctly illustrate my writing, for he not only illustrates the text, but he also illustrates my thoughts" (Beard, *Hardly a Man Is Now Alive,* chapter 13).

Connecticut Yankee is arguably the high point of illustration in Twain's works, not only for the quality of the drawings but for their editorial integrity. Subsequent books were either published quickly under financial duress or were published by trade, rather than by subscription, and thus not copiously illustrated. The exceptions were Twain's gift books—artistically produced, thin volumes, the opposite of subscription books. The two notable ones produced in Clemens's lifetime are *Extracts from Adam's Diary*, illustrated by Frederick Strothmann, and *Eve's Diary*, illustrated by Lester Ralph. In both, illustration and text share equal billing and the artists successfully captured Twain's sense of ironic play with biblical motifs. But for the Eve book, Twain wanted a more refined artist, and Ralph's art nouveau style fit the bill perfectly. Other Twain books worth noting for their illustrations show less happy congruence between art and text. Most infamously, the posthumous publication of *The Mysterious Stranger* as a children's Christmas gift book required not only radical bowdlerization, but also ethereal, nostalgic illustrations by N. C. Wyeth. As outrageously inappropriate as these illustrations may be in their effort to interpret a bitter satire as a gentle and nostalgic idyll, there is a certain fitting consistency in that Twain sanctioned much the same approach to the illustrations in *Huckleberry Finn*.

IMPERIALISM. Samuel Clemens's attitudes toward imperialism began as a normal product of his time and place. Of course, the pages of ancient and modern history are filled with accounts of empires, and Europe began its return to imperial prominence with the conquest of the New World in the sixteenth century.

The revolution of the British North American colonies created the United States as the first modern, postcolonial nation, one that was created without concern for natural geographical barriers or the traditional patterns of indigenous peoples, one that was multicultural from its inception. The history of the United States was one of imperial conquest, with movement from east to west justified by an ostensible "manifest destiny" to cover the continent. In the 1830s, when Clemens was born, the borders of the United States were far from fixed, with filibustering expeditions in the Caribbean and South America almost as common as the steady westward flow across what is now the United States. Canada, too, was considered likely territory for U.S. expansion, and the war with Mexico was in part justified as an exercise of destiny. Clemens did not object to any of these imperial ventures in North America. Indeed, he predicated his persistent animosity toward *Native Americans on both his acceptance of American expansion and his belief in *progress as legitimating that expansion. When commissioned by the Sacramento *Union* to tour Hawaii in order to drum up trade, he took the job so seriously that he advocated annexation of the islands to forestall British or other European powers from doing the same.

By the 1890s, though, Twain became an outspoken opponent of American and European imperialism. In part he was responding to a change in the quality of Europe's imperial ventures; in part he was reflecting a change in himself. What had changed in Europe's imperial projects were the rhetoric and the means. After a span of a century in which the language of liberalism masked imperial expansion as progress, the late century witnessed outspoken rejection of the mandate to improve conditions in favor of a new rhetoric of power. After Charles *Darwin, older racisms were given new sanction, leading European nations and the United States to see themselves not only as more advanced, but also as genetically superior. In such terms, many considered violent displacement or eradication a necessity. While *missionaries remained a prominent element in imperial expansion, their presence did no more than take the teeth from some critics.

Moreover, the development of nation-states over the nineteenth century created national patriotism—a powerful political force. Previously Europeans and Americans tended to confine their loyalties to localities where their families had lived for generations. The new nation-states in the age of industrialization had mobile populations that ascribed allegiance to more abstract entities. In the United States, the *Civil War shifted patriotism from individual states to the United States as a whole, making much easier the mobilization of public opinion and national resources for imperial conquest. In Europe, the process of national consolidation made international conquest an alternative to civil war. Germany, for example, militarized in order to create a nation out of a plethora of principalities.

Industrialization also shaped the military technology that allowed smaller numbers of European and American soldiers to subdue populations in other lands. Europeans had long exploited local differences to style themselves as the keepers of the peace. They successfully did so in North America, India, and Africa in the sixteenth, seventeenth, and eighteenth centuries. But the new technologies of breach-loading rifles, rapid-fire guns like the gatling gun, battleships, long-range artillery, and steam locomotives and ships made it easy for industrialized peoples to subdue other lands without even learning much about them. The late-nineteenth-century conquest of Africa, for example, took place without regard to local tribes, with European powers simply carving out territories that they could defend from each other.

While much of the rhetoric of progress hung on to cover this new phase of imperialism, it sounded thin to political radicals and even to many old-fashioned liberals who once accepted it readily. Clemens fell into this latter camp; his conversion to avid public support of anti-imperialism depended substantially on his liberalism. But that alone could not account for the change in his position from publicly supporting annexation of Hawaii to condemning not only the war in the Philippines, but American and European ventures around the world.

The groundwork for the change came in response to his extensive travel. His *tours gradually helped him to develop a cosmopolitan attitude and a kind of cultural ecumenicalism that began to push toward relativism. Yet his liberal ideals continued to encourage him to think that all human beings are fundamentally alike, that obvious differences are in fact superficial. He maintained to the end of his life that introspection could reveal to him the entire human race—his justification for the self-indulgence of the *autobiography—a philosophy very much in keeping with a European liberal tradition of human *identity. The growth throughout his career of sympathetic identification made his around-the-world trip a transforming experience. In spite of the pleasure he took in what he saw as exotic differences between his own culture and those of India and Africa, he substantially saw human nature as consistent across cultures. Thus, *Following the Equator* became a powerful plea to the English-speaking world to see the rest of the world as equal in humanity.

Primed for a new role as political activist by his world travels, Clemens, when he returned to the United States in 1900 after nearly a decade abroad, was lionized in the press for his courage in paying off his debts and for his Americanness in his recent criticisms of Europe. But the American press was not ready for Twain's attacks, grounded in patriotism, on America, given that so much of the media supported President William McKinley and the policy of annexation of the Philippines. Twain's 12 December 1900 introduction of Winston Churchill at a banquet to promote Anglo-American unity called the two nations "kin in sin" for their policies in South Africa and the Philippines. Given Churchill's role as a British hero in the Boer War, the introduction was remarkably caustic. Twain followed that public performance with publication of two of his most biting satires: "A Salutation-Speech from the Nineteenth-Century to the Twentieth, Taken Down in Short-Hand by Mark Twain," published in the New York *Herald* of 30 December 1900, and "To the Person Sitting in Darkness," published in the February 1901 edition of the *North American Review*. In both cases, Twain bypassed the constitutional and practical issues of America's having a far-flung empire, instead concentrating on the moral issues. He used his image as a prototypical American to remind the country that it had long used the rhetoric of its difference from European powers to justify its existence. By linking the United States with Europe, he hoped to play on American patriotism against an expansionist policy promoted in the name of patriotism.

At first the proexpansion press responded cautiously to Twain's satires, though soon, especially after Twain attacked American missionaries, the replies came fast and furious. Twain undoubtedly lost some of his popularity, but at the same time, he gained status as a reformer and a statesman without portfolio. For the rest of his career, he publicly engaged the debate against imperialism, joining the Anti-Imperialist League, along with William *James, Andrew Carnegie, and William Dean *Howells. He railed not merely against American expansionism, as in "To My Missionary Critics" (April 1901), but also against European imperialism. In particular, Twain raised his voice against Belgian activity in the Congo in "King Leopold's Soliloquy" (1905).

While he publicly seemed to enjoy the fight, and even his private letters show him pugnaciously crowing about the fun he was having, several pieces he wrote but did not publish suggest that he had some anxiety about taking such unpopular stands. He did not publish his "Battle Hymn of the Republic (Brought Down to Date)," nor, most tellingly, "Corn-Pone Opinions." He explained his fear in a letter to Joseph Twichell of 29 January 1901: "I'm not expecting anything but kicks and scoffing, and am expecting a diminution of my bread and butter by it." Given these concerns, it is all the more remarkable that his Mark Twain persona gave Clemens the strength and courage to stand up against a tide of public opinion in favor of his deepest ideals.

♦ SEE ALSO Industrial Revolution.

INDUSTRIAL REVOLUTION. For at least a generation now, people have claimed that we live in a time of unparalleled change, with new technologies arising so quickly as to force us into a kind of "future shock." Without dismissing the power and speed of changing conditions in our own time, there is no comparison to the changes that took place in the nineteenth century. The differences between the wired telephone and cellular phones, between analog electronic transmission and digital electronic transmission, are trivial compared to the change from messages sent by "post," that is by horse, and the invention of the telegraph. In short, we hyperbolically term our refinements "revolutions," whereas the period that saw a shift from animal to machine power witnessed a true revolution, one that changed the realm of possibilities for human life and required changes in the structure and texture of work, community, and politics. The industrial revolution in the United States actually encompassed four related revolutions: in transport, the market, industrial production, and finance.

Young Clemens first became conscious of these revolutions when he left home in August 1853, traveling by steamboat and then by rail to New York City. The speed and ease of transit made it possible for him to move away from his small town on the edge of civilization. This first working trip began a pattern of itinerancy by which he not only became a citizen of the world, but also gathered much of the material for his work. He began accumulating material almost immediately in New York when he went to one of the nineteenth century's numerous urban expositions, the Crystal Palace Exhibition. "The visitors to the Palace," he wrote his sister on 3 September 1853, "average 6,000 daily—double the population of Hannibal." His letter home speaks of the technology not only in the "machinery department . . . on the main floor . . . [for which] it would take more than a week to examine everything on exhibition," but especially throughout the city itself, which he could see from

> the Latting Observatory (height about 280 feet) . . . from it you can obtain a grand view of the city and the country round. The Croton Aqueduct, to supply the city with water, is the greatest wonder yet. Immense sewers are laid across the bed of the Hudson River, and pass through the country to Westchester county, where a whole river is turned from its course, and brought to New York. From the reservoir in the city to the Westchester county reservoir, the distance is *thirty-eight* miles! and if necessary, they could easily supply every family in New York with *one hundred barrels of water per day!*

Here he sees with awe the ways that new technologies change the world by allowing transportation of essential goods and services, as well as of people, to provide for new *cities of hitherto impossible size. The growth and quality of cities was a theme of some importance to Clemens throughout his career, with every travel narrative commenting on the physical condition of the people allowed by, or disallowed by, the state of technological *progress attained. Consider, for instance, his comparisons of cities on the Mississippi River in *Life on the Mississippi*, or his descriptions of various European and Middle Eastern cities in *The Innocents Abroad* and *A Tramp Abroad*.

Indeed, for much of his career, Twain equated progress with technology. Perhaps he put it best in his letter to the *Alta California* from shipboard traveling to New York in January 1867:

> "They that go down to the sea in ships see the wonders of the great deep"— but this modern navigation out-wonders any wonder the scriptural writers dreampt [*sic*] of. To see a man stand in the night, when everything looks alike—far out in the midst of a boundless sea—and measure from one star to another and tell to a dot right where the ship is—to tell the very spot the little insignificant speck occupies on the vast expanse of land and sea twenty-five thousand miles in circumference! Verily, with his imperial intellect and his deep-searching wisdom, man is almost a God!

By career's end, even though he never lost his fascination with new *inventions, he had some doubts about whether technology alone meant progress. In "To the Person Sitting in Darkness" (1901) he mentions that nonwestern countries are happy to borrow the technology of war from the West, but efficiency in killing is not an ideal of progress.

As soon as he settled into a job as a typesetter in New York, he discovered another side of the industrial revolution—the changing organization of work to turn human beings into quasi-machines in a system of production governed by machine speeds and standards. As an apprentice in a complete print shop, he worked at a number of jobs at an artisan's pace. But technological developments— new paper, new presses, the technique of "stereotyping" a page of set type—had transformed city shops in the East by 1850 into factories in which the most important skilled job left belonged to the compositor. So, rather than working as a printer in New York and Philadelphia, young Clemens became more narrowly a typesetter. He found the change abstractly fascinating, writing his family about the difference between old presses and new: "What vast progress has been made in the art of printing! This press [i.e., Benjamin Franklin's old press] is capable of printing about 125 sheets per hour; and after seeing it, I have watched Hoes' great machine [i.e., the rotary press invented by Richard Hoe, first used commercially in 1846] throwing off its 20,000 sheets in the same space of time, with an interest I never before felt" (17 and 18 February 1854).

His interest included not only awe but distress:

> The office I work in is John A. Gray's, 97 Cliff street, and, next to Harpers, is the most extensive in the city. In the room in which I work I have forty

compositors for company. Taking compositors, pressmen, stereotypers, and all, there are about two hundred persons employed in the concern.... They are very particular about spacing, justification, proofs, etc. and even if I do not make much money, I will learn a great deal. I thought Ustick [in St. Louis] was particular enough, but acknowledge now that he was not old maidish. Why, you must put exactly the same space between every two words, and *every line must be spaced alike.* They think it dreadful to space one line with three em spaces, and the next one with five ems. (to Jane Lampton Clemens, 31 August 1853)

Forced to learn the discipline to be a machine employee, his creative energies ebbed. Writing to his brother Orion he said, "I will try to write for the paper occasionally, but I fear my letters will be very uninteresting, for this incessant night work dulls one['s] ideas amazingly. From some cause, I cannot set type near so fast as when I was at home. Sunday is a long day, and while others set 12 and 15,000, yesterday, I only set 10,000. However, I will shake this laziness off, soon, I reckon" (28 November 1853). Laziness was his old-fashioned excuse, but over time he rejected such work precisely because it cramped his creativity; he chose instead to return to the editorial side of publishing, a side that was integrated into the entire job in the old-style printing houses in which he had apprenticed.

The tension, then, between the world of the small town and the modern world shows up throughout Twain's writings as a vacillation between *nostalgia and progress, though at times he cannot separate the two. For instance, his "New Dynasty" essay on the value of the *labor movement suggests that the brains of American workers give them their legitimate authority for self-government, ideas echoed in chapter 10 of *The *American Claimant.* There he argues that the technology by which industrialization makes workers—the "true population of this Republic"—more productive, has "reconstructed this nation." In the post–Civil War period, to "reconstruct" the nation would have had powerful political overtones for a northern audience, suggesting a linkage between technological progress and the progress of republican, rather than aristocratic, values. Twain says as much, claiming that this transformation came not from an intellectual elite but from the hands and brains of common workers: "It is not overstatement to say that the imagination-stunning material development of this century, the only century worth living in since time itself was invented, is the creation of men not college-bred" (chapter 10, *The American Claimant*). Here he suggests that the small-town political values with which he was raised are in fact the same values encouraged by industrialization. Yet the perplexing "man factories" of *A Connecticut Yankee in King Arthur's Court* or the fantasy labor army of zombie workers imagined by Colonel Sellers in *Claimant* itself suggest otherwise. Twain's works express profound ambivalence about the political value of industrialization.

Without revolutions in finance and in the market, shifting Americans away from the self-sustaining agrarian ideal espoused so energetically by Thomas Jefferson, these other revolutions in industrial production and transportation would not have developed. Clemens's attitudes to the *economy were even more vexed than those toward the more obvious technological sides of the new industrialism. In politics, his whiggish propensities and his belief in republican virtue interfered with his belief in the market. Of course, his active participation in the industrial economy kept his real *finances actively engaged in capital formation and he regularly speculated in commodities and financial instruments. Nonetheless, in his writings he rarely approves of the very practices of speculation on which he relied in real life. While many commentators call this gap hypocrisy, it may be better explained as a very real manifestation of future shock.

♦ SEE ALSO Imperialism; Paige Typesetter.

INGERSOLL, ROBERT G. (1833–1899). A lawyer, Union soldier, and politician who spent most of his adult life in Illinois, Robert Ingersoll was best known as an orator whose passionate defense of free thought and equally passionate denunciation of *religion earned him significant notoriety. Ingersoll's very popularity was a sign of a change in spirit in America away from a strict Christian orthodoxy and toward an increasingly heterodox spirituality grafted onto a practical materialism.

While both Clemens and Ingersoll were represented on the *lecture circuit by James Redpath, they met just once when they shared the platform in 1879 at a Chicago banquet paying tribute to Ulysses S. Grant. Clemens was taken by their private conversation and awed, as only a fellow professional can be, by Ingersoll's speaking ability. Ingersoll more importantly influenced Clemens's religious thinking. Clemens read significantly in Ingersoll's works, including Ingersoll's twelve-volume collected works published in 1900. In these writings Clemens found support for his own skepticism. Much of the evidence Twain used, especially in his late writings, to condemn what he saw as the narrowness of Christianity he gleaned from Ingersoll's works.

INITIATION RITES. One of the myths of American culture centers around the image of the lone man, the so-called American Adam, facing a new world in glorious isolation, making paradise anew from a state of individual innocence. While some writers pursue such an ideal in their fiction, Twain rarely saw it as an appropriate model. His writings reflect much more the problem of initiation into society, and express Twain's sense of the difficulty of socialization.

The motif of initiation pervades Twain's works. The "innocents" abroad in Twain's best-seller of that name are ironically innocent, as is *Huckleberry Finn. We as readers are not expected to indulge or endorse the same naïveté as either

Twain or Finn. Twain's more characteristic sense of the role of the individual in society comes out in such works as "The *Jumping Frog," *Roughing It*, and *"Old Times on the Mississippi," in which a neophyte to a community either becomes part of the community or is rejected by it through a process of ritual humiliation. In the Frog story, the narrator never even recognizes his humiliation, so he leaves the community none the wiser. In the case of General Buncombe in chapter 34 of *Roughing It*, his virtual inability to recognize not only that a joke had been played on him but what the joke signified, shows his inability to grow, to change to meet the demands of the community around him.

In other words, the initiation rite as a motif serves to make many of Twain's works into *Bildungsromane*. But as a satirist, Twain's interest is less often in the individual growth of a character into a new understanding than in the character of the society itself. The repetition of the initiation motif in *Roughing It* ultimately reflects poorly on the society, which in a state of adolescence does not use its jokes exclusively to social advantage by initiating newcomers, but persists in playing *practical jokes even on those already accepted into the community. As Twain's career developed, he began to see the social coercion in initiation to be as much a problem as a benefit. In "The *Private History of a Campaign That Failed," Twain describes his departure from the military as a failure to be trained in war, but the ironic texture of the piece suggests that his failure is really a success. If Twain ever accepted the American Adam myth, this is the piece that shows it.

Still, as often as he writes of isolated characters who in some way challenge a community to see itself not as the arbiter of value but rather as the corrupter of it, the savior figure is rarely a sympathetic character, precisely because he works his magic on a community through a ritual of humiliation. The title character of "The *Man That Corrupted Hadleyburg" barely intrudes on the story, just enough to display the community's hypocrisy but not enough to provide a moral alternative. Satan in *"Chronicle of Young Satan" acts much as the man who revealed Hadleyburg's corruption, an isolated outsider who demonstrates the shortcomings of a community through ritual humiliation. But Satan, too, is not a sympathetic character. His power as an initiator becomes ironically suspect when the narrator ultimately learns that his own imperfect community provides a better standard for human happiness than does the angel's moral perfection. Thus, even in turning the initiation rite into a comment on society, Twain does not endorse an individualistic alternative to community itself.

INNOCENTS ABROAD, THE (1869). *The Innocents Abroad, or the New Pilgrim's Progress* began as a series of articles for three newspapers: the *Alta California*, the New York *Tribune*, and the New York *Herald*. As a traveling correspondent to Europe and the Near and Middle East, Twain was so popular that

Advertisement for *Innocents Abroad* (Hartford: American Publishing
Company, 1869), placed in many journals throughout the country.
Caricature probably by True Williams (1839–1897).

Elisha *Bliss of the *American Publishing Company actually solicited a book based
on his correspondence. The book's direct origins in *newspaper journalism makes
this first of Twain's best-sellers unique among his works in feel as well as structure.

Clemens had been working as a traveling correspondent for various western
newspapers since he became a full-time journalist in 1862. In 1867, while writing

regular correspondence for the San Francisco *Alta California* from New York City and wherever else in the eastern or midwestern United States his travels took him, he learned that Henry Ward *Beecher's Plymouth Church congregation was planning a trip to Europe and the Holy Lands. With friend and fellow New York *Tribune* writer Edward House, Clemens went to the excursion office sometime in February, and, according to his letter to the *Alta* describing the prospective trip and his inquiries about it, masqueraded as the Rev. Mark Twain, inquiring whether he would be able to share ministerial duties with Beecher on the trip.

Ten years later, the *Quaker City*'s captain, Charles C. Duncan, referred publicly to this hoax, saying that Clemens and House were drunk when they made their visit. Twain responded in an 18 February 1877 letter to the editor in the New York *World*:

> The "captain" says that when I came to engage passage in the Quaker City I "seemed to be full of whiskey, or something," and filled his office with the "fumes of bad whiskey." I hope this is true, but I cannot say, because it is so long ago; at the same time I am not depraved enough to deny that for a ceaseless, tireless, forty-year advocate of total abstinence the "captain" is a mighty good judge of whiskey at second-hand. . . . Why should I worry over the "bad whiskey?" I was poor—*I* couldn't afford good whiskey. How could I know that the "captain" was so particular about the quality of a man's liquor?

In any event, Clemens returned to the excursion office to acknowledge his real identity as well as to book passage, for which he paid $125 "forfeit money." He then asked the proprietors of the *Alta* to fund the trip—passage cost $1,250 and the *Alta* also gave him $500 traveling money—in exchange for a series of letters describing the journey. Before leaving on 8 June 1867, Clemens also agreed with the New York *Tribune* to furnish correspondence for which the paper would pay by the letter. Altogether he published fifty-eight letters about the journey: fifty-one in the *Alta*, six in the *Tribune*, and the final editorial about the journey in the *Herald* after the ship returned to New York on 19 November. He may have written four or more additional letters that were lost in transit.

The letters succeeded admirably, as did the journey itself, as far as Clemens was concerned. Because Beecher and General William Tecumseh Sherman did not accompany the voyage as originally advertised, Twain was the biggest celebrity on board, the one for the nation to follow as the ship made its progress. His letters were widely known on both coasts, stimulating the reception his book would ultimately receive. This boost of popularity was extremely important, as Clemens was disappointed in the sales of his first book, The *Celebrated Jumping Frog of Calaveras County, and Other Sketches*, which failed in part from lack of promotion but also from Twain's more moderate visibility in the spring of 1867.

Clemens also benefited personally from the contacts he made on board, including Dan *Slote, who helped to manage Clemens's business affairs in the years following the journey; Charles Jervis *Langdon, who was to introduce Clemens to Olivia Langdon; and Mary Mason *Fairbanks, who served as Clemens's audience and editor of journalism appropriate to East Coast newspapers.

Within days of his return, Clemens received a 21 November 1867 letter from Elisha Bliss:

> We take the liberty to address you this, in place of a letter we had recently written and was about to forward to you, not knowing your arrival home was expected so soon. We are desirous of obtaining from you a work of some kind, perhaps compiled from your letters from the East, &c., with such interesting additions as may be proper. We are the publishers of A. D. Richardson's works, and flatter ourselves that we can give an author as favorable terms and do as full justice to his productions as any other house in the country. We are perhaps the oldest subscription house in the country, and have never failed to give a book an immense circulation. . . . If you have any thought of writing a book, or could be induced to do so, we should be pleased to see you, and will do so.

Clemens dashed off a reply suggesting that he use the *Alta* letters as the basis of a book:

> I could weed them of their chief faults of con[s]truction & inelegancies of expression, & make a volume that would be more acceptable in many respects than any I could now write. When those letters were written my impressions were fresh, but now they have lost that freshness; they were warm then—they are cold, now. I could strike out certain letters, & write new ones wherewith to supply their places. If you think such a book would suit your purpose, please drop me a line, specifying the size & general style of the volume; *when* the matter ought to be ready; whether it should have pictures in it or not; & particularly what your terms with me would be, & what amount of money I might possibly make out of it. The latter clause has a degree of importance for me which is almost beyond my own comprehension. But you understand that, of course.
>
> I have other propositions for a book, but have doubted the propriety of interfering with good newspaper engagements except my way as an author could be demonstrated to be plain before me. But I know Richardson, & learned from him, some months ago, something of an idea of the subscription plan of publishing. If that is your plan invariably, it looks safe. (2 December 1867)

This correspondence reveals not only Clemens's anxieties about money, but also his anxieties about his kind of writing. These concerns governed his choices in turning his letters into a book.

Regarding the question of money, Bliss offered Clemens either a flat ten thousand dollars or a royalty of 5 percent on each copy. Clemens debated what to do, but as he explained in a 24 January 1868 letter to his mother and sister,

> This great American Publishing Company kept on trying to bargain with me for a book till I thought I would cut the matter short by coming up for a *talk*. I met Rev. Henry Ward Beecher in Brooklyn, & with his usual whole-souled way of dropping his own work to give other people a lift when he gets a chance, he said, "Now here—you are one of the talented men of the age—nobody is going to deny that—but in matters of business, I don't suppose you know more than enough to come in when it rains; I'll tell you what to do, & how to do it." And he *did*. And I listened well, & then came up here & have made a splendid contract for a Quaker City book.

Beecher advised him to take the royalties, a decision that yielded the "*money* in it" that Twain sought. In the first year of sales alone Clemens made fourteen thousand dollars.

But the other concern was the one that preoccupied Clemens in the year it took to write and publish the book. Clemens discovered that the letters he wrote would provide only half of the manuscript he needed. He not only had to rework the letters but also write more, much more, giving him the chance to experiment with style in the new parts, but denying him reflective moments to polish his original correspondence. He wrote to other passengers to get facts and reminiscences that he could use, including the twenty-seven articles written by Mary Mason Fairbanks for the Cleveland *Herald*. In a letter of 24 January 1868 to Fairbanks he said he was "ever so grateful to you for sending me those copies of the *Herald*. I see a good many ideas in your letters that I can steal." But even with help, the composition and production of the book did not go smoothly. Bliss delayed the publication several times while he tried to convince his board of directors to publish a humorous book and to secure enough *illustrations, and Clemens had to contend with the prospect of the *Alta* publishing the original letters in a book of its own.

This horrified Clemens. Not only would such a book require him to write a manuscript from scratch to fulfill his contract with the American Publishing Company, but it would also capture his journalistic style permanently in book form. Unable by mail or telegraph to convince the *Alta* to release its copyright on the letters, Clemens opted to travel to San Francisco in March, precisely when he needed to be writing and editing. But, as he put it to Fairbanks on 10 March 1868, "I *must* go. If the *Alta's* book were to come out with those wretched, slangy letters unrevised, I should be utterly ruined." Clemens uses the terminology equally appropriate to his financial status and to his reputation as a writer. His trip succeeded; the proprietors of the *Alta* agreed to release their copyright and suppress their book for the simple consideration of a notice in *Innocents Abroad* that they had done so.

Clemens agreed to these terms, but begrudged the *Alta* even this, as he felt a proprietary interest in the letters for which the *Alta* had paid.

Under the exigencies of his contract and the distractions of maintaining an income through continued newspaper correspondence, Clemens ultimately revised his original letters remarkably little. Much of what he did do he managed while in California and with the help of Bret *Harte. He intended these revisions to protect his reputation as an author worthy of an audience of respectable ladies and gentlemen. While in California, where his letters had received the greatest play, he was forcibly reminded of the need to edit, as he had become a target of the California ministry, or so he told Fairbanks:

> What did I ever write about the Holy Land that was so peculiarly lacerating? The most straight-laced of the preachers here cannot well get through a sermon without turning aside to give me a blast. The last remark reported to me from the pulpit is "this son of the Devil, Mark Twain!" . . . Don't you distress yourself. It is only the small-fry ministers who assail me. All those of high rank & real influence I visit, dine & swap lies with, just the same as ever. They have complained of nothing save the rudeness & coarseness of those Holy Land letters which you did not revise. (17 June 1868)

In editing, Clemens cut much slang, though he did allow much of what he called "mild" slang to remain. Whether this was a rationalization for the minimal revision he undertook, or a defense of what he knew was part of his basic style, is unclear. Generally speaking, he designed the rest of his revisions to tone down the irreverence toward women, religion, and high culture of the original letters. No longer does he refer to the inconsistencies in the Bible or call the Bible a "guide-book," and the remaining attacks on the "Old Masters" are tame compared to one deleted passage that compared spots of camel dung to frescos by the old masters:

> The sides [of the houses in Magdala] are daubed with a smooth white plaster, and tastefully frescoed aloft and alow with disks of camel-dung, placed there to dry. This gives the edifice the romantic appearance of having been riddled with cannon-balls, and imparts to it a very pleasing effect. Then the artist has arranged his materials with an eye to just proportion—the small and the large flakes in alternate rows, and separated by carefully-considered intervals—I know of nothing more cheerful to look upon than a spirited Syrian Fresco. Nothing in this world has such a charm for me as to stand and gaze for hours and hours upon the inspired works of these old masters. I have seen the *chef d'oeuvres* of Vernet, Tintoretto, Titian and a host of others whose fame is known in every land, but few of them ever affected me like the battle-pieces of these nameless sons of Art. (dated Tiberias, September 1867, published 26 January 1868)

He also cut references to bodily functions and to prurience. Deleted, for example, is a long passage on nude swimming from the *Alta* letter dated "Odessa, Russia, August 22nd": "I was never so outraged in my life. At least a hundred times, in the seven hours I stayed there, I would just have got up and gone away from there disgusted, if I had had any place to go to. . . . Incensed as I was, I was compelled to look, most of the time, during this barbarous exhibition, because it forced them to make a show of modesty, at least" (published 3 November 1867).

Regardless of such deletions, Clemens's revisions themselves made little more than a "show of modesty" as the book's journalistic roots could be neither buried nor disguised. Characteristic of newspaper journalism, Twain's letters described sensational places and events in dramatic and often contentious terms, then moved quickly on, and any book made out of such correspondence could not help but share the scattershot and energetic feel of the originals. The book's persistent irreverence and journalistic slanginess make Twain out to be the original ugly American traveling abroad.

Many reviewers said little else. The negative remarks from such stuffy journals as the *Athenaeum* castigated the American tourist for his skepticism toward anything worthy, and barely saw any humor in Twain's deliberate mistakes. Its review stated that in his errors of fact about cultural icons "there is nothing unusual. Most men who are not learned, and who do not take the precaution of using books of reference before they speak, may fall into the same errors" (24 September 1870). Even quarters that should have been kind were not. The *Tribune*, which had published some of the original letters, chided Twain for his "offensive irreverence" (27 August 1869). Harte's review in *The Overland Monthly* pretended to be positive but contained an insistent note of reserve, subtly criticizing Twain's "lawlessness and audacity" in his "indulgence of a humor that seems to have had very little moral or aesthetic limitation" (January 1870). Clemens feared such negative comments, but must have been relieved when he saw many extremely positive reviews as well, praising his honesty and integrity as a traveler and the originality and power of his comic abilities. The topper was William Dean *Howells's unsigned review in the *The *Atlantic Monthly*: "It is out of the bounty and abundance of his own nature that [the author] is as amusing in the execution as in the conception of his work. And it is always good-humored humor, too, that he lavishes on this reader, and even in its impudence it is charming; we do not remember where it is indulged at the cost of the weak or helpless side, or where it is insolent, with all its sauciness and irreverence" (December 1869).

Such reviews probably helped the sales of *Innocents Abroad*, though the subscription market relied less on reviews than did the trade market.

Certainly the market that Twain did find responded with energy to the skepticism that the *Athenaeum*'s reviewer found so offensive. Furthermore, the market responded to Twain's implicit assertion that America could be the measure of its own greatness. In comparing the Sea of Galilee and Lake Como to Lake Tahoe, Twain tells us, "I measure all lakes by Tahoe, partly because I am far more familiar with it than with any other, and partly because I have such a high admiration for it and such a world of pleasant recollections of it, that it is very nearly impossible for me to speak of lakes and not mention it" (chapter 48). America for Twain becomes the measure of Europe, not the other way around.

Clemens knew that the so-called cultivated in America would not readily accept his new standard. In a letter to the *Alta* dated 5 June 1867, on the very eve of his departure for Europe, Twain wrote,

An educated and highly-cultivated American lady, who speaks French and Italian, and has travelled in Europe and studied the country so faithfully that she knows it as well as another woman would know her flower-garden, said to me yesterday that she had some dear friends in San Francisco and other parts of Idaho, and these Indian rumors gave her unspeakable uneasiness; she believed that for seven nights she had hardly slept at all, with imagining the horrors which are liable at any moment to fall upon those friends; and she said she had friends in Santa Fe and Los Angeles, but she did not feel so worried about them because she believed the Indians did not infest the Cariboo country as much as they did the Farrallone Mountains and other localities further West. I tried to comfort her all I could. I told her I honestly believed that her friends in San Francisco and other parts of Idaho were just as safe there as they would be in Jerusalem or any other part of China.

Here she interrupted me, and told me with a well-bred effort to keep her countenance, that Jerusalem was not in China. I apologized, and said it was a slip of the tongue—but what I had meant to express was that her friends would be just as safe in Santa Fe and other parts of Cariboo as they would be in Damascus, or any other locality in France.

And she interrupted me again, and this time she did laugh a little bit, and told me modestly and in a way that could not hurt anybody's feelings, that Damascus was not in France.

I excused my stupidity again, and said that what I was trying to get at was, that her people might be even in the perilous gorges of the Farrallone Mountains and districts further west and still fare as well as if they were in Hongkong or any other place in Italy.

And then she did not laugh, but looked serious and said, "Are you so preposterously ignorant as all this amounts to, or are you trying to quiz me?" And I said, "Don't you go to Europe any more till you know a little something about your own country." I won. (published 11 August 1867)

With this as his parting commentary on European travel, Twain set out to declare America's cultural independence.

That independence was not to be an independent cultural production so much as an independence of mind that would allow for a new American culture. As the preface to *Innocents Abroad* puts it, Twain intended "to suggest to the reader how *he* would be likely to see Europe and the East if he looked at them with his own eyes instead of the eyes of those who travelled in those countries before him. I make small pretence of showing any one how he *ought* to look at objects of interest beyond the sea—other books do that, and therefore, even if I were competent to do it, there is no need." Yet in saying that he saw Europe with his own eyes, with untrained eyes, he is telling America how to see Europe. His endless refrain throughout the trip is to ask of the culture from which America sprang, "Is he dead?" Twain turns the climax of the trip, the visit to the tomb of Adam, into an exercise in pure bathos, telling us that mourning the past is a waste of time, that it is time to move forward.

To a country that had for nearly a hundred years been repeatedly declaring cultural independence from Europe while imitating and adoring European cultural forms, to a country that had recently finished a Civil War that for the first time insisted on the primacy of a national over a regional identity, to a country that had yet to know what to make of its thousands of war dead, to a country that had yet to know how to record or respect its own past, Twain's question struck a nerve. In asking about Europe's vitality and about the value of Europe's monuments, Twain asked America about its own vitality and *history. The resounding answer was to turn a collective back on the past after one last skeptical laugh.

◆ SEE ALSO Death.

INTERVIEWS. One of Twain's most delightful pieces of nonsense, "An Encounter with an Interviewer" (1874), gives the impression that Twain hated to be interviewed, that he eschewed press publicity. Nothing could be further from the truth. As a former "newspaper reptile" (*Alta California*, 14 July 1867) himself, he understood the reporter's need for good copy and learned to make himself not only available but also colorful in order to secure positive publicity.

But in spite of his connections to journalism, it took Clemens some time in the public eye to learn how best to take advantage of Mark Twain's growing *celebrity. In the 1870s he was somewhat afraid of press notice, in part because short-hand reporters kept transcribing his *lectures, forcing him to write new ones. He also feared the press because, as a humorist, he was as liable to be attacked as praised, and these attacks, beyond mere incursions into the privacy essential to a Victorian gentleman, threatened this arriviste's sense of worth. After he failed to secure enough press notice for *Roughing It*, Clemens learned that any notice was better than none, and that his own personal behavior—or at least his public behavior in his role as Mark Twain—gave him much press notice. He began to make himself available to reporters in order to be sure to receive the coverage he desired.

One of the more famous examples of this occurred in 1891 when, ensconced in his summer retreat in *Elmira, New York, he entertained Rudyard *Kipling, a then-unknown reporter from India. Kipling traded on Twain's celebrity in order to help him publish his accounts of his world tour, but Twain counted, more successfully than he could have imagined, on Kipling's extending Twain's fame at the same time.

Twain's use of the interview blossomed in the 1890s after his bankruptcy, when he needed to stay prominently in the public eye in order to recoup his losses. He remained quiet in public about the hard-nosed negotiations in which Henry H. *Rogers engaged to keep Clemens's creditors from stripping him bare, but when he decided to pay his creditors dollar for dollar, he used the press to make himself seem a moral paragon. In August 1895, he wrote out a statement he hoped would be delivered verbatim. Instead, his nephew, Samuel Moffet, a reporter for the San Francisco *Examiner* who had been sent to Vancouver to see Twain before Twain set out across the Pacific on his around-the-world tour, worked up an interview in which he quoted Twain as saying "Honor is a harder master than the law. It cannot compromise for less than a hundred cents on the dollar" (17 August 1895). A few days later, the *Examiner* also printed Twain's statement in full, but it was Moffet's interview that caught the public's attention. The interview was carried by the New York *Times* and many other papers in America and abroad, and was reprinted at tour's end. It was significantly responsible for the good will Twain experienced throughout the tour.

By this time, Clemens had fully learned the power of the interview and rarely missed an opportunity to take advantage of the press. He wrote out in his notebooks numerous quotable quips that, once memorized, he could deliver to reporters as if they were spontaneous effusions of wit. Since he gave such good copy, he could be assured of plentiful press coverage wherever he went. Indeed, many of Twain's famous *maxims come from 1895 to 1910 in his numerous newspaper interviews.

♦ SEE ALSO False Attributions; Newspaper Journalism; Public Image.

INVENTIONS. "The very first official thing I did, in my administration—and it was on the very first day of it, too—was to start a patent office; for I knew that a country without a patent office and good patent laws was just a crab, and couldn't travel any way but sideways or backwards." So says Clemens, through Hank Morgan, at the beginning of chapter 9 in *A Connecticut Yankee in King Arthur's Court*. So also said Americans almost unanimously in the latter half of the nineteenth century, a time in which every small-scale tinkerer believed he or she would be the next Benjamin Franklin, a time in which the inventor was a folk hero. The United States had had a patent office from the beginning, and the image of

Cover of *Mark Twain's Scrapbook.*

Franklin as an inventor shows how deeply rooted the idea of mechanical invention as *progress was in the American consciousness. But it was not until after the Civil War, when the engineer rather than the shopkeeper became the symbol of commercial success, that American inventiveness hit its professional stride. In 1860, 27,000 patents were registered with the patent office; by the turn of the twentieth century that number had exploded to one million per year. This rise came before the government or industry began seriously and methodically funding research and development. The individual entrepreneurial inventor as folk hero had a basis in reality.

Clemens himself had aspirations as an inventor, actually securing patents on a self-adjusting garter, a history game, and a self-pasting scrapbook, as well as inventing a notebook with tear-away tabs to allow him easily to find his place, an improved bed clamp, and a perpetual calendar. He actually had the notebooks made for his own use, but only the scrapbook ever made any money. He also invested regularly in other people's inventions, most notably in *Quaker City* friend Dan Slote's Kaolatype technique for lithography and in the *Paige typesetter. Clemens ultimately purchased Slote's patents while Slote tried to make the invention commercially viable on Clemens's money. Clemens also employed Slote to manufacture the scrapbook. He ultimately decided that Slote was bilking him, broke off the friendship as well as the investments, and then looked for other ways to waste his money. He did not have to go far—he merely increased his investments in the Paige typesetter, so much so that the strain contributed to his bankruptcy in 1894.

Not surprisingly, inventions and inventors populate his literature. Sometimes he mocks the charlatanism of the nation's patent business, as in a "Patent Universal

Climate-Proof Automatically-Adjustable Oration," which he presented to the Congregational Club of Boston on 20 December 1887. His speech, which he guaranteed to "fit every possible public occasion in this life to a dot, and win success and applause every time," mocked as much his self-adjusting clothing strap as the hucksterism by which such "patent" devices were sold *(Notebooks and Journals* 3:317). More often, however, he wrote in praise of inventions and inventors. *Connecticut Yankee* and *The *American Claimant* both attribute America's wealth to its inventive spirit. "The Austrian Edison Keeping School Again" (1898) promotes the value of Polish inventor Jan Szczepanik's Viennese workshop while mocking the Austrian government's interference in that work.

He loved inventors to his dying day, entertaining the pleas of the unknown and hobnobbing with the famous. Among the celebrated were Nicola Tesla and Thomas Edison, the latter of whom recorded Clemens's image in a moving picture and his voice on wax cylinders. While the film remains, the cylinders were in all probability destroyed in a fire (they remain a Holy Grail to Twain fans who hope that they will turn up someday). For all of his negative financial experiences with inventions, he was unable ever to resist investing in dreams. He had honestly told William Dean Howells in a letter of 22 August 1883, "I must speculate in something, such being my nature," and he chose inventions because he saw inventors as something far beyond the normal run of human being. As he wrote in a letter to his brother Orion, "An inventor is a poet—a true poet—and nothing in any degree less than a high order of poet" (12 June 1870).

♦ SEE ALSO Business Ventures; Industrial Revolution.

IRONY. From the Greek *eiron*, "dissembler," irony is at root a kind of speech in which the actual meaning is the opposite of the literal, though the term is applied to situations as well as words. The irony of situation includes dramatic irony, in which a character in a narrative lacks some knowledge that the audience has so that the audience is able to see a deeper, broader, or contrary meaning in the character's words or actions that the character cannot. The classic example of *Oedipus Rex* suggests that irony has no necessary connection to laughter, though the fact that the reversals of irony develop incongruities makes irony a frequent source of *humor and therefore a staple device in most forms of comedy, especially *satire.

The key to using irony as a device in satire is to establish a firm basis for interpreting the real meaning of the ironic speech. As the case of *Adventures of Huckleberry Finn* suggests, this is not always easy to do, as Huck's use of pejorative terminology to describe enslaved blacks and his outspoken support of slavery even as his actions work to defeat it are often considered signs of Twain's racism. In 1885 Twain assumed his audience would believe that slavery is wrong, and thus he could expect his readers to see the situational irony in Huck's actions belying his words and understand the actions to be in touch with correct belief. Thus, such an audience would read Huck's words against themselves, that is, they would read the author's words as an ironic attack on Huck's racist ideology. But for such irony to work, one must be able to assume the same moral ground as the author; without a shared set of beliefs, irony cannot always be discerned *as* irony. Without a clear sense of what is right, one cannot easily sort out whether to read a statement straight or ironically.

Such confusion actually facilitates the use of some kinds of irony—irony that is meant to be accessible only to an in group and to be rejected by an out group that lacks the frame of reference that would reveal the ironic inversion. This is arguably the case in many of Twain's pieces, as for instance in chapter 53 of *Roughing It*, when Jim Blaine fails to relate the story of his grandfather's ram. The straight direction of the story is that Blaine's entire inside narrative is designed to waste Mark Twain's time. The narrative's rambling, slapstick nature is funny in its own right and successfully "sells" Mark Twain. But as Clemens revealed years later in his *autobiography, the entire piece is designed to ridicule the idea of special providences. This comes clear only in the section in which Blaine tells his hearers that "Providence don't fire no blank cartridges," that all things are planned. His examples cast doubt on the theory, as the character of Blaine himself casts doubt on the reasonability of the doctrine. Only a reader familiar with theological disputes about preordination and providence would grasp the ironic force of the story; other readers would take it at face value.

Obviously, irony can be used to convey serious ideas in a comic wrapper. It is, in fact, a fundamental tool of intellectual discourse, used frequently by the pre-Socratic Greek philosophers in their sophistries, and raised to an art of complete negation by Socrates himself, who asserted that he knew nothing but only sought truth. His persistent questioning of all assumed beliefs left his interlocutors groping for meaning in the face of his devastating irony. As Søren Kierkegaard put it, irony in the hands of a thorough skeptic is "infinite absolute negativity," reading any meaning against itself until all meaning is consumed in a vortex of unending reversals.

Such deep nihilism was always a risk for Twain, whose comic perception worked by reversing commonplace meanings, and then by reversing these again. Much as his *work habits of inverting stories and meanings made it difficult for him to follow a single plot through a linear development, so too they made it difficult for him to settle into comfortable belief. The depth of his skepticism grew out of the power of his ironic turn of mind. His danger, like that of so many idealists whose ideals cannot resist irony, was to replace his idealism with cynicism, confusing skepticism, the refusal to believe, with cynicism, the belief that all is worthless. His recurrent humor, which arose persistently out of his ironic inversions, seems always to have been a counterbalance to cynicism, which equally arose out of his ironic capacity for inversion. Thus, as much as he may have insisted in a 16 February 1905 letter to

Joseph *Twichell that "the man who is a pessimist before 48 knows too much; if he is an optimist after it, he knows too little," he also recognized that his humor returned to him up to his dying days, regardless of how much he knew of the world. In this sense, humor and irony both invert common conceptions of reality in order to challenge conventional points of view, but while irony posits no positive choices, humor is all about alternatives.

♦ SEE ALSO Burlesque.

IRREVERENCE. See Reverence.

 **JAMES, HENRY** (1843–1916). As the other most commonly recognized American writer of the post–Civil War era, Henry James was Twain's antithesis. Clemens disliked James's style and approach to literature, telling William Dean *Howells in a 21 July 1885 letter, "As for [James's] the Bostonians, I would rather be damned to John Bunyan's heaven than read that." But at least he acknowledged James's importance, calling him in another letter to Howells one of America's "literary big fish" (12 October 1876). The very terminology Clemens used to describe James explains why James in turn thought Twain's works were suitable only to primitive minds; the commonplace, slangy metaphor is far from James's range of thought.

Their artistic antipathy notwithstanding, the two crossed paths repeatedly, dining together in London in 1879, meeting again in London in 1900, and twice being entertained in 1904 at the home of George Harvey, editor of the *North American Review* and one of the principals for Harper and Brothers. Their paths crossed figuratively as well, inasmuch as both dwelt on the incongruities of American and European cultures, and both were obsessed with the workings of conscience. For all of their stylistic differences, they share a common interest in writing technique, too; both turned repeatedly to dictation as a way of capturing the flow of the imagination. In this final similarity, though, lies the chasm between them. A typical dictated sentence by James compounds the hypotactic complexity of his written prose. Twain often parodied complex syntax, but his style never, even in its serious imitations of what he called a "literary cakewalk," strayed too far from its roots in oral tradition. As a professional platform speaker, Twain spoke with perfect clarity even when dictating for hours, day after day.

JAMES, WILLIAM (1842–1910). Like his younger brother, Henry, William James was raised as much in Europe as in America, but unlike Henry, William chose to make America his physical and spiritual home. Studying medicine at Harvard, he worked briefly as an instructor in medicine before joining the philosophy department there, rising to full professor in 1885. His interest in psychology as a basis of philosophy helped spawn Pragmatism, the first important American school of philosophy, which influenced George Santayana and John Dewey, as well as much twentieth-century continental philosophy. His ideas recently have had a resurgent influence in the works of Richard Rorty and his followers.

James's philosophy rejected the strict determinism of physics-bound positivism and the radical idealism of Kantian romanticism in favor of a belief that reality is neither transcendent nor absolute, but contingent on the perceptions, biases, and needs of individual human beings: "The knower is not simply a mirror floating with no foot-hold anywhere, and passively reflecting an order that he comes upon and finds simply existing" ("Remarks on Spencer's Definition of Mind as Correspondence," 1878). Such an interest in knowledge as a mediation between external reality and interior desire made James open to the psychology of unusual states of mind, and he carried on his investigations into faith healing, spiritualism, and psychic phenomena with full belief in the believer's needs, without passing judgment on the absolute truth of such beliefs.

Clemens became aware of James's work in his later years, meeting him first in 1892 and probably again when both were members of the Anti-Imperialist League. Clemens's interest in James's philosophy arose in part because the illnesses of Clemens's daughter Jean and his wife Olivia defied conventional cures. He consulted with James by letter to get his opinion of various alternative therapies. Clemens also developed in his later works an interest in subjective states. The cultural relativism of *Following the Equator* and the imaginative fancy of many posthumously published, unfinished works have Jamesian overtones. Some scholars have argued that James directly influenced Twain's works, but the evidence is too sketchy to say more than that their minds occasionally ran in a similar intellectual groove.

♦ SEE ALSO Health and Disease; Imperialism.

JOAN OF ARC (1412–1431). In the last essay Twain published during his lifetime, "The Turning Point of My Life" (*Harper's Bazaar*, February 1910), Twain wrote, "What I cannot help wishing is, that Adam and Eve had been postponed, and Martin Luther and Joan of Arc put in their place—that splendid pair equipped with temperaments not made of butter, but of asbestos. By neither sugary persuasions nor by hellfire could Satan have beguiled *them* to eat the apple." Thus does he explain his fascination with Joan of Arc, a real historical person seemingly immune from human frailties. The fact that she was a young woman made her all the more appealing to Twain, and she became one of the few historical figures used repeatedly in his literature—from passing burlesque references in speeches of 1868 and 1873; to a historical novel, *Personal Recollections of Joan of Arc* (1896); to flattering references in speeches of the 1900s; to an essay, "St. Joan of Arc" (1904). For him, she embodied a very conventional ideal of womanhood: "Gentle and winning and affectionate; she loved her home and friends and her village life; she was miserable in the presence of pain and suffering; she was full of compassion; . . . she was forgiving, generous, unselfish, magnanimous; she was pure from all spot or stain of baseness. And always she was a *girl*; and dear and worshipful, as is meet for that estate" ("St. Joan of Arc"). He considered her talents inexplicable by rational analysis, but his emphasis on her being a girl explains it all to him. He had ultimate faith in an ideal of adolescent femininity, one he clung to all the more energetically in the face of his own daughters' growing up. In his use of her character, Twain expressed his hopes for a much simpler world, even as he depicted a more realistic complexity in his masculine counterpart to Joan, *Huckleberry Finn.

JOURNALISM. SEE Magazines; Newspaper Journalism.

"JUMPING FROG, THE." Clemens never could decide whether his tale about Jim Smiley's jumping frog was "a villainous backwoods's sketch" (letter to Jane Lampton Clemens, 20 January 1866) or "the best humorous sketch America has produced, yet" (letter to Olivia Langdon, 14 December 1869). The way to describe its value to Twain's career, however, might well be from the story itself, as a product of "transcendent genius in *finesse*." It expanded Twain's West Coast reputation into a national one, and he in turn worked that *celebrity repeatedly, with ever greater refinement, into a solid foundation for his position as America's premier humorist.

His own doubts about the piece no doubt arose with his early doubts about his new (in 1865) profession as humorist. In writing to his brother that this new "calling" was decidedly "low" (19 and 20 October 1865), he revealed his own contempt for his talent. Yet the notoriety and income both appealed, and when his friend Charles Farrar Browne wrote repeatedly in 1864 and 1865 for Clemens to contribute a sketch to Browne's new book, *Artemus Ward: His Travels*, Clemens tried to comply. The problem was that he had not decided how to treat the material. His first two attempts to write the Jumping Frog story take an extremely condescending attitude toward Simon Wheeler, the inside narrator, endorsing, as *frame narratives had conventionally done, the values of the gentleman frame narrator. The first of these, "The Only Reliable Account of the Celebrated Jumping Frog of Calaveras County," never even gets to the inside narration, instead only describing "the decaying city of Boomerang," Twain's fictitious name for the mining town of Angels Camp, California. The language is inflated and seemingly nostalgic; comedy intrudes, if at all, only in the narrator's superciliousness toward the town and its inhabitants.

The second draft compensates for the absence of the inside narrator by cutting quickly to Simon Wheeler's narrative after four short introductory paragraphs. The first of these paragraphs, however, gives the reader a clear sense of the narrator's condescension; only the narrator and his correspondent know that Wheeler's stories are funny: "I was told that if I would mention any of the venerable Simon Wheeler's pet heroes casually, he would be sure to tell me all about them, but that I must not laugh during the recital, as he would think I was making fun of them, and it would give him moral offense. I was fortified with the names of some of these admired personages." Nothing about a frog or about a confidence game comes up; the humor remains very much a one-way street, mocking Simon Wheeler without turning the other direction to make fun of Twain. Clemens pigeonholed these two unsatisfactory starts, not writing the third and finally successful version until October 1865. He sent it to New York too late for inclusion in Browne's book. Since the book was already in production, Browne's publisher sent the manuscript instead to Henry Clapp, Jr., for consideration in the *Saturday Press*, which published the tale under the title "Jim Smiley and His Jumping Frog" in the 18 November 1865 issue.

This first publication reveals Clemens's original intention to publish the sketch in Browne's book. He addresses the piece to Artemus Ward, Browne's pen-name, and begins the tale, "Mr A Ward, Dear Sir:—Well, I called on good-natured, garrulous old Simon Wheeler, and I inquired after your friend Leonidas W. Smiley, as you requested me to do, and I hereunto append the result." The opening paragraph ends with a second mention of Ward: "If that was your design, Mr. Ward, it will gratify you to know that it succeeded."

This framing makes Twain the dupe in a joke played on him by Ward, a notorious humorist. Such behavior could be expected from Ward, and that Twain is the butt of the joke makes it likely that Simon Wheeler is merely a tool in Ward's jest. But the story itself contains evidence that Wheeler is a collaborator rather than a pawn. The tale Wheeler tells is about a *confidence game, about a man who could not size up those around him and so ended up gulled. The story suggests the possibility that the stuffy Mark Twain, with his elaborate language and tendency to condescend to the western rough whose coarse speech shows his lack of education, has in reality misjudged Wheeler's shrewdness. In so doing, Twain reveals the inappropriateness of his manners and pretensions in the unrefined democracy of the far West.

The ending of the sketch as written for Ward's volume denies this possibility, though, when Twain takes over, playing with his own self-characterization in the concluding paragraph: "'O, curse Smiley and his afflicted cow!' I muttered, good naturedly, and bidding the old gentleman good-day, I departed. Yours, truly, Mark Twain." In muttering curses that he oxymoronically calls good natured, Twain acknowledges Ward's joke on him, showing his own awareness and ability to take care of himself. In refusing to share the joke with Wheeler, Twain implies that Wheeler is not in on the joke. Instead, by writing to the specific person who set up the gag, he says, in effect, "Yeah, you got me."

In revising the story for publication as the title story of *The *Celebrated Jumping Frog of Calaveras County, and Other Sketches*, Twain heightened the ambiguity of the inside story, making the reader wonder whether Wheeler is in on the joke, and making it clear that Twain is never sure himself. The opening paragraph no longer refers to a specific known joker as the person who sent Twain to see Wheeler, nor is the sketch directed to any specific person. Instead, the reader becomes the audience for a tale of a man forced to suffer out West.

The next time Twain revised the tale, for *Sketches, New and Old* and published under the title "The 'Jumping Frog.' In English. Then in French. Then Clawed

Back into a Civilized Language Once More, by Patient, Unremunerated Toil," he further sharpened the focus on the narrator's tribulations by changing the last paragraph. Instead of speaking to Wheeler at all, the frame narrator merely reports his departure: "However, lacking both time and inclination, I did not wait to hear about the afflicted cow, but took my leave." Inasmuch as the earlier ending showed Twain coming to a clear realization that he had been duped, this ending shows a busy easterner moved to exasperation, not really certain what has happened to him. In these progressive refinements, Clemens built on the initial ambiguity of the tale to make it challenge the putative refinement and superiority of the gentleman narrator, Mark Twain.

Such had become Twain's formula by this point in his career. As an added bonus, in "retranslating" a French translation of his story, he could not only reinforce the idea that learning is contingent on time and place, that language has nuances and exactness that outsiders cannot construe, but he could also brag about the now worldwide popularity American humor, and in particular one American humorist, had attained.

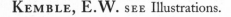

KEMBLE, E.W. SEE Illustrations.

KING, GRACE (1851–1932). A New Orleans–born writer of local color *realism, Grace King's stories were avidly read and appreciated by Clemens and his family. Although King was an ardent Confederate sympathizer who always detested the North, she had to work through northern publishers to make a living as a writer.

Invited to stay at Charles Dudley *Warner's house for introductions to the elite of the publishing world in 1887, she met the Clemens family. She quickly became close friends with Olivia and a confidante of Susy and Clara. When she returned for a visit to Hartford in November 1888, she spent several weeks in the Clemens home. While Samuel was an enthusiastic fan of King, and King relished reporting his doings in her letters home, she remained somewhat circumspect about him, never fully appreciating his literature.

The correspondence from Clemens and his family to King is extensive, and Olivia in particular asked her advice on important matters, like whether to move back into the Hartford house after Susy's death or whether or not to support Clara's singing career. Astonishingly, Albert Bigelow *Paine makes no mention of King in his *Mark Twain a Biography* (1912) and prints none of the correspondence with her in *Mark Twain's Letters* (1917). This may have been one of Paine's attempts to show that Twain had completely shed any sympathy for the Confederacy in his rise to literary prominence.

KIPLING, RUDYARD (1865–1936). A younger contemporary of Twain, Rudyard Kipling began his writing career as a journalist in India. He returned to Britain in 1889 via the United States, where he made a special pilgrimage to Elmira, New York, just to see Twain, a visit Kipling used to further his own career as a reporter. Kipling particularly loved *Adventures of Huckleberry Finn*, which he acknowledged to have influenced his own masterpiece, *Kim*. In writing his *autobiography, Twain played the card the other way, acknowledging Kipling's worldwide *celebrity and recounting his first meeting with the younger man to play off that celebrity: "When he was gone, Mrs. Langdon wanted to know about my visitor. I said, 'He is a stranger to me but he is a most remarkable man—and I am the other one. Between us, we cover all knowledge; he knows all that can be known, and I know the rest.'"

While Kipling's love of Twain's work was diminished slightly with the publication of *Connecticut Yankee*, which Kipling's English patriotism could not countenance, he remained an ardent admirer. Clemens reciprocated the admiration when he read Kipling's first book, *Plain Tales from the Hills* (1888).

While the two came down on different sides of the *imperialism question, their opposition was not total. Kipling was not the jingoist he has been painted to be and Twain was less opposed to the British Empire as a practical expedient than he was to imperialism in the abstract and to America's particular exercises of it in the Philippines and China. Hence, Twain's support of Kipling in "A *Fable" is not as surprising as it might seem at first blush.

Clemens avidly read Kipling's verses, his *Just So Stories*, and, especially, *Kim*; his high praise of these books goes far to belie his professed dislike of reading fiction and *poetry. They saw each other for the last time in 1907 when both received honorary doctorates in literature from Oxford University. Kipling followed Clemens in the procession, and while waiting for the ceremonies to begin, they together surreptitiously violated a ban on smoking. Apparently the English supporter of reverence and custom was willing to bend protocol with the American iconoclast.

KNIGHTS OF LABOR. SEE Labor Movement.

LABOR MOVEMENT. In chapter 33 of *A Connecticut Yankee in King Arthur's Court*, Hank Morgan speaks for Mark Twain in praising the rise of trade unions:

> Thirteen hundred years hence ... the 'combine' will be the other way, and then how these fine people's posterity will fume and fret and grit their teeth over the insolent tyranny of trade unions. Yes, indeed! the magistrate will tranquilly arrange the wages from now clear away down into the nineteenth century; and then all of a sudden the wage-earner will consider that a couple of thousand years or so is enough of this one-sided sort of thing, and he will rise up and take a hand in fixing his wages himself. Ah, he will have a long and bitter account of wrong and humiliation to settle.

Twain had certainly heard the "fine people" of his own day fume and fret, and had contributed to it in ways both subtle and overt. Describing the rise of a riverboat pilots' union in the sixth installment of *"Old Times on the Mississippi" (The Atlantic Monthly*, June 1875), he implicitly praises the union not only for protecting the financial interests of its members, but also for promoting safety on the river by improving the craftsmanship of its members. He published this in the midst of a wave of antiunion agitation following various rail and coal strikes in the early part of the depression of 1873–1879.

Later, during the prosperous middle 1880s when the Knights of Labor became, briefly, a viable national political and economic force, Twain explicitly twitted his prosperous peers in the Hartford *Monday Evening Club with an essay on the Knights entitled "The New Dynasty." Personifying all workers as a single working man, Twain said:

He is the most stupendous product of the highest civilization the world has even seen—and the worthiest and the best; and in no age but this, no land but this, and no lower civilization than this, could he ever have been brought forth. The average of his genuine, practical, valuable knowledge—and knowledge IS the truest right divine to power—is an education contrasted with which the education possessed by the kings and nobles who ruled him for a hundred centuries is the untaught twaddle of a nursery, and beneath contempt. The *sum* of his education, as represented in the ten thousand utterly new and delicate and exact handicrafts, and divisions and subdivisions of handicrafts, exercised by his infinite brain and multitudinous members, is a sum of knowledge compared to which the sum of human knowledge in any and all ages of the world previous to the birth-year of the eldest person here present in this room, was as a lake compared to the ocean, the foothills compared to the Alps; a sum of knowledge which makes the knowledge of the elder ages seem but ignorance and darkness; even suggests the figure of a landscape lying dim and blurred under the stars, and the same landscape revealed in its infinitude of bloom, color, variety, detail, under the noontide sun. Without his education, he had continued what he was, a slave; with it, he is what he is, a sovereign. . . . He is here—and he will remain. He is the greatest birth of the greatest age the nations of this world have known. You cannot sneer at him—that time has gone by. He has before him the most righteous work that was ever given into the hand of man to do: and he will do it. Yes, he is here; and the question is not—as it has been heretofore during a thousand ages—What shall we do with him? For the first time in history we are relieved of the necessity of managing his affair[s] for him. He is not a broken dam this time—he is the Flood!

Perhaps his neighbors worried, perhaps they shared Twain's own patriotic enthusiasm. Regardless, Twain maintained his endorsement beyond the collapse of the Knights as he wrote and published *Connecticut Yankee*.

Connecticut Yankee's praise of trade unions came in the midst of a difficult time for organized labor. While unions were pressing strikes against specific employers with increasing regularity, these actions usually came in response to management-imposed wage reductions or workplace changes that undercut the power and prestige of skilled workers by replacing them with unskilled machine operators. And when laborers did strike, they often found their actions broken by private armies hired by industrialists or troops called out by state governors. So Hank's facts of the nineteenth century were actually Twain's fantasy.

At the same time, Clemens aggressively invested in a machine—the *Paige typesetter—that, if successful, would have thrown thousands of skilled compositors, such as Clemens himself once had been, out of work. From this perspective, Twain's attitudes about labor seem perplexing. However, if one takes a step back and looks at the so-called "labor problem" from an early nineteenth-century perspective, his position, for once, appears remarkably consistent.

Simply put, Clemens was raised in the trades and formulated not only his ideas of work but his ideas of politics in accordance with the principles of the crafts as they developed in the early years of the republic. Such ideas stayed with him throughout his career, and he repeatedly referred to the idea of apprenticeship when writing about steamboat piloting, as in "Old Times"; typesetting, in his 1886 "The Compositor" speech to the Typothetae (a printer's society) and in *"No. 44, The Mysterious Stranger"; and even when writing about writing, as in a 7 April 1887 letter to Grace Trout:

There is an unwritten *law* about human successes, & your sister must bow to that law, she must submit to its requirements. In brief, this law is:

1. No occupation without an apprenticeship
2. No pay to the apprentice.

This law stands right in the way of the subaltern who wants to be a General before he has smelt powder; & it stands (and *should* stand in everybody's way who applies for pay & position before he has served his apprenticeship & *proved* himself.

Here Twain endorses the craft guild's belief in meritocracy, the independence of the worker, a community of manhood, the value of labor, and an idea of *progress. In short, guilds promoted republicanism based on the virtue of independent artisans working in a political community for the common good.

Labor's support of meritocracy arose from its experience of the power of knowledge. The greater the skill involved in a trade, the greater the economic leverage the tradesman had. This was of course also true in preindustrial times, but it became even more salient as industrialization built competition into the trades. As machines took over more and more manual labor, those jobs that remained in the hands of skilled tradesmen often occurred in production bottlenecks. Compositors, for example, retained real economic power long after other aspects of the printing trade—presswork, binding, and so on—were devalued through the development of better machinery. As such, compositors were early able to unionize and set wages, as Clemens discovered in St. Louis and Philadelphia, and to a lesser extent in New York City, where printers, divided among two competing unions, received worse pay.

Craft knowledge, then, created an aristocracy of labor, and the differential status between skilled and nonskilled labor mirrored itself in the hierarchy within a trade itself. Apprentices did the dirty work, were hazed regularly, and received little or no pay for hard work in exchange for the education that would enable them eventually to claim their own position in the hierarchy. But the hierarchy notwithstanding, a deep-seated egalitarianism ran underneath, predicated on the assumption that yesterday's apprentice and today's journeyman would become tomorrow's master. Independence—economic and political—was the goal of the guild system. Even when working in combination for higher wages, guild workers remained touchy about their independence. Again, the sixth installment of "Old Times" speaks to this. Twain begins the section describing pilots as kings without masters even as he tells the story of them creating a closed-shop union that damaged their autonomy. Of course, the creation of the union depended on the grit of some of the best pilots, and was opposed by the equally gritty independence of other excellent pilots. The story is as much about men competing for control of a *political* organization as about the economic value of the union.

Indeed, the political virtue of artisans as the urban equivalent of Jefferson's yeoman farmer is very much a part of the political mythology of the labor movement in the nineteenth century. For example, in *The Labor Movement: The Problem of To-day*, the 1887 volume describing the history, condition, and aims of the Knights of Labor, George E. McNeill puts guild labor at the center of the American Revolution:

> It is a matter of tradition that the idea of overturning the tea in Boston Harbor was first promulgated at a meeting of the ship carpenters and ca[u]lkers, and that these men before that sometimes acted together in political matters. The Revolutionary War naturally tended to the elimination of the class distinctions which had prevailed, and a spirit of individual independence permeated the laboring masses—a spirit that has not yet been wholly obliterated. (p. 71)

This political spirit pervaded the daily routines of tradesmen. Until late in the century strikes were usually spontaneous affairs, prompted by the willingness of an aggrieved craftsman to walk off the job in the full glory of his independence. It was not considered "manly" to consult or wait for others to back one up; but such actions were effective precisely because the "manly" behavior of one respected worker would provoke sympathy strikes on the parts of all others. They boasted, then, of their community, but predicated it on the idea of absolute independence. *Connecticut Yankee* presents this idea when Hank brags that "A man will be his own property ... and he can leave town whenever he wants to, if the wages don't suit him!" (chapter 33).

Guild labor had no affinities with socialism for the simple reason that it had no quibble with private property. The idea of self-ownership on which guild independence stood also buttressed the idea of accumulation of a competence through individual industry. But the guild worker held labor to be the basis of all value. When Twain writes in chapter 33 of *Connecticut Yankee* of the "nobles, rich men, the prosperous generally, ... who do no work," he sees them as parasites, much in the same terms as those used by the early labor activist William Heighton, whose 1827 "Address to the Members of Trades Societies and to the Working Classes Generally" helped develop a class consciousness around a labor theory of value. He lambasted "nonproducers" for stealing "other people's labor" by keeping them "in ignorance and mental blindness." Heighton, like Clemens, owed his political agenda to eighteenth-century rationalists, particularly Thomas Paine, and the inflection of this belief in the value of *education for laborers is particularly revealing when compared with Twain's labor agenda. Throughout *Connecticut Yankee*, he promotes education as the solution to the exploitation of labor; as much as he saw education as the progressive alternative to feudal exploitation, he also viewed it as a buttress against the kinds of political radicalism espoused by William Dean

*Howells. When Howells sent Clemens some anarchist pamphlets, Clemens sent Howells his "New Dynasty" speech. In it, Howells found a rebuttal to his antiproperty position:

> We need not fear this king [i.e., labor]. All the kings that have ruled the world heretofore were born the protectors and sympathizing friends and supports of cliques and classes and clans of gilded idlers, selfish pap-hunters, restless schemers, troublers of the State in the interest of their private advantage. But this kind is born the enemy of them that scheme and talk and do not work. He will be our permanent shield and defence against the Socialist, the Communist, the Anarchist, the tramp, and the selfish agitator for "reforms" that will beget bread and notoriety for them at cleaner men's expense; he will be our refuge and defence against these, and against all like forms of political disease, pollution and death.

While Howells could see the idea of property itself as antithetical to the interests of labor, Twain saw socialism as a new kind of feudalism, and his guild-based idea of progress had no room for such a compromise of individual independence.

Indeed, one of the reasons for the demise of American guild labor stemmed from an idea of progress that included a belief that a true craftsman would always improve the tools of his craft. Thus, artisan laborers, essentially petty-bourgeois in outlook, constantly contributed to the flow of *inventions that transformed the *economy in the *industrial revolution. Twain built a fortune that enabled him to speculate financially, but usually, his investments were in inventions rather than in financial instruments. The most notorious of these was the Paige typesetter, which helped bankrupt him. Even when still in debt from that venture, he put money in an improved loom, about which he wrote to Henry H. Rogers, "My project to put the Jacquard looms of America into the hands of the Standard Oil will furnish me entertainment enough for a spell" (22 March 1898). He wrote this at least partly in jest, but his *notebook entry of about the same date shows Clemens's own affinity with his character Colonel Sellers: "I was born with the speculative instinct." As with Sellers, especially as depicted in The *American Claimant, Clemens was captured by the romance of progress. While that progress as it played out in factories (and for that matter in Sellers's fantasies) was the death of labor as Clemens had known it, it was as a craftsman that he learned the rhetoric of progress and property that fueled his fantasy.

♦ SEE ALSO Work Habits.

LANGDON, CHARLES JERVIS (1849–1916).

Clemens met and befriended Charles Jervis "Charlie" Langdon on the Quaker City in June 1867, and through his friendship with Charlie, ultimately met Olivia, Langdon's older sister, in December of that year. The significant gap in the ages of the two men shows how far Clemens was willing to reach out while onboard the ship in order to find like-minded passengers, which is to say, travelers who were not overly straitlaced. Nonetheless, Clemens's first impression of Langdon was not favorable: He was the model for "The Interrogation Point" in *The Innocents Abroad*. Still, Clemens liked Langdon enough to accept his hospitality; when Clemens first visited the Langdon household in January 1868, it was at Charlie's invitation. When Clemens decided to woo Olivia, Langdon at first felt affronted, though he quickly decided to help Clemens by forwarding love letters to Olivia.

Langdon was, according to his temperance-advocating parents, wild, and when it became clear that Clemens was to become Olivia's husband, the older Langdons hoped Clemens would exercise his influence to help curb the young man. Not relying on this influence alone, they sent him abroad in October 1869 with a professor from Elmira College, Darius Ford, who agreed to supply Clemens with letters that Clemens would work up into a comic around-the-world series, a sort of sequel to *Innocents*. While this trip kept Langdon away from his sister's marriage to Clemens in 1870, Jervis Langdon's ill health forced a summer return. Upon Jervis's death in August, Langdon took over the family business, married Ida B. Clark in October, and settled down. He maintained cordial relations with his sister and brother-in-law, though he disapproved of Clemens's use of Olivia's money and wisely refused to invest in the *Paige typesetter.

♦ SEE ALSO Langdon, Jervis and Olivia Lewis.

LANGDON, JERVIS (1809–1870) AND OLIVIA LEWIS (1810–1890).

Samuel Clemens's in-laws, Jervis and Olivia Lewis Langdon, married in 1832. Jervis was a successful lumber dealer in upstate New York before moving in 1845 to Elmira, where he profitably invested in coal (beginning in 1855) and railroads. The success of his business enterprises enabled him to establish his family as one of the most prominent in Elmira, where he served as a board member for Elmira College and was a founding member of Park Congregationalist Church, of which Samuel and Olivia Clemens were tithing members.

The Langdons had three children—an adopted daughter, Susan Langdon Crane; Olivia Langdon *Clemens; and Charles Jervis *Langdon—and with the help of Jervis's even-handed generosity and Olivia's continuing presence, these children maintained warm relationships through their lives.

The Langdons were politically and socially active. Ardent abolitionists, they were instrumental in establishing a new church when their old one split over the issue of slavery. They used their wealth and influence to help secure Thomas K. Beecher as pastor for their church. They supported abolitionist activists and financed a stop on the underground railroad before the Civil War. They supported the temperance movement and entertained the intellectuals who passed through Elmira during the lecture season. They also supported education, in part by helping to establish Elmira College. Thus, they provided a model of civic engagement for their children, and through the children, influenced the political and social views of Samuel Clemens.

They also helped support Clemens's career in a very material sense; Jervis loaned Clemens $25,000 to help him buy an interest in the Buffalo *Express and bought Samuel and Olivia an expensive house in Buffalo. While the Clemenses took a loss on both of these investments when they moved to Hartford, the proceeds nonetheless helped them establish their home in *Nook Farm.

Jervis took ill suddenly in 1870, dying of stomach cancer in August. His will bequeathed to Olivia Langdon Clemens a substantial interest in his businesses, and the income this property generated went far to supporting the Clemens household. Olivia Lewis Langdon lived until 1890, visiting the Hartford home frequently, as well as entertaining visits from the Clemens family during their many trips to Elmira. Moreover, she frequently gave the Clemenses money, as much as a thousand dollars at a time.

One of the most significant ways in which the Langdon family affected Clemens's career was in simply accepting him as a suitor for their daughter. They were, as a straitlaced, devout, temperance-advocating couple, nervous about their sheltered daughter's interest in a professional funny man, whose humor to that point often turned on burlesque of social convention and jokes about drunkenness. Their concern manifested itself in rather extraordinary efforts to find out more about Clemens. Olivia Lewis Langdon even wrote to Mary Mason *Fairbanks asking about Clemens's character:

> I cannot, & need not, detail to you the utter surprise & almost astonishment with which Mr Langdon & myself listened to Mr Clemens declaration to us, of his love for our precious child, and how at first our parental hearts said no.—to the bare thought of such a stranger, mining in our hearts for the possession of one of the few jewels we have. . . . I desire . . . your opinion of him as a *man*; what the kind of man he *has been*, and what the man he now is, or is to become. I have learned from Charlie & I think the same idea has pervaded your conversation, or writing or both,—that a great change had taken place in Mr Clemens, that he seemed to have entered upon a new manner of life, with higher & better purposes actuating his conduct.—The question, the answer to which, would settle a most weaning anxiety, is,—from what standard of conduct,—from what habitual life, did this change, or improvement, or reformation; commence? (1 December 1868)

Clemens tells the story that Jervis asked him for references from California, and that when Clemens failed to provide any good ones, Jervis declared that he would take Clemens's part himself, but this letter suggests that Clemens's conquest of this bastion of respectability was not so easy. Nonetheless, he did win not only the approval but the good opinion of these fastidious parents. Such a victory was a clear sign to Clemens that he could, on his own terms, earn a place at the table of the eastern establishment, at least that part of it based on new money. But that caveat is important. Jervis Langdon was not part of the eastern establishment as represented by the scions of Brahmin Boston; as a self-made man who built his fortune in lumber and mining in the virtual frontier of Appalachia, he had more in common with Clemens than most of Clemens's biographers are wont to admit.

♦ SEE ALSO Crane, Susan Langdon and Theodore.

LANGUAGE. Mark Twain's mastery of *dialect writing made its use acceptable for subsequent generations of American writers. It is ironic, then, that such a shift should have come from a former typesetter who, when reading books, used to correct the grammar as if he were an after-the-fact proofreader. Raised in an educational climate that stressed correct grammar as an essential element of refinement, Clemens prided himself on perfect fluency with the rules.

Still, the education of his era also insisted that good rhetoric use *style appropriate to time and place. What distinguished Twain as a writer from so many of his contemporaries was that he let this fundamental rule of rhetoric supersede the rules of grammar. In that sense, he kept his ears open, and given the extraordinary range of his experience, travels, and reading, he learned much about variation in language. He listened readily to the voices of African Americans, backwoodsmen, miners, and tradesmen (especially printers and pilots) at the same time that he learned the purified language readers expected from literature. He taught himself the importance of respecting linguistic variation; his own genius in using printed words to create the illusion of hearing different dialects allowed him to translate his experience into works that had a profound influence on American writing.

Moreover, this experience encouraged him to make language itself a thematic component of much of his literature. Juxtapositions between different dialects provided comic material, as in *Roughing It* or *A Connecticut Yankee in King Arthur's Court*. The incapacity of two people, ostensibly speaking the same language, to understand one another creates possibilities for comic misdirection, a kind of verbal slapstick. Twain was good at creating it in his own works and finding it in the world around him. As he wrote in his notebook for 1879, "That dear sweet old German baroness who loved to find similarities between G[erman] & E[nglish]— 'Ah, the 2 languages are so alike—we say Ach Gott, you say Goddam.' To laugh when peop[le] are serious is not a fault of mine, but this 'fetched' me." Indeed, difficulties in translation often fetched him, not only in his own notebooks, but in his writings, such as "The Awful German Language," the oft-reprinted appendix to *A*

Tramp Abroad, and "'The Jumping Frog.' In English. Then in French. Then Clawed Back into a Civilized Language Once More, by Patient, Unremunerated Toil."

This last piece is a delight to anyone who has ever suffered from trying to understand the idiomatic, rather than the literal, meaning of a second language. Twain forcefully depicts language as more than mere words; language is a reflection of a cultural moment, of attitudes, values, and capacities for thought. In this sense, his understanding of language was very much at odds with the prevailing theory of his day, that of the transcendentalists. As Ralph Waldo Emerson put it in section four of his seminal essay *Nature*:

> Words are signs of natural facts. The use of natural history is to give us aid in supernatural history; the use of the outer creation, to give us language for the beings and changes of the inward creation. Every word which is used to express a moral or intellectual fact, if traced to its root, is found to be borrowed from some material appearance.... But this origin of all words that convey a spiritual import—so conspicuous a fact in the history of language,—is our least debt to nature. It is not words only that are emblematic; it is the things which are emblematic. Every natural fact is a symbol of some spiritual fact.

In such a transcendentalist understanding of language, linguistic change is degradation, a moving away from primary spiritual contact with the universe to a merely social one.

Twain saw it just the other way. He had a historical consciousness that was not interested in transcendental spiritual values so much as social ones. His "Concerning the American Language" (1882) goes so far as to describe linguistic changes in Darwinian terms. Describing a conversation with an Englishman who praised Twain's English, Twain replied that he spoke American. The Englishman scoffed, saying the differences amount to little. Twain replied, "The languages were identical several generations ago, but our changed conditions and the spread of our people far to the south and far to the west have made many alterations in our pronunciation, and have introduced new words among us and changed the meanings of many old ones." On the surface, a simple shift in vocabulary and pronunciation as a people migrated means very little, but the key for Twain is that the *social* conditions of the American West have changed the fundamental character of the people. And he describes these changes in a way that suggests an ineluctable progress:

> "In the American language, the *h* is respected; the *h* is not dropped or added improperly."
>
> "The same is the case in England,—I mean among the educated classes, of course."
>
> "Yes, that is true; but a nation's language is a very large matter. It is not simply a manner of speech obtaining among the educated handful; the manner

obtaining among the vast uneducated multitude must be considered also. Your uneducated masses speak English, you will not deny that; our uneducated masses speak American,—it won't be fair for you to deny that, for you can see, yourself, that when your stableboy says, 'It is n't the 'unting that 'urts the 'orse, but the 'ammer, 'ammer, 'ammer on the 'ard 'ighway,' and our stable boy makes the same remark without suffocating a single *h*, these two people are manifestly talking two different languages. But if the signs are to be trusted, even your educated classes used to drop the *h*. They say *humble*, now, and *heroic*, and *historic*, etc., but I judge that they used to drop those *h*'s because your writers still keep up the fashion of putting *an* before those words, instead of *a*. This is what Mr. Darwin might call a 'rudimentary' sign that that *an* was justifiable, once, and useful,—when your educated classes used to say *'umble*, and *'eroic*, and *'istorical*.

For one, in suggesting that the common American speaks in a way that the British must be educated to speak, Twain subtly suggests that Americans have leveled the classes up. The reference to Charles *Darwin suggests that this is a completely natural *progress, and that America's language is a sign of that progress.

For most of his career, his belief in progress shaped the way he viewed language. His fascination with European literature of the fifteenth through eighteenth centuries reflects this interest. Just as W. E. H. *Lecky, one of Clemens's favorite writers, described the gradual development of sympathetic identification as a cultural phenomenon, and Darwin described it in phylogenetic terms, Twain looked at language as reflecting and perhaps influencing this progress. In part, his "Conversation as It Was by the Fireside in the Time of the Tudors" is an investigation of what he saw as the moral degeneracy of the age. As he put it in his notebook for 1879: "I built a conversation which *could* have happened—I used words such as *were* used at that time—1601. I sent it anonymously to a magazine—& how the editor abused it & the sender. But that man was a praiser of Rabelais, & had been *saying*, O that we had a Rabelais—I judged I could furnish him one." So even as Twain acknowledged linguistic difference as cultural and saw the importance of language appropriate to time and place, he maintained a prescriptivist idea of language.

Nonetheless, there are intimations in Twain's works that his use of language in all of its richness and variation was more modern than his prescriptive tendencies would suggest. Even as he complained in his notebook about the vulgarity of this archaic literature, writing that "it defiles literature" as a reflection of a "society [that] should not be preserved," he wrote a page later, "The funniest things are the forbidden" and mentions the delight he took in hearing a hostler utter blasphemy in the presence of Rev. Joseph *Twichell. When Twichell found a tactful way to reveal his calling as a minister, the hostler did not change the color or intensity of his profanity—a circumstance that Twain felt merely heightened the comedy. In this regard, the iconoclastic urge, so central to his creativity, appears.

More importantly, many of Twain's later works, particularly those written in the 1890s and 1900s after he lost much of his belief in moral progress, treat the problem of translation quite differently. In *"Three Thousand Years among the Microbes" the question of language comes up in respect to identity. The narrator is losing his English the longer he stays in Blitzowski, so to retain his language, one of the things that makes him distinctive, he writes his memoirs. But these are still somehow in "microbic" and need to be translated again by Mark Twain. The whole problem, then, is that language goes to the core of identity; that it may in fact not be so much a vehicle of expression as the raw material of thought itself. As in the case of the Jumping Frog story in French, another language cannot do justice to what a first language expresses. Thus, translation is always an exercise in loss. Yet the story also postulates the opposite. While describing a thought recorder, Twain's narrator suggests that thought is prior to language. Such a possibility led to Twain's frequent speculations in telepathy, what he called "mental telegraphy." In this sense, Twain played with the kind of philosophical idealism Emerson expressed.

Clearly Twain could not make up his mind about this fundamental question of language, consciousness, and human identity. But in the unfinished story "The Secret History of Eddypus," Twain comes down on the side of those who believe symbols are the fundamental units of human thought. The rulers of "the world empire" in that story maintain their power by controlling the meanings of words and religious symbols. The subversive historians who try to crack the code are left with the dubious task of translating, without a key, fragmentary texts from the past into the language of their own time, place, and culture. Their gross errors yield the kind of verbal slapstick that always delighted Twain, though this time the slapstick has political and metaphysical resonance. This piece has Twain firmly in the camp of social constructionists and cultural relativists, who see the rules of language as arbitrary but as encoding power structures into the very fabric of thought.

♦ SEE ALSO Off-color Humor; Slang.

LAW. Nevada mining communities indulged themselves in many forms of theatrical entertainment, including mock trials, like the one described in "The *Facts in the Great Landslide Case." Clemens's fellow Virginia City *Territorial Enterprise* reporter William *Wright published an account of one such trial when Judge William Davenport, seeing Clemens and a fellow reporter drinking beer, had them arrested by the city marshal on the charge of "high treason." The judge explained the charge by pointing out that they were "guzzling beer in plain sight of the Court, without inviting it over to take a glass." A crowd enjoyed the spontaneous show and relished the denouement, when Clemens turned the game on the judge, charging him with "malicious prosecution" and ordering him to pay a fine of "beer for the crowd"—which he did ("Making Light of Justice in Virginia City," San Francisco *Morning Call*, 2 December 1865, reprint from *Territorial Enterprise*).

Ever after, Twain made good use in his writing of the humorous as well as dramatic possibilities of competitive oratory in the courtroom. Although Twain often struck a comic pose in describing courtroom antics, his newspaper career put him in constant contact with the instruments of justice as part of his beat, especially in San Francisco. There he learned to despise the manipulations of juries and the political pandering engaged in by police officials and elected attorneys. His reporting was no-holds-barred, more editorial than factual, as when he wrote that San Francisco's assistant district attorney, David Louderback, "affords a great deal less than no assistance to the Judge, who could convict sometimes if the District Attorney would remain silent" (San Francisco *Call*, 29 September 1864). Mostly he learned to detest jury selection in U.S. courts, regularly inserting complaints about "stupid" juries into his books, from as early as *Roughing It* to *"Chronicle of Young Satan."

As much as the earlier book deals with courts in several chapters, the two works share a jury's inquest on a death, passages worth comparing. In chapter 47 of *Roughing It*, Twain tells us, "On the inquest it was shown that Buck Fanshaw, in the delirium of a wasting typhoid fever, had taken arsenic, shot himself through the body, cut his throat, and jumped out of a four-story window and broken his neck—and after due deliberation, the jury, sad and tearful, but with intelligence unblinded by its sorrow, brought in a verdict of death 'by the visitation of God.' What could the world do without juries?" Careful to make sure Fanshaw could not be classed as a suicide, the jury ignores all evidence. In "Chronicle," Satan instantaneously turns a game-keeper into a stone-statue, at the same instant petrifying a fly on the man's cheek. A court inquest leads to a jury concluding that "deceased had come to his death by the visitation of God. Also the fly. The coroner was not willing to accept the verdict, because it included the fly." The jury and coroner argue, with the coroner finally deciding that he cannot accept the verdict because it includes the fly. Thus, "there is no verdict. The absence of a verdict determining the cause of the man's death debars me from issuing the necessary burial-permit; deceased must therefore remain unburied—that is, in consecrated ground. He may be a suicide." In the first case, Twain complains of the soft-headedness of the jury; in the second, he complains of the cruelty of jurisprudence following rules without regard to human needs.

The shift in focus mirrors a career-long complication of Clemens's views about the universe. Early on, he accepted the idea that the law is the essential protector of order. In the Judeo-Christian tradition, the idea of law in covenant with God being powerful enough even to bind omnipotence is central. Clemens was further influenced by the Anglo-Saxon tradition of common law backed up by the Magna Carta's theoretical limitation of monarchical power. This tradition was so strong that the scientific revolution, beginning with Francis Bacon in the early seventeenth century, used the concept of natural law to elevate the idea of natural forces. The metaphorical construction of nature as law-giver made the scientific enterprise easily assimilated in Britain and America. Born into these traditions, Clemens saw the law in these terms and expressed outrage when it was foiled by corrupt human power or, worse, human stupidity.

Throughout his professional career, Clemens turned regularly to the law, expressing in his actions the faith—his experiences as a reporter notwithstanding—that courts would preserve justice. Clemens regularly sued when he felt his rights were being infringed, using lawsuits against former friends, such as Charles Webb or Edward House, as well as against literary pirates, unscrupulous booksellers, and shady manufacturers.

His studies of *history and *evolution over the course of the 1880s and 1890s, however, combined with his growing disillusionment in the idea of progress and his increasingly complex ideas about the nature of divinity, led him to challenge his comfortable faith in law as a principle of order and progress. When he ceased to see nature's god as the eighteenth century's benign clockmaker, he no longer saw nature's laws as principles of balance and order. Instead, as expressed in *"Three Thousand Years among the Microbes," he saw natural law as the law of power. Whether that exchange of power was ultimately benign is an open question in that text, but that it is destructive of individual consciousness and impinges on individual feelings and "rights" is unmistakable. Hence, Clemens's later images of law courts tend to show the pain that rules could cause human beings and that such rules defy the common-sense needs of human nature—as in the resolution of *Pudd'nhead Wilson and Those Extraordinary Twins* or in the inquest in "Chronicle of Young Satan." Of course, the main plot movement in that latter story includes another trial, one in which Satan proves the innocence of Father Peter through careful attention to the physical evidence. But the entire trial only comes about because divine intervention damages the human order of things in the first place, so that the divine resolution, complete with driving Father Peter mad under the false impression that he has been found guilty, complicates the typical idea that a court discovering the truth restores fundamental order. This late Twain work may agree that the universe's order is restored by the trial, but he expresses deep skepticism that this order is worth celebrating.

♦ SEE ALSO Detective Stories; Spectacle.

LEARY, KATIE. SEE Servants.

LECKY, W. E. H.
When in 1900 Clemens dined at William Edward Hartpole Lecky's home in London, he continued in person a conversation he had carried on in literature ever since his brother-in-law Theodore Crane introduced him to Lecky's *History of European Morals from Augustus to Charlemagne* (1869), probably in 1874. Lecky was an Irish-born historian who both trained and then taught at

Dublin's Trinity College, which he represented in the British Parliament from 1895 to 1902. His primary field of interest was the Enlightenment, especially in Britain, with a particular bent toward the interactions between moral ideas, religious institutions, and the progress of political structures. Given these interests, it is no wonder that Clemens read Lecky's works avidly.

While Clemens owned and read most, if not all, of Lecky's books, the *History of Morals* was the most important to Twain's output, for in it Clemens found straightforward descriptions of the two schools of moral philosophy that he found most attractive, *sentimentalism and *utilitarianism. Lecky argued for the sentimental position over the utilitarian. Clemens thought he held the opposite position, as indeed he tries to argue thematically in *Adventures of Huckleberry Finn* by having Huck pursue his own comfort rather than any abstract moral standard whenever he faces moral dilemmas. But one of Clemens's marginalia in the copy of Lecky's *History of Morals* he annotated shows a more complex picture: "It is so noble a book, & so beautiful a book, that I don't wish it to have even trivial faults in it." Clemens wanted to accept Lecky's intuitionist ideas of the moral sense even as he disparaged them, and much of his literary output from *The Adventures of Tom Sawyer* on shows him grappling with this divided loyalty. Indeed even *Huckleberry Finn* can be shown to argue for sentimental morality, as Clemens himself suggested during his 1896 lecture tour when he regularly introduced a reading from the book by saying "that in a crucial moral emergency a sound heart is a safer guide than an ill-trained conscience. I sh'd support this doctrine with a chapter from a book of mine where a sound heart & a deformed conscience come into collision & conscience suffers a defeat." No matter how much Huck may serve his own comfort, his *heart*, rather than utilitarian reason, is what calculates his best interest.

Clemens turned to Lecky for historical fact as well as for philosophical controversy. His books are replete with material drawn from Lecky. *The Prince and the Pauper* and *A Connecticut Yankee in King Arthur's Court* in particular rely on Lecky's accounts of medieval church practices. While he drew at least as much on other crucial sources, he returned regularly to Lecky as one of his guiding lights.

♦ SEE ALSO Crane, Susan Langdon and Theodore; History.

LECTURE CIRCUIT. In the 1830s, a curious blend of democratic ideology, missionary fervor, and the desire for popular entertainment combined into the lyceum movement. Americans raised on sermons and political speeches had long appreciated good oratory, and the new republic came to recognize the value of widespread education as a necessary precondition to the spread of democracy. Josiah Holbrook, one of educational reformer Horace Mann's colleagues, discovered that this blend of forces made his *lectures on science enormously popular, not merely with the school-aged population for whom he originally designed them, but for adults as well. He consequently founded, in 1826, the first lyceum in Millbury,

The Lecture Platform.

1	Rev Talmage	24	E C. Stanton
2	E. Yates	25	S. B. Anthony
3	"Eli Perkins"	26	E. Faithfull
4	"Josh Billings"	27	J. B. Gough
5	W. H. H. Murray	28	Kate Field
6	J. T. Fields	29	A. Livingston
7	Theo. Tilton	30	Wilkie Collins
8	John Hay	31	B. Taylor
9	Bret Harte	32	"Fat Contributor"
10	Scott Siddons	33	E. E. Hale
11	"Mark Twain"	34	Chas. Sumner
12	"P. V. Nasby"	35	J. A. Froude
13	Carl Schurz	36	R. W. Emerson
14	J. M. Bellew	37	A. E. Dickinson
15	Rev. Chapin	38	Elihu Burritt
16	Miss Cushman	39	Sidney Woollett
17	Miss Edgarton	40	Wendell Phillips
18	H. B. Stowe	41	Robt. Collyer
19	J. G. Saxe	42	H. W. Beecher
20	De Cordova	43	Prof. Tyndall
21	Geo. W. Curtis	44	MacDonald
22	Gen. Kilpatrick	45	James Parton
23	Bishop Simpson		

PUBLISHED BY THE
American Literary Bureau,
AGENCY FOR LECTURERS, READERS & SINGERS
COOPER INSTITUTE, N. Y.

Advertisement developed by the American Lyceum Bureau to advertise its line-up of speakers.

Massachusetts, where he gave not only his own educational lectures to a general audience, but also invited lectures on other popular educational topics. His organization proved enormously successful and soon lyceums were cropping up all over New England and throughout the northern tier of states following the Yankee migration westward.

Lyceums were primarily a group of sponsors, well known in their communities, who organized a series of lectures for their towns. In many towns, lyceum societies built halls, complete with reading rooms and libraries; in others, the societies merely rented public halls. In all cases, societies developed subscriber lists and booked series of weekly lectures for the winter months. While the initial point of these lectures was educative, many entertainers made the list of popular lecturers, usually by intermixing their entertainment with content considered uplifting. But some performers, more often after the Civil War, were hired exclusively as entertainment, such as Mark Twain. As Clemens wrote to Mary Fairbanks, who had been encouraging him to perform less as a clown and more as an educator, "What the societies ask of me is to relieve the heaviness of their didactic courses—& in accepting the contract I am just the same as giving my word that I will do as they ask" (12 October 1868).

This combination of didacticism and comic relief proved enormously popular; over three thousand lyceums existed by the mid-1830s, with a steady increase in lyceums or their equivalents into the twentieth century. Those equivalents included various organizations designed to further the education of particular groups, especially working men, as the famous Cooper Union in New York, or religious groups, like the Young Men's Christian Association (YMCA). The Chatauqua movement of the early twentieth century was another offshoot. As the country became more comfortable with entertainment for entertainment's sake, the structure provided by the lyceum system and the appetite for public performance developed by it supported author's readings as well. Charles *Dickens, for example, was able to tour America reading from his fiction, not as a part of a lecture series but as a stand-alone act.

As the country's population expanded and transportation improved, lecturers could cover substantial ground in a season, and the complexity of such tours spawned an industry of intermediaries. Beginning with James Redpath's organizing the Boston Lyceum Bureau, lecture agents oversaw the tours of a stable of lecturers, providing lists of performers from the inexpensive and relatively unknown to world-renowned celebrities. With this infrastructure in place, lecturers could make a substantial livelihood out of itinerant lecturing, with big names, such as Henry Ward Beecher, able to command well over one hundred dollars per performance in the 1870s. Most small communities could not afford a steady diet of big names, but would often pool their resources to capture at least one big act per season.

As lucrative as lecturing was, the profession was grueling. Lecturers often had to make tight schedules, going from the biggest cities to small towns in spite of poor transportation connections and a spate of interruptions from northern winter weather. In the smaller towns, hotel accommodations were notoriously unreliable. Clemens often turned to the platform when he needed a quick source of income, but as much as he relished the money and, for that matter, the accolades, the travel itself exhausted and disgusted him so much that he promised, after virtually every lecture tour he took, never to do it again. As he put it to lecture agent James B. Pond, Redpath's successor, in a 25 April 1887 letter declining a lucrative proposal for lecturing: "No *sir*—I'll never hoof a platform again." But he did in 1895–1896, and, if one includes his many *speeches as well as his humorous lectures as "hoofing a platform," that was one promise he did not keep until he died.

♦ SEE ALSO Browne, Charles Farrar; Cable, George Washington; Leisure.

LECTURES. The beginning of Twain's enormous popularity stemmed from his public lectures as much as from his journalism. In fact, his careers as a writer and platform speaker fed one another; without the two working in tandem it is doubtful either would have developed as well.

As a popular western journalist, Clemens had already given a few public speeches in Virginia City, Carson City, and San Francisco by October 1866. He did not really become a lecturer, that is an itinerant professional speaker on the *lecture circuit, however, until he began a sixteen-engagement tour of *California and Nevada in October and November 1866, giving his first lecture on the Sandwich Islands. This was his initial taste of professional lecturing, and he found himself able to fill houses on the strength of his notoriety as a correspondent for various western newspapers, especially as the Hawaii correspondent for the Sacramento *Union*. When later that year he moved to New York, hoping to build his publishing career there, he tentatively began lecturing as well, but mainly in the provinces. His first lecture tour east of the Rockies took place not in the northeastern center of the lecture circuit, but in the Midwest in March and April 1867, where he visited family while getting used to lecturing and building a reputation. When he returned to New York for his first lecture at Cooper Union in May, he was terrified, writing to his friend and business manager, Frank Fuller, that he had too slim a reputation to be successful as a lecturer.

His concern was unwarranted. Fuller advertised very effectively, not only appealing to the large number of Californians living in New York to support one of their own, but also trading on professional courtesy of journalists. One wrote in the New York *Citizen* of 4 May:

> MARK TWAIN, otherwise known as "The Wild Humorist of the Pacific," whose funny writings have convulsed half a continent, and whose book—"The Jumping Frog," just issued from the press of Webb, is now introducing the accomplished and talented author into new fields, new harvests, and new triumphs, appears before the New York public on Monday evening next, at Cooper Institute, to relate his last year's "Experiences in the Sandwich Islands." There could be no doubt of Mark's ability to be intensely funny, nor of the impossibility of his being anything else, if we were to judge of his quality solely by his humorous publications; but we have the assurance of the San Francisco press that the address contains an immense amount of valuable descriptive matter, not to be found elsewhere, while the quaint similes and expressions are lavished upon the audience in quantity sufficient for an entire course of lectures by any other orator in America.

The reviewer sagely understood that the lecture audience wanted to be amused, but needed the promise of education to justify that amusement. With such advance notices, the lecture was likely to draw, but in his panic, Clemens had Fuller issue free tickets to schoolteachers. The result was a packed house that had to turn people away, and, according to the New York correspondent for the Sacramento *Union*, "I have seldom seen a more intelligent audience anywhere" (4 June 1867). Clemens certainly loved it, saying in his autobiography that the lively and perceptive laughter of that group secured his confidence in his abilities.

With two more nights lecturing in New York City over the next nine days, Clemens was successfully embarked on his lecturing career, in spite of a hiatus warranted by his *Quaker City* trip and the literary work that followed. Beyond the occasional *speeches he gave throughout his life, Clemens went on lecture tours every year between 1869 and 1873, mostly in the United States though twice also in England. In this period, lecturing was one of his primary sources of income; his popularity was such that James Redpath's Boston Lyceum Bureau picked him up as a prime card. Even though he tried to end his lecturing career in 1873, he went on tours again in November 1876, November 1884 to February 1885 with George Washington *Cable, and around the world from July 1895 to July 1896. During the 1876 and 1884–1885 tours Clemens gave readings from his works rather than lectures; in the other tours, he gave Mark Twain's variant of the kinds of lectures popular on the circuit.

Twain's lectures were primarily humorous; he knew that he was hired mainly for comic relief in a series of didactic lectures, but he also knew that he needed some serious content to justify his performance to the more fastidious, and usually vocal, in any audience. Hence, he built his lectures around a counterpoint between comic and serious material: "*Any* lecture of mine ought to be a running narrative plank, with square holes in it, six inches apart, all the length of it & then in my mental shop I ought to have plugs (half marked 'serious' and the other marked 'humorous') to select from and jam into these holes according to the temper of the audience" (to Olivia Langdon Clemens, 21 November 1871). As such, his lectures in fact *burlesqued the typical educational lecture. Late in his career, he ironized his burlesque, presenting himself in his 1895–1896 tour as a moralist delivering a lecture explicitly on morality. In it he combined various readings from his works with a series of bridges attesting to the moral value of the humorous passages he recited, as when he introduced a passage from *Adventures of Huckleberry Finn* by describing it as "a book of mine where a sound heart & a deformed conscience come into collision & conscience suffers defeat." Given that his audience expected burlesque, it may not have recognized that in treating his own persona ironically, he was, in fact, giving a morals lecture.

His platform style depended on deadpan presentation in a southwestern regional dialect. He used a deliberate, low-key drawl, and his presentations were funny as much for the characterization of Mark Twain as a slow-witted bumpkin who did not really understand his own humor as for the wit of his humorous writing itself. He explained this style, with unbecoming modesty, in "How to Tell a Story." In it, he disclaimed the ability to tell a deadpan story himself, but by all accounts, he was the American master of this kind of performance. His style depended on the appearance of spontaneity, but in fact he carefully scripted and memorized his performances. He would write out his lectures, repeating them aloud, canceling passages as he committed them to memory, and often rewriting the lecture from scratch to further impress it on his mind. In this process of memorization, he would fine-tune his scripts, changing words regularly to find a better flow. Even in his author's readings, when he did not have to con the material by heart, he rehearsed it carefully, changing words and marking passages to point out emphases and pacing.

Not surprisingly, each lecture took much time and effort to develop. Thus, when reporters took down his lectures in shorthand, printed them in the next day's paper, and sent the copy via newspaper exchange all over America, Twain was outraged. Each such printing of a lecture required him to change much material, even to write, memorize, and rehearse entirely new material while traveling. He also came to hate the traveling life, not only despising the often poor board and lodging and lousy conveyances, but coming to dislike the often officious courtesy of many of his hosts. They would frequently keep him up late for dinners or social gatherings, regardless of his travel schedule. Worse for a night owl like Clemens was getting up too early. As he wrote to his wife on 4 January 1872:

> A lecturer *dreads* a private house—Oh, more than he dreads 200 miles of railway travel. . . . In *spite* of yourself you respect their unholy breakfast hours—you can't *help* it—& then you feel drowsy & miserable for two days & you give two audiences a very poor lecture. . . . Hotels are the only proper places for lecturers. When I am ill natured I so enjoy the freedom of a hotel—where I can ring up a domestic & give him a quarter & then break furniture over him—then I go to bed calmed & soothed, & sleep as peacefully as a child.

By the end of a lecture trip, Clemens would be exhausted and often out of humor. By the 1872 season he was only lecturing out of financial need, and hoped never to have to do so again. As he put it in an 8 January 1872 letter to Olivia, "Well, slowly this lecturing penance drags toward the end. Heaven knows I shall be glad when I get far away from these country communities of wooden-heads. Whenever I want to go away from New England again, lecturing, please show these letters to me & bring me to my senses." As his writing became more lucrative, he gladly gave up the lecture circuit, only returning to it when he wanted to publicize new books or when—as after his bankruptcy in 1894—*finances made it a necessity.

Even though he saw lecturing and writing as different professional ventures, his lecturing had an incalculable influence on his writing. Much as the associative flow of the "narrative plank" structured his lectures, so, too, did it come to structure the lucrative travel books that made him a best-selling author. Equally important, his lecturing kept his ear attuned to the literary possibilities of common speech as well as to high-style rhetoric. With a lifetime of practice public speaking through a vernacular persona, Clemens never allowed himself to wander from the realities of American *language and speech to the literary styles preached in American schools.

This honesty about the American version of English is one of the reasons his writing *style has been so influential. His stage performances also allowed him to practice his material with audiences who kept him in touch with American concerns, interests, and values. This awareness influenced his writing both for good and ill; while the exhilarating success of speaking to the common people encouraged his democratic idealism, the frustrations of the road and his occasional failures on the platform, as well as his contact with a widespread worship of *celebrity, fueled his pessimism about democracy and human potential.

LEISURE. Most American moralists in the early nineteenth century did not appreciate leisure. Hard work and worship were the acceptable uses of time, and any deviation from those pursuits was socially suspect as a gateway to wickedness. Moralists looked both to the putative excesses and dissipation of the wealthy and the poor to demand that people hew to a straight and narrow path of disciplined behavior. In fact much of the emotional energy of the great religious revivals of the 1830s through 1850s turned on crusades against various recreational vices, such as drinking, tobacco-chewing, and gambling. It was during this period that government revenue-raising lotteries were shut down as immoral and that laws against gambling were first proposed and slowly instituted. The puritanical reforms of the evangelical revivals of the first half of the nineteenth century have been called a "shopkeeper's millennium," suggesting that the impetus in part was to instill in the populace values and habits congruent with a stable economic and political order.

Still, this period saw the beginning of a significant countermovement in the rise of a sentimental alternative religion to revivalist Calvinism. First making inroads in the cities of the East, sentimentalists proclaimed the importance of extending *childhood beyond infancy and envisioning it as a time of healthy balance between moral instruction and recreational play. Similarly, sentimentalists argued, in accordance with precepts of *domesticity, that adults, too, needed a retreat from the serious world of business and politics, and that home was an appropriate place for family recreation. The puzzle was to find ways to structure leisure time that would avoid inculcating vicious habits.

Catharine Beecher in her extremely influential *A Treatise on Domestic Economy* (1841) not only argued for the value of domestic amusements but even prescribed a list. Her suggested amusements included the family's reading wholesome fictional literature. In so arguing, she was both riding and helping to develop a movement that had effectively blossomed by the beginning of the Civil War, at which time the majority of Americans ceased to consider reading novels as an inducement to vice, but rather as a wholesome exercise of the imaginative faculties. Family reading became one of the primary leisure activities of the American public. (In this shift, America was following the lead of Britain, which established the pattern for much of the English-speaking world.)

Such a shift was fortunate for Twain. His own anxiety about the value of literature as a professional calling arose from his small-town background in a revivalist age, but his success as an author depended on his ability to write literature for an audience whose expectations and understanding of literature as legitimate entertainment had shifted over the course of half a generation. His concern with writing for a family audience, of providing the right mixture of comic play and moral uplift, arose substantially out of this shift in cultural expectations. The expansion of *subscription publishing, the kind of publication that reached mass audiences outside the cities, into literature for entertainment rather than exclusively for religious or educational purposes began shortly after the Civil War, with Twain's books among the first representatives of that shift.

The last half of the century saw a steady increase in tolerance for and pursuit of other kinds of leisure activities among Americans. Americans had a church- and politics-trained appetite for listening to speeches, and a commercial *lecture circuit grew around the lyceum movement of the 1830s to satisfy that appetite. Originally structured as a way to bring to small towns speakers who would encourage the edification and uplift of the general populace, the system slowly expanded to include speakers whose primary purpose was entertainment. Before the war, such humorous speakers as Petroleum Nasby and Artemus Ward included significant political content in their lectures, justifying their positions on the lecture circuit. After the war, they often dropped the pretense. Indeed, when Twain spent time on the lecture circuit, he knew that he was not supposed to be an edifying speaker, but rather to provide comic relief from the usual didacticism. The bulk of the course of lectures may still have been designed to educate, but the existence of entertainment for its own sake was new.

The upper classes had long had extensive leisure time, but their leisure became the subject of intense public scrutiny and a mixed censoriousness and admiration after the Civil War. Not only had the war created a plutocracy of millionaires who had supplied war materiel—millionaires Twain called "princes of shoddy" (*Alta California*, 5 April 1867)—but the development of larger circulation city newspapers and newspaper syndicates made the doings of this plutocracy the subject of national interest. Such newspaper gossip both reflected and encouraged decreased anxiety about the moral value of leisure activities. At the same time, popular entertainments were becoming increasingly well attended, with New York City leading the way in sanctioning and supporting museums, theaters, and clubs.

In his early journalism, Twain covered such entertainment as part of his work as a traveling correspondent. Writing from New York for the San Francisco *Alta California*, he wrote about his "pursuance of all the amusements of the metropolis," from the old-fashioned attendance on church, where "all the pretty girls, and also all the young men who dote on them, go to the Sunday afternoon services," to the most extravagant of low-brow theater:

337

When I was here in '53, a model artist show had an ephemeral existence in Chatham street, and then everybody growled about it, and the police broke it up; at the same period "Uncle Tom's Cabin" was in full blast in the same street, and had already run one hundred and fifty nights. Everybody went there in elegant toilettes and cried over Tom's griefs. But now, things are changed. The model artists play nightly to admiring multitudes at famous Niblo's Garden, in great Broadway—have played one hundred and fifty nights and will play one hundred and fifty nights more, no doubt—and Uncle Tom draws critical, self-possessed groups of negroes and children at Barnum's museum. I fear me I shall have to start a moral missionary society here. (28 March 1867)

Twain's outrage was only half joking, as he explained the show's attraction as coming from a spectacular display of

clipper-built girls on the stage . . . with only just barely clothes enough on to be tantalizing. . . . The scenic effects—the waterfalls, cascades, fountains, oceans, fairies, devils, hells, heavens, angels—are gorgeous beyond anything ever witnessed in America, perhaps, and these things attract the women and the girls. Then the endless ballets and splendid tableaux, with seventy beauties arrayed in dazzling half-costumes; and displaying all possible compromises between nakedness and decency, capture the men and boys. (*Alta*, 28 March 1867)

From a prewar culture that tolerated theater grudgingly and only if the melodrama were part of a moral mission, to entertainment for entertainment's sake, America had made a change to which Twain paid attention according to a formula that made his journalistic entertainments quite effective. His reports, complete with the moral coloring that would make such outlandish city events palatable to the less risk-taking among his readers, participated in the gradual acceptance of secular entertainment. Such vicarious experience kept readers buying Twain's travel narratives throughout his career.

Central to Twain's success in selling his version of leisure activity was his awareness—no doubt because Clemens shared in it—of the American ambivalence about pure leisure. Much of the time, Americans masked their leisure as pursuit of self-improvement, as in the case of the lecture circuit, health resorts, or travel. Twain's writings always exploited that conflict, in part by postulating a legitimacy of leisure and in part by moralizing against what he and his public perceived as ethical lapses in certain kinds of leisure.

Twain's defense of leisure itself was explicit and congruent with the American shift toward a view of work as but one part of life's duty. Thus Twain says in *A Tramp Abroad*:

Sunday is the great day, on the continent,—the free day, the happy day. One can break the Sabbath in a hundred ways without committing any sin. We do not work on Sunday, because the commandment forbids it; the Germans do not work on Sunday, because the commandment forbids it. We rest on Sunday, because the commandment requires it; the Germans rest on Sunday, because the commandment requires it. But in the definition of the word "rest" lies all the difference. With us, its Sunday meaning is, stay in the house and keep still; with the Germans its Sunday and week-day meanings seems to be the same,—rest the *tired part* and never mind the other parts of the frame; rest the tired part, and use the means best calculated to rest that particular part. Thus: if one's duties have kept him in the house all the week, it will rest him to be out on Sunday; if his duties have required him to read weighty and serious matter all the week, it will rest him to read light matter on Sunday; if his occupation has busied him with death and funerals all the week, it will rest him to go to the theatre Sunday night and put in two or three hours laughing at a comedy. . . . Such is the way the Germans seem to define the word "rest;" that is to say, they rest a member by recreating, recuperating, restoring its forces. But our definition is less broad. We all rest alike on Sunday,—by secluding ourselves and keeping still whether that is the surest way to rest the most of us or not. . . . We keep [the Sabbath] holy by abstaining from work, as commanded, and by also abstaining from play, which is not commanded. Perhaps we constructively *break* the command to rest because the resting we do is in most cases only a name, and not a fact. (chapter 24)

Twain redefines the terms, using the language of duty itself to promote leisure, which he names rest not in idleness but in active play as recreation.

This language of duty as a defense of leisure pervades Twain's travel writing, allowing him to pass judgment on all he sees from the perspective of a middle-class American's sense of values, all the while granting to that American a broader perspective than his values would otherwise permit. So in Twain's satires of Americans who toured Europe ostensibly for education but in reality to show off, or in his denunciation of the can-can in *The Innocents Abroad*, the American reader could share the experience from a safe vantage point. Mark Twain's persona of studied idleness served the reader similarly; while scorning Twain, the reader could share the experience without compromising his or her own self-image.

♦ SEE ALSO Games; Sentimentalism; Work Ethic.

LETTERS. It is perhaps impossible now to understand what letters meant to nineteenth-century Americans. For centuries, the letter was the basic form of writing in the western world, used not only in its own right, but serving as the primary building block for many other kinds of writing. The first novels, for instance, were epistolary in form; newspapers and magazines modeled their articles on letters and still consider reports from distant places to be the work of "correspondents"; even the New Testament is built in part out of epistles. Indeed, using the very term "letter" to refer to epistolary correspondence suggests the deep connections between literacy and letter-writing. To Americans, living in the first modern culture to strive for universal literacy and in arguably the world's most mobile culture not built on a nomadic economy, letters had value even greater than in the rest of the western world: they were the cord that bound families, communities, and the nation.

Not surprisingly, letter-writing was taken seriously as an art and letters were often treasured as an important part of a person's life-work. When people of even modest stature died, their letters were conventionally returned to their estates, and living relatives would often issue two-volume biographies—one a narrative of the life and the other a collection of edited letters. Twain, as one of the most prominent literary men of the age, warranted a biography printed variously in three or four volumes (1912) and the two-volume *Mark Twain's Letters*, both produced by Albert Bigelow *Paine, a professional writer authorized by first Clemens and then his family to secure Twain's place in history. But Paine only published a small portion of Clemens's correspondence, perhaps five hundred letters total, all edited to create an impression of Twain as a refined gentleman. Clemens may have written as many as forty thousand letters over his lifetime, of which only about twelve thousand are accounted for (though newly recovered letters turn up regularly).

In recent years, many other editors have also published editions of selected Twain letters. The first of these was *Mark Twain Businessman* (1946), edited by Clemens's grand-nephew Samuel Charles Webster in an effort to exonerate his father, Charles Webster, for the failure of Webster and Company, Twain's publishing house. Like Paine, Webster edited the letters to create a biased impression of Clemens, and in so doing distorts both the biographical record and our picture of Clemens as an epistolary artist. Most subsequent editions have tried to present the letters unedited and annotated, in order to let Twain appear as himself, but the selections nonetheless usually show only one narrow slice of Clemens's life and interests. Dixon Wector edited *The Love Letters of Mark Twain* (1949) and *Mark Twain to Mrs. Fairbanks* (1949) to show Clemens's relationships with two women who significantly influenced his work, Olivia Langdon *Clemens and Mary Mason *Fairbanks respectively. Henry Nash Smith and William M. Gibson took a similar tack in selecting Clemens's correspondence with one person, but altered the format by presenting both sides of the correspondence in *Mark Twain–Howells Letters: The Correspondence of Samuel L. Clemens and William D. Howells, 1872–1910* (1960). Lewis Leary took the same approach with *Mark Twain's Correspondence with Henry Huttleston Rogers* (1969). Two more editions of selected letters have come out: *Mark Twain's Letters to His Publishers, 1867–1894* (1967), edited by Hamlin

Hill, and *Mark Twain's Aquarium: The Samuel Clemens Angelfish Correspondence,
1905–1910* (1991), edited by John Cooley. The ultimate edition of Twain's correspondence, an effort to publish his complete letters, is being issued piecemeal, with the
first five volumes of a projected twenty-three carrying Clemens's correspondence
through 1873 published as of 1997 by the Mark Twain Project through the
University of California Press. The Project also intends to produce electronic copies
of the letters to be accessible on the web.

Letters are a wonderful source of information about people's lives, but their value
does not end with their role as historical artifacts. While many nineteenth-century
Americans wrote newsy letters without much concern for their rhetoric, others took
seriously the aesthetic demands of good correspondence. A proper letter needed to
have a shape and order, though it should not look overly studied. Furthermore, a
multitude of different occasions demanded different effects as well as forms. Not
surprisingly, letter-writing form books were common in the century, giving kinds
of letters, turns of phrase, and advice on how to correspond. In the middle of an
ongoing correspondence, letter writers themselves coached, encouraged, and criticized one another's work. For instance, in a 24 October 1879 letter, William Dean
*Howells reported John Hay's reaction to a letter Clemens wrote to Howells: "'Why
don't somebody write *me* such letters,' he sang out. 'Why don't Clemens do it?'"

Not surprisingly, Clemens cared deeply about the art of letter writing, as we can
see in those letters in which he tried to teach his family members how to write the
kinds of letters he wanted to receive. In his early years, he directly complained that
his correspondents did not write often enough or include the appropriate detail: "I
have received one or two letters from home, but they are not written as they should
be; and know no more about what is going on there, than the man in the moon.
One only has to leave home to learn how to write an interesting [letter] to an
absent friend when he gets back" (to Pamela Moffet, 5 December 1853). Ten years
later, he complained to his mother that her habit of writing letters on wayward
scraps of paper made them difficult to read: "Ma, write on *whole* letter sheets—is
paper scarce in St Louis?" (11 April 1863). She apparently did not reform, for in 1861
Clemens wrote an elaborate parody of her habit, writing a gossipy letter on eighteen scraps of paper. Jane Clemens had to read Clemens's hand through the earlier
writing, and had to put the scraps in the correct order to make sense out of the letter. In this case, Clemens even turned a parody of bad letter writing into an art, and
his mother apparently enjoyed the joke enough to save it, carefully marking the
envelope "Sams scrap letter."

Good letter writers in the flow of good correspondence would exchange letters
from friends and family among other people, so it comes as no surprise that letter
writers were often far more self-conscious than the apparent intimacy of a letter
warranted. In the sophisticated and artful correspondence between Clemens and
Howells, this self-consciousness registers in the occasional apology for a "stupid,"

awkward, or brief letter. Indeed, such self-denigration was conventional among letter writers, in part as a way of adding information about one's condition, in part to insist that the letter is spontaneous. For instance, Olivia Clemens, declining an invitation to visit the Howells household on account of her exhaustion in caring for her new daughter Clara, wrote, "If you find misspelled words in this note, you will remember my infirmity and not hold me responsible" (23 April 1875). One gathers she took mild pleasure in having an excuse, for once, for her chronically faulty spelling.

Howells and Clemens carried their correspondence beyond this level of self-consciousness, with Clemens even parodying the conventional humility of such apologies in an addendum to a letter dated 13 May 1886: "P.S. *May 15*. Been interrupted for a day or two. Mrs. Clemens has condemned this letter to the stove—'because it might make Mr. Howells feel bad.' *Might* make him feel bad! Have I in sweat & travail wrought 12 carefully-contrived pages to make him feel bad, & now there's a bloody *doubt* flung at it? Let me accept the truth: I am grown old, my literary cunning has departed from me. I purposed to shrivel you up; & the verdict is as above." Moving beyond the conventional to the liberty of mutual teasing, Howells and Clemens forged a solid friendship that lasted through failed literary collaborations, withstood the hierarchical relationship of editor to contributor, and helped them pass through various family tribulations—in short, that did what a close friendship should do, even though the two men met infrequently. The artistry as well as the candor of their letters was the fabric of their friendship. Such was also the case for friendships Clemens had with correspondents as far flung as California and Europe.

Clemens was a gifted letter writer from the beginning, even though his own educational and social background did not provide auspicious models. The contrast between Clemens's letters and those of his family members is revealed most starkly in his 21 November 1860 letter to Orion Clemens and family, which begins:

> My Dear Brother:
>
> At last, I have succeeded in scraping together moments enough to write you. And it's all owing to my own enterprise, too—for, running in the fog, on the coast, in order to beat another boat, I grounded the [steamboat *Alonzo*] "Child" on the bank, at nearly flood-tide, where we had to stay until the "great" tide ebbed and flowed again (24 hours,) before she floated off.

and ends

> Like all the letters of the family, *this* is to you and Mollie and Jennie—*all*. And as I am "strapped"—and pushed for time, we'll sing the doxology as follows—hoping to hear from all of you soon:
> "In the world's great field of battle,

In the bivuac of life,
Be not like dumb, driven cattle—
Be a *hero* in the strife."
Amen
Votre frere
Sam. L. Clemens

His sister-in-law, "Mollie" Clemens, forwarded this letter to her sister, adding her own comments in the margins. She wrote, in part:

Orion Cliant [client] that was to bring us wood for a fee has disappinted us and Orion has just enguaged 5 cord hicory 2 dollars per cord all write often tell us all the news it is dull.

Orion seams lowe spirited again

I "hooked" [crocheted] Orion a pair of mittens last week, cost 15c

Tell Miss Christfield to be care ful how she uses pain kill her i will write her soon.

While Clemens's quotation from Henry Wadsworth Longfellow's *poetry is uncharacteristic of the mature writer, the letter nonetheless has a sense of style as well as a sense of order, both of which he would develop in professional contexts. Mollie's letter, by contrast, follows a stream of consciousness, not developing any one thought into a story nor ordering the thoughts into a coherent whole. But as much as Clemens's letters were exceptional, so were they appreciated as such, forwarded to a large audience, often reprinted in Orion's newspapers, and carefully saved by their recipients.

The fact that many of Clemens's early letters were intended as much for publication in his brother's newspapers as for family consumption perhaps explains not only why but how he so quickly rose above his surroundings as a writer of letters. It also shows the close proximity between newspaper reporting and familiar correspondence. In another of his early letters to his family complaining about their style of writing, Clemens makes this connection clear: "Pamela, you wouldn't do for a local reporter—because you don't appreciate the interest that attaches to *names*. An item is of no use unless it speaks of some *person*, & not then, unless that person's *name* is distinctly mentioned. The most interesting letter one can write to an absent friend, is one that treats of *persons* he has been acquainted with, rather than the public events of the day" (18 March 1864). So from the first, Clemens's awareness of the importance of detail and of the particularity of intimate human connections drove his writing of both personal and professional letters.

All of Clemens's letters tell much about Mark Twain. They reveal in less public circumstances the concerns that found their way into fiction and essays. They show the rapid development of a literary artist, whose awareness of what would interest his audience quickly translated into effective journalism and ultimately to sketches, short stories, novels, plays, essays, and travelogues. Of the tens of thousands of letters Clemens wrote in his lifetime, many are business letters, many are remembrances of various events—congratulations, condolence letters, thank-yous, invitations. These provide valuable information about Clemens's life and times, often corroborating or disproving the claims he makes in his autobiography and the claims of numerous biographers. In all these ways, the letters are invaluable as sources of information. Most importantly, they deserve appreciation for what they are intrinsically rather than instrumentally. As the entire range of Clemens's correspondence becomes available, the twenty-first century can learn what the nineteenth knew profoundly, that a fine letter is a work of art, and that in Clemens, America has one of the old masters.

LETTERS FROM THE EARTH (1962). One of the most widely available and popular collections of posthumously published works by Twain, *Letters from the Earth* almost never came out. Bernard DeVoto, upon taking over as executor of the *Mark Twain Papers in 1938, selected three volumes from the mass of previously unpublished works, including this volume of short pieces which he assembled first in 1939. He thought these were the best remaining Twain sketches, stories, and satires. Most were written in the last years of Clemens's life, were not intended for publication, and attack *religion, especially Christianity. Clara Clemens Gabrilowitsch objected to publication, fearing that the volume would distort the image of her father that she and Albert Bigelow *Paine had worked so hard to create. She did not withdraw her objection until 1962, and she died before the book was published in September of that year.

This timing was advantageous for the book's popularity. Not only had scholars discovered the depth and value of Twain's works in the intervening years, but the public, which had taken a modest rest from Twain in the three decades after his death (none of the volumes published by Paine sold as well as expected), had rediscovered Twain. At the beginning of a period of social turbulence, Twain's "hidden" protest writings developed a cachet. *Letters* made the New York *Times* best-seller list and has stayed in print steadily thereafter. This volume helped make Twain an icon for a decade of protest.

♦ SEE ALSO Posthumous Publications.

LIFE ON THE MISSISSIPPI (1883). In 1882, Clemens arranged to visit the *Mississippi River valley in order to collect information to write a book. He intended to turn his successful travelogue formula on his home turf, the part of the country where he was born, learned two trades, and prospered until the coming of the Civil War. He had already found the valley imaginatively profitable in *"Old Times on the Mississippi" and *The Adventures of Tom Sawyer*, but in 1875 he had a revulsion against the *nostalgia with which he had first approached the material. In this mood, he began, pigeonholed, returned to, and pigeonholed again the manuscript of *Adventures of Huckleberry Finn*. In the interim, he had turned to a study of history in order to write *The Prince and the Pauper*, and now he intended to focus this more critical eye on the scenes of his youth and early manhood.

The Mississippi book was not a new idea. He had planned to make this trip as early as 1866, and his ambitions for the book were substantial, telling his wife in an 1871 letter that as good as *Roughing It* was, "When I come to write the Mississippi book, *then*, look out! I will spend 2 months on the river & take notes, & I bet you I will make a standard work" (27 November 1871). By the time he got around to making that trip his circumstances had changed in a way that reinforced his ambition but undercut his ability to succeed. For one thing, his status and resources were much more substantial, making his trip not that of an anonymous reporter but of the *celebrity returning home. He could not hide in the anonymity that would give him a chance to see things from the bottom up. For another, he found his perspective had significantly changed. He had traveled, read, thought, and lived much, and his experiences made his homecoming more complex than he originally intended. Rather than writing a celebration of America's great inland waterway and its culture, he wrote an exposé of what was wrong with America, and in particular what was wrong with the South.

Even when leaving on his trip, though, he expected to hew to his original intentions. The shock of the return to the scenes of his youth showed him how much he had changed and helped him realize that his intentions, too, had to change. He wrote home indulging not in the pleasant nostalgia that had sustained *Tom Sawyer*, but rather with dismay: "That world which I knew in its blossoming youth is old and bowed and melancholy now; its soft cheeks are leathery and wrinkled, the fire is gone out in its eyes, and the spring from its step" (to Olivia Clemens, 17 May 1882). Much of the resultant book, then, deals with loss, sometimes with a sense of personal loss but more often from a political and moral point of view, seeing not so much a loss of innocence, but lost opportunities for progress.

Indeed, much of the book derides the South for its backwardness. The famous chapter 46 in particular is unrelenting, viewing the South's propensity for feudal ornamentation as a symbol of its profound retrogression. But this section merely follows from a chapter on southern sports, which begins with a discussion of the Civil War:

> In the South, the war is what A.D. is elsewhere: they date from it. All day long you hear things "placed" as having happened since the waw; or du'in' the waw; of befo' the waw; or right after the waw; or 'bout two yeahs or five yeahs or ten yeahs befo' the waw or aftah the waw. It shows how intimately every individual was visited, in his own person, by that tremendous episode. It gives

the inexperienced stranger a better idea of what a vast and comprehensive calamity invasion is than he can ever get by reading books at the fireside. (chapter 45)

The closing lines suggest a sympathy with the southerners' obsession, but the framing of this concern ironizes it. Not only is this the first topic in a chapter on southern *sports*, but it is followed by a discussion—at first neutral in tone—of cock-fighting. In reading of the cockpit, the reader's own disgust is put in surprising abeyance by Twain's neutrality—until he says, "I did not see the end of the battle. I forced myself to endure it as long as I could, but it was too pitiful a sight; so I made frank confession to that effect, and we retired." Low key, but certain, Twain passes judgment against this practice and, by association, the preceding southern interest in blood.

In this context, Twain's exposure of southern chivalry makes sense, as does even his semiserious blame of Sir Walter Scott for causing the Civil War by encouraging false ideas of chivalric heroism. This exercise in explicating causes of historical events has not only the humorist's touch of exaggeration, but also the writer's belief in the power of ideas. He ends the chapter: "A curious exemplification of the power of a single book for good or harm is shown in the effects wrought by *Don Quixote* and those wrought by *Ivanhoe*. The first swept the world's admiration for the medieval chivalry-silliness out of existence; and the other restored it. As far as our South is concerned, the good work done by Cervantes is pretty much a dead letter, so effectually has Scott's pernicious work undermined it." Pernicious precisely because it masks barbarism in the guise of civilization. Chivalry, as Clemens's reading in history had led him to believe, was merely the justification of institutional violence.

Much of *Life on the Mississippi* details violence as the sign of barbarism, which while passing in modern, technological America, still persisted in the South. Chapter 26, detailing the Darnell–Watson feud, and chapter 29, recounting the historical activities of the Murrell gang, are the other most conspicuous examples of Clemens's attack on southern violence. These chapters surround his discussion of foreign tourists' travels in the United States. He implies something of the violence of the past in order to, for a change, endorse European criticism of America. Passages in the original manuscript but not printed in the book reveal this intention more explicitly:

[Mrs. Trollope] found a "civilization" here, which you, reader, could not have endured; and which you would not have regarded as a civilization at all. Mrs. Trollope spoke of this civilization in plain terms—plain and unsugared, but honest and without malice, and without hate. Her voice rises to indignation, sometimes, but the object justifies the attitude—being slavery, rowdiness, "chivalrous" assassinations, sham Godliness, and several other devilishnesses which would be as hateful to you, now, as they were to her then. She was holily hated for her "prejudices;" but they seem to have been simply the prejudices of a humane spirit against inhumanities; of an honest nature against humbug; of a clean breeding against grossness; of a right heart against unright speech and deed.

In this, Clemens at least implies that time has civilized America in the due course of progress.

Such is the tenor of his comments in chapter 46, suggesting that northern civilization is not jejune enough to fall for chivalric sham. So as Twain's pilgrimage takes him north to St. Paul, Minnesota, his praise of the tidy, modern city implies the progress that could come if the South would accept the present in order to move on to the future. Indeed, Clemens did have high hopes for progress, but he had less sense of the North's superiority than the book as published suggests. In another passage that remains in the manuscript but that did not make it into the published book he describes the difference between the sections:

> In one thing the average Northerner seems to be a step in advance of the average Southerner, in that he bands himself with his timid fellows to support the law (at least in matters of murder), protect judges, juries, and witnesses, and also to secure all citizens from personal danger and from obloquy or social ostracism on account of opinion, political or religious; whereas the average Southerners do not band themselves together in these high interests, but leave them to look out for themselves unsupported; the results being unpunished murder, against the popular approval, and the decay and destruction of independent thought and action in politics.

On the one hand this passage denounces the post-Reconstruction turn of southern whites to terror against blacks and dissenters to secure racial supremacy. On the other, it implies a northern cowardice and bigotry in abandoning the South to its violence. He thus saw civilization in the North as merely incipient, the first step in progress, not the millennium come. His scorn for the North would only increase in the next year, when he found himself attacked for turning *Mugwump.

All of this serious content and historical perspective on American civilization came packaged in a large subscription book sold as *humor. The book is replete with humor, of course, because Clemens used his associative style to pack his "standard work" full of everything—anecdotes, history, geology, politics, anthropology, literary criticism, and mythology. As Lafcadio Hearn put it in his review in the New Orleans *Times-Democrat* of 20 May 1883, "The author has taken pains to collect and set forth almost every important fact connected with the Mississippi

River—historical or geographical. These positive data rather gain than lose in weight by their humorous presentation; and it may safely be said that many persons who read the opening chapters will obtain from them a better knowledge of what the Mississippi is, than they could gain by laborious study of physical geographies." When Clemens finished his tour and returned east to write the book, he succeeded over the course of the summer and autumn to put together enough manuscript, coupled with the "Old Times" articles, to flesh out 624 pages. Few of his books came together so quickly, but the result was, from Clemens's point of view, a disaster. He had agreed to use James Osgood as his publisher again, in spite of his disappointment with the sales of *The Prince and the Pauper*, but Osgood made the colossal blunder of using the "Old Times" material in the sales prospectus. Many prospective buyers, Clemens believed, assumed the book would be entirely reprinted material and were uninterested.

Even so, Osgood sold over thirty thousand copies in the first year. By most writers' standards, such a sale would have been a smashing success. Clemens, on the contrary, saw it as a failure. On 21 December 1883, he wrote to Osgood that the book "could not have failed if you had listened to me. . . . The Prince & the Pauper & the Mississippi are the only books of mine which have ever failed. The first failure was not unbearable—but this second one is so nearly so that it is not a calming subject for me to talk upon. I am out $50,000 on this last book—that is to say, the sale which should have been 80,000 (seeing the Canadians were for the first time out of competition,) is only 30,000." As he put it in the opening line of chapter 1, "The Mississippi is well worth reading about," and he expected his book to become a standard.

Generations of readers have not agreed. Early reviews were mixed. Most judged the "Old Times" part of the new book by far the best, and while some nonetheless praised the weaker part, many berated it as dull padding. Most twentieth-century readers have agreed with this verdict. The critical attention paid to the book has generally focused on the impact Clemens's trip to the Mississippi had on his completion of *Huckleberry Finn*. Without doubt that contrast makes *Life on the Mississippi* more interesting than otherwise, but for anyone who appreciates the leisurely pace with which Twain ambles over a large expanse of material, burying his substance in a pile of anecdotes and digression, *Life on the Mississippi*, like the travelogues that preceded it, has plenty of life on its own.

♦ SEE ALSO Cable, George Washington; Subscription Publishing.

LITERARY COMEDIANS. SEE Comic Journalism.

LOCKE, DAVID ROSS (PETROLEUM V. NASBY) (1833–1888). Like Clemens, David Ross Locke began his working life as a printer before becoming a journalist, editor, and platform speaker. Unlike Clemens, he stayed on as an editor

in spite of other distractions. As the editor of the Toledo, Ohio, *Blade*, Locke became nationally known for his politics. An ardent Republican, he kept his newspaper far to the Radical Republican side not only during the Civil War but also after, and energetically supported complete equality for *African Americans. In this endeavor he created one of the best-known comic personas of the 1860s, Petroleum V. Nasby, a conservative "Copperhead" who dated his letters from "Confederate X Roads, Which Is in the State of Kentucky." Nasby is in every way repulsive, and his reasons for lending his support to the rebellion were Locke's satiric gibes at the southern cause.

These weekly letters, reprinted regularly by Republican newspapers, were extremely popular among Union partisans. As critic William Matthews put it:

> His rib-tickling irony cheered the patriots, as well as confounded the Copperheads and Rebels. President Lincoln found relief from the weary anxieties of office in reading the letters of the Toledo blade. Grant declared that he "Couldn't get through a Sunday without one," and Secretary [of the Treasury George S.] Boutwell publicly attributed the overthrow of the Rebels to three great forces,—the Army and Navy, the Republican Party, and the Letters of Petroleum V. Nasby. (quoted in Walter Blair and Raven I. McDavid, Jr., *The Mirth of a Nation*)

Locke took his satires on the *lecture circuit, where even after the war he continued to promote the cause of the freed slaves as well as to support *women's rights.

Clemens met Locke on the lecture circuit in March 1869, where they became instant friends. As Clemens wrote to Olivia Clemens on 10 March, "Nasby called at my room at 10 last night & we sat up & talked until 5 minutes past 6 this morning...I took a strong liking to this fellow, who has some very noble qualities." At this meeting, Locke invited Clemens to join the *Blade*, an offer Clemens considered briefly before ultimately rejecting it. But the two did correspond at least through 1874, and their contact on the lecture circuit may have been influential in helping change Clemens's mind about women's suffrage.

LYON, ISABEL (1863–1958).

Isabel Lyon worked as Clemens's private secretary and general factotum from 1902 to 1909. She spent much time with him not only in her professional capacity helping him to organize his correspondence and his business and social affairs, but also as part of his household entourage particularly after the death of Clemens's wife and later when his remaining family members were present less frequently. In fact, Lyon may have played a role in isolating Clemens from his remaining family. If her journal is to be trusted, she even took it upon herself to shield Clemens from bad news, keeping from him letters from his daughter Jean. Certainly, Lyon took on the role of female head of Clemens's household, supervising household management, overseeing the construction of the new house in Redding, Connecticut, in 1907, and spending long evening and nighttime hours playing cards or billiards with Clemens, Ralph W. *Ashcroft, and Albert Bigelow *Paine.

Along with Paine and a stenographer, Lyon served as Clemens's audience when he was dictating his *autobiography. Clemens had always when writing relied on quick responses to his work, depending substantially on his wife and children for the first reaction to the material he had written in a day. In the last years of his life, absent that audience, he turned to Paine and Lyon as surrogates. Lyon in particular fulfilled this function poorly, as she had little sense of literary discrimination and a sycophant's admiration of everything Clemens did. Her nickname for Clemens, "The King," did not stem from her reading of *Huckleberry Finn*, but was rather a sign of her adulation. If Clemens's output was even more irregular than usual in his last years, the irregularity may be attributed as much to his reliance on an unreliable audience as on a decline in his powers.

Lyon kept a journal that, while biased by her self-aggrandizement and adulation of Clemens, nonetheless reveals much about the pain of Clemens's last years. She wrote in September 1907 of Twain's obsessive fear of being alone: "The King cannot bear to stay alone in this house or any house. If I stay away the night he cannot eat, for it is solitude." She also wrote of late nights playing cards and billiards, and of not infrequent drinking bouts:

> Ashcroft came to dine and for cards. We played Hearts until after 3 in the morning, and the King got drunk. He sailed around the room trying to reach the door and landing up in the corner by the Joan of Arc. He cast a gay little eye over at me in his unsteady gait, and said "I'm just practicing," as he sailed with light footsteps over to the door, and up to the bath room. Ashcroft began to spill his cards on the floor, and I picked up a discard of 27 cards and tried to arrange it as my hand—so much for the whole quart of scotch they— we—drank. (16 January 1908)

Not surprisingly, Clara Clemens viewed Lyons with suspicion, believing that Lyons, taking advantage of Clemens's loneliness and lack of circumspection, was trying to become his new wife. Certainly Clara's suspicions were fueled when Clemens gave Lyons and Ashcroft power of attorney over his business affairs. Ashcroft married Lyon in 1909. Lyon wrote in her diary that the marriage had been arranged to "formalize" her role in the household, though if that had been the inducement, the consequence was just the opposite. Shortly after the wedding, which Clemens attended in apparent good will, Clemens accused Lyon and Ashcroft of financial malfeasance and fired them both.

♦ SEE ALSO Work Habits.

MAGAZINES. Today, most magazines are narrowly focused to appeal to niche markets, just the opposite of what they were when publishers borrowed a word for storehouses to apply to a periodically produced miscellany. The subtitle of one of America's earliest magazines, the *Massachusetts Magazine* (1789–1796), carries the idea to the point of absurdity: "Monthly Museum of Knowledge and Rational Entertainment, Poetry, Musick, History, Biography, Physicks, Geography, Morality, Criticism, Philosophy, Mathematicks, Agriculture, Architecture, Chemistry, Novels, Tales, Romances, Translations, News, Marriages and Deaths, Meteorological Observations, Etc., Etc." Early magazines were often one of many ventures engaged in by a single printer, and they usually folded within a few years, if not a few months. They did so in part because Americans who had the leisure, taste, and wherewithal to indulge in *belles lettres*, including magazines, usually purchased them from England.

By the time Clemens was born in 1835, American magazines were finally developing a basis for their own survival at least, and, by the end of the century, for spectacular profitability. They began their rise in part by following the British formula, including pirating British literature in order to have celebrity headliners, but at the same time by appealing to nationalism, suggesting that their magazines were creating and supporting an indigenous culture. The most long-lived and culturally influential of these was the **North American Review*, founded in 1815 by the Anthology Club of Boston, early associated with Harvard College, and edited by such cultural heavyweights as Jared Sparks and Edward Everett. Published either quarterly or monthly until its demise in 1940, the *North American Review* never gained exceptionally wide circulation, but it always maintained its status as one of the premier American periodicals, an arbiter of taste in literary and cultural matters as well as a firm champion of American culture.

From the 1830s through the 1850s, a number of successful magazines—following this formula of mixing politics, science, gossip, and the arts, and targeting families as audiences—created a market for American writers beyond *newspaper journalism. The magazines in fact helped create certain genres of writing, such as the short story, which evolved from the "tale" and the *"sketch," and novels themselves developed—in England first—through magazine serialization. Most American magazines began with a regional focus, including the *Knickerbocker* (New York, 1833–1865), the *Southern Literary Messenger* (Richmond, 1834–1864), and The **Atlantic Monthly* (Boston, 1857 to present), but most of the successful ones, like *Putnam's*, expanded to have a national focus and helped to create a national identity. The most important of these was *Harper's New Monthly Magazine*, founded in 1850. Twice the size of most American journals and filled with woodcuts, this periodical quickly developed a national circulation of 200,000 copies per month, becoming one of Harper and Brothers publishers most successful ventures. They followed their success with *Harper's Weekly: A Journal of Civilization* and *Harper's Bazaar*, which was more tightly focused on fashion.

Indeed, the success of fashion magazines in the antebellum period led to the trend toward niche marketing. *Godey's Ladies Book*, founded in 1830 in Philadelphia, targeted women by printing hand-colored fashion plates (which today are collectors items). It included the lighter fare of other magazines, but eschewed partisan politics and went easy on science (though *Godey's* did report on technological marvels, such as the Philadelphia Water Works). It had one of the largest national circulations, with a subscriber list of 150,000 shortly before the Civil War. Similarly, the New York *Spirit of the Times*, a gentleman's magazine devoted to sport, deliberately eschewed politics and inadvertently helped created *southwestern humor. So while magazine culture took off in the antebellum years substantially because of its political content, publishers also discovered the value of politically neutral entertainment, a discovery that gradually moved general circulation magazines away from politics into the early twentieth century.

Magazines became lucrative enterprises by 1860, so much so that their numbers skyrocketed during the immediate postbellum years, at precisely the same time that Twain's career was taking off. Between 1865 and 1872, the number of magazines doubled from about 700 to roughly 1,400. A few of these were sufficiently capitalized and paid their writers well, such as *The Galaxy Magazine* (1866–1878). It early on sought Twain as a highly paid contributor. While most magazines were based in the Northeast, even San Francisco had its literary magazines, the *Golden Era* (1852–1893) and the *Overland Monthly* (1868–1876). Twain contributed to both, and his pieces in the *Overland* published during Bret *Harte's editorship (from 1868 to 1870) helped him to formulate the Mark Twain persona. Another major magazine founded between 1865 and 1872 was *Scribner's Monthly*, which became the *Century Magazine* in 1881 and was an important venue for Twain's writings.

Besides the earliest women's and men's magazines, other periodicals pushed the trend toward special interest magazines. Some concentrated on particular trades, organizations, or religions, or insisted on fighting the tendency toward broad appeal by trying to maintain a high literary tone. Such magazines, which often bordered on newspapers or newsletters, struggled between the needs to serve a particular community and to broaden circulation to the point of profitability. Twain often used this struggle as a subject of his fiction, for example, in "How I Edited an Agricultural Newspaper" and in his remarks on a literary magazine in chapter 51 of *Roughing It*. But growing specialization of journals had an even more significant impact on Twain. When he was under financial duress in 1892, his decision to close a contract with *St. Nicholas Magazine* for children to publish **Tom Sawyer Abroad* is only the most obvious case of Twain's writing a story to fit a particular journal's editorial policy. More importantly, his efforts to make his writing worthy of the very literary *Atlantic* nearly twenty years earlier when he published **"Old Times on the Mississippi"* had an enduring impact on his *style.

The general magazines and the women's magazines remained the most lucrative, especially from the 1880s on when dramatic advances in the printing of illustrations made the large monthlies more like modern magazines. *Harper's*, *Century*, and a new *Scribner's* reached national audiences with subscription lists between 100,000 and 200,000, but the newer, less prestigious, and less expensive journals like *Cosmopolitan*, *Collier's*, and *McClure's* had even larger audiences. With circulations that substantial, they were able to pay the best American and European writers and artists excellent prices for their contributions. Not surprisingly, then, after 1890 with the decline of the subscription book, Twain turned increasingly to magazine publication as a major literary outlet and source of income.

♦ SEE ALSO Reading, Clemens's.

"MAN THAT CORRUPTED HADLEYBURG, THE."

"MAN THAT CORRUPTED HADLEYBURG, THE." One of Twain's most widely reprinted short stories, this moral fable was written in 1898 while Clemens was living in Vienna, watching the immoral, anti-Semitic populist politics of Vienna Mayor Karl Luegar and brooding on the ills of late–nineteenth-century culture. Similar in theme to **"Chronicle of Young Satan,"* "Hadleyburg" depicts a normal, morally corrupt town asleep to its hypocrisies and self-complacency, awakened by the arrival of a mysterious stranger whose malevolent machinations expose the town's conformity, greed, and self-deception. The moral touchstones of the piece are for the most part outsiders in the town's hierarchy: the loafer Jack Halliday, the shamed and ostracized minister Burgess, a deceased iconoclast allegorically named "Goodson," and the unnamed stranger whose desire for revenge drives the plot. In an elaborate *practical joke that plays on the greed of the town's nineteen most reputable families, the stranger arranges a court of derision, presided over by Burgess and the ghost of Goodson, with Halliday serving as foreman of the jury. Halliday leads the world in derisive, ritual laughter at the exposed moral hollowness of eighteen of the town's nineteen first families.

The one exception, Mary and Edward Richards, provides a countermoral to the piece. While the exposure of the town's artificiality, conformity, and greed seems for the most part fitting and proper, the story paints the Richards' situation in specific detail to complicate this assessment. Their moral shortcomings are patent, but the pressures that lead them to such failures are so overwhelming and out of their control that the story has a countertext of sympathy for the wrong-doers. As such,

"Hadleyburg" develops the moral double-vision of many of Twain's late works, recognizing and scorning human shortcomings while simultaneously sympathizing with individual human beings for the impossible demands placed on them by a morally indifferent universe.

In other words, Twain cannot decide whether to condemn humanity or extend charity, but the hidden thrust of the story suggests the latter. While the court excoriates the town for lying, the question of the town's honesty is merely a red herring diverting attention from its real failing—its lack of charity. Everyone in the town knows that the only person capable of giving money to a destitute stranger was Goodson. The Richards, who had inadvertently exercised charity toward Burgess in the past, are treated charitably by him in turn when he refuses to identify them as liars. But neither Richards gets the point. Wrapped up in an obsession with a narrow honesty, they cannot accept Burgess's charity toward them, nor can they find any for themselves. Without the capacity to forgive and to love, they are as doomed as the rest of the town.

♦ SEE ALSO Anti-Semitism; Money; Moral Sense.

MARK TWAIN. One of the most famous pseudonyms in literature, Mark Twain served its owner, Samuel Clemens, as a comic persona, alter ego, and conduit for creative energies. It was not the first of Clemens's many *pseudonyms and personas, nor the last name he used to mask his own *identity, but it was the most enduring, the one that signaled his permanent decision to be a professional writer, the one that he sued repeatedly to protect and finally registered as a trademark in the *Mark Twain Company. How Clemens used the name and what it meant both to him and his public opens an important window onto the life and writings of Samuel Clemens.

The first known use of the name "Mark Twain" by Samuel Clemens was on 3 February 1863 in the Virginia City *Territorial Enterprise*. In early 1873, in a biographical sketch for his friend Charles Dudley Warner, editor of the Hartford *Courant*, Clemens claimed that he filched the pseudonym from an old riverboat pilot, Captain Isaiah Sellers, whose real name Clemens borrowed for Colonel Sellers in the novel he cowrote with Warner, *The Gilded Age*. Clemens said that the old man wrote river correspondence over the name "Mark Twain" when Clemens was a cub pilot. Later, when he needed a pseudonym for his own travel writing in Nevada, he borrowed the name. Clemens repeated the account often, most conspicuously in chapter 50 of *Life on the Mississippi* and most succinctly in a form letter he drafted to handle common questions:

> Dear Sir: "Mark Twain" was the nom de plume of one Capt Isaiah Sellers, who used to write river news over it for the New Orleans Picayune. He died in 1863, & as he could no longer need that signature I laid violent hands upon

it without asking permission of the proprietor's remains. That is the history of the nom de plume I bear.

Ys Truly

Saml. L. Clemens

Scholars debate the truth of this story. Some point out that Sellers did not die until 1864 and that no one has ever located correspondence by Sellers under the name "Mark Twain" in the New Orleans *Picayune*. Yet much circumstantial evidence suggests that the name did indeed originate from Clemens's days as a steamboat pilot.

In any event, if this story is correct or even substantially correct, then the name simply refers to the riverboat leadsman's cry of "mark twain," meaning that the water in the river at that point is two fathoms deep, the depth necessary for the safe passage of a typical Mississippi River steamboat. Of course, while Twain wanted his name to denote safe water, that would depend on whether "mark twain" was the last or first reading of a patch of shallow water.

But there is another equally telling story about what "Mark Twain" signifies. Clement T. Rice, Clemens's good friend and rival reporter for the Virginia City *Union*, referred to Clemens in a 29 January 1864 article as "Mark Two," a reference to Clemens's putative habit of always ordering two drinks at once and marking them both on his bar tab. Certainly Clemens drank heavily in Nevada, and men like Rice, who enjoyed chaffing Clemens as much as Clemens enjoyed returning the favor, would have loved punning on the name. Thus, it is unlikely that this second meaning of "Mark Twain" was of Clemens's origin, but insofar as the name denominated a comic persona, the role of heavy-drinking wild man became very much part of the pose. Early Twain sketches, especially those naming Rice as "The Unreliable," often depend on drunkenness for their humor. While the Mark Twain of the East tended to rely less on such spirited humor, references to *alcohol are a central part of the Twain persona.

Both of these origin stories reveal characteristics of Mark Twain not so much as pseudonym as persona. On the one hand, Twain is an image of ambiguously safe fun. It is a mask that offers safe passage from one mood to another while flirting along the way with dangerously unsettling ideas. On the other hand, it is a carnival mask behind which the staid and proper can shed inhibition to revel in extravagant feelings. The Twain persona serves his readers as much as it served his creator—it is a mask of freedom and imagination, the traits that Clemens most needed to cultivate in order to make a serious living as a public clown.

While these fundamental characteristics remain constant throughout Clemens's career as Mark Twain, Twain is not a static comic character but rather exists in several distinct manifestations, each dominant in different periods. When first created by Clemens, Twain was a rambunctious, arrogant, disputatious, slangy, hard-drinking journalist, who functioned primarily as a reporter. Often this Mark Twain uses the editorial "we" and arrogates to himself complete editorial righteousness, even as he describes his drinking bouts. He readily mocks his reportorial duties by staging elaborate journalistic hoaxes, such as "My Bloody Massacre" or "Petrified Man," and creates news by picking fights with public persons or with other reporters. Such wholesale dealing in insults, or what nineteenth-century writers euphemistically referred to as "personalities," made Twain's position as the socially correct "Reliable" in juxtaposition to Clement Rice's "Unreliable" completely ironic, but it did reveal to Clemens the comic potential of Mark Twain as straight man.

In this second pose as straight man, which had three distinct incarnations, Twain plays the gentleman only to have his airs revealed as fruitless at best. In this pose, Mark Twain is not so much the originator as the target of Clemens's comedy, and it tends to be the comedy of humor rather than wit. He hit accidentally on this formula in his third draft of "The *Jumping Frog" story and then developed it as Twain's main mask for much of the rest of his career. In one incarnation of this pose, Twain is paired with an underling sidekick, such as the Mr. Brown of the travel letters to Hawaii, New York, and Europe of 1866 to 1867, or the Harris of *A Tramp Abroad*. In the 1866–1867 letters, the gentlemanly Mr. Mark Twain relishes poetry, landscape, elevated sentiments, and propriety while Mr. Brown undercuts all of Twain's high-blown rhetoric. The counterpoint between the two positions did not allow enough flexibility for Clemens to handle all of his travel reporting, so the mask was far from consistent. In these letters, the original Twain would often erupt to handle his opinions directly, scorching anything and anyone he pleased in high style or low whenever the Twain-Brown pas de deux no longer served. Later, in *Tramp Abroad*, Clemens developed a better sense of the possibilities of a persona, and so held character much better, in part by reducing the gap in *social class between Twain and Harris as that between Twain and Brown, and in part by showing how thin was the veneer of gentility covering Twain's selfishness and vulgarity.

Another incarnation of this second pose does away with the sidekick entirely, setting up the contrast between the narrator's romantic, refined expectations and reality from a retrospective point of view. In *Roughing It*, *"Old Times on the Mississippi," and "The *Private History of a Campaign That Failed," for examples, the older, wiser Mark Twain recounts the story of his own callow youth, allowing himself to serve not only as the butt of the humor but as the wise man who reveals humor in folly. Often in this mode, Twain is the gull in a *confidence game, a *practical joke, or an *initiation rite, and his wiser retrospective point of view serves at some points to put his readers on guard against the deceptions of the world, at others, against self-deception. Not far from this use is Mark Twain as the audience of someone else's tale, in which a credulous Twain becomes the willing stand-in for his readers, enabling them to enjoy outlandish stories but protecting them from being fooled as badly as is Twain himself.

While this humorous "Twain as straightman" dominated the middle part of Clemens's career, his later career saw a shift back toward wit, with Twain posing as the wise man of the world, a philosopher born of experience rather than bookishness. This return to wit, however, does not reveal Twain as a boisterous youth again, but rather as a sage, dealing not so much in insults as in *maxims. As first-person and framed narratives were characteristic of both the early and middle phases of the Mark Twain mask, the third-person narrative characterizes this later phase.

As much, however, as the maxim-maker or the third-person narrator of *Pudd'nhead Wilson and Those Extraordinary Twins* seems to understand the world completely, another Mark Twain mask began to find its way into Clemens's writing in the 1890s and 1900s that suggests just the opposite. In the published diaries of *Adam and Eve and in many unfinished tales, such as *"Three Thousand Years among the Microbes," Twain poses not as an omniscient narrator nor as a willing audience to an oral tale, but as translator of a narrative from another time, place, or condition. As such, Twain is both in a position of authority, as the person who has broken a code to bring us an outlandish tale, and in a position of tentative knowledge, fully aware that his translations themselves are mere approximations. In these translations, Clemens again uses the Mark Twain pose as a conduit for imagination and humor rather than for judgment and wit.

♦ SEE ALSO Public Image.

MARK TWAIN CIRCLE OF AMERICA.

Until recently, Twain was one of the few major American authors not to have a society of academics banded together to aid study of his work. The Mark Twain Circle of America was formed in 1986 to fill that need, substantially under the impetus of Everett Emerson, then a professor of English at the University of North Carolina at Chapel Hill. While Emerson felt that the group should include nonacademics as well, and that its function should be to support the appreciation of Twain's works rather than merely to provide a forum for professional scholarship, scholars have been the driving force behind this very active group since its inception, and its meetings are, for the most part, affiliated with two of the largest academic organizations in the United States, the Modern Language Association and the American Literature Association. The Mark Twain Circle holds regular meetings concurrently with the annual meetings of both of these groups, in late December and late May respectively, and also coordinates with the American Literature Association to hold occasional conferences elsewhere. Still, the group does actively work to connect the worlds of scholarship and of wider interest in Twain, inviting nonscholars to contribute to its functions and using its newsletter, the *Mark Twain Circular*, to inform members of the wide variety of events associated with Twain in the United States and abroad.

♦ SEE ALSO Critical Reception; Public Image.

MARK TWAIN COMPANY AND MARK TWAIN FOUNDATION. Throughout his career, Clemens sought ways to protect his financial interests in his writing against literary piracy. He found copyright to be too weak to provide adequate protection against Canadian pirates Belford and Brother in particular, and even found it difficult to protect his interests in the United States. Thus, when business manager Ralph W. *Ashcroft suggested using trademark laws to protect the interests of a Mark Twain Company, Clemens agreed. The company became the holder of Clemens's copyrights and his trademarked image. At Twain's death, the company was under the direct control of Clara Clemens Gabrilowitsch *Samossoud. Upon her death in 1962, her second husband Jacques Samossoud surrendered partial control to Clara's daughter, Nina Clemens *Gabrilowitsch, and willed the rest to his friend Dr. William E. Seiler. Both Gabrilowitsch and Samossoud died in 1966. When Seiler died in 1978, the company was formally ended. It was replaced by the Mark Twain Foundation, a charitable trust that holds the remaining copyrights on Twain's works and distributes portions of the annual proceeds to various organizations dedicated to preserving Twain's legacy, such as the museums in Hannibal, Missouri, and Hartford, Connecticut, and the Mark Twain Project.

♦ SEE ALSO Public Image.

MARK TWAIN FORUM. Founded in 1992 by Taylor Roberts, then a graduate student at the Massachusetts Institute of Technology, the Mark Twain Forum is an electronic list server. The subscriber list fluctuates around 450 members who share an interest in Twain. Members post questions and opinions about Twain as well as mentioning upcoming events—such as television specials, appearances of Twain impersonators, and museum exhibitions—pertaining to him and his writings. The forum also posts reviews of books, videos, and electronic media by or about Twain. The forum not only actively sends new postings to members, but also maintains a web-site with a searchable database in which all postings are logged.

While the forum has proven to be long-lived in this new electronic world, its address has changed more than once and its server has also moved. The best way, then, to join is to search for the forum's web-site using a search engine and then follow the instructions for logging on.

♦ SEE ALSO Critical Reception; Public Image.

MARK TWAIN JOURNAL. Founded in 1936 by Cyril Clemens, a distant cousin of Samuel Clemens, the *Mark Twain Journal* from its first number in 1936 to 1983 was a strange mix of gossip, Cyril Clemens's posing with famous people on the pretext of getting their opinions about Twain, and useful reprints of difficult to find Twain items. Its editorial standards were at best amateurish, and its publication was infrequent and unreliable.

In 1983, Thomas A. Tenney took over editorship of the journal. He focused and improved editorial standards significantly. The *Journal* usually accepts essays dealing with factual matters of biography, bibliography, or historical context rather than with interpretation, though occasionally it publishes special issues that take up interpretive matters directly. The best known of these was a special fall 1984 issue devoted to African-American responses to *Adventures of Huckleberry Finn*, an expanded version of which has been published by Duke University Press under the title *Satire or Evasion? Black Perspectives on Huckleberry Finn* (1992).

◆ SEE ALSO Critical Reception; Public Image.

MARK TWAIN PAPERS. In a 19 and 20 October 1865 letter to his brother Orion *Clemens in which he acknowledged that he felt a "'call' to literature," Samuel Clemens admonished his brother to "shove this in the stove—for . . . I don't want any absurd 'literary remains' & 'unpublished letters of Mark Twain' published after I am planted." Obviously, Orion did not comply, and it was not long before Samuel had cause to thank Orion for being a pack-rat. Indeed, in short order, Samuel began asking his family members to keep scrapbooks of his works, and he borrowed their letters and diaries when he went to write books such as *Roughing It*. His *work habits were such that no scrap of paper lacked value as raw material. While he threatened often to burn manuscripts, and may have destroyed much, he saved his papers for the most part.

His propensity to keep and recycle almost anything he had written had added benefits late in his life. As Twain's fame grew, Clemens came to realize that his manuscripts, letters, and other "remains" were marketable commodities, valuable as an inheritable property for his family.

He occasionally gave manuscripts, or parts of manuscripts, to friends after he published, and many of his manuscripts were destroyed in the process of producing his books and articles. But he collected and preserved much of the rest, as well as any of his correspondence on which he could lay his hands. He also kept most of his working notebooks and a large percentage of his unfinished manuscripts and rough drafts, as well as family papers and many personally annotated copies of his favorite books. He gave this vast quantity of paper into the custody of Albert Bigelow *Paine to be used as raw material for the authorized biography, though ownership and ultimate control remained in the hands of his family. Paine served as literary executor and, while he lost some of the papers and sold others, secured permission from Clara Clemens Gabrilowitsch *Samossoud to publish a small quantity of the *unfinished works.

At Paine's death, he was replaced by Bernard DeVoto, the scholar who had most assiduously attacked the private arrangement between Paine and the estate. DeVoto felt that the papers should be available to an America that needed to know about one of its greatest authors. DeVoto served as steward of the papers from 1938 to

1946, housing them at Harvard University. He tried to make public much of the material, preparing several volumes for the press, though Samossoud's objections prevented publication of some of them until her death in 1962. DeVoto's scholarly professionalism began the process of turning a haphazard and shrinking collection of papers into a growing research library. He worked to acquire thousands of Clemens's letters, to recover much of Clemens's personal library, and to allow limited scholarly access to the papers. In 1946, with Samossoud's blessing, he turned responsibility for the papers over to Dixon Wecter, who was planning a substantial biography to supersede Paine's. Wecter, then chairman of the research group at the Henry Huntington Library in San Marino, California, took the papers west, and shortly thereafter, moved them again when he relocated to the University of California at Berkeley. With this move, he persuaded Samossoud to bequeath the papers to the University of California so that their home would be permanent and secure, rather than contingent on the location of their custodian. Since then, they have been presided over by Henry Nash Smith (1953–1964), Frederick Anderson (1964–1979), and Robert Hirst (1980 to the present).

As the primary collection of documents by and about Clemens, the papers have become the basis of the Mark Twain Project, established in 1980 to publish the definitive edition of Twain's works and papers. With waning financial support from the National Endowment for the Humanities, the project's hopes to finish publishing its projected one hundred volumes in the second decade of the twenty-first century can only be realized if it can find enough donors to establish an endowment.

♦ SEE ALSO Critical Reception; Posthumous Publications.

MARK TWAIN'S LIBRARY OF HUMOR. One of the few literary *collaborations Clemens initiated that finally bore fruit, the *Library of Humor* is an anthology published by Clemens's own publishing firm, Webster and Company, in 1888. The *Library of Humor* is, in its own right, a fine compendium of American *humor, ranging from early humorists such as Washington Irving to Twain's contemporaries. It is also an invaluable resource for understanding Twain, as it shows the context of humorous writing that shaped his understanding of the literary market.

Perhaps, however, the book should not be read with such a narrowly heuristic purpose but rather with ones more congruent with the intentions of the compilers. The man who suggested the idea to Clemens merely wanted to make money. Philadelphia bookseller George Gebbie proposed in 1880 that Clemens compile an anthology for Gebbie to publish by subscription. Clemens was taken with the idea of an anthology of humor, though not with Gebbie himself. While Clemens's inquiries showed Gebbie to be a reputable businessman, the two had different visions of the project. Clemens embraced the idea not only as a money-maker, but also for the pleasure he could have reading and laughing over American humor with two of his good friends. So he made arrangements in 1881 with James R. Osgood, his then publisher, to sell a book to be compiled by Charles H. Clark, a Hartford journalist and member of the *Monday Evening Club; William Dean *Howells; and Clemens himself. Generally speaking, Clark did most of the first screening, Howells made the second pass, and, when most of the *work* was done, Clemens made the final selections, serving as arbiter for differences of opinion between Clark and Howells. In many cases, though, Clemens made his own choices, even going so far as to choose among the works of Bret *Harte, whom by then he had come to hate. What other authors he chose is unknown, though the conspicuous presence of his friend Ambrose Bierce in the book's table of contents is something of a puzzle. Although he liked Bierce personally, he wrote to Chatto and Windus in 1874 that they should not publish bitter Bierce's work because "there is humor in [him], but for every laugh that is in his book there are five blushes ten shudders & a vomit. The laugh is too expensive" (8 April). Still, such expensive laughs made it into the *Library of Humor*. The number of Clemens's friends who appear in the book suggests that in many cases, personal taste in *humor* took second place to the demands of personal friendship. Howells, always trying to defend, explain, and promote American literature, wrote a rather scholarly introduction and carefully arranged all of the selections, but, as he said in *My Mark Twain*:

> When I had done my work according to tradition, with authors, times, and topics carefully studied in due sequence, he tore it all apart, and "chucked" the pieces in wherever the fancy for them took him at that moment. He was right: we were not making a text-book, but a book for the pleasure rather than the instruction of the reader, and he did not see why the principle on which he built his travels and reminiscences and tales and novels should not apply to it; and I do not now see, either, though at the time it confounded me. (chapter 4)

The tensions between the purposes of the collaborators could have confounded the book if Howells had not deferred to Clemens in this project.

The book was also almost confounded by the failure of Osgood's publishing firm, but Clemens's own firm, Webster and Company, picked up the contract and published the book. Clemens wanted to give Howells star billing to acknowledge the amount of work he did and the difficulty of collaborating with so capricious a headliner. Howells, however, had an exclusive contract at the time with Harper's, so his name was left off, though he did receive a hefty five-thousand-dollar payment for his work.

There is some question about how much the book mattered to Clemens, since it took relatively little work on his part and required next to no new writing. Two anecdotes suggest an answer. First, Clemens commissioned E. W. Kemble to illustrate the book, but he found Kemble's widely varied and fascinating drawings lifeless and uninteresting and so severed his connection. His expectations must have been quite high—too high—for him to have formed such a judgment with such consequences. Second, in 1906, Harper's, having a decade earlier purchased the rights to publish all of Twain's books, decided to rework the *Library of Humor* as a much more substantial compendium of American humor. Hiring Burgess Johnson to edit the new book, Harper's kept little more than the title and the "Compiler's apology: Those selections in this book which are from my own works were made by my two assistant compilers, not by me. This is why there are not more." Clemens was far from pleased with the new Harper's anthology under the guise of the old Mark Twain name, as Johnson remembered in a 1937 article entitled "When Mark Twain Cursed Me." Clemens's anger suggests that he had had enough of a hand in building the original book to have his ego tied up in it. Hence, it is reasonable to consider the original *Library of Humor* to be a good barometer not only to the tastes of the day, but also to the tastes of Samuel Clemens.

♦ SEE ALSO Illustrations; Publishing Industry; Subscription Publishing.

MAXIMS. One of the most enduringly popular images of Mark Twain is that of the old man in the white suit looking shrewdly out from under shaggy white brows, ripping out some sharp-edged maxim, like "Nothing so needs reforming as other people's habits" (*Pudd'nhead Wilson,* chapter 15). This Benjamin Franklin with bite, this compassion-free Will Rogers is the man who could say, "There is no distinctly native American criminal class except Congress" (*Following the Equator,* chapter 8); "I don't know of a single foreign product that enters this country untaxed except the answer to prayer" (*Mark Twain's Speeches,* 398); "It was wonderful to find America, but it would have been more wonderful to have missed it"(*Pudd'nhead Wilson,* conclusion); "A man may have no bad habits and have worse" (*Following the Equator,* chapter 1); "There is nothing sadder than a young pessimist except an old optimist" (Notebooks); or, most gloomily, "Pity is for the living; envy is for the dead" (*Following the Equator,* chapter 19).

A cracked cracker-barrel cynic, the old Mark Twain looks the part of the pessimist, dressed in the pristine white of purity but scowling at the vice he sees all around him. Still, the lurking suspicion remains that the gloom is just another act. Some of his maxims—such as "Wrinkles should merely indicate where smiles have been" (*Following the Equator,* chapter 52)—are not bitter and, even more convincingly, Twain's pristine white garb merely proves one of his more famous maxims, "Clothes make the man: naked people have little or no influence in society" (quoted in Merle Johnson, *More Maxims of Mark*). He as much as tells us that the power of image is all surface; we should take that surface as a prop in a performance, not as

(Left) The caption to this photograph, in Clemens's handwriting, reads: "Three of the suspected men still in confinement at Aurora." Clemens (center), then a reporter for the the Virginia City *Territorial Enterprise*, was photographed with William Claggert, representative of the Nevada territorial legislature, left, and A. J. Simmons, speaker of the territorial legislature. *Courtesy of the Mark Twain Papers, University of California, Berkeley.*

(Right) Samuel L. Clemens. Photographed by Mathew Brady in 1870. *Courtesy of the Mark Twain House, Hartford, Connecticut.*

(Left) The Clemens house in Hartford, Connecticut, from a stereoscopic view of the house taken by Richard S. DeLamater in the mid- to late 1870s. *From the Robert Dennis Collection of Stereoscopic Views, Photography Collection, Miriam & Ira Wallach Division of Art, Prints & Photographs, The New York Public Library.*

(Left) The Clemens family on the porch of their Hartford house in a photograph by H. L. Bundy from 1884. From left to right: Olivia, Clara, Jean, Samuel, and Susy. *Courtesy of the Mark Twain Papers.*

(Below) Clemens plays charades with Susy during the summer of 1890 at the Onteora resort in the Catskill Mountains. Clemens, dressed in a swimming suit with a hot water bottle hanging from his neck and capped by a straw bonnet, is impersonating Leander, a character from Greek legend. *Courtesy of the Mark Twain House.*

Clemens lights a cigar in this photograph from 1895. He was frequently photographed with cigars and pipes, and smoking was a significant part of the Twain persona. In his seventieth-birthday-party speech he averred, "It has always been my rule never to smoke when asleep, and never to refrain when awake." *Courtesy of the Mark Twain House.*

(Right) "Mark Twain Lost." Clemens is playing, and losing, a game in which the goal is to stay on a boom on a ship on choppy seas. *Courtesy of the Chemung County Historical Society. Thanks to Marianne Curling for calling this photograph to my attention.*

Visiting the Crane house in Quarry Farm, Elmira, New York, in 1903, Clemens posed for this photograph in the study in which he wrote substantial parts of many of his books. *Courtesy of the Mark Twain House.*

(Right) Clemens poses with a pet in a photograph taken sometime in the summer of 1904 by Joseph Gaylord Gessford of New York. *Courtesy of the Mark Twain House.*

(Below) Clemens's lavish seventieth-birthday celebration at Delmonico's in New York City in 1905. The banquet was staged by Colonel George Harvey, then editor of *Harper's Weekly,* as a publicity stunt to promote his magazines. The guests in this photograph are, from left to right, Kate Douglas Riggs, Clemens, Joseph Twichell, Bliss Carman, Ruth McEnery Stuart, Mary E. Wilkins Freeman, Henry M. Alden, and Henry H. Rogers. All but Twichell and Rogers were authors who had published in Harvey's journals. *Courtesy of the Library of Congress, Pictures and Prints Division.*

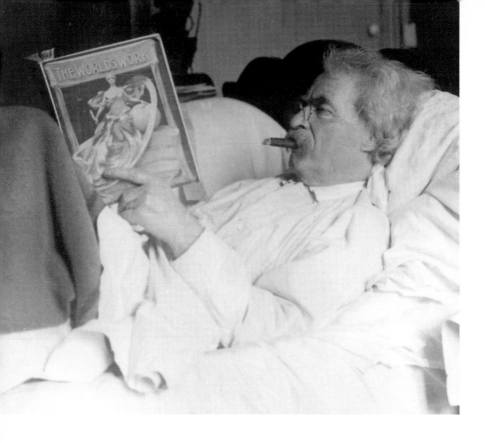

(Left) A 1906 portrait of Clemens in bed. To support his pose of studied idleness, he had numerous photographs taken of himself in bed reading, writing, and, usually, smoking. In this picture his choice of reading matter while he relaxes serves to under-score his indolent image. *Courtesy of the Mark Twain Papers.*

Clemens with his household group, photographed by Alvin Langdon Coburn. Clemens is composing his auto-biography, dictating anecdotes to a stenographer, W. E. Grumman, far left. Also present are Ralph Ashcroft and Isabel Lyon. *Courtesy of the George Eastman House.*

(Right) Clemens teaches Louise
Paine to play billiards, June 1908 at
Stormfield, Redding, Connecticut.
Courtesy of the Mark Twain Papers.

(Left) William Dean
Howells and Samuel
Clemens in 1908.
*Courtesy of the Mark
Twain Papers.*

Portrait of the wedding party at Clara's first wedding, 6 October 1908. Clemens wears the gown and mortar board conferred on him with his honorary doctorate from Oxford University. From left to right: Clemens, his nephew Jervis Langdon, Jean Clemens, Ossip Gabrilowitsch, Clara Clemens, and Joseph Twichell. *Courtesy of the Mark Twain House.*

Clemens admires an automobile at Stormfield, Redding, Connecticut, in 1908. The driver is a Mrs. Enders; Ralph Ashcroft and Mr. Enders (far right) look on. Always quick to use new inventions, Clemens often rode in automobiles in the first decade of the twentieth century. *Courtesy of the Mark Twain House.*

an essential reality. In fact, the dandified posture of pure white clothing belies the image of homespun sage, ironizing the "truth" of the adages he utters. (The irony is perhaps compounded now, since the image of the white-garbed man appears on numerous t-shirts and sweatshirts, only some of which quote him accurately.)

The image of the aged sage does not really cover the range or meaning of Twain's aphorisms. He began spouting them early in his career, but usually to parody the putative authority of pithy sayings. As biblical proverbs, morals to animal fables, and adages from Benjamin Franklin's *Poor Richard's Almanac* or other well-known sources, aphorisms carry the double weight of rhetorical power and authoritative source. Distilled into certain brief rhetorical forms—often relying on rhymes, consonance, alliteration, parallel structure, or chiasmus—aphorisms not only are easy to remember, but sound true. When backed up by an authoritative source, they inspire belief as absolute and eternal truths.

This very function served by the adage is precisely what Twain's maxims play with even at his most cynical. Early in his career, he parodied aphorisms partly to undercut their apparent timeless veracity, as in the sketch "The Late Benjamin Franklin" (1870), in which such understated renditions of Franklin's maxims as "A groat a day's a penny a year" literally belittle Franklin's wisdom. Other parody maxims, distorted through additions that change not only the rhetorical balance of the originals but also their points of view, suggest that maxims may have less to do with eternal truth than with human needs: "Early to Bed and Early to Rise makes a man healthy and wealthy and wise. As if it were any object to a boy to be healthy and wealthy and wise on such terms." So when Franklin utters a maxim, Twain suggests, it is not to tell the truth, but rather to cover his tracks: "If a body, during his old age, happened on him unexpectedly when he was catching flies, or making mud pies, or sliding on a cellar-door, he would immediately look wise, and rip out a maxim." The "flies"–"pies"–"wise" rhyme copies the mnemonic structure of the aphorism, but takes its pleasure in denying us reason with the rhyme. The triviality of the subject further mocks the putative profundity of proverbial wisdom. High-sounding declarations about trivia are commonplace among Twain's maxims: "A use has been found for everything but snoring" (*Notebooks*, May 1892).

Such parody is one pattern of maxim-making that Twain followed throughout his career, especially in his many burlesques of advice literature for children. His early "Advice for Good Little Boys" (1865) and "Advice for Good Little Girls" (1865) make the point but lack pungency, as with, "You should never do anything wicked and then lay it on your brother, when it is just as convenient to lay it on some other boy." Practice made perfect, though; by the 1880s, Twain was coining parody homilies that had just the right rhythm and sound, as in "Advice to Youth" (1882): "Always obey your parents, when they are present"; "Be respectful to your superiors, if you have any"; and "You want to be very careful about lying; otherwise you are nearly sure to get caught." He continued the parody advice in many of his speeches of the 1890s and 1900s, as for example in his "Seventieth Birthday Dinner Speech" (1905). The thrust of the speech is to reject the advice septuagenarians give on how to reach old age. Twain offers a countermaxim: "We can't reach old age by another man's road." He modifies this homily over the course of the speech to, "If you find you can't make seventy by any but an uncomfortable road, don't you go," which he illustrates with his principles about smoking—"I have made it a rule never to smoke more than one cigar at a time"—and exercise—"I have never taken any exercise, except sleeping and resting and I never intend to take any. Exercise is loathsome. And it cannot be any benefit when you are tired; and I was always tired."

The parody maxim stems as much as anything from Twain's definition of *humor as a flavoring that comes from manner of presentation rather than matter, as a mode of digression rather than wit. He developed his humorous style on the basis of circumlocution and *non sequitur*, so that it is far from aphoristic. The maxims he coined in the first half or more of his career serve either to attack the idea of maxims or to help delineate a character in a work of fiction. As a character marker, Twain's maxims as humor work only if the character making the maxim undercuts his authority, turning the maxim from absolute truth into a clearly partisan utterance. Again, Twain used this technique often in the early and middle parts of his career, as in "A Presidential Candidate" (1879), whose narrator characterizes his military virtues by altering a cliché: "If the bubble reputation can be obtained only at the cannon's mouth, I am willing to go there for it, provided the cannon is empty."

Even in his later years when Twain fell in love with the cynical aphorism, he began his love affair in an effort to delineate a character in a novel. When he turned to *Pudd'nhead Wilson and Those Extraordinary Twins* in the 1890s, he ascribed a series of maxims to Wilson in order to establish the character as a "philosopher," although the action had little to do with Wilson. As a way of keeping the character present throughout a complexly plotted novel in which Wilson's role is central only at the book's end, the aphorisms as chapter epigraphs work well. They also show Wilson's intellectual superiority to and distance from the "common herd" in Dawson's Landing. But Clemens's appreciation for maxims came in the dark days that began with his impending bankruptcy. While many of the epigraphs bear on the tale, some others seem to speak directly to Clemens's own circumstances and feelings in the early 1890s. For example, the man whose *finances were sinking under the weight of too many poor investments spoke more for Clemens than for Wilson in the adage, "Behold the fool saith, 'Put not all thine eggs in the one basket,' which is but a manner of saying, 'Scatter your money and attention,' but the wise man saith, put all thine eggs in one basket and—*watch that basket*" (chapter 15).

Clemens seemed to find such pleasure in the role of wise man that he adopted it more for himself, continuing in *Following the Equator* the game of beginning each chapter of a book with maxims. These new chapter epigraphs are ostensibly by Pudd'nhead Wilson, but Wilson's absence from what is really a travelogue makes the attribution transparently false. The sage at the top of the page is Mark Twain—and everybody knows it. This is a new role for Twain, one he relished. Many of his most famous adages come from these epigraphs: "Man is the only animal that blushes. Or needs to" (chapter 27); "It is by the goodness of God that in our country we have those three unspeakably precious things: freedom of speech, freedom of conscience, and the prudence never to practice either of them" (chapter 20); "Be good and you will be lonesome" (frontispiece); "It is easier to stay out than to get out" (chapter 18).

One of these, "Prosperity is the best protector of principle" (chapter 38), is a retelling of a poor Richard adage, "'Tis hard for an empty sack to stand upright." So Twain commits the crime of which he accused Franklin: "sit[ting] up late nights reducing the rankest old threadbare platitudes to crisp and snappy maxims that had a nice, varnished look in their new regimentals" ("Last Words of Great Men"). So from using epigraphs for book chapters, a practice he, Charles Dudley *Warner, and James Hammond *Trumbull had mocked in *The Gilded Age*, to rehashing platitudes, Twain appears to have given up digressive humor for wit.

But his own explanation of the practice of maxim-making, given in an autobiographical dictation of 9 January 1907, suggests that Clemens did not fool himself into thinking that he was peddling eternal truths. He said:

> There has been an incident—an incident of a common sort—an incident of an exceedingly common sort—an incident of a sort which always troubles me, grieves me, and makes me weary of life and long to lie down in the peaceful grave and be at rest. Such incidents usually move me to try to find relief in the building of a maxim. It is a good way, because if you have luck you can get the venom out of yourself and into the maxim; then comfort and a healed spirit follow.

Such a subjective use of maxim-building suggests that Twain was still burlesquing the idea of the maxim even in his most energetic use of it.

No matter how subjective Clemens's use of maxims became, his stage show as sage succeeded to the point that his most banal utterances still carry weight. He is cited with impunity by almost anyone who needs witty authority to promote almost any agenda. Worse, many people invent maxims and ascribe them to Twain, and many of these *false attributions float around backed fraudulently by the authority of the white-haired icon. It just goes to show that even in the very act of parodying aphorisms Twain may have coined one of the most honest of sentiments: "A truth is not hard to kill, but a lie well told is immortal" ("Advice to Youth").

McALEER, PATRICK. SEE Servants.

McWilliams. One of Clemens's recurring characters, McWilliams suggests something of the complex connection Clemens made between reality and fiction. He took the name McWilliams from his Buffalo friends, John James and Esther (Essie) Keeler Norton McWilliams. Married in Elmira, New York, in 1869, they moved to Buffalo, New York, when John's employer, Jervis Langdon, transferred him to the Buffalo office of J. Langdon and Company. The McWilliamses lived in the same boarding house as Clemens and became good friends. In corresponding with his fiancée about whether they should board or keep their own house, Clemens cited the McWilliams's domestic bliss as an argument for the relative simplicity of boarding. When Olivia joined Clemens in Buffalo after their wedding, the McWilliamses helped to arrange the surprise presentation of the house given by Olivia's father. As long as the Clemenses stayed in Buffalo, the two couples remained on excellent terms.

The cordial relations did not translate into a correspondence—at least one of which we have a record—after the Clemenses left Buffalo. Still, when Clemens began a series of articles about his own home life, he used the McWilliams name as a pseudonym for his own family. In "The Experience of McWilliamses with Membranous Croup" (1875), "Mrs. McWilliams and the Lightning" (1880), and "The McWilliamses and the Burglar Alarm" (1882), Clemens elaborately frames burlesques of his own life by having a character named McWilliams relate stories to Mark Twain. While the tales have some connection to his life, the reference to McWilliams complicates the situation, suggesting that Clemens did not intend these pieces merely to burlesque himself and Olivia, but instead to burlesque *domesticity more broadly.

Probably in 1878, in one of his drafts of *"Extract from Captain Stormfield's Visit to Heaven," he inserted the McWilliams name again, this time for Sandy McWilliams, a character whose wisdom about the ways of heaven makes him a tutor for the newly arrived Captain Stormfield (named Wakeman in the 1878 draft). In using the name of a friend as a stand-in for himself, Clemens began to create another writer's mask, a character who would stand for a part of himself, functioning much as the Mark Twain pseudonym itself did. Like other characters, such as Colonel *Sellers, *Tom Sawyer, or *Huckleberry Finn, the McWilliams character began as a caricatured composite of several real people before taking on a larger fictional life of its own.

♦ SEE ALSO Langdon, Jervis and Olivia Lewis; Practical Jokes; Pseudonyms and Personas.

Medievalism. Modern western conceptions, or rather misconceptions, of the age of chivalry were born at the end of the eighteenth century and blossomed in the nineteenth. As part of a Romantic reaction to the Enlightenment, medievalism is a complex ethical and aesthetic phenomenon, manifesting itself in such broadly divergent ways as the anticapitalistic socialism of William Morris on the one hand and as conservative justifications for the French ancien régime on the other. In England and America, nineteenth-century medievalism tended to be reactionary, arising in a post-Napoleonic fear of *revolution and of *democracy more broadly. Political elites in both countries feared the rise of what they considered "the rabble" and sought ideas that would combat the appeal of pure democracy. An idealized vision of the middle ages fit the bill. In America, such ideas were particularly popular in the South, which needed to justify a hierarchical society based on *slavery and, after the *Civil War, the serfdom of sharecropping. Some of the historical romances of Sir Walter Scott provided a pattern by which writers in both countries could create an idealized image of the middle ages as a time when the powerful protected the weak, women were revered as godly, and delicate manners regulated the interactions of all members of society.

Although medievalism was a powerful force in the South through such popularizers as John Pendleton Kennedy, William Gilmore Simms, and other literary advocates of a feudal ideal, it was not as popular in the North until after the Civil War, when the massive concentration of wealth in the hands of a few industrialists and financiers made a plutocratic version of feudalism a reality, and massive immigration threatened the belief of the educated that American culture could level all classes up to gentility. Then, the popularity of Alfred, Lord Tennyson, England's most effective spokesman for medievalism, made the chivalric ideal a commonplace in northern culture as well.

Tennyson, long writing idealized poems about medieval subjects, rewrote the Arthurian myths in his *Idylls of the King* (1833–1891) to glorify *monarchy as an antidote to the factionalism and dissension of an increasingly democratic Britain. Turning to Sir Thomas Malory's *Morte d'Arthur* as his source, Tennyson essentially misinterpreted Malory's lament about the unredeemed violence of chivalry and the immorality of the adultery sanctioned by the code of courtly love. On the contrary, Tennyson used the outlines of the myth to sanction the marriage of Queen Victoria and Prince Albert and to reinvigorate the ancient idea that monarchy is a divinely inspired institution. He dedicated his poem to the memory of Prince Albert:

> These to His Memory—since he held them dear,
> Perchance as finding there unconsciously
> Some image of himself—I dedicate,
> I dedicate, I consecrate with tears—
> These Idylls.
> And indeed He seems to me
> Scarce other than my king's ideal knight,
> Who reverenced his conscience as his king;

Whose glory was, redressing human wrong;
Who spake no slander, no, nor listen'd to it;
Who loved one only and who clave to her—
Her—over whose realms to their last isle,
Commingled with the gloom of imminent war,
The shadow of His loss drew like eclipse,
Darkening the world.

The section titled "The Coming of Arthur" celebrates a powerful monarch as the centralizing force that makes a nation cohere and prosper:

For many a petty king ere Arthur came
Ruled in this isle, and ever waging war
Each upon other, wasted all the land;
And still from time to time the heathen host
Swarm'd overseas, and harried what was left.
And so there grew great tracts of wilderness,
Wherein the beast was ever more and more,
But man was less and less, till Arthur came.
For first Aurelius lived and fought and died,
And after him King Uther fought and died,
But either fail'd to make the kingdom one.
And after these King Arthur for a space
And thro' the puissance of his Table Round,
Drew all their petty pricedoms under him,
Their king and head, and made a realm, and reign'd.

Tennyson and his allies were successful in rescuing the British monarchy. After Prince Albert's death and Victoria's withdrawal into mourning, liberals in Britain thought that they would be able to end the monarchy with her death. But she hung on a long time, and with people like Tennyson building her up as symbol of nationhood, combined with the increasing militarization of British *imperialism, monarchy took popular hold on the imagination once again.

While most Americans did not respond explicitly to Tennyson's praise of monarchy, they did respond to his idealized notion of chivalry as a manifestation of noblesse oblige, to the image of mannered society holding anarchy at bay, and to Tennyson's fundamental authoritarianism. Such enthusiasm for medievalism sparked Clemens's negative reaction. Sometimes he hid the energy of his disagreement even as he used medievalism's popularity to argue for a developing democracy. *The Prince and the Pauper*, for instance, argues that *progress comes through democratization even as it endorses an ideal chivalry. More often, he mocked the idea that medieval culture was gentle or ideal, as in "An *Awful ---- Terrible Medieval

Romance," "1601," and, most importantly, *A Connecticut Yankee in King Arthur's Court*. Even when he glorified individual characters from the middle ages—Joan of Arc or Edward VII, for example—he did so against a backdrop of medieval brutality and barbarism. His knowledge of *history was too extensive to allow him the luxury of historical *romance.

♦ SEE ALSO Lecky, W. E. H.

MERITOCRACY. While Clemens may have moved from a whiggish, modestly aristocratic idea of social order to a more democratic one, he never felt that human beings should all be held on a dead level. Typical of American republicanism, Clemens believed that the meritorious should rule, and that in a free society, they would accrue wealth and power. Thus he railed against *monarchy for limiting natural talent, as in *A Connecticut Yankee in King Arthur's Court*, in which the aristocracy will not allow the talented and well-trained young men Hank Morgan has cultivated in his schools to have any place or station in the military or public life. The sketch "Luck" attacks aristocratic vestiges in the modern world. And as much as he saw oppression as limiting natural talent, he saw talent as generally, over time, superior to circumstance. His "Concerning the Jews," for instance, describes an entire people whom he sees as intellectually superior. He made his point even more explicit in a notebook entry: "The Jews have suffered far severer deprivations, oppressions & persecutions than the Irish; They have endured these oppressions about 2,000 years—& yet . . . they are the world's intellectual aristocracy. There are some things which oppression won't account for" (*Notebooks*, 1879).

Clemens also attacked socialism and communism as impediments to natural hierarchies of talent. As he put it in his notebook of March 1879: "Communism is idiotcy. They want to divide up the property. Suppose they did it—it requires brains to keep money as well as make it. In a precious little while the money would be back in the former owner's hands & the Communist would be poor again. The division would have to be re-made every three years or it would do the communist no good." Clemens's praise of the *labor movement is in fact in keeping with this sentiment. As expressed in his "The New Dynasty" essay delivered to the *Monday Evening Club, he felt that the value of unions, besides consolidating the power of individuals, was to elevate the intellectual level of workers, to give them a chance to use their brain power to advance themselves. Even though he read various anarchist and communist pamphlets given to him by William Dean *Howells, he never saw socialism and communism as any more than a dream of perfect equality—although he could still find the dream inspiring.

Clemens admired, for instance, Edward Bellamy's *Looking Backward*, a book that helped popularize socialism to much larger groups of Americans than had hitherto been the case. As he put it to Sylvester Baxter, who was an avid promoter of Bellamy's political agenda, *Looking Backward* is "the last and best of all the bibles" (19 December 1889). Baxter may have taken this as a perfect compliment, but, coming from a man skeptical of religion, it was probably polite sarcasm. Clemens may have found the vision compelling but doubted its possibility. As he put it in his 1879 notebook, "Religion consists in a set of things which the average man thinks he believes, & wishes he was certain." To Clemens, the enthusiastic individualism of Thomas Paine's *The *Age of Reason* and *Rights of Man* was the system of religion about which he wished to be certain, and as such, he always believed that brains would be rewarded in a free republic. No wonder then that, in spite of the economic depression that prompted thousands of business failures, he took his own bankruptcy to heart as a sign of personal inadequacy.

♦ SEE ALSO Democracy; Medievalism.

MISSIONARIES. When Sabine Baring-Gould, a British Anglican, wrote "Onward, Christian Soldiers" in 1865, he had a receptive audience in both his native England and the United States. Britain was already fully embarked on its imperial program in Asia and Africa, and this Victorian crusading hymn served as a rallying cry to the kind of international evangelism that collaborated so readily with mercantile and military conquest. The United States, in the wake of the Civil War, had slowed its imperial movement considerably and focused its evangelical energies inward—"The Battle Hymn of the Republic" edged out "Onward, Christian Soldiers" in American popularity, but not by much. America had partly been founded by a missionary purpose, to serve as a "city on the hill" that would rekindle Christian evangelism throughout the world. But this initial impulse looked back to Europe and the Near East at first, and then looked toward the frontier, where the spread of European civilization always elicited attempts to Christianize the trappers, hunters, and assorted outlaws who were the culture's vanguard. The missionary spirit of American evangelism was more or less locked in this pattern until well after the Civil War, when U.S. foreign missionary activity and aggressive extra-American *imperialism coalesced.

This is not to say that Americans had not organized missions before the war. As early as the seventeenth century, American Protestant churches organized "foreign" missions to the Native American tribes and "home" missions in the colonies themselves. These foreign missions to the indigenous peoples of the American continent furthered the spread of the American empire on the continent before the Civil War. The distinction between "home" and "foreign" persisted into the twentieth century, but gradually changed focus. Home missions eventually—beginning in the 1870s with the rise of the social gospel and urban evangelicals like Dwight Lyman

Moody—turned to the crises of the inner cities, while foreign missions concerned themselves with the "conversion" of Africa and Asia, and again served substantially as a prelude to imperial ventures.

Twain's contact with such missionary work came about naturally enough as a child belonging to a Presbyterian congregation in which the early extra-denominational missionary societies—most notably the American Home Missionary Society and the American Board of Commissioners for Foreign Missions—raised funds and recruited missionaries. His most significant contact with the results of missionary activity came when he was a special correspondent for the Sacramento *Union* in Hawaii, then called the Sandwich Islands. The American Board had targeted Hawaii for missionary activity in 1820. Their success in Christianizing large portions of the indigenous population, together with their unintended but disastrous importation of diseases such as smallpox, paved the way for the seventy-year colonization and eventual annexation of the Hawaiian Islands by the United States in 1898. Clemens was sent to the islands to promote American mercantile interests and their corresponding political machinations. As such, he had little choice but to support the missionaries' activities as "civilizing" agents. In spite of his praise of the missionary activity in ending various forms of "barbaric" religious and social practices, he found the missionaries themselves self-righteous. Furthermore, even in his youthful inexperience, he expressed reservations about the kind of civilization that would transform a culture in an apparent paradise to one that had to work hard to make money and pray hard to avoid hell. Just a few years later, when writing *Roughing It*, he satirized the missionary impulse in the story of "Jim Blaine and His Grandfather's Ram" (chapter 53), though the satire is subtly disguised. In case anyone should consider him antimissionary, he published a disclaimer in the New York *Tribune* in January 1873: "I am one who regards missionary work as slow and discouraging labor, & not immediately satisfactory in its results. But I am very far from considering such work either hopeless or useless" (to Whitelaw Reid, 14 January 1873).

Much later in his career, when he had developed his own anti-imperialistic attitudes and after America had hypocritically and vociferously embarked on a policy of imperial acquisition in the Philippines and China, Clemens turned savagely against missionaries. In "To the Person Sitting in Darkness" and "To My Missionary Critics," he exposed the behavior of the missionaries as profoundly unchristian. In the latter of these, he prefaced the essay with an account of American inner-city problems in order to suggest that home missions would better serve America's welfare and conscience. Similarly, in "The United States of Lyncherdom," he insists that America's missionaries are needed at home where they might do some good, rather than abroad, where the mischief they cause is at best irrelevant and at worst malicious.

♦ SEE ALSO Food; Reform; Religion.

MISSISSIPPI RIVER VALLEY. No place is of greater importance to Twain's literary imagination than the Mississippi River valley, not merely because he was born there, apprenticed to the printing trade there, and learned to pilot steamboats there, but also because the Mississippi valley was the defining area of the United States over the course of Clemens's life. He turned to it imaginatively in his investigations of America, and his changing reactions to it register the development of his thinking over the course of his career.

The Mississippi valley was the center of the nation geographically, and hence, as the intersection between the country's east-west and north-south axes, it was the nation's central theater politically, economically, and imaginatively. There, over the course of Clemens's childhood and young adulthood, the nation waged its ideological wars over racial identity with respect to both *African American *slavery and treatment of *Native Americans; argued over the kind of society—aristocratic or republican—that would ensue; used technology to transform the *economy; and rapidly colonized a vast expanse of land that ranges from subtropical wetlands in the South, to semi-arid rangeland in the West, to temperate woodlands in the Northeast. American ideals of agrarian independence found their most extreme tests there as the nation as a whole devoted considerable resources to transforming this area to make it fit into a modernizing economy. This vast expanse experienced change from frontier to industrial society in rapid order, and this shift paralleled dizzying transformations in the economy. On the whole, this area's experience typified the strains young America confronted in the nineteenth century, and Twain's imagination capitalized on those tensions.

Twain's *Life on the Mississippi* gives an overview of the physical and demographic elements of the valley, interpolated with a wealth of anecdotes and myths. While he had planned this book from the beginnings of his writing career, he did not complete it until he had learned enough to move from simple praise to a more complex vision of the valley as emblematic of the tensions that constitute America. Hence, his discussion of violence in the Murrell gang or of the Civil War offsets his discussion of orderly northern towns and cities. His depiction of technological power in steamboats stands in contrast to the broken-down, backcountry farmers whose presence the boats reveal. *Life on the Mississippi*, the only one of his Mississippi writings to cover the length of the valley from south to north, marks a midpoint in his examination of the valley's meaning.

His study of the region began with his *newspaper journalism in California papers. In particular, he mentioned the "indian troubles" repeatedly, always in support of the U.S. Army's mission to subdue the tribes of the plains. Over the course of Clemens's life, he participated in the transformation of the Midwest from lands occupied by various Native tribes to those controlled by white farmers. While he was born in Missouri, which had, on the strength of its St. Louis population, been admitted to the Union in 1821, he lived on the northern edge near the Iowa border. Iowa was settled much later, only organized into a territory in 1838. Both Iowa and Missouri had large native populations in their western areas. In the opening days of the Civil War, many of those tribes saw the internecine war between whites as an opportunity to take back lands and power they had lost. In Minnesota and northwestern Iowa, for instance, the U.S. Army quickly quelled uprisings, with many Iowa troops in particular engaged in massacres of Sioux. In Missouri, Arkansas, Texas, and the Indian territories (eventually Oklahoma), the Confederate armies, under the command of Earl Van Dorn, actively solicited Native American allies in the hopes of including Indian territories west of the Mississippi in the Confederacy and to stir up a second front against the Union states of the valley. The battle of Pea Ridge, Arkansas, primarily a battle for control of the southwestern part of Missouri, included a division of "Indian" troops who, when watching the intensity with which the whites killed one another, decided that such a kind of engagement was not for them and effectively withdrew from the Confederacy. After the Civil War, federal armies did not completely demobilize but instead sent significant numbers of troops to the plains. These were the actions on which Twain frequently commented, always in support. To Twain, the elimination of the Native population was a part of *progress. He suggested the need in both *The Adventures of Tom Sawyer*, in which "injun" Joe's villainy is as much cultural as personal, and in the unfinished "Huck Finn and Tom Sawyer among the Indians," a work he intended to have as the sequel to *Adventures of Huckleberry Finn*.

*"Old Times on the Mississippi" is Twain's first extended work in which the Mississippi valley figures prominently. His juxtaposition of natural beauty with the seriousness of technological mastery of nature is a parable of progress, and as much as the nostalgic overtones suggest the loss involved, the overall tenor of the piece praises modern commerce and industry as a transforming power. In a similar vein, *Tom Sawyer* is a hymn to human possibility. In this novel, the Mississippi valley is a boy's paradise, a range of ample opportunity in the as-yet undeveloped lands fully in possession of whites. Tom, though fatherless and virtually self-creating, is the heir to a fantasy land. Called powerfully by both wilderness and society, he is a liminal character in a liminal state of half-civilization. The narrator's sophisticated stance suggests that the town as a whole is in the same boat, and as Tom's essentially social nature binds him to a community and thus civilizes him, the town itself will outgrow its coarseness in the matter of "natural" progress. In a sense, Tom Sawyer's boyhood is symbolic of the transition Twain felt to be taking place in the Mississippi valley.

Such a transition was not all rosy, and the Mississippi trip Clemens took in order to prepare to write *Life on the Mississippi* changed the tint of the glasses through which he had been viewing his own childhood and young adulthood. The consequence of his trip was to raise questions about the other racial divide that characterized the valley's history: black and white, a divide that split North and South no matter that geography insisted on the fundamental connections. The moral, legal, and economic complications of *Huckleberry Finn* and *Pudd'nhead Wilson and Those Extraordinary Twins* show Twain's increasing pessimism about progress, and as much as the river in *Huckleberry Finn* is emblematic of natural powers, the flow leads to danger, not to freedom and moral redemption of the land. As much as the trip in *Life on the Mississippi* moved from south to north to represent civic progress, the movement south in *Huckleberry Finn*, and the movement of David Wilson from the north to a southern town in *Pudd'nhead Wilson*, symbolizes Twain's fear that progress is an illusion.

Significantly, while *Life on the Mississippi* does extensively discuss the great *cities of the valley, particularly St. Louis and New Orleans, which Clemens came to know in his brief time as a riverboat pilot, most of the Mississippi stories deal with small-town life, which Americans regularly took to be typical of their nation. Given America's rapid urbanization, which also led to a more heterogeneous population, Twain's examination of the Mississippi valley always had an element of symbolic denial to it, a denial that is fairly typical of America's self-conception. The degree to which his depictions of small-town life became increasingly critical, however, suggests that Twain eventually questioned America's agrarian ideal of civilization.

♦ SEE ALSO Steamboating.

MOFFET, PAMELA CLEMENS (1827–1904) AND WILLIAM A. (1816–1865).

When Clemens's eldest sister, Pamela, married William A. Moffet in 1851, the union provided the first instance of financial stability for the family since the death of their father four years earlier. Moffet, formerly of Hannibal, was a St. Louis commission merchant, a partner in the profitable firm of Moffett, Stillwell, and Company. Not surprisingly, the remaining family members visited the Moffet household as often as they went to Orion *Clemens's struggling households in southern Iowa. When young Samuel turned to steamboat piloting in 1857 (after failing to support himself as a compositor), he looked to his elder brother-in-law for a loan to pay his apprenticeship. His entire time as a pilot, he was in close contact with the Moffet household, where he spent much time teasing his niece, Annie E. Moffet, as well as his mother and sister. Indeed, when the Civil War broke out, Clemens took refuge in his sister's house for fear of being impressed as a riverboat pilot in the service of the Union. When he fled the states for Nevada Territory, his correspondence to the entire family living in the St. Louis household gives us some of the best record not only of his time out west, but also of his opinions about religion, temperance, politics, and life in general. This family grouping was one of Clemens's first audiences, a test-case on which he developed many of his characteristic styles of *humor and *satire.

On William's death in August 1865, Clemens gradually took over supporting not only his mother but also his sister and her two children, helping them to purchase a house in Fredonia, New York, and ultimately hiring Annie's husband, Charles Webster, as first a business agent and then a director of *Webster and Company, Clemens's own publishing firm.

♦ SEE ALSO Webster, Annie Moffet and Charles L.

MONARCHY. One of the primary components of Twain's attack on *medievalism was his persistent assault on the idea of monarchy, which he held to be a remnant of barbarism interfering with *progress. As he put it in his notebook in February 1890, "Monarchy...belongs to the stage of culture that admires a ring in your nose, a head full of feathers, & your belly painted blue." While his faith in *democracy fluctuated over the course of his career, he never was politically conservative enough to label monarchy anything but "the grotesquest of all the swindles ever invented by man" (to Sylvester Baxter, 20 November 1889). As he put it in 1890 in a speech, "On Foreign Critics," "When [the American] revolution began, monarchy had been on trial some thousands of years ... and was a distinct and convicted failure, every time. It had never produced anything but a vast, nearly universal savagery, with a thin skim of civilization on top, and the main part of that was nickel plate and tinsel." Or as he has Huckleberry Finn put it: "All kings is mostly rapscallions, as fur as I can make out" (*Adventures of Huckleberry Finn*, chapter 23).

Given that he lived in a republic, the urgency of Twain's frequent denunciation of monarchy can be difficult to understand. The political and military power of European royal houses, however, was part of nineteenth-century America's reality; most of the century's antimonarchical revolutions had failed in whole or in part. Even in the constitutional monarchy of Britain, the revivification of the monarchy under Queen Victoria had advocates of democracy worried that England was returning to its monarchical past. Part of Clemens's intention in writing *A Connecticut Yankee in King Arthur's Court* was to strengthen the hand of the Liberal party in British politics, though the practical effect was limited. Against this backdrop, Clemens worried that America itself would adopt monarchy sooner or later, especially given the plutocratic tendencies of the *robber barons. As he wrote in the *North American Review*:

> Human nature being what it is, I suppose we must expect to drift into monarchy by and by. It is a saddening thought, but we cannot change our nature: we are all alike, we human beings, and in our blood and bone, and ineradicable, we carry the seeds out of which monarchies and aristocracies are grown: worship of gauds, titles, distinction, power.... We have to be despised by somebody we regard as above us, or we are not happy; we have to have somebody to worship and envy, or we cannot be content. In America we manifest

this in all the ancient and customary ways. In public we scoff at titles and hereditary privilege, but privately we hanker after them, and when we get a chance we buy them for cash and a daughter. (4 January 1907)

Certainly watching the wealthy of America both act like aristocracy and try to marry into it, Clemens's opinion had much merit.

Moreover, he knew that his own fascination with monarchy ran deep, and he believed his own motivations were widely shared in the United States. As much as his literature constantly condemns monarchy, he relished every opportunity of his own to hobnob with royalty. With his *celebrity, he often had the opportunity, meeting the Russian czar, the Austrian emperor, and the German kaiser, among others, events he delighted in discussing in his *autobiographical dictations. So when in his autobiographical dictations he criticized Andrew Carnegie for bragging about having met the kaiser, he was honest

Illustration by Daniel Carter Beard (1850–1941), from *A Connecticut Yankee in King Arthur's Court*, New York: Webster & Company, 1889, p. 419.

enough to turn it back on himself: "We are all like—on the inside.... Scoffing democrats as we are, we do dearly love to be noticed by a duke, and when we are noticed by a monarch we have softening of the brain for the rest of our lives.... When a returned American is casually and gratefully playing the earls he has met; I can look on, silent and unexcited, and never offer to call his hand, although I have three kings and a pair of emperors up my sleeve" (2 December 1906).

♦ SEE ALSO ESSAY ON Etiquette

MONDAY EVENING CLUB. Clergymen Horace Bushnell and Calvin Stowe and scholar and librarian James Hammond *Trumbull founded the Monday Evening Club to promote higher culture in Hartford and, through its artists, the nation. They limited the club's membership to about twenty of Hartford's best known writers, clergy, teachers, businessmen, lawyers, and politicians. Members met from seven to fourteen times a year to read and discuss original essays. During their meetings, the men usually ate light suppers and drank beer, though once, when at the teetotaller Charles Dudley *Warner's house they agreed to do without, the Rev. Joseph *Twichell wrote in his diary that a dry evening was rather difficult to swallow.

The club's serious purpose was balanced by its playfulness, which is fully apparent in much of the correspondence that remains. Naturally, Clemens was at the center of much of this play from the day he accepted admittance, by responding to Trumbull's note of invitation: "I shall be very glad indeed to meet with the Club as a member on next Monday Evening, & am thankful too. And I willingly 'excuse the informal character' of the notice—am even *grateful* for it; for if you had started in to make it formal, you might have got it in Sanskrit, & that would just simply have made trouble with Yrs truly, Samuel L. Clemens" (15 February 1873). Much later, after moving away from Hartford and thus ending his active involvement with the club, Clemens continued to tease club members, as in a brief note sent to Rev. E. P. Parker from Europe. The note, written on a picture postcard of Twain's face, read, "Dear Parker: Motto to chew on: Saintliness is next to Selfishness (being the offspring of it, you see). Truly Yours, Mark Twain" (2 August 1898).

Sometimes the recreational aspect of the club extended to the essays presented at club meetings, with titles like "Moose and Caribou Hunting" (10 January 1876). More often, though, the essays reflect the club's serious purpose, as in "Is Restriction of Suffrage in this Country Desirable?" (29 January 1877), "Reverence" (15 November 1875), "Calvinism" (17 December 1877), "Agnosticism" (14 March 1871), "Some Aspects of Evolution" (27 December 1886), and "Conscience" (20 March 1876).

The group's membership included Horace Bushnell and his theological followers Nathaniel Burton, E. P. Parker, and Joseph Twichell, all Congregational ministers; several faculty members and the president of Hartford's Trinity College; Trumbull, listed in the club's roster as "Historian, Philologist, bibliographer; First Librarian, Watkinson Library of Reference"; the owners and editors of the Hartford *Courant*, including Warner; and five fellows of the Yale Corporation. Given these people and the weight of the topics they discussed, it seems likely that these subjects were treated authoritatively if not exhaustively. If nothing else, Clemens must have learned from club members what to read to approach almost any subject of intellectual importance. It comes as no surprise, then, that in his years of most active participation in the club, the 1870s and 1880s, Clemens began a serious course of *reading that would bring him up to speed in his understanding of science, philosophy, and theology.

Part of the serious point of the club was to enable members to encourage one another and help one another in their work. An exchange of notes between

Clemens and Parker, for instance, has Clemens encouraging Parker as a musical composer and Parker in turn urging Clemens to do some "serious" writing that would display his "genius" to full advantage:

> Now let me say *to* you what I have repeatedly said *of* you—I know no American writer of your generation, who is capable of writing such forcible, sinewy, racy English as you. You are abundantly capable of turning out some work that shall bear the stamp of your individuality plainly enough and at the same time have a sober character and a solid worth and as permanent value. It might not pay in "shekels", but it would do you vast honor, and give your friends vast pleasure.
>
> Am I too bold? Pardon me, but I wish I had your opportunity and your genius. (22 December 1880)

This is the kind of encouragement that Clemens, worried about being dismissed as a "mere" humorist, very much wanted.

Another club member, the politician Henry Robinson (mayor of Hartford, 1872–1874, and later an assemblyman), whom Clemens familiarly addressed as "brer" (as he addressed some other club members as well) and who addressed Clemens as "Brer K," also cajoled him into doing "serious" work. In a 19 July 1885 letter praising a piece on childrearing that Clemens had written for the *Christian Union*, Robinson remarks, "You know that I have often told you that you ought to do more in the line of ethics and philosophy & I want to thank you once more for this very successful effort. *Keep doing it!*"

Clemens relied on this kind of encouragement throughout his career but most especially in the 1870s and 1880s, when he was less sure of his abilities to make his humor carry the weight of moral seriousness. His own essays for the club, while often humorous in presentation, deal with matters of great philosophical, ethical, and political concern. Some of these, like "The Facts Concerning the Recent Carnival of Crime in Connecticut," he published. He incorporated the ideas from some of his other essays into works of fiction: the ideas from an essay on the Knights of Labor, for example, found their way into *A Connecticut Yankee in King Arthur's Court* and *The *American Claimant*.

Often Clemens designed his essays to provoke the club members into strenuous disagreement, but this ensuing contention was usually the constructive antagonism of supportive friends. Cut off from that constructive frisson during the 1890s while living in Europe and unable to attend meetings, Clemens kept in touch primarily with Robinson and Twichell, and they shared a *nostalgia for the community that was. As Robinson put it in a letter of 29 December 1897:

> Dear Brer K:—Sometimes it's so lonesome that I almost feel as if I had been good, according to your maxim, or else it's that you are away & I don't like it,

the months rattle along so fast.... We have had two meetings of the Club. I took in half of each one. At the first one Charlie Clark was as funny as a frog about Mexico, & at the second one General Franklin gave us some Antebellum-Mexicanum reminiscences, 1844–46.... I think you would have enjoyed it exceedingly. But seventy-two years has told a little on the general's tongue. What a gray-haired, limping crowd the Mond Night Club is! Probably they know more than they did 30 years ago, but wouldn't be as attractive to a female boarding school.... Twichell has grown a little deaf, and had hard work to keep awake at the last meeting of the Club.... Strengthen the things that remain, is what we have to write on all our lives.

Clemens responded:

Your picture of the Club! I can see it; & it makes me old. I suppose I attended it for the first time in Nove. or Dec. '71, when I was a lad of 36. Susy was not born then; nor Clara, of course; and Franklin—why Franklin was young in those distant times. What business has Charley Clark to be sporting his irreverent fun in this graveyard? And Twichell—grandfather Twichell in these late years—hard of hearing & asleep under the disconnected mumblings of the mummies. Let's get away from this subject. (13 January 1898)

Their sentimental nostalgia acknowledges the importance of community for these men. For Twain in particular, with his penchant for collaboration and his need for a "sympathetic ear" to help him find his voice, this community was a strong support to sustained creativity.

MONEY. In a culture deeply imbued with biblical values yet increasingly committed to capitalism even over republicanism, the proverb that the love of money is the root of all evil created serious emotional and moral difficulties. In this way, as in so many others, Clemens's attitudes give an excellent window on nineteenth-century America's extreme love-hate relationship with the almighty dollar.

Like many of his contemporaries, Clemens pursued money with fanatical determination, winning and losing fortunes with a recurrent regularity only slightly less volatile than the nation's business cycle. His early life was marred by the destitution of his father, whose great speculations in western lands broke him, as they had so many others. Not surprisingly, then, young Samuel was determined to make a fortune to compensate for that background. But the strain of that task made him alternately love and hate money itself. It is only surprising that after a lifetime of pursuing money much like his father before him, Clemens could nostalgically assert in some autobiographical writings of 1897, "The California rush for wealth in '49 ... begot the lust for money which is the rule of life to-day, and the hardness and cynicism which is the spirit of today," or in an autobiographical dictation of 16 February 1906 claim, "Jay Gould taught the entire nation to make a god of the money and the man, no matter how the money might have been acquired. In my youth there was nothing resembling a worship of money or of its possessor." Given his depiction of money-seeking in both *The Adventures of Tom Sawyer* and *Adventures of Huckleberry Finn*, such assertions are patently absurd.

Clemens's own love of money manifested itself mostly in his conspicuous consumption. As a riverboat pilot, the first time he attained the status of a comparatively rich man, he dressed the part of the dandy. Quick vicissitudes of fortune as a miner then journalist in Nevada gave way finally to the life of a man of letters in Hartford, where he built a lavish house decorated with artifacts collected from America and Europe. Bankruptcy in 1894 led to less extravagant living, but he never really returned to the life of destitution that he had experienced as a child in Missouri or as a young man in Nevada and California. Nonetheless, his debt of almost $200,000 was formidable and depressing, leading him to write not only about the power of money in "The Million Pound Bank Note," but about his hatred of that power in "The *Man That Corrupted Hadleyburg" and "The *Thirty Thousand Dollar Bequest."

These stories are peculiar, however, in their persistent sense that money and property are not real but illusory, that their power is more symbolic than actual. In all three stories, the idea of wealth is more important than the reality, and how one addresses that idea determines the success or failure of the characters. Such an approach was not new in Twain's works. Similarly, in parts of *The Gilded Age*, the dream of wealth is seductive and destructive to many, and those who have money are only transformed by it if they know how to use it. The "real" gentlemen of old but modest money are richer, he suggests, than the parvenus who do not know how to act genteelly. Money itself, he suggests, is the least part of good fortune. Such also is the message of chapter 46 of *Roughing It*, which describes the naïve foibles of the nouveau-riche miners who head east to the capitals of culture. *The American Claimant*, too, argues for the illusory power of wealth, but at least makes constant gestures to the reality that one needs money to live.

In an odd way, Americans currently have grown used to the symbolic nature of money so that its volatility seems fairly unimportant relative to its purchasing power. We are used to translating a sum into constant dollars in order to calculate real profits or losses and to compare standards of living from one time to another. In fact, many people regularly ask how to translate dollar amounts from Clemens's day to ours. Depending on whether one uses a price or wage scale, and granting the impossibility of exact comparisons, it is possible to compute comparable dollar figures in today's money by multiplying by between eighteen and twenty-six. In other words, depending on the standard of comparison one chooses, the $30,000 of the story would become anywhere between $540,000 and $780,000.

During the early days of the modern economy, people were less comfortable with elastic currency. In chapter 33 of *A Connecticut Yankee in King Arthur's Court*, Clemens analogically suggests that most Americans do not even understand that money's value is relative, instead believing a dollar to be absolute. Such a judgment was probably not wholly accurate, but certainly Clemens's intellectual understanding of the symbolic power of money was unusual. One of his favorite terms, applied equally to literature as to banknotes, was "wildcat," meaning notes issued by notoriously unstable frontier banks. In this comparison, Clemens found a way to describe relativity of values—though he was never sure if his own literature was wildcat or gold.

This understanding of money partly showed Clemens's own larger sense of the power of the *economy to determine wealth, even to the point of defining what money is. America at this time had no centralized monetary policy but needed to expand its money supply steadily to provide for a burgeoning population and industrial economy. Without a federal reserve system or a national bank to regulate the supply, Americans developed a patchwork of moneys, including hard money, or specie; notes backed by real property or specie and issued by state-chartered and -regulated banks; or government greenbacks, backed by the government's power to tax. The harder the money, the safer, and hence the greater the value, but hard money was not only hard to the touch but hard to come by. "Wildcat banks," that is banks operating in the same frontier territories in which wildcats still lived, usually kept more specie reserves to cover their notes than did eastern banks, but given their large exposure to the bursting bubbles of frontier land speculation, their notes were usually heavily discounted and quickly traded rather than held. They thus provided a ready money that in its quick motion through the economy helped to fund growth. Big businesses issued notes as well, manipulating equity and banking markets to secure massive amounts of capital. The financial manipulations of the Credit Mobilier led to a major panic and crash that swept not only the United States but also Europe in 1873 and created the longest depression of the post–Civil War nineteenth century.

This depression was exacerbated by the policy of the U.S. government to recall all of the greenbacks issued during the Civil War, when the government went off the gold standard. The resulting wartime inflation hurt the creditor class, which, closely allied with government, encouraged the government to recall the greenbacks in preparation for a return to the gold standard. This recall kept the money supply contracting from shortly after war's end to 1879 when the country went back on the gold standard. The money supply then increased, by 62 percent from 1879 to 1881, finally breaking the depression. Still, the speed with which such hard money changed hands was slower than that of notes. Coupled with the rapid growth of the economy and the population, the government's adherence to the gold standard fueled the deflation of the thirty-year period following the Civil War.

At no time, of course, is a dollar's value constant, but the perception of stability is an important part of a nation's faith in money, and given the steady deflation, even though the nation's standard of living rose on average for nearly every class in the last half of the nineteenth century, a nearly universal lack of trust in anything but hard currency pervaded the nation's economic dealings, making it harder to regulate a flexible money supply.

Such a backdrop influenced Clemens's attitudes about money. In the abstract, he could have Hank Morgan argue energetically in chapter 33 of *Connecticut Yankee* that buying power is the real measure of income, not the dollar number paid in wages, and thus justify low wages. Unskilled urban industrial laborers' wages fell from a high of fifteen cents per hour in 1870 to a low of between eleven and twelve cents before rising to between thirteen and fourteen cents in the mid- to late 1880s. A skilled mechanic did not do much better. By such standards Clemens should have recognized his own extraordinary affluence, even after paying off the debts he incurred in bankruptcy. In fact, the uncertainty of his economic times made him wish always for more money, regardless of its buying power. In this impulse, as much as in his railing against the power of money, Clemens lays legitimate claim to his position as a representative American.

♦ SEE ALSO Finances; Labor Movement.

MOORE, JULIA (1847–1920).

Julia Moore has the dubious distinction of serving as the model for Emmeline Grangerford in *Adventures of Huckleberry Finn*. Moore pretentiously but derivatively called herself "The Sweet Singer of Michigan," following in the footsteps of the very popular Lydia Sigourney, who called herself "The Sweet Singer of Hartford" (from 2 Samuel 23:1–2). Moore composed doggerel obituary verse, sometimes on commission, which she ultimately collected and published. In so doing, she participated in an American tradition of penning such verse, but she had the misfortune of doing it particularly badly. Her efforts brought her a perverse fame—her book has been preserved as a classic of (accidental) American humor. On publication, newspapers took sarcastic notice, such as the Worcester *Daily Press*: "The poet is one who reaches for the sympathy of humanity as a Rhode Islander reaches for a quahaug, clutches the soul as a garden rake clutches a hop vine, and hauls the reader into a closer sympathy than that which exists between a man and his undershirt" (quoted in Walter Blair, *Mark Twain and Huck Finn*, 1960).

Clemens appreciated Moore's verse for its unintentional humor; as he put it in *Following the Equator*, "She has the touch that makes an intentionally humorous episode pathetic and an intentionally pathetic one funny" (chapter 36). This is certainly the case of the sixth and seventh stanzas of Moore's "Little Libbie":

> One morning in April, a short time ago,
> Libbie was active and gay;

Her Saviour called her, she had to go,
E're the close of that pleasant day.

While eating dinner, this dear little child
Was choked on a piece of beef.
Doctors came, tried their skill awhile,
But none could give relief.

Clemens owned a copy of Little Libbie's final resting place—Moore's *The Sentimental Songbook* (1876)—and drew from Libbie at least some inspiration for his "Ode to Stephen Dowling Bots, Dec'd" in *Huckleberry Finn*.

MORAL SENSE. In *sentimentalism the highest of the "finer" sensibilities or tastes is the moral sense, the putative capacity to distinguish between right and wrong not through reasoned judgment but through feeling the inherent quality of an action or prospective action. Closely allied to sympathy—the capacity to feel the consequences of an action to another person—the moral sense was supposed to regulate human behavior for the better. While sentimentalists held that all sensibilities were subject to strengthening or weakening through practice or neglect, the idea of a moral sense requires belief in absolute morality. In this regard, liberal Christians combined the older idea of conscience, the sharing of God's knowledge of the state of one's own soul, with the concept of the moral sense.

Much of Clemens's work grapples with the sentimental understanding of ethical motivation, including whether or not there even is a moral sense or whether our conceptions of morality are all simply the product of culture and "training." Of almost equal importance to Clemens was the question of the connection between moral sense and absolute morality. Although he often wished for that connection to exist, he never found his own ability to believe equal to his desire. As he put it most strenuously in an 1880s manuscript draft of an essay, now published under the title "The Character of Man," he calls a lie the idea "that conscience, man's moral medicine chest, is not only created by the Creator, but is put into man ready-charged with the right and only true and authentic corrective of conduct—and the duplicate chest, with the self-same correctives, unchanged, unmodified, distributed to all nations and all epochs."

Clemens began his critical investigation of the moral sense with "The *Facts Concerning the Recent Carnival of Crime in Connecticut," which juxtaposes Calvinist, sentimentalist, and utilitarian models of conscience in a grotesque tale of Mark Twain murdering his anthropomorphized conscience. While he may have dropped the mask in his succeeding works, Clemens continued his investigation of conscience, finally developing an obsession with the idea of a moral sense. By the time he wrote *Pudd'nhead Wilson*, he seems to have agreed with the sentimentalists that human beings do have a moral sense, though he began to complain bitterly that it did not serve as intended. The epigraph to chapter 16 of *Pudd'nhead Wilson* is the first clear example of what became a leitmotif in his late career: "There is a Moral Sense, and there is an Immoral Sense. History shows us that the Moral Sense enables us to perceive morality and how to avoid it, and that the Immoral Sense enables us to perceive immorality and how to enjoy it." Similar ideas are central to such pieces as *What Is Man?*, the draft stories now known as *The Mysterious Stranger* manuscripts, "Letters from the Earth," "Man's Place in the Animal World," and other late, usually posthumously published works.

MUGWUMPS. In the 1884 presidential campaign between James G. Blaine and Grover Cleveland, Blaine's apparent connection to the Credit Mobilier scandal induced many Republicans to bolt the party to vote for Cleveland, the Democrat. These reformist and liberal Republicans became the target of vitriolic attacks, including an editorial by Charles Dana of the New York *Sun*, who called the party rebels "mugwumps," a word derived from the Algonquin for "big chief." Dana intended the term to deride those who thought themselves more important than their political party. Many of the reformists accepted the word as a badge of honor, including Clemens, who bragged about being a mugwump. His stance, shared by Rev. Joseph *Twichell, was not popular in Hartford, and the two took abuse from members of the *Monday Evening Club and others. Eventually, after passions had cooled somewhat, Clemens took the question of party loyalty to task in his essay "Consistency," which he read to the club, solidifying his position as resident, respected iconoclast.

♦ SEE ALSO Democracy; Politics; Reform.

MUSEUMS. Most towns or small cities in the United States with any reasonable connection to Clemens have some museum or celebratory events in his honor. Florida, Missouri, has a museum for Twain's birthplace, though the house in which he was born has been moved to Mark Twain State Park. *Hannibal, Missouri, where the family moved when Clemens was almost four years old, has a virtual Mark Twain industry, with the house and surrounding areas dedicated as a shrine that brings a substantial number of tourists to the town each year. Virginia City, *Nevada, is now barely populated at all, but the Virginia City *Territorial Enterprise* building has been renovated into a museum, and uses Twain's association with the newspaper to draw tourists. In many ways, the entire town, now lacking any other significant economic base, is a museum, well worth a visit to help understand the mining regions' formative influence on Twain. Less impressive is the so-called "Mark Twain cabin" in Jackass Gulch, Tuolumne County, *California (just south of Angel's Camp, Calaveras County), a replica of the Gillis cabin in which Clemens spent much of the winter of 1864–1865. Angel's Camp also trades on its association with Twain, holding a jumping frog contest during its county fair each year, but lacks regard for historical accuracy. *Hartford, Connecticut, on the other hand, has the Mark Twain Memorial, a foundation which maintains the Hartford *house that Samuel and Olivia Clemens built. It has been painstakingly restored and is open for public tours. The memorial foundation also owns many Twain manuscripts. Less a museum than a research library, Elmira College in *Elmira, New York, houses the Center for Mark Twain Studies. While hosting quadrennial conferences and supporting scholarship is the center's primary focus, it does also have Twain's study on display. The city itself supports an annual Mark Twain celebration, complete with a musical show.

♦ SEE ALSO Critical Reception; Public Image.

MUSIC. Family music was as important as family reading in the repertoire of popular and acceptable Victorian pastimes, and the Clemens family was not unusual in spending *leisure hours singing and playing together. Clemens could accompany his lovely tenor voice with both piano and guitar. He sang regularly in parlor entertainments, as did the rest of the family. The Clemenses, however, took music a step further than the norm. In 1878 they spent four hundred dollars on a very complex music machine. While it worked on the principle of a music box, it played large, changeable disks that produced complex and long pieces of music, and its repertoire was potentially unrestricted. Had the machine caught on, as the phonograph would half a century later, it might have given the family a rich entrée into the repertoire of western music. But the machine's price and limited range ultimately precluded popularity, so the Clemens family had to appreciate music in the usual way, by attending concerts at home and abroad and providing their children with the best available instruction. Not surprisingly, the Clemens children developed an avid interest in music; Olivia Susan aspired alternately to a career as a writer or singer and Clara actually pursued a career as a concert singer.

This interest in and enthusiasm for music appears only sporadically in Twain's writing. Granted, he frequently mentions music in his fiction and travel narratives, but what use he makes is usually negative. He regularly derogates either the performances he reports hearing or the music itself. Such negative comments began early in his career as a journalist covering an arts beat and as a traveling correspondent reporting on foreign places and mores. For instance, on board ship heading out of San Francisco on 23 December 1866, Twain complained that the volunteer choir that practiced late into Saturday night to prepare for the next day's religious services not only butchered "venerable melodies until a late hour," but also, when bid to join the services the next day, needed to be begged. Twain has the captain complain, "D—n that choir! They're like the fellow's sow—had to haul her ears off to get her up to the trough, and then had to pull her tail out to get her away again"

(San Francisco *Alta California*, 24 February 1867). Passages like these comment less on music per se than on the manners and foibles of performance.

In his comments on music itself, Twain typically inverts the received musical hierarchies, calling the music of the cultivated classes "noise" and that of the lower classes heavenly. With respect to Richard Wagner, for instance, he says, "We went to Mannheim and attended a shivaree,—otherwise an opera,—the one called Lohengrin. The banging and slamming and booming and crashing were something beyond belief. The racking and pitiless pain of it remains stored up in my memory alongside the memory of the time I had my teeth fixed" (*A Tramp Abroad*, chapter 9). On the contrary, even though in early works he disparaged Stephen Foster's "Old Dog Tray" and other sentimental, popular music, he often praised popular music, and spirituals in particular, for matching feeling with common human circumstance. In "No. 44, The Mysterious Stranger," for instance, August Feldner, treated to a performance of a spiritual sung by a minstrel in a "clownish and outlandish costume," declares, "There was never anything so beautiful, never anything so heart-breaking, oh, never any music like it below the skies! and by the magic of it that uncouth figure lost its uncouthness and became lovely like the song, because it so fitted the song" (chapter 26).

Such an inversion of artistic hierarchies echoes sentiments Twain frequently uttered about most of the arts, that the artistry of low culture moved him more than that of the learned. Indeed, he went so far as to suggest that art should be judged not by technique and the capacity of the learned to judge, but by effect, the more widespread the better. By this standard, he judged the Fisk Jubilee Singers the best of musicians. Ironically, he came to that conclusion when he heard this African-American choir singing folksongs in Europe, while performing on a fundraising tour to save their college. Clemens wrote that only a European audience could appreciate their artistry, a sentiment he echoed in evaluating his own work, which he felt was dismissed as too low-brow in America but appreciated in Europe. His willingness to accede to the superiority of the cultivated European *taste is, ironically, exactly what he so often disparages by praising folkart.

As with his feelings for the other arts, Twain's professed preference for low music was not easy for him to accept, and he continued to teach himself to appreciate classical music to his dying day, much as he trained himself to appreciate *painting, sculpture, and literature. While he maintained his idiosyncratic tastes in all of these fields, it is impossible, finally, to see him as a simple champion of simplicity.

♦ SEE ALSO Democracy; Food; Patriotism.

MYSTERIOUS STRANGER, THE. In 1916, Harper and Brothers brought out in time for Christmas a beautifully illustrated book, supposedly just discovered among Twain's papers, which they titled *The Mysterious Stranger: A Romance*. The subtitle should have warned any Twain devotee that there was something fishy about the book, but the editor, Albert Bigelow *Paine, was Twain's authorized biographer and custodian of his papers, and Harper's was Twain's official publisher in the last years of his life, so the book was widely accepted as Twain's last finished work. As such, it came under serious critical scrutiny, with Bernard DeVoto even going so far as to accord it special value as the work in which Twain recovered his imaginative powers.

Other critics over the years found the ending peculiar, to say the least, and the obvious discrepancy between the dream ending of the last chapter and the thematic thrust of the rest of the tale called into question the book's importance as a sign of Twain's powers. It was not, however, until 1963 when John Tuckey published *Mark Twain and Little Satan* that the scholarly world learned that *The Mysterious Stranger* is a fraud. Paine and his Harper's contact Frederick Duneka, seeking a Twain book for purely commercial ends, cobbled together the story from a radically edited version of *"Chronicle of Young Satan" and the last chapter of *"No. 44, The Mysterious Stranger." While all but the last chapter is from "Chronicle," they preferred the religiously innocuous latter title. To further protect Twain's commercial image as a grandfatherly romancer, they cut about 25 percent of the original "Chronicle," deleting most of its attacks on religion and God, and inventing a new character, the astrologer, to take the place of Twain's villain, a Roman Catholic priest.

Even though the fraud has been known for over forty years now, the bowdlerized *Mysterious Stranger* is still regularly reprinted as a story by Mark Twain and is far better known than either of the much more powerful and interesting originals from which it was drawn.

♦ SEE ALSO Censorship; Mark Twain Papers; Posthumous Publications; Public Image; Publishing Industry; Tricksters.

NASBY, PETROLEUM V. SEE Locke, David Ross.

NAST, THOMAS (1840–1902). One of America's foremost political cartoonists, Thomas Nast began working for *Harper's Weekly* in 1862. He gave America some of its most enduring representations of the post–Civil War period. Particularly known for his scathing attacks on the Tammany Hall political machine, Nast is often given substantial credit for bringing it down. His efforts were not without personal price, however, as he had to move his family away from New York City after receiving threats while engaged in his anti-Tammany campaign.

Clemens shared Nast's hatred of the Tammany machine and consequently came to admire him tremendously—an admiration that Nast reciprocated enough to develop into a low-level but enduring friendship. Alternately, each wanted the relationship to become something more. Nast first proposed to Twain that they share a lecture platform, with Nast drawing caricatures and Twain supplying running commentary. Twain rejected the idea at first, but he did seek Nast as an illustrator for many of his books, most notably *The Gilded Age*. Later, though Nast had since dropped the idea, Twain revived Nast's plan for a *collaboration on the *lecture circuit. Nothing came of any of their proposals to work together, but Twain's efforts to tie his work to Nast's suggests the degree to which he wanted to be known for *satire rather than *humor.

♦ SEE ALSO Politics; Presidents.

NATIVE AMERICANS. Samuel Clemens outgrew most of the prejudicial racial attitudes of his youth and by his middle years even became a champion of racial tolerance. He did not, however, overcome his animosity toward Native Americans. Granted, the short, posthumously published "The Dervish and the Offensive Stranger" (written in 1902) does mildly condemn European displacement of Native Americans, but it also suggests that the benefits of opening the New World to the Old balance the moral ledger. Compared to his heated writings on imperial conquests in the early 1900s, the criticism here is startlingly cool.

Some critics dismiss Clemens's apparent prejudice, saying that he did not so much attack real Native Americans as James Fenimore Cooper's romanticized ones. Certainly to some degree Twain does use Cooper's "noble savages" as strawmen in his attack on historical *romance. In "Fenimore Cooper's Literary Offenses," Twain even seems to defend the real things against Cooper's characterization:

The ark is arriving at the stream's exit, now, whose width has been reduced to less than twenty feet to accommodate the Indians—say to eighteen. There is a foot to spare on each side of the boat. Did the Indians notice that there was going to be a tight squeeze there? Did they notice that they could make money by climbing down out of that arched sapling and just stepping aboard when the ark scraped by? No; other Indians would have noticed these things, but Cooper's Indians never notice anything. Cooper thinks they are marvelous creatures for noticing, but he was almost always in error about his Indians. There was seldom a sane one among them. . . . In the matter of intellect, the difference between a Cooper Indian and the Indian that stands in front of the cigar shop is not spacious.

Here Twain attacks the romance novel on the grounds that its actions and settings defy human and natural realities. In this sense, Clemens is defending Native Americans.

Nonetheless, in suggesting a substantial difference between a real Indian and a cigar-store Indian, Twain does no more than spare Native Americans his usual animosity. Only one of Twain's Indian characters in his published works, Injun Joe from *The Adventures of Tom Sawyer*, shows intelligence, and even here his intelligence serves his malignity. The other Native Americans are merely squalid, stupid, and impassive. In particular, his characterization of what he calls the "Goshoot" Indians of Nevada and California in chapter 19 of *Roughing It* deals in the most virulent of racist attacks. He calls them "inferior to all races of savages on our continent. . . . Such of the Goshoots as we saw . . . were lean, 'scrawny' creatures . . . their face and hands bearing dirt which they had been hoarding and accumulating for months, years, and even generations, according to the age of the proprietor; a silent, sneaking, treacherous looking race." Again, the chapter ends with a reference to Cooper, but it is clear that Twain's animosity is toward the Natives more than toward Cooper, as is corroborated in his private correspondence from his time in Nevada. He states similar opinions in passages he wrote but later suppressed. In an excised passage from *A Tramp Abroad*, Twain disparaged the French by comparing them to the Comanches, suggesting that sexual immorality is at the root of both cultures' decadence. In the unpublished "Huck Finn and Tom Sawyer among the Indians" (written in 1885), Twain began a parody of a traditional captivity narrative, but stalled when the logic of his own story made murder and rape of whites at the hands of the Indians the necessary outcome of what was supposed to be a humorous story.

Clemens was raised with this prejudice, but unlike his other trained racial antipathies, this one was reinforced in his Nevada days when the so-called Digger Indians threatened Clemens's prospective wealth. In the winter of 1861, when staking claims in the Esmeralda mining district on the border between California and the Nevada territory, Clemens's claims were within easy striking distance of a tribe of Native Americans who took up arms to resist the incursions of a group of white cattlemen in the Owens Valley. The Indians ran the cattlemen off from a small fort, and the cattlemen's efforts to retake their fort also failed. The situation was not resolved for nearly a year until a treaty accomplished for the whites what force of arms could not. Whether this incident was the primary motivation behind Clemens's persistent anti-Indian feelings cannot now be gauged, but the disparity between Twain's portrait of Indian ineptitude and the realities of their effectiveness in Clemens's own experience suggests a compensatory fantasy at work, a counter-romance worthy of Cooper for inaccuracy of observation.

♦ SEE ALSO Mississippi River Valley; Progress; Race Relations.

NATURALISM. Ambrose Bierce defines realism as "The art of depicting nature as it is seen by toads. The charm suffusing a . . . story written by a measuring worm." This definition applies most appropriately, perhaps, to that branch of realism called "naturalism." Naturalistic fiction came into America via translations of Émile Zola, and, with the qualified support of William Dean *Howells, became a literary force for American authors late in the century.

As a kind of realism that professed to follow the model of photography, naturalist fiction is characterized by a painstaking attention to detail. The detail comes across not merely as backdrop, but as a force, because the philosophy of naturalism assumes that individual human beings, mere pawns of social and natural forces, have no free will.

Naturalists often took as their subject matter the daily life of people from the lower classes, as the economic and physical constraints of their existences made the best case for *determinism. While much naturalist literature suggests a need for political reform in order to ameliorate social conditions and ennoble the human experience, there is nothing inherently progressive in naturalism. As part of a Darwinian movement, naturalist literature can just as easily be interpreted as a call to allow the poor to suffer in their conditions in order to purify the race through natural selection. At least naturalist writers, in refusing to sentimentalize the poor, allowed the literature to serve the purposes of social Darwinism, whether or not individual authors so intended. Howells, in advocating naturalism, certainly thought it would serve the purpose of reform, but that may have been merely because he interpreted naturalism as a variant of sentimental realism.

As much as Twain professed to believe in absolute determinism, he only rarely wrote pieces that could be classified as naturalistic. In particular, he tended not to follow his determinism in writing about "low characters"; he instead usually sentimentalized them, and not just in his early years when sentimental fiction was still in vogue. The old miners in "A Californian's Tale" are more sympathetic than the Virginia City "rough" Scotty Briggs from *Roughing It*.

When dealing with social forces, though, Twain did, in his later years, demonstrate an affinity with naturalist literature in such pieces as "The *Man That Corrupted Hadleyburg" and "The *Thirty Thousand Dollar Bequest." In both of these stories, Clemens concerned himself not with the constraints faced by members of the working classes, but with the social power of middle-class society. In this sense, Clemens broadened American naturalism's focus.

Even so, it would be a mistake to consider Twain's writings naturalistic. Clemens's imagination did not run in such a groove, as his humor, engaged with extravagances of imagination, could not really restrict itself to the minute detailing of physical and social circumstance that was central to the naturalist's aesthetic.

NEVADA. Technically acquired by the United States in 1848 at the close of the Mexican-American War, Nevada was practically an extension of the Mormon state, a physically harsh, mountainous, and arid barrier between the Mormon centers of north-central Utah and the more populated regions of the Pacific Coast. But mining interests in *California quickly made inroads, and the discovery of silver in several mining districts, most of which Twain mentions in *Roughing It*, turned Nevada into a prize rather than a booby prize. Organized into a territory separate from Utah in 1861, Nevada served the Union as a source of mineral wealth and by supporting California financial and transportation interests after the first flush of the gold rush wore off. Nevada territory was as much a province of San Francisco as of Washington, D.C.

Clemens's rush to Nevada in 1861 was an escape from the Civil War, which ended his lucrative livelihood as a steamboat pilot, and from steady work, toward an idea of a quickly earned speculative fortune that would haunt his financial dealings for years to come. But in his rush, he learned an entirely new idea of life, one disconnected from the politics of *domesticity, one inviting a person to move on quickly rather than settle and build a world. While such attitudes were typical of mining communities, Nevada provided the extreme since very few valleys in the entire state could support any but the barest subsistence living. The lives of miners completely depended on an extensive commerce with the industrialized world. It was a world of high prices, economic interdependence, and, in spite of the hopes of individual miners to strike it rich, heavy capitalization. In short, the reality of Nevada as a mining region was the antithesis of the American frontier myth of rugged individuals carving civilization out of the wilderness.

And yet it was a frontier. As with each shift of the nation's immigrant population, *Native Americans were demonized, displaced, and killed. Twain's works certainly share in this process. Socially, it was very much a masculine world, exaggerating the western idea of *etiquette as a way of leveling rather than enforcing social distinctions. It was also a place where, in frontier fashion, religion became a private rather than public matter, easier to relinquish than to practice. It was here,

Map of Virginia City, Nevada, Grafton T. Brown, publisher, lithography by C. C. Kuchel, San Francisco, California. *Territorial Enterprise* building as Clemens first knew it in 1861 (before a two-story brick building replaced it in 1863) appears in the top row, fourth image from the right.

and in his later sojourns in California, that Clemens learned habits of drinking and *profanity and developed a taste for ribald humor thoroughly in tension with the proprieties of settled communities, a tension he internalized in his role as Mark Twain, "wild humorist of the Pacific slope." Yet ironically, here, too, he began steady work as a journalist for the Virginia City *Territorial Enterprise*, where he learned much about the craft of writing under the tutelage of Joseph T. *Goodman.

◆ SEE ALSO Alcohol.

NEWSPAPER JOURNALISM. Mark Twain was born as a *nom de plume* for Clemens's fancier newspaper sketches; his straight factual reporting often went under no byline whatsoever, like most newspaper reporting of the nineteenth century. Clemens learned both how to observe and write up his observations and how to spin sketches of fancy while writing for newspapers. As late as 1870 he expected to make a career as a newspaperman; his interest in journalism never waned and Twain never stopped publishing, at least occasionally, in newspapers. But newspaper journalism was not in the nineteenth century what it is today, nor did it remain the same over the course of Clemens's life. His opinions of its value changed, too, both given changes in his political outlook and also in newspaper journalism itself.

When Clemens began his career in publishing as an apprentice typesetter in Hannibal, Missouri, in 1848 for Joseph Ament's *Missouri Courier*, most American newspapers were small, local operations connected to a print shop that produced newspapers as merely one of many printing jobs. Often even the smallest town would have two newspapers, each espousing the partisan opinions of a political party. Such newspapers often published bitter diatribes against each other, creating bad blood between the editors of the papers, which Clemens amply describes with characteristic exaggeration in "Journalism in Tennessee." In his own experience as a newspaperman, such feuds were common matter. One even led Clemens to the point of violence when in 1864 he wrote a squib for the Virginia City *Territorial Enterprise* saying that the Civil War Sanitary Fund campaign was really raising money for a miscegenation society. Here his proslavery political orientation led him to the kind of unbridled *ad hominem* and racist attack that often found its way into the American press. Here, too, as a consequence, Clemens found himself embroiled in "an affair of honor," a duel that ultimately forced him to leave Nevada allegedly to avoid prosecution.

But while much of journalism was vicious out of partisanship, much of the rivalry between newspapers was designed merely to sell newspapers. Especially in big cities by the 1860s, newspapers had increasingly large circulations and had often outgrown the capacity of a single editor and reporter to handle the work. This expansion led to the need for large capitalization to support overhead and a larger staff. Circulation battles transcended papers' partisan positions. On slow days, reporters indulged in written feuds to take up space and add spice. This was the kind of imaginative, rather than reportorial, work that Clemens discovered to be his metier, perfect for the first version of the *Mark Twain guise.

Much of Twain's newspaper badinage has been lost, as the *Enterprise,* the journal that most readily countenanced Twain's frontier journalism, lost its files in a fire. Only articles reprinted in other journals remain. Among these are many pieces about "The Unreliable," Clemens's good friend Clement T. Rice, who worked for the *Enterprise*'s rival, the Virginia City *Union*. On 4 August 1863, Rice agreed to cover Clemens's duties while Clemens nursed a cold. Rice played a joke on Clemens by publishing in the *Enterprise*, under Mark Twain's byline, an apology to the many locals Twain had insulted. He wrote further:

> To 'Young Wilson' and 'The Unreliable', (as we have wickedly termed them), we feel that no apology we can begin to atone for the many insults we have given them. Towards these gentlemen we have been as mean as a man can be—and we have always prided ourself on this base quality. We feel that we are the least of all humanity, as it were. We will now go in sack-cloth and ashes for the next forty days. What more can we do? The latter-named gentleman has saved us several times from receiving a sound thrashing for our impudence and assurance.

Mark Twain in turn replied on 5 August:

Illustration by True Williams (1839–1897), from *Sketches, New and Old*, Hartford: American Publishing Company, 1875, p. 44.

JOURNALISM IN TENNESSEE

We are to blame for giving "the Unreliable" an opportunity to misrepresent us, and therefore refrain from repining to any great extent at the result. We simply claim the right to *deny the truth* of every statement made by him in yesterday's paper, to annul all apologies he coined as coming from us, and to hold him up to public commiseration as a reptile endowed with no more intellect, no more cultivation, no more Christian principle than animates and adorns the sportive jackass rabbit of the Sierras.

When friendship could go to such extremes in mere jest, it is easy to see why unfriendly rivalries often ended in violence.

An 1865 target of Twain's comic sallies was Albert S. Evans, the local reporter for the San Francisco *Morning Call*. Evans occupied the position from which Clemens had been fired in 1864, and in 1865 Clemens exacted some revenge in his position as San Francisco correspondent for the *Enterprise*. Clemens called Evans "Fitz

Smythe," to suggest that Evans was an honorary Irishman in deference to the largely Irish clientele of the *Call*. Of Evans's reporting Twain wrote, "Let Moike Mulrooney, or Tim Murphy, or Judy O'Flaherty, receive a present of raal Irish whisky from the ould country, and it will never let you hear the last of it" (about 15 November 1865). About Evans's notorious lack of a sense of humor, Twain opined:

> Soothsayers were called in at the time of Fitz Smythe's birth, and they read the stars and prophesied that he was destined . . . to arrive to great distinction for his untiring industry in endeavoring, for the period of near half a century, to get off a joke. They said that many times during his life the grand end and aim of his existence would seem to be in his reach, and his mission on earth on the point of being fulfilled; but again and again bitter disappointment would overtake him; what promised so fairly to be a joke would come forth still-born. (*Enterprise*, 24 or 26 December 1865)

Evans was, in his lack of humor, perfectly suited to work as a reporter for a growing daily like the *Call*, which wanted news rather than fancy. In describing his own berth as a reporter for the *Call* Clemens said,

> After having been hard at work from nine or ten in the morning until eleven at night scraping material together, I took the pen and spread this muck out in words and phrases and made it cover as much acreage as I could. It was fearful drudgery, soulless drudgery, and almost destitute of interest. (autobiographical dictation of 13 June 1906)

Insofar as journalism was becoming professionalized to distinguish between news and opinion, Clemens found himself increasingly useless as a reporter but ever more attractive as a columnist.

By the middle of the century, columnists had become the drawing cards for big urban newspapers. In 1855, Sarah Willis Parton, under her pen name "Fanny Fern," received one hundred dollars per column from the new New York *Ledger*. Her column attracted sufficient readership to more than justify her hitherto unheard of salary. Her success, in turn, raised the possibility of the modern newspaper columnist's making a good living. By the late 1860s, Clemens turned his talents in this direction. Newspapers commonly reprinted each others' columns, cutting into the profitability of original work. Ironically, however, this constant piracy spread Clemens's fame enough so that he could move east with the likelihood of making a success at the kind of newspaper sketch that he had perfected out west. Then, with the development of newspaper syndication in the late 1860s, it became possible to make significant money out of a single article. For Clemens this also meant he would no longer be restricted to the drudgery of a single beat, but instead could have a free hand.

By 1868, his reputation was such that he had that license. He wrote to Will Bowen in 1868:

> Mr. Bennett of the New York Herald tells me that if I will correspond twice a week from Washington, I may abuse & ridicule anybody & *every* body I please. Well, I said, "We will just take a drink on that—all I have been wanting, for a year, is to find a paper that will give me room according to my strength—& pay me double price." He said the Herald would do both. I have two weekly Pacific coast correspondence—I'll raise on them, also, & write very seldom for the Tribune—& then I'll sail in and write that book. If it were not for that book I would just show these newspaper men how easy it is to make a stack of greenbacks every week—but the book is going to crowd me some—I shall have to cut off *all* outside work, & it is growing pretty lucrative. I *could* make eight hundred a month so easily if I didn't have the book to write. (25 January 1868)

Here, when faced with the choice between continuing the line of work that he had developed and starting a new direction as an author of books, Clemens was torn between two potentially lucrative angles, one proven, the other merely speculative, the first reasonable in its pay, the other potentially spectacular.

In this same letter to Bowen, though, Clemens exaggerated his prospects as a journalist. In a letter to his publisher, he cited a figure of three hundred dollars per month, and in a letter to his friend Mary Mason Fairbanks, he said he could not afford to marry on the income of a journalist, as "I can't turn an inkstand into Aladdin's lamp" (12 December 1867).

But he may also have been growing out of his love for professional character assassination. Certainly he often criticized the sensational excesses of journalism, writing in his own newspaper correspondence of the special privileges he received because he was a "newspaper reptile" (*Alta California*, 14 July 1867), and complaining that newspapers cash in on "bloody details" so that "I do not know whether I am in the heart of morality and civilization, or not. I begin to waver" (*Alta California*, 21 July 1867). As a newspaper reptile himself, he reports "bloody details" immediately after condemning newspapers for dealing in them.

In this spirit of anxiety about the propriety of his profession, he turned first not to writing books, but rather to working the editorial side of newspapers. He tried to buy into the New York *Tribune*, the Cleveland *Herald*, and the Hartford *Courant* before finally settling on the Buffalo *Express*. Here he hoped to discipline the writers and the compositors to create a dignified tone and appearance. Yet he found the daily demands of editorial work too taxing. His tribute in *Roughing It* to editors in light of his own failure as one reflected his own editorship of the *Express*. When Clemens sold his interest in the *Express* and moved to Hartford, he intended to bid newspaper journalism a permanent adieu.

But it remained a subject of great interest to him. Many of his early sketches decry the excesses of journalism in trying to secure circulation regardless of facts—as in "How I Edited an Agricultural Newspaper Once" (1870)—or at fomenting disagreement—as in "Journalism in Tennessee" (1869)—or at allowing political partisanship to sully objectivity—as in "Running for Governor" (1870). By the 1880s, however, as his politics shifted toward a more democratic outlook, he began to accept the customary justification of a free press. In particular, in *A Connecticut Yankee in King Arthur's Court*, he suggests that journalism progresses with the moral and political growth of a country toward democracy. Similarly, in *The *American Claimant* he argues that the lack of reverence displayed by the American press is precisely what makes it useful, for "its mission . . . is to stand guard over a nation's liberties, not its humbugs and shams" (chapter 10).

By the early 1890s, though, the trends toward consolidation of newspapers into intensely capitalized concerns, coupled with growing urban circulations, bent American newspapers away from independence. American yellow journalism catered to the most prurient and violent of interests with even less restraint than Clemens had complained about thirty years earlier. And with increased circulations, the power a newspaper had to lead public opinion became significantly greater. As Clemens became aware of these trends, he fell away from his admiration of the press as a liberalizing and progressive agent, instead seeing it as an agent of conformity and moral dissolution. In an autobiographical dictation of 1908, he commented on New York District Attorney William T. Jerome's opinion that "a democratic government won't work as long as you have government by the newspapers." Said Twain:

> What we call our civilization is steadily deteriorating, I think. We were a pretty clean people before the war; we seem to be rotten at the heart now. The newspapers are mainly responsible for this. They publish every loathsome thing they can get hold of, and if the simple facts are not odious enough they exaggerate them. (27 April 1908)

Such a complaint could be dismissed as a passing mood, of which Clemens indulged many in his autobiography, but a more trenchant concern had surfaced seven years earlier.

In the posthumously published "As Regards Patriotism" (written in 1901), Twain writes that a citizen cannot buck the power of the press: "Sometimes, in the beginning of an insane and shabby political upheaval, he is strongly moved to revolt, but he doesn't do it—he knows better. He knows that his maker would find it out—the maker of his Patriotism, the windy and incoherent six-dollar subeditor of his village newspaper—and would bray out in print and call him a Traitor." Intriguingly, Twain describes the structure of this kind of political journalism in terms appropriate to that of his younger days, but one outmoded by the urban yellow journalism to which he really refers in this piece as the fomenter of the Spanish-American War. Clemens's closing concerns about American culture and journalism, then, strike a certain nostalgia for a simpler America even as he returns to the same complaints he made when living in that mythical time of simpler journalism.

◆ SEE ALSO African Americans; Chinese in America; Industrial Revolution; Interviews; Public Image; Race Relations; Social Class.

NOOK FARM. George Parsons Lathrop, describing *Hartford, Connecticut, as "A Model State Capital" in *Harper's Monthly Magazine* (October 1885), focused much of his space on the elite Nook Farm neighborhood, best known for its literary circle. In his tour of Nook Farm he described how

> A few steps only from Mrs. Stowe's brings you to Mr. Clemens's house, and still fewer, if you take the short-cut through the lawn and shrubbery, by which brief transit you pass from old New England to modern America—from the plain quarters of ethical fiction to the luxurious abode of the most western of humorists. It is not difficult to trace, however, the essential kinship between Sam Lawson of *Old-Town Folks* and the equally quaint and shrewd but more expansive drollery of Mark Twain; and, on the other hand, those who see much of this author in private discover in him a fund of serious reflection and of keen observation upon many subjects that gives him another element in common with his neighbor.

Clemens would have approved; there was nothing more that he and his wife wanted than to belong in this exclusive suburb of one of America's oldest cities.

What it meant to belong differed to some degree between Olivia and Samuel. Samuel's initial impression of Hartford was of its appearance of prosperity and domesticity. His travel correspondence to the San Francisco *Alta California* describes a town

> composed almost entirely of dwelling houses—not shingle-shaped affairs, stood on end and packed together like a "deck" of cars, but massive private hotels, scattered along the broad straight streets, from fifty all the way up to two hundred yards apart. Each house sits in the midst of about an acre of green grass, or flower beds, or ornamental shrubbery, guarded on all sides by the trimmed hedges of arbor-vitae, and by files of huge forest trees that cast a shadow like a thundercloud. (6 September 1868)

But when he first stayed in Hartford at the Nook Farm house of Thomas Hooker, Clemens felt, as he would have Huckleberry Finn put it years later, "cramped and smothery." He wrote to Mary Mason *Fairbanks:

I am the guest of Mr. Hooker's (Henry Ward Beecher's brother-in-law) family here for a few days, & I tell you I have to walk mighty straight. I desire to have the respect of this sterling old Puritan community, for their respect is well worth having—& so I don't dare to smoke after I go to bed, & in fact I don't dare to do *anything* that's comfortable and natural. (24 January 1868)

In 1868 and 1869, then, Samuel was attracted to Nook Farm's means and cramped himself to fit the atmosphere.

Olivia, on the other hand, saw the opulence as nothing unusual; she had grown up in it and expected it. She felt the community's atmosphere was the essential element in domesticity. As Clemens explained it to his newly made Nook Farm friend, Rev. Joseph *Twichell:

My future wife wants me to be surrounded by a good moral & religious atmosphere (for I shall unite with the church as soon as I am located,) & so she likes the idea of living in Hartford. We could make more money elsewhere, but neither of us are much fired with a mania for money-getting. (14 February 1869)

Of course, to get to Hartford, Clemens first had to prove a capacity to make money, which he did selling subscription books, and the family finally moved to their first-choice town in 1871.

The Nook Farm community in which they resided was not, finally, the straitlaced Puritan corner that Clemens had feared or Olivia had hoped. It was instead an exclusive suburb founded by Joseph Hooker who subdivided his holdings in order to sell lots to a few select families, including his sister-in-law, Harriet Beecher Stowe, several Hartford families of fortune and power, several ministers, and college professors from nearby Trinity College. Hooker established a community in which the life of the mind would find common ground with political and industrial leaders.

One of the early institutions of the community, the *Monday Evening Club, was founded to facilitate this exchange between the elite of Hartford. Later, a similar club for girls, the *Saturday Morning Club, was established to extend the influence of education and connections into the next generation. Less regular events included amateur theatricals as well as frequent formal dining, with various Nook Farm residents hosting celebrities from around the nation and the world.

The families, for all of their prestige and wealth, and the imposing distances between their houses, kept a remarkably relaxed social life, exchanging frequent informal visits. When the Clemens family first lived in town, Olivia and Samuel had about equal social distance to travel to be comfortable: Olivia had to relax her Victorian formality as much as Samuel had to tighten up his western gregariousness. In an early visit to Harriet Beecher Stowe, Sam made his call without wearing a necktie. When he returned home, Olivia chided him for not appearing properly clothed, so he had a servant send over his necktie in a box. Nook Farm was informal enough not to have noticed the original deviation from Victorian social standards, and friendly and vital enough to appreciate such jokes.

The ease with which the Clemens family fit in is in part the measure of Clemens's own powers of mind and popularity as well as of the family's material prosperity. But as much as both wanted to be accepted by such a prestigious community, they had social interests more personal in their original decision to move to Hartford. One of Olivia's oldest and closest friends, Alice Hooker Day, was a resident, as was one of Clemens's newest but ultimately dearest friends, Joseph Twichell. They made new friends in Nook Farm, too. The friendship between Susan Warner and Olivia Clemens was warm and enduring; the friendship between Charles Dudley *Warner and Samuel Clemens endured less well but was very important to Clemens in the 1870s. For both, the people were the ultimate wealth of Nook Farm.

♦ SEE ALSO Etiquette.

NORTH AMERICAN REVIEW. Founded in 1815 under the auspices of Boston's Anthology Club at a time of intense nationalism and associated with Harvard University, the *North American Review* was one of America's most important and prestigious *magazines. Editors such as Jared Sparks and Edward Everett gave it its pre–Civil War stature, and James Russell Lowell and others maintained its standards during and after the war. It moved to New York City and switched from quarterly to monthly publication in 1878, helping to signal New York's victory over Boston as the nation's publishing center.

Twain's professional connection to the magazine began in the 1890s during his period of greatest financial distress. His connection with the journal was a bright spot in this otherwise gloomy period, in part because appearing in its pages gave him status even as he was cranking out potboilers purely for money. When George *Harvey purchased the magazine in 1899, the same year he became president of Harper and Brothers in a major reorganization of that venerable firm, Twain's connection to the *North American Review* was strengthened by his contract with Harper's. He developed a strong friendship with Harvey and used Harvey as his primary editor in selecting passages from his *autobiography for publication in the *North American Review* in 1906–1907. As important, the magazine gave Twain an outlet for his anti-imperialist writings, including "To the Person Sitting in Darkness" (1901).

NOSTALGIA. In the wake of the Civil War, which significantly altered the nation's character, and given an American culture that mythologized childhood and motherhood as the cradle of morality, nostalgia was a particularly potent political, social, and artistic force.

As a political tactic, appeals to a sentimentalized past preceded the Civil War, with many politicians harking to the days of the heroic founding fathers in an effort to quell regional conflict. In particular, and corresponding to a new American attitude about *death that led to the creation of cemetery parks, Americans raised money to turn George Washington's grave into a national shrine. Edward Everett made a career out of fund-raising for such a shrine between 1856 and 1860, giving an oration entitled "The Character of Washington" over one hundred times to massive crowds. In it he recited familiar myths of Washington's life, suggesting that if Americans were to remember their simpler, earlier days in the spirit of Washington, their sectional troubles would evaporate. During the war, too, appeals to a mythologized feeling of the past had their popular place, as when Everett's nephew and namesake, Edward Everett Hale, published in The *Atlantic Monthly "The Man Without a Country," about a fictionalized historical character whose nostalgia for the nation he renounced turns him into an ultra-patriot. Building on such solid foundations, the nostalgia industry grew substantially after the war, with much local color *realism memorializing bygone folkways and regional peculiarities; with an extensive, now mostly forgotten literature, song, and art of death and disasters; and with a rash of tales about childhood. At its worst, this literature included obituary verse as bad as that of Julia *Moore and apologetics for a mythic antebellum South of chivalric men and sweet belles. At its best, it grappled with changing mores and manners.

Clemens's response to popular manifestations of nostalgia followed four general periods, with significant variation within each. His early journalism is skeptical of any *sentimentalism, political or personal. His 1864 sketch "A Touching Story of George Washington's Boyhood," for instance, attacks both personal and political uses of nostalgia, relating a reminiscence about a "conversion" experience of sorts before failing to tell the story of Washington and his cherry tree. This story suggests something of personal reminiscence's self-indulgence, though not nearly as successfully as "'Mark Twain' on the Launch of the Steamer 'Capital'," which equates moralistic nostalgia with the maudlin ramblings of drunks:

> We took pure, health-giving water, with some other things in it, and clinked our glasses together, and were about to drink, when Smith, of Excelsior, drew forth his handkerchief and wiped away a tear; and then, noticing that the action had excited some attention, he explained it by recounting a most affecting incident in the history of a venerated aunt of his—now deceased—and said that, although long years had passed since the touching event he had narrated, he could never take a drink without thinking of the kind-hearted old lady. Mr. Nickerson blew his nose, and said with deep emotion that it gave him a better opinion of human nature to see a man who had had a good aunt, eternally and forever thinking about her.

Many other pieces of the period, such as "Lucretia Smith's Soldier" (1864), suggest that nostalgia is morbid.

When courting Olivia Langdon, Clemens's attitudes took a decided turn that lasted six years. Upon his marriage, he sent wedding announcements to a large circle of family and friends, including many people in Missouri, from which he had moved permanently a decade earlier. Old friends sent their good wishes, and one in particular, childhood friend and fellow riverboat pilot Will Bowen, wrote a long letter filled with childhood memories. Clemens replied energetically with his own gush of nostalgia, saying that Bowen's letter had

> stirred me to the bottom. The fountains of my great deep are broken up & I have rained reminiscences for four and twenty hours. The old life has swept before me like a panorama; the old days have trooped by in their old glory, again; the old faces have looked out of the mists of the past; old footsteps have sounded in my listening ears; old hands have clasped mine, old voices have greeted me, the songs I loved ages & ages ago have come wailing down the centuries! Heavens what eternities have swung their hoary cycles about us since those days were new! (6 February 1870)

Here Clemens sets up an impossible distance between himself and his childhood in order to mythologize his own past.

This change of perspective bore fruit in two important, concurrent works: *"Old Times on the Mississippi," written in 1874 and 1875 and published serially in 1875, and *The Adventures of Tom Sawyer*, written between 1872 and 1875 and published in 1876. The sixth installment of "Old Times" speaks of a relatively recent past in virtually archaeological terms: "Behold, in the twinkling of an eye, as it were, the association and the noble science of piloting were things of the dead and pathetic past." That distance allows Clemens to make *Tom Sawyer into a hero. Each of his scrapes, through the rosy glow of memory, comes out to Tom's advantage, and every mean trick he plays appears as a manifestation of an ultimately pure heart.

On finishing *Tom Sawyer*, Clemens had another change of perspective. He recognized his false interpretation of that character, and began almost immediately to capture the same time and place, without the mythic purification, through first-person narrative in *Adventures of Huckleberry Finn*. After his first summer's writing on *Huckleberry Finn* in 1876, he received another letter from Bowen, which detailed some of his recent business reverses and asked for a bit of sympathy: "I feel that a letter from my old time friend would be a sweet morsel and when you have the leisure I hope that you will recall some of the old feeling, that distance and time and their duties have perhaps dimmed a little and write me a word or two" (25 August 1876). Clemens turned on him savagely, telling him that indulging in nostalgia was "mental & moral masturbation": "As to the past, there is but one good thing about it, & that it, that it *is* the past—we don't have to see it again. There is nothing in it worth pickling for present or future use. Each day that is added to the past is but an old boot added to a pile of rubbish—I have no tears for my pile, no respect, no reverence, no pleasure in taking a rag-picker's hook & exploring it" (31 August 1876).

This overreaction to Bowen's letter exaggerates Clemens's scorn for the past, but not his feeling about how to treat it. Rather than revere the past nostalgically, he turned to a study of *history in order to see how human beings could progress into a better future. *Huckleberry Finn, The Prince and the Pauper, Life on the Mississippi, A Connecticut Yankee in King Arthur's Court,* and to some degree *Pudd'nhead Wilson and Those Extraordinary Twins* belong to this period.

The period came to a close gradually through the 1890s, both with Clemens's business and personal losses and his loss of faith in progress itself. If history does not reveal possibilities for improvement, then perhaps it is best to hang on to and improve, through memory, life's best times. "A Californian's Tale" is the harbinger of this retreat, and *Personal Recollections of Joan of Arc* and Clemens's *autobiography are the most substantial expressions of his return to nostalgia.

NOTEBOOKS AND JOURNALS. Among the richest sources of information about Twain's professional development and Clemens's personal life are his notebooks and journals. He kept them throughout his career and, remarkably, preserved most of them. While there are some significant gaps—most conspicuously from 1868 to early 1873 and then again from later in 1873 to 1877—they cover at least some part of almost every year from 1865 to 1910. They show something of every aspect of the man who was both Samuel Clemens and Mark Twain. He jotted down lists of books he bought or borrowed and sometimes added comments about them. He listed stocks and bonds he had purchased. He noted appointments. And most importantly from the literary point of view, he jotted down ideas for novels, short stories, *essays, *sketches, *dramas, *lectures, and *maxims. The notebooks help us to understand the contexts that motivated his writing and to analyze his *work habits.

Albert Bigelow *Paine published a mere quarter of the notebooks, savagely edited without any concern for temporal sequence, in a volume he called *Mark Twain's Notebook* (1935). All forty-nine extant originals from which Paine drew his volume are now kept in the *Mark Twain Papers in Berkeley, California. The Mark Twain Project plans to publish all 450,000 words of these notebooks in five volumes. Three of them, covering the years 1855 to 1891, are already in print.

The notebooks make no pretense to literary polish, and indeed they are often so cryptic as to be meaningless. Twain himself wrote in his notebook for 1879 when he was working on *A Tramp Abroad,* "One often finds notes in his book which no longer convey a meaning—they were texts, but you forget what you were going to say under them." If he had trouble, no doubt we do, too. Nonetheless, they are entertaining reading, giving a backstage glimpse into an astonishingly prolific public life.

"No. 44, The Mysterious Stranger." The second of two *unfinished works woven into the spurious *The *Mysterious Stranger*, "No. 44" begins in manuscript with basically the same opening. In 1902, after Twain had abandoned the first version, he used the opening manuscript pages, with minor revisions, to set the scene for yet another tale of the intrusion of a supernatural stranger into the life of an adolescent boy. He wrote but never revised the remainder of the tale, complete with a conclusion, in at least four stages through 1908.

In contrast to *"Chronicle of Young Satan," "No. 44" is a gothic story, set in an ancient and crumbling castle in which the newly invented printing press is lodged with its supporting guild labor. The symbolic implications of the gothic, in which a house itself represents a child's origins and need to find him- or herself in coming of age, coupled with the press as an image of enlightenment, led Twain to explore the psychology of enlightenment, the powers of the imagination to overcome strangling fear and conformity. In this context, the stranger, No. 44, plays a different role than Satan in "Chronicle," as can be seen in the way the two play out a pageant of human history. Satan emphasizes the inexorable march of time revealing an unchanging human depravity and violence. No. 44 plays the pageant backwards as well as forward, revealing his concerns with showmanship and color and creativity, as well as with finding human community. He refuses to engage in moral debates, and instead encourages the narrator, August Feldner, to release his mind into a divine realm of absolute freedom in pure creativity. It is a fantasy of release from adult responsibility into a world of boyhood companionship in play.

**OFF-COLOR HUMOR.** Scholars have called Twain the Victorian of *Southwest Humor because his public humor, even at its raunchiest, is not as interested in bodies and bodily functions as that of many of his predecessors, most notably George Washington *Harris. Nor did he approve of any fundamental assault on Victorian proprieties. When writing to his fiancée about what books she should read, he displayed a profound prudery quite out of keeping with the image of Mark Twain the iconoclast:

You would not like the volume [*Gulliver's Travels*], Livy—that is, a part of it. Some of it you would. If you would like to read it, though I will mark it & tear it until it is fit for your eyes—for portions of it are very coarse & indelicate. I am sorry enough that I didn't ask you to let me prepare Don Quixote for your perusal, in the same way. . . . You are as pure as snow, & I would have you always so—untainted, untouched even by the impure thoughts of others. . . . Read nothing that is not *perfectly pure*. . . . Neither it nor Shakspeare [*sic*] are proper books for virgins to read until some hand has culled them of their grossness. No gross speech is ever harmless. "A man cannot handle pitch & escape defilement," saith the proverb." (2 March 1869)

He likewise hoped to meet these standards in everything he published for an audience that would include women and girls.

Nonetheless, Twain's humor is often "gross," by which he meant calling attention to the body in ways that lead to an earthy train of thought. Especially when writing or speaking privately to men, or publicly to the western newspaper audiences that by convention were assumed to be masculine, he allowed himself what William Dean *Howells called, with substantial embarrassment, "Elizabethan breadth of parlance." Howells, almost despite himself, enjoyed Mark Twain's *[1601]. . . Conversation as It Was by the Social Fireside, in the Time of the Tudors*, the subject matter of which is alternately scatological and sexual. Written in 1876 as a letter to Rev. Joseph Twichell, first privately printed in 1880 and again in 1882 but never published with Clemens's explicit permission, *1601* was an exercise not so much in pornography as in ideas, in violating the expectations of Victorian propriety at the same time that it challenged Victorian idealizations of the medieval past.

And that is where Clemens's off-color humor rises beyond the level of mere male bonding. Much of his early journalism, with frequent reference to drinking, vomiting, and less often to voyeurism and sexuality, endorses Victorian propriety by propagating the double standard by which men were allowed transgressions in part to prove the value of the purity of their women. Later in his career, his 1879 speech to the Stomach Club in praise of masturbation, "The Science of Onanism," is exactly this kind of thing. No women were allowed to hear the speech; no harm was considered done. But with *1601*, even granting that Clemens kept the piece for male audiences, what he and Twichell laughed about was not so much the bawdry, but the narrator's reaction to the conversation. The narrator, the queen's cupbearer, is offended by the mixture of *social classes that is the precondition for the conversation, rather than the conversation itself. He cannot accept that the queen would consort with the baseborn, such as William Shakespeare. The two knew that most of their peers would not be outraged over nobility hobnobbing with Shakespeare, but that they would be outraged at the explicit references to sex and flatulence. In laughing at the cupbearer's outrage over what, to a Victorian audience, was the wrong thing, Clemens and Twichell relished their sense of the artificiality of propriety. Such knowledge was what always had Twain pushing the limits of *taste and decorum.

Sometimes that testing of limits took the character of sly interpolations of inside dirty jokes in otherwise clean entertainment, as when he had the king and the duke in *Adventures of Huckleberry Finn* perform the "King's Camelopard." In his *autobiography, he credits this tale to James Gillis, who, Twain mistakenly says, invented it to pass the time in Dick Stoker's cabin in Jackass Gulch, Calaveras County, California. In fact, it was a standard of southwestern oral bawdry, the tale of a man who dances around a stage while using his anus as a candlestick—hence its usual title, "The Burning Shame." In a 26 January 1870 letter to Gillis Twain recalled Stoker acting out the gag, but acknowledged in his autobiography that he "had to modify it considerably to make it proper for print" (dictation of 26 May 1907). In fact, no amount of editing could make it proper by Victorian standards; Twain could get away with the gag only by counting on the ignorance of most of his readers. The very presence of the escapade in the book is an act of terrorism against a system that imbued mere etiquette with absolute moral value.

Throughout his career, Clemens occasionally made his attacks on Victorian propriety explicit. In "About Smells," Twain suggests that much of Victorian propriety is really about social snobbery, about constraining by disdaining the lower classes. In this sense, his persistent use of slang—though now considered a mark of his artistry in finding the literary power in the speech of the common person—was his most prevalent form of off-color humor. The success of his humor demonstrates how much of Victorian manners were political and accidental, not, as so many of his contemporaries believed, part of a seamless fabric of moral thought and action. At least that is how his off-color humor developed over time; the prudery of his early years gave way ultimately to an understanding of the contingency of culture and the simultaneous need for convention and to occasionally transcend that convention in order to more fully express oneself. As he put it in his autobiography, "The world loses a good deal by the laws of decorum; gains a good deal, of course, but certainly loses a good deal." For Twain, humor writing became a game of gaining what he could when he could.

♦ SEE ALSO Dialect; Medievalism.

"Old Times on the Mississippi." This series of seven pieces, published in *The *Atlantic Monthly* between January and August 1875, inextricably tied the public image of Mark Twain to the Mississippi River. Despite Clemens's discomfort with the title, they ran under the heading "Old Times on the Mississippi," which became the title used in several pirated book editions of the articles. Twain himself reprinted the series with minor changes as chapters 4 to 17 in *Life on the Mississippi*, but the series is best known in English and in translations by the pirated version's title. In his *autobiography, Twain bragged about this series when he spoke of its reputation in Germany; he reported that everyone from the lowly porter in his German boardinghouse right up to the kaiser considered it to be his best work. Many American commentators have long agreed, praising the book's rich humor of situation, character, and tone, and seeing the series as one of Twain's best efforts at turning the American scene into literature.

This enduring response echoes the immediate reaction to these sketches. On receiving the first installment for publication William Dean *Howells wrote to Clemens, "The piece about the Mississippi is capital—it almost made the water in our ice-pitcher muddy as I read it" (23 November 1874). Right after publication of the first piece, John *Hay wrote to Clemens, "I have just read with delight your article in the Atlantic. It is perfect—no more nor less. I don't see how you do it. I knew all of that, every word of it—passed as much time on the levee as you ever did, knew the same crowd and saw the same scenes,—but I could not have remembered one word of it all. You have the two greatest gifts of the writer, memory and imagination" (16 December 1874, copied by Clemens in a letter to Howells, 18 December 1874). Hay here welcomes Clemens into the ranks of literary artists for whom the effort to capture reality is a complex interaction between the real and the ideal, mediated as much by imagination as by recalled observation. The effect, however, is not a fictional resemblance, but an accurate depiction of the appearance and feel of the Mississippi, exactly as expected of the then fashionable local color *realism.

Yet the attention paid to this nostalgic realism obscures two other, perhaps more important points. First, Twain published this detailed portrait of labor conditions in antebellum America at precisely the moment when these conditions were moving to the center of American political consciousness. The series of articles may begin with a portrait of a time and a place, but they move on to describe an apprenticeship in a trade guild, the system of labor control and privilege that governed relations between labor and capital in America before the development of large-scale industrial concerns. While the growth of unskilled labor began early in the nation's federal period in New England's textile mills, skilled labor guilds remained the primary mode of organization for labor in the nineteenth century. After the Civil War, intense labor strife occurred because guild labor resisted centralized control in factory systems and the depreciation of their skills through machine fabrication.

"Old Times on the Mississippi" describes a guild's control over a modern but decentralized industry, then depicts the failure of the guild system—a consequence of its own success—leading to the rise of a trade union that extends beyond the shop-by-shop (or in this case, ship-by-ship) organization to an industrywide one appropriate to modern business. Twain describes in brief the dissolution of the union's power when the more cost-efficient technologies of railroads and barges challenge the steamboat's place. In this portrait of a worker as a young man, "Old Times on the Mississippi" provides a précis of American labor history to 1875, with a prescient picture of what was to come in the next twenty-five years. Remarkably, Twain's vision is without obvious bias either for or against unions. At the beginning of America's political engagement in the "labor question," Twain presents an open mind, one that would take both sides at different times.

Second, these articles also remain powerful as an allegory of learning. The sketches describe the cub pilot's move from apprenticeship to mastery at precisely the moment when Twain felt that he was making a transition from lower-class clown to literary man. As such it reveals much about his own sense of vocation and status.

The articles began not in Clemens's mind as an inspiration that needed to be realized, but rather in Howells's repeated plea for contributions to the *Atlantic*. After the success of Twain's first contribution, "A *True Story, Repeated Word for Word as I Heard It," Howells pestered Clemens repeatedly for "another of those little stories" (5 October 1874), the kind that readers like J. W. De Forest, who wrote to Howells on 5 January 1875, called "a really great thing, amazingly natural & humorous, & touching even to the drawing of tears" (quoted in *Mark Twain–Howells Letters*, 25). As editor of the *Atlantic*, Howells sent this praise on to Twain to encourage him to continue contributing.

Twain needed such encouragement. He was not sure he could write "literature," at least not of the high order suited to the *Atlantic*, and he kept stalling until he wrote Howells in despair on 24 October 1874: "My Dear Howells: I have delayed thus long, hoping I might do something for the January number, & Mrs. Clemens has diligently persecuted me day by day with urgings to go to work & do that something, but it's no use—I find I can't." Liberated by his refusal, he then struck an idea. Later that same day he wrote again, "I take back the remark that I can't write for the Jan. number. For Twichell & I have had a long walk in the woods & I got to telling him about old Mississippi days of steamboating glory & grandeur as I saw them (during 5 years) *from the pilot house*. He said, 'What a virgin subject to hurl into a magazine!' I hadn't thought of that before. Would you like a series of papers to run through 3 months or 6 or 9?—or about 4 months, say?" He indeed had not thought of it before as a magazine subject, although he had been contemplating a book on the topic since at least 1866. But he had not considered it for literary magazines substantially because it was a part of his working-class past, a past that he did not associate with his aspirations to climb into the august company of the *Atlantic*. Only with the encouragement of his closest Hartford friend did he have the courage to try to bridge the gap between his past—which he had no qualms about putting into subscription books like *Roughing It*—and his future.

Even so, he found it difficult to establish the right tone and style for his Mississippi articles, sending his first installment to Howells with the plea: "Cut it, scarify it, reject it—handle it with entire freedom" (November 1874). Howells did not, instead praising it energetically, but when he requested the next installment, he cautioned Clemens, "Don't write *at* any supposed Atlantic audience, but yarn it off as if into my sympathetic ear. Don't be afraid of rests or pieces of dead color. I fancied a sort of hurried and anxious air in the first" (3 December 1874). Clemens's 8 December attempt to deny such fears in fact confirms Howells's insight: "It isn't the Atlantic audience that distresses me; for *it* is the only audience that I sit down before in perfect serenity (for the simple reason that it don't require a "humorist" to paint himself stripe'd & stand on his head every fifteen minutes)." Here is the lament of an insecure man tackling a new kind of project with false bravado, revealing in his desire to appeal to the *Atlantic*'s audience not his confidence, but the novelty of his situation.

The second installment begins the story not with the science of piloting, but rather with the *initiation into the mysteries of a guild. As Clemens threw himself before his master Howells to be cut, scarified, and rejected, so Twain writes of an earlier apprenticeship, in which he threw himself before Mister B— to be humiliated and corrected. Not surprisingly, Twain makes his cub persona younger and more naive than Clemens was in fact, suggesting that the power dynamic between master and apprentice is similar to that between adult and child. And as the cub pilot's motives for joining the guild stem from a childlike, romanticized view of the power and prestige of piloting—ultimately undercut by drudgery and feelings of inadequacy—so Clemens in these very articles metaphorically voiced his admiration for the literati and worried whether he had the brains to acquire the craft he needed to become a bona fide literary artist. The cub does learn that the sweat of work has its compensation in the comradeship of professionals, but in "Old Times" the cub never reaches that pleasure. When Twain finally finished this allegorical history in chapters 18 to 20 of *Life on the Mississippi*, the cub physically beats his master and ends in gentlemanly equality with a colleague whose pleasures are reading Shakespeare and playing a flute. Clemens did apparently get over his sense of inferiority as a literary artist, but it took him nearly another decade to do so.

♦ SEE ALSO Labor Movement; Social Class; Work Habits.

OSGOOD, JAMES (1836–1892). James Osgood was one of American publishing's leading figures. His career parallels the decline of Boston and rise of New York City as the center of publishing. Originally with Ticknor and Fields starting in 1855, by 1868 Osgood had become a name partner in Fields, Osgood and Company. With a list including some of New England's most famous authors, the firm was an established and reputable trade publication house and publisher of the prestigious *Atlantic Monthly and *North American Review. But Boston's 1872 fire, followed by the panic of 1873, cramped the business. The firm sold the magazines, but Osgood merged his still-indebted company with Henry Houghton's house in 1878. He remained there until 1880, when he was forced out and decided to form his own firm. Several of his best known authors, including William Dean *Howells, followed him.

Shortly before Osgood's brief connection with Houghton, Clemens, frustrated beyond tolerance with Hartford's American Publishing Company, struck a deal with Osgood to publish his books. Together they published four titles: *A True Story and the Recent Carnival of Crime* (1877), *The Prince and the Pauper* (1881), *The Stolen White Elephant and Other Stories* (1882), and *Life on the Mississippi* (1883). While Clemens expected little of *The Stolen White Elephant*, which he called, in an autobiographical dictation of 24 May 1906, "a collection of rubbishy sketches," he had very high hopes for the last two books. Osgood had no experience with subscription publishing, however, and achieved only modest success with both. Twain subsequently left Osgood to found his own publishing firm, *Webster and Company. Unlike most business associates, Osgood comes off well in Twain's *autobiography, in which he called Osgood "one of the dearest and sweetest and loveliest human beings to be found on the planet anywhere.... He was a sociable creature and we played much billiards and daily and nightly had a good time" (24 May 1906). But at the time, his disappointment amounted to outrage. When Osgood's firm failed in 1885, Clemens seemed almost satisfied, especially since his own publishing firm was thriving.

With his failure in 1885, Osgood went to work for Harper and Brothers, first in New York and then in London as Harper's agent. While he did try to start another firm of his own in 1891, he died before the depression of 1893 could lead to yet another failure. Meanwhile, Harper and Brothers made a contract with Howells, inducing him to move from Cambridge, Massachusetts, to New York City. Eventually, Harper's became Twain's publisher as well. By century's end, the shift of America's literary center was complete.

PAIGE TYPESETTER. If it hadn't been for the potential profits of the Paige typesetter, Clemens might never have dreamed that *A Connecticut Yankee in King Arthur's Court* would be his last book, and he would doubtless have modified his message significantly. But then, if it hadn't been for the devastating drain the typesetter put on Clemens's financial resources to the tune of $200,000, he might not have had to write any books after *Connecticut Yankee*, either. For better or worse, the typesetter was the albatross that prevented a major change in Clemens's career, forcing him to accept his vocation as a writer when his role as investor came to naught.

Clemens explained his continuing investments in the typesetter as a result of Paige's spell-binding arguments: "When he is present I always believe him; I can't help it." But Clemens needed no salesman to attract him to such an *invention. He had begun his working life as a compositor himself, and excepting brief stints as riverboat pilot and as silver miner, he had spent his career in *publishing. He knew well that there was much money to be made in the industry, one of the nation's biggest, and that typesetting was the needle's eye through which all publishing riches had to pass. It was skilled-labor intensive and therefore expensive. It was also a slow process and liable to multitudinous errors, as each letter, punctuation mark, and space had to be transferred from a copy text to the composer's stick, in reverse order. But from the beginning of printing with movable type in the fifteenth century to nearly the end of the nineteenth, no significant advances had been made in typesetting. The inventor who came up with a better way would be able to print his own money, so to speak.

James W. Paige (1842–1917) hoped to be that inventor. He had taken his first patent out on a mechanical compositor in 1872 while working as a machinist in Rochester, New York. He moved to Hartford, Connecticut in 1875, where he rented workshop space at the Colt Arms Factory. Paige by all accounts was brilliant at contriving complex devices, but his compositor began on the faulty premise that a composing machine should duplicate typesetting as human beings do it. While the human operator of Paige's machine had little to do but punch keys, the machine drew movable type from racks above each key and moved each piece to a track equivalent to a composing stick. The machine sorted type in racks above each key, and sorted used type in bins below from which they were moved to the appropriate racks above. Such a machine required over eighteen thousand parts, many of them movable and subject to wear—and they had to work precisely to keep the machine from jamming. While the machine did, when operating, set and justify type quite well and quickly, its complexity made it break down frequently. Paige spent years trying to "perfect" his fundamentally flawed design, all the while trying to raise the money he needed to capitalize his enterprise.

When he met Clemens in 1880, he convinced Clemens to invest. Spending modest amounts at first—he was then focusing his investments on Dan *Slote's Kaolatype process for printing illustrations—Clemens grew more enthusiastic with Paige as he grew disenchanted with Slote. One of the greatest ironies, though, is that Clemens should have known that Paige's design was flawed; as early as 1867 he saw a machine that set type on principles similar to those that ultimately proved successful. As he wrote from New York to the *Alta California* (18 February 1867):

> I have been examining a machine to-day ... which will greatly simplify, cheapen and expedite stereotyping. With a single alphabet of type, arranged around a wheel, the most elaborate book may be impressed, letter after letter, in plaster plates, ready for the reception of the melted metal, and do it faster than a printer could compose the matter. It works with a treadle and a bank of keys, like a melodeon. It does away with cases of types, setting up and distributing, and all the endless paraphernalia of a printing office.

But having forgotten this glimpse into the future, in 1886 he negotiated with Paige for a half interest in Paige's invention and began spending three thousand dollars per month to support Paige and the machine. He hired Frank G. Whitmore to oversee Paige, and used Whitmore as his general agent to watch over Webster and Company as well. With his business concerns multiplying, Clemens was distracted from his income-generating literary work. Clemens counted on Paige's machine to make him a multimillionaire who would not have to write, but the financial drain of the endeavor forced the issue. Paige finished a working prototype in 1889, encouraging Clemens to believe that his fortune was soon to be made, but the financial strain was such that Clemens was forced to return to writing at a feverish clip, producing a number of poorly conceived and poorly executed stories, essays, and novels, only one of which, *Pudd'nhead Wilson*, continues to receive significant critical attention.

Paige secured a contract to test the machine with the Chicago *Tribune*, a test that, even as it proved the shortcomings of Paige's machine, might yet have made Clemens a fortune had it not been for the competition. Ottmar Mergenthaler had recently invented the Linotype, a compositor that worked on a radically different plan. Rather than set movable type, the Linotype uses steel dies to strike impressions of letters into copper sheets, which in turn are used as molds for molten lead. When hardened, the lead serves as set type, entire lines set in blocks. When a line is no longer needed, it needs only to be remelted rather than resorted. With fewer moving parts and no small type pieces to jam, the Linotype proved reliable. When running, Paige's machine set type faster, but the Linotype's reliability made it faster in practice. With progressive improvements made in the years to come, it served as the primary typesetter for nearly a century. The *Tribune*, in fact, had already put some of Mergenthaler's machines in use by the time it tried Paige's machine. When Paige's proved unreliable in December of 1894, it was without commercial value.

In the meantime, Clemens had found a financial angel, Henry H. *Rogers, to help him deal with Paige. Rogers himself invested, modestly, in the Paige machine, used his own stock plus that of Clemens and other friends Clemens had encouraged to invest as leverage to reorganize the company, and drove Paige from control. From this position of power, Rogers was able to negotiate for the Merganthaler company to buy Paige's patents, which they did to ensure the end to their competition. That left Clemens with the uncomfortable job of recouping not only his own losses, but the losses of various friends he had induced to invest, such as Bram Stoker, Henry Irving, and Dr. Clarence C. Rice. He paid his friends as quickly as he could, and faced up to the need to pay off his many creditors. With Rogers playing bad cop to prevent the creditors from destroying Clemens entirely, Clemens returned to the lecture platform and to the pen, not ever really retiring from writing until he died.

♦ SEE ALSO Business Ventures; Finances, Money.

PAINE, ALBERT BIGELOW (1861–1937). A writer who introduced himself to Samuel Clemens in 1906 with a plan to write an authorized biography. Clemens agreed and used Paine as part of his audience when dictating his *autobiography, efficiently creating what he expected to be his most enduring work at the same time he gave Paine much useful information. On Clemens's death, Paine became, with the permission of Twain's one surviving daughter, the executor of Mark Twain's literary remains, with the intention of maintaining the marketability of Twain as long as possible. With Clara's approval, Paine tried to recreate Twain's image, highlighting his genteel aspirations and downplaying the manic, cynical, and iconoclastic sides.

Perhaps nowhere is this more clear than in Paine's bowdlerization of several of Twain's manuscripts, concocting a story he titled The *Mysterious Stranger* (1916) out of three related but drastically different satires. Paine reduced a biting anticlerical satire into a putative children's Christmas book, complete with idyllic illustrations by N. C. Wyeth and the wholesale removal of the villain of one of the satires, to be replaced by a character not to be found in Twain's works. In other Paine-edited works ostensibly by Mark Twain, *Mark Twain's Autobiography* (1924), *Mark Twain's Letters*, and *Mark Twain's Notebook*, the editorial practice is just as ruthless, though more subtle, consisting primarily of excisions rather than additions.

More influential and damaging as a distortion of Mark Twain's image is Paine's multivolume *Mark Twain: a Biography* (1912). Inasmuch as Paine had access not only to records, some of which he damaged during his executorship, but also to people whom Twain had known, his work still is a source of much raw information. But the distortions Paine exercised limit the book's usefulness.

From the beginning, the book failed in its purpose, coming under attack as biography and bringing Mark Twain under attack as a writer. The perceptive Edna Kenton, for example, in reviewing the biography in the *Evening Mail*, attacked Paine's hypocritical prudery for keeping the best of Twain out of the public eye. She found glimmers of the vitriolic Twain in some of the excerpts Paine published, but denounced Paine for editing after the "usual Anglo-Saxon manner, not for himself, but for others." More influentially, Van Wyck Brooks accepted Paine's analysis at face value in *The Ordeal of Mark Twain*, which attacks Twain for capitulating to what Brooks felt was an attenuated, feminized high culture. Much Twain criticism in the twentieth century has moved in these two grooves, established early by the critical reactions not so much to Twain as to *Mark Twain: A Biography*.

♦ SEE ALSO Censorship; Critical Reception; Mark Twain Papers; Posthumous Publications; Public Image.

PAINTING. In *Modern Painters* (five volumes, 1843 to 1860), John Ruskin denounces what he considers a lack of perceptivity induced by technological progress. He condemns travel by train, or even by coach, because "all travelling becomes dull in exact proportion to its rapidity"; we should, on the contrary, walk when we travel, so that

> every yard of the changeful ground becomes precious and piquant; and the continual increase of hope, and of surrounding beauty, affords one of the most exquisite enjoyments possible to the healthy mind; besides that real knowledge is acquired of whatever it is the object of travelling to learn, and a certain sublimity given to all places, so attained, by the true sense of the spaces of earth that separate them. A man who really loves travelling would as soon consent to pack a day of happiness into an hour of railroad, as one who loved eating would agree ... to concentrate his dinner into a pill. ("Of Many Things," vol. 3, pt. 4)

It is likely that Twain's decision to structure *A Tramp Abroad* as a pedestrian tour gone awry is a response to Ruskin's view, with Twain parodying Ruskin's pedestrianism in a pun suggestive of how pedestrian Ruskin's snobbery really is.

At any rate, much of the book is a deliberate criticism of Ruskin's elitism, of Ruskin's belief, again from *Modern Painters*, in the danger of

> the setting [of] Beauty above Truth, and seeking for it always at the expense of truth. And the proper punishment for such pursuit—the punishment

which all the laws of the universe rendered inevitable—was, that those who thus pursued beauty should wholly lose sight of beauty.... One desert of Ugliness was extended before the eyes of mankind.

Here Ruskin requires of the reader a spiritual education, one versed in Ruskin's own doctrinaire understanding of art; he insists that no spontaneous or conventional reaction to painting is spiritually adequate, just as no expedient mode of transportation is spiritually adequate. The pragmatic, American side of Twain, the one that knew no American could even get to the great paintings of Europe without the aid of modern technology, bridled at Ruskin's snobbery, and much of Twain's commentary on painting is a direct reaction to Ruskin.

So it begins, anyway, in chapter 23 of *The Innocents Abroad*, in which an educated American expatriate teaches Twain to disparage painting of the Renaissance, which Ruskin, a pre-Raphaelite sympathizer who preferred the art of the Middle Ages, disparaged for its *realism. Yet realism—or at least a resistance to what he felt was the false spirituality of Roman Catholicism—was what Twain's art criticism professes. When he did not mention Ruskin in chapter 23 of *Innocents*, Twain was attacked as a philistine for his attacks on the "Old Masters." He chose not to repeat the mistake when he returned to the game in *A Tramp Abroad*. In case his readers missed his satirical gibe at Ruskin's pedestrianism, or even missed Twain's own "primitive" art that taunts Ruskin's praise of the primitive art of the Middle Ages, Twain refers directly to Ruskin in chapter 24:

> What a red rag is to a bull, Turner's "Slave Ship" was to me, before I studied art. Mr Ruskin is educated in art up to a point where that picture throws him into as mad an ecstasy of pleasure as it used to throw me into one of rage, last year, when I was ignorant. His cultivation enables him—and me, now—to see water in that glaring yellow mud, and natural effects in those lurid explosions of mixed smoke and flame, and crimson sunset glories; it reconciles him—and me now—to the floating of iron cable-chains and other unfloatable things; it reconciles us to fishes swimming around on top of the mud—I mean the water. The most of the picture is a manifest impossibility—that is to say, a lie; and only rigid cultivation can enable a man to find truth in a lie.... A Boston newspaper reporter went and took a look at the Slave Ship floundering about in that fierce conflagration of reds and yellows, and said it reminded him of a tortoise-shell cat having a fit in a platter of tomatoes.

If this isn't enough, chapters 48 and 50 finish the job, parodying a critical passage on Bassano done by Ruskin with Twain's famous description of a picture of a hair trunk.

But of course chapter 50 also backtracks from Twain's interest in realism, showing that at least in matters sexual, he would rather have a purified ideal than any blunt reality. He attacks Titian's Venus as "the foulest, the vilest, the obscenest picture the world possesses" not for its nakedness, but for "the attitude of one of her arms and hand."

In this, Twain is not consistent in his art criticism, and in fact, his early appreciation for impressionism suggests that *realism was not at all his primary concern in painting. Instead, he seems to have spent inordinate amounts of time attacking Ruskin and the "Old Masters" because he opposed the pretensions of an educated elite in aesthetic matters. Partly, he wished to carve out the possibility that Americans could be great artists, and that American themes, though not those sanctified by the tradition Ruskin and his ilk praise, were worthy of representation. In having his portrait done by Whistler, he was one of many Americans who supported American art. Partly, too, his attack on artistic snobbery cut closer to home in that, as a humorist, his own writing was not considered artistic by those who cleaved to "educated" standards. In this, at least, whether addressing painting, *music, or writing, Twain was consistent in suggesting that the tastes of the common person were self-justifying, regardless of what any critic had to say. As he put it in his 28 May 1867 letter to the *Alta California*:

> I am thankful that the good God creates us all ignorant. I am glad that when we change His plans in this regard, we have to do it at our own risk. It is a gratification to me to know that I am ignorant of art . . . [b]ecause people who understand art find nothing in pictures but blemishes. . . . The very point in a picture that fascinates me with its beauty, is to the cultured artist a monstrous crime against the laws of coloring. . . . Accursed be all such knowledge. I want none of it.

♦ SEE ALSO Medievalism; Photography.

PARODY. Parody is mockery through imitation, imitation that is slightly distorted to create or to highlight comic elements. *Burlesque is a broad form of parody, broad both in its degree of exaggeration and in the target of mockery. Parody, in the narrowest sense, targets a specific literary or artistic work, whereas burlesque targets a kind. Parody given a moral edge is a device often used in *satire.

Twain often practiced parody in the narrowest sense, imitating specific works. For example, in "A Couple of Poems by Moore and Twain," Twain reprints Thomas Moore's original poem "Those Evening Bells" and then prints his parody, "Those Annual Bills," immediately after. The parody follows with very slight variation the stanzaic structure, rhyme scheme, and meter of the original. Compare, for instance, the first stanza of each:

> Those evening bells! Those evening bells!
> How many a tale their music tells

Of youth, and home, and that sweet time
When last I heard their soothing chime."

These annual bills! These annual bills!
How many a song their discord trills
Of "truck" consumed, enjoyed, forgot,
Since I was skinned by last year's lot!

Parodists rarely make their models so absolutely accessible, because they usually choose targets that are well known.

Twain most often parodied specific works when handling *poetry. His prose writings usually tend more broadly toward burlesque than narrowly toward parody of specific works or authors. For example, in his lifelong play with obituary poetry, he mocked the genre rather than specific artists. Twain's best known burlesque obituary verse, "Ode to Stephen Dowling Botts, Dec'd," from *Adventures of Huckleberry Finn* may have been in part inspired by Julia *Moore's "Little Libbie," but scholars have also proferred other poems as the models Twain drew on. The point is that the structure of Twain's verse is general to a type, rather than specific to an author.

♦ SEE ALSO Humor.

PATRIOTISM. Samuel Clemens was born in a patriotic age, yet the fires of patriotism, or at least the factional loyalties that passed for patriotism, rarely burned very bright for him. When the Civil War began, the cry of patriotism to Union or to state motivated many a man to enlist; it moved Clemens halfway across the continent to mine silver in Nevada. Even there, when local men and women tried to raise money for the relief of the Union war wounded, Clemens mocked the effort in private, even as he publicly supported it.

But to say this is not to say that Clemens was without his own patriotic impulses. Especially in the aftermath of that war, Clemens got caught up in the rush of patriotism, demonstrated most clearly in *The Innocents Abroad*, which mocks almost every aspect of European in favor of American culture, and especially reviles those Americans who willingly surrender their nationality:

> Think of our Whitcombs, and our Ainsworths and our Williamses writing themselves down in dilapidated French in foreign hotel registers! We laugh at Englishmen, when we are at home, for sticking so sturdily to their national ways and customs, but we look back upon it from abroad very forgivingly. It is not pleasant to see an American thrusting his nationality forward *obtrusively* in a foreign land, but Oh, it is pitiable to see him making of himself a thing that is neither male nor female, neither fish, flesh, nor fowl—a poor, miserable, hermaphrodite Frenchman! (chapter 23)

It is in this vein that so much of Mark Twain's work defends American speech and mores against the attacks of Europeans and of Americans who revere Europe over America. Much of the agenda of the two European travel books, *Innocents Abroad* and *A Tramp Abroad*, serves this kind of low-level patriotism, as does the essay "Concerning the American Language," in which Twain explains that the conditions of a culture create a language that is peculiar to that place and time. All of Twain's efforts to capture dialect could be construed as patriotic in this sense.

But in the sense of defending a country, in the sense of "my country right or wrong," Clemens's coolness grew absolutely cold as his life progressed. Knowing that his audience revered patriotism, he often tried to turn the bloody-mindedness of patriotism around from a cosmopolitan perspective. In *Following the Equator*, for instance, he challenges British—and by extension, all countries'—*imperialism by challenging the British monopoly on patriotism. In response to two British monuments in New Zealand at Wanganui, Twain opined:

> One is in honor of white men "who fell in defense of law and order against fanaticism and barbarism." Fanaticism. . . . If you carve it at Thermopylae, or where Winkelreid died, or upon Bunker Hill monument, and read it again— "who fell in defense of law and order against fanaticism"—you will perceive what the word means, and how mischosen it is. Patriotism is Patriotism. Calling it fanaticism cannot degrade it; nothing can degrade it. Even though it be a political mistake, and a thousand times a political mistake, that does not affect it; it is honorable—always honorable, always noble—and privileged to hold its head up and look the nations in the face. (chapter 35)

Such public remarks use the language of patriotism to resist imperialism in the name of country.

Twain used the same tactic more energetically in his attacks on the United States' imperialism in the Philippines in "To the Person Sitting in Darkness," in which he ironically undercuts revered ideas about the American government in order to fire up a patriotic passion against imperialism. But the most energetic attacks he did not publish. "The Battle Hymn of the Republic (Brought Down to Date)," for instance, contains the stanza

> I have read his bandit gospel writ in burnished rows of steel:
> "As ye deal with my pretensions, so with you my wrath shall deal;
> Let the faithless son of Freedom crush the patriot with his heel;
> Lo, Greed is marching on!"

Continued on page 426

Performance

Arthur Miller

One cannot read Mark Twain's anguished record of his daughter Susy's death and its effects upon him without admiring not only his stoicism in being able to write at all on so painful a subject, but his maintaining so fine a balance between a flow of genuine feeling and the restraint of a man trying to stay lucid after a mortal blow to his sanity. He seems always to have been an observer of himself, albeit an often mystified one, as well as of the world. "I was born reserved as to endearments of speech and caresses, and hers [his young wife's] broke upon me as the summer waves break upon Gibraltar. I was reared in that atmosphere of reserve. . . . I never knew a member of my father's family to kiss another member of it except once, and that at a death-bed." And indeed, it was only to ask to be allowed to die that the kiss was given by the dying man.

Twain admits to his feelings, and in full-throatedly doing so he often moves us just before he makes sure to mock himself. But what supports this acerbic distancing is his announced role as a lifelong witness to his experience rather than a participant. I suppose what also keeps his sentiment from overflowing is his incredible truthfulness. One never feels one is being worked over, pumped for sympathy or anything else. He seems to be saying, quite simply, Here are the facts of myself on this occasion. And of course he manages to express this distancing through what might be called his confessional laughter. Speaking of the large prices paid at auction for some of his old letters, and comparing them to the lower prices brought by General Grant's: "I can't rise to General Grant's lofty place in the estimation of this nation, but it is a deep happiness to me to know that when it comes to epistolary literature he can't sit in the front seat along with me." He has not only beaten Grant out but is enjoying it, and that's funny because its truth threatens our defenses against admitting the pleasure of besting someone we respect.

Clemens was an alienated man, but with the difference that he admits to sharing the absurdities which he has observed and often ruthlessly criticizes in others. He seems to have seen his role, and probably the role of literature in general, differently than most cultural observers presently see theirs. He is not using his alienation from the public illusions of his hour in order to reject the country implicitly as though he could live without it, but manifestly in order to correct it.

I can think of two possible reasons that he stops short of giving up on the whole human race, including its corrupted politics; first, because doomsday thinking was not yet the style which would come on after the two world wars, plus the Fascist

421

and Communist depradations and the dawning awareness among the civilized of the physical and psychic damage of racism; and second, because Clemens wrote much more like a father than a son. He doesn't seem to be sitting in class taunting the teacher but standing at the head of it challenging his students to acknowledge their own humanity, that is, their immemorial attraction to the untrue. Nor does he spare himself, except indirectly by virtue of bringing up, time and again and in a host of disguises, the whole matter of lying.

He can't stop his boasting, quickly following up by puncturing whatever balloon he has just inflated. Tracing his lineage, whose distinction in Britain he has just been bragging about, he quickly comes down to earth with "But I am forgetting the first Clemens—the one that stands furthest back toward the original *first* Clemens, which was Adam."

Clemens, a second son, writes as though he were the eldest. His older brother, Orion, was a touchingly inept man who flew from perch to perch all his life and never found one where he felt comfortable, and Henry, two years younger, was apparently a rather dull fellow whose role in the family was to bore their mother with his tedious goodness until she turned for relief to Sam and his pranks, wise-cracks, and unexpectedness. Looking back over his seventy years, Clemens seems to see himself as the preferred child, and maybe this helps account for the air of confident, abundant love we find just below the surface of many of his recollections. If a more skeptical author would be hard to find—"Carlysle said 'a lie cannot live.' It shows that he did not know how to tell them"—he can speak in almost the same breath of his daughter's death in some of the most nakedly painful prose imaginable: "It is one of the mysteries of our nature that a man, all unprepared, can receive a thunder-stroke like that and live." His hard-edged, hard-eyed contempt seems not to have interfered with admissions of grief, empathy, limitless affection and weakness. Perhaps this accounts for the devotion he seems never to have lost among his countrymen. In the end readers love love.

Clemens was always the artist first and foremost, and the artist is a liar who, in Harold Clurman's phrase, tells lies that are like truth. Throughout Clemens's canon there are a number of charming, innocuous-seeming stories which, intentionally or not, are metaphors of the artist's moral situation. There is his story of the mesmerist who performed in Hannibal when he was a boy of fourteen and wanted to stand before the town dripping with glamor. The mesmerist would select members of the audience, put them in trances, and control their actions by his commands. The young Clemens eagerly submitted himself, but unlike others, he could never manage to escape his stubborn consciousness. Finally, in order to astound the credulous audience, he faked a hypnotic state, pretending to carry out the mesmerist's orders. So convincing was his spirited acting that he quickly became a favorite subject for the mesmerist, who obviously knew a good thing when he saw it. But not everyone in the audience was convinced. A clutch of elderly men thought he was faking until in one of his trances he began recalling the details of a long-forgotten theater fire which he had once overheard them talking about, unbeknownst to them. Amazed by his "vision" of an event which only they were old enough to have witnessed, they rallied to his side and helped lift him triumphantly over any doubters in the audience.

But having hit once, he had to repeat. One evening, spotting a local bully who had been making his life miserable, he fell into his usual trance and then suddenly grabbed a rusty revolver off a prop table, leaped from the stage and took out after his persecutor, who fled in terror. Uproar! But the mesmerist assured the frightened audience that the Clemens boy could not possibly have done any damage because he had been under mesmeric control the whole time and would have been stopped by the great mind-pilot before he could shoot anybody. Clemens had now become a veritable star in the mesmerized-performer business, walking proof of the power of hypnosis. "It is curious," he writes. "When the magician's engagement closed there was but one person in the village who did not believe in mesmerism, and I was the one." And here speaks the artist surrounded by his trunks filled with stringed puppets, his technique, and his bag of tricks which sweep the public imagination as mere fact never can. Again, the human mind loves the lie which ironically can be made beautiful in the shape of art.

It needs no special psychiatric sensibility to note that his first subject after this public triumph of his boyhood is his mother, and how he entertained her with his lies. Visiting the lady thirty-five years after these "evil exploits of mine"—and after an unexplained hiatus of more than ten years during which he failed to visit her—he is filled with remorse, not only for having ignored her but for having convinced her, his own mother, with the lie that he was so famously mesmerized so long ago. He resolves to confess himself. The consequence is typical Clemens, and a bit strange.

By this time he had long felt revulsion at his ill-earned fame in Hannibal, based on fraud as it indeed had been. It is very odd, the depth of this self-revulsion at what would seem a boyish prank, and stranger still that he sustained the sensation for nearly four decades. "How easy it is to make people believe a lie, and how hard it is to undo that work again!" Only after much anguish can he bring himself to tell her the truth, in dread "of the sorrow that would rise in her face and the shame that would look out of her eyes," but "after long and troubled reflection" he makes his confession.

Naturally, being Clemens's mother, she rejects the confession, calmly insisting that after so many years he can't possibly remember accurately what happened, and that as a witness to his victory she is sure he earned it honestly and was certainly under the mesmerist's control. Her turning his guilt away alarms him. He protests that he had no "vision" at all of the theater fire as he pretended, but merely overheard the men talking about it some time earlier. And more, the mesmerist's trick of pushing needles into his arm while he showed no pain was also a fraud, for he was in fact in agony, just as he would be now if she stuck pins into his flesh.

But she is tranquilly adamant in her belief in him. "I was nettled, to have my costly truthfulness flung out of the market in this placid and confident way when I was expecting to get a profit out of it." In short, she denies him absolution in favor of his artistic triumph, his power and fame which she loves, and fare more than she loves his picky purity. In effect, she rejects the real him and the bared soul he has offered her. And here is the artist's complicated disgust with his art, the disgust mixed with equal amounts of pride plus the feeling of control over the imaginations of other people and his guilt at having planted images in their minds which he alone knows are hot air molded to beautiful and sometimes meaningful forms. It is all a lie, a lie like truth. Again, there is a certain indefinable sadness an inch beneath Mark Twain's happy art, like a painful longing for some elusive reconciliation which lends it an indefinable depth. There is hardly a story in this autobiography which does not pose the lie against the truth; and the victory of the lie leaves everyone basking contentedly in life's normative stasis. The victory of untruth and illusion simply doesn't matter one way or the other in the long scheme of things, and yet it is important to Clemens that there be honest people in the world.

Mark Twain was a performer, obviously, a man drawn happily toward center stage. Almost from the start of his career he moved about the country from one lecture platform to another, telling his stories, cracking his jokes. It was years before he was taken seriously—or took himself seriously—as an artist, let alone a major one who would be looked to for insights into America's always uncertain moral life and its shifting but everlasting hypocrisies. One has to wonder what would have become of him in our television age, when he may well have found fame as essentially a comedian, like Will Rogers, or a character with his own program, perhaps like Jack Benny or Bob Hope. Sam Clemens did not disdain money, not at all, and TV could have made him very rich, could have addicted him to the compromises that come and must come with that territory, could have fed his appetite for soft celebrity rather than the hard bed of art. He would have been pressured to round the edges of his satire so as to emphasize uplift for the folks, perhaps to spare some fraudulent politician his lash whose subcommittee might make trouble for the broadcasting industry. Or even simpler, he would have been told in very clear tones, as I and doubtless other writers have been told by a network producer, that American television does not want "art." (They pronounce the quotation marks.) And that he must eliminate diversions from the main drive of his stories and simplify his syntax lest the audience lose track of a too-lengthy sentence. One way or another he would surely have ended in a head-on crash on the information superhighway, there can be no doubt of that.

It isn't easy to say how strong his resistance would have been to the suborning of his talent by his own declared wish to capture the big audience rather than settling for a far easier triumph with a narrower and more elegant supportive clique that already agreed with him. That big audience today is facing the TV screen, not the book or the lecture platform. My own inclination is in his favor; I think he would certainly have fallen for the power and emoluments of national TV celebrity, but would have found his way home again. Because he was an artist, and one who fed upon his soul as much as on what he observed, and the call of the soul was the most powerful emotion he knew.

Of course this estimation may be wrong. Orson Welles, another man of brilliance and also a performer, was basically neutered by the American entertainment business, and spent most of his creative powers at poolside thrilling other artists with his culture, his knowledge, and the spectacle of a greatness that was always on the verge of retaking the stage but could not be reborn, at least in my opinion, because it had no spiritual support in a country where few people know enough to want what he could give. All that is certain is that the country by and by would have tired of listening to the Mark Twain Weekly Hour; and if he wanted to remain a national prime-time asset, the bubbling up of his genuine material would have slowed in due time and he would have had to begin clawing at himself, scouring his memories to feed into the television maw, and would have ended in a wealthy, self-contemptuous defeat.

We had Mark Twain when it was still possible to have him as an artist intent on addressing the whole country without having to pay the price of celebrity and the inevitable desiccation of his talent. We had Mark Twain when it was still possible to have him as the celebrity he was and the respected artist at the same time; the culture would support such a phenomenon still. That he might have survived intact the crush of the bottom line of mass communications—which in theory would have attracted him—is not easy to imagine. So the treasure is intact, and our American luck, at least in this case, has held.

Continued from page 420

Again, Clemens seems happy to endorse the Filipino's patriotism while condemning American aggression as mere greed. Patriotism he values over other human motives.

In two other unpublished pieces, he seems to doubt the value of patriotism at all. In "As Regards Patriotism," he says "Patriotism is merely a religion—love of country, worship of country, devotion to the country's flag and honor and welfare. . . . [I]n England and America it is furnished, cut and dried, to the citizen by the politician and the newspaper. The newspaper-and-politician-manufactured Patriot often gags in private over his dose; but he takes it, and keeps it on his stomach the best he can. Blessed are the meek." In "Man's Place in the Animal World," he more explicitly describes Patriotism as a violent alternative to the more important value of universal humanity: "For many centuries 'the common brotherhood of man' has been urged—on Sundays—and 'patriotism' on Sundays and week-days both. Yet patriotism *contemplates the opposite of a common brotherhood.*" So while his early objections to American patriotism derived from divided loyalties between opposed causes, he came finally to object to national patriotism on universal grounds.

♦ SEE ALSO Arnold, Matthew; Civil War; Food; Music; Newspaper Journalism; Painting.

PERSONAL RECOLLECTIONS OF JOAN OF ARC (1896). Most readers of Mark Twain's works find *Personal Recollections of Joan of Arc* anomalous, wondering what interest the notorious critic of Catholicism, of French culture, and of *romance could have in the idealistic tale of a devout Catholic French girl. The key lies in the word "Personal" in the title. As much as Clemens distanced himself from the story by calling it a translation 1of Sieur Louis De Conte's history by a contemporary Frenchman, Jean Francois Alden, and by first publishing it anonymously in *Harper's,* his personal involvement in the tale is what explains the apparent anomaly. While the book follows history, it is not so much the history of Joan as the history of Clemens through De Conte, commenting on disillusionment and a sense of personal failures, both practical and moral.

Clemens felt failure keenly when he first turned to drafting the novel in August 1892. His financial affairs were disastrous and growing worse, with *Webster and Company insufficiently capitalized to fulfill its obligations, and with investments in the *Paige typesetter swallowing money Clemens no longer could afford to lose. The Clemens family was living in Florence (and would stay in Europe for years), in part to save money, in part to avoid the shame of the poverty they felt. The feeling of shame only increased as bankruptcy struck in 1894. In traveling back and forth between Europe and America to attend to business affairs, Clemens came deeply to regret that he had even tried to become a businessman instead of an author. On one of these trips, he pledged to his wife that when he finally worked his way out of debt, when—in his analogy—the anchor would finally drop that would see him safely in a permanent port, he would say:

> "Farewell—a long farewell—to *business!* I will *never* touch it again!"
> I will live in literature, I will wallow in it, revel in it, I will swim in ink! Joan
> of Arc——but all this is premature; the anchor is not down yet.

Here he reveals his hope to become, finally and fully, a literary man, willing to live in the land of fiction and imagination rather than in the hard-edged world of business, where he had discovered himself insufficiently sharkish.

In 1893, Clemens fortunately found in Henry H. *Rogers a financial advisor— and ultimately business manager—to rescue him from his own financial missteps. In his extensive correspondence with Rogers about business dealings, he at first recorded his efforts on *Joan* as the deliberate creation of a commercial property. He wanted Rogers to see him as working his way out of his financial hole. Hence, letter after letter comments on how many words he has piled up, how far into the story he has made it, how much remains to do; these letters alternately show Clemens pleased with his output or anxious over how little he was able to produce. A 2–3 September 1894 letter, for instance, says:

> Joan. I hadn't any trouble there. That is a book which writes itself, a tale which tells itself; I merely have to hold the pen. At 7 yesterday my aggregate on that book for the 6 days was 10,000 or 11,000 words—plenty good enough, considering how much time was daily lost in freshening-up on history, and in thinking. I think the mill is fairly started for a long grind; I hope so, anyway.

Such hopes, in the context of his gloom over financial matters and over the precarious *health of his family and himself, were false. In his very next letter he says, "I drove the quill too hard, and I broke down."

On again, off again, but steadily piling up pages, Clemens wrote as much to keep his mind off his bankruptcy as to make a salable book. As he wrote Rogers on 17 December 1894: "I must go right to work and bury myself deep down in it and among the phantoms flitting vaguely through the mists of the Middle Ages, or there will be a sudden inquest and a verdict of 'died of the blues.'" He helped lift his family's spirits, too, by sharing the pages with his wife and daughters, among whom Susy was a particularly active editor. While Clemens always needed an audience for his writing, the circumstances of this book's production made it almost a collaborative effort between Sam, Olivia, and Susy, who was old enough now to have an adult's reactions, rather than the child's reactions she had to *Prince and the Pauper* over a dozen years earlier.

While writing this book Clemens faced not only the bankruptcy of Webster and Company in early 1894, but the full failure of the typesetter in December. Just about a month later, he finished a draft. On 29 January 1895, he wrote to Rogers from Paris:

> At 6 minutes past 7, yesterday evening, Joan of Arc was burned at the stake.
>
> With the long strain gone, I am in a sort of physical collapse to-day, but it will be gone to-morrow. I judged that this end of the book would be hard work, and it turned out so. I have never done any work before that cost so much thinking and weighing and measuring and planning and cramming, or so much cautious and painstaking execution. For I wanted the *whole* Rouen trial in, if it could be got in in such a way that the reader's interest would not flag—in fact I wanted the reader's interest to *increase*; and so I stuck to it with that determination in view—with the result that I have left nothing out but unimportant *repetitions*. Although it is mere history—history pure and simple—history stripped naked of flowers, embroideries, coloring, exaggerations, inventions—the family agree that I have succeeded. It was a perilous thing to try in a tale, but I never believed it a doubtful one—provided I stuck strictly to business, and didn't weaken and give up; or didn't get lazy and skimp the work. The first two-thirds of the book were easy; for I only needed to keep my historical road straight; therefore I used for reference only one French history and one English one—and shoveled in as much fancy-work and invention on both sides of the historical road as I pleased. But on this last third I have constantly used five French sources and five English ones, and I think no telling historical nugget in any of them has escaped me.
>
> Possibly the book may not sell, but that is nothing—it was written for love.

Much of this self-assessment is true, especially the understanding that it might not sell. It did not, as Clemens remarked in a mild postscript to Rogers in a 14 April 1897 letter: "The Harpers have done first-rate with the old books. Joan didn't take with the public." With no other of Clemens's books did he react so mildly to even modest sales. He did indeed write for love.

But love of what is not so obvious to readers over a century later. Clearly he wrote for love of his wife and daughters. The book's dedication to his wife "in grateful recognition of her twenty-five years of valued service as my literary adviser and editor," makes it clear that much of the love is for a particular woman. What is a bit harder for the modern reader to see is that Clemens wrote it at least as much in praise of an ideal of woman: of woman as pure, innocent, and morally powerful, an ideal that a mere man, as Clemens saw it, could not even understand, much less attain. The book's narrator does not ever comment on the source of Joan's voices, which she claims come from God. He makes it clear he does not see himself as in a position to judge a faith beyond his mere masculinity. Instead, he idealizes Joan as perfect in herself, as a product of the nature he and other children from Joan's village revered in pure simplicity. The church merely taints that pure faith in casting out the fairies from "l'arbre fee de Bourlemont," the fairy tree that the children worshiped and tended, and that is their talismanic symbol of eternal bliss. Joan is the tree's ultimate defender, the one villager in perfect accord with its magic and purity.

That is the ideal of womanhood that Clemens held, almost without change, throughout his life, the ideal, commonly held in his day, that first made him oppose *women's rights, and then support them. In many ways, *Personal Recollections of Joan of Arc* argues in fiction what Clemens said directly in his 1901 speech "Votes for Women"—that, if given power, women would clean up the moral mess made by men.

Such a stance was a simplistic reaction to the more complicated reality of the women's movement, which by the 1880s had given rise to what was being called the "New Woman," one willing to define herself by her own public professional accomplishments rather than simply through her domestic role. In seeking public lives of their own, both of Clemens's older daughters were already by the 1890s challenging his simplistic conception of women's roles and rights, but in expanding that conception to include work outside the home while maintaining feminine purity, Clemens may have been trying to acknowledge and accept his daughters' growth without changing his understanding of who they were.

Nonetheless, the reality of their growing intellectual powers and ambitions confronted him daily, even as he saw himself as declining under the weight of a failed public life as a businessman. Hence, much of the love he expresses in *Personal Recollections* is a love for the past. The narrator's tone is one of unrelieved *nostalgia for a simple purity of childhood, for idealism untainted by the realpolitik of adulthood. As much, then, as most of Clemens's works argue for the importance of watching reality in order to master it, when he turned his mind to a work of love, reality was the last thing he wanted to see.

♦ SEE ALSO Domesticity.

PETROLEUM V. NASBY. Pen name of David Ross *Locke.

PHOTOGRAPHY. In December 1874, at an *Atlantic Monthly*–sponsored dinner of literary notables, Thomas Bailey Aldrich asked Clemens for a photograph. Clemens responded extravagantly by preparing fifty-two photos of himself in order to send one a week for a year. He decided, then, that the joke would be more enjoyable if handled more quickly, so he sent one a day for two weeks before sending a deluge of about twenty on New Year's day. Judging by Aldrich's reply that "the police are in the habit of swooping down upon a publication of that sort," the two men enjoyed the joke. But the serious request that precipitated it was part of a Victorian tradition of exchanging photographs, which were still a recent enough innovation to enjoy the benefit of novelty. Clemens's letters, like those of many of his contemporaries, are replete with requests for photographs and with references to enclosed photographs.

Clemens grew up with this new art and participated in the fads that accompanied it. While the first photograph produced on a metal plate was made in 1827; the first photographic negative was made in 1835, the year of Clemens's birth. Shortly after 1845, when photography was first used for portraiture, daguerreotypy (i.e., the taking of photos on tin plates) became commercially viable and was soon in wide use. The first photograph we know of Clemens was taken in 1851, in Hannibal, when he was an apprentice printer in straitened economic circumstances. That he would spend money on a photograph says much about the allure of this technique. The allure never disappeared for a man fascinated with *inventions. Clemens had hundreds of photographs taken of himself and his family and even made himself the subject of one of the earliest moving pictures. The photograph for Clemens was not just a social novelty or a way to record family history, it was a central part of his professional life in two ways. First, in developing his ideas about writing, Clemens used the photograph as his metaphor for *realism, seeing in the photograph a representation of reality superior to the long-standing literary metaphor of the *sketch. This is not to say that the metaphor of photographic fidelity to life dominated the works of Mark Twain, whose humor more regularly followed in the metaphoric footsteps of caricature.

Second and more important, Clemens used photographs to create *Mark Twain. With a canny sense of self-promotion, Clemens helped fashion the image of Twain by staging various photographs that were then published widely. In particular, the images of himself in his white suit or smoking in bed were carefully crafted to create the image of an iconoclastic yet avuncular sage. He allowed his image to be used to advertise various products, helping to make his image one of the best known in all America. In this sense, Clemens was a trendsetter in using new technologies to create the modern idea of *celebrity.

PIRACY. SEE Copyright.

POETRY. In a 1906 speech to the Manhattan Dickens Fellowship, Mark Twain said:

> I always had taken an interest in young people who wanted to become poets. I remember I was particularly interested in one budding poet when I was a reporter. His name was Butter. One day he came to me and said, disconsolately, that he was going to commit suicide—he was tired of life, not being

able to express his thoughts in poetic form. . . . He put [a] revolver to his fore-head and blew a tunnel straight through his head. The tunnel was about the size of your finger. You could look right through it. The job was complete; there was nothing in it. Well, after that that man never could write prose, but he could write poetry. He could write it after he had blown his brains out. There is lots of that talent all over the country, but the trouble is they don't develop it. (*Speeches* 347–348)

Such a jest would garner more agreement in America today than it would have a century ago, as poetry is in danger of becoming a coterie genre, cultivated in schools and repudiated by the masses.

In Clemens's own day, though, his denigration of poetry was a minority opinion, an opinion voiced in comic irreverence, an outrageous gesture designed to elicit nervous laughter. For America in the nineteenth and early twentieth centuries was a land, if not of poetry, at least of verse. Of the literary celebrities of the generation preceding Twain—Emerson, Whittier, Lowell, Longfellow, Holmes, Stowe, Hawthorne, Sigourney, Bryant, Irving, Cooper—most were known for their poetry, and of the mid-nineteenth-century figures now considered great but not at the time well-known or appreciated, many—Whitman, Thoreau, Dickinson, Melville—wrote poetry. Poetry was the great genre, the genre that would secure an American's reputation as a serious writer.

Poets who turned their talents to writing song lyrics could make serious money. Sharing Hartford with Stowe and Twain, for instance, was the famous songwriter Henry Clay Work, some of whose songs are standards in the canon of American music, and whose popularity depended as much on his lyrics as on his music. It was an age in which lyric poetry had not lost its connection to music.

The great popularity of various poems made them easy targets for burlesque humor, as Twain often rewrote famous verses for different purposes. From the mild reworking of Thomas Moore's poem "The Bells" into Twain's "Those Annual Bills," a lament about how painful it is to discharge debts, to the biting "Battle Hymn of the Republic (Brought Down to Date)" in which Twain satirically attacks imperialism, Clemens's primary creative connection to poetry was through parody. Nothing in parody necessitates any condemnation, though his supposedly mild parodies of Holmes, Emerson, and Longfellow in the *Whittier Birthday Dinner speech were construed by many as an attack on such revered poets.

The many defenders of the Fireside Poets against Twain's burlesque were right with respect to Henry Wadsworth Longfellow. Twain enjoyed a particularly mean-spirited burlesquing of Longfellow above all other well-known and highly touted poets, as seen not only in the Whittier Birthday Speech, but in several other very public parodies, as in his Buffalo *Express* poem "Sorosis," parodying Longfellow's "Excelsior."

> The shades of night were falling fast,
> As through an eastern city passed
> A blooming maid in bloomers dressed,
> With this device upon her crest,
> Sorosis

And so on for several gleefully lurid stanzas, the most striking, perhaps, being:

> "Beware the baleful company
> Of Francis Train and Susan B!"
> This was old Greeley's warning knell.
> A voice replied, you go to—well,
> Sorosis!

At the conclusion, Twain signed the poem "Somefellow," confirming that Twain's target was at least as much the poet as it was advocates of *women's rights. (In particular, the poem mocks journalist Jane Cunningham Croly, well-known contributor to women's magazines under the pen-name Jennie June, who in 1868 founded the Sorosis Club in protest of the existence of all-male *clubs.) A *Galaxy* piece of August 1870, "The Story of a Gallant Deed," has no other purpose than to mock Longfellow by putting a business contract in blank verse "roughly after the meter of *Hiawatha*."

But it is wrong to impute Twain's disdain of Longfellow to his opinion of all the Fireside Poets, at least one of whom came off quite well in Twain's hands. Twain acknowledged an early familiarity with and respect for the poetry of Oliver Wendell Holmes, even to the point of cribbing the dedication to *The Innocents Abroad* from a volume of Holmes's poetry. Twain, then, was not opposed to verse per se. His use and abuse of poetry seems as much to have been an attack on a mood, a result of his discomfort with certain kinds of serious emotion, especially as wrought, or overwrought, in conventional channels. In particular, he usually pushed imitation into bathetic mockery when dealing with romantic or sentimental verse. While his most frequent and arguably best-known attacks on poetry may have been on obituary poetry—as in the "Ode to Stephen Dowling Bots, Dec'd" from *Adventures of Huckleberry Finn*—he also wrote parodies of more substantial, though still popular, verse such as the entire subgenre of sentimental ballads about ocean disasters. His "The Aged Pilot Man," in chapter 51 of *Roughing It*, for instance, mocks Longfellow's "The Wreck of the *Hesperus*" and Henry Clay Work's "When the Evening Star Went Down," while also satirizing Coleridge's "The Rime of the Ancient Mariner."

As uncomfortable with feelings of connection as with loss, he also mocked love poetry, as in his 1892 "Love Song," a bit of occasional verse composed during a visit to a German health resort, which appeared in the St. Louis *Medical Fortnightly*:

I ask not, "Is thy hope still sure,
Thy love still warm, thy faith secure?"
I ask not, "Dream'st though still of me?—
Long'st alway to fly to me?"—
Ah, no—but as the sun includeth all
The good gifts of the Giver,
I sum all these in asking thee,
"Oh Sweetheart, how's your liver?"
For if thy liver worketh right,
Thy faith stands sure, thy hope is bright,
Thy dreams are sweet, and I their god.
Doubt threats in vain—thou scorn'st his rod.
Keep only thy digestion clear,
No other foe my love doth fear.
But Indigestion hath the power
To mar the soul's serenest hour—
To crumble adamantine trust,
And turn its certainties to dust—
To dim the eye with nameless grief—
To chill the heart with unbelief—
To banish hope, & faith, & love,
Place heaven below & hell above.
Then list—details are naught to me
So thou'st the *sum*-gift of the Giver,
I ask thee all in asking thee,
"O darling, how's your liver?"

Bathos is Twain's typical poetic mode, perhaps his typical comic reaction to any situation in which powerful feeling finds vent through conventional forms of expression.

Given his denigration of conventional romantic and sentimental verse it is easy to explain at least some of his poetic affinities, particularly his avid appreciation for the poetry of Robert Browning, whose verse was more abstruse and difficult than most Victorian poetry. Usually as ironic in tone as it was unconventional in structure, Browning's poetry never yielded to Twain's facile complaints that poetry is cliched and bathetic, but the difficulties presented by Browning's verse opened it to the equally powerful charge of elitism. The putative champion of *dialect and vernacular values, Clemens nonetheless also became a champion of Browning's verse, going so far as to give public readings.

In spite of his anxiety about poetry as a genre for expressing powerful emotions, Clemens often turned to verse when he needed to express to himself the emotions that he mistrusted—especially ironic in light of his mockery of obituary verse. In the last years of his life he wrote poems to his dying wife, about the death of his daughter Olivia Susan (Susy), and even about death in the abstract. Some few of these he published, but many others he kept to himself in his notebooks, as his 1905 poem "Apostrophe to Death." The ending of this poem explains much about Clemens's conflicted feelings about poetry:

> O Death, O sweet & gracious friend,
> I bare my smitten head to Thee, & at thy sacred feet
> I set my life's extinguished lamp & lay my bruised heart.
> I worship thee, & thee alone;
> I lay my bruised heart. I worship thee, & thee alone;
> Would kneel to thee, were't meet to offer, where one loves,
> The attitude that shames both him that kneels & him that suffers it.

His sense of shame over his fear of and fascination with death manifested itself in parody, but the depth of his feeling also manifested itself in the very kind of poetry that he spent a lifetime fleeing.

♦ SEE ALSO Moore, Julia; Style.

POLITICS. Given America's current low voter turnouts and professed disaffection with politics, it may be difficult now to realize that, in the nineteenth century, politics was America's favorite pastime. And while elections of *presidents symbolically defined the direction the nation was taking, politics was fought at the local level over local issues in ways our now mobile and electronically connected republic can only dimly remember. In a country weaned on sermons, people saw political oratory as entertainment. As such, speeches were not restricted to the many election campaigns for local as well as national offices; they were as much a part of regular holidays—such as militia musters or Independence Day—as parades and heavy drinking. Indeed, American politics of the nineteenth century had a carnival atmosphere, and as such, the level of discourse was often extravagant and vitriolic, as often satiric as patriotically maudlin. Twain's descriptions of the election rallies in *Pudd'nhead Wilson* are exaggerated, but not by much.

America's tradition of political rhetoric carried over into *newspaper journalism and belletristic literature. This is not surprising in the field of journalism, especially given the partisan biases of most newspapers. It is a bit more so in literature, given that belletristic narratives—sketches and novels—had developed in Europe primarily for a female audience and addressed courtship above all. Not that American narratives, in spite of what some critics have opined, never touched sexual relations, but belles lettres in America developed a very popular tradition of discussing the public sphere, in part because of a nationalistic cry to develop a literature appropriate to America, in part because most American *magazines, the places where most belletristic writing found its first home, were quite explicit in including political writing in their contents, and in part because most of America's writers of fiction were journalists first.

Samuel Clemens gave birth to Mark Twain in newspapers, so naturally Twain often took politics as his subject matter. His political gibes were often as much a matter of personality as policy, as when he wrote "The Petrified Man" to attack Humboldt County, Nevada, judge G. T. Sewall; at least, the attack itself does not make explicit any political rationale, though private letters suggest that the men's mutual animosity was based on their differing attitudes toward the *Civil War. Other times, the politics clearly engendered the animosity, as when Clemens tackled the San Francisco police department for its corruption in such pieces as "Policemen's Presents" (*Golden Era,* 1866) or "What Have the Police Been Doing" (*Territorial Enterprise,* 1866). These were early efforts to attack machine politics in favor of civil service reform, an agenda Twain pursued throughout his life, as in his attacks on the Tammany Hall machine in New York City.

Like most political writers of his day, Twain occasionally addressed particular political campaigns in support of or in disparagement of individual candidates. In "The Secret of Dr. Livingstone's Continued Voluntary Exile" (1872), for instance, Twain backs Grant's reelection by attacking Horace *Greeley:

> Hold on! [says Livingstone] I am a simple, guileless, christian man, and unacquainted with intemperate language; but when you tell me that Horace Greeley is become a democrat and the ku-klux swing their hats and whoop for him, I cast the traditions of my education to the winds and say, I'll be d—d to all eternity if I believe it. (after a pause.)—My trunk is packed to go home, but I shall remain in Africa—for these things *may* be true, after all; if they are, I desire to stay here and unlearn my civilization.

But such pieces are relatively rare. What is remarkable in Twain's political writing is that it tends to address general political issues and the nature of politics itself rather than support particular agendas of particular political parties.

The general success of the *Republican party at the national level did not thwart Clemens—a stalwart Republican himself, by the time he moved East—from attacking corrupt Republicans, as he and Charles Dudley *Warner did, in thinly veiled form, in *The Gilded Age.* No wonder, then, that Twain turned *Mugwump; his biases toward good government over partisan victory were as old as his invention of Mark Twain as the voice through which he could speak his political mind. And this agenda persisted regardless of the changes in his political orientation; whether he was promoting oligarchy as in "The Great Revolution in Pitcairn" (1879) or "The Curious Republic of Gondor" (1875) or radical *democracy as in

Caricature of "pork-barrel politics," *The Gilded Age: A Tale of Today*, Hartford: America Publishing Company, 1873, p. 92.

portions of *A Connecticut Yankee in King Arthur's Court*, his essential concern seemed to be that government be fair and honest.

This concern carried over into Twain's interest in international politics—one of the allegorical aims of *Connecticut Yankee* is to support the hand of the Liberal party in England at the time. Other writings, such as "Stirring Times in Austria" (1898) show his concern that demagogues can manipulate popular passions to create great injustice, whether a government is democratic or not. Much of this material made its way into fiction in *"Chronicle of Young Satan." His concern for good government also carried over into his attacks on newspaper partisanship, as in "Running for Governor" (1870), in which Twain, running for the office on an independent ticket, is falsely accused of heinous crimes by the journals of the two major parties. Twain suggests that politics cannot be fair or honest unless newspapers are independent and honest.

The centrality of politics to Mark Twain's writings helps explain why he seldom pursued pure realism. Twain's political writings follow tradition in their structure and approach, a Whiggish tradition imported into American political discourse from eighteenth-century Britain, tending substantially toward allegorical *satire. The humor of the southwestern United States developed in this tradition. Indeed, if one views *southwestern humor as part of this larger set of conventions it seems less an expression of southern culture and more in the American mainstream. In this sense, James Russell Lowell's *Bigelow Papers* are not that different from Augustus Baldwin Longstreet's *Georgia Scenes* or the many Crockett Almanacs. While all have been Americanized with the particular idiom of particular American places, and thus contribute to a nascent *realism in writing, and while all, in addressing immediate political concerns, have a realistic motive behind them, none is essentially realistic in design. Most American political satire works metaphorically or allegorically, postulating an ideal against which to measure an exaggerated caricature of reality. And while American political satire often uses a homegrown traveler, the traveler motif as a way of providing satiric contrast comes from Europe.

Twain makes this explicit in his "Goldsmiths' Friend Abroad Again" (*Galaxy Magazine*, November 1870–January 1871) by reference to Oliver Goldsmith's *Citizen of the World*, the narrator of which, ostensibly Chinese, describes the foibles of London society from an outsider's point of view. Twain uses a Chinese narrator more narrowly to explore the hypocrisy of America's treatment of Chinese labor in light of its ostensible appreciation of the rights of all human beings. This traveler motif is much older than Goldsmith, going back into the European Renaissance with such allegories as More's *Utopia*; American political satire gave the motif a new and energetic life. Among Twain's allegorical travel narratives are *The Prince and the Pauper*, *Connecticut Yankee*, *The American Claimant*, the unfinished *"Three Thousand Years among the Microbes,"* and arguably *Life on the Mississippi*, *Adventures of Huckleberry Finn*, and *Following the Equator*.

Another traditional satiric motif common both to American political writing and to the works of Twain is the beast fable. G. T. Lanigan, author of *Fables by G. Washington Aesop* (1878), and Ambrose Bierce were perhaps the best known animal fabulists of the day, working the fable's traditional moralism into ironic twists commenting on contemporary affairs. These tended, in good satiric tradition, to treat general cultural patterns rather than specific political actions. Similarly, Twain's beast fables, which tend to be embedded in larger stories, comment more broadly on general rather than specific problems, and the politics tend to be tangential rather than central. The *"Bluejay Yarn"* for instance mentions the dishonesty of politicians only in passing, and the references to Andrew Jackson and Daniel Webster in "The *Jumping Frog*" don't make easy political sense. But the basic thrust of the piece, to exalt democratic values—much like the episode of the coyote and the town dog in *Roughing It*—moves the fable in a generally political direction.

Finally, of great importance to Twain's output are the conventions of political caricature, of exaggerating either particular individuals or, more commonly, of exaggerating a type of individual in order to make a political point. Mark Twain's self-description in "A Presidential Candidate" (1879) is perhaps the best example of this game, though the depictions of Pap, the King, and the Duke in *Adventures of Huckleberry Finn* are not far behind. Certainly the technique of caricature is not limited to political discourse, and equally certainly Twain used it in many humorous, rather than satirical pieces, but the patterns of political discourse encouraged—indeed expected—in American culture gave Twain an obvious and important

437

venue, one that built his skills as a writer and spread his fame to a large audience. In this sense, the importance of politics in forming Twain's style as well as supplying much of his subject matter cannot be overstated.

♦ SEE ALSO Reform.

POSTHUMOUS PUBLICATIONS. Given the large volume of publications still coming out under the name Mark Twain, it would seem appropriate to ask his famous question from *The Innocents Abroad*: "Is he dead?" Dead though he may be, new Twain writings keep appearing for two reasons. First, much of the writing Twain did was in the form of *letters dispersed among thousands of correspondents all over the world. These keep turning up in an unsteady stream. Second, because his work habits were such that he left boxes of papers behind—some of *unfinished works, some of discarded works deemed unfit by Twain himself or by one of his advisors or editors, some of private writings never intended for publication—scholars at work in known archives are steadily editing and publishing what was left unpublished at Twain's death. In particular, the Mark Twain Project has among its tasks the responsibility for publishing all of Mark Twain's notebooks and journals, letters, and previously unpublished stories, sketches, satires, articles, novels, plays, and *autobiography.

Given the chaos Twain left his papers in, often cobbling scraps from one aborted piece to another, it is impossible accurately to catalogue all of this material, and sometimes even at this late date, a scholar looking for evidence to support a particular point will uncover and publish an unknown work or one only partially published before.

As time passes, such events become rarer, but it is nevertheless unlikely that arguments about what constitutes the complete works of Mark Twain will ever end for the simple reason that editorial standards are themselves subject to debate. The *Autobiography*, for instance, exists in four different editions right now, none of which follows Twain's full intentions for the work, intentions that changed even as he compiled the extensive manuscript.

Similarly, many works long regarded as Twain's, such as The *Mysterious Stranger*, are arguably as much the work of editors as of Twain himself. Most of the posthumous publications of new material released before the 1960s have prompted serious questions of editorial accuracy. Early editions of Twain's letters, for example, were significantly yet silently emended.

It is not, however, just the works first published after Twain's death that come in for editorial scrutiny. Many modern reprints of the major works published in his lifetime have significant questions surrounding how well they really convey the impact Twain expected them to have, too. Many editions published during Twain's own life were not fully under his control, leaving modern editors to decide whether or not to include excised passages. However, even modern editions that have reliable texts are not necessarily true to Twain's intentions. It is debatable whether any book Twain published as an illustrated text is really what Twain intended when published without illustrations, as most modern editions are. Indeed, the Mark Twain Project decided that its first effort, in 1972, to publish a definitive edition of *Roughing It* was a failure, in part because it did not include the original illustrations. Hence, the project reissued *Roughing It* in 1993.

Often, too, the words themselves may not be exactly what Twain wrote. As with the letters, many of his books have been silently edited for particular audiences. *Adventures of Huckleberry Finn*, for instance, has been expurgated for children in more than one edition, and these editions are still to be found circulating in school libraries. But even unexpurgated editions are not always reliable, and even the best efforts to determine a reliable text are often controversial. For instance, when the Mark Twain Project released its edition of *Huckleberry Finn* in 1985, it restored the raftsman chapter originally written for the book but first published in *Life on the Mississippi* and left out of the first edition of the later work. The decision to include this chapter could only be argued, never proven, to be in line with Twain's original intention. Thus, an arguably new *Huckleberry Finn* became the standard edition a century after original publication. This new version was based substantially on a careful collation of existing manuscript materials (roughly the second half of the manuscript), working notes, printer's copy, and the first edition. Then, in 1990, the previously missing first half of Twain's holograph manuscript of *Huckleberry Finn* was found in an old trunk. By 1996, Random House came out with a new edition incorporating passages Twain had deleted from his edition. Again, the inclusion of these passages may cast light on Twain's intentions, but the character of the book changes with these inclusions. The editors of this edition make no hard claim that the newly discovered passages should be in a definitive edition of *Huckleberry Finn*, but by including them, they are suggesting as much. It is doubtful whether such an extreme alteration will make a place for itself as the new standard, especially since the Mark Twain Project published in 2001 a revised edition based on the complete manuscript. Regardless, the competing editions certainly breed confusion among readers.

While it may be impossible ever fully to decide on definitive editions of many of Twain's works, it is reasonable to demand editions that explain their editorial principles. What is inexcusable about the Paine edition of the letters, say, or any of a number of popular anthologies of Twain's works is the degree to which editorial selection silently alters Twain. Caveat emptor.

PRACTICAL JOKES. In the part of his *autobiography published in the **North American Review*, Twain wrote:

> When grown-up persons indulge in practical jokes, the fact gauges them. They have lived narrow, obscure, and ignorant lives, and at full manhood they still retain and cherish a job-lot of left-over standards and ideals that would have been discarded with their boyhood if they had then moved on into the world and a broader life. (chapter 11, 1 February 1907)

In typical satirist's fashion, he condemns what he practices, even as his condemnation is absolutely sincere. While the kind of practical joke that relies on physically humiliating someone was indeed far from his repertoire, his published humor often verged on practical jokes. In playing with the border between factual reporting and fictional invention, much of Twain's oeuvre depends on tricking his audiences. His 1870 *Galaxy Magazine* piece titled "A Couple of Sad Experiences" makes an elaborate apology to those deceived by his play:

> When I published a squib recently, in which I said I was going to edit an Agricultural Department in this magazine, I certainly did not desire to deceive anybody. I had not the remotest desire to play upon anyone's confidence with a practical joke, for he is a pitiful creature indeed who will degrade the dignity of his humanity to contriving of the witless inventions that go by that name.

He tries to pass off his hoaxes as *satire, justifying his fooling as educational. Yet when he inserted the names of friends into his sketches, as in "Cannibalism in the Cars" (1868), or in the *McWilliams tales, or when he used his access to the press as a *newspaper journalist to humiliate his enemies, either to promote a cause or to exact revenge, he stretched the bounds of satire—justified as a public service—right to the edge of practical joking.

♦ SEE ALSO Initiation Rites; Tricksters.

PRESIDENTS. As is true of most Americans, Clemens found presidential elections to be both compelling dramas and signs of the health or disease of the American republic. Unlike most Americans, his *celebrity and power as a man of letters gave him access to presidents, enabling him to influence political appointments as well as simply to hobnob with the most conspicuous politicians of his day.

Of course, he gained that access after becoming famous, though his interest in *politics began much earlier, when working with his brother Orion publishing newspapers. Both were active in the election of 1856, aligning themselves with the Know-Nothings. Given this background, it is not surprising that Orion worked energetically early on for the *Republican party and was rewarded with a political appointment in the Nevada territory. By then, Samuel was working as a steamboat pilot. Given that his livelihood depended on north-south trade and on the viability of the South's cotton-based economy, he voted for Bell and Everett on their pro-south, pro-Union platform. His early journalism of the 1864 election suggests some dislike of Lincoln and the Republican party, but he kept such feelings for the most part secret.

Immediately after the war, Clemens's political positions were very pragmatic. As a journalist, he tried to use his influence to secure patronage for himself and his family, and succeeded in getting close to the center of power during his stay in Washington as private secretary of Senator William Stewart of Nevada, who introduced him to then Secretary of War Ulysses S. *Grant. As close as he was to the center of power, his public interest in politics had less to do with the content of the squabbles within the Republican party than with the drama of Johnson's impeachment trial. His dispatches from Washington show almost no partisanship, merely fascination with the political machinations and personalities.

His fascination with personalities never vanished, but his lack of interest in partisanship quickly reversed when he married and settled down. He became a loyal supporter of the radical wing of the Republican party, anonymously supporting Grant's reelection in a Hartford *Courant* sketch of 20 July 1872, "The Secret of Dr. Livingstone's Continued Voluntary Exile," and writing a letter praising Thomas *Nast's campaign of caricature against Horace *Greeley in the 1872 campaign: "[Y]ou more than any other man, have won a prodigious victory for Grant—I mean, rather, for Civilization & progress" (10 December 1872). With the typical fervency of partisan politics of his day, Clemens simply equated everything desirable with the victory of his party's candidate, everything evil with failure. Such certainly was the case with the Hayes-Tilden election of 1876. Responding to Howells's news that he had been commissioned to write a campaign biography for Hayes, Clemens replied, "Get out your book quick, for this is a momentous time. If Tilden is elected I think the entire country will go pretty straight to Mrs. Howells's bad place" (9 August 1876). But he retained some reticence about using his pen to support a particular candidate. When asked by Howells to "come out with a letter, or speech, or something, for Hayes" (20 August), Clemens replied:

> I'm glad you think I could do Hayes any good, for I have been wanting to write a letter or make a speech to that end. I'll be careful not to do either, however, until the opportunity comes in a natural, justifiable & unlugged way, & shall not then do anything until I've got it all digested & worded just right. In which case I *might* do some good—in any other I should do harm. When a humorist ventures upon the grave concerns of life he must do his job better than another man or he works harm to his cause. (23 August)

Such was the explanation for his reticence, knowing that as a humorist he was not taken seriously, and as a satirist, he could attack the opposition but not support his own side directly.

Certainly this was the case in his "Mark Twain as a Presidential Candidate," published in the New York *Evening Post* of 9 June 1879. Something changed in his attitude about politics, perhaps because the Hayes/Tilden election was stolen, as he described later in his autobiographical dictations, perhaps because in the compromise that allowed Hayes's election, the very thing the Radical Republicans sought in the presidency, namely the preservation of Reconstruction, was bargained away. Whatever the cause of his disillusionment, Clemens no longer saw guaranteed salvation in his own party and the political destruction of the country in the other; he instead came to see the need for good government arising out of choosing the best candidate. Hence his parody of the moral quality of any person running for president in parties that favor expediency over platforms; hence his willingness to turn *Mugwump in the Cleveland election of 1884.

During the Blaine-Cleveland campaign, Clemens renounced his earlier practice of participating in the spoils system. He had always actively solicited consulships and minor offices for literary friends and often for his brother. For instance, after campaigning for Garfield in 1880, he helped secure a position for Frederick *Douglass. But as a Mugwump, he saw the spoils system as corrupting, and decided that political support should be given without reference to patronage in order to maintain true independence. Nonetheless, as he described in the 7 December 1906 installment of his autobiography in the *North American Review*, he did work to keep a friend of his in a consular position in Germany.

Clemens's increasing celebrity made him a desirable consort of politicians, but after Cleveland, with whom Clemens became quite friendly, Clemens grew reticent. He increasingly believed that presidents were becoming too powerful, using their celebrity to turn the presidency into an American monarchy. He did not blame the presidents themselves exclusively, suggesting that monarchy is the natural form of government for human beings: "In our blood and bone, and ineradicable, we carry the seeds out of which monarchies and aristocracies are grown: worship of gauds, titles, distinctions, power" (*North American Review*, 4 January 1907). But as much as this installment of his autobiography exhorted the American people to "obstruct these encroachments and steadily resist them" so that "the monarchy can be postponed for a good while yet," he noted in private that the monarchy had already come. In his dictation of 16 July 1908, he said, "For fifty years our country has been a constitutional monarchy, with the Republican party sitting on the throne. Mr. Cleveland's couple of brief interruptions do not count; they were accidents and temporary, they made no permanent inroad upon Republican supremacy."

Acknowledging the collaboration of the American people in their own debasement before this imperial presidency, he mostly blamed the plutocracy of *robber barons—the power behind the throne, as he saw it—and men like Theodore Roosevelt for the moral turpitude necessary to assume the power of kings behind the masquerade of a republic. He accused Roosevelt of buying his election through outright bribery of voters, of habitual dishonesty, of cowardice, of having policies but no principles, of cruelty, of crudeness, of bombast, of megalomania—"He was once a reasonably modest man, but his judgment has been out of focus so long now that he imagines that everything he does, little or big, is colossal." In ultimately rejecting Roosevelt as a president, Clemens passed his final judgment not just on the presidency but on the people who allow the presidency to be more than it should:

> Mr. Roosevelt is the most formidable disaster that has befallen the country since the Civil War—but the vast mass of the nation loves him, is frantically fond of him, even idolizes him. This is the simple truth. It sounds like a libel upon the intelligence of the human race but it isn't; there isn't any way to libel the intelligence of the human race.

At least not when it comes to a presidential race.

♦ SEE ALSO Reform.

PRINCE AND THE PAUPER, THE (1881). On 22 December 1880, Clemens's neighbor and fellow *Monday Evening Club member E. P. Parker wrote, "I want you to do something! Your rank as a writer of humorous things is high enough—but, do you know, Clemens, that it is in you to do some first-class serious or sober work." Clemens must have loved to receive such a letter. Not only had he been delighted to be accepted as a serious literary man by the Hartford community, but also his long-standing anxiety about being a mere comic journalist had steadily pushed him to try his hand at different kinds of writing. So when he received this letter, he took it as an opportunity to ask Parker to read the manuscript of the serious book he had in hand, *The Prince and the Pauper*. Of course, as much as Parker found it to be the kind of book he hoped to see under the name Mark Twain, another of Clemens's readers grew worried merely reading advance notices of the book. Joseph *Goodman wondered, "But what could have sent you groping among the driftwood of the Deluge for a topic when you would have been so much more at home in the wash of today?" Later when the book appeared, he berated Clemens for forgetting not only his characteristic material, but also for abandoning his characteristic style, which Goodman rightly understood to be not only serious in ultimate intention but revolutionary in value.

All three men felt that *The Prince and the Pauper* was a departure for Clemens, but in retrospect, it is easy to see that the book is right in the mainstream of Clemens's characteristic interests and ambivalences, as the history of its composition and publication suggests.

In a letter of 5 February 1878 to Mary Mason *Fairbanks about the manuscript in progress, Clemens wrote, "I have been studying for it, on and off, for a year & a half," suggesting that he had begun this new novel about the same time that he finished *The Adventures of Tom Sawyer* and was already at work on the opening chapters of *Adventures of Huckleberry Finn*. While the notebooks Clemens kept from 1873 to 1877 are lost, we can assume from his working notebooks for 1878 that he first intended to write *The Prince and the Pauper* as a play rather than as a novel, and that his studies were designed not only to give him the necessary historical background for the political events around which this historical romance would turn, but to get the necessary sense of mores, manners, and language.

Indeed, he immersed himself as much in *Shakespeare for the language as in Hume for the history. Not surprisingly, the first literary fruit of his study was the bawdy *1601* written in the summer of 1876. Never intended for publication, except in manuscript among a few select male friends, *1601* is a linguistic tour de force, a long riff on *dialect. In the process, Clemens discovered some of his animosity toward the elitism of feudal society, and, in spite of his professed anglophilia of the early 1870s, a distinctly American faith in meritocracy over aristocracy. These themes were to play out in later years in his mockery of claimants and his vicious satire of feudalism and monarchy in *A Connecticut Yankee in King Arthur's Court*.

Certainly these satirical tendencies found much support in his historical studies for *The Prince and the Pauper*. His preparatory *reading treated not only English history in Hume's histories, it covered the history of monarchy and feudalism more generally in Taine's *Ancien Regime*, Trumbull's *Blue Laws*, Carlyle's *French Revolution*, and in many other historical sources. All of this study was a by-product of his reading of one of his favorite works, W. E. H. *Lecky's *History of European Morals from Charlemagne to the Present*, perhaps the most formative work of history and ethics on Clemens's mind.

Clemens's interests in history, in the idea of progress, in individual *identity as arising out of social conditions, in moral development, and in the burdens of history shape not only *The Prince and the Pauper*, but *The Adventures of Tom Sawyer*, which preceded it, and *Adventures of Huckleberry Finn*, which he wrote concurrently. Not surprisingly, then, all three deal with the passage from boyhood innocence to dawning moral consciousness, and all three deal with discrepancies between individual feelings of compassion and social cruelties. All three are not only novels of development, but are also novels of manners.

Of course, *The Prince and the Pauper* is the only one of these three boyhood novels set in Europe as opposed to America, but again, this is not out of Twain's usual groove, especially considering that his first major work, *The Innocents Abroad*, concerned America's confrontation with its European past, and that another book he composed while working on *The Prince and the Pauper*, *A Tramp Abroad*, treated much of the same subject matter as *Innocents*, but found a deeper satire. *The Prince and the Pauper* is one step on the way to Clemens's disillusionment with Europe even as it is the most optimistic about the potentials for progress arising from historical processes in concert with individual moral growth.

The big difference between *The Prince and the Pauper* and the other two novels is that Clemens was trying hard to achieve a level of respectability that his status as comedian did not afford him. As such he turned to a genre that he had once vigorously burlesqued, the historical romance. As part of his preparation for *Prince and the Pauper*, Clemens read the children's historical romance *The Little Duke* (1854), by Charlotte Yonge, and turned also to Scott's historical romances. Scott's novels in particular served as benchmarks of literary respectability. When initially published, they were among the first novels to break down the English-speaking world's "holy horror" of novels as immoral lies. Scott's insistence on placing heroic, moral action in specific historical contexts helped make pleasant fictions serve socially approved didactic functions. In trying to learn from Scott, Clemens was indeed trying to achieve a different effect than his usual comically iconoclastic one. Perhaps some of the critics' enduring disappointment with the book is that it seems strange for the author of "An *Awful ---- Terrible Medieval Romance" to create an implausible romantic plot set in medieval England, worked out at the end with fantastic deus ex machina precision. Be that as it may, the stage properties of *The Prince and the Pauper*, while on the surface supporting the ideas of rank and privilege, are set in their fantastic motion to challenge the medieval systems of privilege even as they teach something of the history of that privilege.

Clemens may have begun writing the novel in the summer of 1876 while he was doing research on English and European history; he certainly had written some of the early chapters by the next summer and was already testing them among various audiences, as he reported to Mary Mason Fairbanks in a letter of 5 February 1878: "What am I writing? A historical tale, of 300 years ago. . . . I swear the Young Girls' Club to secresy [*sic*] & read the MS to them, half a dozen chapters at a time, at their meetings." He temporarily abandoned the project shortly thereafter when he took his family to Europe, partly to save expenses in the midst of a temporary diminution of the family's income, partly to dig up materials for another European travel book, partly because families of the Clemens's social class spent significant amounts of time in Europe on a regular basis, and perhaps partly to leave the scene of what he felt to be his great social crime, the *Whittier Birthday Dinner speech. In any event, the circumstances of the European trip were not the happiest, vexed as Clemens was by money concerns and preoccupied by the need to write the book that was to alleviate those concerns, *A Tramp Abroad*. His return to America and his return to historical fiction were both happy escapes from a period of embarrassment and drudgery.

In any event, he returned to the project in 1880 after finishing *A Tramp Abroad*, and completed the first draft of the manuscript by September of that year. But obviously concerned about what he perceived as the novelty of the work, he submitted it for review to Parker, Rev. Joseph *Twichell, and William Dean *Howells. Howells assiduously edited the manuscript, cutting significantly, not so much to make the book more respectable, but to make it flow better. In particular, he advised Clemens to cut lengthy descriptive passages, so as much as some critics blame Howells, Fairbanks, Parker, and Olivia for the book's "respectability," Howells, at least, is off the hook.

For that matter, the others probably are, too. After all, Clemens himself demonstrated his own editorial censorship in his choice of topic, his decision to use archaic language, and in his use of test audiences to confirm his choices. In his *autobiography, he reports how he made his own anxiety about respectability into a compositional game. Knowing that his family would read his day's work in manuscript, he would put in "remarks of a studied and felicitously atrocious character" in order to create an uproar, with Olivia demanding the passage be cut and the children complaining about her editing. If, by chance, Olivia missed something, Clemens later cut it himself (*North American Review*, 2 November 1906). But none of these playful abominations ever made it out of the family. By the time he began reading the manuscript to the *Saturday Morning Club, he had cleaned it once. In asking Parker to read it to his family, he was doing market research: "Will you, too, take the manuscript and read it, either to yourself, or, still better, aloud to your family? Twichell has promised me a similar service. I hoped to get criticism from Howells's children, but evidently he spared them, which was carrying charity too far!" (24 December 1880). Parker certainly did not expect to offer criticism. As he put it in his letter of 29 December 1880, "It will give me pleasure to read the manuscript you describe, and I rejoice in your project. I can, at least, find pleasure in the continued successes of my friends."

With responses from neighbors, neighbors' children, and his own family circle, Clemens edited the manuscript once more before he put it in the hands of his publisher. Having given up on the American Publishing Company, which he was convinced had systematically cheated him, he had arranged to have his Boston friend James R. *Osgood, a trade publisher, bring out his works, including *The Prince and the Pauper*, as subscription books. Osgood put the book in production in February 1881, delivering proofs to Clemens and Howells in September, and securing copyright in November, just in time for Christmas sales. Osgood, however, had no knowledge of the subscription business and did not adequately promote the book. The sales were not horrendous—twenty thousand copies had been sold by February 1884, when Clemens's own publishing company took over the job of selling the remaining five thousand copies from the initial press run—but they were very disappointing to Clemens. After all, this was the book that had received almost universal praise in the press for its uplifting character, that had delighted the neighborhood children, that was praised by his daughter Susy as his best book, one that fulfilled her hope that he would "write a book that would reveal something of his kind sympathetic nature, and 'The Prince and the Pauper' partly does it. [T]he book is full of lovely charming ideas, and oh the language! [I]t is *perfect*" (Twain quoting

Susy, "Chapters from My Autobiography" 5, *North American Review*, 2 November 1906). To have such a book not sell out its first run bothered Clemens greatly.

The book was very well reviewed, praised for its attention to detail, its wholesomeness, its high moral purpose, its delightful story. Parker himself wrote the review for the Hartford *Courant*, some sentiments of which he echoed in his letter of 28 December 1881 to Clemens: "It is a noble piece of work. The scholarly reader will see it at once [*sic*] what studious pains you have taken in your indirect but faithful delineation of the manners, habits etc. etc. of the times in which your story is laid." Such, not surprisingly, was exactly Goodman's complaint:

> You went entirely out of your sphere. The laboriousness is apparent every-where by which you endeavor to harmonize irreconcilable improbabilities, to manage the obsolete customs and parlance of the times, and to wrestle gener-ally with a condition of things to which you feel yourself alien and unsuited. And after all you don't succeed. The impression of a skillfully wrought-out improbability is still uppermost when the volume is closed; we feel that all the pomp and pauperism has been a masquerade, and not the genuine article, and we are conscious of not having heard the real language of the age and person-ages, but a stilted imitation that never did and never will have existence out-side of a book.

Critics have traditionally looked to the book's early slow sales as confirmation that Goodman was right to pan it. But the novel has been one of Twain's perennial best sellers, primarily as a children's book. *Tom Sawyer* always appealed as much to adults as to children; *Huckleberry Finn* is not really a children's book at all. But Clemens intended *Prince and the Pauper* to be a children's book, and admirably real-ized his intentions—it has been one of Twain's most frequently republished and translated novels. Adapted for other media, numerous film and television versions keep the work current and popular. As a transitional work in the development of an important writer, *Prince and the Pauper* deserves critical study; as a good story in its own right, it has never needed any justification in the eyes of its extensive public.

♦ SEE ALSO Work Habits; ESSAY ON Etiquette.

PRINTING. When *Adventures of Huckleberry Finn* was in production, a profes-sional proofreader caught an error that Twain, Howells, and several other readers had missed for years—that the canoe, lost in chapter 16, suddenly was no longer lost in chapter 19. It was a problem central to Twain's original dilemma in plotting the novel, that as soon as Huck and Jim found out they had missed the Ohio River in the fog, they should have turned back in their canoe. They did not because Twain conveniently lost the canoe for them. He then had a steamboat run over their raft, after which he set the book aside for about three years. Not surprisingly, the detail of the lost canoe escaped his memory when he returned to the book with new and richer ideas for social satire. The proofreader's good catch allowed Twain to change the offending line from "I took the canoe" to "I found a canoe." Such attention to detail is what printing is all about, and as much as Twain could sometimes be careless as a writer, he owed much of the development of his talent to the skills he developed as a printer. One of those was to pay attention to details of language. That attention to detail stood him in good stead as he developed his *style. The care he usually took in editing his own copy and in correcting proofs helped him develop great artistry in rendering vernacular voices and cadences into print.

The print shops where Clemens learned the trade were not all about setting and correcting type. They were guild shops in the old traditions of labor, where workers learned all aspects of printing, from editorial to production work. Such knowledge helped Clemens negotiate the business side of authorship. The print shop also taught him a complex social reality. That reality intrudes into his writing in the frequent use of metaphors from the print shop and in the frequent use of the thematics of apprenticeship and *initiation, as in *"No. 44, The Mysterious Stranger." Finally, the print shop gave a small-town boy access to the world through print. The habit of small-town printers to scavenge copy from miscellaneous sources brought a wide range of books and journals through young Clemens's hands as he worked. In such a position, education was augmented rather than supplanted by work. Even lacking an extended formal education, Clemens's first work introduced him to the world of letters. This was such a common path to education—indeed, the list of American men of letters in the nineteenth century who began as printers rather than attending college is astonishingly long—that it was generally accepted that those who came into the world of letters through the print shop were fully deserving of their reputations as educated men.

♦ SEE ALSO Industrial Revolution; Labor Movement; Newspaper Journalism; Paige Typesetter.

"PRIVATE HISTORY OF A CAMPAIGN THAT FAILED, THE." This essay blossomed in popularity during the Vietnam War years when protesters latched onto it as an antiwar satire. It may indeed be that, but in a more complicated way than its 1960s supporters understood. Clemens wrote the essay—a partly fictionalized account of his brief 1861 stint as an irregular soldier in a states-rights militia—in 1885 after Robert Underwood Johnson, editor of the *Century Magazine*, asked Clemens to contribute to the *Century's* series of articles on "Battles and Leaders of the Civil War." Clemens had long been interested in the series, proposing to Charles L. *Webster that Webster and Company should negotiate for rights to publish the series in book form. Later, when the *Century* had already published several installments of Ulysses S. *Grant's memoirs, Clemens negotiated with Grant to publish the completed memoirs as a subscription volume, a deal that threatened the *Century's* return on the series.

Clemens did not want to upset any of these possible commercial ventures, even as they were in potential conflict with each other. As he wrote Webster in the summer of 1884, "We want the Century's warbook—keep on the best of terms with those folks," and in March 1885, "Keep on good terms with the Century people. We will presently prove to them that they can't *afford* to publish their war book themselves—we must have it." Thus, when in May 1885 Johnson asked Clemens to contribute, Clemens willingly obliged, sending a comic article that greatly pleased Johnson, who published it in the November issue of the magazine.

Given the reading public's glorification of the twenty-years-past war, and given Clemens's own financial stake in that glorification, Clemens's memoir pulls its punches by making Mark Twain's conscientious objection laughable rather than noble. While making fun of the first person narrator was one of the ploys he often used behind the mask of *Mark Twain, he had more than usual at stake in making fun of himself here. He was, after all, trying to publish the memoirs of U. S. Grant, and Twain felt a need to co-opt any criticism that a former southern soldier would be profiting from the union hero's story. So in "Private History," he made himself out to be much younger and more naïve than he was in 1861 in order to excuse his behavior.

Still, the sketch does suggest contempt for war. For one, it describes how those who stuck with the military learned to become machines. Moreover, the story's one, probably fictional, encounter with killing does challenge war in its essentials. So Clemens did make his pacifist point, but in undercutting his own authority as a commentator, he denied his contemporaries the grounds for taking his satire seriously. Perhaps only a different generation, one distanced from the history of that particular war, could see through the smoke screen.

PROFANITY. In the very religiously observant America of the nineteenth century, to follow the third commandment not to take the name of the Lord in vain was held a bound duty as well as a requirement of etiquette; by the standards of taste that held slang to be a breach that would lead to moral corruption, the idea of profanity was broadened significantly beyond explicitly religious profanation. By the same token, given the culture's sexual double standard that held men to be worldly, capable use of profanity was often considered a sign of manliness and rhetorical prowess. Across the *social class spectrum, breaches of taste, especially the most serious breach—profanity—were allowed to men in masculine company. As William Dean *Howells put it in a 10 May 1903 letter trying to comfort Clemens during an illness, "What you need all the time is some good appreciative contemporary to swear to."

Certainly Clemens, in spite of promises to his mother and in spite of the remonstrances of his devout brother, developed a knack for profanity when working in the mines of Nevada. His letters home to his mother tease her with the suggestion that his ears are at least assaulted by the degrading and immoral sounds of blasphemous remarks, which he implicitly includes through his careful use of dashes to only partially obscure the profanity:

First and foremost, for *Annie's*, Mollie's, and Pamela's comfort, be it known that I have never been guilty of profane language since I have been in this Territory, and Kinney hardly ever swears. But *sometimes* human nature gets the better of him. On the second day we started to go by land to the lower camp, a distance of three miles, over the mountains, each carrying an axe.... [W]e wandered four hours over the steepest, rockiest and most dangerous piece of country in the world.... After we would get over a dangerous place, ... he would draw a long sigh, and say: "Well—could any Billygoat have scaled that place without breaking his ———— neck?" And I would reply, "No, — I don't think he could. "No—you don't think he could — " (mimicking me,) "Why don't you *curse* the infernal place. You know you *want* to. *I* do, and *will* curse the ———————— thieving country as long as I live." (18–21 September 1861)

His 1860s letters to fellow miners, however, are replete with profanity and references to it, as in a 28 February 1862 letter to William Clagett: "Damn the day I left Unionville before there was any necessity for it. For I have been sitting here swearing like a trooper ever since I arrived."

In many ways he learned to swear much more creatively than a trooper, a talent of which he was inordinately proud. In a notebook entry of October 1889, he brags:

I dropped a strong phrase, in the presence of [theater] manager K (some others present.) He rebuked me. I was surprised out of my self-possession for two or three awkward moments; then I said, seriously: "I ought to explain. I have often used profane language in the presence of God. As he has always put up with it, I had an idea that maybe a damned theatre manager could stand it." It caught him unexpectedly, & his sudden explosion of laughter shot his false teeth across the corner of his desk, & they fell at my feet like a trophy.

To use profanity to gain power, prestige, or a business edge was to Clemens a highly masculine art.

This was the context in which Mark Twain tried to negotiate American language, pulling the "vigorous" language of the West and of masculine enterprise into the literary realm governed by eastern standards of respectability and by the highest standards of speech that were de rigueur when women and children were part of the audience.

Twain's writings rarely employ direct profanity, though references to hell and damnation occur frequently through euphemism and periphrasis. But Twain makes profanity itself a constant subject of his writing, suggesting that profanity is a social art worthy of respect for its capacity creatively to convey emotion. References to swearing appear in *"Old Times on the Mississippi," repeatedly in *Roughing It*, and in the *"Bluejay Yarn," in which Jim Baker cites the jay's ability to "out-swear any gentleman in the mines" as the strongest evidence of the jay's essential humanity.

What's more, Twain challenges the basis of the injunction against profanity, suggesting often that the words do not entail the sinfulness of profanity—it's the thought behind them that counts. In the case of Scotty Briggs and the Parson in *Roughing It*, Scotty uses slang, including profanity, without self-consciousness, without intent to profane the "sacred proprieties." When he becomes a Sunday school teacher, his ability to speak to his charges "in a language they understood" secures more converts than would a purely respectable language.

Twain used his disagreements with his wife over his strong language to make similar points. For instance, he once mocked his wife for the repressed purity of her speech. In a letter to Howells, he wrote of Olivia's reaction to the news that the Howells would have to visit the Warners in Hartford before they could visit the Clemenses:

> When Mrs. Clemens read about your being so "many promises deep," she made that noise which one creates by suddenly detaching the tongue from the roof of the mouth, & which expresses aggravation. That did not deceive the Recording Angel a bit; I knew the entry that was being set down in the great book opposite the name Livy L. Clemens, to wit: "March 24, 1880—at breakfast—unarticulated remark reflecting the thought, '*Damn* those Warners.'"
>
> To get this woman to give up the baneful habit of underhanded swearing, is one of those things which I have long ago been obliged to give up, as being among the reforms which cannot be accomplished. But the poor children don't suspect, I thank God for that.

Making the same point from an opposite tack, he describes in his *autobiography the first time his wife overheard him swear energetically. To punish him, she repeated his remarks,

> the language perfect, but the expression velvety, unpractical, apprentice-like, ignorant, inexperienced, comically inadequate, absurdly weak and unsuited to the great language. In my lifetime I had never heard anything so out of tune, so inharmonious, so incongruous, so ill-suited to each other as were those mighty words set to that feeble music. I tried to keep from laughing, for I was a guilty person in deep need of charity and mercy. I tried to keep from bursting, and I succeeded—until she gravely said, "There, now you know how it

sounds." Then I exploded; the air was filled with my fragments, and you could hear them whiz. I said, "Oh Livy, if it sounds like *that* I will never do it again!" (*North American Review,* 2 November 1906)

PROGRESS. An August 1847 article in *Scientific American* entitled "The Utility and Pleasures of Science" captures one dominant strand of American thinking:

> The progress of human knowledge has accomplished within a century revolutions in the character and condition of the human race so beautiful and sublime as to excite in every observing mind feelings mingled with the deepest admiration and astonishment. No age has illustrated so strongly as the present the empire of mind over matter. . . . It is a happy privilege we enjoy of living in an age, which for its inventions and discoveries, its improvement in intelligence and virtue, stands without a rival in the history of the world.

Twain voices a similar opinion frequently in his career, which began in Enlightenment optimism that science, both pure and applied, would lead to the ultimate moral as well as physical progress of human beings. From his 1850s descriptions of the waterworks in New York and Philadelphia right up to his essay "About All Kinds of Ships," he expressed delight in technology and suggested that the improvements in the physical conditions of human beings allowed for a corresponding improvement in their moral being as well. Nowhere does he make this case more strenuously than in *The American Claimant,* in which he incorporated his rebuttals to Matthew *Arnold's attacks on American civilization.

In his speech "On Foreign Critics" (1890), he focuses less on technology than on moral progress, but the thrust of his argument still supports the idea that progress is possible:

> What is a "real" civilization? . . . Let us say . . . that any system which has in it any one of these things, to wit, human slavery, despotic government, inequality, numerous and brutal punishments for crimes, superstition almost universal, ignorance almost universal, and dirt and poverty almost universal— is not a real civilization, and any system which has none of them, is. If you grant these terms, one may then consider this conundrum: How old is real civilization? The answer is easy and unassailable. A century ago it had not appeared anywhere in the world during a single instant since the world was made. If you grant these terms—and I don't see why it shouldn't be fair, since civilization must surely mean the humanizing of a people, not a class—there is today but one real civilization in the world, and it is not yet thirty years old. We made the trip and hoisted its flag when we disposed of our slavery.

Clemens's faith in progress to this point was buttressed by his extensive reading in *history, especially in W. E. H. *Lecky's *History of European Morals*, and while Lecky's book insisted on the power of technology to make democracy possible by equalizing power and eliminating poverty, its primary focus was on moral development, a focus Twain's works share.

This faith in moral progress was in keeping with a liberal Protestant progressivism, very much in keeping with the ancient Christian idea of the progress of souls. Liberal, sentimental Christians, however, insisted that this progress was not simply a function of a Calvinist conversion experience, but was a moral and practical concern that required ameliorating the human condition to create a version of heaven on earth. Thus, liberal Protestants were incorporating ideas of the Enlightenment, including the idea of *evolution.

In this sense, progress was defined in opposition to Romantic ideas of "primitive" virtue, ideas that gave rise to popular *medievalism, which Twain regularly opposed, or to the idea of the "Noble Savage." Promoters of progress, then, were quick converts to theories of evolution, and many promoted *imperialism as a progress of civilization. Twain's early embrace of this idea of progress led him to support America's policy of Indian removal, support that Twain voiced explicitly in his letters to the *Alta California* and over the course of his career in a series of attacks on James Fenimore Cooper, including passages attacking *Native Americans in *Roughing It* and in his two later essays on Cooper's works, *"Fenimore Cooper's Literary Offenses" (1895) and "Fenimore Cooper's Further Literary Offenses" (1895). His later turn against imperialism signaled his substantial disillusionment with the idea of moral progress.

His turn against this idea can substantially be explained by his motivations for embracing the idea of progress in the first place. As much as the idea of progress is central to American culture, and as much as it fits with a part of Christian belief, the *Calvinism of Clemens's youth is predicated on a belief in the total depravity of all things natural and the insufficiency of human powers to cause "regeneration." In this sense, belief in moral progress is the sin of pride, and the jeremiad, a sermon taking believers to task for backsliding from appropriate humility, is, paradoxically, as deeply resonant in the American public consciousness as is the idea of progress. Clemens worked hard to shake this Calvinist belief in fundamental moral depravity, and his turn to an Enlightenment idea of progress, in which human control of nature is inextricably bound to moral as well as physical progress, regularly served him in his efforts to free himself from Calvinist dogma.

A journal entry of late 1881 or January 1882 suggests as much:

Men are more compassionate/(nobler)/magnanimous/generous than God; for men forgive the dead, but God does not. Men are more noble-natured than

453

Steam printing—

Railway—

Telegraph

Telephone

Stereoscope

Anaesthetics

(Electric light. & motors (future)

Steamship.

Sewing machine

Photography.

Wooden legs.

14 photos in a second.

Chromos.

Geology. Paleontology. destroyed Genesis

There is a difference between invention & application.—The ancients invented; the modern spirit invents & applies. Destruction of the personal devil.—a great victory. Destruction of infant damnation.

Pneumatic tubes.

The medical & surgical science.

Here Twain postulates human *inventions as breaking down a Calvinist idea of God and religion, and lumps physical with moral ideas in his category of compassionate and generous inventions.

But his persistent deep affinity with a Calvinist idea of depraved human nature would not be appeased by simple appeals to the technological sublime. As much as the ideas sketched in this notebook entry found their way into *A Connecticut Yankee in King Arthur's Court*, the novel's cataclysmic ending reveals Twain's sense that progress may not be all that it's cracked up to be. This concern became pervasive in his late works, as he developed an idea of cultural relativism in *Following the Equator*, and began to see greed, a lust for power, a willingness to defer to the powerful, and an abiding hunger for approval as ineradicable human traits that impeded fundamental moral progress. Thus, several pieces written in 1901, such as "To the Person Sitting in Darkness," "The Battle Hymn of the Republic (Brought Down to Date)," "As Regards Patriotism," and "The *United States of Lyncherdom," all suggest that human moral progress will always falter, backsliding into savagery. As he puts it in the mouth of Satan in *"Chronicle of Young Satan," by the end of the nineteenth century "the pagan world will go to school to the Christian: not to acquire his religion, but his guns." Moral and technological progress have, by the late 1890s, been divorced in Twain's imagination.

Nonetheless, Twain tried to have it both ways in *What Is Man?* Even though he there argues that human beings are mechanical contrivances, incapable of inventing anything because totally controlled by external circumstance, he argues that human beings can use their worst weakness, the desire for approval, to lead to gradual moral amelioration. Through scrupulous training "upwards," the entire culture can progress, more or less in spite of human nature. In this deterministic version of progress, Twain cribs many of the ideas of Herbert *Spencer, and like Spencer, he sees this new kind of biological and moral determinism as the only satisfactory rejoinder to the fundamental conservatism of Calvinism.

♦ SEE ALSO Industrial Revolution; Nostalgia; Religion.

PSEUDONYMS AND PERSONAS. Nineteenth-century humorous writers conventionally used comically significant pseudonyms to distinguish the comic character from its author. The practice is similar to the use of the *frame narrative as a way of insulating the author from the socially suspect, often lower-class behavior of the comedian, and also gives the audience cues to the interpretation of the comedy. Robert Henry Newell's "Orpheus C. Kerr" (a pun for "office seeker"), Henry Wheeler Shaw's "Josh Billings," Clemens's Nevada friend William *Wright's "Dan DeQuille" (for dandy quill), and Charles Farrar *Browne's "Artemus Ward" (after a Revolutionary War general, Artemas Ward) all served these purposes.

Clemens learned, especially from Ward, the commercial value of a single pseudonym, which he cultivated when he finally settled on *"Mark Twain." Indeed, his book contract with the American Publishing Company dated 22 June 1872, stipulates that if Clemens wrote a book on the diamond mines of South Africa under the name "Mark Twain" he would receive an 8.5 percent royalty, but if were to use a different nom de plume, he would receive only 5 percent. Such a concrete difference was persuasive, even at times when he worried that his pseudonym would detract from the literary value of his writings, as when he reluctantly published "A *True Story, Repeated Word for Word as I Heard It" in The *Atlantic Monthly under the name "Mark Twain."

Clemens went through several pseudonyms before "Twain," including "W. Epaminondas Adrastus Perkins," "W. Epaminondas Adrastus Blab," "Rambler," "Grumbler," "Thomas Jefferson Snodgrass," and "Josh." After finally settling on "Mark Twain," he also invented the persona of *McWilliams as a first person narrator who often speaks for Clemens from behind the Mark Twain mask.

PUBLIC IMAGE. While the *Mark Twain persona served Samuel Clemens's psychological needs in sparking his creativity, giving him leverage on his culture and a certain mental and moral freedom to explore ideas beyond the pale of Victorian society, he cultivated it primarily to serve his professional needs. Comic personas were a convention of the literary world when Clemens first became Mark Twain; what is extraordinary is the way Clemens expanded the value of a comic *pseudonym into a commercial image. He borrowed pages from P. T. *Barnum's book of tricks, turning almost anything he did publicly as Mark Twain into a publicity stunt, even if it served him differently in his private life as Samuel Clemens.

For instance, he and Joseph *Twichell regularly took long rambling walks, during which they talked, talked, talked, talked. It was the essential activity of their deep friendship. Nonetheless, when the two of them decided to walk to Boston from Hartford in November 1874, Clemens used his lecture agent, James Redpath, to alert the world. He telegraphed Redpath: "Rev. J. H. Twichell and I expect to start at 8 o'clock Thursday morning, to walk to Boston in 24 hours—or more. We shall telegraph Young's Hotel for rooms for Saturday night, in order to allow for a low average of pedestrianism." Redpath of course gave the telegram to the press, and the Associated Press documented the journey, making sure its correspondent papers across the country could publish accounts of Twain's progress. This was the perfect opportunity for Clemens to project Twain as lazy jokester. After two days of walking, he telegraphed Redpath, "We have made thirty-five miles in less than five days. This demonstrates the thing can be done. Shall now finish by rail. Did you have any bets on us?"

Even though Clemens had a proprietary right in his name and image, he freely let businesses use his name to endorse their products. For instance, Clemens let the Mark Twain name be associated with packaged wheat flour, with cigars, with whiskey. Henry Ward *Beecher had already broken the endorsement ground by taking money to endorse Pears' soap. Clemens was less concerned about the immediate cash than the free advertising. He knew that it was important not to flood the market with his product, but that his product's value would slip if he fell too far or too long out of the public eye. So he appreciated pervasive advertisement on products.

He was a master at manipulating the press, working interviews always to his satisfaction. He also frequently wrote letters to newspaper editors, knowing that they would be published. Early in his career, when he cared deeply about a cause, he would either submit such letters under his own name or anonymously, worried that the humorist Mark Twain would carry no serious weight. But as his career advanced, he realized that *celebrity carried its own sway. He thus worked his image more broadly, not just as America's funny fellow, but as political commentator, as family man, as man of letters, as international diplomat, as philosopher, as quintessential American.

All of these images have endured. *National Geographic* in September 1975, without concern about potential disagreement, could title an article "Mark Twain:

Mirror of America." Perhaps a manufactured image is the best mirror of America; at least it is an image many Americans, in their great diversity, use as an icon of their ideas of Americanness. Twain's image appears regularly in high and popular culture, alluded to in everything from serious literature to movies like *It's a Wonderful Life* and television shows like *Star Trek: The Next Generation*. If a writer can put a Mark Twain spin on a story, so much the better, as the San Francisco *Chronicle* tried to do in its coverage of the "Heaven's Gate" mass suicide in its 6 April 1997 issue. In its way, this journalistic reach was as bizarre as the events themselves.

Writers and storytellers not surprisingly gravitate toward Twain; what's a bit more surprising is the breadth of the image's appeal. Americans regularly attach his name to products for sale, including such unlikely candidates as pizza and banking services (though why anyone would put money in the Mark Twain Bank is a deep mystery). More importantly, his name is attached to any kind of idea that anyone wants to promulgate. Because he wrote and spoke voluminously and publicly for about half a century, he weighed in on almost every imaginable issue, often reversing ground over the course of his career. As such he is eminently quotable and has become the political darling of anyone with an axe to grind, and if he didn't say something usable, it is easy enough to find a *false attribution that will serve as well. He is used either to defend or disparage capitalism, labor, communism, revolution, American patriotism, or just about any cause imaginable simply because his image and sayings are so recognizable and so quickly convey authority. Sometimes, however, that is precisely why he and his books come under attack. Inasmuch as he is often considered the archetypal American man, those who see America's flaws are quick to use his image as a lightning rod for their discontent. Many, for example, hold him to be the paradigmatic American racist, even while others see in him a prophet of antiracism.

The image of Twain as a person who celebrates leisure is at least as popular as the image of the elder statesman whose political pronouncements carry weight. *Tom Sawyer is one of America's—and perhaps the world's—favorite images of boyhood, and the elderly Mark Twain's picture is regularly juxtaposed with an idealized Tom, suggesting, as Twain himself often publicly implied, that he and Tom Sawyer are one. In private, Clemens denounced Tom Sawyer as a "one-horse" character, but in public, he played the Tom Sawyer card with great finesse.

Twain's images as iconoclast and as devoted family man also seem able to coexist in the enduring image of Twain. On the one hand, the cigar smoking, whiskey-toting, western rowdy image appeals to many readers, readers who have kept "1601—Conversation as It Was in the Time of the Tudors" and other Twainian *off-color humor alive and well, among the most talked about, though not most readily found, of Twain's writings. On the other hand, few used bookstores that carry any Twain lack copies of *The Family Mark Twain*, a collection of his works deemed uncommonly wholesome. To the audience for such a collection, the image of Twain as devoted father and husband appeals. Of course, consumers of these two different images often disparage one another. The partisans of Twain the iconoclast often blame Olivia Langdon *Clemens for censoring Twain, thereby crippling him. Such an image misses the complexity of Clemens's own ambivalence about Victorian culture and helps such readers miss the persistent Victorian paradoxes in our own day. At the same time, the purified family Twain misses out on the tortured feelings of each of his close relations as they individually and collectively tried to negotiate the ideal image of family promulgated by Victorian society against the ideal of American individualism. Simplified images prevent us from seeing the real value to us of the complex life and art of Samuel Clemens as Mark Twain.

Nonetheless, Clemens was so effective at giving Americans what they want that many different kinds of Americans have adopted some image of Twain as a favorite emblem. It seems that Clemens's skill in manufacturing an image was so great that his portrayal still has more resonance in the popular imagination than the picture produced by half a century of painstaking scholarship.

♦ SEE ALSO Mark Twain Company and Mark Twain Foundation.

PUBLISHING INDUSTRY. Throughout Samuel Clemens's life, publishing was one of the top five largest American industries. The industry changed significantly over that time, and the changes had a profound impact on Mark Twain's career. At the beginning of his life, publishing, like most American industries, was radically decentralized, with almost every small town having at least one printer who published a newspaper and town directories, and handled the printing needs of the community. Such printers usually also worked as stationers. Samuel Clemens began his working career in such print shops, and learned attitudes toward labor and business in this artisanal climate.

Book publishing was international in scope, however, and small printers usually did not publish books. By the time of Clemens's birth, book publishing in the United States was concentrated in five cities: Boston, Hartford, New York, Philadelphia, and Cincinnati. By the nineteenth century's end, New York was the acknowledged center of the book publishing industry. At century's beginning, the primary book market was in religious texts, but a growing interest in novels, histories, travel narratives, and educational texts mirrored changing attitudes toward *religion, *leisure, *education, and the arts generally. The nation's increasing appetite for books of all kinds pushed commercial book publishers to the forefront of the industry by the end of the century.

The revolutions in transportation and communication that developed over the middle of the century, coupled with improvements in printing technology, radically changed the publishing industry. Transportation and communication improved national markets; developments in press and binding machinery as well as in techniques for producing inexpensive paper enabled huge economies of scale that made book and *magazine publishing possible in large orders, and that made large-circulation daily newspapers possible as well. Consequently, publishing, like most industries, became concentrated into fewer hands as large concerns forced small ones out of business. With advances in size came the need for specialization, and publishers split editorial, sales, and production. In fact, there ceased to be a necessary connection in a single house between editorial work and printing. While old publishers, like Harper & Brothers, continued for some time to stay in the printing as well as publishing business, many new publishers were merely editorial and sales agencies that farmed out press and bindery work.

Such was the case with most of the publishers Clemens contracted with over the course of his book publishing career, for better and for worse. On the one hand, this division of labor made it possible for a publisher to be much more flexible in responding to new markets. On the other, economic downturns left publishers in narrow niches with no diversification and little or no physical plant as part of their capitalization. The evaporation of a market would mean the loss of all capital and goodwill, totally bankrupting many a publisher.

The history of the American publishers for Mark Twain's books contains many a bankruptcy. Charles Henry Webb, who published Twain's first book, *The Notorious Jumping Frog of Calaveras County*, lacked the resources effectively to promote the book. Twain's second publisher, the American Publishing Company, thrived under Elisha *Bliss, but by the 1890s, under Elisha's son, Frank Bliss, the company was struggling. The problem was that *subscription publishing itself was no longer an economically viable system. James *Osgood, the publisher Clemens turned to after he left the American Publishing Company and before he formed his own imprint, went bankrupt as he tried to straddle the worlds of trade and subscription publishing. *Webster and Company, which Clemens formed himself after Osgood's failures with his books, had a brief flowering in the 1880s, before quickly running aground in the 1890s because it was undercapitalized and had taken on too many subscription commitments at exactly the moment that trade publishing began to out-compete subscription publishing. Even Harper & Brothers, the company that Twain went to in his last years, struggled through the last years of the century, though it righted itself to survive as an independent publisher until the 1980s.

In spite of the volatility, there was much money to be made in publishing, though at the beginning of Twain's career, writers realized relatively little of that money. Printing may have been considered an industry, but writing was considered a gentlemanly avocation. *Newspaper journalism helped change that, with popular columnists on large dailies, particularly in New York City, being among the first American writers able to earn large incomes for their writing alone. Book publishing followed as the market expanded into a national one, and by the end of the century, when American magazines were publishing large quantities of original material, writing for magazines became quite lucrative. The arc of Mark Twain's career follows this pattern, beginning in journalism, moving into book publishing, and then balancing between magazine articles and books.

Part of the lag in pay for writers was an outgrowth of a *social class hierarchy in publishing. The small market literary magazines like the *North American Review and The *Atlantic Monthly were the organs of greatest prestige, but the prestige that seemed a corollary to small circulations meant low rates of pay for the most part. The larger circulation periodicals, the books sold by subscription, and the many dime novels paid much more but gave their authors little or no status. Twain's own career was one that helped modify these distinctions, but the lack of prestige that attended his large sales was always a source of anxiety to both him and his wife. Indeed, in the 1890s, when the lower prestige Cosmopolitan magazine offered to pay Twain large sums for various articles, he and his wife debated whether it was an appropriate venue for him, Olivia writing, "I should greatly prefer appearing in the Century or Harpers" (16 April 1893). But money had its attractions. As Clemens put it in a letter to his business manager, Fred J. Hall, "I like the Century and Harper's, but I don't know that I have any business to object to the Cosmopolitan if they pay as good rates" (3 February 1893).

Cosmopolitan could in fact pay better rates because it found a formula for making more money than the staid old monthlies while putting pressure on the older journals' circulations. Harper's and the Century Magazine cost thirty-five cents per copy, whereas Cosmopolitan, following McClure's lead in 1893 and joining other magazines like Collier's and Munsey's, dropped to fifteen cents and then to ten shortly thereafter. These cheaper monthlies made their profits by selling much advertising, and their lower rates helped them build huge circulations—at the expense of the more respectable competition. Still, while Cosmopolitan in particular had made strenuous efforts to be on par with the older journals, hiring William Dean *Howells as editor in December 1891 (though he quit by June 1893) and buying work from the best of America's writers, its equal flair for the provocative and scandalous made it, like the other ten-cent monthlies, less respected among America's literary and culture elites.

Clemens met and liked Cosmopolitan's owner, John Brisben Walker, in April 1893, while Howells was still editor. That personal contact, plus the high sums Walker was willing to pay, convinced Clemens to publish in Cosmopolitan and to try to entice Walker to buy his share of Webster and Company. Walker wisely stayed out of the firm, but the high prices he paid for Twain's work—eight hundred dollars, for example, for "The Esquimaux Maiden's Romance"—helped Clemens significantly in the dire financial pinch of 1893. Still, Harper's, the Century, and the North American Review were his preferred venues in his later years.

While most of Mark Twain's sales, *celebrity, and income were made in the United States, the characteristics of international publishing had a significant impact on his career. Much of that impact was negative. Given the lack of effective international *copyright, Mark Twain lost income on sales of pirated books through much of the English speaking world. The pinch came especially from Belford & Brothers publishers in *Canada, who specialized in pirating American authors and then selling the books they legally printed in Canada back across the border into the United States. British publisher John Camden Hotten was another foreign publisher who took advantage of copyright to steal much of Twain's early work. To prevent Hotten from continuing his piracy, Clemens contracted with George Routledge from 1871 to 1876. After Hotten's death in 1873, the much more scrupulous Andrew Chatto bought the firm. Before the publication of *The Adventures of Tom Sawyer*, Chatto approached Clemens with an offer better than that of Routledge, and Chatto's firm, Chatto & Windus, then became, under British copyright law, Twain's British publisher. This arrangement secured Clemens royalties on books Hotten already had published, on ones Chatto bought from Routledge (excluding *The Innocents Abroad*), as well as on every subsequent Mark Twain book. This relationship proved so productive that, for many years, British royalties made up about a quarter of Clemens's annual royalty income.

Chatto and Routledge were not the only publishers outside the United States who paid Clemens for Mark Twain's books. Leipzig publisher Christian Bernhard von Tauchnitz approached Clemens for the rights to issue English language editions of Twain on the continent for modest fees. As Clemens explained the arrangement to Howells:

> Tauchnitz called the other day—a mighty nice old gentleman. He paid me 425 francs for the Innocents—I think he paid me about 6 or 700 fr for Tom Sawyer (it being new); he is going to print Roughing It by & by, & has engaged advanced sheets of my new book. Don't know what he will pay for the two latter—I leave that to him—one can't have the heart to dicker with a publisher who won't steal. (15 April 1879)

While these sums were hardly more than pocket money for Clemens and his family, considering that Tauchnitz could have more easily—and profitably—pirated the works, Clemens was content to take anything.

In spite of the tendency in publishing, as in so many other industries, toward concentration into fewer large companies, it is worth noting that almost every one of the publishing firms Clemens dealt with, in newspaper, magazine, or book publishing, was run by its founder or by its founding family. Clemens preferred all his life to take business, as he took politics, on a very personal level. So in spite of the large scale and impersonal forces affecting the *economy at large, and even though publishing was as affected by those forces as any industry, Clemens never was forced to see his work in any but the very personal terms he preferred. As much, then, as he was at the forefront of changing literary tastes, and as much as he preferred to consider writing to be vocational rather than avocational, he was able to live the myth of the individual republican businessman as long as he stayed in the gentlemanly business of publishing.

PUDD'NHEAD WILSON AND THOSE EXTRAORDINARY TWINS (1894). Like most of the Twain novels now taken seriously, *Pudd'nhead Wilson* is notorious for and considered fascinating because of its discontinuities of plot and theme—exactly the opposite traits praised in most novels. As Twain himself wrote in the preface to *Those Extraordinary Twins* about this strangest of Twain's novels:

> A man who is not born with the novel-writing gift has a troublesome time of it when he tries to build a novel. I know this from experience. He has no clear idea of his story; in fact he has no story. He merely has some people in mind, and an incident or two, also a locality. He knows these people, he knows the selected locality, and he trusts that he can plunge those people into those incidents with interesting results. So he goes to work. To write a novel? No—that is a thought which comes later; in the beginning he is only proposing to tell a little tale; a very little tale; a six-page tale. But it is a tale which he is not acquainted with, and can only find out what it is by listening as it goes along telling itself, it is more than apt to go on and on and on till it spreads itself into a book. I know about this, because it has happened to me so many times.

Of course, when a man's *work habits allow him to dawdle over a novel for years at a time, discontinuities come naturally, but in the case of this novel, the complexity in the manuscript and the corresponding confusion in both the main novel of *Pudd'nhead Wilson* and its auxiliary farce, *Those Extraordinary Twins*, arose in short order. From composition to full publication in a volume was at most a matter of just over two years, with serial publication of the *Pudd'nhead* part taking place nearly a year earlier. By Twain's standards, this was lightning-quick work, yet in that time he compressed the confusions of a lifetime under the pressures of imminent bankruptcy.

The book began, he claimed, on his seeing an advertisement in 1891 for "Siamese twins" on tour. He did not discuss the possibility of turning this idea into account until the summer of 1892, when he discussed a possible new book for publication by *Webster and Company with Fred Hall, then running the firm. Hall was trying to save the company, in part by shifting its focus to trade publication from *subscription publication, which was losing steam as an economically viable business over the course of the 1890s.

Perhaps when he jotted the first intimations of the twins' story in his notebook in 1891, he did think of it as no more than another magazine article, not that different from his old sketch "The Personal Habits of the Siamese Twins," pub-

ROXY AND THE CHILDREN.

Illustration by Louis Loeb for the serialization of *Pudd'nhead Wilson*, *Century Magazine*, January 1894, p. 328.

lished in 1869. By the time he began writing, however, he knew it would be much more. In fact, he assumed that he would write the tale to be a typical subscription book, which is to say, large, when he discussed the idea of a new book with Hall in July 1892. By January 1893, he claimed the book was finished, writing to Hall on the 28th: "I have written 1800 MS pages since the 5th of last August, and 1500 of them are still here in my possession (one completed book and one half-complete make 1350 of the 1500)." The complete book was *Pudd'nhead*; the other was *Personal Recollections of Joan of Arc*, and the remainder was a number of magazine pieces. This letter suggests that the earliest he began serious work on *Pudd'nhead* was in August 1892, as part of an absolute blur of writing.

His output was staggering because he was writing in a white heat to make money. The publishing firm was floundering; Clemens's expenses on the *Paige typesetter were still overwhelmingly heavy, and with the family in Europe economizing after closing the Hartford house in 1891, Clemens turned with a vengeance to the writing he had once sworn he would retire from with *A Connecticut Yankee in King Arthur's Court*. A notebook entry describes even more astonishingly the energy Twain poured into the book: "Dec 20/92. Finished 'Pudd'nhead Wilson' last Wednesday, 14th. Began it 11th or 12th of last month, after the King girls left. Wrote more than 60,000 words between Nov. 12 and Dec. 14. One day, wrote 6,000 words in 13 hours. Another day wrote 5,000 in 11." Perhaps he had written only desultorily on the novel until November; if so, the book's discontinuities may actually be the result, for once, of too fast rather than too slow composition.

At any rate, the book began as a burlesque of the life of some European conjoined twins who for reasons unexplained decide to live in the town of Dawson's Landing on the Mississippi River. The opening sketch of Dawson's landing prepared the way for a travesty of small town values and virtues. As such, the book was an antipastoral romp, as well as a send-up of aristocratic values. The themes were old, the spirit of comedy one that Twain needed professionally—he wanted the book to sell well. More importantly, perhaps, he needed the light touch for personal reasons; the weight of possible failure distressed the entire Clemens family, and their dislocation from their Hartford home was quite a blow. As he put it to Hall on 14 August 1893: "I mean to ship 'Pudd'nhead Wilson' to you—say tomorrow. It'll furnish me hash for a while I reckon. I am almost sorry it is finished; it was good entertainment to work at it, and kept my mind away from things."

The evidence of composition, though, suggests that he was never able to devote his entire mind to the story. Right in the middle of his compositional flurry of November, he changed the story from a simple farce of southern manners to a *detective story with racial overtones. He explained to Hall in a letter of 12 December 1892:

> The last third of it suits me to a dot. I begin, to-day, to entirely re-cast and re-write the first two-thirds—new plan, with two minor characters made very

prominent, one major character dropped out, and the Twins subordinated to a minor but not insignificant place. *The* minor character will now become the chiefest, and I will name the story after him—"*Pudd'nhead Wilson.*"

The shift apparently came about when Clemens hit on the idea of fingerprinting as the plot device to structure a detective story.

He came to this idea when he read *Finger Prints*, a new book by Francis Galton, a scientist interested in genetics. Galton's discovery that each person has unique and enduring fingerprints suggested to Twain a way to build an entirely new plot around David Wilson, Rowena, and a new conception of Tom Driscoll. Right up to publication, Twain felt that his use of this new knowledge made his book salable. In a letter to Fred Hall of 30 July 1893, asking him to arrange publication in a magazine, Twain wrote: "Now then, what is she worth? The amount of matter is but 3,000 words short of the American Claimant, for which the syndicate paid $12,500. There was nothing new in that story, but the finger-prints in this one is virgin ground—absolutely *fresh*, and mighty curious and interesting to everybody."

The interest, though, quickly moved beyond a mere quirk of human anatomy into a thematic deepening. Originally, Twain had no concern for racial motifs in his burlesque; Driscoll was simply the child of rich white parents. But the new idea sent Twain backwards into a field of interest that presented some of the most intricate of moral tangles presented by antebellum society. Only then did he come up with the idea of having Tom be the changeling child of Roxana. He thus wrote the last third of the book knowing that he would have to change the first part to accommodate the last. His solution was merely to add some new material at the beginning to explain the action, and change as little as possible in the rest of the novel. But even though the composition was compressed in such short time by Twain's standards, his usual pattern of moving from simple humor to ironic satire held true. The newest material is the most intensely satiric of the book, yet its position at the beginning of the story makes the quick lapse into simple farce puzzling in its tonal inconsistency, an inconsistency matched by the divided focus in plot. When writing to Hall about the book, Twain's own confusion about its content is reflected in his ambivalence about what to title it: "My book is type-writered and ready for print—'Pudd'nhead Wilson—A Tale.' (Or, 'Those Extraordinary Twins,' if preferable)" (3 February 1893).

Twain must have had some sense of the difficulty he had created for himself by changing plans in the middle of composition. He wrote to Laurence Hutton on 2 January 1893, "I've finished that book & revised it. The book didn't cost me any fatigue, but revising it nearly killed me. Revising books is a mistake." In fact, he had barely revised at all, and the knowledge that he would have to revise more stringently was what was bothering him, not the minimal labor he had actually expended.

At this point, Twain put aside his concerns about the book's impossible disjunctions. He instead turned his mind from composition to publication, wanting to make as much money on the book as possible, but knowing as well that Hall had converted Webster and Company to a trade firm. His letter to Hall continues:

> It makes 82,500 words, 12,000 more than Huck Finn. But I don't know what to do with it. Mrs. Clemens thinks it wouldn't do to go to the Am. Publ. Co. or anywhere outside of our own house; we have no subscription machinery, and a book in the trade is a book thrown away, as far as money-profit goes. I am in a quandary. Give me a lift out of it.
>
> I will mail the book to you and get you to examine it and see if it is good or if it is bad. I think it is good, and I thought the Claimant bad, when I saw it in print; but as for any real judgment, I think I am destitute of it.

Indeed under duress as he was, he did lack judgment, not only about the quality of the tale but about the advisability of publishing by subscription, about which he was intransigently obsessed. Just four days earlier he had written to Hall on the same topic, claiming, "There is no money for a book of mine (or anybody else's for that matter) in the 'trade.' . . . I would like to pocket $30,000 again on a book as I used to do. And I don't a bit like 'serial' publishing."

Hall's reply accurately stated what Clemens did not want to admit, that publishing had changed: "While I have not read 'Those Extraordinary Twins' I am sure, judging from the condition of the book trade in all its branches, that to get the book up in handsome style, as you suggest, illustrating it fully and putting a high price on it, would merely mean to sink money in it. I doubt if we could get our money back out of it." He further explained that "there is a good and profitable sale in the trade for any of your books that strike the public fancy. There is no sale at present by subscription for any book that you could write." Hall noted that even the American Publishing Company was earning Twain's current royalties on old books now sold in the trade, but he also understood that Twain's last book, *The American Claimant*, had sold so poorly that it damaged Twain's chances in the marketplace: "The 'Claimant' has not sold at all well, and it would make the booksellers a little chary of any new book you might write" (10 March 1893).

On 22 March, Clemens returned to the United States in order to transact pressing business, and, in all likelihood, to press Hall to arrange for publishing the new book. While he was there, the Panic of 1893 began in earnest in April, ultimately sending the U.S. economy into a prolonged depression. The immediate need for Clemens and Hall was to keep their banks from calling their notes—something they had done five years earlier in relatively good economic times. Sometime during this visit Hall convinced Twain that his large new book was more *Claimant* quality than up to his old standard. Upon returning to his family in Europe at the end of May, Twain finally went to work editing the original manuscript into a streamlined *Pudd'nhead Wilson*, leaving out the scraps of the original farce, changing the twins from conjoined to separate, and making their role minimal rather than central. He wrote Hall from Germany on 30 July 1893:

> *This* time "Pudd'nhead Wilson" is a success! . . . I have pulled the twins apart and made two individuals of them; I have sunk them out of sight, they are mere flitting shadows, now, and of no importance; *their* story has disappeared from the book. Aunt Betsy Hale has vanished wholly, leaving not a trace behind; aunt Patsy Cooper and her daughter Rowena have almost disappeared—they scarcely walk across the stage. The whole story is centered on the murder and the trial; from the first chapter the movement is straight ahead without divergence or side-play to the murder and the trial; everything that is done or said or that happens is a preparation for those events. . . . Consequently, the scenes and episodes which were the strength of the book formerly are stronger than ever, now.

Indeed, the tale as Twain had now edited it has proven itself to have enduring power, but his editing was nowhere close to as diligent as he claimed to Hall. A careful reader of the story will discover many editorial lapses, places, for example, where it is clear that the twins are still referred to as a single being. In other places, the streamlining was incomplete, as when the twins play the piano. Their performance has nothing odd in it unless they are conjoined twins; the persistence of this scene in the final cut shows that Twain really did not have a sure sense of what "movement straight ahead without divergence" would entail. Surely he exaggerated in boasting to Hall: "When I began this final reconstruction the story contained 81,500 words; now it contains only 58,000. I have knocked out everything that delayed the march of the story—even the description of a Mississippi steamboat. There ain't any weather in, and there ain't any scenery—the story is stripped for flight!" His word count here shows how much he judges his editing quantitatively rather than qualitatively, seeing his task primarily as shifting the book from a subscription-sized to a trade-sized volume. In concentrating on elements of plot, he ignored not only details that would make the plot smooth and consistent, but also problems of tone and theme that he created in the very first rush of composition.

Again, the press of money kept Twain's mind off the greatest potential virtues of his story, pushing him instead to see it in purely commercial terms. He begged Hall to arrange for serial publication, knowing that it would provide him immediate income even though he felt that the ultimate proceeds from the book would be harmed: "[D]o you best for me, for I do not sleep, these nights, for visions of the poor-house. This in spite of the hopeful tone of yours of 11th to Langdon (just received from him with approving words)—for in me hope is very nearly expiring. Everything does look so blue, so dismally blue!" (30 July 1893). Clemens refers here to the Mount Morris bank calling Webster and Company's loans, and his brother-in-law stepping in to pay notes due in mid-August. At this time, Clemens returned to the United States for about six months to help Hall manage the company's finances, as well as to place *Pudd'nhead*. This he did in September, arranging with the *Century Magazine* for serial publication, in seven installments from December 1893 through June 1894.

He had met Henry H. *Rogers in November 1893, and in short order, he had thrown his problems on Rogers, who by April 1894 convinced Clemens to allow Webster and Company to go bankrupt. Clemens's hopes to have Webster publish *Pudd'nhead* after the *Century* finished serializing it were dashed, and he instead turned back to the American Publishing Company to have the book published by subscription. Ironically, it now needed to have its original bulk back. Clemens penned a new introduction, explaining that people might find his confused methods of composition interesting, and then cobbled together the scraps left over from the original farce into "Those Extraordinary Twins," writing a few new bridge passages to restore some semblance of continuity.

Even though the American Publishing Company enabled Twain to recover his original intention to lavishly illustrate a large volume for subscription, Hall was right about the changes in the publishing business. Overall sales were modest by comparison to earlier books, even though they were not disastrous enough to turn Twain finally away from the American Publishing Company. These modest sales came in spite of good publicity. Early reviews were on the whole complimentary, even if often expressing some puzzlement. For example, the *Athenaeum*'s 19 January 1895 review notes that while "the idea of the change of babies is happy, and the final trial scene is a good price of effect, . . . the story at times rambles on in an almost incomprehensible way. Why drag in, for example, all the business about the election, which is quite irrelevant? And the Twins altogether seem to have very little *raison d'etre* in the book. . . . Still, the book well repays reading just for the really excellent picture of Roxana." Modest sales and good publicity notwithstanding, the book slipped quickly into an extended period of obscurity.

Fairly well ignored in its own day and for much of the time since, over the past three decades this novel has become one of Twain's most studied, primarily because of its treatment of what chapter 2 calls the "fiction of law and custom," racial identity. Critical opinions vary significantly, with many critics holding the opinion that Twain satirizes racial attitudes by inverting the conventional sentimental tale's happy ending with the rediscovery of lost family bonds and the reestablishment of social order. The restored heir, Thomas Driscoll, having been raised a slave, is unable because untrained to exercise his privileges as an aristocrat. And while

David Wilson no longer suffers ostracism, the town's recognition of his value merely incorporates him into a corrupt social system, compromising his ironic distance from that corruption.

Other critics deny the effectiveness of the satire, suggesting that Twain's fascination with science as a surefire technique for discovering absolute truths merely reinforces prevailing cultural ideas about racial identity. Many such critics point out that Galton's work, which was Twain's source for fingerprinting as a plot device, was intended originally to prove racial distinctiveness in order to help buttress his argument for white superiority.

A dissenting position suggests that the book is not worth the critical attention it has recently garnered, because it lacks the aesthetic, intellectual, and moral integration essential to a book meant to speak cogently to any issues of critical concern. This, of course, is a critical argument that crops up over most of Twain's longer works, with some critics complaining that Twain never could maintain focus long enough to make his points consistent and clear. But in the case of *Pudd'nhead Wilson*, the compositional discontinuities are of many orders greater magnitude than in *A Connecticut Yankee in King Arthur's Court* or *Adventures of Huckleberry Finn*, for example. Those who see the book as valuable and interesting reply that Twain's confusions reflect cultural ambiguities, that his very perplexities are of value because he distilled them in ways that allow Americans to perceive and understand divergent attitudes and ideals common to the culture as a whole.

PUNCH. A London weekly humor magazine founded in 1841, *Punch* featured, from its inception, illustrations as well as text. While in its early days it was associated with British radicalism, it gradually grew less political and less sharp in its comedy, which was certainly the case by the time Twain came into professional contact with it.

Twain did not write for *Punch*, and in the early days of Twain's career, *Punch*'s writers tended not to speak highly of Twain. As a professional humorist and satirist, though, Twain kept his eye on *Punch*, recognizing the power of its publicity. In the story "The £1,000,000 Bank-Note" (1893), Twain mentions *Punch*'s power not as the power of *satire to destroy a reputation but as the power of *amiable humor to endear a person to the public. The story's first-person narrator mentions that he had received much publicity from the newspapers but that this was "only notoriety. Then came the climaxing stroke—the accolade, so to speak—which in a single instant transmuted the perishable dross of notoriety into the enduring gold of fame: 'Punch' caricatured me. Yes, I was a made man, now; my place was established. I might be joked about still, but reverently, not hilariously, not rudely; I could be smiled at, but not laughed at." Twain achieved the same fame in 1907 when visiting England to receive an honorary doctorate from Oxford, but *Punch*

Caricature of Mark Twain being toasted by Mr. Punch, by Bernard Partridge for the cover of the June 1907 issue of *Punch* magazine.

took the accolades a step further by not only caricaturing Twain being toasted by "Mr. Punch," but by hosting a dinner in his honor, supposedly the first time it feasted—though not the first time it feasted on—a foreigner.

♦ SEE ALSO Reverence.

QUAKER CITY. A 1400-ton side-wheel steamer, the *Quaker City* was built in Philadelphia in 1854, served as a Union supply ship in the *Civil War, and was bought and converted to a passenger ship by Charles C. Leary. Charles Duncan, a parishioner of Henry Ward *Beecher's Plymouth Church, arranged to lease the ship and to serve as captain for an 1867 tour of the Holy Land. After convincing Beecher and Gen. William T. Sherman to go, he published a prospectus for a pleasure cruise with religious overtones. Not surprisingly, the Beecher congregation was heavily represented on the tour's roster, but when both headliners withdrew, Duncan's plan to make a substantial profit on the voyage dissolved. His hoped-for 110 passengers dwindled to a mere 64, not counting Duncan's family or Charles Leary, who went along in search of a buyer for his ship. The side trip to Yalta to visit the czar of Russia, which Twain describes in chapter 37 of *The Innocents Abroad*, was in fact an effort to convince the czar to buy the ship.

At any rate, the cruise's substantial cost, $1250 per person, and its planning through a church congregation biased the passenger list in favor of older, well-to-do churchgoers. Clemens, taking the trip as a professional journalist in the pay of a California newspaper, did not fit the profile. He was a heavy drinker, heavy smoker, a purveyor of *slang, and, in general, a notorious rowdy. The contrast created some of the tensions that energize Twain's correspondence and that found their way into *Innocents* even after he edited the original letters.

This is not to say that Clemens found no congenial spirits on the voyage. He made important connections to Mary Mason *Fairbanks, who helped guide his developing literary *style, with Charles *Langdon, whose sister would ultimately marry Clemens; and to Dan *Slote; with whom Clemens would have long-standing business relations that eventually soured. He made other friendships with John A. Van Nostrand, Julius Moulton, and Dr. Abraham Reeves Jackson, who appear, along with Slote and Langdon, as some of the boys in *Innocents*. He also enjoyed the company of Julia Newell, who met Jackson on the voyage and married him in 1871. Clemens visited the pair that year in their Chicago home. Clemens also stayed on good terms with and respected Moses Beach, owner of the New York *Sun*; Clemens especially liked Beach's teenaged daughter, Emeline, with whom he corresponded into the twentieth century. Solon Long Severance, a banker from Cleveland, and his wife, Emily Severance, round out the list of those whose company he enjoyed on the trip.

QUARRY FARM. SEE Crane, Susan Langdon; Houses.

RACE RELATIONS. For most of Clemens's life, racial discrimination in America was legally sanctioned; for all of his life, racial discrimination was socially sanctioned. The South's need to rationalize the institution of chattel *slavery—a practice far more encompassing than most historical slave practices—fueled anti-black racism. Because slavery in the United States was race-based, slave codes argued that blacks were an inferior race, either on the pseudoscriptural grounds that *African Americans were the descendants of the biblical Ham and therefore deserving of eternal servitude, or on the psuedoscientific basis that they were a genetically inferior people, deserving the treatment due animals, not human beings. Considering that most Americans of African descent were by the 1860s partially of European descent as well, this argument was easily challenged by antislavery advocates. Regardless, race-based laws and customs in slave states made manumission for most slaves a dim possibility and the "liberty" of even the few free blacks in the South a bitter irony.

But as much as slavery contributed to racist attitudes, it was not the only, or even the primary cause of such bigotry. Indeed, much antislavery agitation, north and south, was predicated on racist fears. Many Northerners worried that the practice of concubinage, common in the South, would dilute the white race. This fear was so prevalent that even Frederick Douglass, whose ultimate objective was social and political equality between blacks and whites, played the miscegenation card in his attack on slavery: "[T]his arrangement admits of the greatest license to brutal slaveholders, and their profligate sons, brothers, relations and friends, and gives to the pleasure of sin, the additional attraction of profit" (*My Bondage and My Freedom*, chapter 3). Many Northerners who attacked this arrangement had no genuine concern for African Americans, as the widespread hope that freed slaves could be returned to Africa attests.

Many Northerners, however, were sincere advocates of political and social equality for African Americans; the *Civil War put their demands on the nation's agenda, temporarily radicalizing American politics. With the Radical Republicans in ascendance in Congress and the North's victory in the Civil War, the nation endorsed a spate of civil rights legislation, culminating in the ratification of constitutional amendments eliminating slavery (13th amendment, adopted 1865), guaranteeing equal protection under the law (14th amendment, adopted 1868), and protecting voting rights regardless of "race, color, or previous condition of servitude" (15th amendment, adopted 1870). But such victories for racial equality were soon overshadowed and undermined. With the end of the Civil War, Union troops were dispatched to the Great Plains to battle *Native Americans; many tribes were virtually wiped out in the "Indian Wars" of the era. No civil rights legislation addressed the status of Native Americans, who became the scapegoats that enabled many Americans to see North and South unified without slavery. Then, as soon as the disputed Tilden-Hayes election of 1876 was resolved in a bargain that would end Reconstruction, enforcement of civil rights guarantees quickly ceased throughout the South. Jim Crow laws were enacted across the region, and occasionally in the North and West, and were ultimately sanctioned nationally in 1896 when the Supreme Court ruled, in *Plessy* v. *Ferguson*, that separate and equal accommodations were legal under the Fourteenth Amendment. It took two generations of legal maneuvering to overturn that decision; in the meantime, legal racism had virtually no impediments.

Among the primary inducements to racism in both antebellum and postbellum America were economic arrangements—a chronic cyclical labor shortage encouraged immigration, and recent immigrant groups usually felt threatened by the groups succeeding them. Religious and cultural concerns further provoked suspicion and isolation between various racial and ethnic communities. During the colonial era, chattel slavery coexisted with indentured servitude, feeding the insatiable demand for agricultural labor in a frontier, agrarian economy. Yet bound labor of immigrants and slaves threatened the yeoman population. Given a broad definition of "race" to include what would now be considered ethnicity—the Irish, for instance, were often considered to be a distinct race—Americans of British extraction masked their class concerns behind race concerns, first displaying animosity against "Beer-guzzling" Dutch (that is, German-speaking immigrants). Later, as industrialization changed the nation's labor needs and encouraged new waves of immigration, quondam British and "Dutch" alike railed against the Irish, later yet against Southern and Eastern Europeans, while virtually every group discriminated against blacks. On the West Coast, labor shortages in railroad construction encouraged the importation of *Chinese, who were subject to persistent legal and extralegal discrimination, including the imposition of selective "foreign" taxes on mining and transportation.

Not surprisingly, such economically inflamed racism intensified when the economy put pressure on labor. Beginning with the depression of 1873–1880, most of the rest of the century saw steady deterioration of the condition of labor, with steadily decreasing wages and fewer opportunities for skilled workers. This period has come to be known as the nadir in American race relations.

On top of deep-seated clannishness and economic anxiety, new pseudoscientific arguments further aggravated racist attitudes. Darwin's theory of natural selection encouraged the idea that the races represent different stages of advancement—a notion now disproved if not dead. Beginning in the 1870s, many of the Western world's most prominent scientists had no compunction about declaring African and Asian peoples "inferior," and there was no shortage of popularizers to spread such ideas.

E. W. Gilliam, for instance, writing in the July 1886 edition of the *North American Review* on Chinese immigration, advanced such an opinion as if it were received fact: "The three great families into which mankind is divided—black, yellow, white—(the debasing effects of amalgamation across color lines indicate this) should develop *within themselves*, and toward what apparently are their respective bounds, a half-civilized, civilized, and enlightened condition" (34).

Such was the environment in the late 1860s in which Clemens began to shed his own racist beliefs, particularly concerning blacks and Chinese. (He held to some bigoted opinions about the Irish and never overcame a racist outlook on Native Americans.) In a letter to William Dean *Howells (15 July 1886), Clemens mocked Gilliam's hierarchy as absurd, ironically calling Gilliam's belief in white "enlightenment" a manifestation of "delicious unconsciousness." Consciousness was, finally, what Clemens pursued, bringing to mind the failures of civilization to live up to a compassionate ideal and showing that "there are many humorous things in this world; among them the white man's notion that he is less savage than the other savages" (*Following the Equator*, chapter 21).

♦ SEE ALSO Anti-Semitism.

RAILROADS. Because railroads destroyed the glamour and profitability of riverboat piloting, Samuel Clemens may have had a particular animus against them; his charge in an 1873 Fourth of July speech delivered in London to a group of Americans, however, was calculated to appeal to a set of prejudices more broadly held by his countrymen:

> I refer with effusion to our railway system, which consents to let us live, though it might do the opposite, being our owner. It only destroyed 3,070 lives last year by collisions, and 27,260 by running over heedless and unnecessary people at crossings. The companies seriously regretted the killing of these 30,000 people, and went so far as to pay for some of them—voluntarily, of course, for the meanest of us would not claim that we possess a court treacherous enough to enforce a law against a railway company. But thank heaven the railway companies are generally disposed to do the right and kindly thing without compulsion. I know of an instance which greatly touched me at the time. After an accident the company sent home the remains of a dear, distant old relative of mine in a basket, with the remark, "Please state what figure you hold him at—and return the basket."

The remarks were funny because, though overstated, they had a near relation to the truth. Clemens, like most Americans, did admire the technology of railways, bragging about American sleeping cars, for instance. But such admiration could not counterbalance his disgust with the corrupting influence railway corporations had on

American politics, established quite powerfully by the Credit Mobilier scandal, which helped bring down the world *economy in a significant and long-lasting depression beginning in 1873.

Whatever the degree of Clemens's animus, it didn't stop him from investing in railroads, nor from living off his wife's substantial interest in those railroads built by her father to move his coal to market. Clemens relied on them professionally in his many *lecture tours and made them a common feature of his writing. Railroads figure prominently, without irony or humor, in many of his travel narratives. In particular, passages in *The Innocents Abroad* and *Roughing It* use the quality of railroads as touchstones for describing the material civilization of faraway lands. In this sense, as much as Twain may have decried the railway corporations' power over the United States' political and economic life, he viewed the railroad, as did most of his countrymen, as a symbolic measure of *progress.

As much as horses were the mode of transportation most often referenced in the humor of the previous generation, and as much as automobiles and airplanes figure in the humor of our own day, railroad stories and jokes were a mainstay of Twain's era, and his works often employ railroad travel as either the setting or as a crucial component of a comic story. Among these comic pieces are "The Danger of Lying in Bed," "Punch Brothers, Punch," "The Invalid's Story," and "Travelling with a Reformer." In this last, the railroad serves a larger point as being the representative of an increasingly complicated, bureaucratic society, a point Twain makes in other pieces like "The Man That Put Up at Gadsby's" or *"Extract from Capt. Stormfield's Visit to Heaven." In this sense, the railroad serves not only as a symbol of progress, but also as a symbol for progress's attendant discomforts.

♦ SEE ALSO Industrial Revolution; Inventions.

READING, CLEMENS'S. In his public persona as *Mark Twain, Samuel Clemens tried to appear unlettered, as a natural genius whose sage advice came exclusively from his observations of human life, not from book learning, or at least not from "high brow" belletristic literature and religious writing. In an 1889 interview with Rudyard *Kipling, for instance, he told Kipling, "I never care for fiction or storybooks. What I like to read about are facts and statistics of any kind. If they are only facts about the raising of radishes, they interest me." But while the stance served him well in public, he in fact read much fiction—as well as statistics. He lived in print, reading voraciously across every conceivable genre, about every imaginable topic.

In this he was a normal man of letters and fairly typical of his class and era. Before the inventions of radio and television, print media were *the* mass media. *Publishing was by 1900 the country's third largest industry—behind machinery and lumber and ahead of steel production—and, as it does today, publishing served diverse purposes: educational, business, and entertainment. While literacy was not quite as widespread as it came to be in the early twentieth century, it was the key to belonging in national political, economic, and social arenas. People marked their *social class in part by what and how they read, but in all classes, public reading was a primary entertainment—even if it was communal Bible reading in a family that scorned belles lettres.

It was to such a family that Samuel Clemens was born. Despite her visible pride in her son's accomplishments, Clemens's mother had little interest in literature. His repeated references to his solitary reading as a "dissipation" suggest that as a boy he was chastised for his habit of reading novels. Even so, he was encouraged to go into *printing, for though it entailed manual labor, its association with letters gave it an aura of gentility.

In his training as a printer, Clemens acquired habits of concentration on texts that stood him in good stead all his life; in his marginal notations in many of his books, he corrects grammar, style, and page layout, working as an after-the-fact copy editor and proofreader. That attention to detail shows in his own *work habits, as he often meticulously edited his own drafts to create precise stylistic effects.

More importantly, as a printer he was exposed to a heterodox and voluminous flow of print matter, facilitating the wide-ranging tastes that helped make him such a successful writer. Newspapers, while serving local audiences and the political inclinations of their backers, nonetheless kept an eye on the world of print, always stealing from a variety of sources in order to fill pages with salable matter. Much of the briefest of this matter was humorous, sometimes anonymous, circulating from paper to paper. Clemens's fondness for such squibs is marked by his inclusion of a few in *Mark Twain's Library of Humor*. His work on newspapers helped cultivate not only his taste in humor but his devotion to a wider range of reading, including in books and journals designed to be edifying, rather than merely diverting. Writing home from New York on 31 August 1853, Clemens described the range of journals printed by his employer, John A. Gray, and mentioned further that his entertainment as a printer was to read: "The printers have two libraries in town, entirely free to the craft; and in these I can spend my evenings most pleasantly. If books are not good company, where will I find it." One of these libraries, the Printers' Free Library and Reading Room, had about three thousand books as well as files of major newspapers.

At this stage of his life he developed a lasting taste for nonfiction in addition to his earlier love of fiction, and like his contemporaries he read in *science and history along with philosophy and theology, seeing these subjects not as separate, but as profoundly connected. For instance, he read *Darwin's *Descent of Man*, Paley's *Natural Theology*, and *Lecky's *History of European Morals*, essays by William Graham Sumner (whom he had invited to speak to the *Saturday Morning Club), some philosophy by Herbert *Spencer, David Hume's "Of Miracles" from *Inquiry Concerning Human Understanding*, Amédée Victor Guillemin's *The Heavens*, Thomas Huxley's *Hume*, and John Fiske's 1882 *Atlantic* essay "Charles Darwin," all in a study of moral philosophy. None of this reading was pointedly in service of his writing, though much of it influenced not only his general outlook and ideas, but also specific arguments he would make in his works.

Clemens read as widely and avidly in fiction—of both his contemporaries and his antecedents—as he did in nonfiction. But while he addressed nonfiction primarily from the point of view of an interested outsider, he addressed fiction as a professional writer commenting on his own craft. Of course he did not begin reading fiction that way, and his early tastes ran toward *romance. Early in life he relished Scott, Dickens, Poe, and Cooper, as well as writers of lower status, such as the gothic writers George Lippard, author of *The Monks of Monk Hall*, or Robert Montgomery Bird, author of *Nick of the Woods*. He spent much of his own career as a writer renouncing his earlier tastes, and at the same time extended his passionate attacks on fiction to many of the greats of his and preceding generations. In praising William Dean *Howells's *Rise of Silas Lapham*, Clemens wrote:

> You are really my only author. I am restricted to you; I wouldn't give a damn for the rest. I bored through Middlemarch during the past week, with its labored & tedious analyses of feelings & motives, its paltry & tiresome people, its unexciting & uninteresting story, & its frequent blinding flashes of single-sentence poetry, philosophy, wit, & what-not, & nearly died from the overwork. I wouldn't read another of those books for a farm. I did try to read one other—Daniel Deronda. I dragged through three chapters, losing flesh all the time, & then was honest enough to quit, & confess to myself that I haven't *any* romance-literature appetite, as far as I can see, except for your books. . . . You make all the motives & feelings perfectly clear without analyzing the guts out of them, the way George Eliot does. I can't stand George Eliot, & Hawthorne & those people; I see what they are at, a hundred years before they get to it, & they just tire me to death. And as for the Bostonians, I would rather be damned to John Bunyan's Heaven than read that. (21 July 1885)

Of course, his resistance to romanticism never fully succeeded; he found himself, as much as his literature attacked romance, repeatedly succumbing to it, never sure whether reality should be protected against romance, or the other way around.

As much as Clemens tried to resist romance, he only pretended resistance to high literature, in part to maintain Mark Twain's image as a man of the people, in part merely to tease his friends. In describing a ship's library in chapter 62 of *Following the Equator*, for instance, he glibly distinguishes his taste from that of the literary upper crust: "Jane Austen's books, too, are absent from the library. Just that one omission alone would make a fairly good library out of a library that hadn't a book in it." To Howells on 29 April 1903 he wrote: "Putnam Place did not much interest me; so I knew it was high literature. I have never been able to get up high enough to be at home with high literature. But I immensely like your literature, Howells." Clearly he took as much pleasure in twitting Howells as in declaring his allegiance to "low" literature. Howells responded on 1 May in the same spirit: "Though it isn't quite down to your level, I don't wonder you like my literature—it's nearly all about you. But you'd better take a brace, and try to get up as high as 'Putnam Place.' Now you're sick, I've a great mind to have it out with [you] about Jane Austen. If you say much more I'll come out and read 'Pride and Prejudice' to you."

This idea that Clemens could not appreciate high literature was a joke. He did indeed detest Austen as much as Howells loved her, but he had read and relished many of the classics, including works by *Shakespeare, Cervantes, Cellini, Defoe, Johnson, Voltaire—such a list could stretch for pages.

And as much as he professed not to like high literature, Clemens only liked the really low in order to mock it. He kept a "library of literary Hogwash," filled with writers like Julia *Moore. His knowledge, too, of what he called "wildcat" literature—dime westerns and other inexpensive sensation fiction—may have influenced his writing, but it was not literature he endorsed.

What he did endorse was literature he both enjoyed and enjoyed sharing. To Clemens, as to many of his day and place, reading was a social practice. He courted his wife over books, marking a copy of Holmes's *The Autocrat of the Breakfast Table*, as well as discussing in his letters Coventry Patmore's *The Angel in the House*. A 27 February 1869 letter suggests that there were other books they shared in courtship as well: "I am glad I marked those books for you, since the marking gives you pleasure, but I remember that the pencilings are very meager—for which I am sorry. I have marked many a book for you, in the cars—& thrown them away afterward, not appreciating that I was taking a pleasure of any great moment from you. I will do better hereafter. . . ."

He marked books all his life, and in sharing books back and forth among family and friends, apparently hoped that such markings would both inform and entertain.

Reading was social in a more direct sense than swapping books to be read privately. Family readings were very much a part of the Clemens family life, including Clemens's own daily reading of his literary output. Clemens also read and was read to in larger circles, from the small groups gathered to hear Clemens read Browning, to the reading of essays at the *Monday Evening and Saturday Morning Clubs, to the large gatherings for author's readings, such as the one given by *Dickens when Clemens first met Olivia Langdon, or such as the many Clemens gave from his own works, either for pay or for *charities. While entertainment was certainly part of the point of such reading, the purpose was equally to stimulate edifying discussion. Clemens's communities of readers shared newspapers, novels, history, literary criticism, poetry, sketches, short stories, *essays, science, philosophy, theology, sermons—in short, anything that could remotely stimulate public discussion of the issues of the day. Warner and Clemens made teaching such reading practices part of their message in writing *The Gilded Age*.

As a professional writer, though, Clemens did not see reading merely in this social sense; he also used his reading directly for his writing. In preparing his travelogues, he read extensively about the places he visited, reading accounts not only in English but also in German and French. He also did research for his historical novels, *The Prince and the Pauper*, *A Connecticut Yankee in King Arthur's Court*, and *Personal Recollections of Joan of Arc*, again reading in French and German as well as in English.

The surprising thing is not that Clemens saw reading as professional preparation but that he persisted to his dying day in seeing reading as recreation, a feeling that few professional writers are able so completely to hold. But Clemens did, regularly whiling away whole days in bed, smoking, drinking, and reading, as if idleness, *tobacco, *alcohol, and books were all dissipations. His physician of many years, Dr. Clarence C. Rice, wrote in a 1924 memoir: "Sometimes he stayed in bed all day because he enjoyed reading and writing lying down. He was always reading, and seemed to enjoy any kind of printed page, from a child's school book to an almanac." Clemens developed this habit early in bachelor days, reading when traveling on ship or train, reading when his work was done, sometimes reading entire nights through. He wrote Olivia in November 1873 about his sea voyage to England on board the S.S. *City of Chester*, "I have read all night in this [rough] weather—sleep would only tire me." As a man who had to travel often on business and who also traveled often on pleasure, Clemens felt it necessary to always be well stocked with books, and his friends and relations helped him satisfy this need. On 12 May 1893, just before embarking on a transatlantic journey, he wrote Howells: "I am very glad to have that book for sea entertainment, & I thank you ever so much for it. . . . You have given me a book, Annie Trumbull has sent me her book, I bought a couple of books, Mr. Hall gave me a choice German book, Laffan gave me two bottles of whisky & a box of cigars—I go to sea nobly equipped."

And reading was not merely a pastime for traveling; it was Clemens's favorite pursuit on any occasion. Whenever he needed to take a break from writing, he would lounge a day in bed reading. When he reached old age and considered himself retired, he would spend entire weeks in bed reading, or hours in the billiard room reading, alone or to company. He tried to live out the motto he first wrote in his notebook in 1898: "Good friends, good books & a sleepy conscience: this is the ideal life."

♦ SEE ALSO *Age of Reason, The*; *Arabian Nights Entertainment, The*; "Fenimore Cooper's Literary Offenses"; Journalism; Lecture Circuit; Magazines; Newspaper Journalism; Realism.

REALISM. Paradoxical by definition, since no account of reality is ever fully congruent with reality, the term "realism" defines no single kind of literature, but rather defines a struggle throughout the nineteenth century to argue for the value of various kinds of fiction. In trying to validate their work, the writers of any school of fiction attached to it the label "realism." So to say Twain was a realistic writer, as he often declared himself to be, says merely that he was participating in the battles of definition, not what his literature actually entailed. Discounting his newspaper reporting, Twain wrote at various times in his career four kinds of realistic fiction— sentimental realism, local color realism, social realism, and *naturalism—sometimes in full congruence with the precepts of one of these schools, more often in some tension with them.

Sentimental realism may now appear to be a contradiction in terms, but it was perhaps the dominant mode of fiction until late in the century, practiced in the historical romances of James Fenimore Cooper, in the sketches of Bret *Harte, in the novels and short stories of Harriet Beecher *Stowe, and by Charles Dudley *Warner among other American writers whose work influenced Twain. Sentimental realists believed that fiction needed to depict not merely the physical realities of human life, but the emotional and spiritual core of human experience. In service of moral uplift, their literature began from real scenes and circumstances, but accepted a need to purify nature of its distractions in order to depict pure examples of emotional states or moral actions. The metaphors most often used by sentimental realists to explain their technique and purpose derived from painting and sketching. Warner, coauthor of *The Gilded Age* with Twain, explained the precepts of sentimental realism clearly when he argued against the social realism and naturalism that came into prominence in the last quarter of the century. According to Warner in his April 1883 *Atlantic Monthly* essay "Modern Fiction," "Art requires an idealization of nature. . . . When we praise our recent fiction for its photographic fidelity to nature we condemn it, for we deny to it the art that would give it value. We forget that the creation of the novel should be . . . a synthetic process, and impart to human actions that ideal quality which we demand in painting" (p. 464).

To Warner and like-minded writers, fiction must give models for upright behavior, and models cannot afford the precision of unadulterated nature, even as their essential lineaments are abstracted from nature.

Local color realism grew out of sentimental realism, as can be deduced by the fact that the "sketch" was one of the dominant genres of local color fiction. While *sketches designed to convey a spirit of place had long been popular, especially in series of sketches about travel, in the years after the Civil War local color sketches found a new popularity for a new purpose. The centralization and economic disruption of both the Civil War and of industrialization in the aftermath of the war led to a *nostalgia for a dying or lost American past. That this past was usually idealized was precisely the point. The preservation, or at least memorialization, of republican virtue and simplicity in the face of postbellum social complexity and political corruption had an easy appeal, and dovetailed with political movements to return government power to the states and to resist homogenization in an industrial economy. Ironically, the demands for a return to the decentralized government of the antebellum years created the power vacuum that encouraged the corporate growth and political corruption that fueled the nostalgia in the first place.

Arising in this context, the literary movement of local color sketches was one of the dominant modes of fiction throughout Twain's career, and he capitalized on it incessantly, even as he partly resisted the conventions of the school. The cachet of his early California sketches derived in part from the reading public's desire to read about regional peculiarities, and no matter what his ultimate purposes were in *"Old Times on the Mississippi," Twain cashed in on postwar nostalgia in the very title, which suggests an ideal past. His opening line of the first number begins wistfully, "When I was a boy. . . ." Later he touches a nostalgic chord when he explains how the glory of steamboating came to an end:

> First, the new railroad stretching up through Mississippi, Tennessee, and Kentucky, to Northern railway centres, began to divert the passenger travel from the steamers; next the war came and almost entirely annihilated the steamboating industry during several years . . . and finally, the railroads intruding everywhere, there was little to do, then the war was over, but carry freights; so straightway some genius from the Atlantic coast introduced the plan of towing a dozen steamer cargoes down to New Orleans at the tail of a vulgar little tug-boat; and behold, in the twinkling of an eye, as it were, the association and the noble science of piloting were things of the dead and pathetic past.

Such moralizing was in concert with the school of local color realism.

But the entire agenda of "Old Times" does not follow the thrust of these occasional passages of moralizing; the bulk of the collection of sketches seems to be looking away from the influence of Warner toward the influence of Howells, who, as new editor of *The Atlantic Monthly*, had commissioned the sketches. Howells had been hired to expand the magazine's appeal, and, with a largely free hand, he did so by attracting a new kind of realism, a realism that idealized less and described in more minute detail the complexities of life. To Howells, and to Twain in their growing correspondence of the 1870s and 1880s, idealization led to lies. Said Howells in a 20 January 1882 letter to Twain, "The ideal perfection of some things in life persuades me more and more never to meddle with the ideal in fiction: it is impossible to compete with the facts." Under this standard, both men came to reject the sketch and the painting in favor of the photograph as their model of representation. Said Twain to Howells in a letter of 21 January 1879 praising *The Lady of Aroostook*, "It is all such truth—truth to life; everywhere your pen falls it leaves a photograph."

Continued on page 485

Realism

Frederik Pohl

The cluster of talents that go into writing a story are not equally distributed among writers. Some writers are particularly good at constructing tightly woven plots, so that the reader is drawn on to find out how it all comes out. That isn't Twain's style. His best stories have little detectable plot. They are a series of loosely connected incidents, and to the extent that they are structured at all—if I may borrow an analogy from Hollywood—they are more like a television sitcom than a feature film.

But so is real life. The main difference between your life or mine and the lives of Tom, Huck, Captain Stormfield, and all the rest of Twain's wonderful human beings is that the fictional incidents are a lot more entertaining than the drab and frequently unpleasant things that happen to ourselves. We may expect that a novel will come to a point, but only the most innocent expect it of our own lives. *War and Peace* has a natural ending built in; the novel ends when the war does. *Moby Dick* stops when Captain Ahab finally goes one on one with the great whale. Mark Twain's best work does not allow itself such machineries. Twain permits himself many artistic liberties—coincidence when it is helpful, bodacious exaggeration whenever he finds a tall story to tell—but not the one of shaping events to a formulaic plot.

We might regret the absence of that convention of the novel, if it were not for what we get in return. By being as episodic as life itself, Mark Twain gives us the feeling of life.

A few years ago my wife and I found ourselves on the Iowa shore of the Mississippi, in possession of the unusual treasure of a few unbudgeted days to spend as we chose. We decided at once that there was only one thing to do with them. We drove down along the riverside to Hannibal, Missouri, and there immersed ourselves in the world that Tom and Huck had once inhabited. We clambered through the cave where Injun Joe tried to scratch his way to freedom before he died. We took a boat out into the river and cruised past the island where the two boys hid when they pretended to be drowned, and where Huck and Jim found the raft that took them on their long, slow downstream voyage. (Our boatman told that that was the only part of the books he couldn't believe. No one could have spent a night on that island unprotected, he said, because the mosquitoes would have drained him dry in the first hour.) We ate catfish (farm-raised, to be sure) in a restaurant that had Tom Sawyer's name over its door, and we even browsed tolerantly through the endless assortment of mugs, postcards, guidebooks, T-shirts, and baseball caps that were for sale all over the village—the whole thing a festival of commercial hype, of course, but we didn't mind. What made all these enterprises profitable for the town's merchants was exactly the same thing that had brought us there. It was love.

There are many novels I esteem highly but few writers who have made their characters a part of my life in the way that Mark Twain's stories have. It has never occurred to me, while in Paris, to seek out the streets Marcel Proust's people walked, or in the Italian lakes to try to retrace the flight of Hemingway's army deserter. These are all good characters, splendid ones, but I have never thought of them as real.

Twain's people are quite different. Not being demented, I do know that the man made them up and they never actually lived, but they are as solid in my mind as, say, Caesar or Mary of Scotland. They are family, dearer to me than most of my cousins, and I will always love and honor Mark Twain for bringing them into my life.

Continued from page 482

At about the same time, Twain was turning his satirical eye on *painting itself in order to attack idealized representations. In *A Tramp Abroad*, for instance, much of which parodies high art, he unleashes his famous attack on Turner's "Slave Ship," and John Ruskin's admiration of it: "The most of the picture is a manifest impossibility—that is to say, a lie, and only rigid cultivation can enable a man to find truth in a lie" (chapter 24). (SEE ALSO Painting.) Here Twain rejects the sentimental conception of a moral truth abstracted from nature. Twain wants the facts to speak for themselves, or at least to be fully present when the artist tries to speak through them.

To Twain, then, realism had to rely on experience and observation, as he puts it in another letter complimenting Howells on his work. In response to chapters 23 through 26 of *A Modern Instance*, Twain wrote on 22 June 1882, "That's the best drunk scene—because the truest—that I ever read. There are touches in it which I never saw any writer take note of before. And they are set before the reader with amazing accuracy. How very drunk, & how recently drunk & how altogether admirably drunk you must have been to enable you to contrive that masterpiece!"

Not that, in his jest here, Twain felt that realistic writing was to have no moral purpose, but he was coming to agree with Howells that idealistic fiction designed to present moral models tended to obscure not only the complexities of moral questions, but to ignore unpleasant realities in favor of idealized happy ends and false models of heroism.

Perhaps this shift to Howells's brand of social realism, a realism that describes complex social problems in order to imagine workable solutions, explains much of the difference in tone and tenor between *The Adventures of Tom Sawyer* and *Adventures of Huckleberry Finn*. *Huckleberry Finn* does not whitewash the past in a comfortable nostalgia, nor does it offer a comfortable happy ending with a simple, heroic resolution to intractable problems.

In Howells's kind of social realism, the growing emphasis on social problems allowed for the development of an American naturalism, a kind of realism that Ambrose Bierce described as "reality as seen through the eyes of a toad" (*Devil's Dictionary*). The naturalist's emphasis on social forces as larger than the individual never sat comfortably with Twain, but in his later years he often professed to accept the idea of social and natural *determinism. *Pudd'nhead Wilson*, *What Is Man?*, and "The Turning Point of My Life," for example, all bear the influence of literary naturalism.

Such a survey of kinds of realism and Twain's attitudes toward them gives the impression that Twain was a realist. He would have his readers believe so according to his literary criticism of historical romances in *Life on the Mississippi*, in which he blames the Civil War on Sir Walter Scott's fantasies of feudal valor, or in *"Fenimore Cooper's Literary Offenses," where he charges Cooper with crimes against art for failing to observe nature before trying to write about it. But in Twain's case, the paradox of "realism" grows proportionately more complex when the extravagance of his humor is considered; in spite of his best theoretical intentions to stick to the facts, he wandered almost always into realms of fancy.

♦ SEE ALSO Politics.

REFORM. Samuel Clemens was born in a period of incredible social ferment, in which reform movements blossomed in tropical profusion. The title of historian Alice Felt Tyler's *Freedom's Ferment* appropriately connects the enthusiasm for reform to the new nation's efforts to define itself, and even though many of the era's reforms were imported from England, American enthusiasm for them was predicated on an idea of American exceptionalism. If America were to become all that God intended it to be, the general argument ran, it would have to improve the men and women in it by stamping out vices such as spitting, swearing, gambling, drinking *alcohol, smoking *tobacco, desecrating the Sabbath, prostitution, dueling, ignorance, *slavery, women's subjection before the law, and so forth. The general thrust of all of these reforms was to improve individual character, held to be the foundation of the republic. So most reform movements concentrated not on large-scale political or social institutions, but rather on individual behavior. Labor unions, for example, stressed sobriety and "manliness" of character as much as they stressed improved working conditions.

There were significant exceptions. *Women's rights agitation, while it included educational reforms to elevate the character of individual women, also included appeals for changing laws regarding property, child custody, and suffrage. Much antislavery agitation sought changes in laws, though the colonization movement also saw itself as a voluntary organization that would put a stop to slave trading, and the Garrisonian effort to end slavery through moral suasion disparaged institutional reform as both impossible because corrupt and inadequate because not changing individual character. Prison reform, which sought changes in order to "reform" the character of felons, necessarily focused on institutions. Similarly, *education reform, though all about building the character of young Americans, devoted itself to changing laws—in particular, to require early education and to attack child labor.

Many reform movements recapitulated the early puritan movement of withdrawal, setting up utopian communities of like-minded people. Most of these were religiously based, and most shared a distaste for capitalism. The Oneida, Shaker, Amana, and Mormon communities all practiced socialism to one degree or another, building their life practices around interpretations of sacred scriptures. Less explicitly religious utopian communities included the industrial experiment of New Harmony,

Indiana, and the agrarian Brook Farm experiment. The latter had significant impact on northeastern literary culture through participants like Nathaniel Hawthorne, Margaret Fuller, and George William Curtis as well as through well-wishers like Ralph Waldo Emerson. Fuller later became one of America's preeminent feminists, downplaying full equality with men in favor of advocating greater freedom for women so that they could develop individual character and religious affinities. Curtis was one of America's most influential magazine editors through *Putnam's* and *Harper's* as well as one of America's most significant advocates, both in his writing and in his work on the *lecture circuit, of women's suffrage, broadening access to higher education, and civil service reform.

An ambivalence about freedom characterized most reform movements. While praising the free exercise of individual Americans, most reformers stressed the dangers lying in wait to destroy that independence of mind and morals. Hence, as much as these movements tried to build character, they had a top-down emphasis suggesting that the reformers themselves had the keys to the kingdom of morality. For example, the antigambling movement first attacked state and local lotteries as a revenue source that encouraged vice before moving on to outlaw private gambling as well. The *temperance crusade that began with an emphasis on self-control as a feature of moral strength transformed, in the early twentieth century, into a temporarily successful campaign to nationalize legal prohibition. Reformers often crossed the line between self-control and legal control.

Clemens's contact with reform movements in his childhood had a profound influence on his character and in turn on the works of Mark Twain. And as much as the antebellum period in which Samuel Clemens grew up may have been the most fecund period for reformism in U.S. history, the postbellum years in which Twain's works were published were not far behind. Mostly he wrote of his contact with movements concerned with smoking, swearing, and temperance.

Throughout, Twain's works express a revulsion with the paternalism of most reform movements, best expressed in his *maxim from *Pudd'nhead Wilson*: "Nothing so needs reforming as other people's habits." He bridled against the curtailment of freedom implicit in reform as well as against the futility of what he saw as a crusade against nature. From chapters 32 and 33 of *Roughing It* to the *Seventieth Birthday speech, Twain rails against constraint, mocking those who would reform his bad habits. In a telling moment in the first chapter of *Following the Equator*, he describes how when ill, his doctor forced him to give up his drinking, smoking, caffeine, and immoderate eating:

> At the end of forty-eight hours the lumbago was discouraged and left me. I was a well man; so I gave thanks and took to those delicacies again. It seemed a valuable medical course, and I recommended it to a lady. She had run down and down and down, and had at last reached a point where medicines no

longer had nay helpful effect upon her. I said I knew I could put her upon her feet in a week. It brightened her up, it filled her with hope, and she said she would do everything I told her to do. So I said she must stop swearing and drinking, and smoking and eating for four days, and then she would be all right again. And it would have happened just so, I know it; but she said she could not stop swearing, and smoking, and drinking, because she had never done those things. So there it was. She had neglected her habits, and hadn't any. Now that they would have come good, there were none in stock. She had nothing to fall back on. She was a sinking vessel, with no freight in her to throw overboard and lighten ship withal. (chapter 1)

The conjunction he makes with swearing as part of a general reform agenda is gratuitous in the context of health, but Twain knew well that to his audience, the entire moral agenda was what was really at stake.

As often as these individual behavioral reforms appeared in Twain's works as fodder for humor, the more politically charged movements made their way in as well. He was not an abolitionist as a young man, but he came to understand the travesty of justice perpetrated in Jim Crow segregation after Reconstruction, and wrote regularly, in a veiled, satiric way, in support of improving conditions for *African Americans. He had a similar change of heart with respect to women's rights, frequently advocating women's suffrage in speeches and in *Following the Equator*, but basing his advocacy as much on his belief in fundamental moral differences between men and women as on his conception of the justice of universal suffrage.

One reform movement in which he consistently participated over the course of his literary career was the good government movement of the late nineteenth and early twentieth centuries. Not advocating many specific reforms so much as denouncing corruption wherever he found it, he operated on the assumption that men of letters justified themselves by serving as public watchdogs. From his attacks on the police in San Francisco, to his attacks on Tammany Hall in the 1870s, to his share in *The Gilded Age*, to late speeches and essays about New York City *politics, he regularly attacked political malfeasance, and praised others, like Thomas *Nast, who did the same. But in not seeking major institutional changes, Twain's works fit into the general pattern of nineteenth-century reformism, putting the entire onus of public morality and honesty in the hands of individuals. The agenda of Warner and Twain in *The Gilded Age* is to have individuals insist on their rights, and to work in concert as the aristocracy of the "middle ground." By the time he wrote and published "Travelling with a Reformer" (1893), he may have had some doubts about the humorlessness of this agenda, but he still seemed to believe that individuals insisting on their rights was the only way to improve the moral caliber of not only government, but of all bureaucratic institutions.

◆ SEE ALSO Labor Movement; Revolution; Social Class.

REID, WHITELAW (1837–1912). A journalist who came to national prominence for his war correspondence, Reid was hired by Horace *Greeley to work for the *New York Tribune* in 1868, a year after Clemens started writing regularly for it. Reid took over editorship of the paper on Greeley's death in 1872 by purchasing a half interest for $500,000, in part backed by Jay Gould. Reid held the editorship until 1905 when named U.S. ambassador to Great Britain. From his prominent position on the *Tribune*, Reid participated in the nation's political life, even running (unsuccessfully) as vice presidential candidate in 1892 after serving as ambassador to France (1889–1892).

Clemens and Reid corresponded regularly and cordially up to the publication of *The Gilded Age* in 1873, when Reid refused to allow Clemens's friend Edward House to review the new novel for the *Tribune*. Their falling out reveals the intense animosities of which both men were capable, very much in tune with the intensity of nineteenth-century *journalism. The two blackguarded each other publicly and privately for the next decade, ignored each other for the next quarter century, and finally publicly acknowledged each other's eminence only in 1907 when Clemens received an honorary doctorate at Oxford University. Clemens said they resumed communication "not cordially, but merely diplomatically."

Each apparently detested the other's arrogance and cultural power; each threatened to dethrone the other; neither followed through. Reid, for instance, wrote to Kate Field on 17 July 1873, "If Twain gives us trouble, I'm very much tempted to make him a more ridiculous object than he has ever made anybody else." Nearly a decade later, Clemens, believing on hearsay that Reid had been slandering him not only in private letters but also in the pages of the *Tribune*, planned a calumnious biography of the man he called "Outlaw Reid." In an entry in his 1882 notebook, he explained his need to do so as follows: "When the naturalist finds a new kind of animal, he writes him up, in the interest of science. No matter if it is an unpleasant animal—he wrote up the skunk (Latin name.) R[eid] is a new kind of animal—& in the interest of society must be written up. He is the (skunk) of our species."

In all likelihood, Twain's animus was refueled by his friend and *Tribune* employee Edward House and perhaps by former *Tribune* managing editor John Russell Young. Both of these men, like Twain, worked for the *Tribune* before Reid arrived and hated Reid as, in Young's words, a "gigantic donkey—with none of the donkey's redeeming qualities" (letter to Clemens, 11 January 1882). In any event, Clemens dropped his plans when he investigated the slander charges and found them baseless.

RELIGION. When Samuel Clemens was born in 1835, Low Church Protestant Christianity dominated every aspect of culture in the United States; by the time he died in 1910, the culture as a whole was significantly more secular, religious feelings were spread more widely among Christian and non-Christian religious beliefs, and religious intensity had waned significantly, though it still was a powerful force in American life. Mark Twain's works both reflect this shift and encouraged it. Yet to say this about Twain and American religion is to say too little in saying it all. It does not explain the varied nature of American religious experience even early in Clemens's lifetime, nor does it explain how a man whose fundamental beliefs were quite skeptical of the religion of his youth could count among his best friends many ministers, including Henry Whitney Bellows of San Francisco, Thomas K. Beecher of Elmira, Horace Bushnell and Edwin Pond Parker of Hartford, and perhaps his best friend of all, Joseph Hopkins *Twichell, also of Hartford. That story lies in the nature of American Protestantism and how it developed during the nineteenth century.

When Mark Twain was born, the United States was experiencing the second Great Awakening, a widespread revival of Low Church Protestant religiosity. Like the first Great Awakening, it was a reaction to the falling away from religion of the educated elites, and like its predecessor, it turned to energetic fundamental- ist *Calvinism in response to a gradual rationalizing trend among the religious congregations of the eastern seaboard. While these urban congregations were making their peace with Enlightenment rationalism to one degree or another, accepting latitudinarianism, Unitarianism, and figurative interpretations of the Bible as part of a general belief in a benign, rational, and relatively distant God, congre- gations through the rest of the country were insisting on the tenets of Calvinism, and in the process, returning to the long-standing rejection of Roman Catholic, High Church liturgies. Low Church congregations tended to return, though not as desperately perhaps, to the asceticism of the original puritans, disdaining novels as lies, dance and music as seductions, and ornamentation of body or home as worldly.

Ironically, such attitudes toward art pervade the works of Mark Twain, whose anxiety about working as a humorist took its shape in a letter in which he lamented his "calling," the Protestant term for the task God has called one to perform in this world. There is throughout Twain's early writings a persistent resistance to art generally and to fiction specifically. *The Innocents Abroad* and *A Tramp Abroad* con- tinue a pose Twain developed early in his work as a reporter, commenting with dis- dain on art as something unworthy of reverence. As for fiction, the *burlesque mode that governed so much of Twain's work suggests his ambivalence about fiction—he was attracted to it enough to understand its workings, but anxious enough about its power that he wanted to deflate it. In particular, *The Gilded Age* argues that modern novels corrupted youth, and even classic fiction needed to be taught carefully so as to convey proper values. Such an opinion could be chalked up to Clemens's relative youth as a writer in 1873, but that he would return to such a theme in *Adventures of Huckleberry Finn* over a decade later—with Tom Sawyer misreading *Don Quixote* in the beginning of the book and misusing countless fictions in the last third—suggests that Clemens's anxiety about fiction ran quite deep, as deep as his roots in Calvinism.

The early nineteenth century's great period of revivalism saw its greatest successes in the trans-Appalachian regions of the country. The second Great Awakening first took root in the 1820s in upstate New York, which became known as the "burned-over district" for the intensity and frequency of its revivalism. Charles Finney and similar evangelists promised the new millennium if believers would accept their power as God's agents of transformation. In his belief in human power, Finney was not an orthodox Calvinist, and the impact of his brand of revivalism throughout the North blended to some degree with the softening of Calvinism that was already underway. Olivia Langdon Clemens's family came from this area, and its religious and social practices—including a principled resistance to slavery—reflected the attitudes of the region. From upstate New York the Awakening spread into the Midwest and the South. In the South, which had been the hotbed of deism during the eighteenth century, revivalism spread quickly via the newer sects, especially Baptists. Mostly, these newer sects preached consistent Calvinism, and thus, ironically, the South became the new home of the religion that formerly characterized New England.

This diffusion in rural districts and especially in the South among the children of pioneering families heightened long-standing *social class distinctions among the churches. The more prestigious churches, Congregationalist, Presbyterian, and Episcopalian, insisted that each new congregation have a college-trained minister. Hence, they were slower to evangelize than the Baptists, who not only used lay preachers as a matter of course, but encouraged revival meetings led by circuit riding ministers, who, by virtue of their itinerancy, could cover much more ground than could settled ministers. The Methodists were somewhere between the Baptists and the other denominations, proselytizing through circuit evangelism, but holding a much tighter reign on the ministry.

These distinctions in social class are very much part of the picture Twain's works paint of the rural south in the 1840s and 1850s. In *Adventures of Huckleberry Finn* in particular, Twain mocks the Baptist reliance on lay preachers in the character of Silas Phelps, who, when confused by the "evasion" practiced on him by Tom and Huck, "preached a prayer meeting sermon that night that give him a rattling ruputation, because the oldest man in the world couldn't a understood it" (chapter 42).

The most significant difference between the second Great Awakening and the first was the nineteenth-century insistence on moral reformation as a part of regeneration into the body of the church. Earlier Calvinism had insisted that good works were completely ineffectual as agents of grace and so downplayed works as part of devotion. After the religious controversies of the eighteenth century, many American congregations followed the Arminian line, that is, the belief that "since faith without works is a dead faith," works must be a legitimate means to grace.

This belief was a large part of the eighteenth-century relaxation of American Calvinism that the second Great Awakening was reacting against. The social prestige of those liberal congregations weighed heavily, however, so the new revivalists had to demonstrate some tangible results—hence, the conjunction between revivalism and campaigns against idleness, drinking, smoking, gambling, swearing, dueling, and spitting tobacco. Historians have interpreted the second Great Awakening as "a shopkeeper's millennium," a movement that inculcated values appropriate to a growing petty-capitalist economy. In any event, moral reformism has a constant place in Mark Twain's literature, sometimes merely as mockery of any effort to perfect human nature, as in chapters 32 and 33 of *Roughing It*, other times more seriously when Clemens wanted to investigate the sources of moral behavior, as in "The *Facts Concerning the Recent Carnival of Crime in Connecticut."

Nineteenth-century revivalism also rekindled a long-standing Protestant prejudice against Roman Catholicism, the Protestant's dread "whore of Babylon." This revival of bigotry slightly preceded the first major wave of non-Protestant immigration into the United States when the Irish potato famine began in 1845. In Northeastern Missouri in 1845, young Samuel Clemens was living close to the old Catholic population of St. Louis, with its French and German populations. The influx of the Irish over the next two decades, while it concentrated primarily in the cities of the East, gave Clemens, among others, another target for the expression of anti-Catholic hostility, a hostility that manifests itself in Mark Twain works from *The Innocents Abroad* through *A Tramp Abroad* to later pieces written while in Austria—*"Chronicle of Young Satan," *"No. 44, The Mysterious Stranger," and the reportage "Stirring Times in Austria." He also combined an attack on Roman Catholicism with one of many attacks on Christian Science in "The Secret History of Eddypus."

By 1835, while the Awakening continued to spread further into the rural districts of the West and South, the intense asceticism of the revivalist movement limited its ultimate appeal. While the rural Presbyterian congregations tended to hew to the Calvinist line, their connection with an educated clergy tended to keep them in touch with the meliorating tendencies of East Coast, urban religion. In these and like-minded congregations, an appreciation for art coupled with a persistent Arminianism created a powerful alternative to fundamentalist Protestantism, an alternative that would become America's mainstream religion by 1870. Sentimental Protestantism argued that the Bible should be read not for its literal facts, but for the feelings it engenders, and that as a wellspring of religious feeling, it should be seen as complementary to all of the arts. Novels, poems, music, the plastic arts—all could and should be used as goads to devotion, as ways of developing the tastes to understand the beauty and harmony of God's world. Christianity, according to *sentimentalism, is not a rebirth into grace after the sinful natural man has been struck dead, it is a process of gradual growth into spiritual understanding from an infancy of innocence through human experience. Cultivate the tastes correctly and innocence yields perfection of the soul. Fail to cultivate them correctly, and the results are catastrophic enough in this world to suggest what they would be in an afterlife.

Such was the position taken by Harriet Beecher *Stowe in the dominating book of nineteenth-century America, *Uncle Tom's Cabin*. Her success shows the depth of resistance to fundamentalist Protestantism by the 1850s, especially on two points—the sinful nature of children and the immorality of fiction. But the advocacy of sentimental Christianity was not restricted to writers of fiction; a significant number of influential clergymen came to prominence in the 1850s and 1860s who challenged the hegemony of orthodox Calvinism. Among these prominent advocates of such a gentler form of Christianity was Clemens's Hartford neighbor Horace Bushnell, whose *Christian Nurture* (1861) was exceptionally popular, not only in the cities of the East, but ultimately throughout the country. Bushnell's disciples included Joseph Twichell and E. P. Parker as well as Henry Ward *Beecher and Thomas K. Beecher. All of these clergymen construed Biblical truth broadly. All kept up on current discoveries in *science, and felt that a reasonable and compelling religion had to embrace modernity in all of its dimensions. No wonder Clemens found such clergymen to be pleasant company. They indulged the skepticism he had arrived at concerning the tenets of Calvinism and they endorsed the social practices—particularly writing fiction—about which he was ambivalent. Not surprisingly, when the Bushnell brand of religion appears in Twain's works, it is not subjected to the same energetic derision applied to fundamentalist Calvinism on the one hand or Roman Catholicism on the other. The widow Douglas in *Huckleberry Finn*, for instance, appears gracious and gentle in her sentimental Christianity by contrast to the rigid fundamentalism of her sister, Miss Watson. This is not to say that Clemens did not mock sentimental Christianity, too, but only that he spared it the greater intensity of his attacks on other forms of religion.

One of the unintended outgrowths of sentimental Christianity was the idea of sentimental *domesticity, in which women were given the task of moral preceptor in the American family. Over the course of Clemens's life, patterns of church membership and attendance began a steady change that perhaps has not yet seen its culmination. Men began to attend church much less regularly and to express religious *faith much less certainly. In Clemens's case, his adult attempts to find religion were wrapped up in his courtship of Olivia Langdon, whom he addressed as the angel who would lead him to belief. While he may temporarily have found faith in this sentimental rendition of woman as savior, his faith was short lived, as he became increasingly skeptical about any Christian idea of God, no matter how figurative that divinity might be.

The relative drop in church attendance by men that took place especially after the Civil War had many causes, not least of which was the influence of the war itself on the faith of many of those who fought in it. Commerce, too, had claims that pulled men away from the demands of piety toward more worldly concerns.

Equally importantly, the discoveries of science made any religious faith, no matter how ecumenical, deistic, or figurative, ever more difficult. Addressing all of these trends, Twain's writings comment regularly on the state of American religion, sometimes arguing against the hypocrisy of a worldly approach to life, other times finding religious doctrines completely incompatible with the world as it really is. As much as conventional Christianity was put under strains in a modernizing culture, alternatives were promulgated with increasing frequency. *Spiritualism, which began as a serious alternative religion in the 1840s, grew increasingly popular by the end of the century. Mark Twain showed remarkable tolerance toward spiritualism, accepting the idea of telepathy, which he called "mental telegraphy," and seeing in faith healers a group of practitioners who found ways to tap into the unconscious powers of the human mind. But he was also skeptical of any absolute belief, reporting that he had proven the fraudulence of a mesmerist who visited Hannibal in his youth and uncovering the schemes of various fortune-tellers throughout his career.

In these kinds of alternative religions Clemens did not usually have much emotional investment, so the level of his rhetoric rarely rose to the fever pitch of so much of his unfinished and posthumously published diatribes against Christianity, many of which appear in the Mark Twain Papers volumes *Fables of Man*, *What Is Man?*, and *The Great Dark*. On the contrary, most of Mark Twain's remarks on *spiritualism, mesmerism, faith healing, mental telepathy, and the like are either open-minded explorations or simple caveats against *confidence games. An exception is the case of *Christian Science, which hit a particular nerve with Clemens, perhaps because he encountered its promises of physical wholeness in return for pure belief at exactly the time when the illnesses of a number of women close to him had angered him at the plan of the universe. He could not accept that those he cared for were responsible for their own diseases, as Christian Science preached.

♦ SEE ALSO Health and Disease.

REPUBLICAN PARTY. Given that Samuel Clemens was a Southerner and briefly enlisted in the Missouri militia, it may seem astonishing that he became a staunch member of the Republican party by 1868. It is less of a surprise if one looks into the birth of the party. Built strangely out of the fragments of the old Whig party, the Free-Soil party and the Know-Nothings, the Republican party embraced many of the political positions Clemens was born into or had developed. His father was an old-style Whig voter, believing in the importance of an elite governing through representative bodies in order to check the barbarism of the mob. The Whigs were largely the party of the landed and wealthy, and they often confused their ideas of noblesse oblige with their own economic interests. As a printer, Clemens developed strong sympathies with the Know-Nothings, whose anti-immigration stance played well among laborers who saw a threat to their status and wages in the influx of skilled labor from Europe. Only the Republicans' antislavery plank kept Clemens out of their camp in the 1860 election, when he voted not with the Democrats, but with the Constitutional Union party.

After the *Civil War, Clemens had a change of heart about his slavery position, and readily became a supporter of the Republican party, fitting in to the Hartford community that had been so instrumental, especially through the *Courant, in building the party's original platform. Clemens became such the perfect convert that in the Hayes-Tilden presidential contest of 1876, he worried that Tilden's election would mean the end of the republic. It was in this period that he wrote "The Curious Republic of Gondor" (1875), which advocated oligarchy, and "The Great Revolution in Pitcairn" (1879), which exposes his distrust of pure *democracy. His hopes for good government—which meant to him a government in which "foreign" influence was diminished by depriving newly arrived immigrants of full voting rights—were fully congruent with the fundamental beliefs of a significant faction of the Republican party.

It was in this hope for good government that his ardor for the party cooled when he turned *Mugwump in the 1884 election. He ultimately chastised his Hartford neighbors for being politically retrograde in his essay "Consistency" (1887), suggesting that the Republican party had ceased to be a progressive force for good government, or—an increasingly important issue to Clemens—for the rights of individuals. His growing belief in democracy over the 1880s pitted Clemens, like other influential Mugwumps such as George William Curtis, against the Republican party's entrenched connection to big business. By the end of his life, he worried that the Republican party's grip on power had ended the possibility of American democracy. As he put it in his *autobiography, concerning Theodore Roosevelt's endorsement of William Taft as his successor:

> For fifty years our country has been a constitutional monarchy, with the Republican party sitting on the throne. Mr. Cleveland's couple of brief interruptions do not count; they were accidents and temporary, they made no permanent inroad upon Republican supremacy. Ours is not only a monarchy but a hereditary monarchy—in the one political family. It passes from heir to heir as regularly and as surely and as unpreventably as does any throne in Europe.... Formerly our monarchy went through the form of electing its Shadow by the voice of the poll, but now the Shadow has gone and *appointed* the succession Shadow! I judge that that strips off about the last rag that was left upon our dissolving wax-figure republic. It was the last one in the case of the Roman Republic. (16 July 1908)

Partly what had happened was that Clemens's Whiggish ideas had softened as his hopes for democracy deepened, but his cynicism about power had hardened so that he felt it was impossible to unseat the party once it was firmly in power. As such, he never really lost his belief in a republic nor in good government, but he did abandon his belief that a party could achieve any but ignominious ends.

♦ SEE ALSO Politics.

REPUTATION. SEE Critical Reception and essay on following page.

REVERENCE. One of the higher sensibilities in the psychology of *sentimentalism, reverence is often at odds with comedy, which frequently dethrones revered people, objects, and ideas in order to provoke laughter. Sentimentalists therefore endorsed laughter only if and when it did not challenge ideals of reverence:

> Either never attempt ridicule upon what is every way great ... ; or, if our wit must sometimes run into allusions, on low occasions, to the expressions of great sentiments, let it not be in weak company, who have not a just discernment of true grandeur. And ... concerning objects of a mixed nature, partly great, and partly mean, let us never turn the meanness into ridicule without acknowledging what is truly great, and paying a just veneration to it. (Frances Hutcheson, "Reflections on Laughter")

By such standards and by Victorian standards of gender roles, laughter needed either to sequester itself for "low occasions" among men, or to pursue a delicacy and refinement that is intrinsically ennobling. This is a difficult line to walk, and for much of Mark Twain's career, he found the difficulty a source of frustration and fear.

Early in his career, Mark Twain's ridicule appeared in newspapers, and in particular in western newspapers, which, by conventional agreement, were primarily a masculine venue and therefore considered appropriate for low comedy. Even so, his *burlesques upon "great" things often elicited scathing attacks, most notably his 1864 newspaper squib suggesting that the Sanitation Commission in Nevada was actually sending funds not to the relief of wounded Union soldiers, but to a "miscegenation society." Such an attack, which touched the honor of the ladies who were deeply involved in running the Sanitary Commission, pushed well beyond the bounds of acceptable irreverence, and helped precipitate Clemens's departure from Nevada as persona non grata.

For much of the rest of his career, Mark Twain struggled to find a comedy that would be reverent enough to pass muster as *amiable humor; he worried that he often failed, a worry supported by repeated suggestions in reviews of his work that he showed inadequate reverence for sacred things. Most painful of these to Clemens was the lashing he received in the press after his *Whittier Birthday Dinner speech in 1877.

Continued on page 511

Mark Twain's Reputation

Louis J. Budd

Mark Twain, we can safely infer, accumulated a reputation far sooner than most persons of eventual renown. As a bright, quirky boy, Samuel Clemens doubtless aroused comment outside his family. Then the slam-bang humor of his sketches for the Hannibal *Journal* set off a wider sharing of judgments about him. After he left home, his travel letters published in Iowa newspapers raised him further above the human leaves of grass. As a steamboat pilot whose peers admired his flair for writing he had higher status between St. Louis and New Orleans than his Sunday-School teachers would have expected. Driven to the far West by the Civil War he projected himself, with rising éclat, as a recklessly comedic reporter in Nevada, a bohemian freelancer in San Francisco, an ebullient yet focused correspondent from the Sandwich Islands, a humorous lecturer, and—in total—a unique personality whose name earned exposure well beyond the West Coast. By the age of thirty-one he felt enough buoyancy to try navigating the East Coast again. But he brought along a realistic sense of the risks. On leaving Nevada in 1864 he had felt disgraced, and he had learned that his freewheeling ways could antagonize both sober-sides and official San Francisco. When his prospective father-in-law checked with western sources about his character—in effect, his reputation—he rightly felt anxious.

In besieging Manhattan and Brooklyn he offered to enliven any kind of subject with risk-taking humor. But the jumping-frog yarn had already made him so visible that promoters for the *Quaker City* cruise rated him a colorful asset. On getting back, he was surprised to hear that his travel letters had made him far better known. The resulting *Innocents Abroad* would stay his best-selling work until his death. In 1893 a poll in the *Critic* for "The Best American Books" picked it as his leading candidate. If a single work seldom propels its author's name for decades ahead, many readers long identified Twain with the personality that rears up throughout the text—shrewd, irreverent, impulsive, doggedly humane, egalitarian, humorous by nature, and proud to represent the New World. Persons who should have known better would misspell his family name. Appropriately, Twain wanted to call his last house, where he would die, "Innocence at Home."

Of course, many more books followed at short intervals, and Twain's fame climbed unstoppably, sometimes almost flattening and sometimes soaring but never dropping insofar as such a process can be charted. As an insider he knew how easily the winds of public favor could be shifted. So late as 1898, in a letter to Henry Huttlestone Rogers, he worried that "a literary reputation is a most frail thing." But his fame rose even as he challenged the American imperialists after 1900. However much it verged toward notoriety in the early years, it eventually steadied into not just celebrity but herohood.

The dogged analyst can challenge any pattern for its details. In a multilayered, mobile, partly illiterate United States, hero to whom? In a population seething with immigrants, celebrated for what? Just why did the newspapers, increasingly profit-driven, give Twain so much play? When did the magazines chime in and in what key? Just what magazines, in fact? What can any review mean unless we know about its author (maybe an overworked hack), to some degree controlled by the policies of his outlet or, rather, employer, in turn dependent on advertising in varying degrees? And just how effectively did Twain, always both hungry and aggressive in the marketplace, push himself? He was cannier about the ongoing transaction than most writers who manage to hold on to fame during their lifetime. Yet if Twain masterminded his ascent, how do we account for his reputation still booming after he was no longer alive to leverage his friendships with reporters, editors, and critics? Or, from the other side, how much did geopolitics drive his indisputably highest honor, the doctorate from Oxford University, or why did an American-financed bimonthly in a devastated Berlin feature him in its opening issues after World War II? Such questions can almost dissolve Twain's fame into his tactics or others' purposes. Nevertheless, he did become and remains one of the best-known American writers. The evolution of that fact, whatever its causes, is worth knowing on its own terms.

Focusing on the gears of public opinion and on Twain as their engineer blurs the trickiest question: the appeal of his humor that moved those opinions. Despite a long history of theorizing and, finally, some clinical research, nobody has diagramed definitively the mental-emotional genome for humor. Twain's career exemplifies the difficulties in pinning it down. Perhaps the core of his genius was his own complexity of purpose (multiplied by the complexity of his psyche), which let him appeal to a range of audiences and even to clashing selves of the individual. He ran the gamut of genres or modes, from quick-hit jokes to convoluted, oblique satires. At the start anyway, he played to differing responses at home and abroad. His first American admirers mainly wanted broad brush comedy and tall tales from an irreverent, risk-taking, hyperenergetic westerner whose mock venom often enough subsided into good-heartedness. The emerging persona appealed particularly to the male's ideal of himself as a fresh species of humankind with a horse sense for business, politics, and humor; though mostly women bought "literature," Twain still attracted more male readers than any of his contemporaries when he edged into respectability. His early British admirers preferred him as a juggler of paradox or else as a shaggy Yankee democrat come to play court-jester about the unspeakable in colorful dialect. The common denominator of his shifting personas was an irrepressible élan that kept verging on absurdity or mental violence. Readers sighed with relief when the I-narrator of *Innocents Abroad* got back home safely from his overreaching.

Intertwined with the success of *The Innocents Abroad*, Twain's performances on the lyceum circuit also brought favorable notices, multiplied by his ongoing work for the newspapers. Although he would stay alert to their constituency, he started aiming for the magazines. As printed hearsay about his habits and tastes and especially about his marriage accreted another dimension, by the early 1870s Twain already verged on his lifelong image of bouncing and boundless energy, expended prodigally, usually with humor. While most magazines ignored the subscription trade, the major dailies had begun treating books as news. So *Roughing It*, besides adding bulk to Twain's reputation, intensified another side of it. Despite his never getting back to Nevada or California, some of his admirers would always consider him an avatar of the almost Wild or else Golden West. Posturing himself more broadly, Twain continued to raise his visibility in the East as an up-to-the-minute observer. The austere editor of the New York *Tribune*, who gladly published his pro bono letters, smirked over his talent for keeping himself in the public eye and mind. When other newspapers, ignoring stiff-collar disdain, began deploying interviews as a salable genre, he cooperated, as much eagerly as cautiously.

Although *The Gilded Age* got some grumbling reviews, it did associate him literarily with Charles Dudley Warner and, therefore, an amiably refined, refining New England. It fortified his side as a concerned, moralistic citizen, even with British readers who had already bought pirated collections of his sketches entitled *Screamers* or *Eye Openers* and who lionized the flesh-and-blood author, crowding into his lectures. Americans tracked his triumphs in England avidly, proud that one of their own—socially acceptable to John Bull but radiating New World spontaneity—soon had a reputable publisher paying out royalties sometimes higher than those back home. They also knew that the comic melodrama cobbled out of *The Gilded Age* was earning a long run. Even after it collapsed because its lead actor died, Colonel Sellers's insistence for one wildcat scheme after another that "There's millions in it" lived on, until 1900 at least, as a catchphrase from Twain's most memorable character besides himself. His seeming knack for writing popular plays added to his composite reputation for coming up with salable ideas like a genuinely effective embodiment of the Colonel.

Understandably, sensibly, Twain started both taking himself more seriously and wanting the public to do so. Having edged his way, sponsored by William Dean Howells, into the Boston-Cambridge network, he showed up in *The Atlantic Monthly* and soon composed for it seven articles about his learning to pilot a steamboat. They confirmed his reputation for an easy yet hypnotizing style along with a lasting genius for humor. For many a reader they still outclass *Adventure of Huckleberry Finn* in merging him with the "majestic, magnificent" river. Soon pirated as

499

"Old Times on the Mississippi" they charmed readers innocent of bibliography as the best book Twain (n)ever wrote. The obituarist for the Glasgow (Scotland) *Herald*, after dismissing him as the "cleverest and best paid literary clown in the world," was obviously remembering the "Old Times" sequence when he conceded, "I shall certainly reread many times the altogether delightful *Life on the Mississippi*, which as regards sheer writing takes rank with some of the finest prose of the great New England days, and which, like the *Odyssey*, was the first and remains the best of the class to which it belongs" (*Glasgow Herald*, 30 April 1910).

Next *The Adventures of Tom Sawyer* introduced Twain the sentimental romancer about the village nestled in the antebellum heartland. It also widened his reputed insight into errant human nature. To his proper Americans duped by the Old World, motley westerners, and the types swarming around the budget committees of Congress, it added children, especially boys. Furthermore, the narrative voice came out of a basically sensible mind enlivened by cosmopolitan experiences. Twain's operative persona was growing both dazzlingly complex and more pliable than the garment strap he had patented. Naturally, the professional jester who could strain recklessly for a laugh stayed on call. But he was prospering impressively beyond all competitors while diversifying his patterns and moving into mainline forums. As uninhibited as ever—so the eavesdropping columnists kept reporting—Twain had nevertheless matured toward a paterfamilias, close to "settling down." The expensive house in the Nook Farm enclave of Hartford, Connecticut, symbolized the mixed signals: Newspaper wags had competed in jocularity about its showy exterior, but tributes from visitors and guests about its inside decor and amenities started cycling through the nationwide "exchanges."

In the later 1870s Twain's reputation went through its most fluid phase. Culturally aspiring readers could see that *The Atlantic Monthly* continued to prize his work. The solid German firm of Tauchnitz had added *Tom Sawyer* to its "Library," proving that his fame had spread beyond England and helping it further on the Continent. At home he was getting more invitations to speak than he could manage though he tried hard to oblige. Both the importance of the occasion and his handling of it made news, and for an era that admired oratory, editors happily alternated blocks of his period-eloquence and tomfoolery. While genteelists held photographs of themselves as private as their nightshirts, Twain evidently tolerated unpaid uses for likely (cigars) and unlikely ("Stoves, Ranges, Furnace, Pumps . . . ") products—uses that assumed he was a magnetic presence. Eager for fillers, the newspapers and magazines commented more and more often on his doings, deliberate or casual, solemn or frivolous. During a time when routine discourse among the educated could touch on authors, journalists regularly gauged current popularity, with Twain a prime candidate for this thumbnail polling.

His hardcover publications during the later 1870s epitomize his shifting stature. A Boston publisher added *A True Story and the Recent Carnival of Crime* to a series of belles-lettres; a Canadian firm pirated *An Idle Excursion*, his loose travel notes about Bermuda that Howells had allowed into the pages of the *Atlantic*; a crony published the weightless *Punch Brothers, Punch! and Other Sketches*, which carried a clowning pitch for Mark Twain's Patent Self-Pasting Scrap Book. What should the totally alert reader think or feel? The Boston *Literary World* observed that "Mr. Clement's [*sic*] 'happy thought'" had "received more original humorous notices from the press, perhaps, than any work ever issued." The scrapbook was in fact useful, proof of thinking practically, and, since it kept selling into the 1880s, proof of a sense for business. But insistently branding it with Twain's name assumed and then raised other resonances in the public mind too.

For reasons hard to fix, his family's return from abroad in 1879 disclosed a firm upgrading of his status. It turned into a press-event, minor yet covered with noticeable respect. While Twain still struck reporters as instinctively playful, he now came across as more of a somebody who could afford the Grand Tour for his whole family and as an intellect who could aspire to make such a tour but also as an old gogetter who was already shaping up a book about it. Produced with practical speed, *A Tramp Abroad* sold very well in spite of just scattered reviews. With almost presumptuous aplomb, it projected a Twain who was aging only willingly, unique as ever, enlarging his horizons yet bringing his personal and professional selves closer together. For reasons nobody has fixed, *A Tramp Abroad* sold exceptionally well in England, swelling his transatlantic fame and again assuring Americans about their potential for literary genius. More generally, Twain was proving himself capable of the long haul despite his joking about his laziness and anarchical habits.

The Prince and the Pauper impressed reviewers with a distinctly glossier format, a base of authentic details (not awesome yet diligent), and a loftiness of sentiment they dared not deflate. While a rambunctious Twain broke through the decorum often enough to appease devotees of his irreverence, the novel increased the measure and weight of his sensibilities. Next, *The Stolen White Elephant Etc.* seemed to diminish them with its crudely farcical title story. Still, its use of the bookstore channel and its two political homilies reinforced signs of a growing solidity that both the level of binding and overall content of *Life on the Mississippi* soon affirmed. Today's critics take little interest in its dominant subject—the sociocultural and economic activity along the entire Mississippi River valley in the early 1880s—yet reviewers pointed it out. When Twain hired George Washington Cable to tour with him as the Twins of Genius, the press consistently made Twain more equal and hounded him much more for interviews. Meanwhile, his role as publisher of the memoirs that Ulysses S. Grant, weak from cancer, struggled to finish was building toward a front-page display of patriotism, pathos, six- and seven-figure outlays, and hour-tagged bulletins.

Preceding the *Memoirs*, *Huckleberry Finn*, handsomely produced by Twain's own company, got reasonable coverage for a book sold by subscription. Patient searching has surely found most of the reviews, primarily in newspapers. Since it has also laid out the encompassing materials, *Huckleberry Finn* furnishes the best instance for the caveats of estimating Twain's literary reputation solely by the reviews. Although they were mostly favorable, they evidenced, collectively, less empathy or enthusiasm than other current commentary about Twain. Sales after the well-known—then and now—banishment by the board of the Concord Public Library suggest that *Huckleberry Finn* got the reviews that publishers covet most—word-of-mouth endorsement. While the newly organized profession of librarianship dedicated itself to elevating taste rather than satisfying walk-in demand, *Huckleberry Finn* started on its slow rise to eminence—too slowly, nevertheless, to account for the fact that Twain's fiftieth birthday revealed not just a leap in his prestige but fresh sources of its strength.

Twain himself was surprised that the *Critic*, the New York weekly committed to a sustainably high culture, would arrange for greetings from other authors, most notably Oliver Wendell Holmes, who cooperated wholeheartedly with a poem. Did Twain's accumulated writings look as masterful by then as they do now? In 1882 a laudatory essay by Howells for the self-important *Century Magazine* had aroused transatlantic notice. Yet further reasons seem necessary. Gradually, the press had turned the Hartford house into a massive badge of both Victorian domesticity and material success. Twain as ceremonial orator had been granting more and more petitions or turning them down charmingly with letters worth recycling across the country. Newspaper and magazine fillers gloated that his foreign readership was growing in France, German, and Scandinavia, and the *Critic* had reprinted an essay from the London *Daily News* insisting that "surely we appreciate as well as the Americans themselves the extraordinary intellectual high spirits of Mark Twain, a writer whose genius goes on mellowing, ripening, widening and improving at an age when another man would have written himself out" (*Critic* 4 [5 December 1885], p. 274). The Boston *Literary World*, cool toward Twain since starting up in 1870, could not avoid including him in the results of a poll by the Philadelphia *Weekly Press*: In responses to "Who is your favorite living story writer?" Twain had ranked fifth. In 1884, encouraged by a nativist's opinion that the United States could boast of its equals to the French Academy, the *Critic* had invited voting for "Our Forty [living] Immortals." Twain tied for fourteenth place. He was becoming more popular for being popular and successful.

By 1885, more than for any of his contemporaries, Twain's private life, conducted semipublicly, influence how readers (and listeners) took his humor. As with the stand-up comedians today who supposedly build on their experiences, his admirers were responding as much to the (imagined) real-life teller as to the tale. From filler paragraphs in the newspapers they knew far more about him than David R. Locke (Petroleum V. Nasby), Bret Harte, or Marietta Holley (Samantha Allen). Under his panache two facts dominated his thickening image. Journalists even exaggerated his income, spent showily. But they also played him up as conducting a New England household with a proper, poised wife and three daughters. He had migrated from a westerner to a citified insider who spoke through the present-day voice in *Life on the Mississippi* and earlier had made *A Tramp Abroad* tonally more sedate than his breakout book. The series of books in itself raised expectations for a humor weightier than throwaway sketches. More specifically, with *The Prince and the Pauper* and *Adventures of Huckleberry Finn* added to *Tom Sawyer*, a persona as a chronicler of childhood had emerged, and some readers now expected a humorist both more kindly and less guardedly sentimental than the adventurer behind *Roughing It*. As his novels proved that Twain could project characters besides his (presumed) self, his clientele began to esteem him also as a shrewd, amused, ultimately forgiving judge of human nature. Overall, though veteran admirers still preferred his impulsive spontaneity, those more perceptive, sensing a crafty and controlled awareness, enjoyed watching him watch himself performing as Mark Twain.

Twain could not help believing that the public who knew about him at all now took him as more cerebral than a merchant of comedy. Furthermore, tributes to his Americanism, that is, to how he embodied and expressed his country's most typical (and therefore) admirable qualities, had begun to flower. Indeed, Howells offered just that bouquet in *Harper's Monthly* to our "greatest humorist," whose pen name was "as well known, in America at least, as the name of Shakespeare." When Twain added the growing tributes to his push as a businessman in a survival-of-the-fittest economy, he felt ordained to preach with *A Connecticut Yankee in King Arthur's Court*. Resolutely, rightly, he anticipated some hostile reviews in England though various left-liberal groups would thereafter consider him an ally. American reviews, partly by his choice, were relatively sparse; also, some newspapers backed off from a dilemma: either reprimand a popular figure or help his undermining of organized religion. Otherwise, without dimming Twain's luster as a literary comedian, *Connecticut Yankee* intensified his image for a civic commitment enthusiastic about laissez-faire economics yet devoted to Tom Paine's gospels for the rights of man. Still charmed by his preceding books and personal interplay, influential British critics, as soon as Andrew Lang in 1891, indicated they were willing to forget his trashing of the chivalric ideal.

The early 1890s were schizoid for Twain. Privately anxious about solvency, he watched his reputation sweep upward along several tracks. Just when the American ethos started to rank making money as the most heroic of all virtues, rumor had him downright wealthy. Aesthetically, fewer and fewer critics dared to belittle him, and even the *Literary World* printed friendlier tidbits. Without deploring crass standards the *Critic* reported that a "purveyor of fiction to American newspapers" had listed Twain as the leader in "selling value." It helped compare him more

imposingly when it reported that a lament that "there are so few striking personalities among living Americans" exempted Holmes and Twain in literature because
"you don't have to tell anyone who they are" (*Critic*, 17 [16 January 1892] p. 45).

Twain's final cycle of travel letters, welcomed into syndication for newspapers,
reprised the American evaluating Europe idiosyncratically. *The American Claimant*,
little reviewed partly because it was syndicated first, also seemed familiar, this time
in descent from *The Gilded Age*. Although only a few scholars care now about
Merry Tales, it fitted with the sense of Twain as a self-supporting professional,
as did the especially heterogeneous *One-Million-Pound Banknote and Other New
Stories* for British readers. *Tom Sawyer Abroad* catered obviously to a juvenile audience and to adults who enjoyed Twain's way with boys while the realistic-minded
accepted it, like *Tom Sawyer, Detective* later, as resupplying loyal customers.
Pudd'nhead Wilson exemplifies the flaws of gauging Twain's reputation book by
book (*pace* story by story in the magazines). Probably, careful readers wondered
whether it was a call for racial justice or a potboiler, and the deceptively few reviews
didn't help them. Was it upstaged by the almost concurrent melodrama? In 1898 a
critic judged that the "beautiful play" was better known "on account of the prohibi-
tive price put upon" the book after it "had a successful course as a serial" (Paul
Wilstach, "The American Library and the Drama," *Bookman* 8 [1898] p. 137). Furthermore, it sends a warning to check the actual foreign editions. In this case British
reviewers were spared the weakest part, the so-called comedy *Those Extraordinary
Twins*. A final snag in any pattern: Pudd'nhead's Maxims attracted their separate
fanciers and led to a new genre in Twain's repertoire.

No reviewer of *The Tragedy of Pudd'nhead Wilson* had perceived its author as
sinking into gloom. Twain's bankruptcy came as a surprise that overrode any mur-
murs of Schadenfreude. Now all heart, the *Literary World* registered "the sympathy
everywhere felt with Mark Twain ... plainly due as much to his personal as to his
literary popularity" (New York Letter," *Literary World* 25 [5 May 1894] p. 137). The
lecture tour "around the world" to pay off the debts of his publishing house was
launched to editorials on a courage that coped with the aging suddenly perceived in
his face and walk. Then as reports came of how warmly as well as reverentially
Australia, New Zealand, India, and South Africa treated him, Americans swelled
with self-congratulation. Any dry-eyed reviewers of *Personal Recollections of Joan of
Arc* had to demur faintly, and none questioned a jester's fitness to take up so
solemn, so pious a subject. Genteelists, to be sure, welcomed this visit to their
chapel, chaperoned by the House of Harper. Nobody objected noticeably when *The
Library of the World's Best Literature, Ancient and Modern* gave Twain ample pages
(mostly for "Old Times") or Harper—prematurely—announced a uniform edition
of his writings. Meanwhile, newspaper and magazine fillers cheered on the expected
book about the world tour, underlining his heroism in sticking to it despite added
troubles. American reviewers helped the rescue along, and the British tried to

overlook Twain's skepticism about exactly who was toting the white man's burden in their empire. Twain recuperated enough to carry a glittering social burden in Vienna, to the profit of American stringers and the delight of editors back home. After the family returned to London, its establishment, not just literary but political and social, opened all doors to them. Literary academics in the United States, typically Anglophile anyway, did the same in spirit, perhaps happy to stop resisting Twain's genius. An admittedly loose poll for a proposed Academy of American Immortals placed him third. When a collected edition did issue in 1899, it seemed overdue and worthy of its glowing imprimatur from Brander Mathews, ensconced at Columbia University after his own status-climbing.

Charting Twain's rise in Great Britain as well as the United States is easy. Also clear is his emergence in the later 1890s as a celebrity known beyond western Europe and other countries with a readership for American authors, though its speed and strength did puzzle some of his contemporaries. Hindsight shows that the process had been accelerating since 1876 as the Tauchnitz firm in Germany reprinted each major Twain work soon after it came out and also resurrected the two early travel books. Careful to keep its backlist active, vigorous in its marketing, alert to attractive pricing, and quick to finance its reputation for quality and integrity, Tauchnitz had steady sales not only across Germany and nearby Europe but in the Near East and Africa. Furthermore, as reading publics expanded, translators got active in all larger countries. Because publishing had moved more nakedly toward profit, they chose demonstrably popular writers; for Twain they collected the favorites among his short pieces that had already spread his fame among casual readers. Devotees of fiction with memorable characters underrate the appeals of his freestanding sketches.

Meanwhile, new print media were competing more fiercely for the saleable attention of the public. So reputation grew harder yet to measure. How does a review in a dignified *St. James's Gazette* count against a London *Daily News* going all out for circulation? In the professedly literary Boston *Evening Transcript* or the staid New York *Evening Post* against Joseph Pulitzer's *World* scrambling to head off W. R. Hearst's charge eastward? In a slick paper monthly against a flimsy daily even as magazines were straining to look newsier but Sunday editions were developing please-all supplements? Happily for Twain's fame, he could cultivate both gardens and any hybrid as he proved by showily arriving home in 1900 and then handling, selectively yet disarmingly, the demands on his energy. He felt enough in control to challenge American imperialists, militants, missionaries, and chauvinists—combined, the strongest enemy he ever taunted. Although they counterattacked cautiously, if at all, bystanders chuckled that the risk-taking Twain had reared up again. Of course, the factions that benefited sang his praises louder than ever. To nonpartisan readers Twain came across as more righteous than humorous.

Yale University soon thickened his dignity with an honorary doctorate, which encouraged the University of Missouri to follow the next year. Unquestionably, his admirers could now class him as a serious artist though a reviewer still beamed that "Dr. Holmes and Mark Twain are the chief apostles of American humor, the patron saints of the temple of Comus." In those terms Twain towered above mere entertainment just as society was raising the prestige of that commodity anyway. Finally on full throttle, a collected edition kept announcing various formats and offers. While eventually forgettable, new books confirmed the sense of how Twain's creativity meshed with a practical drive for income. His core constituency preferred him to stay characteristic even when understandably claiming seasoned wisdom. They accepted the lead fable of *The Man That Corrupted Hadleyburg and Other Stories and Essays* as sardonic comedy, weightier than before but recognizable; *A Double-Barreled Detective Story* as a self-indulgent revisiting of his burlesques; *Extracts from Adam's Diary* and *Eve's Diary* as whimsical sentiment spiced with bolder free-thought; *A Dog's Tale* and *A Horse's Tale* as ingenious spinoffs of his sympathy for the abused; the soliloquies of Czar Nicholas and King Leopold as updates of Hank Morgan's crusading; and *Is Shakespeare Dead?* as his skepticism charging on into secular heresy. While his hostile quizzing of Mary Baker Eddy raised the most hackles, he had lately been declaring that old age entailed the right to total candor.

Whatever disorderly moves he made, steady reinforcements of his prestige protected him. Howells, his superior by more sedate standards, published an impressively long encomium. In denying that the United States could "boast of a school of fiction distinctively its own," Frank Norris had to grant that Twain was "American to the core" ("An American School of Fiction? A Denial," *The Literary Criticism of Frank Norris*, p. 109 [1964]). Harper's staged a birthday dinner imposing enough for heavy news coverage in 1902. The first seven members elected to the American Academy of Arts and Letters included Twain. For his seventieth birthday in 1905 his publishers orchestrated a much trumpeted banquet for guests more select than the recently anointed Four Hundred. His centerpiece speech was applauded beyond any realistic merits and widely reprinted. While a beloved public figure with a rudimentary talent for humor can get credit for dazzling wit, Twain, with most of his original genius still functioning, drew upon almost forty-five years of establishing his presence and history. For some of his audience, phrases or turns of idea called up a character, event, or punchline of his that they had treasured. An author with a long career has been compounding interest more profitably than war bonds.

The academics who had begun to claim the authority to judge living writers and therefore the contemporary canon added expertise to the consensus. William Lyon Phelps, famously of Yale, had volunteered to lead it before the doctorate from Oxford. After that, superlatives sounded anticlimactic as Twain remained comment-worthy with offhand interviews, strategic outings of the white suit in winter, a last gamut of speeches, breezy statements to the press, and do-good gestures. As cameras improved along with the half-tone process for printing snapshots, he became recognizable on the street or streetcar by people who didn't buy stereographs or remember his oil portraits in galleries or the cartoons at all levels of artistry and circulation. Obviously, the New York *Herald*'s series "Who Are the Ten Greatest Living Americans?" would give Twain his full-page spread (second after Thomas Edison). His death was telegraphed internationally, with banner headlines at home. Only a fearless analyst can encapsulate the reputation driving and then resulting from the torrent of obituaries, roundup stories, anecdotes, and sidebars such as the supposed cooperation of Halley's Comet. An elaborate, eloquent memorial held months later at Carnegie Hall sounded like a huge echo.

Twain's death brought the most compact core-sample of his international reputation. Obituaries and editorials spread across the world as far as South Africa, India, and Australia. They naturally featured his American qualities but not so intensively as patriots would have liked, even when his commitment to egalitarian humaneness was credited to a native source. More often the eulogies repeated the motifs played during his world tour: besides his popularity in itself, his shrewd yet spontaneous personality and his genius for humor, home-bred yet transnational in its effects. That humor had shipped well through sharply different climates by engaging basic enthusiasms and anxieties. Rather than savoring American distinctiveness, many foreign readers had responded to his delight in the generic absurdities of humankind and its doings, his flouting of workaday rationality, or simply his bursts of irreverent drolling. Translators had expected salability for "My Watch," "Taming the Bicycle," or "The Stolen White Elephant," not just the Tom-Huck books. Monarchist countries evidently found fundamental, apolitical decencies supported entertainingly in *The Prince and the Pauper*, and some non-Christians as well as agnostics enjoyed the elemental psychology in the "diaries" of Adam and Eve.

Twain had prepared for his canonization by accepting A. B. Paine as his biographer and not quite discouraging an academic who maneuvered for the inside track. But indefatigably loyal Howell was ready by July 1910 with an edition of his renowned speeches, and *My Mark Twain* created a homespun yet honorific halo for "the sole, the incomparable, the Lincoln of our literature" (p. 103). The puffing of the collected works, now presumably complete, stepped up. Beginning decades of books, essays, and editions, Paine presented Twain so reassuringly that a version of *The Mysterious Stranger* in 1916 puzzled its few reviewers. He probably hesitated over next using *What Is Man?* to give edge to a shapeless miscellany. But there was no need to worry. As anybody who had met Twain—or dared to claim so—set down the details, sometimes accurately, the stream of reminiscences burbled benignly, virtually free of acids. Because of that blandness, *The Ordeal of Mark Twain* was generally taken as condemnatory though Van Wyck Brooks had granted

Twain's genius, blaming rather his wife and his times for its waste. Anyhow, that same year Twain, finally eligible, mounted to the Hall of Fame administered through New York University. Out in the open air, his reputation survived 1920s cynicism and acquired a Jeffersonian timbre from V. L. Parrington before passing into the formidable care of Bernard DeVoto, who combined it with the enthusiasm for Americana that grew deeper along with the Great Depression.

Official academia mostly ignored the centenary of Twain's birth, though the University of Missouri and Columbia University set up events, and in the New York City area his nonspecialist admirers—still his strongest source of reputation—were more vigorous. Before and after 1935, as Henry Nash Smith observed, literary critics mostly adapted Twain to the broader swings of approach. While their surveys of American culture differed greatly on how much space and homage, if any, to give him, mainstream commentary, overlapping for example with editorials or letters to the editor in the New York *Times*, kept his laurels fresh. Dumas Malone, winding up as chief editor of the *Dictionary of American Biography* and asking "Who Are the American Immortals?" included Twain among the eight men of letters. He was reasonably well positioned for the geopolitical reordering of values after World War II.

Concurrently, and more important for the long run, the reading of his actual words had carried on outside of theories about what had gone right or wrong with American culture. Opinions about specific works regularly turned up in casual as well as organized discourse. At some indeterminate point (after World War I, perhaps), *The Innocents Abroad* sounded more and more provincial. Bonded with the frontier myth, *Roughing It* held its appeal as the Old West grew ruddier in retrospect. *Life on the Mississippi,* or rather its "Old Times" chapters, proved especially suitable for the anthologies that started exerting authority over undergraduate notions of what ranks as the "best" in literature. Many anthologists used "The Man That Corrupted Hadleyburg" if only because its up-front plot functions without bothersome dialect. Its effect supported particularly the image of the down-home philosopher who coined those witticisms that keep recycling both orally and in print.

As the appreciation for egalitarian humor and Americana grew even stronger with the boom following World War II, *Huckleberry Finn* overshadowed *Tom Sawyer*, which struck the higher-browed as shaped for children anyway. So, while *Tom Sawyer* held on in the family circle (which could, however, fuse the two books), *Huckleberry Finn* climbed toward its primacy, already proclaimed memorably by H. J. Mencken and DeVoto. Neither of these robust spirits would have deplored the bootleg editions of "[Date 1601] Conversation . . . in the Time of the Tudors," which increased rumors that Twain's handlers were hiding a trove of raunchy, near-pornographic items. Other suspicions of deviancy hung on among those who heard that some of the unpublished manuscripts dabbled in extreme agnosticism. Of course the Christian Scientists continued to feel slandered. Many kinds of his admirers could, happily, approve the multimedia, perennial reworkings of *The Prince and the Pauper* that reached into the Soviet Union. Otherwise, Cold War monitors couldn't decide how to interpret Twain's popularity there. As ever his reputation had enough mixups to avoid dullness.

Within our skewed yet copious affluence, Twain's reputation has broadened more than deepened as his mere name, face or figure, favored characters, and quotables promote all sorts of services or products. No census can list all the hucksters. For committed readers any comic-book version grows crude after childhood, but they recommend some films, A&E–style biographies, or Hal Holbrook–level imperson-ators—accepting a stand-off between dumbing down and acting exclusive. However, the academics who multiplied through the GI Bill tried to take charge of his reputa-tion, an especially attractive exhibit and export for the late-arriving American Century. Although condescended to by some colleagues, they felt feisty after the quasi-official *Eight American Authors* (1956) included Twain. Reinforced now by oncoming scholar-critics they conduct their own "Circle," journals, and Internet "forum." As the cultural skies darkened they have dug harder into his near-nihilistic fables and found sociopolitical gloom overriding comedy in *Huckleberry Finn*; co-conspiring with larger forces, most of them have approved of its (hyper?) canoniza-tion while defending it against charges of latent racism. Today, only the people—as Twain would say—too deaf to see lightning don't know at least that it's a "classic." The thrust of domestic acclaim has finally lifted it into worldwide eminence though many readers who need translations still prefer his less "native" books and short pieces. Scanning UNESCO's *Index Translationum* (which covers 1932–1940 and 1948–1986) leads to a more complicated sense of his appeal than cultural imperialism allows for.

Because American pop-culture has proved so seductive, we tend to assume that Twain's global readership responds to his indigenous qualities, however defined. At least that's more plausible than inferring eagerness to learn about American society. Twain's fictional world—in his times seldom contemporary, much less mainline—is long gone. Instead, many of his foreign admirers find transhistorical qualities, as in other figures of world literature. Stated combatively, those qualities center on his resistance to social hierarchy, routine, sober practicality, pressures for coherent behavior, or just the shackles of tidy conversation. Stated positively, those qualities center on taking kinetic pleasure in life, on keeping alert, flexible, hopeful, and ven-turesome. Often with illustrations that strike Americans as strange, *Tom Sawyer* has accumulated a wide, deep record of translations because its hero is imaginative, indomitable, and—yes—successful. Although Ecclesiastes already decided that "all is vanity and vexation of spirit" (1:14) (and one side of Twain would agree), *homo sapiens* keeps resonating to a rising rather than dying trumpet. Ordinary readers everywhere get more fun out of Twain than do seminars on his tragic mode.

At home *Huckleberry Finn* made the century's turn the richest years for Twain's reputation since 1910. The advertising-media-entertainment industry realizes that he remains a grabber also for his (late) physical presence and sayings. More and more people globally know something about his life and could inject a "yes-but" if conversation brings him up. Relative to his prestige he draws surprisingly little backtalk as a dead, white, western male. His reputation will flourish into the predictable future, adapting to the decline of books as the dominant channel of literacy. It is already well-keyed into the World Wide Web.

Illustration from *Following the Equator*, Hartford: American Publishing Company, 1897, p. 516, by F. M. Senior. The chapter opens with a quotation from Puddn'head Wilson's New Calendar: "True Irreverence is disrespect for another man's god."

Continued from page 496

By the 1880s, however, Mark Twain began to challenge the value of reverence, seeing in it a toadying provincialism that supported morally indefensible social practices, and seeing in irreverence a force that could reveal the oppressive shams of revering the wealthy and the powerful. In the 1880s, after reading Matthew *Arnold's attacks on American humor and newspapers for their "irreverence," Clemens began a series of counterattacks defending irreverence as a political necessity for a democratic and modern civilization. Much of this material was too vituperative for Clemens to publish, especially given that Arnold died suddenly of a heart attack right after the publication of "Civilization in the United States." Clemens did have some sense of reverence for the dead, but he still found it impossible to let Arnold's charges go unanswered. While he did not publish any of the nearly one hundred manuscript pages of replies to Arnold, much of this material found its way into *A Connecticut Yankee in King Arthur's Court* and *The American Claimant*, as well as into his speech "General Grant's Grammar," and in his speech accepting an honorary master's degree from Yale (1888).

In suggesting the political importance of irreverence in maintaining democracy, Clemens did not reject reverence, but he did change his conception of how reverence should work and how one should exercise it in service of political change rather than as a conservative force. As demonstrated in *Following the Equator*, Mark Twain came to see reverence working at its highest pitch as an opportunity to exercise the broadest range of sympathy: "True reverence is reverence for another man's god" (chapter 53).

REVOLUTION. To most of America's opinion leaders, the French Revolution was a great bugaboo, the sign that America's "rational" revolution had wisely stopped at representative government rather than moving to pure *democracy. As a person whose politics began Whiggish and who became an avid supporter of the *Republican party in the late 1860s, Samuel Clemens at first shared such a view. "The Great Revolution in Pitcairn," for example, suggests that the revolutionary perspective is really a mask for self-interest, and that any revolution will lead, appropriately, to counterrevolution. By 1887, however, he had changed his mind, passing through the cautious appraisal of *A Tramp Abroad*, in which he called the French Revolution hideous in itself, though yielding positive results, to believing the terror was the right thing. In chapter 13 of *A Connecticut Yankee in King Arthur's Court*, for instance, he called the French Revolution "ever-memorable and blessed" for putting to an end the aristocratic oppression of centuries:

> There were two "reigns of Terror," if we would but remember it and consider it: the one wrought murder in hot passion, the other in heartless cold blood; the one lasted mere months, the other had lasted a thousand years; the one

inflicted death upon ten thousand persons, the other upon a hundred millions; but our shudders are all for the "horrors" of the minor Terror, the momentary Terror, so to speak; whereas, what is the horror of swift death by the axe, compared with life-long death from hunger, cold, insult, cruelty, and heart-break? What is swift death by lightning, compared with death by slow fire at the stake? A city cemetery could contain the coffins filled by that brief Terror which we have all been so diligently taught to shiver at and mourn over, but all France could hardly contain the coffins filled by that older and real Terror—that unspeakably bitter and awful Terror which none of us has been taught to see in its vastness or pity as it deserves.

In this change, Twain was merely catching up to the times, finally accepting the flow of history in the nineteenth century, which witnessed several waves of revolutions. Not least of these were, in America, the *women's rights movement and the anti-slavery battle, both of which were often denounced by social conservatives as of a piece with the revolutions sweeping Europe. These were violent political revolutions against the ancien régime, suppressed ruthlessly.

These European revolutions had an impact on American society by causing corresponding waves of immigration, especially after 1832 and 1848. Both times, foreign workers began radicalizing the American *labor movement. Competition from foreign-born typesetters in the latter wave helped make it impossible for young Samuel Clemens to earn a good living as a typesetter in New York and Philadelphia. While Clemens may have disliked labor radicalism, his early resistance to revolution had roots in his own economic standing.

Still, America celebrated the "ever-glorious Fourth of July" every year, reminding itself that it, too, began in revolution. The gradual radicalization of Twain's expressed opinions of revolution was partly promoted by his growing historical consciousness of how the American Revolution played a part in the world's pattern of increasing democratization. While he never accepted the economic-based arguments of the most radical of European socialist revolutionaries, he did, from about 1887 on, support most revolutionary causes in Europe and those around the world against European *imperialism.

Praise of revolution made it into his works, not only in *Connecticut Yankee*, but also in *The American Claimant* and *Following the Equator*. In the first of these, he has Hank Morgan say, "All gentle cant and philosophizing to the contrary notwithstanding, no people in this world ever did achieve their freedom by goody-goody talk and moral suasion: it being immutable law that all revolutions that will succeed, must *begin* in blood" (chapter 20).

In that reference to moral suasion, Twain is referring to America's antebellum abolitionism under the likes of William Lloyd Garrison, whose pacifism ultimately lost out. Twain here implicitly and in chapter 30 explicitly endorses the North's cause as a just and necessary revolution in favor of moral *progress. In chapter 32 of

Following the Equator, on the contrary, Twain praises the women's rights movement as beneficently violating the Yankee's precept; it accomplished a revolution "without bloodshed."

Notwithstanding Twain's rhetoric in favor of revolution, and his praise of Zola's courage in standing up to the French nation in the Dreyfus affair, one must wonder how deep was Twain's support for revolution. When Maxim Gorki visited the United States in 1906 to drum up financial and political support for Russian revolutionaries, Twain signed on until he learned that Gorki was travelling with his mistress. Gorki's violation of Victorian proprieties was more than Twain felt he could countenance without damaging his own reputation, and he withdrew his support, a withdrawal he feebly explained in "The Gorki Incident." That he wrote the piece in April 1906—shortly after Gorki was evicted from his hotel—but did not publish it in his lifetime, suggests that his renunciation of Gorki and thus of Gorki's cause may have given Clemens at least a twinge of conscience.

♦ SEE ALSO *Age of Reason, The;* Censorship; Unfinished Works.

RILEY, JAMES WHITCOMB (1849–1916). After a varied career that included a stint as an actor with a patent-medicine show, Riley became a writer for the *Indianapolis Journal*, where he contributed comic and sentimental "Hoosier" dialect poetry. Among his more famous are "When the Frost Is on the Pumpkin" and "Little Orphant Annie," suggestive of his niche as a popular, rather than literary, favorite. His writing, however, like that of Mark Twain, had widespread appeal among the literati; heavyweight literary critic Brander Matthews of Columbia University, for instance, praised Riley's poetry for its "elaborate metrical artistry and . . . dexterous command of sound."

Riley appeared on the platform with Twain, George Washington *Cable, and William Dean *Howells in Boston in 1894, virtually stealing the show. Riley was a talented reader of his own works, and he appeared regularly for years with humorist Bill Nye in a platform show that combined Nye's mildly caustic attitude with Riley's sentimentality. Riley's enormous popularity, combined with his great talent as a stage performer, made him the perfect example for Twain's description of what he called American humor in *"How to Tell a Story" (1895).

RILEY, JOHN HENRY (1830?–1872). A veteran of the gold rush in California, John Henry Riley met Clemens in San Francisco when both were working as newspaper reporters. Their paths kept them together in 1867–1868 when both worked as correspondents for the San Francisco *Alta California* from Washington, D.C., where they roomed together. When two years later diamonds were discovered in South Africa, Clemens proposed to send Riley to collect notes that Clemens would work up into a travel book. Clemens was hot on this idea for a *collaboration in spite of his failure to make a book out of the few "Around the World" articles written in collaboration with Darius Ford as the traveler and Twain as the commentator. He blamed the earlier failure on Ford, and believed this effort would succeed because Riley was the right kind of person for the job. He secured a contract with the American Publishing Company and an advance on royalties of two thousand dollars, which Riley used to fund his mining expedition, departing from America in January 1871. Riley developed symptoms of cancer and left the mine fields within three months, and his ill health impeded his utility as a correspondent. He died in Philadelphia in September 1872. With Riley not up to the task and Clemens losing interest as other projects intruded, the South Africa book was never written.

Riley figures in several of Mark Twain's works, explicitly in the 1870 *Galaxy* article "Riley—Newspaper Correspondent," in which Twain praises Riley's "unfailing vein of irony which makes his conversation to the last degree entertaining (as long as the remarks are about somebody else)." This *irony makes Riley the perfect character for the story of "The Man Who Put Up at Gadsby's" in *A Tramp Abroad*.

ROBBER BARONS. While editing the Buffalo *Express* in 1869 and having just married into a family that owned substantial interests in coal mines and railroads in New York state, Clemens attacked in an "Open Letter to Commodore Vanderbilt" the man who had publicly damned the public. Mark Twain expressed his pity for Vanderbilt for the obsequious praise his millions of dollars bought him as well as for his insatiable hunger for more *money:

> I always feel for a man who is so poverty ridden as you. Don't misunderstand me, Vanderbilt. I know you own seventy millions; but then you know and I know that it isn't what a man has that constitutes wealth. No—it is to be *satisfied* with what one has; that is wealth.... [Y]ou *need* five hundred millions, and are really suffering for it. Your poverty is something appalling.... My soul is so wrought upon by your hapless pauperism, that if you came by me now I would freely put ten cents in your tin cup, if you carry one, and say "God pity you, poor unfortunate!"

Such scorn finely began Mark Twain's reputation as a defender of the American bourgeoisie against the new American plutocracy, what Clemens called, in a letter from New York City published in the *Alta California* (5 April 1867), "princes of Shoddy," so called because they made their millions in war contracting, usually by supplying substandard goods at premium prices.

It is worth making a distinction between Clemens's idea of wealth and that of the plutocrats, especially given Clemens's own obvious love of and pursuit of money, enough to enable him to live a life of generous opulence, if not of bloated luxury. He did not, however, dream of watering stock, of manipulating markets, of bilking the public treasury, nor of "selling" his daughters to the scions of the European aristocracy. Nor did he believe, according to the social Darwinist justifications of many of the plutocrats, that anything goes in the struggle for success and that success was a sign of the innate superiority of the rich man over the masses. Stories such as "Cecil Rhodes and the Shark," "Luck," and even much of *Roughing It* challenge the American belief that success is anything other than a fortunate accident, or worse, the result of unscrupulous dealings.

Still, Mark Twain's own celebrity put him in the same public constellation as the superrich, giving him access to the world that he professed to despise. Then, too, the satirist's energy often stems from veiled longing—it is no wonder that Clemens, who had once tried silver mining in search of a sudden fortune and who traded stocks throughout his life in search of an investment that he could retire on, could publish *The Gilded Age* as an attack on the speculative spirit of the times and write, but not publish, the "Letter from the Recording Angel" (also known as "Letter to the Earth"), in which he attacks one of his wife's relatives with as much energy as, and with more concentrated bile than, he spent on Vanderbilt. In a way, he was partly in the pocket of the wealthy and partly under the spell of their example, and he knew and resented it.

Such knowledge and resentment would only grow worse in the late years of his life. Upon his impending bankruptcy in 1893 he was unable to borrow money to rescue his sinking publishing company or to maintain his by now desperate investment in the *Paige typesetter. When introduced by a friend, Dr. Clarence C. Rice, to Henry Huttleston *Rogers, one of the principals of Standard Oil Company, Clemens fell into the hands of his financial angel, the man who more or less became his patron. Rogers took it upon himself to rescue Clemens from fiscal incompetence, advising him how to handle his bankruptcy and then overseeing his *finances. In return, Clemens became a member of Rogers's social circle, which included the likes of John D. Rockefeller, and served not only as entertainer for them, but also helped them in their publicity campaigns.

No wonder that in his autobiographical dictations, which he expected to be published after his death, Clemens wrote scathing denunciations of various plutocrats. Much of his bile he directed at one of the first, Jay Gould:

> Jay Gould had just then reversed the commercial morals of the United States. He had put a blight upon them from which they have never recovered, and from which they will not recover for as much as a century to come. Jay Gould was the mightiest disaster which has ever befallen this country. The people had *desired* money before his day, but *he* taught them to fall down and worship it. They had respected men of means before his day, but along with this respect was joined the respect due to the character and industry which had accumulated it. But Jay Gould taught the entire nation to make a god of the money and the man, no matter how the money might have been acquired. . . . The gospel left behind by Jay Gould is doing giant work in our

days. Its message is "Get money. Get it quickly. Get it in abundance. Get it in prodigious abundance. Get it dishonestly if you can, honestly if you must."

But this opening was merely a temporary displacement. Later in the same dictation, he turned his attack to John D. Rockefeller, Jr., whose company he could not avoid as long as he remained under obligations to Rogers: "Satan, twaddling sentimental sillinesses to a Sunday-school, could be no burlesque upon John D. Rockefeller and his performances in his Cleveland Sunday-school. When John D. is employed in that way he strikes the utmost limit of grotesqueness. He can't be burlesqued—he is himself a burlesque" (16 February 1906).

ROGERS, HENRY HUTTLESTON (1840–1909). From Samuel L. Clemens's point of view, Henry Huttleston Rogers was the man who rescued his financial ship when no other person in the world was able or willing. From the point of view of most Americans of Clemens's generation, Rogers was one of the most ruthless businessmen and financial speculators in the country. Given Clemens's particular bias, it is not surprising that Rogers was the one of America's *robber barons whom Clemens actually supported in public and private.

Born in Mattapoisett, Massachusetts, and raised in nearby Fairhaven, Rogers began his work career as a grocery clerk, paper deliverer, and railroad worker. On the basis of a small savings from that work, in 1861, he and a friend, Charles P. Ellis, founded a small oil refinery in McClintocksville, Pennsylvania. Their business prospered and combined with other refiners until it became one of the founding companies of Rockefeller's conglomerate, Standard Oil. Rogers quickly rose to become vice president of Standard and was one of Rockefeller's most important, trusted, and ruthless associates. His tactics in building monopolies often brought him under government investigation. While he was never convicted of any crime, as Ida Tarbell put it in her memoir, *All in a Day's Work* (1939), Rogers was "as fine a pirate as ever flew his flag in Wall Street." He was at the center of the biggest monopoly in American business and, through exceptionally fortunate and unscrupulous speculation in insurance, transportation, mining, and banking, extended his reach into numerous related or compatible concerns.

Personally, he was, like Clemens, charismatic, a fine raconteur, and devoted to smoking, billiards, cards, and profanity. When his friendship with Clemens began in 1893, he pulled Clemens into his social sphere, entertaining Clemens on his yacht or at his New York or Fairhaven homes. The Rogers circle, in some respects, returned Clemens to the kind of masculine world of business and sporting events in which Clemens began his literary career before he married Olivia Langdon. But while Clemens spent his early years among men on the make with whom he conspired nonstop to find ways to make *money, in Rogers Clemens found a patron. In the years after he proved to himself that he was not a businessman,

Clemens was content to be the artist in Rogers's court. Rogers in turn paid. As Finley Peter Dunne reports, in deciding on the guest list for a literary luncheon club the two were proposing, Clemens suggested:

"How about H. H. Rogers?"
"I thought you said this was to be a literary lunch."
"So it is."
"Then why ask Rogers?"
"Why ask Rogers?" Mark cried. "Why ask Rogers? To pay for the lunch, you idiot." ("Mr. Dooley's Friends," *Atlantic Monthly*, CCXII (1963): 95)

The relationship began with Rogers paying in cash rather than in lunches. In the midst of the financial panic of 1893, neither Clemens's in-laws, nor friends, nor any commercial banks could lend him the money he needed to keep his foundering publishing business, *Webster and Company, afloat. Rogers stepped in to stave off immediate bankruptcy.

In a letter to Olivia, he explained that his friend, Dr. Clement T. Rice, at whose home he was staying while trying to raise money among investors or bankers, "told me he had ventured to speak to a rich friend of his who was an admirer of mine about our straits. I was very glad. Mr. Hall was to be at this gentleman's office away down Broadway at 4 yesterday afternoon, with his statements; and in six minutes we had the check and our worries were over till the 28th" (17 September 1893). Thus began a friendship that Rogers had tried to start two years earlier when the two men first met.

Under these adverse circumstances, Rogers took over Clemens's *finances, arranging to have his son-in-law purchase the *Library of American Literature* from Charles L. Webster and Company for fifty thousand dollars. But despite Rogers's efforts to help the company, it failed in April 1894 when the bank called Webster and Company's loan. He negotiated the bankruptcy for Clemens, arranging that Olivia should be the company's preferred creditor and forcing the other creditors to settle for fifty cents on the dollar. As he told Albert Bigelow Paine years later, the creditors were "bent on devouring every pound of flesh in sight and picking the bones afterward." Clemens was not willing to fight the creditors for favorable terms, believing that he had to pay every dollar owed. His statements to that effect were a public relations necessity for an author struggling to make a comeback, a comeback he could never have achieved if Rogers hadn't bought time with a tough-minded agreement. Rogers, playing hardball behind the scenes, allowed Clemens to act high-minded in public.

Concurrently, Rogers "looked into" Clemens's investment in the *Paige typesetter, becoming Clemens's partner in the business and renegotiating the contract under which Clemens was to make money if the machine ever worked. He helped keep Clemens's bubble alive for a year before the machine proved a failure in December of

1894. Later, he helped arrange a contract with George Harvey of Harper and Brothers to ensure a market for Mark Twain's works for the rest of Clemens's life.

After declaring bankruptcy in 1894, Clemens undertook an around-the-world lecture tour and then wrote a book, *Following the Equator*, based on the tour. As he earned money lecturing, he sent the proceeds to Rogers, whose careful and canny investments paid off handsomely. The results of the tour, the book, and the investments put the Clemens family comfortably back in the black. The intense business cooperation between Rogers and Clemens made the sound basis of a friendship, and Clemens's connections with Rogers from 1893 to Rogers's death in 1909 were among the strongest he had with anybody. Besides sharing drink, smoke, cards, and conversation, they shared philanthropic interests as well, both supporting Booker T. Washington's Tuskegee Institute and Helen Keller's work on behalf of the deaf.

The professional benefits of the relationship were not all in Clemens's favor. Rogers used his friendship with Clemens for good publicity, and occasionally for more. When, for instance, Rogers learned in December 1901 that Ida Tarbell was about to publish an investigative series on Standard Oil in *McClure's Magazine*, Rogers wrote to Clemens about his concern that Tarbell had not consulted with any but "those not disinterested enemies" of Standard Oil and asked if Clemens could do anything. Clemens arranged with *McClure's* to have Tarbell interview Rogers for her series. This was eleven years after the Sherman Anti-trust Act was passed and ten years before Standard Oil was successfully prosecuted under the act. Standard sought positive publicity to protect itself in this environment, and Clemens served that interest.

But this is not to diminish the friendship itself. Rogers stood by Clemens in dark times, and the two shared personal interests. Rogers's magnetic personality was something Clemens especially liked. Used to being the center of every show, he nonetheless enjoyed the company of equally good talkers. They were, however, rare, and in Rogers he found one of the very few men whom he considered a peer as a conversationalist and humorist. As he put it in a letter to Olivia:

> Sometimes when I reflect that our great scheme may still at any moment go to ruin before our eyes and consign me and mine to irretrievable poverty and want, my three months' work are but acts of a tragedy; but all the rest of the time it is a comedy—and certainly the killingest one, the darlingest one and the most fascinating one that ever was. I don't laugh easily, I believe, but there are two men who make me laugh without any difficulty—to-wit, Mr Rogers when he comments on the C[onnecticut] C[ompany], and Frank Jenkins ... when he comments on his opponents' shots in a game of billiards. (27–30 January 1894)

A man who could make Clemens see the bright side of even bankruptcy, who could turn the seriousness of life into a game, helped Clemens more fundamentally than through mere financial manipulations. And Rogers himself seems to have been willing to help Clemens in the first place because he so admired Clemens's writing. Mutual admiration was the real glue for a lifelong friendship that also served mutual interests.

♦ SEE ALSO Publishing Industry; Reform.

ROMANCE. In the introductory chapter to *The Scarlet Letter*, Nathaniel Hawthorne describes the art of the romance writer:

> Moonlight, falling so white upon the carpet, and showing all its figures so distinctly,—making every object as minutely visible, yet so unlike a morning or noontide visibility,—is a medium the most suitable for a romance-writer to get acquainted with his illusive guests. . . . [D]etails . . . are so spiritualized by the unusual light, that they seem to lose their actual substance, and become things of the intellect. . . . [T]he floor of our familiar room has become a neutral territory, somewhere between the real world and fairy-land, where the Actual and the Imaginary may meet, and each imbue itself with the nature of the other.

Such were the artistic tenets of the generation of American writers preceding Clemens's, and such were the ideals held by many of his contemporaries.

While Clemens agreed that moonlight transfigured reality, he did not accept that such transfiguration had value. *The Innocents Abroad* and *Roughing It* are substantially accounts of Mark Twain being disabused of his romantic preconceptions. In *Roughing It* (chapter 18), for instance, when about to cross a Western alkali flat in broad daylight Mark Twain reports that the prospect was "fine—novel—romantic." But the romance "wilted under the sultry August sun and did not last above one hour. One poor little hour—and then we were ashamed we had 'gushed' so. The poetry was all in the anticipation—there is none in the reality." One needs physical comfort, not spiritual disengagement, in order to find the poetry of life: "[I]t was a comfort . . . to sit up and contemplate the majestic panorama of mountains and valleys spread out below us and eat ham and hard boiled eggs while our spiritual natures reveled alternately in rainbows, thunderstorms, and peerless sunsets. Nothing helps scenery like ham and eggs."

By the standard of photographic *realism that Clemens held as his ideal of absolute truth, romantic idealism lies, but Clemens couldn't leave romanticism alone. In spite of repeated attacks on romanticism—in part by way of such attacks—he finds romance anyway, as his adventuresome account in *Roughing It* does not leave a jaded realist so much as a Mark Twain whose capacity for romance always exceeds his experience, and whose tales of romance disappointed are nonetheless romantic. So despite attacks on romantic accounts of Europe in *Inno-*

cents Abroad and *A Tramp Abroad*, on Cooper in *Roughing It* and *"Fenimore Cooper's Literary Offenses,"* on Scott in *Life on the Mississippi* and *Adventures of Huckleberry Finn*, on Tennyson and on the romance of *medievalism in *A Connecticut Yankee in King Arthur's Court*, he could as easily endorse Tom Sawyer's book-inspired imagination in *The Adventures of Tom Sawyer*, the romantic imagination of Colonel Sellers in *The American Claimant*, and the absolute idealism of Joan in *Personal Recollections of Joan of Arc*.

Perhaps Clemens's attacks on romance were in proportion to his own idealism—the gap between imagination and reality was something he experienced with great poignance. In *Following the Equator*, for instance, he describes his disappointment that the Taj Mahal did not live up to the impression he took from his reading:

> I am a careless reader, I suppose—an *impressionist* reader; an impressionist reader of what is *not* an impressionist picture; a reader who overlooks the informing details or masses their sum improperly, and gets only a large splashy, general effect—an effect which is not correct, and which is not warranted by the particulars placed before me—particulars which I did not examine, and whose meanings I did not cautiously and carefully estimate. It is an effect which is some thirty-five or forty times finer than the reality, and is therefore a great deal better and more valuable than the reality; and so, I ought never to hunt up the reality, but stay miles away from it, and thus preserve my own ... ineffable Taj built of tinted mists upon jeweled arches of rainbows supported by colonnades of moonlight. (chapter 59)

In blaming his own habits of *reading, Clemens continues a career-long crusade about the proper use of literature, one that needs to connect reality to reading, mediated by worldly experience and by conversation with others. But he puts this entire discussion in a chapter headed by the motto from Pudd'nhead Wilson's New Calendar, "Don't part with your illusions. When they are gone you may still exist but you have ceased to live."

♦ SEE ALSO Poetry.

ROUGHING IT (1872). The second Mark Twain travelogue, *Roughing It* is Samuel Clemens's first book conceived from the beginning as an original extended narrative rather than as a collection of earlier-written *sketches or tales. As such, it enabled Clemens to finish the process begun in *The Innocents Abroad* of defining the *Mark Twain persona to serve as his narrative voice, and, ultimately, as his alter ego. Clemens consolidated his character primarily by resolving many of the inconsistencies of perspective that had made Mark Twain so useful as a character in sketches, but that made him confusing in *Innocents Abroad*. Not that *Roughing It* lacks inconsistencies, nor that it was written entirely from scratch, nor that the Mark Twain persona remained stable over Clemens's career, but much of the hard work of formulating the character was done over the course of composing *Roughing It*.

Such a consolidation was important in part because, as in all of Clemens's travel narratives—or his novels for that matter—in *Roughing It*, plot takes a back seat to episodes. So coherence, if any, must come from another source. The simple itinerary of a journey provides continuity, a line on which to hang various episodes and digressions, but especially given Clemens's tendency to digress, itinerary alone does not give his travelogues artistic coherence. Mark Twain as narrative persona supplies much of that coherence, as Mark Twain is a mask, a fiction, crafted to provide that center.

This is not to say that the book is fiction, much less a novel. Like all of Clemens's travelogues, it is based on fact, though the discrepancies between Clemens's history and Mark Twain's distorted history are telling. Clemens did leave Missouri for the Far West with the outbreak of the Civil War in order to be the private secretary of his brother, Orion Clemens, appointed by the Lincoln administration to serve as secretary for the new territory of Nevada. Clemens was not, however, an untraveled naïf, nor was he really an Easterner. While he had traveled and worked in New York, Philadelphia and Washington, D.C., he was primarily a Westerner, born in Missouri and, when the story of *Roughing It* commences, last working as a steamboat pilot on the St. Louis to New Orleans stretch of the Mississippi River. He quit his job when river commerce withered with the outbreak of the war, and rather than work for either side as a military pilot, he returned home to northeastern Missouri, where he briefly enrolled in a militia company that sympathized with the Confederate cause. For reasons never fully articulated in any candid, unfictionalized account, he quit the militia to join his Union-sympathizing brother on the trek west, away from the war.

Clemens briefly laid claim to a rich mine in Nevada, but tells us that he lost it out of idleness, an idleness that is central to Clemens's definition of Twain's character. As best as the facts can be discovered, Twain lost his fortune to claim jumpers; he was unable, or unwilling, to risk his life to hold his fortune by force.

Clemens did leave San Francisco, nearly broke and in disgrace, for the gold country of California, where he took potluck with a group of pocket miners. *Roughing It* fails to tell us that he lost his reporter's berth on the *Morning Call* not simply out of idleness, but partly because he had penned an attack on police for their persecution of the *Chinese and for their unwillingness to defend Chinese against illegal attacks by mobs and frauds. Since both the police department and the *Call*'s readership included substantial numbers of Irish Americans and since they could have sensed Clemens's own anti-Irish biases in his reporting, the *Call* censored his work and ultimately fired him. Well connected to San Francisco's bohemian writers' group, Clemens was not at a loss for employment, but wrote a monthly column in the *Californian* and eventually recommenced his regular correspondence with the *Enterprise*. The *Enterprise* correspondence, reprinted in many western newspapers, gave Clemens the forum he needed to attack the police, which he had strong personal

UNEXPECTED ELEVATION.

Illustration by True Williams (1839–1897), from *Roughing It*,
Hartford: Webster & Company, 1872, p. 180.

reasons for doing. In 1864, Lewis P. Ward, one of Clemens's roommates when Clemens was still working for the *Call*, was arrested and beaten by a police officer. Shortly thereafter, another of his roommates, Steve Gillis, was arrested for brawling. Clemens, one of this rowdy bunch, signed a bond guaranteeing that Gillis would appear in court, and then the two skipped town. In short, he left town not out of indolence, but because of his activity, and the kind of activity he engaged in was, to some degree, more scandalous than simple indolence. He developed an antipathy to the police, and he exercised that antipathy with characteristic enthusiasm. When he returned to San Francisco, he used his *Enterprise* correspondence to mock the police and their chief. Given that newspapers exchanged popular writings and that therefore his columns were well known in San Francisco, Twain was not the nonentity he describes in *Roughing It*. Moreover, he kept up his popularity and commercial viability by developing a newspaper feud with his replacement at the *Call*. Clemens's real industriousness does not appear in his semifictionalized history.

The truthful correspondences between Clemens's real motives and behavior and those he ascribes to Mark Twain are equally telling. In prefacing his book with a discreet intimation that he was drunk when writing it ("the tighter I get"), Clemens does at least refer to one of his common conditions when out west. But when writing *Roughing It*, Clemens was in fact trying to *reform himself for his new wife, abstaining not only from *alcohol, but even from the cigars that were one of his life-long trademarks. (He ultimately failed in *both* reforms.)

What these changes add up to is a Mark Twain who in many ways is a reverse image of Samuel Clemens. Over the course of his Western years and his first few years living in the East, Clemens evolved from a boisterous, politically fractious, energetic Westerner to a responsible eastern property holder, editor, husband, and literary moralist. Mark Twain, on the other hand, begins as a more or less respectable eastern gentleman, whose distinguishing characteristics are lack of interest in politics, naïveté about the workings of human nature, especially his own, and a profound aversion to work. His idleness is interrupted only by necessity or by the workings of his curiosity, which, as it rarely leads to any productive ends, is idle in its own right. Under the influence of relaxed western mores, Mark Twain grows less genteel over the course of the book's action.

As a comic character, this Mark Twain is perfect, subject to the whims of his idle humor and to the frauds of a strange new world. And because his point of view is divided between the remembered idiocy of his youthful self and the relatively wise character relating the narrative, Mark Twain allows Clemens latitude for passing moral judgment wherever and whenever he sees fit. The mask has enough consistency to make the book cohere, and enough flexibility to accommodate an incredible diversity of experience and an equally incredible variety of narrative styles.

Clemens's struggle to find this ideal narrative voice explains in part why he had so much difficulty writing this book, though certainly the numerous personal disasters that befell his family in 1871 contributed. After marriage to Olivia Langdon in February of 1870, Clemens settled into a routine of newspaper editing in spite of the huge success of *Innocents Abroad*. However, his enthusiasm for daily *newspaper journalism quickly waned and by mid-July he had signed a contract with the American Publishing Company to deliver a new book within five months. Within three weeks of signing the contract, Olivia's father died of a fast and virulent cancer of the stomach. Olivia was distraught over the death, and her deep depression was augmented about a month later when her visiting school friend, Emma Nye, contracted typhoid and, after several feverish weeks, died in the Clemens's home. Five weeks later the premature birth of Clemens's sickly and short-lived son, Langdon, provided further and continuing distraction. Olivia herself was not well during much of this period, contracting typhoid herself just three months after the birth of her baby. She recovered slowly, and for much time it was unclear whether she would recover at all. During her long convalescence, the family decided to abandon Buffalo altogether, moving to Elmira in March and then to Hartford in October, 1871. Not surprisingly, Clemens had difficulty writing a humorous book during this period.

Yet Clemens did little to make his job easier, as he took on numerous tasks that diverted his attention, including agreeing to write a monthly column for the New York *Galaxy*, which he did from May 1870 to March 1871. He also distracted himself with plans for a book of sketches, with writing and publishing *Mark Twain's (Burlesque) Autobiography and First Romance*, and with a plan to collaborate on a book on South Africa's diamond mines with his friend from his days as a newspaper correspondent in Washington, D.C., John Henry *Riley. Throughout the autumn and winter, then, progress on the new book was slow, partly because Clemens had little faith in the "hackneyed" subject of the West, partly because he had persistent self-doubts about the value of his humor, and partly because he kept searching for an easier alternative in a book composed of sketches already written. Indeed, he ultimately did incorporate many previously written sketches into *Roughing It*, especially in the late sections of the book, when it became clear to him that he had not written as much as he had contracted to write and had therefore to carry the narrative beyond his experiences in Nevada and California. He had on hand, then, a collection of newspaper sketches on Hawaii that he had already arranged into book form in late 1866 or early 1867 but for which he could not find a publisher. Revising once again to fit the collation into the larger book of Western travels, Clemens fleshed out the final section of *Roughing It*.

Over the course of composing *Roughing It* Clemens discovered that his muse could not be forced, that his *work habits often required him to have distractions while he digested material for any number of projects that he usually had pigeonholed. Regardless, Clemens finished the bulk of the manuscript by July, and did much of the revising and proofreading while on a lecture tour in the winter of 1871–1872. Judging from references in letters, it seems likely that Clemens wrote the bulk of the book in the spring of 1871. The burst of creativity was sustained through a visit from his old Nevada friend and editor, Joseph *Goodman, who worked side by side with Clemens for several months in 1871, encouraging Clemens not only with reminiscences, but with critical reading of what Clemens had already drafted. With a sympathetic and knowledgeable audience helping him, Clemens found his stride.

As helpful as Goodman was, Clemens's burst of writing began shortly before Goodman arrived when Clemens finally began to see that the book was not merely a factual account of a journey, but an extended account of a character. In a letter to his brother, then in the employ of his publisher, Clemens wrote: "Just as soon as ever I can, I will send some of the book MS., but right in the first chapter I have got to alter the whole style of one of my characters & re-write him clear through to where I am now. It is no fool of a job I can tell you, but the book will be greatly bettered by it" (4 March 1871).

This letter, explaining and apologizing for having sent so little of the manuscript that was already months late, may have been no more than a delaying tactic, but given that Clemens began writing in a white heat shortly thereafter, it seems likely that he was telling the truth, and that in improving the first eight chapters of the book, he found what he needed to write the rest.

In all likelihood, this reworking of one of his characters was his reworking of Mark Twain himself, the only character whose persistent presence would require such reworking. Here, then, Mark Twain gets his most consistent characterization, as a veteran of the western experience who returns to tell the tale of his own earlier naïveté, to tell us about growing up under duress by making his own gaffs and humiliations the source of his humor. In thus finding his narrative voice and the purpose for the narrative, he found it easier to write. He discovered that he would not be competing with the rash of reportage about the West that spilled from the presses after the completion of the transcontinental railroad. He would be offering not facts about the land and manners of the West, but instead the drama of character that fiction gives. His was to be, after all, a humorous, not a serious book, and as such its competition lay in a different direction entirely. Such a discovery opened doors for Clemens, as not only did it free his muse in writing *Roughing It*, it also enabled him to turn further toward fiction in his next book-length composition, the satiric novel *The Gilded Age*.

Still, as quickly as he wrote the book when he once solidified the Mark Twain persona, *Roughing It* frightened Clemens. Long before production proceeded and canvassing began in the fall of 1871, Clemens began to worry that the book was too slangy, too irreverent, too crude, and that the reviews would destroy his fledgling reputation and his livelihood. These anxieties were probably born with the criticism of *Innocents Abroad* as a book of crude taste and a slangy, corrupting style. While the success of *Innocents* provided a temporary anodyne against these attacks, by the time Clemens tried to write *Roughing It*, the shadow of doubt became nearly debilitating. As early as 26 April 1871, in a letter to Mary Mason *Fairbanks, Clemens expressed the worry that his book would fail: "I am pegging away at my book, but it will have no success. The papers have found at last the courage to pull me down off my pedestal & cast slurs at me—& that is simply a popular author's death rattle. Though he wrote an *inspired* book after that, it would not save him." Strangely, his publisher, Elisha *Bliss, encouraged Clemens's worries, perhaps to try to stimulate Clemens to sustained and inspired production, but more likely to keep Clemens in check, for the overwhelming success of *Innocents Abroad* proved something of a difficulty for Bliss in that Clemens traded his success for greater influence over Bliss's enterprise. Clemens managed to get his brother Orion hired to work for the

American Publishing Company, and Clemens kept pushing for ever better publishing terms. Bliss's steady denigration of Clemens's talents and prospects was probably designed to restore what Bliss perceived as a desirable balance of power between star author and publishing firm.

Whatever the reasons for Clemens's self-doubts even as *Roughing It* neared completion, Clemens consequently adopted the unusual and not to be repeated expedient of trying to keep reviews of *Roughing It* out of major newspapers and magazines unless he could somehow guarantee that the reviews would be positive. His efforts at least partially succeeded in that very few reviews were printed in 1872–1873, though of these few, some commented negatively on the book's slang and "padding." The reviews most critical of *Roughing It*'s taste and style were from English journals, as in the case of the Manchester *Guardian*'s complaint that "Mark Twain ... often falls into the slang of transatlantic journalism, and displays also its characteristic inability to distinguish between the picturesque and the grotesque" (6 March 1872). The American journals, over which Twain was able to exercise greater control, were generally more favorable, but the scarcity of reviews ultimately did at least as much harm to the edition as negative reviews could have. True, canvassing before publication went well, well enough so that when the book finally was printed, bound, and delivered in early 1872, the publisher could not keep up with demand. In America, the book sold very rapidly for a while, with 75,168 copies selling in 1872, but 90 percent of these were sold in the first six months, with sales dropping to 7,831 in 1873 and 5,132 in 1874. English sales followed a similar pattern, with a proportionally smaller drop off in sales. While this pattern was typical for subscription books, it was exaggerated in the case of the American edition of *Roughing It*, as one can see in comparison to *Innocents Abroad*, which outsold *Roughing It* in 1873. This comparison taught Clemens, as he put it in a 4 March 1873 letter to Elisha Bliss, that "if one don't secure publicity & notoriety for a book the instant it is issued, no amount of hard work & faithful advertising can accomplish it later on." So from fearing that notoriety would damage his sales as much as positive press would promote it, Clemens came to understand that any notice was good advertising, at least for his kind of books.

Over time, *Roughing It* has proven to be an enduring favorite. When toward the end of his life Harper and Brothers became Twain's primary publisher, they documented *Roughing it* as the third best seller, behind *Innocents Abroad* and *Tom Sawyer*, among Twain's books. While it would be difficult to trace the continuing popularity of various Twain volumes, there is no doubt that *Roughing It* is one of the best known and most enjoyed. It has not, however, received as much latter-day critical attention as Twain's major novels.

The critical attention it has received has broken down more or less along the lines described by two of the earliest reviews, one by his friend Warner, the other in the California literary magazine *Overland Monthly*. Warner insists that Twain's superficial exaggerations hid a fund of real moral purpose and fundamental *realism:

> Behind the mask of the story-teller is the satirist, whose head is always clear, who is not imposed on by shams, who hates all pretension, and who uses his humor, which is often extravagant, to make pretension and false dignity ridiculous.... [W]e are inclined to think that, on the whole, it [*Roughing It*] contains the best picture of frontier mining life that has been written. The episode of the silver mining in Nevada has certainly never been so graphically described. It is an experience that can, we trust, never be repeated on this continent. In these pages we are made to see distinctly a society that never had any parallel. It would be unpleasant to read about it, if the author did not constantly relieve the dreadful picture with strokes of humor. ("'Roughing It.' Mark Twain's New Book," Hartford *Courant*, 18 March 1872, p. 1)

Warner sees the realism of Twain either lurking in comedy that is fundamentally satiric, or he sees the humor as a sugar-coating to the bitter pill of reality.

Such a line of criticism has dominated large-scale interpretations of Twain's work for much of the second half of the twentieth century, with Henry Nash Smith expanding on the thesis of Walter Blair, Constance Rourke, and George Santayana that American vernacular humor is fundamentally realistic, and that in the hands of Twain it turned into a *satire of inappropriate mores and values of a Eurocentric New England literary hegemony. The narrator arrives at his sense of understanding through a series of rites of passage, changing from greenhorn to old-timer, initiated into the new realities of a vernacular, democratic culture.

The Overland Monthly's review agrees that the humor is humor of the West, and acknowledges that the book has satiric elements, but it sees little of the realism. Instead, it describes Mark Twain as "rioting ... in the drollest and most fantastic exaggeration" of a peculiarly western sort: "The Great West claims him as her intellectual offspring. Artemus Ward, Doesticks, and Orpheus C. Kerr, who have been the favorite purveyors of mirth for the Eastern people, were timid navigators, who hugged the shore of plausibility, and would have trembled at the thought of launching out into the mid-ocean of wild, preposterous invention and sublime exaggeration, as Mark Twain does" (6 March 1872).

The Boston *Advertiser* of 1 May agreed, suggesting "it will be safer, as well as more agreeable, to quote its jokes than its statistics." Such reviews presage the most recent trend in criticism, led by Bruce Michelson, who sees the power of humor in a transgressive encouragement of imagination. According to Michelson, the tenderfoot does not grow, he simply moves from one set of illusions to another. In endorsing the narrator's point of view, the book as whole, then, praises the psychological value of illusion itself.

 **SAMOSSOUD, CLARA CLEMENS GABRILOWITSCH** (1874–1962). The third child of Olivia Langdon and Samuel Langhorne Clemens, Clara was the only of four children to outlive her father. As such, her influence on Mark Twain's estate was profound, and not always for the best. The shape of that influence is explained in part by her position in the family as second daughter, a scant two years younger than Olivia Susan *Clemens, but very much second fiddle to Susy's lead. Most everything about Clara was shaped by Susy's influence; even Clara's nickname, "Bay," came from Susy's pronunciation of the word "baby."

If we were to trust Mark Twain's *autobiography, Clara was Susy's antithesis:

> Clara was sturdy, independent, orderly, practical, persistent, plucky—just a little animal, and very satisfactory. Charles Dudley *Warner said Susy was made of mind, and Clara of matter. When Motley, the kitten died, some one said that the thoughts of the two children need not be inquired into, they could be divined: that Susy was wondering if this was the *end* of Motley, and had his life been worth while; whereas Clara was merely interested in seeing to it that there should be a creditable funeral. (*North American Review*, 7 June 1907)

But the image he presents is suspect when one compares the *Autobiography* with earlier remarks. For example, in the *Autobiography*, he attributes to Clara a remark he attributed at the time to Susy:

> We were in Germany. The nurse, Rosa, was not allowed to speak to the children otherwise than in German. Clara grew very tired of it; by and by the little creature's patience was exhausted, and she said "Aunt Clara, I wish God had made Rosa in English."

In this retrospective depiction, Clemens uses the remark to show Clara's pragmatic resistance to mental processes. Yet in a notebook entry of the time, close to Clara's fourth birthday, Clemens makes a note of her curiosity and mental precision in quoting a conversation between Clara and himself:

> Bay—Why musn't I?
> Because I said *not*.
> Bay—But that's no *why*.

The later depiction in the *Autobiography* shows that Twain was manufacturing a literary family, one that conformed to the convention of sibling opposites. One suspects that this pressure developed early, shaping Clara into a pugnacious child determined to force her way into the family limelight.

That said, Clara was not immune from the family's pressures to have her conform to a Victorian ideal of womanhood. The way Twain develops her in his autobiography suggests as much. Even though he describes her as "just a little animal," he insists that she grew into a conventional woman: "In after years a passion for music developed the latent spirituality and intellectuality in Clara, and her practicality took second and, in fact, even third place." Clara, like Susy, was under duress to conform to an image of femininity as spiritual, artistic, and sensitive. Not surprisingly, she chose a path that her elder sister, too, was considering in following a career in music.

So with Olivia's genteel education—designed to mold the girls into identical forms—and Clara's own longing for a distinct position in the family as the two dominant, largely contradictory forces shaping her young life, Clara moved in and out of Susy's shadow during her teens and twenties. Susy's departure to college could have made independent growth possible, but the family's financial distress and refusal to allow Susy to develop on her own at college kept Susy the center of the family's activities well into the early 1890s. After the family moved to Europe in 1891 to save money otherwise spent in Hartford running the house, Susy was once again in the family center, collaborating with her father and mother in editing *Personal Recollections of Joan of Arc*.

Unable to compete with Susy as a literary collaborator, Clara found her niche in her relative physical strength. As the healthiest of the three daughters, Clara often served as her father's travelling companion, attending him, for example, on one of his business trips to New York from September 1893 to March 1894. After bankruptcy in 1894, Twain proposed an around-the-world lecture tour on which he took his wife and Clara, leaving Susy and Jean behind. From this point forward, Clara figured as the primary filial presence in Clemens's life, in part because Susy died before she had a chance to rejoin the family in England.

At any rate, the family's travels from that point on were as much guided by Clara's needs for training in music as by its search for health care for both Jean and Olivia. The family spent much of the years 1897–1899 in Vienna so that Clara could study piano with Theodor Leschetizky. There she met fellow student Ossip Gabrilowitsch, whom she married in 1909. In the interim, she dropped the study of piano to train as a contralto with the hope of becoming a concert singer. Her career never amounted to much, in part because her mother resisted Clara becoming a public figure. Olivia, with Samuel's complete concurrence, shared the Victorian belief that a woman should be accomplished, but should remain out of the public view. As Olivia put it in a 24 February 1901 letter to Grace King about Clara's decision "to give up her concerts for this Winter. We are very glad. We do not oppose her, for of course that is not best, but we are very sorry indeed that she wants this public life."

Clara, in fact, did not do well under the pressure of stage performance, perhaps because she felt both distracted and undermined by her father's presence. She worried that she could command an audience only because she was Mark Twain's daughter, and as much as she tried to build her career without using his name, she did have to use his pocketbook to subsidize her tours. At any rate, Clara developed a series of psychological and psychosomatic disorders starting in the 1890s, leading her frequently to sanatoriums, most especially after her mother's death in 1904. Suffering both persistent throat and nervous complaints, Clara could never make her career a success in a public sense, but it did allow her an increasing degree of freedom from the family and gained her the attentions of two pianists, her accompanist Charles E. Wark and Ossip Gabrilowitsch.

Between her many concert trips, Clara became the de facto female head of the family after Olivia died in 1904. In that capacity, she helped her father manage his business and domestic affairs. She often served as hostess for Clemens's functions; she chose the land for the house Clemens was to build in Redding, Connecticut; she used her powers of persuasion and coercion to force Isabel Lyon out of Clemens's household when she became convinced that Lyons was taking advantage of her father.

But none of this involvement entailed a particular closeness between Clemens and his daughter. Her interest in *Christian Science, for instance, pulled Clemens into a study of mind-cure that both interested him and raised his hackles, but his expose of the religion was as much an attack on his daughter's interests as on Mary Baker Eddy. Reciprocally, Clara's pursuit of her career violated the wishes of her father, who, in his loneliness, wanted to surround himself with doting family. His idea of doting, apparently, was to keep himself at the center of attention. When Clara married in October 1909, Clemens insisted on wearing his red Oxford robes from his *honorary degree to the ceremony, essentially offering himself as a more conspicuous presence than even the bride. Not surprisingly, Clara opted to live in Europe with Gabrilowitsch, whose career she would now support in lieu of pursuing her own. She gave birth to her only child, Nina *Gabrilowitsch, in August 1910. The First World War drove the family back to the United States, where Gabrilowitsch continued his career in Detroit, Michigan, and where Clara wrote the first of her three books: *My Father: Mark Twain* (1931). Later she penned two others: *My Husband: Gabrilowitsch* (1938) and *Awake to a Perfect Day: My Experience with Christian Science* (1956).

Clara depended on income from her father's properties throughout her life, as did her second husband. After Gabrilowitsch died in 1936, Clara moved to Hollywood, California, to be near her daughter, who was pursuing an acting career.

There Clara was courted by another Russian emigré musician, Jacques Samossoud, who was twenty years her junior. The fifty-year-old Samossoud was directing an opera in Los Angeles when he married Clara in 1944. He apparently saw early retirement in Clara's money, spending it freely on his gambling obsession. He was so anxious to have Clara's money support his impulses that he convinced Clara to rewrite her will to cut her daughter out of any further inheritance than the trust fund already established for her. Samossoud's expenditures were so great that by 1951 he and Clara auctioned off not only Clara's Hollywood, California, house but many of her possessions including numerous Twain manuscripts. They moved to La Jolla, California, where they lived until Clara's death.

When Samuel Clemens died in 1910, Clara was his only heir, and she collaborated with Albert Bigelow Paine to carefully construct an image of her father as a conventional Victorian gentleman. She became one of the directors of the *Mark Twain Company, and maintained veto power over any Mark Twain publications, including holding permission to publish *Letters from the Earth* until just before her death in 1962. After years of fighting with Clara over her efforts to purify her father's image, Bernard DeVoto resigned his position as literary executor of the *Mark Twain Papers in 1946. Subsequent executors worked to create a more autonomous scholarly library for Twain's literary remains, but it wasn't until Clara's death, and then the deaths both of Samossoud (in 1966) and his heir, his friend Dr. William E. Seiler (in 1978), that the Mark Twain Foundation came into full ownership of the Mark Twain Papers.

◆ SEE ALSO Clemens, Olivia Langdon; Health and Disease.

SATIRE. If *amiable humor is moralizing through an indulgent and sympathetic laughter to embrace incongruity, then satire is moralizing through scorn to attack incongruity. Both begin in the amoral pleasure of *humor, but direct the course of humorous perception in radically different ways.

Satire begins with humor, with an incongruous because simultaneous attraction to and revulsion from the object of satire, but moves to choice in negating one possibility. Satire is a directed mode of comedy in which a moral center challenges the purposeless conceptual wandering of humor. Satire requires an audience to recognize two possible constructions of reality, see one as virtuous and one as vicious, and while enjoying both through the passive openness of humor, choose virtue. Usually, satire's audience makes its choice under the fear of the satirist's scorn, which threatens an audience with ostracism if it remains passive in its voyeuristic indulgence of fantasy vice. Thus, through bringing into play additional emotions rather than the passive pleasure of humor, the satirist moves appreciation into moral reformation, into taking the next step toward virtuous action, that step being to choose among possible paths of action. If, however, satire is contextualized in such a way as to strip it of its moral center, or alternatively to encourage the humorous passivity at root, or to encourage criticism as an end in itself, then it loses its power as a bridge toward moral activity because it gives an audience no firm clues how to adjudicate between the simultaneous attraction and revulsion at satire's root.

Traditionally satirists justify the energy and violence of their criticism as a kind of preaching; satire holds up a mirror in which we see our vices, and then, in ridiculing us, encourages us to reform. Thus, satire affirms through negation, yet affirming one trait by negating its ostensible opposite is a dangerous game psychologically and ethically, not because it allows a vicarious indulgence in vice from the moral high ground of judgment but rather because it encourages criticism and negation for their own sakes. Satire needs to have a base of firm moral values to hold up as an ideal; when developed through *irony, satire can spin away from its moral basis into nihilism. This certainly is a risk that Mark Twain ran and often succumbed to in his satire, as in *A Connecticut Yankee in King Arthur's Court* when Hank Morgan suggests that it would be best to "hang the human race and end the farce." The ironic pleasures of criticism at that point have undercut the positive moral values on which Twain originally based the novel.

Traditionally satire has two different modes, the Horatian mode of calm, witty revelation of hypocrisy and the Juvenalian mode of bitter denunciation. In the middle of Twain's career, he seemed to identify only the Horatian mode as potentially successful, as he says in his 30 January 1879 letter to William Dean *Howells:

> I wish I *could* give those sharp satires on European life which you mention, but of course a man can't write successful satire except he be in a calm judicial good-humor—whereas I *hate* travel, & I *hate* hotels, & I *hate* the opera, & I *hate* the Old Masters—in truth I don't ever seem to be in a good enough humor with ANYthing to *satirize* it; no I want to stand up before it & *curse* it, & foam at the mouth,—or take a club & pound it to rags & pulp. I have got in two or three chapters about Wagner's Operas, & managed to do it without showing temper—but the strain of another such effort would burst me.

Twain here suggests two different impulses behind satire: the one, rage, the other, judicious evaluation. This latter, the characteristic of Horatian satire, uses complex ironies in order comically to reveal shortcomings. Satire of this mode can blur into amiable humor.

Juvenalian satire could never be so mistaken as it is transparently aggressive. As Mark Twain describes it through the words of a fictional Satan in *"Chronicle of Young Satan":

> Your race, in its poverty, has unquestionably one really effective weapon— laughter. Power, money, persuasion, supplication, persecution—these can lift at a colossal humbug—push it a little, weaken it a little, century by century;

but only laughter can blow it to rags and atoms at a blast. Against the assault of laughter nothing can stand.

Twain's character here justifies satire by the standard of reformation, but the rage takes center stage. Such anger lurks in much of Twain's satiric output and effloresces in his early journalism and, in spite of his developed belief that Horatian satire is more effective, in many of his late satires.

Juvenalian satire, the satire of railing, uses the crudest, most basic form of irony, the irony of tone, of pure sarcasm. The more sophisticated Horatian satire uses the irony of stance. Hence the tendency toward framed narrative and "character" in Twain's Horatian mode as opposed to the forthright anger in sarcasm of his Juvenalian mode.

While Samuel Clemens's moods and disposition partially explain his various choices of a satire of character and stance on some occasions and a satire of tone on others, American traditions of satire may better explain Twain's choices. Juvenalian satire, no-holds barred, was a commonplace of *newspaper journalism and of the closely related partisan politics that newspapers usually served. Character assassination appeals to fear and loathing; snide cartooning and grotesque caricaturing were staples of political commentary in newspapers, usually partisan in nature. Clemens relished the ability to take such a part, as he says in a letter to Mary Mason *Fairbanks:

> I am tired of writing wishy-washy squibs for the Tribune, & have joined the Herald staff—2 impersonal letters a week. Mr. Bennett says I may have full swing, & say as many mean things as I please. Now don't say a word, Madam, because I just mean to abuse people right & left, in case the humor takes me to do it. There are lots of folks in Washington who need vilifying. (24 January 1868)

In vilifying Washington corruption, Twain can pretend toward virtue, but his political attacks very often served the narrowest of personal interests.

Clemens himself, for all of his interest in promoting governmental honesty, was not averse to helping himself or, more often, his brother, with timely newspaper satire. He helped his brother often in Nevada when his brother worked as secretary to the territory and Sam worked for the *Enterprise*, and later when in Washington, he promised his mother to do all he could to get a clerkship for Orion:

> That cursed, infernal Patent Office Commissionership has changed round again & gone into Cox's hands. I expect that thing is going to take me months to accomplish it. The way I'll waltz into some of those people in the Herald the first they know, will make them think the Devil himself has got loose for another thousand years. If I ever *do* start in, in good earnest, to

fiddle for them I'll bet they'll dance.... If they don't want any clerks in the Departments immediately, I will "show up" their damnable rottenness for *not* wanting clerks. (24 January 1868)

Indeed, in the support of narrow interests, invective is often more useful than judiciously constructed, subtle irony.

Social satire tended toward more complex, usually longer literary forms than the cartoons, newspaper squibs, and political broadsides of partisan politics. In more literary social satires, genres of character sketches, short stories, novels, narrative poetry, and, to a limited degree, drama allowed for more careful development of ironies and gave an audience more time to decipher such ironies. Hence, expectations of form arose from the targets of satire and the forums in which it was published. By shifting from journalism to longer literary forms, Clemens allowed himself to develop his satiric talents in the mode of satire he ultimately held in higher esteem, and culminated in such masterpieces of social satire as *Adventures of Huckleberry Finn*.

♦ SEE ALSO Moral Sense.

SATURDAY MORNING CLUB. Samuel Clemens was one of the main sponsors of the Saturday Morning Club of *Hartford, supporting not only the membership of his daughters, but using his house to host many of the meetings and supplying much organizational help. This club was a sort of girls' auxiliary to the Hartford *Monday Evening Club, sharing much of the same educational and social purpose. The girls' club was organized along the same lines, with the members often making presentations to the group, but the club also invited outside speakers to appear. These included many of the members of the Monday Evening Club, including Clemens himself, and also leading writers and thinkers of the day, including, for example, William Graham Sumner of Yale University. The group also was in correspondence with other Saturday Morning Clubs in other New England cities, and they shared speakers between them.

The careful and extensive records of the Club still exist, giving us a useful portrait of social and intellectual life among the children of Clemens's class and region. While the Club certainly emphasized the *etiquette expected of a properly "finished" young lady of means, the clear expectation that girls should be educated in the latest scientific and political as well as artistic movements challenges current assumptions that women's *education in the nineteenth century was purely ornamental. Clemens's support of the Club also gives a striking picture of his ideas of *childhood, showing him as a deeply involved father who respected the capacities and encouraged the development of his children's minds.

SCHOOLS. SEE Education.

SCIENCE. In his 6 June 1867 letter to the San Francisco *Alta California* from New York City, Mark Twain pretends to assume that "Harry Hill's Club" is a gentlemanly place

> where the *savants* were in the habit of meeting to commune upon abstruse matters of science and philosophy—men like Agassiz and Ericson and people of that stamp. I felt in a reflective mood, and I said I would like to go to Harry Hill's and hear those great men talk much better than to trifle away the time in the follies of gayer localities. We started through a little sawdusted den of a tenth-rate rum-hole, and I said: "This is just like the eccentricities of those wonderful intelligences—we never find *them* surrounded by gilded trappings and pretentious display."

Twain spends the evening, then, consorting with criminals, drunkards, brawlers, cheap showmen, and prostitutes before finally figuring out that the great scientists and philosophers were not present.

Mark Twain could not have exploited such names for comic contrast if they were not the names of celebrities, and celebrities such scientists were to the late-nineteenth-century reader. Like most literate people of his generation, Clemens read extensively in popular accounts of science and technology, like those in *Popular Science*, to which the Clemens family subscribed, and in various volumes like John Fiske's *A Century of Science*, as well as in the primary works of naturalists like Charles *Darwin. Clemens's favorite sciences were geology—having cultivated the interest when he worked as a miner—*astronomy, and biology, which interested him not merely for the theory of *evolution but because he was fascinated with animal behavior. Like his contemporaries, Clemens followed science not merely for its intrinsic interest or practical value, but also for the bearing it had on the nineteenth century's great concern, *religion.

The light science shone on religion was increasingly disturbing to the devout, exciting to the skeptical. As recently as the early part of the century, empirical studies of the natural world were considered a branch of speculative philosophy, called by the name "natural philosophy," and considered subscientific because caught in those epistemological conundrums of empiricism enunciated by Hume and then categorically examined by Kant and his Romanticist followers, including America's Ralph Waldo Emerson. Natural philosophers were, for the most part, gentlemen dabblers whose studies had practical and theoretical consequences, but whose positions as intellectuals were not derived from professional training in rigorous method. Darwin himself to some degree fit this model. Many of these gentlemen philosophers studied the natural world because they saw in nature evidence of divine design. As such, their studies were exercises in devotion, fully conventional along the lines of William Paley's *Natural Theology*, a book that Clemens read and mocked in the 1870s.

Mark Twain's books are replete with parodic references to this kind of amateur science. In the stance of Mr. Mark Twain, gentleman, Twain's early travel letters include experiments, as when he and Brown try to asphyxiate a dog in "The Grotto of the Dog." In other places, such as in "Political Economy," Twain describes gentlemen absurdly distracted by their studies, impractical even as they profess to understand the world. Chapters 37–39 of *A Tramp Abroad* rely on this old idea of the gentleman naturalist as they describe an outrageously elaborate quasi-scientific expedition at the foot of the Matterhorn, run by the idler gentleman Twain ostensibly for the benefit of humankind, but really so that Twain could "show off."

But early in the nineteenth century, many natural philosophers claimed the high ground of "science," a word that had been used primarily for systematic, deductive systems of knowledge, such as mathematics and geometry. In claiming the word "science," they demoted philosophical speculation, challenged the value of intuition and of faith, insisted on mathematical precision in observation and measurement, and claimed that the theories derived from empirical observation had risen to the level of certainty of mathematics itself. Such scientists demoted the gentlemen dabblers from their ranks, discouraged comfortable speculation on the nature of divinity or the divinity of nature, and professionalized their discipline. In these years, American universities began to hire professors in the sciences, as, for example, Agassiz at Harvard.

Clemens had mixed feelings about this shift, following with great fascination as the discoveries of science supported his religious skepticism, but finding, too, that his skepticism about any absolute claims to knowledge extended just as energetically to physical science as to religion. He was a more energetic skeptic early in his career as, when trying to establish himself as a respectable literary man in Hartford, he defended a humanistic skepticism in such works as "Some Learned Fables for Good old Boys and Girls" or "Brief Lectures on Science," or most conspicuously in *"Old Times on the Mississippi" when he describes how the alluvial lower Mississippi occasionally shortens itself by cutting off a bend:

Now, if I wanted to be one of those ponderous scientific people, and "let on" to prove what had occurred in the remote past by what had occurred in a given time in the recent past, or what will occur in the far future by what has occurred in late years, what an opportunity is here! Geology never had such a chance, nor such exact data to argue from! Nor "development of species" either! Glacial epochs are great things, but they are vague—vague. Please observe:

In the space of one hundred and seventy-six years the Lower Mississippi has shortened itself. . . an average of a trifle over one mile and a third per year. Therefore, any calm person, who is not blind or idiotic, can see that in the Old Oolithic Silurian Period, just a million years ago next November, the

Lower Mississippi was upward of one million three hundred thousand miles long, and stuck out over the Gulf of Mexico like a fishing rod. And by the same token any person can see that seven hundred and forty-two years from now the Lower Mississippi will be only a mile and three-quarters long, and Cairo and New Orleans will have joined their streets together, and be plodding comfortably along under a single mayor and a mutual board of aldermen. There is something fascinating about science. One gets such wholesale returns of conjecture out of such a trifling investment of fact.

Here Twain attacks through reductio ad absurdum the methodology of extrapolation, so important to the physical sciences. In so doing, he attacks the epistemological certitude of the enterprise of science itself.

Yet in "Old Times," Mark Twain also uses the language of science to elevate the profession of riverboat pilot. He describes the "science" as well as the "art" of piloting, thereby falling back on an older use of the term "science" to refer to technical skill as well as drawing a distinction between hard knowledge that can be communicated and the intuitive skills that come from experience alone. He uses "science" in this sense and in this way in the sketch "Science vs. Luck," too. But in calling the science of piloting "one of the exact sciences," Twain attaches the newer meaning of the word to the pilot's task, which is to "read" the book of nature for "the amount of usefulness it could furnish toward compassing the safe piloting of a steamboat." Here Twain combines pure and applied science to give the sanctity of science to a mechanical trade.

No matter how much he may have tried to appropriate science's language to borrow something of its prestige, Clemens's own ambivalence repeatedly shows in his alternating evaluations of science. In seeing the utility of scientific knowledge rather than its devotional aspect, Twain here promotes a commonplace opposition between science and beauty: "No, the romance and the beauty were all gone from the river." He then passes judgment on science itself, turning to medicine, the most visible of scientific trades, for his analogy:

Since those days I have pitied doctors from my heart. What does the lovely flush in a beauty's cheek mean to a doctor but a "break" that ripples above some deadly disease? Are not all her visible charms sown thick with what are to him the signs and symbols of hidden decay? Does he ever see her beauty at all, or doesn't he simply view her professionally, and comment upon her unwholesome condition all to himself? And doesn't he sometimes wonder whether he has gained most or lost most by learning his trade?

In expressing his skepticism about scientific knowledge, Twain finds himself accepting Romantic notions of beauty and mystery.

Over the course of his career, however, he seemed to grow more enthusiastic about science because the practical consequences of applied science were both a part of his vision of *progress and congruent with his developing aesthetic and ethics of *realism. The 1905 essay "Dr Loeb's Incredible Discovery" typifies this progressive, realistic view of science.

> In the drift of years I by and by found out that a Consensus examines a new thing with its feelings rather oftener than with its mind. . . . Do those people examine with feelings that are friendly to evidence? You know they don't. It is the other way about. They do the examining by the light of their preju- dices. . . . A consensus consisting of all the medical experts in Great Britain made fun of Jenner and inoculation. A Consensus consisting of all the med- ical experts in France made fun of the stethoscope. A Consensus of all the medical experts in Germany made fun of that young doctor . . . who discov- ered and abolished the cause of that awful disease, puerperal fever. . . . Electric telegraph, Atlantic cable, telephone, all "toys," and of no practical value— verdict of the Consensuses. Geology, palaeontology, evolution—all brushed into space by a Consensus of theological experts, comprising all the preachers in Christendom.

In this empirical realism Twain may reject his earlier Romanticism, but at the same time his underlying skepticism of established "fact" is a consistent component of his attitudes toward science.

Indeed, Twain's skepticism of received opinion coupled with his desire to test things for himself made him a natural devotee of science not as a body of knowl- edge but rather as a method of inquiry. In "Man's Place in the Animal World," he boasted that his conclusions about humanity, his satiric denunciation of human failings, came out of an obligation to follow facts regardless of prejudice, regardless that they may have been "profoundly humiliating to me." But that is what is required when one follows "what is commonly called the scientific method. This is to say, I have subjected every postulate that presented itself, to the crucial test of actual experiment, and have adopted it or rejected it according to the result." Needless to say, his emotional intensity belies his profession of scientific objectivity, no more so than in his intense emotional attraction to the skepticism required of the scientific method.

As much as he often expressed faith in progress that came from science, as much as he saw science as a heroic struggle against prejudice, he also saw in science evi- dence that no progress was possible. Especially in his studies of astronomy and biology, he found evidence to counter the idea of human exceptionalism. In astron- omy he found the infinity of the cosmos, in biology the infinity of the microcos- mos. His fantasy stories "The *Great Dark" and *"Three Thousand Years among the Microbes" turn on the possible parallels between these two realms. Numerous other stories and essays, most of them left unpublished at his death, satirically treat humanity's pretensions to superiority, and in most of these cases he turns to the theories of scientists to rebut the arguments of the devout. In "Was the World Made for Man?", for instance, Mark Twain cites Kelvin, Lyell, and *Spencer in citing the age of the earth and the amount of time human beings had been on it. He is conscious of the debate among scientists about the earth's age, so he takes the most conservative estimates. Even so, he uses these estimates not, as Kelvin did, to discredit the idea of natural selection ungoverned by God's active interposition, but instead to suggest that whatever creative forces spur evolution, they take no particular cognizance of humanity. In this respect, he out-Darwins Darwin.

♦ SEE ALSO Christian Science; Detective Stories; Parody.

SCIENCE FICTION. Because Hank Morgan in *A Connecticut Yankee in King Arthur's Court* says that he traveled through time, Mark Twain has often been touted as one of the fathers of science fiction. Such a claim seems more calculated to find a famous father than it is a legitimate paternity. Among the true progenitors of the science fiction novel, the time travel narratives of Edward Bellamy's *Looking Backward* and H. G. Wells's *The Time Machine*, for instance, are each based on a "scientific" premise. Twain's tale, if one takes Morgan's story seriously, is based not on a scientific premise, but rather on a spiritualist premise, that his time travel, "the transposition of epochs—and bodies" is akin to "transmigration of souls." Twain's agenda here has much more to do with his concerns about *history than about *science.

Which is not to say that Clemens did not share the late-nineteenth-century interest in science nor that his interest did not bear on his fiction. The incomplete manuscripts of *"Three Thousand Years among the Microbes" and "The *Great Dark" are both contingent on his knowledge of discoveries in microbiology. Had he finished and published such works, then devotees of sci-fi could legitimately claim lineage.

♦ SEE ALSO Spiritualism.

SELLERS, COLONEL ESCHOL [MULBERRY BERIAH]. The comic villain of *The Gilded Age*, the main character of the comic melodrama at first titled "The Gilded Age" but renamed *Colonel Sellers*, and a comic hero of sorts in *The American Claimant*, Colonel Sellers was one of the most successful and typical of Twain's comic characters. Twain swore that in creating the character he merely copied from life his mother's cousin, James Lampton. He swore, too, that the dinner of turnips he has Sellers feed young Hawkins in *The Gilded Age* was based on his own experience with Lampton. Nonetheless, Sellers's composition is not so simple, as the character owes a great debt to Twain's brother Orion *Clemens, and an even greater debt to the powers of Twain's own protean mind. Twain's imagination clearly possessed this character, taking him beyond the bounds of possibility into the realm of absurd fantasy.

In *The Gilded Age*, Sellers provides a comic, almost benign version of villainy. He is a penny-ante con man in a world of high-stakes chicanery, clearly unable to comprehend the magnitude of vice around him, but just as clearly wanting his "cut." Sellers is an amiable buffoon, a sort of stand-in for the American dream of getting rich quick without ever questioning the implications of that desire. Sellers spends so much energy dreaming of riches that he keeps his family in abject poverty. The moral of Seller's disposition to fictionalize his own life is pronounced by his wife nearly every time he tries to bolster his wife's spirits through his "speculations":

"Just stop and fancy a moment— ... Bless your heart, you dear women live right in the present all the time—but a man, why a man lives—"

"In the future, Eschol? But don't we live in the future most too much, Eschol? We do somehow seem to manage to live on next year's crop of corn and potatoes as a general thing while this year is still dragging along, but sometimes it's not a robust diet." (Chapter 27)

In this early novel, then, flights of imaginative "speculation" metaphorically serve as the relatively benign counterpart of financial speculation, which the book insists is counterproductive to the economic and moral health of the nation.

From the very beginning Twain had an affinity for the character, a character fundamentally like not only Twain's mother's cousin and his flighty brother, but also like himself. In a sketch of the characters and plot that Warner and Clemens wrote for J. Hammond *Trumbull so that Trumbull could provide chapter mottoes for *The Gilded Age*, they described Sellers as "a gentleman of kindly nature, whose imagination runs away with him, and makes him a conspicuous example of an American visionary, who has the power of illuminating his present poverty with glorious expectations. His untruthfulness is that of the imagination and not of the heart" (quoted in Bryant M. French, *Mark Twain and the Gilded Age*, 273).

In *The Gilded Age*, Twain concentrated on Sellers's "untruthfulness," but gradually shifted his emphasis over time to concentrate on Sellers's good heart. Perhaps this shift in focus came out of a sense of gratitude, since not only did Sellers's presence contribute to the financial success of Twain's first novel, his transformation into a comic stage presence also netted Twain a substantial amount of money, about seventy thousand dollars by 1882.

Not that this money came without some legal difficulties. While the character is clearly Twain's, his name was provided by Charles Dudley *Warner, who, when a law student in Philadelphia, knew of a prominent Philadelphia businessman, George Eschol Sellers. Why it came as a surprise to Warner and Twain that Sellers would have been deeply offended by the use of his name in a novel so clearly based on thinly veiled real events is one of the mysteries of authorship. When the real Sellers threatened a libel suit, however, the authors quickly changed their character's name to Beriah Sellers. Clemens changed the name again to Mulberry when a Beriah Sellers complained of the use of *his* name. It was exclusively as Mulberry Sellers that the Colonel made his final appearances in the minor novel *The American Claimant* and the abortive play of the same name.

In the 1890s when Twain's own fortunes were declining after he had unwisely speculated in the *Paige typesetter, Twain turned again to Sellers, depicting him in *The American Claimant* as a man able to surmount all difficulties through the power of his imagination. Again, his wife provides the commentary: "Well, no doubt it's a blessed thing to have an imagination that can always make you satisfied, no matter how you are fixed. Uncle Dave Hopkins used always to say, 'Turn me into John Calvin, and I want to know which place I'm going to; turn me into Mulberry Sellers, and I don't care'"(chapter 4). In personal financial terms, Twain's own lesson of twenty years earlier about the dangers of economic speculation was more pertinent than ever, but at the same time, in surrendering his image of being a business tycoon for the reality that his fortunes were best made through his ability to imagine, Twain was coming home to his own talents.

♦ SEE ALSO Confidence Games.

SENTIMENTALISM. By the time Clemens began writing professionally, sentimentalism had a long history both as a philosophy and as a style of literature. Originating in the psychology of sensations of John Locke in the seventeenth century and elaborated by such figures as the third Earl of Shaftesbury and Francis Hutcheson in the eighteenth, sentimentalism was founded on the idea that human beings come to know the world through their senses alone, that they have no innate ideas. But while each person may be born a blank slate, a benign God gives each the senses needed to discover happiness in both this world and the next. While the obvious external senses of taste, touch, sight, sound, and smell provide human beings with much information about their world, sentimentalists were more concerned with what they postulated to be finer senses, or sensibilities, of the intangible characters of things. These ostensible sensibilities included senses of compassion, of justice, of beauty, of the sublime, and so forth, with three of particular relevance to Twain: the sense of *reverence, the sense of *humor, and the *moral sense.

Sentimentalists held that these sensibilities were tastes that could be exercised and developed toward refinement or allowed to grow coarse depending on how a person used them. As they held the moral sense to be the highest of these sensibilities, sentimentalists argued that a person's goal in life should be to regulate his or her behavior in accordance with the finest urgings of the moral sense, and that a proper exercise of all sensibilities reinforced the exercise of the moral sense itself. As the Scottish philosopher Hugh Blair, widely influential in American thought, put it: "The exercise of taste is, in its native tendency, moral and purifying."

Sentimentalists held that the faculties of memory and imagination allowed *taste to be developed into morally meaningful habits and *associations. The capacity through sympathy to imagine what another person might feel made social sensitivity—compassion and altrusim—possible. And the ability of memory to attach moral feeling to associated tangible things and places made the tangible world itself a constant goad to the moral action of the sensibilities.

No wonder, then, that sentimentalists stressed the importance of *childhood, holding that when the tastes were in their first contact with life, the impressions they took would shape the moral tendency of the rest of the child's life. The cults, then, of motherhood, childhood, and *domesticity, so strong in the nineteenth century, grew out of this philosophy, as did the belief that *nostalgia, especially for home and for loved ones, was a sure corrective to any person's proclivities toward evil, at least as long as a person's early nurture was properly refined.

Sentimentalism's popularity grew in reaction to the rigors of *Calvinism, which held human beings to be innately sinful and the operations of the senses to be depraved in their worldliness, and in reaction to *utilitarianism, which held that human beings are motivated solely by selfish desires that can be calculated rationally. Sentimentalism stood between these extremes of worldliness and otherworldliness and offered faith in human goodness, in the possibility of altruism.

Sentimental moral philosophy's impact on nineteenth-century art, especially on literature, cannot be overestimated. In breaking down the Calvinist objection to fiction as "lies," sentimentalism rationalized a market in fiction. This rationalization, however, was contingent on the idea that literature must purify the sentiments. As Charles Dudley *Warner put it in attacking the late-century *realism and *naturalism that were coming to replace sentimentalism, "Art requires an idealization of nature ... the creation of a novel should be a synthetic process, and impart to human actions that ideal quality which we demand in painting." This tendency toward idealization in service of moral uplift has led to much criticism of sentimental literature as inappropriately idealistic, simplistic, stilted, stereotypical, emotionally exaggerated, naive, and oppressively serious.

At least those are the criticisms Mark Twain's works often bring to bear against sentimental literature. This is not surprising considering that comedy itself is so often at odds with the reverence at heart of so much sentiment. Granting that sentimentalists postulated a sense of humor, they did not therefore accord comedy very high status. Certainly the crudeness of Twain's early writing might suggest why, as it feeds off of sentimental reverence in its energetic attacks on sentimental convention. In newspaper correspondence of 1866–1868, for instance, sentimental posturing is the target of much of Clemens's comedy. In many of these sketches,

Clemens spoke through two characters, the refined, sentimental Mr. Mark Twain, and his earthy sidekick, Mr. Brown. In his letters from Hawaii, for instance, Mr. Mark Twain gushes over scenery; Brown complains about bugs. When travelling on an interisland schooner, Mr. Mark Twain's sentimental raptures over the sea are interrupted by Brown's groaning complaints of seasickness. To divert Brown from his discomfort, Mr. Twain recites hours of uplifting literature, finally to discover that sentimental, cliche-ridden poetry of his own making lifts up the contents of Brown's stomach. Brown, in his inimitably slangy style praises poetry as an emetic, much to the horror of the refined Mr. Twain.

As his career advanced, Clemens may have tried to write in a less earthy, less vulgar style, but when attacking sentimentalism his early impulses often resurfaced, as in his grotesque parody of obituary poetry in *Adventures of Huckleberry Finn*'s "Ode to Stephen Dowling Bots, Dec'd." In other attacks on literary sentimentalism, he rose to some of his most sophisticated *satire, as when he forever changed the literary status of James Fenimore Cooper in *"Fenimore Cooper's Literary Offenses."

Clemens's attacks also often cut deeper to the philosophical heart of sentimentalism. While he accepted the sentimentalist idea that moral behavior followed from aesthetic practice, he attacked sentimental practice on the grounds that it caused immoral behavior. For instance, in his attacks on what he called, in chapter 46 of *Life on the Mississippi*, "Sir Walter disease," he suggested that idealized literature conditioned people to pursue sensation at the expense of morality. While this is just the opposite of what sentimental moralists felt would happen through the judicious exercise of taste, Clemens argued strenuously that the stimulations of sensation fiction would lead people to misjudge the world or, worse, to pursue false heroism antithetical to the principles of political or individual virtue. He felt that sentimental posturing usually obscured selfish motives that could only be controlled if honestly and realistically represented. *Adventures of Huckleberry Finn* makes this argument repeatedly, as when the new judge tries to reform Huck's father, as when the King and the Duke use "soul-butter and hogwash" to dupe the Wilks girls, as when Tom Sawyer would rather play for effect than accept Jim's and Huck's anxiety to be free.

Clemens's energy in attacking sentimental morality suggests that he felt some need to distance himself from a philosophy that he found attractive, an attraction he admitted in his remarks on W. E. H. *Lecky's energetic exposition and defense of sentimentalism, *History of European Morals*. As Clemens wrote in the margins of his copy, "It is so noble and beautiful a book, that I don't want it to have even trivial faults in it" (vol. 2, p. 39, quoted in Walter Blair, *Mark Twain and* Huck Finn, chapter 10). The attraction certainly shows almost as often in Clemens's works as does the revulsion. Throughout his career, he turned both to sentimental literary conventions and to sentimental ethics on an ad hoc basis, as in the powerfully sympathetic rendition of Rachel Cord's biography in "A *True Story, Repeated Word for Word as I Heard It" or as in later works like "A Californian's Tale," *Personal Recollections of*

Joan of Arc, "A Dog's Tale," and "A Horse's Tale," and in unfinished works like "The Refuge of the Derelicts," or the late additions to "Captain Stormfield's Visit to Heaven" (these last not published in *"Extract from Captain Stormfield's Visit to Heaven," but available in the posthumous *Report from Paradise*). While these are arguably minor works, not central to Clemens's identity as a writer, such cannot be said of perhaps the most sentimental of all of Twain's works, the *Autobiography*. The tenor of this work is perhaps best characterized in an as yet unpublished section: "It is matter for pity, not mirth. No matter what the source of a sorrow may be, the sorrow itself is respectworthy" (10 October 1907). In this late passage, Twain renounces humor, something he in fact did repeatedly in his career, in favor of pure sentimentalism, but what he seems to miss here, as elsewhere, is that his humor itself always required sentimentalism both as justification for humor itself and as target for *burlesque and satire. The ambivalence of humor itself entails Clemens's longing for and rejection of the moral idealism of sentimentalism.

SERVANTS. Like that of any well-to-do Victorian family, the Clemens household included a large number of servants, who made possible not only the daily routines but the regular and rather extravagant entertaining that was a socially expected part of the family's professional and personal life. Among the servants they had were Patrick McAleer, "a brisk and electric coachman, an Irishman," who was hired by Olivia's father as part of the equipage of the house he bought the newlywed Clemenses as a wedding gift. McAleer remained in their employ until they closed their *Hartford house in 1891, and was reemployed by Clemens after Olivia died in 1904. The family moved from Buffalo to Hartford with a stop in Elmira while Olivia lived, and Clemens moved repeatedly in the years after his wife's death; McAleer followed, suggesting that the household was as much the servants in its employ as the buildings in which it lived.

Other servants were even more central to the family than McAleer. In particular, George Griffin (d. 1897), Clemens's own butler, who "came to wash some windows, and remained half a generation," and Katy Leary (1863–1934), Olivia's maid, were particularly close. Griffin was among Clemens's favorite audiences—Clemens delighted in making him laugh when behind his butler's screen and, therefore, supposedly not present. In this respect, Griffin conspired with Clemens to stretch the bounds of Victorian propriety. Which is not to say that he wasn't an upstanding man. Clemens delighted in Griffin's probity, though he found it necessary to train him to serve the family by bending the truth. As Clemens put it in a letter to Howells:

> We have got the very best gang of servants in America, now. When George first came he was one of the most religious of men. He had but one fault—young George Washington's. But I have trained him; & now it fairly breaks

Mrs. Clemens's heart to hear George stand at that front door & lie to the unwelcome visitor. (11 October 1876)

Leary, an Elmira native, was as much Olivia's project as servant. Olivia directed Leary in a course of study, and in time, the family came to entrust Leary with substantial responsibility. It was she who took care of Susy during Susy's fatal illness, on whom much of the burden of care fell during Olivia's terminal illness, who was virtually Jean's guardian when Jean suffered from serious epilepsy, and it was she who had the difficult task of telling Clemens of Jean's death.

Beyond these was a procession of other servants—cooks, gardeners, wet nurses, and nannies. Not all filled their functions admirably. In particular, one of Clara's wet nurses caused great perturbations. As Clemens wrote in a letter to William Dean Howells: "I found it was the wet-nurse who had drank 200 bottles of the 252—so I have been making an awful row in the servants' quarters, this morning, & clearing the atmosphere. My beer will be respected, now, I hope, for I do not wish to resort to bloodshed" (16 March 1875). But much as he complained, Clemens could not control this woman, whom he later, with grudging respect, described in a manuscript titled "A Family Sketch":

> There was never any wet-nurse like that one.... She stood six feet in her stockings, she was perfect in form and contour, raven-haired, dark as an Indian, stately, carrying her head like an empress.... She was as healthy as iron, she had the appetite of a crocodile, the stomach of a cellar, and the digestion of a quartz-mill. Scorning the adamantine law that a wet-nurse must partake of delicate things only, she devoured anything and everything she could get her hands on, shoveling into her person fiendish combinations ... ; and washing the cargo down with freshets of coffee, tea, brandy, whisky, ... —anything that was liquid; she smoked pipes, cigars, cigarettes ... ; and then she would go up stairs loaded as described and perfectly delight the baby with a banquet ... which ought to have killed it at thirty yards, but which only made it happy and fat and boozy. (Written in mid-1897; partially published in *Mark Twain–Howells Letters*, 1960.)

His family's servants rarely appeared in Twain's writings except in his *autobiography and, most significantly, in "A *True Story, Repeated Word for Word as I Heard It," which is based on the biography of Mary Ann Cord, a cook at the Elmira residence of Clemens's in-laws. But questions of service abound in his writings. In *Adventures of Huckleberry Finn*, for example, Huck acknowledges that, unused as he is to having a servant, he treats the slave assigned to him at the Grangerford's well; Buck, on the other hand, makes his "jump." And sketches like "Two Little Tales" (1901) or the passages in *The American Claimant* that mock

Berkeley's supercilious disrespect of the cleaning girl suggest that Clemens opposed aristocratic, which in his terms is to say abusive, treatment of servants.

SEVENTIETH BIRTHDAY DINNER. This giant bash was the bookend to Twain's uncomfortable performance at Whittier's seventieth birthday banquet. When Twain turned seventy in 1905, George *Harvey, then editor of *Harper's Weekly*, threw a banquet for him. He invited over 170 guests, most of whom came, and all but a handful of whom were literary men and women. The five-hour event included more than a dozen speeches, each of which praised Twain as if he were dead. With such an outpouring of support, including, as the *Nation* described it, a "Greeting from forty of the leading men of letters in England," it was easy to conclude that Twain was the greatest writer—perhaps the greatest human being—ever to grace the planet.

At least so one would conclude by reading the press coverage. Daily newspapers were of course alerted to the event in advance, and most New York dailies gave the banquet front-page coverage. Major papers across the continent also gave the event full coverage, and weekly and monthly magazines wrote stories as well, with many of them extensively quoting Twain's own speech. Harvey in particular cashed in on the event, not only by publicizing it through the newspapers, but by publishing a thirty-two-page report of the event in a supplement to the magazine. James L. Ford, a now forgotten humorist, praised Harvey's "gracious hospitality" and his ability to pursue "the main chance." "Not since," he went on, "round-eyed wonder-seekers looked through the cage-bars at Barnum's 'Happy Family' had such a varied assembly been seen in perfect amity" (*Forty-Odd Years in the Literary Shop*, 1921). Ford's comparison of Harvey to P. T. Barnum is appropriate; Harvey's point was in part to make Twain, whom he was publishing regularly in both *Harper's* and the *North American Review*, a more salable commodity. Not only was Harvey capitalizing on Twain's growing reputation as a major writer—with *honorary degrees from Yale and the University of Missouri as well as a 1904 election as one of the first seven members of the American Academy of Arts and Letters—he was helping to build it. He managed to get the endorsement of the English speaking world's most prominent writers, pretty much ensuring that Twain's reputation would flourish for years to come. Twain had become the Whittier, Emerson, and Holmes of his day.

The weight of all this praise makes Twain's own speech all the more delightful. As soon as a number of renowned writers had finished praising Twain's deep seriousness, Twain gave a light-hearted speech that mostly eschewed the seriousness of the occasion, that even mocked his own importance as a revered and thus authoritative voice. One of his best known speeches, reprinted in numerous anthologies and regularly quoted, it undercuts his own cultural authority. In contrast to the advice, often shared on such occasions, to hew to the straight and narrow path,

Twain praises smoking, drinking, and general immorality, justified with the *maxim, "If you find you can't make seventy by any but an uncomfortable road, don't you go."

♦ SEE ALSO Whittier Birthday Dinner.

SEX AND SEXUALITY. Given the large volume of information we have about almost every aspect of the creative life of Mark Twain and the private life of Samuel Clemens, the gap concerning his sexuality looms large in the imagination. This gap is all the more conspicuous given that many married couples of the era did discuss their sexual desires and practices in their letters, as Karen Lystra's *Searching The Heart: Women, Men, and Romantic Love in Nineteenth-Century America* points out. Lystra, relying substantially on a wealth of diaries and letters, debunks many stereotypes about Victorian sexuality, showing that, in private, men and women often had quite open attitudes toward a full and robust sexuality. But Lystra could not have used Clemens's papers to further her study simply because his papers reveal so little.

Nonetheless, Clemens discusses sex and sexual practices in a few letters and creative works, most of which he either suppressed entirely, circulated privately, or gave as speeches that went unreported. These give us some idea of his acceptance or resistance to commonplace public ideas about sex and sexuality. For example, in a letter to William Bowen, he refers to *nostalgia as "intellectual and moral masturbation" that should be left to the period of life when one physically masturbates. This letter tells us at least that, before marriage, he masturbated, which in fact tells us little. What is lacking is a sense of shame over it, a shame that Victorians supposedly felt over any sexual pleasure, but especially over the "secret vice." By the same token, Clemens implicitly suggests that heterosexual copulation is the natural mature expression of sexuality. Yet he could make masturbation jokes to an audience of men in "The Science of Onanism," a speech he gave to "The Stomach Club" in the spring of 1879. This club was an unpublicized, but not unknown, group of English-speaking men that met irregularly in Paris to enjoy *off-color humor. The speech shows Clemens's awareness of the commonplace moral and "hygienic" injunctions against masturbation and his lack of regard for those injunctions.

Similarly, in looking at *Letters from the Earth*, we can assume that he took great pleasure in sexual intercourse, and thought that the Victorian denial of it as an essential part of human happiness was absurd. On the other hand, we know that he supported the Victorian idea that sex outside of marriage was an affront to the social order. In 1877, he discovered that one of the Hartford housemaids in his employ had been entertaining her unemployed lover in the basement of the Clemens house. When confronted with the evidence of their escapades, she confessed, saying, however, that she had been seduced and was pregnant (neither of which, Clemens learned later, was true). He coerced the two into marriage and dismissed the maid, sending the couple away with one hundred dollars apiece. Apparently, he doubted the man would stay with his new wife, so Clemens gave money to *each*, but he also apparently felt that the social ritual of marriage was an absolute necessity to sanction their sexuality.

In such episodes and in his many works in which he mentions sexuality, we know something of Clemens's public and quasi-public attitudes toward sex, but we still have no evidence of his private attitudes or practices. Of course, our post-Freudian presuppositions of Victorian culture make us assume that all such public statements are hypocritical. Thus, scholars have speculated for years that Clemens must have had some kind of sex life beyond the pale. Yet few have ever speculated that Clemens was unfaithful to his wife. This is remarkable given how quickly such rumors spread. For instance, Charles Dudley *Warner was rumored to have had a longtime mistress (at whose house he died of a heart attack—ostensibly suffered during coitus). No such rumors have ever attached to Clemens, and, indeed, the Warner rumor is often used to explain the cooling of their friendship. The suggestion is that Clemens learned of Warner's behavior and distanced himself in protest. Of course, the way Clemens froze Warner out of profits from the drama *Colonel Sellers*, based on their jointly authored novel, provides a better reason for their social distance. Still, as an explanation of human behavior, sex has a greater allure than business.

Given the apparent exclusivity of the relationship between Samuel and Olivia Langdon *Clemens, what Clemens did before he married has been the subject of much speculation. Some of it is quite ingenious given that it stands on no direct evidence. Andrew Hoffman's biography of Mark Twain, for instance, suggests that Clemens had long-standing homosexual relationships with at least two men when he lived in Nevada and California. Other scholars suggest that Clemens did in fact sleep with his servants. This latter suggestion is made in response to another possibility, that Clemens frequented prostitutes when out west. Certainly Clemens himself was worried that such an assumption would be made of him, and his letter to his prospective father-in-law of 29 December 1868, in which he tries to assure the Langdons that he is worthy to marry their daughter, implicitly says that he has not. He deliberately forces their attention to his drinking and lack of religion, concluding, "I never did anything mean, false or criminal. . . . [T]he same doors that were open to me seven years ago are open to me yet; . . . all the friends I made are still my friends; . . . wherever I have been I can go again—& enter in the light of day & hold my head up." The list of references he gives will, he is sure, back up his assertion. Again, though, we have no direct evidence, only the evidence sculpted by a man whose powerful creative imagination shapes his past in order to get what he wants in the present. Perhaps that gives us license to indulge our own imaginations in reconstructing the sexuality modern readers wish Twain to have, that is, sexuality worthy of legend.

SHAKESPEARE, WILLIAM. The Rev. Henry N. Hudson, nineteenth-century America's most popular critic and editor of Shakespeare, lectured and published widely in praise of Shakespeare's works as second only to the Bible as a repository of moral truths. Hudson praised Shakespeare for having perfect insight into human nature, and even though he ruthlessly cut almost every reference to sexuality from his 1870–1871 edition of Shakespeare's plays for "home and school," he declared in the preface to his edition of *Othello* that he "holds Shakespeare's workmanship to be everywhere free from the least blame of moral infection or taint: he knows of no passage that can be hurtful to any fair mind, if taken in its proper connection with the whole." Hudson is representative of a major movement in America's reaction to Shakespeare over the course of the century. Early American commentators who saw Shakespeare more as a literary artist than as a dramatist praised Shakespeare so much that his name became synonymous with literary genius. This elevation helped secure a place for imaginative literature and, to a limited degree, *theater in American high culture. But as much as critics like Hudson tried to elevate Shakespeare, Shakespearean *drama was a very lively part of American popular culture, too.

Staged with comic afterpieces and entr'actes, performed as readily on the road by traveling troupes as in big city theaters, Shakespeare was naturalized for an American audience as popular entertainment, much as it was originally intended. As such, it had elements to appeal to the most ignorant as well as the most educated tastes. Through most of the century, acting styles favored heroic bombast, turning Shakespeare's plays into screaming melodramas, and *burlesque performances of Shakespeare were as popular as serious ones. But toward the close of the century, under the influence of such critics as Hudson and with the discovery of literature as an academic subject, with Shakespeare as the guiding light, Shakespeare was gradually pulled out of the popular realm and into the realm of the classics. Acting styles changed as well, moving toward quieter, subtler performances designed to educe the complex textures of the plays.

This is the context in which Clemens came to Shakespeare's works. He was aware of them early in his life, and certainly saw many screaming performances both in the Mississippi valley in the 1850s and in the far West in the 1860s. He himself tried to cash in on the burlesque movement, but his reticence shows something of his own feeling of awe for Shakespeare, that he bought into the movement elevating Shakespeare beyond mere entertainment. As he put it in a letter to William Dean *Howells about his burlesque *Hamlet*:

> [A]n old idea came again into my head . . . of adding a character to Hamlet. I did the thing once—nine years ago; the addition was a country cousin of Hamlet's. But it did not suit me, & I burnt it. A cousin wouldn't answer; the family could not consistently ignore him; one couldn't rationally explain a *cousin's* standing around the stage during 5 acts & never being spoken to: yet

of course the added character must *not* be spoken to; for the sacrilegious scribbler who ventured to put words into Shakespeare's mouth would probably be hanged. But I've got a character now, who is all right. He goes & comes as he pleases; yet he does not need to be spoken to. (3 September 1881)

Worried about sacrilege, yet drawn to it irresistibly, Twain created this new character as a subscription book agent, whose very presence challenges the high status of Shakespeare, and whose speeches make the point explicit, as for example in his soliloquy at the beginning of scene 3:

They're on the high horse all the time, then: they swell around, and talk the grandest kind of book-talk, and look just as if they were on exhibition. It's the most unnatural stuff! why, it ain't *human* talk; nobody that ever lived, ever talked the way they do. Even the flunkies can't say the simplest thing the way a human being would say it (*striding, stage-fashion, and imitating them.*) "Me lord hath given commandment, sirrah, that the vehicle wherein he doth of ancient custom, his daily recreation take, shall unto the portal of the palace be straight conveyed . . . " Now what d — d rot that is! Why, a man in his right mind would simply say, "Fetch the carriage, you duffer, and *hump* yourself!"

The agent goes on to explain that these people talk normally enough when they're not in the parlor, but there, perfect propriety must reign.

On the one hand, Twain's burlesque, which he never finished or published, expresses anxiety about the formality of high Victorian culture, of which the Shakespeare cult was a part. But he also expends his animus on the degradation of Shakespeare in bombastic acting. That is what the target is in his rendition of Hamlet's soliloquy in *Adventures of Huckleberry Finn*, in which he mocks not Shakespeare per se so much as the strenuous, shallow performance of Shakespeare on the popular stage.

Clemens's own reverence for Shakespearean drama, or at least his ultimate acquiescence in its continuing elevation, explains in part his *Is Shakespeare Dead?* (1909), in which Twain weighs in on the authorship controversy in favor of Bacon. Given that Clemens's own educational background proved the possibility of a man of limited education becoming a serious writer, his support of Bacon's authorship of Shakespeare's works suggests a continuing doubt about his own value.

SIMON WHEELER. The character to whom Mark Twain applies for information in "The *Jumping Frog," Wheeler is a conundrum, representing the inscrutability of the West to an Easterner. The Easterner assumes Wheeler is an old fool, but the tale he tells suggests otherwise, that Wheeler is trying to teach the Easterner about the shrewd *confidence games of a democratic West, in which simple appearances mask a much more complex reality. Twain picked up the character again in *Simon Wheeler, Amateur Detective*, first written as a drama that, though copyrighted, was never performed, and then edited and expanded into a novel that was never published. This tale was a *burlesque *detective story in which he turned the enigmatic Wheeler into a true simpleton. While the target of this book was the detective story, the reduction of Wheeler into a stock character, the likes of which peopled Bret *Harte's fiction, may have been one of the reasons Twain did not publish the book.

SKETCH. The sketch as a genre is rarely mentioned now, being subsumed by two other genres, the short story and the *essay, but in Twain's day, the sketch was one of the most important and vital of literary forms. Beginning in the eighteenth century with the rise of newspapers and magazines that needed large volumes of short pieces, the sketch took its name from the visual arts. It was meant to be a quick, incomplete rendition of some place or character. The sketch could thus include a fictional or nonfictional tale, but was not primarily interested in plot. Its descriptive purpose did not have time to develop the cause and effect relationships of plot, nor was it interested in character change and development so much as in revealing essential and static characteristics.

Developed in England, the sketch was early naturalized in America, with one of America's first successful professional writers, Washington *Irving, eschewing the novel in favor of the sketch. The shorter form's flexibility allowed him in *The Sketchbook of Geoffrey Crayon* not only to describe exotic European scenes for his audience, but also to develop the character of his narrative persona. Irving mastered the forms of Addison, Steele, and other English journalists who used the sketch equally well to reveal the artist as to reveal what the artist took as his subject. Hence, even the narrator's choice of short narratives, narratives verging on the short story, reflects back on the narrator in the manner of *frame narratives. In this aspect of literary sketching, the eighteenth- and nineteenth-century practice of taking on literary *pseudonyms as character masks was born. Clemens from the outset of his career used such pseudonyms to project a comic image, most conspicuously in the character of Mark Twain.

Twain wrote sketches from the beginning of his career to the end, but the balance of his output shifted away from sketches toward essays and narrative forms, including the short story and the novel, later in his career, partly because the literary market was shifting toward longer works, partly because he was no longer connected to particular newspapers or magazines—such as the Virginia City *Territorial Enterprise*, the San Francisco *Alta California*, or the *Galaxy Magazine*—that demanded a steady stream of journalism. Nonetheless, even in his longer works, including his novels, the episodic character of his plotting bears the marks of his penchant for writing sketches.

It is now perhaps impossible to say if Twain wrote sketches because he had so much difficulty contriving plots or if he had so much difficulty contriving plots because he began his career writing sketches. Either way, the sketch's brevity and emphasis on character, place, or situation fit Twain's literary imagination perfectly. Moreover, it allowed him to worry little about the distinctions between fact and fiction inasmuch as the sketch traditionally blended both realms without any compunction and apparently without causing any anxiety for readers. Sketches such as Twain's "The Late Benjamin Franklin" treat historical subjects fictionally not so much to create a plot about the past, as historical romance did, but rather to crystallize an idea about the present. This is another reason the sketch was so popular as a genre—it opened itself easily to political and social *satire, which was entirely congenial both to American culture and to Twain's temperament.

♦ SEE ALSO Newspaper Journalism; Realism; Sentimentalism.

SKETCHES, NEW & OLD (1875). First suggesting a new volume of *sketches to Elisha *Bliss in January 1870, and beginning to select the contents and signing a contract for the volume by the end of December, Twain did not deliver the completed manuscript until 1875, after he had put the turmoil of Buffalo behind him, but more importantly, after he had finished *Roughing It* and *The Gilded Age*. Author and publisher feared that the sketches would interfere with sales of the bigger books, and they also wanted to figure out how to secure copyright on the old, hitherto uncopyrighted material. Clemens in part made his selections of the earlier sketches in such a way as to downplay the more scandalous side of his western image. When the book was in press he wrote to William Dean Howells, "I destroyed a mass of sketches, & now heartily wish I had destroyed some more of them" (14 September 1875). But in part he made selections to secure his property rights in what was to him primarily a source of income. When the final manuscript was delivered, fifty-six of the sixty-three sketches were previously published material, but only ten of these were from his western journalism. Twain drew the bulk of the book from his more recent work, including about one third of the book from his contributions to the *Galaxy*. While by 1875 Twain thought of himself as having moved beyond the style and content of these sketches, many remain perennial favorites, regularly reprinted in anthologies.

SLANG. Samuel Clemens, at first frightened by the literary standards of the East, worried about his love of slang, but no matter how much he tried to cramp his style, nonstandard expressions bubbled out of him. He simply could not escape the fact that, as literary language, slang often has no equal because, as he metaphorically put it in the *"Bluejay Yarn," it is often "just bristling with metaphor . . . —just bristling!" So as much as he tried, when first writing for an eastern audience, to revise the slang out of his style, he found himself inveterate. And as much as his writing was regularly attacked for its slang, he also heard it praised on the same grounds. When, for example, Richard Watson Gilder, editor of the *Century Magazine*, solicited serialization of *Adventures of Huckleberry Finn* for his journal, he confessed that he would have to edit some to fit the taste of his audience, but that "I have a pretty 'robustuous taste,' (for a pharisaical dude) and wouldn't mutilate your book you may be sure" (10 October 1884). Even among literary brahmins, slang had a sub rosa vitality that Mark Twain's literature helped bring to light.

♦ SEE ALSO Comic Journalism; Dialect; Goodman, Joseph T.; Language; Profanity; Style; Taste.

SLAVERY. Trying, in *"Old Times on the Mississippi," to illuminate the power a riverboat pilot had, Clemens explained that, excepting pilots, "every man and woman and child has a master, and worries and frets in servitude." For a man living in Hartford, Connecticut, in the 1870s to use such a trope to describe human connections and responsibilities argues not only for Clemens's power of hyperbole, but also for the hold over his imagination the idea of slavery had. Given Clemens's childhood in a slave state when slavery was the nation's most hotly contested moral and political issue, his need somehow to reconcile the idea of a father who had held slaves and a brother who was an abolitionist, his simultaneous awareness of the violence that upheld the system and of the familial connection between slave and slaveholder, it does not surprise that slavery, as historical fact and as literary symbol, recurs frequently and intensely in his writings.

Slavery was, after all, a system of violent coercion centered in families and household economies. Few slaves worked in industries—most were either household servants or, predominantly, field hands. Most slaveholders were small farmers who held no more than one or two slaves, though most slaves were held on large plantations, working in gangs, governed by overseers. That dichotomy explains what to Clemens was the puzzle of slavery: how can an ostensibly civilized people live in a community that sanctions slavery—or any other gross evil for that matter—while maintaining for the most part civil relations with one another and with the world? Depending on his mood and general outlook at any given period, he solved that puzzle in radically different ways.

One answer was that slavery in Missouri—at least the familial slavery that he knew in Missouri—was not overtly brutal enough to call attention to its inconsistency. An argument could be made for such a position. In a religious community in which children were regularly beaten as a form of discipline, the difference between beating a slave and a child was easily elided. In such a community, slaves and children could be companions, much as an aged Clemens suggested through the glow of *nostalgia in his *autobiography. His depiction of his Uncle Quarles's farm is nearly bucolic, describing a companionship among the young, regardless of color. Frederick *Douglass, in *My Bondage and My Freedom*, suggested something similar, describing how his white childhood companions, as yet untutored in the ways of slaveholding, helped teach him to read. Such was the history that enabled Clemens to have the Wilks girls in *Adventures of Huckleberry Finn* cry when their putative uncles sell their slaves.

In such a familial variant of the "peculiar institution," many slaves lived by a hierarchy within families as well as between, vaunting themselves or denigrating others by their associations with fine families or fine positions. Hence Clemens describes Aunt Rachel in "A *True Story, Repeated Word for Word as I Heard It" as puffing herself by her claims to fine origins; hence he describes Roxana in *Pudd'nhead Wilson* bragging about her ancestry among the First Families of Virginia.

Yet Clemens was aware that such a tidied picture of slavery told only a very superficial tale, one that left out the important differences between slave and slave-holder even in the most compassionate and gentle of families. In his autobiography he acknowledges that the differences of "color and condition interposed a subtle line which both parties were conscious of, and which rendered complete fusion impossible." This line was reinforced by violence, a violence that Clemens came to hold to be the basis of slaveholding cultures.

He had personal experience of that violence, observing it regularly as a child in Hannibal. Memories of it come up regularly in his fiction, especially in *Adventures of Huckleberry Finn* and *Pudd'nhead Wilson*, but also displaced in time and space in *A Connecticut Yankee in King Arthur's Court*. In some places he spoke directly of these childhood memories, as when in chapter 38 of *Following the Equator* he describes a man striking his Indian servant in Bombay:

> I had not seen the like of this for fifty years. It carried me back to my boy-hood, and flashed upon me the forgotten fact that this was the *usual* way of explaining one's desires to a slave.... When I was ten years old I saw a man fling a lump of iron-ore at a slave-man in anger, for merely doing something awkwardly—as if that were a crime. It bounded from the man's skull, and the man fell and never spoke again. He was dead in an hour.... Nobody in the village approved of that murder, but of course no one said much about it.

This moral passivity among the best people, and the concomitant moral numbness that slavery engendered, became central topics for Clemens, expressed most directly, perhaps, in "My First Lie and How I Got Out of It" (1899):

> It would not be possible for a humane and intelligent person to invent a rational excuse for slavery; yet you will remember that in the early days of the

emancipation agitation in the North the agitators got but small help or countenance from any one. Argue and plead and pray as they might, they could not break the universal stillness that reigned, from pulpit and press all the way down to the bottom of society—the clammy stillness created and maintained by the lie of silent assertion—the silent assertion that there wasn't anything going on in which humane and intelligent people were interested.

Of course, he also saw such moral numbness become active rather than passive in the behavior of his own father, who served on a jury that convicted two Northerners of encouraging a slave to escape. For all of John Marshall *Clemens's moral uprightness, he saw such service as supporting law and order, whereas Samuel Clemens came to see it as merely endorsing injustice through organized violence. He ultimately saw in slavery the violence that he held to be central to all civilizations, and his attacks on *imperialism in "To the Person Sitting in Darkness" and "King Leopold's Soliloquy," among others, rely on this understanding. Ultimately he suggests that the moral blindness of accepting such gross violations of humanity is the most debilitating slavery of all.

♦ SEE ALSO Moral Sense; Race Relations.

SLOTE, DAN (1828?–1882). Slote, a New York City manufacturer of stationery, met Clemens on the *Quaker City* expedition to Europe and the holy lands. Dan was one of "the boys" who figure so prominently in *The Innocents Abroad* as one of the alter egos of the sanctimonious pilgrims. Not surprisingly, fast-living Clemens appreciated Slote in the tight quarters of a ship. As he wrote to his family, he could put up with a bigoted minister on board because "I have got a splendid, immoral, tobacco-smoking, wine-drinking, godless room-mate who is as good & true & right-minded a man as ever lived." At first, Clemens relied on his impression that Slote was "right-minded." When they returned to New York City, Clemens used Slote as his "banker" and Slote's home as his New York address frequently in 1868, and kept in touch for years, having Slote manufacture his self-pasting scrapbook *invention, and investing in a lithographic process Slote developed. Clemens ultimately invested so heavily that he came to own the process, and his dealings with Slote over this Kaolatype and the scrapbook convinced him that Slote was indeed "immoral," specifically, a liar and a thief. In fact he commissioned his nephew-by-marriage Charles *Webster to investigate, leading to another infamous link in the chain of Clemens's disastrous *business ventures. "Webster," said Clemens, "could always select a fool." Fine words from a man who had a talent for being fooled.

"SOCIABLE JIMMY." While on a lecture tour in the winter of 1871–1872, Clemens stopped in Paris, Illinois, where one of the hotel staff, "a bright, simple, guileless little darkey boy," absolutely captured Clemens's imagination with his energetic dialect conversation, or rather monologue. Clemens transcribed the conversation, and set it in a newspaper *sketch published in the New York *Times*, 29 November 1874. The sketch is significant as a marker of Twain's interest in African-American vernacular and as a sign of his interest in a child's perspective. It is his first sustained experiment with a child's voice as worthy of exposition. Yet while the child's voice is prominent, the framing is extremely patronizing in ways quite conventional for a *frame narrative. The nearly contemporary publication of Twain's "A *True Story, Repeated Word for Word as I Heard It," shows a much more sophisticated play with dialect in frame. Still, "Sociable Jimmy" is an important step on Twain's way to the dialect and point of view of *Adventures of Huckleberry Finn*.

♦ SEE ALSO African Americans.

SOCIAL CLASS. American travelers in England, when inquiring about some peculiarity of social class, often hear that they should not try to understand because only an English native can fathom the complexities of the English class system. Most Americans are satisfied with that answer for they know how complex social class can be: in the United States, class patterns are so confused that not even a native can understand them. Indeed, sociologists who study the idea of social class constantly debate how to classify Americans. Americans themselves tend to hide behind such clumsy categories as lower, middle, and upper class. The problem, of course, is that by these standards, nearly everyone thinks of him- or herself as middle class. That is, excepting in the South, which always complicates any discussion of social class in America, and excepting, too, the self-identified upper-middle class, which cannot stand to be average, but does not dare identify itself as purely upper class—a term that is anathema in America.

These terms, grossly inadequate as they are in describing American class, were not regularly used in the nineteenth century. Early in the century Americans spawned one of their favorite myths to distinguish America from *Europe. According to this myth, in a country of hereditary caste and distinction, social class is who you are; in America, social class is what you make of yourself. Yet the American idea of class was substantially complicated by the hangover of hereditary status that was especially prevalent on the Atlantic seaboard, home to many of the nation's opinion leaders. Many of these continued to look to European, aristocratic models to define social class. In part they did so because they were stung by repeated European attacks on the putative crudeness of American society. These Americans struggled to define the impossible: a democratic ideal of hierarchy that would look good in European eyes. The result was that American opinion elites usually *defined* social class by a standard of gentility, by a standard of *etiquette and cultivation. Formality and correctness of language and deportment as well as cultivation of taste in literature (especially *poetry), *music, *painting, architecture and other arts, knowledge of French, Latin, and perhaps another European language, familiarity with European *history, and ideally an extended *tour in Europe were generally expected as requirements for gentility. At the same time, those elites recognized that *money undergirds almost all real power in America, and that while money needed a veneer of gentility, and while gentility had its own class rewards regardless of wealth, money was becoming the primary standard of class.

According to republicanism, the quasi-official standard of the opinion elites who wrote regularly in newspapers, magazines, and books, there was nothing wrong with amassing wealth, but to use it to buy power over others while pretending to European aristocratic manners was a betrayal of American values. Yet these educated men and women had traditional standards of gentility that were passed on through generations and that earned them easy entrée into the best circles. Regardless, by these republican standards, the European idea that a gentleman or lady had avocations rather than vocations came under regular attack, even as it persisted as an ideal. At the same time, Americans generally accepted that, while labor was intrinsically noble, some kinds of labor were more ennobling than others. Americans developed an idea of the "professions" as superior to manual labor. Merchants, while looked down upon by European nobles, came early to be respected as professionals by many in the United States.

No outline of American class ideas of the nineteenth century can be complete without mentioning regional variations. The trans-Allegheny West had a much more democratic conception of republican mores, and the consequent difference in manners between East and West was noted by most travelers in America. Western etiquette was much more open, much more familiar, and many Easterners, as well as most European visitors, saw such familiarity as boorish. But by the standards of the West, any other approach to one's social equals, no matter how wealthy or well educated, was a mark of either snobbery or flunkyism. In the South, this openness was complicated by the pseudoaristocracy of a slaveholding society. Elaborate racial hierarchies were necessary to justify slavery; the correlative idea that whites, too, were stratified on the basis of physical, mental, and moral superiority or inferiority was widely held. Such ideas, latent in much of the United States in the face of immigration and internal migration, gained new traction after the *Civil War when *evolution began to be widely accepted. Mark Twain's works of the 1880s and beyond regularly parody such ideas, most notably in *Adventures of Huckleberry Finn*, in which Twain has Huck mouth such platitudes about quality:

> Col. Grangerford was a gentleman, you see. He was a gentleman all over; and so was his family. He was well born, as the saying is, and that's worth as much in a man as it is in a horse, so the widow Douglas said, and nobody ever denied that she was of the first aristocracy in our town; and pap he always said it, too, though he warn't no more quality than a mud-cat. (chapter 18)

Huck learns the same attitudes from the top of the social scale to the bottom, so he has no reason to doubt them, but the reality of Grangerford's violence and

THE CHURCH, THE KING, THE NOBLEMAN, AND THE FREEMAN.

Illustration by Daniel Carter Beard (1850–1941), from *A Connecticut Yankee in King Arthur's Court*, New York: Webster & Company, 1889, p. 218.

touchy honor belies his pretensions toward gentility in the satirist's eye. Similarly, in *Pudd'nhead Wilson*, by having Roxy berate her son for not living up to the First-Families-of-Virginia blood in his veins, Twain belittles the entire idea of innate gentility.

The ambivalence educated Americans felt, then, about a republican version of gentility, complete with all of its aristocratic trappings, made its way into much literature of the nineteenth and early twentieth centuries, and it is a staple of Twain's work, much of which could be categorized as comedy of manners. From the beginning, the *Mark Twain persona played on ideas of cultivation and vulgarity, at first when Mr. Mark Twain was the refined counterpoint to the vulgar Mr. Brown. Later, Clemens collapsed the distinction, sending Mark Twain into the hallowed realms of Europe and the holy lands in *The Innocents Abroad* and then again in *A Tramp Abroad*. Much of *Roughing It* is built on the gradual education of refined Mark Twain in the ways of the West, including in its less-than-genteel *work ethic and the rawness of its *leisure, but as much as the book mocks the pretense of eastern gentility, it also endorses the idea that a true gentleman is marked by his fundamentally decent behavior. Speaking of the poor treatment the *Chinese receive out west, Twain writes:

> They are a kindly disposed, well-meaning race, and are respected and well treated by the upper classes, all over the Pacific coast. No California *gentleman* or *lady* ever abuses or oppresses a Chinaman, under any circumstances, an explanation that seems to be much needed in the east. Only the scum of the population do it—they and their children; they, and, naturally and consistently,

the policemen and politicians, likewise, for these are the dust-licking pimps and slaves of the scum, there as well as elsewhere in America. (chapter 54)

The spin Twain gives class here is that true gentility is fundamentally humanitarian in spirit, setting up a paradox long an element in social activism in the United States—much *reform to broaden access to the institutions of power and prestige in the United States has been instigated by the elites in the name of "improving" those below them.

Given that Clemens himself was among those scum in that he and his roommate, Steve *Gillis, used to hurl empty beer bottles on the roofs of the houses in San Francisco's Chinatown in 1864, this 1872 diatribe against "scum" is remarkably energetic. But Clemens had been trying to climb, socially, for some years, turning his back on his working-class past. After Anson *Burlingame befriended him in Hawaii in 1866, Clemens began the task of social climbing that was to engage him for some time. Courting Olivia Langdon, editing the Buffalo *Express*, building a substantial *house in Hartford, publishing in the *Atlantic Monthly*, feeling intense remorse about his *Whittier Birthday Dinner speech: all were emblems of his desire to rise, efforts Annie *Fields noted with astonishment in watching "this growing man of forty—to see how he studies and how high his aims are."

But the Mark Twain persona, dubbed "The Wild Humorist of the Pacific Slope" in his early eastern lecture tours, gave Clemens a vent for his ambivalence about his own climbing. To a large degree, Twain's humor expresses anxiety about hard work, education, manners, and the entire Victorian exercise of self-control in the name of gentility. Given that Clemens's own aspirations were widely shared, and given that Americans remained anxious not only that they were not cultivated enough but that they might become too cultivated, Twain's popularity comes as no surprise. Americans appreciated a homespun wild man telling the truth about high society, "[t]hat," as Twain puts it in the epigraph to chapter 62 of *Following the Equator*, "there are no people who are quite so vulgar as the over-refined ones."

♦ SEE ALSO Food; Race Relations; ESSAY ON Etiquette.

SOUTHWESTERN HUMOR. Mark Twain's works owe much to the *humor of the old Southwest as expressed in a body of writing mostly antedating the Civil War and taking as its subject matter the people and places of that region of the South extending from inland Georgia to the Mississippi River. With roots as varied as classical *satire, the eighteenth-century character *sketch, and folktales and myths, southwestern humor became a distinctive and very popular type of humor in the middle of the nineteenth century precisely because it reflected the national interest in and anxieties about *social class distinctions and the transformation of a frontier culture into "civilization."

One significant source of this humor is a tradition of folktale and folk mythology that grew up on the nation's frontiers over the eighteenth and nineteenth centuries as westward migration rose to a flood from the settled eastern seaboard into the trans-Appalachian interior. The confrontation with a natural landscape that was inhospitable to European forms and customs led to, among other things, a kind of storytelling that captures the ambivalent exhilaration and terror of the move into the wilderness. Heroes of these tales tend to be much larger than life, even as their occupations are among the most mundane, as in the case of Mike Fink, a river raftsman, and Daniel Boone and Davy Crockett, woodsmen. The stories of these folk heroes revolve around impossible strength and prowess surpassed only by the heroes' capacities to brag about that prowess. One Davy Crockett tale, for instance, has Crockett awake to a morning so cold that the earth has frozen to its axis. With the earth no longer turning, the sun won't rise and life itself is at risk. Crockett, recognizing the problem, sets out for the north pole to fix matters. Along the way, he kills and carries away a bear. When man and dead bear arrive at the pole, Crockett squeezes enough bear grease onto the pole to break the earth free on its axis. The world turns, the sun rises, creation is saved, and Crockett walks home with a piece of sunshine in his pocket. Central to most such stories is a self-consciousness of the story itself, lending a sense of skepticism that suggests deceit and the discovery of deceit is the real pleasure of the tale. In the words of Simon Suggs, arch villain/hero of a series of southwestern tales, "It is good to be shifty in a new country."

Tall tales of the folk tradition are, if not always a source, often a model for the many tall tales in the works of Mark Twain. Similarly, the political use of animal fables, and of anecdote as parable is exemplified in this tradition. Davy Crockett in particular was self-consciously developed by the Whig party to serve as a folk-hero counterbalance to Andrew Jackson. Crockett, a real woodsman, was recruited to run for the Whigs on the platform of genteel resistance to Jacksonian democracy. While the earthy appeal of Crockett was essentially democratic, the use to which the Whigs put his tales was the opposite. For instance, in suggesting that the blandishments of a Democratic opponent were really self-serving and demagogic, Crockett tells the tale of how he could grin so well that he could grin a raccoon to death. Rather than waste precious bullets and powder, then, he would simply smile whenever he saw a raccoon he wished to kill. One night, he saw what he took to be the eye of a raccoon in a tree and he began his malevolent grin. When the raccoon did not immediately drop dead, Crockett was perplexed but determined, so he stood there grinning until dawn made it clear that the ostensible raccoon was nothing more than a knothole in a tree, but that Crockett had grinned so hard that he had grinned the bark off that part of the tree. Crockett then admitted that when it comes to dangerous grinning, he doesn't hold a candle to his political opponent. The apparent friendliness of the Democratic candidate, and by extension, the apparent friendliness of the democratic western culture, is a real threat.

This antidemocratic impulse is central to another major source of southwestern humor, Augustan satire. In a significant majority of published sketches in the southwestern tradition, a gentleman narrator describes the barbarism of the country. Often using a *frame narrative to allow the country bumpkins to speak for themselves, often using third person narration to describe the brutalities and ill manners of the people from a position of unmitigated superiority, such stories reenforce aristocratic values in the face of burgeoning democracy. The importance ofsuch stories to a southern culture that needed to uphold a myth of aristocratic superiority in order to support *slavery helped give such antidemocratic satires, which were common in the North as well, their special virulence and longevity in the antebellum South. Particularly significant practitioners of this satiric strain of southwestern humor are Augustus Baldwin Longstreet, whose *Georgia Sketches* are among the earliest of the school; Johnson Jones Hooper, whose Simon Suggs stories are among the most bitter; Henry Clay Lewis; and Joseph Glover Baldwin. In a special class are the sketches of George Washington *Harris—perhaps the most important to Twain—whose antebellum satires are quite conventional but whose tales of the 1860s, published as humor rather than as satire under the title *Sut Lovingood's Yarns*, break down the hegemony of the gentleman narrator's voice, turning the mockery as much on the frame narrator "George" as on the illiterate "Sut" whose powers as a raconteur would be lost without George as his amanuensis.

A third strand in the tradition of southwestern humor owes its existence much more to the Atlantic North than to the old Southwest in that it was discovered and promoted by William T. Porter's *Spirit of the Times*, a New York–based gentleman's magazine devoted to leisure and sports in deliberate avoidance of politics. Porter's hope was to alleviate sectional rivalries by promoting the common interests of gentlemen of leisure throughout the country, and as such, his magazine devoted much space to hunting and to horse racing, both of which had avid followings in the South and West. Porter solicited work from correspondents in all regions, and in the process discovered the vitality and popularity of character sketches that captured regional peculiarity. Porter's magazine thus used the conventions of *amiable humor to develop what was to become a major literary mode after the Civil War, the *realism of local color.

The most important work in this particular vein is T. B. Thorpe's "The Big Bear of Arkansas," a frame tale told by a gentleman whose business took him on a brief trip on a Mississippi steamboat, where he met men from all states of the union and from Europe as well. Among these, the loudest, friendliest, most vulgar, and most interesting was Jim Doggett, a.k.a. the Big Bear of Arkansas, who regales the crowd with tall tales of hunting before finally relating a mythic story of his hunt of a "creation b'ar," whose time to die had come with the progress of civilization. Again, the allegorical value of the tall tale as a cultural myth in this narrative served Clemens as a model of the literary potentials in a tradition of humor.

♦ SEE ALSO Animals; Vernacular Humor.

SPECTACLE. From the time around 1845 when he deliberately became a traveling mesmerist's favorite subject—or so he said—to his wearing his scarlet Oxford robes to his daughter's wedding in 1909, Clemens had an appetite for spectacle, an appetite that was not only part of his personality but was also encouraged by his job as a reporter to write up all the entertainments he could find. His sensitivity to spectacle finds its way into much of his writing, but with an ambivalence that suggests something of a Protestant reticence about show in the face of a culture that was always hypocritical about its craving for display.

The adherents of mainstream *Calvinism rejected most aspects of *leisure as sinful, and such grand entertainments as the circus or the *theater were anathema. As Edward Eggleston (1837–1902) put it in his 1878 novel *Roxy*, "A man in that time might be a miser . . . dishonest in a mild way . . . censorious and a backbiter . . . and the church could not reach him. But let him once see a man ride on two bare-back horses, and jump through a hoop!" And the increasing censoriousness of fundamentalist Protestants in the reformist spirit of the second Great Awakening made complaints about the immorality of spectacles all the more energetic and common. In describing his mother's response to spectacle, Twain describes a typical reaction of the churchgoing population of rural America:

> Like my mother, Aunt Betsey Smith had never seen a Negro show. She and my mother were very much alive; their age counted for nothing; they were fond of excitement, fond of novelties, fond of anything going that was of a sort proper for members of the church to indulge in. They were always up early to see the circus procession enter the town and to grieve because their principles did not allow them to follow it into the town. They were always ready for Fourth of July processions, Sunday-school processions, lectures, conventions, camp meetings revivals in the church—in fact, for any and every kind of dissipation that could not be proven to have anything irreligious about it—and they never missed a funeral. (autobiographical dictation of 30 November 1906)

Religious scruples notwithstanding, the generally rural populace of the United States had plenty of diversions to attend. For the most sanctimonious, there was always the funeral, which, in a rural country made up of a highly mobile population, was often the most important event for gathering family and friends together. Clemens's mother was this kind of devotee of funerals, or so said his niece Annie Moffett *Webster in her 1946 reminiscence published in *Mark Twain, Business Man*: "Her interest in funerals was not morbid, but the result of having lived in a remote mountain community in Tennessee where funerals were the only occasion of a general get-together. Sometimes the funerals were saved up, and would be held for three or four persons when the preacher came around. Sometimes a man would go to his wife's funeral with his second wife." That Moffett feels a need to defend her grandmother from the charge that her interest *might* have been morbid suggests something about the American cult of *death that made funerals into grand celebrations.

At least Mark Twain's works often suggest as much. He opens chapter 47 of *Roughing It* with the line, "Somebody has said that in order to know a community, one must observe the style of its funerals and know what manner of men they bury with most ceremony." His elaborate description of Buck Fanshaw's funeral is meant to illustrate the point. A similar point is made implicitly in *Adventures of Huckleberry Finn* at the funeral for Peter Wilks, in which an oily undertaker makes everyone feel fine by explaining why a dog was barking during the ceremony. "There weren't," says Huck, "no more popular man in town than what that undertaker was."

Other socially acceptable spectacles were militia musters, Fourth of July celebrations, and election campaigns. These earned their status as events of citizenship, but each was marked by a carnival atmosphere in which men drank heavily. The comic literature of the nineteenth century is replete with such episodes, and Twain's literature is no exception, especially in *Pudd'nhead Wilson*, in which a brawl during a campaign is one of the events on which the plot turns.

Reformers themselves understood that parades and pageants were good selling points. As such, temperance crusades regularly organized such public events, or participated in Fourth of July pageants. In his *autobiography, Twain claims that he joined a temperance group as a child solely to participate in a parade:

> In Hannibal, when I was about fifteen, I was for a short time a Cadet of Temperance, an organization which probably covered the whole United States during as much as a year. . . . It consisted in a pledge to refrain, during membership, from the use of tobacco; I mean it consisted partly in that pledge and partly in a red merino sash, but the red merino sash was the main part. The boys joined in order to be privileged to wear it. . . . The organization was weak and impermanent because there were not enough holidays to support it. We could turn out and march and show the red sashes on May Day with the Sunday schools, and on the Fourth of July with the Sunday schools, the independent fire company, and the militia company. But you can't keep a juvenile moral institution alive on two displays of its sash per year. (13 February 1906)

The parade or procession that he claims to have been so seductive in his youth maintained its hold on his imagination, with descriptions of pageants and parades working their way into too many of his works to mention here.

Other amusements were not so readily accepted among the religious communities of rural America, but they did well regardless. Circuses were roundly denounced in pulpits, but widely frequented. Given how often they make it into Twain's works—most conspicuously in *Huckleberry Finn* and *A Connecticut Yankee in King Arthur's Court*—one assumes he saw as many as he could.

The traveling showman, too, made his rounds throughout America, often using the show as a sidelight to selling some product, like patent medicines. Phrenologists, mesmerists, and various other traveling performers sold themselves as men of science and gave their performances in town lecture halls. Others would simply set up a wagon or tent and begin their proceedings. The successful ones found some way to suggest that their shows had a moral bearing. Twain's King and Duke in *Huckleberry Finn* are this type of character, and Twain's equation of their showmanship with chicanery suggests that he was not too far from his mother's position about the moral quality of spectacle even as he shared her fascination.

One of the kinds of shows most popular and yet most roundly attacked in America was the minstrel show. Invented in 1828 by Thomas D. "Daddy" Rice, it caught on in the forties, and remained a major attraction through the 1850s. Many of the nation's favorite songs, including many of Stephen Foster's best-known pieces, were written for minstrel shows. Clemens loved these shows, not at all concerned about the denigration of *African Americans implicit in the schtick. The typical minstrel company consisted of white men wearing blackface and red painted lips that looked, as Twain describes in his autobiographical dictation of 30 November 1906, like "slices cut in a ripe watermelon." Their costumes were outlandish caricatures of fine clothing, set off in contrast to the one man not in black face, the "middle-man." "He," Twain explains, "was clothed in the faultless evening costume of the white society gentleman and used a stilted, courtly, artificial and painfully grammatical form of speech, which the innocent villagers took for the real thing as exhibited in high and citified society." At either end of a row of chairs, arranged in semicircle for the performers, were the two "end men," Brer Bones and Brer Banjo (or Tambourine). These two would engage in mock arguments that parodied school rhetoric. Such arguments set off conversations with the "white" interlocutor, with the "black" characters making jokes out of malapropisms. Throughout, the entire troupe would play music and sing songs; the show concluded with a fancy dance, a "cakewalk."

The minstrel show itself had a powerful influence on Twain's writing. He used the term "Cake-walk" in the essay "In Defense of Harriet Shelley" to describe an over-written book, and a minstrel character appears in chapter 26 of *"No. 44, The Mysterious Stranger." Roxy's argument with Jasper in chapter 2 of *Pudd'nhead Wilson* owes much to minstrelsy. But in no place does the model of the minstrel show have a greater influence than in *Huckleberry Finn*. The argument between Huck and Jim over Solomon, for instance, is a *burlesque version of a minstrel routine. As is so often the case with Twain's works, however, he turns over the original value of what he burlesques. In this case, while the minstrel show suggests that the end men are stupid and inarticulate and representative of all blacks, Twain's use of the pattern turns its meaning over, showing Jim's intellectual superiority to Huck, asking the reader to draw the unexpected conclusion. Perhaps Twain's willful refusal to see the denigration of blacks in minstrelsy stems from his insistence that folk forms of art are superior to high forms; at least he makes such a case in his autobiographical description of minstrelsy, which he compares favorably to grand opera. He liked that the minstrel show was "extravagant," an adjective suited to much of his own literature for its equal willingness to push the bounds of decorum in order to achieve spectacular effect.

More importantly, perhaps, Twain's very role as humorist was closely tied, psychologically, to the idea of festival. Carnival days in most cultures are sanctioned times of release from decorum and seriousness, and it is in the release of carnival experience that humor and satire flow. It is not surprising, then, that Twain tried to tap the feelings of carnival by referring to spectacular events, everything from funerals, to elections, to royal processions, to college graduation ceremonies, to minstrelsy. In creating such events in the reader's mind, Twain opened the reader to laughter.

♦ SEE ALSO Speeches.

SPEECHES. In an age when rhetoric was considered the queen of the arts, speech making took many forms for many occasions, ranging from the one-person shows of the *lecture circuit, to campaign speeches, to long public performances on important occasions, such as dedications or Fourth of July celebrations, and so forth. None so typifies the age as the short speech at the semipublic banquet, held either in honor of a guest or to raise money for a cause.

Until late in the nineteenth century, invitations to such banquets were usually extended to men only, though women were allowed to observe from a gallery, which they shared with reporters. Invariably formal, often held at restaurants like Delmonico's in New York City that catered to such events, or at private clubs, these banquets would begin as early as 7:30 and run until at least midnight. Toward the end of the century and in the first years of the twentieth, after-dinner dancing would run into the wee hours of the morning.

Beginning with multicourse meals, replete with wine and cigars, the real focus of such events was the after-dinner speaking, usually a series of ten or more "toasts" of about five to twenty minutes in length, on topics assigned in advance by a toastmaster, who would also introduce the many speakers, and move things along with his own patter. His responsibilities included introducing the topics of the various toasts, and Twain, at least, found it valuable for a toastmaster to give enough substance to work from. A purely laudatory introduction made it more difficult to launch into a comic speech or to create the impression, through an impromptu reply, that the festivities were really a conversation rather than a series of set pieces. But spontaneous they were not. If a man not scheduled to speak tried to interject a toast of his own, he would often be heckled into silence.

Whether these toasts were to be directed at a guest of honor, or to a cause, their topics were usually quite general and usually varied around a series of conventional subjects, as, as for instance, "To Woman," which Mark Twain addressed on 11 January 1868 at a Washington, D.C., Newspaper Correspondents Club banquet, and at the 209th Anniversary Festival of the Scottish Corporation of London, in November 1873 under the title "The Ladies." A brief list of such topics opens Twain's widely reprinted toast to "The Babies" in November 1879: "I like that. We haven't all had the good fortune to be ladies; we haven't all been generals, or poets, or statesmen, but when the toast works down to the babies, we stand on common ground. . . . It is a shame that for a thousand years the world's banquets have utterly ignored the baby."

Perhaps no performer was more celebrated at such events than Mark Twain, with that popularity attested to by three separate, though overlapping, volumes: *Mark Twain's Speeches* (compiled by F. A. Nast and introduced by William Dean *Howells) of 1910, *Mark Twain's Speeches* (compiled by Albert Bigelow *Paine) of 1923, and *Mark Twain Speaking* (edited by Paul Fatout) of 1976. The last of these three, a scholarly edition published by the University of Iowa Press and containing the texts of nearly two hundred speeches, carefully explains the difficulties we have now of collecting Twain's speeches, for many of our texts are derived from newspaper accounts rather than from manuscripts. And, of course, Twain's manner of delivery was at least as much of his humor as the matter, so we'll never know fully one of most heralded parts of Mark Twain's art.

As with his *lectures, Twain carefully prepared his speeches, writing them out in their entirety and committing them carefully to memory. Yet he delivered them in an off-hand way, creating the impression that he always spoke impromptu. Indeed he often allowed himself tremendous latitude, especially in later years, to add or subtract from his speeches according to audience mood. This comes as no surprise considering that in the last years of his life he received more invitations to banquets and *charity events than he could possibly attend, and he attended as many as he possibly could. While he found these events exhausting—in later years he would skip the banquet part of the evening, arriving just for the speeches and postspeech festivities—he also found them exhilarating, which explains in part why he went to so many.

Two particular banquet speeches count in any tally of Twain's most humiliating and most triumphant public performances: the *Whittier Birthday Dinner speech of 1877, in which he found his humor uncomfortably irreverent, and the celebration of Ulysses S. *Grant at the thirteenth Reunion Banquet, Army of the Tennessee, Chicago, 13 November 1879, in which his irreverence delighted even Grant, a man notoriously unwilling to show emotion in public. In fact this latter event was not entirely in honor of Grant, though he gave the first toast as the *guest* of honor at about 10:30 P.M. Five hours later, delivering the last of the fifteen speeches, Twain gave his toast, of his own devising, to "The Babies." It is difficult to imagine anyone, after all those hours and all that alcohol still paying attention, but by almost all accounts, Twain's was one of the three best speeches of the night, though Robert *Ingersoll was generally credited with the most powerful. Twain himself, in his 17 November 1879 letter to William Dean Howells describing the event, wrote, "Bob Ingersoll's speech was sadly crippled by the proof-readers, but its music will sing through my memory always as the divinest that ever enchanted my ears." Yet even after such praise for the substance and delivery of Ingersoll's speech, he reserves the ultimate bragging rights for himself:

> Gen. Grant sat at the banquet like a statue of iron & listened without the faintest suggestion of emotion to fourteen speeches which tore other people all to shreds, but when I lit in with the fifteenth & last, his time was come! I shook him up like dynamite & he sat there fifteen minutes & laughed & cried like the mortalest of mortals. But bless you I had measured this unconquerable conqueror, & went at my work with the confidence of conviction, for I knew I could lick him. He told me he had shaken hands with 15,000 people that day & come out of it without an ache or pain, but that my truths had racked all the bones of his body apart.

Here the *Civil War deserter suggests that the banquet room was his battlefield, and if making people laugh was victory, then Twain was usually victorious.

♦ SEE ALSO Spectacle.

SPENCER, HERBERT (1820–1903). A materialist philosopher whose efforts to synthesize a comprehensive philosophical system predicated on *utilitarianism, Spencer is best known as a popularizer in Britain and America of the theory of *evolution. Spencer was particularly influential among those who came to espouse naturalist principles, either the social Darwinists who held that Spencer's exposition of evolution showed that charity weakened the human race, or liberals such as Clarence Darrow, who often argued that individuals could not be held responsible for their criminal actions when social circumstances caused those actions through a necessary and inevitable chain of events. Spencer would have been surprised at either extreme, as he felt that his philosophy proved the value of conventional morality when stripped of Christian guilt. The extreme competitiveness of social Darwinists and the extreme social *determinism of naturalists like Darrow would have struck Spencer as immoral.

But perhaps such mistakes were only fitting interpretations of a philosophy that promulgated a tremendous mistake. Spencer copied Lamarck's model of evolution, not *Darwin's, and in ascribing the proof to Darwin, he helped misinform the American and British publics about the theory of natural selection. Clemens was one such misinformed reader. His theory of heredity, central to his own determinism, was cribbed from Spencer, not Darwin, though he read widely in both.

Clemens met Spencer in London in 1873, and maintained an interest in him that spanned his career. He published some of Spencer's works through *Webster and Company, and made mention of him in many late works, often parodying his style, but usually referring to him as a significant intellectual force.

SPIRITUALISM. Samuel Clemens's first known letter, written in 1853, refers to spiritualism in the sentence, "Rochester, famous on account of the 'Spirit Rappings' was of course interesting," though the neutrality of the adjective "interesting" tells us nothing of his attitude toward spiritualism. Part hoax, part alternative spirituality, spiritualism has a deep history in various religious movements that believe in ghosts, spiritual visitations, and communication with the dead, but began as a quasi-organized "ism" in 1848 in Rochester, New York, when teenaged sisters Kate and Margaret Fox embarked on a career as mediums, holding seances in which the spirits of the dead ostensibly "rapped" on tables, walls, floors, and doors in response to questions. Late in her life, Margaret revealed that the show was a hoax; the sisters merely popped their knuckles and other joints to create the noises. But the simplicity of their hoax was not enough to prevent the energetic belief of large numbers of people, among them Horace *Greeley, though most mainstream Christians found spiritualism either absurd or morally reprehensible. In spite of such resistance, the Fox sisters created a craze that peaked in the 1850s and again in the 1870s in part because such practices as mesmerism and faith healing had gained credence in the first half of the century, in a confluence of spiritual practices that were as much scientistic as pietistic.

In any event, Clemens had a life-long interest in spiritualism and similar unorthodox, quasi-psychological phenomena. He regularly consulted fortune tellers "when other amusements fail[ed]," and while he usually debunked their prophecies—skepticism toward prophecy appearing repeatedly in his literature—he at least once, in a 6 February 1861 letter to Orion about his visit to a New Orleans soothsayer, expressed surprise at her apparent accuracy: "Although of course I have no faith in her pretended powers, I listened to her in silence for half an hour, with the greatest interest, and I am willing to acknowledge that she said some very startling things, and made some wonderful guesses."

Considering his usual skeptical bent toward all things religious, Clemens was remarkably open-minded toward spiritualism and other marginal spiritual practices. He and Olivia, for instance, consulted psychics to communicate with their dead daughter Susy, and Clemens was a believer in mental telepathy, which he called "mental telegraphy." His late interest in *dreams as alternative states of the soul owes much, too, to spiritualism, and many of his late stories built around dreams investigate these ideas.

♦ SEE ALSO Confidence Games; Faith; Religion.

STEAMBOATING. When Robert Fulton invented the steamboat in 1807, America's population was mostly located along the Atlantic seaboard or along rivers navigable by sloop. "Road" was a polite name for a track that would become a quagmire in bad weather, so cross-country travel by any route but water was avoided whenever possible, and moving goods by road was often an exercise in futility. Canals were an alternative for any location wanting cheap and certain transportation, but for the many backwoods settlers, the only possibility of taking goods to market was the nearest river, which meant that flatboats could move goods to market, but that the return trip was a burden making trade more or less a one-way street. By 1815 when steamboats proved their worth with the trip of the *Enterprise* from Pittsburgh to New Orleans and back to Louisville, Kentucky, a new age in transportation dawned, helping to spawn America's *industrial revolution both by creating the steamship-building industry and by making possible two-way transportation of goods anywhere in reach of a moderate-sized river.

While steamships were plying all navigable American waterways by the 1830s, nowhere did the steamship make more of a difference in the lives of Americans than in the great inland waterways of the Mississippi valley, where neither canal barges nor sailing ships could compete. While eastern steamships used low-pressure engines for safety, the boats on the western rivers used high-pressure engines, which were lighter and smaller and so allowed more cargo and passenger space per boat. The disadvantages were that the high-pressure engines were very loud, vibrated excessively, and were much more susceptible to explosion. But the profits to be made in quick transport of high volumes of freight on the western rivers made the drawbacks trivial. Boats were expected to last no more than five years before either snagging, exploding, burning (from sparks emitted from the smokestacks landing on the wooden decks or the flammable cargoes of cotton, etc.) or falling to pieces, yet the profits were more than enough to pay for such a short life expectancy. So boats were built to minimum standards, with most expense lavished on ornamentation rather than on substantial construction. If human life was lost because shortcuts were taken in safety, that was considered a small price to pay in the early days of America's laissez-faire *economy.

Among those who died when a western steamship exploded was Samuel Clemens's younger brother Henry *Clemens. In describing his brother's death in *Life on the Mississippi*, Twain mentions that he and his brother discussed what they would do in the case of an accident; they both knew well that they were in a dangerous profession.

Dangerous, but also glamorous and profitable. Clemens's pay as a pilot put him in elite company in the antebellum South, about which he gloated in a 27 June 1860 letter to Orion *Clemens:

> I can "bank" in the neighborhood of $100 a month . . . and that will satisfy me
> for the present. . . . Bless me! . . . what respect Prosperity commands. Why, six

months ago, I could enter the "Rooms," [of the Western Boatmen's Benevolent Association] and receive only the customary fraternal greeting—but now they say, "Why how *are* you, old fellow—when did you get in?" And the young pilots who used to tell me, patronizingly, that I could never learn the river, cannot keep from showing a little of their chagrin at seeing me so far ahead of them. . . . I must confess that when I go to pay my dues, I rather like to let the d—d rascals get a glimpse of a hundred dollar bill peeping out from amongst notes of smaller dimensions.

Even the lowliest workers in the industry did well. Wood sawyers, who provided the fuel that ran the boats on the western rivers, were able to turn their notoriously low-status profession into lucrative business, a business as much about chicanery in stacking wood sold by the cord as in cutting the wood itself. As Twain has Huck describe it in chapter 19 of *Adventures of Huckleberry Finn*, the wood often was "piled by them cheats so you can throw a dog through it anywheres." Perhaps the very name Tom Sawyer suggests something of the boy's character.

STOWE, HARRIET BEECHER (1811–1896). In 1869, when Samuel Clemens was first seriously considering a move to *Hartford, Connecticut, Harriet Beecher Stowe was the largest literary figure not only there, but in the country. Her *Uncle Tom's Cabin* (1852) held sales records for the United States, if not for the world, selling in the first sixth months in the United States alone over one hundred thousand copies. Clemens used Stowe's sales as a benchmark for his own, bragging, for instance, in a letter of 6 February 1870 to Horace Bixby that *The Innocents Abroad* "has met with a greater sale than any book ever published except Uncle Tom's Cabin," though *Innocents'* 39,000 in six months ran a distant second.

While Clemens may have measured Stowe's stature by book sales, and while Stowe became a consummately professional author as concerned about the sales of her books as Clemens was about his, her real influence cannot be measured in sales figures. *Uncle Tom's Cabin* is a watershed in American political, cultural, and religious history. Politically, it galvanized the antislavery movement at a crucial moment. Prior to 1850, antislavery agitation was tainted, in the eyes of many Americans, by its association with New England parochialism or with radical abolitionists like William Lloyd Garrison. The cause as a whole was found guilty by association with its most extreme advocates. But in Stowe, America found a member of one of its best-known families, the Beechers, advocating the antislavery cause in intensely human terms, making the argument that *slavery was wrong because it separated parents from their children and because it violated the golden rule. Questions of property interests, states' rights, popular sovereignty, and the whole range of political arguments engaged in the slavery debate she swept away with this starkly fundamental human argument.

In religious terms, Stowe's forceful advocacy of *sentimentalism over the stern *Calvinism of her father struck a national chord. Again, part of the attractiveness of sentimentalism as opposed to Calvinism is that sentimentalism encouraged loving bonds between parent and child, seeing the infant not as a damned soul whose will needed breaking, but as an innately innocent soul whose purity could be protected only in the care of loving, intact nuclear families. Culturally, as the daughter of a Calvinist who forbid the reading of all novels except those of Sir Walter Scott, Stowe helped change American attitudes toward fiction when she chose to use a novel for political and religious advocacy.

Her Nook Farm neighbor, the Rev. E. P. Parker, summed up these three dimensions of Stowe's influence in his biography of Stowe for *Eminent Women of the Age* (1868):

> It was a perfectly natural, thoroughly honest, truly religious story, with nothing unwholesome in its marvelous fascinations, but contrariwise, fairly throbbing in every part with a genuine Christian feeling. No wonder that ministers, and deacons, and quiet Quakers too, and all the godly folk who had always been accustomed to frown with holy horror upon novels, did unbend themselves to read, and diligently circulate the words of this woman. . . . Great statesmen like Mr. Seward and Mr. Sumner had argued the question of slavery. Able divines had given the testimony of the Scriptures upon it. Eloquent platform orators, and vigorous writers had discussed all its aspects and relations. And still a mist of romance, and an atmosphere of sanctity, or at least of privilege, enveloped and concealed its real features. Mrs. Stowe treated the subject, not as a question of law, or of logic, or of political economy, or of biblical interpretation, but as a simple question of humanity; not as an "abstract theory of social relations, but as a concrete reality of human life." She does not tell, but shows us what it is. She does not analyze, or demonstrate, or describe, but, by a skilful manner of indirection, takes us over the plantation, into the fields,—through the whole Southern country in fact,—and shows us not only the worst but the best phases of the slavery system, and allows us to see it as it really is. And all the while the power of her own intense sympathy for the oppressed millions whose cause she pleads, is felt throbbing in every line of the narrative. (pp. 316–318)

Still an active writer in 1868 when Parker thus lionized her, Stowe continued to be a crusader as well as a professional writer, though her cultural power was about to decline.

Having spent most of her writing career espousing sentimental *domesticity, she was, in the late 1860s, finally beginning to see much sense in the feminism of her half sister and Nook Farm neighbor, Isabella Beecher Hooker. When she became convinced of the truth of Lady Byron's charges that Lord Byron had had an adulterous, incestuous affair, she first counseled Lady Byron to keep quiet for fear of damaging herself further. As she became more convinced that *women's rights in marriage were in fact damaged by the conventional code of silence, she not only advised Lady Byron to make her story public, she helped by publishing a defense of Lady Byron in *The *Atlantic Monthly*. The nation's reaction to Stowe's new cause was one of cautious outrage. Here was America's literary icon mentioning in public taboo subjects. Many *Atlantic* subscribers cancelled their subscriptions on the grounds that a family journal should not even mention such things.

The literary world was more cautious, but among newspapermen who understood the feminism behind Stowe's newest crusade, Stowe became a target of derision. Clemens as an editor of the Buffalo *Express* wrote an editorial defending Stowe against at least one such editor, Ausburn Towner, for his editorial in the Elmira (New York) *Advertiser*. In doing so, he was siding with the Beecher clan, to which his fiancée's family had strong connections. At the same time, he wrote a *burlesque of the Byron scandal, suggesting that he thought Stowe's charges were a bit overblown. At any rate, he did not publish this burlesque, writing in his *Galaxy Magazine* column:

> There are some things which cannot be burlesqued, for the simple reason that in themselves they are so extravagant and grotesque that nothing is left for burlesque to take hold of. For instance, all attempts to burlesque the "Byron Scandal" were failures because the central feature of it, incest, was a "situation" so tremendous and so imposing that the happiest available resources of burlesque seemed tame and cheap in its presence. ("Memoranda," July 1870)

Clemens's reticence on this issue shows his affinity with those *Atlantic* subscribers whose Victorian morality precluded even mention of things sexual for fear of tainting *childhood innocence, a morality congruent with the sentimentalism that Stowe had so long and so successfully preached.

Stowe tried to recover her reputation after the Byron article, but her intellectual powers were to wane before she could fully succeed in her campaign. During her last years in Hartford she suffered from senile dementia. As Clemens later explained:

> Harriet Beecher Stowe ... was a near neighbor of ours in Hartford, with no fences between. And in those days she made as much use of our grounds as of her own, in pleasant weather. Her mind had decayed and she was a pathetic figure. She wandered about all the day long in the care of a muscular Irishwoman. Among the colonists of our neighborhood the doors always stood open in pleasant weather. Mrs. Stowe entered them at her own free

will, and as she was always softly slippered and generally full of animal spirits, she was able to deal in surprises, and she liked to do it. She would slip up behind a person who was deep in dreams and musings and fetch a war whoop that would jump that person out of his clothes. (autobiographical dictation of 23 March 1906)

Nonetheless, in his autobiography Clemens referred to Stowe with great respect:

[Isabella Beecher Hooker] and her sister, Harriet Beecher Stowe, were near neighbors of ours in Hartford during eighteen years. I knew all the Beecher brotherhood and sisterhood, I believe. . . . There was not an ungifted Beecher among all those brothers and sisters, and not one that did not make a considerable name. (1 March 1907)

This is his fitting, though broadly couched, tribute to the literary giant whom he came ultimately to replace as the best-known literary resident of Nook Farm.

STYLE. Many writers and critics have praised Mark Twain's style as the most important legacy he left to American culture, but such praise says little if it doesn't specify *which* of Twain's many styles is being extolled. Twain was, above all else, a stylistic mimic with the writer's equivalent of a perfect ear, and his use of a multitude of styles arose partly from his need as a humorist to generate comic incongruities and partly from his divided sympathies between different aesthetic values.

Mimicry was the basis of much of Twain's early humor, with stylistic juxtapositions yielding comedy, as in his many letters describing the contrasts between the high-flown Mr. Mark Twain and his lowbrow companion Mr. Brown. Mr. Twain speaks constantly in a style derived from literary models, which he often quotes, and as often misquotes. But Mr. Twain always strives for elevation of sentiment in elevated language. Mr. Brown, as an earthy man, has no patience for Mr. Twain's pretension.

In one place, when having to wait for a becalmed schooner and suffering from acute hunger and thirst, Mr. Twain and Mr. Brown try to harvest "coco-nuts," with Brown doing the work and Twain superintending. Having had no success in getting Brown to secure a meal, Mr. Twain says,

I glanced over my shoulders, as we walked along, and observed that some of the clouds had parted and left a dim lighted doorway through to the skies beyond; in this place, as in an ebony frame, our majestic palm stood up and reared its graceful crest aloft; the slender stem was a clean, black line; the feathers of the plume—some erect, some projecting horizontally, some drooping a little and others hanging languidly down toward the earth—were all sharply cut against the smooth gray background.

"A beautiful, beautiful tree is the coco palm!" I said fervently.

"I don't see it," said Brown resentfully. People that haven't clumb one are always driveling about how pretty it is. . . . I don't see what there is about it that's handsome; it looks like a feather duster struck by lightning." (Sacramento *Union,* 30 August 1866)

Mark Twain's language is filled with the clichéd metaphors of travel writing, comparing leaves to feathers, gaps in clouds to doorways to heaven, speaking of the palm's fronds as a "crest," using many adjectives, elevated diction, as in "observed" for "saw," and even inverting common syntax, as in "A beautiful, beautiful tree is the coco palm." Brown's responses are mundane in diction and syntax, but are not without their own use of literary tropes, as in the witty simile that caps the exchange. In finding the rhetorical power of the homespun, as opposed to the erudite, comparison, Clemens finds the poetry and power in common speech.

Brown usually gets the best of these exchanges between highbrow and lowbrow, suggesting Twain's affinity for the vernacular. Yet make no mistake, Twain's mockery of *literary* style shows his perfect familiarity with it, a familiarity that suggests his appreciation. His letters from his early manhood support this conclusion, showing extensive reading in fine literature, with an eye seemingly less on content than on style, as in his 18 March 1861 letter to Orion:

Your last has just come to hand. It reminds me strongly of Tom Hood's letters to his family, (which I have been reading lately). But yours only *remind* me of his, for although there is a striking likeness, your humour is much finer than his, and far better expressed. Tom Hood's *wit*, (in his letters) has a savor of *labor* about it which is very disagreeable. Your letter is good. . . . Its quiet style resembles Goldsmith's "Citizen of the World" and "Don Quixote,"—which are my *beau ideals* of fine writing.

Through a lifetime of eclectic and incessant reading, Clemens learned the power and limitations of conventional literary language as much as he studied ways to incorporate unconventional language into literature. In both cases, his capacity for mimicry not only allowed him the comic pleasure of juxtaposition, as in the speech of Mr. Twain versus that of Mr. Brown, or the speech of Hank Morgan versus that of Sandy in *A Connecticut Yankee in King Arthur's Court*, but it also served him when he chose to write pieces that would earn the immediate approval of book reviewers who sought "fine writing."

In this regard, two pairs of books written simultaneously suggest something of Mark Twain's stylistic flexibility. On the one hand, the pseudoarchaic English of *The Prince and the Pauper* is as characteristic of Mark Twain as is the Missouri slang of *Adventures of Huckleberry Finn*. Both are roughly contemporary and deal with many of the same themes, but stylistically, they are radically different. Consider, for example, early passages from each describing the relationship between a boy and his abusive father:

> All Offal Court was just such another hive as Canty's house. Drunkenness, riot and brawling were the order, there, every night and nearly all night long. Broken heads were as common as hunger in that place. Yet little Tom was not unhappy. He had a hard time of it, but did not know it. It was the sort of time all the Offal Court boys had, therefore he supposed it was the correct and comfortable thing. When he came home empty handed at night, he knew his father would curse him and thrash him first, and that when he was done the awful grandmother would do it all over again and improve on it; and that away in the night his starving mother would slip to him stealthily with any miserable scrap or crust she had been able to save for him by going hungry herself, notwithstanding she was often caught in that sort of treason and soundly beaten for it by her husband. (*The Prince and the Pauper*, chapter 1)

> We lived in that old cabin, and he always locked the door and put the key under his head, nights. He had a gun which he had stole, I reckon, and we fished and hunted, and that was what we lived on. Every little while he locked me in and went down to the store, three miles, to the ferry, and traded fish and game for whisky and fetched it home and got drunk and had a good time, and licked me. . . . It was pretty good times up in the woods there, take it all around. But by and by pap got too handy with his hick'ry, and I couldn't stand it. I was all over welts. (*Adventures of Huckleberry Finn*, chapter 6)

Similarly, *Personal Recollections of Joan of Arc* and *Pudd'nhead Wilson and Those Extraordinary Twins* share a period in Mark Twain's life, express many of the same concerns, and appear, on stylistic analysis, to be the work of different authors.

Stylistically consistent internally, none of these four novels relies primarily on stylistic incongruity for comic effect; in each case Clemens made stylistic decisions depending on his allegiance to a vernacular or to a literary style, decisions contingent as much on Clemens's own ambivalence about the implications of these styles as on his sense of appropriateness to audience and to content. The debate over whether an ornate, Latinate style or a plain, Anglo-Saxon style is the best style for literature in English goes back at least to Chaucer, and the grounds for the debate remained essentially the same. The advocates of a plain style appealed to national pride and to the moral value of a direct, simple language, while the supporters of an ornate style argued for the value of a connection to the traditions of classical rhetoric and learning, which emphasized the values of sophistication, appropriateness, hierarchy, and formal structure.

The American nineteenth century witnessed a revival of this debate, with peculiar twists. While high style in classical terms was a mark of nobility as well as erudition, in a republic the idea of a hereditary nobility was anathema, at least west of the Alleghenies. But rhetoric as the queen of the arts suited a republic in which power came from the ability to persuade. As such, traditions of rhetorical sophistication, whether based on a vernacular or on a scholarly vocabulary, were very much part of the American scene, with the puzzling contradiction of a popular art of rhetorical sophistication.

American journalism, too, reflected the lack of consensus about an appropriate American style. The degree to which newspapers touted themselves as organs of democracy led them to puzzle over whether they should use a direct language or a rhetorically elaborate one, though until American schools began to teach plain style, most journalists wrote prose that is, by current standards, overwrought. Still, as long as newspapers had to appeal to immediate constituencies, they were grounds for stylistic experimentation. Clemens's beginnings in Western journalism may well have exposed him to the rhetorical possibilities of a relatively plain style.

As much as America's politics influenced American ideas about rhetorical style in contradictory ways, so its religious background created a confusion over what should constitute an American style. The Calvinist heritage that nineteenth-century Protestantism shed with difficulty considered ornament of any kind to be worldly and sinful; language was to be stripped of ornamentation to keep it honest. A young Samuel Clemens heard enough about the excesses of Roman Catholic ornamentation to launch into lifelong diatribes against Catholic aesthetic sensibilities. In works from *The Innocents Abroad* to unfinished late pieces such as the *"Chronicle of Young Satan" and "The Secret History of Eddypus," Twain attacks the show for covering up the substance of Catholicism. The last of these in particular suggests that rhetoric, merely an art of deception, leads inexorably toward tyranny and religious superstition. In such terms, then, Clemens advocated a plain style.

But out of the Protestant tradition of evangelism came a respect for emotional preaching, for finding a vocabulary and presentation that would pierce the hearts of listeners. From this tradition of artistic, emotional language came the Victorian rejection of Calvinist asceticism. Not only in the ornamentation of Victorian plastic arts and architecture, but in rhetoric as well, the progressive stance against puritan narrowness affirmed the value of ornament and emotionalism, which in writing and rhetoric translate more or less into complex syntax built around periodic sentences and chiasmus and complicated diction utilizing periphrasis in a Latinate vocabulary that did not reflect ordinary English.

In the usual American confusion over conservatism and progressivism, such a progressive move against Calvinist authoritarianism was the move of a highly educated, urban elite against the rural majority and the growing urban working class.

As such the political as well as aesthetic implications of any particular use of any particular language were never clear. This was certainly the case with the writers of *realism who were Twain's professional contemporaries. Some reacted against the elitism of classical rhetoric to seek in *dialect a truly American style.

In such a complex situation, it is not surprising that from the beginning Clemens found his sympathies divided between the languages of Mr. Mark Twain and Mr. Brown, though the bulk of his commentary on style comes down on the side of Mr. Brown. The best known of these published comments refer specifically to diction or rather vaguely to "grammar," as in his essay "Concerning the American language," his attack on Cooper's diction in *"Fenimore Cooper's Literary Offenses," and in his *aphorisms about diction—"The difference between the *almost* right word and the *right* word is the difference between the lightning bug and the lightning" (in a letter to George Bainton, 15 October 1888) and "As to the adjective: when in doubt, leave it out"(*Pudd'nhead Wilson*, chapter 11)—leading to the easy conclusion that diction was the aspect of style that concerned Twain the most, and that the recovery of commonplace diction is the stylistic innovation he should be known for. But Twain's fine ear was at least as well attuned to the syntax of common speech as to diction.

American vernacular was also simpler in syntax than the models in school rhetoric books. Perhaps Twain's most important influence was to shed the elaborate syntax of rhetoric taught in American schools for cleaner, more direct structures. In particular, the single most characteristic point of Twain's plain style is the use of paratactic structures not only in dialogue, but also in discursive prose. In the process, Mark Twain elevated common rhythms to literature.

Consider, as an example of the rhetorical standards of the day, a typical passage from William Dean *Howells, whose prose Twain publicly praised as nearly ideal:

> Her total distrust of his judgment in the matters cited and others like them consisted with the greatest admiration of his mind and respect for his character. She often said that if he would only bring these to bear in such exigencies he would be simply perfect; but she had long given up his ever doing so. She subjected him, therefore, to an iron code, but after proclaiming it she was apt to abandon him to the native lawlessness of his temperament. (*A Hazard of New Fortunes,* chapter 11)

Each sentence breaks neatly into two parts of roughly equal weight, with a mirrored rhythm that demonstrates the author's complete rhetorical control.

Twain, on the other hand, tends to use shorter sentences, with greater variation in the length between sentences. When he uses long sentences, they tend to be lists strung together with "ands," suggesting a spontaneous flow of ideas rather than a carefully premeditated and crafted set piece. In dialogue, such a sense of spontaneity realistically represents conversation; in discursive prose, it is an aesthetic and intellectual argument for thinking, suggesting that the realities of a mind's action are simpler than ornate rhetorical forms suggest. It is an argument for intellectual honesty, for congruence between form and content.

Twain often put this argument, both explicitly in the content of his writing and implicitly in the style of his prose, in nationalistic terms. In "General Grant's Grammar," a speech defending the style of *Grant's memoirs against the attacks of Matthew *Arnold, Twain justifies Grant's style as "flawless" because powerful and vivid:

> There is that about the sun which makes us forget his spots; and when we think of General Grant our pulses quicken and his grammar vanishes; we only remember that this is the simple soldier, who, all untaught of the silken phrase makers, linked words together with an art surpassing the art of the schools, and put into them a something which will still bring to an American ear, as long as America shall last, the roll of his vanished drums and the tread of the marching hosts.

Forgetting for a moment that his own speech seems to challenge the silken phrase makers on their own turf, Twain's claim for a plain style depends on an implicit argument that such a style is plainly appropriate for America.

Of course, Mark Twain was not alone in advocating a prose style suitable to American English and American circumstances. Calls for a national literature were already as old as the nation when he developed his characteristic syntax. But manifestos are one thing; practice quite another. No Charles Brockden Brown, no James Fenimore Cooper, no Ralph Waldo Emerson, no Henry David Thoreau, and no William Dean Howells, preaching to the contrary, ever shed his formal training in style to find a style true to colloquial American syntax and diction. Mark Twain did. Several times.

♦ SEE ALSO Calvinism; Newspaper Journalism.

SUBSCRIPTION PUBLISHING.

SUBSCRIPTION PUBLISHING. Well into the 1890s, Mark Twain published his books through subscription publishing houses, houses that would canvas the public to secure sales before actually printing, binding, and distributing a book. Subscription publishing actually goes back well into the early days of *publishing, especially in America where the dispersal of the population made the usual system of trade publication—the sale of finished books at wholesale prices to bookstores, on the hope that a market would exist—only modestly profitable. The urban elites who read regularly and who frequented bookstores gave the trade a higher profile that offset the low volume in many ways, but for a man like Clemens who wanted to make serious money as a writer, the high volume of subscription publication was the way to go. As he defended his choice to William Dean *Howells and Thomas

Bailey *Aldrich, "Anything but subscription publishing is printing for private circulation" (*My Mark Twain*, chapter 2).

Of course, for publication of any kind to achieve the volume necessary for high profits, not only does the market need to exist, but it must be reached and it must be supplied. All three elements converged briefly in the approximately forty years following the Civil War. First, the market expanded significantly over the course of the nineteenth century as strictures against reading for *leisure and entertainment slowly relaxed at the same time that the literacy rate soared. Subscription firms had long catered to that expanding class of relatively new readers, though they first purveyed family bibles, encyclopedia, religious tracts, compendia of medical advice, and similar no-nonsense literature. Soon after the war they found a growing niche in lighter literature, the category into which Twain's writing was cast, and which ultimately became the industry's cash cow.

Second, this vast market beyond the range of bookstores had to be reached. Traveling salesmen canvassed door to door selling subscription books on the basis not of catalogues with brief descriptions, but by showing prospectuses of the books they had to sell. Each prospectus included judicious selections of text and illustrations, enough to catch a reader's interest but far from enough to satisfy. Prospective purchasers could choose quality of binding and pay accordingly, but while the books as a rule were more expensive than trade books, they also tended to be substantial in size (usually over five hundred pages), loaded with illustrations, and with embellished covers that made them look fancy. Purchasers were encouraged to believe that they would more than get their money's worth. The product and the method of selling were exactly right for the market, but the need for a large pool of labor to transact the business was another limiting factor until the end of the war, when large numbers of war widows and former soldiers found bookselling fit their financial and personal needs.

Third, the technologies of book production advanced significantly over the course of the century with the development of cheap paper made of wood pulp and with the development of a system—called stereotyping—of replicating forms of hand-set type into metal printing plates that could be run on fast and efficient steam presses. Such major improvements in print technology enabled publishers to produce enormous numbers of books quickly, and to realize significant enough economies of scale to make bookselling very profitable.

These conditions of industrial production and mass marketing were what deprived subscription publishing of status. Bulk and a gaudy style may have given a contrary impression, but subscription books were not made to last. The wood-pulp paper was thin and turned brittle quickly; the bindings were light in weight to match. Cost-cutting measures extended to the quality of the illustrations and the quality of printing itself. As Clemens put it in a 24 March 1874 letter to Thomas Bailey Aldrich, "There is one discomfort which I fear a man must put up with when he publishes by subscription, and that is wretched paper & vile engravings," but the payoff, in cash, eased the discomfort. Clemens also had to put up with the lower status that subscription authors were accorded. If Clemens didn't know that when he began, he learned it soon after his first subscription book, *The Innocents Abroad*, was reviewed in the January 1870 *Overland Monthly* by his then friend, Bret *Harte:

> Six hundred and fifty pages of open and declared fun—very strongly accented with wood-cuts at that—might go far toward frightening the fastidious reader. But the Hartford publishers, we imagine, do not print for the fastidious reader, nor do traveling book agents sell much to that rarely occurring man, who prefers to find books rather than let them find *him*.... The book has that intrinsic worth of bigness ... which commends itself to the rural economist, who likes to get a material return for his money. It is about the size of *The Family Physician*, for which it will doubtless be often mistaken—with great advantage to the patient.

Howells, in "The Man of Letters as a Man of Business" (*Literature and Life*, 1902), repeated the general prejudice when he wrote, "No book of literary quality was made to go by subscription except Mr. Clemens's books, and I think these went because the subscription public never knew what good literature they were." Howells's evaluation speaks more to the reputations of both subscription writers and readers, but that reputation had a powerful effect on Clemens. Early in his career, Twain's reputation as a mere humorist bothered him, but as he grew in confidence as a writer, he came ultimately to value his popular appeal as part of his important power as a writer. He wrote in a letter addressed to Andrew Lang (early 1890), "I have never tried ... to help cultivate the cultivated classes. I was not equipped for it either by native gifts or training. And I never had any ambition in that direction, but always hunted for bigger game—the masses." In publishing by subscription, he bagged that game, with all of the attendant ironies and difficulties of writing substantial literature disguised as ephemeral entertainment.

The rise and fall of subscription publication mirrors the rise and fall of Clemens's own financial fortunes. By the 1890s, trade publishing grew more dominant as the country urbanized, as the labor pool for canvassers changed, and as the very popularity of literature, cultivated in part by subscription publishing, expanded the number of bookstores throughout the country. Clemens's own subscription firm, *Webster and Company, failed in 1894, helping drag Clemens down with it. While his last subscription book, *Following the Equator*, helped him recover some of his financial losses, his major outlets for the last fifteen years of his life were trade publishers.

♦ SEE ALSO Finances.

SUMMER RESIDENCES. Considering how many waterborne diseases flourished during the summer in cities before the twentieth century, it is not surprising that those who could afford summers elsewhere made it a habit to leave. But by the late nineteenth century, the impulse to spend summers away from one's primary residence had become more a mark of status than a practical expedient, and fashionable spas and resorts became de rigueur for those who pretended to high *social class.

The first few years after Samuel Clemens married Olivia Langdon were too unstable to let them mimic the patterns of fashionable summering, but by the time they moved to *Hartford in 1872, they tried the game by going to the new summer resort in nearby New Saybrook, Connecticut. The hotel, given the imposing name Fenwick Hall after one of the first English noblemen to settle in the area in the seventeenth century, was built specifically as a summer "watering place" (as Clemens put it in a letter of 10 July) to attract the fashionable residents of nearby cities. Olivia complained in a letter, however, that "the only diagreeableness is that there are so many Hartford people here," suggesting that one of the functions of the summer "watering place" was to provide a cosmopolitan mix of the upper crust from around the nation, or, even better, the world. Regardless, Olivia's recent illness, and recurrent troubles with her back kept her reclusive while Samuel became the sport of the resort. He participated so energetically in games and events as to be conspicuously mentioned in a newspaper account in the Hartford *Courant* as "a great favorite with the ladies, and really the lion of the house." He even participated in tableaux vivants at the hotel, impersonating a *Dickens character, Mrs. Jarley from *The Old Curiosity Shop*.

The following year the family spent the summer and autumn in the British Isles, and then, with the new house in Hartford completed in 1874, the family unfashionably spent the next few summers in town. Apparently the summer whirl of high society was not their style, regardless of how much Samuel had participated in 1872. Instead, with the exceptions of 1878–1879 and 1885, the family took to summering at the Quarry Farm residence of Olivia's sister and brother-in-law, Susan and Theodore *Crane from 1877 to 1889. In this retreat, Clemens was able to escape the social demands of Hartford and his very public life, turning summers into occasions for work, while Olivia was able to spend time with her family. In this particular, the Clemens family resisted participation in one of the rituals of their social class.

In many ways their resistance is surprising considering the degree to which summer resorts were used to build business as well as social contacts. Among artists, writers, and intellectuals, certain summer resorts were frequented as much to solidify group identity as to vacation. William Dean *Howells's 18 July 1880 letter to Clemens expresses a degree of urgency in inviting the Clemens family to join him that year: "Are you going to visit Mr. Norton [Charles Eliot Norton] at Ashfield [Massachusetts], in August? Better do so. Warner is going, and so are Winny and I; and Curtis will be there. We shall have a famous time, and you will enjoy yourself, and make everybody else happy." Norton, the Harvard professor and coeditor of both the *North American Review* and the *Nation Magazine* was one of the arbiters of American culture, as was George William Curtis, editor of *Harper's Weekly Magazine*. Howells, as editor of the *Atlantic*, and Charles Dudley *Warner, coeditor of the influential daily Hartford *Courant*, rounded out the set, making Howells's invitation something of a command performance—which Clemens declined.

Still, the pressure to join a group of literati in the summers was enough to push the Clemens family to consider buying into the resort community at Onteora, New York, where Mary Mapes Dodge, among others, spent her summers. The family spent the summer there in 1890, but financial concerns prevented them from purchasing.

SUNDAY SCHOOL. Samuel Clemens was born during an era of intense Protestant religious activity geared primarily toward evangelizing the American population. At the same time, *childhood was beginning to be treated across a broad spectrum of the population as a distinct phase of human development, separate from both infancy and adulthood, when the child's mind and character needed to be nurtured and protected from adult concerns. The combination of these two trends led to the creation of the Sunday school movement, imported from England, but perhaps nowhere more active—or enduring in its success—than in the United States. Under the coordination of the American Sunday School Union, founded in 1824, American churches of many denominations had easy access to literature designed to teach bible stories and Christian ethics. While such *Bible classes taught adults as part of their evangelical mission, the captive audiences Sunday schools most easily reached were the children of church members, who were trained into Christian adulthood and prepared for conversion and church membership through lessons and books geared to their ostensible levels of intellectual and moral development.

While the homilies taught in Sunday school stories were wholesome in the extreme, they ironically helped break down an orthodox Protestant anxiety about fictions. Such tales as Sunday Schools promulgated were so obviously calculated to lead children onto the straight and narrow path that they were hardly objectionable, even though they could, in the long run, help develop a taste for fiction in their readers.

These kinds of tales were a source of unending pleasure to Mark Twain in a very different sense. He did, in fact, find these tales immoral to some degree because the lessons they inculcated tended to be so insipidly presented and so geared, not to the level of a child's mind, but to the level of an adult's imagination of what a child's mind should be like that they taught nothing so much as rebellion. Twain's *burlesques of Sunday school morality are one of his own longest-lasting rebellions, one that became intensely public starting in 1865 with "Advice for Good Little Boys," followed by "Advice for Good Little Girls" and "The Christmas Fireside for Good Little Boys and Girls. By Grandfather Twain. The Story of the Bad

Little Boy That Bore a Charmed Life," and continued with "Reflections on the Sabbath" (1866), "Colloquy Between a Slum Child and a Moral Mentor" (1868), "Mamie Grant, Child Missionary" (1868), "The Story of the Good Little Boy Who Did Not Prosper" (1870), "The Story of Poor Little Stephen Girard" (1872), culminating in *The Adventures of Tom Sawyer* (1876). The point to this collection can be summed up in a paragraph from the first:

> Good little boys must never tell a lie when the truth will answer just as well. In fact, real good little boys will never tell lies at all—not at all—except in cases of the most urgent necessity.

In using the adjective "real" instead of the adverb "really," Twain imitates the condescending pseudochild's language of graded books while punning on the grammatically correct way of reading the line: real boys do tell lies whenever they feel the necessity, broadly construed. Such real boys are, nonetheless, good, or at least as good as can be expected.

Rarely, Twain uses the generally accepted morality of the Sunday school book to make his points, as in his ninth Washington letter to the *Territorial Enterprise* (7 March 1868):

> Right here in this heart and home and fountain-head of law—in this great factory where are forged those rules that create good order and compel virtue and honesty in the other communities of the land, rascality achieves its highest perfection. Here rewards are conferred for conniving at dishonesty, but never for exposing it. . . . I meet a man in the Avenue, sometimes, . . . [who] was a clerk of a high grade in one of the Departments; but he was a stranger and had no rules of action for his guidance except some effete maxims of integrity picked up in Sunday school—that snare to the feet of the unsophisticated!—and some unpractical moral wisdom instilled into him by his mother, who meant well, poor soul, but whose teachings were morally bound to train up her boy for the poor-house.
>
> Well, nobody told this stranger how he ought to conduct himself, and so he went on following up those old maxims of his, and acting so strangely in consequence, that the other clerks began to whisper and nod, and exchange glances of commiseration—for they thought that his mind was not right.

Here, even though Twain sets absolute honesty as the moral standard by which he condemns Washington corruption, the irony is that he makes his same old point about those who follow Sunday school morality, namely, that they are not in their right minds. Most people seem to find a balance between integrity and self-interest.

By the time he wrote *The Adventures of Tom Sawyer*, this balance is what Twain describes. The purpose of Sunday school in the novel is not so much piety as social connection, and Tom Sawyer, though he fails miserably at the ostensible lessons the

Sunday school inculcates, succeeds admirably at achieving social distinction. He may not obey, but he never is really apostate in his small town. Perhaps, then, by 1876, Mark Twain had made his peace—at least temporarily—with the moral absolutism of the Sunday school, seeing in the social rituals of small town America compensations for the moral rigidity it professed.

♦ SEE ALSO Education; Moral Sense; Religion.

SUPERSTITION. A review of nineteenth-century magazines and books will turn up a fair number of treatises on superstition, which turns out to be a fairly good touchstone for some of the hot issues of the era. Most print accounts of superstition took a kind of anthropological approach, assuming that the educated nineteenth-century reader would reject superstitions on principal, but would nonetheless be fascinated by them. Often, especially in the antebellum period, writers went to great lengths to list current superstitions in order to discourage them, working on the Enlightenment assumption that no rational being would let superstition govern behavior. In this spirit, William T. Coggleshall in the *Ladies Repository* (November 1857) wrote:

> History teaches us that when nations are young faith in omens and charms prevails most widely among them; though in the period of the highest refinement it was not eradicated by the Romans, nor has it yet been by Celts, Germans, or Anglo-Saxons. Individuals are like nations in respect to superstitions. Upon early impressions—indeed, convictions before we reason—depend superstitious fears; and often, in middle or later life, when we know that we are the victims of superstition, we are none the less surely victimized. Therefore, parents should have exceeding care concerning the impressions made upon their children's minds before they have experience and observation from which to reason for themselves.
>
> Confidence between parents and children should always be free, that whatever erroneous impressions young minds receive may be removed. Instruction respecting familiar things should frequently be imparted in the family circle; and, that common superstitions and pernicious errors respecting our ordinary relations to air, earth, and water, may be prevented, many books which popularize science ought to be widely circulated. We have a few good ones, but we might have many. They will be written and published whenever families and schools practically demand them. (p. 676)

Notice, here, the Enlightenment idea that individual lives parallel the lives of cultures, an idea of *progress that provided fertile ground for the idea of *evolution. Notice, too, the anxiety that both cultures and infants begin life in superstition only to have reason not fully capable of rising above all traces of superstitious power. The power, then, of early training, of *childhood *association to govern rational adulthood, is equally important for children and nations, requiring careful *education.

Clemens certainly shared these opinions. His reading in *history or in Thomas Paine's *The Age of Reason* made him a strong believer in the value of growth toward rationality. In no work, perhaps, is this belief more centrally important than in *A Connecticut Yankee in King Arthur's Court*, though his attack on *Europe in *The Innocents Abroad* is also predicated on his belief that America has done a better job of rising above superstition. Twain's famous *maxim from chapter 51 of *Following The Equator*, "Let me make the superstitions of a nation and I care not who makes its laws or its songs either," suggests that by 1897 he despaired of the possibility of progress and regarded superstition as one of the insuperable barriers to the growth either of a culture or of an individual.

Implicit in both Coggleshall's attack and Twain's repeated gibes at superstition is the idea that *religion itself is too often tainted by superstition. Indeed, Twain goes so far as to imply, by juxtaposing in *Adventures of Huckleberry Finn* Huck and Jim's superstitions with the literalist *Calvinism of Miss Watson, that religion is nothing more than superstition. Twain was not alone in making the connection, so he could assume his readers would understand his satiric point. But many writers of the period, recognizing that rationalists would use scorn of superstition to attack Christianity, defended superstition in order to support religion. Indeed, a number of essays written about superstition in the nineteenth century defend it as at worst a harmless naïveté, at best, a manifestation of the highest religious impulse.

Finally, many writers of the period who addressed superstition did so in a study of America's infancy. One of the impulses of local color *realism was to capture those aspects of America that were part of its infancy but that were quickly passing. In this spirit, magazines carried articles about superstitions of regions, such as the South, or simply listed a number of superstitions as if they were quaint antiquities. It was in this spirit, perhaps, that Mark Twain depicted youthful superstitions in *The Adventures of Tom Sawyer*. In the preface, he states, with the dispassionate air of an anthropologist studying what he thinks is a primitive culture, "The odd superstitions touched upon were all prevalent among children and slaves in the West at the period of this story—that is to say, thirty or forty years ago." Over the course of the story, however, Twain's tone shifts to suggest a certain idealized fondness for the foolish pleasures of childhood superstition. Only through the gentle gaze of *nostalgia did Clemens abandon his contempt and fear of superstition.

Sut Lovingood. see Harris, George Washington.

TASTE. In *"Old Times on the Mississippi," Mark Twain treats a consummate symbol of Victorian America's taste, the steamboat, with typical ambivalence. In one place he calls the highly ornamented boats "cheap, gaudy," but a few lines later he says:

> The boat *is* rather a handsome sight, too. She is long and sharp and trim and pretty; she has two tall, fancy-topped chimneys, with a gilded device of some kind swung between them; a fanciful pilot-house, all glass and "gingerbread," perched on top of the "Texas" deck behind them;

the paddle-boxes are gorgeous with a picture or with gilded rays above the boat's name; the boiler deck, the hurricane deck, and the texas deck are fenced and ornamented with clean white railings; there is a flag gallantly flying from the jack-staff; the furnace doors are open and the fires glaring bravely; and so on, with everything designed to make a grand show, to have an overwhelmingly sensational effect.

Whether one found such a show beautiful or merely gaudy is a question of taste; but to Clemens and his contemporaries, a question of taste was never "mere."

To Americans of the last half of the nineteenth century, questions of taste were intimately connected with questions of morality, and the fanciful and ubiquitous ornamentation of American plastic, musical, and literary art was in part the external manifestation of a baroque ethos. In the Protestant world's reaction to the asceticism of its Calvinist past, liberal Christians of the nineteenth century, following the ethics and aesthetics of both *sentimentalism and romanticism, came to believe that God gave human beings tastes for the physical world in order to have the world's beauty move humankind to love creation and the Creator. In that sense, any exercise of taste was an exercise in devotion, and any degradation of taste was considered sin. By such standards, taste was a profoundly moral concern, and careful categorizations of what constituted good taste became an obsessive Victorian exercise in morality.

In this sense, arbiters of taste and morality were always arguing about hierarchies of good taste, and about what kind of ornamentation was ennobling, what kind indifferent or worse. Mark Twain took part in this argument throughout his career, casting his moral vote against what he at times felt was spurious and meretricious ornamentation in the very title of his book *The Gilded Age*, which has served as one of the most enduring names for the era. But such a complaint obviously did not exhaust Twain's feelings, inasmuch as he could find the beauty in "gaudy" steamboats, and could relish ornamentation as assertively as anyone. We cannot understand Twain's tastes without surrendering twentieth-century ideas of Victoriana. Victorian standards of taste were not absolute; they were a source of cultural contention precisely because Victorians loaded them with such moral imperatives.

It is safe to generalize to some degree with the enduring caveat that exceptions abound. Victorian tastes could be called baroque in that they violated earlier, classical conventions of taste in architecture and decorative arts, in part by heaping on ornamentation in defiance of older rules of balance and order. Ornamentation served as a physical sign of optimism in the congruence between God's eternal plan and the human manifestation of it, as a way to relish the sensation of beauty as a path to reconciliation with God. And at the same moment that Victorian taste promoted human arts, it encouraged a studied appreciation of nature and of the picturesque. Romantic taste and sentimental taste are virtually indistinguishable in this sense, and Victorian plastic arts drew as readily on folk art and the gothic past as they did on natural motifs. Indeed, an extreme eclecticism marked Victorian taste, not only including classical ornamentation along with gothic (a conjunction Americans of a mere generation earlier would have held, by European standards of classical propriety, to be barbaric), but also embracing the trade of an imperial era to include "oriental" motifs.

The key to assembling all of this eclectic ornamentation was that the plastic arts were falling out of the hands of craftsmen into the hands of machine operators. Lathes, jigs, presses, casts, looms, and other machines enabled factories to reproduce ornamental moldings, "gingerbread," railings, sculpture, ceramics, glass, fabric, carpet, flooring, and so forth in precise profusion, enabling builders and designers to have a free hand not only in combining forms from different traditions, lands, and historical periods, but in making such forms affordable on very large scales. Cast metal ceilings, for example, made it possible to imitate or even outdo the fanciest of plaster ceilings at a fraction of the cost and in places where skilled artisan labor was not available. The world of forms and styles was no longer dependent on the work of individual, specialized craftsmen.

The result was an exuberant architecture, marked by free-flowing spaces decorated in mixed styles, as for instance in the famous high Victorian houses as readily ornamented with classical cornices on windows as gothic turrets and garrets, folk art–inspired "gingerbread" under the eaves, or "oriental" screens on porches. Interior decoration, too, was marked by a radical eclecticism and a love of the ornate and plush. Whereas American styles of the previous generation looked to either pure classical restraint, or to the even greater austerity of Protestant aesthetics, many Victorians went in for overstuffed chairs, tasseled lamp shades, statuary and miniatures, sketches, watercolors, chromolithographs, and the like in an outpouring of decorative ornamentation.

Of course, decorative touches on houses and in personal adornments had long been a sign of wealth; in Victorian America the impulse to ostentation was also connected to economic well-being. The wide availability of ornament was considered by many a sign of America's virtue; that material prosperity had spread so far somehow marked America's superiority to the rest of the world. Americans held their land to be a bastion of good taste, a land in which the middle classes lived in an opulence once reserved for the elites of *Europe or Asia. In *The *American Claimant*, Twain makes much the same argument, connecting the ingenuity of America's mechanical classes with their productivity, their wealth, and their willingness and ability to engage in activities that lift them into a higher class. In this sense, American taste, in all its exuberance and opulence, was considered by many to be not only a sign of America's morality, but also a sign of the virtue of *democracy.

Ironically, the very conjunction of an idea of democracy with machine culture and material prosperity did lead to a reaction among the truly wealthy, of whom there was an increasing number in the age of *robber barons. The tastes of the economic elite complicated arguments about the moral value of a machine aesthetic. Before machine production, quality of workmanship was judged by how flawlessly the workers could erase signs of their workmanship. No human workman can compete with the precision of machine reproduction, so that the machine age made perfect reproduction of art and of design elements in architecture and interior design accessible to wide ranges of the population. Thus, it was in the late Victorian period that handcrafts were coming to be perceived as more valuable than machine crafts, and the mark of handiwork was its imperfection, rather than its approximation to perfection, or its uniqueness, rather than its reproducibility. Ironically, then, the wealthy, whose exercise of conspicuous consumption was meant to separate them from the masses, gave weight to a new aesthetic movement that was begun as a socialist alternative to capitalist industrialism. Romantic reactionaries to machine reproduction, like William Morris, argued for a socialist utopia based on craft production. But Morris's design style and his emphasis on artisanal production became fashionable among the very rich; his work had a major influence on twentieth-century ideas of high versus low taste and, perhaps ironically, is regarded as emblematic of the former.

These trends show in the Clemenses' *Hartford house. The exterior is typical high Victorian in its love affair with machine-produced ornamental effects, and the interior, too, has woodwork unattainable without machine tooling. But the hand-painted Tiffany wallpaper is designed to demonstrate a different aspect of the Clemens family's taste and economic power.

In any event, the class confusion of democratic middle-class but elevated taste encouraged many of the anomalies in Victorian aesthetics. For one, the long-standing concern that a democratic culture could not be well mannered created a heightened concern with *etiquette, a concern that spilled over into Victorian taste.

Victorian silverware and the highly mannered table etiquette governed by the profusion of utensils produced by the silverware industry are obvious manifestations of the American aspiration to high-class taste.

Less obviously, but of more central concern to Twain's works, the American interest in cleanliness was, in part, a novelty of class climbing, a way to show American taste as civilized, in contrast to its recent frontier past. Twain's own incessant joking about the dirt and squalor of the Nevada mining district, of Hawaii, of poor stretches of the rural South or Appalachia in *Roughing It*, *Life on the Mississippi*, and *The Gilded Age*, for example, shows his sense of an American middle-class progress of taste. Similarly, in describing Euorpean dirt and squalor in *The Innocents Abroad*, he was showing that American culture had developed a taste for cleanliness. Of course, underneath this concern for cleanliness was the reality that improved hygiene, especially at the public level, improved *health. Some of Twain's writings make that point, but usually he addresses hygiene as a matter of taste.

Even though class consciousness did move Victorian Americans away from their traditional taste for simplicity, Americans never reached a baroque sense of *fashion in personal ornamentation. Clothing remained remarkably somber, especially for men. Watches and watch chains, canes, hats, and the jewelry necessary to button shirts were the extent of masculine ornamentation considered tasteful. "Loud" clothing and excessive jewelry were considered vulgar for men. Women's clothing and personal decorations were much more elaborate, but they were still remarkably subdued by historical standards. The continued plainness in clothing showed the persistent power of Calvinist ideas about personal ornamentation being sinful and suggests something of the connection between *Calvinism and business ethics, since it is the business suit mentality that held (and still holds) men's clothing to a subdued standard of taste. Still, women's clothing did grow more elaborate in accordance with Victorian ideas of femininity and *domesticity. In a culture that considered women to be civilizing agents because they ostensibly had a more refined sense of beauty, women were expected to want to dress beautifully as well as to be the primary organizers of domestic ornamentation.

In this history, then, we can see some of Twain's own ambivalence about Victorian taste. A residual Calvinism appears in much of his early journalism in which he mocks fashion generally, but as he came to appreciate Victorian concepts of taste, he instead began to jump into the game of adjudicating what was and what was not in "good taste." One of his recurring standards through much of the middle of his career was that "effeminate" beauty should be restricted to women and to the home, and his mockery of feminine standards of beauty was as often as not a way of demarcating masculine and feminine spheres. Yet in his own home, he took an active part in

Continued on page 600

Technology

Bruce Michelson

Every American writer born after 1820 has lived in the whirl of industrial and technological revolutions, decades in which powerful new machines and light-speed communications systems have overhauled nearly every aspect of public and private life in the United States, including the nature and consequences of authorship. However, no major American author of the nineteenth century participated more actively and imaginatively in that revolution than Samuel Clemens. His direct engagement began in his thirteenth year when his cash-strapped family arranged for his apprenticeship to a Hannibal, Missouri, printer named Joseph Ament. That involvement with technology continued full force throughout his life, to the last consequential texts that he authored. Technology is so extensively intertwined with the story of Mark Twain that it must be sorted arbitrarily into five subject areas:

1. Clemens's own professional experience with significant new technologies, most notably innovations in printing and publishing and in book illustration. His experience as a licensed pilot of a Mississippi River steamboat is also a strong early indication of his wish to understand and control new mechanical powers that were transforming his world.

2. Clemens's repeated and ultimately disastrous investments in complex inventions directly related to the industry of printing and publishing, most notably Kaolatype and the Paige Typesetter.

3. His long-term enthusiasm for technological innovation in his private life: telephones, typewriters, bicycles, and so on. His delight in new domestic apparatus spills over into his major fiction and into one of his hobbies, the invention of low-technology personal and home contraptions. These included three devices he actually patented: an "elastic vest strap," a "bed clamp" for keeping sheets and blankets tucked in, and Mark Twain's Self-Pasting Scrapbook, which enjoyed some commercial success.

4. His unprecedented exploitation of new communications and production technologies to invent himself as a worldwide celebrity and to reinvent the published text, first as a commodity and later as an artifact for political and moral education.

5. The literary themes within his writings related to mechanical and industrial innovation as a transformative cultural force.

Early and Professional Life

When Clemens began his working life as a "printer's devil" or roustabout apprentice in Ament's small shop in 1848, and continued working in this capacity, largely unpaid, for his cash-strapped brother Orion in a succession of failed local newspaper ventures, he was entering an industry that in major cities had already undergone a quantum change in speed and productivity. In the year of his birth, the technology of a big New York printing operation was little different from that of small towns in the outback: the central device remained the hand operated bed and platen press, somewhat improved from the days of Benjamin Franklin and Johannes Gutenberg but essentially the same in its basic workings. Larger publishing operations made use of stereotyping, which allowed an array of set type to be reproduced in metal casts for multiple simultaneous print runs, but most of the labor was still Renaissance: hand-pulled presses, hand-dampened and positioned sheets, inking by hand, removal, cutting, folding—all by hand. When Clemens reached his teens, the technological gap between metropolitan and small-town printing was suddenly immense, thanks to a spate of inventions, chief among them the Adams Press, a powered press that made possible a dramatic increase in book-quality printing; the Hoe "Type Revolving" machines, a series of rapidly improving rotary presses, which by the 1850s were capable of output approaching twenty thousand sheets per hour; and the Bullock Sheet Feeder, which kept up with the breathtaking speed of the Hoe machines.

The difference between what was possible technologically in Philadelphia, New York, St. Louis, and other cities and what was possible in Hannibal, Missouri, was nothing less than astounding—and in Ament's *Missouri Courier* and Orion Clemens's *Western Union* and *Hannibal Daily Journal*, the economic and cultural pressure can be clearly seen. The power presses were already up and running in St. Louis, less than a hundred miles down river, but Hannibal had nothing quicker or easier than Columbians and Washingtons—standard, hand-operated, one-sheet-at-a-time presses. The telegraph network had reached East St. Louis by December 1847, but news from the East, which now arrived in hours, took several more days to move from St. Louis to Hannibal by river. A railroad connecting Hannibal to the outside world would not be completed until 1859. Regarding the news to print, Hannibal papers were gleaners and beggars, and the best source for advertisements remained the new national weeklies and monthlies, which arrived on the Hannibal docks literally in stacks and bales, thanks to the railroads, steamboats, vast improvements in the production of cheap wood-pulp paper, and of course the quantum jump in printing technology. Charging less for more and better things to read, the national weeklies were provisional life-support for Orion's little four-page issues, even as they wooed away subscribers and drove him under.

In January 1853, at the age of seventeen, having learned all he could from local printing operations and tired of its hard, old-style manual labor and starvation-level pay, Clemens fled to St. Louis to find the real action in the American publishing industry. A stint at the printing shops for the St. Louis *Evening News* was just the start; over the next few months, Clemens used his saleable skills to work his way to the major publishing hubs on the East Coast, serving as a journeyman printer in New York and Philadelphia. From New York he wrote back to his family with enthusiasm about seeing the "New Hoe machines" turning out twenty thousand impressions per hour as a main attraction at the Crystal Palace Exposition in the summer of 1853. His subsequent dreams of becoming a tycoon in the publishing industry, and his association of the printed word with potential wealth, fame, and cultural power, were probably rooted in these teenage experiences with type, ink, paper, and unprecedented machines for mass production.

Steamboats

In our popular culture, the nineteenth-century sternwheeler or side-wheeler steamboat is an object of nostalgia; it takes a bit of imagination to see them as they must have appeared to Clemens and other boys along the Mississippi River in the late 1840s and 1850s. Chapter 14 of *Life on the Mississippi* (one of the best of the "Old Times on the Mississippi" chapters, originally published in *The Atlantic Monthly*) includes a famous prose hymn to the power and glory of piloting; however, this retrospective account, written more than twenty years after Clemens's experiences as a cub pilot, does not present the steamboat fleet as a recent, powerful, and dangerous technology. Along with the power came peril—to crews, passengers, and even cities along the shore. On 17 May 1849, a fire aboard the steamer *White Cloud*, moored at the crowded landing in St. Louis, spread fast and burned not only twenty-three other steamboats along the river but also fifteen blocks of the city itself. Wrecks and catastrophic boiler explosions were common, so much so that in his apprentice-printer days young Clemens, perhaps in a cynical mood about wire-service "news" and its impact on country papers, included the following squibs in his brother's newspaper:

> The telegraph wires between the East and St. Louis surely do not work well. The St. Louis papers of yesterday contain no accounts of further loss of life by railroad or steamboat. Accordingly to lately established custom, something of the kind should happen every day. (*Hannibal Daily Journal*, 13 May 1853)

> Terrible Accident!
> 500 Men Killed and Missing!!
> We had set the above head up, expecting (of course) to use it, but as the accident hasn't happened yet, we'll say
> (To Be Continued) (*Hannibal Daily Journal*, 14 May 1853)

This adolescent humor would come back to haunt him in 1858 when Clemens's younger brother Henry, who had followed Clemens into work in the Mississippi fleet, was scalded to death in a boiler explosion on the steamer *Pennsylvania* not far from Memphis, Tennessee. Nonetheless, these treacherous boats offered Clemens membership into his first professional elite and pay that made him the envy of his old friends in Hannibal. The boats taught Clemens about the glory and terror that could come of a relationship to big new machinery—they helped him to escape provincial life, took him on adventures, and fired his imagination, even as they killed a member of his immediate family. If we seek for sources of Clemens's ambivalence about the industrial age unfolding around him, the mix of fascination and fear that characterizes his meditations on technology, culture, and human prospects, we can find roots of that ambivalence in these pilot years before the Civil War.

Investment Fiascoes

When the Clemenses moved to the new "Nook Farm" house in Hartford in May 1874, they were establishing themselves in a city of celebrities, tycoons, industry, and ingenuity. The Gilded Age was moving into high gear, and grandiose plans and big, dangerous investment schemes were everywhere. If Clemens had an inventor-tycoon dream lurking in his psyche from his formative years in printing and piloting, the dream became virulent now; and in the early 1880s it focused on the one phase of the printing process which had not yet been successfully automated: typesetting. Endlessly redesigned, fabricated, and tested and re-tested less than two miles from the Clemens home, the Paige Compositor was a catastrophe in Mark Twain's life, consuming most of his personal fortune and much of his wife Olivia Langdon's inheritance as well. Driving him into virtual bankruptcy, the Paige forced the aging Clemens into a world lecture tour, into publishing inferior and potboiler work, into selling his cherished Nook Farm house, and into loss of control over the format and even the content of many of the volumes that were sold under his name. These traumas all occurred as part of the recovery deal Henry Huddleston Rogers, Clemens's friend and a Standard Oil executive, worked out with Harper and Brothers in the wake of Clemens's bankruptcy. The story of James Paige's dream and Clemens's embroilment in it has been told often, frequently with the implicit or explicit judgement that there was something mad about the project. Critics described the machine as a white elephant of runaway complexity with nearly eighteen thousand parts, a gross weight of over seven thousand pounds, and a price tag that eventually soared to more than three times the cost of the competition, most notably the simpler, reliable Merganthaler Linotypes.

Contrary to myth, the final model of the Paige successfully did its job in a light sixty-day test at the Chicago *Herald*. But that was in September and October 1894, by which time, after ten years of development and huge investment, the Paige had been beaten to the potential market. Its problems were at least as much financial and interpersonal as they were technological: as the engineer who proposed the machine, held the patents, and oversaw the development, Paige refused to surrender majority control of the company's stock. His authority was a major disincentive in attracting other investors, broader support, and additional minds to review and question the machine's ambitions.

For there were technological problems here too. Paige intended his machine not just for composition but for distributing type as well. In other words, unlike the Linotype, which cast the type on demand for a single use (after which the type was melted down again), the Paige tried to be a complete replica of a good journeyman printer, collecting the used type and sorting it accurately back into sets for subsequent projects. For human printers this was a time-consuming and enervating task; any mistakes here could foul up the next print run. It is not hard to see, then, how a veteran "printer's devil" and "jour printer" like Clemens could be intoxicated by the idea of one elegant machine literally doing it all, taking not only the art but the sheer drudgery out of the professional life. The Linotypes went in an entirely new direction, abandoning altogether the use of durable type for printing.

What the Paige attempted, in other words, was what Henry Rogers called the "mechanical replication of a human being," in other words, a robot complete and capable in all major duties. This strategy might seem like benighted engineering, but as an imaginative stimulus, it had a great impact on Clemens. The Paige represented not just a labor-saving device, a high-tech variation on Tom Sawyer's fence-painting scheme: it was a duplicate self (a theme that Twain explored before and after the Paige years); a blow against unionized labor (about which Clemens had several outbreaks of rage); and ultimately a kind of immortality, a human-made simulacrum than was checked by neither sleep nor death, that could go on and on doing what it was made to do, perfectly.

Kaolatype and the Illustration Revolution

Compared to the Paige investment, Kaolatype was a minor debacle, lasting longer as a nuisance in Clemens's career but consuming only about $50,000 compared to the estimated $300,000 or more that Clemens lost on the Paige Typesetter. Dan Slote, a traveling companion with Clemens on the *Quaker City* excursion that produced *The Innocents Abroad*, drew Clemens into investing in this new technology for book and magazine illustration. Other processes of the time involved steel, stone, copper, wood, grease, wax, and other media; Kaolatype's innovation was a surface of fine clay. Its advantages included material that was easy to mark and work with; the disadvantages centered around durability and the clarity of the impression.

After *The Innocents Abroad*, Twain almost always wrote his words to be accompanied by pictures, so there is little surprise that he was infatuated with a new way to get those pictures reproduced. The Kaolatype experiment failed amid a flurry of new strategies for illustrating the printed page, a revolution that was as rapid and many-faceted as the printing-press revolution in the middle of the nineteenth century. Beverly David has published wonderful research into the artists who illustrated the first editions of Twain's books and his variable involvement with the choice and quality of those pictures. A story that remains largely untold, however, is the outburst of technological innovation that simplified, cut the cost, and greatly improved the processes by which illustrations were situated on the printed page. Two key developments particularly revolutionized book illustration from the 1870s to the turn of the twentieth century. First, it became feasible and cost-effective for publishers to utilize photographs printed directly onto wood or zinc plates. This breakthrough allowed engravers to do their work on the original material rather than copy it, and because photographs could enlarge or reduce the work of artists, the artist could work in virtually any size or medium. The second development was the so-called "half-tone" process, which reproduced photographs with unprecedented accuracy in shading. There were many variations on "half-tone" technology; what they all made possible, however, was photographs from life as part of the printed text, the visual "reality" merged with the narration and the commentary. Three of Twain's works particularly reflect the new print environment: *A Connecticut Yankee in King Arthur's Court*, which melded Hank Morgan's story with illustrations of unprecedented grace and sophistication, and with a pre-Raphaelite lyricism that balanced and countered Hank's wild and sometimes-grisly tale; *Following the Equator*, in which half-tone illustrations give veracity to Twain's adventures in exotic India; and *King Leopold's Soliloquy,* in which shocking, untitled photographs of Leopold's mutilated Congo workers resist and overthrow the hypocritical bombast of the imagined King.

Private Life

Clemens boasted more than once about being the first to take advantage of the latest gimmick: by his own reckoning, he was the first major author to compose a manuscript on a typewriter and the first private citizen in Hartford to have a telephone connection to his home. In his domestic life, he liked toys—and when he wrote sketches about domestic life, he often described the effects of these innovations. One of the funniest and most astute of these sketches is "A Telephonic Conversation" (1880), an insightful glimpse of how the newly disembodied voice of the telephone was transforming communication in several dimensions at once—between the caller and the called and among the phone-talkers and others within earshot. Soon we would all be subjected to a new kind of discourse, a dialogue in which only one participant is audible. This is a cognitive anomaly that we take for granted now; Twain's sketch recovers for us its strangeness at the inception. Other stories play with the enforced enigmatic terseness of telegraph messages, laconic reports out of the ether. Some are cadenzas about the comfort and amusement conferred by new-fangled luxuries, for example Hank Morgan's nostalgic paean to the "chromos" as household decor in his Connecticut home. Finally, a number have gags about railroads, carpet-weaving machines, automatic electric burglar alarms, and other technological advantages and intrusions in American private life.

Technology, Authorship, and Celebrity

Mark Twain was America's first world-renowned media star, and his savvy exploitation of the technological revolution played a great role in raising him to that unprecedented level of fame. He quickly and effectively used most of the major developments in communications. When the railroad network linked up the nation coast to coast, he rode it far and wide as a comic lecturer. When a plunge in production costs and an array of new printing technologies made possible the nationwide sale of big, gaudy, heavily-illustrated books sold door to door, Twain immediately became a central figure in that trade, writing with pictures in mind, hiring illustrators himself and doing some illustrations by himself, and padding books shamelessly in order to reach the page-quantities that would assure better sales and higher prices. When photographs became standard features in large-circulation newspapers, Twain became an early master of the photo-op, working up a personal style that showed up strikingly in black and white. Using the telegraph, the rails, the transatlantic cable, and the quick succession of faster and more comfortable passenger ships, he toured Europe often and was one of the first major western authors to circle the world, spending months in Australia, India, South Africa, and other places where high-profile American celebrities had not appeared before. By 1900 he had made himself the best-known face that the United States had ever produced and the best-selling writer before 1900, eventually surpassing even Harriet Beecher Stowe.

All of this provides an interesting episode in the history of American celebrity, the manufacture and worldwide worship of images and reputations, an industry that brings the United States an inordinate share of both love and hate in other countries and cultures. That interest increases, however, when we reopen some of Clemens's major works as meditations on the effects of mass-produced, mass-marketed, fast-moving storms of words and images—effects upon the self, human relationships, and communities small and large. Mark Twain returns to this issue again and again from his first book to his last major manuscript, and the complications and reach of his thinking are so rich that they can only be sampled and summarized here.

In the travel books, especially *The Innocents Abroad, A Tramp Abroad,* and *Following the Equator,* Twain writes uneasily about his visits to the familiar places—"familiar" in the sense that these sites had already been lithographed, described, and venerated in a profusion of printed pages. When he describes the Holy Sepulchre in Jerusalem, the Vatican, the Acropolis, the Taj Mahal, or the Matterhorn, his prose tries hard to defy expectations and conventions, because these places were such standard fare in American books and magazines from the 1850s onward. Of the hundreds of illustrations in

597

the American Publishing Company editions of *The Innocents Abroad*, many are strictly conventional: engravings of facades and panoramas, pictures that were little different from those in travel books written by others. However, when Mark Twain himself appears in our field of vision—either in the prose or in the foreground of an illustration—he animates and refreshes the perspective. By placing himself incongruously in *our* field of vision, he humanizes the scene, makes it personal—for himself, and for us as readers. His text resists the power of the printed picture while also exploiting that power. In *Following the Equator*, Twain's own celebrity further complicates the situation. By 1896 (the year of his world tour), he was an icon visiting icons, encumbered as much by his media-tech fame as by the mobs of present and former visitors to the great attractions. An additional source of interest—and trouble—in *Following the Equator* is the advent of half-tone illustrations, printed photographs. Visual truth—or something that seemed very much like truth—was strengthening its dominion in books about sightseeing; and the diminished whimsy in Mark Twain's final travel book may be an effect of that change.

In the narrative fiction about life along the Mississippi (most notably *The Adventures of Tom Sawyer* and *Adventures of Huckleberry Finn*), the pressure of the new communications technology takes a different form. Set in the years of Clemens's own boyhood and adolescence—there are several embedded clues in *Huckleberry Finn* that the action unfolds in the late 1840s or early 1850s—these stories are in part about sparsely settled villages and a relatively simple culture coming suddenly under the effects of an onslaught of print, words, and pictures from an Elsewhere so exotic as to disrupt everyday life and imagination. Tom Sawyer is the most conspicuous victim of this communications onslaught; he has been reading British and translated French romantic fiction, fair and foul, either in the new, cheap American editions or serialized in the national weeklies and monthlies. However, other people and places along Huck Finn's river journey show the effects of this unprecedented encounter: the pretensions and mass-market decor of the Grangerford household; the theatergoers of Bricksville, who are drawn to fraudulent performances by half-remembered misinformation gathered from newspaper and magazine stories about Drury Lane and the London West End. And everywhere there seem to be printing presses, which can be hired or commandeered for handbills, tickets, wanted posters, a flood of dubious print from dubious characters.

The most sustained and complex meditation on modern technology, and its contents and discontents, is *Connecticut Yankee*, whose message about industrialism and modernity scholars have debated for decades. Is the book a cautionary fable about high-tech exuberance gone mad, an ordinary modern man swept to his doom—and the doom of a whole society—by an intoxication with new ways of building and blowing things up? Is it a preadolescent fantasy of ultimate power, the euphoria felt by small boys in the opposite experiences of creating and wrecking? Is Hank an expression of Twain's exasperation at Anglo-European stodginess and entrenched class structures and belief systems? Is the book so thoroughly nihilistic that it destroys not only the Arthurian myth, modern England, and Hank himself, but also its own basic coherence as a story? No critic has sorted this out in a way that satisfies all readers, or even some solid majority. But here, at the core of this headlong and vigorous fantasy, the machines of Twain's time are brought together: the telegraph, the printing press, the dynamos, the Gatling guns, the high explosives, and the factories churning out the consumer goods which enliven and disrupt the world that Hank Morgan creates and destroys. Did Mark Twain make up his mind firmly about the value and dangers of "technology"? Not likely. But his major works make it clear that the enigma of powerful modernity was often in his thoughts and imagination, and that his career as an author and American celebrity were deeply connected to the technological upheavals of his time.

Continued from page 590

planning and decorating the Hartford house, even though the primary responsibility for collecting the ornaments fell to Olivia on their many trips to Europe or, for that matter, to New York City.

More importantly, Twain attacked the romantic *nostalgia for things gothic. In *Life on the Mississippi*, for instance, he blames the Civil War on Sir Walter Scott's *medievalism, and sees persistent signs of it in the prevalence of gothic architecture. In this sense, Twain is not so much attacking ornamentation as he is a particular manifestation of it, paying close attention to the symbolic significance of a specific standard of taste; that is, he attacked that kind of ornamentation that he felt to be backward and antidemocratic. By this standard he also promoted an American vernacular. It was not that slang was unadorned; he was well aware that the slang he loved was, as he put it in the *"Bluejay Yarn," "bristling with metaphor, just bristling." So his standard of taste in language was not finally for a plain *style so much as for a democratic style.

In all such arguments about taste, Twain publicly accepted the conjunction between taste and morality. Toward the end of his career, he came to doubt that conjunction, and when he did, he found himself much freer to follow caprices of his own taste without concern for moral consequences. His famous praise of fanciful clothing in *Following the Equator* could only come after he had surrendered his belief that "good" taste showed a laudable march of civilization by some morally absolute standard of progress. Instead, he turned the conjunction of taste and morality around, most notably in "Corn Pone Opinions," in which he argues first that matters of taste are accidents of cultural conformity, and then suggests that matters of morality and *religion are too.

♦ SEE ALSO Money; Social Class.

TELEPHONE. One of many revolutionary technologies invented in the nineteenth century, the telephone is one in which Clemens did not invest money. In a 24 May 1906 yarn from his *autobiography, he explains that through the 1870s he had been investing and losing mountains of money when, in 1877, his friend and fellow member of the *Monday Evening Club, Joseph R. Hawley, invited him to listen to an

> agent for a new invention called the telephone. He believed there was great fortune in store for it and wanted me to take some stock. I declined. I said I didn't want anything more to do with wildcat speculation. Then he offered the stock to me at twenty-five. I said I didn't want it at any price. He became eager—insisted that I take five hundred dollars' worth. He said he would sell me as much as I wanted for five hundred dollars—offered to let me gather it

up in my hands and measure it in a plug hat—said I could have whole hatful for five hundred dollars. But I was the burnt child and I resisted all these temptations, resisted them easily, went off with my check intact, and next day lent five thousand of it on an unendorsed note to my friend who was going to go bankrupt three days later.

About the end of the year ... I put up a telephone wire from my house down to the *Courant* office, the only telephone wire in town, and the *first* one that was ever used in a private house in the world.

Even discounting for Clemens's customary hyperbole, it is true that he declined what would have been a fortune on an invention that would ordinarily have charmed his pocketbook wide open, an invention so enticing to him that he became an early user and advocate.

The phone caught on fairly quickly, and Clemens may have helped boost it with his 1878 *Atlantic Monthly* *romance "The Loves of Alonzo Fitz Clarence and Rosannah Ethelton," in which the affair is conducted entirely by telephone—transcontinental telephone at that. While Twain may have been jumping the gun on the technology available, in this sketch he plays with what he found most exciting about such technologies, the transfer of the human essence—character and spirit—over long distances. As much as he professed to disdain *spiritualism, he did believe in the capacity of human beings to project thought, as his interest in what he called "mental telegraphy" attests, and he saw the telephone as an almost magical technological equivalent.

♦ SEE ALSO Inventions.

TEMPERANCE. The temperance movement, often called by its promoters the temperance crusade, really took off in the early nineteenth century with the second Great Awakening, when ideas of self-control under the banner of *reform became associated with spiritual redemption. Through colonial times, *alcohol was an essential part of American life, as a primary way of preserving foodstuffs and of purifying water, which in its natural state was often the carrier of disease. But with the second Great Awakening emphasizing a program of self-improvement as a goad toward godliness at the same time industrialization made working conditions too dangerous for anyone not sober, temperance became one of the dominant movements of the century, culminating, eventually, in Prohibition in the twentieth.

Even though Samuel Clemens as a young man joined the Cadets of Temperance briefly—he tells us in his autobiography that he liked the red sashes they were issued and the *spectacle they made on parade—by the time he became a riverboat pilot, his abstemiousness, advocated by most of his family, became a dead letter. He recovered his pledge only when he wanted something, like the hand of Olivia

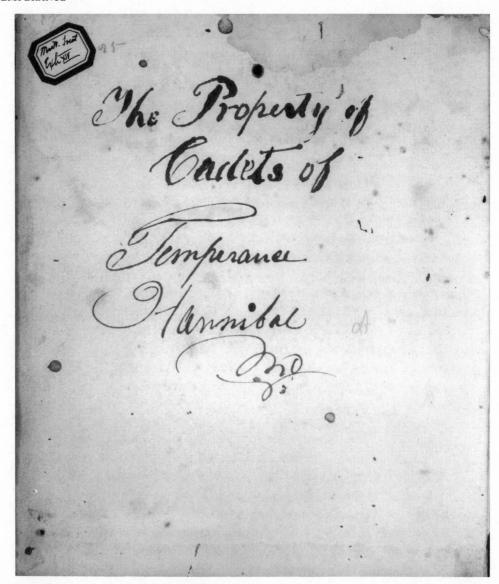

The register of the Cadets of Temperance that features Samuel L. Clemens's name. Original in the Hannibal Home Museum, Hannibal Missouri.

Langdon, whose parents were avid temperance advocates. As is shown by a 23 July 1875 letter to his sister Pamela, Clemens could be vehement in his opposition to the crusade:

> Nothing can persuade me to read a temperance tract or be a party to the dissemination of such injurious publications.... I never would be able to make you comprehend how frantically I hate the very name of total abstinence. I have taught Livy at last to drink a bottle of beer every night; & all in good

time I shall teach the children to do the same. If it is wrong, then, (as the Arabs say,) "On my head be it!"

As much as anything, Twain hated the hypocrisy of the movement that could attack men who drank explicitly for pleasure, but could find surreptitious ways to supply alcohol to almost anyone who wanted it. Virtually every patent medicine had a base in alcohol, whether it was laced with opiates, as was laudanum, or some other psychoactive substance. The "Pain-Killer" forced on young Sam by his mother and that made its way into fiction in *The Adventures of Tom Sawyer* was likely to be as potent as whiskey. Moreover, he suspected that those who espoused temperance were unlikely to be honest in their own dealings. Nowhere does he better make this point than in his rejoinder to Captain Charles Duncan's public attack on Mark Twain as a drunkard, or at least as drunk when he applied for passage on the *Quaker City*'s expedition to Europe and the holy lands. Duncan accused Clemens of presenting himself while reeking from the "fumes of bad whiskey." Interviewed in the New York *World* for 18 February 1877, Twain replied, "For a ceaseless, tireless, forty-year advocate of total abstinence the 'captain' is a mighty good judge of whiskey at second hand." But as much as Clemens disliked the temperance crusade, he had no choice but to cater to it, or criticize it lightly, as say, in "The Temperance Insurrection" (1874), or else lose popularity. His appreciation for alcohol, then, is veiled in his writings, which promote instead the idea that it is not the drink, but the drinker who is the problem, and that the real point of temperance should be just that, temperate use, rather than professed abstinence entwined with hypocrisy.

♦ SEE ALSO Religion.

TERRITORIAL ENTERPRISE, **VIRGINIA CITY.** While young Samuel Clemens had written a number of letters for his brother's newspapers and an occasional column while a riverboat pilot, he began writing as his primary profession in the autumn of 1862 for the Virginia City *Territorial Enterprise*. The *Enterprise* had begun its life as a small newspaper in the hands of Jonathan Williams, who moved it around various small Nevada towns from 1858 to 1859 before settling in Virginia City, site of the newly discovered (1859) Comstock Lode. Williams sold shares on 2 March 1861, to Joseph T. *Goodman and Denis E. McCarthy, both of whom had been working for San Francisco newspapers and were looking for an opportunity to do more. Williams sold his remaining shares to Dennis Driscoll, the *Enterprise* bookkeeper, later that year, who in turn surrendered his share of the paper to Goodman and McCarthy in October 1863. Goodman ran the editorial side of the paper, while McCarthy handled production.

When the silver boom began in earnest in 1861, the *Enterprise* benefited from extensive advertising and quickly became, by American standards, a major daily newspaper. From a small one-story building that housed the editorial offices, press, and living quarters for its worker-owners, it moved to a large rented building and then to its own three-story building in 1863. With huge cash flow, it was able to buy steam presses and hire a significant staff, turning it into one of the nation's most technologically sophisticated and lucrative daily newspapers.

But as much as its position might already have seemed ideal for profitability, the new proprietors were excellent businessmen, always in search of ways to improve the operation. After Sam Clemens published a series of letters for them under the *pseudonym "Josh," Goodman decided to offer Clemens a berth on the paper as a reporter. He made the decision in part because of his need to temporarily replace his editor and writer William *Wright (pen name Dan DeQuille), who was about to take a leave of absence for a trip east in the autumn of 1862, in part because of Clemens's family connection to the territorial government. Indeed, shortly after Clemens began working for Goodman, the *Enterprise* secured from Orion Clemens the contract as printer for territorial business.

Clemens took the job, which at first paid twenty-five—later forty—dollars a week, because his mining had driven him into debt and yielded no income. In despair over his cash-flow problem, he opted for reporting as a stopgap until his mining investments could come in. Of course, what happened instead was a complete change in his career. Clemens learned the ropes of reporting and came to love the energetic and convivial life led by the staff of a major newspaper in a boom town.

Not surprisingly, one of Clemens's assignments was to cover the territorial legislature when it was in session, but when not in Carson City, Clemens spent his time learning the trade from Goodman, Wright, and the other experienced writers on the *Enterprise* staff. While they did teach him the job of regular reporting, they also gave him tremendous latitude for fancy sketches. Indeed, in the work of "DeQuille" Clemens found an example of how to write fanciful satires and burlesques. Clemens enjoyed his work at the *Enterprise* immeasurably, as he relates, in a lightly fictionalized way, in chapters 42 to 55 of *Roughing It*. His letters bear out this portrait—their tone changes quickly from brooding and bitter during the last days of his stint as a miner, to effervescent and confident once he became well-known as a reporter.

After Clemens left daily reporting for the *Enterprise* when he departed Virginia City for San Francisco in 1864, he became an occasional correspondent for the *Enterprise*. He came to rely on what the *Enterprise* paid, especially after he quit his daily work on the San Francisco *Morning Call* and instead tried to patch together a livelihood working for the literary magazines *The Golden Era* and *The Californian*. The *Enterprise*, essentially, saved him from destitution for a second time.

The *Enterprise*'s fortunes quickly fell with those of its hometown. Devastated by a fire in 1875, and then starved after 1878 when the mines played out, Virginia City became a shadow of its former self. The *Enterprise* died with the town, ending regular publication in 1893. The paper has made a minor, tourist-inspired comeback; the building that housed it has been restored and now houses a museum that trades on the popularity of Mark Twain.

♦ SEE ALSO Gillis, James N. (Jim) and Steve; Newspaper Journalism.

THEATER. In a 23 May 1867 letter from New York to the San Francisco *Alta California*, Mark Twain writes of one of his experiences as a theatergoer:

> I attended the Old Bowery Theatre in the evening, and there, in the pit, I found the whole tribe [of boot blacks]. I suppose there were three hundred of them present, closely packed together in their rags and dirt, and the way they guyed the actors and criticized the performance was interesting. They applauded all the "ranting" passages furiously, and hurled uncompromising scorn and contempt upon the sentimental ones. I asked one of them what he thought of the lead man as an actor? "Oh, he ain't no force. You'd ought to hear Proctor—Oh, geeminy! why, you can hear Proctor f'm here to Central Park when he lays hisself out in Richard Third."

American theater in the late nineteenth century was changing from its disreputable past to its current status as high-brow, expensive art, but the change was slow, primarily because the theater had not yet divided itself into subcategories attracting different kinds of crowds. Theaters in America still had an Elizabethan openness, with groundlings taking cheap tickets for standing room near the stage, expensive seats in the dress circle and lower balconies, and an upper gallery, often entered by a separate door, that had a bar and was prime work space for prostitutes soliciting clients. Such space had no *social class or racial restrictions; it was open to anyone interested in what it had to offer.

Twain himself goes on in his *Alta* letter to describe this area:

> Up in the fifth tier—the gallery—there was a multitude of negroes, and a sprinkling of bootblacks and women of the town. There was a bar up there, and two of the women came forward and asked us to treat. A bootblack, who had just blacked my boots and perhaps felt a personal interest in my welfare on that account, tipped at me a wink of wonderful complexity and mystery, and I went and asked him to translate it. He said: "You keep away f'm them women. I've been around here four years, and I know all about 'em. Don't you go no where with that curly-headed one, nor 'other one either— they'd go through you for everything you've got. That's their style. You ask any cop (policeman,)—they'll tell you. Why, that curly girl's rid in the Black Maria (conveyance for prisoners) oftener that she's rid in the street cars. And don't you touch that liquor in there ... don't you drink that dern swipes—it's pison."

Twain's description accurately describes the run of theaters in the antebellum years and those also established in Western mining camps. It also explains to a large extent the persistent religious resistance to the establishment of theaters in many parts of the United States.

In fact, the dissenting Protestant tradition, so influential in all local governments throughout colonial times as well as the nineteenth century, fairly well kept the theater out of the colonies altogether. It wasn't until the very end of the eighteenth century that theaters were established in New York, Boston, Philadelphia, Baltimore, and Richmond. As much as they were frequented by fashionable young men in these cities, they were under nearly constant attack until after the Civil War. That attack came about in part because theaters did not really discriminate between the kinds of attractions they would offer; they were merely large public houses for staging entertainments. While plays were among their staples, they also staged minstrel shows, musical entertainments, juggling acts, *lectures, or anything else available that would draw a paying crowd. This mix may have kept the big cities in the forefront of the nascent *leisure industry in the United States, but their viability relied on the viability of the visiting troupes who passed through—and most entertainers were traveling as much in the provinces, creating any kind of *spectacle that would attract an audience, as they were between big cities.

Regardless of the shaky social status of actors and acting in America, the plays of William *Shakespeare were considered the highest caliber of literature by the educated classes in the early days of the United States. Moreover, the widespread belief in education and uplift made Shakespeare's plays widely known and appreciated among the working classes as well. In chapter 19 of *Life on the Mississippi*, Twain describes his riverboat pilot partner, George Ealer, as a devotee of Shakespeare who awakened Twain's interest in the bard.

The cultural importance of Shakespeare in some ways opened the door for theater more broadly, with American theater managers in the first half of the nineteenth century developing the tradition of importing renowned British Shakespearean actors to U.S. stages for presentations of the most famous tragedies and, to a lesser extent, comedies. Such tours were extremely lucrative to both the actors and the playhouses precisely because Shakespeare's works brought respectability to the theater.

Still, with the pit and gallery so inexpensive as to make theatergoing a popular entertainment, the social organization of the theaters affected the kinds of shows put on. Even Shakespeare's tragedies were performed sandwiched between vaudeville acts at the beginning and end of the plays, and with song and dance routines between the acts. No theater manager dared let a moment pass in which the audience was present but bored for fear that the groundlings would riot. Not surprisingly, melodrama and comedy, as well as variety shows, were the principal styles of American theater for much of the nineteenth century. Even Shakespeare's plays were often cut up into reviews, with famous actors performing a series of favorite scenes from a variety of plays.

The style of acting was, by today's standards, bombastic in the extreme. And just because Americans flocked to the theater to see famous actors and actresses fresh from Europe does not for a minute suggest that acting was considered more important than stage properties. Productions were expected to be opulent to match the energy of the most fervid performers. Given this context, it is no surprise that *burlesque—of Shakespeare as well as of contemporary literature and current events—was also a very popular form. Among Twain's ultimately unrealized plans was a burlesque *Hamlet* in which he introduced the anachronistic character of a book subscription agent into the tragedy. And in *Adventures of Huckleberry Finn*, the burlesque Shakespeare performed by the King and the Duke is right out of the American theatrical tradition. Indeed, Twain's own most successful play, *Colonel Sellers*, works as a burlesque of American capitalism and optimism. And when he and William Dean *Howells tried to collaborate on a play, "Colonel Sellers as Scientist," they continued in the burlesque vein. Howells in his own works tried to write serious *drama during a period in which there was virtually no commercial outlet for the homegrown variety, but Twain always counseled Howells to stay in a burlesque vein, as for example when he suggested to Howells that he rewrite his magazine sketch "The Parlor Car" as a play:

> Of course the thing is perfect, in the magazine, without the train-boy; but I was thinking of the stage & the groundlings. If the dainty touches went over their heads, the train-boy, & other possible interruptions would fetch them every time. Would it mar the flow of the thing too much to insert that devil? I thought it over a couple of hours & concluded it wouldn't, & that he ought to be in for the sake of the groundlings. (14 Sept 1876)

As much as Twain was partly teasing Howells here, he did know the realities of American theater.

After the Civil War, the separation of theatrical performances into occasions of different social standing began with the importation of ballet and French *opéra bouffe*. These brought a sexual raciness to theater in the immediate post–Civil War years that threatened to debase further the theater's reputation; American theater managers recognized their appeal, and created a homegrown version that would capitalize on sexual display. The trend took off with the success of *The Black Crook*, in which a conventional melodrama was used as the medium for dancing girls to strut their stuff in what were then considered scandalously skimpy costumes. As Twain described the show to his California readers in his 2 February 1867 letter to the *Alta*:

> The scenic effects—the waterfalls, cascades, fountains, oceans, fairies, devils, hells, heavens, angels—are gorgeous beyond anything ever witnessed in

America, perhaps, and these things attract the women and the girls. Then the endless ballets and splendid tableaux, with seventy beauties arrayed in dazzling half-costumes; and displaying all possible compromises between nakedness and decency, capture the men and boys. . . . The scenery and the legs are everything; the actors who do the talking are the wretchedest sticks on the boards. . . . Those girls dance in ballet, dressed with a meagerness that would make a parasol blush.

Still, as much as theater's origins were socially suspect, and as much as its licentious traditions persisted through the postwar era, the growing middle- and upper-middle-class interest in leisure that could be considered wholesome began developing some countertrends in the theatrical world. While serious drama did not regain a foothold in the English-speaking world until very late in the nineteenth century, and American dramatists did not have much success in staging their own serious plays until the twentieth, the period from 1855 to 1900 saw a gradual improvement in the status of theater among the elites and the gradual confinement of the racier kinds of entertainment to music halls. This is not to say that farce and comedy gave way to literary drama; they did not, as Twain complained in "About Play-Acting" (1898).

It was this shifting context that allowed Twain to move into drama himself in securing the copyright on *Colonel Sellers* and then to conceive of many of his works as sliding between literature and drama. While *The Prince and the Pauper* and *Pudd'nhead Wilson* both made their first public appearances as novels, both were dramatized. *Prince and the Pauper* probably began in Twain's mind as an idea for a play; certainly *The *American Claimant* did, taken, as it was, from the script that Clemens had written with Howells before Howells got cold feet and backed out of the production.

The shift in the social respectability of theater also enabled Clemens to make friends with those in the theatrical world—such as Bram Stoker and Henry Irving—without damaging his own carefully nurtured image. After all, as a comic lecturer and writer of humorous literature, Clemens was himself often held by some of America's opinion leaders in the contempt reserved for clowns and showmen. His efforts early in his career to distance himself from such a reputation gave way over the course of the century in part because the rise of *celebrity made it less difficult for him to maintain both his career as showman among showmen as well as his status as gentleman.

♦ SEE ALSO Sexuality.

"THIRTY THOUSAND DOLLAR BEQUEST, THE."

"**THIRTY THOUSAND DOLLAR BEQUEST, THE.**" Written in late 1903 to early 1904 in Italy, where the Clemens family had moved in an effort to prevent Olivia's health from deteriorating further, this short story was published in the 10

December 1904 issue of *Harper's Weekly*, and again as the title story in *The $30,000 Bequest and Other Stories* in 1906. Many commentators draw biographical connections between Saladin and Electra Foster, the main characters in the story, and Samuel and Olivia Clemens. Others find a parallel between the story and Clemens's father's hopes for wealth from his Tennessee land. Perhaps most fruitful, though, is to see it as one of a number of Twain tales dealing with the American dream of *money suddenly come by. Of course, in this story, Twain takes money's power a step further, treating it not as a reality, but as a vision, for Electra and Saladin destroy their lives not over a real bequest, but over a promised inheritance that is merely a practical joke. This strain is common in Twain's works, from *Roughing It* and *The Gilded Age* toward the beginning of his career to "The *Man That Corrupted Hadleyburg," "The Million Pound Banknote," and "The Esquimau Maiden's Romance" near the end. That Clemens shared the dream of making a fortune and spent much of his time imagining fortunes he never realized enabled him more readily to write a series of parables denouncing the power of money, either as fact or as fantasy.

"THREE THOUSAND YEARS AMONG THE MICROBES." Clemens wrote the entirety of this fantasy in thirty-five days of May and June 1905. Clemens dropped it *unfinished. Though he had Jean *Clemens make a typescript of it and told his Harper and Brothers editor, Frederick Duneka, of the project, suggesting that he intended it for publication, his inspiration left him. The problem he had with it was typical; he had an idea of how to juxtapose two different conditions in order to highlight the human condition as he understood it, but he had no plot to keep the piece moving once he ran out of episodes. As it stands, it is an extravaganza in which a human being is transmogrified by an experiment gone awry into a cholera germ inhabiting the body of a tramp named Blitzowski. The set-up gives Twain opportunities for metaphysical speculation, for *satire of American culture, for psychological investigations, for examinations of the meaning of time, and for a series of puns and word games.

Published in part in Paine's *Mark Twain: a Biography* (1912) and in full in *Mark Twain's Which Was the Dream?* (1966) and in *The Devil's Race-track* (1980), "Microbes" has attracted the interest of critics who have long debated Clemens's psychological state in his last years. Some cite it as evidence of his despair and lost creativity, others to show signs of his enduring hope and artistic fecundity. Regardless, it is certainly one of the best examples of Twain's interest in scale, juxtaposing images of the cosmic and the microscopic, and playing as readily with time as with space.

TOBACCO. Mark Twain devoted significant space in his *seventieth birthday speech to his favorite habit:

I have made it a rule never to smoke more than one cigar at a time. I have no other restriction as regards smoking. . . . As an example to others, and not that I care for moderation myself, it has always been my rule never to smoke when asleep, and never to refrain when awake. . . . I have stopped smoking now and then, for a few months at a time, but it was not on principle, it was only to show off; it was to pulverize those critics who said I was a slave to my habits and couldn't break my bonds.

He was proud of his capacity for tobacco and proud of the cheap cigars he smoked, telling in several speeches and in his autobiography how he would scare his visitors away with his horrible cigars.

But his vice was not one of unalloyed joy. He says he began with chewing tobacco, though he quickly learned the *social class implications of that habit and graduated to pipes and then cigars. In most of his Mississippi writings and *The Gilded Age*, he uses tobacco habits as a marker of class.

Nor did those many family members who were out to *reform him allow him to indulge his habit freely. Olivia in particular tried to get him to stop, but in a letter of 13 January 1870 he defended his choice in a way that fairly prevented her from forbidding the "habit which is filled with harmless pleasure":

No, Livy dear, I shall treat smoking just exactly as I would treat the forefinger of my left hand: If you asked me in all seriousness to cut that finger off, & I saw that you really meant it, & believed that the finger marred my well-being in some mysterious way, & it was plain to me that you could not be entirely satisfied & happy while it remained, I give you my word that I would cut it off.

With counterarguments like these, no wonder Clemens was nearly immune to permanent reform. In his last two years, he accepted his physician's conclusion that smoking was killing him (he died ultimately from congestive heart failure), yet he remained unrepentant because the habit, which he so enjoyed, took so long to have fatal consequences. Recently, scholars have speculated, on good evidence, that second-hand smoke probably contributed to Olivia's early death.

Tom Sawyer. When introducing Tom Sawyer to the public in *The Adventures of Tom Sawyer* (1876), Twain's preface averred, "Huck Finn is drawn from life; Tom Sawyer also, but not from an individual—he is a combination of the characteristics of three boys whom I knew, and therefore belongs to the composite order of architecture." In all likelihood, Clemens himself was one of the boys in the composite, though the primary model was Will Bowen. Clemens's 6 February 1870 letter to

Frontispiece by Worth Brehm for the 1910 Harper & Brothers edition of *The Adventures of Tom Sawyer*.

Bowen recounts many of their childhood adventures, some of which found their way into *Tom Sawyer*, as for instance his recollection of how they "used to undress & play Robin Hood in our shirt-tails, with lath swords, in the woods on Holliday's Hill on those long summer days." While he may have drawn his adventures from life, Clemens approached the book as "a hymn" to boyhood, coloring all of the incidents in a way that makes Tom's character fundamentally worthy of praise. While Tom violates most minor rules, his good heart keeps him from transgressing his society's basic tenets, and his antics enliven an otherwise dreary town. Tom here is antihero as hero; a bad boy who makes good.

On finishing the book, though, Clemens had a change of heart toward his character, seeing in him not so much a potential to grow up into generous adulthood as a shallow showiness that promised no significant growth. He wrote to Howells:

> I have finished the story & didn't take the chap beyond boyhood. I believe it would be fatal to do it in any shape but autobiographically—like Gil Blas. I perhaps made a mistake in not writing it in the first person. If I went on, now, & took him into manhood, he would just be like all the one-horse men in literature & the reader would conceive a hearty contempt for him. (5 July 1875)

In this mood, he began a sequel, *Adventures of Huckleberry Finn*, in which Huck takes on the role of bad boy as hero and Tom is demoted to the position of puerile respectability. Tom does everything "by the book" even though the books he chooses enforce false moral standards and unearned "respectability." Huck's empirically based morality discovers more honest and humane grounds for social interaction. In this sequel, Clemens ended the hymn by sacrificing his boy angel to the devil.

But as much as Tom's showmanship made him a relief in the first novel and a burden in the second, it was not a trait Clemens could ignore, perhaps because it spoke to his own desire for *celebrity. Much as Tom hijacks the end of *Adventures of Huckleberry Finn*—though the book's ironic structure makes that piracy tragic— Tom persisted in hijacking Huck through three more sequels. One, *Tom and Huck Among the Indians*, Clemens abandoned early on; the others, *Tom Sawyer Abroad* and *Tom Sawyer Detective*, he published in 1894 and 1896 for mercenary rather than literary reasons. Huck narrates in the first person again in both published sequels, but he plays such a decided numbskull to Tom's know-it-all that it is hard to imagine he had been through his own adventures or has his own conscience. In every book, Huck admired Tom as showman. In noting the lack of irony in these last two books, the reader wonders if Clemens returned to his former admiration, too, or merely sold out to a flashy exterior that would sell well.

If Twain's last word on Tom is any indication, then it is this latter. In his *autobiography, he makes his feelings about Tom clear in a comparison he makes between Theodore Roosevelt and Tom:

Mr. Roosevelt is the Tom Sawyer of the political world of the twentieth century; always showing off; always hunting for a chance to show off; in his frenzied imagination the Great Republic is a vast Barnum circus with him for a clown and the whole world for audience; he would go to Halifax for half a chance to show off, and he would go to hell for a whole one. (2 December 1907)

Tom's one horse, apparently, was his need to show off, a need that Twain recognized as fundamentally human and that he had a good share of, but that he despised as a source of weakness and as a compromise to independence.

♦ SEE ALSO Joan of Arc; Tricksters.

TOM SAWYER, THE ADVENTURES OF. SEE *Adventures of Tom Sawyer, The.*

TOM SAWYER ABROAD (1893). In a 10 August 1892 letter from Germany to his business manager at the time, Fred Hall, Clemens wrote about an offer Mary Mapes Dodge, editor of *St. Nicholas Magazine* for children, had made him of five thousand dollars for a story of fifty thousand words. He had not accepted immediately because he wanted more money, but he instructed Hall to

> talk to Alden of Harpers; and the editor of Harper's Youth's Companion; and McClure; and write Howells[.] If they don't raise on Mrs. Dodge's offer, please accept her offer for me.... P.S. I have found *this* out, to wit: That Harper's Magazine paid Charley Warner $100 per 1000 words for those Californian articles.... If my market value is below Charley Warner's, it is a case of Since When? I should multiply it by two or three if required to testify.... The family are *strenuous* that this ... shall appear serially in St. Nicholas. Well, I would prefer that, too, but it seems to me that their offer of $5,000 for 50,000 words is just a considerable trifle moderate. Even Warner gets that.

But burdened by the capital demands of both *Webster and Company and the *Paige typesetter, Clemens settled for Dodge's terms. He dashed off a trivial story of forty thousand words, unsure of whether the focus was on Huck Finn or Tom Sawyer; and sent it to Dodge with permission for her to cut any offending parts—"I tried to leave the improprieties all out; if I didn't, Mrs. Dodge can scissor them out"—and collected four thousand dollars in two installments. After collecting the first payment, he promptly forgot about the quite forgettable piece until November 1893, when the first of six installments appeared.

That is when he discovered that Dodge went further than mere scissoring of references to sweat, drunkenness, and *profanity; she actually changed Huck's grammar and diction. When he discovered this, the inflammable Clemens burned.

According to his illustrator Dan Beard, Clemens stormed into the magazine's editorial office to say "God Almighty Himself has no right to put words in my mouth that I never used." While Clemens then instructed Hall not to use the *St. Nicholas* text in the book version, most of the book was already typeset, and the story was not worth enough to make expensive changes. Only the English edition published by Chatto and Windus was not bowdlerized, but since it was set from a carbon copy of a typescript Clemens had made from his manuscript, it did not include the changes Clemens himself had made on the original typescript. Not until the Mark Twain Project published a corrected text in volume 4 of the *Works of Mark Twain* (University of California Press, 1980) did a correct text appear in public. Corrected or not, this uninspired story is unlikely ever to occupy a significant place in the public imagination.

♦ SEE ALSO Censorship; Finances.

TOURS. De rigueur for any American of high *social class was the "grand tour," a trip through *Europe to see the celebrated monuments of western culture, to learn class-appropriate attitudes toward art, music, literature, language—in short, toward "high culture." Such trips were postulated as civilizing journeys, as efforts to broaden the experience of Americans, reputedly provincial, especially as regarded money. The works of Henry *James, that literary consciousness so appropriately cited as the foil to Mark Twain's, turn incessantly on this motif, but as is so often the case, Twain's work significantly overlaps James's from a radically different point of view. Twain's career as a literary man whose work originated in *journalism set him off on that mercantile footing so opposed to the principles of the grand tour, and his first major book, *The Innocents Abroad*, serves substantially as a parody of the class pieties of those who espouse the grand tour as well as of the objects toured.

Yet in that very trip of his, his contact with Mary Mason *Fairbanks pulled him into the circle of believers. The *lecture he wrote after he returned from Europe and the Middle East played ambivalently with the idea of the grand tour, on the one hand mocking American travelers in the very title of the lecture, "The American Vandal Abroad," but on the other, supplying a moral that "[i]t liberalizes the Van[dal] to travel—you never saw a bigoted, opinionated, stubborn, narrow-minded, self-conceited, *almighty mean man* in your life but he had stuck in one place ever since he was born" (in *Mark Twain's Letters*, vol. 2, 1990, p. 265). As he explained to Fairbanks, this moral "is an entirely gratuitous contribution & will be a clear gain to the societies employing me, for it isn't deduced from anything there is in the lecture" (12 October 1868). In explaining his motives for inserting the moral, he makes it clear that he is not sure whether this idea is true or not, but that he knows Fairbanks believes it, and her belief matters to him.

In his own case, travel to this point in his life was less a journey toward self-development than an escape from a self and life he often found dissatisfying. On the verge of departure for Europe in 1867, he wrote his mother and family, "All I do know or feel, is, that I am wild with impatience to move—move—*Move!* Half a dozen times I have wished I had sailed long ago in some ship that wasn't going to keep me chained here to chafe for lagging ages while she got ready to go. Curse the endless delays! They always kill me—they make me neglect every duty & then I have a conscience that tears me like a wild beast. I wish I never had to stop *any-where* a month. I do more mean things, the moment I get a chance to fold my hands & sit down that ever I can get forgiveness for" (1 June 1867). In this light, the moral at the end of chapter 79 of *Roughing It* seems less comic.

But of course, these bachelor tours of Clemens, his trips from the heartland to eastern cities in search of work, his journey to Nevada, trips to *California, and his journey to Hawaii were not tours in the classic sense, nor really was the trip with the *Quaker City* in that Twain's travel letters were his vocation, not the avocation of a gentlemanly traveler. Through his job as professional writer, Twain became, to a large degree, the stand-in for the great American public that both wanted to travel and could not, and as such, he was never in the position to adopt publicly the persona of a cultivated man. Instead, he needed to denigrate the very idea of cultivation at the same time that he provided an ersatz version of it. This is true not only of *Innocents Abroad*, but also of *A Tramp Abroad*, various short pieces, such as "Travelling without a Courier," and to lesser degrees, because his travels were not to the European fountainhead of Western culture, in "Some Rambling Notes of an Idle Excursion" and *Following the Equator*.

As a professional tourist, his job was to "do" a place, that is, to sweep through it quickly, draw up impressions as if they were based in deep understanding, and move on. He was not unaware of the shallowness of this exercise. In his 1879 notebook, for instance, when drafting materials for *A Tramp Abroad* he spent pages jotting down pithy judgments of France and Germany, including lines like "France has nei-ther winter nor summer nor morals—apart from these drawbacks it is a fine coun-try." Embedded in his list but not altering his practice, he observed, "You see, I generalize with intrepidity from single instances. It is the tourist's custom. When I see a man jump from the Vendome column, I say, 'They like to do that in France.'"

But in Clemens's personal life, once married to Olivia Langdon, the idea of tour as a marker of class and gentility was one he accepted readily. The irony, of course, was that while he was not from Olivia's class background, he had seen much of the world when they married in 1870 whereas she had not. Her first trip abroad came in 1873 during a two-year span in which he made two other working trips to England without his family. The 1873 trip with Olivia, Susy, Susy's nursemaid, Olivia's friend Clara Spaulding, and Samuel's secretary, Samuel C. Thompson, was more stressful on the formally educated Olivia, traveling with a baby, than on her seasoned traveler husband. Her first reaction to England on viewing its countryside from Liverpool to London was joy in having her stereotypes confirmed; she wrote to her sister on 31 May 1873 that "the ride was the most charming that I ever could imagine.... So many things that I had read were made plain to me as we rode along—the little thatched villages, the foot paths by the side of the road—It was like riding for all those hours through Central Park." But it didn't take long for Olivia to become homesick. Part of the problem was that Twain's celebrity was so great that London society drew the Clemens family into its whirl, preventing them from doing any of the sightseeing that Olivia thought of as the point of travel. Samuel concurred from a pragmatic point of view since he needed to sightsee, too, if he were to make a book out of his English journey. Apparently Olivia's tastes were not that far from those of Clemens's home audience, and he knew it.

Yet the Clemens family made lasting friends among the shapers of culture in their brief stay in Britain; they in fact developed the culture that the grand tour was supposed to provide. Not surprisingly, they planned to go back when their children were older, this time to make a significant stay of it so that they could do more than just be tourists in the modern sense. Their second trip to Europe from April 1878 to September 1879 saw the family living for extended periods in various cities in Germany and in Paris, France. While they were spending time in Europe partly to "economize" during the extended economic depression that had so damaged their income from 1873 to 1879, and while Sam partly relished leaving the United States to escape the shame he felt over his *Whittier birthday speech, Clemens was in Europe primarily to gather material for another travel narrative mocking the grand tour as an agent of civilization. Olivia and Sam also saw this trip as an opportunity to raise cosmopolitan children and to acquire artworks for their Hartford home. The gap between Mark Twain's philistinism and Clemens's cultural hunger was never greater. The upshot was that Clemens did acquire a real cosmopolitanism, one not shot through with crass Europhilia, nor with patriotic anti-European sentiment, but a more complex liberalization of sentiments that made Clemens truly a world citizen.

One marker of this shift is the amount of time the Clemens family spent living outside of the United States in the last twenty years of Samuel Clemens's life. The Clemens family lived for extended stretches in Europe from June 1891 to October 1900, and again from October 1903 to July 1904. These European stays were punctuated by brief returns to the United States and by an around-the-world trip from July 1895 to August 1896. Life in Europe made strong economic sense for the family: it was easier to live on a grand scale in countries that were at that time cheaper than the United States. Samuel and Olivia undertook *health regimens, and sought out cultural education for Susy and Clara, both of whom were pursuing careers in *music. On the whole, the Clemens family was comfortable traveling, able to make homes on two continents.

The liberalization that Clemens once mocked did in fact finally affect the works of Mark Twain. *Following the Equator*'s deep cultural relativism is the culmination of that liberalization, and Twain's regular resistance to American *imperialism in his last decade turned an attitude into action. So while in his early years travel may have been no more to Twain than an escape from himself, and while it was a job for him all his life, the moral he once facetiously adopted proved true in his own case: by being almost always on the move, he did finally arrive at a much broader sense of humanity.

TRADE UNIONS. SEE Labor Movement.

TRAMP ABROAD, A (1880). Twain called *A Tramp Abroad* "that most infernally troublesome book" (to William Dean *Howells, 5 March 1880) because the circumstances surrounding its composition and publication were not the happiest (though neither were they as tragic as those of *Roughing It*). But that Twain could produce yet another successful comic travel narrative under the stress he felt at the time is still astonishing. That stress began, perhaps, as early as 1873 when the financial panic and subsequent depression damaged not only the sales of Mark Twain's books but the Clemens family income from Olivia's inheritance. Through the 1870s, residing in their new Hartford home and trying to live at the level of opulence to which Olivia had always been accustomed and to which Samuel had long aspired, they felt constantly pressed for money. They resolved ultimately to live for a while in *Europe to cut living expenses while giving Samuel material for a book. Clemens's shame over his ostensibly failed performance at the *Whittier birthday dinner in December 1877 may have added a sense of urgency to their departure, and they left New York for Hamburg in April 1878. Their idea of cutting expenses had merely to do with the relative cheapness of an equivalent lifestyle in Europe; they did not actually change how they lived. In fact, they took along not only a servant for their daughters, but also as a guest Olivia's good friend Clara Spaulding.

Clemens also paid the expenses for his friend Joseph *Twichell to join them for a portion of the trip. Twichell met them in Heidelberg in August to accompany Clemens through Germany, Switzerland, and France. They had traveled as companions before in a May 1877 trip to Bermuda, a trip Twain turned into "Some Rambling Notes of an Idle Excursion," a series of *Atlantic Monthly* articles published later that year. His payment of Twichell's expenses was a business investment inasmuch as Twichell and Twain shared observations, reminiscences, and anecdotes in ways that helped spur Clemens's literary creativity. In *Tramp Abroad*, Twain renames Twichell "Harris," and downgrades his status from that of Congregationalist minister to that of Twain's factotum and camp follower.

After Twichell left, the Clemens family visited Italy before settling in Munich from November until February and then Paris from March to mid-July; after brief visits to Belgium and the Netherlands, they spent the rest of the summer in England. During all of this hopping around Europe, Clemens worked steadily on the manuscript of *A Tramp Abroad*, but found the writing painfully tedious, perhaps because he did not give himself the usual luxury of pigeonholing the manuscript when inspiration failed. Instead he found himself in a cycle of worry and anger that damaged his humor. He found himself venting his anger in diatribes against everything he found disgusting in Europe, and he found much. This trip returned him to the American nationalism of *The Innocents Abroad* after his intervening European trips had made him much more Europhilic. In particular, he found French culture abominable, primarily because his Victorian sense of propriety was offended by the relative openness of the French about *sexuality. Most of his attempts to attack what he found disgusting he cut, including his chapter comparing the French to the Comanches, as inappropriate to a humorous book.

He did not finish writing until after the first parts of the manuscript had been set and the "proof sheets were piling up." The last of the book proved the hardest, and in a letter to Howells he described the last months of working on the book as

> a life-&-death battle.... I required 300 pages of MS, & I have written near 600 since I saw you—& tore it all up except 288.... I took the 288 pages to Bliss & told him that was the very last line I should ever write on this book. (A book which required 2600 pages, of MS, & I have written nearer four thousand, first & last.
>
> I am as soary (& flighty) as a rocket, to-day, with the unutterable joy of getting that Old Man of the Sea off my back, where he has been roosting more than a year & a half. Next time I make a contract before writing the book may I suffer the righteous penalty & be burnt, like the injudicious believer. (8 January 1880)

Clemens's relief at finishing was exceeded only by Howells's energetic praise of the book in a letter of 22 March 1880:

> I must tell you privately what a joy it has been to Mrs. Howells and me. Since I have read it, I feel sorry for I shall not be able to read it again for a week, and in what else shall I lose myself so wholly? Mrs. Howells declares it the wittiest book she ever read, and I say there is *sense* enough in it for ten books.... Well, you are a blessing. You ought to believe in God's goodness, since he has bestowed upon the world such a delightful genius as yours to lighten its troubles.

This praise encouraged Clemens himself to see that what had become a hated chore was a substantial and valuable book.

Howells naturally would see the sense in it inasmuch as *Tramp Abroad*'s thematic structure reinforces some of the aesthetic and moral principles of social *realism that

Howells espoused and that Twain was now agreeing with. Twain had moved from his earlier agreement with Charles Dudley *Warner's *sentimentalism to Howells's brand of what the two called "photographic realism," of seeing what exactly was there rather than cleaning things up into Warner's "idealization of nature."

The book's structure enables Twain to *parody idealism every step of the way by having a gentleman narrator go to Europe to learn something about the two highest arts according to idealism—*painting and *music—while collecting the lore that gives these arts their poetical, romantic associations. So his primary task, as it was in *Innocents Abroad*, is to cast a realist's eye on Europe. This time, he does it ironically from a different point of view, the point of view of the gentleman who *wishes* to see things not through his own eyes but through the eyes of others. Chapters 2 and 3 warn the reader of his romantic proclivities, asking us to be on guard against his subjectivity, and by that standard, the subjectivity of every European traveler. From then on, he gives us numerous accounts of European legends, some straight, some completely manufactured, but passed off as authentic. The thrust of this legend telling, especially in the context of the *"Bluejay Yarn"'s tall tale structure, is to turn Europe's mythology into mere yarn-spinning, no different from the comic braggadocio of the American frontier—mere pastime, not morally worthy of emulation.

Besides attacking European culture, Twain attacks American sycophants of that culture. Twain as philistine narrator aspires, as do so many of the crass Americans he describes meeting throughout his journey, to move away from the practical civilization of the west, to the Romantic civilization of hierarchy, storied tradition, feudal exploitation, and the ostensible cultivation of Europe. But he insists that such "cultivation" for Americans is fraudulent. Regarding lovers of Wagnerian opera, for instance, he says:

> There is nothing the Germans like so much as an opera. . . . This is the legitimate result of habit and education. Our nation will like opera, too, by and by, no doubt. One in fifty of those who attend our operas likes it already, perhaps, but I think a good many of the other forty-nine go in order to learn to like it, and the rest in order to be able to talk knowingly about it. The latter usually hum the airs while they are being sung, so that their neighbors may perceive that they have been to operas before. The funerals of these do not occur often enough. (chapter 9)

In spite of this kind of frequent, direct denunciation of American pretension, the book usually attacks through ironic parody. As narrator, Twain displays extreme arrogance and laziness, and spends lavishly for mere effect (as in his absurd parody of a gentlemanly scientific expedition in his ascent of the Riffelberg). This behavior sets him up as the kind of American Clemens wanted Americans no longer to be, namely, aristocrats manqué. In thus mocking the idea of the grand tour of Europe as the appropriate way to "finish" a gentleman, he challenged conventional ideals of gentility, instead depicting the gentleman as scoundrel or, rather, as tramp.

He also attacked idealistic aesthetic standards directly in his examinations of painting and music. He attacked, in particular, the music of Richard Wagner and the art criticism of John Ruskin. Of Wagner's music, he wrote:

> A German lady in Munich told me that a person could not like Wagner's music at first, but must go through the deliberate process of learning to like it,—then he would have his sure reward; for when he had learned to like it he would hunger for it and never be able to get enough of it. . . . I *could* have said, "But would you advise a person to deliberately practice having the toothache in the pit of his stomach for a couple of years in order that he might then come to enjoy it?" (chapter 10)

In other words, cultivation of an unnatural, merely ideal pleasure requires an ascetic renunciation, not an aesthetic development.

One pursues such "cultivation," Twain suggests, not for the intrinsic pleasure of moral, intellectual, or spiritual transcendence, all promised in an idealistic hierarchy of the arts, but rather for the base social pleasure of snobbery:

> There are two kinds of music,—one kind which one feels, just as an oyster might, and another sort which requires a higher faculty, a faculty which must be assisted and developed by teaching. Yet if base music gives certain of us wings, why should we want any other? But we do. We want it because the higher and better like it. But we want it without giving it the necessary time and trouble; so we climb into that upper tier, that dress circle, by a lie: we *pretend* we like it. I know several of that sort of people,—and I propose to be one of them myself when I get home with my fine European education. (chapter 24)

So in developing an appreciation of idealistic art, the viewer must learn to cultivate lies. That's exactly Twain's complaint about Ruskin's art criticism, and about much idealistic painting—it lies about nature, and "only rigid cultivation can enable a man to find truth in a lie" (chapter 24).

In seeing the hierarchical nature of sentimental realism and other idealistic art, Twain uncovered what he felt was its greatest lie—that in cleaning up a vision of the world, it allowed the cultivated to become voyeurs of the world, not vital agents in it. Hence, in hiring an agent to do all of his work for him, Twain lives in an attenuated world of imagination unsupported by vivifying experience. In chapter 35, for instance, he hears of some ladders Swiss locals use to climb a precipice. He orders Harris to make the ascent, so I could put the thrill and horror of it in my book, and he accomplished the feat successfully, through a subagent, for three francs, which I paid. It makes me shudder yet when I think of what I felt when I was clinging there between heaven and earth in the person of that proxy. At times the world swam around me, and I could hardly keep from letting go, so dizzying was the appalling danger. . . . When the people of the hotel found that I had been climbing those crazy Ladders, it made me an object of considerable attention.

Here Twain mocks his own readers as well as his hypercultivated self for believing that sympathetic imagination is more valuable than real experience.

In challenging the value of sympathetic imagination, Twain challenges the moral foundation of sentimental literature, which held that human beings could strengthen their *moral senses, and thus become better behaved people, through reading imaginative literature. Twain felt on the contrary that the exercise of sympathetic imagination could become an end in itself and morality an empty abstraction by extension. When he and Harris witness a girl nearly fall off a cliff, for instance, Twain chastises Harris for his relief at the girl's escape. He was

glad the girl was saved because it spared him any anguish, but Harris cared not a straw for my feelings, or my loss of such a literary plum, snatched from my very mouth at the instant it was ready to drop into it. His selfishness was sufficient to place his own gratification in being spared suffering clear before all concern for me, his friend. Apparently, he did not once reflect upon the valuable details which would have fallen like a windfall to me: fishing the child out—witnessing the surprise of the family and the stir the thing would have made among the peasants—then a Swiss funeral—then the roadside monument, to be paid for by us and have our names mentioned in it. And we should have gone into Baedeker and been immortal. I was silent. I was too much hurt to complain. (chapter 36)

Cultivated to appreciate other people's suffering, Twain wants disaster, and even if he doesn't witness it first-hand, he imagines it into his book anyway. His powers of sympathetic imagination have made him bloodthirsty and selfish, rather than compassionate and correspondingly generous. In passages such as these, Twain's behavior ironically makes the case for morality based on experience, not on abstractions made from the superior distance of cultivation.

Such is the sense Howells found in the book, and as much as he appreciated Twain's attack on conventional aesthetics, he also appreciated the wisdom of Twain's alternative. In the "Bluejay Yarn" in chapter 3, Twain posits humor as an avenue to truth and beauty, as a capacity to see what's really there rather than what one wishes. Thus does he offer reality as an alternative to the cynicism attendant on disappointed idealism.

A Tramp Abroad was well received in its time, reversing the trend of declining sales Twain had experienced with each book since *Innocents Abroad*. As difficult as the book had been to write, its success seemed to reinvigorate his creative powers as well as to deepen the moral vision he brought to his work, including to the completion and revision of *Adventures of Huckleberry Finn*. The book sold quite well in Europe as well as in America, and may have been the most popular of Twain's books in England during his lifetime. But as popular as the book was in the nineteenth century, its star has faded since, perhaps in part because the aesthetic debates the book engages are no longer culturally central, perhaps because too many twentieth-century critics took Twain's word for it when he called the book "a gossipy volume" that "talks about anything and everything, and always drops a subject the moment my interest in it begins to slacken" (quoted in the *New York Times*, 11 May 1879). Most twentieth-century accounts thus dismiss the book as formless and purposeless and choose to concentrate on the comic gems sprinkled throughout, especially the "Bluejay Yarn" or "The Awful German Language," or approach the text as a window into other of Twain's books. But it's always dangerous to take an ironist at his word about his own writing, and *A Tramp Abroad* took too much work to be a mere Tramp.

TRAVEL. SEE Tours.

TRICKSTERS. On 10 October 1907, Clemens dictated for his *autobiography a lament about the absurdity of human life:

> I must get that stupendous fancy out of my head. At first it was vague, dim, sardonic, wonderful; but night after night, of late, it is growing too definite— quite too clear and definite, and haunting, and persistent. It is the Deity's mouth—His open mouth—laughing at the human race! The horizon is the lower lip; the cavernous vast arch of the sky is the open mouth and throat; the soaring bend of the Milky Way constitutes the upper teeth. It is a mighty laugh, and deeply impressive—even when it is silent; I can endure it then, but when it bursts out in crashing thunders of delight, and the breath gushes forth in a glare of white lightnings, it makes me shudder. (10 October 1907)

Here, the idea of the Christian God laughing at his creation as if it were a *practical joke or *confidence game puts the sardonic Twain out of sorts, precisely because in true satirist's form he accepts a single meaning to creation, a single truth to life, and this single meaning is too painful to bear.

Monotheism has its advantages. It helps a culture cohere by giving it an ideological center. It helps a culture maintain a consistent moral code around that centralizing ideology. But when it comes to *explaining* human life rather than guiding it, polytheism works much better. Competing gods as forces immanent in the universe explain life's chaos in an aesthetically, if not morally, pleasing way, which is another way of saying that *satire is comedy's version of monotheism while *humor acknowledges the many guises of god as trickster.

Twain was always torn between the creative pluralism of humor and the structured meaningfulness of satire; in his early work he usually grounded his humor in the puzzles of human interaction, writing mainly of confidence games and of human self-deception. Until late in his career, he rarely rose to the metaphysical mode of trickster tales, in which supernatural characters vie for supremacy in a world only analogically connected to the human. One of these rare moments is in the *"Bluejay Yarn" from *A Tramp Abroad*, in which Twain invests his unreliable inside narrator, Jim Baker, with supernatural power in describing animal speech. The tale of the jays pursuing their own ends in the face of a world ultimately impervious to their efforts speaks as an existential analog to the human condition. The yarn's ending suggests that humor saves people from the futility of labor, the futility of life.

Incidentally, in having the jays return to the site of a humorous occurrence, Twain seems to be telling a tale out of the traditions of some of the seminomadic Native American tribes of the western and northwestern United States, in which the site of a comic incident becomes a cultural mecca. Insofar as Twain was exposed to *Native Americans and to Euro-American raconteurs who had lived long enough on the frontier to have absorbed Native American mores and humor, Twain was exposed to one of the world's great trickster characters, Coyote, who is more than a mere con artist, something more metaphysical, something more like that described in Maidu Coyote tales, in which Coyote is the great opponent of Earthmaker. Earthmaker wants a stable and ordered world; Coyote wants it to be a place of pleasure and riot. Using his own bodily functions as a source of power, he finds that his very urine and feces give him strength in his battle against Earthmaker for control of the world. Coyote brings mess and death as well as joy, and he pays the price as much as do any. He is a principle of anarchy as a prelude to creativity, of deception as an essential element of growth and change, of divine power not merely divided against the stability and order of Earthmaker, but also against itself in its turbulent self-creation through self-destruction. The coyote in *Roughing It*, one moment a satiric representation of the Native Americans whom Twain despised, rises to a supernatural level, representing powers that the mere Easterner cannot hope to understand.

Twain did not, of course, need Native American tales to give him the idea of trickster gods; they exist in the classical tradition, in European folk traditions, and in the

African traditions Clemens learned in childhood on his uncle Quarles's farm. Twain's outpouring of trickster tales beginning in the mid- to late 1890s about first the Christian god and then about other possible gods suggests this multiple derivation.

In particular, when in Austria in 1897, Twain began writing the first of the so-called *Mysterious Stranger Manuscripts, *"Chronicle of Young Satan," which includes, in its satiric portrayal of a dissipated Roman Catholic priest, one of many versions of European folktales of cheating the devil. But these differ from classical or Native American trickster tales. In all of these, human beings outfox the trickster god of Christianity—namely, the devil himself—suggesting that human wit in combination with God's grace keeps the trickster powers at bay. But when Twain writes the story, he uses it to challenge not only human hubris, but also the concept of grace itself. While the angel Satan who infests Eseldorf is ostensibly God's regent on earth to this town, every bargain he strikes harms human beings. What Twain begins, then, as an attack on human beings, quickly reverses into a lament for human beings, who are the butt of God's merciless joke, a joke defined monotheistically as satire. Satan describes humor as merely the laughter of a superior being at its inferior when he calls laughter humanity's "one really effective weapon. . . . Power, Money, Persuasion, Supplication, Persecution—these can lift at a colossal humbug,—push it a little—crowd it a little—weaken it a little, century by century: but only Laughter can blow it to rags and atoms at a blast." Such laughter reveals and judges confidence games while assuming absolute truth; it is thus not the laughter of the "Blue-jay Yarn," of real trickster narrative, because as much as humanity is the butt of the joke, humanity in these terms cannot laugh at itself. It finds no redemption in its own absurdity. When Satan says that humanity doesn't know how to use laughter to free itself from absurd human institutions, Theodore Fischer, the narrator, says "I was too much hurt to laugh." As he wrote his way into the story, Twain found that, in destroying humbug, satire is more than human beings can stand; some other kind of laughter would have to do the trick, perhaps the laughter of humor, an embracing laughter, one that laughs with rather than at human foibles.

In turning to the next draft, "Schoolhouse Hill," Mark Twain again had an angel come from the Christian god, this time to a Missouri town, where he tries to understand the peculiarities of humanity. This angel does not deride his inferiors, but spurred mainly by curiosity disconnected from human emotions, he can't laugh at all. The tricks he pulls have no substance, they work no deeper magic, and Twain abandoned the story.

His last draft, *"No. 44, The Mysterious Stranger," finds a different kind of god, one not so much an angel representing a distant, ordered, and impervious power, but rather a divinity that incarnates itself in multiplicity rather than unity, in chaos rather than in order, in feeling rather than in reason. No. 44 flaunts his supernatural powers in a way that marks his motivations as distinctly human, which means familiar but still mysterious. Like a boy, he wants to "show off." This is *Tom

Sawyer as god, rather than Tom Sawyer as confidence man, but with significant differences. He despises awe and takes no romantic pleasure in pain. To No. 44, life makes no sense except as spectacle, as pleasure, and he introduces his young companion to the liberating pleasure of chaos. Like the Bluejay, he uncovers redemption in distance from seriousness, and like the lazy gentleman narrator of *Roughing it*, he finds life's gusto not in work directed toward serious ends, but rather in taking advantage of other people's purposes to drive his leisure.

In this final sense, then, Twain sees God as divided rather than monolithic, immanent rather than transcendent, and such conceptions pervade many of his late literary extravaganzas, such as "The *Great Dark," with its trickster Superintendent of Dreams, and *"Three Thousand Years among the Microbes," in which the outside frame makes fun of the very idea of a monolithic truth by suggesting that life's meaning is always a translation through subjectivity, and in which the inside story suggests that divinity is merely the cycle of feeding and being fed upon that channels force in the natural world.

To surrender to such images is to deny the moral force of satire, as Twain does in the *unfinished, *posthumously published "The Secret History of Eddypus." The tale's action, a serious effort of scholars to uncover true history in the face of religious *censorship, seems ripe for satire, which this piece threatens to become at the outset, becoming one more outpouring of Twain's bitterness at the "damned human race." But instead, he humorously turns the piece inward, laughing at posterity's translation of Twain himself:

> Mark Twain, Bishop of New Jersey, . . . the most ancient writer known to us by his works, . . . The Father of History. . . . The Father of History had many gifts, but it is as a philosopher that he shows best. But he had a defect which much crippled all his varied mental industries, and impaired the force and lucidity of his philosophical product most of all. This was his lack of the sense of humor.

Such mistranslation, in the words of the heroic rescuer of a past buried and condemned, turns the laughter back on the very enterprise of truth seeking. Truth itself becomes subjective and creative and multiple, and fractures and errors become more pleasing than the truth itself. Such a world ruled by the trickster spirit became one of Twain's alternatives to despair.

♦ SEE ALSO Animals; Frame Narrative; Religion.

"True Story, Repeated Word for Word as I Heard It, A."

This is the first piece Clemens published in the *Atlantic Monthly,* and he at first proposed to publish it under his own name rather than under his comic *pseudonym precisely because he wanted it to be taken seriously as literature rather than as comic ephemera. He feared that his subtitle would have been discounted as ironic had he printed it under the name *Mark Twain, and for once he wanted the biographical underpinning of his piece to outweigh the fictional trappings. In this case, the facts were of the life of Mary Ann Cord, a former slave who after the Civil War went to work for Susan and Theodore *Crane in Elmira, New York. Clemens and his family regularly spent summers at the Crane's Quarry Farm home, where he learned of Cord's history.

Such a grounding in biographical fact does not, however, diminish for a moment the artistry with which Clemens constructed the piece, for he used Cord's tale not merely as a source of local color, but more significantly, to attack the racial prejudices held as much by northern liberals as by southern apologists for *slavery. Specifically in this case, Clemens attacks the widely held white belief that the mask of good humor worn by blacks revealed their real emotional interiority.

To see how he does this, it is useful to compare "A True Story" to its slightly earlier contemporary and companion in subject matter, the newspaper sketch titled *"Sociable Jimmy." In both, Clemens reveals his fascination with *dialect, particularly with African-American dialect, and with the power of a spoken performance to captivate an audience. But in "Sociable Jimmy," Mark Twain as narrator remains in a comfortable position as distant observer. His admiration is the admiration of a superior intelligence for some fascinating new discovery, but the play of the piece is entirely on the surface. "A True Story" begins with the narrator—here named "Misto C" by "Aunt Rachel"—assuming the same position of fascinated superiority in observing the verbal performance of a servant. But the action opens with the frame narrator asking the performer what her performance means, and in the process, this outside narrator gets his comeuppance. He is humbled in learning his error, and the staging of the piece, with Aunt Rachel beginning her story while sitting on a step below her interlocutor, but quickly, as she warms to her story, looming over him in the growing darkness of twilight, reveals the inversion of expected status.

This inversion is reinforced in the way the frame narrator plays his part. Unlike in "Sociable Jimmy" in which the frame narrator gives repeated stage directions, finally closing the sketch with a description of Jimmy's actions, in "A True Story," the frame narrator fades out, leaving Rachel the task of giving her own stage directions in the story and of having the last word.

In publishing this story in the *Atlantic*, Clemens knew he was writing for a staunch northern audience, most of whom had been abolitionists, readers familiar with the slave narratives that made such an important part of the antislavery rhetoric of the antebellum years. In this context, what Clemens does not report is as important as what he does. Whether Cord told her story in just this way or not, Clemens's refusal to concentrate on her sufferings in slavery would have stood out to a reader of the *Atlantic* as a violation of the conventions of slave narratives. Cord speaks of the disruption of her family and of her beatings in a matter-of-fact way that, in belying the emotional intensity of her experience, allows her her dignity. Clemens does not require her to parade her sufferings; rather, he allows her the depth of positive feelings, of reconnection to a member of her family, while showing her as a subject capable not only of self-directed action but of emotional discretion. What she reveals over the course of the story is the seriousness of real emotion, both negative and positive, in direct contrast to the mask of "happy darky" that she wears in the typical course of social relations with whites.

Clemens as outside narrator stands in for his expected readers, serving as the lightning rod for their own humiliation and for expiating their ignorance. In so doing he uses the same technique of ignorance revealed that he learned to play to such comic effect in *Roughing It* and that became central to his guise as Mark Twain. Here, he revealed to himself the serious potentials in the same dramatic structure, and while at this point he did not trust the Twain name to carry that seriousness—though he did, finally, sign the piece with his nom de plume—from this point forward, his repertoire included a new capacity for depth, in the words of Mark Twain.

♦ SEE ALSO Frame Narrative; Race Relations.

TRUMBULL, JAMES HAMMOND (1821–1897). Linguist, bibliographer, chief librarian of the Watkinson Library of Trinity College, and Connecticut secretary of state from 1861 to 1866, J. Hammond Trumbull was a friend and fellow *Monday Evening Club member of Clemens in *Hartford. Trumbull's massive erudition served Clemens numerous times in his writing, most particularly when Clemens and Charles Dudley *Warner asked Trumbull to supply chapter mottoes for *The Gilded Age* and when Clemens used Trumbull's *The True-Blue Laws of Connecticut* as a source for chapters 15, 23, and 27 in *The Prince and the Pauper*. Clemens also drew on Trumbull for literary counsel. Occasionally Trumbull's replies show his sense of humor, as when Clemens asked Trumbull for advice on whether or not a projected dream ending to a play had ever been done before and then telegraphed to say that he no longer needed the advice as he had changed his mind about the play's ending. Trumbull replied:

> My dear Mr. Clemens, You never got a wronger sow by the ear than when you came down on me for knowledge of the modern drama and I was greatly relieved by the telegram that came an hour after your call. I did, to be sure, remember, dimly, some such device for a denouement as the one you proposed to use, but I had lost my copy of the play—it was Tchan-Kin's "casket of Five Pearls, or the Princess Lu-Pu's slipper"—and I didn't like to quote it from memory. Ferdusi has, I believe, a similar conceit in one of his poems—which has not yet been translated to English; and the Persian commentator

suggests that he has borrowed it from the Sanskrit, but the Sanskrit original appears to have been lost before the time of Panini. I may be mistaken in fancying that there is something like your back-action dream in the Hawaiian Kaao of "Laieikawai," for you would yourself have remembered it if it was in that charming legend. The plot somewhat resembles that of the Zulu—no, I am wrong; it is the Efik "Kpupru or uk nkpo"—but *there* the heroine doesn't wake up till *after* she has been executed—which relieves you of the suspicion of plagiarism. On the whole—the question was a troublesome one, and I'm glad you have unasked it. I am gladder yet, that you have changed your wind-up. Yours truly, J. H. Trumbull. (22 July 1874)

TWICHELL, REV. JOSEPH HOPKINS (1838–1910).

Joseph Twichell, pastor of *Hartford's Asylum Hill Congregationalist Church from 1865 until he retired in 1910, was probably Samuel Clemens's closest and longest friend, a man who shared Clemens's life in almost every particular from shortly after their first meeting in 1868 to when Twichell officiated at Clemens's funeral more than forty years later. Their closeness could have been expected when Clemens, while courting Olivia Langdon, was trying to convert to Christianity, but it persisted long after Clemens turned apostate against *religion entirely. While Clemens often befriended clergymen, his relationship with Twichell was exceptional in part because Twichell was exceptional in an era when Americans were coming to expect an increasingly fastidious character from their ministers. Twichell had a breadth of vision that enabled him to accept Clemens's most outré behavior, including his theological ruminations, as the efforts of an earnest seeker.

Unlike many Congregationalist clergymen, Twichell was not bred to the cloth, though his deacon father cared deeply about religion. Twichell's early life suggested a different path. In his undergraduate years at Yale, he was an active member in the secret society Scroll and Key, rowed on the crew, and once was the leader of a traditional undergraduate festivity that got out of hand, accidentally killing a fireman. He was nonetheless an excellent student, winning a prestigious prize in English composition. After graduation in 1859, he enrolled in the Union Theological Seminary, interrupting his studies during the *Civil War to enroll as a chaplain in the New York Zouaves, the roughest regiment he could find. He finished his divinity degree after the war at Andover Theological Seminary.

His war experiences took him through some of the hardest fighting in the eastern theater under General Daniel E. Sickles. While not called to the ministry out of a love of doctrine, Twichell found his already capacious ideas about Christianity broadened during the war, ministering to a largely Roman Catholic regiment, and sharing his blanket with a Jesuit priest, Rev. J. B. O'Hagan. This background may explain his tolerance of Clemens's own heterodox theological musings. Indeed,

Twichell's own broad-mindedness may have influenced Clemens, for Twichell introduced Clemens to O'Hagan, beginning a friendship that challenged Clemens's anti-Catholic prejudices. As Clemens wrote to Charles Warren Stoddard on 1 February 1875, Twichell was taking him

> to have a "time" with a most jolly and delightful Jesuit priest who was all through the war with Joe. . . . I sent the Padre word that I knew all about the Jesuits, from the Sunday-school books and that I was well aware that he wanted to get Joe and me into his den and skin us and make religious parchment out of us after the ancient style of his communion since the days of good Loyola, but that I was willing to chance it and trust to Providence.

In this humor, Clemens both acknowledges and belittles an old prejudice that is dying hard. Typically for Twain, such a prejudice had to die through friendship with a person whose very being undercut the stereotype. Such a friendship with a practical-minded priest who shared Twichell's belief that Christianity was intended to ameliorate the asperities of men's lives as much as to save their souls may have spurred Clemens's remarks in *A Connecticut Yankee in King Arthur's Court* that, while the church may be rotten from power, many priests serve their flocks well.

Certainly Twichell was a generous pastor for Clemens, going beyond the duties of officiating at Clemens family marriages, christenings, and funerals. Having a broad, earthy sense of humor, Twichell was Clemens's favorite regular conversation partner. The two of them took frequent long walks during which they discussed everything that could come to the minds of two men who had seen much of the world and were interested in it all. In these walks, Twichell provided the audience that galvanized much of Twain's writing. It was Twichell who gave him the idea for turning his Mississippi experiences into a series of magazine sketches. The resultant *"Old Times on the Mississippi" is one of Twain's greatest accomplishments. It was with Twichell, too, that Clemens walked to Boston on a publicity stunt. He wrote in his *autobiography of their contact, then, with a hostler whose *profanity was so unconsciously artful as to delight but whose blasphemy was so intense that Twichell, as a minister, could not countenance it even as he could find no tactful way to discourage it.

Clemens may have loved the company of clergymen precisely because their conflict between propriety and humanity was so intense, and this conflict not only deviled Clemens in his own life, it delighted him to see it in the lives of others. In this spirit he shared much *off-color humor with Twichell and wrote *1601* with Twichell as his first audience. Twichell loved it, apparently with no embarrassment, which could not be said for William Dean *Howells's vexed appreciation of Clemens's "Elizabethan breadth of parlance."

Clemens so appreciated Twichell as walking and talking companion that he paid for Twichell to accompany him on several *tours, including one of Bermuda in

1877 that resulted in "Some Rambling Notes of an Idle Excursion," in which the character Peters is a modestly fictionalized Twichell. Twichell also joined Clemens in Europe for six weeks in 1878, six weeks that were crucial for Clemens's work on *A Tramp Abroad*, in which a radically fictionalized Twichell serves as the character Harris.

Clemens also appreciated Twichell as an intellectual companion and moral guide. Twichell was an early member of the *Monday Evening Club, so central to Clemens's intellectual development, and he also suggested books for Clemens to read. Especially in his later years when he was raging at the universe and castigating its maker, Clemens allowed Twichell generously to guide and cajole him back toward accepting his membership in the human race. Alarmed at Clemens's pessimism, Twichell tried to use Clemens's anticlerical bias as leverage to get Clemens to rethink his position: "Mark, the way you throw your rotten eggs at the human race doth arride me. We preachers are extensively accused of vilifying human nature, as you are aware; but I must own that for enthusiasm of misanthropy, you beat us out of sight" (24 August 1900). In this vein, he encouraged Clemens to reread Jonathan Edwards's *On Freedom of the Will*, hoping to turn Clemens away from an essentially Calvinistic *determinism by calling attention to its roots. Twain's reply shows a brusqueness and insensitivity to Twichell's intention, but a serious engagement with the issues:

> Until near midnight I wallowed and reeked with Jonathan in his insane debauch; rose immediately refreshed and fine at 10 this morning, but with a strange and haunting sense of having been on a three days' tear with a drunken lunatic.... He seems to concede the indisputable and unshakable dominion of Motive and Necessity (call them what he may, these are exterior forces and not under the man's authority, guidance or even suggestion)—then he suddenly flies the logic track and (to all seeming) makes the man and not these exterior forces responsible to God for the man's thoughts, words and acts. It is frank insanity. (February 1902)

While Twichell may have minded the brusqueness, he did not let it show. He instead served as both friend and pastor in lending an ear to Clemens's outbursts, all the while gently remonstrating about the targets of Clemens's attacks:

> All right, Mark, go ahead, I give you free leave to syphon out to me all such secretions whenever they accumulate to the pitch of discomfort.... 'Tis an old saying that "Some men's oaths are more worshipful than some men's prayer." The *motive* of your automatic curses, is, I allow, pure, though the *object* of them might, in my opinion, be more judiciously selected. (3 July 1905)

Such was the strength of Twichell's calling to minister to an anguished soul, but more importantly, such was his love for a dear friend. He wrote in a 13 June 1905 letter: "I love you, old fellow, in spite of all your bad behavior, very, very dearly." Though he didn't say it in so many words, Clemens reciprocated the sentiment.

♦ SEE ALSO Calvinism.

TYPEWRITER. Christopher Scholes made the first practical typewriter in 1867, patented it in 1868, and sold the patents to the Remington Arms Company in 1873 for $12,000. Remington had the wherewithal to improve, manufacture, and market typewriters, which came into wide use by the 1880s. Clemens's fascination with machines and with type made him early quite interested in typewriters, and he bought one for himself in December 1874 for $125. One of his first two letters he produced on it, to his brother on 9 December, praises the machine's virtues of saving paper, being faster than writing, and producing clean copy. But the other letter of that day, to Howells, expresses doubt: "I DONT KNOW WHETHER I AM OGING TO MAKE THIS TYPE-WRITING MACHINE GO OR NTO." The answer for himself was "not," and he turned his failure into a running gag in his letters to Howells, to whom he promised the machine. Before Howells could accept, Clemens had given it to Elisha Bliss. Clemens wrote:

> The machine is at Bliss's, grimly pursuing its appointed mission, slowly & implacably rotting away another man's chances for salvation. I have sent Bliss word *not* to donate it to a charity (though it *is* a pity to fool away a chance to do a charity an ill turn), but to let me know when he has got his dose, because I've got another candidate for damnation. You just wait a couple of weeks & if you don't see the Type-writer come tilting along toward Cambridge with the raging hell of an unsatisfied appetite in its eye, I lose my guess. (25 June 1875)

His personal failures with an early model notwithstanding, Clemens well enough understood the typewriter's value in literary endeavors to have copies of holograph manuscript put into typewritten form for typographers to work from. He was if not the first author then at least one of the first to do this when, in 1882, he presented a typewritten copy of *Life on the Mississippi* as a copy text for typesetting, and his use helped legitimize the typewriter as a tool for business.

♦ SEE ALSO Autobiography; Inventions; Progress; Technology; Work Habits.

U & V

UNFINISHED WORKS. At his death, Samuel Clemens left thousands of manuscript pages in hundreds of different works. The *Autobiography* in particular Twain left to be published after his death, so he teased the public with installments and the promise that the good stuff would come later. Twain's first literary executor, Albert Bigelow *Paine, taking his cue from Twain's marketing pitch for the autobiography, tried to do the same for the reservoir of unfinished works, hoping that he could string them out into a series of publications that would earn him and the *Mark Twain Company a steady income over a long time. So Paine, in *Mark Twain: a Biography* (1912), deceptively tantalized the public, suggesting that works of great power lay in the papers, complete but seen by his eyes only. This prepared the way for his publication of the bowdlerized *Mysterious Stranger* (1916), an edited composite of two separate and unfinished works.

The fantasy Paine created would not die, leading Bernard DeVoto, Paine's successor as literary executor of the *Mark Twain Papers, to bring out a couple of volumes he culled from the papers, acknowledging that relatively little was finished or, to his mind, worthy of publication. DeVoto, while using much more honest standards than Paine and never foisting his own work off on the public as Twain's, was also a rigorous editor, changing our perception of the unfinished work by how he handled it. Thus, *Mark Twain in Eruption* does not publish the entirety of a nearly finished experimental autobiography, but instead prints excerpts as if the papers were a very rough draft of the autobiography Twain would have written had he lived long enough or maintained interest long enough to do so. Another of the volumes, however, was suppressed by Clemens's one surviving daughter, Clara *Sammousoud, until 1962, again creating the idea that the unpublished works were the great outpourings of Twain's late years.

Not until the Mark Twain Project began publishing volumes of previously unpublished material did the wider scholarly world and the public at large learn that the bulk of the papers unpublished at Clemens's death were unfinished and either were never designed for publication or were awaiting authorial inspiration before being readied. Moreover, while the bulk of these were written in the last fifteen years of his life as catharsis of the pain he felt when his eldest daughter died, many date back to the earliest years of Twain's career as a writer.

Quite simply, Twain's *work habits made it impossible for him not to leave many unfinished pieces at his death. As he put it in an autobiographical dictation for 30 August 1906 (published under the title "My Literary Shipyard" in abbreviated form in *Harper's Magazine* in August 1922 and in a more complete text in *Mark Twain in Eruption* under the title "When a Book Gets Tired" in 1940):

> There has never been a time in the past thirty-five years when my literary shipyard hadn't two or more half-finished ships on the ways, neglected and baking in the sun; generally there have been three or four. This has an unbusinesslike look, but it was not purposeless, it was intentional. As long as a book would write itself, I was a faithful and interested amanuensis, and my industry did not flag; but the minute that the book tried to shift to *my* head the labor of contriving its situation, inventing its adventures and conducting its conversation I put it away and dropped it out of my mind. Then I examined my unfinished properties to see if among them there might not be one whose interest in itself had revived, through a couple of years' restful idleness, and was ready to take me on again as amanuensis.

While he minimizes the degree of control he exercised over his writing, he accurately describes his basic pattern of composition. Naturally, many ships were caught in the shipyard when Clemens died.

Twain also often wrote without any intent to publish, as in the years following Susy's death with *"Chronicle of Young Satan," "The *Great Dark," "Which Was It?," "Which Was the Dream?," *"Three Thousand Years among the Microbes," and *"No. 44, The Mysterious Stranger," among others. These were private exercises in purgation, designed for no eyes but his own. They included not only blasphemous rantings, but also daring thought experiments and extravagant fantasies about human creativity.

These were not the only kinds of unfinished works. Many had been begun and had stalled decades earlier. Some, like the burlesque "Hamlet," were the products of some momentary silliness—sometimes in *collaboration with a good friend—and couldn't be sustained too far beyond the first impulse. Still others struck Clemens as too important to give up on, but too controversial to publish, so even if he had virtually finished a piece, he kept on tinkering indefinitely. Most conspicuous among these is "Captain Stormfield's Visit to Heaven," begun in 1869, and worked on at least five times before Twain published a small portion of it as *"Extract From Captain Stormfield's Visit to Heaven" in installments in 1907–1908. With these extracts he followed the pattern of publication he had used for "installments" from his autobiography. He had become so comfortable with his technique of writing over time that he dared inflict it on his public by publishing unfinished works over time as well.

The unfinished works have become the center of a significant scholarly controversy over Mark Twain's creativity. Many critics, following the lead of Van Wyck Brooks in 1920, saw Twain losing his creative power in his late years and point to all of the half-finished manuscripts as evidence. Others see in the effusion of flamboyant and creative pieces a sign of Clemens's artistry and genius working at full bore right to the end. How one responds to the controversy is now, fortunately, no longer dependent on the intermediary of scholars who have read the works in the Mark Twain Papers because much of the unfinished work has been made public in a series of *posthumous publications from the Mark Twain Project, which has given us annotated, unbowdlerized editions from which we can make our own judgments.

UNIONS. SEE Labor Movement.

"UNITED STATES OF LYNCHERDOM, THE." In an 1879 notebook entry, Clemens classified himself as a "humanitarian" opposed to capital punishment, following up on an 1871 satiric editorial, never published, that he submitted to the New York *Tribune*, which mocked the entire concept of justice through retribution. He instead understood organized violence to be a form of coercion that needed to be reformed through the exposure of its hypocrisy and cruelty. It is in that spirit that he opposed the late-nineteenth-century outbreak of organized lynchings of blacks that swept the American South and West. Lynchings were very much a part of the racist terror campaigns in the South during Reconstruction—these illegal executions took place largely at night with white perpetrators generally disguised in Klan outfits. Beginning in the 1880s, lynching in the South became a socially acceptable extension of legal authority, with mobs not only doing their work in daylight and undisguised, but often led by politicians and endorsed by newspapers. In the late 1890s, lynching was epidemic, with newspapers noticing planned lynchings, extra railroad cars being commissioned to carry the crowds, and schoolchildren sometimes getting holidays to attend. Rebecca Latimer Felton, a former slaveholder from Georgia, appeared on the *lecture circuit in 1898 promoting lynching "a thousand times a week, if necessary." In the South, those blacks and whites who raised voices against this terror were subject to it.

In this context Clemens wrote in 1901, but did not publish, his attack on lynching, insisting, perhaps against hope, that the participants did not really enjoy the practice, and that simple moral courage on the part of a few was enough to end this, and all, social barbarism. Ironically, as much as the subject exercised Clemens—he even planned to write a subscription book attacking lynching—he published nothing on it in his lifetime, perhaps for fear of the backlash against him and his family.

♦ SEE ALSO Missionaries; Race Relations; Reform.

UTILITARIANISM. Utilitarian ethics were very much a part of the intellectual climate of Clemens's day, and he was exposed to them explicitly during his years in *Hartford if not before. We know for certain that the *Monday Evening Club had several papers delivered about utilitarianism and its exponents, including John

Stuart Mill. One of Clemens's favorite books, W. E. H. *Lecky's *History of European Morals*, included a fine capsule summary of utilitarian ethics as a position Lecky felt history was moving away from. Ironically, Clemens found the position as Lecky articulated it to be intellectually, if not emotionally, compelling.

Utilitarianism as Clemens confronted it and endorsed it was not Jeremy Bentham's insistence on cost-benefit analysis. In his play with utility as a social force, Clemens was not interested so much in the greatest good for the greatest number as he was in the utilitarian's idea of what motivated human behavior. He accepted the utilitarian idea that human beings were motivated exclusively by the desire to seek pleasure and avoid pain. He further accepted the idea that morality is socially conditioned, and that people follow social dictates in order to avoid the pain of ostracism or to secure the pleasure of social approval. In this sense, utilitarianism played into a rationalistic cosmos, one in which Clemens easily saw human beings as machines, and in which *determinism made sense.

More importantly, the idea that morality is selfish and socially contingent fascinated Clemens both because he found it true and because it disturbed his belief that transcendent selflessness was the only legitimate basis for moral behavior. By utilitarian standards he believed no act was selfless, but by his emotional attachment to various romantic and sentimental ideas of morality, he could not accept utilitarian motivations as morally valid. The double bind he thus fashioned for himself helped fuel his frequently manifested and deep, though not all-encompassing, cynicism about human beings. It also formed, in the byplay between his rational utilitarianism and his emotional *sentimentalism, the creative tension that yielded many of his best and most interesting books, including *Adventures of Huckleberry Finn* and *A Connecticut Yankee in King Arthur's Court*. While many of his utilitarian *aphorisms—such as "Training is Everything: the peach was once a bitter almond, the cauliflower is nothing but a cabbage with a college education"—are cited regularly, most works in which he argued for utilitarianism more directly and without much or any qualification, such as *What Is Man?* or "The Turning Point of my Life," have not remained popular. Such, too, is the case with most of his purely sentimental works, such as "The Californian's Tale," or "A Dog's Tale." Only when Clemens tried to reconcile his divided sympathies did he capture complexities in ways that keep readers coming back for more.

♦ SEE ALSO Darwin, Charles; Moral Sense; Spencer, Herbert.

VERNACULAR HUMOR. SEE Dialect.

VIRGINIA CITY TERRITORIAL ENTERPRISE. SEE *Territorial Enterprise, Virginia City.*

WAKEMAN, CAPT. EDGAR (NED) (1818–1875). Wakeman was a commercial sea captain under whose command Clemens sailed as a passenger in 1866 from San Francisco to Nicaragua. As men with west coast celebrity and shared interests in storytelling and ship piloting, Clemens and Wakeman struck up a friendship, short-lived, but significant to Clemens for the literary material Wakeman provided. Clemens found Wakeman's self-taught approach to the *Bible hilariously blasphemous, his abilities as a yarn-spinner excellent, and his commanding presence worthy of admiration. In Clemens's account to the San Francisco *Alta California* of his journey to New York, Wakeman figures prominently, and even though Wakeman was well known in San Francisco, Clemens took liberties in his dispatches with Wakeman's stories, as can be seen by comparing his finished work with his notebook entries. As time passed, Clemens strayed further from biographical fact as he let Wakeman's character and tall tales work their way into his writings. The character of a blustery, domineering, gentle-hearted old sea hunk appears often in Twain's works, closely resembling the original in such cases as Captain Ned Blakely in chapter 50 of *Roughing It* and Captain Hurricane Jones in "Some Rambling Notes of an Idle Excursion," less closely in other places, as in chapter 16 of *The *American Claimant*, and in the *unfinished works "Refuge of the Derelicts" and "The *Great Dark" and the long suppressed *"Extract from Captain Stormfield's Visit to Heaven." In the latter, Clemens altered details of Wakeman's life in creating his title character, describing a sea captain who was born at sea (rather than in Connecticut) and lived to sixty-five years old. In his autobiographical dictations concerning Wakeman and the fictional Stormfield, Clemens misapplied the details of the fiction to the fact, a telling mistake for a man whose career depended on slippage between literary *realism and fantasy.

When Wakeman suffered a stroke in 1872, he appealed to Clemens for help, asking Clemens to collaborate on Wakeman's life story. Clemens refused, suggesting that his brother Orion do the job instead. Nothing came of this proposed collaboration. Clemens did, however, publish a letter in the *Alta* appealing for donations to help Wakeman's family.

WAR. "I have been reading the morning paper," Clemens wrote William Dean *Howells on 2 April 1899. "I do it every morning—well knowing that I shall find in it the usual depravities and baseness & hypocrisies & cruelties that make up Civilization, & cause me to put in the rest of the day pleading for the damnation of the human race." Such was the extreme aversion Clemens came to have to violence toward the end of his career. Besides publishing several essays against *imperialism, he penned numerous manuscript pages denouncing militarism and war, few of which were published in his lifetime. Perhaps the most memorable of these is "The War Prayer," which, rejected for publication in *Harper's Bazaar* in 1905, was finally published posthumously.

A simple list of some events he found in his newspaper from 1895 to 1900 might explain his obsession. In 1895, the Armenian massacres began; the Japanese defeated the Chinese in Manchuria and appropriated Port Arthur before international pressure forced them to give it back in exchange for an exorbitant "indemnity"; the Italians continued their war against Ethiopia; Cuban nationalists fought their Spanish overlords; Jameson and company started their ill-fated raid in South Africa; and indigenous people in Mozambique fought against European domination. In 1896, the so-called Kruger telegram precipitated an Anglo-German crisis that helped spur the naval arms race between Germany and England; the Cretan revolution against Turkey began; France annexed Madagascar; the British suppressed the Ashanti for the fourth time; and the Matabele uprising began in the recently organized state of Rhodesia. 1897 saw a native insurgency in the Philippines; more Armenian massacres; the British conquest of the Sudan; the Greco-Turkish war; a French advance into the Sudan; and various native battles against imperial conquest in Africa. Relatively tame 1898 saw vigorous action in the European partition of Africa and China; the Spanish-American War; and the first German Navy Bill, which sealed the fate of any attempts at rapprochement between England and Germany. In 1899, the Filipinos under Aguinaldo, having been denied independence by the United States, were obliged to fight for it—thus confirming the hypocrisy of the Spanish-American war—and the *Boer War began. In 1900, the British invented the concentration camp in their efforts to suppress Boer resistance; the Chinese "Boxers" rose against foreign domination only to be ruthlessly subjugated; the Ashantis once again fought for their freedom; and the Russians occupied Manchuria. It was a period in which international affairs were defined by imperialism and militarism, against which relatively few in the Western world spoke out.

This is the backdrop of Twain's horror at war, his contempt for its exaltation, in *Following the Equator* (1897), "To the Person Sitting in Darkness" (1901), and the *posthumously published *"Chronicle of Young Satan" and "The War Prayer," among others. It solidified the position he had begun to develop in the 1880s in "A *Private History of a Campaign That Failed," in which he described the frequently glorified American *Civil War as being like any war, not the defense of a great cause, but rather "the killing of strangers against whom you feel no animosity; strangers whom, in other circumstances, you would help if you found them in trouble, and who would help you if you needed it." In "The War Prayer" he took this analysis further, explaining that war was not about securing victory so much as ensuring the destruction of other human beings, and that people whooped into enthusiasm for victory are too insane to understand the consequences of their actions.

None of this is to say that Twain disliked soldiers or was an adamant pacifist. He was friends with several generals, including Ulysses S. *Grant and William T. Sherman, and he relished his many visits to West Point. He readily supported anti-monarchical *revolution and native self-defense against imperialism, even going so far as to play the glory card in such support. For instance, in *Following the Equator* he praises Maori patriotism: "Even though it be a political mistake, and a thousand times a political mistake, that does not affect it; it is honorable—always honorable, always noble—and privileged to hold its head up and look the nations in the face" (chapter 35). To some degree Twain did approve of *patriotism; he was not fully immune to one of his era's obsessions. And to some degree Twain even relished war in his love of military pageantry, of courage, of strength. But mostly he understood war as a violation of courage, at least of moral courage, and as a triumph of conformity. As he put it in "Chronicle of Young Satan": "[Y]our race . . . is made up of sheep. It is governed by minorities, seldom or never by majorities. It suppresses its feelings and its beliefs and follows the handful that makes the most noise. . . . Look at you in war—what mutton you are, and how ridiculous."

In preaching moral courage, he found his resistance to his era's glorification of war.

WARD, ARTEMUS. Pseudonym of Charles Farrar *Browne, newspaper humorist and comic lecturer.

WARNER, CHARLES DUDLEY (1829–1900). Warner was, along with Joseph *Goodman, Bret *Harte, Mary Mason *Fairbanks, and William Dean *Howells, one of the five most important of Twain's mentors in writing. Not that Warner was more experienced than Clemens when they met, but Warner's confidence, his education, and his connections were all seductive. Clemens was pulled into Warner's *Hartford circle as early as 1869, the year they met and two years before the Clemens family moved to the city.

Warner's confidence and connections came naturally to a college graduate (Hamilton College, 1851) who, after a brief postgraduate flirtation with speculative work in railroading, turned to studying law. After practicing briefly, he was invited by Joseph Hawley, the owner of the Hartford *Evening Press*, to be assistant editor. Warner took the position working as coeditor of the *Press* and then of the Hartford *Courant*, with which the *Press* combined in 1867. Hawley's political career left Warner with effective control of one of America's most important newspapers, one which had a strong hand in establishing the *Republican party and whose voice in all matters political and literary carried national weight.

As the editor of this paper, Warner had easy access to the best literary journals and publishers, publishing a string of travel books and essays, contributing literary criticism as well as essays to significant national journals, and eventually serving as a contributing editor to *Harper's Magazine* between 1884 and 1889.

Warner's literary biases were confidently conservative, as he espoused the genteel commonplaces of sentimental *realism, shared by most other members of the *Monday Evening Club to which Hawley and Clemens also belonged. In Warner's collaboration with Clemens on *The Gilded Age* (1874), this conservative moral philosophy shaped the structure and moral outlook of the book. While not, then, an influence on Twain's writing *style, Warner's understanding of the moral value and purpose of literature guided Twain's efforts in his first novel.

The Clemens and Warner families were particularly close during the first years the Clemenses spent in Hartford, and Olivia Clemens and Susan Warner maintained the closeness of their friendship to the end. The two men, however, had a cooling in their connections. According to rumor, the estrangement began when Clemens learned that Warner kept a mistress (in whose house he died of a heart attack in 1900). Whether this is true or not, they did have ample intellectual grounds for drifting apart. As Clemens grew more confident in his powers and more theoretically disposed to the kind of literary realism William Dean Howells promoted, he had every reason to see Warner's aesthetic limitations for what they were. By 1883, when other American writers were experimenting with new ways of describing the changing conditions of American society, Warner ineffectually complained about changing definitions of realism, seeking instead an idealized vision of human possibility. Clemens, too, always held human behavior up to an ideal, but as a satirist, he believed that literature's task was to hold a mirror up to humanity, not to soften the picture before literature's work was done. By this point in their respective careers, Clemens had left Warner behind.

♦ SEE ALSO Sentimentalism.

WASHINGTON, D.C. In 1854, young Samuel Clemens made a brief trip to Washington, D.C., while he was working as a typesetter in Philadelphia. He describes disdainfully a raw city of shabby houses sprinkled around the monumental architecture that housed the federal government: "The public buildings of Washington are all fine specimens of architecture, and would add greatly to the embellishment of such a city as New York—but here they are sadly out of place looking like so many palaces in a Hottentot village" (17–18 February 1854). The only place he describes with pride is the Museum of the Patent Office. The rest comes in for substantial criticism, the Congress most especially.

> I passed into the Senate Chamber to see the men who give the people the benefit of their wisdom and learning for a little glory and eight dollars a day.

> The Senate is now composed of a different material from what it once was. Its glory hath departed. Its halls no longer echo the words of a Clay, or Webster, or Calhoun. They have played their parts and retired from the stage; and though they are still occupied by others, the void is felt.

The contrast to his letters from Philadelphia, "[r]ich in Revolutionary associations" (28 October 1853), is striking, suggesting that he already had lost faith in the national government, reserving his *patriotism for a heroic past.

His return in November 1867, nominally as secretary to Nevada Senator William M. Stewart but actually as a reporter, did nothing to change his opinions. He witnessed up close the corruption of Washington *politics, and even bragged, as in a 24 January 1868 letter to his mother and sister, that as a journalist he had significant influence over politicians. While working as a reporter he was fully in the fray, reporting both for western and eastern newspapers, but what he most wanted to do was to act as muckraker exposing the corruption at the heart of national politics. To that end, he began a correspondence with the New York *Herald* in which he would, as he wrote Mary Mason *Fairbanks, "have full swing, & say as many mean things as I please. Now don't say a word Madam, because I just mean to abuse people right & left, in case the humor takes me to do it. There are lots of folks in Washington who need vilifying" (24 January 1868). He further promised himself that he would write a book that would reveal the truth about Washington, a promise he substantially kept in 1873's *The Gilded Age*.

♦ SEE ALSO Newspaper Journalism; Reform.

WEBSTER, ANNIE MOFFET (1852–1950) AND CHARLES L.

(1851–1891). Annie Moffet, Samuel Clemens's niece by his sister Pamela Clemens *Moffet, was something of a favorite with Samuel for many years—he went so far as to name a mining claim after her in the winter of 1862. In person or in his letters to his sister's family, he often teased his niece by telling her "to trade her testament for lager beer," and playing stupid whenever she tried to teach him *Bible stories:

> I was very fond of Uncle Sam, but I did not think he was the genius of the family. I remember when I was about eight I thought he needed a little religious instruction and started to tell him the story of Moses. Uncle Sam was strangely obtuse, and finally I went to my father and said, "Papa, Uncle Orion has good sense and Mama has good sense, but I don't think Uncle Sam has good sense. I told him the story of Moses and the bullrushes and he said he knew Moses very well, that he kept a secondhand store on Market Street. I tried very hard to explain that it wasn't the Moses I meant, but he just *couldn't* understand. (Quoted in *Mark Twain, Business Man*, chapter 5)

It became a running joke with the two, and perhaps in *Adventures of Huckleberry Finn* Huck's lack of interest about Moses in the "bulrushers" is an inside joke for Annie's sake.

The financial help Clemens gave his sister after her husband died took Annie to Fredonia, New York, where she met and in 1875 married Charles Webster, a Fredonia native who became a civil engineer. Given Clemens's involvement in Annie's life, it is not surprising that in 1881 Clemens hired Webster to investigate the Kaolatype process, which Clemens thought was being mismanaged by Dan *Slote. Clemens quickly heaped more responsibility on Webster, turning him into his general business agent and then, when he founded his own publishing firm, made Webster the name partner in the firm.

At first, Webster was deferential, but after the successes of *Adventures of Huckleberry Finn* and of Ulysses S. *Grant's memoirs, Webster grew tired of appeasing his uncle-in-law. The two grew ever more abrasive in their correspondence until Clemens began to develop Fred Hall into an alternative partner in *Webster and Company. As the company's fortunes began to ebb in the late 1880s, Webster's health began to decline until, in 1888, Clemens forced Webster to take a leave of absence from the company. Webster never returned and, in 1891, died of "neuralgia."

Clemens recorded his hatred of Webster in his autobiographical dictations, though these were not published until 1940 in *Mark Twain in Eruption*. Webster's son, Samuel Charles Webster, attempted to exonerate his father in *Mark Twain, Business Man* (1946), which selectively uses family and business records to paint Clemens as a tyrant. A more balanced portrait comes out in the full correspondence between the two, published in *Mark Twain's Letters to His Publishers* (1967).

♦ SEE ALSO Business Ventures; Finances.

WEBSTER AND COMPANY. Webster and Company was born when Clemens decided that his connection with James *Osgood's *publishing firm had deprived him of profits on his books. He had already used his nephew-in-law, Charles *Webster, as a business agent—in particular, as the general agent for the New York area for the last book he published with Osgood—so he took the next step toward self-publishing by establishing Webster as titular head of a publishing house that was designed to sell Mark Twain's books by subscription. As Twain explained in the Elmira, New York, *Herald* of 6 July 1885, "I am Webster & Co., myself, substantially." The point was to give Twain a regular outlet for his own books that would cut out the middleman, leaving Clemens the profits.

Webster learned the ropes not only of marketing but also of manufacturing a book on *Adventures of Huckleberry Finn* (American edition, 1885), which was so enormously successful as to convince both Clemens and Webster that the publishing house itself was a viable concern. Their production of Ulysses S. *Grant's memoirs (1886) reinforced that conclusion. But inasmuch as Webster and Company was Clemens, Clemens had to furnish all the capital and shoulder all the risk. Under an 1885 formal contract of partnership, Webster would receive a $2,500 annual salary, one-third of profits up to $20,000 per year, and one-tenth of anything further. Clemens was to receive the rest of the net, 8 percent interest on the capital he advanced, and 70 percent royalty on his own new books, 60 percent from those old ones he brought from Osgood. When the firm was making money, these terms seemed fine, indeed fine enough to Clemens that in 1886 he agreed to increase Webster's salary to $3,000 and cut his own interest on capital to 6 percent.

While the two early successes made the firm one of America's most prominent publishers nearly overnight, the firm never duplicated those early successes. Instead, it took on numerous other projects that failed to realize the profits expected. Many were projects from Clemens's friends; others were expected block-busters that turned out to be no more than ordinary. The authorized biography of Pope Leo XIII, published in 1887, for instance, merely broke even. Clemens solicited the book in the first place because he believed almost every Roman Catholic would buy one, as he put it in a letter to Webster, "with the priesthood to help" (28 December 1885). Sales were disappointing, but rather than challenging Clemens's ideas of the power of the priesthood or the obedience of Roman Catholics, he appears to have merely decided that the clergy preferred its flock to remain ignorant. So he suggested in *A Connecticut Yankee in King Arthur's Court* (1889), anyway, and his opinion was seconded by Fred Hall, who had by then taken over managing the company. Hall assured Clemens that the anti-Catholic diatribes in *Yankee* would cause no harm because it was "the Catholic church that would . . . attack, and that they were not book buyers anyway" (Hall to Clemens, 8 October 1889).

The firm also took on the multivolume *Library of American Literature*, which proved to return money on investment painfully slowly. While the books did sell, they were sold on installments, so that expenses were front-loaded but revenues merely trickled in. The strain on capital was far too enormous to allow Clemens to receive the returns he expected. Indeed, he found that he was plowing royalties on his own books back into the firm. Coming at a time when he was also investing heavily in the *Paige typesetter, this reinvestment of royalties put him in a consider-able financial bind. Nonetheless, the Paige machine did not drain capital from Webster and Company, as Webster's son argues in *Mark Twain, Business Man*.

At any rate, Webster's oversight of the company was sufficiently lax to enable a bookkeeper to abscond with $25,000. The embezzlement was discovered in 1887, by which time the firm could recover less than a quarter of the loss. That coupled with Webster's increasing physical debility encouraged Clemens to force Webster from the company and replace him as manager with Fred Hall. Hall worked hard to rescue what was already a sinking ship, keeping up a steady stream of publications well into the 1890s, and trying to shift the company from subscription publishing into the trade.

Twain's early fascination with the publishing company as something larger than an outlet for his own works came to backfire not only because the company drained his royalties out of his own pocket, but because he had to work his own books into the larger publishing schedule. He complained in a letter to Kate Field (turning down her book, one of numerous exposés of Mormonism), "I think I could write a very good moral fable about an author who turned publisher in order to get a better show, and got shut up entirely." Of course, he exaggerated in order to suggest that he was refusing Field's book merely because of other obligations, but in fact, Hall did see the publishing company as coming first, and Twain's books as only part of that business. When Twain submitted an unwieldy draft of the book that was to become *Pudd'nhead Wilson*, Hall rejected it.

Still, Webster and Company published two of the Twain books most studied now, *Adventures of Huckleberry Finn* and *A Connecticut Yankee in King Arthur's Court*. It also published several minor works and collections: *Merry Tales* (1892), *The *American Claimant* (1892), *The £1,000,000 Bank-Note* (1893), *Tom Sawyer Abroad* (1894), and the *Howells-edited *Mark Twain's Library of Humor* (1888). Many of these were dashed off and were intended to create cash flow for the firm as its finances grew more precarious in the nineties. Such stopgaps ultimately failed, however, as the firm, deeply in debt to fund its ongoing operations, found its loans called after the panic of 1893 dried up credit. In 1894, the firm declared bankruptcy, and as Clemens was its principal capitalist, its bankruptcy forced his own.

♦ SEE ALSO Business Ventures; Religion.

WHAT IS MAN? (1906). Always concerned with cosmology, theology, and moral philosophy, Clemens nonetheless as a humorist rarely ventured into direct philosophizing, usually couching his ideas indirectly in fiction or satire, and reserving his essays for less sweeping matters of politics or society. But in his notebooks and in many unfinished works, he turned to ultimate questions. Having over the years contemplated humanity and its place in the cosmos, Clemens turned, in 1898, to writing what he called his gospel, the philosophical dialogue *What Is Man?* The title, taken ironically from Psalms 8:4, belittles human exceptionalism, preparing the reader for a book that depicts human beings as mere machines in a mechanical universe. His gospel denies human beings any responsibility for their behavior—good or bad—at the same time it suggests, in spite of its contemptuous tone, the possibility of human progress through deliberate training toward higher moral purposes.

Olivia hated the doctrine and implored Clemens not to publish it. Clemens himself was convinced that it was a brilliant and novel exposé of the human condition that if published would ruin his reputation and livelihood as well as the future comfort of his children. In fact, his *determinism was merely of a piece with the *naturalism of the age, and much of what he argued in *What Is Man?* he had already asserted in *A Connecticut Yankee in King Arthur's Court*. When after Olivia's death he had the dialogue privately printed by DeVinne press and distributed copies to select friends, he discovered that many of them accepted the ideas as commonplace.

What they didn't see was the degree to which Clemens built into his deterministic philosophy a relativistic alternative. The Old Man in the dialogue reveals that his desire for an absolute truth stems from a subjective condition:

> I said I have been a Truth Seeker. . . . I am not that now. I told you that there are none but temporary Truth Seekers; that a permanent one is a human impossibility; that as soon as the Seeker finds what he is thoroughly convinced is the Truth, he seeks no further, but gives the rest of his days to hunting for junk to patch it and caulk it and prop it with, and make it weather-proof and keep it from caving in on him. . . . Having found the Truth; perceiving that beyond question Man has but one moving impulse—the contenting of his own spirit—and is merely a Machine and entitled to no personal merit for anything he does, it is not humanly possible for me to seek further. The rest of my days will be spent in patching and painting and puttying and caulking my priceless possession, and in looking the other way when an imploring argument or a damaging fact approaches. (chapter 5)

In this, Clemens leaves open the possibility of human freedom; the Old Man merely chooses not to investigate a more complex reality the existence of which he acknowledges. Given this acknowledgement, it is not surprising that when Clemens began writing this deterministic tract he had recently published investigations into social relativism in *Following the Equator* and that shortly before publishing *What Is Man?* he was flirting with extreme solipsism in *"No. 44, The Mysterious Stranger." His own behavior shows that the Old Man is wrong; Clemens himself was a permanent Truth Seeker.

♦ SEE ALSO Bible; Utilitarianism.

WHITMAN, WALT (1819–1892). For all of his putative dislike of *poetry and for all of his prudishness on questions of *sexuality, Clemens responded enthusiastically to a request for *charity for Walt Whitman. In response to a letter soliciting funds to buy Whitman a cottage in the New Jersey countryside, away from insalubrious Camden summers, Clemens wrote:

> My Dear Mr. Baxter:
> You did not mention any particular sum; so I enclose $50, with the request that if you should have to issue another call before you accomplish your object, you be not diffident about extending it to me.

You perceive that in signing, I have mentioned no sum. That is because I would a little rather no sum were mentioned—for these things get into print, you know. What we want to do, is to make the splendid old soul comfortable, & do what we do heartily & as a privilege. My name can indicate that attitude for me, by itself; & so let us leave my contribution unspecified. (1887)

Clemens's fifty dollars was significantly higher than the sums given by other signatories, most of which are either five or ten dollars.

Clemens also penned an encomium to *progress titled "To Walt Whitman" (1889) for Whitman's seventieth birthday celebration. Clearly something about Whitman—perhaps his interest in a vision of progress, perhaps his faith in the power of the American language and the value of the American common person—touched a chord in Clemens.

WHITTIER BIRTHDAY DINNER. "The Story of a Speech," often republished as an excerpt from Mark Twain's *autobiography, turns one of Samuel Clemens's greatest humiliations into an after-the-fact triumph. Early critics of Twain take the story of Brahmin Boston's refusal to accept any humor at its expense as a sign of its ossified stuffiness. Still other critics accept at face value the assumption that Twain's speech really was transgressive and thus a sign of his burning hatred of the literary generation that preceded him. Both partial truths hide a more complex reality about the humorist's imagination; he allowed a lack of reaction to turn, in his own imagination, into a deserved punishment of the highest order.

The Whittier birthday dinner of 17 December 1877 was one of those semipublic celebrations called banquets, at which invited guests would eat, drink, and listen to *speeches, while a gallery of reporters took down the events to circulate to the American public at large. The *Atlantic Monthly*, like many other American magazines, held such banquets regularly in order to get free advertising as well as to fete distinguished guests. In the year of John Greenleaf Whittier's seventieth birthday and on the twentieth anniversary of the founding of the *Atlantic*, the publishers invited about fifty contributors to the magazine, among them America's best revered writers—Oliver Wendell Holmes, Ralph Waldo *Emerson, and Henry Wadsworth Longfellow—who sat at the head table next to the guest of honor. Emerson was growing senile, Longfellow was hard of hearing, but along with the other literary lights at the table of honor they subjected themselves with good will to the endless speech making characteristic of such occasions. Nonetheless, the evening was not the gayest; as the Boston *Advertiser* described it in its next day's issue, the honored guests "gave a reverent, almost holy, air to the place."

Not surprisingly, Clemens lost some of his nerve when he delivered his comic representation of three Western reprobates who pass themselves off as Holmes, Longfellow, and Emerson. The thrust of the speech is really quite reverential, suggesting that the poetry of all three has touched even the most distant and impoverished reaches of America, and suggesting further that Twain, in their company, is an "imposter." But in describing three men who took the names of these revered figures—and in a context that was not effervescent enough to stimulate humor—Twain's delivery was relatively poor. Or perhaps the guests of honor just didn't hear him very well. They did not, anyway, break into laughter, and the room took its cue from them. William Dean *Howells, responsible for bringing Twain into this august circle, immediately commiserated with Clemens in such a way that the speaker's shame at failure turned into guilt for having "insulted" the icons. In an outpouring of angst, his letters to Howells in the weeks following worked guilt into humiliation.

If Clemens should have felt guilty only for real harm done, then his contrition was entirely unnecessary. None of the three men concerned took offense, and literary Boston seemed cosmopolitan and confident enough to take Twain's speech in the proper spirit of fun. Boston newspapers, at any rate, did not really take Twain to task when they reported his speech. But when the provincial papers received reports of the evening, several began to blow up a storm of protest, accusing Twain of a debased irreverence and challenging his legitimacy as a peer of the three hallowed authors. This press, from middlebrow middle America, the realm of readers who buttered Twain's amply coated bread, was the one that Twain heard when excoriating himself for his grievous breach of decorum, showing how completely in tune he was with the broadest reaches of the American audience.

The public damage was short-lived. Two years later Howells invited Twain to another *Atlantic* celebration, this time a breakfast in honor of Holmes's seventieth birthday. Clemens saw this as an opportunity to atone for his earlier blunder and asked Howells to vet his entirely reverential speech, "Unconscious Plagiarism." The speech was entirely successful, and Clemens apparently learned better how to judge the temper of an occasion; within a decade, Twain was invited to give a speech in a benefit for a Longfellow Memorial Fund, and from then on he only grew in popularity as a maker of speeches on public occasions.

♦ SEE ALSO Public Image.

WILLIAMS, TRUE. SEE Illustrations.

WOMEN'S RIGHTS. In chapter 32 of *Following the Equator* Mark Twain gives a thumbnail sketch of the history of women's rights in America by contrasting that history to what he saw in New Zealand after that country legalized women's suffrage in 1893:

> I take it from the official report: "A feature of the election was the orderliness and sobriety of the people. Women were in no way molested." At home, a

standing argument against women suffrage has always been that women could not go to the polls without being insulted. The arguments against woman suffrage have always taken the easy form of prophecy. The prophets have been prophesying ever since the woman's rights movement began in 1848—and in forty-seven years they have never scored a hit. Men ought to begin to feel a sort of respect for their mothers and wives and sisters by this time. The women deserve a change of attitude like that, for they have wrought well. In forty-seven years they have swept an imposingly large number of unfair laws from the statute books of America. In that brief time these serfs have set themselves free—essentially. Men could not have done so much for themselves in that time without bloodshed—at least they never have; and that is argument that they didn't know how. The women have accomplished a peaceful revolution, and a very beneficent one; and yet that has not convinced the average man that they are intelligent, and have courage and energy and perseverance and fortitude. It takes much to convince the average man of anything; and perhaps nothing can ever make him realize that he is the average woman's inferior—yet in several important details the evidences seems [*sic*] to show that that is what he is. Man has ruled the human race from the beginning—but he should remember that up to the middle of the present century it was a dull world, and ignorant and stupid, but it is not such a dull world now, and is growing less and less dull all the time. This is woman's opportunity—she has had none before. I wonder where man will be in another forty-seven years?

Twain's awe at the sea change in human relations that was occurring before his eyes, and to which at this stage in his career he contributed by advocating women's suffrage, registers well both the increasingly effective and energetic advocacy of women's rights through the nineteenth century and the continued double standard—an argument from women's moral superiority—that fueled that advocacy.

What Twain does not acknowledge here was that early in his career, he was one of those conservative prophets whose attacks on women's suffrage were equally founded on a sexual double standard, a standard that accepted women's moral superiority at the same time it postulated her weakness, mental and physical, that would enable her easy corruption were she to participate in worldly affairs outside the home.

Indeed, Twain retailed all the mocking and contemptuous bromides against women's suffrage in his letters of March 1867 on the subject. The first of these, to the St. Louis *Democrat* on 12 March, was a crude satire suggesting that women voting, and worse, in public office would destroy the republic; they would, he claimed, ignore questions of state in favor of going "straight after each other's private moral character," that is, when they weren't paying attention to dress and ornamentation. Their homes would go to the dogs, and neglected husbands like Mark Twain would even have to bear "the one solitary thing I have shirked up to the present time [falling] on me[,] and my family would go to destruction; for I am not qualified for a wet nurse."

When a woman reader responded seriously to these flippant charges, Twain replied that he would "for once drop foolishness, and speak with the gravity the occasion demands." He argues against justice in favor of expediency, acknowledging that it would be just to let women vote, but claiming that it would not be politically expedient:

> An educated American woman would ... vote with fifty times the judgment and independence exercised by stupid, illiterate newcomers from foreign lands, ... the ignorant foreign women would vote with the ignorant foreign men—the bad women would vote with the bad men ... [and] a very large proportion of our best and wisest women would still cling to the holy ground of the home circle, and refuse to either vote or hold office— ... and, behold, mediocrity and dishonesty would be appointed to conduct the affairs of government more surely than ever before. (13 March 1867)

While if this were the only consequence, Twain would still have to acknowledge that justice should prevail, he expressed the hackneyed position that women themselves would be tainted by acting in public:

> That must be a benefit beyond the power of figures to estimate, which can make us consent to take the High Priestess we reverence at the sacred fireside and send her forth to electioneer for votes among a mangy mob who are unworthy to touch the hem of her garment. ... There is something revolting in the thought. It would shock me inexpressibly for an angel to come down from above and ask me to take a drink with him (though I should doubtless consent); but it would shock me still more to see one of our blessed earthly angels peddling election tickets among a mob of shabby scoundrels she never saw before.

His argument here is completely conventional and, while expressed to the extreme under the pen name Mark Twain, is ultimately of a piece with his social and domestic attitudes toward women as expressed in his courtship of Olivia Langdon.

In that courtship, Clemens encouraged Langdon to read Coventry Patmore's "The Angel in the House," and used various passages in it to encourage her to see her feelings for him—which apparently were couched at first as those of a Christian for a sinner or, at strongest, of a sister for a brother, as necessary steps on the way to full romantic love. Patmore's ideas of the role of a woman in marriage are highly idealized presentations of woman as domestic evangel.

Ironically, it was partly through the Langdon circle that Clemens was exposed to more progressive ideas about women's roles. At that time Langdon was struggling, in her own modest way, with feminism, especially in her conversation with her friend Anna *Dickinson. Clemens met Dickinson on the *lecture circuit, where he also met many other politically engaged speakers who confronted the topic. The Boston Lyceum Bureau, for instance, listed ten speakers on women's rights as among its lecturers for the 1870–1871 season, including Susan B. Anthony on "The Woman Question," Anna Dickinson with "A New Lecture on the Woman Question;" and Petroleum V. Nasby (David Ross *Locke, pseudonymously) on the "Struggles of a Conservative with the Woman Question." Locke may have been particularly influential on Clemens, as the two were friends on the circuit, and as satirists used the same rhetorical devices to confront political questions. Locke used Nasby ironically as a conservative whose selfish and bilious opposition to *reform cast conservatism in an ugly light.

In spite of, or perhaps in reaction to, this exposure, Clemens frequently ridiculed women's suffrage, as in a 10 June 1871 letter to David Gray, in which he writes a parodic lecture notice:

> MARK TWAIN IN THE LECTURE FIELD. —Mark Twain is going to make a short lecturing tour in the early part of the coming season. Subject—"An Appeal in behalf of Extending the Suffrage to Boys." He says he thought he had retired permanently from the lecture field, but upon looking into things and finding that Woman is less persecuted, and is held in a milder bondage than boys, he thinks it incumbent upon somebody to "lift up a voice for the poor little male juvenile."

About this time, however, he changed his mind, surrendering expediency to justice. He had obviously told Locke sometime in the 1871–1872 lecture season that he had become an advocate of women's suffrage because Locke, when asked in April 1872 by the Michigan Women Suffrage Association to write a play to satirize the foes of women's suffrage, suggested the association ask Clemens: "I am not certain but that Mark Twain would do it, as he is not busy at the present time. Write him and say that I suggested him. He is thoroughly in sympathy with th[e] cause and Can do it (if he will) splendidly."

This is the earliest mention of Clemens's change of mind, and the fact that he turned down the commission may say something about the depth of his commitment. At any rate, he kept his opinions, in flux as they were, fairly much to himself for the next twenty years, with occasional exceptions, as in "The Temperance Insurrection," published in the London *Standard* in March 1874. When he finally became a regular and persistent public advocate of women's rights, he dated his conversion to the early to mid-1870s, as in his 1901 speech, "Votes for Women," in which he declared, "For twenty-five years I've been a woman's rights man."

In part he may have been simplifying his past, as in his autobiographical dictation of 1 March 1907 in which he praised Isabella Beecher Hooker's work on women's rights: "She labored with all her splendid energies in that great cause all the rest of her life; as an able and efficient worker she ranks immediately after those great chiefs, Susan B. Anthony, Elizabeth Cady Stanton, and Mrs. Livermore." This is a far cry from his letter to Olivia Langdon Clemens of 3 October 1872, when he complained that "this pleasant lady, under the impression that she was helping along a great & good cause, has been blandly pulling down the temple of Woman's Emancipation & shying the bricks at the builders." Here Clemens clearly supports women's "emancipation," but is uncomfortable with Hooker's position, which was at this point in concert with the positions taken by Tennessee Claflin and Victoria Woodhull, that women's subjection begins not so much in the polling place as in sexual relations with men.

In his disagreement with Hooker's position, then considered extreme, Clemens showed that his conversion to women's rights did not include a shift in attitude about women's moral and sexual differences from men. In his private remarks on women's rights in "Man's Place in the Animal World," one of his strongest arguments about man's depravity stems from his sense of the debased character of masculine sexual appetite:

> Roosters keep harems, but it is by consent of their concubines; therefore no wrong is done. Men keep harems, but it is by brute force, privileged by atrocious laws which the other sex were allowed no hand in making. In this matter man occupies a far lower place than the rooster.

In this sense, Twain uses "man" not to describe the race but only the sex. His attitude, held by many in the women's rights movement, supported his belief in women's suffrage. In short, his argument for women having the vote ultimately came down to his belief that women would vote with more wisdom and with greater moral conviction than would men, and thus would clean up politics. In his speech "Votes for Women," he prophesied that when women finally gained "that whip-lash, the ballot," "they would rise in their might and change the awful state of things." Perhaps he should have kept in mind the usual inaccuracy of political prophecy.

♦ SEE ALSO Democracy; Domesticity; Sexuality.

WORK ETHIC. In his 30 April 1867 correspondence from New York City to the *Alta California*, Mark Twain wrote with astonished pride:

> By some wonderful process or other the soldiers of both armies have been quietly and mysteriously absorbed into civil life, and can no more be distinguished from the children of peace. It is hard even for an American to understand this. But it is a toiling, thinking, determined nation, this of ours, and little given to dreaming. It appreciates the fact that the moment one thing is ended, it must be crossed out and dropped, and something else begun. Our Alexanders do not sit down and cry because there are no more worlds to

conquer, but snatch off their coats and fall to shinning around and raising corn and cotton, and improving sewing machines.

No doubt Clemens did for the most part admire this national attribute, but it was not the habitual stance of Mark Twain. In a country with the unofficial motto "Idle hands are the devil's playthings," and with its favorite spokesman of industriousness, Benjamin *Franklin, eternally extolling the virtues of hard work and savings, Twain's running gag of total idleness was a startling and pleasant comic contrast to convention. No man in America, perhaps, could better understand the longing for idleness in the face of a relentless work ethic than could Samuel Clemens, because in his upbringing and professional life, all of the paradoxes of America's work ethic flourished in their most intense, productive, and psychologically stressful forms.

In his *autobiography, no doubt with characteristic hyperbole, Mark Twain tells us that he was not raised to work, that he shared his father's belief that his speculation in a plot of land in Tennessee would ultimately allow the family to live in the idleness of sufficient wealth. He tells us that his father, allegedly a scion of southern aristocracy, aspired to the leisure of the landed gentry, finding in wealthy leisure not an impetus to dissipation, but an opportunity to cultivate the higher capacities of a person in pursuit of a virtuous independence. This may have been the aristocratic ideal, widely espoused in the South, but virtually nothing in Clemens's own life suggests that he expected or knew how to appreciate such leisure. His early letters suggest an obsession with work. His first trip from home, for instance, was an effort not merely to see the world, but also to make his own way, and in the process to send money back home to his mother. He in fact could not do so, finding employment scarce in New York City after Harper and Brothers, Publishers, suffered a fire that put most journeymen compositors in the city out of work, and finding it impossible to secure a permanent berth in Philadelphia. Nonetheless, in a letter dated 26–28 October 1853, from Philadelphia, he declared his determination: "I fancy they'll have to wait some time till they see me downhearted or afraid of starving while I have strength to work and am in a city of 400,000 inhabitants." The very next paragraph refers to a visit to the grave of Benjamin Franklin, Clemens's idol at this point in his life. On this first working tour from home, he had made Franklinian vows to remain sober and industrious, promises he seems to have kept.

In making these promises, he seems to have accepted two different aspects of the American cult of work, namely, that hard work was a source of virtue and perhaps salvation and that hard work would lead to material success. He was still under the spell of Franklin, whose autobiography was a second bible to both Samuel and his brother Orion, who each imitated the life of secular saint Ben much as he suggested young men might:

From the poverty and obscurity in which I was born and in which I passed my earliest years, I have raised myself to a state of affluence and some degree of celebrity in the world. As constant good fortune has accompanied me even to an advanced period of life, my posterity will perhaps be desirous of learning the means, which I employed, and which, thanks to Providence, so well succeeded with me. They may also deem them fit to be imitated, should any of them find themselves in similar circumstances.

In Franklin's autobiography and in his *Poor Richard's Almanacs*, Americans found a creed mixing a belief in the greater good with the pursuit of individual fortune.

Along the way, they found a powerful statement of the dignity of labor. According to Franklin, his father, trying to thwart Benjamin's rebellious inclination to go to sea to pursue his own pleasure away from the controlling hand of civil society,

> sometimes took me to walk with him and see joiners, bricklayers, turners, braziers, etc., at their work, that he might observe my inclination and endeavor to fix it on some trade that would keep me on land. It has ever since been a pleasure to me to see good workmen handle their tools; and it has been useful to me to have learned so much by it as to be able to do little jobs myself in my house, when a workman could not readily be got, and to construct little machines for my experiments when the intention of making these was warm in my mind.

Here, perhaps, is the best expression of the American spirit of hearty independence and self-reliance in labor. Mark Twain's Hank Morgan traces his lineage to this kind of Yankee inventiveness:

> My father was a blacksmith, my uncle was a horse-doctor, and I was both, along at first. Then I went over to the great Colt arms-factory and learned my real trade; learned all there was to it; learned to make everything: guns, revolvers, cannon, boilers, engines, all sorts of labor-saving machinery. Why, I could make anything a body wanted—anything in the world, it didn't make any difference what; and if there wasn't any quick new-fangled way to make a thing, I could invent one—and do it as easy as rolling off a log. ("A Word of Explanation" from *A Connecticut Yankee in King Arthur's Court*)

In this Franklinian heritage, too, was a profound belief that a life of leisure was a life of corruption. Even the independently wealthy needed to follow a profession in order to maintain their status; as Henry *James put it in *Washington Square*, America is a "country in which, to play a social part, you must either earn your income or make believe that you earn it." This belief was true to Clemens's essential sense of himself, as can be seen by his manic pace of work through most of his career, and his periodic disgust with kinds of work that he did not see as legitimate. For instance, after frantically working as a prospector and miner in Nevada in 1861 and 1862, Clemens finally had exhausted the money he had saved as a riverboat pilot. When he turned then to writing to make a steady wage, he explained his new profession in a 23 July letter to Orion as an expedient to tide him over until his investments in mines and mining stock should pay off: "[M]y board must be paid." Yet in the same paragraph, he suggested that such work was legitimate whereas his speculations were not: "[N]ow it has been a long time since I couldn't make my own living, and it shall be a long time before I loaf another year." He implies that his speculations were idle, an idea that comes up repeatedly in his literature, for example in *The Gilded Age*, one of the primary themes of which is that legitimate work eschews speculation because speculation produces nothing, and merely exploits those who do work in productive enterprises. Ironically, though, his prospecting speculations entailed incredibly hard work, as he acknowledged in one of his letters to Orion (17 and 19 April 1862): "No, don't buy any ground, anywhere. The pick and shovel are the only claims I have any confidence in now. My back is sore and my hands are blistered with handling them to-day. But something must come, you know."

The moral intensity of America's work ethic suggested that work was the secular equivalent of salvation. Certainly in Clemens's own life, work was the key to his ideas of worldly redemption; he saw in his success as a writer the possibility of marriage to an "angel" who would redeem him. His task, very much according to the commonplaces of nineteenth-century *domesticity, was to make the worldly livelihood that would support a home as haven. But repeatedly over the course of his career, Clemens found work to be psychologically redemptive, too. During his *Washington years he wrote his brother, "I am most infernally tired of Wash. & its 'attractions.' To be *busy* is a man's only happiness—& I *am*—otherwise I should die." In the 1890s, when his financial troubles grew overwhelming, Clemens turned to his writing with a vengeance, and a bit later, with the death of Susy, he redoubled his efforts to find, if not solace, at least escape in work. As he put it in a 22 January 1898 letter to William Dean *Howells:

> I couldn't get along without work now. I bury myself in it up to the ears. Long hours—8 & 9 on a stretch, sometimes. And all the days, Sundays included. It isn't all for print, by any means, for much of it fails to suit me; 50,000 words of it in the past year. It was because of the deadness which invaded me when Susy died. I have made a change lately—into dramatic work—& I find it absorbingly entertaining. I don't know that I can write a play that will play; but no matter, I'll write half a dozen that won't, anyway. Dear me, I didn't know there was such fun in it. . . . I get into immense spirits as soon as my day is fairly started.

Certainly this sense of work as salvation found its way into the works of Mark Twain. In *The *American Claimant*, for instance, the hero, Berkeley, raised as an aristocrat with no trade but idleness, finds himself down and out in the big city before stumbling upon a trade as a dauber of comic paintings. In so doing he discovers for the first time in his life the pleasure and dignity of work.

Clemens was extremely conscious of the paradoxes in America's work ethic. First, as much as Americans professed a belief in the dignity of all work and a political appreciation of work over aristocratic idleness, Americans pursued wealth in order not to have to work any more. This was true of Clemens himself, first in his frantic efforts to secure a fortune in mining, then in his persistent speculations in various machines and businesses. When writing *Connecticut Yankee*, Clemens turned up the satiric volume in part because he expected not to have to worry about the consequences to his literary reputation, believing his investments in the *Paige typesetter would relieve him of the need ever again to work for a living. Though this dream long motivated Clemens personally, he spent much of his literary life mocking it. He had seen the ravages of failed speculation among the miners of the West, ravages he had barely escaped himself. In 1862 he rashly wrote to his brother, "I shall never look upon Ma's face again, or Pamela's, or get married, or revisit the 'Banner State' until I am a rich man" (24 and 25 April), and when by 20 October 1865 he had not fulfilled that promise, he wrote Orion:

I have a religion—but you will call it blasphemy. It is that there is a God for the rich man but none for the poor. You are in trouble, & in debt—so am I. I am utterly miserable—so are you. Perhaps your religion will sustain you, will feed you—I place no dependence on mine. Our religions are alike, though in one respect—neither can make a man happy when he is out of luck. If I do not get out of debt in 3 months,—pistols or poison for one—exit *me*.

Transmuting his own experience into fiction, this melancholy about failing to strike it rich makes its way often into Twain's writings, as in the case of misanthropic Dick Baker in the *"Bluejay Yarn" from *A Tramp Abroad*, a miner whose failure to return home wealthy meant a life of lonely exile.

On the other side of the coin, Twain mocked those whose speculative wealth put them beyond labor but did not give them commensurate resources to make their leisure dignified or culturally valuable. In *The Gilded Age*, his scathing attack on the "Parvenus" suggests a kind of elitist belief that most people should remain as laborers. Less mean-spirited, but still expressing anxiety about the consequence of work that leads to wealth, are his portraits in *Roughing It* of working-class miners whose sudden wealth never elevates them beyond their narrow horizons. At the same time, Twain recognized that bromides about the dignity of labor and about its political value as an antidote to aristocratic pretension were highly suspect. Especially as business circumstances changed in the late nineteenth century with massive accumulations of capital dividing the permanent working class from the capitalists whose decisions governed the living as well as working conditions of their employees, the old belief that in labor was independence became an archaism. On the one hand, *"Old Times on the Mississippi" is a paean to the past power and dignity of labor, with Twain suggesting that the pilots' kingly independence vanished under the industrial conditions of the post–Civil War era. On the other hand, his "Letter to the Earth" suggests that the old nexus between Calvinistic faith and the work ethic leads to unscrupulous business behavior based on a narrow self-righteousness.

In this context, the stance of idleness that Clemens cultivated for Mark Twain becomes an idyllic escape. He discovered this idyll first in his letters home from Nevada, where he dropped the pose of earnest and sober young man to tease his mother and sister with an image of young Sam as dissipated idler. Every chance he got he suggested that he did no work. Even in describing his horse, he suggests his infirmity: "I am sorry you do not know him personally, ma, for I feel towards him, sometimes, as if he were a blood relation of our family—he is so infernally lazy, you know" (30 January 1862). All the while he was working frantically to secure wealth, but in the stance of idler, he took pleasure in violating the shared expectation that he would apply himself unceasingly to his prospects.

This background helped as Clemens developed the character *Mark Twain. At first Twain was merely the gentleman narrator, whose refinement was comic in counterpoint to the earthiness of his imaginary sidekick, Mr. Brown, and to a generally accepted western egalitarianism that scorned the pretensions of "gentlemen." When he began to solidify that character in *Roughing It*, he recovered the playful value of the stance he took in his letters home. Mark Twain became an inspired idler, one whose idleness arose not from independent wealth, but from a remarkable ability to shirk work while finding comrades to do it for him. The stance held, with refinements, in *A Tramp Abroad*, in which the narrator's pretensions toward gentlemanly idleness are challenged in the punning title. Is he tramping for recreation, or is he a tramp? *Following the Equator* took a strange turn in a different direction, for the book was well known to be a work—in both senses of the word—designed to recoup Clemens's financial losses. The stance of idler could hold very poorly, but that interlude did not stop Clemens from returning to the pose as soon as possible, with the last years of his life governed by the trope that Mark Twain had retired. His refusal to lecture for money, even as he lectured and spoke repeatedly for various charities, coupled with his persistent habit of holding court to photographers and reporters while in bed solidified the old image of Mark Twain as America's sanctioned idler. If the rest of America had to work, as least it could relax vicariously through the studied lounging of Mark Twain, who appeared relaxed no matter how hard Clemens had to work at the pose.

♦ SEE ALSO Calvinism; Finances; *Letters from the Earth*.

WORK HABITS. In a letter to William Dean *Howells dated 15 July 1874, Clemens reveals his basic outlook on his work as a writer:

No doubt you & I both underrate the worth of the work far enough; but that you are warrior enough to stand up & charge anything above a week's board is gaudy manliness in a literary person. Our guild are so egotistically mock-modest about their own merits.—We make a wretched bargain—caressing our darling humility the while—& then when we come to think how much more we could have got, we go behind the house & curse.—By George I admire you. I suppose "consuling" is not without its uses—it breeds common sense in parties who would otherwise develop only the uncommon.

Here Clemens argues against the popular idea that writing was an avocation for gentlemen, insisting instead that it is a legitimate vocation worthy of pay. In this sense, he found writing to be much more a trade than an art. Given that he learned his first two trades—printer and riverboat pilot—within tightly controlled guilds, he continued to use the metaphor of guild *labor to describe and organize his work, seeking not only mastery of his craft but to be his own guild master, controlling sales and distribution of his works.

He used the idea of the guild to elevate his status as a writer in his own mind, equating his "literature of a low order, i.e. humorous," with the serious literature of men like Howells. While current standards of literature accept the similarity, Clemens feared his contemporaries did not. Hence, his guild metaphor leveled the field in his own mind, enabling him to see himself as a legitimate worker in a broadly legitimate field. Such a metaphor enabled him psychologically to distance himself from the larger field of quasi-amateur writers who had achieved local celebrity and who wished to achieve national reputation and comparable pay. When approached by his brother Orion for help in publishing a parody of Jules Verne, Clemens replied:

Every man must *learn* his trade—not pick it up. God requires that he learn it by slow & painful processes. The apprentice-hand, in blacksmithing, in medicine, in literature, in *every*thing is a thing that can't be hidden. It always shows. But happily there is a market for apprentice-work, else the Innocents Abroad would have had no sale. (23 March 1879)

He used this argument to prevent his brother from using his name to help secure a publisher, and he used a similar argument from time to time against unsolicited manuscripts from people asking his opinion or advice. He characteristically replied that only the public could judge a book and, in so saying, betrayed his guild metaphor—he, the master, would not take on apprentices. Taking this position, he practically demonstrated the difference between a freelance writer and a shop master in a conventional guild. The rest of his 1879 letter to Orion shows further divergences between his actual practice of writing and his metaphorical justification of his work. He goes on to explain that he has worked on a piece for years that has not satisfied him:

Illustration by True Williams (1839–1897), from *A Tramp Abroad*, Hartford: American Publishing Company, 1879, p. 16.

Nine years ago I mapped out my "Journey in Heaven." I discussed it with literary friends who I could trust to keep it to themselves. I gave it a deal of thought, from time to time. After a year or more, I wrote it up. It was not a success. Five years ago, I wrote it again, altering the plan. That MS is at my elbow now. It was a considerable improvement on the first attempt, but still it wouldn't do. —Last year & year before I talked frequently with Howells about the subject, & he kept urging me to do it again. So I thought & thought, at odd moments, & at last I struck what I considered to be the right plan! Mind, I have never altered the *ideas*, from the first—the *plan* was the difficulty.

No journeyman would wait for inspiration to finish a piece of work. Even as he was trying to explain to his brother the amount of time it takes to get a piece right, he was also suggesting that he was as much an artist as a craftsman.

A confused sense of himself as both craftsman and artist shows in Clemens's many attempts to describe his technique for writing long fictional narratives. In a letter written in May 1887 but never sent, he wrote:

It is my habit to keep four or five books in the process of erection all the time, and every summer add a few courses of bricks to two or three of them; but I cannot forecast which of the two or three it is going to be. It takes seven years to complete a book by this method, but still it is a good method: gives the public a rest. I have been accused of "rushing into print" prematurely, moved thereto by greediness for money, but in truth I have never done that. . . . In twenty-one years, with all my time at my free disposal I have written and completed only eleven books, whereas with half the labor that a journalist does I could have written sixty in that time.

Again, the tasks he compares to writing books show something of his confused sense of the status of his work. As a gentleman artist, he takes his time in contrast to the journeymen journalists, yet he compares himself metaphorically to a journeyman mason.

This strange mixture of artistic and mechanical conceptions of his work never left Clemens, as he often considered inspiration a mechanical process of "filling up his tank," but he nonetheless usually waited for inspiration—he did not for the most part write according to a predetermined plan. As he put it in a letter to his Edinburgh friend, Dr. John Brown:

I have been writing fifty pages of manuscript a day, on an average, for some time now, on a book (a story) and consequently have been so wrapped up in it and so dead to anything else, that I have fallen mighty short in letter-writing. But night before last I discovered that that day's chapter was a failure, in conception, moral truth to nature, and execution—enough blemish to impair the excellence of almost any chapter—and so I must burn up the day's work and do it all over again. It was plain that I had worked myself out, pumped myself dry. (4 September 1874)

Clemens struggled constantly between spontaneity and craft in writing his longer works—and a craftsman he was, setting aside regular working hours for writing, and keeping notebooks the rest of the time as a way to collect raw material. He developed the habit of keeping journals before he turned to writing as a vocation—we still have a notebook from 1855, showing the young printer trying to learn French, studying phrenology, and a notebook from 1857 showing the apprentice pilot trying to memorize the Mississippi River. By 1865, the next notebook that survives, he was using his memorandum books not only to record daily events, but also to capture ideas for sketches. From then to the end of his life, he kept notebooks, and in these we see much of Clemens's life, from notations about business dealings to the record of a writer at work.

From these notebooks, we can also see that the first germs of ideas for books and articles often preceded the execution by years. Often they show how an idea was born in one key before shifting to a completely different key under the pressure of composition. Once a book moved from idea to execution, Clemens would write until inspiration failed him, when he would pigeonhole the manuscript for as long as it took for inspiration to strike again. Over the years, his habits of writing shifted to some degree, but after he dropped full-time *journalism in 1871, he wrote most during summers or during times he otherwise carved out from social and business obligations.

He usually wrote in his notebooks in pencil, on his manuscripts in ink. He wrote a clear hand on very good, but not exceptionally fine, writing paper, usually on single sheets of about four and one-half by eight inches. By contrast, he often wrote letters on folded letter paper. He tended to buy his writing supplies in bulk and keep records of the purchases, so that we can now often date manuscripts by the color ink—black, brown, or purple—or the brand and kind of paper he used. Sometimes, alterations in manuscripts can be dated by the discrepancies in ink between first draft and later revision.

He would usually write for several hours on a stretch, tossing finished leaves on the floor. At the end of a stint of writing, he would collect the leaves, order them, and calculate roughly how many words he had written in a day. He learned this habit as a journalist filling columns of particular length, and found the habit useful when he was laboring on large subscription books for which he had to provide a minimum number of words in order to fill his contracts. Such conditions encouraged padding, which Clemens often secured by cribbing information from other sources. Astonishingly, his *style remained economical in spite of this pressure toward verbosity.

Clemens did much of his best writing during summers spent in Elmira with his brother- and sister-in-law, Susan and Theodore *Crane. On the farm there the Cranes had built for Clemens an octagonal study, separated from the house. When in Hartford, he usually wrote upstairs in his billiard room, separated from all distractions. When he went to Europe to write, he often rented extra rooms to serve as writing studios. In any event, he needed privacy to draft his books. But he found inspiration as much in community as in isolation. He could not work without regular contact with an actively engaged, responsive audience. He began his work as a professional writer under the tutelage of Joseph *Goodman, whose editorial eye looked over Clemens's work daily. We cannot reconstruct their Nevada conversations, but we do have two accounts of Goodman reading *Roughing It* during his visit to Elmira in 1871. According to Goodman himself:

> I recollect his giving me the manuscript of "Roughing It" to read one afternoon when I was visiting him in the early seventies. He had made a great hit with "The Innocents Abroad," and was afraid he might not sustain his newly acquired reputation.... When I began to read the manuscript Sam sat down at a desk and wrote nervously. I was not reading to be amused, you understand, but was studying critically the merits of his writings. I read along intently for an hour, hardly noticing that Sam was beginning to fret and shift about uneasily. At last he could not stand it any longer, and in despair he jumped up exclaiming, "Damn you, you have been reading that stuff for an hour and you have not cracked a smile yet. I don't believe I am keeping up my lick." ("Jos. Goodman's Memories of Humorist's Early Days," San Francisco *Examiner*, 22 April 1910)

Albert Bigelow *Paine adds that Goodman responded, "Mark . . . I was reading critically, not for amusement, and so far as I have read, and can judge, this is one of the best things you have ever written" (*Mark Twain: A Biography*, 435).

If this picture is accurate, Goodman was a serious and exacting critic, and the correspondence we have from Goodman also suggests that he was an honest, insightful, and supportive reader of his friend's work; certainly Clemens credited him as a source of instruction in the trade of writing. So from the beginning, Clemens had an audience to help him gauge his day's output, and he sought to replicate such an audience in every phase of his career. In San Francisco, he identified Bret *Harte as his preferred reader; on board the *Quaker City* it was Mary Mason *Fairbanks; in Buffalo, David Gray. Once in Hartford, his circle of close respondents grew to include Charles Dudley *Warner, Joseph *Twichell, and many members of the *Monday Evening Club. More important with each passing year, he found in William Dean Howells an ideal audience. With many of these people, Clemens tried to reconstruct the cooperative and convivial environment of his newspaper days, proposing *collaborations with Howells, actually cowriting a novel with Warner and a play with Harte, enlisting Twichell's aid as traveling companion whose conversation inspired Clemens's writing, and borrowing notes on his travels from everyone he could think of, including Fairbanks for *The Innocents Abroad* and his brother for *Roughing It*.

No other audience was more important than his family, especially in the middle years of his career. At the end of a day's work, he returned to the household, collated pages in hand, and read the result to his assembled family, much as he describes in his autobiography:

> The children always helped their mother to edit my books in manuscript. She would sit on the porch at the farm and read aloud, with her pencil in her hand, and the children would keep an alert and suspicious eye upon her right along, for the belief was well grounded in them that whenever she came across a particularly satisfactory passage she would strike it out. Their suspicions were well founded. The passages which were so satisfactory to them always had an element of strength in them which sorely needed modification or expurgation, and were always sure to get it at their mother's hand. For my own entertainment, and to enjoy the protests of the children,
> I often abused my editor's innocent confidence. I often interlarded remarks of a studied and felicitously atrocious character purposely to achieve the children's brief delight, and then see the remorseless pencil do its fatal work. I often joined my supplications to the children's for mercy, and strung the argument out and pretended to be in earnest. They were deceived, and so was their mother. It was three against one, and most unfair. But it was very delightful, and I could not resist the temptation. Now and then we gained the victory and there was much rejoicing. Then I privately struck the passage out myself. It had served its purpose. It had furnished three of us with good entertainment, and in being removed from the book by me it was only suffering the fate originally intended for it. (*North American Review,* 2 November 1906)

While the outlines are accurate, Clemens here indulges his usual coloration in suggesting that he was in complete control of his improprieties. While he may well have added a few delicious indelicacies for sport, he needed his audience in part because he had such a poorly calibrated sense of propriety. As a humorist, his job was to push the boundaries of propriety without going too far, but in spending so much of his time dancing over the boundary, he found that the line tended to blur. Without regular feedback, Clemens had no confidence in his ability to transgress within acceptable limits.

Such a fear was one of the things that kept him from finishing books quickly. The "Journey to Heaven" that he mentioned to Orion in his 1879 letter never did get finished, though he finally published a part of it as *"Extract from Captain Stormfield's Visit to Heaven" in *Harper's Monthly Magazine* of December 1907 to January 1908, and slightly more of it in book form in 1909. In a 12 July 1908 letter to James Tufts of the San Francisco *Examiner*, who had inquired about the recently published *Harper's* installments, Joseph Goodman explained:

> During one of my visits to Mark Twain, at Hartford . . . he showed me the MS of this article. . . . I asked Mark why he hadn't published. . . . He said because it might hurt his literary reputation; that the public wasn't yet advanced enough for that sort of thing; but that he intended to amplify it and leave it to be published posthumously.

Certainly neither Goodman nor Howells discouraged publication, though apparently Olivia did, and Clemens accepted her judgment as his own. Only after her death, without her voice seconding his own fears, did he dare to publish.

Like most writers, Clemens found the physical act of writing to be uncomfortable, something he occasionally made much of in his writing. A 10 May letter to James B. Pond makes a joke out of a writer's typical complaint:

> Dear Pond:
>
> O, b'gosh, I can't. I hate writing.
> Ever thine,
>
> Mark

And in his autobiography, he said repeatedly that having discovered dictation in the early 1900s, he would never return to the hard work of writing by hand. Yet he had tried dictation before, first in 1873 and later in 1882, finding it no replacement for putting pen to page, however tedious a process that was. And for all the success he had with dictation in the 1900s, he still turned to the pen to work on letters, essays, sketches, and novels, as well as the occasional chapter for his autobiography. Earlier in his career, he tried the *typewriter, hoping that it would be a comfortable alternative, though he early discovered, as have many writers since, that it was not. Still, he found the clarity of the typewritten page a great benefit, often having typists turn his manuscripts into clean copies suitable for revision and better for typesetting.

As for revision, as much as Clemens wrote remarkably clean drafts rapidly and well, he revised extensively at all levels. In some cases, revision was a question of trying several times to work out an idea. He wrote in his notebook around 1902, "The time to begin writing an article is when you have finished it to your satisfaction. By that time you begin to clearly and logically perceive what it is that you really want to say." Yet he rarely really took this advice, being loathe to throw unsatisfactory material away, instead preferring to revise through addition, taking old material to work into the new, or letting the old stand, while new episodes ironize what went before. He wrote novels not to follow a clear plot development so much as to work, like much music, around a single theme, varying its meaning by varying its tone. The inversions of *irony easily led Clemens's *humor astray in these variations, turning from *burlesque to *satire and back in the course of a single story, such as in *Adventures of Huckleberry Finn*.

Clemens also usually revised his works at the smallest level of detail, carefully playing with diction and punctuation to capture the exact feelings and sounds he intended to convey. Sometimes such revisions made his language more conventional, as when he revised much of the slang of his journalism to make *Innocents Abroad* more literary. At other times, he worked just the opposite way, as with *Adventures of Huckleberry Finn*, for which he consistently revised Huck's language down. As much care as he could take with such detail, however, he often, as he approached the end of a project, tired of the tedium. At that point, his final revisions and his proofreading were capricious. While sometimes he proofread meticulously, he tried to shirk this work as much as possible, occasionally enlisting the aid of Howells, often doing a quick, cursory job on his own, especially when new projects called. In this caprice, varying between absolute meticulousness and pure nonchalance, Clemens again revealed his ultimate confusion over what kind of work he did—the work of an artist or the work of a craftsman.

♦ SEE ALSO *Arabian Nights Entertainment, The.*

WRIGHT, WILLIAM (1829–1898). After an unsuccessful career as a prospector in Nevada, Wright turned to journalism, becoming city editor of the Virginia City *Territorial Enterprise* in 1861. Under the pen name Dan De Quille ("dandy quill"), William Wright wrote fanciful sketches for the *Enterprise* and for other western journals, and as both straight reporter and as sketch writer, he was one of Twain's early tutors in the possibilities of *comic journalism.

Wright was born in the Midwest, beginning his life on a farm in Ohio. He moved with his family to Iowa in 1847. Married in 1853, he left his wife and three children for the mining districts out west. When in 1862 Wright took a trip to visit his family, the *Enterprise* hired Clemens to serve as a temporary replacement. When Wright returned, Clemens remained on the staff and the two became fast friends, eventually rooming together. In spite of the intensity of their friendship in Nevada, the relationship was not as important to Clemens as was his connection with Joseph *Goodman, owner of the *Enterprise.* While Wright and Clemens did correspond some over the years, Clemens quickly outgrew Wright's mentoring. By 1876, Clemens was helping Wright, encouraging his publication of *The Big Bonanza* (1876), a history of the Comstock mining region in Nevada.

Researching Mark Twain

Primary Sources

Given the number of inaccurately edited and bowdlerized reprints of Mark Twain's works, any effort to research Mark Twain should begin with good copies of the works themselves. The most carefully edited modern reprints are in the Mark Twain Project volumes published by the University of California Press and, soon, online. See the Mark Twain Project's web site for a current description of what is published where. This edition is probably as close to an accurate publication of what Samuel L. Clemens intended in his various writings as it is humanly possible to get. Many Mark Twain Project texts are available in lower-cost copies in the Mark Twain Library series. These include all of the same illustrations as in the Project editions but lack the scholarly appendices that explain how the text was derived.

No texts are as accurate as the Mark Twain Project texts. That said, as much as the Mark Twain Project's texts are determined according to the most advanced textual scholarship available, they still do not fully capture the *feel* of the originals. In the case of Mark Twain's published writings, there is no substitute for first editions if one is trying to recreate a sense of what it might have been like to have been a contemporary reader of Twain. Remarkably, first editions of many of Twain's works are quite accessible. Many older college and public libraries have early or first editions of some of Twain's—usually lesser known—books. Often these are housed in special collections but, surprisingly often, such volumes are in open stacks. Many used booksellers, of course, routinely offer Mark Twain volumes. Depending on the condition and popularity, some of these are little more expensive than comparably sized brand-new hardbound books, though a first edition of *The Adventures of Tom Sawyer* will cost thousands of dollars. Before buying expensive first or early editions, it is probably worth looking in the standard bibliography of Twain's works, Merle Johnson's *A Bibliography of the Works of Mark Twain* (rev. edition, 1935). In the absence of the Johnson, Jacob Blanck's *Bibliography of American Literature* (1957) covers the same ground. Most university libraries carry the Blanck; the Johnson is less common, but should be accessible via interlibrary loan.

In the absence of used imprints, facsimiles are available, most notably in the *Oxford Mark Twain,* Shelley Fisher-Fishkin, ed., a series of photographic reprints of all of Twain's books published in his lifetime. Some electronic facsimiles are available, too (see Electronic Resources, below).

Of course, much of Twain's original output was published in journals, and nineteenth-century journals are harder to find. Many college and university libraries house old magazines, but these collections grow less accessible with each passing year as time takes its toll on paper and bindings. Newspaper collections are almost nonexistent except on microfilm. Luckily, the Internet is preserving a pale version of many journals and a few newspapers (see Electronic Resources). The biggest advantage of locating Twain texts in nineteenth-century journals is that one can get a sense of the context in which Twain's writings appeared. For instance, the first excerpts of *Adventures of Huckleberry Finn* appeared in the *Century Magazine* in the same volume (29) as excerpts from William Dean Howells's *The Rise of Silas Lapham* and Henry James's *The Bostonians*, numerous poems, short stories, and various illustrations as well as articles on the electoral system, voting patterns in the South, the Civil War, discoveries in astronomy, architecture, education, and family life. One sees the appropriateness of fictional social commentary in magazines that contain such a wealth and diversity of social commentary.

In supplementing a contextual approach to studying Mark Twain, it is useful to know how his contemporaries reacted to his works. Of course, much of that reaction will never be known except insofar as his books sold well, but the published reviews in newspapers and magazines say much about what Twain's contemporaries saw in his books. Louis J. Budd has compiled an excellent, extensive collection of such reviews in *Mark Twain: The Contemporary Reviews* (1999). Other less comprehensive collections are still useful, such as *Mark Twain: The Critical Heritage* (1971), Frederick Anderson, ed., or the collections of reviews of particular books in the Norton critical editions series.

For researchers looking merely for reliable texts, there are many reprints that do no serious violence to Twain's words. The Library of America volumes in particular fit this bill. Indeed, the Library of America's *Mark Twain: Collected Tales, Sketches, Speeches, & Essays*, Louis J. Budd, ed., is the most reliable of any readily available collection of Mark Twain's shorter works. Penguin editions, too, tend to be of high quality, and most Riverside editions are acceptable as well.

Secondary Sources

Literary criticism can be viewed best, I believe, not as a collection of definitive statements of fact, but rather as a series of ongoing conversations that develop the value of literature. This book as a whole is a redaction of and contribution to many threads of that conversation, and the essay on *critical reception in the body of the book gives an overview of the dominant patterns in Mark Twain criticism. *A reading of that essay is perhaps the best place to begin a study of the extensive secondary literature on Mark Twain.* That said, there are literally hundreds of other conversations in literary criticism, some centrally and others tangentially addressing Mark Twain's works, and no single article (in this or any other book) covering the main trends could possibly do justice to such an abundance of material. Nor could a simple list of the works I have consulted. What the reader needs to do is to use bibliographies of literary criticism in order to follow his or her own interests.

The conversation in Twain studies has been so prolific, however, that no one bibliography can do everything a researcher could need. The most complete Mark Twain bibliography is Thomas A. Tenney's *Mark Twain: A Reference Guide* (1977), with annual supplements in *American Literary Realism* from 1977–1983 and in the *Mark Twain Circular* from 1984 to the present. The *Circular* is readily available online (see Electronic Resources). Tenney's bibliography is wide-ranging and as close to complete as is imaginable. It is not simply a listing of essays and books; Tenney includes brief descriptive comments. For comments that evaluate rather than describe, see *American Literary Scholarship*, an annual critical review that solicits bibliographic essays from specialists. Each year's volume has a chapter devoted to Mark Twain studies, and while these chapters are not quite exhaustive, they do cover the most influential works in a year's output.

Both of these bibliographies suffer from their format as annuals. For a researcher who wishes to cover many years by topic, any of the many electronic humanities databases available in almost all libraries will serve. The most comprehensive review of literary studies is the *MLA Bibliography*; other electronic databases that cover the humanities more broadly are useful for finding historical and cultural contexts. The downside of these is that they are mere listings with neither description nor evaluation, but coupled with Tenney's descriptions or *ALS*'s evaluation, a researcher can get a good picture of what is available on any topic. Finding the articles and books listed in these bibliographies may take patience but should be possible for anyone who has access to a public library. Most university libraries subscribe to most of the journals in which essays on Mark Twain appear, and most of these libraries are now beginning to keep these journals in electronic form, too. Public libraries tend not to subscribe to scholarly journals, but a patient researcher can use interlibrary loan to find almost anything that has ever been in print. Which brings up the most important trick in a researcher's repertoire: when in doubt, ask a reference librarian.

Other reference sources worth noting are compendia of Mark Twain quotations, of which there are many. One of the most common, Alex Ayres's *The Wit and Wisdom of Mark Twain* (1987), is amusing but not very accurate. Far better are two other books: Paul M. Zall, ed., *Mark Twain Laughing: Humorous Anecdotes by and about Samuel L. Clemens* (1985), and R. Kent Rasmussen, ed., *The Quotable Mark Twain: His Essential Aphorisms, Witticisms & Concise Opinions* (1997). Zall's book is organized by year, with a fine index giving access to quotations by subject. Rasmussen's is organized by topic, and it also has an index that allows one to refine subject searches.

Many researchers wish to begin a study of an author's works with a study of the author's life. Unfortunately, Mark Twain biography is a vexed field. The extraordinary amount of information available about this complex life makes any biographer's task almost impossible, so that almost all of them narrow their scope in some significant way. Consequently, each biography has been the subject of substantial criticism, criticism that says as much about current readers as it says about Mark Twain (though see above for widely held criticisms of *Mark Twain: A Biography* in the entry on Albert Bigelow *Paine). As much as all of these biographies have their weaknesses, most have strengths as well, so perhaps a collection of biographies does the best job of capturing the complexity of this famous life. A good way for the new researcher to decide which biographies he or she would like to read is to look in Jason G. Horn's bibliography of biographies, *Mark Twain: A Descriptive Guide to Biographical Sources* (1999). Biographies are not the only way to learn about Samuel Clemens's life; much literary criticism is based substantially in biography, such as James M. Cox's *Mark Twain: The Fate of Humor* (1966), Henry Nash Smith's *Mark Twain: The Development of a Writer* (1962), and my own *Sentimental Twain: Samuel Clemens in the Maze of Moral Philosophy* (1994). The advantage of such criticism *as* biography is that it reveals its biases. Yet another approach for those patient and confident enough to draw their own conclusions is to read the Mark Twain Project's various volumes of Mark Twain's letters and the Harvard University Press edition of the *Mark Twain–Howells Letters* (1960), Henry Nash Smith and William Gibson, eds. Finally, a book that is implicitly a biography of Clemens's mind is Alan Gribben's *Mark Twain's Library: A Reconstruction*, which is also an invaluable resource for studying almost any aspect of Mark Twain's works.

Secondary sources on the times rather than the life of Mark Twain are overwhelmingly numerous, and a search of the appropriate bibliographic databases of American history and culture would be a first step toward turning a researcher into an expert on American culture. But given the focus here on Mark Twain, I will provide a reading list that I find helpful in building a social context whenever I need to. It is useful to have a good college-level American history survey to cover the broad sweep of American politics and culture as well as a time line of modern world history; these abound and it would therefore be fruitless to specify. More narrowly covering the political history of Twain's early years as a writer are Eric Foner's *A Short History of Reconstruction, 1863–1877* (1990) and Kenneth M. Stampp's *The Era of Reconstruction, 1865–1877* (1965). Shifting from political to social history, the wonderfully engaging *The Americans: A Social History of the United States 1587–1914* (1969), by J. C. Furnas, will amply repay the time spent reading it. For a broad social history specifically of the Reconstruction years, see Daniel Sutherland's *The Expansion of Everyday Life, 1860–1876* (1989).

Mark Twain's career was constantly affected by shifting economic and industrial conditions; his fortunes rose and fell with each turn of the business cycle, and he found many of the subjects for his works in changing economic conditions. For the history of America's economy and the reactions of people to the changes brought on by industrialization, see Stuart Bruchey's *Enterprise: The Dynamic Economy of a Free People* (1990), Walter Licht's *Industrializing America* (1995), Bruce Laurie's *Artisans into Workers: Labor in Nineteenth-Century America* (1989), T. J. Jackson

Lears's *No Place of Grace: Antimodernism and the Transformation of American Culture, 1880–1920* (1981), and Leo Marx's *The Machine in the Garden: Technology and the Pastoral Ideal in America* (1964).

One of the most prolific fields in both literary and cultural studies in recent years has been gender studies. This topic became of special importance to Mark Twain studies almost from the beginning with the publication of Van Wyck Brooks's *The Ordeal of Mark Twain* (1920), which postulated that Twain's talent had been emasculated by a feminized culture. Bernard DeVoto's defense of Twain, *Mark Twain's America* (1932), besides being a wonderful social history in its own right, defended Twain's masculinity without challenging Brooks's demeaning picture of women's cultural influence. Not surprisingly, then, with the recent development of gender studies in critical circles more broadly, much new information about gender identity and literary culture that has come to light is useful in Mark Twain criticism. See Mary Kelley's *Private Woman, Public Stage: Literary Domesticity in Nineteenth-Century America* (1984), Ann Douglas's *The Feminization of American Culture* (1977), Christopher Lasch's *Haven in a Heartless World: The Family Besieged* (1977), Karen Lystra's *Searching the Heart: Women, Men, and Romantic Love in Nineteenth-Century America* (1989), Anthony Rotundo's *American Manhood: Transformations in Masculinity from the Revolution to the Modern Era* (1993), Gail Bederman's *Manliness and Civilization: A Cultural History of Gender and Race in the United States, 1880–1917* (1995), and Michael Kimmel's *Manhood in America; A Cultural History* (1996).

Many of these histories of gender, particularly Douglas's *The Feminization of American Culture,* touch also on religion, which became primarily the province of women over the course of the nineteenth century. Certainly Twain examined contemporary ideas of female spirituality, but he also examined questions of faith in his own right, and thus a broader history of religion helps us understand Twain's output. Sydney Ahlstrom's *A Religious History of the American People* (1972) fills the bill admirably. From Samuel Clemens's point of view, and he was not alone, the most important single influence on religion in the nineteenth century was the publication of Darwin's *Origin of Species.* To get a sense of Darwin's place in the English-speaking world and the impact his work had, see *Darwin's Century* (1958) by Loren Eiseley.

One of the topics of greatest interest to students of Twain is the problem of race and how Twain reacted to it. Once again, this is an enormous topic, one worthy of a book-length bibliography. Certainly all of the general histories I mentioned above are good beginning sources of information. For historical background specifically on the African-American experience, John Hope Franklin's *From Slavery to Freedom: A History of Negro Americans* (3d edition, 1967) is still highly respected. The development of late-nineteenth-century pseudoscientific racism is the topic of George M. Frederickson's *The Black Image in the White Mind: The Debate on*

Afro-American Character and Destiny, 1817–1914 (1971). More narrowly literary in scope but giving substantial background information on the role of race in American culture are Eric J. Sundquist's *To Wake the Nations: Race in American Literature and Culture, 1830–1930* (1993) and Henry Louis Gates's *The Signifying Monkey: A Theory of African-American Literary Criticism* (1988).

Even though Mark Twain's works almost entirely postdate emancipation, slavery does figure prominently in many of his books. Thus, many who study Twain wish to know more about slavery itself, especially as it bears on Twain's depiction of African-American characters. The modern debate over the impact of slavery was formulated around Stanley Elkins's controversial thesis in *Slavery: A Problem in American Institutional and Intellectual Life* (2d edition, 1968) that many slaves out of necessity became collaborators, adopting the outlook of their masters. In response to this strong position, many scholars proposed the opposite, that the slave community had integrity in its own right and influenced the slave-holding class. In this debate, many scholars unearthed detailed information about the lives of slaves in many different circumstances in order to assess the impact of African-American culture on American culture as a whole. Best known among these, perhaps, are John W. Blassingame's *The Slave Community: Plantation Life in the Antebellum South* (1972) and Eugene Genovese's *Roll Jordan Roll: The World the Slaves Made* (1974). The two opposing perspectives on slave "character" are reflected in interesting ways in the extensive literary criticism of Twain's treatment of race.

Of equal interest to a study of Mark Twain is how European Americans responded to slavery. James Oakes's *The Ruling Race: A History of American Slaveholders* (1982) may do the best job of depicting the circumstances of slaveholders when Samuel Clemens was a child. On a larger scale, David Brion Davis's classic *The Problem of Slavery in Western Culture* (1966) gives an overview of the traditions of thought that had a profound impact on Clemens's reaction against his own past, and Ronald G. Walters's *The Antislavery Appeal: American Abolitionism after 1830* (1976) details the movement that captured the hearts and energies of both the Howells and Langdon families, both of which were so influential on the development of Twain's thinking about slavery.

In order to understand Mark Twain's works, one must know something of his complicated relationship to high culture, and excellent studies of the culture industry shine much light on this context. A pairing of Russel Nye's *The Unembarrassed Muse: The Popular Arts in America* (1970) and Lawrence W. Levine's *Highbrow/ Lowbrow: The Emergence of Cultural Hierarchy in America* (1988) gives a good picture of Americans' changing attitudes toward art and the people. William Charvatt and Matthew Bruccoli's *The Profession of Authorship in America, 1800–1870* (1992) shows how the development of popular and middlebrow audiences enabled the development of writing as a lucrative profession. As a companion to Mark Twain's extensive journalism, Frank Luther Mott's five-volume *A History of American*

Magazines (1938–1968) will give a picture of where in the hierarchy of cultural production various magazines fit.

Humor, in magazines or in books, usually fits on the lower rungs of the cultural ladder, which is one reason that Twain's relationship to high culture was so tortuous. Much good work has been done on humorous literature, and a list of such works must begin with the scholarship of Walter Blair, whose *Native American Humor* (1937) virtually founded the field. An astonishingly large amount of work on American humor revolves around Mark Twain, so a good search in the databases I mentioned above will turn up a substantial bibliography. Humor studies more broadly speaking, though, disappoint in their explanations of this most puzzling of human phenomena. Humanists tend to latch on to one of five general theories— the classical theory of humor as nothing but aggression, Freud's theory that humor provides relief from psychic repression, Henri Bergson's idea that laughter developed as a form of social control, Mikhail Bakhtin's theory of humor as liberation, and the incongruity theory of humor popularized during the eighteenth and nineteenth centuries. A good compendium of these theories is to be found in John Morreal, ed., *The Philosophy of Laughter and Humor* (1987). None of these approaches is less than a half century old. While age is not intrinsically a problem with good scholarship, none of these theories and few of their current followers have caught up to the substantial leaps cognitive science has recently made in understanding the way the mind works. Two recent literary studies make the effort to update humor studies in the humanities: Bruce Michelson's *Literary Wit* (2000) and the last chapter of my own *Necessary Madness: The Humor of Domesticity in Nineteenth-Century American Literature* (1997).

No essay on researching Mark Twain can be complete without acknowledging that Twain's language is one of the things that makes his literature so effective. Given that he was an advocate of using that most difficult to find of literary raw materials, the right word, a dictionary is the most useful of all reference tools in Twain studies. Of course, not just any dictionary will do. Oxford University Press puts out one or two fine dictionaries, and Merriam-Webster has a solid reputation on the western side of the Atlantic, so dictionaries by either of these publishers will serve for the run-of-the-mill words in Twain's vocabulary. But when the tough ones cross your path, pick up the Random House *Historical Dictionary of American Slang*, edited by J. E. Lighter, who has the last word on American English.

Electronic Resources

Most of my discussion to this point has referred to electronic resources only in passing. This is in part because, as I write this in 2001, the Internet as a medium of communication is still in its infancy and suffers intense growing pains. It has only recently become useful and is still far from fulfilling its promise. Be that as it may, the Internet is now becoming an excellent source for doing primary research on

American culture broadly and on Mark Twain specifically. I give many web addresses below; though I know that many of these will change many times in the coming years. It is always possible to use search engines to find sites when their addresses have changed, though of course, some of these sites may not last. I have chosen to discuss only those that I find useful and likely to last, but my crystal ball works only tolerably well at best.

Many nineteenth-century journals are available online through "The Making of America" sites supported by the Universities of Michigan and Cornell. Each has a number of journals available in three formats—photographic facsimile, text, or pdf. Each site's database also includes many books, and each database is searchable. Unfortunately, the sites have several downsides. One, while the photographic and pdf facsimile files are excellent, the text files have not been corrected, so that these are replete with scanning errors. Furthermore, since searches are done in the text files, the number of scanning errors makes the searching only partially reliable. Moreover, searching is further complicated by the fact that the two sites are not connected, so that a search of any one topic needs to be done twice. Finally, each page image is in a separate, unconnected file, so that printing of, say, an article from a journal has to be handled one page at a time. These negatives are trivial, however, when one considers the wealth of information these databases bring to anyone with an Internet account. And while searches may not be fully reliable, to be able to search at all allows scholars to take a quantum leap over the old approach of finding and surveying annual indexes one magazine at a time.

There are many other excellent resources scattered over the Internet, and the number is likely to grow quickly over the coming years. Many of these are supported by universities, including sites at the University of Virginia, the University of North Carolina, and the University of California; others are supported by commercial outlets or by aficionados. At this stage, reliability and longevity are still not easy to predict, and finding access is not always easy. One disinterested search engine is the On-line Books page of the University of Pennsylvania. The scholars who tend the site simply make links to as many electronic books as they can find online and make their collection of links searchable. They do not vouch for the quality of the texts, nor is it possible for them to remove dead sites quickly enough for their service to be as effective as one would hope, but these are quibbles hardly worth noting in contrast to the value of the service. Of course it is always possible to use commercial search engines to find literary and cultural resources, but the odds are that your searches will be gummed up with much commercial drivel, distractions that make the Internet often exasperating.

e-Twain

Mark Twain has a substantial web presence, and given the fact that much of it is sponsored by universities and museums, it is likely to remain. The first of these to note is the web site for the Mark Twain Papers and Project, www.lib.berkeley.edu/ BANC/MTP, which describes the Project's ongoing efforts to produce a definitive edition of Twain's works. It also has links to many other Twain sites, as, for that matter, do most of the other sites I list here. By using these links it is possible to visit all of these sites after typing in but a single address. The University of Virginia "Electronic Text Center" sponsors an excellent site, "Mark Twain in His Times," by Stephen Railton, http://etext.virginia.edu/railton/index2.htm. The site is beautifully produced, one of the gems of the Internet. It also includes facsimiles of some of Mark Twain's books.

The Center for Mark Twain Studies, which supports many programs in support of Mark Twain research, maintains an informational site: www.elmira.edu/ MarkTwain/twainhom.htm. Similarly, the Mark Twain House museum in Hartford, Connecticut, supports research into Mark Twain. It, too, has an informational site: www.MarkTwainHouse.org.

A different kind of site is the one maintained by the *Mark Twain Circular*, the newsletter of the Mark Twain Circle of America. This site includes the online text of the *Circular*, which is useful not only for its essays and its notices of Mark Twain conferences and other events, but also for its publication of Thomas A. Tenney's bibliography of critical work on Mark Twain (see above). The address: www.citadel.edu/faculty/leonard/mtcircular.htm.

One of the first entrants into the field of e-Twain was the Mark Twain Forum, a moderated discussion group run by e-mail (see *Mark Twain Forum in the body of the book). While one can belong to the forum without ever approaching the World Wide Web, the forum does have a web presence called "TwainWeb" at www.yorku.ca/twainweb. This site includes information on how to subscribe to the forum, a research guide, a number of photographs, the forum's archives, and even a selection of Mark Twain merchandize.

Two commercial sites are worth mentioning for their quality and likely longevity. Jim Zwick, a well-known Twain scholar and early supporter of the web as a research tool, has developed an array of Mark Twain materials for his site at http://boondocksnet.com/twainwww/index.html. This is an especially good site for finding information on Twain's fight against imperialism. Another web wizard is Barbara Schmidt, who has the patience and tenacity to use e-mail and Internet resources to track down facts that have escaped scholars for years. Her work demonstrates the value of scholarly collaboration and of the web for facilitating collaboration, as she is constantly asking questions of various Twain scholars and sharing the information she gathers. Schmidt's site, www.twainquotes.com, is an especially good resource for finding Mark Twain's newspaper journalism, much of which she has transcribed into html.

A Bibliography of Works by Samuel L. Clemens

To the uninitiated, it will be surprising that such a major author as Mark Twain does not have a complete, authoritative bibliography of primary materials nearly a century after his death. But for anyone who has tried to work with the scattered, multifarious writings of Clemens, the possibility of a complete bibliography is an unrealized dream. Twain wrote for dozens of newspapers, the files of some of which—most importantly, the Virginia City *Territorial Enterprise*—are lost, and much of his work as a regular reporter was not signed. Moreover, before he took the pen-name "Mark Twain," Clemens irregularly contributed to a host of newspapers and magazines under many pseudonyms. What exactly he wrote is therefore often open to debate. Once, the Quintus Curtius Snodgrass letters that appeared in the New Orleans *Crescent* in early 1861 were attributed to Clemens, but careful study has almost certainly excluded these letters from the oeuvre. More difficult are items in the Buffalo *Express* in 1869 and 1870. Clemens was a part owner of the paper, and sometimes wrote over his nom-de-plume, but many more unsigned humorous pieces in the paper have been attributed to him. Scholars argue over these attributions, and while our steadily improving knowledge of where Clemens was when helps us decide on some of these, much work remains to be done.

It is my hope here to help Mark Twain scholars get closer to an authoritative bibliography, though I do not claim to have produced one. Instead, I have collated a number of bibliographies and tables of contents so that scholars can add to the list and challenge many of the attributed items here. Oxford University Press will mount this bibliography on-line at www.oup-usa.org/twain, and I will update it as new information becomes available. With this as a starting point, we should be able to create as good a bibliography as possible.

Of course, I began with Merle Johnson's *A Bibliography of the Works of Mark Twain* (rev. edition, 1935) and Jacob Blanck's *Bibliography of American Literature* (1957). As thorough as Johnson and Blank were, their works cannot account for the large number of posthumous works that issued over the last half of the twentieth century, nor do they account for the larger number of attributed journalistic pieces. For Clemens's earliest writing, I turned to Edgar M. Branch's "A Chronological Bibliography of the Writings of Samuel Clemens to June 8, 1867," *American Literature* 18 (May 1946): 109–59. Beyond that, I have collated tables of contents of posthumous publications and the reference tables of the Mark Twain Project volumes. Indeed, the core of my work was provided by the Project, a nearly 800-item list that the editors have drawn from various sources over the years. I also used various on-line resources, consulting Barbara Schmidt's list of Clemens's contributions to the New York *Times*. What remains, and the task is large, is to search the various Hartford newspapers, especially the *Courant*, and to make an effort to attribute unsigned items in the San Francisco *Dramatic Chronicle*. Certainly too, as the remaining unpublished manuscripts find their way into print, this list will need further additions.

I have chosen to leave out both personal letters and speeches, though I have included a large number of letters that were published in Clemens's lifetime when it seemed reasonable to assume he intended them to be published. Otherwise, the *Union Catalogue of Clemens's Letters,* now available on-line at the Mark Twain Projects site, is the best place to find information about the thousands of letters Clemens wrote in his life. Speeches present a more difficult problem. Insofar as he presented them in public, they were, in a sense, published works, but very few of them survive in manuscript, and the various newspaper reporters who preserved the texts rarely transcribed the speeches accurately enough for us to credit them as Mark Twain's writings. However, I have included those speeches that Clemens himself preserved and published.

The bibliography is given in chronological order. In the case of most *Enterprise* sketches, because our copy-texts are usually reprints from other western newspapers, the dates of original publication are speculative, though usually accurate to within a few days. In most cases, the dates listed are dates of publication, not composition, though I have put posthumous publications in order of composition and have also given the date of first publication.

Abbreviations used in this bibliography

(A)	attributed	MTS	*Mark Twain Speaking*, ed. Paul
alt.	alternative		Fatout (1976)
d.	dated	(P)	Published posthumously
MTB	*Mark Twain: A Biography*, by		
	Albert Bigelow Paine (1912).		

Periodicals

A	Aldine	Cal	Californian
AC	Alta California, San Francisco	CSF	Call, San Francisco
AP	American Publisher	CB	Carpet-Bag
AM	Atlantic Monthly	CM	Century Magazine
BA	Boston Advertiser	CR	Chicago Republican
Br	The Broadway: A London	CU	Christian Union
	Magazine	CEC	Cincinnati Evening Chronicle
BE	Buffalo Express	CBR	Cleveland Bazaar Record
CA	California Advertiser	CH	Cleveland Herald
CY	California Youths' Companion	CPD	Cleveland Plain Dealer

CW	Collier's Weekly		MEC	Monday Evening Club Paper
Cos	Cosmopolitan		MC	Morning Call
CH	Courant, Hartford		MJ	Muscatine Journal
DP	Denver Post		NCR	Napa County Reporter
DC	Dramatic Chronicle		NO	Naples Observer
EA	Elmira Advertiser		NOC	New Orleans Crescent
EB	Evening Bulletin		NPR	New Princeton Review
EE	Evening Express		NYEP	New York Evening Post
ES	Every Saturday		NYEW	New York Evening World
Ex	Examiner		NYG	New York Graphic
F	Forum		NYH	New York Herald
Fr	Friend, The		NYS	New York Sun
G	Galaxy		NYSM	New York Sunday Mercury
GC	Gate City		NYT	New York Times
GE	Golden Era		NYTr	New York Tribune
HC	Hannibal Courier		NYW	New York World
HJ	Hannibal Journal		NAR	North American Review
HM	Harper's Monthly		OM	Overland Monthly
HB	Harper's Bazaar		PS	Pacific Spectator
HW	Harper's Weekly		PM	Packard's Monthly
HEP	Hartford Evening Post		PAC	Philadelphia American Courier
HH	Hawaiian Herald		SU	Sacramento Union
ILN	Illustrated London News		SFN	San Francisco New Letter
KP	Keokuk Post		SP	Saturday Press
KSP	Keokuk Saturday Post		ST	Spirit of the Times
LS	Liber Scriptorum		SLD	St. Louis Dispatch
LDN	London Daily News		SNM	St. Nicholas Magazine
LMP	London Morning Post		SM	Sunday Mercury
LSp	London Spectator		TE	Territorial Enterprise
LSt	London Standard		Tw	The Twainian
LL	Lotos Leaves		VHR	Volcano House Register
MS	McClure's Syndicate		WMC	Washington (D.C.) Morning Chronicle
MF	Medical Fortnightly			
MDA	Memphis Daily Appeal		WES	Washington Evening Star
MD	Missouri Democrat		WR	Weekly Review
MR	Missouri Republican		WU	Western Union
MSJ	Missouri State Journal			

Title • Notes	Month/Day	Location
1850		
Humorous Comment Upon the Excellence of a Wedding Cake • Byline: "Devil."	11	WU (A)
1851		
Gallant Fireman, A	01/16	WU
New Costume, The	07	WU (A)
1852		
Dandy Frightening the Squatter, The	05	CB
Paragraph on a Military Company Formed by Town Boys	07	HJ (A)
Blabbing Government Secrets • Byline: "W.E.A.B."	09	HJ
Family Muss, A • Byline: "W. Epaminondas Adrastus Perkins."	09	HJ
For the Journal. Letter to "Mr. Editor" • Byline: "W. Epaminondas Adrastus Blab."	09	HJ
Letter to "Mr. Editor" • Byline: "A Dog-be-Deviled Citizen."	09	HJ
Local Resolves to Commit Suicide • Byline: "A Dog-be-Deviled Citizen."	09	HJ
Editorial Agility	09/16	HJ (A)
Historical Exhibition-A No. 1 Ruse	09/16	HJ
Local Resolves to Commit Suicide • Byline: "A Dog-Be-Deviled Citizen."	09/16	HJ
Blab's Tour • Byline: "W. Epaminondas Adrastus Blab."	09/23	HJ
Pictur' Department • Byline: "A Dog-Be-Deviled Citizen."	09/23	HJ
Connubial Bliss	11	HJ (A)

Title • Notes	Month/Day	Location
1853		
To Jennie	03/06	Early Tales and Sketches, 1979
For the Daily Journal • Byline: "Rambler."	04	HJ
News item about two stolen hams • Byline: "Rambler."	04	HJ
On Miss Anna Bread	04	HJ (A)
About "Rambler and His Enemies"	05	HJ (A)
Burial of Sir Abner Gilstrap, Editor of the Bloomington Republican • Parodies "The Burial of Sir John Moore." In "Our Assistant's Column."	05	HJ
Drunken Spree on the Ferry Boat	05	HJ (A)
Editor Left Yesterday . . . , The	05	HJ (A)
Editorial comment on Abner Gilstrap	05	HJ (A)
Editorial note praising "Oh, She Has a Red Head" • See below, 1853/05.	05	HJ (A)
For the Daily Journal • Byline: "Peter Pencilcase's Son, John Snooks."	05	HJ
For the Daily Journal • Byline: "Rambler."	05	HJ
For the Daily Journal • Byline: "Rambler."	05	HJ
Heart's Lament, The • Byline: "Rambler."	05/04	HJ
Increase of the Population of England for 1853	05	HJ (A)
Letter to "Mr. Editor" • Byline: "Grumbler."	05	HJ
Love Concealed • Byline: "Rambler."	05/04	HJ
Married in Podunk . . .	05	HJ (A)
News item about steamboat arrivals • Byline: "Rambler."	05	HJ

Title ♦ Notes	Month/Day	Location
Nonsense riddle	05	HJ (A)
Oh, She Has a Red Head ♦ Byline: "A Son of Adam."	05	HJ
Our Assistant's Column	05	HJ
Our Assistant's Column	05	HJ
Our Assistant's Column	05	HJ
Separation ♦ Poem. Byline: "Rambler."	05	HC
Terrible Accident! ♦ Headline hoax.	05	HJ
To Rambler ♦ Byline: "Grumbler."	05	HJ
Two paragraphs ridiculing Abner Gilstrap	05	HJ (A)
Two short editorials on Abner Gilstrap	05	HJ (A)
Heart's Lament, The ♦ Byline: "Rambler."	05/05	HJ
Sunday Amusements	05/10	HJ (A)
Friday Evening, May 27, 1853	06/02	HJ (A)
Saturday Evening, May 28, 1853	06/02	HJ (A)
Monday Evening, May 30, 1853. Small Pox Gone	06/02	HJ (A)
Tuesday Evening, May 31, 1853	06/02	HJ (A)
Letter to Mrs. Jane Clemens ♦ Letter d. 31 August.	09	HJ
Letter from New York ♦ Letter to Mrs. Jane Clemens, d. 08/24.	09/05	HJ
Letter from Philadelphia. ♦ Letter to Orion Clemens, d. 10/26.	11	MJ
Original Correspondence ♦ Letter for publication from Philadelphia, d. 12/04.	12	MJ

1854

Title ♦ Notes	Month/Day	Location
Correspondence ♦ Letter for publication from Philadelphia, d. 12/24.	01/06	MJ

Title ♦ Notes	Month/Day	Location
Correspondence of the Journal ♦ Letter for publication from St. Louis, d. 02/16.	02	MJ
Correspondence of the Journal ♦ Letter for publication from St. Louis, d. 03/05.	03	MJ
Washington Correspondence ♦ Letter for publication d. 02/18, 02/19.	03	MJ

1856

Title ♦ Notes	Month/Day	Location
Great Fair at St. Louis, The	10	KP
Snodgrass' Ride on the Railroad ♦ Byline: "Thomas Jefferson Snodgrass."	11	KP
Correspondence ♦ Byline: "Thomas Jefferson Snodgrass."	11/01	KSP
Ju'lus Caesar ♦ Date conjectural, mid-1855–late 1856.		(P) Early Tales and Sketches, 1979

1857

Title ♦ Notes	Month/Day	Location
Snodgrass, in an Adventure ♦ Byline: "Thomas Jefferson Snodgrass."	04	KP

1858

Title ♦ Notes	Month/Day	Location
My Brother, Henry Clemens ♦ Clipping from an unidentified newspaper in Clemens's Scrapbook 1:15.	?	unknown
Our Special River Correspondence	09/01	MD
Memphis-The Cotton Trade-Illinois Politics-What Tennessee Thinks of Them	10/22	MR
Correspondence	10/24	MDA

Title • Notes	Month/Day	Location
1859		
River Intelligence • Byline: "Sergeant Fathom."	05	NOC
Soleleather Cultivates His Taste for Music	07	NOC
1860		
Pilot's Memoranda	08/30	MR
Colloquy between a Slum Child and a Moral Mentor • Date conjectural, 1860s.		(P) Fables of Man, 1972.
1861		
Report on the Hannibal Home Guards	06	MSJ
Nevada Correspondence • Letter d. 10/26.	11	GC
Ghost Life on the Mississippi		(P) PS, 1948
1862		
Josh Letters, The • Written 02–07/1862. No copies have been located. Byline: "Josh."	02	TE
Model Letter from Nevada • Letter d. 1/30.	03	GC
Hannibal, Missouri	05/08	PAC
Letter d. 03/20	06	GC
Late from Washoe • Reprinted in SU d. 07/13.	07/20	TE (A)
Reports of the Second Territorial Legislature of Nevada	10	TE (A)
Spanish Mine, The • Text from reprint in the Butte Record, 11/01.	10	TE
Gale, A • Reprinted in the Butte Record, 10/11.	10/01	TE (A)
Indian Troubles on the Overland Route • Reprinted in the Marysville (Calif.) Appeal, 10/05.	10/01	TE
More Indian Troubles • Reprinted in the Marysville (Calif.) Appeal, 10/05.	10/01	TE (A)
Petrified Man • Date conjectural.	10/05	TE
Washoe Joke, A • Reprinted in EB, 10/15. The traditional title of Clemens's hoax is "The Petrified Man." The traditional date of first publication is 10/05 in the Virginia City Territorial Enterprise.	10/05	TE
Letter from Carson City • Clipping in Scrapbook 1:60.	12/08	TE
Particulars of the Assassination of Jack Williams • Reprinted in CSF 12/14.	12/10–12	TE (A)
Pah-Utes, The	12/13–19	TE
Letter from Carson • Clipping in Scrapbook 1:60.	12/15	TE
Blown Down • Clipping in Scrapbook 4:14.	12/30–31	TE
1863		
Reportorial • Appears in Early Tales and Sketches.	?	TE
Letter from Carson City • Clipping in Scrapbook 4:11.	01	TE
Sunday in Carson, A • Internal evidence dates this piece shortly after 01/23.	01	TE
Big Thing in Washoe City, A • Reprinted in Placer Weekly Courier, 01/17.	01/15	TE
In Carson City • Article is part of Clemens's feud with Clement T. Rice and may be d. after 02/02.	02	TE

Title • Notes	Month/Day	Location
Election in Virginia City, Gold Hill, Carson and Dayton, N.T., Yesterday-Splendid Union Triumph-Suicide of a Pioneer-Jack McNabb Shooting Policemen-Talk of a Vigilance Committee, etc., etc., The • Dispatch d. 09/02.	09/03	CSF
Mark Twain's Letter • Letter d. 08/30.	09/03	CSF
Bigler vs. Tahoe • Text follows a 09/13 GE reprinting.	09/04–05	TE
Literary Manifesto of Clemens and William Wright • Date conjectural, but no earlier than 09/05.	09/05	TE
Letter from Mark Twain • Letter d. 09/13.	09	TE
How to Cure a Cold • In Sketches New and Old as "Curing a Cold."	09/17	GE
Lick House Ball, The	09/27	GE
Great Prize Fight, The	10/11	GE
First Annual Fair of the Washoe Agricultural, Mining and Mechanical Society • Letter d. 10/19.	10/20	TE
Latest Sensation, The • Reprinted in the EB, 10/28.	10/28	TE
Clemens's reply to the Gold Hill (Nev.) News • Text from reprint in EB 11/03.	10/30	TE
'Ingomar' over the Mountains. The Arguments. • Date conjectural. Reprinted in GE 11/29.	11	TE
Letter from Dayton • Date conjectural, between 11/1863 and 03/1864. Reprinted in Glasscock, 122–23.	11	TE (A)
Play Acting over the Mountains. The Play of 'Barbarian,' by Maguire's Dramatic Troupe at Virginia City • Date conjectural. Reprinted in GE 11/29.	11	TE
Tide of Eloquence, A • Date conjectural. Reprinted in GE 12/06.	11	TE
Letter from Mark Twain • Letter d. 11/07.	11/10	TE
Letter from Mark Twain • Letter d. 11/15.	11/17	TE
Mark Twain's Letter • Letter d. 11/14.	11/19	CSF
Announcing Artemus Ward's Coming • Date conjectural; from 11/29 GE reprint.	11/20	TE
Lives of the Liars, or Joking Justified • Not extant, but referred to extensively in the Gold Hill (Nev.) News, 11/21.	11/21	TE
Still Harping • Not extant, but referred to and digested in the Reese River (Austin, Nev.) Reveille, 11/21.	11/21	TE
Mark Twain on Murders	11/22	CSF
Chinatown • Date conjectural, not extant, but probably 1863 or early 1864. Appears as chapter 54 of Roughing It.	12	TE
Death-Robbery, Carson, Dec. 1	12/02	CSF
Letter from Mark Twain • Letter d. 12/05.	12/08	TE
Assassination in Carson • Dateline Carson, 12/10.	12/11	CSF
Our Carson Dispatch-Second Session	12/13	TE

Title • Notes	Month/Day	Location
Third House-Reported by Mark Twain in "Phonographic Short Hand" • Letter d. 12/13.	12/13	TE
Letter from Mark Twain • Letter d. 12/12.	12/15	TE
Nevada State Constitutional Convention. Third House • Report d. 12/13.	12/19	TE
Report of Artemus Ward's lecture in Virginia City • Date unknown, not extant, but quoted in the Virginia City EB, 12/28.	12/28	TE
Christmas Presents	12/29	TE
Bolters in Covention, The	12/30	TE
Gorgeous Swindle, A	12/30	TE

1864

Title • Notes	Month/Day	Location
Letter to S. Pixley and G. A. Sears • Letter d. 01/23.	?	TE
Washoe Wit. Mark Twain on the Rampage	?	TE
Letter from Mark Twain • Letter d. 01/10.	01/11	TE
Legislative Proceedings	01/14	TE
Legislative Proceedings	01/14–27	TE
Letter from Mark Twain • Letter d. 01/14.	01/19–20	TE
Message to the "Third House," delivered in Carson City, 27 January	01/27	TE
Satirical account of Bill Stewart's party. • Not extant. Described in Lyman, Saga of the Comstock Lode, 269.	02/01	TE
Letter from Mark Twain	02/05	TE
Doings in Nevada • Letter d. 01/04.	02/07	NYSM
Letter from Mark Twain • Letter d. "Saturday night." Reprinted as "Concerning Notaries" in Walker.	02/09	TE
Legislative Proceedings. . . . House-Thirty-first Day	02/12	TE

Title • Notes	Month/Day	Location
Removal of the Capitol, The	02/16	TE
Legislative Proceedings	02/16–20	TE
Those Blasted Children	02/21	NYSM
Reviews of Adah Isaacs Menken's performances • Not extant. Menken opened in Virginia City on 03/02. SC is said to have written a series of eulogistic reviews and then some severe criticism of other companies playing in Maguire's Opera House.	04	TE
Another Traitor-Hang Him! • Reprinted under the editorial title "Another Goak."	04/01	TE
Frightful Accident of Dan De Quille • Reprinted in GE 05/01 as "Mark Twain and Dan De Quille-Hors De Combat-Counter Statement-Just Retribution."	04/20	TE
Letter from Mark Twain • Letter dated "Monday."	04/28	TE
Burlesque Life of Shakespeare	05	TE
Anticipating the Gridley Flour-Sack History • Date conjectural, from a reprint in EB 05/26.	05/20	TE
Washoe-Information Wanted • Reprinted in GE 05/22, and in Jumping Frog as "Information for the Million."	05/01–14	TE
History of the Gold and Silver Bars-How They Do Things in Washoe	05/16	TE
Grand Austin Sanitary Flour-Sack Progress through Storey and Lyon Counties	05/17	TE (A)

683

Title	Month/Day	Location
• Notes		
Editorial on the use of the Sanitary Fund proceeds in Carson City	05/18	TE
• Not extant, but quoted in a letter d. 05/18 from Mrs. W. K. Cutler and others, printed in the Virginia Daily Union, 05/27.		
How Is It? in "How Is It?'-How It Is."	05/18	TE
Travels and Fortunes of the Great Austin Sack of Flour	05/18	TE (A)
• Reprinted in EB, 05/20.		
Editorial, continuing the controversy with Virginia Daily Union over the Sanitary Fund proceeds.	05/20	TE
• Not extant, but answered in an editorial and letter in the Virginia Daily Union, 05/21.		
Miscegenation	05/24	TE
Personal Correspondence	05/24	TE
Burglar Arrested	06/07	CSF (A)
Another Chapter in the Marks Family History	06/12	CSF (A)
Beasts in the Semblance of Men	06/12	CSF (A)
Parting Presentation	06/13	AC
Petty Police Court Transactions	06/15	CSF (A)
Mark Twain in the Metropolis	06/17–23	TE
• Reprinted in GE 06/26.		
Short-Hand Law Reporter	06/21	CSF (A)
Another of Them	06/23	CSF (A)
Charge against a Police Officer	06/25	CSF (A)
Trip to the Cliff House, A	06/25	CSF (A)
The Evidence in the Case of Smith vs. Jones	06/26	GE
Accessions to the Ranks of the Dashaways	06/28	CSF (A)
Board of Supervisors	06/28	CSF (A)
Charges Against an Officer	06/28	CSF (A)

Title	Month/Day	Location
• Notes		
Hackmen Arrested	06/28	CSF (A)
Missionaries Wanted for San Francisco	06/28	CSF (A)
Swill Peddlers	06/28	CSF (A)
Kahn of Tartary, The	06/29	CSF (A)
Police Court	06/29	CSF (A)
Municipal Records	06/30	CSF (A)
Sacrilegious Hack-Driver, The	06/30	CSF (A)
House at Large	07/01	CSF (A)
More Steamship Suits Brewing	07/01	CSF (A)
Old Thing, The	07/01	CSF (A)
Police Commissioners	07/01	CSF (A)
School Children's Rehearsal	07/01	CSF (A)
Chance for the Hotels	07/02	CSF (A)
Policeman Suspended	07/02	CSF (A)
Stole a Shirt	07/02	CSF (A)
Swindle Case, The	07/02	CSF (A)
Early Rising, As Regards Excursions to the Cliff House	07/03	GE
Nabbed	07/03	CSF (A)
Secesh Highwaymen, The	07/03	CSF (A)
Theatrical Record City	07/03	CSF (A)
Those Thieves	07/03	CSF (A)
Young Thieves	07/03	CSF (A)
"Altagraph," An	07/04	CSF (A)
Original Novelette	07/04	CSF (A)
Sheep-Stealer Caught, A	07/04	CSF (A)
Banner Presentation	07/06	CSF (A)
Fourth of July	07/06	CSF (A)
Racing Stock in the Procession, The	07/06	CSF (A)
Shirt Stealing	07/06	CSF (A)
Homicide-Coroner's Inquest	07/07	CSF (A)
Arrested for Bigamy	07/08	CSF (A)
Bigamist, The	07/08	CSF (A)
En Route	07/08	CSF (A)
Insane	07/08	CSF (A)
Swill Music	07/08	CSF (A)
Bigamist, The	07/09	CSF (A)
Break in the Water Works	07/09	CSF (A)

Title • Notes	Month/Day	Location	Title • Notes	Month/Day	Location
Burglary-The Burglar Caught in the Act	07/09	CSF (A)	State Prisoners	07/19	CSF (A)
Opium Smugglers	07/09	CSF (A)	Lunatic	07/20	CSF (A)
United States Circuit Court	07/09	CSF (A)	Poetic Rabies, The	07/20	CSF (A)
Young Offender	07/09	CSF (A)	Police Court	07/20	CSF (A)
Bigamist, The	07/10	CSF (A)	Stage Robber Amongst Us, A	07/20	CSF (A)
Green-back Theft	07/10	CSF (A)	Amazonian Pastimes	07/21	CSF (A)
Astounding Cheek	07/12	CSF (A)	Attempted Mayhem	07/21	CSF (A)
Bigamy Case, The	07/12	CSF (A)	Detective Rose Again	07/21	CSF (A)
Chinese Slaves	07/12	CSF (A)	More Young Thieves	07/21	CSF (A)
Police Court Testimony	07/12	CSF (A)	Police Applicants	07/21	CSF (A)
United States Circuit Court	07/12	CSF (A)	Arrest of a Secesh Bishop	07/22	CSF (A)
Board of Education	07/13	CSF (A)	Astonishing Freak of Nature	07/22	CSF (A)
Insane	07/13	CSF (A)	Boss Earthquake, The	07/22	CSF (A)
Its Opponents	07/13	CSF (A)	First Regiment Election	07/22	CSF (A)
New Board Rooms	07/13	CSF (A)	Good Effects of a High Tariff	07/22	CSF (A)
Calaboose Theatricals	07/14	CSF (A)	Police Court Besieged, The	07/22	CSF (A)
Inspection of the Fortifications	07/14	CSF (A)	Rough on Keating	07/22	CSF (A)
Not Insane	07/14	CSF (A)	Scene at the Police Court-The Hostility of Color, A	07/22	CSF (A)
Runaway	07/14	CSF (A)			
Wife-Smasher in Limbo, A	07/14	CSF (A)	Demoralizing Young Girls	07/23	CSF (A)
Disposed Of	07/15	CSF (A)	Discharged	07/23	CSF (A)
Camanche, The	07/16	CSF (A)	False Pretences	07/23	CSF (A)
"Coming Man" Has Arrived, The	07/16	CSF (A)	Nose-Biter, The	07/23	CSF (A)
Gross Outrage, A	07/16	CSF (A)	Oh! That Mine Enemy Would Make a Speech!	07/23	CSF (A)
Moses in the Bulrushes Again	07/16	CSF (A)	Rape	07/23	CSF (A)
Remarkable Clock	07/16	CSF (A)	Merited Penalty, A	07/24	CSF (A)
County Prison, The	07/17	CSF (A)	"Nina Tilden," The	07/24	CSF (A)
Independent Candidate for Stockton	07/17	CSF (A)	Obscene-Picture Dealers	07/24	CSF (A)
Juvenile Criminals	07/17	CSF (A)	Police Court Doings	07/24	CSF (A)
More Cigar Smoking	07/17	CSF (A)	Startling!-The Latest General Order	07/24	CSF (A)
Progress of the Camanche-Libel	07/17	CSF (A)	Concerning Hackmen	07/26	CSF (A)
Too Infernally Accommodating	07/17	CSF (A)	Lewd Merchandise	07/26	CSF (A)
Assault	07/19	CSF (A)	Vending Obscene Pictures	07/26	CSF (A)
Camanche Matters	07/19	CSF (A)	Bail Forfeited	07/27	CSF (A)
Police Court	07/19	CSF (A)	Family Jar	07/27	CSF (A)
Real del Montel	07/19	CSF (A)	Police Court	07/27	CSF (A)
			Munificent Donation	07/28	CSF (A)

Title ◆ Notes	Month/Day	Location	Title ◆ Notes	Month/Day	Location
It Was True	08/10	CSF (A)	Unprofitable Operation, An	08/16	CSF (A)
Murderer Kennedy-A Question of Jurisdiction, The	08/10	CSF (A)	Sarrozay letter from the unreliable	08/16–22	Forty Tales and Sketches
New Star, A	08/10	CSF (A)	Aggravating a Pawnbroker	08/17	CSF (A)
Our U.S. Branch Mint	08/10	CSF (A)	Bella Union Imbroglio, The	08/17	CSF (A)
They Got Her Out	08/10	CSF (A)	Conjugal Infelicity	08/17	CSF (A)
Accumulation of Copperheads, An	08/11	CSF (A)	Judge Shepheard's School of Discipline	08/17	CSF (A)
Meteoric	08/11	CSF (A)	Peace-Maker, A	08/17	CSF (A)
Police Judge's Budget	08/11	CSF (A)	School Director Pope and the Call	08/17	CSF (A)
Small Business	08/11	CSF (A)	Damages for Personal Injury	08/18	CSF (A)
Young Celestial Derelicts	08/11	CSF (A)			
Growing	08/12	CSF (A)	Daring Attempt to Assassinate a Pawnbroker in Broad Daylight!	08/18	CSF (A)
Sanitary Fund	08/12	CSF (A)			
School Children's Rehearsal	08/12	CSF (A)	Fire at Hayes' Valley	08/18	CSF (A)
War of the Fruit Dealers	08/12	CSF (A)	Insolent Hackmen	08/18	CSF (A)
What a Sky-Rocket Did	08/12	CSF (A)	Launch of the New Stockton Steamer	08/18	CSF (A)
Billy the Boatman	08/13	CSF (A)	Man Run Over	08/18	CSF (A)
Camanche, The	08/13	CSF (A)	Soap Factory Nuisance, The	08/18	CSF (A)
Dr. Bellows' Address Last Evening	08/13	CSF (A)			
Drunken Duodecemvirate, A	08/13	CSF (A)	Washoe Congressional Gossip	08/18	CSF (A)
Fruiterers Fined	08/13	CSF (A)	New Chinese Temple, The	08/19	CSF (A)
More of the Fine Arts and Polite Literature	08/13	CSF (A)	What Goes with the Money?	08/19	CSF (A)
Sundries	08/13	CSF (A)	Wounded Boy, The	08/19	CSF (A)
Won't You Walk into My Parlor	08/13	CSF (A)	Mary Kane	08/20	CSF (A)
Another Clothing Thief	08/14	CSF (A)	More Abuse of Sailors	08/20	CSF (A)
Hotel Thief Arrested, A	08/14	CSF (A)	Revolutionary Patriot, A	08/20	CSF (A)
Washoe Convention, The	08/14	CSF (A)	Same Subject Continued, The	08/20	CSF (A)
Enlargement of the Spleen	08/16	CSF (A)	Suit Against a Mining Superintendent	08/20	CSF (A)
Hotel Thief, The	08/16	CSF (A)	Who Lost Them?	08/20	CSF (A)
Ill-Advised Prosecution, An	08/16	CSF (A)	Arms Taken in Charge by the Authorities (A)	08/21	CSF
Lively Times at the Bella Union	08/16	CSF (A)	Chinese Temple, The	08/21	CSF (A)
Manes of an Old Ejectment Laid	08/16	CSF (A)	False Rumor	08/21	CSF (A)
			It Is the Daniel Webster	08/21	CSF (A)
Rival Water Companies	08/16	CSF (A)	Still Improving	08/21	CSF (A)
Sharp Woman, A	08/16	CSF (A)			

Title • Notes	Month/Day	Location	Title • Notes	Month/Day	Location
Board of Supervisors	08/23	CSF (A)	Enthusiastic Hard Money Demonstration	08/30	CSF (A)
Camanche Items-Sanitary Contributions	08/23	CSF (A)	Fined	08/30	CSF (A)
Inexplicable News from San Jose	08/23	CSF (A)	Police Calendar	08/30	CSF (A)
New Chinese Temple, The	08/23	CSF (A)	China at the Fair	08/31	CSF (A)
No Earthquake	08/23	CSF (A)	Good and Bad Luck	08/31	CSF (A)
Rain	08/23	CSF (A)	Henry Meyer	08/31	CSF (A)
Sentenced Yesterday	08/23	CSF (A)	Mayhem	08/31	CSF (A)
Birney and Bunsby	08/24	CSF (A)	Pueblo Case, The	08/31	CSF (A)
Dark Transaction, A	08/24	CSF (A)	Shiner No. 1	08/31	CSF (A)
Ingratitude	08/24	CSF (A)	Strong as Sampson and Meek as Moses	08/31	CSF (A)
Police Contributions	08/24	CSF (A)	Cannibalistic	09/01	CSF (A)
Police Record	08/24	CSF (A)	Cosmopolitan Hotel Besieged, The	09/01	CSF (A)
Supernatural Impudence	08/24	CSF (A)	Doubtful Case, A	09/01	CSF (A)
Henry Meyer	08/25	CSF (A)	Fine Picture of Rev. Mr. King	09/01	CSF (A)
Judgements Against the "Sir George Grey"	08/25	CSF (A)	Kane Presentation	09/01	CSF (A)
Ladies' Fair, The	08/25	CSF (A)	Mechanics' Fair	09/01	CSF (A)
Theatres, Etc.: Metropolitan, The	08/25	CSF (A)	Police Subjects	09/01	CSF (A)
			Rincon School Militia	09/01	CSF (A)
War of the Races	08/25	CSF (A)	Strategy, My Boy	09/01	CSF (A)
Confederacy Caged, A	08/26	CSF (A)	Theatres, Etc.: Mr. Massett's Lecture- "Drifting About," The	09/01	CSF (A)
Good from Louderback	08/26	CSF (A)			
Mechanics' Fair	08/26	CSF (A)			
Who Killed Him?	08/26	CSF(A)	Art Gallery, The	09/02	CSF (A)
Arrest of Another of the Robbing Gang	08/27	CSF (A)	Camanche, The	09/02	CSF (A)
			Lost Child	09/02	CSF (A)
Fair, The	08/27	CSF (A)	Mechanics' Fair, The	09/02	CSF (A)
Forlorn Hope, The	08/27	CSF (A)	Rewards of Merit, The	09/02	CSF (A)
How to Cure Him of It	08/27	CSF (A)	Roll of Fame, The	09/02	CSF (A)
More Hawaiian Donations	08/27	CSF (A)	Afloat Again	09/03	CSF (A)
Who Lost Evangeline?	08/27	CSF (A)	Another Pawnbroker in Trouble	09/03	CSF (A)
Chicken Case, A	08/28	CSF (A)			
Determined on Suicide	08/28	CSF (A)	California Branch of the U.S. Sanitary Commission	09/03	CSF (A)
Don't Bury Your Money in Oyster Cans	08/28	CSF (A)			
Fair	08/28	CSF (A)	Contempt of Court	09/03	CSF (A)
Red, Black, and Blue, The	08/28	CSF (A)	Labyrinth Garden	09/03	CSF (A)
Board of Supervisors	08/30	CSF (A)	Lost Child Reclaimed, The	09/03	CSF (A)
Chinese Railroad Obstructions	08/30	CSF (A)	Marine Nondescript	09/03	CSF (A)
Dismissed	08/30	CSF (A)	Suicide out of Principle	09/03	CSF (A)

Title • Notes	Month/Day	Location	Title • Notes	Month/Day	Location
Wrecking Party in Luck, A	09/03	CSF (A)	Discharged	09/10	CSF (A)
Brutal	09/04	CSF (A)	Doing a General Business	09/10	CSF (A)
Californian, The	09/04	CSF (A)	Philanthropic Nation, A	09/10	CSF (A)
Criminal Calendar	09/04	CSF (A)	Race for the Occidental Hotel Premium	09/10	CSF (A)
Domestic Silks	09/04	CSF (A)	Attempted Assassination of a Detective Officer	09/11	CSF (A)
Hurdle-Race Yesterday, The	09/04	CSF (A)	Large	09/11	CSF (A)
Looks Like Sharp Practice	09/04	CSF (A)	Abolition Outrage, An	09/13	CSF (A)
Opening of the Fair	09/04	CSF (A)	Camanche, The	09/13	CSF (A)
Terrible Monster Caged, A	09/04	CSF (A)	Lost Children	09/13	CSF (A)
Conjugal Infelicity	09/06	CSF (A)	Plethoric	09/13	CSF (A)
Long Fast, A	09/06	CSF (A)	Police Target Excursion	09/13	CSF (A)
Mechanics' Fair	09/06	CSF (A)	Sad Accident-Death of Jerome Rice	09/13	CSF (A)
Peeping Tom of Coventry	09/06	CSF (A)	Sent Up	09/13	CSF (A)
Pound-Keeper Beheaded, The	09/06	CSF (A)	Board of Education	09/14	CSF (A)
Promising Artist, A	09/06	CSF (A)	Two Hundred Dollars Reward	09/14	CSF (A)
Set for Wednesday	09/06	CSF (A)	County Hospital Developments	09/15	CSF (A)
Small Piece of Spite, A	09/06	CSF (A)	Ingenious Contrivance, An	09/15	CSF (A)
Turned Out of Office	09/06	CSF (A)	Interesting Litigation	09/25	CSF (A)
Amende Honorable	09/07	CSF (A)	Mining Machinery	09/15	CSF (A)
Christian Fair	09/07	CSF (A)	Specimen Case, A	09/15	CSF (A)
Come to Grief	09/07	CSF (A)	Strange Coincidence	09/15	CSF (A)
In Bad Company	09/07	CSF (A)	Alleged Swindling, The	09/16	CSF (A)
Police Court Sentences	09/07	CSF (A)	Extraordinary Enterprise	09/16	CSF (A)
Terrible Calamity	09/07	CSF (A)	For the East	09/16	CSF (A)
Beautiful Work	09/08	CSF (A)	More Donations	09/16	CSF (A)
Captain Kidd's Statement	09/08	CSF (A)	Night Blooming Cereus	09/16	CSF (A)
Democratic State Convention	09/08	CSF (A)	Officer Rose Recovering	09/16	CSF (A)
Earthquake	09/08	CSF (A)	Suicide of Dr. Raymond	09/16	CSF (A)
Ladies' Fair, The	09/08	CSF (A)	Vegetable Bouquets	09/16	CSF (A)
Mark Mayer Ahead on the Home Stretch	09/08	CSF (A)	Blunder Corrected	09/17	CSF (A)
Charitable Contributions	09/09	CSF (A)	Dr. Raymond Not Removed	09/17	CSF (A)
Cross Swearing	09/09	CSF (A)	Late Suicide-Coroner's Inquest, The	09/17	CSF (A)
Democratic Ratification Meeting	09/09	CSF (A)	Chinese Banquet	09/18	CSF (A)
Mrs. Hall's Smelting Furnace	09/09	CSF (A)	Cruelty to Animals	09/18	CSF (A)
Curiosities	09/10	CSF (A)	Due Warning	09/18	CSF (A)
			Election of Coroner, The	09/18	CSF (A)

Title ◆ Notes	Month/Day	Location	Title ◆ Notes	Month/Day	Location
Suffering for Opinion's Sake	09/18	CSF (A)	Fair at the Fair, The	09/25	CSF (A)
Take One!	09/18	CSF (A)	Gilbert's Museum	09/25	CSF (A)
Theatrical Record: Maguire's Opera House	09/18	CSF (A)	Mint Troubles, The	09/25	CSF (A)
			Monitor's Progress, The	09/25	CSF (A)
Board of Supervisors	09/20	CSF (A)	Mortimer Again	09/25	CSF (A)
Board and the Rincon School, The	09/20	CSF (A)	Professional Garroter Nabbed	09/25	CSF (A)
Camanche Matters	09/20	CSF (A)	Rioters, The	09/25	CSF (A)
Chinese Banquet, The	09/20	CSF (A)	Boat Salvage	09/27	CSF (A)
Mayhem	09/20	CSF (A)	Narrow Escape	09/27	CSF (A)
Theatres, Etc.: Maguire's Opera House, The	09/20	CSF (A)	Nuisance	09/27	CSF (A)
Theatres, Etc.: Wilson-Zoyara Circus, The	09/20	CSF (A)	Whale Beached, A	09/27	CSF (A)
			Answer to a Mining Company's Suit	09/28	CSF (A)
Board of Education	09/12	CSF (A)	Advice to Witnesses	09/29	CSF (A)
Earthquake	09/21	CSF (A)	After Mortimer	09/29	CSF (A)
Judgments Against a Steamship Company	09/21	CSF (A)	Deaf Mutes at the Fair, The	09/29	CSF (A)
New Poundkeeper, The	09/21	CSF (A)	Demonstrative Anatomy	09/29	CSF (A)
Out of Jail	09/21	CSF (A)	Day of Atonement	09/30	CSF (A)
Stabbed	09/21	CSF (A)	Dog Theft	09/30	CSF (A)
Street Obstructions	09/21	CSF (A)	For the Santa Barbara Sufferers	09/30	CSF (A)
Terrible Weapon, A	09/21	CSF (A)	Jewish New Year, The	09/30	CSF (A)
Consequences of Indefiniteness, The	09/22	CSF (A)	More Children	09/30	CSF (A)
Female Assault	09/22	CSF (A)	Robbery	09/30	CSF (A)
Queer Fish	09/22	CSF (A)	Damages Awarded	10/01	CSF (A)
Stabbing Case	09/22	CSF (A)	Great Excitement	10/01	CSF (A)
Strike of the Steamer Employees	09/22	CSF (A)	Notable Conundrum, A	10/01	Cal
Trial of a Hackman	09/22	CSF (A)	Benefit for the Santa Barbara Sufferers	10/02	CSF (A)
Very Foolish Policy	09/22	CSF (A)	Everybody Wants to Help	10/02	CSF (A)
Weller's Bust	09/22	CSF (A)	Important Arrest	10/02	CSF (A)
Arrested for Riot	09/23	CSF (A)	Last Hitch at the Mint, The	10/02	CSF (A)
Dedication of Bush Street School	09/23	CSF (A)	Last Night of the Fair	10/02	CSF (A)
Farewell Address of Dr. Bellows	09/23	CSF (A)	Burglary-Two Men Shot	10/06	CSF (A)
Ah Sow Discharged	09/24	CSF (A)	Great Seal of Nevada	10/06	CSF (A)
Children at the Fair	09/24	CSF (A)	Interesting Correspondence, An	10/06	CSF (A)
Ellen French Fined	09/24	CSF (A)	Trial of the Folsom Street Wharf Rioters	10/06	CSF (A)
Accommodating Witness	09/25	CSF (A)			
African Troubles	09/25	CSF (A)			

Title / • Notes	Month/Day	Location
Concerning the Answer to That Conundrum	10/08	Cal
Convicted	10/08	CSF (A)
Judicial Change	10/08	CSF (A)
Police Court	10/08	CSF (A)
Rough Customer, A	10/08	CSF (A)
Camanche, The	10/09	CSF (A)
Miscegenation	10/09	CSF (A)
Nuisance, A	10/09	CSF (A)
Roderick Case, The	10/09	CSF (A)
Had a Fit	10/11	CSF (A)
Still Further Concerning That Conundrum	10/15	Cal
Whereas • Also known as "Love's Bakery"; "Aurelia's Unfortunate Young Man."	10/22	Cal
Touching Story of George Washington's Boyhood	10/29	Cal
Daniel in the Lion's Den—and Out Again All Right	11/05	Cal
Killing of Julius Caesar "Localized," The	11/12	Cal
Full and Reliable Account of the Extraordinary Meteoric Shower of Last Saturday Night, A	11/19	Cal
Lucretia Smith's Soldier	12/03	Cal
Excursion to Sacramento • Title supplied. Date conjectural, 1864–1865.		(P) Early Tales and Sketches, 1981
Mysterious Chinaman, The • Date conjectural.		(P) Tw, July–August 1947

1865

Title / • Notes	Month/Day	Location
Mark Twain On the Ballad Infliction • Reprinted in Cal., 11/04.	?	TE
Page from a Californian Almanac, A	?	DC
San Francisco Letter • Letter d. 12/29.	01/03–10	TE

Title / • Notes	Month/Day	Location
Romance in Real Life • Reprinted in County Gazette, 01/06.	01/02–04	TE
Unbiased Criticism, An	03/18	Cal
San Francisco's New Toy • Reprinted in CSF 05/16, reprinting the Virginia City TE of unknown date, sometime after 04/06.	04	TE
Important Correspondence	05/06	Cal
Further of Mr. Mark Twain's Important Correspondence	05/13	Cal
How I Went to the Great Race between Lodi and Norfolk	05/27	Cal
Voice for Setchell, A	05/27	Cal
Advice for Good Little Boys	06/03	CY
Answers to Correspondents	06/03	Cal
Answers to Correspondents	06/10	Cal
Answers to Correspondents	06/17	Cal
Enthusiastic Eloquence	06/23	DC
Advice for Good Little Girls • In $30,000 Bequest, slightly revised version under the title "Advice to Little Girls."	06/24	CY
Answers to Correspondents	06/24	Cal
Just One More Unfortunate • Reprinted in Downieville (Calif.) Mountain Messenger, 06/27–06/30.	06/27–30	TE
Answers to Correspondents	07/01	Cal
Smith Brown Jones	07/02	GE (A)
Answers to Correspondents	07/08	Cal
S. Browne Jones	07/09	GE (A)
S. Browne Jones	07/16	GE (A)

Title • Notes	Month/Day	Location
Mark Twain on the Colored Man • Reprinted GE 07/23.	07/07–19	TE
Facts, The	08/26	Cal
Cats! • Date conjectural. Reprinted in GE 10/29.	10	TE
Cruel Earthqake, The • Reprinted in Gold Hill News, 10/13.	10/10–11	TE
Popper Defieth Ye Earthquake • Clipping in YS, 38A-39.	10/15–31	TE
Earthquake Almanac	10/17	DC
Bob Roach's Plan for Circumventing a Democrat • In TE, lost date.	10/21–24	Ex
Attention, Fitz Smythe	10/26	DC (A)
Real Estate versus Imaginary Possessions, Poetically Considered • Includes the burlesque poem, "My Ranch."	10/28	Cal
Lisle Lester on Her Travels	10/30	DC (A)
Steamer Departures • Unidentified newspaper reprinting the Virginia City TE of unknown date, probably between 10/31 and 11/02. Clipping in Yale Scrapbook.	10/31–11/02	TE
Grand Theatrical Banquet	11	TE
Scriptural Panoramist, The	11	Ca
More California Notables Gone	11/01	DC (A)
'Chrystal' on Theology	11/03	DC (A)
Oh, You Robinson	11/06	DC (A
Explanation	11/07	DC (A)
Word from Lisle Lester, A	11/07	DC (A)
San Francisco Correspondence • Letter d. 11/08.	11/08	TE
Surplusage	11/08	DC (A)
Stand Back!	11/09	DC (A)
Pleasure excursion	11/09–12	TE
Cheerful Magnificence	11/11	DC (A)
Exit Bummer	11/11	Cal
In Ecstasies	11/13	DC (A)
Ye Ancient Mystery	11/16	DC (A)
Ambiguous	11/17	DC (A)
Improving	11/17	DC (A)
No Verdict	11/17	DC (A)
Bad Precedent	11/18	DC (A)
Jim Smiley and His Jumping Frog	11/18	SP
Mark Twain on the Launch of the Steamer Capital	11/18	Cal
Old Thing. "What Cheer Robbery," The	11/18	TE
Pioneers' Ball, The • Date conjectural, perhaps 11/21. Reprinted in GE 11/26 as "'Mark Twain-The Pioneers' Ball." Alt. title "'After' Jenkins" in The Celebrated Jumping Frog of Calaveras County.	11/19	TE
Goblin Again!, The	11/20	DC (A)
Wangdoodle Mourneth, The	11/24	DC (A)
Great Earthquake in San Francisco, The	11/25	WR
Letter-San Francisco, Nov. 23, 1865	11/25	NCR
Uncle Lige • Reprinted in Cal. 12/02 under title "Mark Twain Overpowered."	11/28–30	TE
Bribery! Corruption!	11/30	DC (A)
Drunk?	11/30	DC (A)
Shame!	11/30	DC (A)
Too Terse	11/30	DC (A)
Letter on the Mexican Oyster • Not extant.	12	TE

Title • Notes	Month/Day	Location
Story of the Bad Little Boy	12	Cal
How Is That?	12/01	DC (A)
Mark Twain's Letters • Letter d. 11/30	12/02	NCR
Delightful Romance	12/05	DC (A)
Rich Epigram, A	12/08–10	TE
Graceful Compliment, A	12/10–31	TE
San Francisco Letter	12/11	TE
Our Active Police	12/12	DC (A)
San Francisco Letter	12/13	TE
Celebrated Jumping Frog of Calaveras County, The • Version of "Jim Smiley and His Jumping Frog."	12/16	Cal
San Francisco Letter	12/19	TE
Grand Fete-day at the Cliff House • Reprinted in San Francisco Ex 12/23.	12/19–21	TE
San Francisco Letter • Letter d. 12/20.	12/20	TE
San Francisco Letter	12/20	TE
San Francisco Letter	12/22	TE
Christmas Fireside, The • Appeared under title "The Story of the Bad Little Boy Who Didn't Come to Grief" in Celebrated Jumping Frog of Calaveras County, and Other Sketches.	12/23	Cal
Enigma	12/23	Cal
San Francisco Letter	12/23	TE
San Francisco Letter • Letter d. 12/23.	12/26–27	TE
San Francisco Letter	12/29	TE.
Letter to the Californian • Title supplied; date conjectural.		(P) Early Tales and Sketches, 1981

1866

Title • Notes	Month/Day	Location
Fitz Smythe's Horse	?	TE

Title • Notes	Month/Day	Location
Honored as a Curiosity in Honolulu • Extracted from Sandwich Island Letters by Bret Harte for publication in Cal.	?	SU
Il trovatore	?	(P) Satires and Burlesques, 1967
Mark Twain	?	TE
Mark Twain on the Signal Corps. Equal to Spiritualism	?	TE
Mark Twain. What Have the Police Been Doing?	?	TE
Mark Twain's Kearny Street Ghost Story	?	TE
Mark Twain's New Year's Day	?	TE
Mysterious Newspaper Man • Reprinted in GE 02/16, with title "The Russian American Telegraph Company."	?	TE
New Biography of George Washington, A • Reprinted in GE 03/04. Reprinted in New York Weekly Review, 02/05, as "A New Biography of Washington." Reprinted in Jumping Frog as "Brief Biographical Sketch of George Washington."	?	TE
Policeman's Presents	?	GE
Presence of Mind. Incidents of the Down Trip of the 'Ajax.' • Reprinted in Jumping Frog.	?	TE
Short and Singular Rations • Extracted from Sandwich Island Letters by Bret Harte for publication in Cal.		SU

Title • Notes	Month/Day	Location
Spiritual Séance, The	?	TE
Steed "Oahu," The • Extracted from Sandwich Island Letters by Bret Harte for publication in Cal.	?	SU
San Francisco Letter	01/08	TE
San Francisco Letter	01/11	TE
San Francisco Letter • Letter d. 02/23.	02/25–28	TE
Letter from Mark Twain • Letter d. 02/25.	02/27–03/01	TE
Take the Stand, Fitz Smythe	02/06–07	TE
Mark Twain on Spiritual Insanity	02/08–11	TE
Mysterious Bottle of Whiskey, The	03/03	SP
Mark Twain on Boot-Blacks	03/11	GE
Reflections on the Sabbath	03/18	GE
Complaint about Correspondents, A	03/24	Cal
Complaint about Correspondents, dated in San Francisco, A	03/24	Cal
On Linden, etc.	04/07	Cal
San Francisco to Sandwich Islands-No. 1 • Letter d. 03/18.	04/16	SU
San Francisco to Sandwich Islands-No. 2 • Letter d. 03/19. Reprinted in Cal 04/21 and New York WR 06/02 as "Mark Twain at Sea."	04/17	SU
San Francisco to Sandwich Islands-No. 3 • Letter dated March.	04/18	SU
Scenes in Honolulu-No. 4 • Letter d. March.	04/19	SU
Scenes in Honolulu-No. 5 • Letter d. March.	04/20	SU
Scenes in Honolulu-No. 6 • Letter d. March.	04/21	SU
Scenes in Honolulu-No. 7 • Letter d. March.	04/24	SU
Mark Twain on His Travels	04/28	Cal
Scenes in Honolulu-No. 8 • Letter d. April.	05/21	SU
Scenes in Honolulu-No. 9 • Letter d. April.	05/22	SU
Scenes in Honolulu-No. 10 • Letter d. April.	05/23	SU
Scenes in Honolulu-No. 11 • Letter d. April.	05/24	SU
Mark Twain on His Travels	05/26	Cal
Mark Twain on a Singular Character	06/02	Cal
Strange Dream, A • Reprinted in Cal 07/07.	06/02	SP
At the Volcano • This entry in the Volcano House Register was torn out sometime after 1912, but was transcribed before lost.	06/07	VHR
Two Views of Honolulu • Excerpts from SU letters including "The Steed 'Oahu'" and "Etiquette."	06/09	WR
Scenes in Honolulu-No. 12 • Letter d. 05/23.	06/20	SU
Scenes in Honolulu-No. 13 • Letter d. 05/23.	06/21	SU
Mark Twain at the Islands	06/23	Cal
Scenes in Honolulu-No. 13 • Letter d. 06/22.	07/16	SU
Letter from Honolulu • Letter d. 06/25.	07/19	SU
Short Rations	07/21	Cal
Scenes in Honolulu-No. 14 • Letter d. 06/30.	07/30	SU
San Francisco Letter	08	TE
Mark Twain at the Confessional • Letter d. 07/19 to the Reverend Mr. Damon.	08/01	Fr
Scenes in Honolulu-No. 15 • Letter d. 07/01.	08/01	SU
Letter from Honolulu • Letter d. July.	08/18	SU
From the Sandwich Islands • Letter d. July.	08/24	SU

Title • Notes	Month/Day	Location
Letter to the Editor of the Californian	08/25	Cal
Moral Phenomenon, The	08/25	Cal
From the Sandwich Islands • Letter d. 1866.	08/30	SU
Mark Twain on His Travels	09/01	Cal
From the Sandwich Islands • Letter d. July.	09/06	SU
From the Sandwich Islands • Letter d. July.	09/22	SU
Mark Twain at the Islands	09/22	Cal
From the Sandwich Islands • Letter d. 09/10.	09/26	SU
How, for Instance? • Reprinted in TE 10/28 [?], as "An Inquiry About Insurance."	09/29	WR
Mark Twain at the Islands	09/29	Cal
Origin of Illustrious Men	09/29	Cal
Advertisement	10/02	DC
Epistle from Mark Twain, An	10/17	HH
From the Sandwich Islands • Letter d. June.	10/25	SU
Card from Mark Twain • Letter d. 11/01.	11/04	TE
Card to the Highwaymen	11/11	TE
Letter from Honolulu • Letter d. 06/03.	11/16	SU
Story of a Scriptural Panoramist, The • Extracted from "On the Launch of the Steamer Capitol," 11/18/1865.	11/17	Cal
Mark Twain's Interior Notes	11/30	EB
Forty-Three Days in an Open Boat • Author's name mis-spelled as "Mark Swain."	12	HM
Mark Twain's Interior Notes-No. 2	12/06	EB
Mark Twain Mystified	12/07	EB
Mark Twain's Interior Notes-No. 3	12/07	EB
So Long	12/14	AC

Title • Notes	Month/Day	Location
Depart, Ye Accursed • Reprinted in Cal 01/19/1867, as "Mark Twain on Chamber-maids" and in Jumping Frog as "Concerning Chambermaids."	12/15	WR
Mark Twain's Farewell • Speech delivered at Congress Hall, San Francisco, 12/10.	12/15	AC
Miss Slimmens	12/31	(P) On the Poetry of Mark Twain

1867

Title • Notes	Month/Day	Location
Cholera in Nicaragua • Telegram d. 01/12.	01/13	AC
Letter from Mark Twain • Letter d. 12/20/1866 on "Steamship America."	01/18	AC
Mark Twain On Chambermaids	01/19	Cal
Letter from Mark Twain. Number II. • Letter d. 12/20/1866 on "Steamer Columbia."	02/22	AC
Letter from Mark Twain. Number III. • Letter d. 12/23/1866.	02/24	AC
Winner of the Medal, The	03/03	SM
Barnum's First Speech in Congress	03/05	EE
Female Suffrage: Views of Mark Twain	03/12	MD
Volley from the Down-Trodden	03/13	MD
Iniquitous Crusade against Man's Regal Birthright Must Be Crushed	03/15	MD
Letter from Mark Twain. Number IV. • Letter d. "Christmas Eve" 1866.	03/15	AC
Letter from Mark Twain. Number V. • Letter d. "New Year's Day."	03/16	AC

Title · Notes	Month/Day	Location
Curtain Lecture Concerning Skating, A	03/17	SM
Letter from Mark Twain. Number VI. · Letter d. 01/01.	03/17	AC
Letter from Mark Twain. Number VII. · Letter d. 01/06.	03/23	AC
Barbarous	03/24	SM
Mark Twain in New York. Letter Number VIII. · Letter d. 02/02.	03/28	AC
Mark Twain in New York. Letter Number IX. · Letter d. 02/18.	03/30	AC
Mark Twain in New York. Letter Number X. · Letter d. 02/23.	04/05	AC
Female Suffrage	04/07	SM
Mark Twain in New York. Letter Number XI. · Letter d. 03/02.	04/09	AC
Official Physic	04/21	SM
Aurelia's Unfortunate Young Man · Variant of "Whereas," edited for Celebrated Jumping Frog.	05	Celebrated Jumping Frog of Calaveras County, and Other Sketches
Celebrated Jumping Frog of Calaveras County and Other Stories, The	05	Charles Henry Webb
Curing a Cold · Variant of "How to Cure a Cold," edited for Jumping Frog book.	05	Celebrated Jumping Frog
He Done His Level Best	05	Celebrated Jumping Frog
Remarkable Instances of Presence of Mind	05	Enterprise
Mark Twain in St. Louis. No. XII. · Letter d. 03/15.	05/13	AC
Letter from Mark Twain. No. XIII. · Letter d. 03/25.	05/19	AC

Title · Notes	Month/Day	Location
Letter from Mark Twain. No. 14. · Letter d. 04/16.	05/26	AC
Letter from Mark Twain. No. 15. · Letter d. 04/19.	06/02	AC
Letter from Mark Twain. No. 16. · Letter d. 04/30.	06/10	AC
Letter from Mark Twain. No. 17. · Letter d. 05/17.	06/16	AC
Letter from Mark Twain. No. 18. · Letter d. 05/18.	06/23	AC
Letter from Mark Twain. No. 19. · Letter d. 05/19.	06/30	AC
First Interview with Artemus Ward (alt title: "A Reminiscence of Artemus Ward")	07/07	SM
Letter from Mark Twain. No. 20. · Letter d. 05/20.	07/07	AC
Reminiscence of Artemus Ward, A	07/07	SM
Jim Wolf and the Tom-Cas	07/14	SM
Letter from Mark Twain. No. 21. · Letter d. 05/23.	07/14	AC
Letter from Mark Twain. No. 22. · Letter d. 05/26.	07/21	AC
Letter from Mark Twain. No 23. · Letter d. 05/28.	07/28	AC
Mediterranean Excursion, The · Letter d. 06/23.	07/30	NYTr
Mark Twain in Quarantine · Letter d. 08/02.	08/03	NO
Letter from Mark Twain. No. 24. · Letter d. 06/02. Reprinted in AC, 09/16.	08/04	AC

Title • Notes	Month/Day	Location
Letter from Mark Twain. No 25. • Letter d. 06/05.	08/11	AC
Letter from Mark Twain. No 26. • Letter d. 06/06.	08/18	AC
Holy Land Excursionists, The • Letter d. 08/01.	08/20	NYH
Holy Land Excursionists, The • Letter d. 08/02.	08/22	NYH
Holy Land Excursion. Letter from Mark Twain. Number One, The. • Letter d. 06/19.	08/25	AC
Holy Land Excursion. Letter from Mark Twain. Number Two, The. • Letter d. 06/30, num- ber 16 in the sequence.	08/27	AC
Holy Land Excursion. Letter from Mark Twain. Number Three, The. • Letter d. 07/01 at "Tangier, Africa."	08/31	AC
Holy Land Excursion. Letter from Mark Twain. Number Four, The. • Letter d. 07/01 at "Tangier, Africa."	09/01	AC
Holy Land Excursion. Letter from Mark Twain. Number Five, The. • Letter d. 07/12.	09/05	AC
Mediteranean Excursion • Letter d. July "At Large in Italy."	09/06	NYTr
Holy Land Excursion. Letter from Mark Twain. Number Six, The. • Letter d. 07/16.	09/08	AC
Holy Land Excursion. Letter from Mark Twain. Number Seven, The. • Letter d. July at "Milan, Italy."	09/15	AC
American Excursionists, The • Letter d. 08/27.	09/18	NYH

Title • Notes	Month/Day	Location
Americans on a Visit to the Emperor of Russia. • Letter d. 08/26.	09/19	NYTr
Holy Land Excursion. Letter from Mark Twain. Number Eight, The. • Letter d. July at "Lake of Como."	09/22	AC
Holy Land Excursion. Letter from Mark Twain. Number Nine, The. • Letter d. July "Abroad in Italy."	09/26	AC
Holy Land Excursion. Letter from Mark Twain. Number Ten, The. • Letter d. August at "Naples, Italy."	09/29	AC
Holy Land Excursion. Letter from Mark Twain. Number Eleven, The. • Letter d. August at "Naples."	10/01	AC
Holy Land Excursion. Letter from Mark Twain. Number Twelve, The. • Letter d. August at "Naples."	10/06	AC
Holy Land Excursion. Letter from Mark Twain. Number Thirteen, The. • Letter d. August at "Naples."	10/10	AC
Holy Land Excursion. Letter from Mark Twain. Number Fourteen, The. • Letter d. 07/29.	10/13	AC
Holy Land Excursion. Letter from Mark Twain. Number Fifteen, The. • Letter d. 08/15.	10/18	AC
Holy Land Excursion. Letter from Mark Twain. Number Sixteen, The. • Letter d. 08/20.	10/20	AC
Holy Land Excursion. Letter from Mark Twain. Number Seventeen, The. • Letter d. 08/23.	10/23	AC

Title • Notes	Month/Day	Location	Title • Notes	Month/Day	Location
Yankee in the Orient, A • Letter d. 08/31.	10/25	NYTr	Holy Land Excursion. Letter from Mark Twain. Number Twenty-six, The. • Letter d. 09/08.	11/24	AC
Holy Land Excursion. Letter from Mark Twain. Number Eighteen, The. • Letter d. August at "Constantinople."	10/27	AC	Holy Land Excursion. Letter from Mark Twain. Number Twenty-seven, The. • Letter d. 09/11.	12/01	AC
Holy Land Excursion. Letter from Mark Twain. Number Nineteen, The. • Letter d. August at "Constantinople."	10/29	AC	Holy Land Excursion. Letter from Mark Twain. Number Twenty-eight, The. • Letter d. 09/12.	12/04	AC
Holy Land Excursion. Letter from Mark Twain. Number Twenty, The. • Letter d. 08/22 at "Sebastopol."	11/01	AC	Holy Land Excursion. Letter from Mark Twain. Number Twenty-nine, The. • Letter d. 09/17.	12/08	AC
American Colony in Palestine, The. • Letter d. 10/02.	11/02	NYTr	Holy Land Excursion. Letter from Mark Twain. Number Thirty, The. • Letter d. September at "Banias."	12/15	AC
Holy Land Excursion. Letter from Mark Twain. Number Twenty-one, The. • Letter d. 08/22 at "Odessa."	11/03	AC	Letter from Mark Twain: The Facts in the Case of the Senate Door Keeper. • Letter d. 12/15.	12/15	NY Citizen
Holy Land Excursion. Letter from Mark Twain. Number Twenty-two, The. • Letter d. 08/27 at "Yalta."	11/06	AC	New Cabinet "Regulator," A • Letter d. 12/14.	12/16	WES
Holy Land. First Day in Palestine. • Letter d. September at "Baldwinsville, Galilee."	11/09	NYTr	Information Wanted • Letter d. 12/10.	12/18	NYTr
Holy Land Excursion. Letter from Mark Twain. Number Twenty-three, The. • Letter d. 08/27 at "Yalta, Russia."	11/10	AC	Holy Land Excursion. Letter from Mark Twain. Number Thirty-one, The. • Letter d. September at "Banias."	12/22	AC
Holy Land Excursion. Letter from Mark Twain. Number Twenty-four, The. • Letter d. 09/05.	11/17	AC	Mark Twain's Letters from Washington. Number I. • Letter d. 12/04.	12/22	TE
Cruise of the Quaker City, The • Undated letter written 11/19.	11/20	NYH	Facts Concerning the Recent Resignation, The	12/27	NYTr
Holy Land Excursion. Letter from Mark Twain. Number Twenty-five, The. • Letter d. 09/06.	11/21	AC	Holy Land Excursion. Letter from Mark Twain. Number Thirty-two, The. • Letter d. September at "Banias."	12/29	AC
			Quaker City Holy Land Excursion, The • Unfinished script for a play.		(P) Privately printed for M. Harzof, 1927

Title	Month/Day	Location
◆ Notes		
Goodbye		(P) CPD 04/27/1910
Who Was He? A Novel		(P) Satires and Burlesques, 1967

1868

Title	Month/Day	Location
Fine Old Man, A	?	BE
Holy Land Excursion. Letter from Mark Twain. Number Thirty-three, The. ◆ Letter d. 09/1867 at "Williamsburgh, Canaan."	01/05	AC
Mark Twain's Letters from Washington. Number II. ◆ Letter d. 12/16/1867.	01/07	TE
Letter from Mark Twain. Home Again. ◆ Letter d. 11/20/1867.	01/08	AC
Mark Twain's Letters from Washington. Number III. ◆ Letter d. 12/20/1867.	01/11	TE
Holy Land Excursion. Letter from Mark Twain. Number Thirty-four, The. ◆ Letter d. 09/1867 at "Williamsburgh, Palestine."	01/12	AC
Woman-an Opinion	01/13	WES
Mark Twain in Washington. (Special Correspondent of the Alta California.) ◆ Letter d. 12/10/1867.	01/15	AC
Holy Land Excursion. Letter from Mark Twain. Number Thirty-five, The. ◆ Letter d. 09/1867 at "Capernaum."	01/19	AC
Colloquy between a Slum Child and a Moral Mentor	01/20	(P) Fables of Man, 1972
Letter from Mark Twain. (Special Correspondent of the Alta California.) ◆ Letter d. 12/14/1867.	01/21	AC
Information Wanted ◆ Undated letter to the editor.	01/22	NYTr

Title	Month/Day	Location
◆ Notes		
Holy Land Excursion. Letter from Mark Twain. Number Thirty-six, The ◆ Letter d. 09/1867 at "Tiberias."	01/26	AC
Mark Twain in Washington. (Special Correspondent of the Alta California.) ◆ Letter d. 12/17/1867.	01/28	AC
Mark Twain's Letters from Washington. Number IV. ◆ Letter d. 01/10.	01/30	TE
General Washington's Negro Body-Servant	02	G
General Washington's Negro Body-Servant. A Biographical Sketch.	02	G
Holy Land Excursion. Letter from Mark Twain. Number Thirty-seven, The. ◆ Letter d. 09/1867 at "Nazareth."	02/02	AC
Gossip at the National Capital ◆ Special Correspondence of the Herald. Letter d. 02/01.	02/03	NYH
Mark Twain in Washington. (Special Correspondent of the Alta California.) ◆ Letter d. 01/11.	02/05	AC
Letter from Mark Twain ◆ Letter d. 01/31.	02/08	CR
Holy Land Excursion. Letter from Mark Twain. Number Thirty-eight, The. ◆ Letter d. 09/1867 at "Nazareth."	02/09	AC
Washington Gossip ◆ Special Correspondence of the Herald. Letter d. 02/08.	02/10	NYH
Mark Twain in Washington ◆ Delayed Letter. Letter d. 12/23/1867.	02/11	AC
Facts Concerning the Recent Important Resignation, The ◆ Letter d. 02/09.	02/13	NYTr

699

Title ♦ Notes	Month/Day	Location
Mark Twain in Washington. (Special Correspondent of the Alta California.) ♦ Letter d. 01/16.	02/14	AC
Holy Land Excursion. Letter from Mark Twain. Number Thirty-nine, The. ♦ Letter d. 09/1867 at "Nazareth."	02/16	AC
Mark Twain's Letters from Washington. Number V. ♦ Letter d. 01/11.	02/18	TE
Washington Gossip ♦ Special Correspondence of the Herald. Letter d. 02/15.	02/18	NYH
Mark Twain in New York ♦ Letter d. 01/20.	02/19	TE
Mark Twain in Washington. (Special Travelling Correspondent of the Alta California.) ♦ Letter d. 01/12.	02/19	AC
Mark Twain's Letter ♦ Letter d. 02/14.	02/19	CR
Holy Land Excursion. Letter from Mark Twain. Number Forty-three, The. ♦ Letter d. 09/1867.	02/23	AC
Concerning Gideon's Band ♦ Undated letter to the editor.	02/27	WMC
Mark Twain's Letters from Washington. Number VII. ♦ Letter d. 01/30.	02/27	TE
Holy Land Excursion. Letter from Mark Twain. Number Forty-four, The. ♦ Letter d. 09/1867 at "Jerusalem."	03/01	AC
Mark Twain's Letter ♦ Letter d. 02/21.	03/01	CR
Mark Twain's Letters from Washington. Number VIII. ♦ Letter d. 02/05.	03/01	TE
Mark Twain on His Travels. (Special Correspondent of the Alta California.) ♦ Letter d. 02/01.	03/03	AC
Rock Him to Sleep	03/04	CEC
Mark Twain's Letters from Washington. Number IX. ♦ Letter d. February.	03/07	TE
Holy Land Excursion. Letter from Mark Twain. Number Forty-five, The. ♦ Letter d. 09/1867 at "Jerusalem."	03/08	AC
Chinese Mission, The ♦ Undated letter to the editor.	03/11	NYTr
Mark Twain's Letters from Washington. Number X. ♦ Letter d. 02/22.	03/13	TE
Holy Land Excursion. Letter from Mark Twain. Number Forty-six, The. ♦ Letter d. 09/1867 at "Jerusalem."	03/15	AC
Holy Land Excursion. Letter from Mark Twain. Number Forty-seven, The. ♦ Letter d. 09/1867 at "Jerusalem."	03/22	AC
Holy Land Excursion. Letter from Mark Twain. Number Forty-eight, The. ♦ Letter d. 09/1867 at "Jerusalem."	03/29	AC
Holy Land Excursion. Letter from Mark Twain. Number Fifty-two, The. ♦ Letter d. 09/1867 at "Jerusalem."	04/05	AC
Mark Twain's Letters from Washington. Number XI. ♦ Letter d. 03/02.	04/07	TE
Holy Land Excursion. Letter from Mark Twain. Number Fifty-three, The. ♦ Letter d. 09/1867 at "Jerusalem."	04/12	AC
Holy Land Excursion. Letter from Mark Twain. Number Fifty-four, The. ♦ Letter d. 09/1867 at "Jerusalem."	04/26	AC
My Late Senatorial Secretaryship ♦ Alt. title, "Facts Concerning The Late Senatorial Secretaryship, The"	05	G

Title	Month/Day	Location
• Notes		
Rev. H. W. Beecher. His Private Habits.	09/25	BE
The Last Word • Title added.	09/25	BE (A)
People and Things	09/27	BE
Arthur	09/28	BE
California Pioneers, The	09/29	BE
Latest Novelty. Mental Photographs, The.	10/02	BE
Around the World. Letter No. One. • Letter d. 10/10.	10/10	BE
California Pioneers, The • Letter d. 10/11 to the California Pioneers.	10/14	NYTr
Legend of the Capitoline Venus, The	10/23	BE
Around the World. Letter No. 2. Adventures in Hayti. • Letter d. 10/05.	10/30	BE
Says Gossip One to Gossip Two • Title added.	11/02	BE (A)
Good Letter, A	11/10	BE
Around the World. Letter No. 3. California-Continued. • Undated letter to the editor.	11/13	BE
Browsing Around • Letter d. November.	11/27	BE
Lionizing Murderers • Alt. title: "Getting My Fortune Told"	11/27	BE
Back from Yurrup. In "Browsing Around" • Letter d. November.	12/04	BE
Browsing Around • Letter d. November. "Back from 'Yurrup.'"	12/04	BE
Around the World. Letter Number 4. California-Continued. • Undated letter.	12/11	BE
Around the World. Letter Number 5. California-Continued. • Undated letter.	12/18	BE
Ye Cuban Patriot	12/25	BE

Title	Month/Day	Location
• Notes		
Captain Stormfield's Visit to Heaven • SC worked on this piece beginning in 1869, and returned to it repeatedly, at least in 1870, 1873, 1878, 1881, 1883, 1893, and 1906.		Partially published as Extracts from Capt. Stormfield's Visit to Heaven, published in full posthumously in Report from Paradise
Innocents Abroad		AP

1870

Title	Month/Day	Location
Awful ---- Terrible Medieval Romance, An • Alternate title: "A Medieval Romance."	01/01	BE
Mrs. Stowe's Vindication	01/06	BE
Around the World. Letter Number 6. "Early Days in Nevada" • Undated letter.	01/08	BE
Ghost Story, A	01/15	BE
Around the World. Letter Number 8. Dining with a Cannibal. • Letter d. 11/20/1869.	01/29	BE
Around the World. Letter Number IX. The Pacific. • Byline: "D. R. F. (Darius R. Ford)."	02/12	BE
Anson Burlingame	02/25	BE
Blondes, The	02/28	BE
Nasby's Lecture	02/29	BE
Around the World. Letter Number X. Japan. • Letter d. 01/17 and 01/24. Byline: "D. R. F. (Darius R. Ford)."	03/05	BE
Big Thing, A	03/12	BE
Crime of Captain Eyre, The	03/14	BE
Literary	03/19	BE
Mysterious Visit, A	03/19	BE
Facts in the Great Land Slide Case, The	04/02	BE
Mark Twain on Agriculture	04/12	BE

Title • Notes	Month/Day	Location
New Crime, A	04/16	BE
New Crime, The	04/16	BE
About Smells	05	G
City of Hartford • Alt. Title: "Misplaced Confidence." See Collected Tales, Stories, Speeches, and Essays, p. 383.	05	G
Disgraceful Persecution of a Boy	05	G
Engagement Rings	05	G
Facts in the Case of the Great Beef Contract, The	05	G
George Wakeman	05	G
Introductory	05	G
Memoranda • Includes: "Introductory," "The Facts in the Case of the Great Beef Contract," "George Wakeman," "About Smells," "Disgraceful Persecution of a Boy," "The Story of the Good Little Boy Who Did Not Prosper," and four untitled items.	05	G
Oneida	05	G
Professor Silliman	05	G
Story of the Good Little Boy Who Did Not Prosper, The • Published as "The Story of the Good Little Boy" in Sketches New and Old.	05	G
Curious Dream	05/07	BE
Murder and Insanity	05/07	BE
Personal Habits of the Siamese Twins	05/09	BE
Our Precious Lunatic	05/14	BE
Untitled • Composed between 05/14 and 06/08. Albert Bigelow Paine titled it "Chinese Labor &c."	05/14	(P) Mark Twain in Three Moods, 1948
Street Sprinkling • Notice written on 05/26.	05/27	BE
Thanks to the Thoughtful ...	05/30	BE
Breaking It Gently • Untitled in original. Alt. title: "Higgins."	06	G
Couple of Sad Experiences, A	06	G
Higgins • Untitled in original	06	G
Hogwash	06	G
Judge's Spirited Woman, The	06	G
Lady Franklin	06	G
Literary Old Offender in Court with Suspicious Property in His Possession, A	06	G
Memoranda • Includes: "A Couple of Sad Experiences," "The Petrified Man," "My Famous 'Bloody Massacre,'" "The Judge's 'Spirited Woman,'" "Hogwash,'" "A Literary 'Old Offender' in Court with Suspicious Property in His Possession," "Post-Mortem Poetry," "Wit-Inspirations of the 'Two-Year-Olds,'" and four untitled items.	06	G
Murphy	06	G
My Famous Bloody Massacre • Published as "My Bloody Massacre" in Sketches New and Old.	06	G
Patriarch, A	06	G
Petrified Man, The	06	G
Post-Mortem Poetry	06	G
Widow's Protest, The	06	G

Title ◆ Notes	Month/Day	Location
Baby	10	G
Curious Relic for Sale	10	G
Fashion Item, A	10	G
Favors from Correspondents	10	G
How Is This for High	10	G
Johnny Skae	10	G
Memoranda ◆ Includes: "The Reception at the President's," "Goldsmith's Friend Abroad Again," "Curious Relic For Sale," "Science vs. Luck," "Favors from Correspondents" (including "Johnny Skae's Item").	10	G
Obituary	10	G
Obituary	10	G
Reception at the President's, The	10	G
Science vs. Luck	10	G
Some Other Favors	10	G
Goldsmith's Friend Abroad Again	10–11	G
At the President's Reception	10/01	BE
Johnny Skae's Item	10/01	BE
Curious Relic for Sale	10/08	BE
It is said . . . ; And with the . . .	10/15	BE
Mark Twain. His Map of the Fortifications of Paris.	10/15	BE
On Riley-Newspaper Correspondent ◆ Reprinted from "Riley-Newspaper Corespondent."	10/29	BE
Favors from Correspondents	11	G
General Reply, A	11	G
Mark Twain's Map of Paris	11	G
Mark Twain's Map of Paris	11	G
Memoranda ◆ Includes: "Riley-Newspaper Correspondent," "Goldsmith's Friend Abroad Again," "A Reminiscence of the Back Settlements," "A General Reply," "Favors from Correspondents," and two untitled items.	11	G
Reminiscence of the Back Settlements, A	11	G
Riley-Newspaper Correspondent	11	G
Untitled article in "Memoranda"	11	G
Reminiscence of the Back Settlements, A	11/05	BE
General Reply, A	11/12	BE
Present Nuisance, The	11/19	BE
Running for Governor	11/19	BE
My Watch-An Instructive Little Tale	11/26	BE
Art	12	G
Brigham Young	12	G
Divorce	12	G
Entertaining Article, An	12	G
Epitaph	12	G
Favors from Correspondents	12	G
Favors from Correspondents	12	G
Galaxy	12	G
History Repeats Itself	12	G
Map	12	G
Memoranda ◆ Includes: "An Entertaining Article," "'History Repeats Itself,'" "Running for Governor," "The 'Present' Nuisance," "Dogberry in Washington," "My Watch-An Instructive Little Tale," "Favors from Correspondents," and two untitled items.	12	G

Title • Notes	Month/Day	Location
My Watch-An Instructive Little Tale	12	G
Present Nuisance, The	12	G
Running for Governor	12	G
Whitney	12	G
Entertaining Article, An	12/03	BE
Three Aces: Jim Todd's Episode in Social Euchre • Byline: "Carl Byng."	12/03	BE (A)
Dogberry in Washington	12/10	BE
Famous Sanitary Flour Sack, The • Letter d. 12/11.	12/13	NYTr
I Never Played at "Vingt et Un" • Byline: "Ab O'Riginee."	12/13	BE (A)
War and Wittles	12/16	BE
Facts in the Case of George Fisher, Deceased, The	12/17	BE
Waiting for the Verdict	12/19	BE
Mean People	12/24	BE
Sad, Sad Business, A	12/24	BE
Brummel-Arabella Fragment • Begun before 1870, added to and left unfinished in 1870.		(P) Satires and Burlesques, 1967.
Emperor-god Satire, The • Date conjectural, 1870s.		(P) Fables of Man, 1972

1871

Title • Notes	Month/Day	Location
Answer to an Inquiry from the Coming Man	01	G
Concerning a Rumor	01	G
Doggerel	01	G
Facts in the Case of George Fisher, Deceased, The	01	G
Forty-Niner, A	01	G
Goldsmith's Friend Abroad Again	01	G
Mean People	01	G

Title • Notes	Month/Day	Location
Memoranda • Includes: "The Portrait," "The Facts in the Case of George Fisher, Deceased," "A 'Forty-Niner'....," "'Doggerel,'" "Goldsmith's Friend Abroad Again," "Mean People," "A Sad, Sad Business," "Concerning a Rumor," "Answer to an Inquiry from the Coming Man."	01	G
Portrait, The	01	G
Portrait of King William III	01	G
Sad, Sad Business, A	01	G
New Books	01/14	BE
Danger of Lying in Bed, The	01/28	BE
Book Review, A	02	G
Coming Man, The	02	G
Danger of Lying in Bed, The	02	G
Falsehood, A	02	G
Indignity Put Upon the Remains of George Holland by the Rev. Mr. Sabine, The	02	G
Memoranda • Includes: "The Coming Man," "A Book Review," "The Tone-Imparting Committee," "The Danger of Lying in Bed," "One of Mankind's Bores," "A Falsehood," "The Indignity Put Upon the Remains of George Holland by the Rev. Mr. Sabine."	02	G
One of Mankind's Bores	02	G
Tone-Imparting Committee, The	02	G
About a Remarkable Stranger	04	G

Title	Month/Day	Location
♦ Notes		

Memoranda — 04 — G
♦ Includes: "Valedictory," "My First Literary Venture," "About a Remarkable Stranger."

My First Literary Venture — 04 — G

Question Answered, A — 04 — AP

Valedictory — 04 — G

Autobiography, An — 04 — A

Old-Time Pony Express of the Great Plains, The — 05 — AP

Substitute for Rulloff. Have We a Sydney Carton among Us?, A. — 05/03 — NYTr
♦ Letter to the editor d. 04/29.

New Beecher Church, A — 07 — AP

About Barbers — 08 — G

How I Secured a Berth — 08 — G

Brace of Brief Lectures on Science. Part 1, A. — 09 — AP

Revised Catechism, The — 09/27 — NYTr

Brace of Brief Lectures on Science. Part 2, A. — 10 — AP

Big Scare, A — 11 — AP

My First Lecture — 12 — AP
♦ Appears as chapter 78 of Roughing It.

Mark Twain's (Burlesque) Autobiography and First Romance — Sheldon and Co.
♦ "First Romance" is "An Awful ---- Terrible Medieval Romance" (see 01/01/1870).

1872

Mark Twain's Sketches — George Routledge and Sons
♦ Selected and revised by the author. Copyright edition.

New Pilgrims' Progress, The — Author's English Edition

Nabob's Visit to New York, A — 01 — AP
♦ Appears as chapter 46 of Roughing It.

Dollinger the Age Pilot Man — 02 — AP
♦ Appears as chapter 51 of Roughing It.

Roughing It and The Innocents at Home, 2 vols — 02 — George Routledge and Sons

Roughing It — 02/19 — AP

Roughing It — 03 — AP
♦ Appears as chapter 57 of Roughing It.

Horace Greeley's Ride — 04 — AP
♦ Appears as chapter 20 of Roughing It.

Mark Twain on the Mormons — 06 — AP
♦ Appears as chapter 15 of Roughing It.

Mark Twain at the Grave of Adam — 07 — AP
♦ Appears as chapter 53 of Innocents Abroad.

Secret of Dr. Livingstone's Continued Voluntary Exile, The — 07/20 — CH

Mark Twain and His English Editor — 09/21 — LSp
♦ Letter d. 09/20.

Mark Twain — 11/06 — LDN
♦ Departure announcement d. 11/05. Sent to several additional London newspapers.

Daring Deed, A — 11/26 — BA
♦ Letter to the Royal Humane Society d. 11/20.

Concerning an Insupportable Nuisance — 12/06 — HEP
♦ Letter d. 12/05.

Missouri Disaster, The — 12/07 — NYTr
♦ Letter d. 12/05.

Appeal for Capt. Ned Wakeman-Letter from Mark Twain — 12/14 — AC
♦ Letter d. 12/03.

How I Escaped Being Killed in a Duel — 12/21 — ES

New Cock-Robin, The — 12/24 — HEP
♦ Poem d. 12/235.

Title / • Notes	Month/Day	Location
Inquiry about Insurance, An		Celebrated Jumping Frog
Tom Sawyer: A Play		(P) Hannibal, Huck and Tom, 1969
Two Poems-By Moore and Twain (alt. title to "Those Annual Bills")		Sketches, New and Old

1876

Title / • Notes	Month/Day	Location
Some Recollections of a Storm at Sea	01/18	CBR
Literary Nightmare, A • Alt. title: "Punch, Brothers, Punch!"	02	AM
Letter Read at the Dinner of the Knights of St. Patrick	03/18	CH
Facts Concerning the Recent Carnival of Crime in Connecticut, The • Read at Monday Evening Club meeting 01/24.	06	AM
Secret Out, The	07/25	NYEP
Canvasser's Tale, The	12	AM
Adventures of Tom Sawyer, The • English edition through Chatto & Windus had been published in June.	12/08	AP
Ah Sin • Drama co-authored with Bret Harte SC, produced in 1877.		(P) 1961
Date 1601. Conversation, as it was by the Social Fireside, in the time of the Tudors • Composed in 1876, privately printed in 1880.		Privately printed
Murder, a Mystery, and a Marriage, A		(P) 2001

1877

Title / • Notes	Month/Day	Location
Francis Lightfoot Lee		Pennsylvania Magazine
Untitled • "Contributor's Club" regarding Anna Dickinson.	01	AM
Letter to the editor • d. 02/14	02/18	NYW
Tramp of the Sea, A	09/19	CH
Some Rambling Notes of an Idle Excursion	10	AM
Some Rambling Notes of an Idle Excursion	11	AM
Some Rambling Notes of an Idle Excursion	12	AM
Whittier Birthday Speech • First authorized publication in Chapters from My Autobiography XXV (see 12/1907); often excerpted as "Story of a Speech."	12/17	Presented at event in Boston honoring John Greenleaf Whittier
True Story, and the Recent Carnival of Crime, A		James R. Osgood and Co.
Cap'n Simon Wheeler, the Amateur Detective		(P) Satires and Burlesques, 1967
Autobiography of a Damned Fool • Date conjectural.		(P) Satires and Burlesques, 1967

1878

Title / • Notes	Month/Day	Location
Some Rambling Notes of an Idle Excursion	01	AM
Loves of Alonzo Fitz Clarence and Rosannah Ethelton, The	03	AM
About Magnanimous-Incident Literature	05	AM
Lost Ear-ring, The	06	(P) Fables of Man, 1972
Punch, Brothers, Punch! And Other Sketches		Slote, Woodman and Company
Tupperville-Dobbsville • Date conjectural, late 1870s.		(P) Hannibal, Huck and Tom, 1969

Title • Notes	Month/Day	Location
1879		
Recent Great French Duel, The	02	AM
Great Revolution in Pitcairn, The	03	AM
Mark Twain as a Presidential Candidate	06/09	NYEPt
Battle Flag Day	09/11	CH
Our Georgia Visitors	10/17	CH
Mark Twain on the New Postal Barbarism	11/25	CH
Speech delivered at a breakfast honoring Oliver Wendell Holmes's seventieth birthday, on 3 December 1879 in Boston • As reported in "The Holmes Breakfast," BA, 4 December. Variant texts published in the Supplement to the Atlantic Monthly 45 (February 1880); MTS 1910, 56–58; MTS 1923, 77–79; and MTS 1976, 134–36.	12/03	BA
Mark Twain and Postal Matters • Alt. title "Postal Matters" cited by Budd but unlocated.	12/09	CH
French and the Comanches, The • Originally written for A Tramp Abroad.		(P) Letters from the Earth, 1962
1880		
Telephonic Conversation, A	06	AM
Irish Famine Fund, The	05	Art Autograph
Untitled • "Contributor's Club," in reply to a Boston girl.	06	AM
Edward Mills and George Benton: A Tale	08	AM
Mrs. McWilliams and the Lightning	09	AM
Millions in It	09/16	NYEP
Untitled • "Contributor's Club," on obituary eloquence.	11	AM
Letter to Bazaar Bulletin • For charity fair in Buffalo.	12/13	CH
Abner L. Jackson (About to be) Deceased • Date conjectural, 1880–1881.		(P) Fables of Man, 1972
Cat Tale, A		(P) Concerning Cats, 1959
Clairvoyant, A • Date conjectural, early 1880s.		(P) Hannibal, Huck and Tom, 1969
Letter from the Comet, A • Date conjectural, 1880s.		(P) Fables of Man, 1972
Tramp Abroad, A		AP
1881		
Untitled • "Contributor's Club," on German publisher Tauschnitz.	01	AM
Burlesque Hamlet	08	(P) Satires and Burlesques, 1967
Curious Experience, A Burlesque Etiquette	11	CM (P) Partially published in MTB, other parts in Letters from the Earth, 1962
Prince and the Pauper: A Tale for Young People of All Ages, The		James R. Osgood and Co.
Second Advent, The		(P) Fables of Man, 1972
1882		
Why He Didn't • Might be a reprint from Childhood's Appeal, 1880.	05/18	Youth's Companion

Title	Month/Day	Location
Stolen White Elephant and Other Stories, The		James R. Osgood and Co.
McWilliamses and the Burglar Alarm, The	12	HM Christmas Supplement
Concerning the American Language		Stolen White Elephant and Other Stories
Invalid's Story, The		Stolen White Elephant and Other Stories
Legend of Sagenfeld, In Germany		Stolen White Elephant and Other Stories
On the Decay of the Art of Lying		Stolen White Elephant and Other Stories
Paris Notes		Stolen White Elephant and Other Stories
Speech on the Babies ◆ Speech given at the Army of the Tennessee Reunion in 1879.		Stolen White Elephant and Other Stories
Speech On The Weather		Stolen White Elephant and Other Stories
Stolen White Elephant, The		Stolen White Elephant and Other Stories

1883

Title	Month/Day	Location
Life on the Mississippi	05	James R. Osgood and Co.
Mark Twain Aggrieved ◆ Alt. title: "Why a Statue of Liberty When We Have Adam?"	12/04	NYT
1002'd Arabian Night		(P) Satires and Burlesques.

1884

Title	Month/Day	Location
Tragic Tidings	?	SF Wasp
Ye Equinoctial Storm ◆ Written spring 1868.	01/19	SF Wasp
Carson Fossil-Footprints, The	02/16	San Franciscan

Title	Month/Day	Location
Huck Finn and Tom Sawyer among the Indians ◆ A 228-page manuscript begun in July 1884 and abandoned probably in mid August. Some was set on the Paige typesetter in 1889 or 1890.	07	(P) Hannibal, Huck, and Tom, 1969; corrected with additions in Huck Finn and Tom Sawyer among the Indians, 1989
Hunting for H—	08/24	NYS
Adventure of Huckleberry Finn: With an Account of the Famous Grangerford-Shepherdson Feud, An	12	CM
My Dog Burns	12	Every Other Saturday

1885

Title	Month/Day	Location
Jim's Investments, and King Sollermun	01	CM
Royalty on the Mississippi: As Chronicled by Huckleberry Finn	02	CM
What Ought He to Have Done	07/16	CU
Accepting a Pension	07/18	BA
Future National Capital, The	07/30	NYS
Private History of a Campaign That Failed, The	12	CM
Wanted-A Universal Tinker ◆ Byline: "X.Y.Z."	12	CM
Adventures of Huckleberry Finn ◆ English edition through Chatto & Windus was published in December 1884; American edition delayed until early 1885.		Charles Webster and Co.
Character of Man, The		(P) What Is Man? And Other Philosophical Essays, 1973

Title · Notes	Month/Day	Location	Title · Notes	Month/Day	Location
Slovenly Peter · Twain's translation of Der Struwwelpeter, a children's book in German.	09	(P) Harper and Brothers, 1935.	Affeland (Snivelization)		(P) Satires and Burlesques, 1967
Mark Twain at Aix-les-Bains · Alt. titles: "Tramp Abroad Again I. Paradise of the Rheumatics" in Illustrated London News in 11/14 and 11/28. Also "Aix-les-Bains," cited in Skandera, p. 96. See also: An Austrian Health Factory, NYS 02/07.	11/08	Chicago Tribune	American Claimant, The		Charles Webster and Company
			Californian's Tale, The		LS
			Merry Tales		Charles Webster and Company
			The Late Reverend Sam Jones's Reception in Heaven · Written winter of 1891–1892.		(P) Mark Twain's Quarrel with Heaven, 1970
Mental Telegraphy	12	HM			

<table>
<tr><td colspan="3">1893</td></tr>
</table>

Title · Notes	Month/Day	Location
One-Million-Pound Banknote, The	01	CM
Cure For The Blues, A	02	
Enemy Conquered; or, Love Triumphant, The	02	
Is He Living or Is He Dead?	09	Cos
Esquimau Maiden's Romance, The	11	Cos
Tom Sawyer Abroad	11	SNM
Pudd'nhead Wilson	12	CM
Tom Sawyer Abroad	12	SNM
Travelling with a Reformer	12	Cos
Concerning Tobacco		(P) What Is Man?, 1917
Extracts from Adam's Diary, The Earliest Authentic Mention of Niagara Falls · Variants reprinted under the title "Extracts From Adams Diary."		Niagara Book
Some National Stupidities		(P) Europe and Elsewhere, 1923

Title · Notes	Month/Day	Location
Playing Courier	12/19 & 12/26	ILN Entire piece ran in the San Francisco Ex 01/03/1892.
Innocents Adrift, The · MS of 174 pages, published in part in Europe and Elsewhere as "Down the Rhone."		(P) Europe and Elsewhere, 1923

<table>
<tr><td colspan="3">1892</td></tr>
</table>

Title · Notes	Month/Day	Location
About All Kinds of Ships · Collected in The One Million Pound Bank-Note And Other New Stories	?	MS, NYS
Austrian Health Factory, An	02/07	NYS
Mark Twain in the Cradle of Liberty	03/06	Chicago Tribune
Love Song	05/15	MF
German Chicago, The	10/01 & 10/22	ILN
The Earth Invoketh the Sun	11/27	(P) On the Poetry of Mark Twain, 1966

<table>
<tr><td colspan="3">1894</td></tr>
</table>

Title · Notes	Month/Day	Location
Pudd'nhead Wilson	01	CM
Tom Sawyer Abroad	01	SNM
Pudd'nhead Wilson	02	CM

Title / • Notes	Month/Day	Location
Tom Sawyer Abroad	02	SNM
Pudd'nhead Wilson	03	CM
Tom Sawyer Abroad	03	SNM
Private History of the "Jumping Frog" Story	04	NAR
Pudd'nhead Wilson	04	CM
Tom Sawyer Abroad	04	SNM
Pudd'nhead Wilson	05	CM
Pudd'nhead Wilson	06	CM
Scrap of Curious History, A	06	HM
In Defence Of Harriet Shelley	07–09	NAR
Derelict, The • Privately published Jervis Langdon, 1938, p. 23–24.	12	(P) Scott
Macfarlane		Mark Twain's Autobiography, 1924
Tragedy of Pudd'nhead Wilson and the Comedy of Those Extraordinary Twins, The		AP

1895

Title / • Notes	Month/Day	Location
What Paul Bourget Thinks of Us	01	NAR
Fenimore Cooper's Literary Offences	07	NAR
Contract with Mrs. T.K. Beecher	07/31	NYTr
Mental Telegraphy Again	09	HM
How to Tell a Story	10/03	Youth's Companion, 3 October, 464
Fenimore Cooper's Further Literary Offenses • Alt. title: "Cooper's Prose Style." In Letters from the Earth		(P) New England Quarterly, September 1946

1896

Title / • Notes	Month/Day	Location
Tom Sawyer, Detective	08	HM
Tom Sawyer, Detective	09	HM
Enchanted Sea Wilderness, The • Date conjectural.		(P) Which Was the Dream? 1968

Title / • Notes	Month/Day	Location
Love Came at Dawn • Date conjectural.		(P) On the Poetry of Mark Twain, 1966
Man's Place in the Animal World • Alt. title: "The Lowest Animal."		(P) Letters from the Earth, 1962
Personal Recollections of Joan of Arc		Harper and Brothers
Tom Sawyer Abroad, Tom Sawyer, Detective, and Other Stories		Harper and Brothers
Ancients in Modern Dress • Date conjectural, 1896 or 1897		(P) Fables of Man, 1972

1897

Title / • Notes	Month/Day	Location
Queen Victoria's Jubilee	06/22	NY Journal (and syndicated)
Riot in the Vienna Parliament, A	11/29	NYW
Chronicle of Young Satan • Unfinished. Composed 11/1897–09/1900.	11	(P) The Mysterious Stranger Manuscripts, 1969
In Memoriam	11	HM
James Hammond Trumbull	11	CM
Hellfire Hotchkiss		(P) Satires and Burlesques, 1967
Villagers of 1840–3		(P) Hannibal, Huck and Tom, 1969
Following the Equator: A Journey around the World		AP
In My Bitterness		(P) Fables of Man, 1972
More Tramps Abroad • British edition of Following the Equator; superior text.		Chatto
Tom Sawyer's Conspiracy		(P) Hannibal, Huck and Tom, 1969

715

Title • Notes	Month/Day	Location
Which Was the Dream? • Unfinished.		(P) Which Was the Dream? 1968

1898

Title • Notes	Month/Day	Location
Zola and Dreyfus	01/30	NYH (Paris Edition)
Dueling	03	(P) Europe and Elsewhere, 1923
Stirring Times In Austria	03	HM
Word of Encouragement for Our Blushing Exiles, A	05/24	(P) Europe and Elsewhere, 1923
Spanish American War, The	06/18	Critic
My Platonic Sweetheart • Date conjectural; written before August 4.	07	(P) HM, December 1912
Anglo-American Unity	07/24	NYT
Fourth of July in Berlin	07/24	NYT
At The Appetite-Cure	08	Cos
Austrian Edison Keeping School Again, The	08	CM
Memorable Assassination, A	09	(P)
What Is Man?, 1917		
About Play-Acting	10	F
From the "London Times" of 1904	11	CM
Schoolhouse Hill • Composed November to December.	11	(P) Mysterious Stranger Manuscripts, 1969
Great Dark, The • Unfinished.		(P) Letters from the Earth, 1962
Wapping Alice • Date conjectural.		(P) Friends of the Bancroft Library, 1981

1899

Title • Notes	Month/Day	Location
Austrian Parliamentary System or Government by Article 14	02	Lords and Commons
Diplomatic Pay and Clothes	03	F
Concerning the Jews	09	HM
Christian Science and the Book of Mrs. Eddy	10	Cos
My Debut as a Literary Person	11	CM
My First Lie and How I Got Out of It	12	NYW
Man That Corrupted Hadleyburg, The	12	HM
Goose fable • Date conjectural, 1899–1900.		(P) Fables of Man, 1972
How to Make History Dates Stay		(P) HM, December 1914
Indiantown		(P) Which Was the Dream? 1968
Simplified Alphabet, A		(P) What Is Man?, 1917

1900

Title • Notes	Month/Day	Location
My Boyhood Dreams	01	McClure's
To the Above Old People	01	McClure's Magazine
Tribute to Gutenburg	06/25	NY Journal and Advertiser
Salutation Speech from the 19th Century to the 20th	12	NYH
Mock Marriage • Date conjectural, early 1900s.		(P) Fables of Man, 1972
Passage from Lecture • Date conjectural, early 1900s.		(P) Fables of Man, 1972
Passages from "Glances at History" (suppressed) Date, 9th century • Date conjectural, early 1900s.		(P) Fables of Man, 1972
Passages from "Outlines of History" (suppressed) Date, 9th century • Date conjectural, early 1900s.		(P) Fables of Man, 1972
Recurrent Major and Minor Compliment, The • Date conjectural, early 1900s.		(P) Fables of Man, 1972
Synod of Praise, The • Date conjectural, early 1900s.		(P) Fables of Man, 1972

Title • Notes	Month/Day	Location
Mark Twain, Able Yachtsman, on Why Lipton Failed to Lift the Cup	08	NYH
Order of Acorns, The	10/22	NYEW
Dog's Tale, A	12	HM
You've been a dam fool, Mary. You always was!	12	(P) Fables of Man, 1972
As Regards the Company's Benevolences		(P) Mark Twain's Correspondence with Henry Huttleston Rogers, 1969
Was the World Made for Man?		(P) Letters from the Earth, 1962
Which Was It? (unfinished)		(P) Which Was the Dream? 1968

1904

Title • Notes	Month/Day	Location
Italian Without a Master	01	HW
Goodnight, Sweetheart, Goodnight • Title added.	02	(P) My Father, Mark Twain, 1931
Italian With Grammar	08	HM
Thirty-Thousand Dollar Bequest, The	12	HW
Extract from Adam's Diary • Variant of 1893 version. Lightly edited by SC to make it a companion piece to "Eve's Diary."	12	Harper and Brothers
Saint Joan of Arc	12	HM
Fable of the Yellow Terror, The • Date conjectural, 1904–1905.		(P) Fables of Man, 1972
Flies and Russians		(P) Fables of Man, 1972

1905

Title • Notes	Month/Day	Location
Concerning Copyright	01	NAR
First Writing-Machines, The. • Alt. title: "From My Unpublished Autobiography."	03/18	HW

Title • Notes	Month/Day	Location
Czar's Soliloquy, The	03	NAR
Dr. Loeb's Incredible Discovery • Written after 03/02.	03	(P) Europe and Elsewhere, 1923
Humane Word from Satan, A	04	HW
Apostrophe to Death	06/26	(P) Scott
As Concerns Interpreting the Deity • Paine published this under the title "As Concerning the Deity."	06	(P) What Is Man? 1917
Lantern for Sale	08/05	HW
Lantern for Sale	08/12	HW
Petition for W. T. Jerome, A	08/26	HW
Treaty of Portsmouth, The	08/30	Boston Globe
Christian Citizenship	09	CW
Russian Envoys who Negotiated the Treaty of Portsmouth, The	09/10	NYT
Helpless Situation, A	11	HB
Overspeeding	11	HW
For Ivins and Jerome	11/04	NYH, NYT, and NYTr
Eve's Diary Translated from the Original MS	12	HM
Old Age	12	(P) Mark Twain's Fables of Man, 1972
Refuge of the Derelicts, The • Date conjectural, 1905–1906.		(P) Fables of Man, 1972
A B C Lesson		(P) Mark Twain in Eruption, 1940
Adam's Soliloquy		(P) Europe and Elsewhere, 1923
Eve Speaks		(P) Europe and Elsewhere, 1923
In the Animal's Court		(P) Letters from the Earth, 1962

Title • Notes	Month/Day	Location
Intelligence of God • Date conjectural. Alt. title: "God."		(P) Letters from the Earth, 1962
King Leopold's Soliloquy: A Defense of His Congo Rule • Pamphlet produced for the Congo Reform Association.		P.R. Warren Company
Ten Commandments, The • Date conjectural, 1905–1906.		(P) Fables of Man, 1972
Three Thousand Years Among the Microbes		(P) Which Was the Dream, 1966
War Prayer, The		(P) Europe and Else-where, 1923
Zola's "La Terre" • Date conjectural.		(P) Letters from the Earth, 1962

1906

Title • Notes	Month/Day	Location
Lincoln Farm Association, The	02/10	CW
Comments on the Moro Massacre	03/12 & 03/14	(P) Mark Twain's Weapons of Satire, 1992
For the Russian Revolution	03/30	NYH, NYT, and NYTr
Carl Schurz, Pilot	05/26	HW
William Dean Howells	07	HM
When a Book Gets Tired • Version, with some text deleted, appeared under the title "My Literary Shipyard" in Harper's Monthly, August 1922.	08/30	(P) Mark Twain in Eruption, 1940
Chapters from My Autobiography I	09/07	NAR
Chapters from My Autobiography II	09/21	NAR
Innocent Endorsers of Quackery, The	09/22	CW
Chapters from My Autobiography III	10/05	NAR
Chapters from My Autobiography IV	10/19	NAR

Title • Notes	Month/Day	Location
Chapters from My Autobiography V	11/02	NAR
Chapters from My Autobiography VI	11/16	NAR
Hunting the Deceitful Turkey	12	HM
Chapters from My Autobiography VII	12/07	NAR
Chapters from My Autobiography VIII	12/21	NAR
Birthplace Worth Saving, A		Lincoln Farm Association Pamphlet
Captain's Story, The • Extracted republica-tion from "Some Rambling Notes of an Idle Excursion," 1877.		$30,000 Bequest and Other Stories
Deception, A • Also in Merry Tales		$30,000 Bequest and Other Stories
Gorky Incident, The • After 04/15.		(P) Letters from the Earth, 1962
Introduction to "The New Guide of the Conversation in Portuguese and English"		$30,000 Bequest and Other Stories
Monument To Adam, A • Written 1879.		$30,000 Bequest and Other Stories
Simplified Spelling		(P) Letters from the Earth, 1962
$30,000 Bequest and Other Stories, The		Harper and Brothers
What Is Man? • Anonymously pub-lished in SC's life-time; authorship revealed shortly after his death in 1910. Republished under the name Mark Twain in What Is Man? And Other Stories, Harper and Brothers, 1917.		DeVinne Press

1907

Title • Notes	Month/Day	Location
Chapters from My Autobiography, IX	01/04	NAR

Title • Notes	Month/Day	Location
Chapters from My Autobiography, X	01/18	NAR
Chapters from My Autobiography, XI	02/01	NAR
Chapters from My Autobiography, XII	02/15	NAR
Chapters from My Autobiography XIII	03/01	NAR
Chapters from My Autobiography XIV	03/15	NAR
Chapters from My Autobiography XV	04/05	NAR
Chapters from My Autobiography XVI	04/19	NAR
Chapters from My Autobiography XVII	05/03	NAR
Chapters from My Autobiography XVIII	05/17	NAR
Chapters from My Autobiography XIX	06/07	NAR
Private Secretary's Diary, The	06	(P) Fables of Man, 1972
Chapters from My Autobiography XX	07/05	NAR
Chapters from My Autobiography XXII	09/08	NAR
Chapters from My Autobiography XXIII	10	NAR
Christian Science, with Notes	10	Harper and Brothers
Chapters from My Autobiography, XXIV	11	NAR
Mental Telegraphy?	11	(P) Mark Twain's Quarrel with Heaven, 1970
Chapters from My Autobiography, XXV • Excerpt from this frequently reprinted as "The Story of a Speech."	12	NAR
Extract from Captain Stormfield's Visit to Heaven	12	HM
Cushion First		(P) Mark Twain, a Biography, 1912
Little Nelly Tells a Story Out of Her Own Head		(P) Fables of Man, 1972
Poem to Margaret • Date conjectural.		(P) Mark Twain Quarterly, Summer 1942
Robert Fulton Monument		Extracts from the Minutes and Report of the Robert Fulton Monument Association
Things a Scotsman Wants to Know • Byline: "Beruth A.W. Kennedy."		(P) What is Man?, 1917

1908

Title • Notes	Month/Day	Location
Extract from Captain Stormfield's Visit to Heaven	01	HM
Fund for Feeding Needy School Children	06/09	NYT
Support for Red Cross Stamps	12/28	NYW
About Asa Hoover • Date conjectural.		(P) Fables of Man, 1972
Little Bessie • Unfinished. Date conjectural, 1908–1909.		(P) Fables of Man, 1972
Number 44, The Mysterious Stranger • Unfinished. Date conjectural, 1902–1908.		(P) The Mysterious Stranger Manuscripts, 1969
Something about Repentance		(P) Letters from the Earth, 1962

1909

Title • Notes	Month/Day	Location
Is Shakespeare Dead?	?	Harper and Brothers
New Planet, The	01	HW
Death of Jean, The • Possibly early January, 1910.	12	(P) HM, December
Fable, A	12	HM

Title ◆ Notes	Month/Day	Location
Marjorie Fleming	12	HB
International Lightning Trust: A Kind of Love Story, The		(P) Fables of Man, 1972
Letters from the Earth		(P) Letters from the Earth, 1962
Official Report to the I.I.A.S.		(P) Letters from the Earth, 1962

1910

Title ◆ Notes	Month/Day	Location
Turning Point of My Life, The	02	HB
Parody on Swift, A		(P) Mark Twain's Margins on Thackeray's "Swift," 1935

UNIDENTIFIED

Title ◆ Notes	Month/Day	Location
Etiquette for the Afterlife: Advice to Paine ◆ Year Undetermined		(P) The Bible According to Mark Twain, 1996
Tom Sawyer's Gang Plans a Naval Battle ◆ (after 1900)		(P) Hannibal, Huck and Tom, 1969
More Maxims of Mark	Various times	Compiled and privately printed by Merle Johnson, 1927
Miner's Lament ◆ Undated newspaper clipping from unknown newspaper, signed Mark Twain. See Scott, On The Poetry of Mark Twain.		unidentified

A Chronology of Samuel Clemens's Life, Work, and Times

	Samuel Clemens's Life and Works	Literature and Other Arts	The World
1835	SC born 30 November in Florida, Mo.	Alexis de Tocqueville, *Democracy in America*. Hans Christian Andersen publishes first fairy tales. Nathaniel Hawthorne, "Young Goodman Brown." First Crockett Almanacs. b. Camille Saint-Saëns (d. 1921).	Andrew Jackson is president during a period of economic growth. Second Seminole War (1835–1842). Samuel Morse builds first version of the telegraph. Halley's comet visible from earth. New York *Herald* begins publication. b. Andrew Carnegie (d. 1919).
1836		Ralph Waldo Emerson, *Nature*. Thomas Chandler Haliburton, *The Clockmaker*. Oliver Wendell Holmes, *Poems*. First *McGuffey's Eclectic Reader*. b. Thomas Bailey Aldrich (d. 1907). b. Bret Harte (d. 1902).	Texas "Lone Star" Republic founded. Arkansas admitted to the union. Martin Van Buren elected president. Colt revolver invented. Mount Holyoke Seminary (first women's college in U.S.) founded. Construction of Washington Monument begins.
1837		Emerson, "The American Scholar." Hawthorne, *Twice-Told Tales*. Thomas Carlyle, *The French Revolution*. b. William Dean Howells (d. 1920). b. Algernon Charles Swinburne (d. 1909).	Financial panic begins economic depression. Michigan admitted to the union. Canadian rebellion. Victoria becomes queen of the United Kingdom. Mob kills abolitionist Elijah P. Lovejoy in Alton, Ill. Horace Mann begins work as an educational reformer. b. Sitting Bull (d. 1890). b. Grover Cleveland (d. 1908).
1838		Emerson, "Divinity School Address." John Greenleaf Whittier, *Ballads and Anti-Slavery Poems*. Edgar Allan Poe, *Pym*. Harriet Martineau, *Western Travel*.	Iowa Territory organized. Underground Railroad active. 14,000 U.S. troops forcibly remove Cherokee Indians from Georgia to what would become Oklahoma. John James Audubon, *Birds of America*, vol. 4. Daguerreotype photography first exhibited. b. John Muir (d. 1914). b. Victoria Woodhull (d. 1927).
1839	Moves with family to Hannibal, Mo. Sister Margaret dies.	Henry Wadsworth Longfellow, *Hyperion* and *Voices of the Night*. Kirkland, *A New Home*. Poe, *Tales of the Grotesque and Arabesque*. b. Henry Adams (d. 1918). b. John Hay (d. 1905). b. Paul Cézanne (d. 1906).	Depression deepens. Aroostook War. Britain and China begin "Opium War." Mormons establish city-state of Nauvoo, Ill. Boers found Natal. Baseball invented. First bicycle made. b. John Rockefeller (d. 1937).

	Samuel Clemens's Life and Works	Literature and Other Arts	The World
1840	Begins schooling.	Richard Henry Dana, *Two Years Before the Mast.* b. Thomas Hardy (d. 1928). b. Émile Zola (d. 1902). b. Thomas Nast (d. 1902). b. Claude Monet (d. 1926). b. Pierre-Auguste Renoir (d. 1919). b. Auguste Rodin (d. 1917).	William Henry Harrison elected president. Wilhelm IV crowned king of Prussia.
1841		Cooper, *The Deerslayer.* Brook Farm founded. *The Dial* magazine debuts.	Harrison dies; John Tyler becomes president.
1842	Brother Benjamin dies. Brother Orion moves to St. Louis to find work as a compositor.	Poe, "Masque of the Red Death." Charles Dickens, *American Notes.* Honoré de Balzac, *La Comédie Humaine.* b. Ambrose Bierce (d. 1914).	Webster-Ashburton treaty defines U.S.–Canada border. Orange Free State founded. Amana Colony founded. Barnum's Museum opens. b. William James (d. 1910). b. Peter Kropotkin (d. 1921).
1843	Father sells property to pay debts.	Tennyson, "Morte d'Arthur." Dickens, *Martin Chuzzlewit* and *A Christmas Carol.* John Ruskin, *Modern Painters,* vol. 1. First minstrel show produced by D. D. Emmett. b. Henry James (d. 1916).	U.S. economic recovery begins. Maori fight British in New Zealand. Migration to Oregon begins.
1844	Father elected justice of the peace.	Emerson, *Essays, 2nd Series.* J. M. W. Turner, *Rain, Steam, and Speed* displayed, Tate Gallery.	James K. Polk elected president. Morse exhibits the telegraph. Young Men's Christian Association (YMCA) founded in England.
1845		Frederick Douglass, *Narrative of the Life of Frederick Douglass.* Poe, *The Raven and Other Poems.* Margaret Fuller, *Woman in the Nineteenth Century.* Richard Wagner, *Tannhauser.*	Texas annexed, admitted to union. Irish potato blight sparks massive Irish migration, especially to U.S. Florida admitted to union. Anglo-Sikh War (to 1849).
1846	Mother starts taking boarders to supplement income; family sells furniture to pay debts.	Emerson, *Poems.* Hawthorne, *Mosses from an Old Manse.* Holmes, *Poems.* Poe, "Cask of Amontillado" and "Philosophy of Composition." Melville, *Typee.*	Mexican-American War begins. Iowa admitted to union. Mormon migration to Utah begins. Richard M. Hoe's rotary printing press in use.
1847	Father dies.	Longfellow, *Evangeline.* Melville, *Omoo.* Prescott, *Conquest of Peru.*	Liberian Republic founded.
1848	Begins printing apprenticeship with Joseph C. Ament.	James Russell Lowell, *The Biglow Papers.* Poe, *Eureka.* Stephen Foster, *Songs.* b. Joel C. Harris (d. 1908). b. Paul Gauguin (d. 1903).	Mexican-American War ends with Treaty of Guadalupe Hildalgo, ceding territory that would become much of the SW U.S. Zachary Taylor elected president. Revolutions in many European cities. Seneca Falls women's rights convention. Gold discovered in California. Karl Marx and Friedrich Engels, *The Communist Manifesto.* John Stuart Mill, *Principles of Political Economy.*

1849	Ends formal schooling.	Thoreau, "Civil Disobedience." Francis Parkman, *The Oregon Trail*. Amelia Bloomer founds *Lily* magazine. b. Sarah Orne Jewett (d. 1909).	Minnesota territory established. California territorial government formed without congressional authorization. California gold rush. Elizabeth Blackwell becomes 1st woman in U.S. to receive medical degree.
1850		Hawthorne, *The Scarlet Letter*. Melville, *White-Jacket*. Emerson, *Representative Men*.	Compromise of 1850, includes Fugitive Slave Act. Taylor dies in office; Millard Fillmore becomes president. Taiping rebellion in China.
1851	Quits apprenticeship to work for Orion at his print shop and newspaper in Hannibal. Soon begins writing brief sketches for Orion's *Western Union*.	Melville, *Moby-Dick*. Hawthorne, *House of the Seven Gables*. Foster, "Old Folks at Home." b. Kate Chopin (d. 1904).	Indian Appropriations Act concentrates western tribes on reservations. Louis Napoleon's coup d'état in France.
1852	Publishes "The Dandy Frightening the Squatter" in the Boston *Carpet-Bag* and "Hannibal, Missouri" in the Philadelphia *American Courier*. In September, runs Orion's newspaper and supplies pseudonymous satiric sketches.	Harriet Beecher Stowe, *Uncle Tom's Cabin*. Hawthorne, *Blithedale Romance*. Melville, *Pierre*. *Golden Era* literary weekly debuts.	Franklin Pierce elected president. Massachusetts becomes first state to mandate childhood schooling. Napoleon III declares himself emperor (deposed in 1870).
1853	Works as typographer in St. Louis, New York City, and Philadelphia. Some letters published in Hannibal *Journal,* then in Orion's Muscatine, Iowa, *Journal*.	George William Curtis, *Potiphar Papers*. Joseph Baldwin, *Flush Times*. 1st issue of woman's suffrage magazine *Una*. *Putnam's Monthly* debuts. Hawthorne, *Tanglewood Tales*.	Washington Territory formed. Gadsden Purchase agreement signed with Mexico. Growing "nativism" expressed in Know-Nothing (Native American) party agitation. Crimean War begins. World's Fair in New York City. Yellow fever epidemic in lower Mississippi River valley.
1854	Observes Know-Nothing election riots in St. Louis. Works with brothers in a western print shop in Muscatine, Iowa. Works as a typographer in St. Louis. Letters published in Muscatine *Journal*.	Thoreau, *Walden*. Benjamin Penhallow Shillaber, *Mrs. Partington*. Maria Cummins, *The Lamplighter*.	Kansas-Nebraska Act. Republican party forms. Know-Nothing party draws many votes and sparks election riots. Canadian Reciprocity Treaty. Matthew Perry concludes U.S. treaty with Japan. Boston Public Library opens.

	Samuel Clemens's Life and Works	Literature and Other Arts	The World
1855	Works with Orion and Henry in Orion's print shop in Keokuk, Iowa. Tries to arrange an apprenticeship as a steamboat pilot.	Walt Whitman, *Leaves of Grass.* Douglass, *My Bondage and My Freedom.* Longfellow, *Song of Hiawatha.*	Virtual beginning of the Civil War after establishment of two territorial governments, one pro- one antislavery, in Kansas. Czar Alexander II installed in Russia.
1856	Works as printer in Cincinnati, Ohio. Begins apprenticeship as steamboat pilot with Horace Bixby.	Whittier, *The Panorama and Other Poems.* Frances Miriam Berry Whitcher, *The Widow Bedott Papers.*	James Buchanan elected president. Republican party becomes main opposition to the Democrats. Crimean War ends.
1857		Melville, *The Confidence Man.* George Fitzhugh, *Cannibals All.* Hinton Rowan Helper, *The Impending Crisis of the South.* Dion Boucicault, *The Poor of New York,* opens in New York City. *Atlantic Monthly* debuts. *Harper's Weekly* debuts.	Dred Scott Supreme Court decision. Financial panic begins two-year depression. Indian "Mutiny." Irish Republican Brotherhood established. Giuseppe Garibaldi founds the Italian National Association. William Kelley patents economical process for making steel. Mountain Meadows Massacre in Utah.
1858	Brother Henry dies in steamboat accident.	Longfellow, "The Courtship of Miles Standish." Oliver Wendell Holmes, *Autocrat of the Breakfast Table.* b. Charles W. Chesnutt (d. 1932).	Congressional elections; Abraham Lincoln–Stephen Douglas debates. Minnesota admitted to the union; Kansas's bid for admission to the union under the proslavery Lecompton Constitution rejected by Republican House. Overland stage service from St. Louis to San Francisco begins. Colorado gold rush begins.
1859	Acquires pilot's license. Speculates in commodities.	Stowe, *The Minister's Wooing.* Harriet Wilson, *Our Nig; or, Sketches from the Life of a Free Black.* Daniel Emmet, "I Wish I Was in Dixie's Land."	Oregon admitted to the union. John Brown and followers seize federal arsenal at Harper's Ferry; Brown is arrested, tried, and executed. Franco-Austrian War over Sardinia. German unification movement begins. Comstock silver lode discovered in Nevada. Charles Darwin, *On the Origin of Species.* b. John Dewey (d. 1952).
1860		Hawthorne, *Marble Faun.* George Eliot, *The Mill on the Floss.* b. Anton Chekhov (d. 1904).	Lincoln elected president. Shoemaker's strike in New England. Internal combustion engine invented. Printing Office established. Pony express begins.

1861	Joins Masonic Lodge in St. Louis. Brief stint in "Marion Rangers," unit of the Missouri state militia. Moves to Nevada with Orion, who takes up position as secretary to the new territorial government. Begins career as a gold and silver prospector. Speculates in mining securities.	Dickens, *Great Expectations*. Eliot, *Silas Marner*. Holmes, "Elsie Venner." d. Elizabeth Barrett Browning.	Southern states secede from union. Civil War begins. Kansas admitted to the union. First national income tax established. Italian kingdom proclaimed. First transcontinental telegraph message delivered.
1862	Begins work as a reporter for Virginia City *Territorial Enterprise*. Writes both news and sketches.	Charles Farrar Browne, *Artemus Ward, His Book*. Robert Henry Newell, *The Orpheus C. Kerr Papers*. Stowe, *Pearl of Orr's Island*. b. Edith Wharton (d. 1937).	Homestead Act. Morrill Act establishes "land-grant" colleges and universities. Battle of Pea Ridge, Ark., secures Missouri for the union; battles of Shiloh, Second Bull Run, Antietam, and Fredricksburg. Gattling gun patented. First iron-clad warships put into operation. Otto von Bismarck becomes prime minister of Prussia.
1863	Begins using pseudonym "Mark Twain." First visits San Francisco, Calif.	Gettysburg Address delivered. Edward Everett Hale, "The Man Without a Country." Longfellow, "Tales of a Wayside Inn." John Stuart Mill, "Utilitarianism." d. William Makepeace Thackeray.	Lincoln issues Emancipation Proclamation. Conscription act passes. West Virginia admitted to the union. Territories of Arizona and Idaho formed. Battle of Gettysburg; Vicksburg falls to union troops under Ulysses S. Grant. Draft riots in New York City. French capture Mexico City. National Academy of Sciences founded. William Bullock patents continuous-roll printing press. b. George Santayana (d. 1952). b. Henry Ford (d. 1947). b. William Randolph Hearst (d. 1951).
1864	Works as a reporter for San Francisco *Morning Call*; quits to pursue literary work. Publishes sketches in New York and California journals.	David Locke, *The Nasby Papers*.	Battles of the Wilderness, Spotsylvania, Cold Harbor, Petersburg, Atlanta, and Mobile Bay. Montana territory formed. Nevada admitted to the union. Lincoln re-elected. Sand Creek Indian Massacre.

	Samuel Clemens's Life and Works	Literature and Other Arts	The World
1865	Publishes sketches and newspaper correspondence including "Jim Smiley and His Jumping Frog," his first national success.	Whitman, *Drum-Taps*. Mary Elizabeth Dodge, *Hans Brinker*. Lewis Carroll, *Alice's Adventures in Wonderland*. *The Nation* debuts. b. Rudyard Kipling (d. 1936). b. William Butler Yeats (d. 1939).	Civil War ends with Robert E. Lee's surrender at Appomattox. Lincoln assassinated; Andrew Johnson becomes president. Thirteenth Amendment outlawing slavery adopted. Ku Klux Klan founded. Joseph Lister introduces antiseptics in surgery. First oil pipeline built in U.S. John Stetson begins making hats. San Francisco *Examiner* and San Francisco *Chronicle* founded.
1866	Takes job as a traveling correspondent to Sandwich Islands (Hawaii) for the Sacramento *Union*. Goes on first lecture tour. Becomes traveling correspondent for San Francisco *Alta California*.	Howells, *Venetian Life*. Whittier, *Snowbound*. New York *World* debuts. *Galaxy* magazine debuts. b. H. G. Wells (d. 1946).	Revolution in Crete against Turkish rule. German confederation dissolves. First successful transatlantic cable laid. Alfred Nobel invents dynamite. Robert Whitehead invents underwater torpedo. Major cholera epidemic.
1867	Meets Olivia Langdon in New York City. Publishes *The Celebrated Jumping Frog of Calaveras County, and Other Sketches* Writes for *Alta California* on topics including a trip to Europe and the Middle East with the steamer *Quaker City*. Works for New York *Herald* and New York *Tribune*.	Harte, *Condensed Novels*. George Washington Harris, *Sut Lovingood Yarns*. Horatio Alger, *Ragged Dick*. *Harper's Bazaar* debuts. Henrik Ibsen, *Peer Gynt*. .	U.S. purchases Alaska from Russia. Nebraska admitted to the union. Gold discovered in Wyoming. Grange movement founded.
1868	Reports on Johnson's impeachment trial. Lectures in California and Nevada. Befriends Joseph Hopkins Twichell. Courts and becomes engaged to Langdon.	Harte, "The Luck of Roaring Camp." Louisa May Alcott, *Little Women*. *Lippincott's Magazine* debuts. *Overland Monthly* magazine debuts. *Vanity Fair* debuts. b. Mary Austin (d. 1934).	House impeaches Johnson, but Senate acquits. Grant elected president. Fourteenth Amendment adopted, guaranteeing equal protection under the law. Christopher Latham Sholes patents typewriter. SMajor earthquake in San Francisco. Armour meat-packing factory opens. First U.S. professional baseball club founded. b. W. E. B. Du Bois (d. 1963).
1869	Issues *The Innocents Abroad*. Winter lecture tour. Befriends David Ross Locke and William Dean Howells. Buys share of Buffalo *Express* with money borrowed from future father-in-law.	Stowe, *Oldtown Folks*. Aldrich, *The Story of a Bad Boy*. *Appleton's Journal* debuts. b. Frank Lloyd Wright (d. 1959).	National Woman Suffrage Association founded. Suffrage granted to women in Wyoming territory. Prohibition party founded. Financial panic over gold speculation. Transcontinental railroad finished. Heinz food-packing company founded. Mill, "On the Subjugation of Women."

1870	Marries Langdon. Father-in-law, Jervis Langdon, dies of stomach cancer. Mother, widowed sister, niece, and nephew move to Fredonia, N.Y., with financial support of Clemens. Nye contracts typhoid fever and soon dies. Son Langdon born prematurely. Collaborates with Darius Ford on "Around the World" series. Begins regular column in *Galaxy*. Begins work on *Roughing It*.	Harte, "Plain Language from Truthful James." *Scribner's Monthly* debuts. Jules Verne, "Twenty Thousand Leagues under the Sea." b. Frank Norris (d. 1902). d. Charles Dickens.	Fifteenth Amendment guaranteeing equal voting rights to males regardless of race adopted. Department of Justice formed. John Rockefeller founds Standard Oil. Napoleon III deposed. Louis Pasteur invents "pasteurization." d. Robert E. Lee.
1871	Olivia contracts typhoid fever, recovers slowly. Family moves to Elmira, N.Y., then on to Nook Farm, Hartford, Conn. Meets Thomas Bailey Aldrich. Winter lecture tour. Takes out patent on garment strap. Publishes *Mark Twain's (Burlesque) Autobiography and First Romance*.	Harte, *East and West Poems*. Joaquin Miller, *Songs of the Sierras*. William Dean Howells, *Their Wedding Journey*. Whitman, *Democratic Vistas*. b. Stephen Crane (d. 1900). b. Theodore Dreiser (d. 1945).	Indian Appropriation act nullifies treaties with Native Americans and makes them wards of U.S. Treaty of Washington settles difficulties between Britain and U.S. Chicago fire. Barnum opens circus in Brooklyn, N.Y. Henry Stanley meets David Livingstone in Ujiji. Darwin, *Descent of Man*.
1872	b. Olivia Susan (Susy). *Roughing It* issued. In England, meets Moncure Conway and actor Henry Irving. SC invents self-pasting scrapbook.	Eadweard Muybridge's photographs of movement. James Whistler, *The Artist's Mother*. b. Paul Laurence Dunbar (d. 1906).	Credit Mobilier scandal. Grant re-elected. Civil war in Spain. Montgomery Ward issues its first mail-order catalog.
1873	Cowrites (with Charles Dudley Warner) and publishes *The Gilded Age*. Named a director of the American Publishing Company. Purchases lot in Nook Farm. Trip to Britain with family. Lectures in England. Meets Herbert Spencer, Anthony Trollope, Robert Browning, Dr. John Brown. Side trips to Ireland and France. Scrapbook patented and marketed.	Howells, *A Chance Acquaintance*. *St Nicholas* debuts. *Woman's Home Companion* debuts. b. Willa Cather (d. 1947). d. John Stuart Mill.	Financial panic starts depression. Color photographs developed. Philo Remington begins to produce typewriters.
1874	Publishes "A True Story." Begins work on "Old Times on the Mississippi." b. Clara Langdon Clemens. Moves into unfinished house in Hartford. Lectures in Britain. *Colonel Sellers* opens in New York.	First Impressionist exhibition. b. Amy Lowell (d. 1925). b. Gertrude Stein (d. 1946). b. Robert Frost (d. 1963).	Streptococci and staphylococci discovered. Women's Christian Temperance Union (WCTU) founded. Society for the Prevention of Cruelty to Children founded. First U.S. zoo opens.

	Samuel Clemens's Life and Works	Literature and Other Arts	The World
1875	"Old Times" series and *Mark Twain's Sketches, New and Old* published. Finishes draft of *The Adventures of Tom Sawyer*. Visits New York to observe Henry Ward Beecher's trial for adultery. Friendship with Howells blossoms. Hires George Griffin as butler.	Howells, *A Foregone Conclusion*. Georges Bizet's *Carmen* opens in Paris.	Heinrich Schliemann, *Troy and Its Remains*. Mary Baker Eddy, *Science and Health*. b. Albert Schweitzer (d. 1965).
1876	Publishes *Tom Sawyer*. Bret Harte comes on extended visit; SC and Harte work on play, *Ah Sin*. SC helps form Saturday Morning Club.	James, *Roderick Hucson*. Whitman, *Leaves of Grass, Centennial Edition*. b. Jack London (d. 1916). b. Sherwood Anderson (d. 1914). d. George Sand.	Rutherford B. Hayes and Samuel Tilden in disputed presidential election; deals resulting in Hayes's election lead to the end of Reconstruction in the South. Colorado admitted to the union. Custer dies at Battle of Little Big Horn. Alexander Graham Bell patents telephone. World exhibition held in Philadelphia.
1877	Publishes *A True Story and the Recent Carnival of Crime*. *Ah Sin* opens for brief runs in Baltimore, Washington, D.C., and New York City. Harte's visit strains friendship. SC travels with Twichell to Bermuda. Family summers in Elmira. SC gives Whittier Birthday Dinner speech.	Jewett, *Deephaven*. James, *The American*. Sidney Lanier, *Poems*. b. Hermann Hesse (d. 1962).	Rutherford B. Hayes inaugurated. Queen Victoria declared Empress of India. First public telephones appear in U.S. Edison patents phonograph.
1878	Publishes *Punch, Brothers, Punch and Other Sketches*. Family sails to Europe for extended trip. "Walking tour" of Germany and Switzerland with Joseph Twichell to collect material for a travel book.	James, *Daisy Miller*. William Morris, "The Decorative Arts." Gilbert and Sullivan, *H.M.S. Pinafore*.	First bicycles made in America. Canada begins fur farming. Salvation Army becomes known by this name.
1879	Works on *A Tramp Abroad*. Meets Charles Darwin. Returns to U.S.	Howells, *Lady of the Aroostook*. George Washington Cable, *Old Creole Days*. Tourgee, *Fool's Errand*.	Frozen meat from Australia appears in London stores.

1880	b. Jane Lampton (Jean) Clemens. Visits ailing mother. *A Tramp Abroad* issues in March. SC buys controlling interest in Dan Slote's Kaolatype printing process. Meets James Paige; makes investment in Paige typesetter. Elisha Bliss dies, changing SC's relationship with American Publishing Company.	Adams, *Democracy.* Cable, *The Grandissimes.* Lew Wallace, *Ben-Hur.* Fyodor Dostoevsky, *The Brothers Karamazov.* d. George Eliot.	James Garfield elected president. First practical electric lights invented. New York streets first illuminated by electricity. First large steel furnace developed. Bingo developed. Canned fruits and meats appear in stores. b. Helen Keller (d. 1968).
1881	Funds European studies of sculptor Carl Gerhardt. Arranges to have James R. Osgood and Company publish his books. Hires niece's husband, Charles C. Webster, to manage some business affairs.	James, *Washington Square* and *Portrait of a Lady.* Joel Harris, *Uncle Remus. Century* magazine debuts. b. Pablo Picasso (d. 1973). b. P. G. Wodehouse (d. 1975). d. Dostoevsky.	d. Garfield; Chester A. Arthur becomes president. Federation of Organized Trades and Labor Unions of the United States and Canada formed. Booker T. Washington founds Tuskegee Institute. Population of New York City reaches 1.2 million.
1882	*The Prince and the Pauper* issued. Clemens and Osgood travel through Mississippi River valley to prepare for *Life on the Mississippi. Stolen White Elephant* issued. Howells and Clemens begin *Colonel Sellers as Scientist.* Meets Joel C. Harris and George Washington Cable. Jean, Susy, and Samuel Clemens contract scarlet fever; house quarantined.	Howells, *A Modern Instance.* b. Virginia Woolf (d. 1941). b. James Joyce (d. 1941). b. Igor Stravinsky (d. 1971). d. Anthony Trollope.	U.S. bans Chinese immigration for ten years. Triple Alliance begins. Hypnosis used to treat hysteria. American Baseball Association founded. b. Franklin D. Roosevelt (d. 1945).
1883	Publishes *Life on the Mississippi.* Olivia contracts diphtheria. SC meets Matthew Arnold in Hartford.	Ladies Home Journal debuts. b. Franz Kafka (d. 1924).	First skyscraper (ten stories) built in Chicago. Orient Express makes its first run. "Buffalo Bill" begins his "Wild West" show. Brooklyn Bridge opens. d. Sojourner Truth. d. Karl Marx.
1884	SC founds publishing company, to be managed by Charles Webster. Charles Webster and Company begins production of *Adventures of Huckleberry Finn*; British edition issues. During a visit to Hartford in January, George Washington Cable contracts mumps; Clemens hires a nurse to care for him. Begins lecture tour with Cable.	Sarah Orne Jewett, *A Country Doctor.* John Hay, *Bread-Winners. Oxford English Dictionary* begins publication. Auguste Rodin, *The Burghers of Calais.*	Grover Cleveland elected president. Tetanus bacillus discovered. First practical steam turbine engine invented.

	Samuel Clemens's Life and Works	Literature and Other Arts	The World
1885	U.S. edition of *Huckleberry Finn* appears. Ulysses S. Grant agrees to publish his memoirs with Webster & Co.; SC helps Grant finish the work. Grant's death boosts sales of memoir. Susy begins to write biography of her father. SC begins paying board of Warner T. McGuinn, an African-American student at Yale Law School.	Howells, *Rise of Silas Lapham*. b. Ezra Pound (d. 1972). d. Victor Hugo.	Pasteur invents rabies vaccine. Francis Galton proves individuality of fingerprints. George Eastman makes photographic paper. Golf introduced in America. Mormons split into polygamous and monogamous sections. d. Ulysses S. Grant.
1886	Clemens family stages private production of *The Prince and the Pauper*. Henry M. Stanley visits in Hartford. Second volume of Grant memoirs issues. Finishes play *Colonel Sellers as Scientist* with Howells. Makes Frederick J. Hall a partner in Webster & Co. Hires Frank G. Whitmore as business manager to oversee Paige typesetter.	James, *The Bostonians* and *The Princess Casamassima*. Jewett, *The White Heron*. Frances Hodgson Burnett, *Little Lord Fauntleroy*. Howells, *Indian Summer*. *Cosmopolitan* debuts.	Steam used to sterilize surgical instruments.
1887	Reworks *Colonel Sellers as Scientist* as *The American Claimant*. Webster issues *Mark Twain's Library of Humor* and Pope Leo XIII's biography; sales of the latter are poor.	Mary Eleanor Freeman, *A Humble Romance*. *Scribner's* magazine debuts.	Queen Victoria celebrates her Golden Jubilee. Phenacetin discovered. b. Chiang Kai-shek (d. 1975).
1888	Grace King visits in Hartford. Theodore Crane suffers stroke; nursed by Susan Crane and Olivia Clemens in Hartford. Webster driven out of Webster & Co.; Hall takes over management of the company.	James, *Aspern Papers*. Whitman, *Complete Poems and Prose. Collier's* magazine debuts. b. T. S. Eliot (d. 1965).	Benjamin Harrison elected president. Suez Canal convention. Eastman perfects "Kodak" box camera.
1889	Publishes *A Connecticut Yankee in King Arthur's Court*. Dramatization of *The Prince and the Pauper*. d. Theodore Crane in Elmira. Rudyard Kipling visits in Elmira. Prototype of Paige machine appears to be successful.	Howells, *Annie Kilburn*. *Munsey's* magazine debuts.	North Dakota, South Dakota, Montana, and Washington admitted to the union. Frederick Abel invents cordite. Ten states adopt secret ballot. Carnegie, *The Gospel of Wealth*. Barnum and Bailey circus opens at Olympia, London.

1890	Edward Bellamy visits Hartford. Clemens's mother dies. Olivia's mother dies. Edward House sues over rights to dramatization of *The Prince and the Pauper*, ending friendship with Clemens. Critical cash flow problems at Webster & Co.	Emily Dickinson, *Poems.* Howells, *Hazard of New Fortunes.* b. Katherine Anne Porter (d. 1980). d. Vincent Van Gogh.	Idaho and Wyoming admitted to the union. Global influenza epidemic occurs. William James, *Principles of Psychology.* Alfred T. Mahan, *Influence of Sea Power.* Jacob Riis, *How the Other Half Lives.* Daughters of the American Revolution founded.
1891	Family closes Hartford house and moves to Europe to save money. Clemens writes steadily for magazines. Olivia begins showing symptoms of heart disease.	Bierce, *Tales of Soldiers and Civilians.*. Gauguin settles in Tahiti. Henri Toulouse-Lautrec produces movie-hall posters. b. Cole Porter (d. 1964). d. Melville.	Beginnings of wireless telegraph. Trans-Siberian railroad construction begins. Clothing zipper invented.
1892	Dines with Kaiser Wilhelm II. Webster publishes *Merry Tales* and *The American Claimant.* SC contracts pneumonia. Olivia and SC travel in Europe.	b. Archibald MacLeish (d. 1982). b. Edna St. Vincent Millay (d. 1950). d. Walt Whitman. d. Tennyson.	Cleveland re-elected president. Iron and steel workers strike. Rudolf Diesel patents his internal-combustion engine.
1893	*Pudd'nhead Wilson and Those Extraordinary Twins* begins serial publication. Webster publishes *The £1,000,000 Bank-Note and Other New Stories.* Visits Columbian Exposition in Chicago. Staves off bankruptcy by sale of Library of American Literature.	Crane, *Maggie, a Girl of the Streets. McClure's* debuts. b. Dorothy Parker (d. 1967).	Financial panic. Hawaii proclaimed a republic and annexed to U.S.; treaty later withdrawn. Henry Ford builds his first car. Benz constructs his four-wheel car. Frederick Jackson Turner, "Significance of the Frontier."
1894	*Tom Sawyer Abroad* issues. *Pudd'nhead Wilson and Those Extraordinary Twins* publishes in book form. SC moves back and forth between U.S. and family in France. Webster & Co. declares bankruptcy. SC declares personal bankruptcy. Paige Typesetter fails commercial test.	Muir, *Mountains of California.* George Santayana, *Sonnets.* Kate Chopin, *Bayou Folk.* Howells, *Traveler from Altruria.* b. James Thurber (d. 1961). b. Aldous Huxley (d. 1963). d. Oliver Wendell Holmes. d. Robert Louis Stevenson.	Alfred Dreyfus arrested on treason charges in France.
1895	Olivia and Clara accompany SC on lecture tour around the world. Serial publication of *Personal Recollections of Joan of Arc.* Arranges for Harper and Brothers to be primary publisher of works.	Crane, *Red Badge of Courage. Collier's Weekly* debuts. Yeats, *Poems.* Art Nouveau style predominates. Pyotr Tchaikovsky, *Swan Lake.*	Guglielmo Marconi invents radio. Louis Lumiere invents motion-picture camera. First professional football game played in U.S. b. George Herman ("Babe") Ruth (d. 1948). d. Frederick Douglass. d. Thomas H. Huxley. d. Pasteur.

	Samuel Clemens's Life and Works	Literature and Other Arts	The World
1896	Susy dies of meningitis in Hartford. Family secludes itself in London while Clemens works on travel book. Finishes lecture tour. Begins *Following the Equator*. *Personal Recollections of Joan of Arc* issued in book form. *Tom Sawyer Abroad, Tom Sawyer Detective and Other Stories* published.	Giacomo Puccini, *La Bohème*. b. John Dos Passos (d. 1970). b. F. Scott Fitzgerald (d. 1940). d. Stowe. d. William Morris.	William McKinley elected president. Utah admitted to the union. William Jennings Bryan's "Cross of Gold" speech. Evidence for Dreyfus's innocence suppressed. Helium discovered. Niagara Falls hydroelectric plant opens. Nobel Prizes established. First modern Olympics held. Klondike gold rush begins. Thomas Edison shows first motion picture in U.S.
1897	Family moves to Switzerland, then to Vienna; comes out of mourning. d. Orion Clemens. *Following the Equator* and *How to Tell a Story and Other Essays* issues.	Henry James, *The Spoils of Poynton*. Wells, *Invisible Man*. Rodin unveils *Victor Hugo* sculpture. John Philip Sousa, "The Stars and Stripes Forever."	Queen Victoria celebrates her Diamond Jubilee. Electron discovered. William James, *The Will to Believe*.
1898	d. Mary Mason Fairbanks. SC's creditors are paid in full.	Crane, "The Open Boat." Wells, *War of the Worlds*. b. Bertolt Brecht (d. 1956). b. Paul Robeson (d. 1976). d. Carroll.	U.S. declares war on Spain over Cuba. Émile Zola writes "J'accuse" and is imprisoned. Pierre and Marie Curie discover radium and polonium. Photographs first taken using artificial light. d. Bismarck. d. William Gladstone.
1899	Family travels around Europe. Jean treated for epilepsy. SC writes "Christian Science and the Book of Mrs. Eddy."	Oscar Wilde, *The Importance of Being Earnest*. b. Noël Coward (d. 1973). b. Ernest Hemingway (d. 1961). d. Johann Strauss.	Filipinos fight for independence from U.S. First magnetic recording of sound.
1900	James Whistler paints Clemens's portrait. Family returns to U.S. to live. SC attends Hartford funeral of Charles Dudley Warner. Publishes *English As She Is Taught* and *The Man That Corrupted Hadleyburg and Other Stories and Essays*.	Howells, *Literary Friends and Acquaintance*. Joseph Conrad, *Lord Jim*. b. Aaron Copland (d. 1990). b. Thomas Wolfe (d. 1938). d. Crane. d. Oscar Wilde. d. Friedrich Nietzsche.	McKinley re-elected. Boxer uprising in China. Commonwealth of Australia is founded. First trial flight of a zeppelin. Arthur Evans discovers ancient Minoan culture. Cakewalk becomes fashionable dance.
1901	Receives honorary doctorate from Yale. Suffers recurrent attacks of gout. *To The Person Sitting In Darkness* issued.	Booker T. Washington, *Up from Slavery*. Frank Norris, *The Octopus*. Picasso begins Blue Period. b. Walt Disney (d. 1966). d. Toulouse-Lautrec.	McKinley assassinated; Theodore Roosevelt becomes president. Max Planck, *Laws of Radiation*. Marconi transmits telegraphic messages across the Atlantic. John Muir, *Our National Parks*. d. Queen Victoria.

1902	Buys house in Tarrytown, N.Y. Jean's health deteriorates. Olivia becomes critically ill for months. Isabel Lyon becomes Clemens's secretary. In complex dealings with American Plasmon Company, Ralph Ashcroft, the company's treasurer, helps Clemens. SC publishes *A Double Barrelled Detective Story.*	Henry James, *Wings of the Dove.* Arthur Conan Doyle, *The Hound of the Baskervilles.* Kipling, *Just So Stories.* b. John Steinbeck (d. 1967). b. Ogden Nash (d. 1971).	U.S. coal strike. William James, *The Varieties of Religious Experience.* d. Elizabeth Cady Stanton.
1903	Olivia's health improves. SC bed-ridden with bronchitis and gout. Family moves to Italy. Publishes *My Debut as a Literary Person* and *A Dog's Tale.*	W. E. B. Du Bois, *The Souls of Black Folk.* James, *The Ambassadors.* Jack London, *The Call of the Wild.* b. Nathanael West (d. 1940). b. Evelyn Waugh (d. 1966).	Department of Commerce and Labor authorized. Anti-Jewish pogroms in Russia. Orville and Wilbur Wright successfully fly a powered airplane. Henry Ford founds the Ford Motor Company. Alaskan frontier settled.
1904	d. SC's sister-in-law Mollie Clemens. Clara begins concert singing career. d. Olivia. Family returns to U.S. SC publishes *Extracts from Adam's Diary.* Begins autobiographical dictations.	James, *The Golden Bowl.* American Academy of Arts and Letters founded. b. Graham Greene (d. 1991). b. Salvador Dalí (d. 1989). d. Chekhov.	Theodore Roosevelt elected president. Russo-Japanese War breaks out. Work begins on Panama Canal. Thermionic tube used to generate radio waves. Broadway subway opens in New York City. Hellen Keller graduates from Radcliffe College.
1905	Seventieth birthday party at Delmonico's. Publishes *King Leopold's Soliloquy: A Defense of His Congo Rule.*	London, *War of the Classes.* Edith Wharton, *House of Mirth.* Henri Rousseau, *Jungle with a Lion.* Claude Debussy, "La Mer." First regular cinemas established.	Russia surrenders to Japanese at Port Arthur. Attempted Russian Revolution in St. Petersburg crushed. Sinn Féin founded in Dublin. International Workers of the World (Wobblies) founded. Albert Einstein formulates Special Theory of Relativity. Sigmund Freud, *Three Contributions to the Theory of Sex.*
1906	SC suffers from chronic bronchitis and gout. Gives Albert Bigelow Paine permission to write biography; begins publishing extracts from autobiography. Publishes *Eve's Diary, The $30,000 Bequest and Other Stories,* and *What Is Man?*	George Bernard Shaw, *Arms and the Man* published. Upton Sinclair *The Jungle.* b. Greta Garbo (d. 1990). b. Clifford Odets (d. 1963). d. Cézanne. d. Dunbar. d. Ibsen.	Reform laws promulgated in Russia. Dreyfus rehabilitated. U.S. Pure Food and Drug Act. Roald Amundsen determines position of magnetic North Pole. First radio program of voice and music broadcast in U.S. San Francisco earthquake kills 700; $400 million property lost. d. Pierre Curie.

	Samuel Clemens's Life and Works	Literature and Other Arts	The World
1907	Jean sent to sanatorium after seizures. SC receives honorary doctorate from Oxford University. Hires Ashcroft to manage many business affairs. *Christian Science* issues. First of two installments of "Extract from Captain Stormfield's Visit to Heaven" appear. *A Horse's Tale* and *Christian Science* published.	First Cubist exhibition in Paris. Picasso, *Demoiselles d'Avignon*. b. W. H. Auden (d. 1973).	Oklahoma admitted to the union. Vladimir Lenin leaves Russia and founds the newspaper *The Proletarian*. Lumiere develops a three-color screen process for color photography. SS *Lusitania* breaks transatlantic speed record. Henri Bergson, *L'Evolution*. William James, *Pragmatism*. Boy Scouts founded.
1908	Founds "Aquarium Club." Moves into new house in Redding, Conn. d. SC's nephew Samuel Moffett. SC forms Mark Twain Company.	Isadora Duncan becomes popular interpreter of dance. b. Theodore Roethke (d. 1963). b. William Saroyan (d. 1981). b. Richard Wright (d. 1960).	William H. Taft elected president. Union of South Africa established. General Motors corporation founded. Wilbur Wright flies thirty miles in forty minutes. The Ford Motor company produces the first Model T. Jack Johnson becomes first black world heavyweight champion. b. Lyndon B. Johnson (d 1973).
1909	Jean moves into Redding house to take over household management. SC develops clear symptoms of heart disease. Publishes *Is Shakespeare Dead? Extract from Captain Stormfield's Visit to Heaven* issued in book form.	Thomas Mann, *Koenigliche Hoheit*. Ezra Pound, "Exultations." Vassily Kandinsky's first abstract paintings appear. b. Wallace Stegner (d. 1993). d. Swinburne.	Turkey and Serbia recognize Austrian annexation of Bosnia and Herzegovina. Explorer Robert Peary reaches North Pole. First permanent waves are given in London beauty shops.
1910	SC dies 21 April in Redding, Conn. Buried in Elmira, N.Y.	E. M. Forster, *Howard's End*. Stravinsky's ballet *The Firebird* performed in Paris. d. Leo Tolstoy.	W. E. B. Du Bois founds the National Association for the Advancement of Colored People. Marie Curie, *Treatise on Radiography*. d. William James. d. Mary Baker. Eddy. d. Florence Nightingale.

Index

Note: Boldface numbers indicate illustrations.

Picture Acknowledgments

The publishers wish to thank the following who have kindly given their permission to reproduce illustrations as identified by the page numbers. While every effort has been made to secure permissions, we apologize if in any cases we have failed to trace the copyright holder.

5	The Mark Twain House, Hartford, Connecticut
50	Cornell University Library, Making of America Digital Collection
61	California State Archives
67	Cornell University Library, Making of America Digital Collection
74	The New York Public Library
117	The Mariner's Museum, Newport News, Virginia
128	Columbia University Library
138	The New York Public Library
246	The Mark Twain Papers, Bancroft Library, Berkeley, California
296	Yale University Library, courtesy of the Mark Twain Papers
305	The Mark Twain House, Hartford, Connecticut
331	The Mark Twain House, Hartford, Connecticut
393	Library of Congress
463	Cornell University Library, Making of America Digital Collection
470	The Punch Cartoon Library
602	The Mark Twain Museum, Hannibal, Missouri
Cover	Keystone-Mast Collection, UCR/California Museum of Photography, University of California, Riverside.

The last quarter of a century of my life has been pretty constantly and faithfully devoted to the study of the human race—that is to say, the study of myself, for, in my individual person, I am the entire human race compacted together.

—*Mark Twain*